MENTAL HEALTH LAW

Mental Health Law

Policy and Practice

Fourth Edition

PETER BARTLETT

AND

RALPH SANDLAND

OXFORD

UNIVERSITY PRESS

OXFORD
UNIVERSITY PRESS

Great Clarendon Street, Oxford, OX2 6DP,
United Kingdom

Oxford University Press is a department of the University of Oxford.
It furthers the University's objective of excellence in research, scholarship,
and education by publishing worldwide. Oxford is a registered trade mark of
Oxford University Press in the UK and in certain other countries

First edition 2000
Second edition 2003
Third edition 2007

Impression: 1

Published in the United States of America by Oxford University Press
198 Madison Avenue, New York, NY 10016, United States of America

British Library Cataloguing in Publication Data

Data available

Library of Congress Control Number: 2013940316

ISBN 978-0-19-966150-3

Printed in Great Britain by
Ashford Colour Press Ltd, Gosport, Hampshire

Preface

It is now fourteen years since the first edition of this textbook was published, and the time seemed ripe for a full and proper re-writing of the text. In our first edition, it was still possible to frame mental health law as being 'really' about compulsory hospitalisation and compulsory treatment in hospital. Subjects such as capacity could safely be left to a couple of chapters near the end of the book. This is no longer the case. Increasingly, people with mental health problems are spending more and more time in community environments (where they may or may not be subject to compulsion), and capacity has its own statutory structure (now including authority to detain individuals in hospitals and in community settings, most notably care homes). The foundations of the subject are thus shifting, and will no doubt continue to do so in the years to come.

A full re-write also seemed sensible since, for the first time, we can begin by saying that no immediate statutory amendment seems to be in the offing: while no doubt jurisprudence will develop in the years to come, there is no pending government initiative to change the legislative structure. By comparison, the third edition was published just prior to the passage of the Mental Health Act 2007. While that has been frustrating in some ways, the advantage in the delay has been that the 2007 Act has now had some time to bed in, and it is possible to analyse not merely its abstract terms, but also its implementation. Similarly, the Mental Capacity Act 2005 (without the deprivation of liberty safeguards—those were introduced in the Mental Health Act 2007) was just coming into effect when the third edition was published. We now have six years of litigation as to its implementation. The ground is not entirely settled, however. The structure of community care law is, at last, in the process of being reformed. The draft Care and Support Bill (now renamed the Care Bill), discussed in detail in Chapter 3, was introduced into the House of Lords in May 2013, and promises both the simplification and the substantive restructuring of much of community care law.

In tandem with these domestic developments, there have been significant developments in international law. From the early years of the new millennium, the jurisprudence of the European Court of Human Rights relating to mental disabilities (both mental health problems and learning disabilities) has been growing both in volume and in sophistication. Matters relating to guardianship and incapacity, an area barely considered by the Strasbourg court at the time of the third edition, now has the basis of a solid and developing jurisprudence, and cases such as *X v Finland* (see Chapter 9) suggest that the court may be starting to progress on key issues of mental health law as well. These developments are discussed in this edition, but this is an area where the future is potentially exciting.

The United Nations Convention on the Rights of Persons with Disabilities, which came into effect in 2008, presents the most direct challenge to mental health law for a very long time—perhaps ever. It directly challenges the use of state power when laws rely on concepts of disability (including mental disability) to govern detention, involuntary treatment, and decision-making for people identified as lacking capacity. The United Nations High Commissioner for Human Rights interprets the convention in part as follows:

> Legislation authorizing the institutionalization of persons with disabilities on the grounds of their disability without their free and informed consent must be abolished. This must include the repeal of provisions authorizing institutionalization of persons with disabilities for their care and treatment without their free and informed consent, as well as provisions authorizing the preventive detention of persons with disabilities on grounds such as the likelihood of them posing a danger to themselves or others, in all cases in which such grounds of care, treatment and public security are linked in legislation to an apparent or diagnosed mental illness.

United Nations, A/HRC/10/48 (26 January 2009)

This challenges the bases of mental health law that have been accepted for at least 200 years. Fundamental changes in mental health law may be required to comply with the Convention, posing significant challenges to domestic governments.

Such an environment of challenge chimes well with the ethos of this book. At the core of our approach has always been that the purpose of a textbook is to challenge its readers to further inquiry, not to provide snappy answers to snappy questions. Indeed, implicit in our placement of the academic study of mental health law in the context of social and professional practice, has been our view that such simple answers to questions of social regulation do not exist. The CRPD, and the further challenges flowing from the Strasbourg jurisprudence and the developing academic literature relating to disability law provide frameworks for these inquiries. As always, we will have succeeded in our enterprise not if our readers think they have found solutions, but instead if we have inspired them to greater consideration and understanding of the problems.

Many thanks to Mike Sergeant for reading drafts of Chapter 5, and to Arun Chopra for reading drafts of Chapter 9. As always, we would thank our colleagues at Oxford University Press—most notably John Carroll, Sarah Stephenson, and Marie Gill. They have been professional, highly competent and pleasant to work with.

Our thanks are also due to Mandy and Rick, our domestic partners, for the considerable patience they have shown over the grind which the creation of this book has inevitably involved. Once again, we also thank the students who have subscribed to our mental health module since its inception in 1995, and in particular those of them who have shared their experiences of the mental health system with us and with their colleagues, either as patients or staff. They have not merely provided invaluable insights into the law in practice; they have also served as a reminder that the dividing line between 'them' and 'us' is largely illusory.

Peter Bartlett
Ralph Sandland
Nottingham, August 2013.

Outline Contents

Detailed Contents

Table of Cases

Table of Statutes

Proposed legislation

European Union

Finland

Ireland, Republic of

International

Table of Secondary Legislation

Codes of Practice

1

Conceptualising Mental Health Law

In the serene world of mental illness, modern man no longer communicates with the mad-man: on one hand, the man of reason delegates the physician to madness, thereby author-izing a relation only through the abstract universality of disease; on the other, the man of madness communicates with society only by the intermediary of an equally abstract reason which is order, physical and moral constraint, the anonymous pressure of the group, the requirements of conformity. As for a common language, there is no such thing; or rather, there is no such thing any longer; the constitution of madness as a mental illness, at the end of the eighteenth century, affords the evidence of a broken dialogue, posits the separation as already effected, and thrusts into oblivion all those stammered, imperfect words without fixed syntax in which the exchange between madness and reason was made. The language of psychiatry, which is a monologue of reason *about* madness, has been established only on the basis of such a silence.

Foucault, 1965: x–xi

1.1 Introduction

In his usual rather dense style, Foucault encapsulates many of the paradoxes at the root of the study of mental health and illness, and sets the stage for many of the themes which will be of significance in this volume. The centrality of a medical model of insan-ity is asserted, imposing a scientific order onto the profoundly unordered world of the mad. While madness is displayed in the form of a disease, sanity is a constraint, both physical and moral, into which the insane person is confined through pressure of the group, the sane. All this is a construction of the reasoned, and reflects the world of the reasoned; to the insane person, it is an alien landscape.

The situation is yet more complex than Foucault posits here, however, for mental health law, like psychiatry, is also a language 'of reason about madness'. The two lan-guages, law and psychiatry, speak sometimes symbiotically and sometimes in uneasy juxtaposition in the pages which follow. Each are paradigms of rationality in their way, and thus each is faced with the same problem: how to impose order onto madness, a realm which would seem *ex hypothesi* to be lacking order, to be irrational.

This may sound hopelessly abstract, but a few examples will clarify. How exactly, if at all, can mental health (or perhaps more importantly, mental illness) be defined; and are the existing legal and medical definitions clear, consistent with each other, and appropriate? How can we impose reason, rationality, onto the irrational? Does the process of definition not imply a logical structure which cannot be assumed to exist in madness by its very nature? At what point do mad people acquire rights and corresponding responsibilities and authority over what happens to them? Are we content that these languages of mental health and illness remain exclusive of the voices of the people identified as mad, and if not, how are those voices to be included in an understanding of law and policy in the mental health area? And if mental health law and psychiatry are both discourses of reason about madness, what do those discourses tell us about the reasoned people who create them? If, as Foucault claims, the languages of mental health law and psychiatry develop in the silence of those they affect, what do our views of how the insane are understood and when we should intervene in their care tell us, about us, the people who construct the languages about the insane?

These are some of the big issues at the heart of this book. There is no pretence that they will be solved; indeed, it is a fundamental belief of the authors that the purpose of a textbook such as this is not to present solutions, but instead to articulate problems for discussion and investigation.

The questions will be addressed through consideration of the Mental Health Act 1983 as amended (hereinafter, the MHA) and the Mental Capacity Act 2005 as amended (hereinafter, the MCA). By way of introduction, and in very basic terms, the MHA regulates compulsory admission to hospital, treatment for mental disorders in hospital, and, to a limited degree, the control of people with mental disorders in the community. Its key triggering mechanism is a mental disorder (as defined by the MHA, but including mental illnesses, personality disorders, and in some cases, learning disabilities) of sufficient severity (again defined in the MHA) to warrant the compulsion being instituted. The MCA also requires a mental disorder or disability, but its primary triggering factor is instead an individual's incapacity to make a decision at issue. That might well be the result of a mental disorder within the scope of the MHA, but it does not need to be. The MCA is thus about making decisions on behalf of a person lacking capacity, and on its face requires consideration to be given to the wishes and values of that person in deciding what decision should be made. The MHA does not include such a requirement: its agenda, at least on the face of the Act, is providing interventions that are objectively necessary because of an individual's mental disorder. The implementation of the Acts is of course not nearly so stark. No good psychiatrists implementing the MHA will ignore the views of patients, and the judicial decisions under the MCA often show a striking lack of regard for the subjective views of the person for whom a decision is to be taken, but nonetheless, it may be helpful to keep the overall legal bases of the two Acts clear in the discussions that follow.

The first three chapters are essentially introductory, considering how mental disability (here taken to mean both mental health problems, now increasingly referred to as 'psychosocial disabilities', and learning disabilities) is to be understood, and an introduction to how the law is structured overall in this area. Chapters 4 and 5 consider mental capacity both in the realm of general decision-making and when the lack of capacity is used as a justification for depriving an individual of his or her liberty, most frequently in a hospital or care home. Chapter 6 looks at detention under the MHA of people who have not become involved with the criminal system, where Chapters 7 and 8 look at the use of criminal law and related powers to coerce admissions. Chapter 9 considers treatment for mental disorder, and in particular treatment without consent. Chapter 10 follows treatment in the community, and looks at how formal and informal community controls function to govern the lives of people with mental disabilities. Chapters 11 and 12 concern legal safeguards of rights, the former in the form of review tribunals and similar quasi-judicial mechanisms, and the latter in the context of advocacy, both by lawyers and the growing array of lay advocates.

1.2 Who are the insane?

The newspapers would leave us in little doubt. In their eyes, the insane are a threat, a lurking menace in society, a hidden and violent element, which may erupt without notice. The Glasgow Media Group analysed news items about the mentally ill for the month of April 1993, mainly in the tabloid press and on television. It found 323 stories relating to dangerous or violent behaviour by people with mental illness—roughly twice as many as concerned their other categories (stories about harm to self, prescriptive or advice columns related to treatment or care, and stories critical of accepted definitions) combined (Glasgow Media Group, 1996: 47–81). In the subsequent 20 years, little would appear to have changed (see Thornicroft, 2006: ch. 6; Pirkis and Francis, 2012). The portrayals may no doubt be in part a function of the economics of publishing—scaremongering sells newspapers—but the Glasgow Media Group further makes a persuasive case that these representations have their effects on public perceptions. The image is profoundly misleading. The vast bulk of those with psychiatric difficulties are simply not dangerous (Bowden, 1996: 17–22; Thornicroft, 2006: ch. 7). Not only that, but the numbers of persons killed by people with psychiatric problems has been falling since 1970 (Taylor and Gunn, 1999; National Confidential Inquiry into Suicide and Homicide by People with Mental Illness, 2012). The media tends to focus on cases where the assailant was psychotic, or was refusing medical treatment, but these numbers are miniscule. Of homicides committed between 1999 and 2009, only 6 per cent were committed by people with psychosis at the time, or an average of 33 per year. Refusal of medication was even less common—an average of seven assailants per year had refused treatment in the month prior to the homicide: (National Confidential Inquiry, 2012: tables 21, 25).

The images do not stop with violence, however. The mentally ill are perceived as homeless and poor, the deserted of society. There may well be some truth in these allegations in many cases, although much depends on how mental illness is defined, and in particular regarding homelessness, whether substance addiction is considered a mental illness. Certainly, many of those who have been involved with the psychiatric system are poor, although it is a fair question to ask the degree to which this is due to a prejudice of employers against hiring people who have been institutionalised (see Thornicroft, 2006: ch. 3). The image is nonetheless of people who have fallen through the net, tragic figures, lonely, to be pitied rather than valued.

These images cannot tell the whole story. There are countervailing images. When we think of the mentally ill, we might alternatively think of Virginia Woolf, Robert Schumann, Sylvia Plath, or Vincent Van Gogh. The image of the mad artistic genius is in its own way a part of western cultural imagination. The connection between madness and genius excited considerable academic debate in the nineteenth century, and more recently, the American psychologist Kay Redfield Jamison has argued for a correlation between manic depression and artistic genius (Jamison, 1993). The image of the insane person as genius, warranting respect rather than pity or fear, is a refreshing counter-weight to the images of the insane person as dangerous lunatic or homeless vagrant. It becomes possible to ask whether madness is something to be valued rather than dispar-aged. Rather than silencing the mad, should we encourage them to speak?

In the end, all these images must be approached with considerable caution, since the mad artistic genius like the mad killer focuses on the statistically rare exception. The reality in the overwhelming number of cases is likely to be characterised by banality rather than extremes. Current estimates are that mental illness will affect roughly one in six adults in Britain per year, although psychotic illnesses are much less common, closer to one per cent of the population. Depression alone will affect roughly half of women and a quarter of men before the age of 70 (Department of Health, 1998a: 10). This would suggest that it is not appropriate to think condescendingly in terms of 'them', but rather, somewhat more humbly, of 'us'. The frequency suggested by the statistics would suggest that any generalisation may well mislead as much as it informs.

That is perhaps particularly important in so far as it challenges the popular sense that everyone with mental difficulties must somehow be the same. Different difficul-ties affect people differently. It is simply wrong, for example, to expect that people with mental illness will also have intellectual limitations. The fact that an individual is pro-foundly depressed or hearing voices, for example, does not mean they are unable to understand complicated information and process it at a reasonably sophisticated level. Certainly some people with mental illness are not intellectually high achievers, but others are very bright indeed, and most are somewhere in the middle. The experience of people affected would suggest that the stereotype associating mental illness with lack of mental ability remains widespread, a depressing comment on how far society has yet to come in understanding both mental illness and developmental disabilities.

A similar warning ought to be made regarding developmental or learning disabili-ties. Frequently, one hears the phrase 'mental age' used regarding people in this group. It is at best a caricature. People develop in different ways, and at different rates, and the person 'with a mental age of 6' may well have little in common with a 6-year-old child. To refer to a 25-year-old woman in this way is unhelpful: in a very real sense, she is still a 25-year-old woman. Rather than to identify her with the child she manifestly is not, it is far more sensible to consider her actual situation, understanding, and abilities, and proceed accordingly.

Romanticisation of mental illness, whatever image is adopted, is unlikely to be helpful. That said, it is surely appropriate to provide some sort of starting point to understanding what it feels like to be mentally ill. The writings of those who have experienced mental illness first hand provide invaluable reading to the student beginner in the area. A selection is provided in the bibliography (Mays, 1995; Hart, 1995; Dunn *et al.*, 1996; Jamison, 1996; Lewis, 2002; Pegler, 2002; Read and Reynolds, 1996; Styron, 1990, Cockburn and Cockburn, 2011). These readings drive home the point that mental illness, particularly in its more extreme forms, can be a profoundly unsettling and unpleasant experience. Consider U. A. Fanthorpe's description (1996: 52–4) of the experience of depression:

> Again I find myself waking miserably early, even before the summer birds; again I find music unspeakably painful; again my speech becomes slow, and my arms seem grotesquely long; again I'm afraid to go out, because people will see at a glance that there's something wrong, and shun me; I can't face the garden because, although in one part of my brain I know the blackbirds are just making their usual evening calls, I'm convinced that the cats are after them and that it's my fault; above all, my vocabulary shrinks to such an extent that the only word I'm really at home with is 'sorry'.
>
> When I'm badly depressed I long above all things to be a prisoner. I imagine this as a life where you don't make choices, where the pattern of life is plain and involuntary. Life in depression is like this anyway, but it retains the illusion of choice. If you had to do the sad things you are doing because someone had ordered that you should, indeed because you'd deserved it, the despair might (you think) go.

Linda Hart (1995: 19) described the sensations accompanying her schizophrenia as follows:

> The top half of my head feels quite light but the thread that runs down from my head to my stomach is soaked in a deep despair. Maggots in my belly multiply. Rotting flesh. Want to drink bleach to cleanse them or a sharp knife to cut them out. They told me I needed a psychiatrist and not a medical surgeon back in September. They said Graham [the psychiatrist] would get rid of the maggots but he hasn't.

These are not pretty images, and one would be inhuman not to feel considerable sympathy for the individuals affected by these experiences. Yet sympathy is a double-edged sword, for it can easily lead to a paternalist impulse to intervene whether the individual likes it or not, 'for their own good'. The result is a risk of marginalising the person we intend to help, and the reinforcement of the gulf of silence of which Foucault speaks.

This is not merely a civil rights point, nor an abstract issue of discourse construction. It is also a practical point: if intervention is to be successful in the long term, its subject must in the end be supportive of the intervention. In the environment of intrusive surveillance in a psychiatric facility it is possible to force a patient to take drugs they do not wish to take. It is much more difficult outside that environment, and if the patient is not convinced at that time of the continuing benefits of medication, it seems unlikely that he or she will continue taking it.

This marginalisation further pre-supposes a gap between the individual and his or her disorder, or a 'real' person who has been subverted by the disorder into someone else of an unknown character. Such an articulation is contained in the following passage, in which an author describes his first interview with Leslie, the mother of a mentally ill man [Karp, 2001: 3–4]:

> Near the beginning of our first conversation she said that 'so much has happened in three years that I don't even know where to begin…It's overwhelming.' There was, though, one thing that she absolutely wanted to bring up right away and have me understand. […] She went on to explain that 'Mike has the potential for violence. And…because I know this is being recorded, it's really important to me for you to know that he is innately a very, very sweet and kind person. But [because of] the disease he gets very paranoid. His disease has made him a danger to others.… I mean, he wouldn't even step on a bug, you know? But this illness is so [awful] and he has attacked his brother and attacked his sister.' Throughout our nearly ten hours of talk, Leslie repeatedly sought assurance that I would not confuse Mike with his disease.

Such a clear division is presupposed in much of the popular and professional understanding of mental disorder, and articulates the experiences of many people affected by mental disorders. It is further implied in a medical model of mental illness, where imagery in pharmaceutical advertisements, for example, will frequently refer to the drug as allowing for the return of a person, previously 'lost'. At the same time, other accounts call into question whether the disorder is readily distinguishable from the person with the disorder. This ambiguity is apparent in Marie Cardinal's description (1996: 108):

> But for my children, I might let myself go completely, stop fighting, perhaps, for the struggle against the Thing was exhausting. More and more, I was tempted by the medication that delivered me to a nothingness which was dull and sweet.

In this articulation, it is the medication, the alternative to the disorder, which is a void, a nullity. The disorder itself is in Cardinal's reality. This image of mental illness as constructive of self is similarly evident in Sheila MacLeod's description (1996: 81) of her anorexia:

> Two facts emerge immediately from this résumé. The first is that I felt my battle to be with authority, whether in the form of teachers, matrons, parents, or even nature itself. The second is that, up until this point, I was winning. It seems to me that anorexia nervosa acts as a metaphor for all the problems of adolescence. But instead of meeting each problem separately and assessing it for what it is, the anorexic thinks she has a master plan, designed to solve them all at one stroke. She is convinced that it works; it can't fail. It is like a dream come true. It is euphoria.
>
> When I first came across Szasz's dictum, 'Mental illness is a self-enhancing deception, self-promoting strategy', I considered it to be a harsh judgement on a fellow creature. But when I substituted 'anorexia nervosa' for 'mental illness' I could see the truth in what Szasz was saying, and realize at the same time that his judgement was not so harsh. After all, if the self is felt to be nothing, any strategy adopted to enhance or promote it, desperate though it may be, is a step towards what most of us would consider to be health, and an action necessary for survival. The anorexic's skinny body proclaims, 'I have won; I am someone now.'

In this view, the disorder is intrinsic to the self and constitutive of who the individual is. As such, it need not necessarily be viewed in simplistically negative or undesirable terms. Lewis notes (2000: xv):

> If you can cope with the internal nuclear winter of depression and come through it without committing suicide—the disease's most serious side effect—then, in my experience, depression can be a great friend. It says: the way you've been living is unbearable, it's not for you. And it teaches you slowly how to live in a way that suits you infinitely better. If you don't listen, of course, it comes back and knocks you out even harder the next time, until you get the point.
>
> Over twenty years I've discovered that my depression isn't a random chemical event but has an emotional logic which makes it a very accurate guide for me.

A similarly complex vision regarding schizophrenia is discussed by Chadwick (1997). This is not to suggest that either Chadwick or Lewis rejoiced in their disorders. It is instead to suggest that a simplistically dismissive view of the values associated with the disorder may deny an important aspect of the experience of the individual patient.

This view of mental illness as intrinsic to self receives judicial acknowledgement in the case of *B* v *Croydon District Health Authority* (1994) 22 BMLR 13 (HC). That case involved a patient suffering from a personality disorder, not anorexia, which nonetheless manifested itself in the refusal of food to the point of near self-starvation. The primary issue before the trial court was whether the patient had the capacity to consent to treatment, in this case feeding. Thorpe J (as he then was) cites (at p. 19) an expert witness, a forensic psychiatrist, as identifying the relation between the individual and the personality disorder as a factor for the court's consideration:

> The third feature is the patient's necessity to control her own internal world and her relationship with others. In a pathological way, she uses maladapted methods to control distress in herself and to control others around her. Her need to use abnormal coping mechanisms stems from her abnormal development. In relation to this feature, Dr Eastman poses the question: Have we the right to remove the only mechanism that remains to her without the prospect of being able to help her to cope in other ways?

The court gives considerable credence to this concern (at p. 22):

> Here the patient has developed in adolescence an individual personality which can be medically classified as disordered. But the disorder is the person and we must question the justification of depriving such a person of all that is available without the prospect of being able to help her to cope in other ways.

In this formulation, intervention will affect the core of who the individual is. This raises an obvious ethical problem: should the state apparatus be used to enforce this kind of personal alteration?

Various points may be made about this approach. First, the comments occur in an appraisal of capacity. While a similar logic may ethically apply to other branches of mental health law, capacity is a field with its own idiosyncrasies: see Chapters 4 and 5. Secondly, such nuanced assessments are rare in judicial reasoning, and indeed the decision of Thorpe J on capacity was expressly doubted by the Court of Appeal, albeit in comments that are summary and obiter: see [1995] 1 All ER 689. As will be seen in the rest of this book, judges much more frequently uncritically adopt medical approaches, and the factual tensions involve assessments of medical testimony. Normally, and with the important exception of tribunals concerning detention under MHA, courts fail even to hear testimony from the person with mental disability.

Finally, while the relation between the individual and the disorder was clearly a matter considered by Thorpe J, and a factor in his decision that B had the capacity to consent to treatment, it did not in the end preclude him from ordering the provision of tube-feeding as treatment, pursuant to s. 63 of MHA: see further Chapter 9.4.1. In that discussion, there is little of the nuanced consideration of the ethics of forced intervention on the patient.

Even in cases such as *B* v *Croydon*, therefore, the centrality of the disorder to the individual is at best a factor which raises ethical issues regarding intervention; it does not necessarily determine whether intervention is ethically justified. On the question of compulsion, there are a variety of ethical positions. At one extreme, it might be claimed that intervention, and particularly intervention over the patient's objection, is rarely if ever justified on the basis that it constitutes extraordinarily intrusive meddling with an individual's personality and psyche. At the other, it might be argued that intervention is justified on the basis that after the intervention, some people are grateful (this 'thank-you theory' will be examined in more detail in Chapter 6.2.2, in the context of civil confinement), or that the symptoms of the condition are significantly improved by the treatment. Intermediate positions are also possible. Presumably, the wishes of the affected individual may be a significant factor; it would seem positively cruel not to support an individual who wishes to be free of the trait. Thorpe J distinguishes between alterations to an individual's normal personality, and a situation where the disorder is intrinsic to the personality. In *B* v *Croydon*, there was 'no overlay of illness upon the patient's norm' (p. 22). This might be distinguished from a situation where a medically defined variation appears in an already existing personality, where intervention might be justified to restore the pre-existing personality. The difficulty with this approach, of course, is to determine how long the disorder must exist before it becomes integral to personality. In addition, it does not solve the question of what to do when the cure will remove more than the disorder. Marie Cardinal's reference to a 'nothingness which was dull and sweet' suggests a cure removing not only the disorder, but also other parts of her nature as well.

1.3 Mental illness and medicine: A complex relationship

Students of mental health law are often quick to adopt a medicalised model of mental illness, that it is appropriately the realm of a specialised, medical practitioner. Certainly, there is compelling evidence to associate biomedical factors with mental illnesses, but the evidence shows not merely the strengths, but also the limitations of a medical approach. Schizophrenia may be used as an example.

Contrary to popular usage, schizophrenia does not in the overwhelming number of cases have to do with a so-called 'split personality'. It is instead a psychotic disorder: fundamental to its nature is a fractured relationship to reality. This is typically manifested in hallucinations, particularly hearing voices. An interference in the thinking process is common (i.e. 'delusions'), where the individual believes that others are controlling their thoughts, or know what they are thinking. Similarly, a loss of autonomy may be experienced, where strange physical sensations may be felt, or movements occur without the patient's will. A lack of emotional engagement with surroundings, poverty of or minimal speech, lack of drive, lack of pleasure, and poor attention may also appear, generally gradually over a longer period than the earlier symptoms.

Schizophrenia is chosen as an example to explore the medical model in mental illness for a variety of reasons. In the popular imagination, such psychotic disorders are viewed as particularly clear cases of mental illness: people who hear hallucinatory voices are at the centre of the popular understanding of madness and requiring medical treatment in a way that people who are overactive as children or who are depressed, for example, are (rightly or wrongly) not necessarily viewed in the popular imagination as mentally ill, or as medical cases. They are also cases where a medical model seems a relatively good fit: we can conceptualise what a 'cure' for schizophrenia would look like. Schizophrenia is also an example that medicine itself claims: where there are still debates about the role of doctors in the care or control of people with personality disorder, for example, but schizophrenia is taken by psychiatry to be part of its core role. In these ways, therefore, this is an example of the medical model at its strongest.

There is compelling evidence that genetics plays a factor in the occurrence of schizophrenia. The relevant studies are summarised by Thomas (1997: pp. 31–6). If genetics were the sole cause of schizophrenia, one would expect the identical twin of a person with schizophrenia also to have the disorder, since identical twins have the same genetic code. Studies do indicate a much higher probability of this occurring. Thomas cites a study by McGue *et al.*, for example, showing first cousins of people diagnosed as schizophrenic as having a 1.6 per cent chance of developing the disorder, where identical twins of schizophrenics have a 44.3 per cent chance (Thomas, 1997: 33, citing McGue *et al.*, 1985). That is an impressive difference.

While there would thus appear to be a genetic susceptibility, it is not the whole story, as even in the identical twins, sometimes the disorder manifests itself and sometimes not. The reasons for this are not clear. There are biomedical theories, reflected in the medical treatments for the disorder. Anti-psychotic medication tends to inhibit chemical receptors in the brain. Originally, the drugs targeted the uptake of a dopamine, but more recent drugs affect a wider variety of chemicals in the brain. Sometimes (but not always) these drugs are effective at reducing symptoms, although the reasons for this are not yet understood. That suggests, at best, a partial explanation of why symptoms develop. Neuro-developmental models of schizophrenia also exist (Thomas, 1997: 39–44). Here, the idea is that for any of a variety of reasons, be it maternal illness, birth injury, disease, or other factor, an abnormality in the brain occurs and schizophrenia is the result. This, like the genetic factors discussed, seems to apply for a subgroup of the schizophrenic population. In the end, we are left with theories, some more promising than others, but none in the end able to offer a comprehensive explanation.

The search for validation of the concept of schizophrenia can be understood in professional terms: geneticists, neurologists, and medical bio-chemists each attempting to find an explanation for the condition, based on the training they have received and the intellectual structures of their sub-disciplines. Social scientists have made similar enquiries, based on social science methodologies. Reflecting the history of social science research generally, social causes, social reactions, and social constructions of schizophrenia have all been identified. For reviews of the literature, see Thomas (1997: 51–6). Regarding social causes, sociologists have identified class, poverty, and social disintegration as correlatives of schizophrenia. As schizophrenia is geographically centred in inner cities, sociological debate developed around the question of whether it is caused by increased stress in such environments. The alternative explanation, of course, is that the onset of schizophrenia precipitated a fall in socio-economic status, resulting in a disproportionate move by people with the disorder to the inner cities. The social solutions are thus as problematic as the medical ones. In the end, we are left with a variety of partial explanations.

Consistent with this, people affected by mental disorders will often understand their experience in a multi-faceted way. William Styron, for example, writes (1996: 57):

> I shall never learn what 'caused' my depression, as no one will ever learn about their own. To be able to do so will likely for ever prove to be an impossibility, so complex are the intermingled factors of abnormal chemistry, behaviour and genetics. Plainly, multiple components are involved—perhaps three or four, most probably more, in fathomless permutations.

Certainly, those with mental health problems often receive medical attention. Usually this is voluntary on their part, but at the same time, there may be an element of ambivalence to it, even when the treatments work relatively according to plan, and thus alleviate the condition. U. A. Fanthorpe describes (1996: 52) this ambivalence as follows:

> When depression hits me, the last thing I want to do is see the doctor, because it seems hard to define anything 'wrong'. When I have finally made myself go, and the doctor has slotted me back into a medical definition again, the reactions are odd: relief at knowing where I am again and what I have to do, but at the same time resentment that this has happened again, the same symptoms, prescriptions, general fears, and dreariness.

John Bentley Mays describes (1995: xiv, xv) the medicalisation of his condition, in his own eyes as much as those of the doctors, more expressly in terms of alienation, reflecting the Foucauldean vision with which this chapter commenced:

> Yet the forensic language I invoke springs from nothing in my own heart or mind, is no more original than my routine complaining. Rather, it slides down on the page out of clinical case histories and medical records, a portrait of the *nobody*, nameless, extinguished, who is the topic of the technical literature on depression.
>
> I have read the literature now that provides me with terms of order, pretending to study the technical language of depression—but really studying the way of looking, of writing, embodied in such texts. It is a poetry of the scalpel's quick slash, the spurt and stanching of blood, clamping back successive layers of skin, fat, muscle, the probe with a point of

gleaming metal of the nothingness at the centre. Writing myself up as a *case*, I experience myself, pleasurably, obscenely, as object. The former exacerbation of subjectivity is gone, now that the cyst known as *soul* is lanced, and all that remains is flesh, killed by the invasion of medical power, stiffening, cooling.

A similar ambivalence can be seen in attitudes to medication itself. Gwyneth Lewis (2002: 72–3) describes her experience of anti-depressant medication as follows:

After three weeks the anti-depressants began to kick in. These affected the quality of my depression but without changing its nature. What they gave me was some psychic space, a small but crucial distance between me and the horrors. Like a line of crustacean riot police, they pushed back the nightmares clamouring for my attention. This gave me a narrow cordon sanitaire in which to move, some room to breathe. The mental crowds were still there, of course, but they had less power over me, as if the anarchists had turned into paparazzi. The lightning of intrusive cameras was blinding, but at least I was free to move out of their way and into the foyer.

Fanthorpe, Mays, and Lewis describe continuing and successful relations with their respective medical advisors, and acknowledge the benefits they have received from medication: there is no element of sour grapes here. At the same time, they display a real sense of ambivalence to a medical model of their experience, and a resistance to any simplistic association between drugs and cure.

This is significant not merely as an insight into the way those in the affected group perceive their condition; it is also significant because of the way the world, or at least social policy, reacts to this uncertain relationship with the medical model. The silence between the insane and the rational is becoming further enforced, as the failure to follow medical advice is increasingly perceived as an unacceptable act of deviance. The response can take several forms. While mental capacity—the practical ability to make decisions—is not lost simply because an individual has a mental illness or developmental disability, it has long been a matter of concern that disagreement with a doctor may trigger a finding that the psychiatric patient lacks capacity to make treatment decisions. This generally has the effect of removing from the patient the legal right to refuse treatment (see further Chapter 4.4.2). Inpatients detained under the MHA lose the right to consent to most psychiatric treatment whether they have capacity to consent or not (see further Chapter 9.4 and 9.5). This view seems to be a non-negotiable element in government policy. Introducing a process of re-assessment of the MHA in 1998, the then Minister of State for Health, Paul Boateng spoke of the 'responsibility' of patients to comply with the care they were offered: 'Non compliance can no longer be an option when appropriate care in appropriate settings is in place. I have made it clear to the field that this is not negotiable.' (Press release, 22 Sept 98, contained in Department of Health and Welsh Office 1999a: App. C, para. 11). In the White Paper two years later, the point was only slightly softened: 'Care and treatment should involve the least degree of compulsion that is consistent with ensuring that the objectives of the [care] plan are met.' (Department of Health and Home Office, 2000: para. 2.11) Patients were to be as free as is possible, it would seem, as long as they did what they were told. Consistent with this, the legislation finally passed at the end of this process of reform in 2007 did not alter the MHA rules allowing compulsory treatment in hospital. It did introduce community treatment orders. People under such orders still have the right to refuse treatment provided in the community, but can often be recalled to hospital and forcibly treated there if they exercise that right. Given this power, it is fair to wonder whether the consent to treatment in the community of people on these orders necessarily represents their will or desires.

This approach is problematic. Is it reasonable or appropriate to expect unswerving adherence to treatment in a professional context perceived by the patient as alienating? Will this breakdown not be exacerbated if the doctor/patient relationship is not as successful as it appears to have been in the cases of Mays, Lewis, and Fanthorpe? Can the enforcement of treatment be justifiable, when all the indications are that psychiatry is not an exact science? Should the law really be used to enforce compliance with treatment when such levels of uncertainty exist? Many patients embrace the treatments that medicine has to offer, but others are content to live with their disability, even when a treatment exists. The Hearing Voices Network, for example, assists people who hear voices to live with their voices and to get on with their lives (see James, 2001). Many do so, quite successfully. Whether their refusal to take medication is the result of the adverse effects of the medication, a view that the 'cure' affects their self-perception, or because they view their disorder as an integral part of who they are, is it obvious that their views should be subordinated to a medical vision of their condition?

Students new to mental health law sometimes perceive mental illness as something which can be cured permanently, rather like measles, where with appropriate treatment the patient is free of the malady forever. This is often a misleading view particularly in the case of serious mental illness. The better image is of a chronic condition, sometimes controllable but often recurring even if the individual complies with prescribed medication, which may affect the individual for much of their life. This again has social policy implications: if intervention is to be enforced on the individual, is it to be enforced in perpetuity? This seems extremely intrusive to the life of the individual affected, and must therefore be approached with considerable hesitancy.

Viewed in this light, mental health law and policy might be seen as dispiriting subjects. Those affected by mental illness often face a selection of possible courses of action, none of which on balance is particularly appealing. Continuation with the experience of disorder may not be an attractive option, and medicine may either provide an incomplete answer, or entail adverse effects perceived by the individual to be as unpleasant as the disorder. Alteration of the social, cultural, and environmental factors that may contribute to the malady is extremely difficult to achieve in practice. Forced intervention, be it through confinement in hospital, enforced medication, or control of the individual in the community, seems both intrusive and not obviously effective except perhaps in the very short term. One of the difficult things for new students in this area to understand fully is that here, as with many areas of law, there will often be no good solution possible for a client. Instead, there will be a selection of problematic or downright bad possibilities from which a choice must be made.

At the same time, it would be wrong to assume that all persons with mental health difficulties live miserable lives. Again, generalisations are likely to be unhelpful here, but like most of the rest of us, it is reasonable to understand this client group as happy with some parts of their lives, unhappy with others, having some good times and some less good times. While it is inappropriate for the student of mental health law to ignore the realities of the life imposed by the mental condition, it would be equally inappropriate to focus on the mental disorder in a way which obliterates the remainder of the life of the individual.

1.4 The statutory definition of mental disorder and the scope of the MHA

The MHA purports to govern 'the reception, care and treatment of mentally disordered patients, the management of their property and other related matters' (s. 1(1)). The reference to management of property and related matters is a relic from the past, as such matters are now governed by the MCA (see further Chapter 4). Now, the MHA is primarily concerned with hospital admissions (particularly compulsory admissions) and medical treatment of 'mentally disordered patients' and, to a lesser degree, community treatment of such individuals. The phrase 'mental disorder' is thus of importance, as it defines the scope of the MHA.

'Mental disorder' is defined as 'any disorder or disability of the mind' (s. 1(2)). It thus includes the array of mental illnesses such as schizophrenia, depression, bipolar disorder (formerly called 'manic depression') and the like, personality disorders, and learning disabilities (although these last are subject to special provisions in some cases: see further 1.4.1). Notwithstanding this broad definition, dependence on alcohol or drugs is defined not to be a mental disorder (s. 1(3)).

The definition in s. 1(2) was introduced in its present form by the MHA 2007, and there is as yet no jurisprudence on its breadth, but the case law from the earlier legislation suggests it will be accorded a broad meaning by the courts. The Mental Health Act Code of Practice (the Code) (an extensive collection of guidance for practitioners under the MHA) encourages professionals to determine mental disorder 'in accordance with good clinical practice and accepted standards of what constitutes such a disorder or disability.' (Department of Health, 2008: para. 3.2). This suggests a medical frame of reference, and that is consistent with the requirements of the European Convention on Human Rights (ECHR) when the category is used as a justification for detention. For deprivation of liberty of 'persons of unsound mind' under Article 5(1)(e) of the ECHR, *Winterwerp* v *the Netherlands* required that a 'true mental disorder' be shown by 'objective medical expertise' (Application no. 6301/73, judgment of 24 October 1979, (A/33) (1979–80) 2 EHRR 387, para 39). This can be juxtaposed to earlier English jurisprudence which held the phrase 'mental illness', then a sub-category of mental disorder in the MHA, to be not medical, but rather 'ordinary words of the English language [which] should be construed in the way that ordinary sensible people would construe them': *W* v *L* [1974] QB 711 at 719. After *Winterwerp* and subsequent ECHR jurisprudence, the approach in *W* v *L* must be considered doubtful. Where a broader range of perspectives may be relevant to determining whether a mental disorder is sufficiently severe to warrant compulsory intervention such as detention (see, e.g., *R (Ryan)* v *Trent Mental Health Review Tribunal* [1992] COD 157), and while the evidence of doctors should of course be held up to appropriate scrutiny, s. 1(2) does appear to create a diagnostic threshold, to be determined according to medical criteria.

The use of a medical approach to the definitions of mental disorder is problematic for a variety of reasons. The first question is *which* medical approach? There are two primary medical nosologies of mental illness. The one in use primarily in North America is the Diagnostic and Statistical Manual of Disorders, currently in its fourth edition (DSM-IV-TR), published by the American Psychiatric Association. Most of the rest of the world relies primarily on the World Health Organization standard, the International Classification of Diseases and Related Health Problems, currently in its tenth edition (ICD-10), which contains a classification of mental disorders in Chapter 5. Both are currently under revision, with a new ICD expected in 2015 and DSM in 2013. Previous versions of these nosologies had been converging, but initial indications suggest that the new versions may have significant differences, particularly in the areas of autistic spectrum disorders and personality disorders. The development of these diagnostic structures is governed to a considerable degree by medical evidence, but they are also both the products of negotiation, mainly within the medical professions, and will to some degree, at least, reflect the diverse interests and political factors that come to bear in any comparably complex process of negotiation. Occasionally, these become publicly visible, as in the removal of homosexuality from the DSM in 1974 (see discussion, e.g., in Lewes, 1988: ch. 10) (homosexuality was not removed from the ICD until 1993), or the inclusion of self-defeating personality disorder and premenstrual dysphoric disorder into DSM-IV, diagnoses that were perceived to stigmatise women (Caplan, 1995). More frequently, they are internal debates that do not attract public attention; but they still exist.

These debates serve as reminders that even within the medical realm, definitions are contested. The nosologies are used in diverse contexts, ranging from identifying and defining topics of research to identifying disorders on forms required for reimbursement from health insurance companies. It is not obvious that their legal function as one of the borderlines between compulsion and non-compulsion is a significant factor in the development of the medical classificatory structures. That raises a question: if this is not specifically what they are designed for, should they be used this way? But if not, how should mental disorder be defined?

1.4.1 Learning disability

For some provisions of the MHA, a learning disability will be considered a mental disorder only if it is 'associated with abnormally aggressive or seriously irresponsible conduct on his part' (s. 1(2A)). These provisions include:

- compulsory admission for treatment under s. 3 of the MHA (but not for assessment under s. 2, so compulsory detention for up to 28 days may be possible even if a learning disability is not associated with the abnormally aggressive or seriously irresponsible conduct: see further Chapter 6.3.1);

- MHA guardianship under s. 7;
- community treatment orders under Part 2 of the MHA;
- most psychiatric admissions under Part 3 of the MHA of people either accused or convicted of criminal offences.

Learning disability is defined as 'a state of arrested or incomplete development of the mind which includes a significant impairment of intelligence and social functioning' (s. 1(4)). The Code advises that this involves 'a significant impairment of the normal process of maturation of intellectual and social development that occurs during childhood and adolescence' (para. 34.4). People who experience similar limitations that originate after maturity—people whose impairment results from injury as an adult, or who have some forms of dementia, for example—are not within the scope of s. 1(4), and so do not have a learning disability. Such people do still have a mental disorder, but are thus not within the protections of s. 1(2A). Doctrinally, it is not obvious why such categories of people, who may present in notably similar ways to people with learning disabilities, are treated differently by the statute.

The Code notes that there is no defined limit in the statute as to how these terms are to be interpreted, and in particular there is no specific IQ score that determines the matter. Instead, it promotes 'reliable and careful assessment' of the impairment of intelligence, and 'reliable and recent observation' to determine the extent of social competence (para. 34.4). Little further guidance is provided as to how this determination is to be conducted, leaving a considerable degree of professional discretion.

The leading case on the phrase 'abnormally aggressive or seriously irresponsible conduct' is *Re F (Mental Health Act: Guardianship)* [2000] 1 FLR 192. That case involved a young woman nearing her 18th birthday. She had lived all her life, along with seven younger siblings, with her parents in a home where she had allegedly been exposed to chronic neglect, including uncleanliness in the home, sexual abuse by visitors to the home, and the failure of her parents to provide appropriate standards of parenting. All the children including F were removed from the home under a family law emergency protection order.

The remainder of the children were dealt with through family court wardship proceedings, but because of her age, the local social services decided to apply for a guardianship order for F, under s. 7 of the MHA, an application which fell within the scope of what is now s. 1(2A). There was no doubt that F had arrested or incomplete development of mind; the question was whether this resulted in aggressive or seriously irresponsible conduct. Social services took the view that F's desire to return home was sufficient to meet this standard.

It is not difficult to see why they took this view. To them, a desire to return to what they clearly perceived as an inadequate home, a home indeed in which abuse was alleged to have taken place, must indeed have appeared grossly irresponsible. The Court of Appeal did not see it that way. The legislative history of the section suggested that guardianship was perceived by the drafters as a restriction on civil liberties, and this suggested a restrictive reading of the conduct criterion. On this point the court was not guided by the professionals' view. Instead, it was swayed by F's account of her actions, as reported by the trial judge (196):

> What she said to me was that she wanted to go home. Her father is getting old, he is ill and he is dying soon. She has lived with him for 17 years and wants to be with him. She was happy at home, had plenty to do, went to the park. Her mother took her. She had always been with her mother and father and brothers and sisters and wanted to get back.

In the view both of the trial court and the Court of Appeal, this was not irresponsible. There was no question that the social services authorities had acted in good faith and with the best of motives, but their reading of the facts was markedly different from that of F—a reminder of the division between professional and client to which Foucault refers.

It should be noted that these restrictions apply only to learning disability under the MHA. A learning disability that renders an individual unable to make a competent decision may still be within the scope of the MCA, and mechanisms put in place to make the decision on his or her behalf (see further Chapters 4 and 5).

1.4.2 Dependence on alcohol or drugs

Section 1(3) of the MHA provides that 'dependence on alcohol or drugs is not considered a disorder or disability of the mind.' It should be noted that dependence on alcohol or drugs does not preclude an individual from being dealt with under the MHA for other subsisting mental disorders, merely because they are accompanied by a dependence on alcohol or drugs. It states instead that the dependence itself is not a mental disorder. That said, the existence of a mental disorder cannot be used to detain someone to control their use of alcohol or drugs, even if there is some concern that such drug use may eventually result in the individual ceasing to take medication for their mental disorder (*CM* v *Derbyshire Healthcare NHS Foundation Trust* [2011] UKUT 129 (AAC)).

The exclusions created raise the question of when conduct is considered to be mad, and when bad. The fact that dependence on drugs is not to be considered a mental illness does not make that behaviour acceptable. If it constitutes a crime, as much of the behaviour closely related to drug dependency will, it will instead be categorised as criminal.

Prior to 2007, the exclusions also included 'promiscuity or other immoral conduct' and 'sexual deviancy'. These can be understood as flowing from the historical experience of detention as a way of enforcing moral standards, in particular onto the poor. An ambiguity between socially inappropriate behaviour and institutional control may be seen in the Mental Deficiency Act 1913, one of the precursors to the MHA, where 'feeble-mindedness' was not clearly distinguished from immoral behaviour. Feeble-minded unmarried woman giving birth while on poor relief for example were to be subjected to confinement in an asylum, (Mental Deficiency Act 1913, s. 2(b)(vi)) and there are indications that some local authorities required little further proof of mental status, once the fact of the birth on poor relief was discovered (Zedner, 1991: 275). This was consistent with Victorian and Edwardian social policy (see Bartlett, 1999). The rise of the welfare state and the creation of the NHS was intended to constitute a break from this tradition of moral judgment, and the exclusions, originally introduced in the MHA 1959 and expanded in 1983, were to draw a clear line between moral governance, which was outside the MHA, and treatment of illness, which was within.

Promiscuity, immoral conduct, and sexual deviancy disappeared as exclusions in 2007. The government took the view that the mischief they were to remedy was no longer an issue, and were concerned that people were being refused treatment because their underlying disorder manifests itself as sexual deviance (Department of Health, 2006a: A1, 3). While this may be true, it does re-open the ambiguities between mental disorder and bad conduct, particularly in cases of some personality disorders, where the diagnostic criteria are intimately bound up with immoral conduct. Is a serial paedophile a criminal or a person with mental disorder? The removal of sexual deviancy from the list of exclusions makes it easier to define such individuals as persons with mental disorder. Lest that be viewed as a 'light option' relative to criminal sanction, it might be noted that with a criminal sanction, the accused is likely to get a release date set by the court, reflecting the offence committed. That will not occur if he or she is admitted under the MHA. Indeed, it is quite possible that they will be held to have criminal responsibility and therefore first be sent to prison, and then admitted under the MHA as their release date approaches. The changes to s. 1(3) may thus represent an extension of state power over these individuals, rather than a reduction.

1.4.3 Mental disorder, compulsion, and race

The MHA does not affect all groups equally. Black people are just under 3 per cent of the population of England, but they represent almost 10 per cent of psychiatric inpatients, and more than 15 per cent of people on community treatment orders (Care Quality Commission, 2013). Notwithstanding a government policy from 2005 to reduce the prevalence of black people in psychiatric hospitals (Department of Health, 2005b), admission rates actually increased overall, and for almost all sub-categories of black people from 2005 through 2008 (Commission for Healthcare Audit and Inspection, 2008: table 2). Black patients were, further, more likely to be found unable to consent to treatment, held in more secure settings, and kept in hospital for longer periods of time than white people.

The reasons for this are hotly disputed. Singh *et al.* have published a systematic review of the literature (that is, a publication synthesising and analysing the reliability of the range of empirical studies) relating to race and detention under the MHA (Singh *et al.*, 2007). They identify five categories of explanation in the literature:

- 'Patient-related' explanations: these argue that black and minority ethnic (BME) patients have 'higher rates of psychoses, are perceived as being at greater risk of violence and disturbed behaviour, have higher rates of co-morbid drug use and have greater delays in help-seeking'.

- Illness-related explanations: these argue that psychiatric illness manifests itself differently in BME populations, 'with more challenging behaviour or violence, association with offending behaviour, poorer adherence [to medication] and greater denial of illness'.

- Service-related explanations: these involve poor early recognition procedures for BME populations, lower likelihood of early referral for treatment, greater contact with the police as a route of admission, and systemic racial stereotyping and discrimination in the mental health and social services.

- Cultural explanations: these included 'a mixed set of explanations ranging from cultural differences in explanatory models of illness, stigma of mental illness in BME communities, alienation from and mistrust of services due to negative perceptions and experiences, and unwillingness to seek help.'

- Overall racial stereotyping, labelling and discrimination as explanations: These factors in turn led to a breakdown of trust of BME service users in professionals, and increased perceptions by professionals of BME people as violent and as a result of stereotyping failing to provide services of suitable standard.

Singh's analysis finds that none of these have sufficient systematic study, or the studies do not have adequate evidential power, to be probative at this stage. It is also fair to note that the descriptions are not neatly delineated. For example, 'delay in help-seeking' as an explanation begs the question of why the delay occurs. Is it really because the individual does not understand their situation (a patient-related or illness-related explanation), or is it that he or she feels that engagement with the system will create more problems than it solves, as a result of racial stereotyping and discrimination? The explanations are further not mutually exclusive: they may all, or some, be contributors to the differential representation.

It would seem that there is little evidence to suggest that BME populations are at higher risk of serious mental illness in their countries of origin (Fearon and Morgan, 2006), suggesting that the increased incidence is not simply a biological matter. Social factors may however be relevant. There is evidence that mental disorders may for example be affected by social deprivation (see, e.g., Stilo *et al.*, 2012), and if this is the case it would affect representation of BME groups disproportionately (Morgan and Hutchinson, 2010). It is not obvious that they can be a complete explanation, however. Singh's study notes that rates of compulsory detention increase disproportionately for BME populations over time, suggesting that the relationship between BME populations and mental health service providers deteriorates over time. That would suggest that satisfaction with services in this population is a relevant issue.

1.5 Other interests: Mental health care

People with mental disabilities or disorders are of course the client group who are the objects of the psychiatric system, and thus of mental health law, but they are not the only people with interests in the delivery of mental health care. Mental health care is delivered in a system, in part based in the National Health Service, in part elsewhere in the state social services network, and in part in the private sector. A detailed survey of the range of interests operating in this system, and the sociology of how those interests interact, is beyond the scope of this chapter; but a brief survey of some of the players will provide an indication of the complexity of the influences on mental health policymaking.

The prime medical personnel involved in the care of the mentally ill are, of course, nurses and doctors, primarily general practitioners and psychiatrists. These people work in conjunction with social workers, psychologists, community mental health nurses, health visitors, social service agencies and, particularly in recent years, health administrators in the administration of the mental health system.

It is abundantly clear that the vast bulk of these people have a real and honest concern about the people in their care. The power-hungry doctor who has no interest in his patients but merely a desire to control may make good television drama, but it has little to do with the reality of the individuals involved in the mental health system. That said, the individuals listed are all professionals, operating in an administrative system. Vast sociological literatures exist on the way people operate in such bureaucracies, and strive to enhance professional status. The tensions may be within individual professions: psychiatrists, for example, have tended historically to feel undervalued among medical specialisms. The tensions may run between groups: nurses have long been working to see their own profession recognised in the broader medical hierarchy, and social workers have similarly struggled for professional recognition.

Such projects of status enhancement are clearly a part of the sociological and historical fabric of the administration of mental health. They are not generally crass attempts at power-grabbing, but manifest themselves instead primarily in articulation and formation of the values and expertise of the group in question. The group will no doubt sincerely believe, often entirely appropriately, in the value of the expertise it has to bring to a specific set of issues; but the result is nonetheless the privileging of a set of assumptions, or of a specific way of looking at things. It is this process which may result in the person with the mental health difficulty being unable to recognise himself or herself in clinical descriptions. Other ways of looking at things, whether those of the individual with the difficulty or of the other professions, are implicitly challenged or marginalised in the process. Perhaps unintentionally, the knowledge or expertise of the profession becomes the exercise of power, in potential conflict with other professions or ways of looking at things.

On a more mundane note, the professionals noted in this section are also all human, with understandable concerns about job satisfaction and job conditions. The image of the doctor willing to abandon all family or personal life and devote himself or herself entirely to the care of patients has a romantic appeal, but does not represent reality in most cases. The professionals, entirely reasonably and like the rest of us, must balance priorities.

Not all those with an interest in the care and treatment of the mentally ill are contained within the public sector. Overflows of patients from NHS psychiatric wards may be moved to private facilities, simply to alleviate space pressures. Further, many of the facilities such as group homes through which community care is offered are provided by the private sector. Sometimes these private sector providers are non-profit organisations, established through charities such as MIND; in other cases, they are standard businesses, run with a profit motive. Either way, the shift to the private sector means that maintenance of standards and control of staffing are out of direct government control. Regulation is theoretically possible, but complicated by the fact that if unattractive standards are set, the private operator can fold up shop, a possibility the government can little afford given the inability of the NHS to service the demand. This is not a desirable option from the private operator's viewpoint either, since considerable investment will have been made. In this balance policy must be made.

Care is not, of course, the exclusive preserve of the professionals. Families and friends also provide care, and there is considerable American evidence to suggest that the role of families is pivotal to relapse (Dixon and Lehman, 1995; Dixon *et al.*, 2000). The specific role of these informal carers will depend on the circumstances. Sometimes, they provide housing, with or without a day centre providing a formalised programme during the day. Sometimes, the person with mental illness will reside elsewhere, be it in hospital, at a group home, or alone in the community. Here, the role of family and friends may be to provide a sense of community and support, or it may also be to provide some sort of overview, to ensure that the appropriate services are being provided.

These services and the people who provide them have traditionally been largely taken for granted in the administrative structure of mental health. This is difficult to justify, for such carers provide important services, in conditions which may be very difficult. Some public support is available for these activities (see Carers (Recognition and Services) Act 1995) and there are some schemes in place to assist or relieve carers, for example, by allowing them to take the occasional weekend break from their caring duties. Such programmes seem appropriate acknowledgements of services performed which, at their best, provide the person with the mental disorder an optimal home environment at minimal cost to the state.

The family role can also be perceived as much more problematic. Particularly at the onset of an illness, the family may have little understanding of mental disability, and may react with stereotyped views (Thornicroft, 2006: ch. 1). Further, perhaps even more than with the professional actors, the interests of the family member providing care and those of the mentally ill person are difficult to disentangle, suggesting difficulties with formal control of these carers over the decisions that are made about mentally ill family members. Like other service providers, but perhaps more than other service providers, the family and friends of the individual will have an emotional and practical interest in the fate of the individual. The effect of the condition on relations within the family and, if the affected person is a breadwinner forced to cease employment, on the economic life of the family, can be profound. More poignantly, it can be profoundly painful to witness the onset of mental illness in a loved one. Karp comments regarding his attendance at a support group for friends and family of persons with mental disorder (2001: 22):

On any given evening I might hear about the unimaginable pain surrounding the decision to have a child removed from one's home by the police, the powerlessness of visiting
a spouse or child in a hospital who is so muddled by powerful medications that he or
she can barely speak, the shame that accompanies hating someone you love because of
what their illness has done to you and your family, the guilt that lingers from the belief
that you might somehow be responsible for another person's descent into mental illness, the confusion associated with navigating the Byzantine complexities of the mental
health system, the fear associated with waiting for the next phone call announcing yet
another suicide attempt by someone close to you, the disappointment that a talented
son or daughter may never realize even a fraction of their potential, the exhaustion that
accompanies full-time caregiving, or the frustration of being unable to take even a brief
vacation. Pain, powerlessness, shame, guilt, confusion, fear, disappointment, exhaustion,
frustration: these emotions are the currency of conversion among the Family and Friends
group members.

It is difficult to see how family members can be expected to divorce these feelings
from their views of the person with the disorder, and what ought to happen to that person. Unsurprisingly, Karp's study finds family carers building practical and emotional
walls, setting up 'boundaries of obligation', to use his term, in their care relationships.
The result is a paradox: it is the family's intimate knowledge and relationship with the
affected person which creates the appeal of their greater involvement; but at the same
time, this same factor creates the risk that decisions will be made on criteria other than
the best interest of the affected person.

The private interests in the mental health field extend well beyond carers.
Pharmaceutical manufacturers are a particularly clear example of these other interests.
Pharmaceuticals are big business. Roughly 10 per cent of the NHS prescription budget
is spent on drugs for mental disorders—or more than £881 million in 2010 (Ilyas and
Moncrieff, 2012: table 1). Clearly, medication for mental illness has brought considerable benefits in many cases. At the same time, the adverse effects of medication can
be profoundly unpleasant. The precise nature of these adverse effects will, of course,
depend on the patient and medication in question, but they can be significant enough
to dissuade patients from continuing the treatment. Ron Lacey (1996: 118) makes the
point this way, regarding depot anti-psychotic medications, long-lasting medications
injected into patients at intervals of weeks or months.

Whilst they can relieve the torment of the symptoms of serious mental illness for many
people, they can also reduce an individual to an unprotesting zombie-like state. For some
patients the use of depot antipsychotics is little more than an exchange of one form of
human misery for another. Drowsiness, lethargy, loss of motivation, impotence, stiffened
muscles, shaking hands, physical restlessness, severe anxiety and persistent constipation
may be more distressing to some people than a fixed belief that their thoughts are being
controlled by the international brotherhood of Freemasons. For others these side effects are
a small price to pay for the relief that the drugs give them from a much more distressing and
terrifying psychotic inner reality.

The varieties of psychiatric medication and their adverse effects will be discussed in greater detail in chapter 9.3; suffice it here to say that while their benefits should not be ignored or underestimated, they are not problem-free, miracle drugs.

Pharmaceutical manufacturers spend a considerable amount of money advertising their products, particularly in specialist medical, nursing, and health care journals related to mental illness and disability. Unsurprisingly, the advertisements emphasise the potential benefits of the medications, and place the adverse effects in very small print, either at the bottom of the page or off to the side. More interesting are the images used to sell the drugs, often reflecting themes discussed elsewhere in this chapter, although usually with a particularly sugary gloss. Thus images of a patient's return to true self-hood as a result of the drug, or scenes of restored domestic bliss, are common. Perhaps more worrying are advertisements that, often very subtly, suggest the use of medications as an efficient control of patients. These are presumably directed to the harassed doctor, presenting a fast and efficient way to restore order onto their ward or into the local psycho-geriatric nursing home. Are the advertisements effective? The continued use of large advertising budgets by these firms would suggest that they think so. A field trip to the medical library for a critical viewing of these advertisements is instructive to the student who is new to mental health law.

All these groups—patients, the varieties of medical personnel, social workers, hospitals and NHS health trusts, private caregivers, families, and pharmaceutical companies—make use of lobbyists and pressure groups to press their views. Sometimes these roles are performed by professional organisations, such as the Royal College of Psychiatrists, the College of Physicians, or the British Medical Association. Sometimes, they are performed by charities, such as MIND, Mencap, or the National Carers' Association. Sometimes, large organisations such as pharmaceutical companies will hire lobbyists directly. Once again, there is a considerable sociological literature on how these bodies work. If the group represents a variety of different persons or providers, decisions as to what position is to be lobbied for may become complex. This may be particularly complex in some of the groups in the charitable sector, for example, which do not 'represent groups' per se, but exist instead primarily to focus attention on sets of issues. While MIND, for example, endeavours to give particular consideration to the views of users, its mandate and membership is considerably broader than this.

Lobby or pressure groups may further have independent interests involving their reputations or financial integrity that may influence them in addition to, or, occasionally, at odds with the interests of the groups they represent. If a private firm of lobbyists is hired, for example, the firm will have a profit motivation. Even in the charitable sector, the financial integrity of the organisation must remain a factor in its priorities. Amendments to the way in which services are provided has complicated this since, in the last two decades, government has increasingly provided funding in the charitable sector. Nationally, the government provided £175 million of £3,000 million in charitable revenues in 1976, or roughly 6 per cent; by 1984 this had grown to £1 billion of charitable revenue of £10 billion, or 10 per cent (Prochaska, 1988: 4). By 1999, somewhere between 35 and 40 per cent of charitable income was thought to come from government sources (Whelan, 1999: 3). While these figures reflect the entire charitable sector, mental health charities have garnered at least their share of this new money. Indeed, as the charities have found an increasing role for themselves in the provision of community mental health services, the financial relations with government have intensified. The effect on these organisations is ambiguous. On the one hand, government relies on these organisations more than ever before to fulfil government objectives; at the same time, the organisations rely on government increasingly, to provide the funding for their activities. It is difficult to see that this uneasy relationship would not have its effect on the role of these charitable organisations to comment upon and to influence government policy.

Lying across all these interests is the government. It would be an error to think of the government as a monolith; like the remainder of the system, it is composed of parts, which may be characterised as much by competition as co-operation. The clearest of these possibly divergent interests arises between central and local government. The tradition in this country has long been for local government to have a particularly central role in service provision. Thus the actual purchase, and some of the provision, of community care rested at the local authority level, where policy-making rests primarily with central government. The same is true of health care provision, which will be administered at the local level, in the context of central regulation. In each case, much of the core funding will originate with the central government. This suggests that local and central interests may well disagree on a wide variety of issues, from priorities in service provision, to, most pivotally, the appropriate level of funding for service provision. The introduction of commissioning groups in 2013 will remove much of the purchase of services from local government control, to consortia of clinicians. How significant this change will be remains to be seen. It is hard to imagine central government bowing out of regulation, and it will certainly not be ceasing to provide funding. It may well be that the fights will have merely moved to new, quasi-private entities from local government ones.

Even central government must be understood as a complex entity. Mental health care will span a variety of offices and departments. Disability benefits for those living in the community are a social security issue. The Office of the Public Guardian, which has a variety of duties relating to persons lacking capacity, is under the Ministry of Justice. Psychiatric treatment in hospital is of course a matter for the Department of Health, although when such treatment involves people within the criminal justice system, the Department of Justice is also involved (albeit a different part of the Ministry of Justice than that containing the Public Guardian). Within government, status is measured largely in terms of staff allocations and budget. The way in which programmes are divided between departments is thus profoundly relevant to the status of the departments concerned, with corresponding impact on government policy. The interests of a variety of departments in mental health services reinforces that mental health policy may be as much a function of competitive negotiation between government departments as it is of co-operation.

Throughout the system, lawyers can be expected to be active. They will be hired, either to lobby for specific interests or to represent clients in specific situations, by all the parties noted at the beginning of this section. Here again, while the lawyer should of course defend the interests of those clients with all ferocity, limited only by professional standards such as the duty to uphold the dignity of the court, other factors can creep into the picture. Practising lawyers quickly learn that their individual reputations are profoundly significant to the attainment of their career aspirations and, sometimes, to the success of their causes. In practice, this may affect how the lawyer presents a case, and occasionally, what arguments will be made. Similarly, the realities of private legal practice require a cash flow. The lawyer representing clients in mental health, as much as any other, cannot in the end ignore that reality. This is seen with clarity in some of the debates surrounding legal aid. Certainly, availability of legal aid is likely to be vital to many poor psychiatric patients if their rights are to be protected. At the same time, the reason it is vital is because without an appropriate legal aid structure, lawyers simply cannot afford to accept many cases: the issue here is about the economics of running a law office as much as it is about abstract notions of rights.

The resulting picture is of a complex system of actors and interests in the provision of mental health care. It would be unduly cynical to take the view that the people with the mental health problems, the people whom the system ought most to support and assist, are ignored. It would be fair to say that the users of mental health services have not traditionally been as successful as the professional groups in having their voices heard directly. This problem is complicated by the fact that the users of mental health services do not speak with one voice. They range from enthusiastic proponents of medication to people denying the relevance of a medical model to insanity entirely. User views instead tend to be filtered through a professionalised view of best interests. While it would be inappropriate to deny the good faith of much of this professional concern, the other factors noted in this section may distort or influence the message. If it is inappropriate to say that the person with mental health difficulties is absent from policy formation, it is certainly inappropriate to deny the other factors which influence policy formation.

1.6 Sources of law

1.6.1 The roots of the mental health law

Mental health law is as old as law itself. The earliest codified reference in the English statute book is contained in a 1324 statute defining the Royal Prerogative, giving the king jurisdiction over the persons and property of 'idiots' and those who 'happen to fail of [their] Wit' (*De Prerogativa Regis* c. ix, x). Nonetheless, much of the care of the insane in medieval and early modern England occurred outside the realm of statute, and it was not until the eighteenth and particularly nineteenth centuries that the insane became, increasingly, subject to statutory jurisdiction. These statutes may have been the precursors of the MHA and MCA, but they were markedly different in form. Specifically, for much of the nineteenth century, mental health law was not contained in a single Act, but instead in a variety of streams of statutes, each quite distinct from the others (see Bartlett, 2001a). Four nineteenth-century streams, and one additional one from the early twentieth century, warrant particular note, as they combine, in somewhat amended form, to comprise the MHA 1983. The nineteenth century strands were as follows:

- Private madhouse acts. Commencing in 1774, these required privately owned madhouses to be licensed and inspected. These reached maturity in 1845, when a national government body, the Commissioners in Lunacy, were formed to inspect all madhouses in England and Wales. Licensing was done by justices of the peace outside London, and the Commissioners in Lunacy in London. Admission to private madhouses was upon the application of a family member, supported by two certificates of insanity signed by medical practitioners not directly associated with the madhouse.

- County Asylum Acts. These commenced in 1808. They allowed (and after 1845, required) county asylums to be built for the insane poor, financed by the county rates. Throughout the nineteenth century, these facilities were generally restricted to paupers, although in practice a somewhat wide definition of that term might sometimes be employed. Admission was by order of a justice of the peace, upon the application of a poor law relieving officer, supported by one medical certificate, almost invariably signed by the poor law medical officer.

- Statutes concerning the Royal Prerogative, and determination of mental incapacity: originally, the control of 'idiots' and 'lunatics' had rested with the Crown, but this was generally delegated to the Lord Chancellor. Nineteenth-century statutes further arranged that incapacity would be determined initially by chancery judges, then by senior barristers specially appointed to the role (when no jury was requested).

- Criminal lunatics: the first of these statutes was required following *Hadfield's Case* (1800) 27 Howell's St Tr 1281, where it was held that although the insane accused was not to be convicted, he was not to be set free either. A legislative framework to accomplish this came into effect later that year. In the first half of the century, legislation in this area was contained in the County Asylum Acts, but specific statutory regulation occurs in the second half of the century, beginning with the Criminal Lunatics Act 1860.

The Lunacy Act 1890 is sometimes perceived as a watershed statute. In a sense it is, in that for the first time it combines the four legislative streams relating to the laws of insanity into one statute. Further, it was in effect for much of the twentieth century, not being formally repealed until 1959, and the MHA 1983 still resembles it in general structure. In its historical context, however, the 1890 Act is something of an anticlimax, although it did make some changes. For the first time, for example, privately paying patients could not be admitted to psychiatric facilities without the order of a justice of the peace. If the 1890 Act consolidated the various strands into one statute, however, it did not consolidate the strands themselves; for example the paupers who had been under the jurisdiction of the County Asylum Acts continued to be subject to a set of rules quite different from private patients.

The first half of the twentieth century offered two significant developments. The first was to add yet another strand of legislation, the Mental Deficiency Acts, commencing in 1913. These seem to have been given short shrift by legislative historians of insanity. That is unfortunate. Not only did they provide the basis of the current guardianship provisions of the MHA; they also provided the legislative framework for some early care in the community, before the Second World War (Thomson, 1998; Walmsley *et al.*, 1999). This provision was not negligible: by 1939, almost 90,000 people were controlled by these Acts in England and Wales, almost half of which were living in the community (Walmsley *et al.*, 1999: 186). Further, they provided a legislative framework for an increasingly ornate social discourse relating to developmental disabilities. While 'idiocy' was expressly covered under the nineteenth-century legislation, for much of that period little distinction was made between this and 'lunacy'. The Idiots Act of 1886 began to acknowledge the distinctness of problems relating to developmental disability; the differential nature of the issues, and a different set of social responses, was given clearer articulation by the Mental Deficiency Act 1913.

The second development was that the Mental Treatment Act 1930 introduced informal admissions for the first time. In law, this is extremely significant. Up to this time, there was no distinction between admission to and confinement in a psychiatric facility. From 1930, it became possible for an individual to be admitted to a psychiatric facility without a formal and binding order of admission. For the first time, the patient might also be free to leave. While this admission route took some time to gain widespread popularity, it now accounts for around 90 per cent of psychiatric admissions.

It is in this legislative context that we must understand the Mental Health Act 1959. The creation of the NHS in 1948 had largely removed the distinction between public and private facilities, with the incorporation of charitable hospitals into the public sector. The old legislative distinctions appeared to make less and less sense. Where the 1890 Act had left the distinctions largely untouched, but included all legislative strands in one statute, the 1959 Act actually tried to consolidate the divergent strands into one. The solution of the 1959 Act was largely to ram the different processes together. For example, where compulsory admission before that time had been in the hands of poor law/social service officials if the patient was poor and the family if the patient was able to afford private care, under the new system both admission mechanisms were combined for all patients, so that all compulsory admissions required both family and social services involvement.

The 1959 Act did make a few significant changes. First, admissions were now removed from justices of the peace. The process allowed admission instead upon the agreement of a mental welfare officer and the nearest relative of the patient, accompanied by certification of mental disorder by two doctors. This may have reflected existing practice in any event, for there is evidence that in some areas at least, justices of the peace were signing multiple copies of blank orders of admission, in anticipation of applications from poor law relieving officers and medical officers (Forsythe, Melling, and Adair, 1999: 83). Nonetheless, albeit perhaps unintentionally, the 1959 Act is said to have had the effect of moving power from hospital administration and judicial officers directly to treating physicians (Fennell, 1996: 168–9). Secondly, the Act introduced mental health review tribunals. For the first time, a dedicated mechanism was created by which patients could challenge their confinement. Finally, the 1959 Act moved the *parens patriae* power to an entirely statutory footing. Where the previous legislation of this power had functioned as amendments of the common law, the 1959 Act subjected guardianship and conservatorship to a purely statutory regime.

The MHA 1959 once again placed mental disorder and learning disabilities in the same statute, an approach continued under the current MHA. This has not been entirely a success. The combined statute means that the legislative space to consider problems specific to each of these groups has disappeared. This would seem to have worked to the disadvantage of those with learning disabilities, who in discussions related to the current MHA are overshadowed by issues of mental health and illness. This is reflected in the title of the Act: why should people with learning disabilities be subject to a 'mental health' Act, when they are not, per se, mentally ill? Indeed, this book can be justly criticised for this bias. While purporting to discuss the ambit of the MHA as a whole, much of the discussion does show an inappropriate assumption that the prime users of the legislation are mentally ill, not learning disabled.

The MHA 1983, still currently in force, albeit as amended, kept the basic provisions of the 1959 Act. There were some changes in nomenclature: 'mental welfare officers' became 'approved social workers'. Some more substantive changes were also made at this time, however. The new Act was passed in a climate where patient rights had entered the political landscape. Treatment while in a psychiatric facility was for the first time brought into the legislative realm, albeit only for those confined in the facility. That inclusion nonetheless made it equally clear for the first time that those not covered by the provisions, that is, those informally admitted, had the same rights regarding treatment as the common law provides to people outside the facility. In addition, the powers of personal guardians were significantly reduced. The guardian could now only determine where the person could reside (but not require him or her to be returned there, if for example he or she were wandering), and to attend somewhere for treatment (but not to consent on the person's behalf). While they can also ensure access to the individual by social services or medical personnel, they have authority to make no other decisions for the individual. This triggered a process of law reform, eventually resulting in the passage of the MCA. In the interim, the courts expanded common law on an ad hoc basis to fill the apparent gap.

The last decades of the twentieth century saw a forest of policies, guidance, and directives from the Department of Health, introducing best practice policies for a wide variety of matters relating to psychiatric care. While these have been enforced through administrative audit and similar mechanics of government—woe betide a provider who fails to develop the administratively appropriate systems of management—they have no formal legal effect. The courts may look to them, of course, but will not be bound by them when they do not reflect statute or common law: see, for example, *R v Department of Health, ex p Source Informatics Ltd* [1999] 4 All ER 185. The trend towards this form of extra-legal regulation is typical across government, and is certainly prevalent in health matters generally. The move raises questions of accountability: while some of the guidances have considerable effect, they will not have been scrutinised by Parliament.

In the 1995, in response to two *causes célèbre*, significant amendments were made to the Act regarding control of patients released into the community. The MHA 1983 already made the provision of after-care in the community mandatory for people who were released from civil confinement in psychiatric facilities (s. 117). The 1995 amendments began to focus on requiring the person released to accept the care offered. The details are unimportant for present purposes: they are no longer in effect. The relevance of these provisions in an historical context is the blurring of control between the institution and the community and, perhaps more significant, turning the debate surrounding the introduction of these provisions from a language of rights, the predominant discourse in the 1983 debates, to a language of risk. That latter language has become increasingly central to government thinking regarding mental health law since that time.

In the 1990s, various reform projects were undertaken. The Law Commission took up the question of a statutory framework for mental capacity (see Law Commission, 1995). Most of their proposals were eventually passed into law in 2005.

Meanwhile, in the late 1990s, the government introduced a programme of reform to the MHA. This was occasioned in part by concerns that the existing Act would not comply with the Human Rights Act 1998, an ongoing concern raised in numerous contexts later in this book. The reform process cannot be considered to have been a success. An expert committee, well-respected among legal and medical practitioners, reported in 1999 (the Richardson Committee). Its recommendations were rather modest, and reflected the emerging orthodoxies among mental health practitioners, service users, and policy analysts. Thus, for example, service users were to be involved as far as reasonably possible in their own care, and higher requirements for detention would apply if a competent patient was objecting to admission (Department of Health and Welsh Office, 1999a).

At the same time, a second committee was concerned with mismanagement and abuse at Ashworth Special Hospital (the Fallon Committee). Also reporting in 1999, this committee called for stronger controls over people with personality disorders who were perceived as dangerous (Department of Health, 1999b).

The government combined the Richardson and Fallon proposals into one White Paper and draft bill, in 2002. They were not well-received. Service users and their advocates complained about the disappearance of many of the rights-based protections, and the notion that users were to be treated with dignity. Doctors objected that they would be required to warehouse people for whom there was no treatment. Civil rights advocates complained at the demise of due process safeguards proposed by Richardson. The overall direction of change can be illustrated by reference to the guiding principles contained in the bill. The Richardson Committee proposed an array of progressive principles, supportive of patient dignity, liberty, and rights. The draft bill contained three general principles, securing that patients be involved in the making of decisions; that decisions be made openly and fairly; and that 'the interference to patients in providing medical treatment to them and the restrictions imposed in respect of them during that treatment are kept to the minimum necessary to protect their health or safety of other persons' (cl. 1(3)). Unlike the Richardson principles, these simply did not reflect the direction and complexity of discussion and debate in the mental health arena in recent decades. As if this were not enough, the following sub-clause went on to say that the Code of Practice could specify circumstances or decisions or people to which even these minimal principles would not apply (cl. 1(4)). It is unsurprising that the proposals did not receive broad support among users, service providers, and carers, and the government eventually withdrew the bill.

A subsequent draft bill in 2004 was also withdrawn, again attracting little support from stakeholders, and following a highly critical report from a Joint Scrutiny Committee of the House of Commons and House of Lords (House of Commons and House of Lords, 2005).

Eventually, the government abandoned the prospect of a new statute. Instead, it introduced amendments to the existing MHA in 2007. These, like the previous proposals, met with considerable resistance, but the government did manage to get them passed. Most significantly, the 2007 Act created community treatment orders (a manifesto commitment) (see further Chapter 10.4) and introduced procedures by which people without capacity could be detained (the deprivation of liberty safeguards, or 'DOLS') (see further Chapter 5). A variety of other more minor changes were made, and will be discussed as they arise later in this book. The result is an extraordinary disappointment for almost 10 years of effort, and, perhaps most disappointingly, the factors that were the impetus for the reform process in the late 1990s are still there: the MHA is badly drafted, out of date both with modern professional practice and modern views of patient rights, and of doubtful consistency with the ECHR on a variety of points.

In considering the legal developments over the last 200 years, perhaps what is striking is less how much things have changed, as how much they have remained the same. While the distinctions between public and private admissions have disappeared under the current MHA, the structure is otherwise reminiscent of the strands of nineteenth-century law identified in this section: Parts 2 and 6 on admission to facilities, including removal of patients to the various parts of the United Kingdom; Part 3 on criminal confinement. On a more minute level, the continuities are similarly notable. The current role of the approved mental health professional (AMHP) looks remarkably similar to that of the poor law relieving officer, 150 years ago.

At the same time, the context of the MHA has changed markedly, making interpretation complex. When the Act contains the old nineteenth-century clauses, as it often does, their relevance or applicability is no longer clear. Thus s. 1 of the MHA still refers to the Act governing 'the management of [the patients'] property and affairs', although it has not done so since the introduction of the MCA in 2005. Similarly, the provisions defining the right of the nearest relative to insist on the release of a patient contained in s. 23(2) originate in the nineteenth-century statutes. If the confinement was in the private sector, the relative was responsible for paying the patient's upkeep, and therefore was perceived to have the right to demand the release of the patient, to limit their financial exposure. If instead the patient was confined in a county asylum, the right to order release was conditional on an undertaking by the person ordering the release that the individual would no longer be chargeable on the poor law. The right to release was thus a way to enforce public economy in care provision, and to limit the shame of the family at receiving poor relief. Neither of these justifications continues to exist; yet the section remains in relatively unamended form. Justifications may continue to exist for its inclusion, but they are *ex post facto*.

The nineteenth-century rights to order the release of the patient were circumscribed if the patient were 'dangerous to other persons or to himself', a restriction remaining in s. 25 of the MHA; yet how are we to read that section given the standard of confinement introduced in 1959 and still in force, that the civil confinement is 'necessary for the health or safety of the patient or for the protection of other persons'? If it is the same standard, the right of the nearest relative is removed in all cases where the patient is rightly confined, rendering the power a nullity. If the standards are different, how are they different? The answer would have to be to introduce a relatively low standard for 'health' in the 1983 provision, since it is difficult to see how 'safety' of the patient or 'protection of other persons' provides the necessary flexibility to provide a standard different from 'dangerous'; but is that really consistent with the meaning of the 1959 standard as a whole? Does the phrase 'the health or safety of the patient or for the protection of other persons', when read as a whole, not instead imply a relatively high standard of risk to health? And should the determination of modern standards of confinement be based on arcane arguments about nineteenth-century legal history?

The MHA 1983 is full of this sort of difficulty. Its construction and interpretation can be fiendishly difficult. The Code of Practice, most recently revised in 2008, has been issued to assist those charged with the Act's administration (Department of Health, 2008). In a sense, this only complicates matters further, since the Code contains material supplementary to the legal standards of the Act. While the Code is not legally binding on practitioners, they are required to 'have regard' to it (s. 118(2D), introduced 2007) and it is identified as something the Secretary of State is obliged to produce by s. 118 (1) of the Act. As such, while service providers may depart from it, they are required to give the Code 'great weight' and to depart from it only when they have 'cogent reasons' for doing so (*R (Munjaz)* v *Ashworth* [2005] UKHL 58, para. 21). The result can appear to establish ambiguities in the standards to be applied: one is reminded of the Japanese proverb that a person with a clock knows the time; a person with two clocks is never sure. Even without reference to issues of social policy in interpretation, the MHA therefore provides a veritable panoply of difficulties, testing the lawyer's skills in statutory interpretation to their limit.

1.6.2 **Other law and mental disorder**

The MHA and MCA may provide the core of the law for this textbook, but it will be clear from the preceding discussion that they do not stand on their own. Other legal subject areas may come into play in understanding the rights of those with mental health problems. The modern law curriculum, frequently modular, is appropriately criticised for treating legal subjects as self-contained packages, with little to do with each other. The study of mental health law allows the law student an ideal opportunity to think across legal subjects, analysing which approach will yield a desirable result. Mental health law spans almost all legal disciplines. The student of mental health law should see this as an opportunity, not a threat, for it allows a reassessment of those disciplines from a new and different angle from that usually forming the base of law school curricula. A brief survey will show how some of these related areas intersect with mental health law.

The MHA itself involves subjects such as confinement and enforced treatment, performed on statutory justification. These matters tend to be controlled by judicial review, and students should be aware of the relevance of their study of public law to mental health law.

The MHA is not a complete code, and in the silence of the statutes, the common law will apply. The treatment of people with decision-making capacity who are informally admitted to psychiatric facilities is governed by common law, with the standard rules of consent and medical negligence applicable.

Capacity is a threshold whenever people enter into legal relations. The MCA creates prospective mechanisms to allow individuals to make decisions on the incapable person's behalf, but it does not alter the pre-existing legal rules applicable when the incapable person has nonetheless entered into relations with others. Here, capacity law, generally based in common law, reaches into virtually the entire law school curriculum. As an illustrative list, there are rules regarding capacity to marry, to engage in sexual relations, to file for divorce, to sign contracts, to commit crimes and to enter a plea when charged with an offence, to serve as trustee or corporate director, to execute a will, and of course to consent to medical treatment. Some of these will be discussed as they arise in this textbook, most notably in Chapters 4 and 9, requiring some consideration of the broader laws in these areas.

Even regarding mental disorder distinct from incapacity, the MHA does not of course affect all of the individual's life. A variety of other statutory regimes may also be significant. People with mental disorders face, with embarrassing frequency, problems of maintaining jobs and finding places to live (Thornicroft, 2006: ch. 3 and *passim*). The former of these will be subject to employment laws, which articulate the degree to which mental illness can be used to justify dismissal. Similarly, both employment and housing are covered by the Equality Act 2010, which prohibits discrimination on the basis of disability. This may be particularly helpful, as it can require the employer or landlord to make reasonable accommodation to take account of the needs of the disabled person. Disability rights are also noted in the Treaty of Amsterdam 1997, and the Charter of Fundamental Rights of the European Union signed in Nice in 2000 (2000/C 364/01) and strengthened by the Treaty of Lisbon in 2009, suggesting that a European dimension may become increasingly relevant as that treaty is implemented. Particularly if employment fails, the individual may be in need of social services, where a range of disability benefits may be available under social security legislation.

The ECHR has become increasingly relevant to mental disability law in recent years. This is in part because, following the Human Rights Act 1998 taking effect in 2000, the ECHR may be pleaded in the domestic courts of the United Kingdom, so that decisions of the European Court of Human Rights (ECtHR) have a more immediate relevance. It is also because, in the last decade or so, the ECtHR has taken an increasing interest in issues concerning mental disability. Where the first case involving mental disability (*Winterwerp* v *the Netherlands*, (1979–80) 2 EHRR 387) was not decided until almost 30 years after the ECHR took effect, now there is a steady flow of decisions coming from Strasbourg. *Winterwerp* laid down core standards which states must apply when detaining 'persons of unsound mind' if they are to comply with Article 5.1.e. This case has proven extremely important at establishing fundamental standards in the mental health area. The experience since that time has been mixed (see Bartlett, Lewis, and Thorold, 2006). The ECtHR has been strong on ensuring appropriate due process protections, but weak on substantive issues. As perhaps an extreme example, in *Johnson* v *United Kingdom* (1999) 27 EHRR 296, the court held that while an individual who had been but was no longer mentally ill had a variety of process rights to challenge their confinement, the fact that they were no longer mentally ill did not mean that they had a right to an immediate and unconditional release from their psychiatric facility. This does seem to be an extraordinarily conservative reading of the phrase 'person of unsound mind' in Article 5.1.e.

Where early decisions primarily concerned detention, more recent cases cover an increasing range of issues, for example, the right to vote (*Kiss* v *Hungary* Application no. 38832/06, judgment of 20 August 2010); issues concerning the control of people under guardianship because of alleged incapacity (e.g., *Shtukaturov* v *Russia*, Application no. 44009/05, judgment of 27 June 2008; *Stanev* v *Bulgaria*, Application no. 36760/06, judgment of 17 January 2012, *DD* v *Lithuania*, Application no. 13469/06, judgment of 14 February 2012); detentions occurring in care homes rather than hospitals (e.g., *X and Y* v *Croatia* Application no. 5193/09, judgment of 3 February 2012); the failure to protect people with mental disabilities from harassment (*Đorđević* v *Croatia*, Application no. 41526/10, judgment of 24 July 2012); and the appropriateness of psychiatric treatment (*Gorobet* v *Moldova*, Application no. 30951/10, judgment of 11 January 2012, *X* v *Finland* Application no. 34806/04, judgment of 3 July 2012). The growth of this jurisprudence looks set to continue, and students serious about mental health law will need to take account of it.

Also of importance is the work of the Committee for the Prevention of Torture and Inhuman or Degrading Treatment or Punishment (CPT), another body of the Council of Europe. The CPT has taken the view that people who are institutionalised are particularly vulnerable to abuse, and therefore form a particularly important part of their mandate. It has issued standards applicable to psychiatric facilities (see European Committee for the Prevention of Torture, 2011) and routinely visits not merely prisons, but also psychiatric hospitals, social care homes, and similar institutions, to ensure that appropriate standards are met. Their reports are not as influential in domestic English courts as the decisions of the ECtHR, but they may nonetheless be given some consideration: see, for example *R (Wilkinson) v RMO Broadmoor Hospital and MHA Second Opinion Approved Doctor* [2002] 1 WLR 419 (CA) at para. 28 *per* Simon Brown LJ., regarding the rights of persons with capacity to make treatment decisions.

The most recent innovation in international law is the United Nations Convention on the Rights of Persons with Disabilities (the CRPD) (UN General Assembly, A/61/611). This convention was passed by the United Nations General Assembly in December 2006, and took effect in 2008. The CRPD takes a fundamentally different approach to previous international and domestic law. Previous articulations of mental health law had focused on mental disorder, a condition lying in the individual, analogous to a sickness. The CRPD requires a redefinition of the field, placing mental health law (if that is still the appropriate label) in the context of disability law, and adopting a social model of disability: what renders the individual 'disabled' is not something analogous to an illness contained in the individual, but rather the response of society in failing to take adequate account of the person's situation. To pick a somewhat simplistic example, a person in a wheelchair is only disabled if no wheelchair ramp is provided. Similarly for mental disabilities, the disadvantage in the view of the CRPD flows from a failure of society adequately to cater to the needs of people with these disabilities—the failure to provide 'reasonable accommodations', in the language of the Convention.

This has important consequences. Previous international instruments such as the ECHR and the United Nations Mental Illness Principles (General Assembly, 46/119, 1991) had accepted the appropriateness of coercing people with mental disorders in some circumstances; the issue was how to define the circumstances. The CRPD takes no such starting point. It instead starts from the position that coercion in situations where people without disabilities would not be coerced is discriminatory on the basis of disability, and therefore unacceptable. On that basis, much of the mental health and mental capacity law currently existing is in violation, and that appears to be the view of the Committee on the Rights of Persons with Disabilities, the UN body charged with the oversight of the implementation of the Convention: see United Nations Committee on the Rights of Persons with Disabilities, 2011, 2011a, 2012; see also United Nations High Commissioner for Human Rights, 2009 at, e.g., 43–45; United Nations Special Rapporteur on Torture, 2013. At the time of writing the ramifications of the CRPD have not yet been thought through by the government (see discussion in Bartlett, 2012). Certainly, if English and Welsh law are to be made compliant, significant changes will be necessary, and they will be discussed elsewhere in this textbook.

Unlike the ECHR, there is nothing corresponding to the Human Rights Act 1998 for the CRPD. The CRPD is international law, and while the UK is obliged to implement it and comply with it, there is nothing that corresponds to a declaration of incompatibility such as would force the government's hand, as there is for the ECHR. At the same time, it is international law, a Convention that the UK has signed and ratified, and we are meant to implement it. Not only that, but we are required to report every four years on our progress towards implementation, and the Committee on the Rights of Persons with Disabilities comments publicly on those reports. Not only that, but the UK has also signed the optional protocol to the CRPD, which allows individual complaints to the Committee once domestic remedies have been exhausted. While the CRPD may not be directly enforceable by the UK courts the way the ECHR is, we nonetheless cannot assume that non-compliance will go unnoticed.

1.7 Concluding comments

This book views mental health law both as a subject in its own right, and as a case study. In the former context, it provides an opportunity for law students to exercise their skills in statutory interpretation and case analysis, but it requires more. Mental health law and policy is by its very definition an interdisciplinary study. It is not an area where law should be considered independently, divorced from the realities of clinical practice or life for the client in the community. It requires the student to consider how various actors work together, and which interests take precedence over others. Thus empirical research and sociological approaches will often be as enlightening as pure legal analysis.

Mental health law as case study instead requires the student to consider the nature of law. As we have seen, mental health law spans the curriculum. In this, it is typical of other types of law—a secret often kept from students, who seem determined to view law in discrete and unrelated subject packages—and the skills acquired by the student in thinking across these legal areas should be expected to assist him or her in any sort of law they eventually practise. If critical theory and sociology may be required to make sense of what mental health law is about, so mental health law provides a way for the undergraduate student to approach these subjects, and once again, these approaches will prove valuable in other contexts. No law operates divorced from the real needs of clients and the pressures of social policy. Mental health law creates a suitable study of how these interact, and an understanding of this can certainly be applied by students to other areas of law.

In closing, this chapter returns to its beginning: silence. It will be clear that in our view, the silence must be broken. This is, in a sense, a lawyer's conceit, for law glorifies the representation of the individual client: in our professional ideology, based in rights theory and liberalism, the model of the lawyer defending the interests and acting on the instructions of the individual client is pivotal. Yet this is not merely conceit. The more offensive conceit would be to treat mental health law as a set of academic constructs, and ignore the people contained within the system. These are real people with real problems. This is true of everyone in the system, but is perhaps most true of the people with mental health difficulties or developmental disabilities; yet it is their voices that remain largely outside the hearing of judges and policymakers.

If this book argues for the necessity to break down the silence described by Foucault, it should also challenge the reader to question the discourse that has resulted from that silence. If policy has developed through silencing the mad, if it is, as Foucault claims, a discourse of reason about unreason, it then tells us as much or more about the reasonable as the mad. For reason to articulate insanity, it must do it with reference to sanity, for that is the only way the border can be understood. In this way, mental health law and policy can be seen as a mirror, in which we see our own values reflected. For Foucault, this language of reason bears no particularly enhanced status. It is instead 'that other form of madness, by which men, in an act of sovereign reason, confine their neighbors, and communicate and recognize each other through the merciless language of non-madness' (Foucault, 1965: ix). Yet if reason is madness, it is nonetheless our madness, and thus something we should strive to acknowledge and understand.

In the first chapter of *Madness and Civilization*, Foucault uses the imagery of the ship of fools, the *stultifara navis*, as the paradigm of a Renaissance view of madness. Foucault seems to have believed that these ships actually existed, a view which has attracted criticisms from historians (e.g., Midelfort, 1980). He also draws a symbolic meaning from this image: 'It is possible that these ships of fools, which haunted the imagination of the entire early Renaissance, were pilgrimage boats, highly symbolic cargoes of madmen in search of their reason' (Foucault, 1965: 9). This is, in a sense, as appropriately a metaphor for Foucault's view of the result of the enlightenment: the journey of 'that other form of madness' in search of its reason. It is also the project of this book.

2

An Overview of the Contemporary Mental Health System

2.1 Introduction

In an influential paper, Lazlo and Krippner (1998: 54) suggested that 'In the broadest conception, the term [system] connotes a complex of interacting components together with the relationships among them that permit the identification of a boundary-maintaining entity or process'. This is a helpful way in which to begin conceptualising the mental health system. Components of the contemporary system include a series of physical locations—hospitals, care homes, and out-patient facilities such as drop-in centres, for example, provided and maintained sometimes by the state and sometimes by independent providers or charities—and a number of services, delivered by a range of mental health and social care professionals, in those institutions or in the community. The system also has a philosophical aspect to it: it is a system in which competing values have to be reconciled (or not) both at the level of policy and in practice.

Understood in this way, the boundaries of the system may seem fairly well-delineated: a person in hospital, whether on an informal basis or subject to compulsory powers of detention and treatment, is 'in' the mental health system. Similarly, a person in receipt of treatment for mental disorder in the community, again on either a voluntary basis or subject to compulsion, is 'in' the mental health system. But it may be that, from the point of view of the service-user or patient, this is an unduly narrow conception of the mental health system. A user may want to include the benefits system, the housing system, and other things too, such as employment rights, as all being part of the system, in the sense that the availability or efficacy of medical treatment for mental disorder may be significantly impacted on by the housing or financial situation of the service user, and these things may well be part of the package of care that would maximise the mental well-being of the user. For example, there is a clear correlation between homelessness and mental disorder (Rees, 2009): does that mean that the provision of accommodation is a suitable and appropriate response to the mental health needs of a person without suitable accommodation?

If so, what sort of accommodation is suitable: must a person in that situation be prepared to accept accommodation in a care home, hostel, or similar accommodation, or should there be an entitlement to be provided with 'ordinary' accommodation, such as a local authority or housing association house or flat? If it is the latter, it may be that responsibility for providing the accommodation lies with a local housing authority (LHA) rather than with health service providers. Does this mean that the housing system should be seen as part of the mental health system? If not, how do we understand the boundaries between these systems? In short, questions such as this point to the problematic, porous, and uncertain nature of the boundaries of the mental health system.

The role of law within the mental health system is inherently ambiguous. Is it part of the system, or is it an external force, acting on the system? The answer depends, in part, on how 'the mental health system' is understood. If it is seen in primarily medical terms, as part of the broader health care system, then law does seem to function as an external mechanism, which has amongst its functions the placement of limitations on medical discretion. On this view, mental health law upholds the liberty of the individual in the face of medical coercion or over-exuberant benevolence. On the other hand, law is a source of the mental health system in its own right (Fennell, 1986), in terms of discourse, ideas, structures, and so on, and it has had a constructive influence on the contemporary system, so that the 'legal' aspects of the contemporary system cannot easily be distilled from its other components.

Thus it can be said that a psychiatric facility is both a physical structure and a legal entity; there is little point in studying the operation of one without reference to the operation of the other. The same, it must follow, is true of those who enter the system. The patient, or client, is in some sense a product of the legal regime, just as he or she is a product of social and medical policy and practice. The tradition in some of the literature has been to see these approaches as conflicting. This is not necessarily appropriate. As Roger Smith (1981) has shown, legal and medical discourses have displayed considerable similarity in the past. The mutual reliance of these discourses in both the past and present will be a theme of this chapter, and indeed a recurring theme in this text.

We open this chapter with a sketch of the contemporary system. We shall also consider how the system that currently operates came into being. The intimacy of the relationship between past, present, and future in the delivery of mental health services cannot be overestimated. Mental health policy over the last two and a half centuries has tended to be reactive, and as a consequence the system has had continually to live with its ghosts, in terms of physical plant, professional discourse, vested interest and, to a greater or lesser extent, public perceptions. Finally, we shall give some consideration to life inside a psychiatric facility. Unless there is some understanding of the context in which mental health law seeks to operate, there seems little prospect of law and lawyers being able to work effectively for the interests of service users or patients.

2.2 A sketch of the contemporary mental health system

2.2.1 Hospital provision

It is not easy to describe the mental health system, and this is because, as already suggested, the system lacks clear boundaries. To start with what is clear, the mental health system certainly embraces a range of physical locations—hospitals—in which treatment for mental disorder is provided on an inpatient basis. It is the duty of the Secretary of State for Health to promote a comprehensive health service designed to secure improvement in both the physical and mental health of the people of England and to provide for the prevention, diagnosis, and treatment of physical and mental illness (s. 1(1) of the National Health Service Act (NHSA) 2006). Unless charging is specifically permitted, these services must be provided free of charge (s. 1(4), NHSA 2006). The Secretary of State for Health has also been fixed with a raft of new duties—to improve services, reduces health inequalities, promote autonomy, and make provision for research and training, added as ss. 1A–1G of the NHSA 2006 by the Health and Social Care Act (HSCA) 2012, which came into force on 1 April 2013.

In the past, it was also the duty of the Secretary of State to provide specific services, but in practice this duty was always delegated to local providers or commissioners of care. Under the new regime introduced by the HSCA 2012, the relationship between central government and local health care commissioners is clearer. The role of the Secretary of State is now to produce a 'mandate' each year which sets out his or her objectives for that year and the budget which has been allocated to spending on health care (NHSA 2006, s. 13A).

Commissioning of services at national level is the responsibility of the newly-created National Health Service Commissioning Board (NHSCB) (NHSA 2006, s. 1H), which is subject to the same general duty as the Secretary of State (NHSA 2006, s. 1H(2), 1(1)), and which is fixed with a wide range of further duties, including those which apply to the Secretary of State but in addition, amongst others, duties to promote patient choice (NHSA 2006, s. 13I) and patient involvement in decision-making in relation to their care (NHSA 2006, s. 13H), as well as innovation in (s. 13K) and integration of (s. 13N) services. The NHSCB is responsible for the commissioning of primary care, although in practice it works closely with local Clinical Commissioning Groups (CCGs), local social service authorities (LSSAs), and other relevant stake-holders (see NHSCB, 2012).

At local level, commissioning of services is the responsibility of CCGs, again newly created by the HSCA 2012. CCGs are fixed with a wide range of general duties (NHSA 2006, ss. 14P–14Z1). But in particular, s.1I of the NHSA 2006 now provides that CCGs have 'the function of arranging for the provision of services for the purposes of the health service', taking over this function from Primary Care Trusts (PCTs), the difference being that CCGs are local consortia of GP practices and so commissioning of services will henceforth be determined by medical professionals rather than by management professionals, which, it has been claimed by the government, will 'liberate professionals and providers from top-down control. This is the only way to secure the quality, innovation and productivity needed to improve outcomes' (Department of Health (DH), 2010: para. 4.1).

Section 3(1) of the NHSA 2006 places CCGs under a duty to arrange for the provision of a comprehensive range of health services, including hospital and other accommodation, and facilities for preventative and after-care services (there is a power to arrange for the provision of other services: NHSA 2006, s. 3A). From 2012, the commissioning of some mental health services came within the system of 'payment by results' (PbR). The intention is that this will incentivise providers to improve the standards of treatment and care offered, because now, 'For the first time clinicians will have a direct impact on the funding that their organisation receives through their work to deliver high quality care and to achieve better outcomes' (DH, 2012d: para. 1.3). PbR will have a greater role in 2013–14 (DH, 2012d: para. 2.1), and the eventual aim is to establish a national tariff for payment rates, although this stage has not yet been reached (DH, 2012d: para. 2.1).

It has been held that the scope of s. 3(1) should be construed widely, to include, as a 'facility' for the purposes of s. 3(1)(e), a scheme providing advice on welfare and other state benefits to mentally disordered persons (*R* v *Cardiff Local Health Board, ex p Keating* [2005] EWCA Civ 847, [2006] 1 WLR 158), albeit that this was not a health service but a service ancillary to that. Section 2 of the revised NHSA 2006 now provides that the Secretary of State, NHSCB, and CCGs 'may do anything which is calculated to facilitate, or is conducive or incidental to, the discharge of any function conferred on that person by this Act'.

CCGs may purchase secondary (hospital-based and specialist) care from NHS trusts and independent sector providers. Much of, but not all, secondary mental health services are provided by specialist NHS mental health trusts. A NHS trust might have exclusive occupation of a hospital site or a number of separate trusts might provide accommodation and services on the same site. Alternatively, a trust might manage accommodation across a range of sites, perhaps in the form of a psychiatric inpatient facility and a 'satellite' hostel for patients who require some form of assisted accommodation before returning to the community, or perhaps in the form of a number of specialist units.

The trend is towards larger trusts operating a number of sites. The Mersey Care National Health Service Trust, for example, operates 33 inpatient and outpatient facilities of various types. By mid-2013, there were, following some amalgamations, 58 specialist mental health trusts in existence. Of these, 41 had Foundation Trust (FT) status. The concept of a FT was introduced in the Health and Social Care (Community Health and Standards) Act 2003 (see now NHSA 2006, s. 30), as a mechanism to devolve power to those operating services effectively at local level, although all NHS Trusts should have such status by 2014 (See Part 4, HSCA 2012 and Explanatory Notes, para. 22), at which point, the NHS Trust will be abolished: s. 179 of the HSCA 2012. The quality of NHS provision is overseen by the watchdog organisation now known as 'Monitor' (HSCA 2012, ss. 61–71 and Sch. 8).

As at 21 February 2013, the NHS provided 136,076 hospital beds, of which 22,496 were for mental illness and 1,728 for learning disabilities (DH, 2013). Around 60 per cent of inpatients are male (Care Quality Commission (CQC), 2011: 17) and 75 per cent are white British, 4.9 per cent black Caribbean, 2.9 per cent black African, 1.6 per cent Indian, 1.3 per cent Pakistani (CQC, 2011: 15), which is out of line with figures for the general population, certainly in terms of the lower number of white British and the higher number of black Caribbean and black African that appear in these statistics.

In terms of the number of beds, the trend is down: in 2004–05, 31,667 beds were available for mental illness and 4,899 for learning disability (DH, 2006c); in 2002,

34,000 for mental illness and 6,000 for learning disability; in 1995, the figures were 39,000 and 15,000 respectively; in 1990–91 they were 55,000 and 23,000 (Government Statistical Service, 2002: Table B16). Much of the slack has, however, been taken up by expansion in the independent sector, and it has been estimated that there were, in fact, only 5 per cent fewer beds in 2001 than in 1994–95, although the fall in NHS beds was 20 per cent during that period (Mental Health Act Commission (MHAC), 2005: para. 2.51). It is open to debate whether the increased use of the independent sector is bene-ficial. Independent provision can be more expensive than NHS beds and in the past some PCTs have been reluctant to purchase it. More worrying, perhaps, a significant number of transfers of patients from NHS to independent sector providers following the closure of long-term NHS accommodation in the form of the large Victorian asy-lums (see 2.3—48,900 at 31 March 2005, representing 18 per cent of the total council supported residents in England (HC Hansard 3 July 2006, Col. 817W)—were 'out of area', and there is concern that this 'may in effect be re-creating long-stay institutions' (MHAC, 2005: para. 2.22)).

According to the government's published data (DH, 2013), occupancy rates at the end of 2012 averaged 87.2 per cent for mental illness beds and 80.2 per cent for learning disability beds, which is reasonably close to the Royal College of Psychiatrists optimum occupancy rate of 85 per cent (Royal College of Psychiatrists, 2011a: 4, Standard 1; see also Jones, 2011a). Understaffing must be factored in, however, and Garcia *et al.* (2005: Figure 12), found a national vacancy rate of 13 per cent, rising to 22 per cent in London for nursing staff.

The government's figures are, in any case, disputed. In 2005, when occupancy rates were very similar to those in 2012, Garcia *et al.* found average bed occupancy rates of 100 per cent across acute mental health inpatient services in England. The MHAC (2005: para. 2.4) also found occupancy rates in excess of 100 per cent in over half of the 1,591 wards visited between October 2004 and July 2005, and 81 wards had rates in excess of 120 per cent (para. 2.6). More recently, the CQC, which took over the role of the MHAC in 2009, has raised similar concerns, based on its finding in relation to wards surveyed by the Commission, that in 2011–12 only 52 per cent had an occupancy rate of *less than* 90 per cent, with 32 per cent having a rate of between 91 and 99 per cent, 10 per cent having 100 per cent occupancy, 3 per cent had a rate of between 101 and 109 per cent, and 3 per cent had a rate higher than that, with 2 per cent more than 120 per cent full (CQC, 2013: 55, table 5). Whatever the true figures, it is apparent that the system is, to say the least, stretched, and the bed shortages that characterise the NHS generally are particularly acute in some sectors of the mental health estate.

The NHSCB, rather than CCGs, has a specific duty, to be found in s. 4 of the NHSA 2006, to provide high security psychiatric services, for those who 'in the opinion of the Secretary of State require treatment under conditions of high security on account of their dangerous, violent or criminal propensities' (s. 4(1)(b)). These services may only be provided for persons liable to be detained under the MHA 1983, whether under the civil powers in Part II of the 1983 Act (see Chapter 6) or as a result of the exercise by the criminal courts of their powers to send someone to hospital (see Chapter 8) (s. 4(1)(a)).

Such accommodation is provided in high security hospitals, still frequently, although now unofficially, referred to as the 'special hospitals'. There are three such hospitals that provide such services for England and Wales: Broadmoor hospital in Berkshire, Rampton in Nottinghamshire, and Ashworth in Merseyside. These institutions opened in 1863, 1912, and 1989 respectively, although Ashworth hospital is the combination (in 1989) of two earlier institutions, Moss Side Hospital, which opened in 1933, and Park Lane Hospital, the newest special hospital accommodation, built in the 1970s. At the time of writing Broadmoor is being re-built, with new accommodation due to come on stream in 2017. The average population of each of these hospitals is around 250–350 patients, and all three accept patients with all types of mental disorder, although the vast majority of patients are either mentally ill or suffer from a personality disorder.

Other NHS facilities are designated as either 'medium' or 'low' security, although many—psychiatric wards in general hospitals, for example—have no security designation. Within the medium secure unit (MSU) sector, there is in fact a range of levels of security, and, at least until recently, some MSUs were designated as regional secure units (RSUs), indicating a higher level of security. The MSU sector grew markedly in the late 1990s, and by 2000–01, MSUs provided 1,950 beds for mental illness, almost a doubling from the 1,080 beds available in 1994–95, and 430 beds, up from 330 in 1994–95, for learning disability (Government Statistical Service, 2002: tables B22, B23), and there was a further expansion in the early years of the new century to accommodate the programme to relocate patients inappropriately held in the high-security hospitals, through the Accelerated Discharge Programme (ADP), which ran from 2002 to 2004. By 2004–05 there were 2,696 MSU beds for patients with mental illness and 503 for patients with a learning disability (HC Hansard, 20 July 2006, Col. 665W).

Although it is not clear from the data, it seems that this number does not include secure beds for patients with a personality disorder (which at the time was distinct from mental illness under the terms of the MHA 1983), which would add a sizeable number to this total. Many of these places would previously have been provided by the large asylums, which began to close in significant numbers in the mid-1990s (see 2.3). The initiative for the development of secure accommodation has come from within the health service and the Department of Health. Neither RSUs nor MSUs are statutory concepts. In 2007, the Royal College of Psychiatrists developed and published its *Standards for Medium Secure Units* (Royal College of Psychiatrists, 2007), which covers such issues as safety, dignity, patient involvement, professional standards, and inter-agency co-operation in the management of MSUs.

2.2.2 Community care

Primary health-care services are delivered by the NHS. Until recently the unit of delivery has been the PCT, introduced in 2002, but s. 34 of the HSCA 2012 abolished PCTs, which have now been replaced by CCGs. On 31 March 2012 there were 1,079 NHS locations registered to provide 'community health care' services in England (CQC, 2012: 16).

In 2011–12, 1,607,153 individuals received treatment from secondary mental health services for a severe and enduring mental health problem, of which 101,424 were admitted to hospital. For the vast majority—1,505,729—there was some other outcome (NHS Information Centre, 2013: table 1.1). Figures for that year available at the time of writing do not show how many of that number were not offered services, but in 2010–11, of the 1,181,011 seen but not hospitalised, only 86,873 were not offered some type of service as a result (NHS Information Centre, 2013: table 1.1). An even greater number will have consulted their GP and not been further referred. It is important to remember that for most people with a mental health problem, the extent of community care provided by the state reaches no further than their local doctor's surgery and pharmacist, with perhaps some counselling provided in addition.

The duty to secure the provision of services (other than health services) to patients in the community lies primarily with local social service authorities (LSSAs) (s. 46, National Health Service and Community Care Act (NHSCCA) 1990; Local Authority Circular (93)4), although services will also be provided by NHS bodies, local housing authorities, and service providers in the charitable, voluntary, and independent sectors. The NHSCCA 1990 is a co-ordinating piece of legislation and marks the point of entry into a complicated web of services, legislation, delegated legislation, and guidance, but this will be the subject of simplifying reform when the draft Care and Support Bill announced in the Queen's speech in 2012 and reiterated in the 2013 speech (the legal framework for the provision of community care services will be considered in detail in Chapter 3) comes into force sometime in or after 2015. In 2011–12, 2.2 million people contacted or were referred to their local LSSA for an assessment of need for community care services, of whom 1 million were offered ongoing services (CQC, 2012: 26).

A significant proportion of the community care budget is consumed in the provision of residential accommodation of one sort or another. The two main types of unit are homes providing accommodation and personal care, and those providing accommodation and nursing care. Previously known as residential care homes and nursing care homes respectively, all such accommodation is now defined as 'care homes': s. 3(1), Care Standards Act 2000. As at 31 March 2012, there were 13,134 residential care homes with 247,824 beds and 4,672 nursing homes with 215,463 beds registered in England (CQC, 2012: 28). The figures refer to the entirety of the residential accommodation sector, most of which, and almost 90 per cent of nursing home accommodation, provides accommodation for the elderly.

Provision for persons suffering from mental illness was provided by 21 per cent of the total residential home, and 23 per cent of the total nursing home, accommodation in 2011–12 (CQC, 2012: 31 and fig. 16), and for persons sectioned under the MHA in 2 per cent of each type of home (CQC, 2012: 31 and fig. 16), while learning disabilities, including autism, were more frequently catered for by residential care homes, 45 per cent of which offered accommodation to people in this group, but only 11 per cent of nursing homes did likewise (CQC, 2012: 31 and fig. 16). The vast majority of this provision is in the private, charitable, and voluntary sectors (together the 'independent sector'): in 2011–12, 96 per cent of all those placed in a care home by an LSSA were accommodated in the independent sector (CQC, 2012: 28).

It has been policy since 1990 (DH, 1990) that care should be provided to people in their own homes wherever possible, rather than in residential accommodation. Accordingly, the community care system also comprises primary care provision, preventative care, and after-care. For most mentally disordered persons, their GP is the first point of contact with the mental health system. In addition, s. 46(3) of the NSHCCA 1990 requires local authorities to provide (with more or less room for discretion) a wide range of services, which are to be found in any equally diverse number of statutes, to, *inter alia*, mentally disordered persons in their own homes.

The provision of services to people in their own homes is increasing: 16 per cent more home care services were registered with the CQC in 2011–12 than in the previous year, with a further 6 per cent increase in the first six months of 2012–13 (CQC, 2013a: 3). These services are delivered by social workers and other care workers, in tandem with community psychiatric nurses (CPNs), increasingly working out of community mental health centres (CHMCs) or in the form of community mental health teams (CMHTs), which typically comprise, as well as a CPN and social worker, occupational therapists, clinical psychologists, and psychiatrists.

Community care may also be delivered in the form of general social services, for example, domiciliary and other services geared to support independent living. An ongoing cause for concern is the level of abuse of clients which surrounds the delivery of care services to people in their own homes. In 2011–12, there were 133,000 alerts (i.e. situations in which a professional or carer had cause to be concerned about possible abuse of an adult service user and reported those concerns to their local authority), leading to 108,000 referrals (cases in which the local authority decided that the complaint should be investigated) (NHS Information Centre, 2012a: 4).

In the same year, there were 83,500 completed referrals, and in 72 per cent of cases the allegation of abuse was substantiated (41 per cent of the total) or partly substantiated (31 per cent of the total) (NHS Information Centre, 2012a: 5), with physical abuse, neglect, and financial abuse being the three most common findings. A majority of those abused (61 per cent) were female and of pensionable age (60 per cent), and around half were vulnerable by reason of mental disability (NHS Information Centre, 2012a: 5).

The CQC found in its 2012 *Community Mental Health Survey* (CQC 2012a: 7) that the team member seen most recently by service users was a CPN (33 per cent), with 24 per cent having most recently seen a psychiatrist, 16 per cent a Mental Health Support Worker, and 8 per cent a social worker. Psychotherapists and occupational therapists were last seen by service users and were seen least frequently.

CMHCs and CMHTs will also be amongst the forms in which day care provision is made, and will also refer patients to secondary care services and have been influential in this respect. As Rogers and Pilgrim (2001: 147) explain:

> Traditional primary and secondary arrangements between specialist and generalist medical practitioners were disrupted by the introduction of CMHTs. These increasingly became the

main referral point through which GPs and other primary care sources gained access to the secondary sector.

This arrangement replaced that of GPs referring to psychiatrists. Research by Barnes *et al.* (1990) found that, in areas where there are CMHCs, there was a reduction in admissions to hospital. The role of social workers and CPNs in the mandatory provision of treatment and other services, and in exercising powers of surveillance and control over mentally disordered persons in the community, has increased markedly over the last decade, as successive governments have sought to respond to public concerns about the 'failure' of community care in this regard (see Chapter 10).

Between them, inpatient provision and community care, involving a combination of physical locations and staff, comprise what may be thought of as 'the mental health system'. They are certainly designed to be the main mechanisms through which medical treatment and social care are provided to people suffering from mental disorder. But as argued at the beginning of this chapter, this is to understand the 'mental health system' in unduly narrow terms: hospitals and community care do not provide the only sources of help for people with mental disorder and do not constitute the only sites in which treatment is provided. Any survey of the fields of care and control would be remiss if it did not mention at least two further factors: informal care and treatment provided for mental disorder in prison.

2.2.3 Informal care

Considerable numbers of people with conditions that the MHA would identify as 'mental disorders' are primarily cared for informally, by their families or by private facilities. Almost half—45 per cent—of all places in care homes, for example, are privately funded (CQC, 2012: 27). People with developmental disabilities and vulnerable senior citizens are perhaps the obvious examples. The existence of family care for these people may mean that the state has little involvement other than the provision of a GP, or specialised teaching for a child with learning disabilities, or the inspection and licensing of a residential facility for a senior citizen.

This sort of private care provision is a part of state policy, but are these people in 'the system'? The answer to this question may depend on the reason the question is being asked. Thus, if the issue is state encroachment on individual care, the answer may be doubtful, since control of care is largely private, although even here, the existence of some supervision over the nursing home, although not over the specific care of the individual, shows how grey the boundaries of the system can be. If the issue is instead the imposition of power relations onto people who may be vulnerable, these people must be considered a part of the subject class of this book, since such private arrangements for care can be as oppressive as the public, and more visible, psychiatric facilities. A part of the legal tradition involves assuming some responsibility for the protection of such persons; in that context, even purely private care cannot be perceived as outside the system.

Non-professional care provided by family, friends, or others is certainly factored into the assessment of the needs of a mentally disordered person for care. Such provision is recognised in the Carers (Recognition and Services) Act 1995, which gives informal carers the right, in certain circumstances, to require that assistance be provided by a LSSA. Conversely, LSSAs may properly consider care that is being provided informally when assessing a person's need for services, and decide that it can, in a given case, play a residual role, offering respite care to both clients and their carers: *R v North Yorkshire County Council, ex p Hargreaves* (1994) Medical Law Reports 121 (HC); they might also expect that normally a relative will not charge for the care provided: *R v Stockton on Tees BC, ex p Stephenson* [2005] EWCA Civ 960. This 'invisible' element in the system obviously impacts on the pattern of community care expenditure.

2.2.4 The mental health system in prisons

Should prisons be considered as part of the mental health system? The argument that they should is increasingly strong. As discussed in Chapter 8, only a small number of mentally disordered offenders are sentenced to hospital by a court, and the population of our prisons includes a high number of mentally disordered persons. There has long been provision to transfer those in need of treatment for mental disorder to hospital, but even though such transfers have increased in recent years (see Chapter 8, 8.5) it remains the case that around 90 per cent of prison inmates have some form of mental disorder (including substance abuse), rising to 95 per cent for juvenile detainees (HM Prison Service, Department of Health and National Assembly for Wales, 2001: 3; see also Singleton *et al.*, 1998; Rickford, 2003; Rickford and Edgar, 2005; Butler and Kousoulou, 2006: 35), and a significant number have more than one form of disorder: 12–15 per cent of women inmates were found in one study to have at least four out of: neurosis, psychosis, personality disorder, alcohol abuse, and drug dependency (Owen *et al.*, 2004; see also Corston, 2007).

Historically, medical treatment and care for prisoners not ill enough to warrant transfer to hospital, or for whom no hospital place was available, was supplied by the Prison Service rather than the NHS, and was routinely of lower quality than NHS provision (Reed and Lyne, 2000; Reed, 2002). The High Court in *Knight* v *Home Office* [1990] 3 All ER 237 held that prisoners could expect no better, but in 1999 the *National Service Framework for Mental Health* (DH, 1999) made it clear that prisoners should be able to expect the same quality of care as others in need. By 2001, the government had accepted that 'There are too many prisoners in too many prisons who, despite the best efforts of committed prison health care and NHS staff, receive no treatment, or inappropriate treatment for their mental illness, from staff with the wrong mix of skills and in the wrong kind of setting' (HM Prison Service, Department of Health and National Assembly for Wales, 2001: 5).

However, a series of policy developments, beginning in the late 1990s (see DH, 1999; HM Prison Service and NHS Executive, 1999; HM Prison Service, Department of Health and National Assembly for Wales, 2001; HM Prison Service and Department of Health, 2002; HM Prison Service, 2003), culminated in the NHS taking over full responsibility for the health care of prisoners from 2006. At local level, it is now the NHSCB that is responsible for commissioning the provision of health care services for prisoners. Services are delivered to prisoners by mental health in-reach teams (MHIRTs), and funding for 350 dedicated personnel, functioning across over 100 prisons, was made available from 2006 (Brooker and Gojkovic, 2009).

These developments did not prove to be an instant panacea for prison-based health care service delivery, particularly for prisoners requiring treatment for mental disorder. In 2008, a report commissioned by the Sainsbury Centre for Mental Health (Brooker *et al.*, 2008: 2; see also HM Inspectorate of Prisons, 2007) found that prison in-reach had been 'hindered by limited resourcing, constraints imposed by the prison environment, difficulties in ensuring continuity of care and wide variations in local practice' with some NHS areas spending twice as much as others on mental health services for prisoners with no obvious explanation as to why that was the case; that although more is spent per head on prisoners than the national average, this was 'not nearly enough to accommodate [the] much higher level of need' of prisoners compared to the population as a whole. Brooker *et al.* called for 'major investment' to bring services up to the standards available to non-prisoners.

A year later, the Prison Reform Trust commissioned research (Edgar and Rickford, 2009: ch. 7) which came to similar findings, with MHIRTs operating with a lack of definition of their purpose, and with a lack of resources, including staff, particularly for responding to prisoners with a mental health crisis (2009: ch. 4). This research also found that one in three medical appointments were missed by prisoners, but that often there was no attempt made to investigate why an appointment had been missed, notwithstanding that, in one case at least, the prisoner had been hallucinating and that may have explained his non-attendance. Instead, the patient went without treatment or assessment (2009: 26).

Resource shortfall was not the only problem identified however. One illuminating remark was made to the researchers by a member of a prison's Independent Monitoring Board (IMBs monitor the quality of service delivery in prisons) to the researchers (Edgar and Rickford, 2009: 25):

> The unchallenged view within health care is that prisoners try it on all the time. A lot of the drugs we are talking about have similar effects to illegal substances and doubtlessly have a currency within the prison. OK, health care staff have to be careful but they never seem to give anyone the benefit of the doubt and...often seem very uncaring.

Here, we run up against the systemic limits of mental health provision, and the mental health system within the broader, defining, context of the penal system and its construction of the 'prisoner', which can override the health care system's construction, of 'patient'.

The idea of a 'system', as such, is rendered somewhat paradoxical. On the one hand, systemic boundaries, such as that between secure hospital provision and prison, are arbitrary and misleading. The same individual may end up in either system, at least in some circumstances, and in either case he or she is detained and confined. Whether the establishment is a hospital or a prison may not seem to matter much. On the other hand, the mechanisms which constitute the boundaries of each do have real effects. For example, and in particular, it is possible to treat a person detained in a psychiatric hospital without that person's consent (see Chapter 6, 6.3) but there is no such power in prisons.

In the same Prison Reform Trust report, another IMB member explained to researchers that the absence of a power to treat without consent means that 'those exhibiting bizarre behaviour have to be controlled by techniques of restraint rather than medication, altogether a more degrading and less humane response', and such prisoners 'usually end up in the segregation unit, where their disruptive behaviour often continues' (Edgar and Rickford, 2009: 5). But this does not detract from the general point being made here, which is that it is increasingly untenable to regard the prison estate as a system separate from the mental health system. In April 2012 the National Institute for Health and Clinical Excellence (NICE) announced that it would produce guidance on the delivery of health care to prisoners, although this is yet to appear and no date of publication has been confirmed.

2.2.5 Mental health beyond the mental health system

The problematic boundaries of the mental health system extend beyond that border it shares with the penal system. As mentioned at 2.1, if we think of the mental health system from the point of view of the user, then it is not clear why, for example, the housing system or the benefits system, and others too, such as systems surrounding, for example, the protection of employment rights, or the possibilities of obtaining credit or a mortgage, are not seen as within the mental health system, given that they are all systems of governance which can impact on the mental health of individuals.

Some of the boundaries between the mental health and other systems are specified in law. For example, National Assistance Act 1948, s. 21(8), which currently governs the provision of residential community care accommodation provided by LSSAs, provides that an LSSA is not permitted under that legislation to provide accommodation 'by or under any enactment not contained in this Part of this Act'. In other words, a need for housing not linked to the need to be provided with community care services cannot be met by an LSSA. Instead, that is the responsibility of the local housing authority (LHA), charged with duties and provided with powers under the Housing Act 1996.

As will be discussed further at Chapter 3, 3.5.2, although the Housing Act does make some provision for persons with mental disorder who apply to be provided with social housing, the two regimes do not always dovetail well. For the service user, it may not be apparent that there are two systems at work here: LSSAs and LHAs are both 'the council', part of the same system of local government service provision or arrangement. A similar point could be made about the benefits system: to the service user, these services do constitute a 'complex of interacting components' compatible with the definition of a 'system' proffered by Laslo and Kruppner (see 2.1).

As may be expected, the intersection of the mental health system and the benefits system is systematically provided for by legislation and accompanying regulations. There are also benefits designed for persons who have problems with daily living, which are not means-tested, which are available to persons by reason of mental disorder. Disability Living Allowance (DLA) has been payable until recently, but was replaced (although to be phased in) from April 2013 by the Personal Independence Payment (PIP). This is calculated by reference to two components, each of which are payable at a 'standard' or an 'enhanced' rate, depending on the assessment of the payee's condition (see Welfare Reform Act 2012, ss. 77–79 and The Social Security (Personal Independence Payment) Regulations 2013, SI 2013/377 (2013 Regs)). The daily living component is payable from April 2013 at a weekly standard rate of £53 and an enhanced rate of £79.15. The mobility component is payable at a standard weekly rate of £21.00 and an enhanced rate of £55.25 (2013 Regs, reg. 24).

Eligibility for a PIP is assessed by reference to whether the claimant's ability to carry out daily activities is limited by his or her physical or mental condition (Welfare Reform Act 2012, s. 80), and the relevant activities—things like being able to prepare food, wash, bathe and use the toilet, communicate with others effectively, and make decisions—are listed in Sch. 1 to the 2013 Regs. This situation must have existed for at least three months and be likely to continue for at least a further nine months before a claim can be made (Welfare Reform Act 2012, s. 81 and 2013 Regs, regs. 12–14). In a contentious change from the situation with respect to payment of DLA (see Harris, 2011), no payment in respect of the daily living component may be paid to a person residing in a care home (reg. 28), and no payment for either component to a person residing in a hospital or a prison (reg. 29), in either case once that person has been in that care home, hospital, or prison for more than 28 days (2013 Regs, regs. 30(1), 31(1)).

It has been estimated that the removal of care home residents' ability to claim the daily living component will affect 80,000 people and produce savings for the government of £160 million per annum by 2014–15 (HC Debs December 9, 2010, col.393 w and December 16, 2010, col.906 w, cited in Harris, 2011: 107), and overall £2 billion will be saved by the shift from DLA to PIPs. It is clear from the consultation document which preceded the Welfare Reform Act 2012 (Department of Work and Pensions, 2010) that saving money was high on the government's agenda (Barnett-Cormack *et al.*, 2012), and the eligibility criteria, and the requirements to provide evidence, submit to medical examination, and so on, have been generally tightened up by the Act and 2013 Regulations to this end. Mentally disordered persons who are unemployed and do not meet the eligibility criteria for PIPs may claim the new Universal Credit benefit (Welfare Reform Act 2012, s. 1).

Although space does not permit the further exploration of issues around benefits and housing policies and systems, it is clear that these systems can impact as much and, in many cases, more on individuals than does the mental health system, narrowly defined as inpatient and community care services. In these areas, as can be seen, provision has been made with regard to the interface between housing, benefits, and the mental health system. In other areas, outside immediate state control, with the state, rather, acting as regulator not provider, such as employment or access to finance, specific provision is often lacking, and it is necessary for those who feel aggrieved on the basis that they have been treated unfavourably by reason of their mental disorder to ground arguments in human rights law (if applicable) or equality and discrimination law (see Chapter 3, 3.4.2).

Considering things from the point of view of those on the receiving end of the mental health system prohibits us from accepting the easy answer to the question 'what is the mental health system?': tempting as it is, we cannot accept that the only law relevant to understanding the mental health system is to be found in the MHA and clearly related legislation such as the MCA and those statutes which provide explicitly for 'care in the community'. Beyond this, however, the appropriate scope of discussion is ill-defined, and this is because, for a person suffering from mental disorder, and their families, the effects and implications of that disorder can permeate all areas of life.

For ease of digestion and to allow appropriate depth of coverage, the line has to be drawn somewhere, and our primary focus in this book will be on the mental health system, the boundaries of which are set around the provision of treatment and care for mental disorder, either in hospitals or in the community. We will not, however, always be able to stick rigidly within those boundaries: at some points the space between the mental health system and those which border and overlap it is where the issues of legal and policy controversy are to be found. And it is important to remember that the boundaries of the topic, so constituted, are arbitrary, and do not tell the whole story, and that for each patient or service user, 'the system' will be experienced differentially and subjectively.

2.2.6 The mental health system and mental health policy

There are ongoing attempts to pull all of this provision together into a more coherent and uniform, policy and evidence-driven, system. The first such attempt, in 1999, came in the form of the *National Service Framework for Mental Health* (NSFMH) (DH, 1999), listing seven national standards, with a 10-year timescale for implementation:

- The promotion of mental health for all, social inclusion, and the combating of discrimination on grounds of mental health.
- People suffering from a common mental health problem should be able to access necessary assessment and treatments.
- Services should provide round-the-clock coverage.
- All service users with a care plan should receive optimum care, including preventative care, a written care plan, and 24-hour access to services.
- There should be timely access to inpatient care in the least restrictive environment possible.
- Those who provide regular care to a person on the Care Programme Approach (CPA) (see Chapter 3.5.1) are entitled to have their own needs as carers assessed at least once annually.
- By a combination of the above factors, service providers should work to reduce suicides.

Five years on, the pressure and campaigning group MIND issued its report on the first five years of the NSFMH, finding that (2004: 1):

> The picture is mixed. Whilst there is no doubt that increased focus has been placed on specialised community based services, which is welcome, this has in many cases been at the expense of attention on other areas such as mental health promotion and in-patient care. After five years, we would expect more comprehensive improvements to have been achieved. Making high profile improvements in some areas whilst allowing others to be left behind is not acceptable.

Although much of this was accepted by the Department of Health (DH, 2004a), and efforts were renewed, it was reported near the end of the 10-year period that attempts to implement the plan as fully as intended were being undermined by financial limitation (Boardman and Parsonage, 2008).

The NSFMH was replaced by *No Health Without Mental Health, a Cross-government Mental Health Outcomes Strategy for People of All Ages* (HM Government, 2011), launched in February 2011. The strategy, led by the Department of Health acting together with other central government departments, local government, and professional, user, and carer organisations, has lofty aims, and contextualises mental health policy against a broader governmental mission: 'If we are to build a healthier, more productive and fairer society in which we recognise difference, we have to build resilience, promote mental health and wellbeing, and challenge health inequalities' (HM Government, 2011: para 1.6). More specifically, the new strategy is designed to meet the following six objectives (2011: 6):

 (i) More people will have good mental health.

 (ii) More people with mental health problems will recover.

(iii) More people with mental health problems will have good physical health.

(iv) More people will have a positive experience of care and support.

 (v) Fewer people will suffer avoidable harm.

(vi) Fewer people will experience stigma and discrimination.

The strategy is comprised of a variety of messages and agendas. One central message is that mental health has always been the 'poor relation' within the NHS, with priority given instead to physical ailments, notwithstanding that the duties, currently found in the NHSA 2006 (see 2.2.1), require that the NHS secure improvement in both 'the physical and mental health' of citizens. The equal billing in s. 1 of the NHSA 2006 must be accompanied by a 'parity of esteem' (HM Government, 2012: 9).

The accompanying *Mental Health Strategy Implementation Framework* (HM Government, 2012), produced in collaboration with professional and user groups, charities and local government bodies, was published in July 2012. The Framework's mission is 'translating the ideals into concrete actions that can be taken by a wide range of local organisations to bring about real and measurable improvements in mental health and wellbeing for people across the country' (HM Government, 2012: 5), and to this end both organisations directly involved in the provision of services, and those which provide other services for mental disorder—housing, education, benefits, employment assistance and advice—and private entities such as employers, are given advice as to how they can implement the mental health outcomes strategy into their daily operations.

Section 194 of the HSCA 2012 established Health and Wellbeing Boards in every local authority area, membership of which includes top- or high level representatives of public services, along with representatives of user groups and other relevant local actors, with a brief to encourage integrated working across local government (HSCA 2012, s. 195). Health and Wellbeing Boards are intended to be 'at the heart of assessing local needs, agreeing local priorities and planning local actions' and 'central' to improving outcomes locally in accordance with the outcomes strategy (HM Government, 2012: 25). It remains to be seen whether the introduction of the new Boards, and the outcomes strategy in general, is able to connect with those bodies and organisations which do not have the provision of services for persons with mental disorder amongst their core responsibilities and aims, in a way that the NSFMH did not.

Evidently, our mental health system, described here in bare outline, exists in a highly politicised climate. That is because the policy choices involved in running the system are inherently value-driven and political, but the intensity of the situation has increased as the economic recession has taken resources away from service providers. Pressing as these questions of the detail of current provision are, we should not forget to allocate time to the broader and more fundamental questions: is this the system that we want? How, when, and why did it come into being? What is its function or functions (intended or unintended)? To what extent has the 'shape' of the system changed, and with what implications? How well does the system actually work? More pertinently, what is the relevance of such questions for the student of mental health law? Although this book, as a whole, might begin to answer at least some of these questions, it is the questions themselves that will be particularly to the fore in this chapter.

2.3 The rise and fall of asylum-based provision

To say that the interpretation of the historical genesis and development of the contemporary mental health system is a matter of controversy is a substantial understatement. The more one learns of the history of madness and its responses, the better the reasons for this controversy are appreciated. It is both the most fascinating and the most frustrating aspect of this history that, in its detail, one finds the negation of easy generalisation, on more or less any aspect of it. Let us begin with what is not controversial: from its beginnings in a relatively small number of relatively small asylums active at the end of the eighteenth century, specialised institutional provision for the insane grew, over the course of the nineteenth and twentieth centuries, until about the end of the Second World War. From that point, asylum provision has been in a fairly precipitous decline, as public policy has increasingly focused on community care as the primary mode of care provision for people with mental disabilities. The change in provision can be seen

clearly in a few statistical indicators. In 1847, there were 21 county asylums in existence; by 1914, there were 97. The size of the average asylum also grew markedly after
1850: the average population was 1,000 by 1900, with a number of institutions at double
that rate (Prior, 1996: 67).

This growth is matched by the total number of people confined in these asylums. In
1850, total inpatients in county asylums numbered 7,140 (4.03 per 10,000 population).
By 1930, they contained 119,659 people (30.14 per 10,000 population), and by 1954,
148,000 people (33.45 per 10,000 population). At this point, however, the decarceration
movement was beginning to take effect, and the total inpatient population fell more
rapidly than it rose: by 1981, the rate of confinement had more than halved, to 15.5 per
10,000 population. This downward trend continued throughout the 1980s and 1990s.
Between 1980 and 1990, there was a further 25 per cent reduction in the number of hospital beds available. Bed numbers fell below 100,000 by 1990, and by 1997–98 the total
stock of available psychiatric hospital beds stood at 45,878. By 1997–98, there would
remain only two hospitals with more than 1,000 beds (Government Statistical Service,
1998: Table B17). By the end of the century, both of these hospitals had closed.

There are a variety of explanations for these trends. Regarding the growth of asylums, Jones (1972) emphasises the nineteenth-century social reform movements, and
the great men who were their tireless advocates, Sir George Onesiphorus Paul, Charles
Wynn, and, perhaps most significantly, Anthony Ashley Cooper, the seventh Earl of
Shaftesbury, as promoting an increasingly civilised and humane response to the social
problem of madness. The object of these figures was to bring decent and rational provision to some of the most pitiable people of society. Through tireless lobbying, they
brought about the expansion of the county asylum movement to the point where it
became a symbol of nineteenth-century philanthropy, and the provision of standards,
both in those asylums and in private facilities, through the introduction of legislative
standards and an effective system of inspection.

This broadly progressive image of nineteenth-century social policy on asylums cannot entirely be dismissed. Certainly, there was an interest in the legislation of lunacy in
the nineteenth century, such as had not occurred before; the County Asylums Act 1845,
which made county asylum provision mandatory for pauper lunatics, was undoubtedly
a significant boost to asylum construction. But the progressive nature of the reforms is
perhaps open to question. The nineteenth-century commentators were fond of citing
the horrific care provided in environments where reform had not penetrated. A report
from as late as 1845 tells of insane persons outside asylums kept by their families in
that place 'commonly devoted to the reception of coals', this being a 'confined, dark and
damp corner' between the stairs and the ground floor in which 'may be found at this
very time no small number of our fellow-beings, huddled, crouching and gibbering,
with less apparent intelligence and under worse treatment than the lower domestic animals' (Jones, 1972: 12). Was previous provision really so bad? And did it really become
so much better upon admission to asylums?

Certainly, some of the accounts are extremely unpleasant, but modern scholars are
looking to these accounts with an increasingly critical eye. Patricia Allderidge (1985),

for example, has challenged much of the disparaging imagery of Bethlem hospital in the eighteenth and early nineteenth centuries, and Roy Porter (1987a) and Rab Houston (1999) have both painted broadly positive pictures of the care of the insane in the private sector in the eighteenth century. For the poor, provision of care was surely more frugal; research by Akihito Suzuki (1991; 1992) would suggest that it would be wrong to perceive even the poor insane as simply ignored by the system. Instead, they appear to have been treated within the poor law system, much as other paupers were.

The question, therefore, becomes not so much a matter of improvement in treatment on an objective scale, but rather of how the Victorians understood the reforms as progressive. Certainly the perception of improved standards was a part of the concern; equally important was the idea that society could be regulated, and individuals controlled, on a large scale. By 1845, the reforms in their legal form matched a fairly classic Benthamite paradigm. Central legislation was put in place, designed to ensure that poor 'lunatics and idiots' would come to the attention of Justices of the Peace, and would be confined in a new system of county asylums. Both these, and the private madhouses catering to the more monied classes, would be inspected regularly, by a specialised board of inspectors, the Commissioners in Lunacy. And consistent with such a Benthamite model, the asylum itself—both its architecture and the regime it would create—would be pivotal to the conception of the reform of the insane person. Surveillance both of the insane in the asylum and at least of the poorer classes of society became pivotal to the ideology of the statute.

The approach that became symbolic of nineteenth-century asylum care was moral treatment. This form of therapy had diverse origins. In England, it originated in a private facility run by Quakers, the York Retreat, in the years following its opening in 1796 (see Digby, 1985; 1985a). In France, it is attributed to Philippe Pinel, at roughly the same time. In contrast to the intrusive physical treatments of his day, Pinel claimed that 'experience affords ample and daily proofs of the happier effects of a mild, conciliating treatment', and 'giving my most decided suffrage in favour of the moral qualities of maniacs' who would exhibit 'indescribable tenderness' and 'estimable virtue' if treated 'morally'. Although not the first to use such techniques 'Pinel, however, explicitly completed the circle: that which is psychologically caused is most effectively psychologically treated' (Bynum, 1981: 42). A similar philosophy was to be found at the York Retreat, in that 'moral treatment as practised at the Retreat, and elsewhere, meant a concentration on the rational and emotional rather than the organic causes of insanity' (Digby, 1985: 53). This entailed a regime that, although varying from exponent to exponent, essentially comprised the provision of a protective, peaceful, civilised and contemplative environment in which 'to help the patient gain enough self-discipline to master his illness' (Digby, 1985: 53). As the nineteenth century progressed, and scandalous conditions were revealed to exist at asylums, hospitals, and madhouses up and down the country, the York Retreat became a watchword for the humane treatment, and cure, of the insane. By shortly after mid-century, a somewhat mutated form of the Retreat's approach was broadly adopted throughout the country, under the name 'non-restraint'.

The system never worked in the way its framers had intended. The notion of a co-ordinated, centrally directed network of county asylums, and of surveillance throughout the country, whereby the poor insane would be routinely identified and removed to asylums, came up against well-established local interests, and management of, and admission to, asylums remained in local hands. Similarly, while it is certainly true that even in the largest of county asylums few people were subjected to physical restraint, moral treatment was not relied upon to the exclusion of chemical intervention, particularly later in the century when the use of opiates became relatively common. While pragmatic issues will be more relevant at 2.5, it is also appropriate to note the significance of the image of this paradigm of nineteenth-century regulation and care.

As noted, the issues of surveillance, regulation, and control are central to the aspects of the system: surveillance of the community, to ensure the routine diversion of the insane to asylums; surveillance of the insane in the asylum, through appropriate architecture and staffing, to ensure that the insane are properly cared for and appropriately employed; surveillance of the asylum, to ensure that the officers and staff are doing their job properly; surveillance of the insane by themselves, as a method of treatment. Certainly, this can be portrayed as progress. For the insane exposed to the worst of eighteenth-century conditions, there can be little doubt that the nineteenth-century asylum offered an improvement in standard of care: basic comforts, including adequate food, were provided; work was offered to those who were able to do it—generally farm work for men and laundry and needlework for women—but only six hours per day. Perhaps unsurprisingly, there is evidence that some (although not all) individuals wanted admission to this environment (Bartlett, 1999; 1999a). At the same time, there is a sense in which the systemic approach glorified in the nineteenth century implied its own set of particularly intrusive controls and confinements. In theory, the poor were always under surveillance by local officials; there was to be no escape. Asylums were similarly open to the prying eyes of inspectors.

Similarly, the treatment at the centre of the new ideology has not always been portrayed in positive terms. For Castel (1985: 256), moral treatment is 'this authoritarian pedagogy'. For Foucault, moral treatment differed from what had gone before, the lunatic in chains, not so much because of its greater humanity but rather because of its greater, more penetrative, control of the recipient. Now, the mad would police themselves. The moral treatment practised at York was important not so much for its religious element, but rather its more general strategy (Foucault, 1986: 145, 146):

> ...to place the insane individual within a moral element where he will be in debate with himself and his surroundings: to constitute for him a milieu where, far from being protected, he will be kept in a perpetual anxiety, ceaselessly threatened by Law and Transgression...the madman...must feel morally responsible for everything within him that may disturb morality and society, and must hold no one but himself responsible for the punishment he receives.

This may sound harsh, but such apparent harshness in part emphasises the success of the project upon which the new asylums were engaged, a project now completely assimilated into our modern understanding: cure, in the asylum, is to be understood as a journey to normalcy. Where previous approaches to mental illness, based on somatic theories, may have implied such a base line in their diagnostic criteria, moral treatment places a concept of normality at the core of treatment: where previously, it might have been how the insane person was identified, now, it becomes that which the insane person must want. This remains pivotal to our understanding of mental health: success is measured in terms of reintegration into society, and invisibility of the individual when returned to that society.

The nineteenth-century reforms further serve as a marker of a new attitude to people with mental health difficulties: they were a class to be treated differently. This is, in fact, merely a stage on a considerably longer progression, commencing with the Vagrancy Act 1714, which allowed the confinement of the 'furiously mad' poor. The Vagrancy Act 1744 continued this trend, allowing such lunatics to be excused from corporal punishment for failing to work. In this context, the nineteenth-century statutes constitute a continuation of this strategy of classification and differential treatment. This does represent a change from previous legal understanding, however, when the insane poor were dealt with as just another category of deviant. In the eighteenth and nineteenth centuries, they became a unique class, warranting special treatment or attention. It is a theme that permeates our modern view of the appropriate social approach to insanity. It is what makes it somehow socially acceptable to argue for the protective detention of the insane, or for their increased control in the community, in contexts that would be unthinkable in other elements of the population—again, a profoundly important epistemological shift at the root of our understanding of the insane.

While the social reform theory explains much of the theoretical context of asylum provision, both in the nineteenth century and today, it is problematic in that the legislation was not implemented in the way in which it would appear from the statute to have been intended. And the emphasis on the Benthamite model obscures some fundamentally non-Benthamite influences on the shape of the legislation. The control of the new county asylums remained almost entirely outside the scope of the specialist inspectorate, the Commissioners in Lunacy. They were instead managed by the local Justices of the Peace until 1888, when they were transferred to local authorities.

Similarly, Justices of the Peace controlled admission and discharge processes throughout the nineteenth century. The Commissioners in Lunacy could inspect the facilities. They might 'squawk', and squawk they occasionally did in their annual reports, but they had minimal actual power to enforce change. Thus, the City of London did not build a county asylum for its pauper lunatics until 1866, more than 20 years after such provision became mandatory, notwithstanding a continuing series of complaints from the Commissioners. Effectively, if local administrations did not wish to comply with the legislation, there was little to force them. The situation relating to the Commissioners was similar in relation to private madhouses outside London, although inside the metropolis they did have licensing power for such private institutions. As a percentage of asylum provision, however, such private establishments were of minimal significance: the large growth in asylum provision in the nineteenth century was in the county asylum sector, over which the Commissioners had no direct influence.

To understand the actual structure and growth of the nineteenth-century asylum system, therefore, it is necessary to understand the dynamic of the individuals who were actually doing the administration. Here, the presumptions of the previous discussion become almost universally problematic. Certainly, the nineteenth-century statutes appear to create the insane as a separate class of deviant, and in a sense they were; in the county asylum system, they remained a separate class specifically of deviant poor, and pauper status was required in order for admission. Arguably, the county asylum acts of the nineteenth century are appropriately considered to be a branch of the poor law itself (Bartlett, 1999).

This makes sense chronologically. The County Asylums Act 1808 was of limited effect. The 1845 Act was of considerably greater effect, based not only on the numbers of asylums built, but also on the numbers of people confined. Arguably, the significant change occurring between the two Acts is the replacement of the largely voluntary parish officers of the old poor law, with the professional workforce of the new. While the 1808 Act had given poor law officials the duty to enforce the Acts at the local level, it was only with the post-1834 staffing that the admission processes could be run on the scale the Acts intended. If this approach is correct, the question arises as to when the provision of asylum and other services to people with mental disorders really separates from the provision of poor law, or social services, as we would now call it. The question is perhaps whether they have ever become separate. A reasonable case can be made for the separation for asylum provision when the NHS was created, because it was at that time that the final vestiges of the poor law were laid to rest. For community care, however, the argument looks as strong as ever. Thus as will be seen at 2.4.2, it was only when community care services became claimable on social services budgets rather than health budgets that significant provision began to be made for care in the community.

The poor law connection is significant not merely for its administrative relationship to the asylum, but also because it was reformed at roughly the same time as the asylum law, and it too, at least on paper, introduced an institutional solution through the nineteenth-century workhouse. Prisons also grew apace in this period. Institutional solutions were popular throughout social policy at this time. Can these parallels be considered as flowing from the same causes? Can both reforms be related to the economic changes prompted by the industrial revolution? Again, arguments are not straightforward. Certainly, population growth was rapid and unyielding, and there was a shift from rural to urban living for a significant proportion of the population. Traditional communities and social ties were broken. The result was the beginnings of the creation of a great swathe of urban poverty. As Scull has pointed out, however, the asylum had already been adopted as policy when the majority of the population still lived outside new cities, and before the Acts of 1845, the decision, at county level, to construct an asylum bore little relation to the extent of urbanisation and industrialisation.

Scull offers instead an analysis that echoes that offered by Foucault in relation to the previous century. Scull suggests that explanation should focus on 'the effects of the ever more thoroughgoing commercialization of existence' (1979: 29), resulting in 'the abandonment of long-established techniques for coping with the poor and the troublesome'

(1979: 30) without recourse to institutionalisation. For Scull, the new logic of commodification undermined informal methods of responding to insanity based on feudal relations of patronage, essentially converting them from social to economic relations based on waged labour. Madness in the era of capitalism is defined in terms of the requirements of that system, which is to say in terms of the ability to work. Incarceration of the insane freed former carers to work outside the home in the new factories, and in addition 'seemed ideally suited to the means of establishing "proper" work habits among those elements of the workforce who were apparently more resistant to the monotony, routine, and regularity of industrialised labour' (1979: 35).

Proof of such a theory is problematic. It would be naive to ignore the social change that occurred in this period, and the consequent changes to the possibilities of domestic care of the insane. Certainly, the values cited by Scull were significant in the ideology of the new asylums. As we have seen, work was to be provided in the asylum for those able to pursue it. Similarly, an inability to work was one of the factors that might be considered in determining the appropriateness of an asylum admission. It was not, of course, the only one, but Scull's theory is not so crass. It acknowledges that confinement of an insane person may be necessary because of the absence of other care possibilities. It also acknowledges the possibility that those with insane relations might increasingly expect the state to provide care. While certainly an arguable view, such motives are difficult to substantiate. It does not inspire confidence, however, that patterns of institutionalisation of the insane during the period bear no obvious correlation to patterns of economic growth or recession and unemployment in the period, as one might expect if the growth of asylums is to be understood in economic terms.

In all of this discussion of the nineteenth century, doctors, in general, and specialists in mental disorders, in particular, have been conspicuous by their absence. They have long been involved in the treatment of the insane, of course; at some point in the last 250 years, they became particularly central to the administration of insanity. Precisely how and when that colonisation occurred is controversial. Certainly, by the middle of the eighteenth century, the process had begun. Jones (1972: 35) argues that the madness of George III, cured by Dr Willis, gave the image of the mad-doctor a considerable boost. That seems undisputed, although the rudiments of professional formation were falling into place before that time, with the opening of a variety of hospitals for the insane in the second half of the eighteenth century.

First of these was St Luke's in London, opened in 1751. St Luke's was to be a teaching hospital and centre for medical research, and admitted medical students from the start. Other hospitals or asylums, funded, like St Luke's, by way of public subscription, opened in quick succession: Manchester Lunatic Hospital in 1766; others in Newcastle, Liverpool, York, and elsewhere soon followed. Certainly, the doctors running these establishments, and particularly those involved in private madhouses, would complain of low professional status, but, in time, madhouse-keeping became an object of pride rather than shame, 'helping, not hindering, a medical career' (Porter, 1987a: 167). Porter points out that William Battie, the driving force behind St Luke's, was to become President of the Royal College of Physicians.

The movement of medical specialists into the treatment of insanity continued with the development of the county asylums. Andrew Scull (1993) has devoted considerable talent and insight to a claim that the nineteenth century was the period when specialist doctors consolidated their professional status over the insane. Much of his work is extremely perceptive in this regard, examining how the new specialist class of mad-doctors form a profession, complete with professional journals and a professional organisation, the Association of Medical Officers of Asylums and Hospitals for the Insane. It is indisputable that significant medical theory developed in the nineteenth century. That said, for key developments, the medical profession can be seen as followers rather than leaders. Thus, notwithstanding the myth that the policy of non-restraint was introduced by John Conolly at the Hanwell Asylum in London, it would seem instead that it was introduced by the Justices of the Peace in charge of the asylum (see Suzuki, 1995). This is significant of a considerably wider phenomenon: while specialist doctors were appointed as medical superintendents of county asylums for much of the nineteenth century, they had remarkably little power. Specifically, they did not control who came into the asylum; that was the role of Justices of the Peace, poor law relieving officers, and poor law medical officers. They similarly did not control who left the asylum: that, once again, was in the hands of the managing committee of Justices.

In the private sector, things were different, because often the facility would be owned by a doctor. If it was not, however, the relations between the owner and the medical officer might presumably be complex. For both the private and county facilities, medical certificates were, of course, required for admission (two for the former, one for the latter); individuals with an interest in the facility to which admission was sought were specifically precluded from signing the forms. As a result, they would frequently be signed not by specialists, but by general doctors. All of this did not, of course, stop the specialist doctors from developing a professional expertise in the treatment of insanity, but it is difficult to see that this specialist group enjoyed particularly administrative or political influence in the nineteenth century. That would arise instead in the twentieth century.

So why did asylums grow? The centralised theory of Jones is problematic, in that the growth required the acquiescence, if not the outright enthusiasm, of the local officials, and the central authorities had no way of enforcing that. Bartlett's theory may account for that more effectively, but it does not explain why private provision also increased markedly in the nineteenth century (although not as greatly as county asylum provision). The fact that such provision increased outside of the administrative framework Bartlett describes suggests that internal administrative dynamics of the poor law cannot solely account for the growth of the asylum system: this must, at least in part, reflect a broader paradigm shift. The increased promise of cure is similarly problematic as an explanation. The use of data sets by modern historians would suggest that the asylums did have a curative role: roughly two thirds of people admitted were released cured within two years of admission (Wright, 1997). Nineteenth-century observers seemed to be unaware of this fact, however, and their reports tended to read from the earliest times as justifications for the failures of cure (see Scull, 1993). Certainly, the nineteenth century favoured institutional solutions more broadly, but it is difficult to see how that broad principle related to specific causal factors. It would seem that we are left with a selection of partial and not entirely convincing explanations; the issues will no doubt be debated by historians for a long time to come.

Accounts of the retreat from the asylum are no less problematic. Contemporary accounts tended to link the fall-off in hospital inpatient numbers with the emergence of a new generation of major tranquillising drugs in the 1950s. The first and most well-known of these was chlorpromazine, which was first produced in France in 1950. The drug was first used in the UK in 1954 (where it is known as Largactil), and in the USA in 1955 (under the name Thorazine). There is no doubt that there was a 'drug revolution' in psychiatric practice at this time. As Scull (1977: 80) points out, in the USA, in late 1953, Thorazine was only used (in trials) on 104 patients; by 1955, an estimated two million prescriptions were written. Smith Kline French aggressively marketed the drug, and the company's turnover increased from $53m in 1953 to $347m by 1970.

This explanation seems to have a logical ring to it. If drug therapies can, at the very least, hold symptoms in abeyance, and possibly even 'cure' mental illness, the rationale for a general policy of inpatient treatment is undermined. Of course, huge benefits accrued to the status of the psychiatric profession within the medical, and broader, establishment with the advent of the new drug therapies. Here was confirmation of the organic, somatic model of mental illness, which allowed psychiatry to conform more explicitly to a medical model. The drug revolution also precipitated a change in government policy. The Mental Health Act 1959 recast the relation between 'legalism' and 'medicalism' in favour of the latter (although the process had already begun with the introduction of 'informal' admissions by the Mental Treatment Act 1930), and also redrew the map of service provision. From now on, there was to be a greater emphasis, at least at the level of policy, on outpatient and community-based service provision. 'Community care', which had in fact been a constant feature of the social response to mental disorder throughout the age of the asylum, now became government policy.

In 1960, Enoch Powell, then Minister of Health, announced that the old Victorian asylums were 'doomed institutions'. According to his Hospital Plan of 1962, inpatient services were to be relocated to the greatest extent possible within general hospitals (and departments of psychiatry were indeed a feature of many general hospitals from the early 1960s) and, so the theory ran, investment was now to be channelled into community care schemes of one sort or another rather than into the maintenance of the Victorian asylum system (see 2.4.1). Moreover, this was seen to be politically feasible, because there was, by this time, a more tolerant attitude on the part of society in general towards mentally disordered persons.

There is, however, good reason to think that this explanation is altogether too neat. For a start, inpatient numbers in some hospitals began to fall *before* the emergence of chlorpromazine. Mapperly hospital in Nottingham, for example, had started to reduce inpatient numbers from 1948 (1948, 1,310; 1956, 1,060), and this pattern continued 'at an unchanged pace even after drugs arrived on the scene'. This was a pattern that can also be seen in hospitals in the USA (Scull, 1977: 82). In some European countries, asylum numbers continued to rise after the introduction of the new drug treatments (Rogers and Pilgrim, 2001: 62). In the UK, there was little correlation between diagnosis, treatment, and decarceration: so that, although the new treatments were not appropriate for the majority of hospital inpatients this did not prevent their deinstitutionalisation (Butler, 1992: 37). In short, the preponderance of academic opinion today is to the effect that the link between decarceration and the drug revolution is little more than a modern myth (see, e.g., Butler, 1992: 36; Rogers and Pilgrim, 2010: 156; Scull, 1977: 82).

So what does explain the undeniable fact of decarceration? Scull's argument, which is well known, is that asylums did not cure people, but merely institutionalised them; those working in the system did not need radical sociologists to tell them this. Maudsley, for example, was making the point in the late nineteenth century. But the nineteenth-century campaign for a policy of care in the community failed, or rather it lay dormant until its time came, that is, when its interests coincided with wider ideological and political agendas.

Scull's second factor is the development of the welfare state after the Second World War. Scull locates the emergence of decarceration policies in the 1950s in the context of 'the internal dynamics of the development of capitalist societies' (1977: 134). As seen in this section, Scull has offered a similarly economically oriented explanation of the rise of the asylum a century earlier. In respect of decarceration, he argues that, with the emergence of the welfare state and an accompanying rise in state expenditure on the provision of welfare services, the asylum became too expensive to justify when 'out-relief' was as a general rule easier on the state's pocket. Scull points out that expenditure on social services as a percentage of GDP increased from 10.9 per cent in 1937 to 24.9 per cent in 1973, which has led to 'acute budgetary strains' (1977: 138). For Scull, the impact of the drug revolution should be seen as a subset of these broader economic considerations. The virtue of the new drug treatments, as such, is not so much that they 'work' but that they give credence to a strategy of service provision outside the asylum that is geared by considerations of cost rather than therapy.

Scull's analysis cannot easily be dismissed. It has been pointed out, however, that it is an analysis that is easier to apply to the 1960s, when financial problems, the 'sterling crisis' in particular, were a matter of acute concern for the government of the time. The 1950s, by contrast, were not a time of economic crisis, but rather of rapid economic growth (Rogers and Pilgrim, 2010: 158). Rogers and Pilgrim emphasise 'changes in ideological factors not economic factors' (2001: 63), in particular, the link between Nazi concentration camps and other forms of incarceration that had been made, amongst others, by Deutsch (1973). Scull, in turn, has argued that such comparisons represent little more than 'the hyperbole of muck-raking journalism' (1996: 385).

Another undoubtedly important development was the spread of 'open door' policies from the mid-1950s, as psychiatric professionals developed a sensitivity to critical accounts of asylum life, and attempts were made to identify psychiatric facilities more closely with hospitals. The 'open door' policy was itself a function of broader changes within psychiatric practice. Prior (1993) has shown how the objects of psychiatric discourse have changed throughout the twentieth century, as research in the early decades of the century (Rosanoff, 1917; Lewis, 1929; cited in Prior, 1993) revealed both that psychiatric disorder was much more prevalent than had previously been appreciated and that many psychiatric disorders had to be evaluated—and treated—in terms of their social context. As Prior explains, 'the discovery of the reservoir of mental illness in the community suggested that the presence of the asylum wall no longer acted as a natural boundary between the sane and the insane' (1993: 110). Many of the mental health problems identified tended to be minor in nature, and inappropriate for hospitalisation.

Although it may not be immediately apparent how the discovery of greater amounts of mental illness (and learning disability) in the community at large is linked to the policy of decarceration, the point is that there has been a shift in the focus of hospital-based services, from dealing with both acute and chronic cases, to a marked focus on acute cases only. With the closure of the asylums in the late twentieth century, patients with a chronic but not acute condition were thereafter dealt in ways that did not involve long-term psychiatric hospitalisation, other than for brief periods if their condition became acute.

Busfield (1986) has suggested that this shift in orientation from chronic to acute patients can explain the apparent paradox in patterns of hospitalisation in the 1960s, when falling total inpatient numbers coexisted with significant increases in admission rates, from 78,500 in 1955 to 170,000 in 1968 (Scull, 1977: 67). Bott (1976) has argued that the beginnings of this trend are discernible in the 1930s, when first admissions, and numbers discharged, began to rise. It is likely that, as well as reflecting changes in the orientation of psychiatry, these features are a function of the availability, after 1930, of admission to, and discharge from, hospital on an informal basis. Scull is more cynical, arguing that the increase in admissions in this period should be seen in terms of a rearguard action on the part of asylum staff and managers to demonstrate that the asylum was not unable to cure people. A high turnover implies a high cure rate, although in reality, this meant that patients were discharged whether 'cured' or not, and, in the case of long-stay patients, whether 'deinstitutionalised' or not. According to Bean and Mounser (1993: 12) 'everyone gets out, and some, it appears, whether they are ready or not'.

The pattern of ever-increasing admissions continued to be a feature of the system, certainly as far as compulsory admissions under civil law are concerned, throughout the 1990s. There were 16,021 such admissions under Part II of the MHA in 1990–91 (excluding the admission of those already in hospital), rising year on year (save for 1995–96) reaching 26,909 in 1998–9 (DH, 2003: Table 1). Since that time, numbers have moved up or down from year to year, but on the whole have stayed fairly constant. There were 26,752 in 2004–05 (DH, 2006: Table 1), 26, 937 in 2010–12, and 27,855 in 2011–12 (NHS Information Centre, 2012, table 4), the last year for which data are available at the time of writing.

Yet on 31 March 2012, 17,503 persons (including those admitted when already in hospital, who constitute a good chunk of the whole) were detained under Part II (NHS Information Centre, 2012, table 8). This would seem to indicate that duration of stay is relatively short. Ramon (1992: xii) found that 60 per cent of hospital admissions spend less than a month as an inpatient, and more recently, Thompson *et al.* (2004) found that only 3.2 per cent of patients stayed in hospital longer than 90 days, and only 1 per cent were still in hospital a year after initial admission.

This contrasts sharply with the situation when informal patients are included in the picture: the *Count Me In* census for 2008 (CQC, 2009: 3, 4) found, as it had in previous years, that 29 per cent of patients who had been in hospital for treatment for mental illness had been in hospital for one year or more, and almost 20 per cent for over two years, with the median duration of stay being two and a half months for women and five and a half months for men, whilst for patients in hospital by reason of learning disabilities, 68 per cent of patients had been in hospital for one year or more, and 32 per cent for over five years, with a median duration of stay of 33 months for women and 32 months for men. Paradoxically, shorter periods of detention can lengthen the overall time that a patient is, episodically, in receipt of inpatient care. The MHAC (2005: para. 2.14) reported on research conducted in Wales, which found that although 'first admissions were considerably shorter in 1996 than 1896 . . . today's patients will spend longer periods of their lives in hospital than their counterparts a century ago'.

Can the change, at least in part, be attributed to a broader policy shift away from institutional solutions? The beginning of decarceration at the end of the 1940s corresponds to the final end of the poor law and its workhouses, and a move in poor relief generally towards financial assistance to live in the community. If the rise of the asylum can be understood in terms of the favouring of institutional solutions in nineteenth-century social policy, can the twentieth-century move away from the asylum similarly be perceived as just another manifestation of a broader social policy? In this context, it should be emphasised that, notwithstanding the policy focus on asylums in the nineteenth and early twentieth centuries, care in other settings by no means ceased to exist. In part, this emphasises that local practice did not necessarily match official policy discourses. Thus, a steady 25 per cent of those found to be insane in the nineteenth century were cared for in workhouses, and contrary to popular myth, these workhouse wards were not necessarily substandard in accommodation (Bartlett, 1999): many, in fact, became NHS hospitals after 1948.

In addition, care outside institutions continued throughout the so-called heyday of the asylum. Systems of boarding outpatients existed in both Scotland and Wales throughout the nineteenth century, whereby insane persons would be housed with family, friends, or paid carers in the community, or lodged on farms (Hirst and Michael, 1999; Sturdy and Parry-Jones, 1999). In England, arrangements tended to be less formal, but outdoor poor relief (doles) to people identified as insane continued throughout the nineteenth century, albeit on a diminishing scale. In the years between the two world wars, there was increasing experimentation relating to care in the community, particularly of those identified as mentally defective (Thomson, 1996). Indeed, by the Second World War, almost 44,000 people in England were living outside the traditional asylum system under statutory guardianship under the Mental Deficiency Acts of 1913, 1926, and 1939 (Walmsley *et al.*, 1999: 186). On this basis, a move to increased community care can perhaps be seen as a policy reorientation waiting to happen.

2.4 Community care

2.4.1 The development of community care and its impact on hospital-based services

The term 'community care' was first coined by the Royal Commission on Mental Illness and Mental Deficiency (1957, the 'Percy Commission'), which sat from 1954 to 1957. The MHA 1959 lifted the concept of guardianship from the Mental Deficiency Act 1913, giving a 'guardian' the powers 'of a parent over his or her 14-year-old child' over a person subject to an order, the criteria for which were, and remain under the MHA 1983, broadly similar to those for confinement. Although nobody was quite sure what such powers entailed (and their detail was amended in 1983), the intention behind guardianship was to provide a community-based alternative to compulsory institution-alisation. Enoch Powell followed up, a year after his Hospital Plan of 1962, with *Health and Welfare: The Development of Community Care* (Ministry of Health, 1963). All of this seems to fit neatly with the view that the policy of decarceration did not exist in isolation, but rather was the mechanism through which a fundamental change was to be effected in the structure of the mental health system: a relocation of the client base of mental health services from institutions to 'the community'. As with decarceration, however, the actuality is somewhat more complex, even paradoxical. No more than a brief outline of some of the relevant factors at play will be considered here. The current legal framework for community care service provision, which in a state of flux with reform imminent at the time of writing, will be considered in Chapter 3.

The first paradox is concerned with the very existence of community care. On the one hand, the policy document published in 1963 was to be the first of many such government documents with similar sounding names. Amongst the most important of these are: *Better Services for the Mentally Handicapped*, a White Paper published in 1971 (Department of Health and Social Security, 1971a); its companion document *Better Services for the Mentally Ill*, published in 1975 (Department of Health and Social Security, 1975); the Audit Commission report *Making a Reality of Community Care* published in 1986 (Audit Commission, 1986); and the Griffiths Report, *Community Care: Agenda for Action* (Griffiths, 1988). Each of these documents spoke to the failure to translate community care policy into community care practice. As Murphy (1991: 60) pointed out, by 1974 there were 60,000 fewer hospital inpatients than in 1954 'but very few services existed in the community ... in most cases these people simply "disappeared" from the official statistics since no one followed up their progress or knew anything about their fate'.

In the cash-strapped 1960s, the attraction of care in the community as a cheaper option than institutionalisation, buttressed by permissive legislation regarding the provision of services, ensured that the policy was chronically underfunded. The White Paper of 1975 pointed out that, in the year 1973–4, £300m was spent on hospital services and only £15m on community care provision, and by March 1974, 31 local authorities had no residential accommodation for the mentally ill and a greater number—63—did not even have day provision (Busfield, 1986: 348). Although the number of inpatients continued to fall, mental hospitals remained the key locus for the delivery of services. In the early 1980s, all of the hospitals marked for closure by the Hospital Plan of two decades earlier remained open. In part, this is a 'chicken and egg' situation: decarceration policies were delimited by the lack of residential provision 'in the community', but whilst funds remained tied up in hospital services, and hospitals remained willing to admit patients—indeed, as seen in Chapter 6, 6.1 in ever greater numbers, and usually informally—and the public at large continued to construct the mentally ill as 'other', fuelled by a number of notorious cases, there was a lack of political will, both centrally and locally, to make community care a 'reality'. In a very real sense, community care simply did not happen.

On the other hand, recent re-evaluations of the age of the asylum have shown that care in the community has been a constant feature of the social response to mental illness and learning disability: there have always been elements within psychiatry and its (particularly middle-class) client base, which have pursued and sought care outside the asylum (Bartlett and Wright, 1999). In a sense, therefore, 'community care' is nothing new but rather is an approach that existed both before and during the period of the 'great confinement'.

The key to understanding this paradox, which throws much light on the more recent developments, lies in unpacking the concept of 'community'. At a minimum, 'community' is a geographical location, but more importantly, it is also a malleable discursive construct, and is capable of being put to use in a variety of different ways. Bartlett and Wright, for example, use the term as shorthand for care 'outside the asylum', and, in particular, in and by the family. The policy of community care after 1960 was also predicated to a large extent on the assumption that much care that had hitherto been provided in the form of inpatient treatment could be provided—at a fraction of the cost—by and in the family (Lewis, 1989). As women, in fact, provide the vast bulk of 'informal' care (although men may recently have come to play a greater role in this regard, see Arber *et al.*, 1988), whether in a family setting or by way of voluntary work for charitable organisations, the concept of 'community' used here, therefore, implicitly draws on an underpinning set of assumptions about the link between the concepts of care and femininity (Finch, 1984).

Post-1960 community care policy, however, also drew on the notion of 'social reintegration'. 'Community' here is used in a broader sense, to connote not simply the family of the person in need of 'care' but also the community at large. This much is evident from the social work theories that have developed around the concept. Normalisation theory, which emphasises the need for the community to value more highly the contribution that people with mental disorder problems, and learning disabilities in particular, make to society (Brown and Smith, 1992), can be seen as 'treatment' not so much for the client as for the community. The Independent Living Movement argues that community care policy should be geared towards ensuring that persons, who might otherwise be hospitalised, are provided with the means to live independent, participatory lives as members of the broader community (Morris, 1993; Hurstfield *et al.*, 2007;

Disability Action, 2009). Others (see Hume and Pullen, 1994; Holloway, 2005; Wolfson *et al.*, 2009) advocate the 'rehabilitation model', the key elements of which involve helping individuals to (re)learn socially necessary skills, and which, like the Independent Living Movement, emphasises such things as the recognition of the rights of clients, their empowerment in decision-making, and the promotion of normal patterns of life.

At the end of the 1990s the Labour government stated brusquely that 'community care has failed' (DH, 1998; 1998a). One significant reason for this, although not the reason emphasised by the government, was that the 1950s view—that the broader community was prepared for the reintegration of mentally disordered members—was mistaken. And this, in turn, is in significant measure explicable in terms of a failure to understand adequately the multifaceted nature of the concept of 'community' (and its ever-present companion, the 'other', that which is not 'community') before attempting to build a policy on that basis. As early as 1957, research suggested that 'on the whole...people...do not wish to have very much contact with mental illness either on the personal or social level' (Cumming and Cumming, 1957, cited in Prior, 1993: 124).

To say that community care has failed should not, however, be taken to imply that nothing changed. By 1977, one third of admissions into psychiatric hospitals were to wards in general hospitals rather than in mental hospitals (Barham, 1992: 20). Psychiatry became more fully medicalised, and from the start of the 1980s, the old large-scale asylums finally began to close. Initially, this was a painfully slow, ward-by-ward, process, but in the 1990s, the rate of closure speeded up, and was complete by the end of that decade.

Accordingly, the 'shape' of the mental hospital system has changed, although the process is by no means complete. As seen at 2.2.1, the current number of hospital beds available for patients with mental illness or who have learning disabilities (together the 'mentally disordered', as per s. 1(2), MHA 1983)—around 24,250 in England in 2013—represents a significant decrease over previous years, and it is long-stay beds that have been shed by the NHS. Available beds in nursing and residential care homes, by contrast, rose throughout the 1990s, parallel to the asylum closure programme. Residential care beds for persons with a mental illness reached 22,180 in 1994–95 and 37,780 in 2000–01, and in nursing care homes, rose from 24,190 to 28,780 over the same period (Government Statistical Service, 2002: Table B23). Local authorities had long been reluctant to accept fully their responsibilities for the long-term mentally ill and (although to a lesser extent) learning disabled. Various policy initiatives attempted to galvanise local government into action, but it was not until the decision was taken (in 1980) that the cost of residential accommodation could be claimed by way of social security benefits that the residential community care sector finally began to expand, as '[s]uddenly patients could be transferred into the community without burdening the budgets of health and local authorities' (Muijen, 1996: 145). Guaranteed payment by way of benefits provided the incentive required for the rapid development of privately run residential homes (see Commission for Social Care Inspection, 2005: Table 7.1).

These institutions vary in size from a few hundred to a handful of beds. There are four basic types of such accommodation:

- independent flats for patients immediately leaving hospital;
- homes with 24-hour staffing;
- group homes with daytime staffing;
- hostels on hospital sites.

A developing feature of provision is 'extra care', packages of care designed to keep people in independent or semi-independent accommodation rather than needing to resort to residential accommodation (see Darton *et al.*, 2012), although to date most activity surrounds the provision of extra care for elderly people (Darton *et al.*, 2011).

In addition, social service departments and CPNs, combined into CMHCs and CMHTs (see 2.2.2) deliver outreach and other community-based services. The first CMHC opened in 1977, with numbers rising to 54 in 1987, and around 75 ten years later. Today, as the most tangible effect of the implementation of the 10-year NSFMH in 1999, we are approaching national coverage, and although this has been patchy, with out-of-hours services in particular unsatisfactory (Healthcare Commission and the Commission for Social Care Inspection, 2006), improvements in this regard have recently been reported, albeit only slight: in 2012, the number of service users surveyed by the CQC who knew who to contact out of office hours rose to 60 per cent from 58 per cent the previous year (CQC, 2012a: 5). Generally, most users report satisfaction with the service they receive, but a considerable number report problems with either the type, or extent, of support (CQC, 2012a).

There has, then, been a sizeable increase in the provision of mental health services in the form of 'community care', although recent statistics indicate that the exponential growth of residential places that was a feature of the 1990s has now peaked, and the data for the year 2011–12 shows that although the number of nursing homes increased by 1.4 per cent, and the number of beds in such homes by 3.3 per cent, the number of residential care homes reduced by 2.5 per cent, and beds by 5.1 per cent (CQC, 2012: 28), constituting a net reduction from 2010–11. If anything, we can perhaps expect the trend for the balance to shift from residential community care to service delivery to people in their own homes to continue a while yet: that is certainly the direction of travel for current policy. And for most community care users, services are already delivered in the form of care at home or in community-based locations, rather than in residential form.

2.4.2 **Community care: Divergence, convergence, and colonisation**

In order to understand the significance of the contemporary mental health system, it is not sufficient simply to attempt to measure the degree to which there has been a shift from hospital-based to community-based sites of service delivery. An assessment of the degree to which there has been *qualitative* and/or *functional* change in the 'shape' of the system must also be made: and this requires that concepts like 'hospital' and 'community-based' must again be unpacked. It also requires that the provision of community care for those suffering from mental disorder be located in the wider context of the provision of welfare services in the era of decarceration. The services that are the particular concern of this book must be set in the broader context of the development of the welfare state in the period after the Second World War. The establishment of the NHS by the National Health Service Act 1946 drew on consensus-based theories of community and 'cradle to grave' protection for all citizens. Other key legislation, notably the National Assistance Act 1948, which finally abolished the workhouse and ushered in the modern social security benefits system, marks the end of incarceration as the policy response to poverty. Community care for mental disorder must be set against this broader context, not simply in terms of a renewed policy preference for 'outrelief', but also in terms of the material development of the welfare state, in particular, in the form of local authority social services departments.

The assumption built into the Powell scheme of the early 1960s was that, in general terms, the responsibility for the provision of social services in the community was to lie with local authorities, but that the provision of services for the mentally ill was the province of health authorities. The consequence was inertia, because hospital-based spending dominated health budgets and local authorities tended to prioritise poverty and disability rather than mental health. The 1975 White Paper redrew the map to an extent, underlining the point that the appropriate response to chronic mental disorder was small-scale residential units in the community, funded by local authorities, but it was not until the NHSCCA 1990 that the relationship between local and health authorities in the provision of community care services was drawn with anything approaching precision.

The NHSCCA 1990 removed from the NHS the primary responsibility for the provision of non-hospital services for those requiring long-term care. Now, the responsibility for overall planning of service provision was to lie primarily at the door of local authorities, in consultation with health authorities, independent sector providers, and voluntary agencies: s. 46(1), (2) of the NHSCCA 1990 (see now also Health and Social Care Act 2001, Ch. 2, Parts 3 and 4). Although, from one point of view, this might be seen as something of a poisoned chalice, such an arrangement also has the potential to mark a qualitative shift in the shape of the mental health system to the extent that now mental disorder in 'the community' was as much a social work issue as it was a medical one.

This was certainly the intention of the social work profession, and well before 1990. The involvement of social workers in the delivery of mental health policy was slight in the early years of community care. The first psychiatric social worker had only been appointed in London in 1936, although social workers had a presence in American service delivery as early as 1905 (Prior, 1993: 88). But by the 1970s, social work had become a recognised profession requiring training, and its knowledge base began to build up. The British Association of Social Workers (BASW) campaigned for specialist mental health training for social workers to be built into the law by the reforms that took place in 1983, and s. 114, MHA 1983 allocated various statutory functions in relation to detained patients to 'approved social workers', not least being the responsibility to apply to a hospital for a person to be detained in it under the MHA. It is not only hospital-related matters that social workers are concerned with. As discussed earlier, there are now various well-developed social work theories of community care. The post-1990 regime devolved power for the provision of services at ground level to social workers as 'care managers' in social services and 'key workers' in mental health services. Social workers may also take the role of advocate in respect of the entitlement to services of their clients.

Yet to date, in so far as the social work profession has had aspirations to usurp the role of medical professionals in the delivery of community care services, the project must be counted as unsuccessful. The psychiatric profession still dominates, and indeed the exclusive jurisdiction of social work professionals over hospital-related matters was removed by the MHA 2007, which replaced the 'approved social worker' with the broader concept of 'Approved Mental Health Professional' (AMHP), with the intention that 'the role will be opened up to a wider group of appropriately trained and qualified mental health professionals such as nurses and occupational therapists' (DH, 2006a: 2). Further discussion of this point in relation to the admissions process into hospital can be found in Chapter 6. As far as community-based services are concerned, it is clear here too that psychiatry remains the dominant profession (Prior, 1992). There was to be no central funding of specialist mental health training for social workers, and the numbers of such specialists has remained problematically low in the years after 1983. This dominance by the psychiatric profession of services for mentally disordered persons outside of hospital will require further discussion later in this book (see Chapter 10, 10.4.1 and Chapter 11, 11.7.2). Staying for the moment, though, with the NHSCCA 1990, it has to be said that this Act is more often discussed in terms of a definitive moment in the emergence of 'managerialism' rather than that of medicalism in the delivery of health-care services.

In the years following 1979, welfarism was recast, as the concept of 'community' was given a new inflection, emphasising the responsibility of service users and service providers to the broader community in terms of economic efficiency. State services have been increasingly infused with market principles and practices, and the mental health system is no exception. The NHSCCA 1990 was intended not only to systematise the provision of community care, but also to revolutionise the structure of the NHS. The immediate precursors of the NHSCCA 1990 were the White Papers of 1989: *Caring for People* (DH, 1989) was concerned with community care; *Working for Patients* (DH, 1989a) with the NHS. The main concern of each was the same: the cost of community care and the health service, respectively. For instance, in the case of the former, the availability of supplementary benefits (from an uncapped central government fund) for funding residential accommodation had played a large part in causing a rise in expenditure on supplementary benefit from £80m in 1978 to £1.5bn in 1989 (Muijen, 1996: 145). The Audit Commission Report of 1986 (Audit Commission, 1986) pointed out that not only was this a very expensive way of funding community care, but it also built in a tendency for preference to be given to residential accommodation, funded by supplementary benefit, rather than the provision of services to clients in their own homes, the bill for which had to be met from local authority funds.

The NHSCCA 1990 abolished this use of supplementary benefit and set in place a system under which the financing of 'residential care' was to be the responsibility of local authorities, while 'nursing care' was that of health authorities. This was only a small part of the picture. The fundamental change ushered in by the NHSCCA 1990 was the division of both hospital and community care systems along market lines, with players defined as either 'providers' or 'acquirers' (purchasers or, these days, commissioners) of care (NHSCCA 1990, s. 4). Local social service authorities and health authorities (along with fundholding general practitioners and private clients) were to be 'purchasers' of services. Hospitals and local authority social services departments were to be 'providers' of services, now in competition with private sector suppliers. The Labour administration of the late 1990s abolished the single market in health (by way, inter alia, of the Health Act 1999, the Health and Social Care Act 2001, and the National Health Service Reform and Health Care Professions Act 2002); but the devolution of decision-making power and budgetary control to units of provision, and the distinction between primary and secondary care—with the new primary care trusts (PCTs) (which replaced GP fund-holding, and which, as seen above, have now themselves been replaced by CCGs) contracting for the provision of most secondary care from NHS trusts and, increasingly, independent sector providers—remained. The government also adopted a policy of funding trusts according to past performance (Health and Social Care Act 2001, s. 2), and of formalising its policy of public–private partnerships.

The third element of this shift, along with this shift from hospital-based to community-based service provision, and from demand-led to supply-led service provision and managerialism, has been a shift from public to private sector provision. Although the cost of residential care, following the coming into force of the NHSCCA 1990, had to be met by local authorities rather than the social security budget, the shift was sweetened by the availability of grant aid to be spent on acquiring services for persons in need by reason of mental illness (see HC(90)24). The availability of grant aid, which was time-limited to three years, depended on the abilities of local authorities to raise 30 per cent of the revenue, which in practice limited its availability to some local authorities, and could not be spent on capital projects (Butler, 1992: 88–9). Moreover, it was stipulated that 85 per cent of grant provision must be spent on the acquisition of independent sector care. This not only limited the potential of local authorities to work in tandem with health authorities (Muijen, 1996: 147) but gave further momentum to the trend of the 'privatisation' of welfare services throughout the 1990s, and as seen at 2.2.2, it is now the case that the vast majority of accommodation is to be found in the independent sector.

On one view, which tends to be voiced by those who associate with the 'old' communitarian values of the post-war welfare state (Butler, 1992; Cowen, 1999), this process of reform of the mental health system is seen in terms of a betrayal of that ethos. From a different perspective, one that draws on the Foucauldian themes of service provision as 'discipline' and social control, there is an altogether more sinister aspect to these developments. Cohen has provided the most influential and wide-ranging version of this thesis, in his book *Visions of Social Control* (1985). For Cohen, the development of community-based alternatives to institutionalisation in various contexts—poverty, criminality, and mental disorder—should be read as the 'dispersal' of disciplinary strategies, from specialist institutions into society as a whole, involving: a widening of the net of social control; a 'thinning of its mesh', which brings a greater percentage of the population under supervision; a 'blurring' of the distinction between formal and informal methods of control; a greater 'penetration' of the state penal-therapeutic complex into the fabric of society. In its broadest version, this thesis has distinctly Orwellian connotations, of society at large continually under the disciplinary gaze of the state's organs of social control (Mathiesen, 1983). More nuanced versions, however, concede that the target population is limited to society's 'deviant' populations, including persons suffering from mental disorders, but nevertheless argue that the move out of the institution should be seen in terms of the greater 'psychiatrisation' of social problems.

Applied to the context of mental health service provision, this is for some an attractive thesis. The early decades of the twentieth century saw an increase in the scope of psychiatry as new 'illnesses' were discovered in ever-wider sections of the general population. Rose (1986: 83, in Rogers and Pilgrim, 2001: 73) explicitly couples this with the process of decarceration:

> Rather than seeking to explain a process of de-institutionalisation we need to account for the proliferation of sites for the practice of psychiatry. There has not been an extension of social control but rather the psychiatrisation of new problems.

In terms of the present discussion, perhaps the most important point here is that to conceive of community care in terms of new sites for old practises raises the question of the qualitative differences between hospital and community care. It can be argued that, given the rapid growth of residential community-based accommodation, 'decarceration' to date has meant little more than patients being relocated from one institution to another.

Perring (1992) found, amongst former hospital inpatients discharged into community-based residential accommodation in the early 1990s as the old asylums began to close, that although there was a preference for the latter, there were distinctly mixed views. It was widely remarked by residents that the new homes were too much like hospitals. Residents remained under supervision, visits by relatives were not encouraged, and there was a tendency amongst staff to 'infantise' residents: classic traits of hospital life (see further at 2.5). Another feature of the 1990s was that patients made subject to compulsory detention in a hospital under both civil and criminal powers of confinement were being admitted into privately run nursing homes in greater numbers, a trend which has continued subsequently. In 1987–98, there were 281 such admissions, but numbers doubled by 1991–92, doubled again by 1996–97, and again by 2004–05, when there were 1,629 such admissions (government Statistical Service, 2006: Table 1). In 2011–12, following further annual increases, 3,464 patients subject to compulsory detention under the MHA 1983 were held in independent sector accommodation (NHS Information Centre, 2012: table 2b). In the same year, 686 patients were sent to an independent hospital by a criminal court or from a prison under Part III of the MHA 1983 (NHS Information Centre, 2012: table 2b), compared to only 22 in 1987–98 (DH, 1998b: Table 9).

Although such admissions constitute only a small proportion of the whole (see Chapter 6, 6.3.2), they nevertheless raise crucial questions about the qualitative difference between hospital accommodation and community care accommodation. For the purposes of the MHA 1983, 'hospital' is defined broadly in s. 145(1) to include, as well as hospitals as defined by the National Health Service Act 2006, any accommodation provided by a local authority for use as a hospital, and s. 34(1), MHA 1983 explicitly provides that a mental nursing home that is registered to accept detained patients (under the regime found in Part II, Care Standards Act 2000) is to be defined as an 'independent hospital' for the purposes of Part II of the MHA 1983 (s. 2(2), Care Standards Act 2000). Other nursing homes or registered homes are not hospitals for these purposes, but to be registered as a nursing home the establishment in question must offer nursing and personal care to, inter alia, people who have or have had a mental disorder (s. 3(2)(b), Care Standards Act 2000), and are *de facto* hospitals. As Eldergill (1997: 137) pointed out, whether a 'detained' patient is 'discharged' into 'the community' can depend solely on whether local provision of hostel accommodation and the like has been made, or purchased, by the health authority or the local authority: if it is the former, it may be defined as a hospital, but not if it is the latter. It can be suggested, therefore, that what constitutes a 'hospital' is essentially an arbitrary question that, ironically, at least in the context of the compulsory admission of patients into 'hospital', is determined more by the custodial rather than therapeutic qualities of the institution in question. Moreover, the vast majority of residential community-based accommodation is outside the provisions of the MHA 1983, which apply only to 'sectioned' patients, and as such, is a space of virtually unfettered medical discretion.

The 'dispersal of discipline' thesis also garners plausibility from the proliferation of mechanisms for the control and monitoring of mentally disordered persons in their own homes. In the 1990s, 'supervision registers' were introduced, along with systems designed to provide continual monitoring in the form of the 'care plan approach' and 'after-care under supervision', to sit alongside the already existent powers of guardianship (see Chapter 10, 10.3). The power to subject a patient leaving hospital subject to after-care under supervision have subsequently been replaced by the Community Treatment Order (CTO), introduced by the MHA 2007. The CTO comes very close to, but stops short of, introducing powers to give treatment without consent, although it does give various powers of control and coercion of the psychiatrist in charge of patient's care. In practice, the threat of compulsion can often have the desired effect, and it is, in any case, possible to treat without consent in a community setting, if that setting is in the form of accommodation provided by a health authority, because it will count as a 'hospital' for these purposes. The loosening of the judicial embargo on the use of leave of absence from hospital as a way to achieve control over a patient in the community (see *Barker* v *Barking Havering and Brentwood Community Healthcare NHS Trust* [1999] 1 FLR 106, discussed at Chapter 10, 10.2.1) has, in addition, fashioned a *de facto* community treatment mechanism of more general application.

There is no doubt that the 'dispersal of discipline' thesis accurately captures one important element of mental health policy over the last few decades, particularly in respect of the development of control-oriented powers over the last decade. But it also misses some important truths about both policy and, in particular, practice. Dealing first with the policy question, it should be noted that the CTO represents a compromise between the interests of control and the civil liberties of the individuals concerned, and bears the influence of a consideration of the provisions of the ECHR. In other words, it is the case that, if what is meant by 'control' is the medicalisation of those pockets within the wider community that are inhabited by mentally disordered persons, then, 'control' has been hemmed in by the presence of a legalistic discursive input at the level of policy formation.

As far as practice is concerned, the reform process leading to the Mental MHA 2007 had various triggers, but one significant trigger was the alleged reluctance of mental health professionals to undertake responsibility for what Howlett (1998: 3) described as 'chaotic and dangerous' patients. As it was put in the White Paper of 1998 (DH, 1998), 'while [community care] improved the treatment of many people who were mentally ill, it left far too many walking the streets, often at risk to themselves and a nuisance to others'. This was particularly the case with patients diagnosed as suffering from an untreatable 'severe and dangerous personality disorder' or 'SDPD'.

The debate over the non-treatment of Michael Stone, who was found guilty in 1998 (he was retried, and again found guilty in 2001, and appealed unsuccessfully in 2005) of the murder of a mother and daughter in Kent, was an important catalyst for legal change. Stone had previously not been offered psychiatric treatment because his condition (SDPD) was deemed untreatable. Jack Straw, then the Home Secretary, lambasted mental health professionals for their 'refusal' to 'treat' Stone, seeing it as an abdication of responsibility, but the response of professionals was that it was not appropriate to detain and/or treat a person deemed untreatable. The Home Secretary responded by announcing plans in June 1999 for the introduction of preventative custody for such persons (Home Office and Department of Health, 1999; Department of Health and Home Office, 2000a: ch. 2), and although those legislative proposals were subsequently abandoned, £70m was made available to provide accommodation for those with SDPD within the prison estate and £56m for places within the hospital system and in hostels.

The point here is that this is evidence, not of the spread of 'medicine as control' into the community, but of a general reluctance on the part of both psychiatric and social work professionals to undertake the control of such individuals. Returning to the three elements of the shift identified in this section—from hospital to community-based provision, from clinical to managerial control, and from public to private provision—the dispersal of discipline thesis does not always sit easily with the reality of that shift in its first and third aspects. It is hard to see the growth of private sector residential accommodation in the community as 'social control' in any conspiratorial sense, given that it tends to be those who are least in need of control and most in need of treatment that are provided with such accommodation. This is not to dispute that civil liberties issues are absolutely pertinent to the treatment of those who occupy residential or nursing care home beds.

Meanwhile, the second element, the shift from clinical to managerial control, a trend which continued into the first decade of the new century, has been bucked to a certain extent by recent reforms which have, for example, abolished PCTs and replaced them with CCGs, intended to give decision-making power back to clinicians (see 2.2.1), although it may be that, with the emergence of the concept of 'clinical governance' (which was also a feature of the first decade of the 21st century: see for example NHS Executive (1999) *Clinical Governance: Quality in the New NHS*) the opposition between 'clinical' and 'management' decisions has been to some extent collapsed.

The contemporary issues in community care do include the degree to which service provision can, does, or should be seen in terms of a broader trend which can be short-handed as the dispersal of discipline, but such concerns are largely confined to that narrow slice of the mentally disordered population who are thought to pose some risk to the safety of self or others. For the vast majority of service users, and for the government, the availability of services and the manner in which they are funded, and safety in residential accommodation and other community care settings, are more pressing issues.

A root and branch review of funding was carried out by the Dilnot Commission (Commission on Funding of Care and Support, 2011), which reported that 'The current system is neither fit for purpose today, nor for coping with future pressures' (2011: 17) and proposed a number of changes to the way in which community care is funded. The main recommendations of the Commission were that: no person should have to contribute more than £35,000 for their lifetime contribution to social care with all costs above that point met by the state; the means-tested threshold (currently set at £23,250: see Chapter 3, 3.2.2.1.1) should be raised to £100,000; proposals were also made in respect of the eligibility criteria for entitlement to services, the ease with which an assessment of needs is 'portable' from one local authority area to another, and proposals to take the opportunity to improve the integration of social care and other services as part of the review of funding arrangements (2011: 5–7).

Whilst the subsequent government White Paper accepted these proposals in principle (see HM Government, 2012a), it seems unlikely that the detailed proposals with regard to the contributions that users are required to make will be implemented as Dilnot proposed. The Secretary of State for Health, Jeremy Hunt, announced in Parliament in February 2013 (HC Hansard 11 Feb 2013: col. 593) that although ring-fenced assets, currently set at £23,250 as mentioned, would be raised to £125,000 in April 2017, the cap on lifetime contribution would be set at £75,000 (later reduced to £72,000 in the March 2013 budget), double the figure recommended by Dilnot. The announcement was contentious with user groups, although Andrew Dilnot was reported as saying that the proposals '[don't] seem to me that it is so different from what we wanted as to radically transform the basis of the system' (see '£75,000 cap on bills for long-term care disappoints campaigners', *The Guardian*, 11 February 2013).

The Local Government Association, discussing the 2012 White Paper, announced itself 'disappointed the White Paper does not address the reality of the funding pressures councils face' (LGA, 2012) because although the White Paper pledged £200 million for the development of housing for older and disabled persons (HM Government, 2012a: 10), £100 million in 2013–14 and £200 million in 2014–15 to develop integrated working between LSSAs and LHAs (HM Government, 2012a: 11), and £32.5 million in support for developing online information services for users and potential user (HM Government, 2012a: 10), 'All the key funding decisions on implementing Dilnot reforms and addressing the true costs of a reformed care system are postponed until the next Comprehensive Spending Review [in 2015]. There are worrying signals that these issues may have to take their place in consideration of measures to stimulate growth and other public spending pressures' (LGA, 2012: 3). At present, although there is some clarity about the likely operation of the community care system in future years, much is still uncertain. In particular, it remains to be seen whether the extent to which the current activity, in the form of the draft Social Care Bill, does bring about fundamental change or in retrospect will be seen as little more than tinkering with the system.

The safety of, and general standards of care provided for, care home residents is monitored by the CQC, with powers (found in ss. 2(2)(a), (b), HSCA 2008; Care Standards Act 2000, see further Chapter 3, 3.2.2.1.1) to regulate and inspect care homes. And yet, periodically, both before and after the CQC took up its responsibilities in 2008, scandals, such as that concerning the physical abuse and neglect of residents over a period of many years in registered homes licensed and inspected in the Lothians region (*Edinburgh Evening News*, 10 March 2006) and in Cornwall (*The Guardian*, 5 July 2006), or more recently, at a care homes in Bristol (which led to the arrest and imprisonment of a number of staff, who were convicted of abusing and neglecting adults with learning difficulties in their care: see DH, 2012), Lancaster and London (at which staff were covertly filmed abusing a resident with Alzheimer's disease, at a home rated 'excellent' by the CQC: *The Guardian*, 13 November 2012). Reports such as these raise grave doubts about the fitness for purpose of the system of regulation and inspection. This raises the issue of the experience of life as a hospital inpatient or client of community care residential accommodation. Before leaving our discussion of the mental health system, it is necessary to give this topic separate consideration.

2.5 Inside the institutions

2.5.1 'Total' institutions

Within the sociology of medicine, the Weberian model of modernist institutions as bureaucratic organisations characterised by the complexity of their social interaction is a popular way of conceptualising the functioning of hospitals. Such models, although useful, can marginalise the experience of the client population. In this latter respect, one author whose work has provided the template for many people's understanding of life in a mental hospital is Erving Goffman. His highly influential *Asylums* was first published in 1961. The book is the product of fieldwork carried out at St Elizabeth's, a large asylum in Washington DC, in the mid-1950s, although it also draws widely on secondary material to support its general thesis.

Goffman argued that mental asylums have less in common with general hospitals and more in common with other 'total' institutions, such as monasteries or convents. Total institutions are those that erect 'a barrier to social intercourse with the outside and to departure that is often built into the physical plant such as locked doors, high walls, barbed wire, cliffs, water, forests, or moors' (1991: 15–16). These institutions are problematic for Goffman because '[a] basic social arrangement in modern society is that the individual tends to sleep, play, and work in different places, with different co-participants, under different authorities, and without an overall rational plan'. Hence the 'central feature of total institutions can be described as a breakdown of the barriers ordinarily separating these three spheres of life' (1991: 17).

For Goffman, then, the inmates of total institutions have had their lives spatially collapsed and rationalised, and must adhere precisely to a timetable conceived by somebody else, and to a rational plan, to the details of which they may not be privy. They must do this within a confined space and 'in the company of a large batch of others, all of whom are treated alike and required to do the same thing' (1991: 17). Moreover, society within the institutions is split artificially into two groups: the inmates and the staff; '[e]ach grouping tends to conceive of the others in terms of narrow hostile stereotypes' (1991: 18). There is no public/private split here. The most personal or private aspects, not merely of inmates' lives, but of their minds, are public domain: a legitimate target for psychiatric intervention.

This constitutes what Goffman describes as 'a violation of one's informational preserve regarding self' (1991: 32). The most profound or obvious effect of this is 'disculturation' or 'institutionalisation': the inability of inmates to cope with the demands and strains of life outside, i.e. the fostering in inmates of absolute dependency on the system not only to satisfy but also to define their needs. The 'self is systematically, if often unintentionally, mortified' (1991: 24). Institutionalisation signifies a radical departure in the moral career of inmates. The sense of 'self' developed on the outside, in the context of family and other relationships, is left at the gates, along with the inmate's physical possessions and human dignities. Inmates are, quite literally, 'mortified'.

There is an obvious irony here that Goffman is keen to bring out. If the purpose of mental hospitals to cure or rehabilitate inmates for 'life outside', it seems a peculiar way of going about things to suspend 'life outside' as part of this process. This suspension of 'real life', however, is not 'simply' total, but instead plays on the very fact of that suspension (1991: 23–4):

> [T]otal institutions do not really look for cultural victory. They create and sustain a particular kind of tension between the home world and the institutional world and use this persistent tension as strategic leverage in the management of men.

Total institutions are coercive. Goffman talks, for example, about the 'obedience test' that new inmates have to go through (1991: 26–7). This, he argues, consists of the inmate accepting the total authority of the staff. The lesson to be learnt here, however, is not merely obedience but unquestioning obedience. There can be no visible sign that the inmate questions or disagrees with, or feels injustice at, a staff decision. Inmates learn how to keep their facial expressions to themselves, to remain inscrutable, because attitude is as much a target for intervention as is action. The inmate must learn subordination as much as obedience. This is really the key distinction between institutions in general and total institutions: in the latter, the new inmate must make a number of 'primary adjustments' to the self in order to 'fit' appropriately within the institutional world. There are, however, degrees of totality, and this is because inmates also develop 'secondary adjustments': ways to 'buck the system', including, for example, the development of an inmate culture in opposition to that of the institution, the smuggling of contraband of various descriptions, the development of an economic system based on barter, the 'colonising' of vacant space within the institution, and so on. This is done partly to make life more bearable, but partly for the sense of defiance that comes from 'breaking the rules' per se (1991: Parts 2 and 3).

Goffman does not deny that patients do get out of mental institutions, but his point is that, on release, much of what the inmate has learnt inside dissipates (1991: 70) and, from his point of view, this is not surprising, because institutionalisation prepares inmates only for institutionalisation. What those discharged do take with them back into the community is the stigma of their incarceration and an anxiety about being able to cope with the freedoms and responsibilities of life on the outside. Goffman says that, in his experience, it is these factors, rather than those relating to the patient's medical/mental condition, that occupy the thoughts of staff charged with the responsibility of deciding who gets out. The problems, in other words, that face dischargees and decision-makers, are caused by the fact of institutionalisation and not by the reasons for institutionalisation in the first place (1991: 70–1).

This, then, is the general thesis of *Asylums*. The rest of the book adds the detail, but we have already seen enough to realise that Goffman paints a dismal picture of the asylum, as a place where the logic of control has a far greater influence than medical discourse. There is certainly evidence to substantiate the claims that Goffman makes. For example, inquiries at the special hospitals (in 1980 at Rampton (Boynton, 1980); 1988 at Broadmoor (NHS Advisory Services/Department of Health and Social Security Social Services Inspectorate, 1988); and 1992 at Ashworth (Home Office, 1992)) found conditions not too dissimilar from those of the 'total institutions' described by Goffman: 'insular, closed institutions whose predominantly custodial and therapeutically pessimistic culture had isolated them from the mainstream of forensic psychiatry' (DH, 1999b: para. 1.19.7), unable to attract and retain medical staff, with the Prison Officers' Association the dominant professional body. Such institutions cater mainly, although not exclusively, for persons sent to hospital by a criminal court, who can expect to spend a considerable period under detention.

The circumstances surrounding the reports mentioned were similar to those that were at play over the last century, with government action prompted by scandal, concern, and the lobbying activities of a concerned few. This was also the pattern of events preceding subsequent inquiries, at Broadmoor in 1997 and Ashworth in 1997–99, but the nature of the complaint had changed: now the special hospitals were not too austere, but instead too open. Both inquiries were prompted by concerns that security was lax, and that drugs and pornography were widely available. The inquiry at Broadmoor was brief and showed that, on the whole, the regime had improved since the report of a decade earlier, although there were still significant concerns about security. In contrast, the *Report of the Committee of Inquiry into the Personality Disorder Unit, Ashworth Special Hospital* (DH, 1999b) (the Fallon Report) showed that most of the allegations that had prompted the setting up of a Committee of Inquiry in 1997 were, indeed, true. The allegations in question had been made by a former patient of the personality disorder unit (PDU). The most serious concerned the availability of pornography, including child pornography, and the presence in the PDU of the child of a former patient, brought in by him, so the inquiry team found, as part of a plan to have her 'groomed for paedophile purposes'.

There were many other lapses or plain absences of security and of management: patients ran businesses from the hospital and there was very little in the way of the barriers to communication with the outside world that were described by Goffman: Internet access, for example, was freely available. At the same time, the institutions remained isolated in terms of their relation to the rest of the hospital system. The Fallon Inquiry concluded that the custodial, security-inclined regimes that had been detailed in the reports of the 1980s and early 1990s no longer existed, but now 'the pendulum may have swung too far away in the other direction', making a mockery of the notion of a 'high security' hospital. *The Independent* newspaper put the point more bluntly in the headline to its coverage of the publication of the Fallon Report: 'Ashworth run by inmates not staff' (*The Independent*, 6 January 1999: 6).

In Goffman's terms, the Fallon Report detailed the extent to which 'secondary adjustments' can fashion an entirely different regime if 'policy' becomes a vacuum. Following Fallon—indeed, before the report was published—policy moved sharply back in the direction of increased security and control. Fallon recommended that security at Ashworth should be subject to independent and regularly repeated review. The response of the Department of Health was to commission a wider review of security at all three special hospitals by a team led by Sir Richard Tilt (DH, 2000), and this led to 86 detailed recommendations. The Department of Health produced *The Safety and Security in Ashworth, Broadmoor and Rampton Hospitals Directions* (the Directions) in 1999, which have since been revised on a number of occasions, most recently, following consultation (DH, 2011) in 2011. The Directions (*The High Security Psychiatric Services (Arrangements for Safety and Security at Ashworth, Broadmoor and Rampton Hospitals) Directions 2011*) now require routine (monthly) and random searches of patient's rooms and persons (para. 7, 2011 Directions), personal searches for cause (paras. 5, 6) or when the patient moves between areas in the hospital (para. 8), as well as regular (weekly) searches of communal areas (para. 9). There are also stringent requirements for staff and visitors to be searched (paras. 11, 12).

The 1999 Directions had to be amended in 2002 (*The Ashworth, Broadmoor and Rampton Amendment (No. 2) Directions 2002*) to exclude mental health review tribunal members from being searched when entering or leaving hospital premises. This gives some indication of how heavy-handed the Directions were in their initial form and, despite subsequent redrafting, to a considerable extent remain.

Other Directions require 'for cause' and random testing for the use by patients of 'illicit substances', defined as controlled drugs under the Misuse of Drugs Act 1971 and alcohol (2011 Directions, para. 17); only limited and supervised access to computers and games consoles (para.23: this replaces the absolute ban on computers and games consoles which featured in the original Directions); an absolute ban on mobile phones, which applies to staff and visitors as well as patients (para. 30); as well as Directions concerning the opening and inspection of outgoing patient mail and incoming mail addressed to either patients or staff (paras. 26–29); and, when a patient is judged to be 'high risk' following a risk assessment, required by para. 33, various other intrusive actions are possible, such as the routine monitoring of patients' telephone calls. For other patients, such monitoring may be done on a random and routine basis, but in any case telephone calls, which are permitted only by appointment and subject to various security-based measures, should be observed (paras. 32, 33).

Section 134(1) of the MHA 1983 gives the managers of the three high security hospitals a power to withhold a patient's outgoing mail if the managers consider it likely that the item to be posted is likely to cause distress (with no modifier, so that stress need not be, for example, severe or even significant) to the recipient or any other person, and s. 134(2) gives an equivalent power to withhold incoming mail from patients, if the managers deem it 'necessary to do so in the interests or the safety of the patient or for the protection of other persons'. There is a corollary power to open and inspect any item of mail to determine if either ss. 134(1) or (2) apply: s. 134(4). There is a right to appeal to the CQC against a decision to withhold mail, or to monitor telephone calls (s. 134A(3), MHA 1983; regs. 3 and 4 s.134A(3), *Care Quality Commission (Additional Functions) Regulations 2011*, SI 2011/1551), and patients, although in small numbers, have made use of this right. In 2011–12, for example, there were 13 appeals against a decision to withhold mail and one appeal against a decision to monitor telephone calls, 11 of which were successful (CQC, 2013: 41 and table 4). But in the broader scheme of things, these are little victories. Overall it is the object of the Directions to plug all gaps in security identified by the Fallon and Tilt reports.

There is no doubt that the Directions impinge significantly on the rights and liberties of special hospital inmates and move the regimes markedly back in the direction of the 'total institution' model. The security of perimeters, the increase in the use of CCTV, and the strengthening of internal security all also followed in the wake of the Tilt Report, even though Tilt found that absconsions from the special hospitals are rare (23 from 1990–99, and none after 1996: DH, 2000: 8). Legal challenges by patients to the reintroduction of these more draconian policies, that were heard before the coming into force of the Human Rights Act (HRA) 1998, scored little success. In *R v Broadmoor SHA, ex p S and Ors* (1998) *The Times*, 17 February, three patients at Broadmoor sought judicial review of the decision of the hospital authority to introduce a policy of random and routine searching, replacing the 'for cause' policy that had hitherto been applied. Not surprisingly, the application was rejected in the High Court and that decision was upheld in the Court of Appeal. It was held that the power to detain for treatment implied a power to do that which was necessary for the success of that treatment, which included the right to search, as long as that was not exercised unreasonably in the circumstances.

A similarly expansive reading of the MHA 1983 was provided in *R v Mental Health Act Commission, ex p Smith* (1998) *The Times*, 15 May (HC), which relied on the *Broadmoor* decision, and that in *Pountney v Griffiths* [1976] AC 314 (see Chapter 12, 12.4.1.1), to hold that the powers of admission, detention, and treatment necessarily implied broader powers of management and control. After the coming into force of the HRA 1998, the High Court in *R v Ashworth Special Hospital Authority and Anor, ex p N* [2001] EWHC Admin 339 heard an application from a patient that the policy of randomly recording and listening to 10 per cent of patients' outgoing telephone calls, that had been introduced by para. 29(3) of the 2000 Directions, was in breach of the right to privacy protected by Art. 8 of the ECHR. The court laid out the Directions and the evidence from Fallon and Tilt that showed that unimpeded access to telephones constituted a security risk, before concluding that, although the policy did breach Art. 8(1) it was justifiable as proportionate, because, although the patient in question had not been judged to be 'high risk', he was nevertheless a member of a class of dangerous individuals (i.e. special hospital patients) and so the infringement of his privacy was justified by reference 'to the extent of the threat, the established degree of manipulation which can occur and the possible serious consequences to patients, staff and members of the public' (at para. 20). This was so even though N had been conditionally recommended for transfer and so evidently was not dangerous enough to require the conditions of security that pertain in the special hospitals (see also *R v Secretary of State for Health, ex p L* [2000] 1 MHLR 191).

The tenor of these judgments strongly suggest that only rarely will any special hospital patient be able successfully to challenge the substance of the Directions. In *R v Secretary of State for the Home Department, ex p Carroll, Al-Hasan, and Greenfield* [2001] EWCA Civ 1224, [2002] 1 WLR 545, [2001] HRLR 58, 2001 WL 753465, the Court of Appeal upheld the first instance decision, that as long as there is good reason, so-called 'squat searches' (which require the person being searched to strip and squat so that the genital area and anus can be examined for concealed contraband of one type or another) are, in principle, lawful. In that case, the good reason was that sniffer dogs had detected the possible presence of explosives in an area of the prison to which only a limited class, including the two applicants, had access. A search of that area had been carried out and nothing found, after which the decision was taken to search the living quarters of those prisoners, and to carry out squat searches. No particular prisoner was under suspicion, and prisoners were not, out of concerns for security, informed of the reason for the search. C and A-H, two of the prisoners, refused to consent and were subsequently disciplined for failing to obey a lawful order.

The Court of Appeal distinguished earlier case law, which is to the effect that reasons must usually be given for a personal search (*Christie v Leachinsky* [1947] AC 573), holding that 'loss of liberty, security and control are essential parts of the disciplinary process of a prison. Searches, even strip searches, are routine and, for a routine search, reasons need not be given' (para. 68). The only protection the court was prepared to allow was that the decision to carry out a personal search should be taken by an officer of governor grade and that there should be contemporaneous recording of the reasons necessitating the search. Although this case went to the House of Lords on different grounds, on which the Court of Appeal was overruled, this element of its judgment was not challenged, and it is clear that all of this reasoning is equally applicable to the special hospitals. The court did not consider the application of human rights law to this question because the incidents occurred before the coming into force of the HRA 1998, and it was decided by the House of Lords in *R v Lambert* [2001] UKHL 37, [2002] 2 AC 545 that the HRA 1998 did not have retrospective application. Nevertheless, it seems clear from the case law discussed that the HRA 1998 has so far had limited impact on the freedom of regimes to implement the security measures deemed necessary.

Patients have also been unsuccessful in challenging other decisions pertaining to their management. In *R v Ashworth Hospital Authority, ex p E* 2001 WL 1479868 E, a male patient wished to be allowed to dress as a woman in the hospital, but his freedom to do so had been restricted to the extent that he was only allowed to keep and wear a small number of female undergarments, and then only in the privacy of his own room. The reason given for this by E's doctor, Dr S, was that, in his opinion, E was a fetishistic transvestite who was sexually aroused by cross-dressing and the more so in public, and who also had a history of inappropriate sexual behaviour towards women, to the extent that to allow him to wear female clothing in public spaces in the hospital 'would be likely to be associated with unwise behaviour' (para. 8). It was also Dr S's view that wearing female attire might undermine E's treatment plan, inhibit his possible transfer, and increase the risk of an escape attempt, E having previously attempted to abscond whilst dressed as a woman. Although there was evidence from another doctor that to refuse to allow E to wear female clothing subjected him to unnecessary stress, the High Court preferred the evidence of Dr S, to hold that the restrictions of E were *Wednesbury* reasonable (para. 36); and that there was no breach of Art. 8, because although the powers to control such things as mode of dress are not apparent on the face of the MHA 1983 (see Chapter 7), they are nevertheless 'in accordance with the law' as required by Art. 8(2) as being both available and foreseeable in their effect (once the case law already discussed in this section is taken into account) (para. 42).

On the question of necessity, Richards J cited from the speech of Lord Steyn in *R v SSHD, ex p Daly* [2001] 2 AC 532 (HL), and charged himself to conduct an 'appropriately intensive scrutiny' of the decision of Dr S and his colleagues as to whether there was indeed a pressing social need for the infringement of Mr E's rights and whether such action as was taken was proportionate. He reminded himself that 'it must be borne in mind that the hospital authority is the decision maker in this case . . . it is not for the court to engage in a full merits review so as to reach its own independent decision on the matter' (para. 45). His conclusion was that the hospital had made out its case and the restriction was justified.

That decision was applied in *R v SSHD, ex p DB* [2006] EWHC 659 (Admin), a case involving a male-to-female transsexual transferred from prison to Ashworth hospital, which only accepts male patients. Ashworth permitted DB to wear female dress in her room, but demanded that she wear gender-neutral clothes in public areas. DB argued that her rights under Arts. 3 and 8 ECHR had been breached, and pointed inter alia to the fact that the hospital authorities felt that her transfer and continuing detention at Ashworth were inappropriate, both because DB did not require high-security conditions and because, given her transsexualism, the placement was inappropriate. The High Court found that Ashworth had been sufficiently sensitive to DB's situation and there was no breach of either Article, and, indeed, Davies J recorded his disquiet (para. 51) that the claim should have been thought appropriate to have been brought at all.

In *R v Ashworth Hospital, ex p H* [2001] EWHC Admin 872, [2002] 1 FCR 206, H, a carrier of the Hepatitis C virus and claiming to be sexually active within the hospital, challenged the decision of the hospital to refuse to supply him with condoms as in breach of Arts. 2 and 8 ECHR. This decision was made in line with the hospital's 'no sex' policy (see Bartlett *et al.*, 2010), and on the basis that the hospital doubted H's claim to be sexually active. The High Court found in favour of the hospital on both counts, holding that sexual activity between patients was unlikely to occur, and so there was no 'real and immediate threat to life' and hence no breach of either Article, and that the policy was justified on grounds of security (condoms might, in its view, be used as currency or for smuggling purposes). The 'no sex' policy was also justifiable on security grounds. The court also dismissed arguments based on more traditional judicial criteria. Thus, the blanket ban on the issuance of condoms was neither '*Wednesbury* unreasonable' nor 'irrational'.

In *R v Nottinghamshire Healthcare NHS Trust, ex parte G, B and N* [2009] EWCA Civ 795, three patients at Rampton high security hospital challenged, by way of judicial review, both the smoking ban which the hospital had introduced and the underlying legislation (Health Act (HA) 2006, s. 1), which had introduced a prohibition on smoking, inter alia, in enclosed public spaces. Initially, regulations made under the HA 2006 provided for mental health units to be exempt from the effects of the ban, but only for a year after its coming into force in July 2007. In July 2008, therefore, the ban came into force in Rampton as in other mental health facilities. The applicants argued that the ban was in breach of Art. 8(1) of the ECHR in that it violated their right to privacy and home life (the ban does not extend to a person smoking in their own home).

The Court of Appeal, by a 2–1 majority (Keene LJ dissenting) held that it did not: although Rampton was accepted as being the applicants' home, 'it is not the same as a private home and the distinction is of significance. It is a public institution' (para. 40), and 'The degree to which a person may expect freedom to do as he pleases and engage in personal and private activity will vary according to the nature of the accommodation in which he lives' (para. 41), so that although 'a person may do as he pleases in his own home, no one can expect such freedom when detained in a secure hospital' (para. 44).

The conclusion was the Art. 8 was not even engaged in these circumstances (para. 49) because 'Difficult as it is to judge the importance of smoking to the integrity of a person's identity, it is not, in our view, sufficiently close to qualify as an activity meriting the protection of article 8'; but if it is engaged, then the breach of Art. 8(1) could in any case be justified under Art. 8(2) as a proportionate measure justified on grounds of public health (para. 79). Keene LJ, dissenting, held that the ban did engage Art. 8(1), and that it had not been shown that a total ban was necessary to give effect to the policy, of protecting non-smokers from the effects of 'second-hand smoke', that the HA 2006 Act sought to introduce, and so could not be justified under Art. 8(2) because it was disproportionate to the problem it sought to address (para. 107). Whatever one's view on smoking, however, it seems clear that for smokers the decision of the majority in this case does increase the likelihood that institutionalisation will be experienced as 'total'.

Although the ultimate purpose of the 2011 Directions is to ensure a safe and secure environment within the high secure hospital estate, it is not clear that special hospital patients necessarily feel security themselves: bullying, particularly in personality dis-order wards, seems to be a very common but under-acknowledged problem (Ireland and Snowden, 2002; Henson and Ireland, 2009) with 20 per cent of both patients and staff reporting having seen someone been bullied in the preceding week in one sur-vey (Ireland, 2004; see also Ireland, 2006; Ireland and Bescoby, 2004), and there are significant differences between the experiences of women and men, in Ashworth at least, Ireland (2004a: para. 1.3.2.) finding that 3 per cent of men, but 30 per cent of women, reported being bullied in the previous week. Scandalous stories about the rape and sexual abuse of female patients by male patients in Broadmoor broke in March 2003, prompting the Department of Health to pledge the relocation of all female patients out of the hospital within three years (Dillon, 2003), although there were still 42 women amongst the total of 273 patients held in the hospital in January 2006 (West London Mental Health NHS Trust, n.d.). At the time of writing Broadmoor is being rebuilt, and when the new hospital opens in 2017, it will have 210 places for men and 24 'flexible beds'.

It may, of course, be argued that special hospitals are atypical institutions. Indeed they are: yet there is evidence to support a Goffman-influenced understanding of the modern experience of hospitalisation from all sections of the hospital system (Rosenhan, 1973). Research by Bott (1976: 133) discussed by Barham (1992: 8) found that the barrier between staff and inmates was rigidly enforced, because '[t]alking to patients is danger-ous because it threatens to puncture the barrier that keeps sanity and madness in their proper places', while Christine Perring (1992: 134) found that clinical staff take a fatherly role, nursing staff, a motherly role, and that inmates are correspondingly infantised, irrespective of the actual gender of the participants. Although there are no Directions for other hospitals which equate to those which apply to the high security hospitals, the CQC has reported, for example, a blanket ban on the use of mobile telephones in facili-ties (CQC, 2013: 42–43), even though the Code of Practice (DH, 2008: para. 16.6) states that a blanket ban is unlikely to be appropriate 'except in units specifically designed to provide enhanced levels of security in order to protect the public'.

The January 2013 report of the CQC (the report most recently available at the time of writing), reminiscent of earlier reports, and those of the MHAC which preceded it, states bluntly that 'The human rights of patients are often affected by controlling prac-tices that only seem to serve the hospital's needs' (CQC, 2013: 33) before proceedings to note the increasing trend of designating wards as 'locked wards' (CQC, 2013: 33), and that rules that seemed unnecessarily strict about such things as access to bedrooms, or access to outdoor space for smokers (CQC, 2013: 36). In one female forensic ward, the CQC (2013: 39) observed the use by staff of such things as access to food and drink, bedrooms, smoking areas and outdoor space, and personal possessions, dependant on the patient 'displaying controlled behaviour...Such restrictions could be perceived as institutionalised, punitive in nature and even dehumanising'.

Psychiatric hospitals have historically experienced high levels of violence (Shah, 1993). It is difficult to give precise details of the incidence of patient attacks on staff, because abuse is significantly under-reported by staff (Thackrey and Bobbit, 1990), and much of the research tends to be retrospective, based on analysis of reported incidents (Cheung *et al.*, 1997). The attitude of staff to reporting abuse often depends on whether the patient is viewed as morally responsible for his or her behaviour (Crichton and Calgie, 2002). The final *Count Me In* national patient survey (CQC, 2011) found that 11 per cent of patients had been the victim of an assault in the previous 12 months. The CQC did not have information about the identity of the assailants, but Cheung *et al.* (1997) found that patients with schizophrenia and schizo-affective disorders accounted for 80 per cent of physical assaults, and only six patients were responsible for nearly two thirds of all violent incidents. The authors found 'all of them to be suffering from treatment resistant schizophrenia' (Cheung *et al.*, 1997: 51).

In an authoritative survey of 71 studies, published in 13 countries, including 19 studies published in the UK, Papadopoulos *et al.* (2012) found that around four in 10 incidents of patient violence towards staff were precipitated by interaction between the patient and staff member, most often (25 per cent of all assaults) in the form of the denial by the staff member of a patient's request or of the staff member placing some restriction on the patient. In another 25 per cent, however, there was no clear cause for the use of violence. Virtanen *et al.* (2011) found that overcrowding on wards (and as we have seen many wards operate very near to or even above capacity) was firmly correlated with the levels of violence experienced. Best practice is now detailed in NICE guidelines (NICE, 2005).

Around four in every 1,000 persons admitted to a mental hospital will commit suicide (Ganesvaran and Shah, 1997), although the greatest risk is in the days immediately after discharge (Johnson *et al.*, 1993), and 27 per cent of all suicides in the years 2000–10 involved a person who had left a psychiatric hospital less than a year previously (Confidential Inquiry into Suicide and Homicide by People with Mental Illness, 2012: 20). Suicides are statistically more probable for all categories of mental disorder (Ruschena *et al.*, 1998), although those suffering from schizophrenia seem to be more at risk than others (Rossau and Mortensen, 1997). Patients at most risk tend to be young, male, and with antisocial personality traits (Johnson *et al.*, 1993), but over the years 2004–10, suicides amongst those less than 45 years of age fell, but for those above that age, rates increased (Confidential Inquiry into Suicide and Homicide by People with Mental Illness, 2012: 20). Overall, rates fell from 17.4 per cent to 13.8 per cent per 100,000 mental health service users in those years (Confidential Inquiry into Suicide and Homicide by People with Mental Illness, 2012: 20).

There is evidence from Australia that suicide rates in hospitals can be affected by legal changes requiring staff to be more sensitive to the risk (Ganesvaran and Shah, 1997). In Goffman's terms, suicide is the ultimate 'secondary adjustment', but the starkness of the statistics on suicide, and the complexity of the situation, makes one think long and hard about the role of theory. It must not be to offer glib or easy explanations for such problematic issues.

Many more examples of institutions and regimes that exhibit this or that feature of Goffman's model might be drawn from the literature. There is also much autobiographical work that supports Goffman's contention that hospital inpatients must adhere to the regime or suffer the consequences, which places therapy of the mildest kind in a continuum with the use of shock treatment or drugs and, ultimately, when all else fails, straightforward violence and torture-like techniques based on deprivation or segregation, and which sees them as a function of the 'mortification' rather than 'treatment' of patients (Perrucci, 1974). The boredom of institutional life is well documented (see, for example, Anon., 1996). In short, there is little doubt that the characteristics and techniques described by Goffman have been widely deployed in both time and space, and although the view of many ex-inpatients who have been transferred into community-based residential accommodation is that the latter is less 'total' accommodation than that provided by mental hospitals, it is also well documented that many of the conditions of total institutions pertain in such accommodation (see Perring, 1992; Barham, 1992: 21–8; Qureshi, 2009). Two particularly controversial practices are 'restraint' and 'seclusion'.

2.5.2 **Restraint and seclusion**

As discussed at 2.5.1, psychiatric facilities, and other forms of accommodation for people with mental disorders such as care homes, tend to feature greater levels of violence and conflict than are found in or experienced by the general population, whether because a patient or resident is floridly mentally ill, or has learning disabilities and presents challenging behaviour, or is elderly, suffering from dementia, and prone to violent outbursts. Equally, a patient or resident may be reacting to overcrowded conditions, the imposition of non-consensual treatment, or some other aspect of the regime or their treatment by individual members of staff. Wherever possible, strategies of de-escalation that do not involve the use of physical force or the confinement of the patient or client should be used (DH, 2008: para. 15.17; DCA, 2007: para. 6.48). It cannot be disputed, however that on occasion physical intervention or the segregation of the patient or resident will be the only effective short-term response that can manage the risk posed to self or others. The first of these is described as 'restraint', the second as 'seclusion'.

These practices are often described as 'management' in the literature (for example, DH, 2008: para. 15.21). This is not a wholly inaccurate term, but it does not fully capture the reality that these practices are fundamentally about control. There is force in Cohen's point (1985: 2) that 'social control', if defined too broadly, becomes a 'Mickey Mouse' concept, too broad and general to be useful; but the practices of restraint and seclusion fall comfortably within Cohen's truncated criteria of 'organised responses to crime, delinquency and allied forms of deviant and/or socially problematic behaviour which are actually conceived of as such, whether in the reactive sense…or in the pro-active sense' (1985: 3). In this view, 'control' more accurately captures the reality of the situation. As far as the law is concerned, however, these practices constitute 'treatment'. This conceptual ambiguity perhaps reflects our ambiguities, both about mental disorder, and our responses to it. What is certain is that these practices are controversial.

2.5.2.1 Restraint

All hospitals (DH, 2008: paras. 15.21, 15.28–29) and care homes should have written policies on restraint, record its use, and review each instance of use, and all professionals, both in health and residential social care, should follow professional and other guidance (DCA, 2007: para. 6.42). Although there is a fairly clear understanding of what constitutes 'restraint' in both mental health and mental capacity law, only the latter operates around a statutory definition. Section 6(4) of the MCA 2005 defines restraint as the use or threatened use of force in order to secure the doing of an act which the person to be restrained is resisting, or which restricts that person's liberty of movement, whether or not he or she resists.

There is no equivalent provision in the MHA 1983, or in the Code of Practice issued under the Act. The Code simply discusses 'physical restraint' (DH, 2008: paras. 15.21 *et seq.*) and 'mechanical restraint' (para. 15.31) without attempting to define these terms further. This would seem to imply that the MHA 1983 operates with a narrower concept of restraint. Threatened use of force is below the radar for MHA purposes, which is effectively to turn a blind eye to the use of psychological as opposed to physical coercion (although guidance issued by NICE, 2005: 13, does require staff to monitor their own non-verbal behaviour). Even the broader definition in the MCA 2005 seems to cover only the explicit, rather than implicit, threatened use of force. The National Institute for Health and Clinical Evidence (NICE, 2005: 53), having reviewed the evidence, found that the core issues in restraint training courses include 'taking the patient to the floor', 'sitting and standing the patient', 'restraining hold', 'breakaways', as well as blocking punches and kicks, and separating fighting patients, which gives a flavour of what physical restraint comprises.

The legal basis for the use of restraint in respect of persons detained under the MHA 1983 is not found in the Act itself. Rather, it is the decision of the House of Lords in *Pountney* v *Griffiths* [1976] AC 314 (HL), in which it was accepted that 'a hospital's staff has powers of control over all mentally disordered patients, whether admitted voluntarily or compulsorily, though the nature and duration of the control varies with the category to which the patient belongs' (Lord Edmund-Davies at 334). For detained patients, such powers are inherent in the fact of detention, and hence, in the MHA 1983. The MHA 1983 also contains the latest version of the immunity from suit introduced by the Lunacy Act 1890 in s. 139 (see further Chapter 12, 12.4.1). In *Pountney*, it was established that s. 139 protects staff who use reasonable restraint in the course of a patient's treatment.

These days, any use of restraint will also have to satisfy the test of 'medical necessity' required by *Herczegfalvy* v *Austria* (1992) 15 EHRR 347 if a breach of Arts. 3 or 8 ECHR is to be avoided. Even so, a breach may be found, if the particular act of restraint is disproportionate or arbitrary, even if, in general terms, the treatment in question is necessary (Gostin, 2000: 149). But in truth, *Herczegfalvy*, in which a detained patient was fed by force and sedated, as well as, at times, restrained both physically and mechanically (he was variously handcuffed, strapped to his bed, and had a belt strapped around his ankles), offers little protection over and above that of the MHA 1983. The court held that these actions were necessary in order to treat the patient, who was on hunger strike and resisting treatment.

For informal patients, the legal basis for their restraint is murkier. There is Crown Court authority that dealings with informal patients are not covered by s. 139 by reason that such are not conducted 'in pursuance of this Act' as that section requires (*R* v *Runighian* [1977] Crim LR 361), but this may be questionable, because s. 131 does provide for the admission (although only for treatment and not for assessment) of informal patients. There is, in any case, a number of overlapping legal justifications for the use of restraint against an informal patient. There is a common law power exercisable by all citizens to prevent a breach of the peace, which is exercisable in hospitals and residential accommodation. There is a common law right to use force in self-defence, which includes the defence of others. There is also a common law right to confine a person who is insane, as demonstrated by the well-known case of *Fletcher* v *Fletcher* (1859) 1 El.& El. 420. Finally, there is a generally available power in s. 3(1) of the Criminal Law Act 1967 to use force to prevent a crime or to arrest a person unlawfully at large. The precise nature of each of these powers is debatable, but the general thrust of the law is clear, which is that, subject to requirements of reasonableness and proportionality, as well as the test of 'medical necessity' required by *Herczegfalvy*, there will be little difficulty for a staff member in finding a legal basis for the restraint of an informal patient. In addition, of course, if the patient lacks capacity, the powers of restraint available in s. 6 of the MCA 2005 are available.

According to the Code of Practice issued under the MHA 1983, physical restraint should be used 'only as a last resort and never as a matter of course' (DH, 2008: para. 15.23) when it is necessary to take control of a dangerous situation in order to contain a risk to the patient or others, and should 'contain or limit the patient's freedom for no longer than is necessary' (DH, 2008: para. 15.20). This may, exceptionally, be in the form of 'mechanical restraint', although does not define this term. Examples of mechanical restraint include 'supportive chairs' into which the individual is strapped, bed rails to prevent a person leaving their bed, and various other mechanisms to restrain a person. Nottinghamshire NHS Trust (Nottinghamshire NHS Trust, 2011: para. 2.3), for example, lists: Material Handcuffs; Cuffs with belt; Emergency Response Belt (ERB); Velcro Leg Strapping/Belts; Shoulder Restraint; Wheelchair and chair lap straps, amongst mechanisms which the Trust might employ.

The MHA Code does provide that 'Restraint which involves tying (whether by means of tape or by using a part of the patient's garments) to some part of a building or its fixtures [such as a chair] should never be used' (DH, 2008: para. 15.31). It is worrying, and revealing, that this needs to be said at all. Mechanical restraint is rarely used in acute mental health care settings, outside of forensic facilities. It is much more likely to be used in respect of persons with learning disabilities or elderly persons (CQC, 2010: 72), to which the MHA 1983 Code of Practice does not apply (although it does apply to informal hospital inpatients: DH, 2008: para. 15.1).

Any use of restraint must be necessary and proportionate to the harm that its use seeks to avoid or contain (DH, 2008: para. 15.22; s. 6(2), (3), MCA 2005; DCA, 2007: para. 6.41). The MCA Code of Practice (DCA, 2007: para. 6.44) is more expansive than that published under the MHA in this regard:

> Anybody considering using restraint must have objective reasons to justify that restraint is necessary. They must be able to show that the person being cared for is likely to suffer harm unless proportionate restraint is used. A carer or professional must not use restraint just so that they can do something more easily. If restraint is necessary to prevent harm to the person who lacks capacity, it must be the minimum amount of force for the shortest time possible.

Those using restraint in hospitals should be trained in its use (DH, 2008: para. 15.22). The requirement for training is sensible, of course. However, the MHAC warned consistently about 'the proliferation of unregulated training courses' (MHAC, 2001: 4.49), and such warnings are still being issued on a regular basis by the CQC (see, for example, 2013: 47). Moreover, it is very difficult to measure the effectiveness of training. Although there is anecdotal and impressionistic evidence that better training reduces the incidence of violence on wards, there has been, until very recently, little in the way of detailed and comparative evidence about the efficacy of particular techniques, which means that the substantive content of training is not yet evidence-based (National Audit Office, 2003a; Wright, 2003).

In 2003, the report of the inquiry into the death of a patient, David Bennett, who had died following an incident of the use of restraint, reported that methods used including a hand being held to his throat and nursing staff lying across him whilst he was lying face down on the floor (Norfolk, Suffolk and Cambridgeshire Health Authority, 2003: 19–22). When, in consequence, at the request of the Department of Health and Welsh Assembly, NICE produced guidance (still in force) on the use of restraint, it noted that 'there was a dearth of evidence in all areas covered by this guideline and all recommendations and good practice points were arrived at by the [Guidelines Development Group, a multi-disciplinary committee comprising senior health-care professionals, academics and system user representatives] using formal consensus methods' (NICE, 2005: 11). In other words, in the absence of hard research, the guidelines are based on personal experience and anecdote, and are really more 'best guess' than 'best practice'.

The first substantial research on these issues was published in 2006 (Health and Safety Executive (HSE), 2006). This showed that restraint training can have beneficial effects, but often only in the short term. It also found that 'What is clear from the research is that where training does not reflect a sound understanding of need, the impact of training is at best negligible and at worst negative' (2006: viii).

The NICE guidelines do now require that all service providers should provide restraint training, and should have policies that link need for training to risk assessment, and which detail frequency and substance of training courses. NICE is fairly prescriptive in this regard. All staff involved in the administration of restraint, either through physical force or tranquillising drugs, should have training in basic life support. In addition (2005: 13):

> All staff whose need is determined by risk assessment should receive ongoing competency training to recognise anger, potential aggression, antecedents and risk factors of disturbed/violent behaviour, and to monitor their own verbal and non-verbal behaviour. Training should include methods of anticipating, deescalating or coping with disturbed/violent behaviour.

The CQC reports that 'almost all staff will now have some degree of training' (CQC, 2013: 46). This is all well and good, but without evidence as to what works and when, it is not apparent that simply formulating guidelines or requiring training will improve the situation. The knowledge base may be growing (see HSE, 2006: Part 2), but not quickly enough. As the HSE report asks (2006: 30): 'For how long can we continue to operate in this "ad-hoc" manner?' Three years later, however, an authoritative review of the literature found the lack of data on efficacy of outcome 'striking' (Stewart et al., 2009: 13; 2010; see also Stubbs et al., 2009).

If restraint is used on an informal patient, consideration should be given to the invocation of formal powers of detention (DH, 2008: para. 15.34) and if a patient in hospital is subject to the Deprivation of Liberty Safeguards (DOLS), the use of restraint may indicate that the person deprived of their liberty may be objecting to that and so should be detained instead under the MHA (DH, 2008: para. 15.35, and see Chapter 5). On the other hand, if an informal hospital in-patient is not subject to the DOLS, the use of restraint does not necessarily indicate that the DOLS should be considered, on the basis that 'Appropriate use of restraint falls short of deprivation of liberty' (Ministry of Justice, 2008b: para. 2.9).

Although our knowledge of the efficacy of restraint techniques and training remains sketchy, we have a much clearer idea these days of the extent to which restraint is used. In the national survey of inpatients carried out in 2005, it was found that 8 per cent had experienced at least one act of restraint during the previous three months, 1.5 per cent had been subject to five or more acts of restraint, and 0.7 per cent, 10 or more such acts. It was also found that the rate of control and restraint among Afro-Caribbean men was 29 per cent higher than the average rate for all inpatients (Commission for Healthcare Audit and Inspection, MHAC, CSIP and NIMHE, 2005: 23). Smith and Humphreys (1997) found that, of patients requiring transfer to intensive psychiatric care wards, 37 per cent were subject to physical restraint in the four hours prior to transfer, and that restraint was used most frequently on patients admitted under s.4 who resisted admission and acted violently on detention.

A review of the literature from the 1960s onwards conducted by Stewart et al. (2009: 4) found that rates of between nine and 25 incidents per 100 beds per month, in one cluster of studies, and rates of between 12 per cent and 76 per cent of violent incidents leading to restraint in another cluster, with much more restraint employed in high security accommodation, and to some extent medium security accommodation, than in other facilities. This survey, however, did not include restraint carried out in care homes as opposed to hospitals.

The use of restraint has a chequered history, particularly, but by no means exclusively, in the special hospitals, and concerns continue to be expressed about practices, including the use of techniques such as the 'wristlock', which can be effective if applied correctly, but often staff fail to retain skills and techniques in which they have been trained (NICE, 2005). The use of straitjackets (MHAC, 1997: para. 4.5.3) and of mechanical restraint (MHAC, 2003: paras.11.35–11.41; 2005: para. 4.129) on the intensive care wards in the special hospitals has been reported in the past as common. A predominant concern of all CQC reports to date has been the use of restraint as a pretext for the abuse of patients or residents. The Winterbourne view scandal (DH, 2012), which revealed systematic abuse of residents of a care home for persons with learning disabilities was done, as the CQC (2013: 47) notes 'under the guise of restraint'. The CQC reports examples of abuse in its annual reports. Although seen as 'isolated incidents' (CQC, 2010: 72), it is clear that, just as with abuse of staff by patients, some abuse of patients by staff goes unreported.

At the time of writing the most recent report (CQC, 2013: 50) discusses the use by police of Tasers whilst transporting patients on psychiatric wards, in situations which ward staff were unable to de-escalate. It is impossible to know whether such use was proportionate, but it is clear that there is a correlation between the use of restraint and, albeit in a small number of cases, the subsequent death of the patient, the risk of which is greatly increased if the patient has recently been given more than a small dose of antipsychotic medicine. In combination, restraint and medication can cause acute stress and cardiac arrest (see *Buckley* v *UK* [1997] EHRLR 435). The MHAC found (2001a) that, in 22 of 208 deaths of mental hospital inpatients reported to the coroner as involving unnatural causes, the patient was under restraint at the time of death or had been at some time during the week before death. There were 115 deaths from unnatural causes over 2009 and 2010, most of which were attributable to suicide or the consequences of self-harm (CQC, 2011: 66). How many of these (whether or not officially classified as suicide, or even as natural causes, given that cardiac arrest can follow the use of restraint) were preceded by the use of restraint (or seclusion) is not known. However, to not know this information is almost as disconcerting as knowing that there is a correlation.

Sometimes, 'restraint' does not capture the nature of the problem or that of the official response to it. The ninth MHAC report revealed that, 'In this reporting period we have noted a number of uses of the police in full riot gear in response to situations on wards where patients are detained' (MHAC, 2001: para. 4.48). On occasion, nursing staff will also don full riot gear, if deemed necessary in the management of particular patients (see *Brady*, discussed earlier, and Hines, 1999). Those dedicated persons who perform to the best of their abilities in providing treatment to aggressive or disturbed patients deserve a vote of thanks for the difficult and sometimes dangerous responsibility that they shoulder for the general social good; but this does not detract from an argument that it is at this point that the credibility of the medical model of mental disorder begins to look decidedly problematic.

2.5.2.2 Seclusion

Although the MHA 1983 is silent as to the practice known as 'seclusion', the Code of Practice offers the following definition (DH, 2008: para. 15.43):

> Seclusion is the supervised confinement of a patient in a room, which may be locked for the protection of others from significant harm.

If this definition is met, the practice will be defined as seclusion however it is defined by the hospital (DH, 2008: para. 15.44). Another definition was offered by a patient in 2005 (cited in MHAC, 2005: 306):

> Seclusion is the most awful experience: the hopelessness and despair one feels locked in a cell with no knowledge of when one can get out, the powerlessness one feels, the sense of being punished, is overwhelming.

In plain English, seclusion is solitary confinement. It should not be considered as part of a treatment plan (DH, 2008: para. 15.45)—as is implied by its emergency use status—but it nevertheless falls within the definition of treatment in s. 145(1), MHA 1983 (Lord Bingham in *R* v *Ashworth Hospital, ex p Munjaz* [2005] UKHL 58 at para. 19). As Mason (1992; 1993) discusses, however, at a theoretical level, there are at least three possible explanations for the practice of seclusion: therapeutic, containing, and punitive. However guidelines on its use are framed, it will always be an open and empirical question as to which explanation best fits the facts in a given instance.

There is also a lack of consensus as to how seclusion should be defined (Mason, 1992; Exworthy *et al.*, 2001), but there is indisputably a sense in which seclusion that is experienced as punitive *is* punitive. This can be exacerbated by practices such as the use of 'special' clothing whilst a patient is in seclusion, which occurred at least 10 times in medium or high-security facilities during the period covered in a MHAC survey (MHAC, 2005: para. 4.276). This is done on the grounds of removing possible means of self-harm, but there is no escaping the fact that this is also ritualistic degradation that any human being is likely to experience as punitive. This is especially true when patients are stripped by staff of the opposite gender (Mason and Whitehead, 2001). The current Code, however, provides that patients should never be deprived of day-time clothing (DH, 2008: paras. 15.61, 15.67), and should, subject to risk, not be deprived of other aids necessary for their daily living.

Hospitals are enjoined by the Code to draw up guidelines concerning the use of seclusion, and for the monitoring and review of practice, which should be carried out regularly by hospital managers (DH, 2008: para. 15.47). The Code itself, however, is fairly prescriptive of the Department of Health view of best practice. Seclusion should only be used as a last resort for the shortest time necessary. It should not be used as punishment, threat, as a consequence of staff shortages, and should never be used as a response to self-harming behaviour. It should only be used if there is a risk of suicide or self-harm 'when the professionals involved are satisfied that the need to protect other people outweighs any increased risk to the patient's health or safety and that any such risk can be properly managed' (DH, 2008: para. 15.45). The protection of other persons is the 'sole aim' (2008: para. 15.43) of seclusion. It is the view expressed in the Code that seclusion can be ordered by the nurse in charge of the ward, which will usually be a senior nursing officer but may be any nursing officer at that moment 'in charge of the ward', as well as by a doctor, although, if the initial decision is taken by someone other than a doctor, one should attend immediately (2008: para. 15.49).

Seclusion should only take place in a safe, secure, and properly identified room, adequately heated, lit, ventilated, with adequate furnishing, which provides a safe, private environment for the detainee, whilst also allowing complete observation (2008: para. 15.60). There should be a nurse within sight and sound of the room at all times (2008: para. 15.55), and present if the patient has also been sedated (2008: para. 15.57): 'The aim of observation is to monitor the condition and behaviour of the patient and to identify at what time seclusion can be terminated' and the results of observation should be recorded in a documented report every 15 minutes (2008: para. 15.56).

There should be an inter-disciplinary review of the decision to seclude 'as soon as practicable after the seclusion begins' (DH, 2008: para. 15.50), and if it is decided that the seclusion should continue, 'the review should establish the individual care needs of the patient while they are in seclusion and the steps that should be taken in order to bring the need for seclusion to an end as quickly as possible' (DH, 2008: para. 15.50). Thereafter, if the seclusion continues, there should a two-hourly review by two nurses, at least one of whom was not involved with the initial decision to seclude, in the seclusion room, and a four-hourly review by a doctor (2008: para. 15.50), although with a discretion to depart from this during night-time hours when the patient is asleep (2008: para. 15.52). If seclusion is to continue for more than eight hours consecutively, or for 12 hours within a 48-hour period, there should be an independent review by a multidisciplinary team not involved in the patient's care at the time that the period of seclusion began (2008: para. 15.55). If seclusion is used in the case of an informal patient, it should be deemed to be an indication that the use of formal powers of detention should be considered (2008: para. 15.46).

The Code distinguishes seclusion from 'longer-term segregation' but does not discuss when the former becomes the latter. There is something ironic about this, given that the Code is quite clear in its advice to hospitals, that hospitals may not avoid the restrictions placed on the use of seclusion by means of defining a period of solitary confinement as being 'therapeutic isolation', 'single-person wards', and 'enforced segregation' rather than seclusion (DH, 2008: para. 15.44). Longer-term segregation may be used for (DH, 2008: para. 15.63):

> a very small number of patients who are not responsive to short-term management of their aggression and violence and who could be described as "long-term dangerous". By this it is meant that they present a risk to others which is a constant feature of their presentation and

is not subject to amelioration by a short period of seclusion combined with any other form
of treatment. The clinical judgement in these cases is that, if the patient were allowed to mix
freely in the general ward environment, other patients or staff would continuously be open
to the potential of serious injury or harm.

Hospitals intending to use longer-term segregation should develop policies on its use
but there should in any case be 'periodic review' by a senior clinician (para. 15.66). The
frequency of review is not further specified, nor does the Code require that the reasons
for continuing longer-term segregation should be increasingly detailed the longer the
period of segregation lasts, but the ECHR, as interpreted by the Grand Chamber of the
European Court in *Ramirez Sanchez* v *France* no. 59450/00, § 139, ECHR 2006-IX, does.

   Although a seclusion room may be used for this purpose, so too may the patient's
own bedroom (DH, 2008: para. 15.66), and a patient requiring longer-term segregation
should leave that room or have contact with other patients without staff present. Such
a patient should only be removed from longer-term segregation following a thorough
inter-disciplinary risk assessment and should be closely monitored to ensure successful
reintegration into the general ward environment (2008: para. 15.65).

   The extent to which it is permissible for an institution to implement a policy on seclusion at variance from the terms of the Code was argued before the House of Lords in
R v *Ashworth Hospital, ex p Munjaz* [2005] UKHL 58. Following an earlier, partially
successful, legal challenge in 2000 (*R* v *Ashworth Special Hospital, ex p M* (2000) 2000
WL 1480059, (QB)), Ashworth had revised some elements of its seclusion policy. The
revised policy departed from what is now para. 15.50 of the Code, and its requirement
of four-hourly medical reviews, in that it required that, from the second day of seclusion, there would be two medical reviews daily, and from the eighth day, three medical reviews each week, only one of which need involve the responsible clinician (RC).
There would also, from the second week, be two-hourly review by nursing staff, a weekly
multi-disciplinary review, a daily review by the ward or site manager, and a monthly
report to the hospital's seclusion monitoring group. In addition, the hospital would
inform the MHAC (now CQC) of any patient secluded for more than seven days. Under
that policy, M was secluded on several occasions for periods of seven and 15 days. M's
complaint was that the policy departed too far from the requirements of the Code, so that
the infrequency with which his periods of seclusion had been reviewed was unlawful.

   By a 3:2 majority, made up of Lords Bingham, Hope, and Scott, the House, revers-
ing the decision of a unanimous Court of Appeal, held that the revised policy was in
compliance both with domestic law and with the ECHR. As far as the domestic law is
concerned, the issue was the status of s. 118 of the MHA 1983 and the Code of Practice
published under it. If the Code has the force of law, it would follow that a departure
from it is unlawful. Here, the House split 4:1. Lord Bingham examined the terms of the
Code, noted that in its Introduction it is stated that 'The Act does not impose a legal
duty to comply with the Code', and found it 'plain that the Code does not have the binding effect which a statutory provision or a statutory instrument would have. It is what it
purports to be, guidance not instruction' (para. 21, see also Lord Hope at para. 68, Lord
Brown at para. 107, and Lord Scott at para. 101, agreeing with Lords Bingham, Hope,

and Brown). As such, the Code is not a binding document. However (Lord Bingham at para. 21):

> It is much more than mere advice which an addressee is free to follow or not as it chooses. It is guidance which any hospital should consider with great care, and from which it should depart only if it has cogent reasons for doing so.

Moreover, 'these reasons must be spelled out clearly, logically and consistently' (Lord Hope at para. 69).

Applying that *dicta* to Ashworth's policy, all bar Lord Steyn accepted that such reasons had been satisfactorily demonstrated by the hospital. Lord Bingham pointed out (at para. 23) that the Code is silent as to the particular difficulties that attend special hospital patients, and as to the need to seclude a patient for a period of more than a few hours (the Code in force at that time (Department of Health and Welsh Office, 1993) did not contain provision on longer-term segregation). Lord Hope (para. 70) similarly held that 'special considerations need to be applied to the use of seclusion in a high security hospital, bearing in mind that the very reason why patients are there is because they cannot be dealt with by mental health services elsewhere in a way that will protect others from harm'. In this light, Ashworth's policy, to conduct less reviews of a patient in seclusion than stated in the Code, was reasonable, particularly in view of the other mechanisms in place by which a period of seclusion was reviewed and monitored. Indeed, the policy was able to withstand 'a particularly careful and intense scrutiny' (Lord Hope at para. 74, see also Lord Bingham at para. 24) of the type required when the human rights of an applicant are potentially at issue, whether on an application for judicial review or by way of a claim under the HRA 1998.

By a complicated majority, the House also held 4:1 that there was no breach of Arts. 3 or 5 of the ECHR and, 3:2, that there was no breach of Art. 8. Dealing first with Art. 3, Lord Bingham (at para. 29, see also Lord Hope at para. 81) held that Ashworth's policy 'must be considered as a whole' and 'the policy, properly operated, will be sufficient to prevent any possible breach of the Art. 3 rights of a patient secluded for more than seven days'. Lord Hope accepted that Art. 3 imposes a positive obligation on contracting states to act reasonably to safeguard Art. 3 rights, which increases in proportion to the likelihood of the risk in question materialising, but found that 'the risk of ill-treatment is very low if full effect is given to the policy' and that it would therefore be disproportionate to require Ashworth to abandon its policy to eliminate that small risk (para. 82). Hence, there was no breach of Art. 3.

Applying *Ashingdane* v *UK* (1985) 7 EHRR 528, Lord Bingham (para. 30, and see Lord Hope at paras. 83–86) also found Art. 5 to be inapplicable, because the seclusion policy related not to the fact of detention, nor to the type of institution, but only to the particular conditions of detention. Finally Lord Bingham noted 'some difficulty' in appreciating how Art. 8(1) might be said to be engaged by a policy that aimed only to protect third parties and to seclude only for the minimum time necessary to do that (para. 32), but, in any case, went on to hold that, even if Art. 8(1) were engaged, the breach might be justified by reference to several of the grounds listed in Art. 8(2), and

'Properly used, the seclusion will not be disproportionate because it will match the necessity giving rise to it' (para. 33). Lord Hope made substantially the same points, in addition, holding that Ashworth's policy was 'in accordance with the law' as required by Art. 8(2), because, although not made under statutory authority, it did comply with the common law and, as a written and published policy, was sufficiently precise and accessible (paras. 90–92).

For a trenchant critique of this decision, it is necessary to look no further than the dissenting opinion of Lord Steyn, who called it 'a set-back for a modern and just mental health law' (para. 48), which licensed 'a free-for-all in which hospitals are at liberty to depart from the published Code as they consider right' (para. 44). That the majority had upheld a policy, which replaced the 42 reviews called for by the Code in relation to days eight to 14 (and subsequent weeks) of a period of seclusion with the three required by Ashworth's policy, was 'disturbing' (para. 47). Lord Steyn endorsed the decision of the Court of Appeal ([2003] EWCA Civ 1036) that a policy that departs from the Code is unlawful, because, on his analysis, and that of the Court of Appeal, the Code was intended by Parliament to establish 'minimum safeguards and a modicum of centralised protection for vulnerable patients' (para. 44). Departures from the Code should *only* be permitted where a hospital has 'good reason for departing from it in relation to an individual patient' or in relation to a particular class of patients 'who share well-defined characteristics' (para. 46, citing the Court of Appeal at para. 76). Absent good reasons, domestic law is infringed, and there will also a breach of the positive obligation under Arts. 3 and 8 (Court of Appeal, para. 74).

Indeed, Lord Steyn went further than the Court of Appeal, finding that there was also a breach of Art. 5, on the basis that a lawfully detained person has a 'residual liberty'. He cited the well-known Canadian case *Miller* v *The Queen* (1985) 24 DLR (4th) 9, in which the Canadian Supreme Court had held that a prisoner unlawfully subject to solitary confinement had suffered a breach of his residual liberty. He also found support for the concept in the European Court in *Bollan* v *UK* (Application No. 42117/98) (see para. 43).

Subsequently, the European Court in *Schneiter* v *Switzerland* (Application No. 63062/00, 31 March 2005), held that Art. 5 was applicable in a case of solitary confinement for a period of 11 days, although there was no breach in that case, as the use of seclusion in that way was lawful in Switzerland and its use was not arbitrary. In *Munjaz*, however, Lord Steyn's analysis was specifically rejected by Lord Bingham (para. 30). Lord Steyn was joined in the minority by Lord Brown, but only by reason of the latter's view of Art. 8(2)'s requirement that any breach of Art. 8(1) must be 'in accordance with law'. For Lord Brown (para. 127):

> Unless it is to the Code that one can look for regulation carrying the force of law it is not in my opinion to be found elsewhere. Hospital policies themselves provide too insubstantial a foundation for a practice so potentially harmful and open to abuse as the seclusion of vulnerable mental patients.

As seen above, this analysis was also specifically rejected, on this occasion by Lord Hope (para. 98) and Lord Scott (paras. 101–3).

Maybe Lord Steyn's view, that the decision of the majority licenses a 'free-for-all', overstates the situation; there must, after all, be 'cogent reasons' to depart from the Code. On the other hand, although Ashworth clearly developed its policy by reference to the Code, as Lord Brown mentioned (para. 126), 75 per cent of patients in long-term seclusion are not *in fact* in 24-hour seclusion, but are nursed on wards and 'interacting with staff and patients', and so it is clear that 'seclusion' is being used at the hospital in a way very different from that envisaged in the Code. One patient mentioned by Lord Brown had been in 'seclusion' at Ashworth for nine years, before his transfer to Rampton, where he was never in seclusion for more than eight hours at a time (for more information, see MHAC, 2005: para. 4.239). This would seem to suggest that perhaps Lord Steyn is not too far wide of the mark after all.

M took his case to the European Court of Human Rights (*Munjaz* v *UK* [2012] MHLR 351; (2012) *The Times*, October 9) but the Court upheld the decision of the majority in the House of Lords, finding the argument under Art. 3 to be 'manifestly unfounded' (para. 53) and that Art. 8(1) is breached by seclusion (para. 80), but that Ashworth's policy was not arbitrary and so was defensible under Art. 8(2) (para. 95). On the Art. 5 question, the Court was clear (para. 66, 67) that *Schneiter* could not be interpreted as laying down any general rule that seclusion is in breach of Art. 5(1); that rather, it is a question of analysing the extent, duration, and intensity of the restriction of liberty in each case to ascertain whether it was of such a degree that it could constitute a deprivation of liberty within Art. 5(1); and that 'these criteria must apply with greater force when determining whether a person who has already been deprived of his liberty has been subjected to a further deprivation of liberty or merely a further restriction upon their liberty' (para. 67).

The period of detention per se is not sufficient to establish a deprivation of liberty (para. 71), and there was no breach of Art. 5(1) in *Munjaz* because the seclusion was not imposed as a punishment (para. 70); because Ashworth's approach to seclusion was also rather lax compared to the Code, with patients being permitted to be secluded in their own room rather than the dedicated seclusion room and to take meals and otherwise socialise on the ward (para. 72); and because, as a patient detained in a high security facility, M 'even when he was not in seclusion, he would already have been subjected to greater restrictions on his liberty than would normally be the case for a mental health patient' (para. 69).

Although addressed by arguments specifically raising the concept of 'residual liberty', and making mention of *Miller* in its judgment, the Court made no specific ruling on whether it recognised the concept. However, the fact that the court was prepared to accept the applicability of Art. 5(1) in this context, when the person in question is already lawfully detained, does seem necessarily to imply that the concept of residual liberty was endorsed by the Court, and certainly seems to be capable of further development. It is also worth mentioning that the European Court declined to make any ruling in relation to Art. 14, because M, so it was held, had not exhausted all domestic remedies because he had not argued on the basis of Art. 14 before the domestic courts (para. 100), but it remains open for a future applicant to argue that Art. 14 in combination with (most probably) Art. 8 provides a remedy. However, the argument that would have been made in this case was that people in prison in solitary confinement have greater procedural safeguards than do people in hospital in seclusion and, especially, longer-term segregation; and an argument based on a similar comparison in relation to smoking (which is still permitted in prison) fell on deaf ears in *R* v *Nottinghamshire Healthcare NHS Trust, ex parte G, B and N* [2009] EWCA Civ 795.

It is to be hoped that the substance of the decision of the Court of Appeal in the case of *S* v *Airedale NHS Trust*, which it heard together with *Munjaz*, but which was not further appealed to the House of Lords, survives the subsequent litigation. In *Airedale*, S, a patient who had been violent and repeatedly absconded after detention, had been secluded for 12 days in a non-secure hospital because of the unavailability of a bed in a secure unit. His conditions of seclusion were poor: a bare room with no toilet facilities. It was held that the seclusion of S for 12 days in unsuitable conditions, which occurred solely because the facility in question 'could think of no alternative' response to the significant management problems S posed, was unjustified and disproportionate ([2003] EWCA Civ 1036 at para. 81).

In our view, the decision of the House of Lords does not affect this; there was, on the evidence, no 'cogent reason' for the seclusion in this case. In this respect, it is to be noted that in *R* v *MHRT London South and West Region, ex p C* [2001] MHLR 110 (see Chapter 8), Lord Phillips, MR, in determining whether an eight-week wait for a tribunal hearing after an application had been made was in breach of Art. 5.4, cited the decision of the European Court of Human Rights in *Bezicheri* v *Italy* (1989) 12 EHRR 210, to the effect that resource shortages may not be pleaded in mitigation of a breach of that Article. Following *Munjaz*, it seems clear that Art. 5 applies to equally to seclusion, and it is not apparent why the same should not apply to Arts. 3 and 8 when, as here, shortage of resources is clearly the real issue.

Over the years, the reports of the MHAC, and latterly the CQC, have voiced similar concerns about the way in which seclusion is used in practice. The most recently available QCC annual report (2013) discusses: examples of practice which in the view of the Commission amounts to seclusion, such as the use of a 'safe room' in which patients were isolated in order to de-escalate violent or potentially violent situations, but in which the guidance in the Code is deemed not to apply; inadequate implementation of review procedures, in particular doctors not arriving on the scene in good time, sometimes not until the period of seclusion had been ended by nursing staff, and sometimes not at all; reviews were not always conducted with the requisite frequency; some seclusion accommodation was inadequately furnished, heated, lit, and ventilated (with examples of patients being detained in totally empty, sometimes padded, rooms with no access to toilet facilities or even a mattress in day-time hours); and with patients too often not in sight of a clock, which added to the sense of disorientation for the person secluded (CQC, 2013: 44–46).

The MHAC in 2009 (MHAC, 2009: 1.158) discussed one unit for female patients in which women were routinely stripped naked before being secluded to ensure that no concealed weapons or means of self-harm were secreted about their clothing. This may be justifiable for particular cause, but as a routine practice, this seems to us, as it did to the MHAC to be morally indefensible, not to mention legally spurious. The integration of such rituals of degradation into a practice—seclusion—claimed to be therapeutic is arguably enough to undermine fatally what is already seen by many as a problematic claim.

All of this is familiar to readers of earlier reports. The central message seems to be that hospital staff, despite the ruling in *Munjaz* on when it is defensible to depart from the guidance given in the Code of Practice, too often treat the Code as merely advisory. Of course, sometimes this will be warranted, but the failure to meet the basic standards of amenity required in the furnishing of seclusion rooms, for example, seems to be indefensible, as does a failure to comply with requirements as to review and monitoring. As long ago as 1999, the MHAC called for a statutory regime for seclusion and restraint (MHAC, 1999: para. 10.25) and although the important point is not so much the legal status of the controls as whether they work effectively (Taxis, 2002; Gaskin, Elsom and Happell, 2007), it does seem that unless the controls are given statutory force, whatever else needs to be done, they will not work effectively.

The Mental Health Alliance (an umbrella organisation of mental health professionals, social workers, lawyers, religious organisations, and others) campaigned for precisely this in the lead-up to the MHA 2007, but the government was content to leave the situation unchanged. In our view, that was unfortunate. If seclusion is to be practised, then there should be a statutory regime, complete with safeguards and rights of appeal, in place. Moreover, it seems innocuous and inequitable not to acknowledge that detention has different levels of intensity and that seclusion constitutes its most intensive form, and is qualitatively different from detention per se. The concept of residual liberty captures this reality, and so should the law. In our view, the decision of the European Court in *Munjaz* has, at the least, set the scene for this development to occur.

Although the CQC reports annually on the use of seclusion in psychiatric facilities, and its reports certainly give a flavour of contemporary patterns of use and misuse, the CQC reports do not provide information about the extent of the use of seclusion. In this, CQC reports reflect an international paucity of data concerning extent of use (Steinert *et al.*, 2010). Data can be gleaned from the *Count Me In* annual surveys that ran until 2010. The most recent of these (CQC, 2011: 24) found, as had the previous five censuses, that 4 per cent of patients had experienced at least one episode of seclusion in the previous year and that there are significant differences in the use of seclusion by race, with, in 2011–12, white British patients having a seclusion rate (of 9 per cent) below the national average, whilst for White/Black Caribbean Mixed (80 per cent), White/Black African Mixed (90 per cent), Black Caribbean (36 per cent), and Black African (56 per cent) groups, the rates were markedly, even alarmingly higher.

This data does not seem to lend itself to easy interpretation in terms of causality, beyond the clear finding that race influences outcomes. The best data we have on multiple use comes from the 2005 census of hospital inpatients (Commission for Healthcare Audit and Inspection, MHAC, CSIP and NIMHE, 2005: 22), which found that over a three month period, 3 per cent of patients (1,104 individuals) had experienced at least one period of seclusion, 0.3 per cent (112) five or more periods, and 0.1 per cent (42), 10 or more.

2.5.3 Institutions: Conclusion

Goffman's thesis, as might be expected, has not gone unchallenged, on philosophical, methodological, and empirical grounds. Sedgwick (1982), for example, has argued that Goffman's theory is too sweeping and so both underplays the extent to which mental hospitals resemble other hospitals, even from the point of view of the patient, most of whom are not detained, and is insensitive to the historical contingencies that must be taken into account when applying a theoretical model. For instance, Goffman draws, in quick succession, on T. E. Lawrence's description of barracks life in the airforce, practises in a nunnery, and the practice of flogging on nineteenth century warships, to illustrate his thesis, all in the space of a few pages (Goffman, 1991: 37–9), and gives the reader the impression that all are mere examples of a general phenomenon with no particularities or variation to speak of. There is no well-defined qualitative element in Goffman's understanding of a total institution.

There is, for example, as much autobiographical work that contradicts Goffman's views as supports them. Many patients do experience their treatment as beneficial, even if their first impulse had been to resist. Moreover, a central tenet of Goffman's thesis has been undermined by the shift in focus of hospital services to acute care (Cavadino, 1989: ch. 5). In the years of the great confinement, a considerable number of patients spent years, if not decades, inside asylums. The average length of stay in the 1950s had fallen to approximately 10 years, compared to 20–40 years before the Second World War.

As already mentioned, average duration of stay is measured in terms of months, and many patients will spend less than a month in hospital. Rather than being 'total' institutions, contemporary mental hospitals are, not always, but often, better characterised in terms of managed chaos. Over-occupancy of beds results in patients being accommodated in makeshift and impromptu ways—the CQC's most recently available report (2013: 55) discusses a ward with 19 beds and 27 patients, with the overspill sleeping on an otherwise out-of-service and unstaffed ward, raising patient concerns about safety and privacy—as well as inappropriately early discharge or leave of absence, leading to an increase in admissions when patients released too early relapsed and required readmission, as well as delays in admission, as managers and mental health professionals attempt to keep the system running despite overcrowding and insufficient resources (CQC, 2013: 28, 62–63).

2.6 Concluding comments

It is not easy to digest of all this information, and it may be that this is because it sends out conflicting messages. In a very real sense, it is misleading to think of the state provision of mental health services as a singular system. Notwithstanding the move toward statutory integration of administrative structures and standards, with the high security hospitals now integrated into their local NHS trusts, it remains the case that the high security hospitals are as much if not more closely interconnected with the prison system than the national health system.

General psychiatric hospital provision, by contrast, has moved significantly into the mainstream of health care provision and such facilities are very much more part of that general hospital system than was the case, even in the final years of the last century. As such, they share the problems of that system—limited funds, staff shortages, an emphasis on 'throughput', and the dominance of managerial rather than clinical (or social-control-oriented) imperatives. If the problem for patients in the special hospitals is getting out, for those in need of acute care services, the problem can be getting in—and staying in long enough. Similar problems of resource limitations affect the community care system.

Even so, generalisation remains a problem: for example, different wards in the same facility negotiate the balance between treatment and control differently. Wards ostensibly in 'the community' may, in fact, be more secure than those in hospitals; detained patients may be held in conditions of lesser security than 'informal' patients. Work which has unearthed the hidden history of care in the community (Bartlett and Wright, 1999) is a reminder that much of what has passed as 'the' history of the treatment of mental disorder is only a part of that history, and that the role of institutionalisation has been routinely overemphasised by 'traditionalists' and 'revisionists' alike. But are we now at risk of making the opposite mistake: spinning a tale of the shift from institutional to community-based provision, when, in fact, much of that provision in the community is in residential form? The old asylums, as visible icons, may have gone (although many remain and have been converted to other uses), but are they truly 'abolished', or merely rendered more diffuse and opaque, now spread over very many sites, not infrequently 'out of area'; harder to see, maybe, but no less real?

At the same time, we should remember that although for considerable numbers, the mental health system is designed, and experienced, as coercive, for an even greater number it is a system of service provision. This is perhaps a more fundamental divide than that between those housed in the special hospitals and the rest, because it marks the boundary between a system based on coercion and a system based on consent. Here, as discussed at 2.1, the mental health system shares a number of porous borders with other systems for service provision, and at certain points shades into them.

However the mental health system is conceptualised, it is likely that it will continue, as it always has been, to be framed in terms of the negotiation of a balance or compromise between our bi-focal response to mental disorder, prompted both by concern about the plight of fellow human beings and by a desire to control behaviour judged to be dangerous or antisocial. Managerialism and the influence of market principles are vital questions when investigating how the system works. But in terms of function, the overarching perspectives of benevolence and control, medicalism and custodialism *are* accurate: they reflect our motives, and their inherent ambiguity. In large part, the degree to which one or the other is emphasised is a matter of perspective, judgment, and interpretation. But to understand the mental health system fully, in terms of its broader social function and in its microscopic interactions with service users, it is perhaps necessary to learn to live with the paradox that both at once—simultaneously seeking to treat and to control. This is not to say, however, that we all agree about how that system should be constituted, and there is plenty of scope for legitimate disagreement about how the balance between service provision and treatment on the one hand and control on the other should be articulated in law, policy, and practice.

Caught in the middle of this juxtaposition of the mundane, the bizarre and the poignant, as the intended beneficiaries of political and professional initiatives, and of social work and sociological theories, are the users of the service. Although the voices of service users risk being drowned out by those of the others, this must be resisted, if we are not to lose sight of the special contribution to our understanding of our mental health system that its users can make. We shall leave the final words in this chapter to the voice of one user:

> Joe's making a stool
> I'm weaving a basket
> someone's making coffee
> Dee says I can sing
> and she does.
> Jane won't make an ashtray
> Arthur's sulking because the priest wouldn't rechristen him *Jesus*.
> Jane still won't make an ashtray. instead she becomes a dog
> grr Woof!
> Dogs don't make ashtrays.
> Dee's singing the national anthem
> Arthur blesses me.
> Sydney hasn't spoken all morning, or yesterday or the day before, gggrrrr Woof!
> *Shit* said Joe
> *I'm going to discharge myself from this place it's driving me mad*
>
> realising what he had said, he starts to laugh
> i also start to laugh
> the man on my left (who didn't hear Joe) starts to laugh as well. we all laugh
>   except Sid
> who wants to die (and means it)
> then we had coffee

(Lewis, 1996)

3

Community Care

3.1 Introduction

If one considers only the provisions of the MHA 1983, it would seem reasonable to conclude that the defining characteristic of the mental health system is its coercive nature: the MHA 1983 essentially provides for people suffering from mental disorder to be detained in hospital and treated without consent, and to be subject to coercive control after leaving hospital. This is, however, misleading in two ways. First, only a small number of the target population of the mental health system will be treated in hospital, and, secondly, a smaller number still will be subject to coercive control. For many, if not most, people who require some sort of state intervention or assistance with a mental health problem, their first and only port of call is the local GP surgery. For those who require something more than medication or other services which can be delivered by the primary care sector, the issue is rarely coercive control. It is much more likely, instead, to be inability to access the required services.

The essence of community care law, policy, and practice is straightforward. Community care involves, first, assessing the needs of citizens for services, and secondly, meeting those needs assessed as requiring state intervention. The resourcing issues which confront the NHS, LSSAs, and LHAs mean, in practice, however, that access to those services is rationed, and therein lies the complicating factor. The main theme of this chapter, accordingly, is the extent to which those in need of services are able to require the state to provide them, rather than, as for many of the other issues covered in this text, the extent to which a client can free themselves from state control.

As shall be seen, the law in this area, which was by-passed by the reform of both mental capacity law and mental health law in recent years, is complex and confusing, involving a 'maze of interacting statutory provisions' (Lord Phillips MR in *R* v *Wandsworth LBC, ex p Spink* [2005] EWCA Civ 302 at para. 1) providing for health, welfare, and accommodation services, and there have been calls for many years for reform (Clements, 1997). Such calls fell on deaf ears until fairly recently. In 1998, the Labour administration accepted that 'community care has failed' (DH, 1998a), but attempted to improve the situation with policy and other initiatives, and it was not until 2008 that the *prima facie* case for substantial legislative overhaul was accepted, and the Law Commission was charged to investigate and report back on what that reform might entail.

The Law Commission's report (Law Commission, 2011), published in May 2011, endorsed the need for rationalisation of the legal framework and made many (76) recommendations for changes, both big and small. The government accepted the conclusions of the Commission (DH, 2012a), and simultaneously published a draft Bill, the Care and Support Bill (CSB), in July 2012, having already announced its intention to do so in the Queen's Speech in May 2012.

The CSB is partly intended as a consolidating measure, which will finally put all the relevant legislation under one roof, but it seeks also to reorient the system (DH, 2012a: para. 3.4):

> The law is currently built around the provision of State-defined services, rather than around meeting and responding to the needs and goals of individuals. It makes distinctions based on the type of care and support, or the setting in which it is received, often without any clear reason. Moreover, it does not reflect what can be done proactively to support people to maintain their well-being and enable them to make their own decisions about their support. Ultimately, existing legislation does not match our aim for empowering, person-centred care and support.

Meanwhile, as mentioned in Chapter 2 (see 2.4.2), a separate, *ad hoc*, Commission—the Commission on Funding of Care and Support (CFCS)—chaired by Andrew Dilnot, a renowned economist, was set up in 2010 to examine the way in which community care is funded. The CFCS, as was widely expected, concluded that the current system is unfair because 'People are left exposed to potentially catastrophic care costs with no way to protect themselves' (from CFCS website at http://www.dilnotcommission. dh.gov.uk/our-report/). The CFCS made many detailed proposals for reform of the way in which community care is funded, largely accepted by the government in principle (although specific recommendations, concerned with the costs that should be borne by service users, have not been accepted: see Chapter 2, 2.4.2), and the draft CSB also reflects the recommendations of the CFCS, albeit in modified form.

At the time of writing, the draft CSB is undergoing pre-legislative scrutiny by a joint committee of the Houses of Lords and Commons, following the conclusion of which the Committee will report back to both Houses of Parliament and both the future timetable for the progression of the draft Bill into law, and its substantive content, is uncertain, but it does seem probable that new law will come into force within the lifetime of this edition. For the time being, however, the current law remains in place and is likely to do so for some time. Moreover, although the proposals made and accepted will, if and when implemented, improve the legal framework for the delivery of services, many of the issues which have proven problematic in the current law—issues such as the meaning of 'need'; the question of whether resources can be taken into account when assessing and/or meeting needs; the allocation of responsibility as between LSSAs, and as between LSSAs, NHS bodies, and LHAs—will continue to be relevant under any new regime; and much of the substance of the law as it applies to the entitlements of service users and the duties of commissioners and providers will be similar after the parliamentary passage of the CSB to that which currently pertains. In the current, uncertain situation, it seems appropriate, therefore, that this chapter should discuss both the current

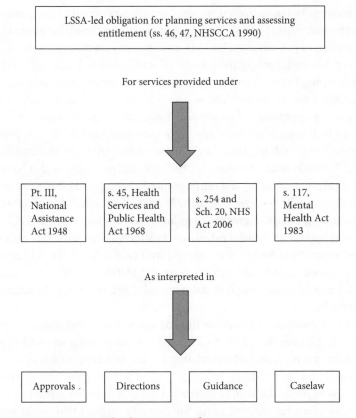

Figure 3.1 The legal framework for the provision of community care services

law (an overview of which is provided in Figure 3.1) and, as far as it can be known, the likely future law.

3.2 Services for mentally disordered persons in the community

3.2.1 Community care planning

The NHSCCA 1990, and the draft CSB, place primary responsibility for the effective delivery of community care services on LSSAs. Section 46(1) of the NHSCCA 1990 requires every LSSA to prepare, publish, and keep under review a plan for the provision of community care in its area. This must be done in consultation with local NHS bodies, LHAs, the voluntary sector (including organisations representing the interests of private carers such as family members, and voluntary housing and community care organisations), and any other persons as the Secretary of State may direct (s. 46(2)).

Despite such local autonomy, there is a significant degree of central government control over service provision at local level. The Secretary of State for Health has powers to provide for the inspection of premises and evaluate management practices, to make regulations, including regulations regarding the transfer of staff between LSSAs and NHS bodies, which must be complied with by LSSAs, and to hear complaints and carry out investigations (NHSCCA 1990, ss. 48–50). The Secretary of State also shapes policy and practice through the use of 'approvals' (which are permissive) and, in particular, 'directions' (compliance with which is mandatory and which are to be found in LAC (93)10, published by the Department of Health in March 1993), made under powers to be found in ss. 7, 7A of the Local Authority Social Services Act 1970. Central government also has control of gross local government funding, and can target funds through the use of grant funding for services for the mentally ill under s. 7E of the Local Authority Social Services Act.

There is also a significant degree of discretion to be exercised at local level, in terms of which services to provide, to what extent, and to which individuals. There is a statutory duty on LSSAs and NHS bodies to co-operate with each other in the delivery of health and welfare services (National Health Service Act (NHSA) 2006, s. 82), and there is law and guidance on co-operation in the assessment and provision of community care services (see 3.5).

The draft CSB contains no provision directly equivalent to the obligation in s. 46(1) but does, in cl. 2(1) require LSSAs to 'establish and maintain a service for providing people with information and advice relating to care and support for adults and support for carers', and 'In providing information and advice under this section, a local authority must in particular seek to ensure that what it provides is sufficient to enable adults to make plans for meeting needs for care and support that might arise' (CSB, cl. 2(3)). An LSSA must also, under the terms of cl. 3(1), 'promote the efficient and effective operation in its area of a market in services for meeting care and support needs' so that potential service users have enough information about the services available and the identity of service providers to be able to make an informed decision. To this end, LSSAs must remain 'aware of current and likely future demand for such services and to consider how providers might meet that demand' (cl. 3(2)(b)) and have regard to 'the importance of ensuring the sustainability of the market' (cl. 3(2)(c)), and in meeting these obligations something very like the current 'community care plan' will necessarily be constituted and published. As under the current law, LSSAs must act in co-operation (cl. 4(1)) with 'relevant partners', defined in cl. 4(5) to include other tiers of local government, NHS bodies, the police, probation service, central government, and any other person specified in regulations (yet to be made). Unlike the current law, however, partners are also placed under a duty to co-operate with LSSAs (cl. 4(1)). There is a specific duty to act co-operatively with LHAs in cl. 4(3).

3.2.2 Community care services

At the moment, out of the many and varied statutory provisions which permit or require the provision of services to mentally disordered persons in the community, only four are defined, by s. 46(3) of the NHSCCA 1990, as sources of 'community care services'. These are:

- Part III of the National Assistance Act 1948;
- s. 45 of the Health Services and Public Health Act 1968;
- s. 254 and Sch. 20 of the National Health Service Act 2006;
- s. 117 of the MHA 1983.

These statutes are concerned with the provision of accommodation services, welfare services, and health services, including after-care, to overlapping groups of clients, the main point of overlap being between services for persons with mental illness or disability and those for elderly persons. Each of the statutory provisions is supplemented by rules, regulations, and guidance, as well as by directions and approvals from the Secretary of State.

Although the draft CSB proposes the abolition of all these statutory provisions, with the exception of s. 117, MHA 1983 (Sch. 4, draft CSB), the nature of the care which an LSSA may provide will not change. Clause 8 of the draft CSB lists the type of ways in which services may be provided:

(a) accommodation in a care home or in premises of some other type;

(b) care and support at home or in the community;

(c) counselling, advocacy, and other types of social work;

(d) goods and facilities;

(e) information and advice.

What will change, however, is the ease with which it will be possible to navigate the new legal framework compared to that which frames the existing law which, as we will now see, is unnecessarily complex, reflecting its history.

3.2.2.1 Part III, National Assistance Act 1948

Part III of the National Assistance Act (NAA) 1948 is concerned with the provision of services by LSSAs. Sections 21–24 and 26 deal with the provision of residential accommodation, ss. 29 and 30 are concerned with welfare services.

3.2.2.1.1 *Residential accommodation under s. 21*

Section 21(1)(a) of the NAA 1948 gives a discretion to LSSAs to provide residential accommodation for persons who by reason of age, illness, disability, or any other circumstances are in need of care and attention which is not otherwise available to them. The scope of the obligations of an LSSA are subject to approvals and directions of the Secretary of State. Directions can be found in Appendix 1 to LAC 93(10), the effect of which is that LSSAs have four duties to make arrangements under s. 21(1)(a). The first is in respect of persons who, by reason of 'age, illness, disability or any other circumstances', are in need of such services and are ordinarily resident in the LSSA's area. The second is in respect of the same classes of persons, who are not ordinarily resident in the LSSA's area but who are in urgent need (LAC(93)10, Appendix 1 para. 2(1)(b)). The third duty, imposed 'without prejudice to the generality' of the first two, is owed to persons in urgent need of temporary accommodation 'in circumstances where the need for that accommodation could not reasonably have been foreseen', and makes no reference to the ordinary residence of the applicant (Appendix 1, para. 2(2)). The fourth, also imposed without prejudice to the generality of the first two, and which applies in respect both of those ordinarily resident in the LSSA's area and those with no settled residence in the LSSA's area, requires LSSAs to make arrangements under s. 21(1)(a) for persons who are, or have been, suffering from mental disorder, and to prevent mental disorder (Appendix 1, para. 3(a), (b)).

In *R v Redbridge LB, Camden LB, ex p N* [2003] EWHC 3419 (Admin), Stanley Burnton J rejected an argument that the duty owed to mentally disordered persons by virtue of para. 3(a) and (b) meant that an LSSA, in effect, owed a duty to the whole world to provide those services, as long as that person was, in fact, present in its catchment area. Rather, he suggested, s. 21 and Appendix 1 must be read subject to s. 24(1), which provides that it is for the LSSA in whose area the applicant is ordinarily resident to provide any necessary residential accommodation. Any other interpretation of the scope of the duty imposed by para. 3 of Appendix 1 would render s. 24 devoid of effect (para. 39) and would 'enable an applicant in arguable need for residential accommodation...to choose which local authority he is to make liable, and possibly in whose area he will live' (para. 40). This does not mean that an LSSA will have to provide services even if an assessment of a person in respect of whom there is a power rather than a duty indicates that person to be in need, because the duty under s. 21 is only to provide care and attention 'which is not otherwise available' and if there is a duty on another LSSA to provide those services this precludes their provision by the LSSA who has carried out the assessment. The duty to assess a person's entitlement, imposed on LSSAs by s. 47 of the NHSCCA 1990, to accommodation under s. 21 of the NAA 1948, however, is not limited in this way (see 3.3.1.1).

The linkage between the provision of accommodation and the need for care and attention indicates that this provision is not concerned with the provision of accommodation per se: s. 21 provides an entitlement to care rather than to housing. A string of cases, culminating in the decision of the Court of Appeal in *R v Tower Hamlets LBC, ex p Abdul W* [2002] EWCA Civ 287, have held that, in limited circumstances, a need identified under s. 21 may properly be met through the provision of 'ordinary' housing rather than residential care home accommodation (see further 3.5.2). An LSSA may provide its own accommodation or avail itself of the provision of another LSSA, for which it must pay (s. 21(4)), although the LSSA in whose area the recipient is ordinarily resident retains the responsibility to provide the accommodation (s. 21(6)). As discussed at Chapter 2, 2.2.2, these days, the vast majority of residential accommodation is purchased by LSSAs, or private individuals, from private providers.

Means-tested charges are payable by recipients of accommodation (NAA 1948, s. 22). Charges should be levied at the standard rate payable by the LSSA for the accommodation in question and that 'shall represent the full cost to the [LSSA] of providing the accommodation' (s. 22(2)). The amount of capital that may be taken into account is regulated by the Community Care (Residential Accommodation) Act 1998 and supporting secondary legislation. A resident is required to pay in full for his or her accommodation if he or she has capital above a specified limit (set at £23,250 from 12 April 2010: see reg. 3 of *The National Assistance (Sums for Personal Requirements and Assessment of Resources) (Amendment) (England) Regulations 2010*, SI 2010/211). Capital of less than £14,000 is disregarded, and those with capital of between £14,000 and £23,250 pay a contribution to the cost of their care (reg. 3(3)).

There is no scope for an individual LSSA to modify these limits, for example by lowering the disregard level to below £14,000 (*R v Sefton Metropolitan Borough Council, ex p Help the Aged and Ors* [1997] 4 All ER 532). It is also provided, in s. 21(2A), that regulations may specify that certain resources must be ignored for the purposes of assessing whether a person is in need of care and attention not otherwise available under s. 21(1)(a), and *The National Assistance (Residential Accommodation) (Disregarding of Resources) (England) Regulations 2001*, SI 2001/3067, provide that the disregard level for the purposes of assessing need is pegged to the capital disregard level under s. 22. The Secretary of State, acting under powers given to him or her, inter alia, by s. 22(5) of the NAA 1948, has also made the *National Assistance (Residential Accommodation) (Additional Payments and Assessment of Resources) (Amendment) (England) Regulations 2001*, SI 2001/3441, which allow a person assessed as needing residential accommodation under s. 21 to pay a 'top up' in order to live in accommodation that is more expensive than the LSSA would usually pay for someone with that person's assessed needs. Policy guidance on charging was issued as part of the Fair Access to Care Services (FACS) initiative in 2002 (DH, 2002; for the most recent version of the *Charging for Residential Accommodation Guide*, known as CRAG, see DH, 2012b). Nevertheless, there remains a considerable discretion, subject to judicial review, to develop policies at local level.

There is also a considerable incentive for those likely to be in need of residential accommodation to divest themselves of their assets, in particular their home, in order to avoid having to pay charges for residential accommodation, and, accordingly, reg. 25 of the *National Assistance (Assessment of Resources) Regulations 1992*, SI 1991/2977, provides that, when capital has been transferred to avoid charges, it may be treated as part of the client's 'nominal' capital for the purposes of assessing liability to charges. In *R v Dorset County Council, ex p Beeson* [2002] EWCA Civ 1812, B had transferred his house by deed of gift to his son. The LSSA saw this as an instance for the application of reg. 25. B's son appealed against this finding and the appeal was heard by a three-person complaints panel (two county councillors and an independent chair), which rejected his complaint. B then sought judicial review. At first instance ([2001] EWHC Admin 986), the High Court held that the regulation did not apply in this case. This was because its application is limited to situations in which there had been a transfer specifically and deliberately to avoid liability, and in this case, the evidence of B and his son, that the house had been transferred to provide B's son with accommodation following the breakdown of his marriage, had not been shown to be inaccurate. The Court of Appeal upheld the High Court on this point.

In a Scottish case, *Robertson v Fife Council* [2002] SLT 951, a decision of the House of Lords, the issue was at what point a consideration of 'notional capital' became relevant. In that case, R, an elderly woman in need of residential accommodation, had transferred her property to her sons, their consideration being 'love, favour and affection', and the relevant LSSA had decided that reg. 25 applied to that transfer. It therefore determined not to provide care to R until such time as her notional capital was reduced to the statutory limit. Lord Hope of Craighead, with whom the other law lords agreed, held at para. 53 that 'Notional capital can be taken into account at the stage when charges are being made for the services. But it must be left out of account at the earlier stage when decisions are being taken to provide these services. This avoids the prospect of very real hardship which this case has demonstrated'. Thus, disagreements about the amount of notional capital available must not impact on the duty of the LSSA to provide services that, by virtue of (in the law of England and Wales) s. 21 of the NAA 1948, they must provide.

Bissett-Johnson and Main (2002) have suggested that, although the practical effect of *Robertson* is sound in policy terms from one point of view—because clients denied access to LSSA-run or commissioned accommodation will often, as in that case, be accommodated in NHS accommodation, which causes 'bed-blocking' in NHS facilities—it is not clear how an LSSA, obliged to accommodate a person that it deems to have notional capital available, will actually be able to extract that capital from third persons lawfully in possession of it, in this case, the client's children. They conclude that 'Without legislative action to afford the local authorities a remedy in this situation, the authorities face serious financial implications' (2002: 282). In *Derbyshire CC v Akril* [2005] EWCA Civ 308, another case in which property had been transferred by an elderly person, A, to his children whilst he was in hospital awaiting a nursing home place, the LSSA sought to use s. 423 of the Insolvency Act 1986 as a mechanism to address this problem. Section 423 empowers the court to order that property transferred in order to defraud creditors be restored to the original owner. The High Court made an order under s. 423 and it was upheld by the Court of Appeal; this seems to go some way to answering Bissett-Johnson and Main's point.

One final question on this issue is whether the complaints panel procedure (outlined in the discussion on *R v Dorset County Council, ex p Beeson*) is ECHR compliant. In *Beeson*, the High Court held that it is not, being in breach of Art. 6 ECHR, because it involves a determination of the applicant's civil rights by a panel that is not sufficiently independent or impartial, which deficits are not answered by the availability of judicial review. The Secretary of State for Health, as an interested party, appealed against this part of the judgment, arguing that Art. 6 is not engaged in such circumstances. The Court of Appeal held that Art. 6 was engaged, given that the panel is charged to decide a matter relevant to the complainant's civil rights, namely the question of where he should live and on what terms, and that the panel procedure per se does not satisfy the requirement of that Article for impartiality, but then, at para. 30, Laws LJ continued:

> That is of course right; but it seems to us to miss the real point in issue here, namely whether, given the quality of the first-instance process such as it is, the addition of judicial review

satisfies Art. 6. If there is no reason of substance to question the objective integrity of the first-instance process (whatever may be said about its *appearance*), it seems to us that the added safeguard of judicial review will very likely satisfy the Art. 6 standard unless there is some special feature of the case to show the contrary. Here there is not.

Although it difficult to dispute that the availability of judicial review renders the system, as a whole, compliant with Art. 6, it is perhaps unfortunate that the court did not take a more robust attitude to the constitution of the complaints panel. Any court or quasi-court that is two-thirds constituted by officers of one of the parties before it is clearly unacceptable and should be reformed. Even without reference to the ECHR, the common law has long demanded as a requirement of natural justice that justice must not only be done, but must be seen to be done, and that is not the case here.

Section 26(1) of the NAA 1948, as amended, authorises LSSAs to make arrangements pursuant to s. 21 for the provision of accommodation with voluntary organisations or 'any other person'—which means privately run care homes—in order to provide care home accommodation with personal or nursing care (s. 26(1A)), as long as those who own and provide services in, and/or manage, such homes are registered in accordance with Ch. 2, Part 1 of the Health and Social Care Act 2008. In practice, most residential accommodation is provided by the independent sector (see Chapter 2, 2.2.2). In *YL v Birmingham City Council* [2007] UKHL 27; [2008] 1 AC 95 the House of Lords held that an independent sector provider of services under contract to an LSSA did not come within the definition of a 'public authority' in s. 6(3) of the HRA 1998, and so there was no direct cause of action in human rights law by a client against the provider of his or her accommodation. This decision was however reversed by s. 145, Health and Social Care Act 2008, which does now provide that independent providers of residential accommodation under ss. 21 and 26 of the NAA 1948 are public authorities for the purposes of s. 6(3) of the HRA 1998.

The Health and Social Care Act 2008, building on provisions currently found in the Care Standards Act (CSA) 2000, and supporting secondary legislation, lays down a detailed regime of registration for care homes, which are defined negatively, as homes that are not 'hospitals' under the terms of s. 275 of the NHSA 2006, but which offer accommodation inter alia for people who are or have been mentally disordered, or who are disabled or infirm, (see CSA 2000, s. 3(2)). The line between a care home and a hospital can be hard to draw. In particular, s. 2(3)(b) of the CSA 2000 provides that an establishment that accepts patients detained under the MHA 1983 is to be deemed an 'independent hospital' rather than a care home. Thus, the definition turns on the type of resident, rather than the type of establishment.

The number of detained patients held in private mental nursing homes has risen considerably since the mid-1980s, from 269 admissions in 1986 to 1,005 in 1996–97 (DH, 2003: Tables 10, 11), 1,629 by 2004–05 (Government Statistical Service, 2006: Table 9), and 2,621 in 2010–11 (NHS Information Centre, 2012: table 2b). In addition, of course, most hospital inpatients are not detained, and in this much larger group, the crossover between 'hospitals' and 'homes' is significantly more substantial. In short, although the MHA 1983 draws a rigid distinction between patients who are in hospital and those who are not (although subject to its provisions on leave of absence—see Chapter 11, 11.2—and s. 2(6) of the CSA 2000 specifically provides that a patient in a care home on leave of absence from a hospital does not convert that care home into a hospital), in practice, the line between inpatient services and community care can be difficult to draw. This has major implications for the way in which the 'shift' to community care should be understood, as does the fact that the DOLS apply equally to persons in care homes as they do to persons deprived of their liberty in a hospital or elsewhere (Department of Health and Office of the Public Guardian, 2009; and see, for example, *A PCT v LDV and B Healthcare group* [2013] EWHC 272 (Fam)).

At the other end of the spectrum, a care home is distinguished from 'ordinary' housing: the former being a place in which accommodation is coupled with personal or nursing care. In *SA v Secretary of State for Work and Pensions* [2010] UKUT 345 (AAC) it was held that a residential college which provided personal care alongside education did constitute a care home, and the fact that the accommodation also fulfilled some other aim besides the provision of care did not preclude that conclusion (with the happy consequence for SA that the costs to the LSSA of providing him with meals as part of his package of care were not to be factored into his claim for income support: see reg. 42(4)(a)(ii) and Sch. 9, para. 66 of the *Income Support (General) Regulations 1987*, SI 1987/1967).

Various bodies have been created and re-created over the years to regulate and monitor the provision of care home accommodation. The latest such body is the Care Quality Commission (CQC), brought into being by s. 1 of the Health and Social Care Act (HSCA) 2008, charged to operate the system for the registration of care homes, and given powers to review and investigate the operation of care homes (HSCA 2008, s. 2(2) (a), (b)) and to monitor the operation of the MHA 1983 (HSCA 2008, s. 2(2)(c)).

It is an offence to provide services in or manage a care home otherwise than in accordance with any conditions that may be attached to a licence to operate (HSCA 2008, s. 33), or to operate following the cancellation or suspension of a licence (s. 34), or to make any false statement when applying for registration or describing the premises to be registered (s. 37). Section 35 of the HSCA 2008 and reg. 27 of the *Health and Social Care Act 2008 (Regulated Activities) Regulations 2010*, SI 2010/781, create a further offence of failure to comply with the terms of regs. 9–24 (which lay down a long list of requirements, to provide for the welfare of care home residents, including protection from abuse, safety, cleanliness, consent to medical treatment and so on). The CQC may refuse to register a care home or may cancel a registration, and the burden of proof is on those alleging that the home and its staff are suitable (*Jones v Commission for Social Care Inspection* [2004] EWCA Civ 1713; *Marshall v Commission for Social Care Inspection* [2009] EWHC 1286 (Admin)).

The CQC has an obligation to cancel a person's registration as a care home manager if there is no person registered as service provider in respect of it or if the registration of a person as service provider, conditional on a manager also being registered, is amended so that the condition is removed (HSCA 2008, s. 17(2)). Beyond that, the CQC has a discretion to cancel the registration of a service provider or manager 'at any time' if that person has been convicted of, or has admitted a 'relevant offence', defined by s. 17(3) to include the offences found in: ss. 33–37 of the HSCA 2008, or the Registered Homes Act 1984 or regulations made under it (although the Registered Homes Act 1984 has been repealed, offences committed under that Act are still relevant); Part 2 of the Care Standards Act 2000 or regulations made under it; and 'any other offence which appears to the Commission to be relevant' (s. 17(3)(d)): s 17(1)(a). It may also cancel registration if some other person has been convicted of any relevant offence in relation to the care provided in the home (s. 17(1)(b)); or that the care home is being, or has at any time been, operated otherwise than in accordance with the relevant requirements (s. 17(1)(c)); or that the registered person has failed to comply with a requirement imposed under Chapter 6 of the HSCA 2008 (which is concerned inter alia with the inspection of premises) (s. 17(1)(d)); or on any other ground specified by regulations (s. 17(1)(e), and *Care Quality Commission (Registration) Regulations 2009*, SI 2009/3112, reg. 25).

Cancellation may be done summarily on the order of a single magistrate, on the application of the CQC, to prevent serious risk to a person's life, health or well-being (s. 30(1), HSCA 2008), and may be done *ex parte* (s. 30(2)). The CQC itself may take an urgent decision to suspend a person's registration if it has 'has reasonable cause to believe that … any person will or may be exposed to the risk of harm' (s. 31(1)). The person affected must be given notice of cancellation or suspension (HSCA 2008, ss.30(5), 31(3)) and must also be informed of their right to appeal to the first tier tribunal (see Chapter 11, 11.4.1), with broad powers to uphold, overturn or vary the decision taken by the CQC or the magistrate (HSCA 2008, s. 32).

The courts have decided that there is nothing wrong, in principle, with LSSAs using the mechanism of contracts with independent providers to impose requirements over and above those specified in the statute, provided that such requirements are reasonable (*R v Newcastle-upon-Tyne City Council, ex p Dixon* (1993) 158 Local Government Reports 441 (HC)). A contractual term will be found to be unreasonable if compliance with it would threaten the continuing viability of the private homes in question, because that constrains the choice of service users and so frustrates the purpose of the policy behind the NHSCCA 1990 (*R v Cleveland County Council, ex p Cleveland Care Homes Association and Ors* (1993) 158 Local Government Reports 641 (HC)).

In recent years, one way in which the question of whether the policy of an LSSA frustrates the purpose of the legislative scheme has shown up is in the form of disputes between LSSAs and providers concerning the fees payable to independent care homes by LSSAs. In *The Sefton Care Association v Sefton Council* [2011] EWHC 2676 (Admin) Sefton Care Association (SCA), an organisation representing the interests of independent care home proprietors in Sefton, sought judicial review of the LSSA's decision, that in 2011–12, for the second year running, it would not increase the fees payable to care homes for residential accommodation provided under ss. 21 and 26 of the NAA 1948. Several arguments were advanced by SCA, but the main argument was that the LSSA's decision was unlawful because it had not calculated its fees accurately.

LSSAs should work out a 'usual cost' for the services it funds at the start of each financial year, and ascertain if there is a 'significant change in the cost of providing care' (DH

2004: para. 2.5.4). This needs to be done for various reasons. One is to be able to assess the amount of money to be paid to a client receiving direct payments to allow him or her to purchase their own care (see 3.6) or to a client who wishes to be accommodated in more expensive accommodation than the LSSA is prepared to fund, but who is able to pay the additional amount themselves. Another is to ensure that the LSSA is able 'to meet the assessed care needs of supported residents in residential accommodation' (also see 3.6) through the payment of fees to care providers. In setting its usual cost, an LSSA 'should have due regard to the actual costs of providing care and other local factors' (DH, 2004: para. 2.5.4). For the purposes of paying providers for contracted care, LSSAs should engage in 'fee negotiation arrangements that recognise providers' costs and what factors affect them (as well as any scope for improved performance) and ensure that appropriate fees are paid (DH, 2001a: para. 6.7). Fees should also be decided upon after consultation with stake-holders, including care providers (DH, 2001a: para. 5.9). SCA argued that the LSSA had not complied with either requirement, and its assessment of costs was unrealistically low, which, it claimed, posed a significant risk of leading to a contraction of service locally, with some care homes being forced to close on financial grounds.

Raynor J accepted that the obligation of an LSSA is not to calculate actual costs, as that would be too time-consuming, but held that nonetheless there should not be 'any significant imbalance between the usual cost of care and the actual cost. If a local authority consciously fixes the usual cost in a sum significantly less than actual costs, then I do not see how it could be said to be having "due regard to the actual costs of providing care" as required by paragraph 2.5.4 of the Guidance' (para. 70). An LSSA may assume that its costings are reasonably accurate. However, once Sefton LSSA was notified by local providers in 2010 that the proposed fees to be paid in 2011–12 were less than actual costs and risked the continued viability of providers (para. 72):

> then at the very least, the [LSSA], pursuant to its obligation to have due regard to the actual costs of care and the provisions of the Agreement referred to above, should, before re-fixing the fees at the 2009 levels, have asked [SCA] to submit a detailed assessment of what they contended were the actual costs of care so as to substantiate (insofar as they were able) their contention that placements were substantially under-funded in relation to the actual cost of care.

As the LSSA did not do this (despite having information itself that standards were likely to fall below statutory minimum quality levels without an increase in the fees paid: para. 75), it was found to have inadequately investigated the actual costs of care, thus rendering its decision as to fee levels unreasonable.

As the LSSA had made the decision to freeze fees before it discussed the matter with SCA, the court also found a failure to consult (paras. 76, 89) and it quashed the LSSA's decision. This decision was followed, on both points, in a very similar situation with, again, a freeze in fees paid to providers for two successive years being questioned by providers on the basis that assessed usual costs did not accurately reflect actual costs, in *East Midlands Care Ltd* v *Leicester County Council* [2011] EWHC 3096 (Admin), with Judge Langham QC holding (para. 55) that, once the issue has been raised with the LSSA by the providers, then the LSSA cannot content itself with a 'general' figure for actual costs: 'A much more analytical, indeed arithmetical, approach was called for'.

The LSSA in *Sefton* denied that it was motivated by financial considerations and the court accepted this, in the sense that it did not seek to justify its decision to freeze fees by reference to its broader budgetary constraints, and was itself satisfied in good faith that the fees it intended to pay were reasonable (para. 92). But there is little doubt that the £25 million shortfall in its overall budgetary scheme, and the fact that £1.4 million could be saved by freezing fees (para. 38) was a very significant factor explaining its decision. This was also the case in *East Midlands* (see para. 38), in which the LSSA needed to make budget cuts of £80 million to keep its spending within centrally prescribed limits. In this financial climate, it seems inevitable that there will be further litigation on this question but, provided that LSSAs heed the advice in these cases and act in accordance with due process, it is likely that in future care providers will be unable to prevent the imposition of real-term financial cuts; at least until such point as the resulting care falls below minimum acceptable standards.

In *South West Care Homes Ltd* v *Devon County Council* [2012] EWHC 2967 (Admin) in which, again, a LSSA decision to freeze fees for successive years was challenged by care providers on the grounds of failure to consult or accurately to calculate costs, the LSSA was able successfully to defend a consultation process involving several meetings with and presentations to providers, even though providers were concerned about the accuracy of some of the supporting data presented to explain the LSSA's decision, and albeit that the information presented was 'complex, sophisticated and technical' (para. 57) and that requests for further explanation made by providers to the LSSA were not responded to. The court found as fact that the consultation had been fair and that there was an opportunity for providers to give a 'meaningful response' (para. 72), and, further, that its methodology for assessing usual costs was not irrational (para. 85–86). The court would not get into the technical detail about the economic models and assumptions used by the LSSA to determine this sum. This seems to suggest that, provided the LSSA has formulated its assessment of usual costs in an analytical, arithmetic way, then its decision will be insulated from challenge by way of judicial review.

3.2.2.1.2 *Welfare services under s. 29*

As far as welfare services are concerned, s. 29(1) of the NAA 1948 provides a wide discretion for LSSAs, subject to approvals and directions made by the Secretary of State, to make arrangements for promoting the welfare of a wide constituency of 'disabled' clients, which includes, inter alia, those 'who suffer from mental disorder of any description'. Section 29 is used for a wide variety of purposes, some of which are listed in s. 29(4), including the provision of home help and meals, recreational facilities such as televisions, organised outings and holidays, and services ancillary to these, such as the provision of transport to and from recreational facilities, holidays, and so on. Such services may also be charged for, to the extent that it is reasonable to do so, under s. 17 of the Health and Social Services and Social Security Adjudications Act 1983.

Charging policy was, until 2000, left to the discretion of individuals LSSAs. The CSA 2000 amended s. 7 of the Local Authority Social Services Act 1970, which gave the Secretary of State powers to issue guidance on the exercise of statutory powers by LSSAs, so that the Secretary of State now has power to issue guidance on charging policy, which was first done in 2001 (DH, 2001), followed by practice guidance in 2002 (Department of Health and Department for Work and Pensions, 2002). The most recently published version of the guidance (DH, 2012c) makes clear that there is no obligation for an LSSA to charge for services provided under s. 29, but that if charges are levied, the net income of the service user 'should not be reduced below defined basic levels of Income Support (now Universal Credit: see s. 1, Welfare Reform Act 2012) or the Guarantee Credit of Pension Credit, plus 25 per cent. Charging policies which reduce users' net incomes below these defined basic levels are not acceptable and undermine policies for social inclusion and the promotion of independence' (DH, 2012c: para. 2). Nevertheless, the statutory requirement is to impose, if charging is imposed, reasonable charges, and this means that LSSAs retain a degree of discretion over their policies at local level.

In *R v Powys County Council, ex p Hambridge (No. 2)* (2000) BMLR 133 (CA), the LSSA had divided service users into three groups: Group A comprised clients whose only income was in the form of Income Support; Group B, which included H, comprised clients in receipt of Income Support and some form of additional disability benefit; Group C comprised clients not in receipt of any state benefit. The LSSA's policy was to charge those in Groups B and C at a higher rate than those in Group A. H challenged this policy on the basis that it was in breach of the Disability Discrimination Act 1995 (see now Equality Act (EA) 2010, ss. 13–15 and 19), in that it discriminated against disabled persons by reason of requiring them to pay higher charges than clients in Group A. The Court of Appeal rejected this argument, on the basis that, although there was 'discrimination', it was based not on disability but simply on ability to pay, as evidenced by the higher charges also imposed on clients in Group C.

3.2.2.2 Section 45 of the Health Services and Public Health Act 1968

Section 45 of the Health Services and Public Health Act (HSPHA) 1968 empowers LSSAs to make arrangements, subject to approvals and directions of the Secretary of State, for promoting the welfare of 'old people', with the limitation, imposed by s. 45(4)(b), that this provision may not be used as a mechanism 'for making available any accommodation or services required to be provided under the National Health Service Act 2006'. Of course, as has been discussed at various points in this text, there are a considerable number of elderly people with mental health problems and so services for the elderly and services for the mentally disordered will inevitably overlap. Department of Health and Social Security Circular 19/71 (Department of Health and Social Security, 1971b) makes it clear, however, that s. 45 of the HSPHA 1968 is designed to catch those elderly people who, because not 'disabled' as defined by s. 29 of the NAA 1948, do not qualify for the provision of services under the Chronically Sick and Disabled Persons Act 1970 (see 3.2.2.5); this means that this is the least relevant provision for present purposes, because the definition of 'disabled' in s. 29 of the NAA 1948 Act will catch most, if not all, of those who are mentally disordered within the meaning of the MHA 1983. The range of services available under s. 45 of the HSPHA 1968 is very similar to that available under s. 29 of the NAA 1948. Again, such services may be charged for under s. 17 of the Health and Social Services and Social Security Adjudications Act 1983.

3.2.2.3 Section 254 and Sch. 20 of the National Health Service Act 2006

Section 254 and Sch. 20 of the National Health Service Act (NHSA) 2006 are the main sources of non-residential community care services for adults suffering from mental disorder provided by LSSAs. Section 254(1)(b) and para. 2(21) of Sch. 20 require LSSAs to provide care and after-care for ill persons, and preventative care. Appendix 3 of LAC(93)10 provides that the Secretary of State has approved the making of arrangements under in connection with all three of these purposes (DH, 1993: Appendix 3, para. 3(1), (3)), with the exception of such services for the purpose of prevention of mental disorder, which are the subject of a direction, in para. 3(2). These services should be provided collaboratively with the local CCG, which is fixed by s. 3(1)(e) of the NHSA 2006 with a duty to arrange care and after-care to 'such extent as it considers necessary to meet the reasonable requirements of the persons for whom it has responsibility'.

LSSAs are specifically precluded from providing residential accommodation to 'any person' using these powers (NHSA 2006, Sch. 20, para. 2(11)) but should provide premises at which facilities are available for people who are or have been suffering from mental disorder as defined by s. 1 of the MHA 1983 or for the purposes of preventing service users from becoming mentally disordered (NHSA 2006, Sch. 20, paras. 2(8), (9)). LAC(93)10 requires LSSAs to make arrangements for the provision of day centres offering facilities for training or occupation, for the provision of an adequate number of approved social workers, and for providing social work support for persons living in their own homes, including the identification, diagnosis, assessment, treatment, and after-care of mental disorder, and for ensuring that guardianship orders (see Chapter 10, 10.3) can be made.

Schedule 20, para. 3 also permits the provision of ancillary services, such as domiciliary assistance, to persons living in their own homes. Individual applicants have no enforceable right to access the services in question, which—the provision of training and day centres, a sufficient number of social workers and social work services—are, by their nature, 'general' provisions; the reference to 'persons' rather than 'any person' supports the view that this is a 'general duty' not enforceable by individuals. This view is further supported by the observation of Lord Clyde in *R v Gloucestershire County Council and Anor, ex p Barry* [1997] 2 All ER 1 (at 16) that, apart from s. 2(1) of the Chronically Sick and Disabled Persons Act 1970 (see further at 3.2.2.5), there was only one other directly enforceable duty to be found in the statutory regime, and that is contained in s. 117, MHA 1983.

3.2.2.4 Section 117 of the Mental Health Act 1983

Section 117 of the MHA 1983 imposes a free-standing, individually enforceable, obligation on CCGs or Health Boards, and LSSAs, to provide (or, as far as CCGs are concerned, arrange for the provision of: s. 117(2D)) after-care to persons leaving hospital after a period of compulsory detention. After many years of uncertainty about whether s. 117 services may be charged for, with around two thirds of areas charging for at least some services provided under s. 117 and the other third providing them free (*R v Manchester City Council, ex p Stennett* [2002] UKHL 34 per Lord Steyn at para. 4), it was established by the House of Lords in *Stennett*, a test case that conjoined several appeals, that s. 117 imposes a freestanding duty, and is not a gateway into other services, and that, because there is no charging provision in the section, it is not permissible to charge for s. 117 services.

This decision, welcome because it ensures free access to these necessary services for those leaving compulsory detention in a hospital, nonetheless produced anomalies in the broader community care framework (Jones, 2012: 478–79). Jones gave the example of a patient leaving hospital who will require long-term residential accommodation to be provided after discharge. If that patient was initially sectioned because he or she would not agree to be hospitalised, then, on discharge, the provision of that accommodation, under s. 117, will be free of charge. But if, at the point of initial admission to hospital, that patient was compliant and so the use of a 'section' was not necessary, he or she will have to pay towards the cost of the provision of residential accommodation, because in that case the accommodation will be provided under s. 21 of the NAA 1948. Lord Steyn in *Stennett* held (at para. 13) that 'this view is too simplistic'; that the legislation has to deal with the 'generality of cases'; and that the distinction between the two cases may reflect the policy view that patients who have been sectioned 'pose greater risks upon discharge to themselves and others than compliant patients'. He also approved the view of Buxton LJ in the Court of Appeal ([2001] QB 370 at 386), that s. 117 applies to an 'exceptionally vulnerable class' of patient.

Our response is: (i) simplistic or not, the anomaly identified by Jones exists; (ii) the distinction between informal and sectioned patients is arbitrary to a large degree—the same patient may be 'compliant' one day but not the next, and the significant use of s. 5 of the MHA 1983 demonstrates this (see Chapter 6, 6.4.1); (iii) as *Bournewood* (see Chapter 5, 5.1.1.2) and its aftermath made clear, exceptionally vulnerable people are often held 'informally' in hospital. The decision in *Stennett* is welcome, however, and Jones' point is not really directed at s. 117, but rather at the regime under ss. 21 and 22 of the NAA 1948, and raises the question of whether continued charging under that regime is a defensible policy, at least when services are provided in the form of after-care, given that the duty under the NAA 1948 is only triggered in cases of 'need', defined restrictively. On the other hand, this would be to set up an equally anomalous and problematic distinction between 'after-care' and 'care', and would impose unmanageable budgetary pressures on LSSAs.

Section 117 has an independent existence outside of the context of community care services as defined by s. 46(3) of the NHSCCA 1990. It functions as part of the raft of provisions which provide for a degree of compulsion in the community, because patients on leave of absence from detention in hospital (see Chapter 10, 10.2) or subject to a Community Treatment Order (see Chapter 10, 10.4) are provided with services under s. 117, and so s. 117 is further discussed in that context in Chapter 10, 10.5.

3.2.2.5 **Other sources of care and assistance in the community**

These then, are 'community care services' as defined by s. 46(3) of the NHSCCA 1990. There is clearly a considerable degree of overlap between the various provisions. Yet these services by no means fill the field, and there are a number of other statutory provisions that, in practice, are as central to the delivery of community care as those singled out by s. 46(3). These various statutory provisions are linked together and weave in and out of the definition of community care services in s. 46(3). A key example is the provision of welfare services under the Chronically Sick and Disabled Persons Act (CSDPA) 1970, access to which is limited to 'disabled' persons.

Section 2(1) of CSDPA 1970 places a duty on LSSAs to identify local needs for services, which is broadly similar to the duty in s. 46(1) of the NHSCCA 1990 Act, and lists a range of welfare services that must be supplied to those in need of them. From one point of view, the role of the CSDPA 1970 after the enactment of the NHSCCA 1990 is to function as a parallel regime, providing services for 'disabled persons', whilst that set up by the NHSCCA 1990 is concerned with providing services to others in need of community care services. Yet things are not that simple, for two reasons.

First, s. 2(1) of the CSDPA 1970, although listing the welfare services in question, refers to s. 29 of the NAA 1948, which gives LSSAs a *power* to supply welfare services. The effect of the CSDPA 1970 Act was to augment that power with a *duty*. Those to whom the duty under s. 2(1) of the CSPDA 1970 is owed are persons defined as 'disabled' in s. 29 of the NAA 1948, and s. 2(1) of the CSDPA 1970 provides that, if it has been assessed as necessary that the LSSA make arrangements in order to meet the needs of the person in question, 'it shall be the duty of [the LSSA] to make those arrangements in exercise of their functions under . . . s. 29 [of the NAA 1948]'.

The point is that s. 29 is to be found in Part III of the NAA 1948, which *is* on the list of community care services in s. 46(3) of the NHSCCA 1990. Therefore, it is arguable that services under the CSDPA 1970 are within the s. 46(3), NHSCCA 1990 definition, through being linked to Part III of the NAA 1948 in this way. This view was rejected by the High Court on a number of occasions (*R v Gloucestershire County Council, ex p Mahfood and Ors* (1996) 8 Admin LR 180, at 193; *R v Gloucestershire County Council and Anor, ex p Barry* (1995) 30 BMLR 20), but the opposite view was taken in *R v North Yorkshire County Council, ex p Hargreaves (No. 2)* (1997) *The Times*, 12 June (HC), and in *R v Powys County Council, ex p Hambridge* [1998] 1 FLR 643 (HC). In the latter case, Popplewell J held bluntly (at 650) that '[w]hen providing welfare services under s. 2 [of the CSDPA 1970] the local authority are exercising their functions under s. 29 [of the NAA 1948]. They are not providing services under s. 2; they are making arrangements under the 1948 Act for the provision of their services'. On appeal ([1998] 3 FCR 190), the Court of Appeal upheld Popplewell J's decision. The practical importance of this question is that, as mentioned at 3.2.2.1.2, services under the NAA 1948 can be charged for under s. 17, Health and Social Services and Social Security Adjudications Act 1983, whereas there are no provisions to permit charges to be levied under the CSDPA 1970.

Second, to confuse matters further still, 'disabled' is defined by s. 29(1) of the NAA 1948 to include, inter alia, people aged 18 or over 'who suffer from mental disorder of any description'. Hence, even if welfare services provided under the CSDPA 1970 are not 'community care services', they may be accessed by persons with mental disorder who would also be *prima facie* entitled to access the same services under the NHSCCA 1990. As might be expected, the complexity of the relationship between the various statutes in this area tends to store up a further set of problems regarding access and entitlement. One significant advantage of the statutory scheme proposed by the draft Social Care Bill is that these legal complexities will be swept away. The Bill proposes a unified system which applies to all service users or potential users in the same way.

3.3 Assessing entitlement, and the nature and scope of the duties owed under the NHSCCA 1990

3.3.1 Entitlement under the NHSCCA 1990

3.3.1.1 Assessing need

In the scheme of the NHSCCA 1990, access to the services listed in s. 46(3) is dealt with in s. 47. This prescribes a two-stage procedure to be used in the assessment of the needs of individuals. Essentially the same procedure also appears as cl. 9 of the draft Care and Support Bill. When it appears to an LSSA that a person may be in need of community care services, the LSSA *must*, first, carry out an assessment of the person's needs (s. 47(1)(a)). It is not open to an LSSA to decline to carry out an assessment, or to hold that a potential service user does not 'appear to be' a person in need, on the grounds that it does not offer the services required to meet any needs that may be identified (*R v Berkshire CC, ex p P* [1997] 95 LGR 449 (HC)), or that it does not have the resources to meet any need that might thereby be identified (*R v Bristol City Council, ex p Penfold* [1998] COD 210 (QB)). But it has been said that an LSSA may refuse to provide a service if it is impossible, for legal reasons, for the LSSA to supply it (*R v Swindon BC, ex p Stoddard* (1998) 2 July, unreported (DC)), in which an LSSA was unable to provide 'community care' accommodation in a regional secure unit, because such facilities only accept 'sectioned' patients.

An assessment of needs will normally require the appropriate forms to be completed by the social worker performing the assessment, but in *R v Kensington and Chelsea Royal London Borough Council, ex parte McDonald* [2011] UKSC 33 it was held that an assessment (or, as in that case, a subsequent review) can be said to have taken place if it has done so in substance albeit that no needs assessment document was completed.

Stanley Burnton J in *R v Camden LBC, ex p B* [2005] EWHC 1366 held that s. 47(1) refers to 'a person who may be in need at the time, or who may be about to be in need', and there is no duty to consider future needs. This was said in the context of patients detained in hospital with little prospect of release in the near future, and should not, in our view, be taken to mean that future needs are not, in general terms, to be considered by a s. 47 assessment. In *R v Islington LBC and Northamptonshire CC, ex parte NM* [2012] EWHC 414 (Admin), a case involving a person in prison but who would need community care services on release, Sales J held (para. 77) that 'it is necessary for a claimant to show that there is a sufficiently concrete and likely prospect of him being in a position where community care services may need to be provided to him if he has relevant needs', such as to convince the relevant LSSA that there is a 'significant possibility' that this is so. In *R v St Helens BC, ex parte Manchester CC* [2009] EWCA Civ 1348 it was said (at para. 31) that 'the threshold for the operation of Section 47(1) is quite low so that local authorities may be under a statutory obligation [to carry out an assessment of need] even if they may not in the end be under an obligation to provide care services'.

The obligation imposed by s. 47 is to carry out a full community care assessment of the applicant's various needs (*R v Islington LBC, ex p HP* [2004] EWHC 7). Guidance on the application of s. 47 was issued most recently in 2010 (DH, 2010a). This advises that 'the depth and breadth of the assessment should be proportionate to individual's presenting needs and circumstances' (para. 69) and should seek to determine 'how these needs impose barriers to that person's independence or well-being' (para. 78).

It has been said that there is no obligation for an LSSA to carry out an assessment of the needs of persons for whom another LSSA has responsibility (*R v Southend BC, ex p J* [2005] EWHC 3457; *R v St Helens BC, ex parte Manchester CC* [2009] EWCA Civ 1348, para. 3), even when, as in *Southend*, those persons have been clients of a service (a day centre) that the LSSA proposes to close. The guidance (DH, 2010, para. 48) advises, however, that although an LSSA owes a duty to provide or commission services only to local residents 'Because local authorities have a power to provide services to people who live outside of their area, the duty to assess is not limited to people who are ordinarily resident in the authority's area'. This, however, is subject to the requirement of s. 47(1)(a), that it 'appears' to the LSSA that the person in question 'may be in need of any such services' as the LSSA provides. The guidance (DH, 2010: para. 50) suggests that this might cover, for example, a person who intends to move into the area of an LSSA to take up a job, but only if his or her needs for care can be met in that area, as well as people leaving hospital and moving from one LSSA area to another in the process.

Section 47(3) provides that if, when carrying out the s. 47(1)(a) assessment, it appears to the LSSA that 'there may be a need for the provision to that person' of health care services or housing, it must then notify the relevant CCG (s.47(3)(za)) or LHA (s.47(3)(b)), 'and invite them to assist, to such extent as is reasonable in the circumstances, in the making of the assessment'; and, in making its decision as to the provision of the services needed for the person in question, the LSSA shall take into account any services which are 'likely to be made available for him by' health or housing services. In *Buckinghamshire County Council v Royal Borough of Kingston upon Thames* [2011] EWCA Civ 457 Patten LJ held, although *obiter*, (para. 48) that this does not amount to a duty for the LSSA to consult those mentioned in s. 47(3) and 'a defect therefore in the s. 47(3) process including a failure to notify is not, in my view, open to challenge by the [CCG] or an LHA. It is at most a ground upon which the service user might be able to impugn the legality of the assessment'.

This view is perhaps debatable. The obligation to notify those bodies mentioned in s. 47(3) once the LSSA decides there may be a need for them to provide services is mandatory—the wording at this point is 'shall'—so there does seem to be a duty to notify and hence there should be an action for breach of that duty. It is true that the second element of s. 47(3) is more permissive in tone, requiring the LSSA to 'invite' those bodies to participate in the s. 47(1)(a) process. The decision in *Buckinghamshire* is compatible with the earlier decision of the Court of Appeal, in *Islington LBC v University College London Hospital NHS Trust* [2005] EWCA Civ 596, in which it was held, for policy reasons (the court not being able to predict the implications had it found the existence of duties), that neither body owes a duty of care to the other. But it seems *prima facie* irrational for the LSSA to have to notify of a suspected need but then not to involve those capable of more precisely identifying, and then of meeting, at least some of the client's needs in the assessment process. Arguably, the better reading is that s. 47(3) places one mandatory obligation—to notify and then work in co-operation with the relevant health or housing provider.

This is the approach taken in the guidance published by the DH (2010a: para. 86), itself based on a commitment to joint assessment made in 2007 (HM Government, 2007: para. 3.3), and developed subsequently, with the use of a common assessment framework by LSSAs and NHS bodies now increasingly common. On the other hand, it is fairly clear that the wording of s. 47(3) does not impose any obligation on the invitee actually to participate in the s. 47(1)(a) assessment. As we shall discuss further at 3.5, these are not simply technical legal questions. Rather, in a time of austerity and shrinking budgets, with incentives for service providers to offload responsibilities onto other provider bodies in its area, or onto those of neighbouring areas, lack of certainty about the precise meaning of the law is likely to be litigated by providers in conflict with each other sooner or later. The draft CSB, following the recommendation of the Law Commission (2011: 183, recommendation 70) is clear that the duty to co-operate is bilateral (see cl. 4(1), CSB), although a 'relevant partner' need not co-operate with a request from the LSSA if to do so would be 'incompatible with its own duties, or otherwise have an adverse effect on the exercise of its functions' (cl. 5(1)). No doubt, the precise meaning and scope of those words will require judicial intervention.

Patten LJ's broader point in *Buckinghamshire* was that the purpose of s. 47(3) is to allow the LSSA carrying out the assessment to do so with as much knowledge as possible of the needs of the client, including those needs which will be met other than through the provision of community care services as defined in s. 46(2). Such an approach is mandated and required by the Care Plan Approach (CPA) (see Ch. 3.5.1) and various general and particular obligations for public service providers to work effectively together and to use resources efficiently. In the *Buckinghamshire* case LSSA1 had placed a client, S, in residential accommodation in the area of LSSA2. Following an assessment under s. 47(1)(a), LSSA1 agreed with S, that she should move out of the residential accommodation and into a flat in the area of LSSA2, as she wished to do. This had the effect of fixing LSSA2 with the duty to provide for S's community care needs from that point, as the law provides (in NAA 1948, s. 24(1), to be re-enacted as cl. 32 of the draft CSB) that it is the LSSA in which the client is ordinarily resident that has the responsibility for meeting that person's needs, on which basis LSSA2 argued that they should have been consulted about LSSA1's plans for S. This argument was rejected by the Court of Appeal. As a matter of statutory construction, the prescription of specific consultees by s. 47(3) indicates that Parliament intended only those listed should be consulted (para. 24), and as a matter of policy, as it was the court's view that the need to consult another LSSA, in situation in which the interests of LSSA1 and LSSA2 are or might be in conflict 'would inevitably complicate the decision making process...The obtaining of information from [LSSA2] is one thing but, if the [LSSA2] were to have a status in the procedure, there would be a large potential for differences of view and for delay' (para. 35 per Pill LJ). In this case, LSSA1 was clearly acting in good faith: 'If, in another case, it were to be established that the motivation for decisions under section 47 as to where to place service users was financial, different considerations would apply' (para. 37).

Oddly, or perhaps tellingly, in that it reflects the mid-twentieth century attitude to welfare provision, s. 47(3) does not require that the potential service user and/or any carer be consulted as part of the assessment process, although in *R v Wandsworth LBC, ex p G* [2004] EWCA Civ 1170 it was held that an assessment must comply with the requirements of natural justice, which included a requirement that the applicant and her representatives should have been allowed to attend meetings relevant to the performance of the assessment. The statutory procedure was amended soon after, and the situation now is that not only must the applicant and any carers be consulted (*Community Care Assessment Directions 2004*, para. 2(2)), but the LSSA must also 'take all reasonable steps to reach agreement with the person and...any carers' (para. 3(3)) as to the services which should be provided. The Guidance (DH, 2010a: para. 79) emphasises that assessment 'should be carried out as a collaborative process', which should also be transparent and comprehensible to the person being assessed. Prior self-assessment may be encouraged to this end (para. 84), as is indeed frequently the case. Some LSSAs have a single point of contact for all applicants for care and support, at which an initial assessment is made, in order to screen out unlikely candidates for service provision at an early stage.

The guidance states that this is acceptable in principle, but LSSAs 'should, however, be aware of risks of screening people out of the assessment process before sufficient information is known about them' (DH, 2010a: para. 76), as this might lead to those inappropriately rejected before a full assessment has taken place re-presenting at a later date with a heightened (and more expensive) set of needs. It should also be pointed out that any 'pre-assessment assessment' is not mandated by the statute and if a person who presents with needs is turned away at an early stage, that pre-assessment or initial screening, as the only assessment undertaken, must be sufficiently rigorous to comply with the requirements of the legislation, case law, and the guidance.

3.3.1.2 Meeting assessed needs

In the second stage of the assessment process the LSSA, 'having regard to the results of that assessment, shall then decide whether his needs call for the provision by them of any such services' (s. 47(1)(b)). The legal obligation to meet needs does not amount to a duty to promote the best interests of the client (Owen J in *Crookdale* v *Drury* [2003] EWHC 1938 at para. 52), and although the duty to provide services is ongoing from the point at which it has been concluded that the applicant does have needs which the LSSA should take steps to meet, it may cease to bind the LSSA if the intended recipient of the services in question refuses to accept them (*R* v *Kensington and Chelsea London Borough Council, ex p Kujtim* [1999] 4 ALL ER 161), but only if that refusal is unreasonable (*R* v *Islington LBC, ex p Batantu* (2001) 33 HLR 76 (QB)). In *R* v *Newham LBC, ex p P* 2000 WL 1741487, Henriques J held that a refusal of accommodation is less likely to be categorised as unreasonable if it were made in the absence of legal advice as to the potential implications of refusal, and that the LSSA should explain the offer to the client and make sure that its terms are properly understood. The court further held that, if the refusal is reasonable, an LSSA that treats that refusal as discharging its duty to assess the client's needs is in breach of s. 47. If the service user lacks capacity, decisions can be taken by any donee of a power of attorney, court-appointed deputy, or by the Court of Protection, or by the LSSA itself (as long as the patient does not object) as provided for by the Mental Capacity Act 2005 (see Chapter 4, 4.2–4.3).

It is likely that a refusal to accept a reasonable offer of accommodation or other services based on a properly carried-out assessment under s. 47 will be unreasonable (*R* v *Southwark LB, ex p K* [2001] EWCA Civ 999, [2001] HLR 31 (CA) per Mance LJ at para. 57). But a refusal to accept offered accommodation has been held reasonable when based on the unsuitability of the location of the accommodation (*ex p K*), or because the property was only available on a short-term basis and was expensive for the applicant (*ex p Batantu*). In the first instance decision in *ex p K* (2000 WL 1791525), Hallett J held that the question of whether a refusal to accept an offer of services was reasonable, in that case, by an elderly Kurdish woman with little ability to speak English who suffered from paranoid schizophrenia and whose capacity was in doubt, 'must involve an objective assessment of the whole of the circumstances, whatever the mental capacity of the claimant or the support they derive from others'. This point was not taken on appeal. It would be unfortunate if Hallett J is understood to have prescribed an 'objective' test of reasonableness, to be applied, by definition, to vulnerable people whose lack of 'objectivity' may well be a symptom of the problem that the community care legislation attempts to address. The better view is that an objective assessment of a refusal must take account of the particular, subjective, circumstances of the client refusing the services offered.

3.3.1.2.1 *'Presenting' and 'eligible' needs*

Although s. 47(4), NHSCCA 1990 provides that a s. 47 assessment 'shall be carried out in such manner and take such form as the local authority consider appropriate', the subsection also provides that this is subject to any directions issued by the Secretary of State. The guidance (DH, 2010a: para. 47) makes a distinction between 'presenting needs' and 'eligible needs', the former being those recognised by a s. 47(1)(a) assessment, and the latter being those presenting needs in respect of which the LSSA will provide services, the implication of which is that 'presenting needs' should be understood broadly: not all such needs will necessarily be met, but full information about the potential client will be needed to make an accurate assessment of eligible needs.

The 2010 guidance acknowledges that LSSAs should develop their own eligibility criteria, but is also fairly prescriptive as to what those criteria should be. It divides the eligibility criteria into four bands, 'which describe the seriousness of the risk to independence and well-being or other consequences if needs are not addressed' (DH, 2010a: para. 54), which are (i) critical, (ii) serious, (iii) moderate, and (iv) low. It should be noted that it is the risk which is subject to banding, not the need as such. The substance of these terms is further defined by the guidance. When the draft Care and Support Bill is passed into law, the eligibility criteria will be put on a statutory basis (cl. 13, CSB) although the substance of the criteria will not change.

There are different risks within each band. For example, included within the 'critical' band are risks of threat to life, or that significant health problems have developed or will develop, but also that 'vital involvement in work, education or learning cannot or will not be sustained'. Similarly, both the risk that abuse or neglect will occur, but also that 'involvement in many aspects of work, education or learning cannot or will not be sustained' are included within the 'critical band' (DH, 2010a: para. 54). The policy in the Guidance is quite clear: 'there is no hierarchy of needs. For example, needs relating to social inclusion and participation should be seen as just as important as needs relating to personal care issues, where the need falls within the same band' (DH, 2010a: para. 61).

The rigidity with which this banding system must be adhered to was underscored in *R v Isle of Wight Council, ex parte JM and NT* [2011] EWHC 2911 (Admin). The LSSA policy had been that it would only fund care when a risk was judged critical or serious. In 2010, because of concerns the LSSA had about the heavy and increasing demand on its services caused by the attractiveness of the LSSA area as a retirement destination, it revised its eligibility criteria, so that henceforth it would only fund care for those in the 'critical' band, and those in the 'substantial' band who were 'very likely' or 'likely' to become 'critical', and within that, it would prioritise those most at risk of being unable to remain at home safely. It also restructured its criteria, so that a risk would only be judged as 'critical' if it was not 'remote', which meant likely to occur less than twice a year. The High Court held that the restructuring of the eligibility criteria was unlawful because, in contravention of the guidance, the revised criteria sub-divided the 'substantial' band by reference to a hierarchy of needs, giving greater weight to the need to remain at home than other needs (para. 72), and because of the limit of 'critical' risk to those likely to occur more than twice a year, which had the effect of treating 'substantial' risks likely to become 'critical' more favourably than 'remote' critical risks (para. 83). Although this decision is understandable as an application of the policy of the guidance, it is not clear that the approach taken by the LSSA, in terms of its construction of the eligibility criteria, was necessarily any more unfair or arbitrary than the statutory scheme from which it was held to have departed.

Sometimes it will be clear which band is most appropriate for the risk in question, but often it will not, and effective assessment will depend on the consideration of contextual factors. The guidance advises (DH, 2010a: para. 51) that 'needs should be considered on a person-centred basis recognising both individual need and taking into account the support that the individual's family or support networks are willing and able to provide'. In *R v Camden LBC, ex p P* [2004] EWHC 55, it was held that P, who suffered from depression, anxiety disorder, and obsessive-compulsive behavioural problems for which he had been hospitalised, was not entitled to be provided with accommodation under s. 21, NAA 1948 on discharge from hospital, inter alia, because he could be provided with support in his own home by his wife, W. This was despite the fact that P and W were not living together at that point as W was unable to cope with P's mental health problems, and P had recently spent time at his parents' home.

The LSSA decided that (1) '[P and W] can live together and if they continue to have relationship problems, these should be capable of resolution with advice and guidance', and (2) 'If for some reason [P] is not able to live with his wife, [P] has support available from his family' (cited at para. 23 of the judgment). The High Court held that this was a reasonable assessment on the facts and therefore P did have care and attention 'otherwise available' to him (para. 29). Whether or not the LSSA assessment was correct, this case does underline the extent to which 'informal' care is seen by LSSAs and the courts as an integral element of the community care 'system'.

In *R v Stockton on Tees BC, ex p Stephenson* [2005] EWCA Civ 960, it was held that an LSSA's policy, that it would not reimburse the cost of care provided by a family member, was lawful in principle, on the basis that family members could be expected to provide services on a voluntary basis. A policy is not a rule, however, and where it can be shown, as in *Stephenson*, that a family member has given up paid employment to care for a relative on the understanding and expectation that payment will be made, such a policy cannot simply be applied without consideration of whether it is fair to apply it in the particular circumstances.

At both stages of the assessment process, the way that 'need' is defined is the crucial factor. It is worth pointing out that a 'need' is not a 'right'. Preferences, in the form of 'aspirations' and 'outcomes' which the client has, should be supported by LSSAs (DH, 2010a: para. 53), and there is specific provision for a client for whom residential accommodation is to be provided to express a preference for particular accommodation, in which case the LSSA 'must arrange for care in that accommodation', provided that it is suitable for the client's needs and does not cost more than the LSSA would usually pay (DH, 2004: para 1.3). If funding is available from a third party or, sometimes, the client, to meet the difference between the LSSA's 'usual cost' and that of accommodation which is more expensive, the LSSA must arrange for the client to receive his or her care in that accommodation (DH, 2004: para. 1.4). However, although the client may express preferences, the final decision is with the LSSA (see *R v Southwark, ex p K*).

On the other hand, the distinction between a 'preference' and a 'need' will not always be clear, and an LSSA which draws the distinction inappropriately may be liable to successful challenge by way of judicial review. In *R v Avon County Council, ex p M* [1994] 2 FCR 259 (HC) M, a learning-disabled client, expressed an emphatic preference for a particular care home, but the LSSA placed him in another home on grounds of cost.

After seeking unsuccessfully to challenge the decision through the LSSA's complaints procedure, M sought judicial review, and was successful, on the grounds that his strong preference constituted a psychological need on his part, that required accommodation in the home of his choice in order for it to be satisfied.

In *R* v *Leicester CC, ex p S* [2004] EWHC 533 (Admin), the respondent LSSA decided to provide residential accommodation for S in Leicester, her home city, notwithstanding that she had, for several years, lived in Newcastle, and wished to be provided with accommodation there. The High Court quashed the LSSA's decision on the basis that it had considered the suitability of the competing placements in Leicester and Newcastle only in terms of the facilities offered, and had not sufficiently, nor sufficiently recently, considered S's particular needs, its last assessment having taken place five years ago. These cases seem to hold out a beacon of hope for client involvement, and while this is accurate in a sense, from another perspective, it merely emphasises that it is what a client needs, rather than what a client wants, that is the decisive factor. Hence, if a want is to be satisfied, it must first be redefined as a need.

An example is provided by *R* v *Southwark LB, ex p K* [2001] EWCA Civ 999, [2001] HLR 31 (CA). K, a Kurdish woman who had been born and lived in Iraq for most of her 91 years, suffered from paranoid schizophrenia, with failing sight and hearing, and various other physical infirmities, rendering her immobile to a large extent. She had been assessed as being in need of accommodation and care, and had been offered, together with her elderly husband, a placement in residential accommodation. This placement was deemed necessary to meet K's needs by the LSSA. It was refused by K and her husband, who wished to be provided with a ground-floor flat, where Mr K, aided by his daughter and other family members, felt they would be able to care for K, who did not speak English (the LSSA had been unable to locate Kurdish speakers to participate in the provision of residential care to K). It was also said in evidence that the use of residential accommodation was antithetical to Kurdish culture, in which family members care for the elderly in their own homes. The High Court held that K's needs had been properly assessed and reasonably responded to by the LSSA, and the Court of Appeal upheld that decision, notwithstanding the views of a social worker and psychiatrist, which supported those of K and her husband. *Avon* was distinguished (at para. 54) on the basis that K's preference did not amount to a need. This is antithetical to the concept of empowerment. Indeed, it may be possible to go further and argue that the assessment procedure under the NHSCCA 1990, as constructed by law, comes close to systematic disempowerment, and *Avon* expresses the exception that proves the rule: that unless clients present as supplicants, which involves clients recasting themselves in the discursive terms of social work as an essentially paternalist discourse, they will be turned away. There is nothing in the draft CSB, which continues to use the language of 'needs', which will change this situation.

Nevertheless, needs are not abstract entities, and a client's needs must be assessed sensitively. For example, services to be provided to clients in their own homes must take account of the particular circumstances of that home life. Obviously, attitudes towards, for example, the use of residential accommodation will vary from client to client and from family to family. A decision to offer a client a care package incorporating residential accommodation, rather than providing services to a client in his or her own home, when that client has a strong preference for staying at home may breach Art. 8 of the ECHR, notwithstanding that there may be a strong financial incentive for the LSSA to prefer residential care (*R v SW Staffs Primary Care Trust* [2005] EWHC 1894). As in *ex p K*, cultural factors, and issues surrounding language skills, may also often be pertinent. There is evidence that mental health services are experienced by actual and potential users from within a particular cultural perspective (Littlewood and Lipsedge, 1997; Sewell, 2008; Fernando, 2010), and the potential of any state system to function as a conduit of racism was underscored by the events that unfolded in the wake of the death of Stephen Lawrence. Gender is also a relevant consideration (Thorogood, 1989; Nasser, 2010; Freeman and Freeman, 2013), and both factors impact on the question of need and how an LSSA makes itself aware of needs in its area (Ahmad and Atkin, 1996). There is also a reported lack of knowledge of available mental health services, particularly amongst Asian women (Hatfield *et al.*, 1996; Akram and Kent, 2010), which calls for more assertive, but also sensitive, outreach, if needs are to be identified as readily as in other sections of the community. This assumes that (more) intervention is necessarily a good thing, which is, in reality, an open question. But the point here is that 'need' cannot be assessed accurately outside its broader social context; in this lies both the potential for empowerment and disempowerment in the assessment process under s. 47.

3.3.1.2.2 *Needs and resources*
The most singularly controversial issue around the question of determining both presenting needs and eligibility is whether and, if so, when and to what extent, questions of resources are relevant to determining these questions. The leading case remains—for now at least—the decision of the House of Lords in *R v Gloucestershire County Council and Anor, ex p Barry* [1997] 2 All ER 1, which was not concerned directly with the NHSCCA 1990 but rather with the CSDPA 1970. As discussed at 3.2.2.5, the CSDPA 1970 is not listed as a source of community care services in s. 46(3) of the NHSCCA 1990, and, even if it does come under that section by virtue of its relation to s. 29 of the NAA 1948, it also and simultaneously functions as a parallel regime, concerned with the provision of services to 'disabled' persons. The wording of the provisions of the CSDPA 1970 that deal with access to services is similar, but not identical, to the wording in s. 47(1) of the NHSCCA 1990, but it is possible nonetheless to apply the implications of the opinions handed down in *Barry* to the question of the interpretation of the NHSCCA 1990.

In *Barry*, the situation was that an LSSA, pleading lack of resources, intended to withdraw cleaning and laundry services, which it had been supplying to B, a pensioner, under the terms of s. 2(1) of the CSDPA 1970. This duty is to provide, where 'necessary', a variety of social services to disabled persons who 'need' them. The central thrust of the opinions of a majority of the House of Lords was that, once (1) a need has been assessed to exist, and (2) it had been decided that it was necessary to meet it (because it was not being met in some other way, for example, through the efforts of informal carers), then (3) there is a duty to meet it. Lord Clyde said that 'a shortage of resources will not excuse a failure in the performance of the duty' (at 16).

To this extent—that there are three stages to the process and at the third stage an LSSA may not plead lack of resources as justification for failing to meet its duty—the decision in *Barry* was endorsed recently by Lord Wilson, speaking on behalf of six members of a seven member court, in the Supreme Court in *R v Cambridgeshire County Council, ex parte KM* [2012] UKSC 23. Lord Wilson held (at para. 15) that under the CSDPA 1970, the three stages can be expressed in the form of three questions:

(i) What are the needs of the disabled person?

(ii) In order to meet the needs identified at (i), is it necessary for the [LSSA] to make arrangements for the provision of any…services?

(iii) If the answer to question (ii) is affirmative, what are the nature and extent of the…services for the provision of which it is necessary for the [LSSA] to make arrangements?

Lord Wilson was of the view that the duty at stage (iii) is 'absolute' (para. 21), albeit subject to the caveat (para. 7) that in meeting that duty, an LSSA may choice the most cost-efficient way of doing so (see further in the rest of this section).

Beyond this, there is less clarity. According to Lord Clyde in *Barry*, the fact that resources are irrelevant at the third stage does not mean 'that a consideration of resources may not be relevant to the earlier stage' of deciding whether or not a need recognised by law could be said to exist and whether it was necessary to meet it. In short, in determining whether or not a *legally* recognised need existed, the issue of available resources was a factor that could properly be taken into account. This was because, in Lord Clyde's view, '[t]he words "necessary" and "needs" are both relative expressions' and their meaning could only be assessed by reference to other factors, such as other, competing needs, types and extent of disabilities, and so on. Once 'external' factors were acknowledged as relevant, the twin issues of cost and resources inevitably became part of the equation. Lord Nicholls of Birkenhead explained (at 12) that:

> Once it is accepted…that cost is a relevant factor in assessing a person's needs…then, in deciding how much weight is to be attached to cost, some evaluation or assumption has to be made about the impact which the cost will have upon the authority. Cost is of more or less significance depending upon whether the authority currently has more or less money. Thus, depending upon the authority's financial position, so the eligibility criteria…may properly be more or less stringent.

Although what was held in *Barry* is disputable, not least because, as Baroness Hale ([2012] UKSC 23: para. 46) noted in *Cambridgeshire*, in *Barry* 'Lord Clyde does break decision-making down into clear stages', the decision of the majority in *Barry* does seems to suggest that *both* the assessment of 'needs' under s. 47(1)(a), *and* the question of whether needs, once identified, must be met under s. 47(1)(b), can properly be answered by the LSSA with reference to the availability of resources: the passage from

Lord Nicholl's speech laid out here does appear to be concerned with 'assessing need' (question (i)) rather than meeting it (question (ii)), for example.

It is arguable that in this situation, the restructuring of the courts' powers of judicial review to take account of human rights obligations that was undertaken in *R* v *Secretary of State for the Home Department, ex p Daly* [2001] 2 AC 532 (HL) would now require something more than the application of the traditional *Wednesbury* approach which was applied in the pre-HRA 1998 case of *Barry*. In *Cambridgeshire*, Lord Wilson noted that 'in community care cases the intensity of review will depend on the profundity of the impact of the determination' (para. 36) on the client, but that in suitable cases the intensity of review should be 'high' (para. 36), although he did also hold that the courts should also afford respect to 'the distance between the functions of the decision-maker and the reviewing court' and 'the court's ignorance of the effect upon the ability of an authority to perform its other functions' if the court placed 'exacting demands' on it in the context of one case (para. 36). But however intense the review, it cannot go behind the law, and so the question of whether resources can be taken into account as a matter of substantive law retains its relevance.

The minority in *Barry*, Lord Lloyd of Berwick, with whom Lord Steyn agreed, was prepared to accept that resources are relevant in answering what in Lord Wilson's terms is question (ii), but dissented on the question of whether resources are also relevant to question (i). Lord Lloyd accepted that 'need' is a relative concept, but decided that it might nevertheless be defined as 'the lack of what is essential for the ordinary business of living' (at 5), which should be 'assessed against the standards of civilised society' (at 6). In practice, this decision is left to the individual social worker, acting in accordance with standards set at local level by his or her LSSA, and although these standards could not be defined precisely, that was no reason to guillotine that judgment through the invocation of questions of resources. His general approach was summed up in his observation that '[e]very child needs a new pair of shoes from time to time. The need is not the less because his parents cannot afford them' (at 6). As far as the words of s. 2(1) of the CSDPA 1970 were concerned, 'there is nothing in the language of the section which permits, let alone suggests, that external resources are to be taken into account when assessing the individual's needs' (at 7). Arguably, the same is true of the NHSCCA 1990.

In *R* v *Kensington and Chelsea Royal London Borough Council, ex parte McDonald* [2011] UKSC 33, in which an LSSA had decided that a client who had been provided with care, inter alia, involving night-time attendance of a carer to help her to use the toilet could instead be provided with incontinence pads, Baroness Hale stated unequivocally that she found (para. 72):

> the reasoning of the minority in *Barry* much more convincing, both as a matter of statutory construction and as a matter of everyday life, than the reasoning of the majority. There is a clear distinction between need and what is done to meet it. We all need to eat and drink. Resources do not come into it. But there are various ways of meeting that need and it is perfectly sensible to choose the most efficient and economical way of meeting it.

Baroness Hale 'wished, therefore, that counsel had taken the opportunity presented by coming to this court to argue that *Barry* was wrongly decided' (para. 73). No such argument was made in that case. But the following year, in *R v Cambridgeshire County Council, ex parte KM* [2012] UKSC 23 the Supreme Court was clearly prepared, at least, seriously to entertain the possibility that *Barry* should be departed from. It invited four charities to intervene and constituted itself as a court of seven (rather than the usual five) in order to hear precisely that argument.

In the event, however, issues of resources were not raised by the *Cambridgeshire* case and so the Supreme Court did not feel able to entertain this argument after all. Lord Wilson, speaking for all members of the court bar Baroness Hale, went out of his way 'to say as little as possible—and certainly nothing controversial—about the decision in the *Barry* case' (para. 7), a view endorsed by Baroness Hale (para. 43), although she did note that 'this wise observation applies as much to any account of what was in fact decided in *Barry* as it does to any observations about whether that decision was a correct interpretation of section 2(1) of the 1970 Act'. In her view, it was not clear that the majority in *Barry* had indeed held that resources are relevant to question (i): Lord Clyde had not made a clear distinction between questions (i) and (ii), and in the view of her Ladyship, it may be possible to read Lord Clyde's speech in a way compatible with the view that resources are only relevant to question (ii) (see paras. 46–48).

Lord Wilson, despite his injunction to avoid discussing *Barry*, did mention in passing that if the House of Lords in that case did hold that resources are relevant to question (i), then 'there are arguable grounds for fearing that the committee fell into error' (para. 5), citing the comments of Baroness Hale in *McDonald*. These comments alone are enough to render the usual view of what the majority in *Barry* had decided uncertain and confused, and although *Barry* survives for now, it does so as a questionable and uncertain authority.

The wording of the assessment procedure, in cl. 9 of the draft CSB, does not differ significantly from that of s. 47, and so the reform of the law which the Bill proposes will not provide an answer to the question of the relevance of resources at stage (i). The Bill does contain provision as to eligibility criteria, and provides that if a need meets the eligibility criteria the LSSA should then 'consider what could be done' to meet those needs (cl. 13(1)(b)). This sounds watered-down compared to the Law Commission's recommendation, which was that there should be a duty for LSSAs to 'meet all eligible needs', and that this should be enforceable by individuals (Law Commission, 2011, para. 6.12 and recommendation 16). This was apparently accepted by the government (see DH 2012a: para. 6.5). At the moment, however, the extent of the duty under the CSB is uncertain: cl. 13(2) of the Bill requires that regulations must be made which 'make provision about the exercise of the duty' under cl. 13(1), and these have yet to be made. If, however it is the intention to allow resources to be considered even at the question (iii) stage, then far from clarifying and settling the law, the draft CSB seems to be set on a collision course with at least some members of the current Supreme Court.

As mentioned, in *Cambridgeshire*, Lord Wilson placed a caveat on the absolute nature of the duty at stage (iii), holding that although the duty must be complied with at this stage, there is a discretion as to how it is complied with, and the efficient use of resources is an appropriate consideration in exercising that discretion. *McDonald* provides an example of how the caveat, seen by Lord Wilson in *Cambridgeshire* as 'an elementary aspect of financial management...better not even included within the debate about...resources' ([2012] UKSC 23 at para. 7), can nonetheless operate problematically. As mentioned, the issue in this case was whether an LSSA could remove from M, who was frail and elderly and who suffered from a neurogenic bladder and so had to urinate two or three times each night, services in the form of a night-time carer who would help M to leave her bed, use a commode, and return to bed, and instead provide her with incontinence pads as a way to meet her eligible need for assistance. The LSSA decided that it would afford M greater privacy, and save £22,000 per annum of LSSA funding, if M was provided instead with incontinence pads, and informed her that it had determined that 'the current provision to be in excess of that required to meet your eligible needs' (cited by the High Court at [2009] EWHC 1582 (Admin), para. 15).

M challenged that decision, inter alia, as a breach of her rights under Art. 8 ECHR. At first instance, although M's needs had initially been assessed as including a need for assistance to access her commode, it was held that M's need had been, and continued to be, a need for safe urination at night, and that it was open to the LSSA to meet that need in a more economical manner than had hitherto been the case, thus applying the caveat on question (iii). M appealed against that decision. In the Court of Appeal, it seems as though the ground shifted. The decision to alter the provisions of M's care package had been preceded by a reassessment of M's needs, and as Rix LJ commented ([2010] EWCA Civ 1109, para. 53) 'they no longer assess M's needs as including assistance to access the commode at night...On the contrary, they refer to M's night-time toileting needs in much more general terms....Thus they speak of a "need for support at night" which "should be managed through the use of incontinence pads"'. In other words, the assessed need had changed, and this was not a case of an existing need being met in a different way.

Although this passage was cited by Lord Brown in the Supreme Court (para. 12) the shift from, in Lord Wilson's terms in *Cambridgeshire*, the territory of question (iii) to that of question (i) is not explicitly discussed by Lord Brown. For him, as for Lord Dyson (see para. 53) it was enough that there has been a reassessment of M's needs which had re-evaluated the nature of the need. Lord Kerr, by contrast, did wrestle with the fact that M's needs after reassessment 'were precisely the same as they had been when originally assessed' (para. 39), eventually deciding that 'The essential question...is whether "needs" partake partly of the means by which the disabilities of the appellant may be catered for' (para. 40), which although 'not an easy conclusion to reach' (para. 39) is 'on reflection...the correct approach': para. 40. He carried on:

> If needs are defined as the issues and problems that the particular individual presents, that would appear to open the way to taking a rather broader view of what needs mean and includes not only the narrow connotation of needs but also how those needs may be met.

It is not absolutely clear whether Lord Kerr is referring to question (i) or question (ii) in this passage; but certainly, the most natural reading of it seems to be that, like the majority in *Barry*, he conflates the two, bringing the resource implications of meeting eligible needs into the question of whether a need is to be officially recognised in the first place. It could be argued that in taking this approach, Lord Kerr in *McDonald* undermines the clear decision in *Barry*, that resources cannot be entertained at the third stage, because if the identification of needs can be tailored by reference to resources at both stages (i) and (ii), it is little compensation to the client to impose an absolute duty at stage (iii). That is a case of shutting the stable door after the horse has bolted.

There was a powerful dissent in *McDonald* from Baroness Hale. She argued that incontinence pads are not a suitable way of meeting the needs of a person like M, who is not incontinent. Baroness Hale in essence applied the reasoning of the minority in *Barry* to the distinction between needs and the meeting of needs, but further held that it was not necessary to decide that *Barry* was wrongly decided to find in favour of M. This was because the decision of the LSSA had to be quashed because 'the need for help to get to the lavatory or commode is so different from the need for protection from uncontrollable bodily functions that it is irrational to confuse the two' (para. 75). She claimed that 'Logically, the decision of the majority...would entitle [an LSSA] to withdraw this help even though the client needed to defecate during the night and thus might be left lying in her own faeces until the carers came in the morning' (para. 77).

The other members of the court absolutely rejected this claim as 'nothing short of remarkable' (Lord Brown at para. 27) and 'rather regrettable' (Lord Walker at para. 32). Lord Dyson claimed (para. 58) that Baroness Hale had confused needs with options for addressing needs, and 'Baroness Hale is only able to say that the [LSSA's] decision is irrational because she has chosen to define the two ways of meeting [M's] needs as needs themselves'. We are left somewhat bemused by this, because on our reading, this is precisely the criticism that Baroness Hale makes of the reasoning of the majority.

At root, although this debate has to occur through the vehicle of the various statutory provisions and so it to some extent a matter of statutory interpretation, the real issue of one of policy. The majority of the Supreme Court noted that evidence had been given that the use of incontinence pads for people who are not incontinent is 'both widespread and accepted practice' (per Lord Dyson at para. 59, see also Lord Walker at para. 31), and this was taken as evidence of the legal acceptability of the practice. For Baroness Hale, by contrast, 'In the United Kingdom we do not oblige people who can control their bodily functions to behave as if they cannot do so, unless they themselves find this the more convenient course. We are, I still believe, a civilised society' (para. 79). It is regrettable that the majority of the court in *McDonald* felt unable to endorse this view.

It is not clear, moreover, that Baroness Hale's assertion regarding the logical consequences of the decision of the majority is incorrect. Although M's claim under Art. 8, ECHR was treated as 'hopeless' by Lord Brown (para. 16), this did not mean that Art. 8 would never be relevant. He endorsed (at para. 18) the decision of the Court of Appeal in *Anufrijeva* v *Southwark LBC* [2004] EWCA Civ 1406 at para. 43, in which the Court of Appeal had held that it was 'hard to conceive...of a situation in which the predicament of an individual will be such that article 8 requires him to be provided with welfare support, where his predicament is not sufficiently severe to engage article 3', but also the decision in *R v Enfield LBC, ex parte Bernard* [2002] EWHC 2282, in which a failure of an LSSA to provide necessary services for a doubly incontinent wheelchair-bound client, causing her to have to defecate and urinate on the floor of the living room she shared with her husband and six children, was found to breach Art. 8 of the ECHR. The fact that Art. 8 does place some lower limits on the quality of care that can be offered is welcome, but the situation in *Bernard* was different from the scenario envisaged by Baroness Hale, in that no care at all was being provided in that case. It seems that Art. 3, and therefore Art. 8, ECHR, according to the majority in *McDonald*, kick in somewhere between being left in soiled incontinence pads until the next morning (*McDonald*) and being left in soiled conditions indefinitely (*Bernard*).

3.4 Alternative mechanisms for securing services

The duties, to assess and meet needs, currently found in s. 47 of the NHSCCA 1990, do not exclude the relevance of other sources of obligation. For instance, an LSSA, CCG and any provider of care, formal or informal, must act in the best interests of clients lacking capacity in accordance with the requirements of s. 4 of the MCA 2005 (see *R v Viridian Housing and LB Wandsworth, ex parte Chatting* [2012] EWHC 2595 (Admin), discussed at 3.4.3, and *R v Croydon BC, ex parte W* [2011] EWHC 696 (Admin)). And of course, the requirements of the Human Rights Act 1998 must be complied with, by both commissioners and public and independent providers of care (Health and Social Care Act 2008, s. 145).

As can be seen from the discussion at 3.3, the NHSCCA 1990 was always more concerned with the *management* of services, and with the putting in place of a coherent framework of responsibility and accountability for service provision, than with questions of *entitlement*. As if the legal situation were not already complex enough, the NHSCCA 1990 did nothing to alter the fact that each of the statutes defined as providing 'community care services' in s. 46(3) of that Act have their own provisions regarding access and entitlement. And, increasingly over recent years, those seeking access to services have bypassed the NHSCCA 1990, using s. 47 only as a mechanism by which to insist that an assessment be carried out, or as a gateway into the legislation to which s. 46(3) refers, under which, it has been argued, stricter duties are to be found than those imposed by s. 47 of the NHSCCA 1990. Most activity has centred around the duties to provide residential accommodation found in s. 21 of the NAA 1948 and the relevant directions, but a more recent phenomenon has been the attempted use of the equality duty placed on LSSAs, as public authorities, by s. 149, EA 2010, as a mechanism to secure services. Both possibilities will now be discussed.

3.4.1 The duty to provide accommodation in s. 21 National Assistance Act 1948

As discussed at 3.2.2.1.1, an LSSA has a duty under s. 21(1)(a) of the NAA 1948 to provide 'residential accommodation for persons who by reason of age, illness, disability or any other circumstance are in need of care and attention which is not otherwise available to them'. The interpretation of this duty and of the relation of its internal components to each other has been the subject of considerable litigation. In *R v Slough BC, ex parte M* [2008] 1 WLR 1808, Baroness Hale in the House of Lords noted that although a construction which linked the words 'not otherwise available' back to 'residential accommodation' was in her view 'grammatically attractive' (para. 16, see also Lord Neuberger at para. 48), this would 'defeat the main purpose of the section, which is to make special provision for those with special needs' (para. 16, see also Lord Neuberger at para. 48) and hence, the better reading is that the words ' "not otherwise available" govern the words "care and attention" and not the words "residential accommodation"... A person may have a roof over her head but still be in need of care and accommodation which is not otherwise available to her in that home and therefore qualify for residential accommodation under section 21(1)(a)' (para. 15).

Conversely, but consistent with this, 'The need for care and attention is a condition precedent to entitlement under s. 21(1)(a). A mere need for housing and support is not a need for care and attention' (para. 21), and a person who needs care and attention, which is not otherwise available, but which can be supplied to that person in their own home, does not qualify for residential accommodation under s. 21(1)(a) (*R v National Asylum and Support Service, ex p Westminster City Council* [2002] UKHL 38 per Lord Hoffmann at para. 26, approving this approach as taken by Hale LJ in *R v Tower Hamlets LBC, ex p Abdul W* [2002] EWCA Civ 287, paras. 30–33).

The meaning of 'care and attention' was subject to further consideration in *Slough*. Baroness Hale noted that 'care and attention' must amount to something more than simply the provision of accommodation, because it is clear that s. 21 is designed as a 'safety net', to apply outside the normal housing legislation (*R v Tower Hamlets LBC, ex p Abdul W* [2002] EWHC Admin 641 per Stanley Burnton J at para. 28) and is not a general power to provide housing (Baroness Hale in *Slough* at para. 33). It should therefore be understood as Baroness Hale, then Hale LJ, had explained it in the Court of Appeal in the *Tower Hamlets* case (para. 32), that is, as 'looking after'. This, as she explained in *Slough* (para. 33) 'means doing something for the person being cared for which he cannot or should not be expected to do for himself', whether that be personal care, household chores, or protecting that person from risks. In *R v Westminster CC, ex parte SL* [2011] EWCA Civ 954 Laws LJ explained (paras. 34, 21) that although there must be 'some nexus between care and attention...and the provision of accommodation...the level of support provided by the [LSSA] does not have to attain any particular level of intensity'.

It was held in *R v Sefton Metropolitan Borough Council, ex p Help the Aged and Ors* [1997] 4 All ER 532 that once it has been decided that a person has eligible needs, the duty owed under s. 21 is enforceable by individuals. As far as the relevance of resources are concerned, Lord Woolf MR, in the light of *Barry*, felt 'compelled to conclude that there is a limited subjective element in making an assessment of whether the ailments of the person concerned do or do not collectively establish a need for care and attention' (at 543). In his view, however, it is 'very much more difficult' for an LSSA to plead lack of resources under s. 21 of the NAA 1948 Act than in the context of s. 29 of that Act or

s. 2(1) of the CSDPA 1970. Part of the reason for this was that the nature of the need—for accommodation—is qualitatively different, by definition of greater severity, from a need for other services. In part also, Lord Woolf emphasised that the requirement of s. 2(1) of the CSDPA 1970—that it must be 'necessary' to provide the services in question—was absent from s. 21 of the NAA 1948, so that, under the latter provision, there is a duty to meet needs even though it is not 'necessary' that they are met.

The qualitative distinction between a need for accommodation and a need for other services is, however, problematic. It tends to break down in practice, because a failure to provide services in the community can increase the likelihood that service users will need residential accommodation. Furthermore, if there is not always a duty, because of limited resources, to meet 'needs' when it has been decided that it is 'necessary' to do so, under the CSDPA 1970, the implication is, surely, that there should be *greater* scope for the exercise of discretion in the case of needs that are *not* defined as 'necessary' under s. 21 of the NAA 1948 and not, as Lord Woolf suggested, *less* scope.

Yet this merely points to the problematic nature of the 'policy' on community care provision, because Lord Woolf was surely correct to the extent that there is no reason, in principle, why it should be have to be 'necessary' that services are provided under s. 2(1) of the CSDPA 1970, but not under s. 21 of the NAA 1948. And although Lord Woolf's reasoning may be somewhat problematic, his view that the scope for consideration of resources is less than under the NHSCCA 1990 or the CSDPA 1970, as interpreted in *Barry* raises the question of the relation between s. 21 of the NAA 1948 and s. 47 of the NHSCCA 1990, to which the Court of Appeal, in the later case of *R v Kensington and Chelsea London Borough Council, ex p Kujtim* [1999] 4 ALL ER 161, gave the response that held an LSSA is not entitled to rely on the discretionary wording of s. 47(1)(b) of the NHSCCA 1990 to justify a decision not to provide accommodation to a client assessed as being in need of services under s. 21(1) of the NAA 1948. Such questions will be rendered redundant if the draft CSB is enacted in its present form, because the Bill would repeal the NAA 1948 in its entirety, and all questions about assessing and meeting needs would be under one roof, with no scope for doubts to be raised about the compatibility or otherwise of overlapping statutory provisions.

3.4.2 The equality duty in s. 149 Equality Act 2010

The appeal in *McDonald* did not rest solely on Art. 8 of the ECHR. M also claimed that the decision of the LSSA breached various provisions of discrimination law, at the time contained in the Disability Discrimination Act 1995, but which are now to be found in the EA 2010, and it has become increasingly common for such arguments to be made in this context.

The EA 2010 prohibits both direct (s. 13) and indirect (s. 19) discrimination for a number of classes of person, defined in terms of 'protected characteristics', which include 'disability'. 'Disability' is defined in s. 6(1) of the EA 2010 to comprise a 'physical or mental impairment' and 'impairment' is defined as 'a substantial and long-term adverse effect on P's ability to carry out normal day-to-day activities'. There is also a duty to make 'reasonable adjustments' so as to prevent or obviate discrimination in s. 20, and specific duties in a diverse range of situations. The EA 2010 has the potential to impact significantly on the provision of services for mentally disordered persons, and indeed has begun to do so (see 3.5.2). The focus here is on the use by persons seeking to obtain community care services of s. 149 of the EA 2010, which contains what is described as the 'public sector equality duty'.

This duty applies to all functions of a public authority, including an LSSA. By virtue of s. 149(2), the s. 149 duty also applies to 'A person who is not a public authority but who exercises public functions' (s. 149(2)), which covers independent sector providers of accommodation commissioned by LSSAs. The duty under s. 149 has three components to it: An LSSA 'must...have due regard to the need to: eliminate discrimination, harassment, victimisation and any other conduct that is prohibited by or under this Act' (s. 149(1)(a)); advance equality of opportunity between persons who share a relevant protected characteristic and persons who do not share it (s. 149(1)(b)); and foster good relations between persons who share a relevant protected characteristic and persons who do not share it (s. 149(1)(c)).

In *McDonald*, an argument based on s. 149 (as it now is) was given short shrift by the Supreme Court. Lord Brown held that the argument was 'hopeless' (para. 24), because, even if there is no specific mention of s. 149 in the documents relevant to the council's decision it may nonetheless be 'absurd' to infer a failure to comply with the equality duty simply on that basis. It is, rather, a question 'of substance, not of form' (para. 24), and here, there was evidence that the duty had been appropriately considered. This *dicta* was applied to a similar fact situation by the Court of Appeal in *Tiller* v *East Sussex County Council* [2011] EWCA Civ 1577, a case in which it was proposed to remove 24-hour on-site care for residential accommodation, and replace it with an on-site service limited to office hours, with an on-call system to carers located off-site being implemented for evenings and weekends. As in *McDonald*, there has been no specific reference to the s. 149 duty or to the fact that due regard had been given to it, by the LSSA decision-maker, but it was nonetheless held that the evidence showed that, in substance, the duty had been complied with. But in other recent case law, arguments based on s. 149 have had more success.

R v *Harrow LBC, ex parte Chavda* [2007] EWHC 3064 (Admin) the High Court quashed the decision of an LSSA to restrict services, previously offered to those in both the 'critical' and 'substantial' risk categories, to those in 'critical' need only, as an equality impact assessment upon which the decision to alter the eligibility criteria was based did not consider the need to comply with the duty now found in s. 149 of the EA 2010. A bullet-pointed reference to 'a potential conflict with the DDA 1995. A change in criteria could be seen as limiting access for some people to services' (para. 34) did not comply with the need to fully consider the factors mentioned in s. 149(1). Similarly, in *R* v *Isle of Wight Council, ex parte JM and NT* [2011] EWHC 2911 (Admin) a proposal to move to a situation where only critical risks would be funded was held to be in breach of s. 149 because the implications of the decision had not been adequately costed (with the council proceedings on the basis that the changes would save £1 million per annum when in fact the saving was only around £55,000: para. 132) and therefore the implications of the decision for disabled persons had not been adequately assessed.

In *Domb* v *LB Hammersmith and Fulham* [2009] EWCA Civ 941, an LSSA made a decision to begin charging for non-residential services provided under s. 29 of the NAA 1948. This was unsuccessfully challenged by three disabled service users, on the grounds, in particular, of what is now s. 149(1)(b), EA 2010. The Court of Appeal held that it was not possible, at the appeal hearing, to go behind the situation whereby, because of a decision made to cut council tax rates by 3 per cent, the LSSA had to either tighten its eligibility criteria or introduce charging. That was because that argument had not been raised at first instance, although Rix LJ did say, *obiter*, (at para. 62) that 'in another case' it may be appropriate to go behind the financial situation into which an LSSA had been put by a prior council decision to reduce its social services budget, and require the council to 'demonstrate...that it had considered, in substance and with the necessary vigour, whether it could by any means avoid a decision which was plainly going to have a negative impact on the users of existing services'.

On the facts, as the LSSA had conducted an equality impact assessment, in which it was emphasised that a decision to impose charges would be 'extremely relevant to disabled people' and which urged councillors to give their 'full consideration' to the impact of the proposal on disabled people, and which was before the council when taking the decision whether or not to impose charges, the Court of Appeal was prepared to accept that 'there is no evidence that it did not do so' (para. 63), on that basis finding compliance with the duty.

There was a similar outcome in *JG and MB* v *Lancashire County Council* [2011] EWHC 2295 (Admin), in which a decision to tighten eligibility criteria so that only 'critical' and 'substantial' risks would be provided for was held lawful because the evidence showed that there had been consideration of the factors mentioned in s. 149 of the EA 2010 and because it was clear that the revised eligibility criteria and corresponding budget allocation would be subject to further equality impact assessment before being implemented.

Rix LJ's obiter statement in *Domb* was applied in *R* v *Birmingham City Council, ex parte W* [2011] EWHC 1147 (Admin). As in *Chavda*, eligibility criteria were revised by an LSSA so that services would only be supplied for those in the 'critical' category, but with no information available or commissioned to explore whether, in the light of the 'drastic consequences' of implementing that policy, it may be possible to save money elsewhere in the council budget as, so the court held (para. 183), was required by general equality duty. If this element of the decision in this case is followed, it has significant implications for the extent to which local authorities must factor the equality duty into decisions taken at council level, as to which services require funding in order to meet the duty, and it will not be easy for a council simply to assert, as happened in *Domb*, that it is too late to revisit the decision as to how much of the total budget of the local authority should be allocated to social service provision.

In a series of recent cases, the equality duty has been considered in the context of disputes between LSSAs and independent sector providers concerning the fees paid by the former to the latter. In *The Sefton Care Association* v *Sefton Council* [2011] EWHC 2676 (Admin) the High Court held that a failure accurately to assess 'usual costs' necessarily meant that the general equality duty had not been complied with (para. 100) in a case (discussed at 3.2.2.1.1) concerning an LSSA decision to freeze fees payable to independent sector providers. But HH Judge Raynor QC in that case also held (see 3.2.2.1.1) that, if there is no dispute about the fees between the LSSA and individual clients (which would raise questions of the duty owed to those individuals), then 'provided that the usual cost of care is properly determined in accordance with the Directions and Guidance, the [LSSA] will be entitled to proceed upon the basis that the requirements of the public sector equality duty have been complied with in the preparation of individual needs assessments and care plans and in my view need go no further when fixing the fees payable in respect of its placements'.

South West Care Homes Ltd v *Devon County Council* [2012] EWHC 2967 (Admin) also concerned a decision by an LSSA to freeze the rate at which it paid fees to care home providers. It was argued that *Sefton* should be confined to its specific facts, and that compliance with the duties imposed by s. 47 of the NHSCCA 1990 and s. 21 of the NAA 1948 cannot in general terms, beyond the specific issue of fixing fees to be paid to providers, relieve an LSSA of the need to comply with its separate duty under s. 149 of the EA 2010, and the court seemed to accept this (see para. 44). In this case, the LSSA thought that a number of care homes in its area were at risk of closure, the risk of which would be exacerbated if fees were frozen. It appreciated that a possible adverse effect of the freezing of fees might be that disabled residents in that accommodation would have to relocate, with possible adverse health consequences. But no measures to mitigate that negative impact were considered by the LSSA, which, instead left it to 'the council's operational managers . . . to safeguard residents when a home closes' (para. 51). That approach, according to HH Judge Harman QC, sitting in the High Court, 'fails to have due regard, in substance or with rigour or with an open mind, to the need to eliminate discrimination and to promote equality of opportunity amongst elderly or disabled residents' (para. 53).

The equality duty has proven useful for some applicants seeking to challenge reductions in the level of service provided by an LSSA, and does have the potential to set some baseline standards for the way in which disabled persons, including mentally disordered persons, as well as those who have other relevant 'protected characteristics' including race, sex, and age are protected from discrimination by LSSA decisions. But the scope of the general equality duty, which, as a duty to have 'due regard' is essentially procedural in character, and offers limited possibilities for providing a challenge to an LSSA decision which will have any longevity. In general terms, a duty will only be absolute and binding on an LSSA when that LSSA has made a promise to an individual or members of a defined group that the services provided to them would be supplied in that form for life.

3.4.3 **Challenging broken promises**

The duty currently found in s. 21 of the NAA 1948 (which will continue after the reform of the law by virtue of the combination of cls. 8 and 9 of the draft CSB, at least in a case in which it is decided that there is an eligible need for residential accommodation) is a potentially onerous one. In *R* v *Kensington and Chelsea London Borough Council, ex p Kujtim* [1999] 4 ALL ER 161, Potter LJ (at para. 30) explained that the duty to provide accommodation subsists:

> on a continuing basis so long as the need of the applicant remains as originally assessed and if, for whatever reason, the accommodation, once provided, is withdrawn or otherwise becomes unavailable to the applicant, then…the local authority has a continuing duty to provide further accommodation.

This enables residents of care homes to challenge decisions to close their particular accommodation, on the basis that the closure puts the LSSA in breach of its continuing duty, if the resident is of the view that his or her needs are no longer being met (Darton, 2004; Netten, Williams and Darton, 2005).

The courts are not generally sympathetic to such arguments, taking the view that as long as the activities of the LSSA are reasonable, the specific details of a care plan, such as which accommodation which will be provided to an eligible person, or the precise details of care provision, such as whether communal dining facilities are provided or not, are not justiciable (*R* v *Barking and Dagenham LBC, ex p L* [2002] 1 FLR 763 (CA) per Schiemann LJ at para. 27). In *Barking*, in which accommodation had been refurbished and restructured, with communal dining facilities removed, the LSSA had given various undertakings, to the effect that the new accommodation would be suitable for L. The Court of Appeal released the LSSA from those undertakings on the basis that they added nothing to their statutory duties. In that case, and in *R* v *Plymouth City Council, ex p Cowl* [2001] EWCA Civ 1935 [2002] 1 WLR 803, the Court of Appeal noted that the LSSA had been willing to settle the matter through its complaints procedure, and held that, until the complaints procedure had been exhausted, there was no cause of action (*Cowl* led to the issuance of a *Practice Direction* to this effect: [2002] 1 ALL ER 633, [2002] 1 WLR 810).

When decisions have been litigated, it has been held that there is a right to be consulted, as a requirement of procedural fairness. In particular, in *R* v *North and East Devon Health Authority ex p Coughlan* [2001] QB 213 [2000] 2 WLR 622, Lord Woolf MR held that (para. 108):

> consultation must be undertaken at a time when proposals are still at a formative stage; it must include sufficient reasons for particular proposals to allow those consulted to give intelligent consideration and an intelligent response; adequate time must be given for this purpose; and the product of consultation must be conscientiously taken into account.

If this is done, and provided that the decision to close a particular facility is not '*Wednesbury* unreasonable', it will be lawful and will not, without more, breach any of the human rights of the residents (*R* v *East Sussex CC, ex p Dudley* [2003] EWHC 1093; *R* v *St Helens BC, ex p Haggerty* [2003] EWHC 803, [2003] HLR 69).

Coughlan has been followed, with varying degrees of success, in a number of subsequent cases in various contexts, including the rights of independent sector providers to be consulted about the level of fees that the LSSA intends to set (*East Midlands Care Ltd* v *Leicester County Council* [2011] EWHC 3096 (Admin); *The Sefton Care Association* v *Sefton Council* [2011] EWHC 2676 (Admin); *South West Care Homes Ltd* v *Devon County Council* [2012] EWHC 2967 (Admin)), and the rights of users of non-residential community care services when services are to be reduced or removed (*R* v *Kensington and Chelsea Royal London Borough Council, ex parte McDonald* [2011] UKSC 33; *R* v *Cambridgeshire County Council, ex parte KM* [2012] UKSC 23), as well in relation to LSSA decisions to close LSSA-run care home accommodation (*R* v *Havering LBC, ex p Johnson* [2006] EWHC 1714), or not renew a contract with an independent provider, resulting in the closure of a care home (*R* v *St Helens BC, ex p Haggerty* [2003] EWHC 803, [2003] HLR 69).

The right to be consulted, as a procedural rather than substantive right, is of limited usefulness. If, however, there has been a promise that 'has induced a legitimate expectation of a benefit which is substantive, not simply procedural', a court may also insist that it be kept, if to break it 'is so unfair that to take a new and different course will amount to an abuse of power' (per Lord Woolf MR in *R* v *North and East Devon Health Authority, ex p Coughlan* [2001] QB 213 [2000] 2 WLR 622). In that case, C and other residents in her care home had been promised that it would be 'their home for life', but later, the LSSA planned to close the home, essentially on grounds of cost. The Court of Appeal held that the closure was not permissible in the face of the promise made to C and the other residents, and that, because few individuals were involved, and because the LSSA had failed to show an overriding public interest, it could not now resile from that promise. In the later case of *R* v *Newham LBC, ex p Bibi* 2000 WL 1544686, the High Court held that a promise was binding even though the LSSA making it thought, wrongly, that it had a statutory obligation to provide accommodation. It is clear that any promise must be 'clear and unequivocal' if it is to bind the LSSA (Lightman J in *R* v *Walsall MBC, ex p P and R* (2001) 26 April, unreported, at para. 8; see also *R* v *Lincolnshire HA, ex p Collins* [2001] EWHC Admin 665).

The Court of Appeal in *ex p Coughlan* also found a breach of Art. 8 of the ECHR, but this was for the particular reason that there had been the promise in question, and when that is absent, *Coughlan* may be distinguished, as it was by Maurice Kay LJ in the *Dudley* case at para. 52. In *CH and MH* v *Merton Primary Care Trust* [2004] EWHC 2984, the residents of an NHS care home (technically, hospital provision, but nothing turns on this) had been given a 'home for life' promise of the sort made in *Coughlan*. The trust sought to close the facility and relocate the residents, all with severe learning difficulties, into the community, on the grounds that that was in the best interests of the residents. The High Court held that (1) there was an entitlement that the applicants have their best interests investigated in family proceedings, such proceedings to run side-by-side with their application for judicial review, at which (2) best interests would also be a live issue, as would the Art. 8 rights of the applicants, and (3) following the decision in *R (Wilkinson)* v *Broadmoor Special Hospital* [2001] EWCA Civ 1545 (see Chapter 9, 9.5.3) the court was therefore bound by s. 6(1) of the HRA 1998 to make a substantive judgment on best interests.

An LSSA (or in this case, PCT, now CCG) may be able to escape from the terms of a 'home for life' promise by demonstrating that Art. 8(2) applies, and that the best interests of the residents are served by the closure of their home, but, as the *Merton* case also makes clear, such a claim cannot be blandly asserted by the LSSA: it must prove its case to the satisfaction of the courts. A 'home for life' promise may be departed from where the medical interests of the client require it (*R v Wandsworth LBC, ex p G* [2003] EWHC 2941; the case was appealed but not on this point).

In *R v Viridian Housing and LB Wandsworth, ex parte Chatting* [2012] EWHC 2595 (Admin) C, who had lived in her care home for 17 years, had through litigation secured a 'home for life' promise from the charitable provider of her accommodation, V. Thereafter, the premises were also sold to a third party, X, which provided both care in line with the new arrangements, and the accommodation. C sought judicial review of the decision to transfer responsibility for her care from V to X as a breach of the promise extracted from V and of Art. 8, ECHR. Her concern was that X would not have to honour V's promise and she would, against her wishes, be moved to alternative accommodation, a concern heightened by her worsening physical health, because it seemed likely that C would soon need nursing care, which could not be provided for her in her current accommodation, as it was not registered as a nursing care home.

The High Court held, in relation to the promise of accommodation for life, that (i) it was subject to the implied condition that it would continue to bind only insofar as C's needs remained unchanged, and a need for nursing care which could not be provided in C's current accommodation permitted V to depart from the terms of the promise (para. 67); that there was no limitation on the identity of the provider of her care (para. 69); and that, generally, a 'promise for life' did not carry any implications as to how the premises in question were to be managed, including whether or not they would be sold (para. 72). In relation to the claim under Art. 8, although it was accepted that the Article did apply to the decision to cease to provide care (para. 80), following the approach of the majority of the Supreme Court in *McDonald* (see Ch. 3.3.1.2), it was held 'the interference in [C's] private life is minor' in comparison to the situation in *Bernard* (discussed at 3.3.2.1), and that Art. 8 did not require that a promise to provide care had to be personally performed by the person or organisation making it (para. 84), and that as, in addition, C had been adequately consulted at each stage (para. 86) there was no breach of Art. 8.

C lacked mental capacity. An argument, that s. 4 of the MCA 2005 required V, and the LSSA who contracted with X for the provision of C's care after X purchased the premises, to have acted otherwise than it did was also unsuccessful, the court holding that 'the fact that [C] is mentally incapacitated does not import the test of "what is in her best interests?" as the yardstick by which all care decisions are to be made' (para. 99), and that the care commissioner and provider acted lawfully if they had due regard for her welfare, this being the duty under s. 21(2) of the NAA 1948. It seems fair enough that a 'home for life' promise should be construed as conditional on circumstances not changing, in particular the nature of the need for care which the service user has, but this apart, this is a disappointing judgment in that it provides LSSAs and care homes with various mechanisms to escape a 'home for life' promise and reveals that arguments based on human rights or capacity law are unlikely to add much to strength of the service user's case.

On the other hand, it is also a realistic judgment. The arrangements for C entailed the creation of a one-bed care home in premises otherwise de-registered and redesigned as sheltered accommodation for those with very low needs for care, with C's care being supplied by a neighbouring provider (albeit part of the same organisation that ran her accommodation), and much as we might wish otherwise, the logistical and financial costs of meeting users' needs in this way are not really viable for other than isolated cases.

3.5 A 'seamless' service?

3.5.1 Working together with NHS bodies

In addition to the requirement of collegiate community care planning currently imposed by s. 46, NHSCCA 1990, assessment imposed by s. 47(3), and the general duty to work together under s. 82, NHSA 2006, policy guidance issued contemporaneously with the NHSCCA 1990 stressed that 'local collaboration is the key to making a reality of community care' (DH, 1990a; Dowling *et al.*, 2004). The DH (DH, 1990) also introduced the care programme approach (CPA) from 1991. According to the NHS Executive, which, in 1994, endorsed the CPA in the form of guidance (DH, 1994), the main aim of the CPA 'is to ensure the support of mentally ill persons in the community, thereby minimising the possibility of their losing contact with services and maximising the effect of any therapeutic intervention' (1994: para. 9), and 'the CPA can and should be applied to all patients who are accepted by the specialist psychiatric services' (DH, 1995: para. 1.3.6), and should be written into contracts with independent and voluntary providers of services.

Box 3.1

KEY ELEMENTS OF THE CARE PLAN APPROACH

- Systematic assessment of health, social care and housing needs, both in the short and long term;
- A written care plan agreed by the patient, relevant professionals, and the patient's carers;
- The allocation of a care co-ordinator to provide a focal point for contact with the recipient of services, to monitor service delivery, and to respond to problems if and when they arise;
- Regular review of the patient's progress and ongoing needs.

(adapted from DH, 2005: para. 10)

Throughout the 1990s, however, the CPA suffered from the limitations of inter-agency co-operation. Research carried out by the NHS Executive, in conjunction with NHS regional offices and the Social Services Inspectorate, in 1997 confirmed that a 'seamless' service was far from being realised in many parts of the country. One reason for this was that LSSAs and NHS bodies 'used different systems for recording information about the processes of treatment and care', and, more often than not, the data accumulated by each was not shared (see DH, 1998: paras. 3.6–3.13).

This lack of inter-agency co-operation can be explained, in part at least, on the basis that each agency, and the professions that dominate the various agencies, functions within different paradigms of care. Equally, in the context of community care, a clash of perspective may be a feature of co-operation at ground level between health professionals and social workers. It was argued, just as it was becoming apparent that the CPA and, especially, joint working was failing to take off, that this is the result of differences in professional ideology, overlain with factors relating to organisational identity, which function as a sort of 'double separation' between LSSAs and HAs (now CCGs) and their respective staff (Dalley, 1993; Onyett *et al.*, 1994). Evidence was also published that suggested that the introduction of managerialist principles by the NHSCCA 1990 impacted negatively on the quality of services, because it encouraged a tendency amongst LSSAs and HAs to budget defensively (Wistow, 1994; 1995), a tendency that accelerated as pressure on resources increased.

There were two main practical consequences of this. First, it led to, or at least exacerbated the existence of, a 'grey area' falling between that which is clearly health care and that which is clearly social care, over which responsibility is ill-defined or agreed (Lewis and Glennerster, 1996). Second, the assessment process, and the implementation of the CPA, was not always the consensual experience that the government's guidance might suggest. In this respect, the seemingly innocuous and straightforward advice from the DH (1995: para. 3.2.10), that a client's key worker will not always act as care manager, and that for clients with complex needs, the functions of care manager may be shared amongst several professionals, often meant that service delivery was experienced by clients as fractured, possibly even as contradictory or incoherent.

The CPA was revised in 1999 (DH, 1999f). The four main elements of the CPA (listed in Box 3.1) were unchanged, as was its coverage (working age adults). As before, 'the key principles of the CPA are applicable to all service users' (1999f: para. 18). There were some superficial changes: key workers have been renamed as care co-ordinators (usually a community psychiatric nurse or psychiatric social worker: see the discussion at DH, 1995: paras 3.1.18–3.1.25); the requirement for six-monthly reviews in all cases was removed, although regular reviews must continue in all cases. A guide for inter-agency working, *Building Bridges*, made clear that a full multidisciplinary assessment should be reserved for complex cases, and the new approach attempted to systematise this, dividing the CPA into two levels, 'standard' and 'enhanced', depending on the needs of the service user, although in either case a multidisciplinary assessment was required, and there should be 'A single assessment [which] should facilitate access to both health and social services' (DH, 1995: para. 38).

The standard CPA was designed for cases in which the need is predominantly for support from one agency, when clients are able to self-manage their mental health problems, when there is an active informal support network, or when patients are more likely to maintain contact with service providers, and when clients 'pose little danger to themselves or others' (DH, 1999d: para. 57). The enhanced CPA, which involved a more interventionist approach, was designed for clients with multiple needs, when continued contact with all agencies is not assured, when agencies such as those that function as part of the criminal justice system may be involved with the client, when more frequent and interventionist management may be required, and when clients are more likely to be at risk of harming themselves or others (1999d: para. 58). Generally, 'Elements of risk and how the care plan manages the identified risk must always be recorded' (1999d: para. 63). The need for joint planning and training of staff was emphasised, together with the development of systems for the sharing of information, and a common approach to risk assessment, which, it was made clear, is 'an essential and on-going part of the CPA process' (1999d: para. 31). Under the old system, the broader Department of Health policy of 'care management', which also entails an individualised approach to the treatment of persons within the NHS generally, ran parallel with the CPA, with the latter seen as 'a specialist variant of care management for people with mental health problems' (DH, 1995: para. 3.2.8).

The CPA was revised again in 2008 (DH, 2008a). The CPA now applies only to patients with 'complex characteristics', which equates with 'enhanced' CPA under the old system. (DH, 2008a: 11 and 13–14, table 2). The intention is to focus inter-agency co-operation more effectively on those who present with needs that require a multi-agency response.

For those removed from the CPA in 2008, or who presented after that date and are not eligible for the CPA, and who need services from only one agency, 'an appropriate professional in that agency' (DH, 2008a: 11) will be responsible for facilitating their care, which will often be that person's GP, if the need is only for medication. Although there need be no formal care plan 'a statement of care agreed with the service user should be recorded. This could be done in any clinical or practice notes, or in a letter, and this documentation will constitute the care plan. It is not necessary to engage in further bureaucracy for these individuals' (DH, 2008a: 11), but there should 'a short central record of essential information' and reviews should take place regularly (DH, 2008a: 11). Those not on the CPA should be given information about services available in crisis situations (DH, 2008a: 15), and as the CPA is not a 'gateway' to other services, and the fact that a person is not on the CPA does not mean that their entitlement to be assessed for and provided with services is lessened in any way (DH, 2008a: 13).

The CPA does not obviate the fact, however, that the various agencies involved in the provision of community care services operate within different statutory frameworks which exhibit differing policy choices, and the interface between the responsibilities of each can be hard to specify. In *R v North and East Devon HA, ex p Coughlan* [2001] QB 213, [2000] WLR 622 [2000] ALL ER 850, the Court of Appeal attempted to specify the border between the responsibilities of NHS bodies (these days, this will usually mean CCGs) and LSSAs with greater clarity. The case concerned the care of C, who had been severely disabled and left with a serious neurological condition following a road traffic accident in 1971. Since that time, she had been resident in accommodation provided by her Health Authority (HA). The HA now wished to close the facility and transfer C to residential accommodation provided by the LSSA.

The case involved several issues, but the pertinent one for the present purposes concerned the question of the financing of C's nursing care in the LSSA-provided facility. If it was to be provided by the HA as 'nursing care' (usually known as 'continuing NHS care' or CHC), then the package of care, including the costs of accommodation in the care home, had to be provided free of charge (under s. 1(4) National Health Service Act 2006), but if it was to be provided by the LSSA, then C was liable to charges (under the terms of the legislation discussed at 3.2.2). The Court of Appeal held that the duty of LSSAs to provide accommodation under s. 21, NAA 1948, because it contemplated that those in need of accommodation by reason of age, illness, or disability, necessarily implied that some nursing care could properly be provided as part of the 'package of care' for which LSSAs are responsible. Such nursing care must be that which is 'provided in connection with the accommodation', as required by s. 21(5) of the NAA 1948.

In C's case, her need for nursing could not be deemed to be part of any 'social care' package, because her disabilities were such that it would not be reasonable for an LSSA to be expected to provide for them. The Court of Appeal held that NHS bodies should develop eligibility criteria to apply to people living in care homes in order to clarify locally the division of responsibility between LSSAs and NHS bodies, which should identify three categories of resident: those with no or low nursing needs, whose care would be provided solely by the LSSA; those whose needs were primarily medical, whose care would be paid for by the NHS, which would also provide the health care components of the overall care package; and those who fell between those two, for whom responsibility would be shared between the LSSA and the NHS (para. 43), but subject to the limitation that such criteria 'cannot place a responsibility on the local authority which goes beyond the terms of section 21' (para. 48). The key point here, however, is that the case shows that inter-agency working has been hindered not only by apathy, or a fear of losing control of local budgets, but also by legal uncertainties.

Consecutive governments since the mid-1990s have attempted to improve co-operation and joint working between LSSAs and NHS bodies (DH, 1995; 1999; 1999e, 2006b), including the introduction of Care Trusts (CTs) by s. 45, Health and Social Care Act 2001, together with the *Care Trusts (Applications and Consultation) Regulations 2001*, SI 2001/3788, which allowed a PCT or NHS trust, already working in tandem with an LSSA, to take over formally the health-related functions of the LSSA if that was likely to promote the effective delivery of those functions by the trust (see *The NHS Bodies and Local Authorities (Partnership Arrangements, Care Trusts, Public Health and Local Healthwatch) Regulations 2012*, SI 2012/3094). By 2013, there were 11 CTs in existence, but from April of that year CTs were abolished, and their functions transferred to local area multi-disciplinary teams, if those CTs had not applied for Foundation Trust status (see Chapter 2, 2.2.1). CTs may have provided examples of best practice, but generally, in terms of working practices, progress towards effective integration was initially patchy. In 2004 the Commission for Health Improvement (CHI) (2004: 15) reported that:

> There are good examples of structural approaches to partnership working with primary care trusts, such as jointly funded posts with responsibilities across primary and secondary

mental health care…There is a range of partnership development between trusts and local authorities…However, there is evidence from one of CHI's investigations to suggest that in some cases, local partnerships have not been sufficiently developed to put these arrangements successfully in place.

Subsequently, efforts to increase co-operation have been renewed. Section 116 of the Local government and Public Involvement in Health Act 2007 imposed an obligation on LSSAs and (now) CCGs to conduct a joint strategic needs assessments for services in their area and Guidance was issued (DH, 2007). The restructuring of the CPA in 2008 was designed to rationalise the system and identify more precisely the target population for inter-agency co-operation in terms of the provision of services.

As far as assessment is concerned, in 2009 (DH, 2009a) the government consulted on proposals to introduce a Common Assessment Framework (CAF) for adults (the CAF for child social service users is well-established), and announced pilot schemes a year later, which ran until 2012. The CAF does not necessarily mean that assessment should always be carried out jointly, but it does mean that information derived from assessments is pooled, which entails technical innovation, in the form of shared databases or systems for the transfer of information from one body to another (in the form of so-called 'CAF messages') and jointly-developed assessment tools, as well as integrated working.

Results from the pilot programme sites indicated that the key to effective co-operation was that the various bodies involved had sufficient levels of trust in each other's ability to generate information in a form that was readily transferable between agencies (meaning that relevant issues are tackled on assessment and information recorded in a form, and using language, comprehensible to those working in different contexts) and that senior staff in each body took responsibility for this (Common Assessment Framework for Adults Network, 2012), which is also the advice given in the implementation framework for the cross-governmental mental health outcomes strategy (HM Government, 2012: 17). At the time of writing the CAF is currently being rolled out, or developed locally. The NHS hosts a website to encourage the pooling and dissemination of information on best practice (see http://www.networks.nhs.uk).

As well as the general duty placed by s. 82 of the NHSA 2006 on health and social service providers to co-operate when performing their functions, s. 76 allows LSSAs to channel funds to CCGs for joint ventures, and s. 75 provides for 'partnership arrangements', under which social service and health bodies may pool resources, staff, and facilities in order to improve the quality of service provision. As seen at Chapter 2, 2.2.6, s. 194 of the Health and Social Care Act 2012 established Health and Wellbeing Boards to foster and oversee joint working locally. Each area should have a joint health and wellbeing strategy (s. 116A, Local Government and Public Involvement in Health Act 2007), and conduct a joint strategic needs assessment, and obligations to co-operate are written into the commissioning obligations of both CCGs (NHS Commissioning Board, 2012a) and LSSAs (DH, 2012e).

Other reforms have helped to clarify with greater precision the allocation of responsibilities between agencies. Section 49 of the Health and Social Care Act 2001 removed the obligation of LSSAs to provide nursing care by a registered nurse: all such nursing is now provided by the NHS free of charge. This partly put into effect the recommendation of the Royal Commission on Long-term Care (1999) to this effect. This lessens the import of the decision of the Court of Appeal in *ex p Coughlan* to a significant extent, although, as the court noted in that case, where the line is to be drawn between 'social care' and 'nursing care' will sometimes be problematic, depending on 'a careful appraisal of the facts of the individual case' (per Lord Woolf MR at para. 30). And it is only nursing care provided by a registered nurse that is to be provided free to LSSA-run care home residents; other nursing remains the responsibility of the LSSA and may still be charged for by a LSSA that provides it. The government has issued guidance as to how CCGs should meet the need for continuing NHS care (DH, 2009a) and how they should assess the needs for nursing care of residents in LSSA accommodation (DH, 2009b).

There is still the potential, and the incentive, for local service providers to construct eligibility criteria that might attract legal challenge, as happened in *R v Bexley NHS Care Trust, ex p Grogan* [2006] EWHC 44. In this case, the High Court found B's eligibility criteria, which assessed clients as being on one or the other side of the line demarcated in *Coughlan* by reference to the nature, complexity, intensity, or unpredictability of their health needs, to be unlawful. This was because the criteria made no mention of the 'primary health need' approach and did not explain the test that was applied to those criteria. The court went on to note that local problems are, at least partly, the consequence of lack of clarity in the guidance issued by the Department of Health following *Coughlan*, in which there seems to be overlap between the factors that point to NHS-provided care and those that point to LSSA-provided care (paras. 63–82: see also *R v South West Strategic Health Authority and North Somerset PCT, ex parte Green* [2008] EWHC 2576 (Admin)).

There can be no doubt, despite such uncertainties remaining, that NHS bodies and LSSAs now function co-operatively with greater efficiency than even 10 years ago. Jointly operated and jointly staffed health and social care teams now operate in many areas of the country. The restructuring of the NHS by the Health and Social Care Act 2012 and of the system for the provision of community care by the draft CSB affords an opportunity to drive these developments further (Kings Fund and Nuffield Trust, 2012). The backdrop to the current reform of the system for inter-agency working also features both the drive towards the 'personalisation' of service delivery, with the focus on the needs of the service user rather than on the duties of commissioners and providers (see 3.6), and reductions in the community care budget (Ham and Smith, 2010; Humphries and Curry, 2011). There are examples of joint working arrangements being severed by local partners unable to agree their various responsibilities (Samuel, 2010). The way in which the interaction of these factors will pan out, following the 'big bang' of restructuring in April 2013, remains to be seen.

3.5.2 Working with housing authorities

According to the LAC 93(10) (DH, 1993): 'no new category of entitlement to housing is created by [NHSCCA] 1990 Act'. The need to consider independent housing had been a feature of the debates about the future direction of community care in the 1980s. But by the time of the Griffiths Report (1988), upon which the subsequent White Paper and the 1990 Act were largely based, the assumption was that the need was for the provision of services to clients already living in their own homes. Although the much-trumpeted intention of the NHSCCA 1990 had been to provide 'the right level of intervention and support to enable people to achieve maximum independence and control over their own lives' (DH, 1990a), LAC(93)10 effectively meant that the role of local housing authorities (LHAs) in the realisation of community care practice would be, at best, marginal. As Cowan (1995a: 216) put it, '[t]his message was crystal clear: either own or occupy your own home or be provided with residential care but do not expect us to provide you with your own independent accommodation'. Contrary to the view expressed in social work theory (see Chapter 2, 2.4.1), the housing elements of the NHSCCA 1990 do not reveal a policy of client empowerment; the point is that this is above and beyond local policies, practices, or failure of communication.

Partly, perhaps in consequence of this, although partly also because of the generic problems facing inter-agency co-operation, discussed in this section, 10 years on from the NHSCCA 1990, whereas LSSAs and NHS bodies had improved joint working, less progress has been made to improve co-operation between LSSAs and LHAs (Social Services Inspectorate and Audit Commission, 2001: 27). The importance of the integration of LSSAs with LHAs was a recurrent theme of the 1999 White Paper (see, for example, DH, 1999a: paras. 2.6, 4.55), but later White Papers, such as *Our Health, Our Care, Our Say: A New Direction for Community Services* (DH, 2006b), although talking in terms of a 'whole system' approach, which acknowledged the need to integrate housing needs into community care provision (DH, 2006b: para. 1.29), and made specific mention of the need to support persons with learning disabilities in 'ordinary housing' (DH, 2006b: para. 4.90), were nonetheless focused very much on the relationship between LSSAs and NHS bodies, and housing needs were lumped together with transport and leisure needs (see for example DH, 2006b: paras. 1.29, 1.45, 2.23, 2.44,and 5.12).

The problem is at least partly legal-structural. As discussed at Ch. 3.3.1, there is no obligation for an LHA to take part in the assessment of a person's needs under s. 47, NHSCCA 1990. If an LHA declines an invitation to assist, it is perfectly possible that an LSSA will nevertheless go on to decide that there is a need for independent housing that it, under the terms of the NAA 1948, cannot supply. Even if an LHA does assist at the stage of need assessment, there is no provision under the NHSCCA 1990 to require it to meet any housing needs that are identified. In sum, this means that for most service users in need of housing, other than residential accommodation, to access provision is through private rental or the general housing legislation. As discussed at 3.1.1.1, the Law Commission (2011: 183, recommendation 70) recommended that there should be a legal duty to co-operate in assessment in place of the current discretionary system. But the Law Commission also recommended that there should be no change to the way in which the dividing line between the responsibilities of LSSAs and NHS bodies, on the one hand, and LHAs, on the other, is currently drawn (2011: 157, recommendation 56). The key provision at the moment is s. 21(8), NAA 1948, which provides that 'Nothing

in this section shall authorise or require a local authority to make any provision authorised or required to be made…by or under any enactment not contained in this Part of
this Act'. This means that those seeking 'ordinary housing' as part of community care
package are required to meet the criteria which apply in housing law in order to be eligible to access housing managed or commissioned by LHAs rather than LSSAs.

Attempts by service users in the 1990s to enlarge the scope of community care in this
regard, by recourse to litigation against LHAs, met with little success, notwithstanding
that 'a person who is vulnerable as a result of mental illness or handicap' is defined as
being in 'priority need' of local authority or social housing (s. 189(1)(c), Housing Act
1996), in which case, the authority 'shall secure that accommodation is available for occupation by the applicant' under s. 193(2) of the same Act. The courts have decided that a
mentally ill or learning disabled person is vulnerable for that reason, when homeless, if
he or she is 'less able to fend for himself than an ordinary homeless person so that injury
or detriment to him will result when a less vulnerable man would be able to cope without
harmful effects' (*R* v *Camden LBC, ex p Pereira* [1998] 31 HLR 317 per Hobhouse LJ at
330; see also *Osmani* v *Camden LBC* [2004] EWCA Civ 1706 and Hunter (2007)).

This test is capable of being applied narrowly, to exclude persons, who are within
the spirit of the legislation, from its protection (see the cases successfully appealed in
Hall and Carter v *Wandsworth LBC* [2004] EWCA Civ 1740). But the main blow came
in the form of restrictions on access to housing, placed on persons in priority need
under what is now s. 189(1)(c) of the Housing Act 1996, by the decision of the House of
Lords in *R* v *Oldham MBC, ex p Garlick; R* v *Tower Hamlets LBC, ex p Ferdous Begum*
[1993] 2 All ER 65 (HL). The latter case on this conjoined appeal, which was heard
before the passage of the Housing Act 1996, although the statutory definition of 'priority need' has not changed, involved an application for council housing made by F, a
learning-disabled woman. This had been rejected by the LHA on the basis, inter alia,
that F lacked the mental capacity to agree to the application that had been made in her
name (the application was for housing for F and her family), or to accept an offer of
housing if one were made.

In the leading opinion on this point, Lord Griffiths confirmed that no duty arose to
provide accommodation unless the applicant, even if both vulnerable and in priority
need, had sufficient mental capacity to agree to the terms of the tenancy, on the basis
that the housing legislation was concerned with housing provision rather than the provision for the severely disabled, which was instead provided under s. 21 of the NAA
1948. As Edmunds aptly summarised in his extended note on the case, 'this significant
and regrettable decision denies people with a mental illness or mental handicap who are
homeless, access in their own right to the complicated network of provisions on local
authority assistance' (1994: 358). This does not mean that all persons who are mentally
disordered will be unable to access entitlement to housing, but it does mean that those
who fail the capacity test (with obscure content), that LHAs are licensed to apply after
Begum, will be excluded. And it is hard to believe that the issue of the resources (in
terms of services provided in the home, that would be required to accommodate many
such persons in 'conventional' housing) was not within the contemplation of Lord

Griffiths in reaching his conclusion on the law (McCabe, 1996), particularly as Lord Slynn dissented, on the basis that there is no reference to a test of capacity on the face of the legislation.

It is an open question whether one or more of the HRA 1998, MCA 2005, or EA 2010, none of which were in existence when this case was decided, has altered this situation. Could it be argued that s. 189(c) of the Housing Act 1996, as interpreted in this case, breaches the Art. 8 ECHR rights of the applicant for accommodation by reason of failing sufficiently to protect the right to home and family life of the applicant? Could it be argued that a person exercising a Lasting Power of Attorney, or a court-appointed deputy, or the Court of Protection itself (or even a person acting under the general authority to act in the best interests of a person lacking capacity) may sign a tenancy agreement on behalf of a person lacking capacity? The only decisions which are expressly prohibited by the MCA 2005 are consent to marriage, civil partnership or divorce or dissolution, or to sexual relations, or to matters concerned with parenting or adoption (s. 27, MCA 2005). It is certainly the case that the steps which the MCA 2005 requires to be taken in order to assist a person of questionable capacity to make their own decision (s. 3(2), MCA 2005 and Department for Constitutional Affairs, 2007, ch. 3) should be taken by LHAs, and the principles in s. 1 of the MCA 2005 must also be observed (see Ch. 4.3).

Alternatively, could it be argued that the decision in *Begum* discriminates against the disabled? Section 33(1) of the EA 2010 provides that a person who has the right to dispose of premises must not discriminate against another either 'as to the terms on which A offers to dispose of the premises to B' (s.33(1)(a)) or 'by not disposing of the premises to B' (s.33(1)(b)), and this does seem at first glance to be indicative that the *Begum* decision should not be allowed to stand today.

Following *Begum*, there were further examples of a failure on the part of the courts to embrace and enforce a notion of joined-up service provision. For example, in *R* v *Brent LBC, ex p Mawcan* (1994) 26 HLR 528 (HC), the court refused to find that it was unreasonable of a LHA to place community care clients in 'bed and breakfast' accommodation, even though concerns have been expressed that such accommodation is unsuitable for mentally disordered persons, risking 'ghettoisation' of mentally disordered persons, because many people are reluctant to share such accommodation with the mentally ill (Jodelet, 1991).

More alarmingly still, in *R* v *Wirral MBC, ex p B* (1994) *The Times*, 3 May (HC), it was held that a LHA was under no duty to contact the local LSSA when contemplating evicting a person known to be in need of community care services. In *Wirral*, B had been evicted from her council property as a result of her awkward and difficult behaviour. She was then held to be intentionally homeless (under what is now Housing Act 1996, s. 191), even though she was acknowledged, by reason of mental illness, to be in priority need. Cowan (1995b) has argued that *Wirral* may be wrongly decided because, in other cases, courts have looked at the background reasons for homelessness when deciding if, in a given case, it can said to be 'intentional'. In *Wirral*, Johnson J held that it is for the client rather than the LHA to contact the local LSSA.

In *North Devon Homes Ltd* v *B* [2003] EWHC 574 (QB); [2003] HLR 59, Steel J accepted a different argument: that the eviction of a mentally ill council tenant on the grounds that her behaviour towards her neighbours, which was indeed offensive, was nevertheless in breach both of s. 22, Disability Discrimination Act 1995 (now EA 2010, s. 33), which prohibits unjustified discrimination against a disabled person (defined to include mental disorder as understood in the MHA 1983) by a landlord, and B's Art. 8 ECHR right to respect for her family life. The decision to evict was held to be unreasonable because B 'cannot help conduct that happens…most if not all of the conduct that is perpetrated is due to her mental problems' (at para. 17), and thus eviction was a response to her disability and hence unlawful.

The same approach was taken by the Court of Appeal in *Lewisham LBC* v *Malcolm* [2007] EWCA Civ 763; [2008] Ch 129, a case in which M, a tenant of the LHA diagnosed as suffering from schizophrenia (although the LHA did not know that), had been given notice to quit his flat because he had sublet it in contravention of his tenancy agreement. M resisted the attempt to evict him, arguing that his breach of his tenancy agreement was caused by his schizophrenia, and that the local authority was consequently in breach of (what is now) s. 35(1)(b) of the EA 2010, which provides that it is unlawful for a person managing premises to discriminate against a disabled person occupying those premises in various ways, one of which is 'by evicting the disabled person'.

The Court of Appeal held that the actions of the LHA amounted to discrimination against M, but on appeal to the House of Lords ([2008] UKHL 43; [2008] 1 AC 1399) that decision was reversed. The House of Lords held that there could be no discrimination because s. 24(1)(a) of the Disability Discrimination Act 1995, which was in force at the time, required that the discrimination be 'for a reason which relates to the disabled person's disability', and as the local authority did not know that M was disabled it could not be suggested that his disability was the reason that he was given notice to quit. The court further held that the appropriate comparator in determining whether a person in M's position had been treated less favourably because of his discrimination is a person without disability who had similarly sublet his or her accommodation in breach of the tenancy agreement. As such a person would also have received notice to quit, there had been no discrimination. In taking this approach, the court overruled earlier case law, in which the appropriate comparator was said to be a person in respect of whom the disability-related reason for the treatment did not apply. Applied to the present case, that would mean a person who had not sublet their accommodation.

The controversial nature of *Malcolm* is illustrated by the finding of Lord Bingham ([2008] UKHL 43 at para. 11), that 'I would accept that, but for his mental illness, Mr Malcolm would probably not have behaved so irresponsibly as to sublet his flat and moved elsewhere.… But Lewisham's reason for seeking possession—that Mr Malcolm had sublet the flat and gone to live elsewhere—was a pure housing management decision which had nothing whatever to do with his mental disability'. In other words, although the court accepted that M's breach of his tenancy agreement was caused by his mental illness, because the local authority's decision was not motivated by it, and because it would have treated a non-disabled person in breach of their tenancy agreement in the same way, there was no discrimination in law. Had the pre-existing test been applied to this fact situation, there would have been a greater chance of a finding in favour of M. It is for this reason that the Equality and Human Rights Commission described this decision as 'worrying' (see http://www.equalityhumanrights.com).

This was also the view of the government, and the EA 2010 responds to the decision in *Malcolm* by adding what is now s. 15 of that Act, which provides that 'A person (A) discriminates against a disabled person (B) if (a) A treats B unfavourably because of something arising in consequence of B's disability, and (b) A cannot show that the treatment is a proportionate means of achieving a legitimate aim'. This provision 'is aimed at re-establishing an appropriate balance between enabling a disabled person to make out a case of experiencing a detriment which arises because of his or her disability, and providing an opportunity for an employer or other person to defend the treatment' (EA 2010, Explanatory Notes: para. 70).

The question now is not whether the allegedly discriminatory action complained of is taken 'for a reason which relates to the disabled person's disability' but rather 'because of something arising in consequence of B's disability', which would include the actions of the appellant in *Malcolm*. On the other side of the equation, if there is unfavourable treatment of a disabled person for this reason, it can nonetheless be justified if reasonable. One element of the decision of the House of Lords in *Malcolm* was not changed by the EA 2010: there can be no claim for discrimination if the LHA did not know that the tenant was disabled (s. 15(2)).

The *Wirral* case underlines the point that patient advocacy (see Chapter 12, 12.9) is vitally important if client empowerment is to develop as fully in practice as it has in various strands of social work theory, just as it underlines the degree to which the law must accept its share of culpability for the 'failure' of care in the community. Decisions such as this buttressed a view amongst LHAs that the onus is primarily on LSSAs acting under the NAA 1948, rather than on LHAs acting under the housing legislation, to deal with mentally disordered persons in need of housing. Conversely, 'LSSAs might also seek to restrict their definitions of the basis that [the Housing Act 1996] should mop up most cases' (Cowan, 1995a: 223). Cowan (1995a) argued that the problem is exacerbated by the failure to integrate the relevant legislation properly. One element of this is that, under the NHSCCA 1990 regime, entitlement is triggered by being 'ordinarily resident' in the LSSA area in question. And this remains the case, despite the ruling in *R v Berkshire CC, ex p P* [1997] 95 LGR 449 (HC) that there is no such limitation of the right to be assessed under s. 47(1), because in the key 'community care service' of residential accommodation under s. 21 of the NAA 1948, the phrase *is* applicable. By contrast, the concept used in the housing legislation is 'local connection', currently contained in s. 199, Housing Act 1996. The two concepts are not coterminous, and the decision about whether an applicant has satisfied the requirement is for the LSSA or LHA respectively. Moreover, s. 198 of the Housing Act 1996 provides that, even if an applicant is in priority need and is not intentionally homeless, an LHA may decline to provide accommodation of any sort, if it is of the view that the applicant does not have a local connection with its area, but does have a local connection with the area of another LHA.

In such circumstances, the duty of the first LHA is only to notify the second one, and the first one need not even offer advice and assistance to the applicants (s. 197, 198(1), Housing Act 1996). In sum, this means that the potential for 'passing the parcel', both as between LSSAs and LHAs, and between different LHAs, is built into the statutory scheme (for an example involving two LHAs 'engaged in a struggle to avoid being fixed with responsibility' for the care of a particularly learning-disabled client with complex needs, described as a 'lamentable state of affairs' by Gibbs J at para. 27, see *RW* v *Sheffield CC* [2005] EWHC 720 (Admin)).

The problems with this situation are twofold: first, there is the potential for a person trying to access residential accommodation to fall between the cracks, with each agency holding the other responsible; second, if the policy behind decarceration and community care is to deinstitutionalise mental health services, the current regime systematically fails, at the level of statutory provision, to permit the realisation of that aim in practice. This is because the legal framework exerts a gravitational pull towards the provision of the community care in care homes. It seems clear that an entitlement to 'ordinary' housing is a prerequisite for any community care policy that has as one of its intentions to reduce the all-too-frequent triadic equation between mental illness, homelessness, and avoidable institutionalisation (Abdul-Hamid and Cooney, 1997).

This type of argument has had some success in litigation. The first relevant decision is that of Moses J in *R* v *Westminster City Council, ex p M, P, A and X* (1997) 1 CCLR 85, who held that 'ordinary' (as opposed to residential) accommodation, rented from a landlord, fell within s. 21 of the NAA 1948. In *R* v *Bristol City Council, ex p Penfold* [1998] COD 210 (QB), before Scott Baker J, an LSSA argued, inter alia, that it could not provide 'ordinary' housing under s. 21 of the NAA 1948. This has certainly been the view that had routinely been taken of the powers in s. 21. The judge rejected this contention, however, holding (at 218) that 'while s. 21(1)(a) is not a basic safety net for everybody, it can in appropriate circumstances extend to the provision of "normal" accommodation', if that is required to meet a need that might otherwise have been met by other community care provisions. There were similar outcomes in *R* v *Wigan MBC, ex p Tammadge* [1998] 1 CCLR 581 and *R* v *Islington LBC, ex p Batantu* (2001) 33 HLR 76 (QB). In all three cases, an LSSA was required by the court to provide suitable 'ordinary' accommodation for a claimant judged to be in need of such.

A dissenting voice was raised by Stanley Burnton J in *R* v *Tower Hamlets LBC, ex p Abdul W* [2002] EWHC Admin 641, on the basis that s. 21(8) of the NAA 1948, which provides that 'Nothing in this section shall authorise or require a local authority to make any provision authorised or required to be made...by or under any enactment not contained in this Part of this Act' precluded the provision of ordinary housing under s. 21. Section 21 should be seen, rather, as 'a safety net provision...to be relied on when all else fails' (para. 28). This was also the right approach in policy terms, because in his view, to hold otherwise would be to create a mechanism to avoid the needs-based system for the allocation of housing that LHAs use. He pointed to evidence given to the court by the local mental health team leader that '[W]'s housing situation is no different from a number of other families in the borough. There are many families in the borough whose unsatisfactory housing impacts adversely on their physical or mental health' (at para. 15).

Despite the reality and legitimacy of these concerns, Stanley Burnton J was overruled by the Court of Appeal ([2002] EWCA Civ 287). Pill LJ pointed out that it has been established, in *R v Southwark LB, ex p K* [2001] EWCA Civ 999, [2001] MHLR 31 (CA), that the need for care and attention is an absolute requirement of eligibility under s. 21 (at para. 20) (see 3.4.1, the leading case is now *R v Slough BC, ex parte M* [2008] 1 WLR 1808). Secondly, he confirmed that, once a duty has been shown to exist because of a need for care and attention, the LSSA might meet that duty as it saw fit, including the provision of 'ordinary' housing (para. 34). Finally, however, he declined to face head-on the argument made on behalf of the LSSA, that, because housing was available (at least in theory) via the housing legislation, W could not be said to be a person in need of accommodation 'which is not otherwise available', as s. 21(1)(a) requires (para. 34).

Hale LJ, giving the other judgment in the Court of Appeal, held that Stanley Burnton's J's analysis of the scope of s. 21 may well have been correct as a matter of historical record. There was substantial reason to think that the original intention behind s. 21(1) was that it should be limited to residential home accommodation, but she went on to say that 'Whatever the words "residential accommodation" may have meant in 1948 ... they are a good example of language which is "always speaking" and can change its meaning in the light of changing social conditions' (at para. 31). As such, it was proper to conclude that, in principle, if the provision of 'ordinary' housing was required as part of a package to meet a client's need for care and attention, it could lawfully be provided under s. 21(1), and s. 21(8) must be read to be compatible with that. Hale LJ did not analyse the import of the words 'not otherwise available' in s. 21(1)(a), but the necessary implication of her judgment, and that of Pill LJ, is that these words should *not* be read to mean that housing cannot be provided under the NAA 1948 because it is dealt with, and hence, in some sense, 'otherwise available' through the housing legislation.

On the other hand, it cannot be assumed that, because there is a need for 'ordinary' housing or rehousing, the duty under s. 21 is triggered (Hale LJ at para. 32). That is dependent upon the presence of an unmet need for care and attention, and 'Ordinary housing is not "care and attention". It is simply the means whereby the necessary care and attention can be made available if otherwise it will not' (para. 32). Hale LJ went on to emphasise that s. 21(8) will ordinarily prohibit the provision of 'ordinary' housing under s. 21, by reason of the fact that there is already a power to meet housing needs through the housing legislation (para. 34); s. 21 reaches only so far as the needs of the applicant, and not to other members of his or her family (para. 34). The needs of children are to be met through the powers available in the Children Act 1989 and should not enter the equation under s. 21 (para. 34), and, if there is a power (not a duty) to provide accommodation for the children of an applicant under s. 21, 'it is not an entitlement or enforceable expectation' (Carnwath LJ in *R v Haringey LBC, ex p O* [2004] EWCA Civ 535 at para. 42).

These dicta were applied in *R v Southwark LBC, ex p Mooney* [2006] EWHC 1912, Jackson J holding that no duty under s. 21 had come into existence in the case of an applicant, M, living in accommodation unsuitable for her because of physical disability, along with her three minor children, two of whom had learning difficulties and emotional and developmental problems. The LSSA had accepted, following an assessment of M's needs, that her current accommodation was unsuitable, and the LHA had accepted her as being in priority need under the terms of the housing legislation. M nevertheless sought judicial review on the basis that the LSSA was in breach of its duty under s. 21 to provide her with suitable accommodation. Jackson J held that no such duty had come into existence, there being 'a substantial gap between establishing a need for housing and triggering a duty under s. 21(1) of the 1948 Act' (para. 51).

Although both *Tammadge* and *Batantu* were distinguished by Jackson J (para. 59), in truth, the difference between this case and those is slight, and the *Tower Hamlets* case should be seen the high-water mark for the development of s. 21 of the NAA 1948 as a mechanism to circumvent the housing legislation and the waiting lists that characterise its functioning. The key distinction is whether a need for accommodation is severable from a need for care and attention, but that is a question capable of being answered differently by different LSSAs. Nevertheless, the case law has now established that it is not permissible to adopt a broad interpretation of 'otherwise available'. It is no longer legitimate for an LSSA to take the view that, as well as housing provided by local authorities, there is always property available to rent through the private sector and so property in the form of 'ordinary housing' will always be 'available'. Such a reading would, of course, totally defeat the intention of s. 21, and it is much better to interpret that phrase narrowly and pragmatically, as being satisfied if the particular client has no other means of securing required accommodation. This reading does not endorse queue jumping; rather, it gives LSSAs to discretion to respond creatively to the identified needs of service users, and is very much in line with the current policy of lessening the reliance on residential accommodation.

The decision in *Tower Hamlets* was followed by the Court of Appeal in *Moore v Care Standards Tribunal* [2005] EWCA Civ 627, [2005] 1 WLR 2979. In this case a charity, F, provided care-home accommodation. F then devolved the provision of accommodation to H, a second charity but one that functioned together with F as part of the same organisation, with F continuing to provide the care. F sought to have a number of its homes deregistered on the basis that it had issued the occupants with assured tenancies, such that they were now tenants of their own 'ordinary' accommodation and so the accommodation in question no longer amounted to a care home, because no care was provided by the lessor, H. If the homes in question were now to be regarded as 'ordinary' accommodation, the residents were no longer in residential accommodation and therefore could claim state benefits including welfare benefits and housing benefits. This would save the accommodation provider a considerable sum, because rent was now being paid by the tenants for the accommodation. The Court of Appeal (Sir William Aldous at para. 21) held that:

> the intention of the legislature was to include within the Act a range of models of care facilities, but I can see no reason why an establishment cannot provide accommodation within

the meaning of that word in section 3 of the [Care Standards Act] 2000 whether or not the accommodation provided is by lease or licence. The crucial consideration is whether the establishment provides the accommodation together with nursing or personal care…The establishment of a lessor and lessee relationship can be an indicator of a situation where an establishment does not provide both the accommodation and the care, but cannot be determinative.

This is an important decision that both challenges care home providers to maximise the possibility for residents to be supported in independent living, and has considerable financial implications for providers, residents, and the Treasury.

To be given full effect, however, the decision in *ex p Ferdous Begum* also needs to be reviewed. As mentioned, it may be that the tools with which to do this are already at hand, in the form of some combination of human rights, capacity, and/or discrimination law. The Court of Appeal in *Tower Hamlets* emphasised that it should be the LSSA rather than a court that decides what needs are present and how they should be met (see Pill LJ at para. 23; Hale LJ at para. 33). And it is perfectly possible that an LSSA might conclude that the needs of a particular client, who lacks capacity, are best met by the provision of ordinary housing and the delivery of various services to the client in that housing. Unfortunately, the decision in *ex p Ferdous Begum* seems to prevent an LSSA from doing just that.

3.6 Personal budgets and direct payments

The model of community care reflected in the current law is essentially one in which an LSSA or an NHS body meets eligible needs through the provision of services to passive recipients of care. This reflects the sensibilities and assumptions that were prevalent at the start of the modern welfare state in the 1940s, which by the consumerist-oriented 1990s were seen as increasingly outdated. The Community Care (Direct Payments) Act 1996 gave LSSAs a power to provide funds directly to certain classes of service user, including mentally ill persons, who would then purchase their own care (Spandler and Vick, 2005; 2006). The Health and Social Care Act 2001 (HSCA 2001) repealed the 1996 Act and introduced a broader scheme, which is still current.

In this scheme—certainly as it has been implemented in recent years, and more so when the draft CSB is passed into law—the key concept is that of the 'personal budget': a sum of money dedicated to the care of a person in need of services. This may or may not be managed through direct payments to the person in need. Underwriting these developments, or running alongside them, is the emergence and rapid growth in influence of the theory of 'personalisation' in social work theory (see Glasby and Rosemary Littlechild, 2009; National Mental Health Development Unit, 2010; Centre for Policy on Ageing Information Service, 2013, for an overview of the literature), which holds, essentially but loosely, that services should be bespoke as far as possible, determined by the needs of the user rather than by the structures of government—divided as between health and social care, for example.

The basic idea in the HSCA 2001 scheme, as before, is that if, following an assessment under s. 47 of the NHSCCA 1990, it is determined that a person is in need of services which may be provided under s. 46 of that Act, then the LSSA *must* make direct payments to or in respect of that person (regs. 7(1)(c), 8(4)(c), *The Community Care, Services for Carers and Children's Services (Direct Payments) (England) Regulations 2009*, SI 2009/1887) subject to various requirements including the need for consent, either of the person in need or some other person (as explained in this section). Although services in the form of residential accommodation may be the subject of direct payments, such care cannot be funded in this way for a period of more than four weeks in any 12 months (reg. 13(1), 2009 Regs), which means that only short-term residential care can be funded in this way, although in the 2012 White Paper *Caring for our future: reforming care and support* (HM Government, 2012) it was announced that the government intends to trial the use of direct payments to fund long-term residential care (HM Government, 2012: 12) and the draft CSB (discussed further elsewhere in this section) contains provision to make direct payments available for all service users, including those in long-term residential accommodation (see cl. 24(1)(e) of the draft CSB).

There is, in addition, a discretion for LSSAs to provide direct payments for a wide array of services, including those provided to a person subject to a guardianship order, or on leave of absence from hospital under s. 17, MHA 1983 (see Chapter 10, 10.2), or in order to comply with conditions imposed on a person subject to a Community Treatment Order under s. 17B of the MHA 1983 (see Chapter 10, 10.4), or as part of a supervision order made under the Criminal Procedure (Insanity) Act 1964 (see Chapter 8, 8.2.3.4), or as part of a community treatment order by a court under s. 177, 189 and 207, Criminal Justice Act 2003, or in a number of further criminal justice contexts (2009 Regs, regs. 7(1)(a), 8(4)(a), and Sch. 2). Direct payments may also be made in respect of persons subject to a restriction order who have been conditionally discharged from hospital by a tribunal or the Justice Secretary (regs. 7(1)(b), 8(4)(b)). There is also provision to make direct payments of sums to which a carer is entitled under s. 2, Carers and Disabled Children Act 2000, to the carer of a person in need under s. 57(2)(b).

Before making any direct payment, the LSSA must be satisfied that the recipient's need for the relevant service can be appropriately met by way of direct payments (2009 Regs, reg. 7(2)). Direct payments may be made either to a person with eligible needs in lieu of service provision, as long as that person consents (HSCA 2001, s. 57(1)) and it appears to the LSSA that he or she is 'capable of managing a direct payment by themselves or with such assistance as may be available to them' (2009 Regs, reg. 2), or to another 'suitable person' (HSCA 2001, s. 57(1A)). A 'suitable person' may be an individual or an organisation (s. 57(1C)), and it is open to an LSSA to appoint itself, or one of its employees, which is in fact commonly done (see further discussion elsewhere in this section). Before an LSSA can accept that a person is suitable, it must consult with any person named by the person in need, that person's carers or anyone interested in his or her welfare, and any representative or surrogate, and must also considers the past and present wishes of the person in need, their values and beliefs, and any other relevant factors, and conduct a Criminal Records Bureau check on that person (reg. 8(2), 2009 Regs) unless the person whose suitability is being assessed is a close relative of the person in need (defined in reg. 8(3)).

Payment should be to a suitable person rather than the person in need if the latter lacks capacity to consent to receipt of direct payments, decided by reference to the test of capacity in the MCA 2005 (s. 57(5A)), although the person in need must consent to the funds being given to that other person (s. 57(1B)(a)), as must a 'surrogate' of the person in need (s. 57(1B)(b)). In addition, a 'suitable person' must, if there is such a person, be a 'representative' of the person in need (s. 57(1C)(a)), defined by s. 57(5B) and reg. 5, 2009 Regs to comprise a deputy appointed for the person in need by the Court of Protection under s. 16(2)(b) of the MCA 2005 or a donee of a lasting power of attorney within the meaning of s. 9 of the 2005 Act created by the person in need.

If there is no representative the funds can be paid to some other person, but only if both the LSSA and any 'surrogate' of the person in need consider that third party to be suitable (s. 57(1C)(b)) and the surrogate gives consent (s. 57(1B)(b)). A 'surrogate' is defined by s. 57(5B) to comprise, again, a court-appointed deputy or a donee of a lasting power of attorney created by the person in need, but only if the powers of that person 'consist of or include such powers as may be prescribed', which means the power to make decisions relevant to the receipt by the person in need of community care services as defined in s. 46 of the NHSCCA 1990, following as assessment under s. 47 of that Act (s. 57(5C) and 2009 Regs, reg. 6). If there is no representative or surrogate, the funds can be paid to another person judged suitable by the LSSA (s. 57(1C)(c)).

The 2009 Regulations also make provision regarding the amount which is payable and the extent to which the means of the person in need may be taken into account (see regs. 9 and 10). Payment may be of the total cost of care, but if the person in need has the means to contribute this may be subject to a condition that a specified sum is reimbursed to the LSSA by that person. Alternatively, payments may be reduced to take into account that the person in need has the means to make a contribution (regs. 3(3)(b), 4, 5), but in any case, the payments should be 'made at such a rate as the authority estimate to be equivalent to the reasonable cost of securing the provision of the service concerned' (HSCA 2001, s. 57(4)(a)). Payments may range from a few hundred to several thousand pounds, and in some cases (*R* v *Cambridgeshire County Council, ex parte KM* [2012] UKSC 23 providing an example), many tens of thousands of pounds per annum, with around one in five being for less than £1,000 and a third being for more than £10,000 in 2011–12 (Association of Directors of Adult Social Services, 2012: 2).

The guidance published in 2009 (DH, 2009) approves the use of models for the computation of approximate costs, whereby points are allocated to various needs and levels of need. These are often described as Resource Allocation Systems (RASs) (DH, 2009: para. 113), and although useful, only give an approximate level of cost, and so RASs should be 'sufficiently flexible to allow someone's individual circumstances to be taken into account' (DH, 2009: para. 113) A challenge to the legality of using an RAS to compute costs was rejected by the Court of Appeal in *R* v *RB Kensington and Chelsea, ex parte Savva* [2010] EWCA Civ 1209, on the basis that the RAS in that case 'was not used as anything other than a starting point or indicative allocation' (para. 18 per Maurice Kay LJ). In *R v Cambridgeshire County Council, ex parte KM* [2012] UKSC 23 Lord Wilson held that 'What is crucial is that, once the starting-point (or indicative sum) has finally been identified, the requisite services in the particular case should be costed in a reasonable degree of detail', and this should preferably be done 'in conjunction with the service-user' (para. 28), and be written up into a 'support plan' (para. 28) from which the person in need can ascertain the services to be commissioned by him or her and the cost of so doing.

Lord Wilson further held (para. 23) that the use of direct payments as a way to meet care needs made it appropriate to add a fourth question to the three which he had identified from his reading of the decision of the House of Lords in *Barry* (see 3.3.1.2):

> (iv) What is the reasonable cost of securing provision of the services which have been identified at (iii) as being those for the provision of which it is necessary for the [LSSA] to make arrangements?

It is at this fourth stage that an RAS is relevant (para. 24), but it is clear that this operates within the same caveat which Lord Wilson had held applies at the third stage (see 3.3.1.2), which is to say, although the most efficient way to meet the duty to provide services can be pursued by the LSSA, at this stage, as at stage (iii), the duty to meet the identified eligible needs is absolute and resource limitations may not be used by an LSSA as a justification for not meeting those needs in full (see para. 21).

Personal budgets have proven popular with many service users (Hatton and Waters, 2011; ADASS, 2011) and in 2010, the Department of Health (DH, 2010b: para. 4.9) announced its intention that all those in receipt of non-residential community care services should be in receipt of direct payments by April 2013. A survey carried out on behalf of the Association of Directors of Adult Social Services (ADASS) reported (ADASS, 2012: 1) that although the total number of personal budgets delivered by LSSAs in 2011–12 was 432,349, an increase of 38 per cent from 2010–11, this constituted only 52 per cent of all those eligible for direct payments. Moreover, over half of those having care provided by way of a personal budget were not themselves in receipt of payments from LSSAs. Rather, LSSAs managed the budget on behalf of the person in need, raising suspicions that the pursuit of the 100 per cent target was prompting some LSSAs to comply with the letter but not the spirit of personal budgets, and merely allocate a person in need with a personal budget although the LSSA would continue, as before, to use that money to purchase services (sometimes from itself) for the person in need. ADASS (2012a: 7) criticised the 100 per cent target because attempts to meet it were putting LSSAs in confrontation with, in particular, older service users who were generally more resistant to managing their own needs, but the 100 per cent target was confirmed when the White Paper on social care (HM Government, 2012a: 54) was published in June 2012. Finally, however, in October 2012, the government reviewed its April 2013 target down to 70 per cent all of cases by that date.

Be that as it may, it is clear that the use of personal budgets and direct payments has become established as part of the landscape of funding and service delivery for non-residential care, accounting for 15 per cent (£2.6 billion) of the total social care budget in 2011–12 (ADASS, 2012: 2). The draft CSB contains provision that all care and support plans (which is how the Bill describes what are currently known as care plans) must include the personal budget (defined in cl. 25) for the person in need (cl. 24(1)(e)), and where the personal budget is to be met by direct payments, the plan must also include information about the amount and frequency of those payments (cl. 24(2)(c)). Direct payments must be used to fund care at the request of the person in need (cl.29) or an authorised person (cl. 30) (this being more or less the same as a 'suitable person' under the HSCA 2001: see cl. 29(4)).

Direct payments were made available in lieu of health-care service provision by NHS bodies by the Health Act 2009, which added new sections 12A–12D to the NHSA 2006. Under these provisions, the Secretary of State, NHSCB, a CCG or an LSSA may make direct payments to a patient or a patient's nominee (NHSCCA 1990, s. 12A(1)), which can include payments in relation to after-care under s. 117 of the MHA 1983 (NHSCCA 1990, s. 12A(4)). The provision of direct payments is subject to Regulations made by the Secretary of State (s. 12B and *The National Health Service (Direct Payments) Regulations 2010*, SI 2010/100), which are similar in content to the 2009 Regulations which apply to the more well-established system for direct payments in community care. To April 2013, direct payments have being trialled in around 60 pilot schemes, provided for by s.12C and reg. 2 of the 2010 Regs, but the government's intention is to roll out direct payments more broadly for patients with long-term conditions (DH, 2013a: para. 10). In early 2013 it consulted (DH, 2013a) on how this might be achieved, and new Regulations are likely to be published by summer 2013.

There is little doubt that one driver of the emergence of direct payments and the concept of the personal budget is, for want of a better word, an ideology, of individualism. *A Vision for Adult Social Care* (DH, 2010b) states that the government's agenda is galvanised by three values: freedom, fairness, and responsibility. As to the first of these, the document states that 'We want people to have the freedom to choose the services that are right for them from a vibrant plural market' (DH, 2010b: 5). This is of course all very well, but the idea that some of the most vulnerable people in society can or do share this vision as it applies to the provision of community care services is debatable. Moreover, to the extent that direct payments can increase the experience of freedom for persons in need, there is some evidence that this risks a diminution of the freedom of those employed to provide care under direct payment arrangements (Leece and Peace, 2010).

Needham (2011) argues that personalisation has been promulgated as a narrative of the development of social services (a shift from the bad old days of centralisation and provider-led decision-making to the new age of freedom of choice) which has obscured questions about the appropriate scope of personalisation. A report commissioned by the think-tank DEMOS (Wood, 2011) highlighted the risk that those with complex needs may not always be best served by the personal budget/direct payment model of service funding; that having a personal budget was not the priority for most people in need of services; and that personal budgets are undermined by lack of adequate funding, and by inadequate integration of health and social care.

Personal budgets have had considerable beneficial impact for some service users, and the availability of direct payments is in principle a good thing, as much of the debate accepts (see Centre for Ageing, 2013); but they cannot solve these other, broader, issues around the funding and provision of care, and if the growth in the use of personal budgets continues to outstrip the use of direct payments, so that LSSAs still in fact buy the services the person in need is eligible for, and the only difference is that they now do so in the name of that person rather than in their own name, it is legitimate to wonder to what extent we are witnessing a change of substance or merely a sleight of hand which seeks to disguise funding shortfalls (Roulstone and Morgan, 2009; Glendenning, 2008; Sang, 2009).

3.7 Concluding comments

The claim of the Labour administration of the late 1990s, that 'community care has failed' (DH, 1998) is, in many ways, no longer accurate. For most of the time, LSSAs and NHS bodies do co-operate at least reasonably effectively in the delivery of community care services, particularly for service users with learning disabilities. There are many more structural mechanisms in place to achieve integrated working than was the case at the start of this century. The draft CSB holds the potential to radically simplify the legal framework in which community care services are delivered, making the system more transparent and intelligible to users and professionals alike. The greater use of personal budgets and direct payments has the potential to empower service users in a way that has not been possible in the past.

At the same time, there is little attempt currently to integrate legal regimes or working practices as between LSSAs and LHAs to any greater extent than at present, which means that some people will continue to fall between the cracks between the two systems. Moreover, reforms of law, policy, and practice cannot abolish what might be described as 'the politics of need' and the related, ever-present issue of resources. In the current economic climate, as the case law reveals, LSSAs have been reducing the availability of services through the restructuring of eligibility criteria and/or charging policies, often determining that only 'critical' risks can be met within existing budgets. The proposals made by the Dilnot Commission (see Chapter 2, 2.4.2) may make the system more equitable for users, even in the modified form preferred by the government, but the final decision as to gross expenditure on community care is with the government of the day, which must balance this against other calls on the public purse. And even the most generous and committed government would not be able to fund community care services to the extent that all identified needs are met. The upshot of this is that litigation generated by financial limitations is likely to continue, involving both service users seeking to access the care they need and care home proprietors and other providers of care seeking to ensure reasonable and viable levels of reimbursement for their services from LSSAs seeking to maximise the purchasing power of their limited resources. Indeed, as the HSCA 2012 encourages even greater involvement of the independent sector in both social care and health, it not unlikely that the amount of litigation will increase.

Finally, we would note that good intentions do not always translate into law and practice. The justification, laid out at 3.1, for reforming the law in 2012 sounds remarkably similar to the sort of things that were being said at the time that the NHSCCA 1990 was being introduced. That, too, sought to bring into being a system of care in the community that was 'much more user driven rather than fitting clients into existing services' (Lord Henley, Under-Secretary of State for the Department of Social Security, Hansard, HL, Vol. 520, Col. 645); and sought to 'ensure that a seamless community care service is available which covers both health and social needs' (Baroness Blatch, Hansard, HL, Vol. 518, Cols. 1537–38). We agree that the current proposals are more likely to achieve these goals than was (and is) the NHSCCA 1990. But revisiting such comments over two decades later is a salutary reminder that legal reform may not always achieve its intended outcomes.

4

The Mental Capacity Act 2005

4.1 Introduction

As we have seen in Chapter 3, it is no longer appropriate (if it ever was) to think of the lives of people with mental disabilities as restricted to hospital care. While certainly many (but by no means all) people with mental disabilities will spend some time in hospital environments, the vast majority will spend considerable periods of time—often virtually all their lives—living in the community. Similarly in hospital, patients continue to have any rights not expressly removed by statute. For example, informal patients, even those admitted to hospital because of mental illnesses or disabilities, continue to have the right to consent to or refuse medical treatment: consent rights are curtailed only if a patient is formally detained under the MHA, and then only for treatments for mental disorder (see further Chapter 9). Otherwise, the individual continues to have the right to decide.

While mental health legislation in the last hundred years has developed some mechanisms to control some of these decisions in specific circumstances (including, controversially and most recently, community treatment orders: see Chapter 10, 10.4), the traditional legal threshold for legal intervention beyond the MHA 1983 is capacity: if an individual has the mental capacity to make a decision, he or she is permitted to make it and is responsible for its consequences.

Capacity is a problematic topic for a book such as this. It cannot be omitted, since it so heavily overlaps, or is perceived so heavily to overlap, with the lives of the people with mental health problems; yet at the same time, it also concerns people who are not mentally ill in the conventional sense. Thus a person affected by a severe stroke may lack mental capacity for a variety of decisions (see, for example, *Re S (Hospital Patient: Court's Jurisdiction)* [1995] 3 All ER 290 (CA)). While we would not expect such a person to be within the purview of mental health law as understood in the rest of this book, he or she is within the scope of the current statutory structure relating to incapacity, the Mental Capacity Act (MCA) 2005. Equally, mental disorder alone does not necessarily render an individual incapable of making decisions. The empirical studies show that even when their disorder is sufficiently severe as to warrant hospitalisation, only a minority of people with mental illness lack capacity to consent to treatment (see Okai, 2007; Cairns, 2005). People with mental disabilities, like all other adults, are presumed to have capacity until the contrary is shown (MCA 2005, s 1(2); *Re C*

(Adult: Refusal of Medical Treatment),[1994] 1 All ER 819 at p. 824; *Masterman-Lister* v *Brutton and Co., Jewell and Home Counties Dairies* [2002] EWCA Civ 1889); and people with mental disabilities, like everyone else, will fall within the powers of the MCA 2005 only if they lack capacity. Precisely what 'lacking capacity' means will be discussed at 4.4,; for the purposes of a general understanding of this introduction, it can be taken to mean that an individual is unable to understand the information relevant to the decision at issue or to appreciate the consequences of deciding one way or another.

4.1.1 The background to the Mental Capacity Act 2005

Some understanding of the legislative history will be helpful in understanding the MCA 2005. Until 1959, the Royal Prerogative power had allowed declarations to be made that an individual lacked capacity in either personal matters or matters of 'property and affairs' (essentially, financial, property, and business matters). These powers were medieval in origin, but subject to considerable statutory regulation commencing in the nineteenth century. The precise effects of a declaration of capacity in either of the personal or property and affairs spheres varied somewhat over time, but by the early twentieth century, a declaration of incapacity removed the individual's right to make decisions in that entire sphere: a decision that the individual lacked capacity for property and affairs meant that all contracts entered into by that individual were void, whether the other party to the contract knew of the incapacity or not: *Re Walker* [1905] 1 Ch 160. Decisions regarding the individual would be taken by a guardian appointed by the court.

The Royal Prerogative (also called the issuance of a 'Commission in Lunacy') therefore gave courts considerable power over persons lacking capacity, but it took effect only if a formal order was made following an application and court hearing, and of course not all persons of doubtful capacity were brought before the courts under this process. The common law therefore developed a range of additional approaches to capacity in individual contexts as they came before the courts. For example, a contract by someone not subject to the Royal Prerogative power would be invalid only if the party lacked capacity and also the other party to the contract knew or ought reasonably to have known of this incapacity: *Imperial Loan Company* v *Stone* [1892] 1 QB 599. The legal tests of capacity also varied in these specific contexts. In contract law, for example, the tests of incapacity were left general, requiring 'such a degree of incapacity as would interfere with the capacity of the defendant to understand substantially the nature and effect of the transaction into which she was entering' (*Manches* v *Trimborn* (1946) 174 LT 344 at 345). This test left considerable latitude to triers of fact in individual cases. For contracts of marriage, to be discussed in greater detail at 4.4.3 significantly more guidance was provided as to what would constitute an adequate understanding of 'the responsibilities normally attaching to marriage' (*In the Estate of Park,* [1954] P 89 at p. 127; see also *Durham* v *Durham* (1885) 10 P 80, *Bennett* v *Bennett* [1969] 1 WLR 431 at 433, *Sheffield City Council* v *E* [2004] EWHC 2808). For wills, the requirement was 'that a testator shall understand the nature of the act and its effects; shall understand the extent of the property of which he is disposing; shall be able to comprehend and appreciate the claims to which he ought to give effect' (*Banks* v *Goodfellow* (1870) 5 QB 549 at 565), suggesting a more overtly moral overtone to the capacity determination than is evident for other contracts. These are examples, and there are as many variations as there are legal contexts in which incapacity could arise. These distinct legal precedents for mental capacity determination continue to exist and develop in their specific contexts.

While common law in its specific contexts has continued to develop incrementally and uninterrupted, the Royal Prerogative powers were abolished by the MHA 1959. Matters concerning property and affairs continued to be dealt with on the basis of capacity, much as had been the case previously. The system was placed on a less formal bureaucratic level, administered by the 'Court of Protection'—not a traditional court at that time, but an administrative office headed not by a judge, but by a Master. Still, capacity determination in this sphere was an all or nothing affair. Either the individual had capacity to make all property-related decisions or none. As this sphere included, for example, all dealings with real and personal property, all business affairs, all contracts, and the right to retain and instruct lawyers, it remained a very wide-ranging and non-nuanced power. These powers were re-enacted as Part VII of the MHA 1983, and remained until the MCA 2005 took effect in 2007.

Originally, there was little scope for advanced planning in anticipation of incapacity. This changed somewhat with the passage of the Enduring Powers of Attorney Act (EPAA) 1985. Previously, a power of attorney was deemed to be revoked when its donor lost capacity. The EPAA 1985 allowed an individual when competent to sign a power of attorney that would continue in effect when the person ceased to have capacity, effectively allowing the individual to select who would control their assets following the donor's incapacity. These provisions applied to matters of property and affairs only however, not to decisions relating to personal welfare; and until the MCA 2005, there was no mechanism by which an individual could determine in advance who would make personal decisions about them if they lost capacity.

The MHA 1959 dealt with personal welfare decisions very differently. It abolished the old Royal Prerogative power, which had in practice not been much used for personal decision-making anyway. Instead it introduced a new set of 'guardianship' provisions (see further Chapter 10, 10.3). Notwithstanding the label that attached to them ('guardianship' is traditionally associated with the care of people lacking capacity or children), these were not capacity-based, but instead grew out of the statutory supervision provisions of the Mental Deficiency Acts 1913, 1926, and 1939. The new powers allowed the appointment of a guardian when a person was suffering from a mental disorder (subject to some further definition) of sufficient severity, and when the appointment was warranted 'in the interests of the patient or for the protection of other persons' (MHA 1959, s. 33(2)). Incapacity thus did not need to be shown. Such guardianship gave the guardian powers over the individual equivalent to those of a father over a child under the age of 14 (MHA 1959, s. 34(1))—essentially, complete control over the individual's life. In 1983, these broad powers were reduced: the guardian could now only require the individual to reside at a specific place (but not detain him or her there), to attend at specific places for treatment, education, occupation, or training (but not to consent to treatment on the individual's behalf), and to require that doctors and specified social care professionals would have access to the individual (MHA 1983, s. 8(1)). The MHA 1983 further changed the relevant prerequisites relating to mental disorder, so that people with most learning disabilities (or 'mental impairments', to use the language of the Act) could only be made subject to guardianship if their condition resulted in 'abnormally aggressive or seriously irresponsible conduct', a requirement that continues in s. 1(2A) of the MHA 1983.

The limitations to MHA guardianship introduced in 1983 were perceived as leaving a lack of clarity as to how decisions could be taken relating to vulnerable people who could not be made subject to guardianship, or which the restricted powers of guardianship would no longer cover. How, for example, would consent to medical treatment be obtained, as this was now expressly outside the MHA guardianship regime? In response, the Law Commission began a project to investigate decision-making for people lacking capacity in 1989, eventually reporting in 1995 (Law Commission, 1995). The Commission proposed a comprehensive statute in the area, including formalising appointment of substitute decision-makers, codifying a test of incapacity and of best interests, providing a set of standards and processes regarding medical research when subjects lack capacity, codifying advance treatment refusals, and providing an enhanced Court of Protection to oversee the new law. The Commission's work and proposals received broadly, although not universally, favourable responses (Carson, 1993; Gunn, 1994; Fennell, 1994, 1995; Freeman, 1994; Parkin, 1996; Bartlett, 1997). Nonetheless, legislative progress was slow, and at times it appeared the project had been abandoned by the government. The MCA was not actually passed into law until 2005, eventually taking effect in 2007.

In the interim, the courts had gone a long way to establishing a prospective declaratory jurisdiction relating to incapacity, which has been named the 'inherent jurisdiction'. In practice, this corresponded broadly to the old Royal Prerogative power, although it was rather different in terms of constitutional theory. By the time the MCA 2005 was passed, the courts had developed powers to make declarations relating to incapacity, and to make binding orders as to what was in the best interests of a person lacking capacity (*Re TF (An Adult: Residence)* [2000] 1 MHLR 120). They had developed jurisprudence as to how incapacity and best interests were to be determined (e.g., *Re A (Male Sterilisation)* [2000] 1 FLR 549, *Newham London Borough Council* v *S and Another (Adult: court's jurisdiction)* [2003] EWHC 1909 (Fam)). They had decreed that the common law allowed acts to be done in the best interests of a person lacking capacity, generally without further authorisation or consent being required (beginning with *Re F (Mental Patient: Sterilisation)* [1990] 2 AC 1), and had found jurisdiction to appoint substitute decision-makers for people lacking capacity (*Re S (Adult Patient) (Inherent Jurisdiction: Family Life)* [2002] EWHC 2278, [2003] 1 FLR 292). Necessary force could be used to ensure that the best interests were achieved (*Norfolk* v *Norwich Healthcare (NHS) Trust* [1996] 2 FLR 613; *TF (Adult: Residence)* [2000] 1 MHLR 120, para 47, per Sedley LJ).

In a sense, it is difficult to fault the judicial activism in this area. At the time, it appeared that the legislature had abandoned any statutory development in the area, and the pragmatic question of how decisions ought to be made for people lacking capacity was perceived as real and pressing. At the same time, the development of the new common law jurisdiction involved doubtful jurisprudence and significant bending of the relevant law (see Bartlett, 2007: ch. 2). Further, the effective recreation of powers expressly abolished by Parliament does raise constitutional questions: in a democracy, even if Parliament gets a decision wrong (as it may or may not have done in this case), is really for the courts to 'correct' Parliament's presumed mistakes?

The MCA 2005 was designed to work in tandem with the common law: incapacity would be determined according to common law standards; the MCA 2005 would provide a mechanism to allow decisions to be made for people who lacked capacity according to the MCA 2005 definitions. Thus for example the probate courts have continued to make decisions about capacity to make a will according to common law standards and without expressly applying the MCA 2005: see *Scammell* v *Farmer* [2008] EWHC 1100 (Ch), *Re Ritchie* [2009] EWHC 709 (Ch), *Carr* v *Thomas* [2008] EWHC 2859 (Ch). Consistent with this, the Court of Protection (whose job it is to interpret the MCA 2005) has taken the position that it does not have jurisdiction to determine whether an existing will is valid: that is the job of the probate court. It can instead determine whether an individual currently lacks capacity and whether a will should be drafted by the court on his or her behalf (a power under the MCA 2005: see s. 18(1)(i)): *Re D (Statutory Will)* [2010] EWHC 2159 (COP). Within the scope of MCA 2005, the MCA definitions apply. Thus whether the individual lacks capacity for purposes of determining whether a will is to be drafted for him or her (an MCA power) will be determined with reference to the definitions contained in the MCA 2005, not the common law. It was hoped that the various common law standards would over time develop towards the MCA standards, so that inconsistencies would be minimised.

This approach was adopted early on in the planning of the MCA 2005, before the development of the inherent jurisdiction by the courts. The inherent jurisdiction raises particular questions, since that jurisdiction so extensively overlaps with the MCA 2005, but not necessarily with the same definitions and substantive and procedural safeguards as the MCA 2005. Consistent with the view that the MCA 2005 did not abolish common law, but was intended to exist alongside it, the courts have held that the inherent jurisdiction continues to exist (see. e.g. *LBL* v *RYJ* [2010] EWHC 2665 (COP) at 62; *X County Council* v *AA* [2012] EWHC 2183 (COP)). Quite how these two regimes will coexist remains to be seen, and the case law is as yet not entirely clear or consistent. There is a significant risk that the inherent jurisdiction will circumvent some of the more nuanced provisions of the MCA 2005. Thus for example a key element of the MCA 2005 is a statutory best interests test; but it was held in *X County Council* v *AA* that the inherent jurisdiction was not bound by this statutory framework (para. 56). It remains to be seen the degree to which the inherent jurisdiction will be used in circumstances when the MCA 2005 would not allow intervention, but it does seem that this is a distinct possibility. Thus the inherent jurisdiction has been held to apply when individuals are not incapable, but are instead vulnerable and either constrained (physically or psychologically), subject to coercion or undue influence, or otherwise unable to express 'real and genuine consent' (*A Local Authority* v *Ma, Na, and Sa* [2005] EWHC 2942 (Fam) (para. 78)). *LBL* v *RYJ* provides authority for the view that the inherent jurisdiction cannot be used to impose a decision on a capable person, but instead can be used only to facilitate the process of unencumbered decision-making (para. 62), but this does appear to be a universal understanding of the authority. Thus in *Ma* itself, the decision to preclude the vulnerable adult from travelling to Pakistan with a view to an arranged marriage was taken on a welfare basis, and in *XCC* v *AA* [2012] EWHC 2183 (COP) the court issued an order of nullity of the adult's marriage, notwithstanding the objection of all parties to the case. In neither *Ma* nor *XCC* were the views of the individual considered. Indeed, it would seem that in both cases the court considered that the individual did not have views worth considering, a rather surprising conclusion given the finding in *Ma* that the individual had capacity to make the relevant decisions. In *Ma*, the decision was taken on the basis of a broadly defined welfare test; in *XCC* the decision involved both welfare and public policy relating to arranged marriages. These cases would suggest an almost unfettered power for the courts in these cases, a rather surprising outcome particularly when the individual, as in *Ma*, has capacity to make the decision in question.

Equally problematic is that there has been no clear cultural break between the development of the inherent jurisdiction and the passage of the MCA 2005. Thus it was held in *MM, A Local Authority* v *MM and KM* [2007] EWHC 2003 (Fam) that there was 'no relevant distinction' between the test of capacity in the inherent jurisdiction and in the MCA (para. 92), and the language of the best interest assessments under the inherent jurisdiction continues to appear in decisions under the MCA (see, for example, the use of the 'balance sheet' approach in *A London Local Authority* v *JH and MH* [2011] EWHC 2420 (COP)). The risk here is that the approach of the inherent jurisdiction is over emphasised, and the nuances of new statutory scheme are sidelined or ignored.

This raises an overarching theme for this chapter: how are common law and the statutory structure interacting, and have the spirit and letter of the MCA 2005 been carried forth into its implementation?

4.1.2 Mental capacity in international law

On its face, the use of mental capacity as a threshold of legal intervention may appear benign. It appears to divide people who are able to make decisions from people who are not, and to allow decisions to be made only for those people who are unable to make them for themselves. Those decisions must in turn be made according to the best interests (a benign-sounding term) of the person lacking capacity. A reading of the MCA 2005 suggests a nuanced approach to questions of incapacity and best interests in the statute, further buttressing this rather rosy image.

The view in international law is much more complex. In many countries, people may be found to lack capacity on limited evidence, in court proceedings of which they may have no notice. The result of the finding of incapacity may involve the loss of all decision-making authority relating to both personal and financial decisions (so-called 'plenary guardianship'). Reassessments of capacity may be infrequent, if they occur at all. While under the incapacity order, the individual may be deprived of virtually all decision-making rights. He or she may be legally prohibited from employment. He or she will often be forced to reside in a large institution, often for the remainder of his or her life, where privacy and human comforts are minimal and where intensive physical and chemical restraints may be in routine use. In some countries, the guardian appointed for the individual's welfare may be the director of the institution, with no acknowledgement of the potential conflicts of interest this entails (on these issues, see further Bartlett, Lewis, and Thorold, 2007: ch. 3; Mental Disability Advocacy Center, 2007, 2007a, 2007b, 2007c, 2007d, 2006).

In the last decade, questions of guardianship and capacity law have begun to be litigated under the ECHR. Unsurprisingly given the use of guardianship in much of Europe, the decisions flowing from the European Court of Human Rights in Strasbourg show significant awareness of the controlling aspects of mental capacity and guardianship regimes. It is now clear that a determination that an individual lacks capacity by the courts is sufficient to engage Art. 8 of the ECHR, and when combined with an absence of meaningful avenues to challenge such incapacitation, constitutes a violation of Art. 8 (*Salontaji-Drobnjak v Serbia* (Application no. 36500/05, judgment of 13 January 2010) para. 144). Even a severe mental disorder will not of itself warrant a finding of full incapacity; the mental disorder must instead be of a kind or degree warranting the deprivation of capacity (see *Shtukaturov v Russia* (Application No. 44009/05, judgment of 27 June 2008) para. 94). For any loss of legal capacity, Art. 6 requires that a fair judicial process must be followed, including the court actually examining the person alleged to be lacking capacity, and the provision of meaningful legal representation (*Salontaji-Drobnjak v Serbia*, para. 127; see also *Shtukaturov*). The Strasbourg court has further held that the exercise of complete and effective control over people lacking capacity can constitute a deprivation of liberty, in turn raising issues of procedural and substantive safeguards under Article 5 (*HL v the United Kingdom*, (Application No. 45508/99, judgment of 5 January 2005); *Stanev v Bulgaria* (Application No. 36760/06, judgment of 12 January 2012)). These cases serve as a salient reminder that incapacity law can be used to enforce choices onto individuals, rather than to buttress autonomy. Typically for the ECHR, the Court's primary response is to require appropriate procedural safeguards.

This range of concerns is carried a step further by the United Nations Convention on the Rights of Persons with Disabilities (CRPD). Article 12(2) requires 'that persons with disabilities enjoy legal capacity on an equal basis with others in all aspects of life'. The word 'enjoy' is important here: legal capacity is not meant to be an abstract concept existing only in a rarefied jurisprudential universe; people with disabilities, including people with mental disabilities, are actually expected to be able to exercise choice in decision-making in their day-to-day lives. Article 12(3) requires states to provide people with disabilities all reasonable support in making decisions, again to ensure that the

auton⌐   ʰt to make choices is protected (on supported
deⁿ·   Ɔ, see Gooding, 2012; Dhanda, 2008). The
                                          ᴜve from a binary system where capacity and
                                          ᴸere increasing support is provided to individuals
                                          ᴜile it may be the case that support mechanisms may
                                          ᴸases, the expectation would seem to be that many people
                                  ᴶacity under the MCA 2005 should be enabled to make deci-
                          ᴸer, 2010: 30; Minkowitz, 2010: 156–58). Article 12(4) requires
                          ᴶstems 'respect the rights, will and preferences of the person'. The
                          ᴸbjective' value systems over the individual's decisions and preferences
                          ᴸ the scope of this supported decision-making system as envisaged by the
                  ᴸnis suggests a very different approach to mentally vulnerable adults than is
coᴸ ᴸned in the MCA 2005 (see Bartlett, 2012: 761–68).

Why has the CRPD taken this different course? Certainly, and consistent with the ECHR jurisprudence, it is in part because of the coercion flowing from capacity law that people with disabilities have experienced under existing legal systems. This coercion has led to serious human rights violations. Internationally, capacity is a severely tarnished brand.

The CRPD's approach also reflects its overarching ethos of maximising the autonomy of persons with disability, and minimising discrimination against them: see Articles 3 and 5. The discrimination point is pivotal to understanding the ethos of the CRPD: equality before and under the law is a core value of the CRPD. People with disabilities are not to be subject to coercive mechanisms that are not equally applicable to people without disabilities. While 'reasonable accommodation' (supportive measures designed to mitigate the restrictive effects of disability) is to be available to ensure the full participation of people with disabilities in society, it does not follow that people with disabilities can be required to use the services provided by way of reasonable accommodation. Thus supported decision-making might be viewed as a clear example of reasonable accommodation, but it is at best doubtful whether it can be imposed on a person with disabilities.

Any temptation to marginalise these issues on the basis that 'it is different in England' should be resisted. Such a position is not sustainable legally: the United Kingdom has signed and ratified both the ECHR and the CRPD, and is bound by them. It is further not clear how different the English situation actually is. It is only with the passage of the MCA 2005 that England and Wales moved away from a plenary concept of incapacity in matters of property and affairs, and introduced any statutory structure for incapacity in personal decision-making at all. It was only in 2007, when forced to do so by the decision of the ECtHR in *HL* v *the United Kingdom,* that any formalised structures regarding the *de facto* detention of people lacking capacity were introduced in England (regarding these detentions, see Chapter 5). Aspects of our very recent past are therefore not dissimilar to the apparently repressive regimes elsewhere. Further, it is questionable how comprehensively the MCA 2005 is actually implemented. In the domestic litigation that led to *HL*, the court was told that roughly 48,000 people who were unable to consent to admission by reason of mental capacity were admitted to hospitals every year (*R* v *Bournewood Community and Mental Health NHS Trust, ex p L* [1998] 3 WLR 107, 112). This estimate did not include people *de facto* detained in nursing homes. In fact, between October 2011 and March 2012, there were only 1,678 requests for deprivations of liberty of people in hospital, resulting in 877 authorisations for deprivation. In the care home sector, 4,255 requests resulted in 2,400 authorisations (DH, 2012f). Even allowing that the figure presented to the court in the *HL* litigation may have been inflated, it would seem that large numbers of people without capacity are still in institutional settings in situations where the MCA deprivation of liberty safeguards should be, but are not being, applied. More broadly, in 2010 there were only 1,263 applications to the Court of Protection based on personal welfare issues, resulting in 218 orders (Court of Protection, 2011: table 2). It must be assumed that the vast bulk of decisions in this area are taken outside of formal judicial oversight. While it may well be unhelpful to overemphasise the value of court processes, their absence is also problematic. For example, while specific English studies on inappropriate prescriptions in nursing homes are hard to find, the literature on America and western Europe generally would suggest that roughly 40 per cent of elderly nursing home residents receive inappropriate medication (Gallagher *et al.*, 2007; Oborne *et al.*, 2003). Issues of human rights relating to mental capacity may well arise in an English context.

The approach of international law raises two additional overarching themes for this chapter. First, to what degree is the law relating to mental capacity to be understood as coercive? Does it buttress or diminish the autonomy of persons to whom it is subject? Second, and related, is the MCA 2005 discriminatory, by inappropriately enforcing values and outcomes onto people lacking capacity that are not enforced on the population more broadly? Are 'good outcomes' inappropriately enforced on this group, when similar coercion is not applied to others?

4.2 An overview of the MCA 2005

While various aspects of the MCA 2005 will be discussed in some detail in this textbook, an overview may assist at this stage. The MCA 2005 refers to a person lacking capacity (or, in some contexts, reasonably believed to be lacking capacity) as 'P', and a person empowered to make decisions on behalf of that person as 'D'. This convention is similarly followed in this chapter.

The MCA 2005 opens with a statement of principles (s. 1) designed to guide interpretation of the remainder of the Act. These are drawn from the common law and from good practice.

The MCA 2005 then defines what it means to lack capacity to make a decision (ss. 2–3; see further 4.4). To lack capacity, P must fail either to understand the information relevant to a decision, to retain it, or to be able to use the information to arrive at a decision. Significantly, the assessment refers to the specific decision to be made: the MCA 2005 envisages that an individual may have capacity to make some decisions, but not others. It is entirely consistent under the Act that an individual will be able to make decisions regarding some or all medical treatments or personal care matters, but perhaps not about some or all financial matters, or vice versa. Thus in *Coventry City Council v C* [2012] EWHC 2190 (Fam), for example, Hedley J notes that the incapacity of an individual to make decisions regarding medical treatment did not determine whether she had capacity to make decisions regarding the adoption of her child (para. 38).

The MCA 2005 places advance refusals of medical treatment on a statutory footing (ss. 24–26) (see also 4.6), defining the circumstances where individuals who have capacity may make refusals of treatment that will have effect if they lose capacity. In general, these are without formalities requirements. If however reliance on them would result in the death of the individual, they must be in writing, signed and witnessed; and they must expressly state that they are meant to apply even if the patient's life is in danger. Advance refusals of medical treatment are unusual, in that the statutory best interests test does not apply to them. If an individual, while competent, makes a valid and applicable advance refusal of treatment and the need for such treatment arises, it is in law as if the individual were competent and refusing the treatment. For somatic treatments, that ends the matter. For treatments for mental disorder, however, P's refusal can be overridden by ss. 63 and 58 of the MHA 1983, if he or she is detained under that Act (see further Chapter 9, 9.5).

There are a few types of decisions to which the MCA 2005 does not apply: voting, consent to marriage or civil partnership, consent to sexual relations, consents relating to new reproductive technologies governed by the Human Fertilisation and Embryology Act 1990, consent to divorce or dissolution of civil partnership based on two years of separation, and consent to placement of a child for adoption or the making an adoption order (ss. 27–29). If the individual is incapable of making these decisions himself or herself, that ends the matter: they cannot be made by others. The specifics of the provisions should be noted, however. Adoptions and divorces may be obtained through a variety of legal mechanisms; the only ones precluded by the MCA 2005 are those requiring P's consent.

For virtually all other decisions (the other arguable exception involves research on people lacking capacity, where more specific criteria are prescribed), the statutory test of best interests applies (s. 4; see further section 4.5). This contains a variety of substantive conditions, not entirely consistent with each other in theoretical approach. Some aspects of the test focus on the subjectivity of P, such as the requirement to take into account P's current wishes, and any wishes expressed while competent. Others are more objective, but focus on the particular situation of P. D is required to take into account the likelihood that P will regain capacity, for example, presumably so that decisions where possible can be structured so they can be reconsidered when P regains capacity. Yet others are entirely objective: D is required to consider 'all the relevant circumstances' in reaching a decision as to best interests. No guidance is provided as to how the various aspects of the test are to be balanced in a given case. The test also includes procedural elements, providing a list of people with whom D must consult in ascertaining best interests. For particularly serious decisions such as those involving medium- or long-term admission to psychiatric facilities or care homes, independent advocates are to be provided for people lacking capacity where others are unavailable to advise on best interests.

The Act specifically holds that D must always act in the best interests of P (s. 1(5)). For substitute decision-makers other than the Court of Protection, a further express limitation is created where the decision would result in the 'restraint' of P, where restraint is taken to mean either doing an act requiring force consequent on P's resistance, or restricting P's liberty of movement. Such actions will only be permitted to prevent harm to P, and where the restraint is proportional to the seriousness and likelihood of the harm prevented (ss. 6, 11, and 20). In the event that the control of P is sufficient to constitute a deprivation of liberty within the meaning of the ECHR, additional statutory provisions apply—see further Chapter 5.

The MCA 2005 envisages several types of substitute decision-maker. Individuals with capacity to do so can sign powers of attorney that will take effect in the event of capacity being lost—a so-called 'lasting power of attorney' (LPOA) (ss. 9–14). The system is broadly similar to the enduring powers of attorney (EPOA) system under the EPAA 1985, but unlike EPOAs, LPOAs can be created for personal decisions as well as for decisions concerning property and affairs. Once the LPOA is registered with the Public Guardian, the donee will be entitled to make decisions covered by the LPOA that the donee lacks capacity to make. These decisions must, however, be made in the donee's best interest, and if the LPOA concerns decisions relating to P's personal welfare, it cannot be exercised for a decision unless the donee of the LPOA reasonably believes that P lacks the capacity to make that decision.

The Court of Protection can make decisions itself on behalf of P, or appoint one or more 'deputies' to do so (ss. 19–20). Deputies are responsible to the Court, normally via the Public Guardian, and are required to make decisions for P according to the best interests criteria. They cannot be given authority over decisions within the scope of an LPOA, and they have jurisdiction only if the individual lacks the capacity to make the specific decision in question, whether that decision relates to property and affairs or personal welfare. In general, the Court prefers to appoint close relatives to these positions, although professionals or local authority social services personnel can be appointed if necessary: *EB* v *RC* [2011] EWHC 3805 (COP), *Re P* [2010] EWHC 1592 (COP).

Absent a decision to the contrary by the holder of an LPOA, a deputy, or the Court, the MCA 2005 provides a broad mechanism where anyone who reasonably believes that P lacks capacity can make decisions regarding P's 'care or treatment' in P's best interests (s. 5). This is the most radical departure in the Act, as it provides a near unbounded authority for altruism. Such flexibility comes at a cost, however: here, as elsewhere in the Act, there are few procedural safeguards to oversee D's exercise of his or her decision-making authority.

A new offence is created by the Act of ill-treating or neglecting a person lacking capacity (s. 44).

The entire process is overseen by the Court of Protection, established by the MCA 2005 and staffed by family court judges drawn from the High Court and county courts. It has broad jurisdiction over matters under the MCA 2005, including disputes regarding whether a person lacks capacity and what the best interests of P are. It can determine the validity and applicability of advance refusals of medical treatment, and can intervene in the event that the donee of an LPOA is not acting in the best interests of P. It can make decisions on behalf of P, including making a will, and as noted, it can appoint a deputy to make decisions on behalf of P.

The research provisions of the MCA 2005 require that any research done on people lacking capacity concerns the impairing condition or its treatment. Such research will be allowed only if the burdens on P will not be disproportionate to the benefits to P of the research, or, where the research is to provide knowledge rather than to benefit P personally, where inconvenience to P will be minimal. A variety of procedural safeguards are introduced to ensure that these standards are met, and if P appears to object to the research, he or she must be withdrawn from it. Further discussion of the research proposals is outside the scope of this book, and readers are referred to discussions elsewhere (e.g., Bartlett, 2007: 3.137–2.149; Jones, 2012).

The MCA 2005 is buttressed by a Code of Practice running to more than 300 pages (Department for Constitutional Affairs, 2007). The deprivation of liberty safeguards (DOLS) introduced in 2007 have their own additional Code (Ministry of Justice, 2008b), running to an additional 125 pages. These Codes are envisaged by the MCA 2005 (ss. 42–43) and often provide helpful guidance, but they are neither statutes nor statutory instruments, and therefore do not have the force of law (see *R (Munjaz)* v *Mersey Care Trust* [2005] UKHL 58 for the comparable point regarding the MHA Code of Practice). The MCA 2005 is binding; the Codes are not. That said, the Codes do appear to be influential in how practitioners understand the Act and are routinely referred to by the courts. As such they are influential.

4.3 The principles of the MCA 2005

The MCA 2005 commences with the following statement of principles, designed to guide the overall interpretation of the Act:

1(1) The following principles apply for purposes of this Act

(2) A person must be assumed to have capacity unless it is established that he lacks capacity.

(3) A person is not to be treated as unable to make a decision unless all practicable steps to help him to do so have been taken without success.

(4) A person is not to be treated as unable to make a decision merely because he makes an unwise decision.

(5) An act done, or decision made, under this Act for or on behalf of a person who lacks capacity must be done, or made, in his best interests.

(6) Before the act is done, or the decision is made, regard must be had to whether the purpose for which it is needed can be as effectively achieved in a way that is less restrictive of the person's rights and freedom of action.

These principles are not new. Those contained in subsections (2), (4), and (5) flow from the common law, albeit with subsection (5) now referring to the statutory definition of best interests, not the common law one. Those contained in subsections (3) and (6) are largely statements of previously existing good practice.

Subsection (2) reiterates the common law presumption of capacity. The relevance of the presumption will be slightly different under the MCA 2005, however, particularly regarding persons of marginal capacity ostensibly agreeing to their care. Prior to the introduction of the Act, it mattered little in practice whether these people had capacity: if they did, they were giving valid consent; if they did not the care would be nonetheless be legal if in their best interests, following the inherent jurisdiction developed by the courts. Under the MCA 2005, if a valid and applicable LPOA has been signed or a deputy appointed by the Court, decisions made on behalf of persons lacking capacity must be made by these substitutes. Whether or not such a substitute has been appointed, best interests will now be determined under the Act, using a procedure considerably more robust than that of common law, with some mandatory elements that must precede the taking of the decision. Whether P in fact has capacity, therefore, may be of considerable significance in ways that were not applicable before the Act. For that reason, it is perhaps appropriate to note that it is a presumption only: at some point, evidence of incapacity cannot be ignored.

The principles in subsections (3) and (4) in effect serve to buttress the general presumption of capacity in subsection (2). Subsection (4) makes it clear that lack of capacity is not to be determined by the outcome of the decision made: capacity is to be determined by functional ability to make decisions, not according to the desirability of the outcome of a choice. Subsection (3) requires that all practicable steps be taken to assist the person to make a decision before he or she is found to lack capacity. This reinforces that the presumption of capacity is not rebutted if obtaining a competent decision would be merely inconvenient. Reasonable steps must be taken to get a competent decision, including, for example, use of alternate methods of communication such as sign language or, in the event that capacity is perceived to vary over the course of the day, asking for a decision at a time when the individual is most likely to have capacity.

Subsection (6) is the principle of least restrictive alternative, and as such has long been at the core of much good practice relating to people with disabilities. Different articulations of the principle of least restrictive alternative have slightly different emphases. This particular version focuses on minimal restriction of the person's 'rights and freedom of action'.

The principles overall appear to reinforce autonomous decision-making, and to restrict the scope of decisions under the Act. In the words of the Code of Practice, they 'aim to assist and support people who may lack capacity to make particular decisions, not to restrict or control their lives' (Department of Constitutional Affairs, 2007: 2.1).

How relevant the principles are to the actual application of the Act is not obvious. This is in part because they are often reflected in more specific sections of the MCA 2005. Thus in 2010, 70 per cent of the applications to bring litigation in personal welfare cases were refused by the Court of Protection. This would appear to be largely because other less restrictive responses were available and applicable in the circumstances, and the Court's approach thus reflects the principle contained in s. 1(6). In the Court's annual report for that year, however, this is explained by reference to more specific sections (the general authority contained in s. 5 and the limitations on the appointment of deputies in s. 16(4)) rather than the principle (Court of Protection, 2011: 7–8), making it unclear how expressly the principle figures in these decisions.

Certainly, the principles are periodically cited in the jurisprudence of the court, but it is not clear how influential they are. If, as the Code suggests, the principles are about assisting people with disabilities to be involved in decision-making, some of the cases discussed in the remainder of this chapter will raise the question of how far this objective is achieved, and thus whether the principles are in fact influential at the level of the court.

4.4 The definition of incapacity

What it means for a person to lack capacity to make a decision is defined in ss. 2 and 3 of the MCA 2005.

Except for a few property provisions (which can apply to children) and the provisions allowing deprivation of liberty without a court order (which apply only if the individual is over 18 years of age), the Act only applies if P is over the age of 16. Children will therefore be dealt with under other legislation or the common law. Much of this other law continues to apply until the individual reaches the age of 18 years, however (*Re R (A Minor) (Wardship: Medical Treatment)* [1991] 4 All ER 177; *Re W (A Minor) (Medical Treatment: Court's Jurisdiction)* [1992] 3 WLR 758). Persons between the ages of 16 and 18 years may be dealt with either under the MCA 2005 or these other legal powers.

4.4.1 The diagnostic threshold

The MCA 2005 imposes a diagnostic threshold: for the purposes of the Act, any incapacity must flow from 'an impairment of, or a disturbance in the functioning of, the mind or brain' (s. 2(1)), be it permanent or temporary (s. 2(2)). The intention was that this would serve as a safeguard to the overuse of the MCA 2005. There is some justification for this concern. Even following the introduction of the Act, with the diagnostic criterion in effect, Williams *et al.* found cases in care homes for senior citizens where people were found not to have capacity based on physical disability and general frailty and vulnerability related to old age, rather than a diagnosis related to mental functioning (Williams *et al.*, 2012: 10.2.1). This would also appear to contradict the requirement that determinations of incapacity must not be established on the basis of a person's age or appearance, or a condition or an aspect of behaviour that would lead to unjustified assumptions about capacity (s. 2(3)). Old age of itself does not imply incapacity (see also MCA Code of Practice: 4.07).

The legislature did not anticipate that the diagnostic threshold would extend to drunkenness and related conditions. This is clear from the Act's amendment to s. 3(2) of the Sale of Goods Act 1979, which previously read:

(2) Where necessaries are sold and delivered to a person who by reason of mental incapacity or drunkenness is incompetent to contract, he must pay a reasonable price for them.

The MCA 2005 itself included analogous provisions (s. 7), and so the words 'mental capacity' were deleted from the Sales of Goods Act 1979 (MCA 2005, Sch. 6 and s. 23). The word 'drunkenness' was not removed, suggesting that it was not to be included in the MCA provisions. Presumably, by analogy, incapacity caused by the effects of drug use would similarly be outside the MCA 2005: the diagnostic criterion was apparently to refer to a clinical illness or learning disability, perhaps broadly construed. The Law Commission perceived such a threshold as a safeguard against the overuse of the statute (Law Commission, 1995: para. 3.8).

This distinction is not reflected in the Code of Practice, which expressly includes incapacity caused by alcohol or drug use within the Act (Department of Constitutional Affairs, 2007: para. 4.12).

While the broader view of the conditions that may give rise to incapacity may be a departure from the legislative intent, it is less obvious that it is an undesirable development. The diagnostic criterion in its restricted form was always criticised in some quarters as being stigmatising of people with mental disabilities (Carson, 1993). Consistent with this, and reflecting the discrimination issues contained in the CRPD, even if capacity can be used as a concept (a complex question under the CRPD), why would people be treated according to different legal regimes according to the cause of their incapacity?

A restrictive reading may further be problematic in practice. Consider the situation of a person with a mental disability, who is taking medication for that disability which has effects which diminish the person's capacity (e.g., by causing confusion or an inability to concentrate). A strict reading of the diagnostic threshold would require analysis of the degree to which incapacity was caused by the underlying disability, as compared to the medication. It is difficult to see that such an exercise would be practical.

Finally, decision-making for people lacking capacity for reasons outside the strict diagnostic criterion would presumably fall if not under the MCA 2005 then under the inherent jurisdiction. As noted, this regime includes remarkably similar powers to those under the MCA, but without the benefit of statutory safeguards (most notably, the nuanced statutory best interests test). It is not obvious why such an approach is desirable.

4.4.2 Processing information

The pivotal definition of incapacity is contained in section 3(1):

3(1) For the purposes of section 2, a person is unable to make a decision for himself if he is unable–
   (a) to understand the information relevant to the decision,
   (b) to retain that information,
   (c) to use or weigh that information as part of the process of making the decision, or
   (d) to communicate his decision (whether by talking, using sign language or any other means).

Precisely what information will need to be understood will depend on the specific decision to be made. There are the beginnings of jurisprudential guidance on this, often relying on common law precedents: see, e.g., *D* v *R* [2010] EWHC 2405 (COP) (concerning capacity to make gifts and capacity to litigate), *A Local Authority* v *A* [2010] EWHC 1549 (Fam) (concerning contraception), and a variety of decisions relating to marriage and sexual behaviour to be discussed at 4.4.3. Often, and perhaps properly, the cases turn on very specific factual situations however, making general requirements for categories of decision difficult to establish.

The individual must be able to understand information relevant to the reasonably foreseeable consequences of deciding one way or another, or failing to make a decision (s. 3(4)). The Act therefore imposes the same standards of capacity for whichever way an individual is to decide: there is no different standard of capacity dependent on whether the individual agrees with professional advice, for example. The information is to be put to the individual in a way that is appropriate to his or her circumstances (s. 3(2)). It may be necessary to use visual aids or simple language, for example. Similarly, it would be necessary to provide the information in a language understood by the individual. The individual need only retain the information for a short time (s. 3(3)).

The individual must be able to 'retain' the information. Section 3(3) makes it clear that a person may have capacity even if only able to retain the information for a short time, but this does not solve the ambiguities around the term. The Code of Practice provides no helpful guidance on this point. Presumably, the information must be retained long enough that the decision can be made. In some circumstances (e.g., instructing an individual to pay a bill on behalf of the individual), that may be sufficient. In circumstances where ongoing consent is required (e.g., consent to medical treatment such as an injection) presumably the understanding of the relevant information is required as long as the consent is required to be in effect.

The requirement that the individual be able to 'use or weigh' the information 'as a process of making the decision' is problematic. Certainly, it may well be the case that to have capacity, an individual should be able to process relevant information to reach a decision; but this criterion, perhaps more than the others, introduces the possibility of clashes between the values of the capacity assessor or decision-maker and the values of the person of marginal capacity.

These clashes can occur in a variety of ways. Most blatantly, it may be the case that a decision that is viewed as inappropriate is taken to bespeak incapacity. This should not occur. The MCA 2005 specifically provides that an individual should not be taken to lack capacity 'merely because he makes an unwise decision.' (s. 1(4)). Nonetheless, there is a persistent set of claims that this standard is, in practice, used frequently. Physicians, for example, are alleged often to be content to treat a patient as competent so long as they are accepting treatment, but incompetent if treatment is refused (see, e.g., Law Commission, 1995: para. 3.4; Gunn, 1994: 16; Roth *et al.*, 1977: 281). More recently, Williams *et al.* note the frequent close connection between capacity determination and best interests assessments, which they call the 'concertina effect', with capacity determination blurring into other issues relating to the individual's care (Williams *et al.*,

2012: 3.2, 3.4). Indeed, in some of Williams' survey, best interests determinations were made under the Act with no reference to a finding of incapacity at all. The risk here is that capacity law becomes a mechanism for care providers to enforce 'right' decisions onto people, suggesting a much more controlling function of the MCA 2005 than was apparently intended by the legislators. The courts have acknowledged this risk. In *CC v KK and STCC* [2012] EWHC 2136 (COP), a case involving the choice between care home and independent living, the court found that the local authority 'may consciously or subconsciously [have attached] excessive weight to their own views of how her physical safety may be best protected and insufficient weight to her own views of how her emotional needs may best be met.' (para. 67).

Issues of the individual's ability to 'use or weigh' information also appear when the individual's choice is perceived not to flow from his or her actual will. Sometimes, this will flow from the effects of a mental disorder itself. In *A Local Authority* v *E* [2012] EWHC 1639 (COP), E suffered from anorexia, and the issue was whether she had the capacity to refuse further treatment for that condition. There was no doubt that she could understand and retain the relevant information. It was held however that she was compelled by reason of her disorder not to allow calories into her system: '[t]he need not to gain weight overpowers all other thoughts.' (para. 49). For this reason, she was unable to use or weigh the relevant information, and lacked capacity.

While the logic of the reasoning is clear, it is not unproblematic. While the reasons for E's refusal of further nutrition are intimately bound up with the nature of her disorder, the diagnostic criteria of the disorder are such that it is difficult to see on this logic how a person with anorexia could ever not be incapable to refuse nutrition. Presumably, such an individual would be competent to decide to eat, however, since this would mean that the disorder would not have the overarching effect it was said to have in E's case. It feels somehow wrong that an individual would almost by definition be competent to consent to, but not competent to refuse, a proposed action. The logic also risks marginalising any competent reasons the individual might have for refusing treatment. In E's case, she had been undergoing treatment for 17 years, and frequent and intensive treatment for the six years preceding the hearing. She viewed the treatment as unsuccessful (with some justification—she continued to have the anorexia and its associated problems), and that it was unlikely that she would successfully attain her goals and aspirations for her life. While she at no time expressed a wish to die, she expressed a firm wish not to be treated under compulsion. While these views make for sad reading, they do not obviously indicate a lack of capacity. E's parents stated (*E*, para. 52):

> It seems strange to us that the only people who don't seem to have the right to die when there is no further appropriate treatment available are those with an eating disorder. This is based on the assumption that they can never have capacity around any issues connected to food. There is a logic to this, but not from the perspective of the sufferer who is not extended the same rights as any other person.

The circular logic referred to can apply to other disorders as well, and one therefore might question whether it is only people who have an eating disorder who are denied the right to die or make other fundamental decisions about their lives. Nonetheless, the sentiment of the parents raises serious challenges to the judicial logic.

In other cases, the will of the individual is taken to be submerged through the overbearing influence of others. In *A Local Authority* v *A* [2010] EWHC 1549 (Fam), for example, the issue was whether Mrs A had the capacity to consent to contraception. The Court held that Mrs A was capable of understanding and retaining the information relevant to making a decision regarding contraception, but because of the overbearing personality of her husband, Mr A, it was not clear whether the decision was really her own. Both Mr and Mrs A had intellectual disabilities. The facts of the case are complex and not entirely clear. It would seem that they both wanted a child, although Mrs A had said that this would be the case only if she were allowed to keep the child (two children, born to her in other relationships, had been put up for adoption). There was further evidence that she feared eviction from Mr A's house if she refused to have a child. Mr A viewed the role of a husband as being the dominant partner in the relationship, and being protective of his wife, and it would seem that Mrs A was content with that. Mr A was increasingly hostile to social services intervention, which he perceived as unduly intrusive in their lives; Mrs A, it would seem, was somewhat less hostile in this regard. There were contested allegations of violence against Mrs A by Mr A. Bodey J held, '[i]n view of what I find to be the completely unequal dynamic in the relationship between Mr and Mrs A, I am satisfied that her decision not to continue taking contraception is not the product of her own free will' (para. 73).

The question here is whether the dominance of one party to a relationship can properly be considered to affect an individual's mental capacity. No doubt in many relationships where neither partner has a mental disability, the decision to have children or to take contraception is complex and fraught with tension. Power dynamics in many relationships place one partner on a different footing than another, and domestic violence, most frequently of men on women, remains a social fact. This may be morally repugnant, but it is not news, and it is not restricted to relationships where an individual has a mental disability. The question is whether capacity law should be used to control some relationships involving people with mental disabilities, when no such controls are imposed on other relationships. To phrase the issue slightly differently, is the appropriate question to be asked in this case not about capacity at all, but instead whether the risks to Mrs A are such as to warrant adult safeguarding interventions? If that is the really the issue in the case, then either there is sufficient evidence for intervention or there is not; and if there is not, is it really appropriate that capacity law be introduced as a mechanism of control when the conditions for safeguarding intervention are not met?

It would further seem to be only pressure applied by family members or occasionally friends that is taken by the courts to vitiate the will to the extent of depriving the individual of capacity. The vulnerable individual may also feel pressured, however, by professional carers such as social services or medical staff. Particularly when the vulnerable person is in an institution or similar environment, such pressure can be felt particularly acutely, but the courts do not appear to view these as affecting the individual's capacity. One hopes that such pressures are not applied maliciously, but equally, it is rare that the courts find the behaviour of the controlling family members to be malicious. *A* may illustrate the ambiguities of professional advice. The court declined to make an order as to Mrs A's best interests, on the basis that compulsory birth control would be 'a horrendous prospect' (para. 74). Instead, it held that '[i]n such a sensitive area, it is difficult if not impossible to envisage any acceptable way forward on these particular facts, other than by an attempt to achieve a capacitated decision from Mrs A, through "ability-appropriate" help and discussion without undue contrary pressure from Mr A' (para. 75). While the provision of support in reaching a capable decision is among the principles of the MCA 2005 (s. 1(3)), the 'help and discussion' here will be provided despite the apparent objections of Mr and Mrs A. In such circumstances, it is difficult to see how they will view it as anything other than coercive, and it is fair to wonder how effectively the professionals will separate their views of Mrs A's best interests from her own capable decision. If the objective is to consider the will of the individual divorced from controlling influences, ought we also to be considering the influence of these professional carers on the individual?

This statutory framework draws heavily on the common law test for capacity to consent to medical treatment (see, e.g., *Re C (Adult: Refusal of Medical Treatment)*, [1994] 1 All ER 819; *Re MB (Medical Treatment)* [1997] 2 FLR 426). The significant departure of the statutory test is that, unlike the common law test, there is no express requirement that P believe the information provided. In *Local Authority X v MM and KM* [2007] EWHC 2003 (Fam), the court held that belief was contained in the statutory test by implication (para. 81):

> If one does not "believe" a particular piece of information then one does not, in truth, "comprehend" or "understand" it, nor can it be said that one is able to "use" or "weigh" it. In other words, the specific requirement of belief is subsumed in the more general requirements of understanding and of ability to use and weigh information.

The first sentence in this quotation is profoundly unconvincing. An individual may well not believe in Darwin's theory of evolution; that does not mean that he or she does not understand or comprehend it. There are further many reasons why an individual may not believe information. In *R (PS) v G (RMO) and W (SOAD)* [2003] EWHC 2335 (Admin), for example, the doctor changed her diagnosis of the patient, and the patient continued to believe the previous diagnosis rather than the revised diagnosis. He may or may not have been correct; but his failure to accept the new diagnosis in preference to the previous one does not necessarily bespeak incapacity. The reason for the non-belief seems pivotal here. If an individual fails to believe his or her doctor on the basis that the doctor is inexperienced, for example, it does not follow that the individual lacks capacity. If, on the other hand, the individual's lack of belief is the result of psychosis (that the doctor is controlled by the CIA, for example), the individual may well lack capacity, and certainly, the false belief would be highly relevant to the determination of capacity.

The requirement of belief again highlights the clash between the values and approach of professional carers in juxtaposition to the individual whose capacity is at issue. The individual is required to adopt the approach of the professional in their understanding of their situation. If they do so, it seems likely that they will do as they are told by the professional. If they do not, they will be found to lack capacity, and the decision will be taken in their best interests. Objective factors in the best interest assessment are likely to give considerable respect to the views of the professional, and P is likely therefore end up doing as the professional wants. Particularly in situations where sensible people may disagree with the information provided, it is difficult to see that this buttresses individual autonomy.

The introduction of belief into the MCA 2005 by the courts is perhaps indicative of the influence of medical treatment decisions in the development of capacity law. There is an established tradition of trusting ones doctor and of judicial deference to the medical profession. The cases about belief seem most convincing when they are in the context of treatment for a mental disorder: if a patient does not believe that he or she is suffering from such disorder, reliance on his or her decision regarding treatment is intuitively discomforting. The MCA 2005 is not limited to medical decision-making, however, but includes other personal decisions, as well as those related to property and affairs. If we expect capable patients uncritically to believe their doctors when they provide advice as to diagnosis and treatment, would we require a similarly uncritical belief in the advice about investments provided by a stockbroker, particularly where the person whose capacity is at issue had significant experience of investments? If not, why would we insist on uncritical belief of medical advice when patients have long experience of their condition, but may view it differently from the doctor?

As noted, belief was included in the common law formulation of the test for capacity. Its omission from the statutory test can hardly be seen as accidental. While the convergence of the MCA 2005 with the common law was foreseen in the development of the legislation, the expectation was that common law would stretch to meet the MCA 2005. This would appear to be an example of the reverse occurring, with the statute being bent to fit the common law.

4.4.3 A case study: Capacity, sex, and marriage

Much of the jurisprudence regarding capacity determination in recent years has occurred in the context of consent to sexual activity and to marriage. These cases warrant consideration not merely because they are interesting in their own right, but also because they present a variety of issues of relevance more broadly in considering and assessing the MCA 2005.

Until 2004, there had been little recent litigation on the level of capacity required to marry. *In the Estate of Park, decd* [1954] P 112 affirmed that to have capacity in this context, one had to understand 'the responsibilities normally attaching to marriage' (127). There had been little jurisprudence on what those responsibilities were since Sir James Hannan held in *Durham* v *Durham* (1885) 10 P 80 (82):

> I may say this much in the outset, that it appears to me that the contract of marriage is a very simple one, which does not require a high degree of intelligence to comprehend. It is an engagement between a man and a woman to live together, and love one another as husband

and wife, to the exclusion of all others. This is expanded in the promises of the marriage ceremony by words having reference to the natural relations which spring from that engagement, such as protection on the part of the man, and submission on the part of the woman.

This passage serves as a reminder that what must be understood in order to have capacity is socially determined. While this passage reflects nineteenth-century roots, it is difficult to see that the more modern articulations to be discussed in this section are any less socially specific. In this sense, capacity cannot be understood in a hermetically sealed legal universe. Even in its nineteenth-century context, the quotation also represents an idealised vision of marriage: Victorian men were not always protective and Victorian women not always submissive. As choices are made about what needs to be understood to have capacity in a specific context, how much should those choices reflect idealised values, and how much the actual experiences that people will encounter in their lives?

While these questions are particularly clear regarding marriage, they apply to the full range of decision-making. For example, clearly the likely clinical outcomes of medical treatment will be relevant to a decision to consent to treatment, but so will a wide variety of other factors relating to social, political, and individual culture and morality. Decisions regarding abortion or birth control are clear examples here, but they are only examples. A perusal of a good medical law text will provide an indication of the complexities relating to treatment availability and consent. Similarly, many people who invest money are influenced by factors beyond a simple calculation of best available return on investment. Whether we restrict the determination of capacity in the former case to purely clinical factors or in the latter to an ability to assess likely financial returns, or expand the required understanding to include an ability to understand the wider array of criteria is a social choice, as much as deciding the responsibilities attaching to marriage is.

The collection of cases relating to sex and marriage commence shortly before the passage of the MCA 2005, with the case of *Sheffield City Council* v *E* [2004] EWHC 2808 (Fam). The case involved an intellectually and physically disabled woman, aged 37, who had moved in with and intended to marry a man who had a significant record of convictions for sexual crimes and sexual violence. Social services had become concerned at the risk that the relationship had become abusive, and commenced proceedings under the inherent jurisdiction to prevent the marriage. This motivation reflects the ambiguities discussed between capacity determination and best interests, and between the MCA 2005 and adult safeguarding. The protection of the vulnerable person from harm in relationships viewed by social services as inappropriate is a consistent theme in the roughly 10 cases relating to sexual and marital capacity since *E*. Often, as in *E*, there are cogent reasons for the concerns of social services; but it does return us to the question raised regarding *A* (see 4.4.2) of whether capacity law in England buttresses the autonomy of people lacking capacity, and how much instead it controls them.

The key question in *E* was therefore whether capacity to marry was to be assessed only in terms of an ability to understand the duties attaching to marriage generally, or also the likely implications of marrying a specific individual. That is a topic that has attracted subsequent litigation, and will be returned to. In addition, however, the Court provided a reassessment of the required understanding of marriage generally. It reasserts that the contract of marriage is a simple one, able to be understood by anyone of normal intelligence (para. 68). After noting the modern views regarding gender equality in relationships, it goes on to hold (132):

> Marriage, whether civil or religious, is a contract, formally entered into. It confers on the parties the status of husband and wife, the essence of the contract being an agreement between a man and a woman to live together, and to love one another as husband and wife, to the exclusion of all others. It creates a relationship of mutual and reciprocal obligations, typically involving the sharing of a common home and a common domestic life and the right to enjoy each other's society, comfort and assistance.

This phrasing certainly represents an advance on the articulation of the duties of marriage in *Durham*, reflecting mainstream modern understandings of gender equality and relationships. As the Court commented in *MAB* about the test in *E*, '[t]he fact is that the wife is no longer the weaker partner subservient to the stronger. Today both spouses are the joint, co-equal heads of the family' (para. 58).

The test in *E* is of course no less socially located than the *Durham* test, and while it reflects the position in much of modern English society, it does not necessarily reflect the modern cultural heterogeneity. A number of the other recent cases relating to marriage concern arranged marriages under Islamic law. In these cases, the courts sometimes acknowledge that the understanding of marriage is culturally distinctive, as in the case of *XCC v AA* [2012] EWHC 2183 (COP) where the court notes that in the Bangladeshi community from which the litigants were drawn, broader family relationships and roles in marriage were highly relevant (para. 9):

> DD lives in a very traditional family in a close-knit community not integrated, by and large, into the non-Bangladeshi local community.... They are devout Muslims. I found that DD is a loved and valued member of her family and that her parents are devoted to her. The family is bewildered and disconcerted that they are seen as having done anything wrong, and that what they have done may be seen as contrary to DD's best interests. In my December 2010 judgment I accepted that in DD's parents' culture it is considered a duty of parents to arrange for their children to be married and that disabled children are found spouses so that they can be provided for when the parents are unable to do so.

This would seem to be a substantively different relationship from that described in *E*. Where the assumption in *E* is of independent and autonomous individuals forming an equal partnership, the context in *AA* and similar cases is of care relationships within an extended family, and the marriage serving to ensure ongoing protective care for a vulnerable family member. The juxtaposition of the two cases reinforces the point made regarding *Durham*: decisions regarding capacity take place in social contexts. This is not the place to enter into a discussion of the merits and problems of either the *E* or the *AA* model of marriage; but it does raise the question of whether the relationships are sufficiently different that different tests of capacity ought to apply. Is the application of the *E* test to the conception of marriage in *AA* as inappropriate as the application of the *Durham* test to *E*? As yet, the courts have not seen fit to establish different tests (see, e.g., *Westminster* v *IC, KC* [2007] EWHC 3096 (Fam), para. 32). The appeal of a common test is its universality of application, and at least superficially non-discriminatory nature. The difficulty is that participants in the culturally different marriages described in the cases may be assessed according to a test that does not reflect the relationship they are about to enter.

The social factors associated with the decision are particularly clear in the case of marriage, but they may extend much more broadly in personal and property-related decision-making. Many people make investment decisions based on a wide variety of factors, for example, not just financial return. The factors involved in deciding where and with whom to live may similarly be multi-faceted, including choices between independence and co-habitation (with family, friends, or romantic partners), the perceived desirability of various locations, and the economic ramifications of various housing possibilities. Whatever choices are made regarding the information required to determine capacity, they will be value-laden, just as the choices for marriage are.

Sex is commonly considered to be part of marital relations, and thus capacity to have sexual relations has been held to be a part of the capacity to marry (*Re MAB, X City Council* v *MB* [2006] EWHC 168 (Fam), paras. 53–4, 84). Capacity for sexual relations is nonetheless subject to its own test of capacity. Here, the jurisprudence presents a variety of different and not entirely consistent approaches. *Re MAB* was another case involving an arranged marriage, this time of a man with pronounced autism. The Court cites with approval the following formulation of what must be understood to have capacity for sexual behaviour (para. 86, approved in para. 91):

> Such information might include basic knowledge about the risks of pregnancy, sexually transmitted diseases; some understanding of what is involved in sexual activity; and an understanding of the nature of the relationship they have with the other party.

This formulation leaves open the key question of what constitutes 'the nature of the relationship'. In *A Local Authority* v *H* [2012] EWHC 49 (COP), it was held that human sexual conduct was distinguishable from that of other animals because of its emotional and moral components, noting that victims of sexual assault refer generally to emotional damage and moral violation more than physical injury (para. 20), although the court shied away from articulating tests in these regards beyond a requirement that the individual understood that he or she had a choice as to whether to engage in the activity (para. 25). In *D Borough Council* v *AB* [2011] EWHC 101 (COP) it was held that 'an awareness that sex is part of having relationships with people and may have emotional consequences' was specifically not required for an individual to have capacity to consent to sexual activity (para. 37). That case further held that capacity does not require an understanding that sexual activity must be consensual, and must only be engaged in by persons over the age of 16 years (paras. 38–40): all that is required, according to the case, is a knowledge of the mechanics of the relevant sexual acts, a knowledge of the health risks, and where the act is potentially procreative, a knowledge that it can lead to pregnancy (para. 42).

The move away from criteria based on morality and emotions in *H* appears to flow largely from questions of practicality: how can one ensure that the law is regulating capacity, rather than morality? Whether by accident or design, this fits with the overall ethos of the capacity test both at common law and under the MCA 2005: it refers to the ability to understand, retain, and use information, and as such it is primarily about the ability to make a rational decision. This undoubtedly has advantages in terms of legal practicality: relevant information can be identified, and reasoning processes analysed. While it should now be clear that these are not value-free exercises, they can be done in a reasonably transparent manner. The sex cases however highlight a limitation of this approach: a visitor to a student pub on a Friday night is likely to get the impression that decisions relating to sexual conduct are not actually made in the detached, self-reflective, and rational way that this capacity model implies. The choice to engage in sexual activity or not tends to involve emotional factors—be that a 'phwoar factor' or an expression of romantic love—much more than a retention and reasoned application of information. Insofar as the test does not reflect how decisions are actually made, it is arbitrary: of people making similar decisions for similar reasons, some will be precluded because they fail a test not related to how the decision is actually being taken. It is difficult to see that this is justifiable.

While sexual behaviour is a particularly clear example of this difficulty, it is a problem that extends much more broadly in decision-making. Psychologists are increasingly aware of the role of emotions in decision-making generally, to the point where the distinction between reason and emotion is almost viewed as irrelevant (see, e.g., Damasio 1994, 2000). Insofar as that is the case, the example of sexual decision-making becomes an example of a much larger problem, and the current concept of capacity is open to question.

Among the most litigated aspects of capacity relating to both sex and marriage is the question of whether the determination of capacity relates to the activity in general (e.g., understanding the nature of marriage, or the sexual activity contemplated) or whether the individual must also understand the likely ramifications of engaging in the activity with a specific person. Here again, the cases flow from situations where the proposed spouse or sexual partner is perceived, generally with considerable justification, as an inappropriate or indeed dangerous choice. In the case of *E*, for example, does the individual merely need to understand what marriage is about, or does she need to understand that marriage to this individual might well result in sexual and other domestic violence?

In *E*, the court holds that the determination of capacity refers to the act in general, and factors relating to the other partner are irrelevant. It finds that no contrary position is to be found in the earlier jurisprudence relating to marriage, and that the contract entered into by spouses was uniform in all cases, containing the same rights, duties, and obligations. Cases concerning consent to medical treatment, where it did seem that one could be competent to consent to some treatments and not others, were distinguishable. First, where the marriage contract was a constant between all marriages, medical treatment varied considerably according to the disorder affecting the individual. Second, medical treatment involved technical information requiring the advice of a professional, where the contract of marriage was a simple one that a lay person could be expected to understand. Perhaps more convincing is the court's concern that a person-specific approach risked collapsing the question of capacity with that of best interests (para. 92): if the court were expected to determine whether E had the capacity to marry one person rather than another, this would almost inevitably become indistinguishable from the question of whether it was a good idea for E to marry one person rather than another.

A similar finding for similar reasons was made regarding consent to sexual activity in *Re MM, A Local Authority* v *MM and KM* [2007] EWHC 2003 (Fam), para. 87. On this authority, one has capacity to consent to the relevant sexual act, irrespective of who the intended partner is.

A different approach was taken in *R* v *Cooper* [2009] UKHL 42, a case arising not under the MCA 2005 or inherent jurisdiction, but under the prohibitions of sexual activity with a person with a mental disorder impeding choice, contained in ss. 30–33 of the Sexual Offences Act 2003. That case involved criminal charges relating to sexual activity with a woman with an intellectual disability, a personality disorder and a schizo-affective disorder. The evidence was that these conditions, coupled with threats from the accused, rendered her unable to refuse consent to the sexual activity. Relying to a significant degree on *MM*, the Court of Appeal held that '[i]rrational fear that prevents the exercise of choice cannot be equated with lack of capacity to choose', and that as capacity is not person-specific, so it was also not situation-specific ([2009] 1 Cr App R 211, para. 53).

Baroness Hale, speaking for a unanimous House of Lords, disagreed (para. 27):

> My Lords, it is difficult to think of an activity which is more person- and situation-specific than sexual relations. One does not consent to sex in general. One consents to this act of sex with this person at this time and in this place. Autonomy entails the freedom and the capacity to make a choice of whether or not to do so. . . . The object of the 2003 Act was to get away from the previous 'status'-based approach which assumed that all 'defectives' lacked capacity, and thus denied them the possibility of making autonomous choices, while failing to protect those whose mental disorder deprived them of autonomy in other ways.

While these comments were made in the context of the Sexual Offences Act 2003, Baroness Hale expressly doubted the correctness of the reasoning in *MM* on this point (para. 24).

Since *Cooper*, a number of cases in the Court of Protection have considered the question, with divergent results. In *D County Council* v *LS* [2010] EWHC 1544 (Fam), the court held that *Cooper* applied to determinations of capacity relating to sex and marriage under the MCA 2005. When the characteristics of the partner were such as would impede or deprive the individual of the ability to make a choice, the individual would lack capacity, but mere unsuitability of a prospective spouse or sexual partner would not be relevant to such a determination (paras. 40–42). In *D Borough Council* v *AB*, [2011] EWHC 101 (COP), the Court held that it did not follow from the fact that sex was person-specific that determination of capacity for sexual behaviour was person-specific, and followed *MM* rather than *Cooper* (para. 36). In *A Local Authority* v *H* [2012] EWHC 49 (COP), the Court based its approach on the difference between the criminal and MCA 2005 contexts (para. 22):

In the criminal law it arises most commonly in respect of a single incident and a particular person where the need to distinguish between capacity and consent may have no significance on the facts. In a case such as the present, however, capacity has to be decided in isolation from any specific circumstances of sexual activity as the purpose of the capacity enquiry is to justify the prevention of any such circumstances arising.

As noted, it declines to introduce an aspect of the determination based on moral or emotional elements, resulting in a finding that the determination is neither person- nor situation-specific.

The reasoning of the Court in *H* has the advantage of considering the relative roles of the criminal law, as compared to the MCA 2005. The Act has a highly limited role in this area. The MCA 2005 was not designed to supplant the existing determinations of mental capacity, but to sit alongside them, providing a mechanism by which decisions could be made on behalf of persons lacking capacity as defined in the Act. Consent to sex and marriage are specifically excluded from the decision-making powers of the MCA 2005 (s. 27(1)(a) and (b)), making it unclear why the MCA is relevant at all. The fact that other decisions in these areas, including *LS, AB,* and *H* itself, purport to rely on the MCA 2005 suggests the Act's expanding influence in the capacity field.

If the MCA 2005 and the Court of Protection have a role in these areas, it is not in the context of substitute decision-making for P (the person lacking capacity). The role, if any, is to ensure the prevention of illegal sex or marriage occurring, as the Court in the quote from *H* states. If however the restriction is focused on the illegality of the sexual activity, however, the test must be the criminal test of the legality of the activity. It is difficult to see that the *Cooper* approach can be avoided. In practice, it would seem that fewer people will lack capacity under *MAB* than under *Cooper*, and *MAB* therefore allows sexual congress that is illegal under the criminal law. It is difficult to see that allowing such activity, as the courts currently appear to intend, is a coherent position.

The resulting position is complex and inconsistent. It would seem that the applications are motivated by adult safeguarding concerns. None of the cases involve activity that, but for incapacity of one of the parties, would be considered healthy or normal. For example, it would seem that sexual activity between elderly married couples, one of whom lacks capacity because of dementia, is fairly common (for a discussion, see Bartlett, 2010). While this activity is as illegal under the Sexual Offences Act 2003 as the activity in *Cooper*, it is conspicuously absent from the Court of Protection case law, presumably because rightly or wrongly, it is not perceived raise the same issues of safeguarding as those where the sexual activity is combined with a risk of domestic violence or similar additional difficulties.

If the motivation for the applications is safeguarding, however, the results are more ambiguous and nuanced. The apparent rejection of *Cooper* in favour of *MAB* appears to limit the safeguarding function of the Court, not to expand it. Even in *A*, while Mrs A was held to lack capacity to consent to contraception, the Court declined to order mandatory contraception [paras. 74–79]. Thus while the motivations of the applications appear to involve safeguarding, and while the Court appears clearly concerned about that, the results are not simply controlling of persons of marginal capacity.

These tensions continue in the discussion of best interests determination, to which this chapter now turns.

4.5 **Best interests**

The definition of best interests in the MCA 2005 is contained in section 4. An analysis of the text of the section shows it to be both nuanced and problematic. The section begins by precluding best interests considerations based on unwarranted assumptions relating to age, appearance, P's condition, or aspects of P's behaviour. It then provides a selection of substantive criteria and procedures that must be followed for best interests determinations under the Act.

The substantive criteria involve a variety of divergent approaches. The decision-maker, D, is required to consider when (if at all) the individual will regain capacity (s. 4(3)). Consistent with the policy of the MCA 2005 to maximise the autonomy of P and capable decision-making, the object here is presumably, where possible, to limit decisions to the period of incapacity, so that P may make his or her own decisions on the issue in question when capacity is regained.

D is further required to involve P in the decision-making. This extends both to requirements to allow P as far as possible to participate in the decision-making, and to take into account P's past and present wishes and feelings (including, in particular, any relevant written statement made while he or she had capacity), the beliefs and values that P would have brought to the decision if capable, and any other factors that P would have considered if he or she were able to do so (s. 4(4) and (6)). The weight given to the factors that P would have brought to the decision if he or she had capacity suggests an acknowledgement of the continuity of P's identity over time: who P was when he or she had capacity is to be reflected in the decisions taken about him or her when capacity is lost. The consideration of P's wishes and feelings at the time the best interests assessment occurs (and therefore, by definition, at a time when P lacks capacity to make the decision in question) in part reflects a gesture of common humanity: if P will find an intervention profoundly emotionally distressing, that is obviously something to be taken into account in assessing his or her best interests, even if P lacks capacity. The provision also allows some acknowledgement to be taken that the abilities of people lacking capacity for a specific decision vary considerably. P may therefore have substantive views that warrant acknowledgement and respect, even if he or she lacks capacity overall for the decision. This statutory provision requires such views to be considered. All these factors require a subjective approach to P's situation: what would P have wanted, and what does he or she want now?

D is further required to take into account 'all relevant circumstances' in the best interests determination (s. 4(2)). This introduces an objective approach, not related to P's current or past views, feelings, or values.

Where the decision to be taken involves restraining P, these objective criteria are expanded by s. 6 (if D is exercising the general authority to act in P's best interests), s. 11

(if D is exercising authority based on a lasting power of attorney), and s. 20(7)–(13) (if D is a court-appointed deputy). These provisions require that the act in question is necessary to protect P from harm, and that the act is proportionate to the likelihood and seriousness of the harm. This test focuses on the best interests of P himself or herself. There is no provision to take account of the best interests of those around P, including his or her carers. Restraint is defined for these purposes as using, or threatening to use, force to secure the doing of an act that P resists, or restricting P's liberty of movement whether or not P resists. Originally, these sections did not extend to include deprivations of liberty, but these restrictions were removed by the MHA 2007, so restraint resulting in a deprivation of liberty is now presumably within the scope of these sections. In any event, the deprivation of liberty provisions themselves introduce an identical provision into their definition of best interests (see MCA 2005, Sch. A1, para. 16(4) and (5) and Chapter 5, 5.4.4).

In determining best interests for purposes of s. 4, D is required to consult with anyone named by P as a person to be consulted on such a decision, P's carers and those interested in P's welfare, any donee of a lasting power of attorney granted by P, and any deputy appointed with responsibilities over P. These consultations are to concern the best interests of P generally, but a specific requirement is made that these people be asked to advise on the subjective elements of P's best interests as described in this section.

The MCA 2005 is also clear that anyone making a best interests decision cannot be motivated to bring about the death of P (s. 4(5)). The MCA 2005 therefore does not alter the law relating to assisted suicide.

The challenge of the statutory test is in the priority given to its divergent aspects: how far should P's current or previous wishes and feelings be given sway, if his or her objective best interests appear to lead to a different decision? The statute itself provides no guidance.

The courts have employed a 'balance sheet' approach (see, e.g., *A London Local Authority v JH* [2011] EWHC 2420 (COP)). This is an approach adopted wholesale from the inherent jurisdiction developed by the courts prior to the MCA 2005, which was in turn adapted from a similar approach used in child welfare proceedings (see *Re A (Male Sterilisation)* [2000] 1 FLR 549 (CA) at 560). Such an approach involves the creation of a notional ledger of advantages and disadvantages of choosing one way or another, and deciding based on the result that provides notionally the best outcome. While the views of P may be factors in this assessment, they are only one factor for consideration, and the degree to which they will be considered will be case-specific.

There is jurisprudence to suggest that these wishes should be taken seriously. HHJ Marshall, for example, in *Re S and S (Protected Persons)* asks rhetorically, 'What, after all, is the point of taking great trouble to ascertain or deduce P's views, and to encourage P to be involved in the decision making process, unless the objective is to try to achieve the outcome which P wants or prefers, even if he does not have the capacity to achieve it for himself?' (unreported; cited in *In Re P* [2009] EWHC 163 (Ch), para. 40). While other cases do not expressly dissent from this view, they are much clearer that the views of P are only one factor for consideration. In *Re M; ITW* v *Z and M* [2009] EWHC 2525 (Fam), Munby LJ provides guidance as to how to gauge the importance of P's wishes in the best interests calculation (para. 35):

a) the degree of P's incapacity, for the nearer to the borderline the more weight must in principle be attached to P's wishes and feelings...
b) the strength and consistency of the views being expressed by P;
c) the possible impact on P of knowledge that her wishes and feelings are not being given effect to...
d) the extent to which P's wishes and feelings are, or are not, rational, sensible, responsible and pragmatically capable of sensible implementation in the particular circumstances; and
e) crucially, the extent to which P's wishes and feelings, if given effect to, can properly be accommodated within the court's overall assessment of what is in her best interests.

Much of this guidance makes sense. Clearly, wishes of P that have been considered and consistently expressed over a long period of time, and of which the courts are certain, should carry more weight than judicial speculation on what P's wishes would have been, particularly when the court reaches a view only with considerable uncertainty.

Item (e) is problematic, however. It would seem to suggest that the court is to make a determination of best interests, and then see if P's wishes and feelings can be accommodated within it. For this to be coherent, it must mean that the court makes an assessment of objective best interests, into which P's views may be given effect only if they do not unduly contravene those objective best interests. This is a reversal of HHJ Marshall's approach: she would determine the individual's values, wishes, and feelings, and where possible try to accommodate objective requirements within the context of those values, wishes, and feelings.

Certainly, there are some decisions of the court that take the subjective situation of P into account (see, e.g., *Cardiff County Council* v *Ross*, 2011 WL 6329190; *A London Borough* v *VT* [2011] EWHC 3806 (COP); *In the Matter of G (TJ)* [2010] EWHC 3005 (COP)). It would nonetheless seem to be Munby's approach that is prevalent in the jurisprudence. Indeed, frequently the Court of Protection makes decisions with no reference at all to the subjective factors in the best interests assessment. For example, *DH NHS Foundation Trust* v *PS* [2010] EWHC 1217 (Fam) involved a proposed hysterectomy as treatment for cancer of the uterus. While the medical evidence of the necessity of the procedure was certainly strong, it is striking in this case that there is no indication of any of the subjective factors of the best interests test: they appear to have been entirely absent from the analysis. In *The Council* v *X, Y and Z* [2011] EWHC B10 (COP) X had dementia and was in a care home. The difficulties in the case concerned her daughter, Y, who was rude and offensive to the care home staff. In addition, when X expressed wishes to leave the home and live with her parents, Y told her frankly that her parents were dead, revelations which X found distressing. Matters reached a point where the care home took the view that either Y's contact with X and access to the home would be terminated, or X's accommodation within the home would be terminated. The court decided that the former was in X's best interests. In the reasons, the subjective factors relating to X's views on the contact and the relocation are absent. While we know that

X was broadly happy in the care home, and found both the altercations between Y and the staff and the revelations that her parents were dead distressing, this does not necessarily provide insight into her wishes and feelings regarding termination of contact with her daughter as compared to moving to a different care home, or what values she would have brought to that choice. Here, as often appears to be the case in the jurisprudence, the dispute appears to be between two sets of carers, typically social services and family. The facts relating to the dispute between the carers appear to be far more significant to the court's reasoning than the subjective factors relating to the person lacking capacity. In many other cases, while the current wishes of P are noted, they do not appear to have a significant role in the decision. This criticism also seems to apply to assessments of best interests by decision-makers outside the courts (see Williams *et al.*, 2012: para. 5.3).

Further, discussions of the beliefs and values P would bring to the decision if competent appear to be almost entirely absent, *A London Local Authority* v *JH and MH* [2011] EWHC 2420 (COP) at p. 43 being a conspicuous exception. Notwithstanding the statutory provisions, the court does not appear to consider them at all. Even in situations where P has previously lived a long and non-disabled life and where therefore his or her values when competent would be readily ascertainable, they are conspicuously absent from the judgments.

The case law tends to focus on decisions relating to personal welfare, where intuitively objective best interests seem particularly relevant. There is certainly an argument that the current wishes of P and the values he or she would have brought to a decision as to where he or she should live are important, but the objective evidence that an individual will be subject to violence or physical or emotional harm in that environment does seem to have a particularly telling relevance. It is more difficult to make the comparable argument regarding financial decision-making. Whatever the likely financial returns to P, can it ever be in the best interests of a life-long vegan to have her funds invested in abattoirs, or a doctrinaire Roman Catholic to have his funds invested in a firm manufacturing birth control pills? There is a wide array of suitable choices for investments that could take account of P's wishes and feelings, and one would expect the subjective factors to be particularly relevant in the best interests assessment.

It is therefore particularly notable that the court appears to be moving away from the relevance of subjective factors in matters regarding property and affairs as well. This is most visible in the jurisprudence in the cases involving the drafting of statutory wills. Before the MCA 2005, the procedure for the drafting of a will for an individual lacking capacity was an attempt to express the presumed wishes of the incapable testator: the court was to imagine what P would do if he or she momentarily regained capacity at the time the will was drafted (*In Re D (J)* [1982] Ch 237). As such, it gave effect to the wishes and feelings of P to the near exclusion of other factors. This approach was not without its problems, particularly in cases where the testator had never had capacity: particularly on a matter so personal and idiosyncratic as the drafting of a will, how can one possibly know what a person would do if he or she had capacity, when he or she has never had capacity?

Since the introduction of the MCA 2005, the courts have however adopted the same approach to statutory wills as to any other best interests determination (*In re P* [2009] EWHC 163 (Ch), para. 38; *Re M; ITW v Z* [2009] EWHC 2525 (Fam), para. 29). As the courts note, this is with reference to a document that will take effect only after P's death, giving rise to a rather bizarre analysis of what the best interests of P will be *post mortem*. The court in *Re P* recognises the relevance of P's wishes, but continues, '[b]ut what will live on after P's death is his memory; and for many people it is in their best interests that they be remembered with affection by their family and as having done "the right thing" by their will' (para. 44). In legal terms, this is a very odd statement. To begin with, by definition, P will be dead. Debate about the nature of the soul after death is a matter for theologians, but it seems at best highly speculative that P when dead will have much actual concern over how he or she is remembered. If he or she would have been concerned about that while alive, it would be a value which he or she would have brought to the decision, and therefore could be taken account of as part of the subjective decision-making factors.

Consistent with this, if the objective factors will only be relevant if the court makes a legacy that P would not have made, will the legatee actually think better of P? It is, after all, not P but the court that is making the will. It may well be the case that the legatee will know that P would not have chosen to make the legacy. Why will they think better of P, because the legacy has been enforced on P through litigation? The court's view would make some sense if they were purporting to give effect to P's views, but this is specifically what it is choosing not to do. While we may be pleased that an apparently deserving legatee receives some property, it is difficult to see that this will change how P will be remembered.

'Doing the right thing' may be morally desirable, but it is difficult to see that it can be articulated in terms of the best interests of P after death. Once again a discrimination question arises: if society wishes to determine that testators must 'do the right thing' in their bequests of property, it is of course open to the legislature to amend the laws accordingly. It is much less obvious that incapacity law should be used to require people who lose their capacity to behave morally, when there is no such stricture on the remainder of society. In *In the Matter of G (TJ)* [2010] EWHC 3005 (COP), a case deciding whether support payments to a family member should be continued notwithstanding the incapacity of the person providing them, the court does not expressly disagree with the reasoning in *Re P* and *M; ITW v Z*, but, much more carefully than in those cases, considers and applies the subjective elements of the best interests test. With respect, the approach in *G (TJ)* is to be preferred, when the previously competent wishes and values of the testator can be reasonably ascertained.

In holding that the weight given to the various factors in the statutory test will depend on the facts of the individual case, the court in *M; ITW v Z* holds that one factor in the case may assume a 'magnetic importance' in influencing or determining the outcome (para. 32). The issue in *LG v DK* [2011] EWHC 2453 (COP) was whether DK, an elderly gentleman with dementia, should be required to provide a DNA sample to determine whether a woman, BJ, was his daughter. The request was made by DK's deputy appointed by the Court of Protection in anticipation of the drafting of a statutory will in which BJ would be a beneficiary, if she were indeed his daughter. BJ had requested DK to have a DNA test when he still had capacity, but he had refused for considered and coherent reasons. The case itself concerned the court's jurisdiction in the matter, but the court did provide a hint as to best interests. Citing the wills cases discussed here, the court held that it was not bound by earlier DK's refusal of the test. While not expressly determining the best interests question, the court states '[i]t would, in my judgment, require unusual facts for DK's best interests to depart from the ascertainment of the truth or the interests of justice' (para. 55). This appears to provide a fairly clear hint that the best interests were likely to be found to be in favour of the test.

Are 'the ascertainment of truth' and 'the interests of justice' in this case the sort of factor acquiring magnetic influence referred to in *M*? Presumably, at least as an initial view, the court thinks so, but while the rhetorical power of the phrases is considerable, it is difficult to see why it should be the case on the facts. The Court makes it clear that BJ herself was not motivated by money, and in any event, would have no obvious expectation of inheritance given that DK had declined the test earlier. Insofar as it was her parentage that she wished to ascertain, she could have asked her mother, who was still alive, but she declined to do so, on the basis that it would upset her (para. 5). We know from DK's previous refusal that he did not wish paternity to be definitively established either way; in what sense, therefore, is the ascertainment of truth in his best interest? The strength of both the ascertainment of truth and the interests of justice suggest again that the court is looking beyond the best interests of the individual, into a broader social vision of best interests. There is nothing in the MCA 2005 that would permit that approach: best interests under s. 4 is the best interests of P, not of carers or family, and certainly not of broader society (unless, of course, these are factors that P would himself or herself consider relevant to the decision, in which case they are relevant as part of the subjective criteria).

It may be that these factors outweigh DK's interests; but if so, it again raises the discrimination question. The justifications for the testing in this case apply as well for people without disabilities as for those that lack capacity. If we wish to make DNA testing mandatory whenever anyone wishes to determine paternity, that is presumably a social choice that can be made; but in the face of a prior and competent refusal of the test, why would it be justifiable to require it of people when they become mentally incompetent, when we would not do so for others?

4.5.1 Best interests, families, and independent living

The competing interests and criteria in best interests assessments are particularly clear in decisions regarding accommodation. Typically, these disputes involve a choice between care in institutional settings (generally care homes) and by family members, although occasionally cases arise involving independent living (for example, in a flat with appropriate support provided).

The tension between family carers and institutional care raises issues relating to the right to private and family life under Article 8 of the ECHR. While the courts have acknowledged the right to family life, attaching both to P and to P's family, they have been hesitant about according it particular priority in making best interests determinations regarding family care. The approach of the courts is that decisions should be taken under the MCA 2005, and then subsequently the analysis should be undertaken as to whether the result is consistent with Article 8: see *K v LBX* [2012] EWCA Civ 79.

The courts have been hesitant about expanding Article 8 rights in this area in any event, at least once the family members reach adulthood and thus have the right to determine with whom he or she will associate. The point was made as follows in *Re S (Adult Patient) (Inherent Jurisdiction: Family Life)* [2002] EWHC 2278 (Fam), a case under the court's inherent jurisdiction (para. 37):

> If a father and his adult daughter wish to enjoy the type of normal family relationship that the State is obliged by the Art 8 guarantees of respect for each party's private and family life not to interfere with arbitrarily, then all well and good. But if for whatever reason, good or bad, reasonable or unreasonable, or if indeed for no reason at all, the daughter does not wish to have anything to do with her father, then he cannot impose himself upon her, whether by praying in aid his Art 8 right to respect for family life or his Art 8 right to respect for that part of his private life which entitles him in principle to establish and develop relationships with other human beings. His daughter can pray in aid against him her Art 8 right to respect for that part of her private life which entitles her to decide who is to be excluded from her 'inner circle' – and in that contest, because she is a competent adult, her Art 8 rights must trump his.

This must be correct: if an individual has capacity, he or she may determine with whom he or she associates. If the both the daughter and the father in the example wish to maintain a close family relationship, however, the state's interference with that would impinge on the Article 8 rights of both.

The S case takes the view that the decision of P, the person lacking capacity, regarding continuation of family relationships and Article 8 rights falls to the state, and is determined pursuant to P's best interests under the inherent jurisdiction of the courts (now, presumably, instead under the MCA 2005). This is not a satisfying approach. P's emotional connections to his or her family or non-familial carers may well be intense and meaningful, and quite separate from his or her capacity to make decisions regarding accommodation or contact. It is at best counterintuitive that P would cede determination of those rights to the decision-maker under the MCA 2005 in those circumstances. It should be noted here that this does not necessarily leave P potentially defenceless in a dangerous situation. Article 8 rights are qualified, and state action would be justified in the event of risk, for example, to P's health. The acknowledgement of P's Article 8 rights would, however, give a different primacy to the family relationship in the event that it was mutual and strong.

There is an ambiguity in the case law as to whether there is any sort of preference to be given in law to care provided within the family. The S case acknowledges that families can bring elements to care that cannot be provided by institutions, leading to a starting assumption that family care is preferable to institutional care, but not a presumption to this effect (para. 48). That said, the traditional position was that any starting assumption was not necessarily strong, as the courts also held that no deficiency in the care provided by a family need be shown for a removal to institutional care, but merely a determination that such a placement was in the best interests of P (see *London Borough of Newham* v *BS* [2003] EWHC 1909 (Fam)). More recently, courts have at least occasionally approached family care with a more sympathetic eye. Thus in *Hillingdon LBC* v *Neary* [2011] EWHC 1377 (COP), the court held (24):

> Decisions about incapacitated people must always be determined by their best interests, but the starting point is their right to respect for their family life where it exists. The burden is always on the State to show that an incapacitated person's welfare cannot be sustained by living with and being looked after by his or her family, with or without outside support.

How secure this apparent shift will be remains to be seen. Recently, the Court of Appeal has returned to the traditional position, that the determination of best interests is focused on the criteria in s. 3, without any express starting point on the desirability or lack thereof of care within the family (see *K* v *LBX* [2012] EWCA Civ 79).

4.6 Advance decisions regarding treatment

The MCA 2005 places advance decisions to refuse treatment on a statutory footing. These may be made by a person over 18 years of age who has capacity to do so, to take effect in the event of subsequent incapacity. While the definition of capacity is that contained in sections 2 and 3 of the MCA 2005, this form of decision-making is unusual in that the best interests provisions of the Act have no application. If a valid and applicable advance decision to refuse treatment applies, it is as if the individual makes a competent refusal of that treatment (s. 26(1)).

The decision must refer to 'treatment'. This is defined in the MCA 2005, rather unhelpfully, as 'includ[ing] a diagnostic or other procedure' (s. 64(1)). Certainly, the term is likely to be taken to include all medical procedures, but nothing express in the Act restricts it to medical treatment. How far it may be read as extending beyond medical care into other forms of personal care remains to be seen.

The effect of a valid and applicable advance decision is the same as if the treatment were refused by a competent person. Two caveats flow from this. First, if the treatment may be provided notwithstanding the competent refusal of consent, it may be provided notwithstanding the advance decision. Most significant for current purposes are treatments provided to detained patients under sections 63 and 58 of the MHA 1983. As consent of the patient is not necessary for these treatments, so they are not precluded by a valid and applicable advance decision, although of course the advance decision would still constitute a factor a doctor might wish to take into account in deciding whether such enforcement of treatment was appropriate under these sections. The advance decision can, of course, preclude treatment of informal patients, or detained patients for treatments other than for mental disorder, as these treatments require the consent of the patient. Second, the effect of the decision can be no more than a refusal of treatment. Nothing in the MCA 2005 creates a power to insist on the provision of a specific treatment—only to refuse it. In this, the Act reflects the common law position: see *R (Burke)* v *General Medical Council* [2005] EWCA 1003. Preferences regarding treatment the individual would want are of course relevant to the best interests determination (see 4.5), but they are not binding.

The advance decision to refuse treatment applies only if it is valid and applicable. The former of these terms refers to whether there is a legally effective decision: has the individual withdrawn it, or done something clearly inconsistent with it (s. 25(2))? Such inconsistency includes, but is not limited to, giving authority to a donee of an LPOA to make the decision in question. Donors of LPOAs may therefore wish to make it clear on the face of those instruments whether they are intended to supersede any advance decision to refuse treatment. Section 25 does not specifically state that the advance decision will be invalid if the individual lacked capacity to make it. Whether one wishes to characterise this scenario as a nullity or as an invalid decision seems a matter of semantics: clearly in such a case the decision has no effect.

By comparison, applicability refers to whether the decision applies to the situation now at issue. The decision will not be applicable if it does not refer to the treatment proposed, or if there are conditions precedent in the decision that are not met (s. 25(4)). The decision will also not be applicable if the individual has capacity to make the decision at the time it needs to be made (s. 25(3)); in that event, the individual consents or not as he or she wishes. The decision will further not be applicable if 'there are reasonable grounds for believing that circumstances exist which P did not anticipate at the time of the advance decision and which would have affected his decision had he anticipated them' (s. 25(4)(c)). A simple example of such a condition would be where an individual makes an advance decision to refuse medication for a specific disorder because of adverse effects of the medications available at the time the decision was made. If medications developed since that time do not have the adverse effects in question, it would be reasonable to think that the individual would not have refused such newer medication. The advance decision might therefore be inapplicable regarding the newer medications.

There is no general requirement that advance refusals be in writing, unless it is a refusal of life-sustaining treatment. In that case, it must be in writing, signed and witnessed, and must state expressly that it is to apply if the life of the individual is at risk (s. 25(5)).

The MCA 2005 provides that practitioners will be not be liable if they provide treatment unless they are 'satisfied' that a valid and applicable advance refusal applies (s. 26(2)). They will further not be liable for withholding treatment if they 'reasonably believe' that a valid and applicable advance refusal applies to the treatment (s. 26(3)). The intention here is to provide legal protection for practitioners in the case of honest and reasonable doubt. In case of doubt, of course, the Court of Protection also has jurisdiction to make declarations regarding validity and applicability, and treatment may be performed to sustain life or prevent a serious deterioration of P's condition pending the court's decision (s. 26(5)).

There is as yet relatively little litigation concerning advance decisions to refuse treatment, but such litigation as there is indicates a marked hesitancy on the courts to uphold the decisions. In the two leading cases to come before the courts, the first under the court's inherent jurisdiction and the second under the MCA 2005, the advance decisions were held not to be valid: see *HE* v *A Hospital NHS Trust* [2003] EWHC 1017 and *A Local Authority* v *E* [2012] EWHC 1639 (COP). Neither of these cases is entirely satisfactory. *HE* was decided in a situation of urgency. At issue was whether HE remained a Jehovah's Witness (as her mother was) or had reverted to the original Muslim faith of her father. The only witnesses were from the Muslim side of the family, and time did not allow the summoning of further witnesses. In such circumstances, it is perhaps unsurprising that the court favoured the provision of life-sustaining treatment, relying on the only evidence before it that HE had reverted to Islam. It is fair to wonder whether further evidence from HE's Jehovah's Witness mother would have differed from this, and at least required an assessment of credibility by the court.

In *A Local Authority* v *E*, E had been undergoing treatment for anorexia for many years, and had reached the view that she no longer wished to be compelled to do so. She provided a long and eloquent statement to this effect in support of her advanced refusal of further treatment. As noted in 4.4.2, it was held that she lacked capacity to make decisions both at the time of the treatment and the time of the making of the advance decision, on the basis that her failure to believe that further treatment could assist her meant that she was unable to weigh the advantages and disadvantages of treatment in a meaningful way. As discussed (see 4.4.2), this is a problematic outcome. On the facts—her views were the result of long consideration and not entirely unreasonable—indeed, they were to a significant degree shared by her parents. On the law, it is difficult to see how persons with anorexia and similar mental disabilities could have capacity, when their views will often so readily be able to be attributed to a manifestation of their disorder.

4.7 Conclusion

Earlier in this chapter (4.1.2), it was noted that the United Nations CRPD marks a new departure, challenging the use of capacity as a legal concept. The use of the category in many other countries has given rise to human rights violations and has worked to undermine the dignity and autonomy of persons with mental disabilities. The movement away from capacity and towards systems supporting people with mental disabilities to make their own decisions is part of the CRPD's agenda to remove discrimination on the basis of disability, to give people with disabilities control over their own lives, and to give practical effect to the human rights that are taken for granted by the rest of the population for disabled people.

The complexities of interpreting the CRPD in the context of mental health and mental capacity law are considered elsewhere and will not be reproduced here (see Bartlett, 2012 and sources therein). Instead, by way of conclusion, this chapter looks to the overarching themes of the CRPD in general and the provisions relating to mental capacity in Article 12 in particular, to provide a framework to consider the overall role and effect of the MCA 2005. To what degree can the Act be seen as promoting, and to what degree inconsistent with, the values of the CRPD?

Certainly, there is an overarching problem that the MCA 2005 does expressly determine capacity on the basis of mental disability. As noted, there is an express diagnostic prerequisite to a finding of incapacity, and the other criteria of capacity determination will affect people with mental disabilities disproportionately to the rest of the population. In the opinion of the UN High Commissioner for Human Rights, this raises a question of discrimination, which would place the MCA 2005 in conflict with the CRPD. In her words, '[w]hether the existence of a disability is a direct or indirect ground for a declaration of legal incapacity, legislation of this kind conflicts with the recognition of legal capacity of persons with disabilities enshrined in article 12, paragraph 2' (United Nations High Commissioner for Human Rights, 2009: paras. 43–45). If this is correct, and it does appear to be consistent many of the academic commentaries, a fundamental change of approach would be required, since the non-discrimination ethos is fundamental to the CRPD.

What of the other values of the CRPD and of Article 12 in particular? The CRPD is intended to buttress autonomy and independent living of people with disabilities. Article 12(2) refers specifically to the *enjoyment* of legal capacity, suggesting that they are expected to be able actually to make decisions, a result to be accomplished through the provision of appropriate supports to decision-making (Article 12(3)). The provision of such supports is not inconsistent with some of the provisions of the MCA 2005. Most notably, s. 1(3) provides that a person is not to be treated as unable to make a decision 'unless all practicable steps to help him to do so have been taken without success', a provision reflected further in the requirement in s. 3(2) that information must be provided to the individual in an appropriate fashion. Even if the individual is held to lack capacity, the MCA 2005 requires the individual to be involved as much as possible in the decision (s. 4(4)), and requires the decision-maker to take account of P's views, values, wishes, and preferences both at the time and when he or she had capacity as part of the decision-making process. There is much here that is consistent with a supported decision-making framework.

At the same time, there is reason for concern. It is a rare case where the court considers whether all reasonable steps have been taken to involve P in the decision-making process, or whether systems of supported decision-making have been attempted. As discussed, this was the eventual approach adopted in *A Local Authority* v *A* regarding Mrs A's decisions about contraception, but the court appears to view this as an exceptional outcome, flowing from the exceptionally personal nature of the decision under consideration. For purposes of the CRPD, it would need to be the norm. Further, reflecting the concerns discussed regarding *A*, structures would have to be put in place to ensure that the supports provided assist P to reach his or her own decision, rather than to lead P to an outcome favoured by the person providing the support. Outside the courtroom, it is not clear how extensively supported decision-making structures are used, or of what they consist: the empirical evidence does not exist.

The CRPD offers no guidance as to how to respond in situations where, notwithstanding support, P is unable to be meaningfully involved in the decision in question. Certainly, it may be possible to involve many more people with mental disabilities in decisions regarding their lives than may be the case at the moment—the impossibility of perfection is not an argument for the status quo—but it seems likely that some people will not be able to make decisions, even given intensive and high quality supports to decision-making. In these circumstances, at least, another individual will have to take a more significant role. What factors should he or she consider in doing so, if the CRPD's requirement that the rights, will, and preferences of that person are to be respected? Presumably, factors such as prior beliefs and values would be factors; but if that is the case, can these factors be relevant more generally for purposes of making decisions under Article 12, or do they only apply in the extreme cases where individuals are unable to be involved at all? If they can be used more generally—a view that would be contested among some scholars—the list of criteria would start to resemble rather closely the subjective factors under the MCA 2005.

Under the MCA 2005, however, while the decision-maker, D, is required to consider the wishes, feelings, beliefs, and values of the person lacking capacity, D is not bound by them. As discussed, D is entitled to make an assessment of P's objective best interests as they appear to D, and to act accordingly. D must consider P's wishes, but often will not decide consistently with them. This does seem directly at odds with the CRPD ethos of buttressing autonomy, and its express requirement that any measures relating to the exercise of legal capacity respect the will and preferences of the person (Article 12(4)). Autonomy is a core value of the CRPD, and this apparent departure thus appears to be in direct conflict with the Convention in an essential matter.

Is it a fatal objection that decisions on behalf of P are technically made by a decision-maker, D, rather than by P himself or herself? Certainly, the CRPD is phrased to place P as the decision-maker, but circumstances can be readily imagined where for practicality, a decision is likely to require implementation by someone other than P, and it may be legally a great deal simpler for that person to have some formal legal authority to do so. The point is perhaps whether D perceives himself or herself as making the decision for P in a paternalistic role, or instead as P's agent, implementing the decision made by P. The latter would seem to be much more consistent with the ethos of the CRPD; but the former appears to be how the courts interpret the MCA 2005.

The marginalisation of the subjective elements of the best interests test reflects the fact that, at least insofar as the reported cases are a guide, the MCA 2005 is used primarily for adult safeguarding. This may in part flow from the non-representativeness of the cases reported: while the bulk of the work of the Court of Protection concerns property and financial matters, the bulk of the reported case law concerns personal decision-making. Safeguarding may be less prevalent a motive in cases involving financial management. Be that as it may, insofar as safeguarding concerns are relevant in the jurisprudence, a successful move towards the CRPD approach would be likely to require new and separate safeguarding measures. Such an approach was in fact suggested by the Law Commission in its 1995 report, but the government declined to give effect to these recommendations. Such safeguarding measures would themselves have to comply with the CRPD, most notably by applying equally to all adults rather than just those with disabilities, suggesting that this might be a difficult legislative exercise. That would in turn allow the main MCA 2005 to return to its original focus of decision-making, rather than protection.

The MCA 2005 is further problematic in its absence of administrative safeguards against misuse of the Act. Article 12 of the CRPD requires that such safeguards be in place to prevent abuse, and must include regular review by an independent and impartial body such as a court. By comparison, the MCA 2005 is designed to keep matters out of court. There is no general obligation for anyone relying on the Act and making and acting on decisions in the best interests of another person even to inform anyone about the decision, let alone for their actions to be scrutinised. Certainly, the Court of Protection has jurisdiction to enquire into the propriety of decisions taken, but actual cases will occur only when they are brought to the attention of the Court, presumably generally by a well-meaning third party, or when there is a dispute between carers. When these triggering situations are absent, it is unlikely that cases will become visible to the Court; but it is in these situations where people lacking capacity will be most vulnerable.

The provision of stronger administrative safeguards is practically problematic, however. A strength of the MCA 2005 is its acknowledgement that capacity is both decision-specific and time-specific: one looks to the individual's capacity to make the specific decision in question, at the specific time that decision needs to be taken. It is difficult to see what administrative structures could be created that could account for the specificity of that decision-making context, without collapsing under their own bureaucratic weight.

The MCA 2005 is still a relatively new statute, and comments regarding its overall effects are correspondingly tentative at this stage. Certainly, it represents progress from the previous legislation. It remains to be seen how it will develop, and how far it will be accepted as a new way forward in decision-making for mentally vulnerable adults.

5

Deprivation of Liberty under the Mental Capacity Act 2005

5.1 Introduction

Chapter 4 discussed decision-making in general for people lacking capacity. The current chapter extends that discussion to situations where the decisions taken involve depriving the person lacking capacity of his or her liberty. The last chapter argued in part that whatever the intent of the Mental Capacity Act 2005 (MCA 2005), the jurisprudence under the Act has been animated by concerns regarding safeguarding of vulnerable adults. The present chapter can be understood in part as a continuation of those concerns, but the resulting deprivation of liberty engages additional legal requirements and legal safeguards. These are embodied in amendments to the MCA 2005 introduced in the MHA 2007, and are generally known as the Deprivation of Liberty Safeguards or more briefly by the corresponding acronym 'DOLS'.

On its face, the DOLS may appear to overlap with detention under the MHA 1983, discussed in Chapter 6. Both are, after all, ways in which people with mental disabilities may be deprived of their liberty. The interplay between the two systems is complex, and will be discussed as it arises both later in this chapter and in Chapter 6. For the present, Table 5.1 provides some general points that may be useful in distinguishing the two systems. Key to the differences are that deprivation of liberty under the DOLS are to be in the best interests of people lacking capacity, and while most frequent in care homes, can occur anywhere. Such detentions are not necessarily with an eye to the provision of medical treatment. Sectioning under the MHA 1983 must be to a psychiatric hospital or psychiatric ward of a general hospital only, either for the treatment for the mental disorder or for assessment with a view to treating the mental disorder. Where the DOLS require that the individual lack capacity to decide on admission, sectioning under the MHA 1983 instead requires the presence of a mental disorder of sufficient severity to warrant detention in the interests of the person's health, safety, or for the protection of others. These are conceptually quite different categories.

Table 5.1 should be read as introductory only. Complications arise for example when a DOLS admission is made to a psychiatric hospital (where the DOLS 'eligibility requirement' comes into play). Similarly, people who are released from hospital where they have been detained under the MHA 1983 may still be subject to MHA controls

Table 5.1 Deprivation of Liberty: DOLS versus MHA 1983

	DOLS under MCA 2005	MHA 1983
Where?	Most usually care homes, but anywhere—restrictions apply to use in hospitals for psychiatric treatment	To psychiatric hospitals and psychiatric wards of general hospitals only
Threshold criterion regarding condition of individual	A mental disorder rendering the person incapable of making a decision regarding admission	Mental disorder of severity warranting detention—individual may or may not lack capacity
Diagnostic restrictions if individual has a learning disability	No restriction—any learning disability resulting in incapacity will suffice to meet this criterion	For detention beyond 28 days concerning a learning disability it must result in abnormally aggressive or seriously irresponsible conduct
Diagnostic restriction: alcohol and drugs	No restriction? (some dispute—see chapter 4.4.1)—if so, lack of capacity flowing from drugs or alcohol would meet this criterion	Dependence on alcohol or drugs is not of itself a mental disorder under the MHA 1983
Threshold criterion regarding appropriateness of detention	Detention is in best interests of person	Mental disorder warrants admission for assessment (for detention up to 28 days); warrants admission for treatment for the mental disorder and treatment is available (if detention extends beyond 28 days)
Medical treatment	DOLS themselves silent, but rest of MCA 2005 applies (see Chapter 4), so person competent to make decision may consent or refuse consent; person lacking such capacity may be treated in best interests under Act	Most treatments for mental disorder may be given without consent, with procedural safeguards taking effect after 3 months. For treatments not related to mental disorder, MCA 2005 applies (see Chapter 9)
Procedural authorisation	If detension to hospital or care home, by DOLS-approved doctor and DOLS-approved best interests assessor. Otherwise by court order.	By two doctors (at least one of whom has special expertise and qualification) and approved mental health professional. After 28 days, 'nearest relative' can challenge detention
Challenges	To Court of Protection	To specialist review tribunal

(either through community treatment orders or requirements flowing from leave of absence provisions, for example), and the MHA may therefore extend into territory where one would expect the DOLS to hold sway. Table 5.1 thus provides a broad starting point only.

5.1.1 *HL*, the European Convention on Human Rights, and the deprivation of liberty

The introduction of the DOLS was enforced onto Parliament by the decision of the European Court of Human Rights in *HL* v *United Kingdom*, application no. 45508/99, (2005) 40 EHRR 32 (also called '*Bournewood*', based on the title of proceedings in the prior domestic litigation). Before this case, there was no formal legal structure controlling the admission of people without capacity to care homes or to hospitals on an informal basis, and no formal constraints on the care of people lacking capacity outside institutional settings such as in private homes. Certainly, the law of wrongful confinement existed, but as the domestic *Bournewood* litigation showed, it had not been applied or considered in the context of the care of people lacking capacity, and its scope had therefore never been tested. Further—and this was the dispute in the *Bournewood* case itself—there was no established mechanism to arbitrate disputes about whether specific institutional care was appropriate or not.

In the *Bournewood* case, HL, an adult with profound developmental disabilities, lived with paid carers who treated him as a family member. HL had a history of becoming agitated coupled with mild self-harm, which the family had been able to control in the three years that HL had lived with them. While at a day centre, he became agitated and was admitted as an informal patient to a psychiatric facility. While agitated in the admission ward, he was generally compliant, and did not attempt to leave the acute ward following the admission. Had he made such a move, formal confinement proceedings would have been commenced, and HL would not have been allowed off the premises; but such formal proceedings had not been necessary. Notwithstanding repeated requests by the family of carers for HL's return, the hospital refused to discharge him into their care, and for a number of months, the family were not permitted to visit HL, in part because of a concern by the hospital that he would try and leave with them at the end of such a visit.

At issue in the domestic litigation was whether individuals such as HL, who acquiesced rather than assented to their admission and who lacked the capacity to make a decision as to where they would reside in any event, could be admitted informally and remain in hospital under these circumstances or whether they had to be sectioned under the formal confinement powers of the MHA 1983. Before the European Court of Human Rights, it was whether these conditions engaged the right to liberty under Article 5 of the ECHR.

The House of Lords held that the MHA 1983 envisaged the informal admission of acquiescing incapable patients: *R v Bournewood Community and Mental Health Trust, ex p L* [1998] 3 WLR 107 (HL). Lord Goff reached this view by citing paragraph 291 of the Percy Commission report, the report that led to the 1959 Mental Health Act (Royal Commission, 1957). Certainly, it does seem that the Percy Commission did advocate informal admission, not merely for assenting patients, but for 'all who need [treatment] and are not unwilling to receive it' (Royal Commission, 1957: para. 291). As a general principle, this interpretation of the Percy Commission is beyond reproach.

The House of Lords then approached the case in the context of wrongful confinement. In that context, Lord Goff held that any question of detention of HL would have arisen only had he attempted to leave the hospital, which he did not. Further, any confinement that would have occurred would in this case have been justified by the developing 'inherent jurisdiction' of the court, the principles of best interests and necessity derived from *F v West Berkshire Health Authority* [1989] 2 All ER 545. It is much less obvious that the House of Lords was correct in these aspects of HL's case (see Bartlett, 2003). The Percy Commission expressly addressed the situation of a family member asking for the release of an incompetent, acquiescing patient. In the event that the family member was the nearest relative, the Commission stated that 'there can be no question of a barring certificate, even on grounds of danger to the patient or to others, in relation to patients admitted informally, whom the hospital has no authority to detain' (para. 305 (ii)). If the person requesting were not the nearest relative, it would seem that the patient should nonetheless be released if the individual had made reasonable plans to care for the patient (para. 305(iv)). The House of Lords was apparently not referred by counsel to this paragraph of the Percy Report, and it is not referred to in its judgment. In any event these aspects of the House of Lords judgment are largely superseded by the decision of the European Court of Human Rights.

The result of the House of Lords decision was the '*Bournewood* gap'—a situation where people lacking capacity could be admitted to intrusive institutional care without the benefit of procedural safeguards. While the House of Lords held on a 3:2 majority that this situation was legal, even some of the judges in the majority were not enthusiastic about the situation: see judgment of Lord Nolan [1998] 3 WLR 107 at 122.

5.1.1.1 Article 5 of the European Convention on Human Rights

An appeal was launched to the European Court of Human Rights on behalf of HL, alleging a violation of the right to liberty under Article 5 of the ECHR. This Article will be at issue on numerous occasions in the central chapters of this book, and a general indication of its scope and core jurisprudence relating to mental disability is therefore appropriate now both for the current discussion and as a basis for those later arguments.

Article 5(1) provides that no one will be 'deprived of liberty' except in specified situations 'in accordance with a procedure proscribed by law'. Two of the situations are primarily relevant for the purposes of mental health law. The first, Article 5(1)(a), allows the detention of persons following conviction. Such detentions will be relevant in discussions of detention of criminals with mental disability under Part 3 of the MHA

1983 (see Chapter 8), but it is not relevant for *HL*. For present purposes, and of primary importance for mental health law generally, is Article 5(1)(e), which allows for the 'lawful detention of...persons of unsound mind.'

Article 5 goes on to provide a set of rights arising when liberty is curtailed. Of present relevance, Article 5(2) provides a person who is arrested the right to be informed, in a language which he or she understands, the reasons for the arrest and of any charge against him or her, and Article 5(4) provides that anyone deprived of liberty 'shall be entitled to take proceedings by which the lawfulness of his detention shall be decided speedily by a court and his release ordered if the detention is not lawful.' Article 5 therefore provides both restrictions to the situations in which a deprivation of liberty may occur, and procedural protections prior to, at the time of, and following the deprivation of liberty.

While the ECHR took effect in 1953, it is not until 1979 that the first case involving persons of unsound mind was decided by the Strasbourg court. What began as a trickle has now become, if not a flood, at least a very significant stream, and a detailed discussion of that case law is outside the scope of the current discussion. Some elaboration will occur as issues arise in the remainder of this volume, but for a fuller and systematic discussion, see Bartlett, Lewis and Thorold (2006). While subsequent case law provides considerable elaboration, that initial case, *Winterwerp* v *the Netherlands* (Application No. 6301/73, judgment 24 October 1979, (A/33) (1979–80) 2 EHRR 387) still provides the basic structure for interpreting Article 5 in the context of mental disability.

Winterwerp requires that 'unsoundness of mind' must flow from a 'true mental disorder', determined by 'objective medical expertise' (para. 39). The expertise does not need to be from a psychiatrist; the view of a general practitioner will suffice (*Schuurs* v *the Netherlands* (1985) 41 D & R 186, 188). The English courts have recently expanded this permitted expertise to include psychologists with relevant expertise in the case of learning disability (*G* v *E* [2010] EWCA Civ 822, para. 60). This extension has not been tested in the Strasbourg court, although if the intent of the *Winterwerp* criteria is to ensure objective and informed expertise, an argument can be made for the position in *G*. While the Strasbourg Court is prepared to take a reasonably wide view of what constitutes unsoundness of mind, an objective basis demonstrating a disorder does appear to be required. Mere eccentricity or social deviance, for example, would not suffice (*Winterwerp* at para. 37). The disorder must be 'of a kind or degree warranting compulsory confinement' (*Winterwerp* at para. 39). This criterion may be met either because the person would be dangerous if left at large, or because of a sufficient need for medical treatment (see *Hutchison Reid* v *the United Kingdom*, Application No. 50272/99, judgment 20 May 2003, (2003) 37 EHRR 9, para. 52). Further, deprivation of liberty must be the least restrictive option available under the circumstances (*Varbanov* v *Bulgaria*, Application No. 31365/96, judgment of 5 October 2000; *Ťupa* v *Czech Republic*, Application No. 39822/07, judgment of 26 August 2011, para. 48) and a proportional response, appropriately balancing the interests of the individual and society as a whole (*Witold Litwa* v *Poland* (2001) 33 EHRR 53, para. 78). In cases of emergency, a reasonable period is permitted following the detention for the medical assessment to occur.

The deprivation of liberty must be in accordance with a 'procedure prescribed by law' (Article 5(1)), taken by *Winterwerp* to mean consistent with the express and implied principles of the ECHR as a whole, being fair and proper, and protecting the individual from arbitrariness (*Winterwerp*, para. 45). This is taken to mean that a person should be able, with appropriate advice if necessary, to foresee the probable consequences of a given course of action (*Kawka* v *Poland*, Application No. 25874/94, judgment on 9 January 2001, para. 49).

The continued deprivation of liberty is justified only if a mental disorder of sufficient severity continues to exist (*Winterwerp*, para. 39). As the nature and degree of mental disorders may change over time, therefore the access to a court or tribunal guaranteed by Article 5(4) must arise on a periodic basis. Quite how frequently has not been finally determined by the Court, but it would seem that a review should be available promptly upon the initial detention (that is, within something like one to two weeks), and something like annually thereafter. There is a right to legal representation at these hearings (*Winterwerp* at para. 60), and while the court has not affirmed a right to universal legal aid in such proceedings, it has been sympathetic in requiring that the state provide representation in a number of cases brought before it (see, e.g. *Megyeri* v *Germany* Application No. 13770/88, judgment of 12 May 1992, (1992) 15 EHRR 584, para. 23; *Pereira* v *Portugal*, Application No.44872/98, judgment of 26 February 2002, (2003) 36 EHRR 49, paras. 58–61).

5.1.1.2 The *HL* decision and the limits of Article 5

In *HL*, the European Court of Human Rights took the view that whether or not the situation constituted a violation of the English law of wrongful detention, HL was deprived of liberty under Article 5 of the ECHR. Article 5 rights were specifically not dependent on whether the individual manifested a wish to leave the facility (*HL* v *United Kingdom*, Application no. 45508/99, judgment on the 5 January 2005, (2005) 40 EHRR 32, para. 90).

The standards in the jurisprudence cited so far in this chapter was therefore relevant to HL's case. In the view of the Court, the existing law did not provide adequate procedures (para. 120):

> In this latter respect, the Court finds striking the lack of any fixed procedural rules by which the admission and detention of compliant incapacitated persons is conducted. The contrast between this dearth of regulation and the extensive network of safeguards applicable to psychiatric committals covered by the 1983 Act [MHA] (paragraphs 36 and 54 above) is, in the Court's view, significant.
>
> In particular and most obviously, the Court notes the lack of any formalised admission procedures which indicate who can propose admission, for what reasons and on the basis of what kind of medical and other assessments and conclusions. There is no requirement to fix the exact purpose of admission (for example, for assessment or for treatment) and, consistently, no limits in terms of time, treatment or care attach to that admission. Nor is there any specific provision requiring a continuing clinical assessment of the persistence of a disorder warranting detention. The nomination of a representative of a patient who could make certain objections and applications on his or her behalf is a procedural protection accorded to

those committed involuntarily under the 1983 Act and which would be of equal importance for patients who are legally incapacitated and have, as in the present case, extremely limited communication abilities.

This must be correct. As the Court notes, there was no procedural structure surrounding HL's deprivation of liberty, and no processes in place for challenges to it, or determining its duration.

The Court's reasoning also shows up limitations of the jurisprudence, however. First, the Court is ambiguous as to whether the existing law was substantively strong enough to meet ECHR standards. It acknowledges that the substantive law relating to the inherent jurisdiction was still under development at the time of HL's detention, but declines to make a finding as to whether it had developed to the point of sufficient clarity to satisfy the ECHR (para. 119). This is an astonishing failure. When the case arose in 1997, the inherent jurisdiction was in its infancy. It had never been subject to judicial comment for the purposes of detention prior to *HL*, and most of the limited jurisprudence on the meaning of best interests antedates the case: there were no substantive rules or standards in effect at the time HL was admitted. It is difficult to see how a stronger set of facts could be found for inadequate substantive provisions for deprivation of liberty. It is bizarre that the Strasbourg court did not find a substantive failing here, but also perhaps telling: the Court's jurisprudence at least when dealing with mental disability is much stronger on requiring procedures than on substance.

The decision was successful at requiring the government to introduce a process to regulate deprivations of liberty of people lacking capacity: the DOLS were introduced in the MHA 2007. The process further appears to meet the *Winterwerp* requirements. Incapacity must be caused by a mental disorder as certified by a medical practitioner. The severity must be such that it is in the individual's best interests to be detained, including the requirements that it must be to protect the individual from harm and that the conditions of the deprivation of liberty must be proportionate to the seriousness and likelihood of that harm. Periodic reviews of detention are put in place, and a representative (generally a family member of the person detained) is appointed to keep an eye on things. Either the person detained or the representative can challenge the detention before the Court of Protection, and legal aid is available.

The government's response has strengths and weaknesses which will be discussed in the remainder of this chapter. The DOLS however provide a good example of the limits of human rights as a model. Post-enlightenment liberal rights, embodied in documents such as the ECHR, tend to pre-suppose an autonomous and self-motivated subject. Classic civil rights can be envisaged as the right of such a subject to be free of government intervention. The right to liberty under Article 5 is a good example of this: it is the right not to be interfered with by the state except in certain circumstances (Article 5(1)), buttressed by a right to be informed of the reasons of any arrest or detention (Article 5(2)), and the right to challenge any deprivation of liberty before a court (Article 5(4)). For the autonomous subject of liberal theory, these are important rights, but what do they mean for people such as HL? Certainly, they provide a system by which one set of officials (the DOLS assessors) checks to make sure that another set of people (the care home administrators, hospital doctors, or social services staff) are acting in accordance with approved professional standards and the best interests of the person detained. That is important, but it is not necessarily empowering of the person detained. Persons deprived of liberty under the DOLS will of course vary in their abilities, and some will be able to challenge their detentions, but many will not. Consider HL himself. He was unable to decide whether or not to attempt to leave the room; it is not obvious what practical benefit will be gained by providing him with information and a right to challenge his detention, since it is difficult to imagine that he will in practice be in a position to use it.

To its credit, the government response goes some way to taking these concerns into account. The person's representative is meant to 'represent' and 'support' the detained person in matters concerning the deprivation of liberty (MCA 2005, Sch. A1, para. 140). Where the individual is likely to have difficulty challenging detention, a lay advocate (an 'Independent Mental Capacity Advocate' or 'IMCA') is to be assigned to the person detained. While this is again an important provision, it begs the question of how far, in practice, such an advocate can provide a voice that reflects the views, wishes, and desires of people with severe impairments such as HL. This is not meant as a criticism of systems such as the DOLS that attempt to provide support in these circumstances; it is instead a reminder that whatever measures are employed, we may be a long way from the self-motivated and autonomous subject of liberal theory.

This in part recalls the questions regarding the UN Convention on the Rights of Persons with Disabilities (CRPD) discussed in Chapter 4, and foreshadows similar discussion in Chapter 6, at 6.2.3 and 6.5.2, regarding the use of mental disability as a justification for deprivation of liberty, an approach the CRPD would apparently prohibit. The CRPD, and indeed human rights law generally, is meant to empower the people under its remit. However laudable that may be as an objective, there may in practice be limits on its achievability. This is of course not an argument against making all reasonable attempts at such empowerment; it is instead a reminder that it is theoretically and practically not straightforward.

5.2 An overview of the DOLS

The DOLS are complex. It is therefore likely to be helpful to provide a relatively brief overview, before launching into the detail.

5.2.1 Deprivations of liberty outside care homes and hospitals, and the residual power of the Court of Protection

The Court of Protection has a general authority to make determinations arising under the MCA 2005, and this includes determinations regarding the deprivation of liberty (MCA 2005, ss. 4A(3) and 16(2)(a)). In the event that the individual detained is subject to a compulsory power under the MHA 1983 (for example, a community treatment order or guardianship), the 'eligibility' requirement contained in Sch. 1A of the MCA 2005 will apply to court determinations regarding deprivations of liberty, but Sch. A1, which contains the bulk of the DOLS processes, does not apply to court-ordered detentions. The DOLS provisions contained in Sch.A1 of the MCA 2005 allow people lacking capacity to be deprived of liberty when specified requirements are met, and it is expected that these will be sufficient for most purposes, but they do not oust the jurisdiction of the court. This is significant in at least two situations.

First, the DOLS processes in Sch. A1 apply only to deprivations of liberty which occur in care homes as defined by s. 3 of the Care Standards Act 2000, or in private or NHS hospitals. Deprivations of liberty occurring in other places (for example, in an individual's home, or in an institution that is not a hospital or care home) are permitted only with an order of the Court of Protection.

Second, while the MCA 2005 in general applies to persons over the age of 16 years (s. 2(5)), the DOLS processes in Sch. A1 apply only to persons over the age of 18 years (MCA 2005, Sch. A1, para. 13). For a person between the ages of 16 and 18 to be deprived of liberty under the MCA 2005, therefore, a court application is required. This may be of particular relevance, since the general law relating to children does not allow the deprivation of liberty of a person over the age of 16, so the court application under the MCA 2005 is the only way this can be done (*C* v *A Local Authority* [2011] EWHC 1539 (Admin), esp. paras. 48 and 64).

5.2.2 **The DOLS: Schedules A1 and 1A of the MCA 2005**

The overall direction of the DOLS is quite straightforward. They apply to persons lacking capacity who are deprived of liberty in a care home or hospital. Subject to some fairly minor tweaking, deprivations of liberty are permitted when in the best interests of the individual. The best interest test is the same as the one in the main MCA 2005, including the requirement that it must be to prevent harm to the individual detained and the detention must be a proportionate response to the severity and likelihood of the harm—a requirement contained for all decisions involving restraint under the main MCA 2005. A 'supervisory body' (the relevant local authority for care homes; the National Assembly for Wales for hospitals in Wales; and for hospitals in England, the detainee's local authority) is to be informed by the hospital or care home when a person without capacity may be being deprived of liberty. That supervisory body will send out two DOLS assessors—one a medical doctor, the other a social worker or similar professional—to ensure that the provisions of the MCA 2005 are being followed. When there is no family member or similar person to consult about the individual's best interests, an IMCA (Independent Mental Capacity Advocate) will be appointed to assist in this determination. If the deprivation of liberty is permitted, a representative (generally, a family member or similar non-professional carer) is to be appointed to maintain contact with the person detained and represent and support the person in matters regarding the detention. Detentions may be permitted for up to one year, at which point the process repeats.

Given the relative simplicity of this approach, the complexity of the provisions is astonishing. Schedules A1 and 1A, where the bulk of the DOLS are located, is longer than the entire MCA (excluding Schedules) as passed in 2005, buttressed by a Code of Practice running to 125 pages (Ministry of Justice, 2008b). The provisions are often needlessly complex. The person thought to be lacking capacity, labelled 'P' in the remainder of the MCA 2005, is for no obvious reason re-labelled 'the relevant person' in the Schedule A1, but not in Schedule 1A, where the usage of the main MCA 2005 is retained. For purposes of consistency, the language of 'relevant person' will be used throughout this chapter, including in the discussion of Schedule 1A. The system is administered through a series of 32 forms. When downloaded together, these run to 172 pages: see http://www.dh.gov.uk/prod_consum_dh/groups/dh_digitalassets/documents/digitalasset/dh_113208.pdf. The form certifying the relevant person to be over the age of 18 years alone runs to three pages. Overall, the provisions are laced with legal jargon, often bordering on the incomprehensible even to lawyers. It is difficult to imagine that doctors, care home workers, and social services staff, the people primarily charged with the administration of the DOLS, will be able to make sense of them. In this, the DOLS differ from the original MCA, passed in 2005, which was a model of clarity and where the key concepts were readily understandable by lay readers. The DOLS amendments to the MCA 2005 are thus a bit like watching a favourite art work being vandalized by thugs.

The process for a DOLS authorisation is commenced by the person in charge of the care home or the foundation trust in charge of the hospital to which the relevant person will be admitted. These are called the 'managing authority' by the DOLS. The managing authority applies to the 'supervisory body' for a 'standard authorisation' to deprive the relevant person of liberty. As noted, the supervisory body is the relevant local authority for care homes, the National Assembly for Wales for admissions to Welsh hospitals, and, since the Health and Social Care Act 2012 came into effect in April 2013, the local authority in which the patient was last resident for hospitals in England (see Health and Social Care Act 2012, s. 136). The supervisory body will send out a doctor (a 'mental health assessor') and a social worker or similar professional (a 'best interests assessor') to decide on the appropriateness of the detention, based on the six 'qualifying requirements' summarised in Box 5.1. The mental health requirement must be assessed by the mental health assessor, who must be a doctor with expertise in treatment or diagnosis of mental disorders, and the best interests assessor must be a social worker, approved mental health professional as defined by the MHA, nurse, occupational therapist, or chartered psychologist: *Mental Capacity (Deprivation of Liberty: Standard Authorisations, Assessments and Ordinary Residence) Regulations 2008*, SI 2008/1858, paras. 4 and 5. The best interests assessor is to carry out the best interest assessment, but also the age and no refusals assessments. The mental capacity assessment may be carried out by either assessor.

Box 5.1

- **Age**: the relevant person must be over the age of 18.

- **Mental Health**: the relevant person must be affected by a disorder or disability of the mind.

- **Mental Capacity**: the relevant person must lack the capacity to decide whether he or she should be accommodated in the hospital or care home for the purpose of being given the relevant care or treatment.

- **Best Interests**: Admission to the care home or hospital on the terms proposed must be in the best interests of the relevant person, and must be necessary to prevent harm to him. The admission must be a proportionate response to the likelihood and severity of the harm the relevant person would suffer if not so admitted.

  - The best interests assessment also contains a determination of whether the relevant person is in fact deprived of liberty.

- **Eligibility**: This requirement determines the dividing line between the DOLS and the MHA 1983. In general terms:

  - If the relevant person is already covered by compulsory powers under the MHA 1983, the eligibility requirement will not be met if the proposed standard authorisation proposed overlaps or conflicts with those compulsory powers.

  - If the relevant person is to be admitted to hospital to be treated for mental disorder and objects either to the admission or to that treatment, the eligibility requirement is not met unless that objection has been overruled by the valid decision of a deputy or donee of an LPA.

- **No Refusals**: This requirement will be met unless (1) the relevant person has made an advance decision refusing some or all of the medical treatment to be provided in the care home or hospital; or (2) if the admission is in conflict with a decision of a donee of an LPA or deputy acting within their authority.

The eligibility assessment may be carried out by either assessor, but if it is by a mental health assessor, that assessor must also be approved under the terms of s. 12 of the MHA 1983, and if by a best interest assessor, that assessor must also be an approved mental health professional (AMHP) (SI 2008/1858, para. 7). The specifics of the roles of s. 12 approved doctors and AMHPs will be discussed in Chapter 6, at 6.3.2.2 and 6.3.2.3. For present purposes, suffice it to say that they are key actors in the processes under the MHA relating to detention, guardianship, and community treatment orders. All assessments, including the eligibility assessment, must be completed for all deprivations of liberty under the DOLS, whether those occur in care homes or hospitals. The result is that anyone deprived of liberty under the DOLs must be seen by someone with a detailed understanding of these MHA provisions.

If all qualifying requirements are certified by the assessors to be met, the supervisory body scrutinises the assessments and may issue the standard authorisation if it considers that the detention is justified. This is meant to be a bona fide scrutiny, and the supervisory body ought not to issue the standard authorisation if it knows or ought reasonably to know that an assessment is insufficient or defective (*London Borough of Hillingdon* v

Neary [2011] EWHC 1377 (COP) paras. 180–184). The detention may be justified for a period of one year, or such lesser period as is approved by the best interests assessor.

Detention under the MHA 1983, like DOLS detentions, requires the involvement both of a doctor with particular expertise in the diagnosis and treatment of mental disorders (a 'section 12 approved' doctor: see 6.3.2.3) and an 'approved mental health professional' (drawn from a range of professions similar to the best interests assessor), as well as a second doctor. The DOLS envisage that the assessors will overlap with these MHA roles, but the appointment processes are separate, so the groups will not overlap completely: some best interests assessors will be AMHPs, but some will not, and vice versa; some mental health assessors will be section 12 approved under the MHA 1983, and some will not, and vice versa.

The DOLS envisaged that the standard authorisation would be applied for either within 28 days prior to the relevant person being admitted, or if already admitted (e.g., in the case of a person whose capacity is failing), within 28 days of the qualifying requirements being met (MCA 2005, Sch. A1, para. 24). This would allow time for the assessments to be completed before any detention begins.

In practice, this pacing does not necessarily occur, and when required, the managing authority can issue to itself an 'urgent authorisation', allowing the detention to occur for one week so as to allow the application and assessments for the standard authorisation (see MCA 2005, Sch. A1, Part 5). The managing authority can request that the urgent authorisation can be extended once, for an additional period of seven days, if the application for the standard authorisation has been made and there are 'exceptional reasons' why the application has not been decided and it is 'essential for the existing detention to continue' (MCA 2005, Sch. A1, para. 84(4)). It cannot be extended a second time, and failure to complete the required assessments by the expiry of the urgent authorisation would result in the relevant person being detained illegally. In the event that the authorisations cannot be completed on time, or of irreconcilable disagreement between the assessors, it would seem that the appropriate response in this situation is an urgent out-of-hours application to the Court of Protection (*A County Council* v *MB* [2010] EWHC 2508 (COP) at para. 89).

A peculiarity of the DOLS system is that local authorities play multiple parts in the system, most notably as the supervisory bodies for the care homes they in fact own and manage, and deciding the appropriateness of deprivations of liberty in situations where the local authority staff has been pivotal in the decision to deprive the individual of liberty. The dual role as managing authority and supervisory body is expressly envisaged in the DOLS (MCA 2005, Sch. A1, para. 184). It is not, however ideal. The role of a supervisory body is quasi-judicial, determining the appropriateness of a deprivation of liberty. The risk is that the local authority staff exercising this role may also become enmeshed in the care planning for the relevant person, ceding (or at least, appearing to cede) their independence from the decision: see, e.g., *London Borough of Hillingdon* v *Neary* [2011] EWHC 1377 (COP) where the person with authority over making DOLS orders was criticised for being involved in the care planning in the case attending a service meeting where the case was discussed (paras. 106 and 112). While this is obviously problematic, it is in a sense unsurprising. The local authority official in question was the service manager—an obvious official to be in charge of the DOLS procedure. This was a case where serious conflict was occurring between the family of the relevant person and the local authority, and it is difficult to see that the service manager could be absent from the meetings relating to those difficulties. The conflict does appear to be real.

Whether the resulting system gives rise to a violation of Article 5 of the ECHR is an open question. Article 5(4) provides the right to challenge a deprivation of liberty before a court, which in turn is understood as an impartial body, independent of the executive and the parties and being of a judicial nature: *De Wilde, Ooms and Versyp* v *Belgium*, Application No. 2832/66, 2835/66, 2899/66, judgment of 18 June 1971, (1972) 1 EHRR 438; *DN* v *Switzerland*, Application No. 27154/95, judgment of 29 March 2001, (2003) 37 EHRR 21. The body does not need to be a court as that is understood in the UK; a tribunal that meets these criteria is within the scope of Article 5(4) (*X* v *United Kingdom*, Application No. 7215/75, judgment of 5 November 1981, (1981) 4 EHRR 188). If the local authority is both detaining the individual and managing the DOLS assessment process, it is difficult to see that there is the required independence to meet the Article 5(4) standard. Probably, it was not intended to: notwithstanding the quasi-judicial nature of the process identified in *Neary*, it does not have the relevant judicial nature. The Article 5(4) point is presumably intended to be addressed by the right of the relevant person and his or her representative to challenge the detention in the Court of Protection. As noted, this is problematic if the relevant person does not have the practical ability to make such a challenge (HL, who was apparently entirely unable to make a decision about his circumstances, is a good example of this). Does Article 5(4) require in these circumstances that a court or similar independent body consider the detention? This issue was considered regarding detentions of people lacking capacity to psychiatric facilities under the MHA 1983, an apparently analogous situation, and the House of Lords considered that such routine judicial (or in *MH*, review tribunal) scrutiny was not required (*R (MH)* v *Secretary of State for Health* [2005] UKHL 60). At the time of writing this case is on appeal to the European Court of Human Rights. Recent jurisprudence of the Strasbourg court suggests that the appeal in *MH* could go either way. In *Stanev* v *Bulgaria*, Application No. 36760/06, judgment of 17 April 2012, the court found a violation of Article 5(4) where there was no routine judicial reviews of peopled detained because of legal incapacity, but this was in a context where the relevant domestic law precluded the detained person from applying for such a review himself or herself (but where family members could apply). In the *MH* case, like in the DOLS processes, the detainee can require a judicial review of the detention. It is not clear how the court will view the situation when there is no realistic prospect of such a review being requested, given the relevant person's abilities.

In reading the jurisprudence, it should be noted that usually when matters relating to deprivations of liberty are contested before the Court of Protection, the Court will be exercising its independent jurisdiction to decide on matters relating to deprivations of liberty. While it is certainly possible to seek judicial review of the people performing assessments under Sch. A1 and of whether the conditions of detailed by Sch. A1 are met (see MHA 1983, s. 21A), these hearings are rare. Much more frequently the Court is focused on the merits of the facts before it, and whether the relevant person ought to be accommodated in the proposed conditions—a matter for them that involves apply-ing the MCA 2005 and the eligibility requirement but not (or at least, not expressly) the requirements contained in Sch. A1—rather than on whether the assessors did their job properly. The relevance of this slightly different role is limited. Key issues in most cases will involve whether a deprivation of liberty is occurring, whether the relevant person has capacity or not, whether the course of action is in the person's best interests and whether, if the relevant person is to be admitted to a psychiatric facility, he or she is 'eligible' for such an admission. All of these will be relevant to Sch. A1 or court-ordered deprivations of liberty. While the court, unlike the best interests assessor, is not expressly required to consider as part of the best interests assessment whether the deprivation of liberty is required to avoid harm to the relevant person and whether the proposed course of action is proportionate to the likelihood and severity of the harm (see *G v E* [2010] EWCA Civ 822), it is difficult to imagine that a court would not do so. Indeed, the obligation of the court to apply the Strasbourg jurisprudence relating to Article 5 imports similar standards of seriousness (see discussion of *Winterwerp* at 5.1.1.1). The most significant difference would appear to be that the court is not required to receive a mental health assessment separate from the diagnostic evidence relevant to mental capacity under the MCA 2005, and generally it would seem does not do so. That said, it will be argued in this chapter that it is at best unclear what in substantive terms the mental health assessment adds, so its absence from the court's process may be of minor importance, except that we will lack judicial guidance on what it means or is for.

5.3 The deprivation of liberty

The triggering issue for the applicability of the DOLS is whether there is a deprivation of liberty. The DOLS define the phrase as having the same meaning as in Article 5(1) of the ECHR (MCA 2005, s. 64(5)), so the Strasbourg jurisprudence is directly on point. Citing that jurisprudence, the English courts have held that there are three elements to deciding whether a deprivation of liberty has occurred: '(a) an objective element of a person's confinement in a particular restricted space for a not negligible time; (b) a subjective element, namely that the person has not validly consented to the confine-ment in question, and (c) the deprivation of liberty must be one for which the State is responsible' (*Cheshire West and Cheshire Council v P* [2011] EWCA Civ 1257, para. 16, citing in particular *Storck v Germany*, Application No. 61603/00, judgment of 16 June 2005; see also *JE and DE v Surrey CC* [2006] EWHC 3459 (Fam), para. 77).

The second two elements of this test may be dealt with relatively briefly. Regarding the subjective element, (b), the courts have accepted that the acquiescence of a person without capacity does not constitute consent to the confinement. After the decision in *HL v the United Kingdom*, the case which was the impetus for the DOLS, this position must be correct. The European jurisprudence further makes clear that the consent to the admission must be ongoing: a person who attempts to leave or escape from the institution and is prevented from doing so can no longer be taken to consent to the admission: see e.g., *Storck v Germany*, para. 76; *Shtukaturov v Russia*, Application No. 44009/05, judgment of 27 March 2008, para. 108. Similarly, a person who consents to admission but subsequently loses capacity must no longer be taken to consent to the admission. This is envisaged by the DOLS themselves (see MCA 2005, Sch. A1, para. 24), which require application for a standard authorisation for deprivation of liberty for those already accommodated in hospitals and care homes 28 days prior to the DOLS requirements being satisfied. This would apply either when increasing controls are becoming necessary (which would be relevant to the objective element—see below), or when the individual is losing capacity (which is relevant to the subjective element).

The court's reference to the relevance of state responsibility for the deprivation of liberty, (c) in *Cheshire West and Cheshire Council v P*, is not as straightforward as the English decisions suggest. It is now clear that the state's duty extends beyond not violating Article 5 by detaining people itself, but also includes a positive obligation more generally to protect the liberty of those within its jurisdiction, whenever the state knows or ought reasonably to know of a deprivation of liberty (*Stanev v Bulgaria*, Application No. 36760/06, judgment of 17 January 2012, para. 118). This does not pose a problem for the current English statutory regime, however, as section 64(6) of the MCA 2005 provides that the definition will not depend on whether the person is deprived of liberty by a public authority or not. This provision applies both to the DOLS regime under Sch. A1 and to the Court's jurisdiction, for deprivations of liberty where Sch. A1 does not apply (most notably, deprivations of liberty outside hospitals and care homes: see 5.2.1).

It is the first element of the determination of deprivation of liberty, the 'objective' element, that has proven problematic. This is in part because the determination has been taken to be heavily fact-specific, and rules of general application may therefore be difficult to develop; but it is also in part because the English courts seem to be keen to limit the scope of cases under the DOLS, where the Strasbourg court seems content to adopt a more expansive approach.

To begin with what is uncontroversial, deprivation of liberty is to be determined according to a wide array of factors, including the type, duration, effects, and manner of implementation of the measure in question. While the ECHR jurisprudence distinguishes between a 'deprivation' of liberty in Article 5 and a 'restriction' on liberty under ECHR Protocol 4, the distinction is one of degree or intensity, rather than nature or substance (*Guzzardi v Italy*, Application No. 7367/76, judgment of 6 November 1980). This reading of the provisions is not entirely convincing. Protocol 4 concerns the right to move freely within ones country of residence, to choose ones residence, and to leave the country. This seems to have little to do with whether the conditions of a given care home are sufficiently strict to constitute a deprivation of liberty under Article 5. Nonetheless the deprivation/restriction distinction is now well-entrenched in ECHR law, and must be taken as here to stay (see, e.g., *Austen v the United Kingdom*, Application Nos 39692/09, 40713/09 and 41008/09, judgment of 15 March 2012, para. 57).

In the context of deprivations of liberty of persons lacking capacity, the detention involves the person's confinement in 'a particular restricted space for a not negligible length of time' (see *Storck*, para. 74). The most important elaboration of this statement by the Strasbourg court is contained in *HL* v *the United Kingdom*: does the care home or hospital exercise 'complete and effective control over his care and movements' (*HL*, para. 91). The exclusion of familial involvement in the admission and visits appears to be relevant to that determination (see, e.g., *Stanev* v *Bulgaria,* para. 122), but it is not determinative (see *DD* v *Lithuania,* Application No. 13469/06, judgment of 14 May 2012, where family visits were allowed and DD's stepfather instigated the admission).

Within that framework, the Strasbourg court seems to include a wide array of people as deprived of liberty. The presence of a locked door controlling access to the ward is not required (*HL*, para. 92), and the Court has recently found a deprivation of liberty to occur when the individual lived in an unlocked ward and, with the permission of care staff, periodically left the facility and visited community (*Stanev*, para. 124). Leaves of absence for a longer period did occur, but at the discretion of the care staff, who had control of the individual's identity papers and finances. Thus while Mr Stanev was able to take journeys, he remained effectively under constant supervision, and could not leave the home without permission whenever he wished. This was enough to constitute a deprivation of liberty. Similarly in *DD* v *Lithuania*, the fact that DD was unable to leave the institution without the management's permission appears to be pivotal to the decision that she was deprived of liberty, although the court notes that management also controlled who could visit DD, and from whom she could receive telephone calls (*DD,* para. 146). The fact that medication was provided to DD, and that she was restrained in the facility (albeit briefly, for only 15 minutes) also appear to be relevant (paras. 148 and 149).

In the *Stanev* case, it held that 'it is unnecessary in the present case to determine whether, in general terms, any placement of a legally incapacitated person in a social care institution constitutes a "deprivation of liberty" within the meaning of Article 5 § 1' (para. 121). The fact that the court was willing to leave this question open suggests a willingness to extend the protections of Article 5 to a wide expanse of people lacking capacity.

While the DOLS Code of Practice contains a list of indicators broadly consistent with the Strasbourg jurisprudence (see Box 5.2), the English courts appear much more hesitant than their Strasbourg counterparts to find a deprivation of liberty. Consider, for example, the facts in *C* v *Blackburn with Darwen BC* [2011] EWHC 3321. In this case, C had a learning disability and a brain injury which resulted in epilepsy. While lacking capacity to make decisions regarding his residence, he did have significant abilities, often being employed as a janitor in his care home. He was able to leave the home only if accompanied by a staff member. While this would often occur on a daily basis, it was subject to the availability of staff. In January 2011, he kicked down the door of the home in an attempt to leave, and the police were called upon to intervene. A standard authorisation issued shortly thereafter, suggesting that at least at that time, the care home and local authority considered that he was deprived of his liberty, since that is a prerequisite for the grant of such an authorisation (see further 5.4.4). In his evidence to the Court of Protection regarding the standard authorisation, he testified that he found the legal restrictions to which he was subjected stressful, making his epilepsy worse. He testified that he wanted to go somewhere else, that he did not get on with other residents, and that he stayed in his room most of the time to avoid them. He testified that he wanted an end to the legal restrictions on his movement (*C*, paras. 8–11 and 19). Notwithstanding this set of facts, the court held that he was not deprived of his liberty.

Box 5.2

Indicators of deprivation of liberty identified by the DOLS Code of Practice (Ministry of Justice, 2008b), para. 2.5

- Restraint is used, including sedation, to admit a person to an institution where that person is resisting admission.
- Staff exercise complete and effective control over the care and movement of a person for a significant period.
- Staff exercise control over assessments, treatment, contacts, and residence.
- A decision has been taken by the institution that the person will not be released into the care of others, or permitted to live elsewhere, unless the staff in the institution consider it appropriate.
- A request by carers for a person to be discharged to their care is refused.
- The person is unable to maintain social contacts because of restrictions placed on their access to other people.
- The person loses autonomy because they are under continuous supervision and control.

The more limited English approach flows in part from considering the 'normality' of the relevant person's life, using a comparison between the life of the person alleged to be detained and that of persons with similar conditions, in assessing whether a deprivation of liberty has occurred. In this way, the English approach does not consider the deprivation of liberty as flowing simply from the conditions in which an individual is accommodated and the behaviour of those providing that accommodation, but asks whether the accommodation is significantly more restrictive than the available alternatives for the individual.

The English approach begins to crystallise with the case of *P (MIG) and Q (MEG)* v *Surrey CC* [2011] EWCA Civ 190. In this case P and Q were sisters, aged 18 and 19, each of whom had a learning disability. P's care was at a foster home, in the care of a foster mother to whom P was devoted. She kept her bedroom door closed there. It was not locked, and P had never shown a wish to leave, but if she had made any attempt to leave, the foster mother would have restrained her. P was provided with intensive support in daily life, including further education, trips, and holidays. She was unaware of danger, so needed help crossing road. She was not on medication. Q lived in a specialist home for adolescents, which accommodated three other residents. Q did have occasional outbursts directed at other residents which required her restraint, but the use of behavioural management techniques had resulted in her behaviour stabilising since her admission. She was subject to continuous supervision and control, but the home was not locked. She had never attempted to leave, so no prevention of that was necessary; she was attended whenever she left home. She attended the same further education college as P, and enjoyed a fuller social life than P. Q was able to communicate wishes in limited manner. She was taking Risperidone for control of anxiety. The Court of Protection held that neither was deprived of liberty, a decision upheld by the Court of Appeal.

P (MIG) and Q (MEG) establishes a variety of points. The trial judge had noted that P and Q were both happy in their accommodation. The Court of Appeal holds that their happiness was certainly relevant to their best interests, but not to whether they were deprived of liberty (para. 24). Any objections by the relevant person to the conditions of their accommodation were relevant to whether a deprivation occurred, and the absence of such objections could also be relevant, insofar as it reduced the confrontations between the relevant person and their carers and reduced the need for restraint and restrictions on behaviour (para. 25). It further holds that the use of medication that has the effect of sedating or tranquilising the relevant person was a pointer towards a deprivation of liberty, as 'it suppresses her liberty to express herself as she would otherwise wish' (para. 26). The relevance of such medication was increased if it was administered by force. Similarly, the absence of medication was a pointer away from a deprivation of liberty. While the specifics of these points have not been litigated before the Strasbourg court, they appear broadly similar to its approach, with the caveat that they are indications, none of which is itself determinative. Thus for example notwithstanding the fact that HL did not appear to object to his care in hospital, the Strasbourg court still found a deprivation of liberty. That said, if the relevant person does object and physical restraint is required, the English court is surely right that this would be relevant to a determination of whether he or she had been deprived of liberty.

The court also, more controversially, notes 'the relative *normality* of the living arrangements under scrutiny' (para. 28, emphasis in original). Just as relevant persons living with their families would not normally be (but might sometimes be) deprived of liberty, so people cared for in fostering arrangements, where the conditions of accommodation were similar to life within families, would often not be deprived of liberty. The court went on to raise but not decide the question of whether the degree of confinement to which P and Q were subject prior to their admission to their foster placements was relevant (para. 30).

The logic in *P and Q* was taken further by the Court of Appeal in *Cheshire West and Cheshire Council v P* [2011] EWCA Civ 1257. That case involved a man with cerebral palsy, Downs' Syndrome, and vascular difficulties, who was housed in supported housing with three other residents. The support in his accommodation included one to one care in the daytime, and two staff on duty to care for the four residents at night. P therefore received intensive support, in virtually all of his daily activity. He was also required to wear clothes which fastened only at the back, to avoid him eating his incontinence pads and their contents. He was able to be in regular contact with his family, and to socialise with the other residents and staff.

In determining whether P had been deprived of his liberty, the court extends the reasoning in *P and Q* by contextualising the factual situations where detention is alleged. It considered by way of example the nineteenth-century case of *R v Jackson* [1891]

1 QB 671, where a man had locked his wife in the matrimonial home until she agreed to restore conjugal rights with him, and compared this to a situation where a man after many years of happy marriage locked his wife in the house because she suffered from dementia and could not safely be allowed out unsupervised. In the court's view, the former certainly constituted a deprivation of liberty under Article 5, but the latter did not (para. 46). The court adopted a variety of approaches to distinguish these situations. All are problematic, both for doctrinal reasons and with reference to the Strasbourg case law (some but not all of which, it should be said, is subsequent to the *Cheshire* decision).

The court noted that in the case of the wife with dementia, there is no legal obligation for her to reside with the husband; it is instead that she has no practical alternative, and that 'it would be absurd to say that she is being deprived of her liberty' in this situation (para. 57). In the court's view, things would be different if the individual had a different option for care, and if the current arrangements were required by the coercive act of a public authority.

The latter point regarding coerciveness is consistent with the Strasbourg jurisprudence, but the concern with the availability of different options for care has its own difficulties, unacknowledged by the court. Consider two persons A and B resident in a supported housing situation similar to P's, and subject to similar conditions of care. Both A and B are unhappy with their residence there, but A has sufficient financial means that other accommodation could be arranged, where B does not. The approach of the court would seem to suggest that notwithstanding identical conditions in their current accommodation, A may be found to be deprived of liberty where B is not. The identical conditions make this an odd conclusion. It also makes little sense in the context of Article 5. The *Winterwerp* decision allows a deprivation of liberty for persons of unsound mind only if it is the least restrictive option available, and is a proportional response to the situation of the individual (*Varbanov v Bulgaria,* Application No. 31365/96, judgment of 5 October 2000; *Ťupa v Czech Republic,* Application No. 39822/07, judgment of 26 August 2011, para. 48, *Witold Litwa v Poland* (2001) 33 EHRR 53, para. 78). It is difficult to see why A should have the benefit of these requirements, where B would not. If alternative accommodation care arrangements for B really could not be found, the current care arrangements might be justified for B but not for A, but a potential defence under Article 5 should not be confused with whether a deprivation of liberty has occurred. Finding that a deprivation of liberty had occurred would oblige the relevant local authority to justify the deprivation by demonstrating that reasonable attempts had been made to find less restrictive arrangements for B.

Limitations of the court's approach can be seen in *C v Blackburn with Darwen BC,* the case noted regarding the epileptic man with learning disability, who notwithstanding an ongoing wish to leave the care home in which he was living culminating in an escape attempt that involved breaking down a door, was held not to be deprived of liberty. Relying on *Cheshire,* the court held (para. 26):

> In the present case Mr C undoubtedly wants to live somewhere else, but this is a reflection of his unhappiness with the care home. He would like to be able to live an unconfined life in the community, but this is not realistically possible due to the extent of his difficulties.

> I distinguish his situation from those where a person has been removed from a home that is still realistically available. While Mr W's suggestion of another unit is consistent with Mr C's wish to leave the care home, it does not represent an actual alternative at the present time.

Mr C's situation is however similar to Mr Stanev's. Both have firm views against their current care arrangements, both are precluded by law from making decisions regarding their placements and the conditions of their care. If anything, Mr Stanev enjoyed a greater degree of freedom than Mr C, as Mr C was only permitted out of the care facility when supervised by a staff member. In neither case was an alternate care placement available. Yet Mr Stanev was held to have been deprived of liberty, and Mr C not.

The *Blackburn* case points up the problematic nature of court's starting point in *Cheshire*. Is it really so 'absurd' to say that people who are required (whether because of disability or not) to live in controlling environments that they may not like should have the benefits of the processes required by Article 5—most significantly, periodic reviews of their care by someone slightly removed from the situation, and the appointment of a representative to watch out for their interests? Options may result from the involvement of family members willing to serve as carers, who may also be watching over the relevant person in the care home. The lack of options may alternatively result from the increased disability of the relevant person. For both these reasons, people without options may be more vulnerable than those with options. Insofar as that is the case, should these more vulnerable people really be deprived of the protections afforded by the DOLS?

The court in *Cheshire* spends considerable effort analysing the relevance of purpose, motive, and intent, eventually holding that the purpose (meaning the pursuit of an objectively justifiable aim) of the alleged deprivation of liberty is relevant to determining whether a deprivation of liberty has occurred (paras. 60–77). This approach has been called into question following the Strasbourg court's decision in *Austin and others v United Kingdom,* Application Nos 39692/09, 40713/09 and 41008/09, judgment of 15 March 2012, 55 EHRR 14, and the best legal view now appears to be that these factors may form part of the overall factual context, but are not directly relevant in determining whether a deprivation of liberty has occurred (see *CC v KK and STCC* [2012] EWHC 2136 (COP), para. 93–96).

The court in *Cheshire* further refines the question of the 'normality' of the conditions of the alleged detention. Citing *Engel and Others v The Netherlands (No 1)* Application Nos 5100/71; 5101/71; 5102/71; 5354/72; 5370/72, judgment of 8 June 1976, 1 EHRR 647, a case which held that to determine whether soldiers were deprived of liberty required a comparison with the life of other soldiers, the court holds that in determining whether people with mental disabilities are deprived of liberty, the court should look not to the population as a whole, but to 'an adult of similar age with the same capabilities and affected by the same condition or suffering the same inherent mental and physical disabilities and limitations' (para. 88). As such, a deprivation of liberty will not occur if the conditions are consistent with 'the kind of lives that people like [the person at issue] would normally expect to lead' (para. 97).

This is a problematic approach. As a test of deprivation of liberty, it would presumably apply to Article 5 as a whole, not merely to people lacking capacity. The comparator group for a murderer undergoing a lengthy prison sentence would presumably thus be other murderers with similar characteristics; but these will most probably also be in prison, leading to the rather surprising conclusion that convicted murderers in prison are not deprived of liberty under Article 5: these are, after all, the kind of lives that such people would normally expect to lead.

The court's approach turns the question of deprivation of liberty into a question of discrimination within a class of people: if all similarly situated people are treated similarly so that there is no discrimination between them, there is no deprivation of liberty. But deprivation of liberty is not a matter of discrimination within a group. It is instead a matter of the intensity of controls applied to an individual, and the fact that everyone within a group may be subject to similarly stringent controls may mean that all of the group are deprived of liberty.

Engel notwithstanding, the language of comparator groups in determination of deprivation of liberty is entirely absent from the Strasbourg jurisprudence. The Strasbourg judges instead look to the degree of control to which the relevant person is subjected, with reference for example to the factors discussed early in this section.

Both *Cheshire* and *P and Q* are currently on appeal to the Supreme Court, with hearings scheduled for October 2013. This will be the first time that the Supreme Court will have had occasion to consider the DOLS; it may well be that the terrain looks quite different following their decision.

5.4 The six requirements

5.4.1 The age requirement

The age requirement is refreshingly straightforward: the DOLS provisions apply only to persons over the age of 18 years (MCA 2005, Sch. A1, para. 13). The MCA 2005 in general assumes jurisdiction once an individual has reached the age of 16, however (s. 2(5)), so such detentions of people between the ages of 16 and 18 may be approved by the court (see 5.2.1). For persons under the age of 16, the MCA 2005 has no application; but this does not preclude the use of relevant child law or the MHA 1983 in appropriate circumstances.

5.4.2 The mental health requirement

The relevant person meets the mental health requirement if he or she is suffering from a mental disorder as defined by the MHA 1983, but explicitly excluding from that definition the restrictions it contains relating to learning disability (MCA 2005, Sch. A1, para. 14). As noted in Chapter 1, 1.4.1, the MHA definition for some purposes requires that a learning disability is associated with abnormally aggressive or seriously irresponsible conduct (MHA 1983, s. 1(2A)). For the purposes of the DOLS, such conduct is not required.

It is difficult to see why the DOLS revert to the MHA 1983 definition of mental disorder, since the MCA 2005 itself includes a diagnostic threshold as part of the capacity determination (and must be used to assess the relevant person as part of the capacity requirement under the DOLS). The MHA refers to 'any disorder or disability of the mind' (MHA 1983, s. 1(1)); the MCA refers to 'an impairment of, or a disturbance in the functioning of, the mind or brain' (MCA 2005, s. 2(1)). It is difficult to see much difference between a 'disability' and an 'impairment . . . or disturbance in the functioning' of the mind. The MCA 2005 definition includes the brain as well as the mind, but can it really be the intent of the legislator that people lacking capacity because of organic neurological disorders rather than psychological or psychiatric ones should be excluded from the DOLS? There is no obvious reason for such an exclusion, but it seems to reflect the divergence in wording.

Is it instead that the MHA 1983 definition excludes dependence on alcohol or drugs from the definition of mental disorder? This makes some sense if the MCA 2005 is taken to include such conditions (see Chapter 4, 4.4.1), but it seems a peculiarly round-about way to achieve this end. If the objective is to keep these conditions outside of the DOLS, it would surely have been simpler to legislate expressly to that effect, rather than approaching the issue obliquely, by incorporating the MHA 1983 definition.

In any event, it is not obvious that any restriction anticipated by use of the MHA 1983 definition will have the desired effect, since people under the MCA 2005 definition will still be within the jurisdiction of the MCA, and therefore will be able to be deprived of their liberty by the Court of Protection (which does not apply Sch. A1 for its decisions regarding detention, and is not therefore required to refer to the MHA 1983 definition). Whether the rationale for the use of the MHA definition flows from a difference between mind and brain, or because of a desire to prohibit deprivations of liberty based on alcohol or drugs, it does seem odd to preclude it in Sch. A1, but to leave it within the jurisdiction of the Court.

There is no threshold for the severity of the mental disorder for purposes of this assessment: simply having one will suffice.

The doctor performing the mental health assessment is also to consider the effects of the proposed deprivation of liberty on the relevant person, and to notify the best interests assessor of any findings in this regard (MCA 2005, Sch. A1, para. 36).

5.4.3 The mental capacity requirement

The DOLS apply only if the relevant person lacks capacity to decide whether he or she 'should be accommodated in the relevant hospital or care home for the purpose of being given the relevant care or treatment.' (MCA 2005, Sch. A1, para. 15). The DOLS are contained in Schedules to the main MCA 2005, and the definitions contained in the MCA are therefore applicable to the DOLS. The discussions relating to the meaning of mental incapacity in Chapter 4 are therefore relevant to this requirement under the DOLS, and will not be repeated here (see 4.4). For a finding of incapacity, the main MCA 2005 requires both a diagnostic condition as the cause of the incapacity and also a functional test—the inability to understand, retain, or use relevant information. The peculiar juxtaposition between the MCA 2005 diagnostic criterion here and the MHA

1983 diagnostic criterion for the mental health assessment have already been noted (see 5.4.2). The remainder of this section will consider the understanding, retention, and use of the relevant information.

The reported case law routinely cites evidence of psychometric testing, often reflected as 'mental age', as relevant to capacity determination. While such tests have the advantage of objectivity, they are not unproblematic in their application to capacity determination. A adult found to have a 'mental age of 7', as was the case in *A Local Authority* v *FG, AG, HG* [2011] EWHC 3932 (COP), does not necessarily have capacity comparable to a 7-year-old child, as capacity will be based not merely on psychological ability but also life experience, a point acknowledged by the court (para. 7). What matters instead is whether the person can understand, retain, and use or weigh the relevant information as part of a process of reaching a decision.

That leads to the question of what the relevant information will be. On this, by way of general guidance, the courts have been remarkably circumspect. If the choice is between local authority and family care, *FG* provides some minimal guidance (para.17):

> That involves an ability to understand what the issues are that determine family or Local Authority provision, what the consequences of any such decision are, and how they are likely to impact on the person's emotional, physical and educational welfare. That is a relatively sophisticated process, and in the context of this case is, it seems to me, a difficult one.

This moves the decision regarding capacity well beyond the ability simply to choose which place one wishes to live in, into a realm where the psychosocial ramifications of the choice must be able to be understood and evaluated. It is not merely the ability to articulate which room, which food, or which cohabitants the relevant person likes better, but which placement will be most beneficial for the relevant person's psychosocial well-being. Given the uncertainties many people of robust capacity have about cohabitation arrangements and the choice of residence, this sets a high bar indeed. This is not necessarily a bad thing. Any standard of capacity will have 'winners' and 'losers', with high thresholds of capacity resulting in the coercion of some people we might like to see left free to make choices but fewer vulnerable people left exposed to the ramifications of bad choices, and low thresholds of capacity the reverse. It does give the lie to any claim that England has a low threshold of capacity, however, at least in this area.

A perusal of the reported case law suggests that a 'realistic' understanding of the risks of the options available (and, most notably, any wish to return home) is required: see, e.g., *FG*, para. 17; *CC and KK and STCC* [2012] EWHC 2136 (COP), paras. 29, 31, and 32; *PH* v *A Local Authority* [2011] EWHC 1704 (Fam), paras. 26, 27, 29, 36, and 45; *RT* v *LT and a London Authority* [2010] EWHC 1910 (COP), para. 30; *WCC* v *GS, RS, JS* [2011] EWHC 2244 (COP), para. 14. The *RT* case is unusual, in that it goes to reasonable lengths to explain how the lack of a 'realistic' assessment is related to the mental disorder experienced by the relevant person; the remainder merely note the 'unrealistic' view of the relevant person. The difficulty with this is, of course, that it fails to distinguish between poor decision-making flowing from the debilitating condition and poor decision-making flowing from other sources. The MCA 2005 is clear that 'a person is not to be treated as unable to make a decision merely because he makes an unwise decision' (s. 1(4)). Without a causal link established between the disorder and the grounds for decision, it is difficult to see why a poor decision would be viewed as evidence of incapacity, rather than merely unwise. Here, as in the discussion of the MCA 2005 generally in Chapter 4, it does seem that a concern for safeguarding is influencing the factual interpretations in determination of capacity.

It is notable and a matter of concern that, notwithstanding disagreements in the evidence regarding the capacity of the relevant person in the cases under discussion, *CC and KK* is notable as the only case in which the court heard face to face the views of the relevant person himself or herself. The court in that case notes that such testimony is unusual (para. 44). In the remainder, the court decided the question of capacity second-hand, by assessing the expert evidence. Finding that one expert is a better witness than another is not a substitute for actually speaking with the relevant person. Direct contact with the relevant person may also be an ECHR requirement. *Shtukaturov v Russia*, Application No. 44009/05, judgment of 27 June 2008, was a case of admission to a psychiatric hospital based on Shtukaturov's incapacity, where all the professional evidence and that of Shtukaturov's family before the domestic court had attested to that incapacity. The Strasbourg court nonetheless found a breach of the ECHR based on the domestic court's failure to see him personally (para. 73):

> The applicant was indeed an individual with a history of psychiatric troubles. From the materials of the case, however, it appears that despite his mental illness he had been a relatively autonomous person. In such circumstances it was indispensable for the judge to have at least a brief visual contact with the applicant, and preferably to question him. The Court concludes that the decision of the judge to decide the case on the basis of documentary evidence, without seeing or hearing the applicant, was unreasonable and in breach of the principle of adversarial proceedings enshrined in Article 6 § 1.

While this finding was made in the context of Article 6 (right to fair trial), the Court notes that the requirements of Article 5(4) are broadly similar (see para. 66). In cases where relevant persons are deprived of liberty after having lived autonomous lives in the community, therefore, it seems likely that the Strasbourg court will require the personal examination of the relevant person in cases before the Court of Protection. While not quite the *Shtukaturov* case, the logic of that case would suggest that where there is contradictory evidence of incapacity before the court, a personal examination of the relevant person would also be required.

5.4.4 **The best interests requirement**

The best interests requirement of the DOLS has two components. The first is that the relevant person is, or is to be, a 'detained resident' (MCA 2005, Sch. A1, para. 16(1)(2)). This component requires the assessor to consider whether the relevant person is (or is to be) deprived of liberty. The second requires that the proposed course of action, including the detention, is in the best interests of the relevant person, with the definition of best interests drawn primarily from the regular best interests criteria of the main MCA 2005 (see Chapter 4, 4.5). This includes the requirement that the proposed course of action is necessary to prevent harm to the relevant person and that the course of action is proportionate to the likelihood and seriousness of the harm, although for reasons best known to the drafters, this requirement is repeated in MCA 2005, Sch. A1, para. 16(1) rather than adopted by reference to the relevant section in the main MCA 2005 (see s. 6 (1)–(3)). While these express conditions relating to harm apply to the best interests assessment under the DOLS, they do not apply to the Court in its exercise of its overarching jurisdiction (*G* v *E* [2010] EWCA Civ 822). The intent of the legislature was therefore apparently that deprivations of liberty that did not flow from a specific harm to the relevant person would be permitted only by the Court, not by the Schedule A1 procedures.

Assessment of the first component requires consideration of whether a deprivation of liberty has occurred, a matter discussed already in this chapter at 5.3. The conduct of that assessment would appear to reflect the tensions in that discussion, with inconsistent results common between best interests assessors. In a study by Cairns *et al.*, five best interests assessors were presented with eight case vignettes, and asked to decide whether the individual described was deprived of liberty. In four of the eight vignettes, they split three to two in this decision (Cairns *et al.*, 2011: table 1). Admittedly, the sample size is small, but the inconsistency of result is reflected in the findings of the Care Quality Commission: there would appear to be significant confusion as to what deprivation of liberty means (see Care Quality Commission, 2011c). The reasons given by these assessors and others asked to provide a view of the vignettes further suggests confusion, even in circumstances where agreement occurred (347):

> Regarding this vignette, psychiatrists, IMCAs and best interest assessors were all in agreement that there had been no deprivation of liberty. The reasons given for this decision included: the acceptable use of restrictions proportionate to the risks; provision of Y's care in the least restrictive setting possible; a care plan that included open access for visits and regular (monthly) outings; the fact that Y had not demonstrated a desire to leave the unit; and the family's belief that he did not object to his situation.

Of concern here is not whether the conclusion is accurate—half the lawyers in the study also considered that the person had not been deprived of liberty—but rather the reasons given. Issues such as the proportionate use of restrictions relative to risk and least restrictive alternative, and to a considerable degree the individual's failure to object to the situation or happiness in it, are matters relevant to best interests rather than the determination of whether there is a deprivation of liberty. As discussed at 5.3, in cases such as *P (MIG) and Q (MEG)* the courts have noted that whether a course of action is in the relevant person's best interests is a different question from whether a deprivation of liberty has occurred. No doubt an assessment should be made as part of the DOLS processes as to whether the relevant person is deprived of liberty, but the inclusion of the deprivation of liberty assessment within the best interests assessment therefore seems bound to confuse, given that they are separate questions.

The second aspect of the assessment is directed to whether it is in the relevant person's best interests to be a detained resident (MCA 2005, Sch. A1, para. 16(3)). The express reference to detention in this provision, along with the requirement noted, that it be proportionate to the potential harm to the relevant person, suggests that questions of safeguarding will be of considerable importance in this aspect of the assessment. At the same time, an apposite note of caution is provided by the court in *CC and KK* (para. 25):

> [I]n cases of vulnerable adults, there is a risk that all professionals involved with treating and helping that person – including, of course, a judge in the Court of Protection – may feel drawn towards an outcome that is more protective of the adult and thus, in certain circumstances, fail to carry out an assessment of capacity that is detached and objective. On the other hand, the court must be equally careful not to be influenced by sympathy for a person's wholly understandable wish to return home.

While this comment is provided in the context of the assessment of capacity, it is equally applicable to an assessment of best interests.

While the questions relating to the potential harm to the relevant person are clearly central issues in the best interests determination, they are not the only ones. The best interests assessor is required in addition to take into account any relevant needs assessment, any relevant care plan, and any views of the mental health assessor regarding how the relevant person's mental health will be affected by the proposed care. In addition to the array of people identified in s. 4 of the MCA 2005, the best interests assessor is obliged to consult with the managing authority—the people managing the care home or hospital (MCA 2005, Sch. A1, para. 39). As such, it would seem that the assessment looks to the entire package of care related to the proposed admission, not merely those involving restrictions directly flowing from the deprivation of liberty.

The deprivation of liberty may only occur to avert potential harm to the relevant person. The proposed course of action should presumably therefore be juxtaposed to a the most reasonable course of action that does not involve such a deprivation of liberty, with the proposed plan being demonstrably preferable both in terms of the overall best interests of the individual and the proportionality of the response in averting potential harm. Such consideration seems appropriate not merely because of the terms of the best interests assessment, but flowing from the principle of least restrictive alternative in the MCA 2005 generally (s. 1(6)). When the alternative choice is care in the family, a full assessment of the family's ability to care for the individual should be undertaken (*LLBC* v *TG, JG, KR* [2007] EWHC 2640 (Fam), para. 33). Often, a simple return to the family home without local authority support will not be a practical option, and this in turn raises the question of what support the local authority is prepared to fund. *A Local Authority* v *PB* [2011] EWHC 502 (COP) shows the sort of difficulty that can arise. That case involved PB, a man in his forties, who was deprived of liberty in a care home. This was challenged by his mother, who had cared for PB all his life and wished to continue doing so. The mother was clear that this would require a package of support, but no concrete plan of support was before the court. The local authority took the view that PB's best interest was to be in the care home, and had thus not prepared an alternative; the mother presumably lacked the expertise to develop and cost such a report and presumably in any event would not have been able financially to commit the local authority to implementing such a plan; and the official solicitor, representing PB, had similarly not developed a plan. The court therefore held that it was insufficiently informed to make a finding relating to PB's best interests (para. 18).

The *PB* case points to an additional set of difficulties with the Court of Protection. The local authority had taken the view pursuant to its statutory mandate that it would refuse to fund any plan that would return PB to his mother's care (para. 19). Whether that was a defensible position was a matter of public law, subject to judicial review, but the Court of Protection has a statutory mandate that does not cover such matters. It cannot therefore require the local authority to fund the care package. Is the court therefore to make a decision based on the options actually available (in this case, care home or care by mother with no support)? This seems undesirable, as it allows local authorities to control the outcome. In *PB* itself, care by the mother without support was manifestly not a workable option, and therefore whatever PB's best interests might have been, had a care package with his mother been funded, he would almost certainly have ended up in the care home. Alternatively, should the court make a finding according to a plan that the local authority says it will not fund, allowing the relevant person to take their chances on judicial review of the refusal of funding? That is equally problematic. Success of such cases is by no means a foregone conclusion (see, by analogy, *Kolanis v the United Kingdom,* Application No. 517/02, judgment of 21 June 2005), and can be a long and costly exercise. And where is the relevant person to live while that is all being sorted out?

5.4.5 The no refusals requirement

The no refusals requirement precludes a deprivation of liberty in the following circumstances (MCA 2005, Sch. A1, paras. 19–20):

- if it is proposed to admit the relevant person for the purposes of providing treatment for which the relevant person has made a valid and applicable advance decision to refuse;
- if the proposed admission would involve the provision of care or treatment in conflict with a valid decision of a donee of a lasting power of attorney.

The first of these situations will prohibit admissions (generally if not always to hospitals) for the provision of treatment which the relevant person has refused (regarding advanced decisions to refuse treatment, see Chapter 4, 4.6). For example, if the relevant person has made a valid and applicable refusal of treatment for cancer, and it is proposed to admit him or her to treat the cancer, the no refusals requirement means that admission cannot occur. This makes sense: why deprive someone of liberty for the purpose of treating them, if the treatment will not be able to be given anyway?

This first situation applies to treatment only. If the cancer patient in question required care rather than treatment and the other conditions of the DOLS were met, he or she could be admitted to receive that care. That said, if there is a valid and applicable refusal of any part of proposed treatment, the deprivation of liberty cannot occur.

The second situation occurs when a donee of a lasting power of attorney acting within their authority decides against the admission of the relevant person to a care home or hospital. This raises the question of what happens when the donee is manifestly not acting in the best interests of the relevant person. In such circumstances, the Court of Protection has jurisdiction to issue directions, as it would for any other decision within the donee's jurisdiction (MCA 2005, s. 23(2)). There have as yet been no reported cases under this power, so it is not clear how much respect and latitude will be accorded to the donee's judgment in these circumstances.

The no refusals requirement provides no exception for admissions or treatment relating to mental disorder. Thus a person who has made a valid and applicable refusal of treatment for mental disorder cannot be admitted for that treatment using the DOLS. The DOLS do not preclude the use of compulsory detention under the MHA 1983, however, when the statutory requirements for such detention are met (see further Chapter 6, 6.3).

5.4.6 **Eligibility**

The substantial provisions of the eligibility requirement are contained in Schedule 1A to the MCA 2005. Unlike the other DOLS requirements contained in Sch. A1, the eligibility requirement applies both to deprivations of liberty by the courts and through the assessment processes in Sch. A1.

The eligibility requirement delineates between the DOLS and the compulsion provisions of the MHA 1983. The Schedule distinguishes between five cases, with slightly different requirements to determine ineligibility (MCA 2005, Sch. 1A, para. 2). The general approach is twofold:

- If the matter at issue in the DOLS determination overlaps with a compulsory power of the MHA 1983 to which the relevant person is already subject, the provisions of the DOLS authorisation must not conflict with the MHA 1983 compulsory power (Sch. 1A, cases A to D, see further 5.4.6.1).

- Otherwise, if it is proposed that the relevant person be admitted to hospital for treatment for mental disorder and meets the substantive criteria for civil detention under the MHA 1983, the DOLS may not be used if the relevant person objects either to the admission or to any of the mental health treatment to be offered in the hospital, unless that objection has been overruled by a decision of a donee of a lasting power of attorney or court-appointed deputy (case E, see further 5.4.6.2).

5.4.6.1 **Where MHA powers are in effect**

The easiest case for the first branch is the individual who is detained in hospital and resident there (case A in MCA 2005, Sch. 1A, para. 2). He or she is already deprived of liberty, and can be treated for his or her mental disorder without consent (subject to exceptions that do not require analysis here) (see Chapters 6 and 9 (9.3)). The ancillary powers of the hospital mean that virtually all aspects of the individual's life are already under the institution's control. Treatment other than for mental disorder falls outside MHA 1983 jurisdiction and therefore is decided under the provisions of the main MCA

2005 if the relevant person lacks capacity, but this is not a DOLS issue. The field is occupied by the powers of coercion under the MHA 1983, and the relevant person is therefore ineligible for a standard authorisation under the DOLS.

The relevant person may alternatively be living in the community either on a leave of absence from a MHA detention (MHA 1983, s. 17) or on a community treatment order (MHA 1983, s. 17A) (respectively cases B and C in MCA 2005, Sch. 1A, para. 2). Typically, these will contain provisions regarding treatment to be given in the community, and sometimes will include other requirements of the individual's life in the community (e.g., where they will live, or what social services they are required to use in the community). Both also allow the individual's recall to hospital, for short or longer periods of time as necessary (see Chapter 10, 10.2 and 10.4). If the relevant person is subject to one of these regimes, the terms of the standard authorisation must be consistent with the terms of the MHA compulsion. Unsurprisingly, since the MHA 1983 provisions provide for hospital admissions for treatment of mental disorder, the relevant person is ineligible for a DOLS authorisation if the proposed course of action consists in whole or in part of treatment for mental disorder in hospital.

MHA 1983 guardianship (case D in MCA 2005, Sch. 1A, para. 2; see MHA 1983, ss. 7 and 37, and Chapter 10, 10.3 in this book) provides limited and specific powers over those under its authority. Most notably, the guardian can determine where the individual will live, and can require the individual to attend as required for purposes of treatment, occupation, education, and training. It does not contain a power to consent to treatment on behalf of the individual, so it does not enforce treatment in the way that detention under the MHA 1983 does, nor does it have provisions regarding hospital admission for a person who does not comply with treatment. If the relevant person is subject to guardianship, once again, any standard authorisation granted must be consistent with the terms of the guardianship. For example, if the guardianship requires the relevant person to live in care home X, the standard authorisation cannot deprive him or her of liberty in care home Y.

A person subject to guardianship may, in principle, be admitted to hospital for treatment of mental disorder by the guardian (see *R* v *Hallstrom, ex p. W* [1986] 2 ALL ER 306 at 312). If a standard authorisation under the DOLS is sought in these circumstances, the relevant person will be ineligible if he or she objects either to the admission, or to any or all of the treatment for mental disorder to be given, unless a donee of a lasting power of attorney or a court-appointed deputy has overruled that objection. In this respect, the person subject to guardianship is in the same situation as a person for whom such admission is proposed, but who is not already subject to MHA 1983 powers: see further 5.4.6.2. The eligibility requirement takes a broad view of objection in these circumstances, requiring consideration to be given to the relevant person's behaviour, wishes, feelings, views, beliefs, and values, both at the time the issue arises and, where appropriate, in the past (MCA 2005, Sch. 1A, para. 5(6)–(7)). It is perhaps appropriate to recall that it is the use of the DOLS that is precluded in this situation. The use of formal powers under the MHA 1983 is permitted, if the conditions specified in that Act apply.

Guardianship provides an example of when a DOLS order may be appropriate, not-withstanding the existence of MHA 1983 powers. The guardian can determine where the individual will reside, and can require the individual's return to that place, but there is no authority in guardianship to deprive an individual of liberty there. Except for hos-pital detentions under the MHA 1983, therefore, if it is necessary to deprive a relevant person of liberty this will only be able to be done under the DOLS, even if the guardi-anship requires the individual to reside at the care home: see, e.g., *C v Blackburn with Darwen BC* [2011] EWHC 3321, para. 30.

This situation also provides an example of the potential difficulties of the system. What if the guardianship requires the relevant person to live in a specified care home, but the best interests assessor, in good faith, thinks that while a deprivation of liberty may be justified, it should not be in that care home? To sign off on a best interests assessment in these circumstances makes a mockery of the protections of the DOLS system. At the same time, if a deprivation of liberty is legitimately required, failure to sign the form may also lead to a vulnerable person coming to harm. Ideally, one would wish that the matter would be referred to a court for adjudication, but which court? The Court of Protection has jurisdiction over the DOLS, but not over the guardianship. The guardianship itself can be challenged through the MHA 1983 procedures in the First-Tier Tribunal (Health, Education and Social Care Chamber), but the jurisdiction only allows cessation or continuation of the guardianship—there is no jurisdiction to challenge the decisions being taken by the guardian. That would presumably be by way of judicial review, but not in the Court of Protection, so the two issues could not be argued in the same place. In any event, the best interests assessor does not have standing to challenge the guardian or the guardian's decision either before the tribunal or by way of judicial review, and even if a way were found to bring the judicial review application, these matters can take considerable time. What would happen to the relevant person in the interim?

5.4.6.2 The DOLS and informal admission to psychiatric facilities

The second branch of the eligibility requirement concerns people who are not already subject to compulsory powers under the MHA 1983, but where it is proposed to admit the individual to hospital for treatment for mental disorder (case E of MCA 2005, Sch. 1A, para. 2). HL, the person whose case was the impetus for the DOLS, is perhaps a clear example: he was admitted to hospital for treatment of his mental disorder, but was not detained in the hospital under the MHA 1983 (and was thus an informal patient under that statute). *HL* forced consideration of the question of how such admissions should be dealt with: when should the MHA 1983 be used, and when the DOLS? This branch of the eligibility requirement addresses that problem.

The relevant person will meet the eligibility requirement for the DOLS if:

- the relevant person is 'within the scope' of the MHA (Sch.1A, para. 2, case E);
- the proposed standard authorisation would authorise the relevant person to be a mental health patient; (Sch. 1A, para. 5(3));

- the relevant person does not object to being a mental health patient or to any of the mental health treatment to be given, unless such objection has been overruled by a valid decision of a donee of an LPOA or a court-appointed deputy. (Sch. 1A, para. 5(4)–(7)).

The relevant person is 'within the scope' of the MHA 1983 if the substantive criteria for detention under ss. 2 or 3 of the MHA 1983 are met. These criteria will be discussed at length in Chapter 6; for present purposes, admissions under s. 2 may occur when the individual is suffering from a mental disorder of a nature or degree warranting detention in hospital for assessment or assessment followed by treatment, and that the person 'ought' to be so admitted in the interests of his or her own health or safety or with a view to the protection of others. Admissions under s. 3 are permitted if the individual is suffering from a mental disorder of a nature or degree making it appropriate for him or her to received medical treatment in hospital, and it is necessary for the health or safety of the person or the protection of others that such treatment be given and it cannot be given without detention under the section, and that appropriate treatment is available.

One of the criteria for detention under s. 3 of the MHA 1983 is thus that appropriate treatment cannot be given without detention under that section. For purposes of determining eligibility under the DOLS, the possibility that such treatment could be provided under the MCA 2005 is not to be considered (Sch. 1A, para. 12(5)). This is presumably to maintain the focus on the treatment in question—is this the sort of treatment that can properly be given under the MHA 1983—rather than becoming entangled in divergent legal possibilities for such provision. The issue, after all, at this point in the assessment is whether the individual is 'within the scope' of the MHA 1983, not whether, in the end, the treatment will be provided under the MHA 1983 or the DOLS and MCA 2005. Indeed, for determining whether the relevant person is within the scope of the MHA 1983, this principle has been extended so that the assessor should assume that whether assessment and treatment under s. 2 of the MHA 1983 can be given without resort to detention should be considered without reference to the MCA 2005 (*GJ* v *The Foundation Trust* [2009] EWHC 2972 (Fam), para. 44).

The detention criteria under the MHA 1983 are open to considerable interpretation in individual cases, and the statutory language allows, rather than requires, the admission of the individual, if the statutory criteria are met. In *GJ*, the court held that the assessor was not required to consider what a reasonable doctor deciding on admission would decide, nor whether the individual would inevitably be admitted. Instead, the assessor was to take their own view, based on the facts, of whether the statutory criteria for admission were met (para. 80).

That view may nonetheless be complex, as the schemes do not always sit easily together. Learning disability provides a good illustration. Under s. 2, anyone with a learning disability who otherwise meets the admission criteria may be detained for assessment, for a period up to 28 days. Under s. 3, people with learning disability may only be admitted if that disability is associated with abnormally aggressive or seriously irresponsible conduct (and, of course, the relevant other criteria are met). This may well mean that a relevant person with learning disability not associated with such conduct may be within the scope of the MHA 1983 for the first 28 days of detention, and then outside it. They would thus be ineligible for a DOLS order for the first 28 days, but then become eligible, until such time as further assessment was required and a new s. 2 admission could be justified, at which time they would once again become ineligible for the DOLS.

As noted, in the event that the relevant person is within the scope of the MHA 1983, he or she is ineligible for detention under the DOLS if he or she is be a 'mental health patient' and either objects to that, or to being given some or all of the proposed treatment for mental disorder, unless that objection is overruled by the holder of a LPOA or a court-appointed deputy.

The term 'mental health patient' is defined as 'a person accommodated in a hospital for the purpose of being given medical treatment for mental disorder' (MCA 2005, Sch. 1A, para. 16). The proposed deprivation of liberty must therefore be in a hospital; no issue of eligibility arises for people not yet governed by the MHA 1983 who are to be deprived of liberty in care homes, even if the admission is to facilitate treatment for mental disorder (*W PCT* v *TB* [2009] EWHC 1737 (Fam)). The admission must further be for the purpose of being given medical treatment for mental disorder. Frequently at the time of admission, the mental disorder may be complicated by a physical disorder requiring treatment. When this occurs, the court has held that the assessor should consider whether, if the treatment for physical disorder did not exist, the hospital admission would be proposed, and on this basis whether the only effective reason for the proposed admission is the treatment of the physical disorder (*GJ* v *The Foundation Trust* [2009] EWHC 2972 (Fam)). If based on this test the proposed admission is essentially for treatment of a physical rather than mental condition, the relevant person is not ineligible and a standard DOLS authorisation may issue.

The same broad view of objection is adopted as was the case for hospital admissions of people under guardianship. Any indication of objection flowing from the relevant person's behaviour, wishes, feelings, beliefs, views, and values is thus to be taken into consideration.

GJ was the first DOLS case to be heard by the Court of Protection. It is still the most comprehensive discussion of the eligibility requirement, but some aspects of it may warrant re-visiting. The case involved a man with diabetes and also vascular dementia and Korsakoff's Syndrome, a memory-related disorder flowing from alcohol consumption. The dementia and the Korsakoff's Syndrome were mental disorders, the diabetes of course a physical disorder, and in determining eligibility, the issues before the court were whether GJ was within the scope of the MHA, and whether he was to be a 'mental health patient' as distinct from a patient admitted for the treatment of his physical disorder. In making this decision, as noted in this section, the court provided a relatively expansionist view of the individuals 'within the scope' of the MHA. It then notes (para. 45; see also para. 59):

> In my judgment, the deeming provisions alone, and together with that view on assessments, are strong pointers in favour if the conclusions that (a) the MHA 1983 is to have primacy

when it applies, and (b) the medical practitioners referred to in ss. 2 and 3 of the MHA 1983 cannot pick and choose between the two statutory regimes as they think fit having regard to general considerations (e.g. the preservation or promotion of a therapeutic relationship with P) that they consider render one regime preferable to the other.

This in turn extends to an obligation on decision-makers under the MCA and DOLS to 'take all practical steps to ensure that this primacy is recognised and given effect to' (para. 65).

Insofar as this means that where the MHA 1983 can be used it should be used in preference to the MCA/DOLS procedures, this interpretation must be incorrect. If a relevant person is within the scope of the MHA 1983 and is to be a mental health patient, Schedule 1A makes it clear that he or she will only be ineligible for a MCA/DOLS deprivation of liberty if he or she objects either to the admission or to some or all of the treatment offered. If the MHA 1983 detention provisions were used whenever they could be used, whether or not the relevant person objected or not would become irrelevant, and that is clearly not the intent of Schedule 1A. There is nothing wrong with taking a broad view of who is 'within the scope' of the MHA 1983 and not allowing this determination to be affected by collateral considerations, but that is quite a different thing to saying that the MHA 1983 must be used whenever possible in these circumstances.

If this is correct, in cases where a relevant person is within the scope of the MHA 1983 but does not object, practitioners could choose whether to use the MHA or the DOLS. The DOLS Code of Practice offers little guidance on this, although it does note that an individual who is likely to regain capacity and at that time object to treatment would sensibly be placed under the MHA 1983, presumably on the basis that MHA compulsion would be required at that time in any event (Ministry of Justice, 2008b: para. 4.48). Notwithstanding the comments in *GJ*, there is no obvious reason why the preservation or promotion of a therapeutic relationship should not figure in this decision. For the relevant person, the DOLS do have the advantage that the rest of the assessments occur expressly, and the best interests assessor can not merely find that the entire deprivation of liberty is unwarranted, but can also require tailoring of the care provided to the relevant person. Issues such as who will be able to visit the individual, or details of the programme of care to be offered, or indeed the actual treatment to be provided, are to be considered by the assessors and in the event of disagreement can thus be challenged before the Court of Protection. Detentions under the MHA 1983 by comparison are challenged before a review tribunal, where the only issue is whether the detention is to continue or not. If that is the issue of concern to the individual, the quasi-judicial nature of those proceedings may be preferable to the more social services ethos of the DOLS assessments, but the continuation of the detention itself is the only matter within the jurisdiction of the tribunal. Challenges to the care or treatment provided under the MHA 1983 are in principle available by way of judicial review, but such challenges have virtually always failed in the past.

5.5 Conclusion

The discussion in this chapter might give the impression that the DOLS are a dynamic new initiative to protect the rights of, and improve decision-making about, some of the most vulnerable people in our society. In fact, they have been something of a damp squib.

The number of people who ought to be subject to the DOLS is not clear, and estimates have shown considerable variation. In the *Bournewood* litigation discussed at the beginning of this chapter, it was estimated before the House of Lords that a finding that HL could not be held informally would result in an additional 22,000 people being subject to MHA 1983 detention on a given day, or an additional 48,000 MHA 1983 detentions per year: *R v Bournewood Community and Mental Health Trust ex p L*, [1998] 3 WLR 107 at 112G. This figure would appear to refer only to psychiatric admissions; persons in hospital where a deprivation of liberty flowed from a physical cause such as a brain injury, where the MHA 1983 is unavailable, would presumably be extra. And the figure refers only to hospital admissions. Care homes, which cater to the needs of the considerable bulk of persons with dementia or learning disability, are similarly not included in this figure. By the time the DOLS were in their planning stages, the usage expected by the government based on existing populations in care homes and hospitals had reduced to 21,000, roughly three quarters of which were expected to come from care home admissions and roughly a quarter of which would be granted. Thus the 21,000 requests for assessment in the first year would yield roughly 5,000 authorisations. The frequency of these was expected reduce over time to roughly 7,000 assessments leading to 1,700 authorisations per year after 2015–16 (DOH, 2008c, paras. 30–32). The Department of Health freely acknowledged that this was an estimate only.

The actual number of applications for standard authorisations in the first year, 2009–10, was 7,157, being 5,393 for care homes and 1,764 for hospitals. Of these 3,297 were granted (2,439 for care homes and 858 for hospitals) (National Health Service Information Centre, 2010). These have gradually been increasing since that time, with 8,982 applications (6,708 for care homes and 2,274 for hospitals) in 2010–11 (of which 4,951 (3,817 for care homes, 1,134 for hospitals) were granted, and 11,393 applications in 2011–12 (8,208 for care homes, 3,185 for hospitals) of which 6,343 (4,697 for care homes, 1,646 for hospitals) were granted (National Health Service Information Centre, 2011, 2012c). Of those applications refused, just over 4 per cent in 2009–10 involved people who were deprived of liberty, a proportion falling to about 2 per cent in the later years. The most frequent reason for the applications being refused would appear to be a finding that the relevant person is not deprived of liberty, but in about 10 per cent of the refusals, there was a finding that the relevant person in fact had capacity.

The result of this is that at the end of March 2012, 1,667 people were subject to standard authorisations under the DOLS—1,421 in care homes and 246 in hospitals (NHS Information Centre, 2012, table 8a). To put that figure in perspective, it is estimated that 304,850 people with dementia in the UK are in long-term care (Luengo-Frenandez,

Leal, and Gray, 2010, p. 19)—admittedly not all in England and Wales, where the DOLS apply. A further, roughly, 43,400 adults with learning disability in England were living in care homes, nursing homes, long-stay hospitals, and similar residential settings (Emerson *et al.*, 2011: 58). No doubt many of these people continue to have capacity, and no doubt many are accommodated in situations that do not constitute deprivations of liberty; but whatever definition of 'deprivation of liberty' one adopts, can it really be said that the 1,667 people under DOLS at this time is anything more than the tip of the iceberg? If the objective of the DOLS was to provide meaningful safeguards for people lacking capacity deprived of their liberty, can it really be seen as a success?

6

Civil Detention under the
Mental Health Act 1983

6.1 Introduction

Each year, roughly 100,000 adults are admitted to psychiatric hospitals in England. Of these, roughly 40 per cent will experience formal legal coercion ('sectioning') under the Mental Health Act (MHA) 1983 in the course of their admission. The use of admissions for assessment (s. 2) and admissions for treatment (s. 3), the sections most relevant to the present chapter, increased from 25,795 to 37,065 between 2006–07 and 2010–11 (DH (DH), 2011e: table 2.1)—a rise of 44 per cent in just five years. While it is certainly true that more people than ever using specialist mental health services are treated in the community without hospital admission—814,252 in 2006–07 rising to 1,094,135 in 2010–11—(DH, 2011: table 1.1) hospital care remains a major component of mental health service provision; and for those admitted, legal compulsion is increasingly prevalent. In 1999, the government could claim that fewer than 20 per cent of psychiatric inpatients were sectioned (DH, 1999a: para. 2.1); the proportion is now more than twice that number.

Detention under these sections of the MHA 1983 has two main effects: the individual cannot leave the hospital without the permission of hospital staff, and, subject to procedures that will be discussed in Chapter 9 (at 9.4 and 9.5), he or she may be treated for his or her mental disorder without consent. If the person is detained under s. 3, he or she may also be subject to a community treatment order when leaving hospital, if the conditions relevant to that order are met (see further Chapter 10, 10.4).

If 40 per cent of persons admitted are at some time detained, it means of course that 60 per cent are not: informal admission under s. 131 of the MHA 1983 remains more frequent than detention under the Act. People admitted informally are not confined in any legal sense. Unlike patients who are sectioned, they may in theory discharge themselves from the hospital if they wish, and they have the right to consent to treatment if competent to do so. At its best, this is no doubt a highly desirable situation, allowing service users greater involvement in their course of treatment and minimising stigma. This rather rosy picture is subject to two practical caveats.

First, the MHA 1983 allows the detention of people who have been admitted as informal patients. Informal patients who wish to exercise their right to leave the hospital or to refuse treatment may find themselves detained under the Act, and indeed it would seem that roughly 28 per cent of the people detained were already informal patients at the time of their detention (Care Quality Commission, 2013: figure 1) For such a high percentage of mandatory admissions, it is surprising that there has been no systematic research on this group of patients. Why do people who did not initially require compulsion on admission come to require it part way through? Are their expectations for treatment and improvement not met? Is there a breakdown in trust between them and their clinicians? Is life on the ward too unappealing? Is the sectioning to facilitate seclusion or other intensive controls, perhaps in response to the patient becoming violent? We do not know.

Second, the absence of formal legal coercion under the MHA 1983 does not necessarily mean that an admission is voluntary in the sense of being freely chosen. Informal patients may acquiesce to admission for example if they feel they have no practical alternative, as when they are dependent on carers in the community who insist on their admission. Such quasi-compulsion may be cloaked in formal law. For example, a guardian appointed under s. 7 of the MHA 1983 (see Chapter 10, 10.3) may require the patient to reside in a specific place. According to R v *Hallstrom (No. 2)* [1986] 2 All ER 306, at 312, there is nothing in the Act to prevent this power being used to admit the patient into a hospital. The patient is not detained under the confinement powers of the MHA 1983, and is therefore an informal patient. Paragraph 26.33 of the Code of Practice argues against the use of this power in this way for anything other than a short stay, but it is difficult to see statutory support for that limitation. The Code further notes that when the admission would result in a deprivation of liberty, MHA guardianship should not be used (para. 26.30). Alternatively, if the patient lacks the capacity to make a decision to be admitted and admission is in his or her best interests, he or she may be admitted through the Mental Capacity Act (MCA) 2005. In this case, if the conditions of admission are sufficiently intense that the individual is deprived of liberty, then legal authorisation for the admission must be sought, either through detention under the MHA 1983 or through the deprivation of liberty safeguards under the MCA 2005 (see Chapter 5). Whether or not the restrictions reach that level of intensity, many of these patients will lack capacity to consent to treatment, and treatment in that case will be given under the terms of the MCA 2005. While that Act in theory requires the involvement of the patient as much as possible in his or her care, implementation of that provision may vary depending both on the capabilities of the patient and the practices of the relevant staff members. In any event, the reality may be a long way from the co-operative decision-making image that is the starting image for informal admission.

When patients acquiesce because they perceive no other alternative to hospitalisation or because of inherent vulnerability that does not render them legal incapable, or because they are afraid of being sectioned if they exercise their rights, no legal processes surrounding the admission apply. Somewhere between 10 and 50 per cent of informal patients feel coerced in this way (Katsakou, 2011; Sheehan and Burns, 2011). The effect of this coercion on clinical outcomes is not clear, but the studies do show that service users find the coercion dehumanising (Newton-Howes and Mullen, 2011). These people may well be highly vulnerable; but they are invisible in law.

While civil detention under the MHA 1983 results in significant reductions in legal rights, patients are often sufficiently uninvolved in the mechanics of the admission that they do not know what their legal status is. This is further complicated by the movement of numerous patients between categories at various times in their hospital stay. Studies suggest that notwithstanding the duty in s. 132 that detained patients be informed of their status and of avenues of redress, 40 to 50 per cent of civilly confined patients did not know they had been confined (Monahan *et al.*, 1995; Goldbeck *et al.*, 1997). Similarly, a survey by the Mental Health Act Commission (MHAC) in 2006 found that more than 30 per cent of detained patients did not recall being told what section of the Act they were admitted under, or how long they were expected to stay (MHAC, 2008: para. 4.53). Studies by Lomax in 2009 and 2010 found that only 60 to 80 per cent of detained patients knew what section they were detained under. Perhaps more significantly, the Lomax studies found that somewhere between 10 and 45 per cent of informal patients were unaware of their informal status, and of those that were, only a third to two thirds understood their right to refuse treatment (Lomax, 2012). Given this limited understanding, it is difficult to see that the rights apparently guaranteed by the statute will be exercised in practice.

Detentions occurring as a result of engagement with the criminal justice system are discussed in Chapter 8. As noted so far, the present chapter concerns instead those who are detained through civil powers—in broad terms, when their mental condition is perceived as sufficiently serious that they require detention, but when they have been neither charged nor convicted of an offence. Once again, while the lines between these are clear in legal terms, they can sometimes be somewhat arbitrary in their application in individual cases. It may well be a matter of discretion whether the police officer called out to address the situation of a person perceived to have mental disabilities proceeds under criminal law powers or instead by short-term detention powers under s.136 of the MHA 1983 that commence the civil detention process (on policing, see further Chapter 7).

6.2 What is it all for?

The decision to section an individual is among the strongest of state powers. Unlike the general criminal law, it carries with it not merely the power to deprive an individual of his or her liberty, but also the power to treat that individual with extremely strong medications—medications that are intended to alter their mood or their perceptions. These are extremely intrusive powers, and require strong and clear justifications.

As discussed earlier in this book (see Chapter 1, 1.6 and Chapter 2, 2.3), the development of mental health law has occurred in an historical context. The justifications have been diverse, and are debated amongst scholars. Scull (1979, 1993) argues that they are located in the processes of industrialisation of the nineteenth century, and in the politics of the rise of the medical profession. Jones (1972) sees them as reflecting from a tension between medical and legal power. Bartlett (1999) sees them as bound up with attitudes to the control of the poor in this period. Foucault (1965, 1977, 1988,

2003, 2006) sees them as flowing from the development of new technologies of power, particularly related to a shift in control strategies from control of the body to control of the self. Rothman (1971, 1980) sees them as flowing from social control. Grob (1994) and Shorter (1998) see them flowing from the rise of medical and social benevolence.

Whatever the history, the voices of people with disabilities themselves were largely absent from the discussion. Indeed, for Foucault, that silencing of the mad was a pivotal aspect of the revolution in and professionalisation of care of the insane in the eighteenth and nineteenth centuries: they became objects of control and treatment, not participants in their own care (Foucault 1965, 2006).

By the late twentieth and early twenty-first centuries, it seems that compulsion had entered the social, legal, and political mindset. The issue, reflected in international human rights instruments such as the United Nations Mental Illness Principles (General Assembly resolution 46/119, 17 December 1991) and the European Convention on Human Rights (ECHR) and its consequent jurisprudence, was not whether compulsion was permissible, but what its appropriate boundaries were. Similarly, the discussions leading to the MHA 2007 in England and Wales (see, e.g., Department of Health and Welsh Office, 1999a; Department of Health, 1999a) included a variety of perspectives on what the guiding principles for compulsion in mental health law ought to be, but did not seriously question whether mental health legislation ought to have compulsory powers at all.

For a serious legal analysis of compulsion, however, it is not enough to say that compulsion is justified because we have long used it. A clearer rationale is required for fundamental removal of civil rights. Ideally, we ought to be able to measure the success of our policies against these justifications, to see what their actual effects are. It is only then that a meaningful debate can occur as to whether the intrusions into civil rights are appropriate.

6.2.1 **'Dangerousness'**

A traditional legal justification for mental health law has been the notion of 'dangerousness to oneself or others'. Indeed, in the debates surrounding mental health law reform in the early 2000s, the government expressly took the view that this was a core function of mental health law (DH, 1999a). While this was controversial at the time (see, e.g., Laing, 2002; Glover-Thomas, 2011; Farnham and James, 2001; Forrester, 2002), dangerousness has long been a justification for detention of people with mental health problems. Brook's abridgement from the sixteenth century refers to restraining the lunatic from killing, or doing mischief such as setting fire to a house (Brook, 1573: 'Faux Imprisonment', pl. 28, vol. 1, 330). In the nineteenth century, confinement criteria were codified by a series of statutes. With minor variations over the century, the standard required that a lunatic, idiot, or person of unsound mind was 'a proper person to be taken charge of and detained under care and treatment' (see Lunacy Act 1890, form 8). Notwithstanding this broad wording, out of a concern for civil rights of the insane, the courts imported the dangerousness language from the wrongful confinement context. The legislation was held to be justified by public order. Thus in *Re Fell, Re* (1845) 3 Dowl

& L 373, 15 LJ (NS) MC 25 QB, Patteson J commented (at p. 29) that 'These statutes were passed for the protection of the public...'. That in turn led to a standard of dangerousness. In *Nottidge* v *Ripley*, (1849) *The Times* (London), 27 June, p. 7, for example, Sir Frederick Pollock CB stated in his charge to the jury, 'it is my opinion that you ought to liberate every person who is not dangerous to himself or others...and I desire to impress that opinion with as much force as I can'. See also *R* v *Pinder, in re Greenwood* (1855) 24 LJ (NS) QB 148 at 151, per Coleridge J.

Certainly, the reduction of violence is generally accepted to be an appropriate role for the state: this premise, for example, forms the basis of much criminal law. Whatever the legal tradition, however, it is much less obvious that mental health law is an effective means to this end. The question of dangerousness of people with mental disorders has been subject to intensive study. While it may be the case that people with severe mental illnesses may be somewhat more dangerous than the bulk of the population, it would seem that most of this difference is attributable to factors unrelated to the mental disorder, most notably substance abuse (Fazel *et al.*, 2009; Elbogen and Johnson, 2009; Van Dorn *et al.*, 2012; Langan 2010). If the policy objective is to reduce social violence, therefore, mental health law seems an odd way to achieve that objective: there is no reason to believe that it will significantly alter the amount of violence in society.

These findings are not new: the evidence has been clear for many years that mental illness is not in itself a good predictor of violence (see, e.g., Monahan 1988, and sources cited therein). The ongoing need to keep proving it raises a question about public perceptions and stigma that in turn raise a question about the appropriateness of a dangerousness criterion. If, as seems manifestly the case, there is an unjustified link in the public's mind between mental disorder and violence, is it ethical to continue using the criterion even in the small number of cases where it may be relevant, since it would seem to give credence to the incorrect association of mental illness with dangerousness, to the disadvantage of the vast bulk of people with mental illnesses who are not dangerous?

Minimal change in the overall pattern of violence in society does not necessarily mean that intervention on an individual basis is unjustified, if people who will be violent can be accurately identified. Sadly, this does not seem to be the case. With the physical illnesses for which quarantine may be imposed, there are generally clear diagnostic tests to ensure that only those people who in fact have the dangerous condition are confined, and clear scientific evidence of contagiousness of a sort that would put the public at manifest risk. The same is not true of dangerousness predictions relating to mental disability.

It has long been known that the intuition of psychiatrists is not a good predictor of dangerousness (see, e.g., Montandon and Harding, 1984, and studies cited therein). If more objective evidence is to be used, it can be of two broad types. Either it is demographic information—information such as race, gender, age, or class—that is relatively clearly definable and may have a statistical correlation with violence, or it is information specific to the individual from his or her past—a history of offending or of violence, for example. In either case, predictions will be made from statistical probabilities: men are more violent than women, or people who have been violent in the past are more likely to be violent in the future. This in turn gives rise to a variety of difficulties.

First, particularly regarding the demographic variables, the empirical base itself may be controversial. Certainly, black people are over-represented in the statistics; but does this mean that black people actually are statistically more violent, or instead that social institutions such as the police respond differently to black people, making their prevalence a statistical artefact? Further, for sound reasons of social policy, it is difficult to see that tests based on race or sex would be permitted under equality legislation. Perhaps for this reason, whatever their predictive value, these criteria do not tend to be used in most structured dangerousness assessments.

Second, the degree of predictive power of many of the variables is limited, and particularly when the predictive power is not strong, it is problematic to use the statistics related to a class of people for predicting individual outcomes. The statistics are clear, for example, that women are better drivers than men; that does not necessarily tell us very much about whether Mary is a better driver than Fred. While the statistics are highly accurate over large groups, they do not necessarily have much predictive value for individuals. In the context of prediction of dangerousness, it may well be the case, for example, that people who lived with both biological parents until the age of 16 are less likely to be violent, to use a question from the Violence Risk Appraisal Guide (VRAG) as an example; but is it really right to use that statistic to predict violence in a given individual, and to detain them, in part, on that basis?

Third, most of the factors in dangerousness assessments are static: if you are male, you will generally remain male, and if your first criminal offence was committed at a young age, it will always have been committed at a young age. If these and similar factors are our predictors of dangerousness, it is difficult to see what changes will occur in the psychiatric facility that will make you cease to be dangerous and allow for release.

The statistical difficulties mean that predictions are inevitably inaccurate to some degree: some people predicted to be not dangerous will be; and some people predicted to be dangerous will not be. The best instrument for prediction is probably that developed in the MacArthur project in the United States (Monahan *et al.*, 2001). Their strongest statistics involved 939 people, at several sites. Of these 176 were in fact violent over the course of the study. Using a variety of statistical methods, they were able to arrive at five risk bands, summarised in Table 6.1.

The level of prediction attained by the MacArthur team is extremely impressive relative to previous risk studies; but it will be clear that even this result is far from perfect. Even in the most dangerous risk category, 5, roughly one quarter of the class did not turn out to be violent in the following year, and would therefore be wrongly confined if subsequent violence were the justification for the imposition of compulsion. If we restricted our confinement criteria so that only those in that most dangerous category 5 were subject to compulsion, we would only have included just over a quarter of the people who would be violent during the following year. To catch half of the violent people, we would have to extend our criteria so that people in classes 4 and 5 would be subject

Table 6.1 Distribution of Dangerous People in McArthur Risk Categories

Risk class	Number of cases in class	% of class violent	Number of people violent	% of total violent people contained in this class	Number of people not violent in class
1	343	1.2	4	2	341
2	248	7.7	19	11	237
3	183	26.2	48	27	135
4	102	55.9	57	32	45
5	63	76.2	48	27	15

(Adapted from Monahan *et al.*, 2001: table 6.7)

to compulsion. That would in fact catch 59 per cent of the people who would be violent in the following year—105 in number—but an additional 60 people, or 37 per cent of those within the criteria, would not in fact have been violent. Even with the MacArthur figures, therefore, a dangerousness standard will result in the imposition of compulsion on a significant number of people who would not, in the end, be violent. We would have severe reservations about a criminal system where 37 per cent of those convicted were not in fact guilty; is there any reason we should lower our standards for mental health compulsion? (See generally Dershowitz, 1970 and Crawford, 1984.)

It should be emphasised that the MacArthur study is the best available. As its authors acknowledge, its criteria are too complex to be used unaided in a clinical environment (Monahan *et al.*, 2001: 127). Any other prediction mechanism used in practice will provide *less* accurate results than those above, compounding the problem of 'false positives' subjected to compulsion. Studies generally find that between one-half and three-quarters of those identified as dangerous by psychiatric professionals do not, in the end, turn out to be violent (studies are surveyed in Langan, 2010; Bowden, 1996; Monahan, 1988; Monahan, 1981).

It is theoretically possible to escape these difficulties if detention is delayed until a violent act is actually occurring. While that escapes the problems of prediction, it has its own limitations. Police are not omnipresent, and delaying to a point where dangerous acts are occurring does mean that some people will get hurt or killed. Even if, as the statistics would suggest, the numbers will be relatively few, it is hard not to feel sympathy for the victims and their families and it is difficult to see that this will be viewed as politically palatable, particularly when even the small amount of violence caused by people with mental health problems can create such a media furore. That said, the general rule in society is that a crime must be committed before intervention occurs; why should crime caused by people with mental disabilities be handled differently?

Certainly, the prevention of public violence is an appropriate role for the state. The philosophical justification for prevention of harm to oneself is not so obvious. The Richardson Committee distinguished between dangerousness to others and risk to self as justifications for compulsion, and specifically did not take a view on whether risk to self was an appropriate ground for intervention, inviting the politicians to consider the matter further (DH and Welsh Office, 1999b). No such consideration was evident in the discussions that followed.

The distinction raised by Richardson is real, however: there is a philosophical difference between putting other people at risk, and putting oneself at risk. If the individual is viewed as an independent and autonomous body, aware of the risks to self that his or her condition implies, it is not obvious why he or she should not be permitted to choose to run those risks.

This argument gives rise to several objections and reservations. First, it suggests a level of understanding by the individual: the individual must have capacity. It is silent when the individual is unable to make a capable choice. Second, it is questionable whether individuals are in fact independent and autonomous bodies. Many people have friends and family and their death will affect those people both emotionally and in some cases economically. Third, human life has a particular value in many ethical codes which allow, and sometimes oblige, interventions that would not otherwise be permitted. If any of these apply, intervention to protect the individual would at least potentially be justifiable. Particularly for the second and third points, however, it is fair to ask why these issues would apply to people with mental disabilities when they are not applied to the general population. An individual with a potentially fatal physical disorder may in principle refuse treatment, die, and leave his or her family bereft; why is the situation different for people with mental disorders?

6.2.2 The need for care and treatment

The use of dangerousness as basis of detention suggests that a key role of psychiatric compulsion is social control. For this reason, clinicians often view the dangerousness standard with considerable scepticism. A particular concern is that confinement without appropriate treatment turns them into gaolers. This reflects a view that psychiatric facilities should instead be institutions of health and care. Anselm Eldergill makes the point as follows (2002: 343):

> The evidence suggests that present medical interventions have, like liberal prison regimes, the reformation of the individual as their aim. This is unacceptable because the proper function of medical science and practice is to treat individual suffering attributable to disease or injury, not to alleviate the suffering of society; and, in the field of mental health, to treat those diseases or injuries which interfere with the development or expression of an individual's personality, not to reform her or his personality by reference to some social or political norm.

The line between these two concepts is however not as clear as Eldergill suggests. People are brought into coercive psychiatric structures when their behaviour becomes sufficiently divergent from social norms as to be perceived to warrant intervention. Whether that is defined in terms of illness or in social terms, the result is still social control. Nonetheless, if the perceived role of psychiatric facilities is provision of care and treatment, it is fair to ask whether this provides a justification for psychiatric detention.

Phrasing the question in this way can be seen as moving towards collapsing the distinction between detention and compulsory treatment: if the point is to enforce care and treatment, there would be little argument for detention if compulsory treatment did not follow. In this, the justification is different from the dangerousness criterion: if the justification for detention is dangerousness to others, the state role can be met through compulsory admission and physical control with the psychiatric institution, with compulsory treatment being a different matter. This is not the case if the justification intrinsically involves provision of treatment.

Does the state have an appropriate role in compulsorily ensuring the health of its citizens? Is there a duty on the part of citizens to be healthy? The current government would seem to think so, with its proposal that benefits be denied to people who are unable to work because of disability but refuse rehabilitative treatment. It must be acknowledged that the state does have an economic interest in minimising its social services budget. Further, in some Communist or communitarian ethical systems there is a duty to prioritise communal benefits over individual choice. If the argument for compulsion is economic, however, it is as yet at best underdeveloped. Hospital admissions are expensive, but the relative costs of detention and treatment in hospital as against not detaining (and perhaps therefore not treating at all, if the patient is refusing all treatment without compulsion) are unclear. Certainly, economic benefit does not have a role in the existing criteria under the MHA 1983 for determining whether individuals should be detained.

Even if the overall argument is sound that the state has a role compelling its citizens to be healthy, the means to enforce that role is notably different for detained psychiatric patients, for it is only they that lose the right to consent to medical treatment. The economic arguments apply equally with non-psychiatric treatments. If the economic arguments are to work in a non-discriminatory fashion, it would presumably follow that the right to consent to medical treatment should be removed much more broadly in the population; and there is no suggestion of that in current politics.

The issues surrounding the desirability of care and treatment would be more convincing if the results of compulsion were better. In a study covering 22 hospitals, Priebe and colleagues followed up detained patients up to a year following their detention. They found that detained patients had high symptom levels on admission, and that these did reduce somewhat, although it was unclear how far this flowed from hospital treatment and how much from spontaneous improvement (Priebe *et al.*, 2011: 383). Social outcomes improved little, and on one measure, actually deteriorated slightly. Indeed, while the authors understood their study as relating to beneficence, they note that perceived coercion was associated with better social effects. They explain, '[i]nvoluntary admission is by definition a coercive process and perceiving a high level of coercion during its process may be an appropriate response and associated with a higher motivation to avoid a repetition of the experience and for positive change in life' (Priebe *et al.*: 284). Insofar as this is correct, it suggests that the beneficial social outcomes may be the result of deterrence—a social control mechanism—rather than with the care itself.

Priebe and colleagues conclude that 'the rather limited clinical and social gains of the patients concerned here might be considered in an ethical debate about involuntary hospital admission.' (Priebe *et al.*: 384). This is broadly similar to Newton-Howe's systematic review of coercion, which notes 'the studies suggest that there is little improvement among patients to offset the negative experience of coercion' (Newton-Howes and Mullen, 2011: 469). If that is the case, it is difficult to see a compelling case in practice for an argument based on beneficence.

Compulsion based on benevolence might alternatively be justified if the service users themselves were appreciative after the fact. While some are, the evidence is not overall encouraging in this regard. It would seem that no more than 40 to 50 per cent of persons compelled later considered their admission to have been justified (Priebe, 2009; Gardiner *et al.*, 1999). Further, Gardiner's study notes that even those who considered their admission to have been justified did not change the way they felt about it. Those that were angry were still angry; they were not grateful.

6.2.3 **The challenge posed by the Convention on the Rights of Persons with Disabilities**

The overall effect of the UN Convention on the Rights of Persons with Disabilities (CRPD) on questions of psychiatric detention will be discussed later in this chapter (see 6.5.2). The challenges it poses are various. Most significantly, Article 14 would appear to require that disability, including mental disability, should form no part of the criteria for deprivation of liberty. Implementation of this would be a major shift in English law, and would require the demise of the MHA 1983 as we know it. This argument will be discussed at greater length at 6.5.2.

Here, it is relevant to note the more general concern of the CRPD in avoiding discrimination based on disability. This creates a challenge for the justifications discussed so far, quite apart from the specifics of Article 14. Absent the actual commission of a crime and a formal criminal trial, we do not detain people without mental disabilities even when there is much stronger evidence of dangerousness than for people with mental disorder. Similarly, people without mental disorder retain the right to refuse medical treatment even when the evidence for positive outcomes of treatment is much more compellingly than for treatments for mental disorder. What justifies this apparent discrimination?

One argument might be that differential treatment is permitted for people who lack the capacity to make their own decisions. This has attracted some enthusiasm amongst progressive policymakers in England, and will also be discussed at 6.5.1. Suffice it here to say that the provisions relating to capacity in Article 12 of the CRPD (discussed in Chapter 4 at 4.1.2 and 4.7), make this a problematic choice in policy terms now.

Rather than compulsion, the CRPD envisages programmes of 'reasonable accommodation'—support mechanisms on individual, policy, and systemic levels that will allow people with disabilities to live full and free lives. The vision of the CRPD is that this will make compulsion based on disability unnecessary. Certainly, this must be a desirable approach as far as possible. If the system is not providing facilities that people want to use, the ethical solution would appear to be to provide facilities they do, rather than to compel them to use facilities they do not. In a survey of English psychiatric facilities, a minority of people with physical illnesses or disabilities felt that these were 'definitely' taken care of enough. A minority always felt safe on the ward, with 16 per cent saying they did not feel safe even to some extent. Less than a quarter said there were sufficient activities during the day on week days all of the time, and only 14 per cent that there were enough activities on evenings and weekends all the time. More than a quarter rated their overall care experience as only fair or poor (Care Quality Commission, 2009). Insofar as these factors and others like them dissuade people from admitting themselves to psychiatric facilities, the response on both ethical and clinical grounds must be to improve the facilities rather than to force people to enter facilities where they do not feel they are receiving proper health care, do not feel safe, are bored, or are dissatisfied with their treatment overall.

It is not controversial that compulsion should be avoided if at all possible; the current MHA Code of Practice makes that point (DH 2008: para. 4.4). What is less obvious is whether accommodations of the sort proposed by the CRPD will be sufficient in all cases. Traditionally, anti-discrimination law has allowed real and relevant differences to be taken into account in tailoring policy responses to individuals and groups. Failure to do so is said to achieve mere formal equality. It can in fact be counter-productive, entrenching patterns of social disadvantage (see further Kayess and French, 2008: 8). If that is the case in the current context, a slavish adherence to the apparently non-discriminatory approach that would seem to be proposed by the CRPD would turn out to be counter-productive for people with disabilities—surely not what the CRPD intended?

6.2.4 **Conclusion**

The tensions relating to justifications for detention are neatly summarised in Patrick Cockburn's discussion of whether his son Henry's section should be renewed (Cockburn and Cockburn, 2011: 158):

> The dilemma facing us was very real. Henry was in DVH [a psychiatric hospital] to protect him from the consequences of his psychosis. But this solution had a massive downside in that the prolonged confinement made him acutely unhappy, and this in turn exacerbated his psychosis. I sometimes used to wonder if he would not be better of wandering the countryside than being stuck in DVH, but I soon realised that if he did this, he would soon be dead. He could display great ingenuity in not taking his medication and escaping from different closed wards, but he showed little ability to survive on his own once he was free. We knew that medication would not cure Henry, but if he took the cocktail of drugs prescribed, they would keep his psychosis under control and give him a chance of returning to full sanity.

There is real concern in this quotation for the well-being of Henry, and the concerns for the risks he poses (in this case, to himself). At the same time, there is the painful apprehension that detention has counterproductive effects. There is acknowledgement of the limited clinical expectations that can be hoped for, but at the same time the perception that it is the best, or least bad, or only, way forward.

One can feel only the deepest sympathy for those confronted by these dilemmas in their own lives, but from a legal perspective, questions remain. Are the theoretical justifications and implementation possibilities for intervention sufficient to warrant state powers of compulsion? And if so, what sort of statutory criteria would provide sufficiently clear guidance? These issues should remain under consideration as we turn to the provisions of the MHA 1983.

6.3 Detention under the Mental Health Act 1983

The MHA 1983 is complex, and an overview in advance may be of assistance in understanding the more detailed discussion which follows. The civil confinement structure is summarised graphically in Figure 6.1. Essentially, civil admissions may be for assessment (s. 2) or for treatment (s. 3). An admission for assessment allows detention of the individual for 28 days. It is not renewable. At the end of that time, the individual must either be released, continued as an informal patient, or admitted for treatment under s. 3. Admission for treatment under s. 3 allows the detention of the individual for up to six months for initial admission and first renewal, and for up to a year for subsequent renewals. Sections 63 and 58 of the MHA 1983 allow patients detained under ss. 2 or 3 to be treated for their mental disorder without their consent (see further Chapter 9, 9.4 and 9.5).

For admission under either s. 2 or s. 3, an application must be made by the nearest relative of the individual or, in practice almost always, by an approved mental health professional (an 'AMHP') (see further 6.3.2.2). The application must in general be accompanied by certificates from two medical practitioners—one a specialist in mental disorders (generally a consultant psychiatrist), the other ideally the patient's general practitioner.

There are several ways for patients to be detained in the short term, to allow for the assessments of the medical practitioners and AMHP to be completed (see further 6.4):

- In an emergency (s. 4), one medical certificate along with the AMHP's application will suffice for a s. 2 admission for assessment, so long as the second medical certificate is furnished within 72 hours.

- An informal patient may be detained for up to 72 hours by a doctor, or, when immediacy is necessary, up to six hours by a nurse (s. 5).

- A justice of the peace, upon application by an approved social worker, may require detention in a place of safety for up to 72 hours of mentally disordered individuals who are being ill-treated, neglected, or not kept under proper control, or who are living alone and unable to care for themselves (s. 135(1)).

- If a police officer finds a mentally disordered individual in a public place to be in 'immediate need of care and control' he or she may remove the individual to a place of safety for up to 72 hours (s. 136).

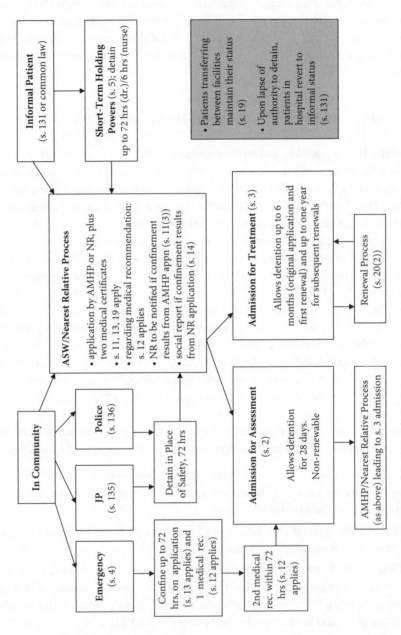

Figure 6.1 An Overview of Civil Confinement

Table 6.2 Confinement Criteria and Resulting Powers under the MHA 1983

Confinement Criteria	For Assessment	For Treatment	Emergency	Urgent Inpatient	Justices of the Peace	Police
Section	2	3	4	5	135(1)	136
Mental Disorder Criteria	Any mental disorder which warrants patient's detention in hospital for assessment for at least a limited period	Any mental disorder which makes it appropriate to receive treatment in hospital. If learning disability, must be associated with abnormally aggressive or seriously irresponsible conduct	As section 2 admission	If application by doctor, no criteria. If application by nurse, as s. 2 admission	Any mental disorder	Any mental disorder
Substantive Thresholds	Ought to be so detained in the interests of his own health or safety or with a view to the protection of other persons	Necessary for patient's health or safety, or for protection of other persons, that such treatment be provided, and it cannot be provided unless detained under this section, *and* appropriate treatment is available	As section 2, but compliance with section 2 would involve undesirable delay	If application by doctor, merely that application 'ought' to be made regarding inpatient. If by nurse, inpatient receiving treatment for mental disorder, and not practical to refer to doctor	Has been, or is being, ill-treated, neglected or kept otherwise than under proper control; or living along and unable to care for him/ herself	In public place, and in need of immediate care and control, and necessary in the interests of the person or for the protection of other persons

(Continued)

Table 6.2 (*Cont.*)

Confinement Criteria	For Assessment	For Treatment	Emergency	Urgent Inpatient	Justices of the Peace	Police
Maximum Detention Authorised	28 days, non-renewable	6 months (original certificate and first renewal); 1 year (subsequent renewal)	Absent second medical certificate, 72 hours. If second certificate, becomes s. 2 admission	By nurse: 6 hours By doctor: 72 hours	72 hours in place of safety	72 hours in place of safety
Compulsory Treatment	Treatment provisions of ss. 58 and 63 apply	Treatment provisions of ss. 58 and 63 apply	Treatment provisions of ss. 58 and 63 do not apply	Treatment provisions of ss. 58 and 63 do not apply	Treatment provisions of ss. 58 and 63 do not apply	Treatment provisions of ss. 58 and 63 do not apply
Other Notes	Discharge under s. 23. Review of detention available under s. 66(1)(b) and (f) and s. 66(2)(b) and (f), once prior to first renewal and once per renewal thereafter. Duty exists to provide after-care under s. 117	Discharge under s. 23. Review of detention available under s. 66(1)(a) and s. 66(2)(a) within first 14 days of confinement	Discharge under s. 23	Designed to allow assessments by AMHP and doctor(s) discharge under s. 23	Designed to allow assessment by AMHP and doctor(s). No statutory provision re discharge	Designed to allow assessment by AMHP and doctor(s) No statutory provision re discharge

In these short-term detentions, the provisions of sections 63 and 58 of the MHA 1983 allowing for treatment without consent do not apply, and the competent patient can therefore refuse treatment for his or her mental disorder if competent to do so, consistent with common law.

The substantive criteria differ for each of these interventions. A brief outline of these criteria, along with the basic effects of confinement under the various categories, is in Table 6.2. There is a curious failure of the academic literature and the case law to analyse in detail the meaning of these criteria. As we will see, the courts have sometimes given relatively broad interpretations to the substantive criteria. Given the intrusion into the civil liberties of those confined, however, the statutes ought instead to be strictly construed (see *In re Dulles' Settlement, In re* [1950] 2 All ER 1013). Careful consideration of the standards is therefore appropriate.

6.3.1 Detention for assessment or treatment: Substantive issues

6.3.1.1 Admission for assessment under s. 2

The substantive criteria for admission for assessment are contained in s. 2(2) of the MHA 1983:

> 2 (2) An application for admission for assessment may be made in respect of a patient on the grounds that–
> (a) he is suffering from mental disorder of a nature or degree which warrants the detention of the patient in a hospital for assessment (or for assessment followed by medical treatment) for at least a limited period; and
> (b) he ought to be so detained in the interests of his own health or safety or with a view to the protection of other persons.

The traditional justifications for admission discussed earlier in this chapter are reflected in these criteria: a mental disorder, that gives rise to dangerousness to oneself or others, or puts ones health at risk. Section 2 admissions do not require that a treatment of the mental disorder is available. This might flow from the fact that this is an admission for assessment: both the short title of the section and the case law say that expressly (see *R (Williamson)* v *Wilson* QBD, 19 April 1995, CO/678/95). If the admission is for assessment, it may well be formulating a treatment plan is part of that process—a view taken by the Code of Practice (DH, 2008: para. 4.26). This argument is problematic, however: if the appropriate treatment has not been identified, why should compulsory treatment powers be available under this section?

What is surprising about the section 2 criteria is not how much litigation they have generated, but how little. The provisions are replete with flexible language—mental disorder 'of a nature or degree which warrants detention' and 'ought to be so detained in the interests of' health, safety, or protection of others being the most obvious—but very little litigation at the domestic or European level provides any further guidance. It would seem clear that the determination that the individual meets the detention criteria must be made prior to the detention, a view flowing both from the terms of the section itself and ECHR jurisprudence (*Gorobet* v *Moldova*, Application No. 30951/10, judgment of

11 January 2012). Detention must be the least restrictive option available, and other less restrictive options must be considered and rejected before an individual is detained (*Varbanov* v *Bulgaria*, Application No. 31365/96, 5 October 2000; *Ťupa* v *Czech Republic*, Application No. 39822/07, judgment of 26 August 2011, para. 48). Detention must be a proportional response to the situation, with the interests of the patient being weighed against those of the public: it is a serious intrusion into individual rights, and can therefore be justified only in serious circumstances (*R (H)* v *London North and East Region Mental Health Review Tribunal* [2002] QB 1, para. 33; *Witold Litwa* v *Poland* (2001) 33 EHRR 53, para. 78). The Code of Practice provides an extensive array of factors for the consideration of the admitting staff in this regard (DH, 2008: Ch. 4).

The mental disorder must be of 'a nature or degree which warrants the detention of the patient in a hospital for assessment (or for assessment followed by treatment) for a least a limited period'. 'Nature' and 'degree' do not have the same meaning. It was held in *R* v *MHRT for South Thames Region, ex p Smith* [1999] COD 148 that the former refers to the particular disorder itself, including the features of the underlying condition and its prognosis, while the latter referred to the current manifestations of the disorder. In the view of the court, these were intentionally listed as alternative requirements in the statute. While the expert evidence was that the degree of Smith's disorder did not warrant confinement, its nature did, and therefore he could be legally confined on the basis that the condition might cease to be static. The *Smith* case itself concerned a patient whose disorder was controlled by medication, but who had a history of ceasing medication and becoming ill. The decision held that patients with such a history could be confined, even when taking their medication. This has led to criticism that patients who ceased their medication with ill effects at some time following a previous release may remain liable to unjustly prolonged detention in subsequent admissions, because of that history (Armstrong, 1999).

If the distinction between nature and degree is taken to its logical end, the situation might be in fact more serious, since 'nature' would appear to refer in the section to the disorder itself, not to the patient's intentions regarding treatment compliance. If that is the case, even patients with no history of ceasing treatment might have disorders of a nature, but not degree, warranting confinement. In that event, section 2(2)(b) might still preclude the confinement, but the safeguards contained in section 2(2)(a) nonetheless appear remarkably weak after *Smith*.

Laws concerning deprivation of liberty must be clearly defined and foreseeable in their application. The standard from the ECHR is that law must be sufficiently precise 'to allow the person...to foresee, to a degree that is reasonable in the circumstances, the consequences which a given action may entail' (*Kawka* v *Poland*, Application No. 25874/94, judgment of 9 January 2001, para. 49). In the context of mental health law, the related proposition is perhaps as useful: law must be sufficiently clear that different people administering the law will reach the same decisions in similar cases. If this is not the case, whether or not an individual is detained will depend not on their individual circumstances, but instead on who does the assessments and fills in the paperwork: human rights becomes a lottery.

It is at best doubtful whether s. 2 meets this standard. The extraordinary flexibility of the language employed—the mental disorder of a 'nature or degree warranting detention', and 'ought' to be detained in the interests of the factors listed provide little guidance to practitioners, and the array of factors listed in the Code of Practice does nothing to reduce what appears to be a very broad discretion. This may render the section adaptable to a wide variety of individual circumstances, but in civil rights terms it is problematic.

6.3.1.2 Admission for treatment under s. 3

The criteria for admission for treatment are contained in s. 3(2):

> 3 (2) An application for admission for treatment may be made in respect of a patient on the grounds that—
> (a) he is suffering from mental disorder of a nature or degree which makes it appropriate to receive medical treatment in a hospital; and
> (c) it is necessary for the health or safety of the patient or for the protection of other persons that he should receive such treatment and it cannot be provided unless he is detained under this section; and
> (d) appropriate medical treatment is available for him.

(Note that the omission of s. 3(2)(b) is not a typographical error; it was repealed by the MHA 2007.)

The structural similarities to s. 2 will be immediately apparent. As under s. 2, the patient must at the time of the application actually be suffering from a mental disorder as defined by s. 1, and the mental disorder must be of a 'nature or degree' that makes it appropriate for him to receive treatment in a hospital. Analogous to the discussion of the criteria in s. 2, this would suggest that some disorders are inappropriate for hospital treatment; and as with s. 2, the assessment must be made on the basis of both clinical and social factors. It must be 'necessary' (perhaps a slightly higher threshold than 'ought' in s. 2?) for the health or safety of the patient or for the protection of other persons that the treatment be given, with the attendant difficulties on how these substantive criteria are to be read.

Much of the analysis of s. 2 will therefore be equally relevant to s. 3. In particular, the ECHR jurisprudence is sufficiently broad to cover both sections, and *Smith* decision applies equally to s. 3 as to s. 2. The concerns about clarity of drafting also warrant consideration for s. 3.

There are however differences from s. 2. First, in the event that the mental disorder is a learning disability, s. 3 can be used only if the disorder results in 'abnormally aggressive or seriously irresponsible conduct' on the part of the person to be detained: see s. 1(2B)(a). The scope of this phrase was discussed in Chapter 1, 1.4.1.

Section 3 is an admission for treatment, and the section requires that the treatment in question could not be provided without detention under the section. The question here is not merely whether the treatment could alternatively be provided in the community without admission to hospital at all; although in that circumstance the conditions in s. 3 would certainly not be satisfied. It is also that the section cannot be used if the patient is content to accept the treatment in hospital as an informal patient.

Section 3 requires that 'appropriate medical treatment' be 'available'. This provision was introduced by the MHA 2007. It replaces a test of 'treatability' (a term subject to further definition) which applied to a small subset of people detained, and attracted significant litigation in particular as it related to people with 'psychopathy' (itself a defined term in the old Act). The new criterion removes some of the complexity of the old, and applies it to all s. 3 admissions. In principle, this means that detention in hospital beyond the 28 days permitted by s. 2 can only occur if there is a therapeutic justification. This is potentially significant. While the use of criteria relating to risk to self and others in the detention criteria means that the social control function of psychiatric hospitals will remain, the requirement that appropriate treatment is available does identify the psychiatric hospital as not simply a carceral institution.

But what is 'appropriate medical treatment'? The MHA 1983 itself is unhelpful, defining the phrase as 'medical treatment which is appropriate in his case, taking into account the nature and degree of the mental disorder and all other circumstances of his case.' (s. 3(4)). This does little more than say that treatment is appropriate if it is appropriate— no doubt true, but not very enlightening. The last phrase does suggest that the assessment is not restricted to clinical factors, but also social factors, an approach reflected in the Code of Practice (DH, 2008: paras. 6.8, 6.10, 6.11). The Code further states that appropriate treatment 'by definition . . . must be treatment which is for the purpose of alleviating or preventing a worsening of the patient's mental disorder or its symptoms or manifestations'(DHDH, 2008: para. 6.8), language which is identical to the pre-2007 treatability test and does speak to an overtly therapeutic purpose for the treatment.

Section 3(4) requires that the treatment in question be 'available': as the Code of Practice notes, 'it is not sufficient that appropriate treatment could theoretically be provided.' (DH, 2008: para. 6.13) Some treatments have long waiting lists—therapies for sexual violence and abusing have for years been notorious in this regard. How available is 'available'? There has been no litigation on this point, but it does seem that placement on a waiting list would not constitute 'available' treatment, although a few days to make necessary administrative arrangements would presumably be unproblematic under the section.

These rather rosy images of therapeutic benevolence and beneficence must be tempered somewhat.

The section requires that 'appropriate' treatment be available, rather than optimal treatment. How effective does treatment need to be if it is to be appropriate, and how predictable do the results need to be in advance? The Code of Practice, citing the definition of medical treatment for mental disorder, notes that treatment must only have as its purpose the alleviation or worsening of the disorder or one or more of its manifestations (s. 145(4)), commenting that 'purpose is not the same as likelihood', and that treatment may be appropriate even if it cannot be shown in advance that a particular effect is likely to be achieved (DH, 2008: para. 6.4). In one sense, this is uncontroversial, Throughout medicine, results can rarely if ever be guaranteed. That said, if it is expected that these treatments will be imposed on the patient without consent (as is permitted when the individual is detained under this section), it is at least arguable that much more certain and positive outcomes should be required than the Code suggests (see further Chapter 9, 9.5).

The question of suboptimal treatment is complicated by the broad definition accorded to 'medical treatment' under the MHA 1983, including not merely treatment with medications but also 'nursing, psychological interventions, and specialist mental health habilitation, rehabilitation and care' (s. 145(1)). The breadth of this definition will be discussed in detail in Chapter 9 at 9.4.1; suffice it here to say that treatment can be minimal in nature. In *MD v Nottinghamshire Healthcare NHS Trust* [2010] UKUT 59 (AAC), the patient was unable psychologically to engage with therapy. He was detained through the criminal system following a variety of major acts of cruelty on young children, but his detaining section, like section 3, required appropriate medical treatment to be available. In this case, while the tribunal held that psychotherapy, the usual treatment for MD's personality disorder, was not appropriate, MD did have the potential to benefit from 'the milieu of the ward both for its short term effects and for the possibility that it would break through the defence mechanisms and allow him later to engage in therapy' (para. 39). Relying in the broad definition of treatment noted in this section, the tribunal held that this was appropriate and available treatment for MD. No particular nursing or other therapeutic input is noted by the tribunal, and as such this case comes perilously close to finding that detention is, itself, appropriate treatment. That in turn goes a long way to undercutting the therapeutic image which the appropriate treatment test was meant to foster.

A more encouraging approach is adopted by the Upper Tier Tribunal in *DL-H v Devon Partnership NHS Trust and Secretary of State for Justice* [2010] UKUT 102 (AAC). This case too involved a person with personality disorder detained through criminal law, this time for arson. In this case, it was contested whether his personality disorder was treatable at all; but in any event, he was not compliant. The Upper Tier Tribunal was concerned that broad language relating to medical treatment should not create the illusion that appropriate treatment was available, masking detentions based on dangerousness alone, and also concerned that treatment refusals (which do not negate the availability of appropriate treatment) should not be cast in argument as unavailability of treatment. It provided the following advice to tribunals (para. 33):

> The tribunal must investigate behind assertions, generalisations and standard phrases. By focusing on specific questions, it will ensure that it makes an individualised assessment for the particular patient. What precisely is the treatment that can be provided? What discernible benefit may it have on this patient? Is that benefit related to the patient's mental disorder or to some unrelated problem? Is the patient truly resistant to engagement? The tribunal's reasons then need only reflect what it did in the inquisitorial and decision-making stages.

This seems as good an approach as is available at this time.

6.3.2 Processes for admission under sections 2 and 3

6.3.2.1 Overview

The compulsory admission of a person into a psychiatric facility is not only a question of diagnosis or of moral justification for the confinement of the dangerous. It is also a matter of compliance with detailed legal processes. The processes involve a number of actors: the nearest relative, the approved mental health professional (AMHP), the 's. 12 approved doctor' (generally a psychiatrist), and another doctor. The precise definitions and roles of these people will be discussed in detail in this section, but an overview of the admissions process will be helpful first.

For admissions for assessment under s. 2, the statute permits either an AMHP or a nearest relative to pursue the detention process (s. 11(1)), but in practice, it is virtually always an AMHP. The AMHP makes an application to the managers of the hospital stating that the relevant criteria are met, and in his or her opinion, the application ought to be made. The AMHP must have interviewed the potential patient in person within 14 days prior to the making of the application (s. 11(5)), and either prior to the making of the application or within a reasonable time thereafter, must inform the nearest relative of the application and of the nearest relative's limited right to discharge the patient (s. 11(3)). The AMHP's application must be supported by two medical opinions (either separate or jointly provided), one coming from a s. 12 approved doctor, and one should, if practicable, come from a doctor with prior knowledge of the patient. In some cases, the s. 12 approved doctor may fulfil this latter role (e.g., if the case involves a re-admission), but more frequently, it will be fulfilled by the second medical opinion, often provided by the individual's general practitioner. The Code of Practice encourages communication and co-operative decision-making between these individuals and joint assessments when possible (DH, 2008: 4.43–46).

Completion of the necessary paperwork gives legal authority to convey the person to be admitted to the hospital in question. While the patient may challenge the detention at a review tribunal following admission, no additional judicial or quasi-judicial order is required at the point of admission in order to detain the individual. Provided that the receiving officer of the hospital is satisfied that the relevant paperwork appears to be in order, the managers of the hospital are legally empowered to detain the subject of the application in the hospital. While the decision to detain is technically that of the hospital managers based on the application (*R (Care Principles Limited) v MHRT, AL, Bartlett* [2006] EWHC 3194 (Admin) para. 45) in practice it seems very unusual that hospital managers second guess the opinions of the doctors and AMHP. In the event of minor or clerical errors on the form, rectification is possible within 14 days of the admission (s. 15; see Keywood, 1996).

In the event that the application is made by the nearest relative rather than an AMHP, it must still be supported by the two medical recommendations. Following these admissions, the managers of the hospital are required to notify the social services authorities, who will dispatch an AMHP to interview the patient and report to the hospital managers on the patient's social circumstances. Admissions based on applications by nearest relatives should now be very rare, however. The Code of Practice provides that doctors approached by a nearest relative with a view to making an application should advise the nearest relative that applications by AMHPs are preferable (DH, 2008: 4.30).

The process and dynamics of admissions for treatment under s. 3 are largely similar to s. 2 admissions. As with s. 2 admissions, the application will almost always be made by an AMHP, who must personally have interviewed the individual within the previous

14 days. The same statutory provisions apply to the two medical recommendations, again one from a s. 12 doctor and one from a doctor with knowledge of the potential patient. Completion of the paperwork itself provides authority to detain the individual, and rectification of clerical or incidental errors in documents is possible.

The main difference in processes for admission under s. 3 concerns the role of the nearest relative. Where the nearest relative is merely to be informed of a s. 2 admission, sometimes after the fact, the process for an admission for treatment under s. 3 requires the AMHP to consult with the nearest relative prior to making the application, unless such consultation would be impractical or involve unreasonable delay. Further, if the nearest relative notifies the AMHP (either in the consultation or otherwise) that he or she objects to the application being made, the AMHP is precluded from making the application (s. 11(4)). In principle, this should mean that the individual is not detained. Data does not appear to be kept on the number of persons who are not detained as a result, but certainly, in some cases, the authorities wishing to detain the individual are sufficiently firm in their views that a logjam results. This appears in a legal setting in applications to replace the nearest relative on the basis that he or she 'unreasonably objects' to the s. 3 admission (s. 29(3)(c)). This, along with the parallel provision that the nearest relative is exercising the power to discharge the patient 'without due regard to the welfare of the patient or the interests of the public' (s29(3)(d)) have attracted litigation, and will be discussed at section 6.3.2.4. To bridge the gap while the legalities work their way through the system, an admission for assessment under s. 2 is deemed to be extended beyond its 28 day usual maximum, until the application to replace the nearest relative is determined (s.29(4)). This can take months or sometimes years: see, e.g., *Lewis* v *Gibson* [2005] EWCA Civ 587, an unusually complex case but nonetheless a case where the process took roughly two years and three months.

Renewal of the s. 3 is governed by s. 20 of the MHA 1983. The substantive criteria are the same as for s. 3, but the process is simplified: the application is made by the responsible clinician. Before making the application, the clinician is required to consult with at least one other person who has been professionally involved with the patient's medical care, but who is of a different profession to the clinician (e.g., if the clinician is a psychiatrist, the second opinion could be provided for example by a nurse). This consultee must also certify in writing that the substantive criteria are met (s. 20(3), (5), (5A)). The AMHP and the nearest relative have no formal function in these renewals.

6.3.2.2 Approved Mental Health Professionals (AMHPs)

As noted, the vast bulk of applications for involuntary admission under ss. 2 and 3 are now made by AMHPs rather than nearest relatives. The role has a long history. Victorian mental health legislation had distinguished between private asylum admissions (where the family of the person detained paid the costs of care) and public admissions (where the costs were paid under the provisions of the poor law—the nineteenth-century social services structure). Where private admissions were organised by the relatives of the detainee, poor law admissions were commenced by the application of a poor law official (a 'relieving officer') to a magistrate. In both cases, medical certificates from doctors were required. Consistent with the ambiguities of Victorian social policy regarding the poor, the role of the poor law relieving officer was to ensure the appropriate categorisation of the individual. To put it crudely, the feckless able-bodied were to be sent to the punitive regime of the workhouse to encourage them to mend their ways; the non-able-bodied could be given 'outdoor relief'—essentially a monetary payment to allow them to live in the community; and the insane were to be sent to the new (and much more expensive) county asylums. It never quite worked that way (see Bartlett, 1999), but that was the theory, and as a result relieving officers had an inconsistent role as agents of moral reform, guardians of the taxpayers' money, and responsibility for people in legitimate need.

The asylums were not transferred to Department of Health control until 1930. At the same time the language and legal ramifications of pauper status were removed from people admitted to asylums and their families, although this did not alter the liability for payment for their care, which remained in the poor law framework (Mental Treatment Act 1930, ss. 18, 20). As important, the Mental Treatment Act 1930 introduced voluntary admissions for the first time (s. 1). Up to 1930, all admissions to county and private asylums had been detentions.

The MHA 1959 merged the various streams of law relating to mental disability then in existence. The foundation of the NHS in 1948 had brought all psychiatric care within the public sphere, and a system based on public/private divide no longer made sense. The previous detention structures were combined: where previously, applications for admission had been launched by either the relieving officer or a relative, depending on whether the admission was privately or publicly paid for, now, as described, both the nearest relative and a 'mental welfare officer' would be involved in the admission process. In 1983, the mental welfare officer was re-labelled again, as 'approved social worker', and consistent with the increasing professionalisation of social work generally, the role was increasingly specialised. By the early 1990s, to attain approved social worker status under the Act, a social worker was required to undergo 12 weeks of training, and to undergo refresher courses at regular intervals (Central Council for Education and Training in Social Work, 1993).

As professional requirements increased, the numbers of social workers with approved status fell. In part, this had advantages. The increasing use of a smaller number of practitioners meant that each practitioner acquired significant experience in the use of the detention criteria, and a study of approved social workers in 2002 noted that all in the study were performing at least a dozen assessments resulting in detention per year. The number of assessments performed can be assumed to be significantly greater, as on average only half of the assessments performed resulted in an involuntary admission (Huxley et al., 2005: 509–10). Approved social workers presumably had a case load sufficient to give them meaningful experience and potential expertise in these assessments. At the same time, the numbers of approved social workers became increasingly inadequate to the task established by the MHA 1983. By 1998, 60 per cent of social services departments reported an insufficient number of approved social workers (Huxley et al., 2005: 509). The same 2002 study found 21 per cent of jobs vacant, with 68 per cent of social service departments reporting recruitment problems and 30 per cent retention problems (Huxley *et al.*, 2005: 511). The study identified better pay and conditions in other forms of social work to be a factor in these recruitment difficulties, as well as the stressful nature of statutory responsibilities under the Act (Huxley *et al.*, 2005: 511; see also Evans *et al.*, 2005).

The government's response in the MHA 2007 was to open the role to professionals other than social workers: nurses (including, perhaps most significantly, community mental health nurses), psychologists, and occupational therapists may now also, following appropriate training, to be registered as AMHPs (*The Mental Health (Approved Mental Health Professionals) (Approval) (England) Regulations 2008*, SI 2008/1206, Sch. 1). This broadening of the role may, perhaps, indicate a shifting of the ground. The argument for the involvement of social workers had been to create a social counterweight to the medical viewpoint in the detention. It was hoped that this would result in a 'creative tension' with medical colleagues (Brown, 2002: 396). While doctors are still specifically excluded from the role (s. 114(2)) the new professions would seem to be generally clinical in orientation. How significant this change will be remains to be seen. A 2012 study found that of 936 candidates trained since November 2008, 84 per cent had been social workers and 15 per cent nurses (General Social Care Council, 2012, cited DH, 2012g: 7). This would suggest that the bulk of AMHPs will in fact be social workers for some time to come.

The inclusion of a social perspective is no doubt a good thing. Research on the old approved social worker system indicated that approved social worker were sometimes able to make a better judgment about the need for hospitalisation than are psychiatrists, perhaps because of their training in issues such as discrimination and disadvantage (Hatfield, Huxley, and Mohamad, 1997) and, no doubt, because of their better knowledge of community-based alternatives. Research by Peay *et al.* suggests that approved social workers did have a reasonable understanding of mental health law (Peay *et al.*, 2001: 52) and are more hesitant than psychiatrists in recommending involuntary admission of individuals (Peay, 2003: Ch. 1). While this is of course very encouraging, it is fair to ask whether some of the conflicting elements of the old receiving officer role remain. The law is not applied in the abstract. Approved social workers were (and AMHPs are) administrators of the health and social services system, and in that role, issues such as budgetary management unavoidably enter the picture, and these factors figure increasingly as budgets are under stretch. The system administered is no longer the Victorian poor law, but the pressures and choices in the system are such that nineteenth-century relieving officers might at least partly recognise.

A social services authority is required to ensure that an AMHP considers making an application for detention if it has reason to think that an application for admission ought to be made (s. 13(1)), or if it is instructed to do so by the nearest relative (s. 13(4)). While this obliges the AMHP to consider the matter, the decision to make an application under s. 2 or s. 3 of the MHA 1983 remains discretionary on the AMHP: he or she is required to make the application only if 'satisfied' that it 'ought' to be made (s. 13(1A)). The Code of Practice lists an array of factors for consideration, primarily related to the health or safety of the individual and the protection of others (paras. 4.4–24). While many of these are no doubt helpful, it is appropriate to recall that the only legal factors are those listed in the statute: the Code of Practice is only guidance (*R (Munjaz)* v *Mersey Care NHS Trust* [2005] UKHL 58).

The AMHP is required to interview the individual no more than 14 days prior to making the application (s. 11(5)), as part of the process of deciding whether the application ought to be made, and in particular satisfying himself or herself 'that detention in a hospital is in all the circumstances of the case the most appropriate way of providing the care and medical treatment of which the patient stands in need' (s. 13(2)). It was said in *St George's Healthcare NHS Trust* v *S* [1998] 2 FLR 728, 3 All ER 673 (CA) that for an admission for assessment (s. 2), an AMHP is not required to be certain that the patient definitely is mentally disordered. Indeed, it 'cannot be a final diagnosis. [An AMHP] is entitled to be wrong: so are the medical practitioners on whose medical recommendations her application is based' (per Judge LJ at p. 690). But his Lordship made clear that an AMHP is required to 'believe' that the person to be admitted for assessment is mentally disordered. This is logical: more precise diagnosis may constitute the need for assessment in hospital. The same reasoning does not apply to admissions under s. 3, however, which would seem to imply that an AMHP or the recommending doctors are *not* entitled to be wrong for such admissions.

Section 13(2) is not concerned solely with medical questions, but rather with the broader question of the 'appropriateness' of confinement. The AMHP must take into account all relevant circumstances of the case, including for example whether detention is the least restrictive option available, and the benefits and detrimental effects that detention is likely to have on the individual. And fundamentally, the AMHP must satisfy himself or herself that the detention criteria in the statute are met.

The breadth of the discretion to make an application has come into question in situations where a patient is successful at a review tribunal: how quickly following the tribunal decision can a new application to detain the individual be made? In *R (M)* v *Managers of Southwestern Hospital* [1993] QB 683, the reapplication was made the day after the tribunal hearing, before it had even come into effect. That case held that the discretion of the applicant social worker was unlimited, and that any good faith application that the detention criteria were met and that an application ought to be made met the terms of the Act. The specific issue was eventually resolved in *R (Brandenburg)* v *East London and the City Mental Health NHS Trust* [2003] UKHL 58, where it was held that a fresh application could only be lodged when there was new information not known to the tribunal, which the applicant honestly believes puts a different complexion on the case. The requirement refers to information not known to the tribunal, not new events following the tribunal decision, so the information could in principle precede the tribunal's decision; but it does seem that a view by the AMHP that evidence was not well-presented to the tribunal does not suffice: (*R(Care Principles Limited)* v *MHRT, AL, Bartlett* [2006] EWHC 3194 (Admin)).

While this certainly limits re-applications following tribunal hearings, it does not obviously extend beyond this. The broad view of AMHP discretion contained in *M* therefore presumably continues to apply more generally.

6.3.2.3 **Medical recommendations**

Two medical recommendations are required to support the application of the AMHP or nearest relative. One of these must be given by a 's. 12 approved doctor'—a doctor approved for the purpose in England by the Secretary of State (a power delegated in practice to Strategic Health Authorities), and in Wales by the Welsh Ministers (who have delegated the power to Local Health Boards). These are generally specialist psychiatrists, but some GPs viewed as having particular expertise in the area are also included. The second recommendation may be given by any physician.

One of the opinions shall, if practicable, be given by a doctor who 'has previous acquaintance' with the patient (s. 12(2)). In practice, this is normally the second medical opinion, often provided by the patient's general practitioner. It would seem that the acquaintance required by the statute may be minimal. In *Ann R (By her Litigation Friend Joan T)* v *Bronglais Hospital Pembrokeshire and Derwen NHS Trust* [2001] EWHC Admin 792, the GP in question had only just accepted R as a patient. His first real connection with her was at a meeting of the local social services department, concerning her potential confinement. Thereafter, he visited her for five minutes and scanned but did not read her medical record when he eventually received it from the Family Health Authority. This constituted his prior acquaintance, prior to a second visit at which he conducted the assessment. Scott Baker J held that the section specifically did not require prior 'personal' acquaintance. The GP had gained sufficient knowledge in the case conference with social services that he was not coming at the matter cold, but with some knowledge of her background. In the court's view, this was all that was required.

The balance contemplated by the MHA 1983 is a mix of substantive expertise, and experience with the particular patient. This may not always be achieved in an optimal fashion. Some people will not have a GP, or will not know their GP: see *Ann R*, and *R (C)* v *South London and Maudsley Hospital* [2003] EWHC 3467 (Admin). If the doctor does not have previous acquaintance with the individual, the Code of Practice recommends that he or she also be section 12 approved (Code of Practice: para. 4.74).

Peay *et al.* (2001) compared the legal knowledge of those involved in the psychiatric process, using a postal questionnaire. The encouraging finding from this survey is that section 12(2) approved psychiatrists and approved social workers (ASW) (now replaced by AMHPs) scored reasonably well. The authors comment that 'put at its simplest, a patient is relatively unlikely to encounter an ASW or s 12(2) psychiatrist with poor legal knowledge' (53). As a patient is required to be examined by both an AMHP and a s. 12(2) approved doctor, normally but not necessarily a psychiatrist, the odds are presumably correspondingly increased that at least one person examining the individual will be aware of the legal standards of confinement.

The findings regarding GPs, be they section 12(2) approved or not, is not nearly so encouraging. While all but 22 of the 573 GPs responding to the survey had participated in a mental health assessment, their knowledge was considerably less than the psychiatrists or ASWs. While the overall findings are comparative between the professional groups rather than purporting to establish absolute scales, answers to specific questions reported by Peay are striking. Only two thirds of the section 12 approved GPs, and half the remaining GPs, knew that criteria for a section 3 admission included that the person needed detention in the interests of their health. Only 59 per cent of the former group and 67 per cent of the latter realised that the admission criteria do not require the individual to lack capacity to consent to treatment (47).

The doctors, like the AMHP, must personally examine the individual. In such examinations, problems arise if the individual is unwilling or unable to be interviewed. In *M v Managers, Queen Mary's Hospital* [2008] EWCA Civ 1112, M was detained under an admission for assessment (s. 2), and her psychiatrist formed the view that this should be continued under an admission for treatment (s. 3). M at this time had been re-located to a regular hospital for treatment of a physical disorder. On the day proposed for her interview by the second doctor and the AMHP, she was unwell and asked through her lawyer that the interview be postponed. This request was refused. The doctor and AMHP attended the hospital for the interview, but M declined to speak with them. The doctor and AMHP nonetheless signed the relevant forms, indicating that the interview had occurred and resulting in the s. 3 detention. The Court of Appeal did not object to this, noting that the form and duration of the interview were not defined in the statute, and were a matter of professional of professional judgment (para. 26). On the facts, this is perhaps a disappointing result. It is also clear that the issues relating to M's physical health were real, although whether they were sufficient to justify postponement of the interview was less clear in the judgment. The section 2 detention had more than two weeks remaining at the time of the scheduled interview; it is not obvious that it could not have been re-scheduled. The approach taken by the AMHP and doctor, however, resulted in an interview in which no conversation with M took place, and which must therefore be considered largely meaningless. The interview is presumably meant to constitute a significant procedural protection against the wrongful detention of a patient; if that is the case, it is difficult to see that the objective was met.

6.3.2.4 Nearest relative

The MHA 1983 provides a variety of roles, duties, powers, and responsibilities for the nearest relative concerning detention of an individual: The duties, powers, and responsibilities of nearest relatives as they relate to admissions for assessment (s. 2) or treatment (s. 3) are listed in Box 6.1.

Box 6.1

- The power to make applications for admission for assessment or treatment under s. 2 or s. 3 (s. 11(1)), although this power is now rarely used.
- The power to require social services to appoint an AMHP to consider whether an application for admission under s. 2 or s. 3 is required, and the right to written reasons in the event that the AMHP decides not to make such an application (s. 11(4)).
- The right to be kept informed of applications for admissions assessment under s. 2 (s. 11(3)).

Box 6.1 (*Cont.*)

- The right to be consulted prior to an AMHP making an application for admission for treatment under s. 3, and to prevent that application by objecting to it (s. 11(4)).
- The power to discharge a patient detained under s. 2 or s. 3 on 72 hours notice (s. 23(2)), although such a discharge may be blocked if the responsible clinician certifies that the patient will act in a manner that is dangerous to others or to himself or herself (s. 25). In this event, the nearest relative may apply for a review tribunal hearing into the detention (s. 66(1)(ii))
- The right to receive information as to the section under which the patient is detained and the patient's rights to request review tribunal hearings, unless the patient objects (s. 132(4)).
- In the event that the nearest relative is replaced as unreasonable (see further in this section), the power to apply for a review tribunal hearing into the detention (s. 66(1)(ii)).
- The power to request an Independent Mental Health Advocate (IMHA—see further Chapter 12, 12.9) to visit and interview the patient (s. 130B(5)(a)).
- The right to be informed of the patient's discharge, unless the patient or the nearest relative requests that this information not be given (s. 133).

Additional powers, responsibilities, and duties relating to persons detained through the criminal process, persons under MHA 1983 guardianship (s. 7), and persons on community treatment orders will be discussed elsewhere in this volume as they arise. The definition of the nearest relative for those purposes however remains as discussed here.

The legal definition of a nearest relative is found in s. 26 of the MHA 1983. The nearest relative of a patient will normally be the person nearest to the beginning of the following list (s. 26(1)):

(a) husband, wife, or civil partner;

(b) son or daughter;

(c) father or mother;

(d) brother or sister;

(e) grandparent,

(f) grandchild;

(g) uncle or aunt;

(h) nephew or niece.

Other persons with whom the patient had been residing for at least five years at the time of admission to hospital are added as a final class on this list by s. 26(7). Those entitled include relatives of both 'the whole blood' and half blood (s. 26(2)). If there is more than one person of the relevant class (e.g., the patient has two children), the elder will be the nearest relative, and relatives of the whole blood are preferred over those of half blood (s. 26(3)). Relatives living abroad, separated spouses, and relatives under age 18 other than parents or spouses are discounted (s. 26(5)), but common law spouses of at least six months' standing are included so long as the patient is separated from anyone to whom they are is married (s. 26 (6)). 'Father' includes an unmarried father only if he has parental responsibility acquired in accordance with the requirements of s. 4 of the Children Act 1989, and members of the father's family similarly can only be the patient's nearest relative if the father has parental responsibility (s. 26(2)(b)). Statutory responsibility acquired under the Children Act 1989 terminates on the child's 18th birthday, and so it would seem that all paternal 'relatives' of the adult offspring of unmarried parents are debarred from being nearest relatives, even if, for example, the unmarried parents do not cohabit and the adult patient is (and may perhaps have been since childhood) cared for by the father or his family.

Notwithstanding the general rule that persons higher up the list take precedence over those lower on the list, where the patient 'ordinarily resides with or is cared for by' one of his relatives listed as (a) to (h), or was so before admission to hospital, that relative is the nearest relative of the patient (s. 26(4)). Both the residence and the care requirement in this subsection have been subject to litigation. The leading case on care is *Re D (Mental patient: habeas corpus)* [2000] 2 FLR 848, but it provides limited assistance. Lord Justice Otton allowed that relevant factors would include duration, continuity and quality of care provided by the relative (para. 14), but otherwise did not expand on the language of the statute. He did hold that the word 'ordinarily' qualified 'resides' only, and not also the care requirement. On the facts of the case, care which was more than minimal, but well-short of long-term and ongoing support, was sufficient to invoke the provision (para. 15).

The requirement that the patient 'ordinarily reside' with the individual is similarly difficult to apply in practice. The test contained in *Shah* v *Barnet London Borough Council* [1983] 1 All ER 226 (HL) at 235 has been used: ' "ordinarily resident" refers to a man's abode in a particular place or country which he has adopted voluntarily and for settled purposes as part of the regular order of his life for the time being, whether short or long duration.': applied in *WC* v *South London and Maudsley NHS Trust and David Orekeye*, [2001] EWHC Admin 1025. The difficulty is that individual lives do not fit into such neat boxes. Thus in *WC* itself, the patient had resided with his wife when his relationship with her was proceeding successfully, and with his mother when it was not. At the time of his admission, he was residing with his mother. As regarding patients already in hospital, the statute refers to the last ordinary residence, suggesting a preference for the mother as the carer; but the court found otherwise on the facts.

There can therefore be difficulties in identifying who is the nearest relative for the purposes of the statute. In practice, these are limited by the requirement that the AMHP consult with the person 'appearing to be' the nearest relative. While the AMHP must make this determination in good faith, there is no requirement that reasonable diligence be used or reasonable enquiries made to identify the nearest relative: *Re D (Mental Patient: Habeas Corpus)* [2000] 2 FLR 848, para. 15. That said, the AMHP is required to apply the statute properly to the facts of which he or she is aware. In *R* v *South Western*

Hospital Managers and Another, ex parte M [1994] 1 All ER 161 (HC), the AMHP consulted the patient's mother, a resident of Eire. The mother could not be nearest relative, as she was living abroad (s. 26(5)(a)). The court held that a person could not appear to be the patient's nearest relative 'where, on the facts known to the social worker, the person in question is legally incapable of being the statutory nearest relative'.

Also problematic is when application of the statutory scheme results in the manifestly wrong choice. *JT* v *United Kingdom* [2000] 1 FLR 909 (ECHR) involved a patient whose stepfather was said to have sexually abused her. Unsurprisingly, Ms T did not wish her nearest relative, her mother who was still living with the stepfather, to be involved in the decisions about her care, nor indeed for the mother to have any knowledge of her whereabouts. The case was settled before the European Court of Human Rights on the basis that the government would amend the Act to allow the patient to challenge the appointment of a given nearest relative.

In response, the MHA 2007 expanded the justifications for replacing a nearest relative by adding a general criterion of unsuitability to act in the role, and allowed patients to apply for replacement of their nearest relatives (MHA 1983, s.29(2)(za), (3)(e)). While this provision will certainly be helpful in particularly clear cases such as *JT*, it does not allow a patient an automatic right to select his or her nearest relative: unsuitability must still be demonstrated, and the person appointed must be, in the opinion of the court, a suitable person to act (s. 29(1A)). These issues are likely to arise in the context of detentions for treatment, situations where frequently if not always there will be a disagreement between the patient and the treatment team as to the appropriate way forward in the patient's care. Is a 'suitable person' one who offers an appropriate but nonetheless possibly robust challenge to the treatment team's proposal, or is it one who accepts relatively uncritically the treatment team's view of the facts and decides according to the treatment team's view of the best therapeutic way forward? If it is the former, the detention is likely to become much more challenging to the doctors; but if it is the latter (and the court's record on replacement of nearest relatives in other contexts suggests that it may well be), it is fair to wonder why the individual would be involved at all. In the reported case law on replacements as a whole, it would appear to be social services staff, sometimes indeed the AMHP himself or herself, who is appointed to the nearest relative role. Unsurprisingly, when this occurs, objections to the course of action proposed by the AMHP tend to disappear; but with them the independent voice that the nearest relative is meant to provide also disappears.

The court's approach to nearest relatives is perplexing. The case law suggests that the court is prepared to take questions of the adequacy of consultation reasonably seriously. Phillips LJ in *Re Whitbread (Mental Patient: Habeas Corpus)* [1997] 39 BMLR 94, focuses on the relationship between the consultation and the nearest relative's right to object to the application:

> No express provision is made as to when consultation should take place. Counsel for the respondents conceded that a nexus must exist between the consultation and the application subsequently made. The consultation must relate to the application. It must place the nearest relative in a position, if so minded, to object to that application.... Provided that

the social worker [now AMHP] explains to the nearest relative that he or she is considering making an application and why, the nearest relative will be afforded the opportunity for objecting to the application that the Act requires.

The AMHP is not required to ask specifically whether the nearest relative objects to the application (*In re GM (Patient: Consultation)* [2000] MHLR 41, *Re M* [2009] 1 MHLR 154, 160), but it does seem at least in circumstances where the nearest relative appears uncomfortable with the detention that he or she must be told of his or her right to object, and the fact that this will stop the detention proceeding (at least pending an application under s. 29 to replace the nearest relative) (*CX* v *A Local Authority* [2011] EWHC 1918 (Admin), para. 65). The objection does not have to be reasonable (although an unreasonable objection can lead to an application under s. 29 to replace the nearest relative): *D* v *Managers of Edgware Community Hospital* [2008] EWHC 3572 (Admin). Misleading information can vitiate consent to the admission. Thus in *CX*, the nearest relative was clearly unhappy with the proposed admission. She was told that if she did not agree, an application would be launched to replace her as nearest relative, and that she would require legal counsel for the resulting hearing. This last point was not correct, and as the nearest relative she knew she was ineligible for legal aid and could not afford a lawyer, her apparent agreement was held not to be valid. The burden of proof is on the detaining authority to demonstrate that the consultation occurred in a proper fashion (*BB* v *Cygnet Health Care* [2008] EWHC 1259 (Admin), para. 50). Inadequacy of consultation results in the application being unlawfully made which in turn renders the detention unlawful and gives rise to damages under Article 5 of the ECHR (*TTM (TM)* v *London Borough of Hackney* [2011] EWCA Civ 4).

While the courts seem thus prepared to give some substance to the nearest relative's right to be consulted and the right to object, a survey of applications to replace the nearest relative under s. 29 is much less encouraging. Applications under this section may be made by the patient, any relative of the patient, anyone with whom the patient is living or was living at the time of admission, or the AMHP, but the reported cases are overwhelmingly applications by AMHPs, with relatives and cohabitants entirely unrepresented in the reported case law. The grounds for replacement are contained in s. 29(3):

(a) that the patient has no nearest relative within the meaning of this Act, or that it is not reasonably practicable to ascertain whether he has such a relative, or who that relative is;

(b) that the nearest relative of the patient is incapable of acting as such by reason of mental disorder or other illness;

(c) that the nearest relative of the patient unreasonably objects to the making of an application for admission for treatment or a guardianship application in respect of the patient;

(d) that the nearest relative of the patient has exercised without due regard to the welfare of the patient or the interests of the public his power to discharge the patient under this Part of this Act, or is likely to do so; or

(e) that the nearest relative of the patient is otherwise not a suitable person to act as such.

The case law concerns almost exclusively (c). To found an application, the court must be given evidence that the proposed application for admission is necessary: *B(A)* v *B(L)* *(Mental Health Patient)* [1980] 1 WLR 116 (CA). The test of the unreasonableness of the objection was established by *W* v *L*, [1974] QB 711. That case involved the objection of a wife to the confinement of her husband, and the test was established by Lord Denning, at 717–8:

> This brings me to the final question: is the wife unreasonable in objecting to the making of an application for the husband's detention? This is a difficult question. One can see that she is pulled both ways: on the one hand, she is devoted to her husband and wants him to be with her; on the other hand, she is devoted to her baby and wants the baby to be with her too. No doubt she feels that she can cope. She says she knows her husband better than anyone else does; she will see that he takes his tablets; she is quite satisfied that neither she nor the baby will be in danger. So if you look at it from her own point of view, she may not be unreasonable. But I do not think it correct to look at it from her own point of view. The proper test is to ask what a reasonable woman in her place would do in all the circumstances of the case....
>
> So we come to this: looking at it objectively, what would a reasonable woman in her place do when faced with this problem? It seems to me that a reasonable woman would say: my husband ought to go in for treatment and he ought to be detained until he is cured. It is too great a risk to have him home whilst the baby is so small. Her objection is therefore unreasonable.

Should such an objective test be used? Is the question what the objective 'reasonable' nearest relative would do, or whether the nearest relative in the case was behaving unreasonably according to a more subjective test? This raises the question, not discussed in the case, as to why the nearest relative should be included in the decision process at all. If it is merely to ensure the provision of relevant information to the doctor, an objective test is defensible; although if this is the purpose, it is not obvious why not merely mandatory consultation but also a veto to admission would be provided. If it is instead to provide an acknowledgement that the nearest relative as an individual family member might have something distinctive to bring to the determination, the case for an objective test is more difficult to make out, as such individuality is removed by the objective test. When such individuality is removed, and when the 'objective' view of the facts is that of the AMHP and the treatment team, any objection is bound to appear unreasonable.

Indeed, the facts of *W* v *L* can be read in that way. Lord Denning presents the case as the wife driven to unreasonableness in the conflicting desires to be near her baby and her husband. Lawton LJ goes so far as to say that the case comes 'to the right conclusion in deciding to safeguard this little baby from the possibility of harm' (719–20). In fact, the baby had been placed in care voluntarily by the wife, so was apparently in no danger whatsoever, at least in the short term. The husband was in fact taking his medication. The husband and wife had been living together for some weeks without dangerous or violent incident. The use of an objective test allowed the court not to consider the balance that the wife had chosen to strike. Objectively, it would seem in the view of the court, the reasonable woman ought to have her baby with her, and she ought to follow the advice of the medical experts about her husband.

The application of this objective test effectively undercuts the independent role of the nearest relative, because it allows findings of fact adverse to the nearest relative effectively to determine the matter. In *Manchester City Council* v *MI*, [1999] 1 MHLR 132, for example, the issue was whether allegedly aggressive behaviour by the patient flowed from mental disorder or from epilepsy. The nearest relative, herself a nurse, had medical evidence from the patient's GP and from an independent expert neurologist attesting to the fact that MI did indeed have epilepsy. The court also had evidence from a senior social worker and two consultant psychiatrists that MI had chronic schizophrenia and Tourette Syndrome. The court preferred the latter evidence, and therefore held that the objection to MI's admission was unreasonable. With respect, this asks the wrong question, since it pre-supposes that the reasonable nearest relative must reach the same view of conflicting medical evidence as the court. If the nearest relative is to have a meaningful role in these circumstances, the question must instead be whether the nearest relative is unreasonable in believing one set of expert medical opinion over another, or was deciding unreasonably given that view of the evidence.

While the courts occasionally deny it, it is difficult to see that s. 29 applications do not in the end collapse into a question of the court's view of the best interests of the patient, and the courts are loathe to take a view divergent from the clinician responsible for the patient's care in the hospital. Indeed, in *McClelland* v *Simon S* [2000] 1 MHLR 6, the trial judge went so far as to find that the nearest relative's 'attack on [the psychiatrist's] opinion is but one indication of the unreasonableness of Mr S's objection to his mother's continued detention in hospital' (p. 6). While Baroness Hale in the Court of Appeal expressly disagreed with that finding, it does suggest an approach of extreme sympathy to medical opinion at trial.

The courts also appear to have abandoned a sense of procedural fairness in these cases. In a number of cases, the application to replace the nearest relative is lodged without notice to the nearest relative (see, e.g., *R (London)* v *London* [1999] QB 1260; *R (Holloway)* v *Oxford* [2007] EWHC 776 (Admin); see also *R (B)* v *Uxbridge* [2000] 1 MHLR 179, where two hours' notice was provided). Interim orders replacing the nearest relative were issued in these cases, and the s. 3 application was completed in this interim period, before the full hearing was held and the nearest relative had a chance to defend his or her position. The rights regarding consultation and objection in the statute were conveniently circumvented. It is difficult to see why this process would be necessary. The commencement of the application will ensure that a s. 2 detention remains in effect pending the outcome of the s. 29 hearing, and adjourning the matter at the initial stage would therefore appear to solve the immediate problem of a s. 2 detention expiring. There is no obvious reason to resort instead to a process that gives the appearance of subterfuge. The court itself indicated in the first of these cases, *R (London)* v *London*, that dealing with the s. 29 issues first was preferable, but while the courts are critical of the conduct of the local authorities in the other two cases mentioned, they did not disallow the orders made.

Consistent with this, the authors of this textbook have located 12 reported cases of local authority applications under s. 29. The nearest relative has lost every one. These are cases where the exercise of professional power over the nearest relative can be seen with particular clarity. That appearance is noted by Hale LJ in *Smirek* v *Williams* [2000] 1 MHLR 38 at paras. 14–15:

> I am bound to say that this case illustrates several aspects of the mental health law which give rise to the greatest possible sense of injustice on the part of patients and from time to time their families....
>
> ... it illustrates the overriding of the views of the nearest relative, and in practice how difficult it is for the nearest relative to avoid being found unreasonable if his views differ from those of the hospital. In this particular case, even more will there be a sense of injustice as his views are the same as those of a Mental Health Review Tribunal. Relatives must in those circumstances wonder why they have any role at all.

Consideration of the consultation and s. 29 cases suggests that in the court's view, the obligation of the AMHP is to engage seriously in the consultation process, and the role of the nearest relative is not to exercise their right to object to the proposed admission.

6.4 Other mechanisms of confinement: Substantive issues

Sections 2 and 3 are the fundamental mechanisms of civil confinement under the MHA 1983. In support of them are a variety of other provisions to facilitate admissions under ss. 2 or 3 in difficult situations. These allow control to be taken of the individual, typically for up to 72 hours, to allow the processes leading to a ss. 2 or 3 admission to take place.

6.4.1 Admission of patients already in hospital

Section 5 allows an application under ss. 2 or 3 to be made in respect of an informal patient already in that hospital. In most cases, this will be used regarding an informal patient in a psychiatric ward, but the section is not formally restricted in that fashion, and it may be used to confine a patient in a different ward of the hospital, being treated for a reason other than mental disorder. The section is restricted to inpatients, however, and persons resident outside the facility but receiving treatment at outpatient clinics are beyond its scope.

The trigger of an application under s. 5 may well be the intent or attempt of an informal patient to leave the hospital. In these circumstances, there may well be insufficient time to follow the regular application processes before the patient leaves. To account for this problem, a 'holding power' is provided for doctors and nurses, giving authority to detain an inpatient who is not yet technically compulsorily admitted.

The provision relating to doctors is notably lax in its requirements. It is available only to the doctor in charge of the patient's treatment, usually a consultant psychiatrist, or in their absence, their named delegate, usually a junior doctor (s. 5(3); Hall *et al.*, 1995). There is no separate substantive standard in the Act for the exercise of this holding power, except that the doctor thinks that an application under ss. 2 or 3 of the Act 'ought' to be made. Consistent with that, the doctor does have to provide reasons why informal status is no longer suitable (*Mental Health (Hospital, Guardianship and Treatment)(England) Regulations 2008*, SI 2008/1184, form H1). The result is that the patient may be confined for 72 hours (s. 5(2)).

Nurses of the 'prescribed class' (s. 5(4),(7); see the *Mental Health (Nurses)(England) Order 2008*, SI 2008/1207), also have a holding power, of six hours' duration (s. 5(4)). Here, there are substantive criteria stated in the section. Unlike the remainder of the section, individuals subjected to this detention must actually be receiving treatment for mental disorder. In addition, it must appear to the nurse:

(a) that the patient is suffering from mental disorder to such a degree that it is necessary for his health or safety or for the protection of others for him to be immediately restrained from leaving the hospital; and

(b) that it is not practicable to secure the immediate attendance of a practitioner for the purposes of furnishing a report under subsection (2) above [the doctor's holding power].

Notwithstanding the similarity in wording between s. 5(4)(a) and ss. 2(2)(b) and 3(2)(b), there are significant differences. Section 5(4)(a) requires the necessity of immediate restraint, for the health or safety of the patient or the protection of others. The necessity of immediate restraint is on its face a stricter test than 'ought' to be detained for assessment (s. 2(2)), and perhaps even than the necessity of treatment (s. 3(2)). It is certainly not a test which will be met simply because a mentally disordered patient wishes to leave the psychiatric ward at a time when no doctor is at hand. The nurse is placed in a position where he or she must make a decision on the criteria. How far this is reflected in practical realities is doubtful. Given the realities of hierarchy in the staffing of psychiatric wards, it is difficult to believe that the criteria prescribed by the MHA 1983 will be the only matters on the nurse's mind.

6.4.2 Emergency admission (s. 4)

Section 4(1) of the MHA 1983 provides a reordering of the s. 2 process in cases of 'urgent necessity'. The application of the AMHP or nearest relative requires medical certification from only one doctor, rather than two. This allows the individual to be detained in a psychiatric hospital for up to 72 hours. If a second medical certificate is provided in this period, the admission becomes a s. 2 admission.

The criteria for admission are as in s. 2, but in addition, the statement of the nearest relative or AMHP must attest that the case is one of urgent necessity, and that resort to the processes of s. 2 would involve 'undesirable delay' (s. 4(2)). While the statute appears to place the responsibility for this matter in the hands of the applicant, the forms place it squarely on the doctor providing the medical certificate. Where the applicant's nearest relative or AMHP must merely certify the urgent necessity, and the undesirable delay, the doctor must estimate the delay which would result from following the procedure in s. 2, and explain the harm which would result to the patient, those caring for the patient, or other persons (SI 2008/1184, form A11).

The Code of Practice makes it clear that the provision is to be used for cases of 'genuine emergency' only, not 'administrative convenience' (para. 5.4–5.5). 'Emergency' is understood by the Code to include an inability of carers to cope (para. 5.6). Evidence of an emergency includes the existence of significant risk of mental or physical harm to the patient or to others, the danger of serious harm to property, and the need for physical restraint of the patient. The Code actively discourages the use of this provision for convenience of doctors to examine the patient inside rather than outside hospitals, and AMHPs unsatisfied with the unavailability of second doctors in these contexts are told to take the matter up with the relevant social services authority (paras. 5.5, 5.8).

6.4.3 Powers of Justices of the Peace in s. 135

Section 4 will be effective in cases of urgency, when an AMHP or nearest relative feels it necessary to act quickly. It will not be successful if an AMHP lacks the information required for an application under ss. 2 or 3, nor if doctors are not given access to the patient, so as to provide the required medical certificates. In such situations, reference should be had to s. 135(1)—this section will be discussed in detail in Chapter 7, 7.3—for present purposes, it is sufficient to note that it applies when a justice of the peace finds that there is reasonable cause to suspect that a person believed to be suffering from mental disorder is being ill-treated, neglected, or 'kept otherwise than under proper control', or is living alone and unable to care for himself or herself. In those circumstances, the Justice may order that the person be detained in a place of safety for up to 72 hours, to allow the appropriate examinations by an AMHP and doctors.

6.4.4 Police powers under s. 136

Section 135 will assist if there is time to arrange an application before a Justice of the Peace. More pressing situations are covered by s. 136. This section allows a constable who finds, in a public place, a person who appears to him to be suffering from mental disorder and to be in immediate need of care or control to remove the person to a place of safety for up to 72 hours, if he thinks it necessary to do so in the interests of that person or for the protection of other persons. Once again, the objective here is to allow time for the required examinations by an AMHP and doctors to be performed.

Section 136 will be discussed in detail in Chapter 7, 7.3. Suffice it here to say that it is not without limits. It is not a general power of the police to intervene in the lives of people with mental disabilities, but instead requires that these people be in immediate need of care or control. It further extends only to places 'to which the public have access'. While the meaning of that phrase is subject to some discussion (see 7.3.2), it is not infinitely malleable. It seems that the section cannot be used to detain an individual apparently in immediate need of control in his or her own home, for example (see, e.g., *R (Sessay)* v *South London and Maudsley* [2011] EWHC 2617 (Admin)).

6.5 New directions?

As we have seen, traditional justifications for detention have focused on dangerousness to self or others and the need for care and treatment. In recent years, a new model has arisen, advocating the combination of mental capacity law and mental health law; and the new United Nations CRPD raises a whole new set of questions about compulsion and detention. This chapter closes with a discussion of these.

6.5.1 Admission and capacity: The fusion proposal

In recent years, there has been a tendency to propose a greater role for capacity in statutory criteria for detention. This has been adopted with apparent success in Scotland, where the criteria for detention require not merely that the detention be necessary in the interests of the patient's health or safety or the protection of others, but also that 'the patient's ability to make decisions about the provision of medical treatment is significantly impaired' (*Mental Health (Care and Treatment)(Scotland) Act 2003*, asp 13, ss. 36(4), 44(4)). Such a greater role for capacity was similarly proposed by the Richardson Committee in its report on reforms to the MHA 1983 (DH and Welsh Office 1999a). While the government rejected this approach, it received considerable academic support at the time (Buchanan, 2002; Gunn and Holland, 2002; Szmukler and Holloway, 2000; cf. Bartlett, 2003a).

These early formulations proposed incorporation of capacity into the structure of the existing MHA 1983. Subsequent academic argument has gone a step further, and proposed the collapse of separate standards of detention in mental health and mental capacity legislation. Under these so-called 'fusion' proposals, a capacity and proportionality test would be applied for all detention and enforced care and treatment related to mental disorder (see Dawson and Szmukler, 2006; Szmukler, Daw and Dawson, 2010; and, somewhat more sceptically, Richardson, 2010; Wand and Chiarella, 2006) The most developed articulation of this approach (Szmukler, Daw and Dawson, 2010) is based on the wording of the MCA 2005. As such, it requires the individual to have a mental disorder resulting in incapacity, understood as an inability to understand, retain, and weigh in the balance the information relevant to his or her care and treatment. Admission would need to be in the best interests of the individual, again taking into account that individual's wishes and feelings, but as under the MCA 2005 also including an objective assessment of best interests. Following the MCA 2005 requirements for restraint, an admission resulting in a deprivation of liberty would only be permitted if it were to be a proportionate response to the likelihood of the individual suffering harm, and the degree of that harm. In this formulation, as under the MCA 2005, there is no express criterion relating to harm to other people. While it is clear that the authors of this proposal would not support such a criterion, there is no reason it could not in principle be included without departing from the overall model, so long as it was included equally for people with mental health problems and people lacking capacity: the foundation of the fusion approach is to consolidate mental health and mental capacity law, so in principle any set of criteria that are consistently applied between these two groups would be consistent with the fusion ideal.

The attraction of the fusion proposal is its non-discriminatory character: we allow intervention in the lives of the general public when they lack capacity; the use of the same criteria in a mental health setting therefore constitutes equal treatment. This is a significant attraction. While the fusion proposal has not been implemented in its entirety anywhere, Scottish mental health legislation has, since 2003, included as a prerequisite to compulsion the requirement of a mental disorder which significantly impairs the individual's ability to make medical decisions: Mental Health (Care and Treatment) (Scotland) Act 2003, ss. 36(4)(b), 44(4)(b), 57(3)(d), 64(5)(d). In practice, this looks much like a capacity criterion, and while it is not the only factor in determining compulsion, it does suggest that as a matter of practicality, a greater role for capacity can be provided in legislation. Further, the limited number of academic studies on the full fusion approach give cause for guarded optimism. A study of 55 patients consecutively admitted to a London hospital gave a high rate of consistency between two independent assessors of treatment capacity, suggesting that capacity might be sufficiently robust to be usable in an admission context (Cairns *et al.*, 2005a). A study of 35 patients in London found a notably high rate of rate of retrospective approval—83 per cent—by those patients regaining capacity for decisions taken for them when they lacked capacity (Owen *et al.*, 2009). While these are obviously small studies, they are certainly encouraging.

At the same time, the fusion proposal has its difficulties. What decision is it that is actually being considered—the decision to consent to admission to hospital, or the consent to psychiatric treatment? Szmukler, Daw and Dawson (2010) specifically do not argue for the separation of these decisions (11), arguing that for the fusion proposals, they should be considered as a single assessment of capacity. Presumably that would mean that an individual would lack capacity and could be within the fusion criteria either if he or she were unable to understand the information relevant to hospital admission or if unable to decide on proposed treatment. This significantly expands the scope of incapacity, and could result in the individual being compelled regarding decisions for which he or she still had capacity. It is also an approach inconsistent with the MCA 2005: there is no suggestion that people who lack capacity to consent to admission to a nursing home necessarily lack capacity to consent to treatment in the nursing home, or vice versa. In this sense, the fusion model of Szmukler *et al.* is a move away from decision-specific capacity, a step that would be perceived by many as retrograde. It is further establishing criteria that are not the same as the broader approach to mental capacity, in contradiction of the foundational idea of the fusion approach.

The mixing together of capacity to consent to admission and to consent to treatment also raises problems under international law. The European Committee for the

Prevention of Torture (CPT) in its standards has since 1998 required that involuntary admission should not mean the loss of rights to make treatment decisions: see 8th General Report, CPT/Inf (98) 12, para. 41; reprinted in the current articulation of CPT Standards, CPT/Inf/E (2002) 1—Rev. 2011, p 53. This view has now been adopted by the European Court of Human Rights (see *X v Finland*, Application No. 34806/04, judgment of 3 July 2012).

Separating the admission and treatment decisions however creates problems of its own. How is the fusion proposal to deal with a person who has capacity to make decisions regarding admission, but not decisions regarding treatment? If the treatment could only be provided in hospital, a patient refusing admission would therefore effectively be refusing the treatment, which he or she lacks capacity to do. If however the patient cannot consent to admission but can consent to treatment, there is the risk that the person could be admitted and not treated, raising the question of whether it is sensible to admit him or her at all.

A significant jurisprudence and academic literature exists on capacity for consent to medical treatment, but much less on what an individual needs to understand to have capacity to make decisions regarding admission (see Bartlett, 2003a). This determination is not necessarily straightforward. Capacity in the context of deprivation of liberty was discussed in Chapter 5, 5.3.4, and will not be repeated here; but there are additional factors that may be relevant to admissions to psychiatric hospitals. Obviously, to have capacity the individual would have to understand that they were being admitted to a psychiatric facility. Presumably the reason for the admission will usually be treatment, and presumably the individual must be able to understand that; but equally this cannot be equated to capacity to consent to the treatment if the distinction between admission and treatment decisions is to be maintained.

Perhaps most difficult is the question of how far individuals would need to understand their psychiatric condition and, in particular, their dangerousness to themselves or others, in order to have capacity to make decisions about asylum admission. If such understandings are required, much of the practical advantage of the capacity standard over the dangerousness one disappears, for all the difficulties of assessment return, and the social control ramifications continue, merely under the guise of a neutral capacity test. If dangerousness is to be a factor in any event, it may perhaps be to the advantage of both patient and clinician to have a clear dangerousness standard placed in the statute, whatever the apparent social control imagery, rather than for the matter to be determined in the murkier twilight of a capacity determination.

Specific problems for the fusion approach arise under the CRPD. Article 12 of the CRPD provides the right to legal capacity, and the right to enjoy that right on an equal basis with others. As discussed in Chapter 4 at 4.1.1 and 4.7, the precise interpretation of this Article is not yet entirely clear, but it would appear to preclude hard line distinctions between people who have capacity and who do not, precisely the distinction on which the fusion proposal is based. Where the fusion proposal views capacity as a way to escape the discriminatory nature of current mental health law, the CRPD views capacity as yet another mechanism by which people with disabilities are subjected to discriminatory control. Given the way capacity is used in much of the world, the CRPD's position here has considerable merit (see, e.g., the reports of the Mental Disability Advocacy Center on Serbia, Russia, Kyrgyzstan, Hungary, the Czech Republic, and Bulgaria, available at http://www.mdac.info; and also *Shtukaturov v Russia*, Application No. 44009/05, judgment of 27 June 2008 and *Stanev v Bulgaria*, Application No. 36760/06, judgment of 17 January 2012). Insofar as the CRPD allows capacity to be used as a concept at all, the view of the UN High Commissioner on Human Rights is that it would need to be separated off from disability. The fusion proposals however apply specifically to people with mental disabilities, and so if the High Commissioner is correct, it is difficult to see that the fusion proposals would be CRPD compliant.

6.5.2 The UN Convention on the Rights of Persons with Disabilities (CRPD)

The challenge posed by the CRPD is much more profound. The potentially discriminatory effect of using standards of detention based on dangerousness to self or others or need for care and treatment was discussed earlier in this chapter, and the potential difficulties of the use of a capacity test in 6.5.1, but the CRPD poses much more fundamental challenges to psychiatric detention. Article 14 protects the right to liberty of persons with disabilities, and Article 14(1)(b) states specifically that 'the existence of a disability shall in no case justify a deprivation of liberty'. The leading interpretation is currently not merely that disability cannot be the sole ground for detention; it is that disability cannot be a factor in determining detention at all. In the view of the United Nations High Commissioner for Human Rights (2009: para. 48):

> Legislation authorizing the institutionalization of persons with disabilities on the grounds of their disability without their free and informed consent must be abolished. This must include the repeal of provisions authorizing institutionalization of persons with disabilities for their care and treatment without their free and informed consent, as well as provisions authorizing the preventive detention of persons with disabilities on grounds such as the likelihood of them posing a danger to themselves or others, in all cases in which such grounds of care, treatment and public security are linked in legislation to an apparent or diagnosed mental illness.

This would seem to mean the end of detention based on mental illness or intellectual impairment, and thus the end of the core of mental health law as it has been understood for more than two centuries. The right to liberty is a civil and political right, and therefore not subject to progressive realisation. Consistent with this, the first three country reports of the Committee on the Rights of Persons with Disabilities, the UN treaty body charged with overseeing implementation of the CRPD, has called on the relevant national governments to amend their laws so they no longer detain on the basis of mental disability (United Nations Committee on the Rights of Persons with Disabilities, 2011: 24–25; 2011a: 35–36; 2012: 28–29), with no suggestion that those reforms are contingent on resources or the prior development of alternative and consensual structures of care in the community, a process that could take years in many countries.

While this appears to be the overall direction of the High Commissioner's report, the subsequent passage introduces a note of equivocation (2009: para. 48):

> This should not be interpreted to say that persons with disabilities cannot be lawfully subject to detention for care and treatment or to preventive detention, but that the legal grounds upon which restriction of liberty is determined must be de-linked from the disability and neutrally defined so as to apply to all persons on an equal basis.

This would appear to suggest that preventive detention is permitted, so long as it does not apply solely to people with mental disabilities and is defined in a disability-neutral way. This view is however problematic on a number of grounds.

For the position to make sense, it must mean more than the removal of the language of mental disability from the statutory criteria. To solve the problem of discriminatory application, it must mean the creation of a statutory regime where mental disability will not be in the mind of the detaining authority, and where apparently neutral criteria will not be applied disproportionately to people with mental disabilities. Otherwise, the criteria would merely move from the realm of direct to indirect discrimination, a result which does not address the question of discrimination at all. It is fair to wonder how practical this is: will people enforcing a preventive detention statute that is on its face disability neutral really put the individual's mental disability out of their mind when enforcing that statute?

Insofar as the High Commissioner advocates a law of preventive detention that applies to everyone, it is difficult to see that this would be a desirable result. It is difficult to see that it would be wise in human rights terms to encourage autocratic governments internationally to pass laws of allowing preventive detention of their citizens: such a law is too manifestly open to abuse. This raises a difficult question, however: if such a law would be too open to abuse for the general population, presumably because concepts such as 'dangerousness' on which it would be based are too malleable and insufficiently precise, why would we consider it acceptable to apply such detention criteria to people with mental disabilities under current law?

Even if such a law of general application were thought to be desirable, there would be problems under the ECHR. Article 5 creates a general prohibition of deprivation of liberty, subject to specific exceptions, including 'lawful detention of...persons of unsound mind' (ECHR, Art. 5(1)(e)), which provides the basis of current mental health law relating to detention. If the law ceases to be based on unsoundness of mind (with the medicalised gloss on that phrase contained in the *Winterwerp* case), it would be necessary to find a different exception under Article 5. It is not obvious what other justification for preventive detention could be found. The ECtHR has not entirely ruled out the use of Art. 5(1)(a) concerning the detention of criminals as a possibility of preventive detention following criminal conviction (see *M* v *Germany* (2010) 51 EHRR 41). When Germany attempted to implement that decision, however, it found itself resorting to criteria based on mental disability, (see Drenkhan *et al.*, 2012), precisely the criteria that the High Commissioner indicates should not be used under the CRPD. The practical possibility for a preventive detention statute not based on mental disability but consistent with the ECHR must therefore be taken to be very narrow indeed.

The response of governments to Article 14 and the High Commissioner's reading of it is likely to be dismissive. Consistent with that is the United Kingdom's response (Office for Disability Issues, 2011: para. 134):

> Under the 1983 Act [i.e., the MHA], a person with a mental disorder may be detained and treated (or be made subject to certain other restrictions) without his or her consent where that is justified by the risk that the mental disorder poses to him or her or to other people. Safeguards ensure that any such deprivation of liberty is not arbitrary and complies with the law (including Article 5 of the ECHR).... Individuals have the right to have their case reviewed by an independent and impartial Mental Health Tribunal. They also have the right to receive support from statutory Independent Mental Health Advocates.

On this basis, the government takes the view that the MHA 1983 is compliant. At least without a great deal more nuanced argument, it is difficult to see that this is a defensible position, given the government's acknowledgement that the law is based on mental disorder, the fundamental point challenged by the High Commissioner's position.

If that is the case, it is necessary to ask whether we could do without preventive detention based on mental disability: could we just abolish the compulsory detention provisions of the MHA 1983? The political realities at this time place such a question in the realm of thinking the unthinkable, but reconsider the questions of justification discussed in Chapter 1, 1.2. Is the abolition of detention based on mental disability really so indefensible?

7

Policing Mental Disorder

7.1 Introduction

This is the first of two chapters which look at the law, policies, and practices of criminal justice agencies and actors when they encounter mentally disordered persons. In Chapter 8, we discuss the operation of the system from the point of court appearance onwards. In this chapter, the focus is on the role of the police, both as agents of the criminal justice system and—for example, in returning detained patients who have absconded from a psychiatric facility—as agents of the mental health system. But first, we consider the broader policy context within which the criminal justice system in all its elements should operate in its dealings with mentally disordered persons, and in this sense this serves as an introduction both to this chapter and Chapter 8.

That policy, in a (confused, ill-defined, and misleading) word, is 'diversion'. Although problematic in application, for a number of reasons (to be discussed further in this chapter), the basic idea seems straightforward. According to a government circular to criminal justice agencies, still in force (Home Office, 1990: para. 2), 'it is government policy that, wherever possible, mentally disordered persons should receive care and treatment from the health and social services'. More recently, in its guidance to the courts on sentencing mentally disordered offenders following the reforms introduced by the Mental Health Act (MHA) 2007, the Ministry of Justice (2008: para. 1.2) explained that 'The Act reflects the continuation of the Government's policy that mentally disordered people who commit offences should receive specialist mental health treatment rather than being punished, wherever that can safely be achieved'.

Such statements are laudable, but problematic. Some of the reasons for this, to do with the intended scope of the policy of diversion, will be discussed shortly. For now, though, the point is that 'diversion' understood in these terms posits two entities, two separate systems, two disposal options, an either/or choice between punishment and treatment (albeit subject to a caveat regarding safety), when in reality it is not clear that there is such clear water between the two. If, instead of thinking about 'treatment versus punishment', which terms do indeed seem very different in emphasis, we think in terms of 'control' and 'protection', then it can be seen that both systems, to this extent at least, pursue the same aim, at least some of the time. Are treatment and punishment two means to the same end, of public safety? Are both systems, ultimately, about control? Are they, in this sense, merely different branches of the same system? In 2010 the

Sainsbury Centre for Mental Health published research (Rutherford, 2010) which demonstrates that the criminal justice and mental health systems are engaged in a process of 'convergence', which offers many benefits, in terms of more efficient joint working between agencies and better outcomes for diversion schemes, but also involves various problematic features: the 'lines between prisons and hospitals may become overly blurred' and '[t]here is a risk that convergence may de-professionalise workforces and that practitioner roles will become increasingly blurred' (Rutherford, 2010: 10).

Public opinion tends to be ambivalent and divided on such questions. For example, a survey conducted in 2010 found that 86 per cent of respondents (although down from 92 per cent the previous year) disagreed with the statement 'People with mental illness don't deserve our sympathy' (Prior, 2010: 20) and 84 per cent of respondents agreed with the statement 'No-one has the right to exclude people with mental illness from their neighbourhood', whilst on the other hand, only 66 per cent agreed with the statement 'Residents have nothing to fear from people coming into their neighbourhood to obtain mental health services' and only 59 per cent agreed with the statement 'People with mental illness are far less of a danger than most people suppose' (Prior, 2010: 25). These findings indicate society's mixed feelings about the mentally ill—seen as deserving of treatment and social inclusion, but also, for many people, a source of danger and fear. One in three of 'us' would rather not have 'them' in our neighbourhood, even if only for the purposes of receiving treatment. Perhaps most revealing was the finding that only 26 per cent of people agreed with the statement 'Most women who were once patients in a mental hospital can be trusted as babysitters' (Prior, 2010: 25), which seems to indicate that, when it comes down to it, 'we' do not really trust 'them', certainly around those of 'us' considered to be most vulnerable. On occasion, negative attitudes towards the mentally ill or persons with learning disabilities manifest in the form of 'hate crimes' committed against such persons (HM Chief Inspector of the CPS, HM Chief Inspector of Probation, and HM Inspector of Constabulary, 2013).

This ambivalence is long-established. Long and Midgely (1992) trace the linkages made in professional and popular understandings of the concepts of criminality and madness in the nineteenth century. The causes of each were understood in much the same way, which meant that the 'two could be viewed together, two sides of a common problem' (1992: 64–65). At the same time, the problem of 'criminal lunatics' was very much in the public eye. When professional disenchantment with the potential to cure either the insane or the criminal set in, towards the end of the century, the view of the 'incurable criminal lunatic' as the archetype of both mental illness and criminality, gained ground accordingly, in popular, as well as professional, discourses (Foucault, 1988).

In part, this mythology (for mythology it largely is) has been maintained to the present day, through a series of folk devils with a roll call that begins with Jack the Ripper, and includes Crippen, Hindley and Brady, Sutcliffe, Nielson, and more recently Fred and Rose West, Harold Shipman, and others. The 'criminal lunatic', and the conflation of the two concepts that such a person is set up to represent, is part of our cultural furniture, a staple in drama, from Norman Bates to Hannibal Lecter and beyond. This figure, this folk devil, continues to exert an influence, both on public opinion and public policy, and sits in tension with our more humanitarian impulses towards the mentally disordered, as fellow citizens in need of medical treatment and other assistance.

For Foucault (2003), this figure is the modern equivalent of the (equally mytho-logical) 'monsters' which spread dread throughout medieval Europe (Cohen, 1999; Mittman, 2006), except that these modern monsters are not marked off by physical 'deformity' (Williams, 1996). Unlike the two-headed, or three-eyed, or other grotesque monsters of the Middle Ages, modern monsters cannot be detected visually. Theirs, rather, is a 'monstrosity of character' (Foucault, 2003: 73), an internal rather than exter-nal monstrosity, a monstrosity which is invisible to the naked eye unless and until it manifests in that person's words or behaviour.

The modern monster is marked not by the evident chronicity of its state but by the sudden, unexpected, and devastating shock of its appearance, its sudden and abrupt reversal of the normal. Harold Shipman's conversion from well-respected long-standing local GP to mass murderer, perhaps even Jimmy Savile's conversion from avuncular, if eccentric, 'national treasure' to predatory child sex offender, amongst others, pro-vide recent examples of the point. The appearance of the monster is always shocking. Whereas the monsters of old stabilised the difference between 'us' and 'them', with 'them' being visually distinct from 'us', the modern monster destabilises that distinc-tion: the modern monster 'appears normal' until their true inner, monstrous, self is revealed. This both makes the modern monster even more monstrous, even more to be feared, and licenses the intervention of psychiatry, as only psychiatry has the tools to detect this hidden monstrosity (see Foucault, 2003: especially, ch. 6).

Hence, it can be argued that the linking of madness and criminality is a profes-sional tactic or technology of professional dominance. Szasz (1970), for example, has famously argued that the emergent profession of psychiatry campaigned successfully for a strategic linkage of the concepts of criminality and madness in the nineteenth century, in order to stake out a professional stamping ground for themselves within the asylum and the prison, and since then has protected that linkage from attempts to separate it. It is certainly the case that the modern prison has been a continuous home for psychiatry. As Long and Midgely point out, right from the start of its life in 1842, Pentonville prison's inmate population featured an over-representation of 'lunatics' by almost ten times more than would have been expected; a feature of imprisonment that, as will be seen, has changed little today.

This ambivalence is present, even in the civil law provisions of the MHA 1983, which reveal a dense and complex weave of medical and criminological ideas. The criteria for civil confinement, as seen in Chapter 6, 6.3.1, treat 'abnormally aggressive or seriously irresponsible conduct', neither of which is a medical concept, as integral to the defini-tion of learning disabilities under the MHA 1983; provide for the detention of persons 'for the protection of other persons'; give Responsible Clinicians (RCs) powers to veto an application for discharge made by a nearest relative of the patient on the grounds of the 'dangerousness' of the patient (see Chapter 11, 11.2.2.1); and so on. In short, although diversion policy assumes a fundamental difference in emphasis as between the mental health system and the criminal justice system, between treatment and pun-ishment, in truth we are more ambivalent about the difference, and this is reflected in law, policy and practice in various ways, as will be seen in this chapter.

The degree of overlap between the two concepts of mental disorder and criminal-ity, in both the popular and the political imagination, and reflected in the law, is such that such interconnectedness can seem inevitable, even natural. But the arguments of Foucault and Szasz entail the conclusion that the extent of the linkage of mental disorder with criminality is a projection, dictated more by the way in which each is constructed and responded to, both by the state and the public at large, than by any innate qualities of the concepts themselves. As Peay (1997: 687) has pointed out, 'the overwhelming correlates of violence are male gender, youth, low socio-economic class, and the use/abuse of alcohol or drugs, and not the diagnosis of major mental disorder'. Yet there is no policy in contemplation to detain men, or the poor (or reckless drivers, or any number of other potentially dangerous and identifiable groups) on preventative grounds of public protection, as there is for mentally disordered persons under the MHA 1983 and, although perhaps to a lesser extent now that Imprisonment for Public Protection (IPP) has been abolished (see Criminal Justice Act 2003, s. 225, as amended by Legal Aid, Sentencing and Punishment of Offenders Act 2012, Sch. 21(1), para. 23), as there is for offenders by the rules which govern sentencing in a criminal court.

It is important always to bear in mind the politicised and partial nature of the con-structions of mental disorder that underpin much governmental and other discourse: we have become so used to thinking of the 'mentally disordered' as being linked with 'the criminal' that we—modern society—tend rather too easily to accept that the response should be similar in either case; and any policy in respect of mentally disordered offend-ers must contend with this historical legacy of prejudice and mistrust. With this in mind, we turn now to consider 'diversion' policy, before turning to the role of the police when dealing with persons who are or appear to be suffering from mental disorder.

7.2 The policy of diversion

The first set of problems with discussing the policy of diversion is that the concept is not well defined. Is diversion a process or an outcome? If the latter, how is outcome to be measured: in mental health system terms, of effective treatment, or criminal justice terms, of prevention of further offending, criminal rehabilitation, and so on? Does diver-sion mean 'diversion from', or does it also include 'diversion to'? For example, is it 'diver-sion' for the police to decided merely to take no further action against a criminal suspect, or for the CPS to decide not to allow a case to proceed to court, or for a court to make an order for absolute discharge, because the accused person is mentally disordered? Or is there also a positive obligation to provide or secure treatment and/or other assistance (which is to link diversion with liaison: Winstone and Pakes, 2010) instead of proceeding with charge, prosecution, or punishment? If both are done at once, so that the prosecu-tion proceeds *and* the accused is provided with other services, is this still diversion?

Underpinning these uncertainties is a set of philosophical questions, the answers to which are equally problematic. What is the moral basis of diversion? One version of diversion can be understood simply as the consequence of the requirements of the criminal law, that *mens rea* be demonstrated in order to convict a defendant. If *mens rea* cannot be demonstrated, there can be no conviction because to convict in such circumstances would be unfair, and there has been no 'crime' if its essential ingredients cannot be made out. But if the 'crime' is a serious one, and the 'offender' is judged to be dangerous, then clearly it is not sufficient simply to disapply the criminal law. Considerations of public protection require an alternative mechanism for such situations, and such mechanisms, such as a finding of 'not guilty by reason of insanity' (the 'insanity plea': see Chapter 8, 8.3), have long allowed the detention of the accused person in a hospital on that basis. Related considerations also apply to a person suffering from mental disorder if that mental disorder renders him or her unfit to stand trial and actively engage in his or her own defence (see Chapter 8, 8.2.3), in which case it is also unfair that the trial should proceed.

The Royal College of Psychiatrists has provided the following typology of the various possible relations between offending or anti-social behaviour and mental disorder (Bradley, 2009: 17):

- The anti-social behaviour is directly related to or driven by aspects of mental disorder;
- The anti-social behaviour is indirectly related to mental disorder;
- The anti-social behaviour and the mental disorder are related by some common antecedent, for example childhood abuse;
- The anti-social behaviour and the mental disorder are coincidental;
- The mental behaviour is at least partly secondary to the anti-social behaviour.

The College goes on to suggest (Bradley, 2009: 17) that in the first case, effective treatment for mental disorder would be likely to reduce the risk of further offending, in the second case, it would contribute to reducing that risk but would not itself be sufficient to tackle the offending behaviour, in the third case treatment for mental disorder would not be expected to reduce offending, and in the fourth and fifth cases, the Royal College says nothing would change, because there is no link, or only a very weak link, between the offending and the mental disorder.

Such considerations do seem clearly relevant to any system of diversion which is justified on the basis of decreasing recidivism, but that is not the basis on which the current system rests. Rather, outside the context of the insanity defence and the issue of fitness to stand trial, a second, more general, version of diversion seems to best reflect current policy and practice. In this version of diversion, there need be no link between the offending behaviour and the mental disorder. Rather, diversion is a humanitarian intervention, based on the fact that the person in question needs medical treatment, and that punishment can only make things worse. The argument is magnified if that person's treatment by the criminal justice system has caused or exacerbated the need for medical treatment as when, for example, a period on remand in prison awaiting trial seems to be implicated in causing the person remanded to become mentally ill.

It is also possible to understand diversion in yet other ways. For example, in terms of citizenship, diversion can be seen as the application of the principle that all public services, and particularly health services, should be available to all citizens irrespective of status or situation. This is the idea behind, for example, the transfer of responsibility for provision of health services in prison from the Prison Department to the NHS (see Chapter 2, 2.2.4). If in the course of such provision, a need for hospitalisation is detected, a prisoner should have no lesser entitlement to that than any other citizen.

A third cluster of issues surround the appropriate target audience for diversion. At the moment, diversion policy essentially (but not always) uses the definition of 'mental disorder' found in s. 1 of the MHA 1983 to mark the population boundaries for diversion, but is this always appropriate? 'Mental disorder', as discussed in Chapter 1, embraces a wide and discontinuous number of unrelated conditions. If for present purposes, mental disorder is divided into three essential sub-categories, of mental illness, learning disability, and personality disorder (particularly severe and dangerous personality disorder or SDPD), then the problem is apparent. For many people, it is by no means evident in terms of the first two possible philosophical justifications for diversion—the 'fair trial' justification and the 'humanitarian' justification—that personality-disordered offenders should be diverted, on the assumption that personality disorder does not usually mean an inability to form an intention to act nor does it mean that the offender is deserving of special dispensation based on humanitarian concerns, even if there is suitable treatment available. Such considerations should be borne in mind when confronted with claims that diversion has failed because our prisons contain high numbers of inmates diagnosed with a personality disorder. It may be naïve to think other than that it was precisely this group of offenders that prisons were primarily designed for in the first place.

All of these problems were canvassed by Lord Bradley in his seismic report (2009) following his *review of people with mental health problems or learning disabilities in the criminal justice system*. Initially, the Bradley Review, which was commissioned by the Labour administration in 2007, was narrowly focused, on 'the extent to which offenders with mental health problems or learning disabilities could, in appropriate cases, be diverted from prison to other services and the barriers to such diversion' (Bradley, 2009: 7). It was expected that the Review would produce recommendations designed to improve court liaison and diversion (Bradley, 2009: 7). However, it soon became clear to Lord Bradley that such a narrow focus would constitute a missed opportunity to examine the whole of the offender pathway, and was likely to repeat past mistakes by focusing on one element of the criminal justice system with no consideration of how the various elements or stages of the criminal justice system impact on each other. The time allocated for the Review was therefore extended from its initial six months to one year, and the remit broadened so as to comprise 'comprehensive consideration of the "offender pathway" and the associated mental health services' (Bradley 2009: 4). Although not notable because it generated great amounts of new knowledge about the operation of the criminal justice system, and was more in the nature of a taking of stock, as its title suggests, the Bradley Report, which generated 82 recommendations for change at all points in the criminal justice system, nonetheless has proven to be the mechanism which has generated much subsequent activity.

Bradley had been preceded by a report published in 2007 under the authorship of Baroness Corston (Corston, 2007), which was focused on the needs of women in the criminal justice system. Baroness Corston, pointing out that most women in prison have not committed a crime of violence, and referring to research which demonstrated that 78 per cent of women received into prison had an unmet mental health need at the time of their reception (Plugge, Douglas, and Fitzpatrick, 2006), suggested that female offenders should be a prime target for improved diversion services at the early stages of the criminal process (Corston, 2007, especially Ch. 7). Baroness Corston (2007: 7.12) found the governmental 'obsession with mapping, gap analysis and evaluating frustrating... I cannot understand the logic in failing to invest modest sums in essential diversion schemes given the cost of keeping these women in prison and the unquantifiable social damage'. Lord Bradley (2009: 20) sought to build on and to integrate Baroness Corston's findings and recommendations into his review.

The immediate response of the government, accepting Bradley's recommendations, was the publication of the national strategy for offender health (Department of Health, 2009d), which recognised that many mentally disordered offenders are vulnerable individuals, frequently unable to access services either in the community or in prison (2009d: para. 1.1–1.3), and sought to instigate the creation of the national system of diversion which the Bradley report envisioned. Reference will be made to specific elements of the delivery plan for the national strategy throughout this chapter and Chapter 8, but here it should be noted that one Bradley recommendation which was immediately implemented was that there should be a national co-ordinating body, now known as the Health and Criminal Justice Programme Board, a cross-departmental body which has responsibility for overseeing the implementation of the delivery plan for the national strategy. The national strategy has various aspects to it. One important aspect is the instigation of a national system of liaison and diversion, due to have been achieved by 2014. To this end, in 2012 the Offender Health Collaborative, a consortium led by Nacro (a crime reduction charity) and comprising the Revolving Doors Agency; Centre for Mental Health; Mental Health Network, NHS Confederation; Cass Centre for Charity Effectiveness at the Cass Business School; and the Centre for Health and Justice, Institute for Mental Health at the University of Nottingham, was appointed to oversee the realisation of the goal of national coverage by that date.

Returning to the question of definition of diversion, Lord Bradley, having considered various possibilities, opted (2009: 16) for the following definition:

> 'Diversion' is a process whereby people are assessed and their needs identified as early as possible in the offender pathway (including prevention and early intervention), thus informing subsequent decisions about where an individual is best placed to receive treatment, taking into account public safety, safety of the individual, and punishment of offence.

For Lord Bradley, diversion itself should be seen as a system, superimposed on the criminal justice system, from the point of early intervention into the offending of young people right through to the prison system.

Diversion in this sense, as a series of mechanisms or opportunities to leave the 'offender pathway' and move onto a different, treatment-oriented, pathway, already exists (see Figure 7.1). As will be discussed, in this chapter and Chapter 8, the police have powers to organise the hospitalisation (or the provision of community care services), rather than arresting and/or charging, a criminal suspect; the CPS may discontinue a case on grounds of mental disorder; the courts can make a guardianship order instead of imposing a criminal sanction and can make a hospital order rather than passing a custodial sentence following conviction; and a prisoner may be transferred to hospital for treatment for mental disorder. Additionally, there are temporary diversion measures, such as remand to hospital for treatment or assessment, at various points along the route. There are also a number of mechanisms which provide for diversion *within* the criminal justice system, whereby the criminal process continues in train but special safeguards are brought into play, designed to ensure that the vulnerabilities or treatment needs of the mentally disordered person are acknowledged and provided for. One example of this is hospital wings in prisons, another, to be discussed shortly, is the system for protecting vulnerable suspects, including mentally disordered persons, in police stations.

The nub of Lord Bradley's recommendations were not that the shape of the system be radically overhauled, but rather that the system as he reviewed it—characterised too often by patchy or inadequate provision, insufficiently developed links and connections, dependent on local initiative and funding rather than central government commitment to a nationally effective diversion system—should start to deliver an effective, efficient, adequately funded, national service. This is an aim with which few could disagree.

As far as the target population was concerned, Lord Bradley eschewed the opportunity to consider the relevance of any links between mental disorder and offending behaviour (2009: 16), opting for the following definition, borrowed from Nacro, of the target population for diversion, namely 'offenders with mental health problems', which means (2009: 17):

> Those who come into contact with the criminal justice system because they have committed, or are suspected of committing, a criminal offence, and who may be acutely or chronically mentally ill... It also includes those in whom a degree of mental disturbance is recognised, even though it may not be severe enough to bring it within the criteria laid down by the Mental Health Act 1983.

This definition does not attempt to link the presence of mental disorder with the alleged offending behaviour as a prerequisite of eligibility for diversion. Beyond that, however, by reason of making reference to 'the criteria laid down' by the MHA 1983, it is not a very clear definition. Presumably, the reference to 'criteria' means the criteria for detention (although under which section is not clear; presumably it would be those in ss. 3

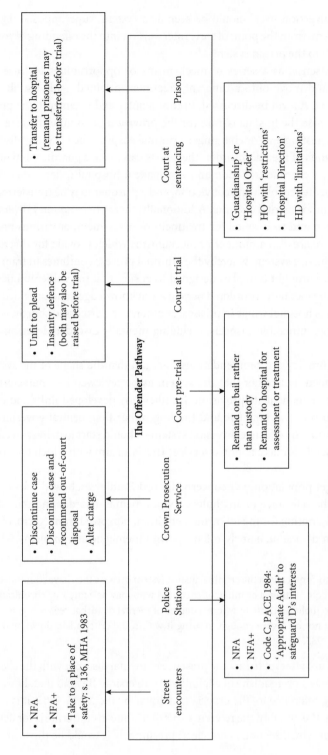

Figure 7.1 Overview of the main diversion routes along the 'offender pathway'

NFA = 'No Further Action', NFA+ = NFA by the criminal justice system but further intervention organised to be provided by health or social services.

and 37). There are no 'criteria' as such which apply to the definition of mental disorder in the revised 1983 Act, which as seen in Chapter 1 (1.4) is extremely broad—'any disorder or disability of mind'—and so it is not clear what other disorders, not covered by this definition, which does not contain any reference to severity, Lord Bradley had in mind when adopting his definition. On the other hand, he is clear that diversion should apply to all categories of mental disorder encompassed by the MHA 1983, including personality disorders of all types. On the question of the purpose of diversion, Lord Bradley favoured an 'outcomes' based approach, but rather hedged his bets: 'I hope that the types of interventions recommended in this report not only improve treatment and outcomes for offenders and their families but also contribute positively to the public safety agenda' (2009: 10).

Although, as will be seen repeatedly over this chapter and Chapter 8, Bradley has galvanised action right across the criminal justice system, his report also underlines the fact that diversion is not (subject to human rights law) a right that any suspect, accused, or offender has. As he noted, 'Safeguarding the public must always remain a top priority' (2009: 10), and as seen in the quotes reproduced here, he built the need to take 'public safety, safety of the individual, and punishment of offence' into this approach at the level of definition. In short, the treatment needs of offenders must always be balanced against the broader considerations of criminal justice.

There is certainly a point at which a failure to divert a severely mentally disordered person into appropriate care or accommodation provided by the mental health system will begin to raise questions under Art. 3 of the ECHR (*Kudla* v *Poland* (2002) 35 EHRR 11); but as the European Court emphasised in *Kudla*, this point is not easily reached, and Lord Bradley's decision, to not consider these more politicised questions, means that the system moves forward on the same shaky philosophical and politicised basis on which it operated previously. Moreover, and consistently with this, despite this discussion of outcomes, in Lord Bradley's conception, diversion is largely seen in terms of processes to identify and assess needs, and it is perfectly possible that, having done so in a particular case, it is decided that those needs do not require diversion of that person, but can be met notwithstanding that that person remains within the criminal justice system.

It is in any case not certain that diversion is a good thing. As Senior *et al.* (2011: 15) have pointed out, although diversion was accepted as such by Lord Bradley, 'most studies do not evaluate anything other than immediate outcomes through, for example, the reporting of short-term routine data, for example number of clients seen and types of immediate disposal' (2011: 15), and papers written by 'diversion clinicians' 'frequently offer...qualitative process-descriptions of the services they offer, often without any meaningful critique of their work' (Senior *et al.*, 2011: 16). In short, at the moment we do not know if diversion works, even in its own terms, partly because we are not certain what those terms are, nor is there any history of attempting systematically to measure such things.

This means that a preference for a policy of diversion cannot be evidence-based, and depends to some extent on the view taken of mental disorder and criminality. Szasz, for example, holds that there should be no diversion, that hospitals should not be places of compulsory confinement; this follows from his understanding of mental disorder as a construction of the psychiatric professions. Lord Bradley (2009: 15) reported 'strong support for the idea that offenders with mental health problems or learning disabilities can benefit from a criminal justice sanction…For some offenders, proceeding with criminal justice sanctions will, at the very least, result in an accurate record of short- and long-term risk factors to others. A further benefit is of setting behavioural boundaries requiring offenders to confront the unacceptability of their offending and to take responsibility for their actions'.

We do not really know what to make of this statement. It is certainly true that offenders may benefit, for example, from being made subject to a community order with a mental health component following conviction (Criminal Justice Act 2003, s. 177), and it is conceivable that some offenders could benefit from imprisonment, if that is used as the mechanism by which to deliver the services needed by that person to improve their mental health (Department of Health, 2009d: para. 1.3) (although the preponderance of evidence is that prison conditions have a deleterious, not beneficial, effect on mental health). But accurate assessments of risk and programmes devised to encourage a person to take responsibility for their actions can be delivered equally effectively by elements of the mental health estate, and so it is not clear why, in principle, such factors militate in favour of a criminal justice disposal rather than the implementation of some diversionary mechanism. However, as long ago as 1989 Carson (Carson, 1989) pointed out that to divert a person may be to deny that person the same rights as other people to test the evidence against him or her in a court, and so can be seen as treating mentally ill persons as second-class citizens, and may amount to the denial of the Art. 6 ECHR right to a fair trial.

All of these difficult questions are bracketed by the current attempts to bring together the various and disparate examples of diversion that have developed, sometimes systematically, sometimes piecemeal and haphazardly, into an integrated diversion system that works effectively. It may be possible to fashion such a system without answering these fundamental questions about its purpose and applicability, but at the sharp end of the system, in face to face encounters with individual mentally disordered suspects or offenders, there is no avoiding these questions; and the various and competing considerations for and against diversion, and as to what form that diversion should take in cases when some intervention is thought desirable, will, or at least should, accompany all mentally disordered suspects, arrestees, defendants, and convicted offenders, throughout their journey along or away from the 'offender pathway'.

7.3 Policing and mental disorder: Street encounters

7.3.1 Policing communities

The police deal with mentally disordered persons on a daily basis. It has been estimated that around 15 per cent of all police encounters with members of the public have a mental health aspect to them (Sainsbury Centre for Mental Health, 2009: 5). Despite this, Lord Bradley found (2009: 34) that 'that the police stage is currently the least developed in the offender pathway in terms of engagement with health and social services, as intervention generally occurs further along the pathway at the court and sentence stages'. Moreover, although Lord Bradley was able to point to examples of mental health training for police officers which included input from both mental health service providers and service users, 'this is not common' (2009: 35). He recommended that 'Local Safer Neighbourhood Teams should play a key role in identifying and supporting people in the community with mental health problems or learning disabilities who may be involved in low-level offending or anti-social behaviour by establishing local contacts and partnerships and developing referral pathways' and that 'Community support officers and police officers should link with local mental health services to develop joint training packages for mental health awareness and learning disability issues' (2009, 36). This, at least, has been achieved, and Safer Neighbourhood Teams are ubiquitous (indeed, most areas had such teams before 2009).

Following Bradley, the *Cross-government Mental Health Outcomes Strategy for People of All Ages* (see Chapter 2, 2.2.6) emphasised (HM Government, 2011: para. 4.32) that the police have a role to play, along with health and education professionals and others, in reducing the national incidence of mental ill health, through its early identification and appropriate intervention. The police should work effectively with other agencies (HM Government, 2011: para. 5.51). The *Outcomes Strategy* suggests that all police officers should receive training in mental health awareness (HM Government, 2011: para. 4.32; see also Cummins, 2012). In 2010 the National Policing Improvement Agency, working with the Department of Health, and acting on behalf of ACPO, published very detailed and thorough guidance (National Policing Improvement Agency and Department of Health, 2010) in response to Lord Bradley's review.

The guidance defines and explains what is meant in law by the term mental disorder, gives advice on how to recognise mental disorder (National Policing Improvement Agency and Department of Health, 2010: Ch. 1), and on how best to interact with persons who appear to be mentally disordered (2010: 29–35). It also requires police forces to establish protocols for joint working with social services, health, and other agencies (2010: 46) and details diversion options (2010: Ch. 3.5), including hospital A&E departments and GPs, as well as more formal diversion mechanisms. All of this should be done in adherence to the mental health principles, of non-discrimination, and good mental health for all, although these principles sit alongside more traditional policing principles such as protecting the public and investigating and tackling offending behaviour (2010: Ch. 4).

There is as yet no significant study of the degree to which the implementation of the *Outcomes Strategy* and the ACPO guidance has changed practice, but recent data, discussed further at 7.4.2, seems to suggest that progress has not yet been as rapid as was intended in 2009. For example, people taken into custody by the police using their powers under ss. 135 and 136 of the MHA 1983 are still, as in the past, commonly taken to a police station rather than a medical facility (37 per cent of all s. 136 cases in

2011–12, amounting to 8,667 instances: NHS Information Centre, 2012: 5), despite the clear advice in the guidance that police stations should only exceptionally be used as a place of safety, and the admonishment of the practice by Lord Bradley (2009: 47). Data obtained by a BBC Radio 4 programme in November 2012 (*The World This Weekend*, 18 November 2012) following a freedom of information request, which led to the disclosure that 347 of those detained in a police station under s. 136 powers were less than 18 years of age, also seems to suggest that further progress is required before the ACPO guidance (and the MHA Code of Practice: see 7.3.2) is reflective of standard practice.

The police should develop policies for dealing with persons who have a mental disorder not just in the context of their offending. There is evidence that crimes against, in particular, persons with learning disabilities, are on the increase that the police, probation, health, and social services are currently ill-equipped, in terms of training and knowledge, inter-agency co-operation and effective leadership, to be able to respond to effectively (HM Chief Inspector of the CPS, HM Chief Inspector of Probation and HM Inspector of Constabulary, 2013). The joint report of the three Inspectors recommended, as a matter of priority (2013: 5) that the police, CPS, and probation services should agree, publish, and disseminate 'a single, clear and uncomplicated definition of a disability hate crime that is communicated effectively to the public and staff', and within six months should develop strategic aims and give consideration to training needs. At the time of writing, these developments are ongoing.

7.3.2 Legal options: s. 136 of the Mental Health Act 1983

When a police officer acting in the course of his or her duty encounters a person who appears to be mentally disordered, and who he or she suspects to have committed, be committing or is about to commit a criminal offence, various options are available. He or she may arrest the individual in question, but may also decide to take no further action (whether or not the crime is recorded) or impose a formal warning. As Lord Bradley (2009: 36) pointed out, '"No further action" in this scenario should mean no further criminal justice action, but officers should signpost to or liaise with appropriate local health and social care services where a mental health or learning disability problem has been identified'. In addition, police officers are empowered by s. 136(1) of the MHA 1983, whether not it is suspected that an offence has been committed, to remove to a 'place of safety' a person found in a place to which the public have access (which therefore includes private premises such as cinemas, shopping malls, or public houses, or, as was held in *Carter* v *Commissioner of Police for the Metropolis* [1975] 1 WLR 507, the communal balcony of a block of flats) if that person 'appears to him to be suffering from mental disorder and to be in immediate need of care or control', and the officer takes the view that it is necessary 'in the interests of that person or for the protection of other persons' that he or she be so removed.

In *Seal* v *Chief Constable of Wales* [2007] UKHL 31; [2007] 1 WLR 1910; [2007] 4 All ER 177, S was arrested at his mother's address for a breach of the peace. Initially, the police intended to take S to his home address, but once outside his mother's house a decision was made by the arresting officers to detain him under s. 136. S was taken to a hospital and subsequently detained there under s. 2 (see Chapter 6, 6.3.1.1) for nine days. Some years later, on the day before the expiry of the six-year limitation period for the bringing of an action imposed by s. 2 of the Limitation Act 1980, S sought to commence an action for wrongful detention, inter alia claiming that the use of s. 136 had been unlawful. He was ultimately unsuccessful, because he failed to obtain leave from the court to bring an action, as required by s. 139 of the MHA 1983 (see Chapter 12, 12.4.1), and by the time this was realised, the limitation period had passed. The Court of Appeal, House of Lords and, ultimately, the European Court of Human Rights, held that failure to comply with the requirement to seek leave within the relevant period meant that the case has been properly struck out by the first instance judge.

The interest of the case here lies in comments made by Baroness Hale. She said at para. 60 that, if the s. 136 action had gone to trial:

> The police may well have an answer to Mr Seal's claim. But their case is not without difficulty. If he was 'removed' under section 136 of the Mental Health Act from his mother's home, he cannot have been 'found in a place to which the public have access'. If he was arrested in her home for a breach of the peace, and then 'removed' under section 136 after they had taken him outside, can it be said that they 'found' him there? (To say otherwise would deprive section 136 of much of its usefulness when an arrested person is later discovered to have a mental disorder.) These are questions which deserve to be addressed at the trial of the claim.

It is to be hoped, if and when this point is fully and substantively addressed by a court, that Baroness Hale's comments in *Seal* will be given full consideration. Our view is that the use of s. 136 in this case may well have been unlawful. Section 136 should not be used to detain a person who is not 'found in a place to which the public have access'. The power to remove a person who is on private premises, contained in s. 135(1), can only be activated following the issuance of a warrant by a magistrate on the application of an AMHP. Thus, the police cannot act alone under s. 135.

Although the criteria under s. 135 are fairly broad—allowing a warrant to be issued by a magistrate who has reasonable cause to suspect that a mentally disordered person is being ill-treated, neglected, 'kept otherwise than under proper control', or unable to care for themselves is on the premises in question—the s. 135 procedure is cumbersome from the police point of view compared to the relatively unfettered discretion given by s. 136. Although there is no reason to think that this was a factor in *Seal*, the possible problem with using the s. 136 power in such a situation is that it allows the police to circumvent the obligation to seek a warrant, and to persuade a magistrate that the criteria for its making, which are (understandably, as the privacy interest of a person in their own home is greater than that of a person in a public place) narrower than those in s. 136. In any case, however, the test under s. 136, which requires an 'immediate need' for care on control, should be construed strictly.

There was a further attempt to avoid the statutory scheme laid down by the combination of ss. 135 and 136 in *R v South London & Maudsley NHS Foundation Trust and The Commissioner of Police for the Metropolis, ex parte Sessay* [2011] EWHC 2617 (Admin). In this case, police officers had been called to an address by a neighbour, claiming that the young girl who lived there was being neglected by S, her mother. The officers were allowed onto the premises by S. They formed the view that S was mentally disordered, and so she was taken, first to a police station, and shortly after to hospital, where she was subsequently, some 13 hours later, detained under s. 2 of the MHA 1983. The question arose, under what authority the officers had acted: s. 135 was not available, as no warrant had been sought to enter the premises, and s. 136 was not available, because S had not been in a public place at the time of her arrest.

S argued that there was no other legal mechanism by which to authorise her removal to a place of safety and then hospital, and so for the 13 hours she had been held in hospital before the authority for detention under s. 2 was completed she had been detained in contravention of Arts. 5(1) and 8 of the ECHR. The officers argued that their removal of S and her subsequent detention were lawful by virtue of ss. 5 and 6 of the Mental Capacity Act (MCA) 2005 which, as discussed in more detail at Chapter 4, 4.3, provide that an act done in connection with the care of another person will be lawful provided that the actor has a reasonable belief that the person in question lacks capacity and that their actions are in that persons best interests and that any restraint involved is proportionate to the necessity to act in that way.

The High Court (Pitchford LJ and Supperstone J), following the decision of the European Court in *HL* v *United Kingdom* [2004] 40 EHRR 761 (see Chapter 5, 5.1.1.2) and that of the House of Lords in *B* v *Forsey* [1988] SLT 572, held that the MHA 1983 lays down a comprehensive scheme for the admission of patients to hospital (para. 45). Having decided that S was in fact detained in the hospital to which she was taken from the point at which she arrived there (para. 53), it followed that her detention, having not been accomplished using the powers available under (ss. 135 or 136 of) the MHA 1983, was unlawful. Sections 5 and 6 of the MCA 2005 'do not confer on police officers authority to remove persons to hospital or other places of safety for the purposes set out in sections 135 and 136 of the Mental Health Act 1983' (para. 54). Moreover, although 'It does not necessarily follow from the fact that there has been detention at common law that there has been deprivation of liberty for Article 5 purposes' (para. 55), the court found as fact that S had been deprived of her liberty in the hospital until such time as the authority under s. 2 was in place (para. 55).

Under the terms of the Police and Criminal Evidence Act 1984 (PACE) a detention under s. 136 is an arrest, even if there is no reason to think that any criminal offence has been committed. The Care Quality Commission (CQC) in the most recent report available at the time of writing (CQC, 2013: 31–32) noted that, because detention under s. 136 counts as an arrest, the fact of its use is recorded by the Criminal Records Bureau and can be disclosed under 'any other relevant information' should that person, for example, later seek employment in a situation in which a CRB check is required, thus effectively undermining the employability of any person who has been the subject of detention under s. 136 in any sector, such as health or social services, or volunteer work with charities or as a counsellor, for example, in which a CRB check is required. The CQC noted that its predecessor, the Mental Health Act Commission (MHAC) had recommended in 2008 (MHAC, 2008: para. 2.149) either that detention under s. 136

should not be entered onto a person's criminal record or should not ordinarily be disclosed, but to date this recommendation has not been acted on. This is unfortunate, unfair, and unnecessary.

The practical implication of detention under s. 136 constituting an arrest for PACE purposes is that the arresting officer has powers, under s. 32 of PACE, to search the person arrested immediately, rather than waiting until arrival at the police station, if he or she reasonably suspects that the person arrested may present a danger to himself or others (s. 32(1)) in order to ascertain whether that person is carrying anything which may be evidence of an offence or may be used to assist that person escape from custody (PACE, s. 32(2)(a), (3), (5)). Necessarily, if these powers are to be effective, but as confirmed in *R v HM Coroner for Inner North Greater London, ex parte Anderson* [2004] EWHC 2729, an officer may use restraint and reasonable force both to effect the arrest under s. 136 and to carry out any subsequent search of that person. Although there is no power to impose medical treatment under the MHA 1983 in this situation, if the person arrested lacks capacity, the power to act in his or her best interests, found in s. 4 of the MCA 2005, would allow treatment to be provided (*Munjaz v Mersey Care NHS Trust* [2003] EWCA Civ 1036, per Hale LJ at para. 46).

A 'place of safety', the immediate destination following the exercise of s. 136, is defined broadly to include a hospital, residential accommodation provided by a local social services authority under Part III of the National Assistance Act 1948, a care home, a police station, or 'any other suitable place the occupier of which is willing temporarily to receive the patient' (ss. 136(1), 135(6)). A hospital is the preferred option, but if that is not possible, it should not be automatically assumed that a police station should be used instead. The MHA Code suggests, that any other suitable place might mean, for example, the home of a friend or relative of the patient who is willing to accommodate them on a short-term basis (Department of Health, 2008: para, 11.22), although the Royal Society of Psychiatrists (2011: 6) has warned that alternatives should not be used 'as an excuse for inadequate staffing of the psychiatric 136 suite'. Lord Bradley (2009: 47) echoed the advice in the Code (Department of Health, 2008: para. 11.21) in recommending that police stations not be used as a place of safety other than in exceptional circumstances.

The Code (Department of Health, 2008: para. 11.21) suggests that detention in a police station should be considered if the detention of that person in a hospital or elsewhere 'would pose an unmanageably high risk to other patients, staff or users', but to date this recommendation has frequently not been acted on (Hampson, 2011; Swift, 2012). In 2011–12, s. 136 was used on 23,569 occasions, and in 8,667 cases (37 per cent of the total), the place of safety was a police custody suite (NHS Information Centre, 2012: 5). This is, however, a marked improvement over the situation in 2008, when it was found that police stations were used twice as often as hospitals as a place of safety (Docking, Grace, and Bucke, 2008: 10).

The reason for removing a person to a place of safety is for the 'purpose of enabling him to be examined by a registered medical practitioner and to be interviewed by an approved mental health professional and of making any necessary arrangements for his treatment or care' (s. 136(2)). A person detained in a place of safety may be removed to another place of safety by a police officer, an approved mental health professional, or a person authorised by that officer or professional (s.136(3)), but the total period may not exceed 72 hours from the time at which the person in question was first detained (s.136(2), (4)). Kemp, Balmer, and Pleasance (2012) analysed 30,921 custody records, and found that the average time spent in a police station as a place of safety by persons detained under s. 136 is 11 hours. Docking, Grace, and Bucke (2008) reported an average duration of nine and a half hours in 2008, and that the actual duration varied widely, and depended largely on the availability of alternative places of safety, which in turn depends on relations between police and mental health service providers at the local level.

The CQC has reported (2013: 54) that pressure on beds, with high ward occupancy rates common in many parts of the country (see Chapter 2, 2.2.1) means that on occasion people are held in a place of safety under what the CQC calls 'police holding powers' under s. 136, awaiting the availability of a hospital bed. The use of this phrase for the powers under s. 136 strikes us as unfortunate: this was not their intended use, and ideally no-one should be held under s. 136 once appropriate disposal has been decided upon, for longer than the time it reasonably takes to put that disposal in place.

MS v UK [2012] ECHR 804, (2012) 55 EHRR 23 provides an example of a case in which the 72 hour limit in s. 136(2), (4) was significantly exceeded. MS was initially arrested and taken to a police station after being found by police officers sitting in a car in the middle of the night continuously sounding the car's horn. At the police station, he was detained under s. 136 because his behaviour was unusual and MS was extremely agitated. It transpired that he had attacked a family member, but there was some uncertainty about whether there was sufficient evidence for MS to be charged. He was assessed as being unfit for interview or charge immediately. In consequence of that, staff from the only local psychiatric facility that was equipped to accommodate MS did not quickly make arrangements for him to be transferred, believing that he would soon be charged and, given the serious nature of the offence MS was accused of, that he would be remanded to prison, rather than being transferred to their facility, which in any case had a waiting list for places. In the event, the CPS decided that there was insufficient evidence to charge MS, but by that time the 72-hour period was largely spent. MS was not finally transferred to a hospital, where he was detained under s. 2 of the MHA 1983, until 103 hours after he was first detained.

Throughout the period of MS's detention in the police station as a place of safety, his mental condition worsened. During the first day of his confinement MS was 'clapping loudly, shouting, banging on the door, lowering his trousers and waving his testicles about, and licking the wall of his cell' and he 'repeatedly hit his head against the wall'. On the second day he removed all his clothing and was observed drinking water from the toilet bowl in his cell. By the third day, MS was 'still naked and was observed during the morning rocking to and fro on a bench, talking to himself, banging his chest and ranting' ([2012] ECHR 804, paras. 13, 16, 17). When assessed on arriving at hospital, to which he was transferred in handcuffs by police on the fourth day following his initial detention, MS was found to be suffering from a manic episode with psychotic features, thought disorders, and persecutory delusions.

The European Court found that MS's treatment violated Art. 3 of the ECHR, not because his detention exceeded the statutory limit, but because of the 'dire' conditions in which he was held and the effect of those conditions on his mental health, holding that, although the police officers involved had clearly done their best to secure a suitable placement for MS, and there was no intention to degrade him, his treatment had 'diminished excessively his fundamental human dignity' (para. 44) to such an extent as to pass the relatively high threshold set for the operation of Art. 3. The events which led to this case occurred in 2004, and the UK government assured the Court (para. 44) that the arrangements for liaison and co-operation had subsequently been reviewed and improved (see 7.4.2). Given the continuing frequent use of police stations (and cells in police stations) as a place of safety under s. 136 it is, however, perhaps difficult to be confident that *MS* is necessarily an isolated incident.

At the expiry of the 72-hour period, the detained person must either be released or detained in a hospital. If the detained person is already subject to some power under the MHA 1983, for example being a detained patient on leave of absence (see Chapter 10, 10.2) or a detained patient released subject to a Community Treatment Order (see Chapter 10, 10.4) thought should be given as to whether that person's leave of absence or Community Treatment Order should be ended and their detention in hospital re-established (DH, 2008: paras. 10.18, 10.40–44).

Most people arrested under s. 136 are not subsequently detained. In 2011–12, 2,142 persons were detained under s. 2, and 440 under s. 3 of the MHA 1983 following their arrival in hospital from a place of safety to which they had been taken by a police officer, this being the highest number in a single year in the last five years, the lowest being 1,753 in 2008–09 (National Health Service Information Centre, 2012: table 1). In practice, diversion at this early stage has historically been something of a lottery, because much will depend on the availability of local alternatives that satisfy the officer in question that a decision not to proceed can be taken (Greenberg *et al.*, 2002), and such local alternatives have frequently not been available. Rowlands *et al.*, (1996) found that the most common form of diversion used by the police is to grant bail to a suspect after having arranged for an outpatient psychiatric assessment, although there was a high rate of failure to attend for such an assessment, particularly amongst substance abusers. Psychiatric services were able, however, to maintain contact with a sizeable number of persons, although most were not formally diverted until the stage of court disposal, when probation orders and discharges were reasonably common.

Research on the detail of the use of s. 136 is thin on the ground, and much of what exists is quite dated. The preponderance of research shows that s. 136 or informal diversion is 'unlikely to be used when evidence of a notifiable crime is present' (Robertson *et al.*, 1996: 176). In such circumstances the police, most often, prefer to leave the decision about diversion to the court. There is also research evidence, although now quite dated, to suggest that, in deciding whether to proceed on the path to prosecution or resort to s. 136, factors such as the practicalities of pressing charges and the perceived seriousness of an individual's mental state are taken into account (Rogers, 1990). A decision not to proceed with criminal charges will often involve officers in negotiation with hospitals or social service departments. Too often in the past, this has been on an *ad hoc* basis, but following the Bradley Report attempts have been made to standardise systems and procedures nationally (see 7.4.2).

There have long been concerns that racial identity is a dynamic factor in the section's use, with those who define themselves as African or African-Caribbean in ethnic origin being more likely than others to be arrested (Dunn and Fahey, 1990; Turner *et al.*, 1992; Simmons & Hoar, 2001). The most common diagnoses are schizophrenia and bipolar disorder (Royal College of Psychiatrists, 2011: 18), but what is not known, as the Royal College also points out (2011: 18) is on how many other occasions it would have been possible (and desirable) to use s. 136, as decisions in this regard are made relatively invisibly and beyond easy scrutiny, by individual officers.

7.4 At the police station

Most mentally disordered persons who enter police custody as criminal suspects are not immediately diverted out of the criminal process, but are instead funnelled into a second variant of diversion, which is found in the PACE, Code of Guidance C, a revised version of which was published in May 2012 (Home Office, 2012), and came into force on 10 July 2012 (*The Police and Criminal Evidence Act 1984 (Codes of Practice) (Revision of Codes C, G and H) Order 2012*, SI 2012/1798, Art. 1(1)). This is concerned with the diversion of mentally disordered criminal suspects, along with other vulnerable detainees, such as juveniles, into an investigative regime with greater safeguards than are ordinarily implemented.

Code C was initially introduced in response to a highly publicised litany of miscarriages of justice involving persons with learning disabilities (PACE uses, and defines in s. 77(1), the term 'mental handicap') or mentally ill persons, based on confession evidence given in police interviews. The Royal Commission on Criminal Procedure was set up in 1978 following the conviction of an 18-year-old man with learning disabilities, with two others, for the murder of Maxwell Confait on the basis of confession evidence later shown not to have been true. Other notable appeals based on pre-PACE practice include those of Stefan Kiszko and Judith Ward. Although s. 77 of PACE continues to apply only to persons with mental handicap, defined by s. 77(3) as a person 'in a state of arrested or incomplete development of mind which includes significant impairment of intelligence and social functioning', PACE otherwise extended the existing system of safeguards to cover all mentally disordered persons. The introduction of Code C has not, however, ameliorated concerns about miscarriages: in 1994, the pressure group, Justice, reported 89 suspected miscarriages by reason of disputed confession evidence (Justice, 1994); for a more recent example, involving a post-PACE case, see *R v J* [2003] EWCA Crim 3309, 2003 WL 22769342.

Continued concerns about the treatment of mentally disordered persons in police custody are partly explicable in terms of uncertainties and gaps in the regime laid out by the Code, as will be discussed. But part of the explanation lies in the fact that Code C is targeted primarily at police officers and has, as its main aim, to ensure that evidence gathered in police interviews can survive challenge under ss. 76–8 of PACE. Section 76(2)(a) requires a court to exclude confession evidence obtained by oppression, and s. 76(2)(b) requires that a confession obtained in circumstances likely to render it unreliable be excluded, unless the prosecution can prove beyond reasonable doubt that it was not, in fact, so obtained. Section 78(1) gives the court discretion to exclude evidence that would adversely affect the fairness of the proceedings if admitted. Section 77(1) places a duty on a trial judge to warn a jury of the dangers of relying solely on the uncorroborated confession evidence of a mentally handicapped (but not an otherwise mentally disordered) person obtained in the absence of an independent third party.

Code C, therefore, is, in a sense, only incidentally concerned to protect the rights of mentally disordered suspects and it is not concerned to divert offenders away from prosecution on grounds of mental disorder. This is a good example of the point that, at the general level, the policy is not diversion per se. Section 77(1) contemplates that a prosecution of a mentally handicapped offender should go ahead, as long as the safeguards therein are adhered to, even if there has been a breach of the Code, and not that there should be no prosecution. In effect, the diversion question is then passed to the court.

7.4.1 The operation of the 'appropriate adult' scheme

7.4.1.1 The role of the 'appropriate adult'

Code C prescribes a particular regime to apply when a 'mentally vulnerable' suspect is detained, or voluntarily attends but is then arrested, at a police station (Home Office, 2012, para. 1.10). A person is mentally vulnerable if a juvenile, or mentally disordered (as defined by MHA 1983, s. 1), or a person 'who, because of their mental state or capacity, may not understand the significance of what is said, of questions or of their replies' (Home Office, 2012: note of guidance IG). Thus, the Code covers a wider constituency of adults than does the MHA 1983.

Code C requires that when such a person is detained or interviewed by police officers in connection with an alleged offence, their interests and rights are protected by the presence of an independent third party known as the 'appropriate adult' (AA). In general terms, the function of an AA is 'to befriend, advise and assist' the detainee (Royal Commission on Criminal Justice, 1993: para. 4.103). According to Code C, the mentally vulnerable person should be told by the custody officer that 'the duties of the appropriate adult including giving advice and assistance' (Home Office, 2012: para. 3.18).

In *R v W* [2010] EWCA Crim 2799, at para. 20, the Court of Appeal explained that 'That role includes a number of matters, ensuring that the detainee fully understands his rights, ensuring that the interview is conducted correctly and ensuring the police do not abuse their position, ensuring that the accused is able to make himself clearly understood and ensuring that the accused clearly understands what is put to him'. The presence of an AA does not, however, depend on whether or not a mentally vulnerable person is to be interviewed. An AA should be asked by the custody officer to attend at the police station in any case (Home Office, 2012: para. 3.15). Specifically, an AA should be present: when a mentally vulnerable person is informed of their rights to have a person informed of their arrest, to legal advice, and to consult Code C (Home Office, 2012: paras. 3.1 and 3.15); or cautioned (paras. 10.11A, 10.12); or charged (para. 16.1); or requested to accept being searched voluntarily (Annex A, para. 2B); or made subject to an intimate body search (Annex A, para. 5); or made subject to identification procedures such as an identity parade (Home Office, 2008: paras. 2.15, Annex B, paras. 2, 8).

A mentally vulnerable person should not be charged if it has not been possible for an AA to attend, and should instead be bailed to return for charging at a time when the AA can attend (Home Office, 2012: note of guidance 16C). An AA has a right to be consulted when it is proposed to extend any period of detention (Home Office, 2012: para. 15.2A); may seek and take legal advice (indeed, the custody officer has a duty to remind both the detained person and the AA of this right: Home Office, 2012: note of guidance 1I), even when the mentally vulnerable person does not wish themselves to take legal advice (Home Office, 2012: para. 6.5A); may inspect the custody record on arriving at the police station in question (Home Office, 2012: para. 2.4); and is entitled to a copy of the record when the mentally vulnerable person is released from police custody or afterwards (Home Office, 2012: paras. 2.4A, 2.5), along with a copy of any document such as the interview records of third parties relating to the offence in question (Home Office, 2012: para. 16.4A) or the charge sheet if the mentally vulnerable person is charged (Home Office, 2012: para. 16.3); has a right to see the finding of any risk assessment made by the police, even though that does not have to be shown to the detained person themselves (Home Office, 2012: para.3.8A); and has a right to read and sign any written record of an interview (Home Office, 2012: para. 11.12). In addition, the detained person has a right to consult privately with the AA at any time (Home Office, 2012: para. 3.18). Case law has established that it is not necessary to await the arrival of the AA before taking bodily samples (*R v Preston, ex p DPP* [2003] EWHC 729), although the mentally vulnerable person may request that an AA be present (Home Office, 2008: para. 6.9).

There will by no means always be an interview. Most persons—around 70 per cent (Robertson *et al.*, 1996: 299)—detained at a police station are not, in fact, interviewed. When interviews do occur, they tend to be of short duration, with half being conducted within 20 minutes and 75 per cent within half an hour (Robertson *et al.*, 1996; McConville and Hodgson, 1993). If there is to be an interview, para. 11.15 of Code C provides that a person who is 'mentally disordered or otherwise mentally vulnerable must not be interviewed regarding their involvement or suspected involvement in a criminal offence or offences, or asked to provide or sign a written statement under caution or record of interview, in the absence of the appropriate adult'.

This not an absolute requirement, however. An interview can proceed in the absence of an AA if an officer of superintendent rank or above (Home Office, 2012: para.

11.18) considers that delay will be likely to lead to interference with, or harm to evidence; or to interference with or physical harm to other people; or to serious loss of, or damage to, property; or might alert other suspects who have not yet been arrested; or might hinder the recovery of property obtained as a consequence of an offence (Home Office, 2012: para. 11.11). The officer making that decision must also be satisfied that the interview would not significantly harm the person's physical or mental state (Home Office, 2012: para. 11.18). A record of the grounds for the decision must be made (para. 11.20). If an interview is held in the absence of an AA on the basis of para. 11.1, it must last only as long as is necessary to avert the risk there referred to (paras. 11.1, 11.19).

Guidance on the role of the AA in interview is found at para. 11.17 of Code C. If an appropriate adult is present at an interview, they shall be informed that:

- they are not expected to act simply as an observer; and
- the purpose of their presence is to:
  - advise the person being interviewed;
  - observe whether the interview is being conducted properly and fairly; and
  - facilitate communication with the person being interviewed.

At the commencement of any interview, the AA should explain his or her role to the detainee while the tape is running. There are clear parallels between the role of AA and that of the attending solicitor, and in *R v Lewis (Martin)* [1996] Crim LR 260 (CA), it was said that the functions of each were essentially similar.

Lawyers do not necessarily have training in mental health matters, however, and legal advice at police stations can be of low quality (Hodgson, 1997: 787, 794; Bradley, 2009: 44), although there is some evidence of improvement (Bridges and Choongh, 1998; Cape, 2002; Cape and Hickman, 2002; Pierpoint, 2011). Surely, the reason that a suspect should have the services of an AA in addition, if wanted, to those of a solicitor, is that it is intended that the AA will bring special knowledge of the particular suspect or expertise in dealing with persons who are mentally ill or have learning difficulties that, by implication, a solicitor is not expected to have. Moreover, it is not obviously the responsibility of a solicitor to 'facilitate communication' with the suspect. In *R v Aspinall* [1999] 2 Cr App R 115, (1999) 49 BMLR 82, this sort of argument was accepted, and the court emphasised that the role of the AA, in safeguarding the interests of the interviewee, is broader than, and distinct from, that of an attending solicitor.

In *Delroy Brown v R* [2011] EWCA 1606, which concerned an unsuccessful appeal against conviction on the basis that B, who had learning disabilities, had not been interviewed in the presence of an AA, the Court of Appeal noted in passing (at para. 40) that 'when it came to legal advice, any appropriate adult would have had to defer to the advice which the solicitor gave him, and the role of the appropriate adult would really have been to give the appellant support and non-legal advice' which indicates a complementary relationship between attending solicitor and AA. It may be, however, that there is not always a clear distinction between 'legal' and 'other' advice, not least, for example, when it comes to advising the detained person whether or not to say anything in the first place.

The detail of the role remains unclear (Williams, 2000) in any case. For example, a solicitor might advise a 'no comment' interview: should an AA still attempt to 'facilitate communication'? As Fennell (1994: 67) has said, the 'danger is that the role of facilitating communication may be over-emphasised to the extent that the [AA] becomes an agent of the interrogating officers'. The situation in *R v Jefferson, Skerritt, Readman and Keogh* [1994] 99 Crim App R 130 (CA) came very close to realising this concern. In this case, the Court of Appeal upheld a decision not to exclude confession evidence obtained by interview of a juvenile suspect in the presence of his father as AA, on the grounds that the father had, on occasion, robustly joined in the questioning of his son, because this, it was held, had not impeded the father's ability to perform a protective role.

Given what has long been known about the suggestibility, or the urge to confess or to please others, that some vulnerable persons exhibit (Royal Commission on Criminal Justice, 1993: 57), this in itself is a questionable decision. It also points to the broader uncertainties about the function of the AA and the interrelationship of that role with that of legal representative: the AA is charged to ensure that an interview is conducted 'fairly', but what does this mean? (See Nemetz and Bean, 2001: 601.) Should an AA take an 'interventionist' or a 'passive' role? If it is the former, how should the demarcation of the role of AA from that of legal adviser be expressed (White, 2002)? What if there is no legal representative? AAs have an independent right to request the presence at the police station of a solicitor (Home Office, 2012: para. 3.19), although this fact does not seem to be well known and, as in *R v Morse* [1991] Crim LR 195, an AA may decline legal advice. How does this affect the role of the AA? What are the implications of the truncation of the 'right to silence' by ss. 34, 36 and 37 of the Criminal Justice and Public Order Act 1994 (see Fennell, 1994a: 58–60, Gray *et al.*, 2001) for AAs? A key distinction between the situation of a solicitor and that of an AA is that there is no privilege in any statements made by the detainee to the AA (Home Office, 2012: note of guidance 1E).

This can create a dilemma for an AA charged on the one hand to protect the rights of the detainee, and, on the other, having no legal right to withhold information from the police, even if the detainee assumed that any information disclosed to the AA would remain confidential. Is it possible to 'befriend' a detainee and pass on his or her confidences to the investigating officers? In summary, although it is possible to give an account in broad terms of the appropriate role of an AA, the more the detail is examined, the less clear the appropriate role becomes; the more clear it becomes that to act as an AA is potentially extremely difficult. The outgoing Labour administration, as discussed at 7.4.1.5, made a number of proposals to improve the functioning of the AA scheme, and the current administration seemed, initially at least, to intend taking a version of those proposals forward, but at the time of writing there is nothing in the proposals to date which would clarify these structural uncertainties in the role of AA.

7.4.1.2 **Who should act as AA?**

Despite the apparent complexities of the role of the AA, there is no requirement that an AA be given suitable training. For mentally disordered and mentally vulnerable persons, Code C provides that the AA must be an adult, and should be a relative or guardian or other person responsible for the care or custody of the mentally disordered or mentally vulnerable person; or a person with experience of dealing with mentally disordered or mentally vulnerable people; or, failing that, some other responsible adult (Home Office, 2012: para. 1.7(b)). A police officer or employee may not act as an AA (2012: para. 1.7(b)) nor may a solicitor or independent custody visitor present in the police station in that capacity (Home Office, 2012: note of guidance 1F), nor may a probation officer (unless specifically requested by the detainee): *R* v *O'Neill* (1990) 16 October, unreported (Crown Court). Also excluded are persons involved in the suspected offence, whether as perpetrators, victims, witnesses, or investigators (Home Office, 2012: note of guidance 1B).

An AA must be able effectively to communicate in English (*H&M* v *DPP* [1998] Crim LR 653 (CA)), and to empathise with the particular suspect (*DPP* v *Blake* [1989] WLR 432 (CA)). If an interpreter is used, that person cannot also function as AA, because an interpreter must be impartial and an AA may not be (*R* v *West London Youth Court, ex p J* [2000] 1 WLR 2368, [2000] 1 All ER 823). An AA should take an active role in events and so needs the mental capacity to fulfil the role. In *R* v *Morse* [1991] Crim LR 195, the father of a juvenile suspect acted as the AA during a police interview, but a psychologist later gave evidence that the father was of low IQ and was probably unable to appreciate the gravity of the situation and what was expected of him as an AA. The confession evidence obtained in the interview was excluded by a Crown Court under s. 76(2)(b) of PACE, holding that the prosecution had failed to discharge its burden, of proving that the unsuitability of the father to act as the AA had not raised doubts about the reliability of the evidence.

There are cases going the other way. In *R* v *W and Anor* [1994] Crim LR 130 (CA), the Court of Appeal emphasised that it is concern about the manner in which evidence was obtained, and not about the truth of the evidence, that triggered consideration of s. 76 (see also *R* v *Cox* [1991] Crim LR 276 (CA)). The court nevertheless upheld a decision to admit evidence obtained by way of police interview of a juvenile suspect in the presence of her mother acting as an AA, even though the mother herself was a person who, if detained, would require the presence of an AA, being 'mentally handicapped' as defined in s. 77 of PACE and suffering from psychosis. This was on the basis that the mother's psychotic thoughts were apparently concerned exclusively with her neighbours, and she was, in fact, capable of acting rationally in connection with the events in question. This is, perhaps, an unfortunate decision. It seems wrong, in policy terms, that a person whom the AA regime is intended to protect can herself act as an AA for a third party.

Although parents most commonly act as AAs in respect of juvenile detainees, there is, in fact, a preference amongst police officers for social workers to be used for adult detainees (Brown *et al.*, 1993), although Bean and Nemetz (n.d.) found that, in one Midlands area, victim support volunteers were preferred, and there is some evidence that contracted private or charitable providers function better than either social work- ers or parents of juvenile detainees (Pierpoint, 2001; Perks, 2010: 9). Code C advises that a trained AA is to be preferred to a relative of the suspect, unless the suspect wishes, as might be commonly the case, that a relative act as AA, which preference 'should be respected, if practicable' (Home Office, 2012: note of guidance 1D).

An untrained AA may do more harm than good, however, by giving the appearance, but not the reality, of third-party protection (White, 2002), yet to secure the services of an AA who is not a member of the detainee's family is not to guarantee that that person has suitable training. For example, some local authorities, unable through pressure of resources to spare full-time staff for this work, use social work volunteers who may well have no specialist training. Not all schemes are run by local authorities; others are in the charitable or voluntary sector, and here it is more likely that non-professionals will operate the scheme.

In a national survey published in 2006, Pritchard (2006: 5,7) found that 49 per cent of all schemes operated solely through the use of volunteer AAs, with training of between 0 and 60 hours, the average being 16.5 hours. Perks (2010) surveyed all 43 police forces in England and Wales. He found that in 14 police areas AA services were provided by a private or charitable organisation, sub-contracted for this purpose; in nine areas AA services were provided by LSSAs; and in a further three there was a mix of contracted services and LSSA provision. One respondent police force stated that there was no organised provision of AAs in its area. The remainder of police forces did not provide data (Perks, 2010: 5). Moreover, because 'very few' (Perks, 2010: 5) forces provided information on referrals to professional or voluntary service providers, or on the fre- quency of relatives and others adopting the role of AA, Perks was unable to conclude either on the extent of or demand for AA services, or on the extent to which dedicated and trained service providers fill that need.

Suitable AAs can be hard to find, as Robertson and his colleagues discovered when researching the use of AAs in London: the researchers were co-opted to act as AAs during their fieldwork 'to avoid lengthy delays for police and detainee' (1996: 309). More recently, the Bradley Review (2009: 43) found that 'in some cases the delay may be sufficient for suspects to forego this service rather than be detained for a longer period in custody' (see also Leggett *et al.*, 2007). Bean and Nemetz, (1997; Nemetz and Bean, 2001) reported the establishment of schemes run by teams of volunteers that, although patchy in terms of national coverage, could in their view provide 'a model for the future' (2001: 603), and by 2004, things had moved on to the extent that the National Appropriate Adult Network (NAAN) was established. In 2005, NAAN promulgated national standards for recruitment, support, training, and service delivery (NAAN, 2005; 2005a; 2005b). It is not clear, however, for the reasons discussed in this section, whether even having dedicated and trained AAs will resolve the more intractable problems inherent in the role. And despite the fact that the NAAN national standards secured approval from the Department of Health and the Home Office in February

2011, there is currently no central authority, no statutory or other legal basis for the NAAN, and no dedicated central funding for AA services.

7.4.1.3 Detecting the need for an 'appropriate adult'

As with diversion out of the criminal justice system altogether, the efficacy of this scheme depends on the ability of police officers to detect the presence of mental disorder. Key to this is the role of the custody officer, usually a sergeant, who has a general responsibility for the welfare of detained persons and to ensure that no person is detained longer than is necessary. It is the duty of the custody officer to activate the particular requirements of Code C in respect of any person about whom he or she 'has any suspicion, or is told in good faith...may be mentally disordered or otherwise mentally vulnerable, in the absence of clear evidence to dispel that suspicion' (Home Office, 2012: para. 1.4).

Code C is not only concerned with the role of the AA. The duty in para. 1.4 also entails that the custody officer initiate an ongoing risk assessment of the mentally vulnerable person. He or she 'should' contact an AA if he or she 'has any doubt' that a person may be mentally vulnerable or mentally disordered (Home Office, 2012: para. 3.5(c)(ii) and note of guidance 1G), and arrange for that AA to come to the police station (Home Office, 2012: para. 3.15). The custody officer should also arrange for a 'forensic medical examiner' (FME) to examine the detainee if it appears to the custody officer that the detainee is suffering from mental disorder (Home Office, 2012: paras. 3.5(c)(i), 9.5).

Two decades ago, research carried out for the Royal Commission on Criminal Justice (the Runcimann Commission) (Gudjonsson et al., 1993) found that very often custody officers missed the presence of disorder, with AAs being present at 4 per cent of all interviews of adult suspects, yet being required in around 15 per cent. Other research has reported even lower AA attendance rates. Bean and Nemetz (1994), in a retrospective analysis of 21,000 police custody records, found that an AA was arranged in only 38 cases, a rate of 0.016 per cent. The expected rate is between 10 and 100 times that. There is, as Pierpoint (2001: 139) has observed, a 'dearth' of more recent research, although Perks (2010: 12) has noted, based on the results of his research, that 'there appears to be a clear disparity between the number of adults identified as vulnerable in police custody and morbidity levels of mental disorder in prisons and offenders with either learning difficulties or disabilities. This would suggest that mental vulnerability is massively under-identified in police custody'.

Perks also found very significant regional variations in the use of AAs. For example, in one police area only four persons requiring AA services were identified by custody officers in an average month, compared to 120 in another police area of similar size (Perks, 2010: 12). The average number of referrals to trained AA service providers across England and Wales varied between police force areas from three to 450 per month (Perks, 2010: 12), although this statistic is based on returns from only 18 of the 43 police forces. Perks also found a significant difference between areas in which local authority social services provided the bulk of AA services, in which there was an average of 26 referrals per month, and areas in which services are largely provided by contracted (private or charitable) providers, where the average was 47 (Perks, 2010: 5).

Of course, it must be recognised that police custody suites can be very busy places, and individuals with no history of mental disorder can react in a bizarre manner to the fact of arrest and detention (Gudjonsson, 1992). The influence of alcohol or drugs can be confused with the presence of mental disorder (Palmer, 1996: 634–5, and see *R v IPCC, ex parte Crosby* [2009] EWHC 2515 (Admin)), and there is evidence to suggest that persons with learning difficulties or who are otherwise vulnerable, for instance by reason of illiteracy, may try to disguise their difficulties (Hodgson 1997: 787). However, there can be little doubt that the current level of false negatives is unacceptably high and risks bringing the AA system into disrepute.

Palmer's (1996) study of police practices in Yorkshire confirmed the findings of earlier research that, although major disorders may be detected, minor disorders frequently are not. Palmer's research also highlighted the frequently made point that the lack of assistance given to police officers by way of a definition of mental disorder results in officers applying their own definitions. As one interviewee said, '[t]here is no test really as far as I can work out' (cited in Palmer, 1996: 634) and so some officers interpret the need for an 'adult' to indicate that it is detainees who exhibit 'childlike' behaviour who are to be defined as mentally disordered. In *Aspinall* (see earlier), the detainee, who was in receipt of medication for schizophrenia, was adjudged by all concerned not to need the presence of an AA, because his illness was not then acute. He was also convicted in the Crown Court and it took the Court of Appeal to affirm that an AA should have been called to attend, even if the detainee appeared to be lucid.

This appears to be a fairly common situation. Bean and Nemetz (1994) found, in their sample of 21,000 cases, 50 examples of detentions in which mental disorder was recognised, but in which an AA was nevertheless not called. It is not surprising, then, that the constant refrain of commentators is to emphasise the need for more and better training of police officers, and custody officers in particular, in matters of learning disability, mental health and illness (e.g. Glover-Thomas, 2002: 182; Perks, 2010). But good training can only follow well thought-out policy. As Nemetz and Bean (2001: 600) pointed out, it may not be readily apparent that a person suffering from psychopathy or anti-social personality disorder and hence covered by the AA scheme, 'who may be highly intelligent, well aware of what is going on, and well able to understand the significance of the questions put to him', is in need of an AA. The police are less likely to be enthusiastic about a system that, from a police perspective, can be seen as offering unnecessary protection and leverage to at least some detainees. More generally, the point is that the AA scheme is poorly thought-out, confusing, or opaque to those who have to operate it at ground level.

Nemetz and Bean's research seemed to suggest that, sometimes, custody officers do detect mental vulnerability as defined in Code C but do not act on that finding, despite the mandatory language which, as we have seen, the Code employs. Evidence from the case law supports this claim. In *R v IPCC, ex parte Crosby* [2009] EWHC 2515 (Admin) C was arrested on suspicion of criminal damage following an altercation with her neighbour, and taken to a police station. Despite suffering from depression and making several suicide attempts, and although the custody officer did secure a visit from a police doctor (or FME), at no time during the 16 hours that C was in custody was an AA called, the custody officer having decided, on the advice of the FME, that to do so was not necessary. C (who was subsequently released without charge) made a complaint about her treatment, including the failure to contact an AA.

This elicited the following response (para. 34) from the Detective Inspector who investigated the complaint:

> Unlike medical personal, police officers are not trained in the assessment of mental capacity. When police consider risk assessments such as in your case, they act where the seriousness or urgency of the situation dictates. Police will then defer to the medical expertise of a medical practitioner, as in your case an FME, and will then provide support as appropriate. From the FME's assessments of your detention, no appropriate adult was advised.

However, although the Code does expressly contemplate that the custody officer should, where appropriate, consult an FME when deciding if an apparently mentally vulnerable person is fit for interview (see 7.4.1.4), there is no such requirement before deciding whether an AA is called for. According to *Crosby*, confirming long-standing research evidence (Palmer, 1996: 638) however, this is what happens; and neither the police, the Independent Police Complaints Commission (IPCC), nor the High Court (*Crosby* was a case of judicial review seeking to challenge the dismissal of C's complaint against the police by the IPCC) can see anything wrong in it. Yet, the wording of the Code is quite clear: where there is any doubt, the custody officer should assume that the person in question is mentally vulnerable and arrange for an AA to attend. That decision is to be made by the custody officer and should not be delayed pending the arrangement and performance of a medical examination.

Crosby is not an isolated example of custody officers failing to follow or rewriting the scheme of the Code. In *Delroy Brown v R* [2011] EWCA 1606, although there was no dispute that B was mentally vulnerable by reason of his learning difficulty, and although he was facing a very serious situation, having been arrested (and was ultimately convicted) for murder, the custody officer did not secure the attendance of an AA but rather consulted B, who declined the offer (para. 39). There is nothing in the Code which indicates that the detained person should be consulted. Instead, it is for the custody officer to 'determine whether the detainee … requires … an appropriate adult' (Home Office, 2012: para. 3.5.(c)(ii)), and for good reason: a mentally vulnerable person may well not be able to protect his or her own best interests because of the presence of mental vulnerability, and the refusal of the offer to have an AA provided, may be a symptom or example of that (B had learning disabilities, but was also described as 'exceedingly assertive and confrontational': para. 28).

The Court of Appeal held that the failure to call an AA did not render B's conviction unsafe: it also pointed out that 'it is worth noting that the force medical examiner did not recommend that [B] required an appropriate adult' (para. 39), which is of course a relevant factor. But the fact remains that in the scheme that Code C envisages, the AA should already have been contacted by the time of any FME examination, and it is unfortunate that the courts do not take every opportunity to insist that the Code is followed to the letter.

7.4.1.4 The role of the forensic medical examiner and the question of 'fitness for interview'

Code C of PACE 1984 requires that, before a mentally vulnerable person can be interviewed, the custody officer must be satisfied, if necessary, having consulted the officer leading the investigation and 'appropriate health care professionals', that he or she is fit for interview, and 'The custody officer shall not allow a detainee to be interviewed if the custody officer considers it would cause significant harm to the detainee's physical or mental state' (Home Office, 2012: para. 12.3). For a long time, an 'appropriate health care professional' has meant an FME, usually GPs who work on a part-time basis for the police, attending to the injuries that police officers sustain in the course of their duties, as well as carrying out physical and mental health checks on detainees when required.

There have long been concerns about the suitability of GPs for this role (Royal Commission on Criminal Justice, 1993: para. 90), and although some forces, including the Metropolitan police force, do require FMEs to undertake relevant training, and one survey commissioned by the Revolving Doors Agency in 2006 found that GPs often provided a high quality of service (Kutchinsky, 2006), in other areas of the country, FMEs will not necessarily have any specialist training in recognising mental disorder. The commissioning of health care services from independent providers has become increasingly common, with Lord Bradley (2009: 47) reporting that around half of all police forces used private contractors rather than employing FMEs directly. Kutchinksy (2006), however, also reported that FMEs supplied in this way are often on short-term contracts with the independent provider and are often unable to provide the same quality of service as traditional FMEs.

This is one issue on which the Bradley review has had a clear impact. Lord Bradley (2009: 48) suggested that the NHS which, as seen in Chapter 2 (Ch. 2.2.4), took over responsibility for the delivery of health care services in prisons in 2006, should explore with police forces whether the NHS might also take over responsibility for providing or commissioning health care services for police forces. The following year, the Home Office (Fox, 2010) announced that 10 'Early Adopters' had been identified (Devon and Cornwall, Kent, West Midlands, Staffordshire, West Yorkshire, Cheshire, Lancashire, Greater Manchester, Northumbria, Derbyshire) in which police and NHS bodies were, within two years, to develop partnership boards to secure the transfer of commissioning to the NHS, in the form of the National Health Service Commissioning Board (NHSCB) rather than CCGs (Health and Social Care Act 2012, s. 15), which from April 2013 has commissioned all health care services provided in police stations (and courts) as well as prisons (see NHSCB, 2013). The shift in commissioning arrangements, which is currently voluntary, is nonetheless well under way. By early 2013, 33 out of 39 police forces in England were involved in the process of transfer of responsibility to the NHS (NHSCB, 2013: 7).

Although the Code does not place an absolute obligation on the custody officer to consult an FME, if there is any doubt about the detained person's fitness for interview there should be consultation, and often that will involve the FME examining that person. There are three possible conclusions that an FME may reach following an examination: that the detainee is not fit for interview; that he or she is fit if there is an AA present; or that he or she is fit without the presence of an AA. What is not clear is *how* any conclusion should be arrived at. Significant harm to the mental or physical health of the mentally vulnerable person is clearly a relevant factor (although it is not clear whether this must be thought to be probable, likely, or whether some other threshold should be used), but this is not the only relevant consideration. There is at least the question of the mental capacity of the vulnerable person to consider. Before 1994, the decision was left totally to the FME concerned, but in that year the British Medical Association and Association of Police Surgeons issued guidance on the meaning of 'fitness for interview' (British Medical Association and Association of Police Surgeons, 1994). This guidance advised that fitness for interview should be assessed by reference to: an assessment of the detainee's competence to understand the situation and questions to be put to him or her; whether there was a need for an AA to be present; and, the expected length and conditions of the intended interview. It also recommended that the detainee be reassessed after interview.

This guidance was less helpful than it might have been, however, because it did not discuss yardsticks, nor how to discern into which of the three categories any given individual fits (Norfolk, 1997). The most recent version (British Medical Association, 2009) has reverted to the pre-1994 position, and whilst giving advice to FMEs on the need to obtain consent, respect confidentiality, and act in accordance with medical ethics, offers no substantive guidance on the meaning of 'fit for interview', leaving that decision to the professional judgment of the individual concerned. In the absence of more specific guidance, it seems probable that the test of capacity found in ss. 2 and 3 of the MCA 2005 should be applied; but the application of this test alone is not sufficient to answer the question of fitness for interview, because Code C clearly requires that the custody officer (who has ultimate responsibility for the decision) must also, as seen, consider the likely effects on the mental health of the detainee of the interview process, and, in turn, the likely effects of that on the credibility and acceptability in court of any evidence which the interview produces.

It is clear that on occasion, perhaps often, there is a failure to identify the presence of mental disorder, an infamous example being that of Travis Clarke (Laing, 1995: 374), who took his own life only hours after having been judged at no risk of suicide by an FME. Gudjonsson (1995) has suggested an approach that asks whether any statement made by the interviewee would be 'necessarily reliable', and if the answer to that question is 'no', then the detainee is not fit to be interviewed. Norfolk similarly advocates a functionalist approach, such that a person should be regarded as unfit if there is a 'substantial risk' that any statement made is likely to be unreliable, and where there is a 'significant risk' any interview should only proceed in the presence of an AA (Norfolk, 1997: 231).

Although there will be problems with any chosen form of words, it is surely correct to emphasise that fitness for interview is concerned with the reliability of any information gathered, as well as the abilities of the interviewee to 'cope with' the experience of being interviewed. It seems that, in practice, custody officers are on occasion more cautious than FMEs and, no doubt with at least one eye on the requirements of ss. 76–78 of PACE, will bail a suspect to return to the police station at a later date if the officer feels that he or she is not at that time fit for interview, or will contact an AA to be present during interview, even if the FME states that the suspect is fit to be interviewed (Robertson *et al.*, 1996). As *Aspinall* shows, however, this will not always be the case.

7.4.1.5 **Should 'appropriate adults' be retained?**

There are examples to be found—*O'Neill* (see 7.4.1.2) is one—of police officers actively impeding a person attempting to assume the role of AA. But it is by far more common to find that persons called on to act in that capacity, in fact, do very little other than observe the proceedings (Littlechild, 1995: 541; Palmer, 1996: 641; Hodgson, 1997: 790). This is perhaps not surprising, given the difficulties of trying to determine exactly what is expected of an AA, and the fact that the AA has trespassed into the heartland of police territory, described by Simon Holdaway as 'an "inner sanctuary" of police stations where police are in total control, and social workers (and others) are potential challengers' (Holdaway, 1983, cited in Littlechild, 1995: 542). The police station, and in particular the interview room, can be a daunting and disempowering environment for those not accustomed to it.

And yet the presence of an AA is constructed in the current scheme of things as a vital mechanism by which the interests of the detainee are protected. There are many reported cases in which evidence obtained at interview has been held inadmissible by a court for want of the presence of an AA (see, for example, *R v Maloney and Doherty* [1988] Crim LR 523; *R v J* [2003] EWCA Crim 3309, 2003 WL 22769342, *R v Blackburn* [2005] EWCA Crim 1349—being appeals referred by the Criminal Cases Review Commission—and *Palmer, Blake, O'Neill* and *Aspinall* discussed in this chapter). But the courts have also consistently held, in the context of appeals based on s. 76 of PACE (see 7.4) that the absence of an AA at the interview of a mentally vulnerable suspect, if a solicitor is present, is not sufficient per se to render evidence obtained at interview inadmissible. Instead, the court should look to the circumstances of the interview and form a view of the effect of the absence of an AA on it (*DPP v Cornish* (1997) *The Times*, 27 January (CA)).

Quite how a court is to ask this hypothetical question of itself is far from clear—does it imply a 'reasonable AA' for example, or should the court consider what the effect of the absence of a *particular* AA may have been? Nevertheless, in *R v Law-Thompson* [1997] Crim LR 674, in *Aspinall*, in *R v Gill* [2004] EWCA Crim 3245; *Julie K v R* [2010] EWCA Crim 914; *R v W* [2010] EWCA Crim 2799 and *Delroy Brown v R* [2011] EWCA 1606, the Court of Appeal reiterated the stance in *Cornish*, and upheld convictions in each case.

In *Gill*, the court explained that on an application under s. 76, the question is not whether the confession made is reliable, but rather, whether a confession made in the prevailing circumstances would be likely to be unreliable. The failure to assure the attendance of an AA, or other breach of Code C, can be caught by s. 76, whether or not the need for an AA was appreciated by the custody officer, and the real question is 'whether, having regard to the purpose for which an appropriate adult is required, the absence on this occasion of the protection which such presence would have provided is likely to have rendered any confession made at that time unreliable. In short, would the presence of an appropriate adult have made any difference?' (para. 68). In *Stanseby v DPP* [2012] EWHC 1320 (Admin) it was held that a conviction of a man, S, suffering from depression, for driving under the influence of alcohol, was safe even though neither an AA nor a solicitor attended S at the police station.

By the same token, in cases such as *Cox* and *Jefferson*, when there is an AA present, the courts have been reluctant to exclude evidence, even if the AA seemed, in fact, to do very little or even 'sided with' the investigating officers, or where there has been a breach of Code C of PACE. In *H&M v DPP* [1998] Crim LR 653 (CA), for example, the Court of Appeal decided that although there had been a breach of para. 11.16 (now para. 11.17) of Code C, because an AA had not been identified formally and the person who acted as *de facto* AA was unaware of the responsibilities attendant on the role, there had been no substantive injustice as a result and the interests of the vulnerable persons (in that case, juveniles) had, in fact, been protected and there was no reason therefore to exclude evidence obtained in interview.

This decision seemed to mark a shift away from the approach taken by the Court of Appeal in cases like *R v Kenny* [1994] Crim LR 284, where it was emphasised that the issue for the court was whether the breach of the Code made it *likely* that evidence obtained was unreliable, but the former position was restored by the 2004 decision of the Court of Appeal in *Gill*, endorsed more recently in *R v W* [2010] EWCA Crim 2799. This is welcome, but it remains the case that when there is an independent third party present, he or she will only be judged not to be an AA if the standard of assistance to the detained person is very poor indeed.

Whether the AA system should continue in its present form is open to question. Gudjonsson *et al.* (2000: 85) found that whilst 58 per cent of police officers thought that the presence of an AA offered significant protection to a detainee, only one in three lawyers shared that view. More recently Perks (2010: 9) found that whilst 50 per cent of police forces expressed satisfaction with local 'professional' (non-relative) AA services, 32 per cent did not (the remaining 18 per cent of forces did not supply data). Forces in areas in which the provision of AAs was sub-contracted to private or charitable providers expressed greater satisfaction than those in areas in which local authority social services departments are the main provider (Perks, 2010: 9), but in many areas dissatisfaction with the time taken for an AA to arrive after being contacted, particularly out of office hours, was expressed (Perks, 2010: 9). It is worth noting that a significant number of police forces provided incomplete data, even though Perks' research was conducted on behalf of the Department of Health and the Home Office.

The inevitable conclusion on reading Perks' report is that the AA scheme continues too often to be 'chaotic and unstructured' as the Joint Home Office/Cabinet Office PACE Review (Home Office/Cabinet Office, 2002) described the situation a decade or so ago. A good part of the reason for this is that the AA scheme nationally continues to run on a shoe-string and is too often a low priority for both the police and social service

departments. Perks (2010: 11) for example found that only eight police forces contrib-
uted at all to the funding of AA services in their area, and the unwillingness of local
authorities to fund out of hours services has been noted already. A second major reason
is that there is no national AA scheme as such, and there has historically been a lack
of central guidance, organisation, and leadership from central government (Palmer,
1996: 643). In consequence, although the NAAN does recommend minimum training
requirements there is no mechanism to either enforce or fund AA training, which is
patchy nationally in consequence. Bean is clear in his view that 'we have to believe that
the Appropriate Adult is the best system there is, and its failings are as much political as
jurisprudential' (2001: 109).

Such views tended to fall on deaf governmental ears for many years, but the Labour
administration, as part of its review of PACE, did, following consultation, produce proposals in 2008 (Home Office, 2008a: 5) the most important of which as far as mentally
vulnerable adults are concerned were:

- The role of the appropriate adult should be limited to those who have received
  adequate training.

- Extend the role of appropriate adult to act as a facilitator between the police and
  the parent, guardian, etc.

- Strongly promote the continued use of the trained volunteer and encourage the
  benefits to be achieved from using professional appropriate adult agencies.

- Give a statutory role to police authorities to ensure that an effective appropriate
  adult scheme is operating in their police area.

- Develop local protocols with voluntary schemes on attendance and response
  times, with social services' departments, and service level agreements with com-
  mercial companies.

- Consider the potential for appropriate adult support through the criminal justice
  system process.

- Provide access to an appropriate adult during voluntary interviews.

- Scope the potential for developing a national support structure for appropriate
  adults and custody visitors on recruitment and retention, communications, learning the lessons and monitoring and accountability.

The wind was rather taken out of the sails of reform, notwithstanding the recommendation subsequently by Lord Bradley (2009: 43) that the role of AA should be reviewed
with an aim to improve the consistency, availability, training, and expertise of those
who act as AAs, following further consultation on these proposals (Home Office, 2010).

Although there was strong support for: the greater use of trained AAs and professional services; the development of local protocols; the extension of the scheme to cover
interviews voluntarily given to the police, rather than just, as at present, to those given
by mentally vulnerable people who are formally detained at a police station; and, the

investigation of the potential for the government to organise or contribute to some sort of national support structure for AAs (Home Office, 2010: paras. 9.1, 9.8, 9.12, 9.18), this is not new knowledge (see Pritchard, 2006). Meanwhile, concern was voiced, by police forces, AA service providers, and others, about the resources implications of extending and formalising the existing AA scheme (Home Office, 2010: para. 9.3), and of extending the use of AAs into other areas of the criminal justice system (Home Office, 2010: para. 9.15).

In addition, police forces expressed wariness in respect of the proposal that they be given statutory responsibility for the provision of AA services locally, suggesting that this might be seen as undermining the independence of AAs (Home Office, 2010: para. 9.9). Several respondents to the consultation preferred statutory responsibilities being placed instead on local authority social service departments (Home Office, 2010: para. 9.11), again confirming what Pritchard (2006) had found some years earlier. The upshot of this second round of consultation was that the Health and Criminal Justice Programme Board was charged 'to consider review of appropriate adult provision by April 2010' (Home Office, 2010: 24). The coalition government which took office following the general election of 6 May 2010 stated an intention to take the review process forward (Pierpoint, 2011: 40, personal communication with the Home Office), but since then things have gone quiet.

As seen, a revised version of Code C was published in May 2012, but it contains no major changes from earlier versions, which seems to indicate that the government has no immediate plans to make any significant alteration to the AA scheme, which, it seems, will continue therefore in its current haphazard manner into the foreseeable future, and the potential protection afforded to mentally vulnerable detainees will remain diminished as a result. Moreover, as Pierpoint (2011: 146, 152 and table 3) has noted, the reform proposals did not in any case tackle the main concern of AAs themselves, which is that the role, and its relation to that of attending solicitor, be clarified.

Almost two decades ago, Fennell (1994a: 67) suggested that the way forward is to abolish the role of AA, and instead put in place a scheme that ensures that mentally disordered or vulnerable suspects are automatically attended at the police station by 'fully qualified solicitors with special training in advising mentally disordered clients'. This has the merit of avoiding the existing overlap in terms of personnel, but it does not necessarily mean that the fundamental tension between the protective and facilitative elements of the role of legal adviser and AA will be any better reconciled. Finally, it should be noted that other substantive changes are required—for instance, the limitation of s. 77, PACE to mentally handicapped persons is anomalous. The protection offered by the section should be extended to all vulnerable interviewees. And if there are to be trained specialist AAs, then it behoves the courts to recognise their worth and to exclude vigilantly any evidence obtained in the absence of the detainee's AA: at present, the courts, like the government, have done little to give shape or definition to the role of AA (Pierpoint, 2006).

7.4.2 **Liaison and diversion after Bradley**

Lord Bradley (2009: 43) noted that AAs:

> would benefit from access to mental health and learning disability specialists within the police environment, such as from liaison and diversion services. This access would provide advice on working with individuals with mental health or learning disabilities, training relating to awareness of the condition and links to organisations outside the police custody suite that may help to enhance their role.

His related proposals (2009: 53, 124), that all police custody suites should have access to liaison and diversion services, and that there should be a national body to oversee liaison and diversion programmes, to cover both police stations and courts, were amongst the most important of his recommendations. As seen (7.2), the Health and Criminal Justice Programme Board was subsequently established, with responsibility for orchestrating the national roll-out of liaison and diversion services allocated in 2012 to the Offender Health Collaborative. By mid-2011, a national network, comprising 101 local liaison and diversion services, staffed by NHS professionals such as Community Psychiatric Nurses (CPNs), was in existence (Department of Health, 2011c), with the intention to achieve national coverage by 2014. The NHS hosts the Health and Criminal Justice Liaison and Diversion Development Network (www.networks.nhs.uk), which functions as a meeting place for sharing knowledge and best practice for those involved in or interested in the development of the liaison and diversion network nationally.

Funding of £5 million in 2011–12 rising to £19.4 million in 2012–13 was made available by the Department of Health to invest in the development of liaison and diversion services (Paul Burstow, Minister of State at the Department of Health, HC Hansard, 12 January 2012, col. 22 WS), designed to allow service providers to 'test different elements of service provision' (Hansard, 12 January 2012, col. 22 WS) in order to develop, by 2013, a business case 'which will inform a ministerial decision on full roll out' (Hansard, 12 January 2012, col. 22 WS). At the time of writing, such a case has not been definitely made to the satisfaction of the government (but see Centre for Mental Health, Rethink, and the Royal College of Psychiatrists, 2011), although it seems clear that the issue is not whether the national network should be fully developed, but rather a need for clarity of the precise details of that development, in terms of funding and the division of responsibilities between the various partners involved.

At the moment, there is no standardised format in which a liaison and diversion scheme is structured. In the past, most schemes have been either police station or court based, with only a small minority covering both (Wish, 2011: 3), some schemes have been reactive, operating on referrals, others have been proactive, services have been provided or commissioned by NHS bodies or LSSAs or the National Offender Management Service (NOMS) and delivered by health, social care, and probation service professionals, sometimes acting alone, sometimes in some combination or other. These logistical questions have to be resolved as a prerequisite to efficient service delivery.

The goals of an efficiently functioning service were spelt out by Lord Bradley (2009: 53) as follows:

- identifying and assessing mental health or learning disability needs swiftly and effectively after arrest;
- ensuring that the police can make a fully informed risk assessment of the offender;
- identifying the need for the attendance of an appropriate adult;
- ensuring that those arrestees with serious mental health problems can be referred to mental health facilities before reaching court, which may have necessitated a period spent in custody on remand;
- providing information for the police and CPS on charging and prosecution;
- providing information and advice for solicitors at the police station;
- ensuring that people with mental health problems who would not necessarily progress to court stage are signposted to mental health services rather than just dropping out of the system; and
- providing information for court services about individuals' mental health or learning disabilities.

As such, Lord Bradley conceived of a liaison and diversion system which would straddle both police stations and courts, and this in itself involves major structural change from the way in which diversion systems have operated in the past (Sainsbury Centre for Mental Health, 2009a, 2009b). Information on best practice, based on research on the operation of the first wave of local schemes created following the creation of the national network, was published by the Offender Health Research Network in 2011 (Senior *et al.*, 2011). Recommendations were made for standardising the target population of schemes (which varied widely from area to area); standardising assessment tools, to be used in face to face evaluations of detainees' needs (rather than, as the researcher commonly found to be the case, basing assessment on paper records); and, standardising procedures for onwards referral and developing care pathways. The researchers found that there was much work still to be done to bring many local arrangements up to the desired levels of efficiency and efficacy.

Senior *et al.* (2011: Ch. 5; see also Dyer, 2011) found that schemes operating in 2011 were often hindered by the same problems which had been identified in the past: lack of adequate funding, with only two schemes operating outside office hours; staff having insufficient time to manage their caseload effectively; services poorly designed and managed; alternatives to custody being too often thin on the ground; and, liaison and diversion services often inadequately integrated with mainstream NHS provision.

It remains to be seen whether the additional funding subsequently made available will improve the situation in this regard. We hope that it does: the failure of police forces to identify and respond to mental disorder has already been discussed (see 7.4.1.3), and this failure will mean that, on occasion at least, and perhaps more frequently, the rules of natural justice are not followed, required treatment is not received, less than optimum outcomes are realised, and generally, the criminal justice system contributes to the sum of mental ill health, with negative consequences for the individuals concerned and for society at large, in direct contravention of the government's *Outcomes Strategy* (see HM Government, 2011; 2012; see also Chapter 2, 2.2.6).

Finally, however, we should sound a note of caution: two decades ago, very similar proposals were made following a similar review of the treatment by the criminal justice system of mentally disordered offenders chaired by Dr John Reed: 'There should be effective local agreements between the police and health, social and probation services as to flexible arrangements for the urgent assessment of people who appear to be mentally disordered' (the 'Reed Report', Department of Health and Home Office, 1992: para. 11.2). Despite the approval with which that recommendation was received at the time, the result was the patchy, hand-to-mouth system which confronted Lord Bradley. The message is clear: without concerted and sustained effort at both local and central level, good aspirations will not be converted into efficient systems.

7.4.3 The decision to prosecute

The decision to prosecute is not taken by the police. Instead, it is a matter for an officer of the Crown Prosecution Service (CPS). Sometimes, the relationship between the two agencies is linear, in the sense that the police assemble a case, which is then handed on to the CPS for a prosecution decision to be made (although often, the decision to proceed is taken quickly, following telephone contact between the responsible police officer and prosecutor); but equally, if not more commonly, the relationship between police and prosecutor cannot be broken down into clear linear stages. As the Code for Crown Prosecutors (CPS, 2013: para. 3.2) notes 'Prosecutors often advise the police and other investigators about possible lines of inquiry and evidential requirements, and assist with pre-charge procedures' and in complex cases 'may be asked to advise on the overall investigation strategy, including decisions to refine or narrow the scope of the criminal conduct and the number of suspects under investigation'. In serious cases, the CPS will decide which charges should be laid against a suspect by the police.

A CPS prosecutor has three options in every case: (i) proceed with the prosecution; (ii) discontinue the case; (iii) recommend that the police organise an out-of-court disposal (which will usually mean a formal police caution, but may also involve referral to other agencies) instead of prosecuting, the second and third of which may be combined. If charges have already been laid against a suspect, the prosecutor may also (iv) alter the charge. As the CPS is a 'public authority', officers must comply with the requirements of the Human Rights Act (HRA) 1998 (HRA 1998, s. 6(3)) and the ECHR. CPS officers are also bound by the requirements of the Equality Act 2010, to promote equality and avoid discrimination on a number of grounds, including disability (see Chapter 3, 3.4.2). More specifically, the prosecution decision involves consideration of two issues, the 'evidential' issue and the 'public interest' issue. The relationship between these two issues is linear: the prosecutor should first consider the evidence for, and then the public interest in, proceeding with a prosecution. These two factors are collectively known as the 'Full Code Test'. Prosecutors should only start or continue a prosecution if the case passes both stages of the Full Code Test (CPS, 2013: para. 3.4).

The evidential test asks whether there is 'sufficient evidence to provide a realistic prospect of conviction against each suspect on each charge' (CPS, 2013: para. 4.4). If so, 'prosecutors must go on to consider whether a prosecution is required in the public interest' (CPS, 2013: para. 4.7). In considering the second of these questions, issues such as the seriousness of the offence and the culpability of the offender should be considered, and if the suspect is known to be 'suffering from any significant mental or physical ill health…this may mean that it is less likely that a prosecution is required', although this must be balanced against the other relevant factors, such as the seriousness of the offence and the risk posed by that person to others (CPS, 2013: para. 4.12). Any negative impact on the mental health of a victim that proceeding to prosecute have should also be considered (CPS, 2013: para. 4.12).

Research conducted on behalf of the CPS in 2008 (Lee and Charles, 2008) found that prosecutors dealt appropriately with cases involving mentally disordered suspects, that in most but not all cases (38 of a sample of 45 discontinued cases) prosecutors learnt of the suspects mental disorder from the police, and that prosecutors requested further information from police about the state of the suspect's health before making a prosecution decision. Twenty of the 45 cases did not pass the evidential test, a further 25 were ended because the public interest test was not met (Lee and Charles, 2008: 18 and table 1).

What this research did not consider, however, is how many cases inappropriately proceed to trial. The National Delivery Plan set up in the wake of Lord Bradley's report required further research on this question (DH, 2009d: 37), which was produced in 2010 (Magill and Rivers, 2010). This found, in a sample of 65 cases, that in only two did the CPS file include information about the nature of the disorder, in the rest it was recorded as 'unknown', and that lines of communication between the CPS, police, and health care professionals were in need of improvement in some areas. Of the 65 cases sampled (on a fairly random basis) only seven went to trial, 46 were stopped by the prosecutor and in 38 of those cases it was the second, public interest, limb of the Full Code Test which was relevant to that decision. A further 11 cases were dealt with by way of conditional caution by the police, the most common conditions being to pay compensation to and apologise to the victim (Magill and Rivers, 2010, Ch. 5). This research seems to indicate that, certainly in cases of evident mental disorder, and minor offending, the CPS acts as an effective gate-keeper against inappropriate prosecution. For serious offences, however, the most common outcome is that the case should proceed to court (Magill and Rivers, 2010, Ch. 5).

7.5 Absence without leave

It is an offence, punishable in the Crown Court with up to two years' imprisonment (MHA 1983, s. 128(4)) to assist or induce a patient who is liable to be detained, or subject to guardianship, or a CTO, to abscond (s. 128(1)), or to harbour a patient who is absent without leave, or to prevent, hinder, or interfere with his or her recapture

(s. 128(3)), or to assist in the patient's escape from custody once retaken (ss. 128(2) and 137). A patient commits no criminal offence by being absent without leave or escaping (*R v Criminal Injuries Compensation Board, ex p Lawton* [1972] 3 All ER 582), but the police do have powers to arrest a Part III patient who has absconded, and the MHA 1983 also gives powers to retake and return all absconded patients to various actors, including the detaining hospital (or LSSA or other guardian if the patient is absent without leave from a place in which they are required to reside under the terms of a guardianship order), various mental health professionals, and the police. As such, to a person who is absent without leave and seeking to evade capture, it may well feel as though they are being treated as though absconding is a criminal offence. It is certainly accurate to describe a person absent without leave as a fugitive from the law.

7.5.1 Defining absence without leave

Section 18(6) of the MHA 1983 defines 'absent without leave' widely, if blandly, as 'absent from any hospital or other place and liable to be taken into custody and returned'. The issue is not necessarily whether a patient has left the premises at which they are required to live but whether he or she can be located by those responsible for her care. Thus, for example, a hospital inpatient given 'ground leave' (that is, permission to leave the ward and visit the grounds, or some other area, of the hospital) will be absent without leave if he or she does not return to the ward at the appointed time, even if he or she has not left the hospital site.

The restructuring of the way in which secondary mental health services are provided within the NHS subsequent to the National Health Service and Community Care Act (NHSCCA) 1990, so that hospital sites may now be split amongst two or more trusts, and one trust will operate a number over a number of different sites, has caused uncertainty about precisely when a patient who stays on the site but not within the area of that site which constitutes the premises of the detaining trust is absent without leave. The MHAC (2003: para. 9.39–9.44) advised that the detaining hospital for these purposes is marked by the boundaries of the shared site, not those of the detaining trust within that site, but the Code of Practice, when revised in 2008 (Department of Health, 2008: para. 21.5) expressed the alternative view, that the boundaries beyond which a patient without leave of absence authorised under s. 17 of the MHA 1983 will be absent without leave are marked by the perimeters of the premises occupied by the detaining trust (although any shared facilities constituted part of each trust which shares them) and this advice is now also given by the CQC (2010a: 3).

A patient will absent without leave within the terms of s. 18 of the MHA 1983 in the following circumstances:

- where, being liable to be detained, he or she:
  - absents him- or herself from the hospital at which he or she is detained without leave of absence being granted under s. 17 (s. 18(1)(a)); or

○ fails to return at the appointed time from leave authorised under s. 17 (s. 18(1)(b)); or

○ fails to return to hospital if leave of absence is revoked (Department of Health, 2008: para. 22.2); or

○ absents him- or herself from accommodation in which it is a condition of leave under s. 17 that he or she resides (s. 18(1)(c)), or

• being a community patient, fails to attend hospital after being recalled (s. 18(2A)), or absconds from the hospital after being recalled (Department of Health, 2008: para. 22.2); or

• being subject to guardianship, absents him- or herself from a place at which he or she is required by the guardian to reside (s. 18(3)); or

• if a restriction order patient conditionally discharged by the Justice Secretary, from the moment that the Justice Secretary decides by warrant recalls the patient to hospital: s. 42(4)(b). In *R v SSHD, ex p S* [2003] EWCA Civ 426, S, detained under s. 3 following his release on licence from prison, absconded from hospital in breach of s. 18(6), unaware that his licence had been revoked by the Secretary of State. It was held that he was also, even whilst detained in hospital, unlawfully at large for the purposes of his recall to prison, under (as it then was) s. 39(2) of the Criminal Justice Act 1991.

The Code of Practice further advises that patients who abscond from a place of safety, having been taken there by the police under the powers in ss. 135 or 136 or who abscond from an escort during a period of escorted leave, should also be treated as absent without leave (Department of Health, 2008: paras. 22.8, 9).

A patient will also be absent without leave if he or she absconds whilst being lawfully conveyed from one place to another. For patients remanded to hospital by a criminal court, whether for assessment or treatment, and those made subject to an interim hospital order, it is specifically provided that a patient who absconds whilst being conveyed to or from hospital following the making of the order in question will be absent without leave (MHA 1983, ss. 35(10), 36(8), 38(7)). For those otherwise detained, s. 137 of the MHA 1983 provides that a person who is being conveyed 'to any place', by those with lawful authority to convey the patient, is in legal custody for the duration of the journey, and so can be retaken if they abscond during that journey (MHA 1983, s. 138).

Although a civil patient is not generally subject to the MHA 1983 until he or she has arrived at the hospital in question and been admitted, it is the making of the application for admission, rather than the admission itself, which justifies the applicant for admission (usually, this will be an AMHP or any person authorised by the AMHP), to take and convey the subject of the application to hospital, and the person so conveyed will be in custody for these purposes (MHA 1983, ss. 6(1), 137(1),(2)) and so will be subject to being retaken if he or she escapes from that custody.

7.5.2 **Responding to an absconsion**

There is a legal obligation on the detaining hospital, if the accommodation is designated as high, medium, or low security (but not if the detaining hospital has no particular security designation) to inform the CQC if a detained patient is absent without leave (reg. 17, *Care Quality Commission (Registration) Regulations 2009*, SI 2009/3112). There is no requirement to inform the CQC if a patient subject to guardianship is absent without leave. Although the relevant CQC form (CQC, 2011b) does ask if the patient in question has a history of absconding, the CQC does not act on the information it receives, other than to keep a central database of absconsions.

The main responsibility for responding to an escape is placed on the hospital or LSSA responsible for the patient's detention, CTO, or guardianship. Hospital managers (for detained and CTO patients) and LSSAs (for patients subject to guardianship) are required to have 'a clear written policy about the action to be taken when a detained patient, or a patient on SCT, goes missing' (Department of Health, 2008: paras. 22.10, 12), which should be agreed with other relevant agencies such as the police, and all relevant staff should be familiar with its terms. The detail of the policy at local level should cover such things as (Department of Health, 2008: para. 22.11):

- the immediate action to be taken by any member of staff who becomes aware that a patient has gone missing, including a requirement that they immediately inform the professional in charge of the patient's ward (where applicable), who should in turn ensure that the patient's responsible clinician is informed;
- the circumstances in which a search of the hospital and its grounds should be made;
- the circumstances in which other local agencies with an interest, including the LSSA, should be notified;
- the circumstances in which the police should be informed, who is responsible for informing the police and the information they should be given (this should be in line with local arrangements agreed with the police);
- how and when other people, including the patient's nearest relative, should be informed (this should include guidance on informing people if there is good reason to think that they might be at risk as a result of the patient's absence);
- when and how an application should be made for a warrant under section 135(2) of the Act to allow the police to enter premises in order to remove a patient who is missing; and
- how and by whom patients are to be returned to the place where they ought to be, and who is responsible for organising any necessary transport.

In addition, all incidents of being absent without leave should be recorded in the patient's notes (Department of Health, 2008: para. 22.11).

Although the MHA 1983 and the Code are concerned only with the situation relating to detained patients, the distinction between informal and detained patients is not so sharply drawn in practice, and it has been reported that the majority of absconders—around 75 per cent—are, in fact, informal patients (Andoh, 1994: 135). In a literature review, analysing 75 research studies over a 40-year period, Stewart and Bowers (2010: 2) found that only one made a distinction between detained and informal patients. There is a sense in which the idea of an 'informal absconder' is paradoxical, but, in hospital, the same recording practices and reactive procedures apply to the unauthorised absences of both detained and informal patients, and the main issue is not legal status but whether the absconding is a matter of 'grave concern' or not (Andoh, 1994). It is perhaps to be expected that most absconders would be informal patients, who comprise the vast majority of annual admissions; and the fact that around 25 per cent of absconders are detained patients means that, as a proportion of the whole, they are markedly more likely to abscond.

Stewart and Bowers (2010: 2) found that a patient is not always immediately deemed absent without leave so as to trigger relevant procedures. Some wards would allow a period of grace, of between one and 72 hours, or until midnight on the day in question, before concluding that a patient was absent without leave. Variables were: whether the patient was absent from hospital or (if on leave of absence, a CTO or subject to guardianship) a home address in the community; the history of the particular patient; but as might be expected, procedures were triggered sooner rather than later in cases where staff had greatest concern (2010: 2).

Andoh (1994) found that the procedure on absconding depends upon the level of concern raised. When there is cause for grave concern—usually when a patient is thought to pose a suicide risk or a risk to the safety of other persons, or to be particularly frail, confused, or vulnerable—nursing staff will first search the hospital and grounds, and then, if failing to locate the patient, contact the duty doctor; a decision is then taken about whether to book the patient as absent and call the police. Nursing staff will also telephone the home address of the patient and, if the patient is there, steps will normally be taken either to compel (if detained) or attempt to persuade (if informal) the patient to return. The patient's home address will also be telephoned in cases causing less-than-grave concern.

7.5.3 Powers to retake a patient absent without leave

There are various general powers which are available for those seeking to retake a patient who is absent without leave. It is possible to use the ss. 4 or 5 of the MHA 1983 powers to compel the return of an informal patient, although the only powers of entry available in the Act are those in s. 135(2) (see 7.3.2), requiring the involvement of the police and the issuance of a warrant. The MHA 1983 provides, in s. 18(1), that a patient who is liable to be detained who is absent without leave and, in s. 18(2A), a community patient who has not returned to hospital following recall, may be taken into custody by any AMHP, any member of staff of the hospital in question, a police officer, and any person authorised in writing by the hospital managers or, for CTO patients only, the patient's RC. If a detained patient is on leave, but with a requirement to reside in another hospital, the staff of that hospital and persons authorised by the managers of that hospital may also retake the patient (s. 18(2)). For persons subject to guardianship, those so empowered are any member of the relevant LSSA staff, or police officer, or a person authorised in writing by the guardian or LASS (s. 18(3)). A retaken patient is entitled to a tribunal review of that decision within the period of renewal (ss. 66(1)(f), (fa), (faa), (2)(f), (fa): see Chapter 11, 11.4.2).

The Code of Practice also encourages those seeking to ascertain the whereabouts of a patient absent without leave to enlist the help of 'people—such as those the patient normally lives with or is likely to contact—who may be able to help with finding the patient' (Department of Health, 2008: para. 22.17), and advises that 'Although every case must be considered on its merits, patient confidentiality will not usually be a barrier to providing basic information about a patient's absence' to such persons (Department of Health, 2008: para. 22.17). The patient's nearest relative should 'normally' be informed once the patient has been missing for 'more than a few hours' (Department of Health, 2008: para. 22.18).

Police should not be involved in taking a patient absent without leave into custody unless necessary (Department of Health, 2008: para. 22.13), although the Code of Practice strongly recommends that the police are informed immediately if a patient is particularly vulnerable, dangerous, or subject to restrictions, and if for some other reason, such as the patient's history, there is particular cause for concern (Department of Health, 2008: para. 22.14). Ideally, where the police are involved it should be in a supportive role, with a mental health professional taking the lead (Department of Health, 2008: para. 22.13). If police are informed, they should be given all relevant information, such as the time limit for taking the patient into custody (Department of Health, 2008: para. 22.15), and should be informed if the patient is subsequently located or returns voluntarily to the hospital (Department of Health, 2008: para. 22.16).

It is not clear to what extent the advice against the routine involvement of the police in the Code is followed. Andoh (1994), looking at practices in three hospitals, found that all three always contacted the police when a detained patient had absconded, although if the case was not one of grave concern this would not be done until the patient had broken the hospital's unofficial curfew (typically 11p.m. or midnight). The police were contacted regarding absconding by informal patients less often, but still perhaps surprisingly frequently, on around 15 per cent of such occasions, although at one hospital, at which there was a relatively small number of absconders, the level was higher, at 55 per cent (Andoh, 1994: 135).

Police procedure on receipt of a report of absconding shows a high degree of consistency across regions. Cases are categorised as either urgent, requiring full inquiry, or non-urgent, requiring limited inquiry. Cases in the first category involve detained and especially restricted patients, and vulnerable patients. In such cases (1994: 132), 'the police would leave no stone unturned in their efforts to find the missing person'. For example, forces other than the one initially contacted, are brought in if necessary. Otherwise, the practice is to go to the home address of the patient, and merely report back to the hospital whether or not the patient was there. The CQC (CQC, 2011: 59) has reported that the police were involved in 37 per cent of returns to hospital in 2010–11.

In *DCD* v *South Tyneside Health Care NHS Trust* [2003] EWCA Civ 878, D, detained in hospital under s. 3 of the MHA 1983, having been diagnosed at various points in the past with both paranoid schizophrenia and bi-polar affective disorder, with behaviour which was frequently and unpredictably agitated, aggressive or, on occasion, suicidal, absconded to her home address. She had absconded on many previous occasions in the course of several periods of compulsory hospitalisation, sometimes returning to hospital of her own accord, sometimes being returned by the police, at the instance of either the hospital or D's family. She had also been given overnight leave to her home address on a number of occasions. On the occasion in question, having requested but not been granted overnight leave, D absconded. Once at home, she swallowed a large number of anti-asthma tablets belonging to a member of her family, and suffered irreversible brain damage as a consequence.

She sued the Trust, arguing that its response to her absconsion had been negligent. Before she absconded, D had been subject to observation at hourly intervals, and claimed that she should have been subject to more frequent observation (every 15 minutes), in which case her absence would have been noted sooner than it was, and, if the hospital had immediately contacted the police (which it did not), the police would have arrived at her address before she self-administered the pills that had caused her brain damage. She also argued, more generally, that the Trust's absconsion policy, which echoed the wording used in the Code of Practice in this regard, providing that although requests to the police to assist in returning an absconder should be kept to a minimum, 'There may be cases where police assistance is required in the retaking of patients who are considered to be at risk of harming themselves or others' ([2003] EWCA Civ 878, para. 7), had not been followed, as the police had not been contacted in this instance, despite the risk that D posed to herself by absconding when her mental state was poor.

At trial, expert evidence given on behalf of D was to the effect that, given her poor and agitated state of mental health, observation at least every 15 minutes was appropriate, whereas evidence given on behalf of the Trust was to the effect that hourly observation was reasonable. Applying the approach to conflicting evidence discussed by the House of Lords in *Bolitho* v *City and Hackney Health Authority* [1997] AC 232, the trial judge had preferred the evidence given for the defendant, and the Court of Appeal reached the same conclusion.

Neither the trial judge nor the Court of Appeal was persuaded that the Trust's absconsion policy, or its implementation, exhibited negligence. The policy was not that the police would be contacted immediately when a person with D's profile absconded. Instead, as Lord Phillips, MR, noted at EWCA Civ [2003] 878, paras. 71, 72:

> The policy gave the hospital considerable latitude as to how to react to an absconsion. It is plain that in Miss D's case the hospital had adopted a policy, perhaps pragmatically, of communicating with her family and giving her a chance to return to the hospital of her own accord. It seems to me that this was a sensible policy. It avoided calling for police assistance when this was not necessary, and it avoided the risk that the exercise of section 18 powers would antagonise Miss D and impair her treatment.... The approach is one of which the Trust's experts approved and, in my judgment, there was good reason to approve it.

Hence, it is legitimate for a hospital to balance a patient's therapeutic needs (in this case to be in hospital and to take her medication) and her safety, against her right to liberty, and to factor in that a confrontational relationship, between the hospital staff and the patient, is counter-therapeutic, even if this means that risks are thereby taken that could have been avoided by a more robust and urgent response to the absconsion, provided that the decisions taken are reasonable by reference to the *Bolam/Bolitho* standard for establishing liability for negligence. In *Lambert* v *West Sussex Health Authority* (1990) *The Times*, which was not cited to the court in *DCD*, a patient who inflicted lower-body paralysis on himself by jumping from a motorway bridge after escaping from a secure ward was awarded damages of £757,114 by the High Court for the detaining hospital's negligent implementation of security measures designed to prevent patients absconding (Andoh, 2004).

The human rights of a person absent without leave were at issue in *Savage* v *South Essex Partnership NHS Foundation Trust* [2008] UKHL 74. S, diagnosed with paranoid schizophrenia and with a history of attempting to abscond, succeeded in doing so from a ward on which she was detained under s. 3 of the MHA 1983. A short time later she was killed by a train. It was evident that her death was the result of an act of suicide, and at the inquest into it, the jury concluded that 'the precautions in place [at the detaining hospital]... to prevent Mrs Savage from absconding were inadequate' (cited by Lord Scott at para. 2). S's daughter sued the Trust, claiming that S's rights under Art. 2 of the ECHR had been violated. The case went to the House of Lords on the preliminary point, of the scope of the detaining hospital's positive obligations under Art. 2 as it related to its policy and practice on absconsion.

The specific question was whether the positive duty imposed by Art. 2, if and when in play, embraces both a 'primary duty, to have proper systems in place for protecting life' (Baroness Hale at para. 76) (which was in principle accepted by both sides) and an 'operational' element 'to protect this particular life' (Baroness Hale at para. 76) (which was contested). On the extent of the primary duty, Lord Rodger summarised the position at para. 69:

> The duty to protect the lives of patients requires health authorities to ensure that the hospitals for which they are responsible employ competent staff and that they are trained to a high professional standard. In addition, the authorities must ensure that the hospitals adopt systems of work which will protect the lives of patients. Failure to perform these general obligations may result in a violation of article 2. If, for example, a health authority fails to ensure that a hospital puts in place a proper system for supervising mentally ill patients and, as a result, a patient is able to commit suicide, the health authority will have violated the patient's right to life under article 2.

Provided that a hospital meets these requirements, there can be no action under Art. 2 based on breach of the primary duty, although it may be possible for a patient to bring a private law action in negligence against a particular individual, and vicariously against the employing Trust, if as a result of that employee's negligence the patient dies (paras. 70, 71). This can be understood as the structural uncoupling of the primary duty imposed by Art. 2 from a private law action in negligence (the High Court in this case having held that Art. 2 would be violated if the actions of the detaining hospital amounted in private law to gross negligence manslaughter).

On the second, and main, issue of dispute Lord Rodger held (para. 72) that 'article 2 imposes a further "operational" obligation on health authorities and their hospital staff'. He proceeded to explain that:

> This obligation is distinct from, and additional to, the authorities' more general obligations. The operational obligation arises only if members of staff know or ought to know that a particular patient presents a 'real and immediate' risk of suicide. In these circumstances article 2 requires them to do all that can reasonably be expected to prevent the patient from committing suicide. If they fail to do this, not only will they and the health authorities be liable in negligence, but there will also be a violation of the operational obligation under article 2 to protect the patient's life.

Baroness Hale reached much the same conclusion (paras. 97–102).

In taking this approach, the House of Lords preferred to apply the line of cases including *Osman* v *UK* (2000) 29 EHRR 245 and *Keenan* v *UK* (2001) 33 EHRR 38, and rejected the application of the decision in *Powell* v *UK* (2000) 30 EHRR CD 362. *Powell* was a case of a patient needing medical treatment, in which circumstances the court would not place a positive obligation on those responsible for treatment to act against their clinical judgement. *Osman* and *Keenan*, by contrast, are cases about the state's duty to protect its citizens in circumstances of identifiable risk, particularly when the person in question is detained by the state, and the House of Lords was clear, taking into account the vulnerability of those detained (citing *Herczegfalvy* v *Austria* (1993) 15 EHRR 437 (see Chapter 9, 9.5) in this regard: see Lord Rodger at para. 54 and Baroness Hale at para. 87), that it was the latter authorities which best reflected the situation in the present case.

Subsequently, when the substantive case went to trial (*Savage* v *South Essex Partnership NHS Foundation Trust* [2010] EWHC 865 (QB)), it was found that S did present a real and immediate risk, both of absconding and of coming to significant harm if she did abscond (para. 88), and that the hospital had not taken sufficient measures to address the risk (para. 89), and the court awarded, by way of 'symbolic acknowledgement' (para. 97) of the wrong done, £10,000 in damages to S's daughter (who had brought the action).

Savage was followed and extended in *Rabone* v *Pennine NHS Trust* [2012] UKSC 2, in which it was decided that the principle which had been applied by the House of Lords to absconding detained patients applied equally to informal patients (in that case) negligently given leave of absence or who, by implication, have absconded. In *Rabone*, R, a patient who had been admitted to hospital because she was judged to be a suicide risk, but who had consented to hospitalisation and treatment and so had not been detained under the MHA 1983, was given leave of absence in circumstances in which, it was agreed by both sides, were such that no reasonable psychiatrist could have concluded were appropriate (para. 107), subsequent to which she committed suicide by hanging.

The Trust argued that the operational duty imposed by Art. 2 was inapplicable because R was not a detained patient and thus no obligation had been accepted by the

hospital. The Supreme Court rejected this argument and applied *Savage*, again rejecting the applicability of *Powell* (Baroness Hale at paras. 106, 105; see also Lord Dyson at
paras. 28–30):

> The analogy with a patient detained under the Mental Health Act is much closer than the
> analogy with a patient admitted for treatment of a physical illness or injury... [R] was admit-
> ted to hospital precisely because of the risk that she would take her own life. The purpose of
> the admission was both to prevent that happening and to bring about an improvement in
> her mental health such that she no longer posed a risk to herself. Although she was an infor-
> mal patient, the hospital could at any time have prevented her leaving [using] ... Section 5(4)
> of the Mental Health Act 1983 ... The experts were agreed that it would have been appropri-
> ate to detain her under the 1983 Act if she had intended to leave the hospital without medi-
> cal approval. The judge in fact found that she would not have done so.

These are welcome decisions, more so if the main consequence is that fewer patients
abscond, and that fewer absconding patients come to harm, than would otherwise have
been the case.

The advice in the Code in respect of the retaking of patients does not distinguish
between Part II and Part III patients, but the MHA 1983 does, and gives the police powers, over and above those available to others, in respect of the latter. For those who have
absconded having been detained under ss. 35, 36 or 38 (remanded to hospital or made
subject to an interim hospital order), MHA 1983, ss. 35(10), 36(8), and 38(7) provide
that a police officer may arrest without warrant. For patients subject to a hospital order,
with or without restrictions, the MHA 1983 contains no similar provision, but s. 72
of the Criminal Justice Act 1967 provides that a hospital order patient who is absent
without leave or who has escaped from custody (MHA 1983, s. 137; Criminal Justice
Act 1967, s. 72(3)), may be arrested, but only if a warrant of arrest has been obtained
from a magistrate.

Although only one magistrate is required by s. 72 of the Criminal Justice Act 1967,
and although a warrant can be quickly organised (albeit more quickly in some areas
of the country than others), a warrant cannot be issued over the telephone, because
the application for a warrant must be 'in writing' (Criminal Justice Act 1967, s. 72(1);
whether this would allow an application by email or text is debatable). It seems peculiar
that greater procedural requirements are placed on those seeking to retake a hospital
order patient who is absent without leave than are placed on the retaking of patients
remanded to hospital or made subject to an interim hospital order.

If the absconder from detention under Part II is found in a public place, there will be
no need to obtain a warrant, as s. 136 of the MHA 1983 (see 7.3.2) is available to police
officers (*R* v *South London & Maudsley NHS Foundation Trust and The Commissioner of
Police for the Metropolis, ex parte Sessay* [2011] EWHC 2617 (Admin)). Another option
for a police officer is to use s. 17(1)(d) of PACE, which gives powers to enter and search
premises for a person 'unlawfully at large and whom he is pursuing'. The House of Lords
in *D'Souza* v *DPP* [1992] 4 All ER 545 held that a person absent without leave under s. 18
of the MHA 1983 is 'unlawfully at large'. As to the reference to pursuit, Lord Lowry held
that this limited the availability of this power to situations where there was a chase, and

it did not provide a general licence to enter premises. If the requirements of s. 17(1)(d) of PACE can be made out, reasonable force may be used in their exercise (PACE 1984, s. 117).

A patient, unless subject to restrictions, will not remain absent without leave indefinitely. The law places time limits on the retaking of the patient. Until the passage of the Mental Health (Patients in the Community) Act 1995, a patient, other than one subject to restrictions, who was not taken into custody within 28 days of the date of absconding, ceased automatically to be liable to be detained. Apparently, around 10 per cent of patients detained under a hospital order achieved discharge in this manner (Walker and McCabe, 1973, in Hoggett, 1996: 166). Section 2(1) of the Mental Health (Patients in the Community) Act 1995 substituted a new s. 18(4) of the MHA 1983, which now provides that persons detained for treatment, including patients on a hospital order s. 37 order (MHA 1983, Sch. 1, Part1, paras. 1, 2, 4), who abscond, may be taken into custody at any time before six months from the first day that he or she was absent without leave, or before the expiry of the period of detention, guardianship order, or CTO, whichever is the later (s. 18(4)(a), (b)). Thus, the maximum period for which a patient may be absent without leave is 12 months, if the authority to detain or guardianship order (s. 20(2)(b)) or CTO (s. 20A(3)(b)) has been renewed (for at least the second time) shortly before the date of the absconding.

A patient who absconds near the end of a period of detention will automatically cause the extension of the period for which he or she is liable to be detained by up to six months. The period of detention, guardianship, or CTO (but not the six-month period: s. 18(4)) may be extended by one week if the patient is absent without leave on the day, or within a week, of expiry, and is recaptured or returns voluntarily before the expiry date (s. 21(1), (2)). This is to allow time for arrangements to be made for the renewal of the patient's detention, guardianship order, or CTO. In addition, s. 21(4)–(5) provides that if a community patient is absent without leave having returned to hospital following recall when the 72-hour period mentioned in s. 17F (discussed further in Chapter 10, 10.4.2) would expire (if, in other words, the patient has absconded following recall), the 72-hour period is abandoned, and will run again in its entirety, if and when the patient is taken into custody and returned to hospital or returns voluntarily. This is to give the RC time to decide how to respond to the reason that prompted the decision to recall (and subsequent events).

The reason why, until the passage of the Mental Health (Patients in the Community) Act 1995, a patient who remained at large for 28 days ceased to be liable to be detained was that it was assumed that a patient who coped for that period of time outside of hospital did not need to be detained. Although that period has now been extended, the 28-day period retains its significance. Section 21A of the MHA 1983 (which, with s. 21B, was also introduced by the Mental Health (Patients in the Community) Act 1995) provides that, if a patient is returned or returns voluntarily to the hospital 'or other place where he ought to be' within 28 days of absconding, the renewal of an order for detention or guardianship under s. 20 or for a CTO under s. 20A may be made as if the patient had not absconded, and, if the period of detention, guardianship, or community treatment has been extended by the operation of s. 21, any examination or report necessary to deciding whether to renew the period further under ss. 20(3) (6) (for detained patients and those subject to guardianship) or s. 20A(4) (for community patients) may take place within the one week extension period (ss. 21A(2), (4)), and any new order made will be deemed to commence on the last day of that week (ss. 21A(3), (5)).

Section 21B lays out a procedure similar to that required for initial admission to be followed in the case of a patient being returned or returning to hospital or other place where he or she ought to be more than 28 days after the date of absconding, and thus maintains something of the philosophy behind the pre-1995, 28-day limit, on liability to recapture. In such circumstances, the 'appropriate practitioner' (who will presumably be the patient's RC) must, within one week of the patient's return, conduct an examination of the patient and, if the patient is liable to be detained or is a community patient, having first consulted with one or more persons professionally concerned with the patient's medical treatment and with an AMHP (s. 21B(3)), must then provide a report to the 'appropriate body' if 'it appears' to the approved practitioner that the criteria for the renewal of the order in question are met.

The appropriate body (which will be the managers of the relevant hospital if the patient was detained in hospital or subject to a CTO before being absent without leave, or the relevant LSSA if subject to guardianship: s. 21B(10)) must then convey that information, or cause it to be conveyed, to the patient (s. 21B(2)). If this is not done within one week of the patient's return, the detention, guardianship, or community treatment order will automatically come to an end, even though the order still had time to run (s. 21B(4)). The obligation to examine and report will not apply, in the case of a community patient, if the CTO is revoked during the one-week period (s. 21B(4A)).

The making of the required report, stating that the criteria in question are met, within the one-week period will extend the period of detention, guardianship, or community treatment in accordance with s. 20(2) (for detention and guardianship) or s. 20A(3) (for community treatment) (ss. 21B(5) and 21B(6A) respectively), that is, for six months if this is a first renewal or one year if it is a second or subsequent renewal. If renewed under these provisions, the new order takes effect from the day on which, apart from any extension of the period by virtue of the operation of s. 21, the earlier order would have expired, and if the earlier order would have expired on or before the date on which the report in question is furnished, the report renews the order retrospectively from that expiry date (s. 21B(6), for detention and guardianship; s. 21B(6B), for community treatment). If there is less than two months to run before an order for detention, guardianship, or community treatment expires when a report is made in accordance with the requirements of s. 21B(2), that report may, if it so provides, 'have effect also as a report duly furnished' for the purposes of renewal of the order (ss. 21B(7), (7A)).

None of the above applies to restricted patients, who remain liable to detention regardless of time absent without leave (MHA 1983, Sch. 1, Part II, paras. 2 and 4), nor to patients held under the short-term Part II powers of detention in ss. 2, 4, 5(2) and 5(4), who may not be retaken once the period of detention has expired (s. 18(5)), nor to patients remanded to hospital for medical reports or for treatment, or on conviction made the subject of an interim hospital order, who may be arrested without warrant by a constable, and returned to the court that made the order, which may (although need not) terminate the order and deal with the offender in some other way (ss. 35(10), 36(8), and 38(7)). There is no time limit on the liability to arrest of absconders in this category.

7.5.4 **Empirical data on absconsion**

Most patients are returned by the police, or by nursing staff, relatives, or friends. Very few absconders remain at large for any length of time. In the research studies surveyed by Stewart and Bowers (2010: 18) most patients were absent without leave for less than 24 hours (89 per cent in Short, 1995: 281; 69 per cent in Huws and Shubsachs, 1993: 51). A sizeable minority of patients return voluntarily (Bowers, 2003). However, a small number were absent for much longer. Huws and Shubsachs (1993) found that 10 per cent of absconders from a high security hospital were still at large one month later. Some patients manage to avoid being taken: 10 per cent in one study in Ireland (Falkowski et al., 1990).

As this short time absent without leave would suggest, most absconders are not hard to find. Homesickness or worry about domestic issues is a common reason for absconding (Stewart and Bowers, 2010: 17)—the patient's view that they do not need to be in hospital is another (Short, 1995: 281)—and many patients are to be found at home (Falkowski et al., 1990; Bowers, 2003). Of course, not all patients go home, and some may not have a home, or any other particular place, to go to (Stewart and Bowers, 2010: 17). Somewhere around one third of patients, possibly more (Short, 1995), will not go somewhere that might easily be predicted by those responsible for retaking them. The hours after noon and before 11 pm constitute the peak time for patients to go absent without leave. For some reason, patients are much less likely to abscond in the morning or (more understandably) late at night (Stewart and Bowers, 2010: 26), and the weekend, Saturday in particular (Stewart and Bowers, 2010: 27), is the peak time of the week for absconding.

The spectre of the 'escaped madman' is a staple of much modern fiction and attracts media attention. Yet the fact is that absconding from the 'deep end' of the hospital system is rare. Huws and Shubsachs (1993) found that, in the period 1976–88, during which a total of 4,909 persons were detained in a special hospital, there were only 36 escapes. Only seven of these were from hospital, the majority occurring on outings from the hospital. Even so, Huws and Shubsachs (1993: 51, 52) compute that there is only a one in 4,000 chance that a patient will abscond when on an outing from hospital. A further 30 high security hospital patients absconded from MSUs, local hospitals, or hostels whilst on leave of absence, at a rate of 1 in 2,800. Young, male, unemployed patients, admitted under compulsory powers with admission requiring police involvement, with a prior history of hospitalisation, and a diagnosis of schizophrenia or personality disorder are most likely to abscond, and more likely to do on two or more occasions (Tomison, 1989; Farid, 1991; Huws and Shubsachs, 1993; Short, 1995), and there is evidence, albeit inconclusive (see Stewart and Bowers, 2010: 21–22) to suggest that Afro-Caribbean patients are more likely to abscond than others (Falkowski *et al.*, 1990).

Many of those who abscond do so in the week or weeks immediately after hospitalisation (Stewart and Bowers, 2010: 24–25). In 2011 the CQC (CQC, 2011b: 59) reported that in the year 2010–11 4,321 incidences of absence without leave were reported to it, of which two thirds (2,908) were from hospitals which had no specified security level. The majority of cases 'just reflect patients returning late from authorised day leave, or staying longer with families during home leave than had been originally authorised by their responsible clinician' (CQC, 2011b: 59). Thus, many incidents of absence will be trivial in nature. The issue is to detect which give cause for concern and which do not.

Even if the absconder is from the 'deep end' of the hospital system, there is good reason to argue that there will very rarely be cause for 'grave concern' for public safety. Offending by patients absent without leave is minimal. Surveys have found an offending rate of between 2 per cent (Short, 1995) and 11 per cent (Kernodle, 1966), although the higher figure is almost 50 years old and a rate of no greater than 7 per cent (Walsh *et al.*, 1998) has been reported since the 1970s. Huws and Shubsachs found that, between 1976 and 1988, absconders from special hospitals committed a handful of petty theft offences. Two very serious offences were committed: a rape, and the shooting of a police officer resulting in a manslaughter conviction. Two serious offences is, of course, two too many, but it comes nowhere near the public perception of the risk. These offences were committed by patients who had absconded from hospital; patients who absconded whilst on leave committed no serious offences (Huws and Shubsachs, 1993: 55). On the other hand, in a study of one independent hospital holding detained patients (Dickens and Campbell, 2001), from which there were 148 absconsions over a three-year period involving a control group of 1,378 patients (potential absconders), of the six crimes committed whilst absent, four were serious crimes involving violence.

Violence is almost never reported to have been a feature of an escape. In the overwhelming majority of instances, absconders pose no significant danger to the public (Brook *et al.*, 1999). There have long been concerns, on the other hand, about the correlation between absconding and risk of suicide or self-harm (Milner, 1966; Falkowski *et al.*, 1990; Morgan and Priest, 1991; Bannerjee *et al.*, 1995, MHAC, 2001; 2005: para. 4.44 and Figure 51), so that best practice is to respond immediately on discovering an escape. It is extremely rare that a detained patient absent without leave is not apprehended, although on apprehension, a small minority are discharged rather than returned to hospital. Of course, prevention is better than cure, and there is a growing literature (Bowers *et al.*, 2003; Stewart and Bowers, 2010) concerned with strategies to prevent absconding in the first place.

7.6 Concluding comments

This chapter has detailed a system in a state of flux with, as has been seen, lots of activity around the project of developing a functioning nationwide system of liaison and diversion, available in all the 600 or so police custody suites across the country, as well as in all criminal courts. It is clear that, following Lord Bradley's report, this issue which, as we have seen, is long standing, has been revisited with a renewed vigour for change and improvement. But as we have also noted, those with long memories may be experiencing a sense of déjà vu: we have been here before and, last time round, good intentions too often foundered on the twin obstacles of ineffective commitment to inter-agency working and shortage of resources, and although there is more of a central steer to current developments from the Health and Criminal Justice Programme Board and the Offender Health Collaborative, funding limitations will remain as an impediment to improvement.

This may explain the retreat from plans to put the role of the appropriate adult on a more secure footing. This is unfortunate: however well-funded and efficient a local diversion scheme may be, the need of mentally vulnerable suspects for high quality assistance in police interviews will remain, and, it seems, will remain unmet too often in future. There are interests and factors here which are hard to quantify and we wonder how they will be factored into the 'business' case for better diversion by the government. We know, for example, that although deaths in police custody have fallen, from 36 in 2004–05 and 28 in 2005–06 to 15 in 2011–12 (Independent Police Complaints Commission, 2012), deaths following other police contact and suicides following release from custody do not show the same decline: there were 47 of the former and 39 of the latter in 2011–12 (Independent Police Complaints Commission, 2012: 9 and table 5).

Of the 15 who died in police custody, two had been detained under s. 136 of the MHA 1983, but seven, that is, virtually half, had been identified as having a mental health problem. Eight of the 15 had been restrained by police prior to their death, including both of those detained under s. 136 (Independent Police Complaints Commission, 2012: 6). The cause of death of five of those 15 individuals was listed as 'excited delirium', which as the Independent Police Complaints Commission (2012: 6, fn. 9) notes, is a controversial diagnosis (not found in either the DSM or the ICD), and indicates the cause of death as cardiac or respiratory failure following intense agitation and stress, often accompanied by hallucinations or other overt signs of mental distress. There are particular concerns about the deaths of black males following the use of restraint by the police (Black Mental Health UK, 2013).

Of those 39 who committed suicide following release from custody (and within 48 hours), 18 were reported to have mental health issues (Independent Police Complaints Commission, 2012: 9). A considerable number of these individuals had been charged with a serious criminal offence, including nine charged with sexual offences against children, and so the reasons for resorting to suicide, and the impact of the actions of the police in this regard, must be treated with circumspection.

The numbers involved here are relatively small, given the 1.5 million or so people arrested each year, but the point is that it is not easy to include these deaths in the quantifiable value-for-money terms that seem to underpin the government's current commitment to improving the quality of services for mentally disordered persons in police stations; but at least some of them would have been avoided if diversion routinely worked effectively. There were also several deaths, including one of a member of the public apparently previously unknown to the attacker, and others involving family members of the released person, at the hands of a person with mental health problems shortly after release from police custody (Independent Police Complaints Commission, 2012: 7).

ACPO (2012) has recently published very detailed guidance on the safe handling of persons in police custody. This applies to all detained persons but makes specific provision for persons suspected of being mentally disordered. The ACPO guidance goes beyond requirements to have effective diversion mechanisms in place, for adequate training of officers and the designation of particular officers as having particular expertise in mental health issues, to suggest that officers should be aware, for example, that touching a mentally disturbed person may be viewed by them as a hostile act, or that confinement to a cell is likely to exacerbate an existing mental illness (2012: 138). Common sense advice this may be, but it is good advice nonetheless. Adherence to its spirit by police officers is as important for effective diversion and optimum 'outcomes' as the successful implementation of the government's current initiative.

That successive governments have attempted for so long to give reality to the policy of diversion from police custody into the mental health system reflects the ambiguities of motive discussed at the start of this chapter. An evaluation of the current system such as has been attempted here reveals the extent to which such ambiguities are inscribed in the applicable law and its implementation. Arrest under ss. 135 or 136 of the MHA 1983, or the powers of arrest available to retake an absconded Part III patient, for example, weave elements of criminal and civil law, of control and benevolence, into patterns which are both complex and perplexing, whilst the appropriate adult system seeks to square the circle by providing benevolent assistance and pursuing a criminal case simultaneously. This is not to doubt the integrity of our benevolent intentions, but it is to remind us that those intentions are always, to a greater or lesser degree, in conflict with our fears and prejudices, and that this will complicate all and every attempt to provide adequate protections for mentally disordered persons when they come into contact with the police.

8

Mental Disorder and Criminal Justice

8.1 Introduction

This chapter looks at the powers given to the criminal courts to make a mental health-based disposal rather than relying on the options available within the criminal justice and penal system when faced with a mentally disordered person accused or convicted of a criminal offence (see Figure 7.1 in Chapter 7). As discussed in Chapter 7(see 7.1 and 7.2), the central philosophical issue is often expressed in terms of an opposition between 'treatment' and 'punishment', and the policy issue in terms of 'diversion', or at least the interaction of that policy with considerations around public safety, and, as will be seen more explicitly in this chapter than in Chapter 7, questions of culpability.

In this chapter, we shall consider the practical shape of diversion policy, in terms of a series of decisions made by criminal courts, at the various stages of the criminal process, as to whether an accused or convicted person should remain within the criminal justice system or instead be diverted into the mental health system. There are a number of legal mechanisms for the diversion of mentally disordered suspects from the judicial process before conviction and sentencing, although these are, in the main, intended to facilitate either the trial—for example, by providing the accused person with treatment to allow the trial to proceed—or the sentencing process—by gathering information relevant to that process—rather than to divert the accused person out of that process.

Nevertheless, on occasion, a defendant may never become fit to be tried, or reports may lead to a more informally engineered diversionary disposal. It is also possible, in certain circumstances, for a court to make a long-term diversionary order for the hospitalisation of an accused person by way of final disposal of the case, without convicting the defendant. The criminal courts also have significant powers, although only infrequently used, to impose a mental health-based disposal rather than a criminal justice disposal at the point of sentencing. These various powers are summarised in Table 8.1 Finally, this chapter will discuss the situation regarding the transfer of both sentenced and unsentenced prisoners to hospital and, sometimes, back to prison.

Table 8.1 Powers available to the Crown Court under the MHA 1983

Section	35	36	37	38	41	45A(3)(a)	45A(3)(b)
Power	Remand for assessment	Remand for treatment	Hospitalisation for treatment following conviction ('hospital order')	Interim hospital order	Adds 'restrictions' to hospital order ('restriction order')	A prison sentence, but the offender is sent to hospital ('hospital direction')	Adds restrictions to a hospital direction ('limitation direction')
Duration	28 days, renewable up to 12 weeks max	28 days, renewable up to 12 weeks max	Indefinite	12 weeks, renewable up to 12 months max	Indefinite	Indefinite	Indefinite
Usage in 2011–12	107 orders	16 orders	459 orders without restrictions attached	143 orders	522 hospital orders made with restrictions attached	8 orders	It is not possible to make a hospital direction without also making a limitation direction

8.2 Court-based diversion before the sentencing stage

Virtually all criminal prosecutions open in a magistrates' court. Much of the throughput of magistrates' courts is in terms of one-off court appearances at which the case against the defendant is proven, or, more commonly, there is a guilty plea, and the defendant is convicted and sentenced immediately. Such cases are typically trivial in nature and most are dealt with by way of a fine. In such a case, it is very rare that the defendant will have any further contact with officers either of the criminal justice system or the mental health services after conviction.

In a significant minority of cases, however, progress through the system is less rapid. More serious offences, known as 'indictable offences', can only be heard by the Crown Court and often require that the defendant is remanded, on bail or in custody, for considerable periods of time awaiting a court date. For middle order ('either way') offences, either the defendant or the bench may elect for Crown Court trial. In some cases, magistrates will convict but then pass the case to the Crown Court for sentencing. In others, for example, if a court is considering passing a community sentence or a prison sentence in certain circumstances or is dealing with a member of a class of offenders, such as a mentally disordered offenders, reports of various types, including psychiatric reports, must be called for (Criminal Justice Act 2003, s. 157), and cases adjourned for that purpose. This means that the engagement with the trial process can, for some, be a protracted experience.

8.2.1 Bail or remand? Questions of policy, practice, and resources

In strict theory, remand in custody is the exception not the rule. Virtually all accused persons have the same entitlement to bail. It is not possible to grant bail where a defendant, having a similar conviction or one for culpable homicide, is charged with murder, attempted murder, manslaughter, rape, or attempted rape (Criminal Justice and Public Order Act 1994, s. 25), nor is it possible to remand a person convicted of murder to hospital for assessment (MHA 1983, s. 35(3)) or a person accused of murder for treatment (s. 36(2)). But this apart, s. 4(1) of the Bail Act 1976 introduced a statutory presumption in favour of granting bail to accused persons, including persons whose case is adjourned after conviction to enable reports to be made (s. 4(4)).

The presumption can be rebutted for various reasons, to do with the likelihood of reoffending, absconding, interfering with witnesses, causing physical or mental injury to a family member, or having previously committed offences whilst on bail (Bail Act 1976, Sch. 1, Part I, paras. 2, 2ZA, 2A). An accused person may also be remanded to prison rather than bailed if the court is satisfied that this is required for his or her 'protection', which is capable of wide definition (Bail Act 1976, Sch. 1, Part I, para. 3); if it has not been practicable to carry out reports so as to enable a decision about bail to be made (para. 5); or if it appears to the court that it would otherwise be impracticable to complete any necessary inquiry or report (para. 7).

Even when a defendant has been identified as a potential candidate for bail or some other form of diversion by a court-based scheme or otherwise, the Bail Act nevertheless requires the balancing of the needs of the individual concerned for treatment with the considerations in the Act. The court should also consider the nature of the offence, the strength of the evidence, and the strength of the accused person's community ties (Bail Act 1976, Sch. 1, Part I, para. 9), and it is easy for these factors to conspire in the direction of remand to prison for mentally disordered suspects. The experience of James *et al.* (1997: 39) was that '[t]he most serious cases of violence would in any case be remanded into custody for reasons of public safety'.

It is possible to attach conditions to a bail order, relating, for example, to attendance for medical report or treatment, place of abode and so on, or to submit to electronic monitoring if bail would not otherwise be granted (Bail Act 1976, ss. 3(6), 3(6) A, 3AA–3AC). Home Office guidance (1990) urges magistrates to work in co-operation with the health service, and para. 8(1) of the guidance requires magistrates to give consideration to alternatives to remand in hospital, such as the attachment of a condition to an order granting bail that the defendant stay in a hospital or attend as an outpatient. Moreover, according to para. 7, 'a mentally disordered person should never be remanded to prison simply to receive medical treatment or assessment', and the power to remand instead to hospital rather than to prison 'should be used wherever possible to obtain a medical report on an accused person's condition' (para. 8(2)).

The remand prison population has, however, continually been found to contain a high number of mentally disordered persons (Taylor and Gunn, 1984; Birmingham *et al.*, 1996; Brooke *et al.*, 1996; Hardie *et al.*, 1998; Gunn *et al.*, 1991; Williams *et al.*, 2005). Lord Bradley, writing in 2009 (2009: 98), cited an Office of National Statistics survey from the late 1990s (Singleton *et al.*, 1998), which found, in a sample of 3,000 prisoners, that 10 per cent of remand prisoners (and 7 per cent of sentenced prisoners) were suffering from a psychotic disorder. This research also found that only 10 per cent of prisoners did *not* have at least one of personality disorder, drug or alcohol dependency, neurosis, or psychosis, and 78 per cent of remanded males prisoners were diagnosed as having a personality disorder, most commonly an anti-social personality disorder (Coid *et al.*, 2002: 248).

Lord Bradley lamented the fact that no further national data had been produced since that time, and called on the government to commission a repeat of the ONS survey (2009: 138), noting that 'Information is particularly poor in relation to those on remand or serving very short sentences, due to the fact that they are not subject to the current offender management system'. Although this situation changed thereafter, in 2012, HM Inspectorate of Prisons (2012: para. 135) noted that the National Offender Management Service (NOMS) 'has since removed remand prisoners from the new offender management model to be rolled out', and so it seems that the relative dearth of information about remand prisoners compared to those under sentence is set to continue.

More recent, but not such wide-ranging, data on the extent of mental disorder in prison was published in 2009. The study conducted by Shaw *et al.* (2009: 40 and table 3), the focus of which was prison in-reach teams, and therefore provides data only on those receiving services rather than all prisoners, but which does cover both remand and sentenced prisoners, found that:

- 32 per cent of patients had a severe and enduring mental illness (SMI);
- 26 per cent had an SMI together with either a personality disorder (9 per cent) or a substance misuse problem (17 per cent);
- 16 per cent had a diagnosis of personality disorder alone;
- 12 per cent had a diagnosis of personality disorder combined with substance misuse.

In 2012, HM Inspectorate of Prisons (2012: paras. 1.26, 7.59, table 24) reported that 36 per cent of those remanded had a mental illness or a welfare problem. These figures match closely the data generated by previously conducted research. Brooke *et al.* (1996), for example had also found that a quarter of people remanded to prison in their sample suffered from an SMI.

This does not mean that all of these people should necessarily be in hospital rather than prison: Brooke *et al.* (1996) were quick to point out that, although 55 per cent of their sample was in immediate need of medical treatment '[m]ost... could be provided by health services in prison'. Yet in the view of the researchers, 9 per cent of the sample (64 individuals) should have been in hospital (1996: 1526), which, extrapolating to the remand prison population as a whole (10,661 on 31 December 2012, amounting to around one in eight of the then total prison population of 83,757: Ministry of Justice, 2012: table 1.1a.) suggests that, on any one day, there are several hundred persons remanded into custody who need to be in hospital. This does not mean that these remand decisions are necessarily inappropriate, but some will be, and recent evidence is that improvement in the functioning of diversion policy in this corner of the criminal justice system is required.

For the system to operate as intended, the key is to develop efficient mechanisms for information provision at all stages of the process. Those arrested and remanded need information about the possibility of bail and how to apply for bail, which at present is too often not forthcoming from prison authorities utilising staff with no training in this regard (HM Inspectorate of Prisons, 2012: para. 7.5). Prison authorities need to become more adept at detecting the presence of mental disorder at the point of admission. As Lord Bradley (2009: 101) noted, 'Theoretically, there should be a whole wealth of information on an individual's health needs that can be made available to prison reception to inform and support their assessment'. In practice, however, this is often not the case, and prison reception medical staff must make a judgement solely or largely on the way in which the new arrival presents him- or herself.

The system for screening for mental disorder in one UK prison was subject to particular criticism in *Edwards* v *UK* (2002) 35 EHRR 19. E, a remand prisoner, who at the time of his arrest had acted violently and shown indications of developing schizophrenia, was housed in a prison cell with another remand prisoner, L. L was also schizophrenic, and with a known history of violence and who had, in fact, been violent immediately before being placed in the cell with E. A few hours later, L violently assaulted and killed E. The European Court found the UK to be in breach of its positive obligation to protect the right to life, imposed by Art. 2 of the ECHR, because in these circumstances the prison authorities should have known, or ought to have known, that their decision to house L and E together constituted a real and immediate risk to E (para. 60). The Court found a further breach of Art. 2 on the grounds that the subsequent inquiry into the incident had been carried out in private and without satisfactory procedures with respect to powers to compel witnesses.

Although this case revealed deficiencies in the ability of criminal justice personnel to recognise significant mental illness, or to act when mental illness is recognised at various points of the process from arrest to prison reception, the court found specific fault with the system for screening receptions (at para. 62): 'The defects in the information provided to the prison admissions staff were combined in this case with the brief and cursory nature of the examination carried out by a screening health worker who was found by the Inquiry to be inadequately trained and acting in the absence of a doctor to whom recourse could be made in the case of difficulty or doubt.' It also cited the findings of the inquiry into the incident, which had concluded that there had been 'a systemic collapse of the protective mechanisms that ought to have operated to protect this vulnerable prisoner' (para. 33).

The quality of the screening for mental disorder which occurs when there is a remand to prison has long been subject to criticism for the brevity of the typical screening and for the lack of training in mental disorder of those conducting screening. Birmingham *et al.* (2000) argued that the 'one size fits all' system of screening of prison receptions that then operated should be abandoned in favour of a more tailored and focused approach that provides a fuller assessment of those most likely, based on past psychiatric history, to be mentally disordered on reception to prison. The Prison Service, which issued a Prison Service Order, PSO 0500, in 2004, subsequently updated (HM Prison Service, 2012), and the Department of Health (Department of Health and National Institute for Mental Health in England, 2005) subsequently attempted to initiate a more nuanced system.

PSO 0500 lists a number of procedures and service standards said to be 'mandatory' for all prison receptions. Chapter 6 of the Order deals with screening for mental disorder, and at para. 6.1 requires screening procedures 'to determine whether [new arrivals] have any immediate health-care needs and whether they present a risk of harm to themselves or to others'. This must be done by 'appropriately trained member of the healthcare team' (para. 6.3). Thereafter, within a week, there should ideally be another screening, which should be in the form of 'a general health assessment' (para. 6.7). A new screening tool was also developed, with questions set by the Prison Service.

A few years later, in 2008, all prison screening processes in English and Welsh prisons were analysed by Shaw and colleagues (Shaw *et al.*, 2008b). They found (2008b: 21) that although the new screening tool (often modified locally, however) was working effectively to an extent, there were still numerous problems with the screening process nationally. These included:

- confusion over the purpose of the initial screening;
- over-reliance by screeners on historical factors instead of making an assessment at that time;
- pressure from other parts of the reception process—the requirement to search new arrivals, confirm their identity, and so on—limited the time available for mental health screening;
- screening carried out in inappropriate locations with insufficient regard for privacy;
- low rates of compliance with the discretionary second screening.

Lord Bradley (2009: 102) made two specific recommendations:

- An evaluation of the current prison health screen should be undertaken in order to improve the identification of mental health problems at reception into prison.
- Urgent consideration should be given to the inclusion of the identification of learning disabilities as part of the screen.

Subsequently, the national strategy for offender health care, articulated through the Department of Health's (DH) *Improving Health, Supporting Justice: The National Delivery Plan of the Health and Criminal Justice Programme Board* (DH, 2009d: 12) committed to review and strengthen screening for mental health problems and begin screening for learning disabilities within 18 months, and this is what PSO 0500, in its current and modified form, now requires. At the time of writing it remains to be seen what impact, if any, these recent developments have on the rate at which mental disorder is detected at the point of entry to prison.

If there is better information earlier in the process, available to the court considering how to dispose of an accused person pending trial, the commissioning of reports, and so on, the pressures on prison reception suites may well be alleviated, either because less people with mental disorder would be remanded to prison than is currently and histori-cally the case, or because better information at the point of entry to prison would be of assistance to those medical professionals screening at the point. In 2009, two specialist mental health courts (at Brighton and Stratford Magistrates' Courts) began to operate on a trial basis, involving a mental health professional operating in the court buildings, rapid assessment and effective options for liaison and diversion, involving both health and criminal justice partners, principally the probation service. The courts 'yielded innovative multi-agency collaborations that addressed needs which probably would have gone unmet' (Winstone and Pakes, 2010a: iv), often in the form of a community disposal rather than the use of custody, and also offer the opportunity to practice effec-tive 'therapeutic jurisprudence', by factoring health considerations systematically into sentencing decisions (Ryan and Wheelan, 2012). Despite the apparent success of the pilot schemes, and the support of Lord Bradley (2009: 77–78) there has been no roll out of mental health courts to date. Instead, the emphasis has been on establishing a national network of liaison and diversion schemes.

Diversion, as a set of practices rather than sentencing options, was, however, late to reach the criminal courts. A number of 'bail information schemes' were set up from the mid-1980s, but detecting persons suffering from mental disorder, out of the constant stream of people who pass through the court system, can be like looking for a needle in a haystack (Brabbins and Travers, 1994). Accordingly, the spread of court-based diversionary schemes specifically aimed at mentally disordered defendants has also been a noticeable development in recent years. Schemes vary in form from area to area, but the basic idea is that mental health professionals should be available in the court building when courts are sitting to take referrals from court staff, police, probation, and social professionals when there is reason to suspect that an accused person may be mentally disordered, and be able to engineer an appropriate diversionary option when appropriate, whether that involves remand to hospital, or, as is more often the case, referral of the accused person to community services of one type or another.

In the mid-1980s, such schemes were unknown; by the turn of the decade, 48 schemes were in existence (Blumenthal and Wessely, 1992), increasing to more than a hundred by 1995 (DH, 1995a, cited in Peay, 1997; see also Greenhalgh *et al.*, 1996; Austin *et al.*, 2003; Cooke, 1991; Evans and Tomison, 1997; Exworthy and Parrott, 1997; James *et al.*, 1997) and 136 by 2005 (Centre for Public Innovation, 2005: 16). By 2005, however, 'The national picture is far from ideal. Many areas have no provision at all. Many others rely on one lone worker, most often a community psychiatric nurse' (National Association for the Care and Rehabilitation of Offenders, 2005: 14); and in 2009 the Sainsbury Centre for Mental Health (Parsonage *et al.*, 2009: 14–18) reported that too little had improved subsequently. Of schemes surveyed by Nacro in England and Wales in 2004, one third operated with only one community psychiatric nurse (CPN), and although 42 per cent had three or more staff members, 50 per cent had no input from a psychiatrist or psychologist (Nacro, 2005: 5). Over two thirds (69 per cent) of schemes were 'reactive', only assessing those referred to them (2005: 9).

Nacro found that 'each of the schemes visited differed in set up, composition and working practices; there was no "norm" in place. The schemes had developed over varying lengths of time and had evolved in relation to service provision from local mental health and criminal justice agencies' (Centre for Public Innovation, 2005: 33: and see Parsonage *et al.*, 2009: ch. 3; Macleod *et al.*, 2010, for information on some currently functioning schemes). *Breaking the Cycle*, the Green Paper published in 2010 (Ministry of Justice, 2010: 36) announced the implementation of a national liaison and diversion scheme, to be fully operational by 2014, as discussed in Chapter 7: the liaison and diversion scheme described at 7.4.2 is intended to cover both police stations and courts.

An efficiently functioning local scheme does not mean that all those referred to it will be diverted. In the scheme analysed by Kingham and Corfe (2005), for example, there was no recommendation to divert 52 per cent of those referred, but it does mean that the possibility of diversion is appropriately considered in all relevant cases, and there is also long-standing and more recent evidence that the court process can itself function more efficiently, with average disposal times, adjournment rates, and associated costs significantly reduced for all defendants (James and Hamilton, 1991; Parsonage *et al.*, 2009; Winstone and Pakes, 2010a).

This is welcome, but even with an efficient national system for identifying mental disorder in court, a court which wishes to remand an accused person to hospital rather than prison may be constrained by the fact that it is not always easy to find a hospital place, particularly if secure hospital accommodation is required, as Greenhalgh *et al.* (1996), Nacro (2005: 5), and Parsonage *et al.* (2009: 18) amongst others, have discovered. Partly, this is because there is a general shortage of beds, but in addition, there is a certain degree of resistance within the mental health system towards accepting offender patients, who are viewed as more 'difficult' than others (Coid, 1988), and partly because of the pressure that criminal justice admissions place on already oversubscribed local hospital accommodation (James *et al.*, 1998).

8.2.2 **Remand to hospital: The law**

Section 35 of the MHA 1983 provides a general power to remand a defendant in a magistrates' court or the Crown Court to hospital 'for a report on his mental condition'. Section 36 confers a power, exercisable only by the Crown Court, to remand to hospital for treatment. In many ways, the two sections are similar: in either case, a court shall not remand an accused person to hospital unless satisfied, on the written or oral evidence of the intended approved clinician (AC) or manager at that hospital, that a bed will be available within seven days and that the accused can be detained in a place of safety in the meantime (ss. 35(4), 36(3)). In both cases, there is a right for the person remanded to obtain an independent medical report which can be submitted to the court in support of an application to have the remand to hospital terminated (ss. 35(8), 36(7)).

A period of remand may not last more than 28 days, renewable to a maximum of 12 weeks (ss. 35(7), 36(6)). An order under either section may be renewed if written or oral evidence is provided by the relevant AC (although in the case of a person remanded under s. 36 only, this must be the patient's RC) of the need to remand further to complete the process of assessment (s. 35(5)), or treatment (s. 36(4)); the accused person need not be brought back before the court on such occasions provided that he or she is represented at the renewal hearing by an 'authorised person' MHA 1983, (ss. 35(6), 36(5), 55(1); Legal Services Act 2007, s. 18) who will usually be a professional lawyer but may also be a paralegal or equivalent. There are, however, also significant differences between the two sections, although the import of these has been lessened by decisions of the Court of Appeal.

8.2.2.1 **Remand of an accused person to hospital for treatment under section 36**

Section 36 is only applicable to an accused person in respect of whom the Crown Court is satisfied, on the written or oral evidence of two doctors, at least one of whom must be 'approved' under s. 12 (s. 54(1)), that the accused 'is suffering from mental disorder of a nature or degree which makes it appropriate for him to be detained in a hospital for treatment' (s. 36(1)) and that 'appropriate treatment is available for him' (s. 36(1)(b)).

The wording of this test is identical to that to be found in relation to civil detention for treatment under s. 3. A patient detained under s. 36 is subject to the powers of compulsory treatment without consent contained in Part IV of the MHA 1983 (ss. 56(2), (3)). Section 36 is used rarely: 16 occasions in England in both 2010–11 and 2011–12, down from 30 in 2009–10, although that was an unusual year: in 2008–09, 19 orders were made, and there were 17 in 2007–08 and 19 in 2006–07 (NHS Information Centre, 2012: Table 1).

The long-term trend is downwards: there were 25 orders made in 2001 (Government Statistical Service, 2006: Table 1), 33 in 1996–97, and 48 in 1990–91 (DH, 2003: Table 1). Although the falling use of s. 36 is in line with the pattern in respect of other diversionary measures, which show a general decline over recent years, the infrequency of use of s. 36 is also partly explained by the increased use of the Justice Secretary's powers in s. 48 to transfer unsentenced prisoners from prison to hospital, used with greater frequency from the mid-1990s (see 8.5), and the tendency of court-based diversions schemes to come into play somewhat earlier in the process in magistrates' courts (Blumenthal and Wessely, 1992), when it is s. 35 that is the relevant provision. Before 2007, only mentally ill and severely mentally impaired persons could be remanded under this section. Its extension to all forms of mental disorder has evidently done little to encourage its greater use, and when the numbers remanded under both sections are compared to the thousands of mentally disordered people remanded to prison for medical assessments, the underuse of the powers to remand to hospital is truly shocking.

8.2.2.2 Remand under section 35

Section 35 is indeed used more frequently than s. 36, although long term trends are hard to predict. There were 107 orders made in 2011–12, up from 85 in 2010–11, but 106 orders were made in 2009–10, down from 145 in 2007–08 (NHS Information Centre, 2012: Table 1), and remarkably down on the 419 such orders made in 1990–91 (DH, 2003: Table 1). The powers contained in s. 35 are exercisable in respect of an 'accused person', defined in s. 35(2). In respect of the Crown Court, an accused person is one who is awaiting trial or has been arraigned but not sentenced for 'an offence punishable by imprisonment' (s. 35(2)(a)), with the exception of the offence of murder (s. 35(3)). So far as magistrates' courts are concerned, an accused person is defined in s. 35(2)(b) to include:

> any person who has been convicted by the court of an offence punishable on summary conviction with imprisonment and any person charged with such an offence if the court is satisfied that he did that act or made the omission charged or has consented to the exercise by the court of the powers conferred by this section.

Thus, a person may be remanded to hospital by magistrates without the bench being satisfied that he or she did the act alleged, if that accused person consents to the remand. But if that person has not been convicted, he or she cannot be remanded under this provision without consent unless the bench is satisfied that the defendant did the act or omission charged. If the defendant refuses or lacks capacity to consent, a magistrates' court may, when there is a firm diagnosis by two doctors, one of whom is 'approved' under s. 12, that the defendant is suffering from mental disorder, make a full hospital order (discussed at 8.2.4) under s. 37(3) instead of remanding the defendant to hospital under s. 35.

This may be done without convicting the accused if the court 'is satisfied that the accused did the act or made the omission charged' (s. 37(3)), and does not require the consent of the offender (*R* v *Lincoln (Kesteven) Justices, ex p O'Connor* [1983] 1 WLR 335 (DC)). This mechanism can achieve the same effect as an order made under s. 35, which provides an identical test (s. 35(2)(b)), with the important differences that a s. 37 order will not be time-limited and a patient detained under s. 37 is subject to the powers of treatment without consent contained in Part IV of the MHA 1983, whereas persons detained under s. 35 are not (s. 56(3)(b)).

In order to circumvent the disapplication of the powers to treat without consent to those held under s. 35, it has long been the practice that, if it was deemed necessary by the responsible clinician to treat such persons without their consent, then they would, during the duration of the remand, also be sectioned under ss. 2 or 3 of the MHA 1983, despite long-standing doubts about the legality of such 'dual detention' (Fennell, 1991b). In *Dlodlo* v *Mental Health Review Tribunal for the South Thames Region* (1996) 36 BMLR 145 and *R* v *North West London Mental Health NHS Trust and Ors, ex p Stewart* [1997] 4 ALL ER 871, [1998] 2 WLR 189, however, the Court of Appeal decided that there is no embargo on the application of the provisions of one part of the MHA 1983 to a person already detained under another part. Jones (2011, 1–429; see also Fennell, 1991b) has laid out a number of strong arguments against the holding in *Stewart*, the following of which continue to resonate:

- 'dual detention' defeats the clear intention of Parliament that there should be no compulsory treatment of persons remanded for reports, as evidenced by s. 56(3)(b);

- a person detained under Part II could be 'discharged' by a tribunal (see Chapter 11, 11.5) but would still be liable to be detained under s. 35;

- the powers of the responsible clinician, for example, to grant leave of absence, in respect of patients detained under Part II would not, in fact, be exercisable;

- the duty of hospital managers under s. 132(1) to ensure that the patient understands the legal basis for detention and the avenues open by way of challenge to continued detention could only be carried out with difficulty.

In short, the argument is that the MHA 1983 is clearly not set up to contemplate all the myriad complications relating to the legal status of a patient subject to dual detention. Nevertheless, the Court of Appeal has ruled in favour and there is little objection from within psychiatry (Gunn and Joseph, 1993).

The Mental Health Bills of 2002 and 2004 would have given explicit powers to treat those held on remand for assessment, but the 2006 proposals made no mention of this and the MHA 2007 initiated no change. It is our view, however, that this is a necessary reform. There is little reason to object in principle, particularly if the alternative is remand in prison (although it is possible to remand a person under s. 35 who would not have otherwise remanded to prison, if the court decides that it would be impracticable for a report on his or her mental condition to be made if that person was bailed: s. 35(3)(b)). Other proposals fell with the 2002 and 2004 Bills. For example, a person remanded in hospital cannot be given leave of absence by his or her RC. A common complaint of RCs is that the constraints of a remand order impact negatively on the ability to construct a satisfactory care plan, if leave of absence is seen as an important part of that plan. The proposal, now abandoned, to relax the time limits on remand might have encouraged the greater use of remand in hospital, as one reason for the current underuse of these powers is that the time limits imposed by ss. 35 and 35 of the MHA 1983 are thought by some medical professionals to be too short to allow satisfactory treatment to be given (although, as the European Court held in *Kudla* v *Poland* (2002) 35 EHRR 11, remand cannot be for any longer duration than is reasonable in the circumstances).

In addition, the MHA 2007 was not used as an opportunity to amend the potentially problematic wording of s. 35(2)(b) of the MHA 1983, the general thrust of which is to allow magistrates to remand to hospital both convicted, and in the circumstances detailed, unconvicted defendants. In one important respect, it seems that the wording of the provision frustrates that intention. The problem is with the reference to 'an offence punishable on *summary* conviction' because this comprises only summary offences (triable only in a magistrates' court) and offences that are 'triable either way' (which may be dealt with in either a magistrates' court or the Crown Court), which comprise petty and moderately serious offences. The most serious of offences are triable *only* 'on indictment', that is, only in the Crown Court. Such offences, as a matter of law, simply *cannot* result in a 'summary conviction', which means that a person charged with such an offence cannot be remanded to hospital by magistrates. This was the view of the law taken in *R* v *Chippenham Magistrates' Court, ex p Thompson* (1995) *The Times*, 6 December (DC), in which it was held that a 'hospital order' in s. 37, which uses the same phraseology as s. 35, could not be made by magistrates in relation to an indictable offence. There would seem to be no good reason for the narrow scope of this provision as a matter of policy and it is unfortunate that the opportunity was not taken to revise it.

The chronic under-use of the option of remand to hospital rather than to prison by the courts is partly explicable in terms of the ability to recognise mental disorder at remand hearings, partly about lack of funding (although funding has recently been increased: see Chapter 7, 7.4.2.), but it is also an indication that the courts and service-providers have not been convinced by the merits of the policy of diversion. A case which demonstrates the interconnectedness of these factors is *R* v *West Allerdale Magistrates Court, ex p Bitcon* [2003] EWHC 2460, in which a magistrates' court made an order under s. 35, for B to be remanded to a private nursing home. B's local PCT refused to fund his placement, however, basing its decision on the view of a psychiatrist, that only remand in prison would be appropriate. The court then revoked its order. When B sought judicial review of that decision, the High Court held that the magistrates' court had no choice but to act as it had.

In consequence of scepticism about the use of the powers to remand to hospital, it is vital that the quality of medical care for mental disorder in prisons is of good quality, and that the system for transfer from prison to hospital (see 8.5) works effectively. But the need to encourage the more systematic use of the power to remand to hospital rather than prison is, if anything, more vital, if the remand to hospital system is not to become *de facto* obsolete. More resources are necessary, but attitudinal change, both on the part of the courts and psychiatrists too often unwilling to accept remanded patients, is the real key.

8.2.3 **Fitness to stand trial**

Remand to hospital is not the only pre-trial diversionary mechanism available for consideration, if the situation is that the accused person may be mentally unfit to be tried. The conviction of a person who was unfit to plead at the time of trial will be unsafe and will be set aside (*R v Lewis-Joseph* [2004] EWCA Civ 1212), although the Court of Appeal is unlikely to allow an appeal on the grounds that the defendant was unfit at the time of trial if the issue was not raised at trial unless there are compelling reasons (*R v Erskine* [2009] EWCA Crim 1425; [2010] 1 WLR 183, paras. 82–83).

The prohibition on putting a person unfit to plead to trial reflects the long-accepted wisdom of common law, and now of Art. 6 of the ECHR, that, because it is unfair, there should be no trial of a person who is unable to understand the proceedings, and so cannot respond to the charge against him or her 'with that advice and caution that he ought' (Blackstone, 1793, in Mackay, 1995: 216). It is perhaps for this reason that unfitness is usually uncontested by the prosecution (Mackay and Kearns, 2000). At the same time, though, society needs to be protected from those who 'present a continuing danger' to it (per Lord Bingham CJ in *R v Antoine* [1999] 2 Cr App R 225 (CA) at 227; see also the speech of Lord Bingham in *R v H and SSHD* [2003] UKHL 1 at para. 2).

Section 2 of the Criminal Lunatics Act 1800, which put this view on a statutory basis, provided that a person found to be insane, by a jury empanelled for that purpose, should not be tried but instead 'kept in strict custody'. This was more or less the position until recently, with the caveat that the triggering concept was subsequently widened and is now that of 'disability' rather than 'insanity' (Criminal Procedure (Insanity) Act (CPIA) 1964, s. 4) as substituted by s. 2 of the Criminal Procedure (Insanity and Unfitness to Plead) Act (CPIUPA) 1991. An overview of the current system is provided by Figure 8.1. There is a right of appeal against any order made under these Acts, and a decision that the accused is under disability, or did the act, may be set aside if the Court of Appeal considers it unsafe (Criminal Appeals Act 1968, ss. 15, 16).

This area of law has seen reform in 1991 and 2004, which inter alia widened the choice of disposal available following a finding of unfitness, and in 2010 the Law Commission consulted on provisional proposals it had formulated for further reform. At the time of writing, that consultation has closed and the Commission is analysing responses. There must be a good chance that a significant number of the proposals consulted on will result in legislation sooner or later, not least because they address

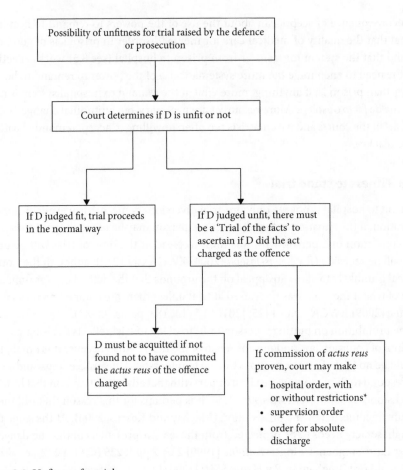

Figure 8.1 Unfitness for trial

*if the offence charged is murder, the court must make a hospital order and a restriction order

long-standing problems with the law in this area and have widespread, albeit conditional, support from those whose views are influential in this field (Peay, 2012: Mackay, 2011) and the relevant professional bodies (Royal College of Psychiatrists, 2011c; Law Reform Committee of the Bar Council and the Criminal Bar Association of England and Wales, 2011).

8.2.3.1 The test for unfitness

The possibility that a defendant is under such disability as prevents him or her being tried may be raised by the defence 'or otherwise' (CPIA 1964, s. 4(1)), in any case, before a Crown Court. In *R v Robertson* (1968) 52 Cr App R 690, [1968] 1 WLR 1767, it was held that, if the issue is raised by the defence, the burden of proof is on it to establish on a balance of probabilities that the defendant is unfit, but in *R v Podola* [1960] 1 QB 325

(DC), it was held that the criminal law burden of proof—beyond reasonable doubt—applies when the issue is raised by the prosecution. A court may not find a defendant unfit to plead except on the written or oral evidence of two or more doctors, at least one of whom must be 'approved' (CPIA 1964, s. 4(6)), although in *R v Ghulan* [2009] EWCA Crim 2285 the Court of Appeal held that s. 4(6) applies to a finding of unfitness but not to a finding of fitness, and a judge may therefore declare, provided that the decision is reasonable (as it was in *Ghulan*, being based on the judge's observations of the accused at trial), that an accused is fit.

This in our view is a problematic decision, particularly as the Court of Appeal made clear that a judge can so decide in the face of medical evidence suggesting unfitness. The Court of Appeal's reasoning (and that of the trial judge) was that it should not be possible to raise the possibility of unfitness merely as a mechanism to engineer an adjournment. This is understandable, but if there is good prima facie evidence of the possibility that the accused is unfit, this interpretation of s. 4(6) should not be used by judges as a mechanism to guillotine further exploration of that question. Recourse to the CPIA 1964 and CPIUPA 1991 is not possible in a magistrates' court (*R v Barking Youth Court, ex parte P* [2002] EWHC (Admin) 734; [2002] 2 Cr App R 19, para. 8), although magistrates may use their powers in s. 37(3) of the MHA 1983 to achieve much the same ends (see 8.2.4).

There is no statutory definition of the concept of 'disability' or 'unfitness to plead' as it is commonly, but misleadingly, described. The leading case remains *R v Pritchard* (1836) 7 C & P 303, in which it was held, per Baron Alderson, that a defendant is unfit for trial if unable to plead to the indictment, or if not 'of sufficient intellect to comprehend the course of the proceedings in the trial so as to make a proper defence, to challenge a juror to whom he might wish to object and to comprehend the details of the evidence' (see also *R v Friend* [1997] 2 Cr App R 231, CA). That this 'cognitive' test is capable of allowing departures from its spirit is evident from *Podola*, in which a person suffering from amnesia about the events relevant to the charge was held not to be unfit. It may well be that such a person can understand the proceedings, and so on, but without a memory of the relevant events, it is not clear how he or she could decide on a plea, instruct a lawyer effectively, provide evidence or testimony to contradict that of the prosecution and its witnesses, or make any number of other decisions that are required of a defendant in a criminal trial.

In *R v M (John)* [2003] EWCA Crim 3452, the Court of Appeal did not disagree with a judge's direction given to a jury, which comprised the following six factors (at para. 20). To be fit to plead, the defendant must be capable of: '(1) understanding the charges; (2) deciding whether to plead guilty or not; (3) exercising his right to challenge jurors; (4) instructing solicitors and counsel; (5) following the course of the proceedings; (6) giving evidence in his own defence.' This test seems to move closer to the 'decisional competence' approach long advocated by some commentators (Duff, 1986; Grubin, 1993; Mackay, 1995) and more recently by the Law Commission (2010: para. 1.34), which is a much more wide-ranging concept than 'disability' as developed by the common law, and which would include some assessment of the defendant's ability not merely to understand but also their capacity to make relevant decisions before and during the process of trial.

The trial judge in *R* v *M* elaborated on various aspects of the test. He explained, for example, that the sixth point required that, to be found fit, 'the defendant must be able (a) to understand the questions he is asked in the witness box, (b) to apply his mind to answering them, and (c) to convey intelligibly to the jury the answers which he wishes to give' (para. 24), which does seem to require something more than simply cognition. But it is possible that a defendant might 'go through the motions' without being decisionally competent. It seems that an ability simply to answer questions from counsel, even if the answers reveal little understanding of the those questions, will be acceptable as evidence of fitness to stand trial. The judge in *R* v *M* went on to explain that: 'It is not necessary that [the defendant's] answers should be plausible or believable or reliable.' For Mackay (2002: 733), decisional competence constrasts with 'competence to assist counsel', or 'a rudimentary understanding of the trial process'. He (2002: 732) cites research (Polythress *et al.*, 2002) to show that, in order to take a truly proactive part in proceedings, it is decisional competence that is required.

In *R* v *M*, as in *Podola*, the substantive outcome was that a defendant with significant short-term memory problems was found fit for trial. If the defendant proved unable to remember events referred to in cross-examination, 'He is entitled to say that he has no recollection of those events, or indeed of anything that happened during the relevant period' (para. 24). It is not clear that this is necessarily the best course for a defendant in this position to take, and raises prior questions, for example, about whether to give evidence in one's own defence or not, which would be required by a full-blown 'decisional competence' approach but which are not relevant under the current approach (Gray *et al.*, 2001). The implication of this is that some defendants are undergoing trial on the basis that they are, applying *Pritchard*, fit to do so but in circumstances which do raise questions about compliance with Art. 6 of the ECHR. This concern finds some support in the empirical literature, as does the concern that *Pritchard* is in any case applied inconsistently by those medical professionals required to do so (see Rogers *et al.*, 2009: 816).

Several recent cases illustrate the point that a defendant may in fact be unable to conduct his or her defence because his or her decision-making capacity at trial is undermined by the mental disorder from which he or she is suffering. In *R* v *Murray* [2008] EWCA Crim 1792 (and see also *R* v *Diamond* [2008] EWCA Crim 923) M had persistent paranoid schizophrenia. She stabbed her young daughter many times, causing her death, and was charged with murder. She pleaded guilty, notwithstanding that the defence of diminished responsibility was accepted by all parties as available to her, and was convicted. The medical evidence was the M was fit to plead by reference to the *Pritchard* test: she 'is able to comprehend the details of the evidence against her, and follow the court proceedings, is able to instruct her solicitors and on questioning understood that she can challenge a juror' (medical evidence given at trial and accepted by the Court of Appeal, para. 4). But it was also clear that (para. 5):

> she does not appear to be able to weigh up appropriately the contribution of her mental illness to her behaviour. Either this is because she lacks insight or (and I think this is more

likely) she does have some memory still of her thoughts and emotions during the period leading up to the killing of her daughter, but does not wish to discuss this with anyone as she wishes to be punished for her crime. She would see a conviction of murder as entirely appropriate.

In other words, M was fit to plead as a matter of law but her mental disorder dictated her approach to her trial to such an extent that she was not in fact able to conduct her defence with, in Blackstone's words 'that advice and caution that he ought'. For Toulson LJ, the case 'illustrates in acute form the problems of the potential mismatch between the legal test and psychiatric understanding in these matters' (para. 6). Following conviction, M was persuaded to appeal, and the appeal was allowed on the basis that the conviction was unsafe, but not on the basis that M had been unfit to plead. The appeal court replaced the conviction for murder with a conviction for manslaughter by reason of diminished responsibility. Yet there is a good argument that M should not have been tried in the first place.

In *R v Moyle* [2008] EWCA Crim 3059, M, who was diagnosed with paranoid schizophrenia, was convicted of murder and appealed on the grounds that he had been unfit to plead at trial. M had refused to co-operate with psychiatric assessments which may have allowed a finding of unfitness. This decision, and others taken in relation to the trial, was coloured by M's delusional belief that the psychiatrist appointed to assess him 'was part of a larger conspiracy that involved the courts, the police, the prison system' (para. 22). He also believed that God had informed him that he was innocent, that the Queen of Sheba was the real culprit, as well as various other delusional interpretations of his situation.

The Court of Appeal allowed the appeal against conviction, substituting a conviction for manslaughter by reason of diminished responsibility, but would not allow the appeal on the basis that M had not been fit to plead. The Court of Appeal unanimously held that there can be no 'proposition of law that a person suffering from delusions is thereby necessarily unfit to plead' (Pill LJ at para. 37) and then went on to say (para. 38):

> Each case, of course, depends on its own facts but delusions as to the court's powers of sentence, or as to the objectivity of the court, or as to the evil influences which are thought to be present in the proceedings, do not necessarily require a finding that a person is unable to give instructions and to understand the proceedings.

Commenting on this case, Taylor's view (2009: 588; see also Howard, 2011) is that 'Intuitively one has to have doubts about the fitness of a defendant who believes the court to be under the influence of Satan, but on reflection this state of mind does not necessarily impinge upon an individual's ability to participate in the proceedings and understand them, and one must make the consideration as to fitness within the context of the public's right to see an accused person tried'.

We would agree with this: the link between delusion and ability to participate needs to be explored empirically rather than having any necessary implication, and the public interest in seeing justice done is unarguable. However, in *Moyle* the court did seem prepared to accept that fitness is demonstrated if the accused can 'certainly understand, for example, what was being said in court on an, if you like, grammatical level' despite the fact that 'at a more distal level the way that he would interpret that and manipulate that information and make use of it, I think, was almost certainly corrupted by his illness' (medical evidence cited by Pill LJ at para. 30), and our view is that understanding in this sense amounts to little more than going through the motions, and undermines at least the spirit of the notion of a fair trial (see also *R v Diamond* [2008] EWCA Crim 923).

In subsequent cases the issue has surfaced again. In *R v Erskine* [2009] EWCA Crim 1425 [2010] 1 WLR 183 E killed a number of people. There was strong evidence at trial that diminished responsibility was present, but E refused to plead guilty and was convicted of murder. As in the earlier cases the Court of Appeal replaced a conviction for murder by one of manslaughter by reason of diminished responsibility but would not accept an argument that E had been unfit at trial, even though his decision not to advance the defence of diminished responsibility at trial was 'irredeemably flawed', rendering the murder conviction unsafe, 'as a result of reduced mental acuity, not amounting to unfitness to plead, but part and parcel of his mental illness' such that 'there was nothing his legal advisors could do about it, and in reality nothing he could do about it himself' (para. 95).

Erskine was followed in *R v Walls* [2011] EWCA Crim 443; [2011] 2 Cr App R 6, in which it was held that a person with significant learning difficulties and an IQ in the range 63–71, who had been convicted of sexual offences against a young girl following a trial at which no party had raised the issue of fitness to plead, had not been unfit to plead, as a medical report undertaken after conviction suggested. This was on the basis that W 'was able to explain the function of the judge and jury in the court; he understood that the Magistrates' Court tried less serious offences; he was able to understand the charges against him, he was able to understand he could challenge a juror when put in simple language' and so satisfied the *Pritchard* test, even though he 'struggled to understand the concept of pleading on issues rather than facts' (para. 31). In this case, the court also emphasised (para. 37) that it is open to a court to take various steps, such as appoint an intermediary to assist an accused person to meet the *Pritchard* criteria.

In all of these cases, there is potential injustice because the *Pritchard* test focuses on ability to understand in a narrow sense, which incorporates little which allows the mental capacity of the accused person fully to engage in the trial process to be evaluated. The Law Commission (2010: para. 3.13) proposed that *Pritchard* be replaced with a test similar to that found in ss. 2 and 3 of the MCA 2005 (see Chapter 4, 4.4). Section 3(1) of the MCA 2005 provides that 'a person is unable to make decisions for himself if he is unable (a) to understand the information relevant to the decision, (b) to retain that information, (c) to use or weigh that information as part of the process of making the decision, or (d) to communicate his decision (whether by talking, using sign language or any other means)'. Although s. 3(3) of the MCA 2005 does provide that 'The fact that a person is able to retain the information relevant to a decision for a short period only does not prevent him from being regarded as able to make the decision', it would seem at least arguable that a defendant such as that in *R* v *M* would have been classified as unfit under this test, on the particular grounds of not satisfying the requirements of s. 3(1)(b) and therefore also s. 3(1)(c). But arguably, decisional competency would require something more than simply replacing *Pritchard* with a test similar to that in the MCA 2005. A functional test still carries the risk that an accused who can 'go through the motions' of participation will (wrongly) be judged fit. As such, any replacement of *Pritchard* 'should be broad enough to cover reasoning difficulties which are caused by matters other than cognitive deficiency or mental illness' (Law Commission, 2010: para. 3.38) such as an emotional or psychological deficit.

In the view of the Law Commission, although this does not mean that the unfitness to plead criteria should encompass consideration of the rationality of decisions made by an accused person (Law Commission, 2010: para. 3.57), this 'is not to say, however, that the rationality or otherwise of a decision is irrelevant' (Law Commission, 2010: para. 3.54). This must of course be correct, but it is a fine line to tread. In Jersey, in *Attorney General* v *O'Driscoll* (No. 2) [2003] JRC 117, the Royal Court of Jersey decided not to follow *Pritchard*, emphasising the importance of capacity and decisional competency in determining unfitness (see further Mackay, 2004 and *A-G* v *Harding* [2009] JRC 198). However, the Jersey court did not replace *Pritchard* with a capacity-based test. Rather, it modified it. The substantive content of the modification is that in addition to being able to understand the nature of the proceedings so as to instruct a lawyer, make a proper defence, understand the substance of the evidence, and give evidence on his or her own behalf (which is the *Pritchard* test), an accused must also be able 'to make rational decisions in relation to his participation in the proceedings, (including whether or not to plead guilty), which reflect true and informed choices on his part'. As Mackay (2011: 436, emphasis in original) has explained, the precise nature of the requirement is not that the accused should act rationally, but rather that he or she should have '*the ability*' to make rational decisions, and it is thus possible to be found fit even if one's substantive decisions are patently irrational.

This may or may not be dancing on the head of a pin. In any case, Mackay proceeds to argue against the abolition of the *Pritchard* criteria on the basis that the law should recognise two levels of capacity, 'foundational competence' to instruct counsel, and 'decisional competence' to actively participate in proceedings. The current, foundational, *Pritchard* criteria do operate to identity and divert several hundred people each year 'without the need to resort to the complexities of decisional capacity or the issue of special measures' (2011: 445) such as the appointment of an intermediary. The Law Commission's proposals would be 'leaving decision-making capacity to do all the work when the role of the latter should be limited to those cases where "decisional competence" is of specific relevance' (2011: 445). Mackay's suggestion may be a simpler route to the same destination as that sought by the Law Commission.

Historically, it has been for a jury to determine whether a defendant is unfit, but s. 22 of the Domestic Violence, Crime and Victims Act 2004 altered this, and it is now provided that the question of unfitness is to be decided 'by the court without a jury' (CPIA 1964, s. 4(5)). The issue is usually raised early in the trial process, at arraignment. If unfitness is raised at any later stage, such as in the course of trial, it 'shall be determined as soon as it arises' (s. 4(4)), but this is subject to a discretion in the court to delay consideration of the issue until the opening of the defence case (s. 4(2)). This may be a suitable option if there is reason to believe that the prosecution case is weak, such that the court may direct, or the defence submit, that there is no case to answer. In such circumstances, the defendant must be acquitted and the question of unfitness 'shall not be determined' (s. 4(3)).

8.2.3.2 The 'trial of the facts' procedure

If the accused is judged fit for trial, the trial will proceed. If not, it will not, or, if it has already commenced, it must be halted, and a jury must determine whether or not it is satisfied that the accused did the act or made the omission with which he or she is charged (CPIA 1964, s. 4A(1), (2)). This is to be done either on the evidence that has already been heard, or on the prosecution evidence and that given by a person appointed by the court to act for the defence (s. 4A(2)(a), (b)). This is described in the long title to the CPIUPA 1991 as a 'trial of the facts'. Its purpose is to protect an accused person who would not have been found guilty of the offence charged from the consequences of a finding of unfitness. A jury that is not satisfied—and the test seems to be that which is usually applied in criminal courts, of 'beyond reasonable doubt' (Home Office, 1991: para. 9; see also the speech of Lord Hutton in *Antoine* in the House of Lords [2001] 1 AC 340 at 376)—that the defendant did the act or made the omission in question must acquit (s. 4A(4)).

The courts have been posed with some problems by the apparently mandatory nature of ss. 4(4) and 4A(2) of the CPIA 1964, coupled with s. 5(2) (discussed further later in this section), under the terms of which the court 'shall' determine the question of fitness as soon as it arises, the jury 'shall' then determine whether the accused did the act or omission in question, and the court 'shall' then make one of the orders available to it. If the accused is found, and remains, unfit, there is no problem, but in cases where the mental state of the accused fluctuates, things have not been so straightforward. In *R v Omara* [2004] EWCA Crim 431, the Court of Appeal held that, once a finding of unfitness has been made, a trial of the facts must follow, even if, as in that case, the defendant had in the meantime become well. In *R v DPP, ex p Ferris* [2004] EWHC 1221, Maurice Kay LJ, sitting in the Divisional Court, held that the wording of s. 4A(2) is mandatory, in a case in which a trial had recommenced after an earlier finding of unfitness and a trial of the facts which found that D did the act charged, and had then stopped a second time, again on grounds of unfitness. The court held that the statute required that there must be a second trial of the facts, and the jury charged to determine whether D did the act in question must not be informed of the earlier finding.

In both of these cases, the court expressed a dissatisfaction with the statute as it is presently worded, and made the policy argument, that there is nothing to be gained by finding for a second or subsequent time that the defendant did the act or made the omission in question. The policy reasons did seem to prevail, however, in *R v Hasani* [2005] EWHC 3016 (Admin), [2006] 1 ALL ER 817. The Divisional Court held that 'the ss. 4A and 5 procedures are inapplicable if, following a further s. 4. hearing, the court has found the accused person fit to plead' (para. 14), noting that it would be 'a quite absurd waste of time and money' for a trial of the facts to take place when it is known that the accused is fit to stand trial, as it would if the court had to make an order for absolute discharge because of an earlier, and now out-of-date, finding that the accused was unfit.

The court in *Hasani* accepted that it had departed from the literal rule of statutory interpretation in reaching this conclusion, instead following the rule that statutory provisions must where possible be given a sensible meaning (para. 14). It is submitted that the approach in *Hasani* is to be preferred, notwithstanding that judicial rewriting of the statute is entailed. As the Court of Appeal noted in *Omara*, the statute, as it is currently constructed, risks breach of the Art. 6 rights of the defendant. After some uncertainty in the case law, the Court of Appeal in *R* v *K, M and H* [2001] EWCA Crim 2024, [2002] 1 WLR 824 held that the wording of s. 4A(2), which provides that once a finding of unfitness has been made 'it *shall* be determined by a jury [emphasis added]' is procedural rather than mandatory, and does not limit the inherent powers of the courts to stay proceedings, at any stage of the process, but 'An abuse application, whenever made, must be founded on matters independent of the defendant's disability, such as oppressive behaviour of the Crown or agencies of the State, or circumstances or conduct which would deprive the defendant of a fair trial e.g. destruction of vital records…'. It is no abuse of process to continue proceedings notwithstanding that the accused is mentally disordered.

When *K, M and H* reached the House of Lords (*R* v *H and Secretary of State for the Home Department* [2003] UKHL 1) the sole issue was whether the trial of the facts procedure breaches the protection provided by Art. 6 of the ECHR to those involved in criminal proceedings. The appellant argued that a trial of the facts was no fairer to a defendant found to be unfit than was a full trial. In a trial of the facts, just as in a full trial, the defendant would be unable to participate in the proceedings rendering a trial of the facts 'unfair' within the meaning of Art. 6(1). It was further argued that a trial of the facts is to be conceptualised as a criminal trial, thus bringing Art. 6(2) into play, and allowing the argument that the presumption of innocence guaranteed by Art. 6(2) was not adhered to, and that the defendant in such a hearing would not have 'adequate time and facilities for the preparation of his defence', or be able to defend him or herself, or examine witnesses, or cause that to be done by counsel of his or her own choosing, as required by Art. 6(3).

Lord Bingham, giving the opinion of the House, rejected these arguments. He applied the three-part test developed by the European Court in *Engel* v *The Netherlands* (No. 1) [1976] 1 EHRR 647. This provides that, in order to determine the status of proceedings, it is necessary to consider (1) if the proceedings in question are categorised as criminal under domestic law, (2) the nature of the offence, and (3) the severity of any penalty. Lord Bingham noted that the proceedings are not categorised as criminal by the CPIA 1964 and CPIUPA 1991, which provide, as seen in this section, that a trial of the facts occurs only when a criminal trial has been halted. On the second and third points, Lord Bingham said (at para. 18) that: 'Whether one views the matter through domestic or European spectacles, the answer is the same; the purpose and function of the section 4A procedure is not to decide whether the accused person has committed a criminal offence. The procedure can result in a final acquittal, but it cannot result in a conviction and it cannot result in punishment.' As such, although 'the procedure under section 4A must always, of course, be conducted with scrupulous regard for the interests of the accused person...if properly conducted [it] is fair' (at para. 20) and compatible with Art. 6.

This is perhaps an unfortunate decision. In support of his conclusion that there is no punitive disposal available following a trial of the facts, Lord Bingham emphasised that an absolute discharge (as had been ordered at first instance in this case) is not a punishment, but an alternative to punishment according to the definition in s. 12(1) of the Powers of Criminal Courts (Sentencing) Act 2000. But, as will be discussed further at 8.2.3.3, a court has, since 1991, had the option of making a 'supervision order' following a trial of the facts, which in substance is remarkably similar to a psychiatric probation order; probation has, since 1991, been defined as a punishment (before that date it was conceptualised as an alternative to punishment). Thus, it can be argued, the distinction between what is or is not, at an abstract or principled level, 'punitive' under the CPIA 1964/CPIUPA 1991 regime is perhaps more problematic than Lord Bingham, sticking closely to technical definitions that may have scant relationship to how any particular disposal is experienced by the person subject to it and the facts of the case before him, suggests.

Moreover, although it is true that a trial of the facts does not 'determine any criminal charge' against the defendant (see further in the rest of this section) as required to bring the criminal law elements of Art. 6(1) into operation, it is only because a defendant has been charged with a criminal offence that the trial of the facts procedure will have been activated. The court does, in most circumstances, make a final disposal following such a trial, and so there is in truth a 'determination', just as in truth the punitiveness of any disposal is in the eye of the beholder.

The slippery quality of this question is underlined by the fact that subsequently, in *R v Bradford Crown Court, ex p South West Yorkshire Mental Health NHS Trust* [2003] EWCA (Civ) 1857, the Court of Appeal held that the s. 4A procedure could be classified as involving 'a criminal cause of matter' for the purposes of determining the applicability of the right to appeal under s. 18 of the Supreme Court Act 1981, and in *R v Chal* [2007] EWCA Crim 2647, [2008] 1 Cr App R 247, for the purposes of admitting evidence under s. 134 of the Criminal Justice Act 2003. In *R v DPP, ex p Ferris* [2004] EWHC 1221, Maurice Kay LJ, at para. 17, provided a rather bemusing explanation:

> when classification is necessary proceedings under Section 4A may be civil for some purposes, as was found in the case of *H*, and essentially criminal for other purposes, as was found in the *Bradford Crown Court* case. On any basis, the proceedings...bear some of the hallmarks of both civil and criminal proceedings: civil to the extent that they do not and cannot involve conviction or punishment in the penal sense; criminal in the sense that the rules of criminal evidence, including those relating to the burden and standard of proof, apply, and the result may be loss of liberty.

The implication of this seems to be, in essence, that a court may choose to emphasise either the criminal or the civil aspects of the s. 4A procedure as it wishes, and the implication of that is that it was open to the appellate courts in *H* to have bestowed a greater degree of protection on those subject to that procedure than was the case.

Rose LJ in the Court of Appeal in the *H* case ([2001] EWCA Crim 2024, [2002] 1 WLR 824) gave further consideration to the question of 'fairness'. The court noted that although the right to a fair trial in Art. 6 is 'an absolute right, the content of that right varies'. The ability of defendants to pursue their defence actively varies, and for some, age or unfitness will constitute a disadvantage. The court 'should do its best to minimise that disadvantage, but it may be unable to remove it totally'. In *T* v *UK* and *V* v *UK* [2000] Crim LR 187 (see also *SC* v *UK* (2005) 40 EHRR 10), the European Court required national law and process 'to reduce as far as possible' the disadvantages of the defendants, also recognising, in the words of Lord Bingham in *Brown* v *Stott* [2001] 2 WLR 817 at 836, cited by Rose LJ in *K, M and H*, 'the need for a fair balance between the general interest of the community and the personal rights of the individual'.

The Court of Appeal in the *H* case concluded that 'If Article 6 applies, it has not been infringed in any of the cases before us'. This means that only if there is some departure from or abuse of the ss. 4 and 4A procedures, which pushes the disadvantage to a particular defendant beyond that which is reasonable in the circumstances, will the ECHR rights of the defendant be at issue. An example of such a case is provided by *R* v *KM* [2003] EWCA Crim 357, in which the Court of Appeal found a breach of Art. 6(3) in a trial of the facts at which it had been found that K had committed the act (of murder), based largely on a witness statement, which was not subject on a trial of the facts to cross-examination, made by another party who had a vested interest 'in pinning the murder on the defendant' (para. 61).

The trial of the facts procedure remains controversial in terms of its scope, particularly the meaning of the words 'did the act or made the omission charged against him as the offence' in s. 4A(2) of the CPIA 1964. The view of the government, at the time the CPIUPA 1991 was passed, was that a trial of the facts should be limited to an inquiry into whether the defendant had committed the *actus reus* of the offence in question, because otherwise there would be little to distinguish a trial of the facts from a full trial, for which the defendant is not meant to be fit (Mackay and Kearns, 1997: 650). As White (1992) pointed out, however, the *actus reus* of some offences—he gave the example of theft—embraces elements of intention. Subsequently, in *R* v *Egan* [1997] Crim LR 225 (CA), the Court of Appeal held that this meant that, for the offence of theft, 'did the act or made the omission' meant *all* the ingredients of the offence, so that on a trial of the facts on a charge of theft, a defendant is entitled to be acquitted unless the prosecution can show both that he or she took the property in question, and that this was done dishonestly and with an intention permanently to deprive. Soon afterwards, however, in *Attorney-General's Reference (No. 3 of 1998)* [1999] 3 ALL ER 40, a differently constituted Court of Appeal reached the opposite conclusion.

In *R* v *Antoine* [2001] 1 AC 340, in which the appellant had been found on a trial of the facts to have committed the act of murder, the House of Lords approved

Attorney-General's Reference and disapproved *Egan* (at 372). The reasoning of Lord Hutton, giving the leading opinion, is deceptively simple. Section 4A(2) of the CPIA 1964 requires the jury to consider whether the accused 'did the act or made the omission charged against him as the offence'. 'Act' is accordingly counter-posed to 'offence', the difference between them being the presence of *mens rea*. Hence a trial of the facts is concerned only with the questions of whether the accused committed the *actus reus* of the offence. To this, he added a policy consideration (at 373): 'The risk would be that if a defendant who killed another person and was charged with murder was insane at the time of the killing and was unfit to plead at the time of his trial by reason by that insanity, then *mens rea* could not be proved because of the insanity existing at the time of the alleged offence, and the jury would have to acquit the defendant and he would be released to the danger of the public'.

The policy consideration is valid, but the distinction between *actus reus* and *mens rea* that underpins Lord Hutton's analysis of the statutory provisions is, with respect, problematic. The point is that the two elements of a crime—*actus reus* and *mens rea*—derive their legal significance from each other. An act is only a constituent part of a crime if accompanied by the necessary mental element. It is not a crime for A to kill B. It is only a crime if A kills B unlawfully, that is with intention, recklessly, or negligently. As Smith (2000: 622) noted, the decision in *Antoine* 'seems to be a novel departure. No other occasion when the *actus reus*, standing alone, has been held to have any legal consequences comes to mind'. Moreover, there is a certain logic to the argument that when a defendant has been found not guilty by reason of insanity, as required by the special verdict, it is perverse to investigate his or her *mens rea* at the time of the offence. But the argument is less persuasive in the context of unfitness to plead. This is because such a finding carries no implications about the defendant's state of mind at the time of the offence, but only at the time of trial.

This is unfortunate whatever the offence charged, but the most serious consequences are felt when the approach in *Antoine* is combined with the requirement of s. 5(3) of the CPIA 1964, which, as mentioned, requires the imposition of a hospital order and unlimited restriction order if the offence charged is murder, and if the grounds for a hospital order are present. The key issue remains the accessibility of defences that would have been available had the case gone to trial. In *Antoine*, Lord Hutton did say (at 376) that 'If there is objective evidence which raises the issue of mistake or accident or self-defence, then the jury should not find that the defendant did the "act" unless it is satisfied beyond reasonable doubt on all the evidence that the prosecution has negatived that defence' (although the availability of self-defence in a trial of the facts was left open by the Court of Appeal in the later case of *R v Jagnieszko* [2008] EWCA Crim 3065 at para. 65). These defences cannot be raised 'in the absence of a witness whose evidence raises the defence' (377). In other words, they cannot be raised by reference to the state of mind of the accused. 'Objective evidence', accordingly, means the evidence of persons other than the accused.

These defences, if successful, lead to acquittal, and therefore partly answer the objection made, but it remains the case that it is possible that a defendant, who would have been able to plead self-defence, mistake, or accident on the basis of his own evidence had the case gone to trial, can be found to have done the act on a trial of the facts. Moreover, the defences of diminished responsibility and provocation introduced by the Homicide Act 1957 cannot be accessed on a trial of the facts. These defences, which apply only when a defendant is charged with murder, can, if successfully pleaded, reduce a conviction from murder to manslaughter; a finding on a trial of the facts, that the act of manslaughter is proven, frees the court to choose the most suitable disposal as per s. 5(2) of the CPIA 1964. But these defences go to the question of *mens rea* rather than *actus reus*, and it is clear from the authorities that they cannot be accessed on a trial of the facts.

In *Antoine*, the argument of the defendant was that he should be able to put the defence of diminished responsibility to the jury. Lord Hutton, in rejecting that argument, pointed out (at 365) that, following a finding of unfitness the defendant is no longer liable to be convicted of murder—as decided in *H*, a trial of the facts is not a criminal trial and does not seek to establish whether or not a criminal offence has been committed. And it is only when all the ingredients of the offence of murder have been made out that the defence of diminished responsibility can be triggered, thus reducing the conviction for what would otherwise be murder to manslaughter. Because the s. 4A procedure does not require all the ingredients of the offence to be made out, the process never reaches the point at which diminished responsibility becomes a relevant consideration. The court also pointed out that, if a person found to have done the act of manslaughter on a trial of the facts subsequently became fit for trial, he or she could not be tried at that stage for murder because the finding of manslaughter at the trial of the facts would also have entailed an acquittal on the charge of murder (at 367).

Lord Hutton left open the question of the category into which the defence of provocation fell (376). Was it an 'objectively' verifiable defence, or did it go to the forbidden territory of *mens rea*? In *R v Grant* [2002] 1 Cr App R 38, the Court of Appeal decided that it was the latter. G killed her partner. She was subsequently found unfit to plead. Before a trial of the facts took place, defence counsel submitted that he should be allowed to place a defence of provocation before the jury. The judge rejected that request, and G was subsequently found to have committed the *actus reus* of murder and a hospital order and a restriction order were duly made. G appealed on the basis that the judge was wrong to refuse to allow the defence of provocation to be put to the jury. The Court of Appeal applied *Antoine*, holding that although 'the distinction applied in *Antoine* between *actus reus* and *mens rea* is not clear-cut . . . in our judgment provocation falls clearly on the *mens rea* side of the dividing line' (at para. 45), and that the considerations relevant in that case were equally relevant to the defence of provocation (at para. 46).

There is thus, on the law as it stands at present, no way for a defendant charged with murder and subsequently found to be unfit to plead to access the defences of diminished responsibility or provocation. There is currently no *charge* known to law of 'diminished responsibility manslaughter' or 'manslaughter by reason of provocation'. Given the harsh consequences of a finding that the defendant committed the *actus reus* of murder following a finding of unfitness to plead, it is to be hoped that prosecutors keep the possibility of injustice in mind when laying charges, and that a charge of manslaughter rather than murder is brought in appropriate cases (see *R* v *Cox (Maurice)* [1968] 1 WLR 308). This would allow the courts access to a broader range of disposals.

It is arguable whether the distinction between objective and subjective, and the distinction between *actus reus* and *mens rea*, is sustainable. The defences of accident, mistake, and self-defence can be understood as subsets of the general defence of 'no *mens rea*' and so it can be suggested that, by allowing these defences, the House of Lords in *Antoine*, maintaining the distinction between an act and its meaning on the one hand, deconstructs or undermines that distinction on the other. Shortly afterwards, the Divisional Court was forced to concede that, if a mental element is part of the *actus reus* (in that case, the *actus reus* of the offence, under s. 7(1) of the Financial Services Act 1986, was 'concealing' material facts, and to conceal, rather than, say mislay or overlook, requires intention), then the state of mind of the defendant can be inquired into to that extent (see *R* v *Central Criminal Court, ex p Young* [2002] EWHC 548 QBD), and more recent case law has continued to find that the *actus reus/mens rea* distinction is problematic to apply for particular crimes (such as voyeurism, defined by s. 67 of the Sexual Offences Act 2003 as observing another person doing a private act, but only if that observation is for the purpose of sexual gratification: see *R* v *B* [2012] EWCA Crim 77; [2013] 1 WLR 499).

Clearly, to say the least, the core distinction between 'act' and 'offence', is one beset with difficulties. This was further made apparent in *R* v *KM* [2003] EWCA Crim 357, in which the Court of Appeal upheld the trial judge's view that the accused 'did the act' if he or she took part in a criminal enterprise either as a principal or a secondary party. The upshot of this decision was that KM should be found to have committed the act of murder if he had inflicted one of the two fatal knife wounds during a group attack on a young boy, or if he had inflicted one of the other non-fatal wounds or, most controversially, if 'he was a person who took part in what he knew at the time was a knife attack' (per Potter LJ at para. 47), that is, had been a member of the group even if he had not actually used a knife against their collective victim.

Our humanistic concern with this decision is that it allows, as in this case, a young man unfit for trial on the grounds of having the 'intellectual capacity of a young child' and who 'was so suggestible and lacking in understanding that he could not follow the court processes' and 'would have been unable to give intelligent or coherent evidence' (Potter LJ at para. 3) to be stigmatised as having committed the act of murder, when it is *possible* that his actual involvement and his understanding was minimal. Our legalistic concern is that *KM* provides a further example of the problematic policy of attempting to determine whether a criminal act has been committed without recourse to questions of *mens rea*. The requirement that 'he knew at the time it was a knife attack' entails consideration of the state of mind of the accused. This was, according to Potter LJ at para. 42 'a matter of inference from the independent evidence of witnesses and not from the evidence of the defendant', but this only dissimulates the fact that the defendant's *mens rea* is absolutely pertinent to this determination, and the evidence of any third party is in reality evidence, once-removed, of what the defendant him- or herself understood to be the situation.

The Law Commission has recognised these difficulties, noting a number of offences in which the distinction between *actus reus* and *mens rea* might well prove to be problematic if litigated (2010: para. 6.28) and has suggested (2010: para. 6.9) that the trial of the facts be replaced with a two-stage procedure. At the first stage, there should be an investigation which is in all ways equivalent to a criminal trial in terms of the defences which are permissible. If the result of that hearing is that the accused person is acquitted, there may, at the discretion of the judge (because sometimes it will be clear that the reason for acquittal was mental disorder and a further hearing would add nothing: 2010: para. 6.142), be a further hearing to determine if the sole reason for that acquittal related to the accused's mental disorder. Such a procedure would appropriately balance the competing considerations (2010: para. 6.138):

> By requiring the prosecution to prove all elements of the offence, it ensures greater fairness to an unfit accused. It also means that the difficulties resulting from the decision in *Antoine* are avoided and would mean that an unfit accused would benefit from the protection of article 6 of the European Convention on Human Rights. The provision for a qualified acquittal, however, ensures that the public can be protected from an accused who may be dangerous.

This is not the only option for reform: various other formulas for dealing with the unfit to plead can be founded in common law jurisdictions (see Mackay and Kearns (1997: 650–1); Mackay, 2011; Law Commission, 2010: ch. 6), but at the very least it seems clear that this proposal if implemented would constitute an improvement on the current situation.

8.2.3.3 Disposals following a trial of the facts

If an accused person is found to have done the act or made the omission charged, it is then for the court to decide on disposal. In some instances, it will be appropriate, at least in the first instance, for courts to use the powers in s. 5A(2) to remand an accused to hospital under ss. 35 and 36 of the MHA 1983 (discussed 8.2.2), or to make an interim hospital order under s. 38 (discussed further 8.4.3). These powers are available if an accused has been found unfit and a trial of the facts has concluded that he or she did the act in question, even if the offence that the accused is found to have committed the *actus reus* of is murder, but a disposal under s. 5 has not yet been made.

Before 1991 there was only one possible disposal: a hospital order with a restriction order attached. The situation now is that long-term disposal options are laid in s. 5(2) of the CPIA 1964: the court may make a hospital order, with or without restrictions, or a 'supervision order', or order the absolute discharge of the accused. There is a right to appeal against the making of a hospital order or a supervision order following a finding of unfitness (Criminal Appeals Act 1968, s. 16A) which if successful allows the appeal court to quash and replace the original order (Criminal Appeals Act 1968, s. 16B), but there is no discretion allowed for the court to order a retrial (*R v Norman* [2009] 1 Cr App R 13 and *McKenzie v R* [2011] EWCA Crim 1550).

Research by Mackay (2010: 232), looking at all uses of disposals following a finding of unfitness to plead, found that supervision orders and absolute discharges make up around a quarter of all disposals (with absolute discharges rising from 3.6 to 6.3 per cent of the total orders made over the research period), the rest involving a hospital order, and around half of hospital orders have restrictions attached. Findings of unfitness are made across a wide variety of offences, but most commonly in non-fatal assault and sexual offences (Mackay, 2010: 204–216 and table 7).

Before the court may make a hospital order, which has the same meaning as an order made by a court following conviction under s. 37 of the MHA 1983 (CPIA 1964, s. 5(4)), in addition to meeting the criteria for unfitness to plead, the requirements for admission under s. 37(2)(a), which are very similar to those which apply under s. 3 for civil admission, must also be satisfied. This was not the case before 2004, and the medical evidence necessary under s. 4(6) of the CPIA 1964 applies only to evidence of unfitness to stand trial, and so it was possible that an accused be made subject to a hospital order although the criteria for the making of such an order were not met, which could frustrate the intentions of the court because a patient in that position would be entitled to discharge from hospital by his or her RC, hospital managers, or nearest relative. It also meant that a person could be admitted to hospital without objective medical evidence of the need for hospitalisation, in apparent breach of Art. 5(1) of the ECHR. The making, by a Crown Court, of an order for admission to hospital requires the managers of the hospital specified in the order to admit that person (MHA 1983, s. 37(4); CPIA 1964, s. 5A(1)(c)).

A 'restriction order', designed to protect the public (see 8.4.2) can be attached at the discretion of the court, even if medical evidence does not support that option, as long as it can be said that the decision of the court is a reasonable one given the totality of the circumstances (*R* v *Isleworth Crown Court, ex p Jones* [2005] EWHC 662 (QBD)). There are no criteria governing the making of a restriction order in addition to a hospital order on the face of the CPIA 1964 and CPIUPA 1991, but s. 5(4) of the CPIA 1964 provides that reference to a restriction order in s. 5(2)(a) carries the meaning given by s. 41, so that the same criteria, and requirements as to medical evidence (discussed in detail at 8.4.2.1), apply under both routes into a restriction order.

Whether or not a restriction order is made is crucial to the accused, not simply because restriction order patients will be subject to a more restrictive hospital regime and to greater restrictions on release, but also because, when, and only when, a court makes a restriction order in addition to a hospital order, can the accused be remitted directly to court, or to a prison, or remand centre, for trial, if, following treatment, he or she is well enough to stand trial (CPIA 1964, s. 5A(4)). The power to remit is vested solely in the Justice Secretary, and may only be exercised if, after consultation with the defendant's RC, he or she 'is satisfied that that person can properly be tried', which, presumably, should involve a reapplication of the *Pritchard* test.

If the offence that the defendant is found, on a trial of the facts, to have committed is murder, there is no option but to make a hospital order and a restriction order without limit of time (CPIA 1964, s. 5(3)), but *only* if the criteria for a hospital order are made out (CPIA 1964, s. 5(3)(b)). If they are not, 'the court's options are limited to a supervision order or absolute discharge' (Home Office, 2005: para. 12).

Supervision orders are only available under the CPIA 1964. The details of the scheme are found in Sch. 1A to the Act. Supervision orders are similar to guardianship orders (see Chapter 10, 10.3) in some respects, but provide for considerably more nuanced control over the subject of the order (the availability of guardianship orders under the CPIA 1964 was removed in 2004). A supervision order (which can only be made if the court is satisfied that it is the most suitable means of dealing with the accused or appellant: Sch. 1A, para. 2(1)), is an order requiring the person in respect of whom it is made to be under the supervision of a social worker or probation officer, from within a specified social service or local justice area (para. 3(1)) for up to two years (Sch. 1A, para. 1(1)).

An order can include a treatment component for all or some of its duration, if there is medical evidence from at least two doctors, at least one of whom is 'approved', that the subject of the order is in need of treatment but his or her condition is not such as to warrant hospitalisation (paras. 1(2), 4, 5). Treatment may only be given on an outpatient basis (paras. (3), 5(3)) in a specified hospital or other place, and under the direction of a specified doctor (para. 4(3)), but there is also provision for an order to include a requirement as to residence (para. 8), and so the subject of a supervision order may be *de facto* hospitalised by the terms of an order. There is, however, no sanction for any breach of the terms of an order, and this is because the supervision order, new in 2004 (although replacing the similar 'supervision and treatment order'), 'is designed to enable support and treatment to be given to the defendant to prevent recurrence of the problem which led to the offending' (HM Stationery Office, 2004: para. 96).

If an order for absolute discharge is made, s. 12(1) of the Powers of Criminal Courts (Sentencing) Act 2000, which provides the jurisdictional basis to make such an order, applies, but is modified by s. 5A(6) of the CPIA 1964, to the effect that the sentencing court must be of the opinion that it is inexpedient to inflict punishment, and that an absolute discharge 'would be most suitable in all the circumstances of the case'. There is no guidance about when a community-based disposal is to be preferred over the making of a hospital order. It is, however, not possible to make a hospital order unless there is medical evidence in support of that option, and so, provided that the decision to make a hospital order rather than a supervision order or an order for absolute discharge is bona fide, the law as it now stands is in compliance with the requirements of Art. 5(1)(e) of the ECHR. If a hospital order is made instead of a community-based option for inappropriate reasons, such as a lack of resources to fund a particular defendant's care in the community, the situation may be different (*R, on the application of Mohammed Latif* 2002 WL 31422140, para. 12).

8.2.3.4 The use of unfitness to plead

In both *Erskine* (para. 84) and *Walls* (para. 38) the Court of Appeal noted that increasing numbers of appeals were raising unfitness to plead, with the court in *Erskine* noting that this seemed to be particularly the case when there had been a tactical decision not

to raise the question of fitness at trial. The numbers of patients entering hospital subject to a restriction order following a finding of unfitness to plead has been uneven. In
2011, there were 62 cases, but only 37 in 2010. For the five years previous to that there
were between 29 and 32 cases each year, with 51 in 2004 and only 22 in 2000 (Ministry
of Justice, 2012: table A6.5). The numbers detained show a clearer pattern, with a year
on year rise throughout this century, from 124 in 2000 to 327 in 2011 (Ministry of
Justice 2012: table A6.2). Mackay's data (2010: 208, table 2a), which concerns the years
2002–08, shows a broadly similar pattern, with around three in 10 of all disposals under
s. 5(2) of the CPIA 1964 involving a restriction order in a typical year, although not all
years are typical.

The Law Commission's proposals for law reform extend beyond the test for disability
and the trial of the facts. The need to develop a defined psychiatric test for unfitness
(2010: para. 5.17); to make greater use of 'special measures' in both determining unfitness and in assisting those struggling to achieve capacity to do (2010: para. 4.27; see also
McEwan, 2013); and to give the courts powers to remit a case back to hospital when it
has been remitted from hospital to court by the Justice Secretary (2010: para. 7.21), are
all discussed by the Commission. It is to be hoped that these proposals, at least those
which enjoy a consensus of support, will be taken forward into legislation.

8.2.4 Magistrates' courts and unfitness to plead

Although the CPIA 1964 and CPIUPA 1991 are not generally applicable in magistrates'
courts, magistrates' courts do have powers to revoke or amend a supervision and treatment order, as does the court which made the order (CPIA 1964, Sch. 1A, Part 3, paras.
9(1), (2), 11). An application for an order to be revoked can be made by a supervising
officer or a supervisee, and may be revoked if 'having regard to the circumstances which
have arisen since the order was made, it would be in the interests of the health or welfare
of the supervised person that the order should be revoked'. It is difficult to know what a
magistrates' court would make of this provision, because there are so few cases, but it is
likely that, in practice, the opinion of the supervisor would be determinative, whether
the application was for a revocation or an amendment. An order cannot be 'amended' to
extend its duration beyond two years from the date on which it was made (CPIA 1964,
Sch. 1A, Part 3, para. 11(2)).

Magistrates can, in fact, achieve much the same effect as an order made under the
CPIA 1964 and CPIUPA 1991. This is because magistrates may make a hospital order
under s. 37(3) of the MHA 1983 without convicting the defendant if satisfied that
the defendant did the act or made the omission that constitutes the *actus reus* of an
offence punishable on summary conviction with imprisonment. This includes offences
triable 'either way' even if the defendant wishes to elect for Crown Court trial (*R v
Ramsgate Justices, ex p Kazmarek* (1985) 80 Cr App R 366 (DC)), but not offences that
are triable only on indictment, since such offences are not punishable on *summary*
conviction (*R v Chippenham Magistrates' Court, ex p Thompson* (1995) *The Times*,
6 December (DC)).

It has been said that magistrates will only very rarely have need to use this power (*R v Lincoln (Kesteven) Justices, ex p O'Connor* [1983] 1 WLR 335 (DC)), but on the other hand, should not be reluctant to do so when appropriate (see *R v Redbridge Magistrates' Court, ex parte Varma* [2009] EWHC 836 (Admin)). When it is used, it must be used in accordance with the diagnostic criteria employed by the MHA 1983 rather than the *Pritchard* test. There is also a power to remand a person in the same circumstances if satisfied that the accused did the act or made the omission charged and the court 'is of the opinion that an inquiry ought to be made into his physical or mental condition before the method of dealing with him is determined' (Powers of Criminal Courts (Sentencing) Act 2000, s. 11(1)(b)), for a maximum of three weeks if remanded into custody or four weeks if remanded on bail, although in either case the period of remand is renewable (Powers of Criminal Courts (Sentencing) Act 2000, s. 11(2)).

The Court of Appeal has held that if unfitness is raised as a possible issue before a magistrates' court, the question of whether the accused did the act or committed the omission constituting the offence should then be decided, so that if acquittal is a possibility, it will be arrived at sooner rather than later (*R v Stratford Magistrates' Court, ex parte Singh* [2007] 4 All ER 407). However, if acquittal is not the outcome of the trial of the facts procedure, the court may have no choice at that stage, by reason of s.11 of the Powers of Criminal Courts (Sentencing) Act 2000, but to adjourn (*Blouet v Bath and Wansdyke Magistrates' Court* [2009] EWHC 759 (Admin)).

A guardianship order was usefully made in *Bartram v Southend Magistrates Court* [2004] EWHC 269. B, suffering from paranoid schizophrenia and having failed to take prescribed medication, stabbed and killed his dog, believing it to be possessed by an evil spirit. He was charged with causing unnecessary suffering to an animal. It was clear to all that B was unfit to plead and the court, being satisfied that B did the act of killing the dog, made an order under s. 37(3). B's condition responded well to treatment in hospital and his mental state became stable and co-operative. The magistrates' court took this to mean that B was no longer mentally ill and held that there was therefore no scope for the further use of s. 37, and it proposed to try his case. B sought judicial review of that decision, which was successful, the Divisional Court holding that, although B was stable and not now in need of hospitalisation, psychiatric reports indicated that he remained liable to further acute attacks and that the continued use of s. 37, now to make a guardianship order, was not merely legally possible, it was also the best way to dispose of the case.

8.3 The special verdict

The 'special verdict' offers an alternative to conviction. The legal basis of the special verdict remains s. 2 of the Trial of Lunatics Act 1883, which now provides that a person who was 'insane' at the time the alleged offence was committed may be found 'not guilty by reason of insanity'. Like the law relating to disability to stand trial, the special verdict is subject to the regimes laid down by the CPIA 1964, CPIUPA 1991 and Domestic

Violence, Crime and Victims Act 2004 discussed in 8.2; as with unfitness, before the CPIUPA 1991, the only disposal available was indefinite detention in a hospital. The situation now is that the range of disposals discussed earlier in the context of unfitness are also available if a special verdict is returned (CPIA 1964, s. 5), again with the exception that an order committing the defendant to hospital with restrictions must be made if the offence in question is murder and the grounds for a hospital order can be made out (CPIA 1964, s. 5(3)). As with unfitness, the issue of insanity may be raised by defence, prosecution, or the court, and must be demonstrated by the defence on the balance of probabilities (*R* v *Constantini* [2005] EWCA Civ 821). It is established that the defence is available both in the Crown Court and on summary trial in magistrates' courts (*R* v *Horseferry Road Magistrates' Court, ex p K* [1996] 3 All ER 733 (CA)).

Neither the CPIUPA 1991 Act nor the Domestic Violence, Crime and Victims Act 2004, however, did anything to change the definition of insanity, and the leading authority remains the infamous *M'Naghten's Case* (1843) 10 C & F 200, in which Tindal CJ (at 210) laid out the '*M'Naghten* rules'. That is, to establish the defence of insanity:

> it must be clearly proved that, at the time of the committing of the act, the party accused was labouring under such a defect of reason, from disease of the mind, as not to know the nature and quality of the act he was doing; or if he did know it, that he did not know that what he was doing was wrong.

If the court determines that the defendant is insane in the *M'Naghten* sense, the court then moved on to consider disposal without any requirement to hear objective medical evidence of a mental disorder warranting hospitalisation (Howard, 2003).

This situation was changed in 2004 and now medical evidence is required (CPIUPA 1991, s. 1(1)). But it can be argued that the latest round of reforms did not go far enough. If the function of the *M'Naghten* test is to differentiate the dangerous (in need of detention in a hospital) from those who are not (and so are able to access the alternative of non-insane automatism, which provides a complete defence), or the morally blameworthy from those who are not, there is general agreement that it fails (Baker, 1994; Kerrigan, 2002). From a psychiatric point of view, the problem is that the *M'Naghten* test focuses on cognition (understanding) rather than conation (motivation or volition, reasoning), and would, for example, label children as insane rather than as, on a conational model, merely immature.

In addition, at present, the definition of insanity is premised on an internal/external causes model: if the cause of the actions in question is 'internal', insanity is the issue. This distinction has produced manifest injustices, such as that in *R* v *Sullivan* [1984] AC 156 (HL), in which it was held that psychomotor epilepsy came within the *M'Naghten* definition of insanity, or in *R* v *Hennessey* [1989] 2 ALL ER 9, in which it was held that hyperglycaemia was also caught by the concept of a 'disease of the mind'. Bizarrely, the courts have always insisted that the definition of insanity to be used in criminal trials is a matter of law, yet, of course, in reality *M'Naghten* constitutes the legal 'freezing' of a particular phase in the development of psychiatric knowledge and theory, and in consequence, the legal definition of insanity is not coterminous with modern medical knowledge.

Situations like those in *Sullivan* or *Hennessey* will not generally be problematic in practice under the current law: the broader range of disposals and the need for medical evidence in support of hospitalisation means that, in such cases, a hospital order need not, or cannot, be made. Additionally, despite their rigidity as a matter of legal doctrine, the research evidence is that, although the rules are usually (but not always) referred to by psychiatrists reporting to the court, 'wrong' is more often than not (68 out of 100 cases: Mackay *et al.*, 2006: 405–6) interpreted to mean, given the defendant's (often confused or deluded) understanding of the events in question, 'morally wrong', rather than the, stricter, 'legally wrong'. As Mackay *et al.* (2006: 407) state, 'psychiatrists may in many respects be adopting a pragmatic approach by augmenting the strict scope of the *M'Naghten* rules and the courts by accepting this interpretation are in reality continuing to accept a wider interpretation of the rules', which does embrace notions of conation.

Yet there is still an argument to be made that any test that catches such cases is in need of reform. In 2002, the government stated its intention to redraw the test as part of the reform of mental health law (Department of Health and Home Office, 2002: para. 4.3), but this did not occur as part of the reform of mental health law in 2007 or otherwise. In Jersey, in *Attorney General v Prior* (2001) (see Mackay and Gearty, 2001), the argument that the *M'Naghten* rules breach Art. 5(1)(e) has been accepted (although on the equivalent of the pre-2004 Act law). The Royal Court of Jersey instead adopted the definition of insanity offered to the court by Professor Mackay, namely that a person is insane for the purposes of the insanity defence if at the time of the offence 'his unsoundness of mind affected his criminal behaviour to such a degree that the jury consider that he ought not to be found criminally responsible'. A jury (or judge, as is now the case) might only reach such a conclusion if there is medical evidence to support that view. Given that the *M'Naghten* test is 'offensive, and no longer meaningful in either a clinical or a common language context' (Mental Health Act Commission, 2005: para. 5.21), it is difficult, in our view, to dispute the preferability of this test over the *M'Naghten* approach.

Before the CPIA 1991 reforms, the insanity defence, with its mandatory and inflexible consequences, was used no more than two or three times annually, if that. Even after 1991, the inflexibility of the defence, the harshness of the consequences of its use, and the availability of a preferable alternative of the defence of diminished responsibility, introduced in 1957, and the abolition of the death sentence for murder in 1965, together meant that it was no longer clear that indefinite detention in a psychiatric hospital was preferable to a criminal disposal from the point of view of the accused. It remains the case that the insanity defence is successfully pleaded in only a very small number of cases each year. This reached double figures in 1995 and has continued to rise subsequently. Mackay *et al.* (2006: 2) point out that there were more cases (72) in the second five years of the operation of the CPIA 1991 (1997–2002) than there had been in the whole of the period 1975–91 (69). The numbers placed on a hospital order with restrictions has remained low: there were 8 such cases in 2011, and 7–9 for most of the last decade, apart from 2006 when 10 order were made, and 2003 when only 2 were made (Ministry of Justice, 2012: table A6.5).

In their research, Mackay *et al.* found that, in 1997–2001 there were such orders were made in 27 cases, comprising 37.5 per cent of the total (2006: Table 8), which would suggest that there are around 20 uses of the defence annually, although Mackay (2012: E6) has reported that the number hit 30 for the first time in 2011, with over half involving a community-based disposal. The defence is used for a broad number of disorders, but Mackay *et al.* (2006: tables 2, 3 and 5) reported that 50 per cent of all cases involved a primary diagnosis of schizophrenia, and it is most often used in cases of homicide or serious offences against the person, overwhelmingly involving male defendants aged 20 to 40, and Mackay's more recent research (2012: E8, E10, tables 3a, 3b, 3c, 6a) confirms the continued accuracy of this data. It is also apparent that all ethnic groups other than white Caucasians are significantly over-represented in their use of the defence (2012: table 4). The numbers involved are so small that it is difficult to talk of trends, and it is clear that the use of the special verdict is a rare event.

In 2012 the Law Commission (2012) published a scoping paper on insanity (and the defence of automatism), in which the Commission announced itself 'convinced' that 'there are significant problems with the law' (2012: para. 1.4). Some of these problems parallel the concerns regarding unfitness to plead—the problems of building the disposal options around the act/omission distinction (Law Commission, 2012: paras. 2.3–2.6) and the poor match between the archaic legal criteria for insanity and contemporary professional understandings of mental disorder (paras. 2.12–2.15). Others, such as the meaning of 'defect of reason' and the internal/external factors distinction (paras. 2.16–2.25) are specific to the insanity defence. The plan at the time of writing is that the results of this consultation should be integrated with the more advanced Law Commission project to review the law on unfitness to plead.

8.4 Sentencing as diversion

The relevance of mental disorder to the substantive criminal law is beyond the scope of this text, as is detailed discussion of the sentencing options open to a court on convicting an offender. Nevertheless, it is appropriate to point out that the principles of punishment, crime reduction, public protection, reform, rehabilitation, and reparation that are to be found in s. 142 of the Criminal Justice Act (CJA) 2003 apply to all offenders, mentally disordered or not (although these considerations do not apply if a court makes a hospital order: s. 142(2)(d)).

The CJA 2003 contains a graded system of sentencing, which attempts to engender proportionality in sentencing practice. A prison sentence, and a community sentence, must not be passed unless the court is satisfied that the offence committed is serious enough (defined in s. 143) to warrant it, and the sentence passed must be the shortest that is commensurate with the seriousness of the offence (CJA 2003, ss. 152(2), 153(2), 148(1)). Before a person who is, or appears to be, mentally disordered can be imprisoned, the court must first obtain a medical report from a s. 12 MHA approved doctor

(CJA 2003, s. 157(1), unless the court considers that to do so it not necessary: s. 157(2)) and must also consider any information about that person's mental condition (whether given in a medical report, a pre-sentence report or otherwise), and the likely effect of such a sentence on that condition and on any treatment which may be available for it (s. 157(3)). A court may decide, on the basis of such evidence, that a defendant's mental disorder amounts to mitigation, in which case it may pass a lesser sentence than it otherwise would have done (s. 166) and may, in particular, make a community-based disposal even if the seriousness of the offence in question would normally result in a custodial sentence (s. 166(2)).

There are exceptions to these general rules, however, and in particular s. 224A and Sch. 15B of the CJA 2003 provide for the mandatory imposition of a life sentence on a person convicted of a second serious crime of violence or sexual crime, and ss. 224 and 225 (or s. 226 for people below the age of 18) require a life sentence to be passed for a serious sexual or violent offence if 'the court is of the opinion that there is a significant risk to members of the public of serious harm occasioned by the commission by him of further specified offences' (s. 225(2)); a life sentence is available for the offence in question; and the offence, alone or in combination with others, justifies the imposition of a life sentence. In a case where s. 225(2) does not apply, the court may nonetheless pass an extended sentence under s. 226A (or s. 226B for people below the age of 18). In addition, ss. 110 and 111 of the Powers of Criminal Courts (Sentencing) Act 2000 prescribe mandatory minima for third-time drug trafficking and domestic burglary offences.

These considerations apply to all offenders, whether or not mentally disordered. However, the CJA 2003 also amended s. 37(1A) of the MHA 1983, so that the availability of a hospital order to a sentencing court is not affected by the passage of ss. 224–226B of the CJA 2003 or other legislation which prescribes mandatory minimum sentences. This means that sentencing courts will always, unless the defendant has been convicted of murder, have the option of making a hospital order instead of sending a convicted person to prison, if the conditions for the making of such an order (on which, see 8.4.1) can be made out.

In addition to the standard sentencing options, including the making of a 'community order' (formerly a probation order) with a requirement to accept treatment for mental disorder attached (CJA 2003, ss. 177, 207), the courts can send a mentally disordered person to hospital instead of prison by making a 'hospital order', which can be given additional bite by the addition of a 'restriction order', or to prison with immediate reception into a hospital, in the form of a 'hospital direction' coupled with a 'limitation direction' (see Table 8.1). These additional orders, which can only be made if the offender constitutes a threat of serious harm to the public, place the hospital order patient under the control of the Justice Secretary, who has powers to override and veto the patient's RC on decisions relating to discharge, leave of absence, or transfer. These are significant powers although, as will be seen, such orders are only made rarely.

8.4.1 **Hospital orders**

The power to make a 'hospital order' is contained in s. 37 of the MHA 1983. The order is an alternative to imprisonment, and a court making an order under s. 37 may not also impose a punitive criminal justice disposal on the defendant (s. 37(8)), although there is some lack of clarity about what orders can be appropriately attached (see *R v Taher Ahmed Chowdhury* [2011] EWCA Crim 936 at paras. 17, 18). The court has the discretion to make a guardianship order rather than a hospital order (s. 37(1)). This is only rarely done, however (see Chapter 10, 10.3), and in a case in which a community-based disposal is deemed preferable to detention, a community order is likely to be preferred over guardianship, because conditions relating to the acceptance of treatment can be attached (*R v Clare T* [2003] EWCA Crim 17, 2003 WL 1202680 (CA)) (although the order requires the consent of its subject). Whenever a s. 37 order is made, then, unless a 'restriction order' (see 8.4.2) is also made, the defendant passes out of the criminal justice system altogether, and cannot be brought back into that system.

In the leading case on the use of hospital and restriction orders, *R v Birch* (1989) 11 Cr App R(S) 202 (CA), Mustill LJ explained (at 210) that the option for sentencers of being able to sentence an offender to hospital:

> is intended to be humane by comparison with a prison sentence. A hospital order is not a punishment. Questions of retribution and deterrence...are immaterial. The offender who has become a patient is not kept on any kind of leash by the court.

Nor does the Ministry of Justice monitor the subsequent history of patients sentenced to hospital under s. 37 if restrictions are not also imposed under s. 41 (Home Office Research, Development and Statistics Directorate, 2005: 26). The criteria for making an order under s. 37 are substantially the same as for civil confinement under s. 3, and psychiatrists, hospital managers, and tribunals have similar powers to discharge hospital order patients as apply to patients detained under Part II of the MHA 1983 (see Chapter 11, 11.3).

Unrestricted hospital orders were made on 459 occasions in 2011–12, down from 493 in 2010–11. There were 456 such orders made in 2009–10, 392 in 2008–09 and 352 in 2007–08 (NHS Information Centre, 2012, table 1). By contrast, 522 hospital orders coupled with restriction orders were made in 2011–12 (NHS Information Centre, 2012, table 1). The published data no longer includes information about the offence committed. In 2004, the last year for which such data is available, 215 had been convicted of a violent offence, including 19 convictions for homicide other than murder (Home Office Research, Development and Statistics Directorate, 2005:Table 18: it is not possible to make an unrestricted hospital order in respect of a conviction of murder: s. 37(1)). Of the rest, 124 had been convicted of criminal damage including arson. A further 37 had been convicted of a sexual offence. A similar number had been convicted of burglary (40), robbery (44), or for theft or handling (40), 62 had been convicted of other indictable offences, and 94 of summary offences (Home Office Research, Development and Statistics Directorate, 2005: Table 18).

Although information on the average period spent by hospital-order patients in hospital is hard to come by, it is unlikely that all are discharged within the first six months following the making of the order by the court. There is much else we do not know about the making of hospital orders: for example, which courts make the orders in question, or whether there are significant regional variations in orders made as a percentage of total convictions.

The statistics do, nevertheless, indicate that, although, as might be expected, a good number of persons in respect of whom hospital orders are made have been convicted of an offence with an element of actual or potential dangerousness to others, the range of offences in respect of which hospital orders are made is relatively broad. This suggests that the courts do see the order as a therapeutic response, and its use is not linked to the offence but the need for hospital treatment. In *R v Paul Lee S* [2001] EWCA Crim 743, the Court of Appeal held that the making of a hospital order does not depend on demonstrating any link between the offending behaviour and the disorder, and even where there is such a link a hospital order need not be made for reasons to do with risk to the public or the culpability of the offender (*R v Drew* [2003] UKHL 25, [2003] 1 WLR 1213, [2003] 4 All ER 557; *R v Dass* [2009] EWCA Crim 1208, paras. 46–47). Each case will turn to a large degree on its own facts.

Before making a hospital order, the court must be satisfied, on the written or oral evidence of two doctors, one of whom must be approved (MHA 1983, s. 54(1)), that the defendant is suffering from mental disorder of a nature or degree that makes it appropriate for him or her to be detained in a hospital for treatment, and that appropriate treatment is available (MHA 1983, s. 37(2)(a)(i)). There have long been concerns about the treatability of persons diagnosed as suffering from psychopathic disorder or an anti-social personality disorder or a similar personality disorder, with the result that many such persons have received a prison sentence rather than a hospital order. It was this perceived problem with the operation of s. 37 that provided the initial impetus to introduce in 1997 what are now known as 'hospital and limitation directions' (see further at 8.4.3), and, later, was part of the thinking behind the removal of the subcategories of mental disorder from the statutory definition and the replacement by the concept of 'appropriate treatment' of the old 'treatability' requirement by the MHA 2007. This does not, however, seem to have had any noticeable impact on the rate at which hospital orders have subsequently been made, with or without restrictions.

Similarly, a court may not make a guardianship order under s. 37 unless the court is satisfied that an LSSA or other suitable person is willing to act as guardian (s. 37(6)). Section 39 gives the court powers to require (s. 39(1)) from the relevant CCG or local health board (which by default will be that which has responsibility for the area in which the defendant lived or last lived, but may also be any other as in the court's view is appropriate: s. 39(1)), information as to the availability of hospital accommodation, and s. 39A contains similar provision by which the court can require the relevant LSSA to provide information about the provision for guardianship in its area.

As with orders made under ss. 35 or 36, an order under s. 37 'shall not be made' unless the court is provided with evidence (which may be written or oral) from the doctor who will be in charge of the patient's treatment (the 'approved clinician' or AC), or from the managers of the intended recipient hospital, that arrangements are in train for the admission of the defendant within 28 days of the making of the order, and that, if admission cannot occur immediately, that there is a suitable place of safety in which the defendant can be detained in the meantime (s. 37(4)). A 'place of safety' for these purposes is any police station, prison, remand centre, or hospital willing to receive the patient (s. 55(1)). If a hospital order is made under s. 37, s. 40(1) gives authority for the defendant to be conveyed to and detained in the hospital named in the order by any police officer, AMHP, or 'other person directed to do so by the court'. If a guardianship order is made under that section, a guardian will be appointed with the same powers as provided to the guardian of a patient by ss. 7 and 8 of the MHA 1983 (see Chapter 10, 10.3), which means that that person (or, more likely, LSSA) has authority to require the person subject to the order to reside in a particular location.

In either case, but in practice of most concern in relation to hospital orders, a problem may arise if, after an order has been made and the assurance of a hospital place has been given, that place is then withdrawn. The 28-day limit is absolute, and if the patient is not in the allocated hospital accommodation within that time, the s. 37 order provides no lawful basis for the subsequent admission of that patient into hospital (*R v Nottingham Healthcare NHS Trust, ex parte B* [2008] EWCA Civ 1354; [2009] 2 All ER 792). In such a situation, the Justice Secretary may, but not must, direct, before the expiry of the 28-day period, that the patient be admitted to another specified hospital (s. 37(5)), or the sentencing court may substitute a sentence under s. 155 of the Powers of Criminal Courts Act 2000 or s. 142 of the Magistrates' Courts Act 1980. Section 155(1) of the Powers of Criminal Courts Act 2000 requires a Crown Court to exercise this power within 56 days of the original sentence, but in order to ensure that there is no lapse in the authority to detain the patient, the 28-day limit in ss. 37(4) and 40(1) of the MHA 1983 will have to be complied with.

There has been an acknowledged problem, since at least the mid-1970s, of hospitals refusing to take some hospital order patients (see *R v Officer* (1976) *The Times*, 20 February; *R v Gordon* (1981) 3 Cr App R(S) 352 (HC); *R v Harding* (1983) *The Times*, 15 June (CA)), which does not appear to have abated, because despite the subsequent expansion in medium-secure provision, the pressure on beds both in medium-security and high-security accommodation remains high (see Chapter 2, 2.2.1). In *R v Galfetti* [2002] EWCA Crim 1916, the defendant had been convicted and the court wished to make a hospital order, but it took nine months before a bed could be found, at which time the hospital order was eventually made. The Court of Appeal, although finding this to be an 'excessive delay' (at para. 43), held that there was no breach of any of Arts. 3, 5, 6 or 8 of the ECHR in the delay itself, because the court is able to monitor the delay and take action if required, thus satisfying the 'reasonable time' requirement of Art. 6 (para. 48). Nor was there any breach of an ECHR right in activating the order so long after it had originally been made, because there was evidence before the court when the order was finally made that justified its making, and the defendant had been transferred to hospital where he had received appropriate treatment in the meantime (para. 49).

The court did say, however, that if a hospital bed cannot be located within an appropriate time, the sentencing court may have to consider the use of another disposal (per May LJ at para. 48). The court bemoaned the lack of powers available to it to secure a hospital bed with promptitude, and drew attention to the fact there is no mechanism to enable a person in Galfetti's position to appeal against an order adjourning his sentence indefinitely. In *Brand* v *The Netherlands* [2001] Hudoc reference REF00006531, the Court declared inadmissible the argument based on Art. 3, of a person held in prison awaiting the availability of a hospital bed, because he had, on the facts, not suffered adversely or been denied treatment whilst in prison, and thus could not be said to have suffered inhumane or degrading treatment. The Court distinguished the decision in *Aerts* v *Belgium* (2000) 29 EHRR 50, in which it had unanimously found breaches of Art. 5(1)(e) when a defendant sentenced to hospital had waited for seven months in *unsuitable* surroundings in prison for a hospital bed to become available.

In addition to the requirements of s. 37(2)(a) of the MHA 1983 being met, s. 37(2)(b) provides that before a court may make a hospital order it must be 'of the opinion, having regard to all the circumstances including the nature of the offence and the character and antecedents of the offender, and to the other available methods of dealing with him' that a hospital order is the most suitable disposal. In *Birch*, the Court of Appeal suggested the following order of deliberations. First, a sentencing court should decide, on normal sentencing principles, whether the defendant should be compulsorily detained or whether some form of community-based sanction such as probation with treatment-related conditions would be more appropriate. This is known as the 'custody threshold'.

If it is decided that detention is required, the second question is whether the conditions contained in s. 37 are satisfied and, if so, whether the making of such an order is preferable to the imposition of a prison sentence. According to the court in *Birch*, there are only two reasons for sending a mentally disordered person in respect of whom the conditions in s. 37 are satisfied to prison: (1) 'the offender is dangerous and no suitable secure accommodation is available' and; (2) where 'notwithstanding the offender's mental disorder there was an element of culpability in the offence which merits punishment' (Mustill LJ at 215). In short, the court must decide whether the offender perpetuated a crime primarily 'of illness' or 'of wickedness' (Mustill LJ at 215).

The thrust of the court's approach, though, was in favour of diversion from prison, Mustill LJ holding that 'even where there is culpability, the right way to deal with a dangerous and disordered person is to make an order under section 37 and 41' (s. 41 is considered at 8.4.2), and that it is inappropriate to pass a prison sentence out of a concern that the defendant will be released earlier from hospital than would be the case if sent to prison. In this, the Court of Appeal in *Birch* was following its own earlier authorities, *R* v *Howell* (1985) 7 Cr App R (S) 360 and *R* v *Mbatha* (1985) 7 Cr App R (S) 373, which are to the same effect. *Birch* has subsequently been followed on many occasions, the Court of Appeal consistently taking an approach that holds, in essence, that if the conditions

for a hospital order are made out, and there is a bed available, then, subject to considerations of security and culpability, that is the course that the court should ordinarily take.

In cases involving a successful appeal against the passing of a prison sentence, it is
often the case that an order under s. 41 (which is focused on questions of culpability
and risk) is made alongside the s. 37 order. But if the Court of Appeal is satisfied that
the defendant has little culpability and does not pose a danger to the public, an order
under s. 37 alone will be substituted for a prison sentence, recent examples of which
include *R v Heinz* [2010] EWCA Crim 3121; *R v Lavender* [2012] EWCA Crim 1179;
and *R v Searles* [2012] EWCA Crim 2685 (where the Court of Appeal was so satisfied even though S's crime was robbery involving a degree of violence). The Court of
Appeal may also remove s. 41 restrictions from a s. 37 order on appeal (see *R v Cooper*
[2009] EWCA Crim 2646; *R v Taher Ahmed Chowdhury* [2011] EWCA Crim 936; for
unsuccessful appeals, see, for example, *R v Anderson* [2009] EWCA Crim 405; *R v Steele*
[2010] EWCA Crim 605; *R v Chiles* [2012] EWCA Crim 196). Of course, most of the
hospital orders that are imposed without restrictions are made at first instance, and in
most cases there is no appeal.

8.4.2 Restriction orders: s. 41

8.4.2.1 The making of a restriction order

A restriction order will be of indefinite duration and is the equivalent in mental health
law to the life sentence in penal law. As a serious deprivation of liberty, an order under
s. 41 cannot be made by a magistrates' court (MHA 1983, s. 41(1)), although that court
may commit to the Crown Court if of the view that a hospital order, coupled with a
restriction order, is required (ss. 43, 44). The profile of offending of those given a hospital order with restrictions leans more noticeably towards the more serious offences than
that of those given hospital orders without restrictions. In *Birch*, Mustill LJ explained (at
211) the effect of a 'restriction order' being added to a hospital order:

> No longer is the offender regarded simply as a patient whose interests are para-
> mount . . . Instead, the interests of public safety are regarded by transferring the responsibil-
> ity for discharge from the responsible medical officer and the hospital . . . to the Secretary of
> State and the Mental Health Review Tribunal. A patient who has been subject to a restric-
> tion order is likely to be detained in hospital for much longer than one who is not, and will
> have fewer opportunities for leave of absence.

Even when a restriction order patient leaves hospital, it is overwhelmingly likely that
that discharge will be conditional in the first instance, and a conditionally discharged
restriction order patient remains liable to recall to hospital (see Chapter 11, 11.3.2).
A hospital order made under a s. 37 order, coupled with a restriction order made under
s. 41, can therefore be understood as the conceptual intersection between treatment
and punishment or protective custody. This option is designed to accommodate those
who are both 'mad' and 'bad', or dangerous.

This can be a fine line at the best of times, and the tendency of the higher courts has
been to emphasise that the balance between therapeutic and punitive objectives, and

consequences which flow from that initial choice, such as whether it is appropriate that a defendant be placed in the mental health system (from which discharge is governed, ultimately, be medical criteria) or the penal system (where the parole focuses much more on questions of risk) is 'a matter to which sentencing judges and appellate courts should try to give appropriate weight' (Lord Bingham, expressing the unanimous view of the House of Lords in R v Drew [2003] UKHL 25 at para. 22). However, Lord Bingham proceeded then to point out that the policy of diversion which ss. 37 and 41 embody was not designed merely for the benefit of those diverted: 'The difficulties caused to prison managements by the presence and behaviour of those who are subject to serious mental disorder are, however, notorious, and we would need to be persuaded that any significant change in the prevailing practice was desirable.'

Where the alternative to making orders under the MHA 1983 is a fairly short prison sentence, there may be little dispute that orders under ss. 37 and 41 are to be preferred (see for example R v Walton [2010] EWCA Crim 2255), but the implications of Drew are that even in a situation where a serious offence has been committed and the sentencing court would otherwise impose a long sentence or discretionary life sentence on the offender, if the criteria for detention under ss. 37 and 41 are made out, it is those orders which should be imposed (R v Mitchell (1997) 1 Cr App R (S) 90 (CA); R v Hutchinson (1997) 2 Cr App R (S) 60 (CA)). If this is not done at the time the Court of Appeal may substitute orders under the MHA 1983 for a life sentence if new evidence subsequently comes to light that the defendant was disordered to the extent required by the criteria for those orders at the times of the offence or trial (R v Da Silva (1994) 15 Cr App R(S) 296; R v Hughes [2010] EWCA Crim 1026; R v O [2011] EWCA Crim 376; R v Channer [2012] EWCA Crim 1667; R v Fletcher [2012] EWCA Crim 2777). This can be so, even if the reason that evidence of the defendant's mental disorder was not available at the time of trial was because of the defendant's refusal to co-operate with any attempt to undertake a pre-trial psychiatric assessment of him (R v Shulman [2010] EWCA Crim 1034).

If there is substantial culpability, however, the presence of mental disorder, and the detrimental effect of a prison rather than a hospital environment, will not save the defendant from being given a discretionary life sentence rather than being made subject to hospital and restriction orders, even though he may well remain more dangerous than would otherwise be the case. This was the decision in Walsh v R [2011] EWCA Crim 73, the Court of Appeal emphasising both the defendant's culpability and the 'important factor' of 'public confidence in the approach of the court' (para. 14) when dismissing W's appeal against a discretionary life sentence. Similar comments were made in R v Dass [2009] EWCA Crim 1208 (para. 46). A prison sentence is also more likely if the evidence is that the offending behaviour was not linked to the defendant's mental disorder (R v Nafei [2004] EWCA Crim 3238, [2005] 1 Cr App R (S) 24, distinguishing Birch on this basis).

These questions of policy can only arise, however, if the criteria for the making of an order under s. 41 are satisfied; and they arise precisely because those criteria are similar to those which determine whether a prison sentence should be imposed. A s. 41 order is not freestanding, but must be attached to a s. 37 order. The requirements of s. 37 must therefore be met as a prerequisite to the making of a s. 41 order. In addition, a s. 41 order can only be made where the court is of the view, given the nature of the offence, the history and antecedents of the offender, and the risk of reoffending (s.41(1)), that 'it is necessary for the protection of the public from serious harm'. This question must be addressed explicitly by the sentencing court (*R v Czarnota* [2002] EWCA Crim 785).

The meaning of 'serious harm' was considered in *Birch*. Mustill LJ held that 'harm' here is 'not limited to personal injury. Nor need it relate to the public in general' (213). The condition may be met where there is a risk of serious harm to 'a category of persons, or even a single person...Nevertheless, the potential harm must be serious, and a high possibility of a recurrence of minor offences will no(t)...suffice' (213). The court overruled earlier cases where orders had been made on this basis, but did approve the case of *R v Khan* (1987) 9 Cr App R (S) 455, in which, although the offences in question were fairly minor (reckless driving), the risk that was thereby posed to the public was serious.

In *R v Cowan* [2004] EWCA Crim 3081, hospital and restriction orders had been made following C's conviction for common assault. Although the harm caused in that case was fairly minor, hence the offence charged, it was in the view of the sentencing judge merely good fortune that C's victims had not sustained greater injuries. The Court of Appeal upheld the first instance decision, accepting that, although the case was marginal, it was 'on the side of the margin calling for a restriction order' (Douglas Brown J at para. 10). In *R v Pemberton* (1996) 24 June, unreported (CA) an appeal was allowed against the making of a s. 41 order because the trial judge had considered there to be a 'serious risk' of harm. The Court of Appeal, citing *Birch*, pointed out that it is the potential harm and not the risk of its occurrence that must be serious. It is clear that harm includes psychological harm (*R v Macrow* [2004] EWCA Crim 1159). A court may conclude that there is such a risk even if the defendant has no history of violence, if the medical evidence supports that conclusion (*R v Kamara* [2002] EWCA Crim 1559). Nevertheless, as Street (1998: 14) found, in his analysis of all restriction orders made in 1992 and 1993, there do appear to be cases, which are not appealed, in which a s. 41 order has been made although 'the risk of serious future harm was not readily apparent'.

In arriving at its decision, s. 41(2) requires that the court hear oral evidence from at least one of the doctors who have already given evidence about the suitability of a s. 37 order, and although this need not as a matter of law be a s. 12 approved doctor it should, as a matter of good practice, be a doctor on the staff of the hospital at which the defendant will be detained if the order is made (*R v Blackwood* (1974) 59 Cr App R (S) (CA)). As Akinkunmi and Murray (1997: 55) have noted, however, this is not always easily possible. For example, staff at the Bentham Unit (a specialised unit designed to accept persons remanded to hospital by a court under ss. 35 and 36) have found that a problem has arisen on sentencing subsequent to a period of remand, because only they have the expert medical knowledge of the patient that the court needs to decide whether or not a hospital order should be made but they do not intend to accept a patient on a long-term basis under a hospital order.

It is the responsibility of this doctor or doctors (it is unusual in practice for a sentencing court to hear only the evidence of one doctor) to advise the court on the question of risk. Although risk assessment is a technical matter, Street found that 'psychiatrists largely took the straightforward view that those offenders who committed the most serious offences were the most likely to pose a risk to others in the future' (1998: 24). Recommendations to the court come in various shades, from a firm recommendation that a restriction order is required, through to a recommendation that a hospital order be made with no opinion expressed about a restriction order, although it is rare for psychiatrists who recommend a hospital order to oppose positively the making of a restriction order. In a number of cases, there will be no express recommendation, because some psychiatrists feel that it is not the role of the doctor to become too closely associated with the sentencing process. But in the majority—70 per cent—of cases in which a restriction order is made, there had been a preponderance of medical evidence to the effect that the defendant did pose a risk of significant harm to others, even if there was not always a positive recommendation that a s. 41 order be made (Street, 1998: 28).

This still means, however, that 30 per cent of restriction orders are made even though there is no consensus amongst medical witnesses that the defendant poses a significant risk. As the facts of *Birch* demonstrate, medical evidence does not need to be followed by the sentencing judge. In that case, three approved doctors gave evidence that the defendant who, acting under diminished responsibility as a result of her mental disorder, had killed her husband, did not present a danger of significant harm to the public or any individual. Nevertheless, the trial judge made a restriction order and his decision was upheld by the Court of Appeal, where it was pointed out that, under the terms of s. 41, unlike those of s. 37, the trial judge need not follow any medical recommendations that are made. The decision, ultimately, is one for the court.

The Court of Appeal, in the later case of *R v Reynolds* [1999] 2 Cr App R (S) 5, made comments that might be seen to contradict this: 'On hearing the evidence there must be at least some basis upon which the doctor is able to say, and persuade the court, that a restriction order is appropriate.' But we do not regard these comments as incompatible with *Birch*: the judge is entitled to make his or her own decision, which may depart from the medical views and recommendations expressed before the court, but the judge's reasons cannot be arbitrary: as was said by the Court of Appeal in *R v Haile* [2009] EWCA Crim 1996 at para. 12 (see also *R v Anderson* [2009] EWCA Crim 405; *R v Parkin* [2012] EWCA Crim 856), for such a decision to survive appeal, the judge's reasons for doing so must be 'persuasive'. In *Birch*, the Court of Appeal approved, as good law under the MHA 1983, the dicta of Parker CJ in *R v Gardiner* (1967) 51 Cr App R 187 that, for crimes of violence, particularly where there is a prior history of such offending, or of mental disorder manifesting as violence, 'there must be compelling reasons to explain why a restriction order should not be made'.

Each case, however, must be decided on its own circumstances, including the seriousness of the offence, the medical evidence and prognosis, and any other relevant factors. It would seem to follow that, because there is a general discretion to ignore medical advice in the interests of public safety, a decision to add a restriction order will be harder to appeal than the making (or not making) of a s. 37 order in the first place, and indeed this is generally the case. If there is a medical recommendation in favour of s. 41, an order can be made even though some, or even the preponderance, of medical opinion is against it (see, for example, *R* v *IS* [2004] EWCA Crim 957, *R* v *Jones* 2000 WL 976077 and *R* v *Daniel O* 2001 WL 1476329).

Even when there are no medical recommendations in favour of s. 41, the court may, if it is reasonable to do so, make an order. For example, in *R* v *Goode* [2002] EWCA Crim 1698, four doctors were unanimous in their view that a s. 37 order alone was required, and that there was no risk of reoffending. The judge nevertheless made a s. 41 order, and that decision was upheld by the Court of Appeal, because there was evidence from which it was reasonable for the court to conclude that there was a low risk of serious reoffending. In an unusual case, *R* v *Martin* 2000 WL 877792, the defendant, already detained in hospital under s. 37, was sentenced to ss. 37/41, having been convicted of criminal damage for setting fire to a mattress in the hospital. He appealed against the sentence because he wished to leave the hospital and preferred the option of prison. As the first instance judge had followed medical advice as to the desirability of a s. 41 order, the appeal was held to be without substance.

The Court of Appeal has, however, made plain that it will allow an appeal and rescind a s. 41 order if the trial court falls into error on the law (*Pemberton*), if the judge bases the decision on his or her own views in contradiction of the medical evidence (*R* v *Daniel F George R* 2000 WL 1544620, in which the judges' views about the effects of long-term cannabis use were found to have coloured his judgment) or, as in *R* v *Slater* (1996) 7 October, unreported, and *R* v *St Leonce* [2004] EWCA Crim 1154, where the Court of Appeal was satisfied that there had not, in fact, been a serious risk of harm if the order had not been made. The court has also been prepared to allow an appeal when, on the evidence then available, a s. 41 order was properly made at first instance but has subsequently been shown to have been unwarranted in reports ordered by the appeal court (*R* v *Maria TK* [2001] EWCA Crim 400; *R* v *Hughes* [2010] EWCA Crim 1026) or because the restrictions that attend s. 41 impact negatively on the treatment plan for the defendant whilst in hospital (*R* v *Ayan M* 2000 WL 544040, a case in which the RC wished to use leave of absence as part of the defendant's care plan, which intention would have been hindered if a restriction order had been made, because of the powers given to the Justice Secretary (see Chapter 10, 10.2.2) to veto leave of absence if a restriction order is made: see also *R* v *Osker* [2010] EWCA Crim 955).

As already mentioned, 522 restriction orders were made by a court in 2011–12. This is up drastically from the 156 made in 1991 (Home Office Research, Development and Statistics Directorate, 2002: Table 3) and the 198 made in 2003, and although 2003 was a low point, no more than 250 restriction orders were made in the years before then (Home Office Research, Development and Statistics Directorate, 2005: Table 3). Since 2003, numbers have in percentage terms risen faster than the prison population. The highest number of transfers in recent years was in 2008–09, when 565 orders were made.

Until the four sub-categories of mental disorder were removed by the MHA 2007, annual data published by the Ministry of Justice included information about the type of disorder with which those sentenced to ss. 37 and 41 were diagnosed. Data for 2007, published in 2009, showed that of all the 333 admissions of patients subject to restrictions imposed by a court in 2007 the vast majority—259—were diagnosed as suffering from mental illness, and a further 32 had a mental illness coupled with another disorder. Numbers for psychopathic disorder, mental impairment, and severe mental impairment were 32, 23, and 1 respectively, and three defendants had a dual diagnosis of mental impairment and psychopathic disorder (Ministry of Justice, 2009: Table 4).

As with hospital orders, both property offences and offences of violence feature in the statistics, although the latter are more prominently represented here, with 35 offences of manslaughter and 93 of 'other violence' amongst the 288. There were 19 restriction orders made following conviction of a sexual offence and 43 following conviction for arson. There were 39 restriction orders following property offences of various kinds, and 59 orders were made following a conviction for other offences, which would no doubt include some of a minor nature (Home Office Research, Development and Statistics Directorate, 2005: table 5).

Street (1998) found that, apart from restriction order patients being more likely to have committed a dangerous offence and more likely to have, or likely to have more, previous convictions than hospital order patients, there was very little to distinguish the two groups in terms of age, sex, or age at first conviction. The majority of all patients are in the 21–39 years age range (Ministry of Justice, 2012: table A6.3), and 90 per cent were male, being first convicted at around twenty years of age (Street, 1998: 31). *Within* the group of restriction-order patients, however, there were significant variables. Men were much more likely to be sentenced to a restriction order than women, but women were twice as likely as men to have a main diagnosis of psychopathic disorder, and less likely to be diagnosed as mentally ill (which echoes the finding of Milne and Milne, 1995). Black defendants were nearly all (96 per cent) diagnosed as mentally ill, compared with 69 per cent of white defendants (Street 1998: 10). Other research has found a wide discrepancy in the frequency with which black defendants have a diagnosis of schizophrenia. In general terms, Street found a significant over-representation of black African or Caribbean people (21 per cent of those given a restriction order) compared with the population as a whole (at around 2 per cent). The reasons for this are complex and disputed, and the arguments have been rehearsed at various points throughout this text. Street did find that white defendants made subject to a restriction order were less likely than black defendants to have committed a crime of violence, at 75 per cent compared with 85 per cent, although this hardly explains the width of the discrepancies that exist; other studies, such as that carried out by Shubsachs *et al.* (1995) at Rampton found no significant differences on a number of indicators, including offence.

In a helpful although now quite dated review of the literature and issues, Boast and Chesterman (1995) concluded that the high incidence of black people at the deep end of mental health services represents the outcome of social disadvantage, and both direct and indirect discrimination at various decision-making points 'lower down' the system, from the diagnosis of disorder to the perception of the police and the courts of the (perceived) relation between ethnicity, dangerousness, and risk. Equally depressing statistics, however, cut across barriers of race. Street (1998: 12) found that the typical recipient of a restriction order is long-term unemployed (90 per cent of all orders made in 1992 and 1993), long-term single (68 per cent) and, with the exception of mentally impaired persons, a high percentage (41 per cent) lived alone. Around 20 per cent, rising to almost 40 per cent of mentally impaired defendants, lived in hostels, bed and breakfast establishments, or were homeless. Restriction orders, in short, are overwhelmingly made in respect of some of the most economically and socially disadvantaged in society.

8.4.2.2 The nature of the restrictions and the restricted patient regime

Until 1997, there was no legal requirement that a s. 41 patient be held in secure accommodation such as a special hospital, although the situation now is that the court may specify not only the hospital but also the unit within the hospital in which the subject of the order is to be detained (Crime (Sentences) Act 1997, s. 47(1)). Only a small number of restriction order patients—92 in 2010—begin their time in hospital in one of the three high security hospitals. The vast majority—1,453 in 2010—are received into conditions of lesser security (Ministry of Justice, 2011: table 10.4). It is not only the patient who is subject to restrictions: the clinical freedom of the RC is curtailed by a restriction order (Baker, 1992: 32).

As such the restriction order is one of the best examples of the legal institutionalisation of a hierarchy of concerns that places control above treatment. The restrictions are set out in s. 41(3) of the MHA 1983, and s. 41(3)(a) provides that 'none of the provisions of Part II of this Act relating to the duration, renewal and expiration of authority for the detention of patients shall apply'. The patient cannot be given leave of absence, or be transferred or discharged, by the RC without the consent of the Justice Secretary (s. 41(3)(c)). If leave of absence is granted the patient can be recalled to hospital at any time by the Justice Secretary (s. 41(3)(d)). These restrictions of course impact significantly, too, on the patient, and in addition there can be no application to a tribunal except in circumstances specified (s. 41(3)(b): see further Chapter 11, 11.4.2.1.2).

Whilst a restriction order is still in effect, any hospital order will also continue (s. 41(4)), although the bringing to an end of a restriction order (by the Justice Secretary or a tribunal) does not mean that a patient is no longer liable to be detained. Instead, such a patient is treated as though on a s. 37 order from the date of the cessation of the restriction order by virtue of s. 41(5), known as a 'notional s. 37', a term which is also applied to a prisoner transferred from prison to hospital under s. 47 of the MHA 1983 without restrictions (see 8.5; and Mental Health Act Commission, 2005: paras. 5.66–5.70 for further discussion).

It is perhaps misleading, however, to explain the effect of a restriction order simply in terms of a list of restrictions on discharge, leave, or transfer. Restricted patients are subject to ongoing monitoring by the Mental Health Casework Section (MHCS) in the Ministry of Justice, by way of mandatory annual reports that must be made to the MHCS by each patient's RC (s. 41(6)); and the MHCS and the Secretary of State tend towards caution in their attitude to the release of restriction order patients. A restricted patient will feel the state breathing down his or her neck much more keenly than other detained patients. Moreover, the effects of a restriction order continue after release from hospital, because virtually all restricted patients are, in the first instance, discharged conditionally, and unless and until discharge is made absolute, are liable to recall to hospital (see Chapter 11, 11.3).

The restricted patient regime does not only apply to those sentenced to a restriction order by a court, but also includes most patients transferred to hospital from prison, and restrictions can also be attached to those hospitalised after having been found unfit to be tried, and those found not guilty by reason of insanity. The total number of restricted patients has risen continually year on year for well over a decade. On 31 December 2011, 4,347 restricted patients were detained in hospital (Ministry of Justice 2012: table A6.1), compared to 3,601 in 2006 and 2,858 in 2000 (Ministry of Justice 2012: table A6.1). Many can expect to spend long periods in hospital before being considered for release: of the 3,282 restricted patients detained on 31 December 2004 (the last year for which such data is provided) 83 had been in hospital for more than 30 years, 200 for between 20 and 30 years, 593 for between 10 and 20 years, 643 between five and ten years, 639 between two and five years and 927 (including 192 patients on remand) less than two years (Home Office Research, Development and Statistics Directorate, 2005: Table 15). Of those detained for long periods, a numerically small, but statistically significant, number of patients with psychopathic disorder—33 out of a total of 412—had been detained for more than 30 years. By way of comparison, 30 mentally ill patients had been detained as long, but this was out of a total of 1,970 (2005: Table 15). Another 125 psychopathically disordered patients had been detained for between 10 and 20 years, and 48 for between 20 and 30 years.

Yet what is more remarkable is that many patients in all disorder categories spend a considerable number of years in hospital. It is clear that a restriction order is by no means a 'soft option' compared with imprisonment, at least in terms of time served. Although the more recent data does not give this detail about length of stay, we do know that of the 4,347 restricted patients detained on 31 December 2011, 2,087 were aged 21–39, 328 were aged 60 or older, and 1,817 were aged 40–49 (Ministry of Justice, 2012: table A6.3). This seems to suggest, given that most offences are committed by those in the younger age bracket, that a similar pattern of length of stay continues to be the case, although there is evidence that for some mentally disordered offenders, offending behaviour is life-long (O'Sullivan and Chesterman, 2007).

8.4.3 Hospital and limitation directions

Under the regime contained in Part III of the MHA 1983, as initially enacted, a patient sentenced to hospital could not be transferred to prison at a later date. Although s. 38 provides for interim hospital orders (see further discussion elsewhere in this section), this provision, as the Court of Appeal noted in *Birch*, has not been popular with sentencers. There were calls for a number of years for greater flexibility to be crafted into the system. In addition, there has long been concern about the particular problem of psychopathically disordered offenders, in the rather awkward language of the pre-2007 law, which in reality pertains to a broader group of personality disordered offenders including, but not limited to, those diagnosed with a severe and anti-social personality disorder (SAPD), given the dubious treatability of this condition, making it unclear that a hospital order under s. 37, rather than a prison sentence, was appropriate.

In such cases, in the years after 1983, the accused person would, on conviction, receive a prison sentence, and although there is the possibility of transfer to hospital from prison, this is not a realistic prospect for the majority of offenders, Moreover, when transfer does occur, it may be late into the sentence of imprisonment, one signifi-cant reason for which is that 'it is only when a prisoner reaches his tariff that he can be considered for admission for psychiatric rehabilitation' (*R v House* [2007] EWCA Crim 2559), and so unless a prisoner is floridly mentally disordered its presence may not be detected until late in his or her sentence. One consequence of this is that the prisoner following transfer continues to be detained in a hospital after the expiry of the sentence given, which raises its own set of ethical and legal problems. Conversely, in some cases, ss. 37/41 orders have been made, only for those charged with treating the subject of the order to discover that he or she is not, in fact, treatable, with the consequence that the function of hospitalisation, in practice, is purely custodial.

Sentencing courts have also sometimes displayed concern that a defendant sentenced to hospital may be released inappropriately early. Hospital orders were (and still are) rarely made in cases involving personality disorders. In 2007, the last year such stat-istics were collected—the sub-categories of mental disorder having been abolished by s. 1, MHA 2007—only 23 patients diagnosed as psychopathic were admitted to a hos-pital under ss. 37 and 41, compared with 259 mentally ill offenders (Ministry of Justice, 2009: Table 8); a ratio which had been consistent for many years. Psychopathically dis-ordered offenders are also more likely to be recalled after discharge than are other cat-egories of mentally disordered offenders. In practice, most psychopathically disordered offenders are given a punitive disposal that frequently means that there is little further involvement by the mental health services, during or after custody, until, in those few cases where it does, disaster strikes.

The White Paper, *Protecting the Public* (Home Office, 1996) and an ensuing con-sultation document (Department of Health and Home Office, 1996) signalled govern-mental acceptance of, at least some version of, these arguments, and s. 6 of the Crime (Sentences) Act (C(S)A) 1997 inserted new sections—ss. 45A and 45B—into the MHA 1983, which provide for 'hospital and limitation directions' to be made by a sentencing court. Now, a court is not faced with a stark choice between sending a defendant either to prison or to hospital, but may instead pass a sentence of imprisonment, but direct that the disposal is initially to a hospital, but with the reassurance that, if hospitalisa-tion proves unsuccessful or successful, so that in either case no further treatment is intended, the prison sentence passed can be activated. A 'hospital direction' is defined in s. 45A(3)(a) as 'a direction that, instead of being removed to and detained in a prison, the offender may be removed to and detained in such hospital as may be specified in the direction'.

A hospital direction can only be made following the conviction of the defendant in a Crown Court for a crime other than murder (s. 45A(1)), and in circumstances in which the court considered making a hospital order under s. 37 but decided instead to impose a sentence of imprisonment (s. 45A(1)(b)). Section 45A, in subsection (3)(b) also introduced the 'limitation direction', which is 'a direction that the offender be subject to the special restrictions set out in s. 41'. There is no scope to make a hospital direction without also making a limitation direction.

Confusingly, however, the conditions that must be met before a hospital direction can be made are the same as those relevant to the making of a hospital order under s. 37. As under that section, a court contemplating making a hospital direction must be satisfied on the written or oral evidence of two doctors (at least one of whom must be 'approved': s. 54(1)) that the defendant (i) is suffering from mental disorder of a nature or degree that (ii) makes it appropriate for him to be detained in a hospital for medical treatment (s. 45A(2)(a), (b)) and (iii) that 'appropriate medical treatment is available for him' (s. 45A(2)(c)). Section 45A(4) requires the court to hear oral evidence from at least one of the two doctors who gave evidence under subsection (2) before making the two directions, but as the wording of s. 45A(4) is similar to that of s. 41(2) (see 8.4.2.1), it would seem clear that, as under that section, the final decision is for the court.

One difference between the hospital and limitation directions and hospital and restriction orders when the former were first introduced was that hospital and limitation directions could only be made in respect of offenders suffering from psychopathic disorder. Although there was a certain logic to this, in that it was this group of offenders who, as explained, were thought most likely to be imprisoned rather than made subject to a hospital order, it seems that the limitation was in fact based more on financial and resource considerations (Eastman and Peay, 1998: 98). In addition, although the 1996 consultation document explained that a hospital direction and limitation direction would be appropriate where the outcome of treatment was uncertain, a treatability requirement was included in the criteria for the making of hospital and limitation directions, which rather undermined this rationale.

This mismatch between a focus on patients of uncertain treatability and a requirement that appropriate treatment be available may well go some way towards explaining the minimal use made of hospital and limitation directions in the years after their introduction. Hospital and limitation directions were made on only three occasions in 2000 and 2001 (Home Office Research, Development and Statistics Directorate, 2002: Table 4), only twice in 2004 (Home Office Research, Development and Statistics Directorate, 2005: Table 4), and not at all in 2004–05 (Government Statistical Service, 2006: para. 5.13). By then, the appellate courts had begun to voice dissatisfaction with the limited constituency eligible for consideration for hospital and limitation directions. In *Drew*, Lord Bingham (para. 21) expressed the 'hope that further thought may be given to exercise of the power conferred by section 45A(10)' (now repealed) which gave the Secretary of State powers to extend the scope of hospital and limitation directions, and the Court of Appeal added its voice in *R v IA* [2006] Cr App R (S) 91 and *R v Staines* [2006] EWCA Crim 15.

The MHA 2007 included the asked-for reform. Hospital and limitation directions are now available in respect of a person suffering from mental disorder rather than only a person suffering from the species of mental disorder known to the pre-2007 Act law as psychopathy. The effect of this is to narrow even further the difference between hospital and restriction orders and hospital and limitation directions, which now have the same criteria and apply to the same constituency of offenders. However, the government view, according to the consultation document which preceded the introduction of the hybrid order, was that there were two distinct situations in which hospital and limitation directions might properly be made when a hospital order, even with restrictions attached, is felt to be inappropriate. The first is when it is not clear that the making of a hospital order, with or without restrictions, would 'sufficiently address the risk to the public posed by the defendant' (Department of Health and Home Office, 1996: para. 1.4).

This is because, on discharge from hospital, a patient detained on a s. 37 order, even one with restrictions attached, has to be discharged into the community. Although discharge is almost always conditional in the case of restricted patients, and even though there is a certain logic in the discharge of patients from hospital who have apparently responded successfully to treatment or are found not to be treatable, it was thought that this prospect might incline sentencers into opting for the perceived safer option of imprisonment, with release controlled by a parole board and the focus very much on the extent to which the offender is still thought to pose a risk to public safety. In consequence, s. 45B(2) provides that a hospital direction is to have effect as a transfer direction and a limitation direction as a restriction direction, which means that, on discharge, a s. 45A patient may (as happened in *R v House* [2007] EWCA Crim 2559) be transferred to prison to serve out his or her sentence (s. 50(1)). Alternatively, and apparently more commonly (*R v Cooper* [2010] EWCA Crim 2335, at para. 19), the patient in this situation will remain in hospital unless and until he or she is able to convince the Parole Board that release from detention is justified.

Laing (1996: 138) argued that the ever-present prospect of transfer to prison may undermine the doctor/patient relationship for s. 45A patients, either by offering patients who do not wish to confront their problems an escape route from hospital (Mental Health Act Commission, 1995: 72) or by providing a disincentive to respond as well as might otherwise have been the case for patients who do not wish to return to prison. But within the frame of reference in which the hospital and limitation directions were concocted—the need to convince sentencers that detention in a hospital would not increase the chances of early release back into the community—this problem seems to be unavoidable. Simply, without the backstop of prison, there would be no meaningful distinction between these powers and the established orders, and so no encouragement for sentencers, who were historically reluctant to make hospital orders in cases involving psychopathically disordered offenders, to make hospital and limitation directions.

The other main difference between hospital and limitation directions and hospital and restriction orders, according to the 1996 consultation document, is that hospital and limitation directions would be appropriate in cases where 'a punitive element in the disposal is required to reflect the offender's whole or partial responsibility' (para. 1.4). Subsequently, although the reference to 'responsibility' was conspicuous by its absence from the Home Office Circular that accompanied the C(S)A 1997 (Home Office Mental Health Unit, 1997), culpability has become a key factor in determining when hospital and limitation directions should be used in preference to hospital and restriction orders. At the same time, however, the decision-making process that a sentencing court should go through before getting to the point of being able appropriately to consider making hospital and limitation directions is such that they will only be appropriate in very few cases.

In order to get to that point, the sentencing court must first go through the process laid down by the Court of Appeal in *Birch*. As discussed earlier, this requires the judge to consider: first, the making of a non-custodial disposal; second, if detention in some form is required, whether a hospital order can and should be made. And the only reasons to decide against making a hospital order when the criteria are satisfied are to protect the public when there is no secure hospital accommodation available, or to recognise the culpability of the offender when punishment is warranted. According to the Mustill LJ in the Court of Appeal in *Birch*, this must be culpability to a particular (although unspecified) degree, because in his view orders under ss. 37 and 41 are, 'even where there is culpability, the right way to deal with dangerous and disordered persons...'. This means that persons eligible for consideration for hospital and limitation directions must, by definition, be either particularly dangerous or particularly culpable. In short, only a small constituency of offenders will meet both the medical and the sentencing criteria for hospital and limitation directions.

This helps explain why, after the extension of the constituency in 2007, this sentencing option has proven little more popular than it was previously. In 2011–12 eight orders were made under s. 45A, there was only one order made in 2010–11, in 2009–10 there were five, and in 2008–09 there were three (NHS Information Centre, 2012: table 1). In the two years immediately preceding the broadening of the constituency from psychopathy to mental disorder, noticeably more, although still very few, orders were made: eleven orders in 2007–08 and twelve—the highest in any year since their introduction—in 2006–07 (NHS Information Centre, 2012: table 1).

It is not surprising, in view of the rarity of use of s. 45A, that little case law has been generated. The first case to reach the Court of Appeal, *R v Staines* [2006] EWCA Crim 15, does perhaps demonstrate the potential usefulness of the section for its limited target group. S, 18 years of age and whose life had been an 'unmitigated and profound tragedy' (Tomlinson J at para. 2), killed a man who had befriended her. She told police officers and social workers that she had heard voices that had told her to carry out the attack. S was convicted in December 2000 of manslaughter by reason of diminished responsibility and given a discretionary life sentence. The judge made an order under s. 45A, partly because of doubts about her diagnosis and treatability, partly because of concerns for public protection, and partly to mark her culpability for the offence. This was a case, then, in which all three of the original justifications for making an order under s. 45A were, in the view of the sentencing judge, present.

Three and a half years later, S successfully applied for leave to appeal against her sentence. Her argument was that orders under ss. 37 and 41 of the MHA 1983 should have been made in her case. Her grounds were (i) that she had responded to treatment following her arrival in hospital (S was, in fact, already in Broadmoor at the time of her trial, having been transferred from prison whilst on remand) and therefore there was no need for the possibility of her transfer to prison, concerns about which would also have a deleterious effect on her treatment; (ii) that she had been wrongly diagnosed as suffering solely from a personality disorder. She also suffered from a mental illness that had been present at the time of the offence and therefore reduced her culpability to a greater extent than appreciated by the sentencing court; and (iii) the fact that S was technically a prisoner meant that her release was a matter for the parole board rather than, as would be the case if she had been merely a patient, a mental health tribunal, with the consequence that there was less scope to fine-tune the supervision and treatment of S if, and when, released into the community.

The Court of Appeal rejected all three arguments. It was not satisfied that the option of return to prison had, in fact, proven any significant impediment to S's treatment in Broadmoor (para. 27). It was not satisfied, although there was conflicting evidence, that the diagnosis of psychopathic disorder, accepted by the sentencing court, was incorrect (para. 23). Nor, therefore, would it accept that S's culpability was less than that judged by the sentencing court and, following *Drew*, a prison sentence was appropriately given to mark S's culpability. Finally, the court held that the parole board was able to impose conditions, relating to medical treatment, similar to those that could be imposed by a tribunal, and that the fact that S was a prisoner whose release would be considered by the parole board 'affords to the public a significantly enhanced and desirable degree of protection from the risk of danger from the appellant' (para. 30). There was, as such, no reason to interrupt the sentencing decisions made at first instance.

There is little doubt that the availability of the hybrid order kept S out of prison. At first instance, it was found that, despite her disorder, S bore 'a considerable degree of responsibility for this savage killing'. She had a long history of being abused and abusing others, and had been convicted of a previous, serious, attack on the same victim. She had been subject to a 'very urgent transfer' to hospital whilst on remand in prison because of fears for her own safety and that of others in the prison, and had responded to treatment whilst in hospital. At the same time, the safety of the public had been assured. There can be little surprise that her appeal was unsuccessful, or that it appeared to the appeal court that the availability of the hybrid order had allowed a win–win outcome in this case.

The approach taken to s. 45A in *Staines* was followed in *R v House* [2007] EWCA Crim 2559, *R v Cooper* [2010] EWCA Crim 233, *R v Fox* [2011] EWCA Crim 3299, and *R v S* [2012] EWCA Crim 92, all of which involved persons mentally disordered at the time of their offence but who, it was felt, retained a significant degree of culpability for their actions nonetheless. In *House* and *Cooper*, a s. 45A order had been made by the sentencing court, reflecting the judge's views regarding culpability and risk (and in *House*, the uncertain treatability of the defendant) and in both cases the Court of Appeal refused to depart from the decision of the trial judge, as he or she 'was in the best position to reach conclusions about what the psychiatrist said and the responsibility of the appellant' (Leveson LJ in *Cooper* at para. 23). In *R v S*, the defendant, S, 18 years of age and diagnosed with Asperger's Syndrome, had raped a 15-year-old boy and been sentenced to ten years in prison. He was transferred to hospital three months into his prison sentence under s. 47 (see further 8.5). He successfully appealed against sentence, the Court of Appeal holding that the criteria for orders under s. 45A were met in his case and so such orders should have been made by the sentencing judge, particularly as it would be difficult to deliver the treatment S required in a prison setting. Interestingly, although counsel for the defendant had raised the possibility of a hospital order at trial, which the judge had rejected for reasons to do with culpability and risk, the possibility of orders under s. 45A had not been raised by any party. If this is common (and, if so, it is unfortunate), it might explain the relative dearth of orders under s. 45A. Defence counsel should take note: s. 45A can in appropriate cases keep your client out of prison.

In lieu of the failure of the C(S)A 1997 to provide for the originally intended target population of patients of uncertain treatability, sentencers should be encouraged to make greater use of their powers, contained in s. 38 of the MHA 1983, to make an interim hospital order. There is evidence that sentencers need such encouragement (see *R v Beeby* [2012] EWCA Crim 2636 at para. 13). An order under s. 38 can be made provided that an offender is suffering from mental disorder (s. 38(1)(a)), and that two doctors, one of whom must be an AC (s. 54(1)), and one of whom must be employed at the hospital to be specified in the order (s. 38(3)), have given evidence to the court's satisfaction that there is 'reason to suppose that the mental disorder from which the offender is suffering is such that it may be appropriate for a hospital order to be made in his case' (s. 38(1)(b)). An order under s. 38 can only be made by a court on convicting a defendant of an offence punishable with imprisonment. As with an order under s. 37, it must be certified that the arrangements have been made for the reception of the defendant into hospital within 28 days of the making of the order and that there is a place of safety available if necessary (s. 38(4)).

The idea of the interim order is to give adequate time to assess the treatability of the defendant's disorder, which may not be available under the remand powers. An interim order should not, however, be used as a holding device until a suitable long-term hospital placement can be made, if it is clear at the outset that the preferable order is one under s. 37 (*R v Galfetti* [2002] EWCA Crim 1916, per May LJ at para. 7). If, following the making of a s. 38 order, the defendant is judged suitable for hospitalisation, a full hospital order may be made without the defendant being brought back before the court, provided that his or her authorised representative has the opportunity to be heard (s. 38(2)). If not, the defendant may be sentenced to a term of imprisonment. Until 1997, the maximum duration of an interim hospital order was six months (s. 38(5)), but this was extended to 12 months by s. 49(1) of the Crime (Sentences) Act 1997—the same legislation that introduced the hospital and limitation directions. An order may initially last for a maximum of 12 weeks (s. 38(5)(a)), but can be renewed thereafter every 28 days up to the 12 months maximum duration (s. 38(5)(b)), which can be done in the absence of the defendant as long as he or she is represented at renewal hearings by counsel or a solicitor (rather than the broader category of 'authorised representative')(s. 38(6)).

An order under s. 38, as amended, should be able to deal satisfactorily with the initial justification for the introduction of hospital and limitation directions, which view is bolstered by the fact that, according to government statistics, 143 persons were admitted to hospital in 2011–12 by virtue of either s. 38 or ss. 44 or 46 (NHS Information Centre, 2012: table 1). Section 44 deals with persons committed to Crown Court by a magistrates' court, with a view to a restriction order being passed, and is unlikely to be used much, and s. 46, which dealt with members of the armed forces, was, in fact, repealed by the Armed Forces Act 1996, Sch. 7, Part III, para. 1, so this number is largely made up of interim orders under s. 38. The use of s. 38 also seems to be increasing: 69 persons were admitted to hospital in 2004–05 by virtue of either s. 38 or ss. 44 or 46 (Government Statistical Service, 2006: Table 1). It is tempting to conclude on this basis that hospital and limitation directions as currently structured have little practical value over and above the other available orders, and should be seen to reflect (confused) political imperatives. In retrospect, the main significance of the introduction of hospital and limitation directions may be as a sign of the increasing political emphasis on control over treatment.

8.5 Transfer from prison to hospital

If the measure of the success of the policy of diversion is the number of mentally disordered persons who end up in prison, then there is a good argument to say that the policy has failed. As Peay (1997: 668) succinctly states '[m]any, if not most, "disordered" offenders do not receive the therapeutic "hospital order" disposal, even though their culpability may be mitigated, if not absolved, by their mental state'. Despite the policy of, and mechanisms to secure the practice of, diversion of offenders suffering from mental disorder from the penal to the hospital system, the numbers of such persons amongst sentenced prison populations has, as discussed at 8.2.1, been consistently well-documented. In some instances, this will be because an offender's mental health is negatively affected by prison conditions, but there is little doubt that some if not most of those in prison suffering from mental disorder were suffering at the time of their arrival.

The current system of transfer does not aim to transfer each and every person who is in prison and is mentally disordered to hospital. Rather, as the Department of Health explains (2011d: 4), 'The vast majority of prisoners who experience mental illness whilst in custody are successfully treated by prison health services. However, some acutely mentally ill prisoners will require inpatient care as their clinical treatment needs cannot be met in a prison setting'. Even with this limited focus, however, as will be discussed further, the system of transfer has continually struggled to work effectively.

The current law is to be found in ss. 47–53 of the MHA 1983. Section 47 provides for the transfer of sentenced prisoners. The medical criteria to be satisfied are identical to those contained in ss. 3 and 37. Two doctors, at least one of whom must be 'approved' (s. 54(1)), must examine the patient and agree that he or she is suffering from mental disorder to a nature or degree that makes it appropriate for him or her to be detained in a hospital for treatment, and that appropriate treatment is available for him or her (s. 47(1)(a)–(c)), and report their findings to the Justice Secretary.

In *South West London and St George's Mental Health NHS Trust* v *W* [2002] EWHC 1770, a prisoner diagnosed as suffering from psychopathic disorder was transferred under s. 47 to a hospital near the end of his prison sentence under a care plan that proposed staged introduction of leave and eventual further transfer to a hostel, and then release into the community. The court held that this plan amounted to 'treatment', even though there would be no more than 'psychological supervision' of W whilst in hospital, because graduated release would be more likely to prevent a deterioration, or allow less of a deterioration, of W's condition than would be the case if he were not transferred but were released immediately into the community from prison. This is an expansive concept of 'treatability', although it does not look out of place amongst the other case law on this question (see Chapter 9, 9.4.1), and although the treatability test is now phrased differently there is no reason to suppose that this approach would not be followed today.

The decision whether to transfer a prisoner lies with the Justice Secretary who, assuming the above criteria are met, 'may, if he is of the opinion having regard to the public interest and all the circumstances that it is expedient to do so by warrant direct that that person be removed to and detained in such hospital as may be specified in the direction', which is known as a 'transfer direction' (s. 47(1), MHA 1983). This provision is very widely worded. It is clear for example that 'all the circumstances' includes such things as the availability of a hospital bed. When he or she does act under this section, it must first be decided in good faith that a proposed transfer is expedient (*Birch* per Mustill LJ at 210; see earlier), but that apart, the courts have traditionally been reluctant to interfere. In *R* v *SSHD, ex p K* [1990] 1 All ER 703 (DC), McCullough J, in a wide-ranging discussion of the powers given to the Secretary of State by Part III of the MHA 1983, said, *obiter*, that 'the Secretary of State is never obliged to act under s. 47, even if he thinks that the necessary preconditions are fulfilled' (716).

This view should arguably now be modified in the light of the decision of the European Court in *Aerts* v *Belgium* (2000) 29 EHRR 50, where it was held to be a breach of Art. 5(1)(e) of the ECHR to hold a person judged suitable for hospital treatment on remand in a prison, in which suitable treatment was not available, for seven months. The case of a prisoner awaiting transfer is essentially similar to that of a person held in a prison until a hospital bed is found. If this view is correct, then given the numbers of mentally disordered persons held in prisons, its implications for the Ministry of Justice may be considerable: Rickford and Edgar (2005) estimated that there are between 3,000 and 3,700 acutely mentally ill people in prison who are in need of urgent transfer, and nowhere near that number are transferred into hospital (see statistics later in this section).

The opposing view is that Art. 5 is not engaged by transfer decisions because it deals only with the initial detention and not with the conditions in which detention is served (*R* v *Deputy Governor or Parkhurst Prison, ex p Hague* [1992] 1 AC 58 (HL)). In *R* v

Mersey Care NHS Trust, ex p Munjaz, R v Airedale NHS Trust (Appeal) ex p S [2005] UKHL 58, [2005] 3 WLR 793, [2005] HRLR 42, at para. 30, Lord Bingham held that, although Art. 5 'cannot found a complaint directed to the category of institution within an appropriate system', it 'may avail a person detained in an institution of an inappropriate type', which seems clearly to support the view that, on a suitable fact situation, Art. 5 might provide relief, and the decision of the European Court in the same case seemed to confirm that (see *Munjaz* v *UK* [2012] MHLR 351; *The Times*, October 9, 2012, discussed at Chapter 2, 2.5.2). Lord Bingham also observed, in *R* v *Drew* [2003] UKHL 25, [2003] 1 WLR 1213, [2003] 4 All ER 557 at para. 18, that the Home Secretary (now Justice Secretary) is bound to act in compliance with the ECHR, and in *R* v *SSHD and National Assembly of Wales, ex p D* [2004] EWHC 2857 (Admin), Stanley Burnton J held that s. 47 is more than simply permissive (para. 33):

> once the prison service have reasonable grounds to believe that a prisoner requires treatment in a mental hospital in which he may be detained, the [Justice] Secretary is under a duty expeditiously to take reasonable steps to obtain appropriate medical advice, and if that advice confirms the need for transfer to a hospital, to take reasonable steps within a reasonable time to effect that transfer . . . The steps that are reasonable will depend on the circumstances, including the apparent risk to the health of the prisoner if no transfer is effected.

He then linked a failure properly to utilise s. 47 to a possible breach of Art. 8 of the ECHR (para. 33), although there was no breach on the facts of that case, the delay in D's transfer being explained by legitimate reasons, namely difficulty in arriving at a diagnosis and the lack of a suitable hospital placement (para. 48). There is always, in addition, as Stanley Burnton J noted, Art. 3, but the attitude of the European Court, in cases such as *Kudla* v *Poland* (2002) 35 EHRR 11, is that Art. 3 is not easily engaged.

A transfer direction made under s. 47 is deemed to have the same effect as a hospital order (s. 47(3)). An order made under s. 47 can be accompanied by an order made under s. 49, (a 'restriction direction') by which the restrictions contained in s. 41 may apply to a transferee (s. 49(1), (2)). It is the policy of the Justice Secretary to impose restrictions in all cases, except when a patient is transferred within days of his or her release date and is not judged to constitute a threat to the public. This policy was challenged in *R* v *Secretary of State for the Home Department, ex p T* [2003] EWHC 538. T argued that an order under ss. 47 and 49 is analogous to one made under ss. 37 and 41, and hence should only be made when there is a demonstrable need for public protection. The High Court, although accepting that no one had suggested that T was a danger to the public (para. 12), rejected this submission, because ss. 47 and 49 deal with sentenced prisoners and hence there is no reason why the policy of the Justice Secretary under s. 49 should reflect the approach of the courts when deciding the appropriate sentence at trial. Maurice Kay J held that the policy of the Justice Secretary properly emphasised the need for public protection and was lawful.

There were 41 transfers under s. 47 alone in 2011–12 (NHS Information Centre, 2012: table 1), and there have been no more than 45 and no less than 40 such transfers for each of the past five years apart from 2008–09 when there were 74. Transfer under s. 47 with a s. 49 restriction direction attached occurred on 427 occasions in 2011–12,

430 in 2010–11 and 458 in 2009–10 (NHS Information Centre, 2012: table 1), that being the highest number of ss. 47/49 transfers in a single year. The long-term trend is up: there were 346 transfers under ss. 47 and 49 in 2004, 296 in 2003, and 223 in 2002, having hovered at around an average of 250 annually for the previous decade (Home Office Research, Development and Statistics Directorate, 2005: Table 3). The rising numbers in part reflect the rising numbers of persons sent to and detained in prisons, which stood at around 85,000 in early 2013, compared to around 75,000 in 2003, and around 45,000 in 1993 (Ministry of Justice, 2013: 7). But it also reflects attempts, undertaken with renewed vigour following the Bradley Report (Bradley, 2009), to improve the operation of the transfer system. Even so, the numbers involved remain very small compared to the prison population and in light of the high rates of acute disorder which research has continually found to be present in that population (see 8.2.1).

There is also provision for the transfer of other than sentenced prisoners under s. 48, defined by s. 48(2) to include remand prisoners, civil prisoners, and those held under the Immigration Act 1971 or s. 62 of the Nationality, Immigration and Asylum Act 2002. Section 48 applies only to a prisoner suffering 'from mental disorder of a nature or degree which makes it appropriate for him to be detained in hospital for medical treatment' (s. 48(1)(a)), for whom appropriate treatment is available (s. 48(1)(c)) and, imposing more restrictive criteria than s. 47, who 'is in urgent need of such treatment' (s. 48(1)(b)). A patient so transferred is treated as though on a hospital order (ss. 48(3), 47(3)) and, again, it is unusual for an order to be made under s. 48 without an accompanying direction being made under s. 49(1): no more than 10 such orders have been made in any year in the last four years (NHS Information Centre, 2012: table 1).

There were 398 ss. 48/49 transfers in 2011–12 and 403 in 2010–11, this being the highest number in a single year for some years, although this longer-term trend is down. From very infrequent use in the 1980s—only 77 ss. 48/49 transfer directions were made in 1987—by 1994 this had increased to 536. It is clear that the rise in numbers through the 1990s was linked to the increase in the number of regional and medium-secure unit beds. Two out of three transfers were in respect of persons charged with violent or sexual offences in Mackay and Machin's research (1998; 2000). Thereafter, the rate fell back unevenly but steadily, against the backdrop of an ever-increasing prison population. There were 392 transfers in 2000, after which numbers began to rise again, reaching 421 transfers in 2002 and 485 in 2004 (Home Office Research, Development and Statistics Directorate, 2005: Table 3), before dipping back to the figure of around 350–400 annually we have seen in the last few years. That the rate of transfer under these provisions is going in the opposite direction to the total numbers incarcerated gives cause for concern.

For all transfers, the receiving hospital should be specified in the direction (ss. 47(1), 48(3)) and although it does not follow from this that the agreement of that hospital must be obtained before a direction is made, this has been the normal practice of the Justice Secretary (see *R* v *Secretary of State for the Home Department, ex p T* [1994] 1 All ER 794 (DC)). This is understandable, particularly because, under the terms of s. 47(2), a transfer direction under either ss. 47 or 48 will cease to have effect if the person named in the direction has not been transferred within 14 days of its making. Delays in the execution of a decision to transfer a prisoner to hospital have been constantly reported since at least the 1970s (Tidmarsh, 1978; Cheadle and Ditchfield, 1982; Grounds, 1990; Dolan and Shetty, 1995; Hargreaves, 1997; National Institute for Mental Health in England, 2003). Grounds, for example, found that in the decade 1974–83, the mean wait was 7.5 months, with a quarter of patients waiting a year or more.

Although there was some sign of improvement in the late 1990s (Huws *et al.*, 1997; Mackay and Machin, 1998, 2000), by November 2005 the situation seems to have worsened again. At that time, Louis Appleby, the National Director of Mental Health, and John Boyington, the Director of Health and Offender Partnerships, wrote (Appleby and Boyington, 2005) to all strategic health authority prison leads and mental health leads, PCT commissioners, and care service improvement partnerships prison mental health regional leads, in bald terms, stating that 'there are currently some unacceptable delays in the transfer of acutely mentally ill prisoners to and from hospital under ss. 47 and 48 of the Mental Health Act 1983'. They were referring to the 'prison traffic light' reporting system, which, in September 2005, stated that there were 51 prisoners waiting, after acceptance by an inpatient mental health service provider, for more than 12 weeks for transfer to hospital under the MHA (HM Prison Service, 2006: 2).

In *R* v *SSHD and National Assembly of Wales, ex p D* [2004] EWHC 2857 (Admin), Stanley Burnton J, although holding that there was no breach of Art. 8 in the delayed transfer of D in that case did also say, by way of observation, that the lack of a national database of available hospital beds hindered the process of transferring D, commenting that 'the Claimant has not suggested that the lack of such a database caused an infringement of his Convention rights, and the practicalities of establishing and maintaining such a database have not been investigated. The position might be otherwise in future' (para. 60).

The Royal College of Psychiatrists, the Royal College of Nursing, and the members of Her Majesty's Prison Service also brought pressure to bear (Shaw *et. al*, 2008: 17), and the result was the issuance by the Department of Health in 2005 of guidance on transfer (DH, 2005; see also DH, 2005a). Subsequent research showed that this guidance, which sought to impose clear demarcations of responsibility, better procedures for inter-agency working, and target times for transfer to occur, with a 14-day time limit being trialled in some areas, had improved the situation (see McKenzie and Sales, 2008; Shaw *et al.*, 2008; Rickford and Edgar, 2009, ch. 5). However, when Lord Bradley produced his Report in 2009, delays remained at an unacceptable level.

Lord Bradley (2009: 105) identified a number of reasons for delay:

- communication breakdowns within and between prisons and hospitals;
- difficulties in obtaining the required paperwork held within different departments across the criminal justice system;
- lack of administrative support in prisons;
- lack of bed availability and, on closer inspection, lack of through-care/step-down facilities to provide fluidity and movement between different levels of security;

- problems establishing responsible PCT commissioners and getting PCTs to accept responsibility for payment for prisoners' treatment;
- disputes over the level of security required for the prisoner; and
- different attitudes and perceptions of prison and hospital staff towards mental illness and offenders.

Bradley (2009: 106) concluded that 'to make real progress in this area this issue must become a higher priority and be made one of the mainstream requirements' and recommended that a 14-day time limit be imposed on all transfers, from the point of the need for transfer being identified to the relocation of the prisoner in hospital.

Subsequently, and following consultation, the guidance issued by the Department of Health was revised (DH, 2011). The guidance covers commissioning issues—designed to prevent disputes arising between agencies as to which of them is responsible for which elements of the transfer process—and inter-agency co-operation (see also Olumuyiwa et al., 2009; Wilson et. al, 2010; Royal College of Psychiatrists, 2011b), and provides detailed information about how the transfer process should take place, the information required, and the parties it is required from, and explains the relevant law (which, as Shaw et al. (2008) found, is poorly understood by many relevant actors). On this last point, it is slightly disconcerting that the guidance refers throughout to 'mental illness' rather than mental disorder, and its focus is very much on the acutely mentally ill in prison. Whilst the vast majority of those in need of transfer will indeed be mentally ill, this will not always be the case, and in this respect the guidance is likely to confuse those to whom it is addressed.

The main innovation is that the 14-day time limit has now been rolled out nationally. The guidance uses the concept of the 'transfer clock' (DH, 2011d: para. 3.6). Within two days of the need for transfer being identified by a doctor (whose report will constitute one of the two reports required by s. 47(1)) the prison health care team should contact the MHCS to establish the level of security that will be required to house the prisoner in hospital, gather together all the information needed to establish the need for transfer, contact the relevant service commissioner, and organise a second medical opinion (DH, 2011d: para. 4.5). Within a further seven days, that medical opinion must be given following an assessment of the prisoner by the second doctor, a hospital bed should be identified, and all information provided to the MHCS (2011d: para. 4.5). Within a further five days, the MHCS should approve the transfer and issue the warrant to effect it, the recipient hospital should confirm the admission date with the prison, and the prison should organise the removal of the patient to hospital (2011d: para. 4.5).

At the time of writing it remains to be seen to what extent it proves possible for this timetable to be complied with. In its final report, the MHAC (2009: para. 4.24) noted continuing 'serious delays in arranging transfers' from prison to hospital, the main causes of which were inefficiency of inter-agency liaison and delays on the part of commissioners to fund transfers. There has subsequently been no significant increase in the numbers being transferred (see statistics earlier in this section), which indicates that there is still a significant amount of unmet need. In 2012 HM Chief Inspector of Prisons for England and Wales reported that 'Transfer times for patients accessing secure NHS facilities continued to improve but in certain areas of the country, including London, they remained problematic. At the time of our inspection of Brixton, for example, 14 patients were awaiting transfer to NHS mental health beds, one of whom had been waiting over six months. This was unacceptable' (HM Chief Inspector of Prisons for England and Wales, 2012: 48). It was announced in 2012 that commissioning intentions for 2013–14 include 'Taking more effective action to tackle mental health and addiction, including drug recovery wings in prisons, and early identification and intervention to support diversion from the justice system where appropriate and inform sentencing' (Ministry of Justice/National Offender Management Service, 2012: 6).

It is to be hoped that the practice, prevalent in the past, of obscuring delay in the process of transfer by not organising for the transfer direction to be signed until a bed had been found, with patients not officially recognised as in need of transfer by the prison authorities until that point, will be ended by the new guidance. This had the associated problem that the underpinning medical recommendations would be stale by the time transfer was finally organised. In *R* v *Secretary of State for the Home Office, ex p Gilkes* [1999] 1 MHLR 6 (HC), it was held that, if there is fluctuation in the medical condition of the person in respect of whom transfer is being contemplated, it is unreasonable for the Justice Secretary to rely on dated medical reports. In addition, it was held in *Varbanov* v *Bulgaria*, Application No. 31365/96 (2000) that reliance on outdated reports could amount to a breach of Art. 5(1)(e) of the ECHR, whilst as already suggested, not to act within a reasonable time in that situation may also constitute a breach, if suitable treatment is not forthcoming in prison (*Aerts*).

There are other concerns with the operation of the transfer provisions. The most significant is the effect that a transfer to hospital has on the length of time that the individual spends in custody. It is established that a determinate prison sentence, and the tariff for those given a discretionary life sentence, continues to run whilst the prisoner is in hospital following transfer for prison (*R* v *Secretary of State for the Home Department, ex p H & Ors* [1994] 3 WLR 1110 per Rose LJ at 1120C); but there has been a long-standing issue regarding prisoners transferred late in their sentence (Grounds, 1990: 57). This was considered by the Court of Appeal in *R* v *SSJ, ex parte TF* [2008] EWCA Civ 1457, a case in which a prisoner was transferred to hospital on the day of his expected release from prison. The court noted, first, that it hoped that transfer on or near the prisoner's release date would only occur in 'very exceptional cases' (para. 31).

The guidance issued by the Department of Health (2011d: para. 3.10) refers to the judgment in *TF* and notes that 'The Mental Health Casework Section (MHCS) in the Ministry of Justice (MoJ) advise that where a prisoner is sufficiently close to their release date that admission to hospital could be appropriately achieved using civil powers of the 1983 Mental Health Act, it is unlikely that directing a transfer under s. 47 can be justified'. Section 47 will be used, however, when (DH, 2011d: para. 3.13):

- admission to hospital is an urgent necessity;
- it is necessary for the prisoner's own health and/or safety; and

- the urgency of need is such that it is not safe to wait until the release date for admission to hospital.

The law reports do nonetheless continue to reveal cases in which transfer under s. 47 occurs within days of the end of the prison sentence (see for example *MP* v *Mersey Care NHS Trust* [2011] UKUT 107 (AAC)).

The Court of Appeal in *TF* went on to suggest, secondly, that where there is a transfer near the end of the prisoner's sentence, this 'heightens the scrutiny' (para. 13) that any claim that it was done unlawfully should be given by a court hearing an application for judicial review, both in terms of making sure that the transfer is procedurally correct, and based on substantive reasons which address the grounds for transfer in s. 47 such as enable the court to police the requirement (para. 18) that 'a decision to direct a transfer cannot simply be taken on the grounds that a convicted person will be a danger to the public if released (as understandable as that concern must be) but can only be taken on the grounds that his medical condition and its treatability (to use a shorthand) justify the decision'.

The application in *TF* was successful before the Court of Appeal, the court finding (as had the High Court) that the Justice Secretary, via the MHCS, had made the decision to authorise transfer based on inadequate recent evidence about TF's treatability for his condition, diagnosed as Dissocial Personality Disorder. This diagnosis chimes with research which found that psychopathically disordered offenders featured strongly amongst those transferred late in their sentence (Huws *et al.*, 1997: 77), and with earlier case law on this issue, such as *R* v *Rampton Hospital Authority, ex p W* [2001] EWHC Admin 134 and *South West London and St George's Mental Health NHS Trust* v *W* [2002] EWHC 1770. It may well be, as Huws *et al.* suggested, that prisoners suffering from a personality disorder, unlike mentally ill prisoners, do not come to the attention of prison medical services until they are assessed prior to their proposed release from prison (1997: 82), because those suffering from such disorders do not necessarily appear to be 'mad'. Nonetheless, it seems odd that personality disorders feature so largely in this group, when elsewhere their treatability is, at best, suspect. It is difficult not to feel a lurking sense of unease that, when release is imminent, personality disordered offenders are suddenly deemed (deploying a problematic definition) 'treatable', albeit not in large numbers. Of course, such suspicions can be hard to prove, but it is noteworthy that in *R* v *Nottingham Healthcare NHS Trust, ex p M* [2002] EWCA Civ 1728, at para. 37, Pill LJ held that: 'The treatability test must of course be applied in good faith and not used as a cover for decisions taken on other grounds.'

If, as is usual, a transfer to hospital under s. 47 has restrictions attached under s. 49, that person can be transferred back to prison if, before the expiry of that prison sentence (measured by reference to the patient's earliest release date (ERD) on licence, ignoring for these purposes any powers of the parole board: s. 50(3)), the patient's RC, or any AC, or a tribunal, notifies the Justice Secretary that the person concerned no longer requires hospital treatment or has proven to be untreatable (s. 50(1)(a)). The question of whether the two criteria in s. 50(1) are mutually exclusive—so that the information to be provided to the Justice Secretary should state either that the patient no longer requires any treatment in hospital or that no effective treatment can be given in the particular hospital at which the patient is currently detained—was raised in *R v Larkin and SSJ, ex parte W* [2012] EWHC 556 (Admin), a case in which the RC of a patient transferred from prison to Broadmoor hospital had stated in his report to the Justice Secretary that both criteria in s. 50(1) were satisfied.

The patient argued that this was an unlawful notification, as was the order to transfer the patient back to prison made subsequently by the Justice Secretary, because the first limb implies that the patient need not be detained in any hospital whereas the second limb is concerned only with the actual hospital at which the patient is currently detained, and as such when both limbs are claimed to be satisfied the Justice Secretary is unable to tell if it was more appropriate for the patient to be returned to prison, or should instead be transferred to another hospital at which there is treatment available for him or her.

The court rejected this argument, whilst accepting that there might in some situations be a conflict between the two limbs in s. 50(1), because as Ouseley J explained (para. 38):

> The two limbs can go together to cover precisely the sort of circumstance which arises here. The claimant does not require to be treated in hospital for mental disorder because the sort of treatment for his mental disorder, from which he would benefit, is available in prison. It may be appropriate for him to receive such treatment in a hospital, and that treatment may be effective, but that treatment cannot be given in Broadmoor. So, in circumstances where it may be appropriate, but not required, for someone to receive treatment for a disorder in a hospital, notwithstanding its availability to a considerable degree in the prison state, but, where it is not available to the hospital where he is currently detained, both boxes can sensibly be ticked "no", as was done here.

In *R v Shetty, ex p IR* [2003] EWHC 3022, the High Court held, on a judicial review application, that its role in respect of claims by IR that the decision of the Secretary of State to recall him to prison breached his rights under Arts. 3 and 5 of the ECHR, was to conduct a 'heightened' review of that decision, but did not extend to the court deciding for itself that there had been a breach. The court concluded that the Secretary of State's decision, itself based on a 'most anxious scrutiny' of the situation, was in breach of neither Article. The decision in this case was applied in *ex parte W.*

The Justice Secretary may alternatively release that person on licence (which allows conditions that cannot be attached to an order for discharge from hospital) or discharge him or her if that would have been possible had he or she been in prison (s. 50(1)(b), and see *R v SSHD, ex p Abdul Miah* [2004] EWHC 2569 (Admin)). In either case, the restriction direction automatically lapses (s. 50(1)). The Justice Secretary also has the option to use his or her powers under s. 42(2) to discharge any person held under restrictions (see further Chapter 11, 11.2.4).

The nature of what is entailed by the requirement that the RC notify the Justice Secretary was litigated in the *Nottingham* case (already discussed in this section). M had been transferred to Rampton hospital from prison for treatment early in 2000. In

March 2002, his RC, following a case conference at the hospital at which the preponderance of opinion was the M should be returned to prison, made an urgent request under s. 50(1) on the grounds that M was no longer treatable, and was actively resisting and/or trying to dictate his treatment and undermine his RC and named nurse. M sought judicial review of this decision, on the basis that some of those involved in his treatment did not share the view of his RC. The Court of Appeal held that the RC did not have to provide an inventory of the various views of his or her colleagues to the Secretary of State (para. 39). Nevertheless, 'there is a duty upon an RMO [now RC] before giving a notification to make proper enquiries within the hospital as to whether the treatability test is satisfied and to consider views expressed, as well as his own first-hand knowledge and experience, before making a recommendation. The extent of enquiry and of disclosure of information will depend on the circumstances of the particular case and will normally be judged as at the moment of decision' (para. 41).

M had also argued that he should have been allowed to make formal representations to the Secretary of State in order to dispute the view as to his treatability expressed by the RC. On this point, the court held that 'There will be cases in which circumstances, including information available to the Secretary of State, either in the documents by which the notification is given, or from other sources, create a duty in the Secretary of State to make further enquiries or take further action or both' (para. 47), but this was not such a case. Nor was there any right for the patient to make representations to the Secretary of State, or to be consulted about a proposed transfer. Finally, the court dealt cursorily with the relevance of Art. 8 of the ECHR, holding that 'Transfer from prison to hospital and hospital back to prison, as a part of a high-security custodial regime, cannot in present circumstances be said to breach the Article notwithstanding the differences in medical treatment which may occur. I do not of course exclude the possibility that some aspects of a custodial regime might attract a case for a breach' (at para. 49).

If the patient was on remand before transfer to hospital under s. 48, the transfer direction, and any accompanying restriction direction, is automatically brought to an end if, and when, that individual is returned to court and his or her case disposed of. 'Disposal' here means a final disposal, so if a person was remanded by magistrates the transfer direction will continue in force if on the case returning to that court the accused person is 'sent in custody' to the Crown Court for trial or other disposal (s. 52(2)). If an accused person is further remanded by a magistrates' court this can be done without the accused person being brought before the court (s. 52(3)) unless the accused has not been before the court in the previous six months (s. 52(3)), in which case he or she must be present at the hearing. Magistrates may end a transfer direction made by them under s. 48 if notified by the RC that the criteria for making a direction are no longer satisfied (s. 52(5)). If this does not happen and the accused is sent to Crown Court for disposal under s. 52(2), the provisions of s. 51 shall apply (s. 52(6)).

Disposal may be by means of a hospital order, in addition to the other options open to a sentencing court (s. 51(2)). A hospital order can be made if, on a reapplication of the criteria and procedures for s. 37, this is warranted and the court, after 'considering any depositions or other documents' thinks it 'proper' to make a hospital order (s. 51(6)). In

R v Snaresbrook Crown Court, ex p K 2001 WL 1422891, Pill LJ held that, even with the aid of depositions, it is difficult to know what is 'proper' because it cannot be known if the information in the depositions would have been accepted as evidence, and to sentence a person without convicting him or her is 'a drastic step, one that should only be taken in exceptional circumstances' (at para. 35).

If, before the time that the case of the person remanded comes before a court for disposal, the RC (or another AC or a tribunal) notifies the Justice Secretary that the patient no longer requires treatment or is untreatable, the Justice Secretary has a discretion to order by warrant the return of the individual to prison (s. 51(3)), which can also be ordered by the court having jurisdiction to try the case if the Justice Secretary declines to act (s. 51(4)). If there has been no action under either ss. 51(3) or (4), the court having jurisdiction over the case may make a hospital order (with or without a restriction order) without convicting the defendant, and this may be done in his or her absence if the conditions in s. 51(6) apply (s. 51(5)(b)) and it is 'impracticable or inappropriate to bring the detainee before the court' (s. 51(5)(a)). In *ex p K*, the Divisional Court (Pill LJ at para. 32) held that:

> the word 'inappropriate' in section 51(5) must be construed restrictively. The section must not be used as a routine and easy way of avoiding a potentially troublesome trial...I would not necessarily restrict the word 'inappropriate' so as to mean 'physically impossible' but a high degree of disablement or relevant disorder must be present. The section does not apply in a situation in which all that is involved is possible inconvenience for the Crown and inevitable distress for the defendant and others likely to be concerned in a trial.

If this is only done in 'exceptional' circumstances, it will also be no breach of the right to a fair hearing that is protected by Art. 6 of the ECHR (at para. 37). But, in any case, the Court of Appeal decided, in the later case of *R v Griffiths* [2002] WL 1311144, the s. 51(5) powers are only applicable before a trial has begun. If doubts about whether it is appropriate for the defendant to attend the trial surface after it has begun ('beginning, broadly with the swearing in of the jury' per Tomlinson LJ, in *Snaresbrook*, at para. 48) the appropriate mechanism is that of unfitness to plead (per Keene LJ, in *Griffiths*, at para. 21).

8.6 Concluding comments

As was noted at Chapter 7, 7.1, in 2008 the Ministry of Justice (2008: para. 1.2) reaffirmed 'the continuation of the long-standing policy that mentally disordered people who commit offences should receive specialist mental health treatment rather than being punished, wherever that can safely be achieved'. And indeed, in this chapter we have discussed a fairly comprehensive, and still developing, 'all-points' legal framework of diversionary mechanisms, from the point of initial contact with a court, to transfer from prison after sentence, which does seem to give reality to that claim.

However, it is equally clear that the way in which the system of diversion actually operates, and is intended to operate, does not really fit with the government's claim.

Only a very small number of those who come before the criminal courts are actually 'diverted' out of the criminal justice system and into the mental health system, and safety is by no means the only factor explaining the very low use of the orders available to sentencers in Part III of the MHA 1983, or the very low number of prison transfers: culpability is often a more important consideration. In practice, the opposite of the Ministry of Justice's claim is really true: provided that a mentally disordered person is deemed to be sufficiently safe in prison, then that is where that person will be held, in all but the most acute and serious cases of mental illness.

In philosophical terms there are two diversion systems: the insanity defence and the law relating to unfitness for trial, as well as the powers to remand to hospital, are underpinned by the need to make sure that trials are fair. Hospital orders, by contrast, are underpinned by humanitarian considerations, and function with a much more expansive concept of 'fairness'. Sometimes it will be clear that diversion is driven by such considerations. But most of the time things are more complicated. For example, is the purpose of court-based mental health assessment facilities to ensure that prosecutions are fair, or is it to identify those who should be diverted from the trial process?

The answer, of course, is that such schemes seek to do both, and the tension between treatment and punishment as such is built into diversion at the micro-level of individual assessments. The expansion in coverage of, and the apparent increase in funding for, court (and police-station) based diversion, as well as new timetables for prison transfers, which are welcome on one level (although less attention has been paid to some issues, such as the operation of the appropriate adult scheme in police stations), will nonetheless be hampered by this structural ambiguity, both about the aim of diversion and about the balance between diversion as humanitarianism on the one hand and the obligation to punish all offenders equally, as a matter of fairness or justice on the other. When these factors are overlain with further layers of ambiguity about, for example, the appropriate target population for diversion, the potential for confusion, inconsistency, and lack of clarity is great.

The Labour government that left office in 2010 attempted to square the circle of post-sentencing diversion by improving the quality of medical treatment in prisons and again, whilst this is in and of itself welcome, it demonstrates that diversion from the criminal justice system to the mental health system is not, in fact, the default position for the vast majority of those sentenced to prison. It also provides an example of the 'convergence' described by Rutherford (2010), as the gap between hospitals (which particularly in the higher security bands are as much custodial as therapeutic in orientation: see Chapter 3, 3.4) and prisons narrows, which raises a new set of questions about what we mean by 'diversion' and how we should measure its success, as does, for example, the introduction of hospital and limitation directions (which Rutherford also identifies as an example of 'convergence').

For the moment, however, the most pressing issues are not so much these theoretical questions about the trajectory and future interrelationship between the mental health system and the criminal justice system, or the diversion system as the bridge between the two, but about the chronic under-use of all diversionary mechanisms at all stages of the court, sentencing, and penal processes. In this sense, the substantive law can be positively misleading. On reading the decision of the Court of Appeal in *Birch* (see 8.4.1), for example, an intelligent reader might easily conclude that the making of hospital orders, or hospital orders together with restriction orders, would be a regular and routine occurrence in the criminal courts and yet, of course, they are measured in the hundreds whilst prison sentences are measured in the tens of thousands. The explanation of the law in *Birch* has been routinely ignored ever since by the vast majority of courts, such that the law as explained in that case, some might want to argue, is little more than a fiction.

This is not a matter which, at root, can be addressed by better funding or more efficient liaison and diversion services. These things can make a difference, but really, to borrow the rhetoric of modern day politics, the key issue in diversion is a 'battle for hearts and minds': until police, sentencers, mental health and criminal justice professionals, not to mention the government and the general public, resile from the reality that the criminal justice system largely processes mentally disordered persons, things will not change very much. As we suggested in Chapter 7 (7.1), there are deep psychological attachments to the 'criminal lunatic', the offender who is both mentally disordered and culpable, both 'mad and bad', as a prime figure of the Other, the monster, the antithesis of normality, and therefore the mechanism by which the 'normal' is defined, and hence a comforting and reassuring figure, as well as a figure to be feared (on this, see, from an extensive literature, Shildrick, 2002; Dendle, 2007).

These impulses incline us, as a society, towards punishment rather than treatment, even in the most trivial of cases, because the quality of the crime is not the prime consideration. Rather, it is the risk of the appearance of the monstrous in the mundane, the 'dynasty of abnormal Tom Thumbs' descended from 'the great monstrous ogres' of the medieval period, as Foucault (2003: 109) puts it, which is the main concern. The consequence is that the diversion system, presented as wide-ranging (going as we have seen, even beyond the very broad definition of 'mental disorder' found in s. 1, MHA 1983: see Chapter 7, 7.1 and Bradley, 2009: 16), functions in reality as an emergency service for the acutely mentally ill who come into contact with the criminal justice system, with a residual use as a mechanism to 'divert' some personality-disordered offenders very near the end of their prison sentence. For those who are not so acutely ill, and sometimes even for those who are, the punitive impulse is stronger than the humanitarian impulse. In summary, the point is that at the moment most mentally disordered offenders are not 'diverted' in the sense implied by the Ministry of Justice (2008) in its guidance to the courts, and, as things stand, it seems as though that was never the intention of diversion policy.

9

Medical Treatment

9.1 Introduction

Key points related to treatment of people with mental disabilities are contained in Box 9.1. They are provided with some hesitancy, since all are more complex than they appear at first glance, but they should provide an overall structure to make sense of the more detailed discussion that follows.

Box 9.1

TREATMENT FOR MENTAL DISORDER: KEY POINTS AND OVERVIEW

- Treatment in the community is governed generally by common law and the Mental Capacity Act (MCA) 2005. The exception to this rule involves people on leave of absence from detention in hospital. This basic position is also not so simple for people on community treatment orders or conditional discharge from criminal detentions.

- Informal inpatients can be treated only on their competent consent or under the MCA 2005.

- For disorders *unrelated* to mental condition, detained patients can be treated only on their competent consent or under the MCA 2005.

- Detained patients can be treated for their mental disorder without their consent for the first three months of their detention.

- After the expiry of this three month period, detained patients can be treated with medicine for their mental disorder only on their competent consent, or else if the treatment is approved in a second opinion provided by a doctor appointed through the statutory scheme (a 'SOAD').

- Electro-convulsive therapy (ECT) and psycho-surgery are subject to special rules.

- Notwithstanding the previous points, detained inpatients can be given most treatments for their mental disorders if it is immediately necessary to preserve life, prevent a serious deterioration of their condition, prevent serious suffering by the patient, or prevent violence or dangerousness.

9.2 Treatment outside the scope of the MHA

Absent statutory authority to the contrary, the legal conditions concerning the treatment of people with mental disorders are the same as that for anyone else: adults with capacity may make treatment decisions themselves, and adults without capacity can be treated if there is compliance with the Mental Capacity Act (MCA) 2005 (see Chapter 4). This starting position has real application. It applies for all informal patients in hospital. For detained patients, it applies for all treatments except those that are for the individual's mental disorder. It also applies for the vast bulk of people with mental disorder in the community, including people on MHA guardianship (see Chapter 10, 10.3). 'Community patients' (i.e., those living in the community subject to a community treatment order under s. 17A of the MHA 1983) can in principle consent to treatment, but in the event of a refusal can in some circumstances be forcibly returned to hospital and treated there without consent (see further Chapter 10, 10.4). Further, people living in the community who are on leaves of absence from their detention in hospital under s. 17 of the MHA 1983 are in law still subject to detention, and are subject to the same rules regarding consent and treatment compulsion as other detained patients. In practice, if restraint or other force is required for the treatment of these patients they, like the community patients, are returned to hospital, even if briefly, for the treatment.

Even where treatment could legally be provided without the consent of the patient, the MHA Code of Practice states that consent should be sought if practicable (para. 23.37).

When treatment is provided on the consent of the patient, the issues that arise mirror those elsewhere in health care law, including whether the consent is voluntary and informed. These topics are covered at length in the standard texts on health law (see, e.g., Herring, 2012; Jackson, 2010; Kennedy *et al.*, 2010) and that general analysis will not be repeated here. There are, however, a number of issues relevant to that larger literature that play out slightly differently in the context of mental disorders.

One of these is knowledge of rights. As noted, the right to refuse treatment for mental disorder is dependent on whether the individual is informal or detained. The Code of Practice makes it clear that there is an ongoing obligation on staff to provide patients with 'sufficient' information about proposed treatment and alternatives to it (para. 23.33). It does seem that these efforts are not always successful. As noted in Chapter 6 (at 6.1), somewhere between 10 and 45 per cent of informal patients are unaware of their informal status, and of those that are, somewhere between a third and two thirds are unaware of their right to refuse treatment (Lomax, 2012; see further Chapter 6, 6.1). This lack of knowledge extends into knowledge about treatments as well. A survey of people on acute or intensive psychiatric wards by the Care Quality Commission (CQC) in 2009 found that only a third of these people had been as involved in their care as they would have wished, and half were not given explanations of adverse effects of medications that were comprehensible to them (CQC, 2009). The CQC survey does not distinguish between those with formal or informal status on the wards (itself an interesting omission, given the legal importance of this distinction), but it seems likely that significant numbers of informal patients will be contained in these findings. When the legality of the treatments is contingent on the patient's consent, it is a matter of some concern that the consent is provided by individuals who do not understand the potential adverse effects of the proposed drugs. Certainly, the pragmatics of explanation on a psychiatric acute ward may be complex, and the patient may not be in a position to make a considered reflection and decision on information immediately following admission; but this is not an argument for failing to repeat the information at a later time, when the patient is in a more suitable frame of mind.

It is further fair to wonder how far the consent of the individual in fact represents that individual's real choice. This is perhaps easiest to see in the example of community patients. As noted, these patients have the right to consent to treatment, but can often be forcibly readmitted and compulsorily treated if they refuse treatment. Given this implied threat of compulsion, how real is the consent of these patients? This is however merely a particularly clear example of a much more pervasive problem. As we have seen (see Chapter 6), informal patients who are in hospital may nonetheless be detained if the requisite conditions under the MHA 1983 are met. We know little about these detentions, but it is fair to surmise that many may be triggered by a refusal of the patient to take the prescribed medication. Insofar as this is believed to be true by patients, the threat of such detention and enforced treatment for mental disorder may similarly result in consent of reluctant informal patients in much the same way that the thread of readmission may induce consent among community patients.

The express or implied threat of detention is not the only coercion that may be experience by service users. In recent years, attention has been turned to other forms of 'leverage'—requiring treatment compliance as a condition of community accommodation, or of retaining custody of one's children, or as a condition of reduced sentencing, for example, or offering financial incentives to accept treatment—all of which seem to be common in America (see Bonnie and Monahan, 2005). While these pressures seem somewhat less common in England, it is still the case that one in three people with mental health problems in this country report such leverage in at least one of these areas. Housing is the largest of the areas identified, with roughly a quarter of people with mental health problems (here including people with substance abuse problems) having been required to comply with treatment as a condition of their community-based accommodation (see Burns *et al.*, 2011). The requirement that people give up their right to consent to treatment—a fundamental civil right—in these leverage situations on its face raises ethical problems. The legality and justifications of such requirements will depend on the circumstances of each case. Where failure to comply with a treatment regime in the past has been demonstrably associated with risk to a child, it seems reasonable for courts to make compliance with such treatment a condition of ongoing custody of the child, for example. On the other hand, a requirement by a private landlord that people with mental disabilities will comply with treatment when such a requirement is not made of people without those disabilities may well give rise to issues of discrimination under the Equality Act 2010. In either case, however these restrictions are understood legally and ethically, the point for current purposes is that the 'consent' of the individual to treatment when such leverage has been employed must be viewed with a critical eye: it may or may not represent the real wishes of the individual regarding the treatment in question.

9.3 Treatment for mental disorder

As noted, consent is in some circumstances not required for detained patients, when the treatment is for their mental disorder. The legal scope and requirements for such involuntary treatment will be discussed later in this chapter, but by way of introduction, it may be helpful to provide an indication of the sorts of treatment that are commonly or notably offered to patients.

9.3.1 Medication

Medications are often prescribed for psychiatric difficulties. While there is no doubt that medications are successful on some patients, results are not universally positive, and the drugs do have adverse effects.

For schizophrenia and similar disorders, an antipsychotic medication (also called a 'neuroleptic' or, occasionally in older literature, a 'major tranquiliser') will generally be part of the treatment provided. The first of these was discovered in the 1950s. The early ('older generation') drugs of this type functioned by inhibiting dopamine receptors in the brain. So-called 'second generation' or 'atypical' antipsychotics, which inhibit a broader range of receptors in the brain, were discovered from the late 1970s. A systematic review of second generation antipsychotics showed benefits in 41 per cent of patients with schizophrenia, as compared to 28 per cent showing benefits with a placebo (Leucht *et al.*, 2009). Efficacy may decrease over time—a significant problem, since schizophrenia and similar disorders may require long-term treatment. Adverse effects of antipsychotic drugs include obesity, diabetes, cardiovascular irregularities, sexual dysfunction, drowsiness, apathy, confusion, headaches, blurred vision and sensitivity to light, and dizziness. They also cause 'extra-pyramidal' symptoms, including parkinsonian symptoms (including tremors), dystonia (abnormal face and body movements), akathesia (restlessness), and tardive dyskinesia (rhythmic involuntary movements particularly of the tongue, lips, face, hands and feet). These effects can be permanent (Joint Forumlary Committee, 2012: s 4.2.1). Extra-pyramidal effects are meant to be less common in newer drugs, but even in the second generation antipsychotics, they occur in 35 to 55 per cent of cases (Bobes *et al.*, 2002). Clozapine, a fairly common antipsychotic, also causes changes in levels of white blood cells in roughly 3 per cent of patients. In a third of those, the decreases can result in dangerously low levels which can in turn result in the collapse of the immune system, and sometimes death. For this reason, ongoing blood tests must accompany its administration.

Usually, antipsychotic drugs will initially be administered orally in tablet form, but particularly when the patient is to be discharged into the community, many can be administered by injection in longer-lasting doses ('depot' medication), typically lasting one to four weeks. This may be convenient for the patient, but it also allows clinicians to ensure that the patient is indeed taking the drugs, allowing for forms of community control that would be much more problematic when medications are taken daily in tablet form in environments where the clinician may not be present.

Medication is used for moderate or severe depression. While it is no longer the preferred treatment for mild depression at least initially, it is still used in practice, particularly when talking therapies, the preferred response, are unavailable. Antidepressant medications are of three main types—tricyclics, selective serotonin reuptake inhibitors (SSRIs), and serotonine and norepinephrine reuptake inhibitors (SNRIs). Three months after commencing treatment, roughly half to two thirds of patients will experience significant improvement, although in most cases the depression will dissipate within eight months or so even without treatment (Royal College of Psychiatrists, 2012). The specific adverse effects will depend on the category of drug taken. SSRIs may cause gastro-intestinal problems such as vomiting, nausea and digestive problems; anorexia and weight loss; and also nervousness and anxiety, sexual dysfunction, insomnia, headaches, mania, hypomania, and hallucinations. Rarely, they have been linked with suicidal behaviour, particularly in children (Joint Formulary Committee, 2012: s 4.3.3). Tricyclic medication shares many of these effects, but also carries a risk of cardiovascular difficulties and a higher incidence of blurred vision and dry mouth than SSRIs.

In all these cases, there are a variety of medications in each class, each of which will have different positive effects and adverse effects, and will work differently on different people. Similarly, the required dosage of drugs will vary depending on the individual. The process of determining what will be effective or optimal for a given patient may be a matter of trial and error. Sometimes, these medications may be prescribed in combination ('polypharmacy'), or in excess of the dosages recommended by the manufacturers ('megadosing'). These practices are associated with increased adverse effects, including, perhaps, mortality (Carnahan *et al.*, 2006; Ray *et al.*, 2009). In the UK, it would nonetheless seem that roughly 40 per cent of people in hospital receiving antipsychotic medication on a given day are in receipt of more than one such drug, and more than one third are in receipt of dosages above the maxima listed in the British National Formulary (BNF) (Paton *et al.*, 2008). Polypharmacy among inpatients would appear to be particularly prevalent in men and detained patients, and it seems to decrease with age at least up to age 65 (Lelliott *et al.*, 2002). These situations are not necessarily restricted to hospital. A recent study found that 16 per cent of people taking antipsychotics on discharge were prescribed more than one such medication, and 7 per cent discharged on dosages in excess of BNF standards (Tungaraza *et al.*, 2011). In the community generally, it may be that prevalence is higher. Tungaraza's 2010 study of prescribing practice in Wales found that only 37 per cent of those on antipsychotics were on one such drug, and almost a third were receiving three or more. Fourteen per cent were on dosages above BNF maxima (Tungaraza *et al.*, 2010).

These figures for polypharmacy include only combinations of antipsychotics. When other psychiatric medications are included (for example, antidepressants and mood stabilisers) Tungaraza's figures rise to about two thirds of people on combinations of psychiatric medications on discharge. In Tungaraza's community study, more than half those receiving antipsychotic medication had been prescribed antidepressants in the previous year, and 15 per cent mood stabilisers. Sometimes, combinations can be much more complex, particularly when medications for physical disorders are included in the mix. The median number of medications overall prescribed for patient's on discharge in Tungaraza's study was two, but the maximum number was 24. The presence of large numbers of medications raises obvious questions as to how the medications may be interacting with each other, but it also serves as a reminder that some cases are actually very complex.

Psychiatric medications comprise 8.6 per cent of prescriptions in England, accounting for 10 per cent of the cost of prescription drugs, or a total of £880 million per year. While antidepressants account for a little more than half the prescription amounts and antipsychotics just under 10 per cent, antipsychotics account for roughly one third of the cost (£282 million), and antidepressants for an additional quarter (£220 million) (Ilyas and Moncrieff, 2013: table 1). A result of these numbers is that psychiatric medication is big business in England and internationally. Drug companies are often huge. GlaxoSmithKline, for example, had a turnover of £27.4 billion in 2011, of which £18.7 billion was pharmaceuticals. Psychiatric medication accounted for a little less than 10 per cent of that, £1.7 billion (GlaxoSmithKline, 2012: 2). The company turned a profit in 2011 of £8 billion. AstraZeneca made a profit of $13.2 billion on sales of $32.6 billion in 2011. Its turnover on its main antipsychotics, Seroquil IR and Seroquil XR, was $5.8 billion worldwide in 2011 (AstraZeneca, 2012: 5). This is the world of major capitalism, and as one would expect in a highly competitive market, drug companies operate on the logic of the market. Inevitably, this will lead to tensions with health promotion objectives. A particularly clear case involves Seroxat (a trade name for the drug paroxetine), an antidepressant medication. The manufacturer, GlaxoSmithKline, chose in the late 1990s not to disclose evidence to the drug regulator that there was no evidence of the drug's efficacy in children and adolescents, and indeed that there was a risk of increased suicidal behaviour in this population. They eventually disclosed this information in 2003. In the interim the drug had been widely prescribed to children, with 32,000 prescriptions issued for children in the UK in 1999 alone. It would seem, according to their internal emails, that the decision not to disclose in the 1990s flowed from a concern that to do so would 'undermine the profile' of the drug, and out of a concern for 'potential negative commercial impact' (McGoey and Jackson, 2009: 107–08). Drugs are developed by large corporations in market environments; it is unreasonable to expect that they will be governed by the public good or health care optimisation rather than profit motives. At the same time, the pharmaceutical companies are major lobbying forces that have tremendous effects on health policy, and they provide the information on which prescription choices are made. It would be naïve to deny that this constitutes a real conflict.

The recitation of even the most common adverse effects may give an overarching negative impression of the medications. That is not intended. Re-read the user accounts of their disorders in Chapter 1. If the antipsychotics or antidepressants make those highly unpleasant experiences go away, that is likely to be perceived as beneficial by patients. Roughly 80 per cent of people who take antipsychotic medication will have a therapeutic response (although even if they stay on the medication, 80 per cent of people with schizophrenia will also suffer at least one relapse within five years) (Jones and Grey, 2008: 344) In a study by Gray *et al.*, roughly 45 per cent of patients with schizophrenia were satisfied with their antipsychotic medication, and an additional 23 percent very satisfied. Roughly 20 per cent were dissatisfied or very dissatisfied (Grey *et al.*, 2005). Consistent with this, as mentioned earlier, more than 8 per cent of prescriptions in England and Wales are for psychiatric medication (Ilyas and Moncrieff, 2012: table 1). Large numbers of people with mental health difficulties therefore take these medications, and most will not be under the compulsory powers of the MHA 1983. They may or may not take the drugs with enthusiasm, but many patients presumably consider that on balance taking the drugs is preferable to not doing so.

That said there does seem to be a strain in the political and legal discourses that psychiatric mediations are unproblematic. In 1998, when the process for reform was commenced that eventually resulted in the MHA 2007, health minister Paul Boateng stated that there was 'a responsibility on individual patients to comply with their programmes of care' and that '[n]on compliance can no longer be an option when appropriate care in appropriate settings is in place' (Department of Health and Welsh Office, 1999b: 142). The impression is that there is no downside to treatment, and that patients should therefore just say yes. Similarly, as will be clear in the discussion that follows, courts are content to adopt readings of law and views of evidence that favour the provision of compulsory treatment. In *R (JB)* v *Haddock* [2006] EWCA Civ 961, for example, Auld LJ held that ECHR safeguards should not be interpreted 'to cut across the grain of good medical practice' (para. 33). While the potential benefit of the drugs to at least some people is clear, the problematic aspects of the drugs must also be acknowledged. In Grey's study, two thirds of patients were experiencing adverse effects, and 22 per cent of patients were experiencing adverse effects that they considered intolerable, that is, not something they could put up with (Grey *et al.*, 2005: 34). These are complex drugs, with significant benefits and significant detriments that affect different people differently. While there are certainly reasons why a patient might wish to take the medications, there are also cogent reasons in many cases why they would wish not to do so. This is an important point in a chapter on an area of law that is largely concerned with forcing people to take these drugs when they do not wish to do so.

9.3.2 **Electro-convulsive therapy (ECT)**

Electro-convulsive therapy (ECT) involves running an electrical current through the patient's brain for approximately four seconds, to induce an epileptic seizure. For reasons that are not clearly understood, this can have a positive effect on a patient's mood, and ECT is in England, and internationally, an accepted treatment for severe depression, particularly in cases where medications have proven ineffective, and it may also be used in emergency situations where an individual's life is at risk as a result of refusal of food or drink or, occasionally, an ongoing wish to commit suicide (Greenhalgh *et al.*, 2005). A typical treatment plan consists of around 12 'doses' of the treatment. It has been estimated that 'around 20,000 people have ECT every year' (Farrell, 1997: 130). In the Department of Health's (DH's) two month (January–March 1999) survey of the use of ECT there were 2,835 patients (1,900 or two-thirds of whom were female) in receipt of 16,482 doses of ECT. In the days following its discovery in 1938, adverse effects included bone fractures (including spinal fractures) flowing from the seizures, but these have been largely eliminated with the use of anaesthetic and muscle relaxants prior to treatment. While Greenhalgh *et al.* note the paucity of study of adverse effects of ECT, it would now seem that the primary adverse effect is memory loss. While this is often temporary, anecdotal reports do suggest that it can be long-term. The treatment seems to be used particularly in older people. In the DH 1999 survey for example, 5.8 people per 100,000 in the population as a whole underwent ECT, but this rose to 15.1 per 100,000 in the population over the age of 65.

Much psychiatric treatment provokes strong views among service users, but ECT appears to have been particularly controversial. Personal testimony from patients both for and against ECT can be found. Perkins (1996), for example, details how her depression prevented her from functioning, as she was 'unable to think properly' (1996: 66) and yet, after receiving a course of six doses of ECT was back at work within a week. Perkins experienced little in the way of side effects although she did suffer from memory problems whilst having the course of treatment. In a survey involving 54 patients, 85 per cent thought themselves slightly, or much, better for having received a course of ECT treatment (Benbow and Crentsil, 2004). In contrast, Taylor (1996) describes the course of 12 ECT treatments given to him as 'barbaric or inhuman'. He experienced a number of side effects, including severe headaches, neck ache, memory loss, disorientation, and 'total confusion and a confused sense of time and space', which left him in a 'vegetative, numb or stupified condition' (1996: 64). Taylor reports that although the intensity of these effects lessened over time, memory problems, low self esteem and a state of confusion were semi-permanent effects of the treatment. Such stories are fairly common.

ECT is subject to particular legal provisions in the MHA 1983 (see further below 9.4.3.2).

9.3.3 **Psychosurgery**

Psychosurgery (or 'neurosurgery') involves the destruction of brain tissue, or the creation of lesions to separate the frontal lobe cortex from the limbic lobe (a process called 'lobotomy' or 'leucotomy'), to reduce unwanted emotions. It was once viewed as a highly promising treatment; indeed, the Nobel Prize for Medicine in 1949 was shared by António Egas Moniz for the discovery of its therapeutic effects. It is legally important, as the MHA 1983 requires both a competent consent from the patient and also the approval of an independent doctor provided by the CQC (a 'SOAD'— a second opinion approved doctor, see further 9.4.2 prior to its performance (MHA 1983, s. 57)— again, see further 9.3.2.1). It is of minimal practical importance, however, as it has now almost completely fallen out of use. There were only 45 cases in England between 1997 and 2010, and in 2009–10, the CQC received only one request for the treatment to be authorised (CQC, 2010: 93).

9.3.4 **Talking therapies**

In addition to these physical interventions, there is a wide array of psychotherapeutic therapies available. They occur most commonly in one-on-one settings (the patient and a therapist) or group environments (a group of patients and one or more therapists), but cognitive behavioural therapy (CBT) is now also available on computer, and it is recommended by NICE for mild depression in this form (alongside other CBT provision). The therapy will normally involve some form of discussion between therapist and patient, either individually or in a group setting, but it may contain other activity as well, as for example in music or art therapy. The objectives of the psychotherapy will depend on the situation of the patient and the type of therapy in question, but they tend to encourage self-examination by services users of their situation, sometimes with a view to cure (e.g., identifying a cause of an individual's depression and addressing it) or sometimes, more modestly, helping the individual to understand their situation and encourage productive (or, at least, less destructive) responses to it. It is this self-reflexive quality, coupled with therapeutic goals, that distinguishes psychotherapeutic regimes from other activity that may be good for the patient. Thus there is a growing body of evidence that exercise is beneficial for people at risk of depression (Rimer *et al.*, 2012) and might well be recommended by a doctor, but going to the gym of itself is not psychotherapy, as it lacks the quality of structured self-reflection. Similarly, simply playing in a band is not in itself music therapy, and going out to sketch the countryside is not art therapy.

For some disorders, psychotherapy will be at the core of the treatment programme, sometimes to the exclusion or near-exclusion of other interventions. This is the case for many personality disorders, for example, and as noted also for mild depression. In other cases, psychotherapy will be in conjunction with other treatments. Thus for example, NICE now recommends that CBT be provided as an adjunct treatment for schizophrenia, to encourage people to associate their thoughts and feelings with current or past symptoms or behaviours (NICE, 2009: para. 1.3.4.12).

Psychotherapy is legally interesting because it relies on the active engagement of the patient, and may well not involve any physical contact. These factors make the standard law relating to medical treatment difficult to apply. If consent is understood as a defence to a battery (non-consensual touching), it is doubtful whether consent is necessary for psychotherapy, where no such touching occurs (see *R (B)* v *Ashworth Special Hospital* [2005] UKHL 20, para. 10). It is therefore largely outside the scope of common law regulation. At the same time, as it is based on the active engagement of the patient, it is difficult to see that it can be successfully administered without the patient's positive co-operation. As such, it is difficult to see that it can effectively be administered under legal compulsion, although 'leverage' mechanisms may induce co-operation, much as they do in cases of apparent consent, discussed at 9.1.

9.4 Compulsory treatment of detained patients for mental disorder: The statutory provisions

9.4.1 **The scope of s. 63**

The basic rule regarding compulsory treatment of detained patients is contained in s. 63 of the MHA 1983:

> The consent of a patient shall not be required for any medical treatment given to him for the mental disorder from which he is suffering, not being a form of treatment to which section 57, 58 or 58A above applies, if the treatment is given by or under the direction of the approved clinician in charge of the treatment.

'Patient' is defined by s. 56 of the MHA 1983 to include, for purposes of s. 63, only patients who are detained under the MHA 1983, but not if:

- the patient is detained under, s. 5(2) or 5(4) (emergency holding provisions for informal patients pending assessment), s. 35 (remand of accused by court for assessment), s. 135 or s. 136 (short-term detentions pending assessment), or under one medical certificate under s. 4 (emergency admission) (for all these, see further Chapter 6, 6.4);

- the patient is detained in a place of safety pending detention in hospital under ss. 37(4) or 45A(5) (see further Chapter 8);

- the patient has been conditionally discharged from detention under ss. 42(2), 73, or 74 and has not been recalled to hospital (see further Chapter 11, 11.3).

The first two of these cases refer to people in very brief detentions, pending initial assessment or actual admission to hospital. Section 63 thus applies to people detained following actual hospital admission on the major sections (e.g., for assessment (s. 2) or for treatment (s. 3), by a court in the criminal process (ss. 37, 38, 45A), or on a prison transfer (ss. 47, 48)). The third case precludes the application of s. 63 only when conditionally discharged patients have not been recalled; upon recall, s. 63 does apply. This places these patients in the same situation as community patients, who are expressly included in the remit of s. 63 if they have been recalled (s. 56(4)) (see further Chapter 10, 10.4.2). The exclusion does not expressly cover patients living in the community on leaves of absence from hospital under s. 17. This is illogical, as the situation of a patient on leave of absence may be very similar to that of a community patient. Further, one of the consistencies in the exclusions would seem to be that enforced treatment should only happen in hospital. The failure expressly to exclude patients living in the community on s. 17 leave seems arbitrary.

The general rule for detained patients is therefore that they can be treated for their mental disorders without their consent. A corollary is that, while valid and enforceable advance decisions to refuse treatment for mental disorder under the MCA 2005 must be respected for informal patients, they are not effective for detained patients. There is a logic to this: an advance decision puts an individual in the same situation as a person making a capacitous refusal of treatment (MCA 2005, s. 26(1)). If a capable refusal can be overridden by s. 63 of the MHA 1983, it is logical that the advance decision is similarly unenforceable. The exception is a valid and applicable advance refusal of ECT (see further 9.4.3.2).

The general rule that consent is not required is subject to the exceptions in ss. 57, 58, and 58A: electro-convulsive therapy (s. 58A) and treatments under s. 57 (most notably psychosurgery) have special rules. Section 58 limits the general rule of no consent for treatment with medication after three months, requiring either that the patient consent to the treatment or that it is approved by in a second opinion provided by a doctor appointed under a statutory scheme (a 'SOAD'—a second opinion approved doctor). Each of these exceptions will be discussed further in this chapter (s. 57 at 9.4.3.1, s. 58 at 9.4.2, and s. 58A at 9.4.3.2).

The issue at the moment is the scope of s. 63: what is 'medical treatment given to him for the mental disorder from which he is suffering'? The point is important because treatment within s. 63 can be given without consent, where treatment outside s. 63 requires consent (or compliance with the MCA 2005, if the patient lacks capacity to consent).

'Medical treatment' is defined in s 145 of the MHA 1983, including 'nursing, psychological interventions and specialist mental health habilitation, rehabilitation and care' (s. 145(1)), the purpose of which 'is to alleviate, or prevent a worsening of, the disorder or one or more of its symptoms or manifestations' (s. 145(4)). This is a remarkably broad definition. Clearly the medications and psychotherapy commonly prescribed for mental disorders and described earlier in this chapter would be within its remit.

The courts have moved considerably beyond such core treatment, and pushed the boundaries of the definition to the maximum. In *B v Croydon Health Authority* [1995] 1 All ER 683, for example, a manifestation of B's personality disorder was a refusal of food, and the question in the Court of Appeal was whether force-feeding her was within the scope of s. 63. The evidence was clear that her personality disorder could only be treated by psychotherapy, and it was argued on B's behalf that the provision of food was not treatment, but at most rather a prerequisite to treatment. The court viewed this approach as 'too atomistic', and after noting the breadth of the definition in s. 145, held (at 687):

> It does not however follow that every act which forms part of that treatment within the wide definition in section 145(1) must in itself be likely to alleviate or prevent a deterioration of that disorder. Nursing and care concurrent with the core treatment or as a necessary prerequisite to such treatment or to prevent the patient from causing harm to himself or to alleviate the consequences of the disorder are in my view all capable of being ancillary to a treatment calculated to alleviate or prevent a deterioration of the psychopathic disorder.

The finding in *B* is puzzling, in that all inpatients are provided with food and similar requirements of life when they are admitted to hospital, whether for mental disorder or other cause. Certainly, treatment can only continue if the patient remains alive, but is that enough for the provision of this care to constitute treatment for the disorder? Cancer patients also receive food; does that make the food treatment for the cancer? Is it instead the fact that it must be compelled that makes the food provision treatment in B's case? That would be peculiar: why would something that was not treatment already become treatment because it is compelled? There is no suggestion of that approach in the B case, although there may be some sense of that in *R (Brady) v Collins and Ashworth Special Hospital* (2001) 58 BMLR 173 (QB), where the refusal of food by a patient on hunger strike was understood in part as part of a set of complex power relations with the medical authorities flowing from the patient's personality disorder.

If feeding can constitute treatment for mental disorder, can the overall conditions of detention do so as well? This was the question for the court in *Reid v Secretary of State for Scotland* [1999] 2 AC 512 (HL). For present purposes, the Scots legislation at issue in that case did not differ from the English MHA. In that case, the patient was not receiving treatment for his personality disorder, apart from his detention in a high security environment. His doctor took the view that Reid's anger management improved in the structured environment of the ward, and that since this environment was under the supervision of a clinician, this constituted treatment. The court agreed (531, 541, 552). The MHA Code of Practice (DH, 2008) further allows for this possibility, noting that treatment does not necessarily involve medicines or psychological therapy and that '[t]here may be patients whose particular circumstances mean that treatment may be appropriate even though it consists only of nursing and specialist day-to-day care under the clinical supervision of an approved clinician, in a safe and secure therapeutic environment with a structured regime' (para. 6.16). It then goes on to state that '[s]imply detaining someone—even in a hospital—does not constitute medical treatment' (para. 6.17). While after *Reid* this seems a correct reading of the case law on the point, it is fair to wonder quite what the difference is between care on the ward, where neither psychotherapy nor medication is available, and mere detention.

Perhaps the most startling of the cases on the meaning of treatment for mental disorder in s. 63 is *Tameside and Glossip Acute Services Trust v CH* [1996] 1 FLR 762 (Fam). In that case, CH was 38 weeks pregnant and suffered from schizophrenia. Complications in the pregnancy developed, such that delivery by Caesarean section was considered necessary by the care team, and the question was whether the Caesarean section operation was within the scope of s. 63. Following the B case, the court held that it was, on the basis that a stillbirth would involve a deterioration of CH's mental state and interrupt the treatment of her schizophrenia. This interruption would arise both from the grieving process for the child, and, the care team believed, her consequent blaming of the medical staff for the stillbirth. In addition, her schizophrenia treatment had been interrupted, as the relevant medication could not be used during her pregnancy. This finding does seem to push the statutory language beyond reasonable limits. The evidence that failing to give birth to a healthy baby would increase her schizophrenia was at best speculative. Certainly, she would be expected to have a grief reaction, but it is not obvious from the evidence that this would have been more extreme than anyone else in similar circumstances. No evidence was given that she had an immediate need for the stronger medications that could not be given to her during pregnancy, drugs she had apparently not been using for some months. The motivation for the intervention appears to have been the well-being of CH and her prospective child—a laudable motivation, no doubt, but not obviously one which converts a Caesarean section operation into treatment for schizophrenia.

What are we to take from these cases? It does seem that the court has been prepared to stretch the scope of s. 63 a very long way. Whether this will continue to be the case is less obvious. The leading cases pre-date the MCA 2005, and it may well be that capacity arguments will supplant some of the s. 63 arguments. In *CH*, the court specifically held that CH lacked capacity to make the relevant decisions, and in *B*, the Court of Appeal specifically doubted the first instance finding that B did indeed have capacity. It may be that the MCA 2005 is perceived as the new way forward for these rather peripheral treatments under s. 63. Further, at least regards pregnancy, the Court of Appeal in *R (S) v St. George's Healthcare NHS Trust* [1998] 3 WLR 936 criticised robustly the use of the MHA 1983 to enforce Caesarean section operations onto women who did not want them. That was a case, however, where there was no credible evidence that the mother had a mental disorder of any sort. The court in *S* makes no express criticism of the approach in *CH*, suggesting that the broad approach to the scope of s. 63 may yet be good law.

Once the treatment has been held to be within the scope of s. 63, and unless the treatment provided is either ECT or a treatment regulated by s. 57 (most notably, psychosurgery), the MHA 1983 provides no procedural safeguards of any sort to the administration of compulsory treatment under s. 63 for three months, at which point the provisions of s. 58 will apply in most cases. The patient can of course challenge his or her detention before the review tribunal, but the tribunal in those cases is focused on the criteria for detention, not the specifics of treatment. There are no express treatment-related requirements for detention under s. 2, and under s. 3, the requirement is merely that 'appropriate treatment is available' (see further Chapter 6, 6.3.1.2). An application for judicial review is in principle possible (a *Wilkinson* hearing: see further 9.5.3), but no such hearing has been successful, and indeed while there are certainly cases where the applicability of s 63 has been challenged (most notably, the cases discussed in this section regarding its scope), there are no reported cases of a *Wilkinson* hearing occurring prior to the expiry of the three-month period that triggers s. 58.

9.4.2 **The safeguards of s. 58**

The safeguard provided by s. 58 applies to the administration of medicine after three months have elapsed since he or she was first treated with medicine for his or her mental disorder as an involuntary patient (MHA 1983, s. 58(1)(b)). In that event, the administration of medicine can occur only if either the patient is capable and consents to its administration or a second opinion in support of the treatment is provided by a SOAD. The section specifically does not apply to ECT and s. 57 treatments (most notably psychosurgery), which are subject to different and more stringent rules (see further 9.4.3.2 for ECT and 9.4.3.1 for s. 57).

The safeguard under s. 58 applies only to 'the administration of medicine'. It therefore does not apply to aspects of treatment or care that may be quite intensive, but do not involve the administration of medicine. Thus is does not apply to psychotherapy unless medication is administered in addition to the talking elements of those regimes, and if that is the case, it applies only to the medication. It would seem that it does not apply to force-feeding, since food is not considered to be a medicine (*B v Croydon HA*) and the tentative view of the Mental Health Act Commission (now subsumed into the CQC) in 1999 was that it did not extend to placebos either: (Mental Health Act Commission, 1999: para. 6.17). This position makes some sense if, following *B*, 'medicine' is defined in terms of its chemical composition.

In all these examples, however, one might equally ask what purpose the safeguard in s. 58 is meant to achieve. If it is meant to protect patients against physical harm from adverse effects, a restrictive reading of 'medication' makes sense: feeding through a tube, psychotherapy, and placebos are all low risk in terms of adverse physical effects (although in the case of tube feeding, not necessarily zero risk, and in the case of psychotherapy, there may be psychological risks). If instead the purpose is meant to be providing a more rounded reassessment of the course of action in a situation where, after three months, the patient is not consenting to the treatment, the restrictive reading of s. 58 is not so convincing. This is perhaps most obvious in the case of *Brady*, who continues to be force-fed 14 years after his case was decided. Can it really be the intention of the statute that force-feeding should continue for this length of time, with no mandatory outside assessment of its ongoing appropriateness? Treatment by placebo raises a different set of questions, since by definition the patient will not know that he or she is being treated by placebo, and therefore cannot offer consent within the meaning of s. 58, since he or she will not know the 'nature, purpose and likely effects' (s. 58(3)(a)) of the substance being ingested. It seems fair to ask in this circumstance whether it was really the intention of the legislator to allow the ongoing deception of the patient, again with no mandatory outside assessment of the appropriateness of that deception.

The three-month period technically runs from the first time medicine is given as treatment for mental disorder during the patient's detention, not from the commencement of the detention itself. Often, this will make only a small difference, since many detained people are treated with medication promptly on admission.

Beyond the three month initial period, the treatment may continue if the patient consents to it (s. 58(3)(a)). In this event, the patient's responsible clinician must certify that the patient is capable of understanding the nature, purpose, and likely effects of the treatment and consents to it; or a SOAD must certify either that the patient lacks the capability to consent to the treatment or that he or she has capacity but refuses it, and also that it is nonetheless appropriate that the treatment be given (s. 58(3)). There is further elaboration on this threshold in s. 64(3), which states that 'it is appropriate for treatment to be given to a patient if the treatment is appropriate in his case, taking into account the nature and degree of the mental disorder from which he is suffering and all other circumstances of his case.' It is difficult to see that this advances understanding much, saying as it does that the treatment is appropriate if it is appropriate. It perhaps leaves the argument that the determination is not simply a clinical assessment, but should include a broader assessment of the patient's situation.

Prior to so certifying, the SOAD must consult two people professionally involved in the patient's care other than the responsible clinician. One of these consultees must be a nurse, and the other neither a nurse nor a doctor (s. 58(4)). In practice, this 'other' consultee appears often to be a social worker, although there is no requirement that it be so.

The SOAD system is administered by the CQC. The panel of SOADs consists of consultant psychiatrists of at least five years standing. While the CQC provides general guidance to SOADs and assigns a SOAD to the particular case, once assigned the SOAD acts independently, rather than under the direction of the CQC, and is expected to form an independent view of the situation (R (Wilkinson) v Broadmoor Special Hospital Authority [2001] EWCA 1545, paras. 32–33, 71; R (B) v S [2006] EWCA Civ 28, para. 71). Reasons for the SOAD's decision must also be provided (R (JW) v Feggetter and MHAC [2002] EWCA 554).

The SOAD system was introduced by the mental health legislative reforms of the early 1980s, and it remains the only significant procedural safeguard relating to compulsory treatment. In practice, it offers little protection. To begin with, as noted, it takes effect only after three months of psychiatric treatment under detention. This is significantly longer than the bulk of detentions last. In 2009–10, 45,755 people were detained under the MHA 1983; SOAD opinions were given regarding these people in 8,781 cases—just under 20 per cent (CQC, 2010:19 and 83). This means that for more than 80 per cent of detentions, there was no external monitoring of compulsory treatment at all. This limitation in itself was enough to raise the concerns of the Mental Health Act Commission, the then administrator of the SOAD scheme, in its final report prior to its merging into the CQC (Mental Health Act Commission, 2009: 3.17):

> It is seems quite possible that the absence of an external safeguard in relation to the imposition of medication without consent for such a period will, at some future point, be found incompatible with human rights obligations, given modern medical practice and pharmacopoeia.

Even for those patients within the SOAD system, it is not obvious how much of a safeguard is provided. In 2008, SOADs made some alteration to about one in four treatment plans, but the considerable bulk of these were 'slight'. Significant alterations were made in only four per cent of cases (Mental Health Act Commission, 2009: fig. 50). There may of course be many reasons for such a low rate of amendment; but nonetheless the level of agreement is striking.

Concerns regarding the efficacy of the SOAD system have been long-standing (see, e.g., Fennell 1996). It is therefore perhaps surprising to see the substantive standard of the opinion required of the SOAD weakened in the 2007 legislation. Prior to that time, the SOAD had been required to attest that 'having regard to the likelihood of its alleviating or preventing a deterioration of [the patient's] condition the treatment should be given' (s 58(3)(b)). It is now merely that 'it is appropriate for the treatment to be given'. The new wording does make clear that the SOAD's decision is not solely a clinical appraisal, but requires the balancing of clinical and social factors (see DH, 2008: para. 24.57–8); but it equally appears to water down the clinical aspect. The word 'appropriate' suggests not a clear assessment of whether the treatment will work, or whether the SOAD views it as the right choice, but instead a more *Bolam*-like assessment of whether it is within the bounds of reasonableness. It is difficult to see that this standard will strengthen the SOAD's role. The Code of Practice advised SOADs regarding the old wording that the test was whether proposed treatment was 'reasonable in light of the general consensus of appropriate treatment', a phrasing criticised by the Court of Appeal (see *R (Wilkinson)* v *Broadmoor Special Hospital Authority* [2001] EWCA 1545, para. 32–3, 71; *R (B)* v *S* [2006] EWCA Civ 28). The rewording in 2007 can perhaps be seen as undoing the rather limited gain that patients had made through litigation. While the current Code of Practice continues to note that the decision is an independent one for the SOAD (para. 24.56), the language of the new standard suggests a weakening of the independent assessment to be made.

9.4.3 Exceptional cases

The preceding rules of general application are overlaid by more specific rules relating to ECT, treatments governed by psychosurgery, and urgent treatments.

9.4.3.1 Section 57 treatments

Treatments within the scope of s. 57 may be provided only if both the patient offers a competent consent to the treatment and also if a SOAD certifies that the treatment is appropriate to be given. As in s. 58, this certification may only occur following consultation with a nurse and a non-medical professional, both of whom are involved in the patient's care. The SOAD must also certify that the patient understands the nature, purpose, and likely effects of the treatment, and consents to it (s. 57(2)–(3)).

Section 57 covers all patients, not merely those who are detained (see s. 56(1)).

The section covers psychosurgery ('any surgical operation for destroying brain tissue or for destroying the functioning of brain tissue'—s. 57(1)(a)) and such other treatments as may be specified in regulation by the Secretary of State. To date, there has been one such additional treatment, the surgical implantation of hormones for the purpose of reducing the male sexual drive (see *Mental Health Regulations 2008*, SI 2008/1184, reg. 27(1)). The relevance of this addition has been effectively annihilated by the decision of the court in *R* v *Mental Health Act Commission, ex p X* (1988) 9 BMLR 77, where the court held that the term 'hormone' did not include hormone analogues, and the phrase 'surgical implantation' did not include administration by syringe. This is a somewhat surprising finding as hormone analogues have much the same chemical function and purpose as actual hormones, although the one at issue in the case, Goserelin, was roughly one hundred times as powerful as natural hormones. Memorably putting the letter of the statute before its spirit, Stuart Smith, LJ held that '[i]f Parliament passes legislation on the control of leopards, it is not to be presumed that leopards include tigers on the basis that they are larger and fiercer' (p. 83). Now, hormone analogues are virtually always used instead of natural hormones, and they are administered orally rather than surgically. The result is notwithstanding the apparent parliamentary intent that hormonal alterations of male sex drive be subject to particular scrutiny, the treatments as practised are outside the scope of s. 57. There have been no requests for a SOAD opinion for hormone treatments since 1988 (Jones, 2011: para. 1–664).

Of interest under this section is also a new technique, deep brain stimulation. Unlike psychosurgery, this does not involve the destruction of brain tissue. Instead, it involves the surgical implantation of stimuli that sent electrical impulses to various parts of the brain—essentially a 'brain pacemaker'. There has been some experimental usage of this technology in the context of treatment for mental disorder, particularly treatment resistant major depression and Tourette's Syndrome. The Scots legislation has for some years provided similar safeguards for this treatment to those provided under s. 57 of the MHA 1983 (see Mental Health (Medical treatments subject to safeguards) (Section 234) (Scotland) Regulations 2005 (SSI No.291)) and the Mental Health Act Commission and its successor body, the CQC, have been pressing for its inclusion in s. 57 since 2007 (Mental Health Act Commission, 2008: para. 6.89–91). As yet, the government has declined to respond to the Commission's recommendations.

As a question of law, treatments governed by s. 57 may be given in urgent situations: see s. 62, discussed at 9.4.3.3. That said, given the nature of the treatments, it is difficult to imagine circumstances where this would be appropriate. If the patient has capacity and consents, it is difficult to imagine circumstances sufficiently pressing that a SOAD could not be made available. If the patient refuses to consent or does not have capacity, the clear intent of s. 57 is that the treatment should not be given. It is difficult to see that s. 62 should be used to end-run the clear intent of the statutory provision. Further, the terms of s. 62 only justify treatment which is not irreversible, unless the patient's life is at risk. Psychosurgery, the key treatment under s. 57, involves the cutting of brain tissue, and that is irreversible. It would thus in practice be justified under s. 62 only if the patient's life were at risk, and it is difficult to see that as a likely scenario.

9.4.3.2 ECT

The statutory provisions regarding ECT cover detained patients (as defined at 9.4.1), and persons under the age of 18 years (whether or not they are detained) unless they are subject to a community treatment order (s. 56). This means that regarding ECT, informal patients over the age of 18 years remain outside the scope of the MHA 1983 and can be treated only either with their capable consent or, if incapable, under the terms of the MCA 2005.

For detained patients over the age of 18 years who have capacity to consent, ECT may only be administered with the consent of the patient. Prior to such administration, the clinician providing the ECT, or a SOAD, must certify that the patient is capable of understanding the purpose, nature, and likely effects of the treatment and has consented to it (s. 58A(3)).

For adult detained patients lacking the capacity to consent to ECT, the treatment may proceed if a SOAD certifies that the patient is not capable of understanding the nature, purpose, or likely effects of treatment, that it is appropriate that treatment may be given, and that the treatment does not conflict with a valid and applicable advance decision to refuse the treatment, or a decision made by a donee of an LPOA or a court-appointed deputy under the MCA 2005 (MHA 1983, s. 58A(5)). As under s. 58, the SOAD must, prior to certifying the appropriateness of the treatment, consult with a nurse and a non-medical professional who have been professionally concerned with the patient's treatment.

These provisions regarding ECT are one of the significant changes introduced by the MHA 2007. For the first time, competent patients can refuse ECT, and can sign binding advance decisions under the MCA 2005 to refuse the ECT. Usually, such advance decisions can be overridden in the case of detained patients by the compulsory treatment provisions of the MHA 1983. Section 58A makes it clear that this is not the case for valid and applicable advance decisions refusing ECT.

For patients under the age of 18 years with capacity to consent, ECT may be given only if a SOAD certifies that the patient is capable of understanding the nature, purpose, and likely effects of the treatment and consents to it, and also that it is appropriate for the treatment to be given (s. 58A(4)). This means that competent minors cannot be given ECT without their consent. This is a significant departure from the common law position, which allows either parent or child to consent to treatment, whether or not the child has capacity, until the child reaches the age of 18 (*Re W (A Minor) (Medical Treatment: Court's Jurisdiction)* [1992] 3 WLR 758).

If the minor lacks capacity to consent to the ECT, authority for treatment must be obtained through parental consent or, if the patient is over the age of 16, through the MCA 2005 (MHA 1983, s. 58A(7)). Paragraph 36.60 of the Code of Practice recommends that court authorisation should be sought in these cases, but there is no obvious legal requirement to do so. In addition, a SOAD must certify that the patient is not capable of understanding the nature, purpose, and likely effects of the treatment, and that the decision is not inconsistent with the decision of a deputy or of the Court of Protection, as for an adult lacking capacity. Advance decisions to refuse treatment and lasting powers of attorney will not be relevant in this circumstance, as these can only be made by people over the age of 18. Perhaps surprisingly, the objection of a parent to the provision of ECT to an incompetent minor over the age of 16 does not appear to be preclude the SOAD from certifying the appropriateness of the treatment.

Notwithstanding any of the preceding rules, ECT may be given without consent in urgent situations (see s. 62, discussed at 9.4.3.3).

9.4.3.3 Urgent treatment (s. 62)

Section 62 states that sections 57 and 58 do not apply to a treatment (s 62(1)):

(a) which is immediately necessary to save the patient's life;
(b) which (not being irreversible) is immediately necessary to prevent a deterioration of his condition; or
(c) which (not being irreversible or hazardous) is immediately necessary to alleviate serious suffering by the patient; or

(d) which (not being irreversible or hazardous) is immediately necessary and represents the minimum interference necessary to prevent the patient from behaving violently or being a danger to himself or to others.

The scope of s. 62 is limited to treatment which is immediately and minimally necessary, which has been defined tightly at common law in *Devi* v *West Midlands AHA* [1980] 7 CL 44 (HC). There is no other limitation on life saving treatment, but for lesser emergencies the treatment must not be 'irreversible', or 'irreversible and hazardous', as the case may be. These terms are defined in s. 62(3). Treatment is classified as 'irreversible' if it has unfavourable irreversible physical or psychological consequences and 'hazardous' if it entails significant physical hazard. Although all physical treatments potentially carry the risk of unfavourable irreversible consequences, it is unlikely that the emergency administration of clinically indicated drugs would be so classified by a court, or else s. 62 would be otiose. Consistent with this view, as will be discussed in this section, ECT is specifically included within the scope of s. 62.

The section is phrased in such a way that ss. 57 and 58 do not apply. This is easiest to understand in the context of detained patients, where the situation reverts to the general rule of s. 63: detained patients may be treated for their mental disorder without consent. When the circumstances in (a) to (d) are satisfied, the treatment can be administered without the consent of the patient and without a SOAD authorisation, whether or not the three-month period described in s. 58 has expired, and whether or not the treatment is within s. 57.

As noted at 9.4.1, s. 63 does not extend to all detained people. People detained in places of safety pending assessment under ss. 135 or 136, or people detained in emergency situations under s. 2, for example, are outside the scope of s. 63. Section 62 does nothing to change this, and although these may be people in the most immediate need of urgent treatment, it cannot be given under s. 62. In the event that the individual lacks capacity, the treatment could be provided under the MCA 2005, if, as seems likely, the treatment would be in the patient's best interests. If restraint (using or threatening to use force, or doing an act that the patient resists) were required to administer the treatment, however, the MCA 2005 requires that the treatment be to avoid risks to the patient himself or herself (see MCA 2005, s. 6(2) and (3)). Insofar as the risks in question are to others in situations where restraint is necessary, or where the patient has capacity, the MCA 2005 offers no assistance. In the event of serious risk to others, common law may allow some restraint, but it is less obvious that it allows enforced medication.

The situation of informal patients largely mirrors that of detained people outside the scope of s. 63: they cannot be treated under s 63, so the urgency provisions in s. 62 has little effect on them. If they lack capacity, they can be treated under the MCA 2005, subject to the same restrictions noted in the previous paragraph. The point of difference is that s. 57 applies to informal patients, and s. 62 says that in situations of urgency, s. 57 does not apply. It is an interesting academic point what this means. Certainly, a SOAD authorisation would not be required for treatment. Section 57 treatments are presumably medical treatments for mental disorder and thus within the substantive scope of

s. 63, so that a detained patient could be treated without consent; but s. 63 provides no such power for an informal patient. It would seem that the best view is that the effect of s. 62 here is to revert to the basic position for informal patients, that treatment can be provided either with the competent consent of the patient, or under the terms of the MCA 2005. The question is, however, of minimal practical relevance at this time. The only relevant treatment is psychosurgery which, for the reasons outlined at 9.3.3, is in practice unlikely ever to meet the requirements of s. 62.

ECT once again has slightly special rules. It may be given to detained patients on an urgency basis, but only when immediately necessary to save the patient's life or if immediately necessary to prevent a serious deterioration of his condition (s. 62(1A)). In these circumstances, ECT can be given even if a competent patient objects, or has signed an advance decision refusing the treatment, or if the patient lacks capacity and the treatment is refused by a holder of an LPOA or a court-appointed deputy (s. 58A(2)). In the event that the patient lacks capacity, a SOAD authorisation is not required in these circumstances. In practice, it would seem that emergency ECT is used primarily when a severely depressed patient's life is at serious risk, either because of self-neglect or a determined and uncontrollable wish to commit suicide.

9.5 Involuntary treatment of detained patients for mental disorder: Jurisprudence and analysis

In general, the MHA 1983 offers few safeguards to the compulsory treatment of detained patients for their mental disorders. As noted in 9.4, except in unusual cases, such treatment may be given without consent for three months, and after that either with consent or following certification by a SOAD. While the statute thus permits treatment without consent, nothing in the MHA 1983 requires a clinician to enforce treatment on a given patient. It is instead a matter of discretion by the clinician. While some minimal obligations to provide treatment may exist in negligence law, that does not fundamentally alter matters, as the test of negligence is also one of reasonable professional judgment (*Bolam* v *Friern Hospital Management Committee* [1957] 2 All ER 118; *Bolitho* v *City and Hackney HA* [1997] 4 All ER 771). This raises the question, therefore, as to how a doctor should exercise this discretion: when should treatment be enforced?

9.5.1 The substantive criteria for involuntary treatment and the ECHR

The MHA 1983 is notably silent on substantive criteria in this regard, and the Code of Practice similarly offers no significant guidance. This silence is increasingly untenable, as international instruments increasingly call into question the use of enforced treatment. Thus the published standards of the European Committee for the Prevention of Torture (CPT) have, since 1998, provided the following with regard to psychiatric patients (extract from 8th General Report, CPT/Inf (98) 12, para. 41; rpt in current articulation of CPT Standards, CPT/Inf/E (2002) 1–Rev. 2011, 53):

> Patients should, as a matter of principle, be placed in a position to give their free and informed consent to treatment. The admission of a person to a psychiatric establishment on an involuntary basis should not be construed as authorising treatment without his consent. It follows that every competent patient, whether voluntary or involuntary, should be given the opportunity to refuse treatment or other medical intervention. Any derogation from this fundamental principle should be based upon law and only relate to clearly and strictly defined exceptional circumstances.

Other international instruments are consistent with this view. The United Nations Mental Illness Principles (now largely superseded by the more robust provisions of the Convention on the Rights of Persons with Disabilities (CRPD)) has required prior approval by an independent authority of non-consensual psychiatric treatment since 1991 (General Assembly res 46/119 (1991)). Increasingly, internationally, this is being reflected in the provision of rights regarding consent to people with capacity to make the relevant treatment decision. In America, the right of competent detained patients to make decisions regarding treatment has been a constitutional principle for more than thirty years (see *Rennie* v *Klein* 653 F 2d. 836 (USCA, 1981); *Rogers* v *Okin* 634 F 2d 650 (USSC, 1980); *Rogers* v *Okin* 738 F 2d 1 (USCA, 1984)). A similar approach has been adopted in the Republic of Ireland (Mental Health Act (Ireland) Part IV; see Donnelly 2005) and in Ontario (see Bartlett, 2001). The appropriateness of this approach in international law will depend on the degree to which capacity may continue to be used, following the United Nations CRPD (see discussion in Chapter 4, 4.1.1 and 4.7). Indeed, the non-discrimination approach of the CRPD (see the right to treatment based on informed consent without discrimination based on disability, contained in Article 25(d) and the right to integrity in Article 17) raises the question of how far the MHA approach can be continued at all: see further at 9.6. Even ignoring the CRPD issues for the moment, it is difficult to see that the current MHA provisions, with their limited safeguards, minimal procedures, and near-unfettered discretion, are remotely compatible with even the previous international standards and legal norms.

Notwithstanding the CPT's standard, the jurisprudence before the European Court of Human Rights has so far been of minimal assistance, although there are some recent indications that they are beginning to take these matters more seriously. Of particular relevance would seem to be Article 8 of the ECHR, which provides the right to privacy and family life. As the Code of Practice notes, any non-consensual medical treatment engages this Article (para. 23.40); see also, e.g., *Glass* v *the United Kingdom*, Application No. 61827/00, judgment of 9 March 2004, para. 70; *YF* v *Turkey*, Application No. 24209/94, judgment of 22 July 2003, (2004) 39 EHRR 34. Article 8 allows restrictions on such rights, however, when the restrictions are 'in accordance with the law' and 'necessary in a democratic society in the interests of…the protection of health' (Art. 8(2)). The latter of these requirements creates a substantive threshold. While 'necessary' does not mean indispensible, it does mean more than ordinary, reasonable, or desirable (*Handyside* v *the United Kingdom* (A/24) (1976) 1 EHRR 737). Given the CPT standard and the other international and foreign domestic law noted, it is difficult to see that the blanket removal of consent provisions relating to treatment of detained patients meets this standard. Further, the requirement that the interference be in accordance with the law does not, as the paragraph in the Code of Practice suggests, mean merely that the interference has a basis in domestic law, although that is certainly a requirement (*Silver* v *the United Kingdom*, Application No. 5947/72, judgment of 25 February 1983). In addition, the law 'must afford adequate legal protection against arbitrariness and accordingly indicate with sufficient clarity the scope of discretion conferred on the competent authorities and the manner of its exercise' (*S and Marper* v *the United Kingdom*, Applications No. 30562/04, judgment of 4 December 2008, para. 95; see also *Malone* v *the United Kingdom*, Application No. 8691/79, judgment of 2 August 1984, paras. 66–68. The MHA 1983 provision provides unlimited discretion, with no guidance as to how it is to be exercised, over a detained and (as noted in *Herczegfalvy* v *Austria*, Application No. 10533/83, judgment 24 September 1992, (A/242-B) (1993) 15 EHRR 437, para. 82) potentially highly vulnerable population. It is difficult to see that this meets Article 8 requirements.

The engagement of Article 8 further raises the issue of discrimination: why is it permitted to remove the right of consent for people under the MHA 1983, when we do not do so for other ill people? The answer cannot be that they lack capacity (and are thus treated similarly to other ill people without capacity, who lose the right to consent under common law and the MCA 2005), since the MHA 1983 provisions also apply to people who have capacity. It is not obvious why people with mental disabilities are a special case in this regard. Certainly, some people with mental disabilities will make therapeutically poor choices, sometimes with very unfortunate results; but that will also be the case for people with other illnesses. Such bad choices may be expensive in terms of the provision of health care services; but that may also be the case for other illnesses. Sometimes, the choices will have difficult ramifications within the family; but that will also be the case for other illnesses.

Article 14, the anti-discrimination provision of the ECHR, applies only to the provisions of the ECHR itself (although a broader anti-discrimination provision contained in Protocol 12 has been signed by some states, not including the UK), but once Article 8 is engaged, as it is here, Article 14 can be invoked in aid. While disability is not an explicitly prohibited ground of discrimination under Article 14, the list of prohibited grounds is not closed, and disability has now been included by implication by the European Court of Human Rights: see *Glor* v *Switzerland*, Application No. 13444/04, judgment of 6 November 2009. It is not obvious why the current English law, applying as it does to people with mental health problems but not to others, would be consistent with Article 14.

Article 3 prohibits torture and (more relevant for present purposes) inhuman or degrading treatment or punishment. The leading case on psychiatric treatment and Article 3 is *Herczegfalvy* v *Austria*. The treatment at issue in this case included enforced psychiatric medication and physical restraint, most notably handcuffing the patient to a security bed for more than two weeks. The following statement by the court has become the benchmark for interpretation of Article 3 in psychiatric contexts since that time:

> 82. The Court considers that the position of inferiority and powerlessness which is typical of patients confined in psychiatric hospitals calls for increased vigilance in reviewing whether the Convention has been complied with. While it is for the medical authorities to decide, on the basis of the recognised rules of medical science, on the therapeutic methods to be used, if necessary by force, to preserve the physical and mental health of patients who are entirely incapable of deciding for themselves and for whom they are therefore responsible, such patients nevertheless remain under the protection of Article 3 (art. 3), whose requirements permit of no derogation.
>
> The established principles of medicine are admittedly in principle decisive in such cases; as a general rule, a measure which is a therapeutic necessity cannot be regarded as inhuman or degrading. The Court must nevertheless satisfy itself that the medical necessity has been convincingly shown to exist.

No violation of Article 3 was found.

Herczegfalvy was primarily a case concerning detention, and its reasoning regarding Article 3 and enforced psychiatric treatment is at best cursory. While Herczegfalvy had at some time in the past been held to lack at least some capacity, it is not clear whether he had capacity to make the relevant decisions at the time in question. In any event, and notwithstanding the reference to 'patients who are entirely incapable of deciding for themselves', it would seem that capacity is not pivotal to the court's current approach to Article 3 (see *Nevmerzhitsky* v *the Ukraine*, Application No. 54825/00, judgment of 12 October 2005). Measures that are a therapeutic necessity, it would seem, do not violate Article 3 even if a competent patient refuses the treatment in question.

The approach in *Herczegfalvy* is very sympathetic to the medical approach to disability and, certainly until recently, there was little evidence that the court was prepared to look behind a claim of medical necessity in this area. Fundamental issues, such as the meaning of 'therapeutic necessity' and what it would mean for this to be 'convincingly shown to exist' have remained unexplored in the jurisprudence. The absence of case law may perhaps flow from the *Herczegfalvy* itself. The court was not prepared to look behind the medical view that handcuffing an individual to a bed for over two weeks was a therapeutic necessity (para. 83). That cannot have inspired optimism amongst potential litigants.

The beginnings of a more robust approach by the court can perhaps be seen 20 years later, in the case of *Gorobet* v *Moldova* (Application No. 30951/10, judgment of 11 January 2012). In that case, both Mr Gorobet's detention and his enforced treatment were challenged. Regarding the detention, very unusually, the court rejected the evidence of the admitting psychiatrist that the detention was based on an examination prior to the detention occurring (para. 41). The court therefore held that there was no independent medical evidence of mental disorder prior to the detention, and therefore that the detention was in violation of the right to liberty under Article 5. It continues (para. 42):

> It is true that after his confinement in the Bălți psychiatric hospital he was diagnosed with paranoid depression by the doctors treating him; however, it was not argued by the

Government that those records contained information according to which the applicant presented any risk to himself or to other persons, and that therefore his mental disorder was of a kind or degree warranting compulsory confinement.

When it came to the Article 3 point, after citing *Herczegfalvy*, the court held (para. 52):

> The applicant argued that his confinement and forced psychiatric treatment in the Bălți psychiatric hospital caused him severe mental suffering amounting to inhuman and degrading treatment. In the circumstances of the present case, the Court sees no reasons to disagree with the applicant and notes that no medical necessity to subject the applicant to psychiatric treatment has been shown to exist and that his subjecting to psychiatric treatment was unlawful and arbitrary (see paragraphs 41 and 42 above). Moreover, the Court notes the considerable duration of the medical treatment which lasted for forty-one days and the fact that the applicant was not allowed having contact with the outside world during his confinement (see paragraph 8 above). In the Court's view such unlawful and arbitrary treatment was at the very least capable to arouse in the applicant feelings of fear, anguish and inferiority.

On this basis, the court found a violation of Article 3.

It is not clear how the court's reasoning is to be understood. On one reading, the Article 3 violation appears to be bound up with the Article 5 violation: Mr Gorobet should not have been in the psychiatric hospital; the intrusive measures he suffered were thus unjustified; and there was therefore a violation of Article 3. By implication on this reading, had he been correctly detained, there would have been no Article 3 violation. While this is a relatively weak reading in that it would not be furthering an understanding of what 'therapeutic necessity' means for people who are detained consistently with the law, it would still be a significant result, in that it would establish a precedent that people wrongfully detained have an Article 3 claim for what happens to them in hospital, as well as a claim under Article 5.

That reading implies a nexus between the Article 3 and the Article 5 claim, and in principle that should not necessarily be the case. They are, after all, separate rights, and as noted, the move in international law is towards increased consent rights for people in psychiatric hospitals. If that is understood to be the logic, the point is not that detention was unjustified; it is instead that the evidence following admission that he was in need of treatment was not strong enough: he may have been diagnosed with paranoid depression, but there was no evidence that this was such as to present a risk to himself or other persons. Such a finding would still be sympathetic to the medical perspective: it is the treating physicians' own evidence that shows no risk. It would nonetheless suggest that the court is moving beyond a standard where 'medical necessity' means merely clinically appropriate in the honest view of the doctor. If the court is insisting that evidence of risk be required to justify a finding of 'therapeutic necessity', that would be a significant development, in that it would be starting a process of bringing clarity to an otherwise very nebulous concept.

In recent years, the court has also made it clear that even if the treatment itself does not violate Article 3, its mode of administration may (see *Nevmerzhitsky* v *the Ukraine*, Application No. 54825/00, judgment of 12 October 2005). This is consistent with jurisprudence that the use of any force not strictly necessary on a detained person may constitute a violation of Article 3: see, e.g., *Mouisel* v *France*, Application No. 67263/01, judgment of 14 November 2002, (2004) 38 EHRR 34 (handcuffing a prisoner during chemotherapy); *Van der Ven* v *the Netherlands*, Application No. 50901/99, judgment of 4 February 2003, (2004) 38 EHRR 46 (strip searches conducted in an intrusive manner). The mode of administration may be particularly significant in the case of people with mental disabilities, given their particular vulnerability noted in *Herczegfalvy*. This was acknowledged in *Keenan* v *the United Kingdom* Application No. 27229/95, judgment of 3 April 2001, (2001) 33 EHRR 38 (para. 111):

> In particular, the assessment of whether the treatment or punishment concerned is incompatible with the standards of Article 3 has, in the case of mentally ill persons, to take into consideration their vulnerability and their inability, in some cases, to complain coherently or at all about how they are being affected by any particular treatment[.]

In the event that treatment is provided in an unduly intrusive fashion, therefore, an Article 3 issue may arise.

The standard of therapeutic necessity, the cornerstone of the ECHR jurisprudence is in any event under increasing challenge internationally. In his 2013 Report, the United Nations Special Rapporteur on Torture considered, in particular, rights abuses in health-care settings. Regarding enforced treatment in a psychiatric context, he stated (Report to UN General Assembly, A/HRC/22/53, 1 February 2013):

> Forced interventions, often wrongfully justified by theories of incapacity and therapeutic necessity inconsistent with the Convention on the Rights of Persons with Disabilities, are legitimized under national laws, and may enjoy wide public support as being in the alleged "best interest" of the person concerned. Nevertheless, to the extent that they inflict severe pain and suffering, they violate the absolute prohibition of torture and cruel, inhuman and degrading treatment. Concern for the autonomy and dignity of persons with disabilities leads the Special Rapporteur to urge revision of domestic legislation allowing for forced interventions.

This still requires a minimum threshold of pain or suffering to ground a finding of inhuman treatment, but the reference to therapeutic necessity must be taken as a direct challenge to the *Herczegfalvy* jurisprudence. It remains to be seen how the Strasbourg court will respond.

9.5.2 The substantive criteria for involuntary treatment under ss. 63 and 58: Jurisprudence

The statutory scheme imposes no explicit substantive standard for involuntary treatment of detained patients for the first three months, and then a standard of 'appropriateness' under s. 58 thereafter. This standard is overlaid by the 'therapeutic necessity' standard contained in the jurisprudence surrounding Article 3. The present question is how to make sense of these differing standards. This is something of a guesswork exercise at this time, as there has been no litigation on the scope of discretion to treatment under the 2007 s. 58 criteria, and none at all under s. 63. There was some litigation concerning the ECHR criteria and the previous MHA criteria (see discussion in Bartlett, 2011), where the SOAD was to approve the treatment if 'having regard to the likelihood of the treatment alleviating or preventing a deterioration of the patient's condition, the treatment should be given', (s. 58(3)(b), as unamended) and this may provide some guidance, in as far as it goes.

On its face, the current standard in s. 58 appears lower than the Article 3 one: it is not difficult to think of treatments which may be appropriate, but are not necessary. Medication which attacks symptoms, but does not attack the underlying disorder is perhaps an obvious example. For physical disorders, these might include painkillers: they do not address the cause of pain, and do not speed healing; they may nonetheless be appropriate for prescription in that they make the patient feel better. The difficulty with psychiatric illness is that specific biological bases of the disorders are unknown, making it impossible to know whether it is the disorder or merely the symptom that is being attacked. While this view is of some force if 'therapeutic necessity' is taken to mean attacking the disorder, rather than its manifestations, it is not obvious that this is what the phrase means in the context of Article 3. There is little guidance in the current jurisprudence, but as noted in 9.5.1, the *Gorobet* case may understand therapeutic necessity in terms of removing risks posed by Mr Gorobet to himself or others. Those risks would be caused by manifestations of the disorder, and it would seem their control by medication could be within the scope of 'therapeutic necessity'.

More problematic are treatments that will improve the patient's condition, but only to a limited degree. Examples might include treatments that reduce the severity of delusions but do not remove them completely, or treatments that reduce risk factors associated with patients, but not to a degree that allows them to be cared for in less intrusive environments. These treatments may well be appropriate; are they therapeutically necessary? The Strasbourg jurisprudence offers no obvious guidance.

As noted, the appropriateness test is expanded somewhat in s. 64(3), where it is defined as 'appropriate in [the patient's] case taking into account the nature and degree of the mental disorder from which he is suffering and all other circumstances of his case.' Perhaps this means that the determination is not a strictly clinical one, instead including a wide array of factors relevant to the patient and his or her life. This is certainly the position adopted by the Code of Practice in interpreting identical wording in the context of the 'appropriate' treatment required as a condition of detention under s. 3 (see s. 3(4), Code of Practice, paras. 6.08, 6.10, 6.11; see further Chapter 6, 6.3.1.2). As well as the usual therapeutic criteria, the Code provisions in this other context require cultural, ethnic, and religious circumstances to be considered, as well as the patient's gender, gender identity, sexual orientation, and age; the implications for the patient's family and social relationships, including his or her role as a parent; and the implications for the patient's work or education. Notwithstanding the identical wording of s. 3(4) and s. 64(3), these factors are not repeated or cross-referenced in the guidance to SOADs in chapter 24 of the Code. Including them by implication in the context of enforced treatment has the advantage of moving outside a narrowly medical universe, to a consideration of the patient's whole situation—an approach the Code favours at least in other contexts. However desirable this broader assessment may be, it is difficult to align with the medical language of the ECHR jurisprudence. It is further not obvious why this broader approach, if it is intended, is to be assessed solely by a SOAD—always a consultant psychiatrist—rather than in conjunction with a social worker or AMHP, who has greater professional expertise and experience of potential non-clinical factors.

Can one use the identical wording of s. 3(4) and s. 64(3) to elucidate the standard of compulsory treatment, so that the treatment that can be compulsorily administered is the 'appropriate medical treatment' under s. 3? On a superficial level there is a certain conceptual neatness to this approach: it would mean that s. 3 of the MHA 1983 would identify appropriate treatment to justify detention, and Part IV would allow the administration of that treatment by compulsion if necessary. The patient could be required to take the treatment he or she needed in order to become well enough that detention under section 3 would no longer be justified. Indeed, compulsory treatment in this interpretation can be seen as an adjunct to detention. In the words of Baroness Hale, '[o]nce the state has taken away a person's liberty and detained him in a hospital with a view to medical treatment, the state should be able (some would say obliged) to provide him with the treatment which he needs' (*R (B)* v *Ashworth Special Hospital* [2005] UKHL 20, para. 31). On this view, detention without treatment would be ethically questionable.

Attractive though this interpretation may be on its face, it is problematic on closer analysis. To begin with, the timings are different. The appropriate treatment test applies to detentions under s. 3 but not to s. 2, and therefore applies either immediately upon admission (if the admission is under s. 3), or when the patient moves from a s. 2 to a s. 3 (generally at the end of 28 days). The appropriateness test in the context of compulsory treatment applies under s. 58 after 3 months of detention or, if it is also the test under s. 63, immediately to both compulsory treatment under ss. 2 and 3. Either way, there may be periods where the concept would apply for compulsory treatment but not detention, or vice versa.

Secondly, this approach would presumably mean that only the treatment identified as 'appropriate' on admission could be enforced. In a sense, this is the reading's attractiveness: compulsion would be available only for treatments that are sufficiently significant as to be a ground for detention. Beyond this, treatment would presumably be either on consent or under the terms of the MCA 2005. This would move some distance towards the CPT requirement that boundaries be placed on non-consensual treatment. The difficulty is that it would also create seemingly arbitrary boundaries between what could and could not be compelled: if the treatment were directed to the identified justification for the detention, it could be compelled; if not, it could not. Such distinctions did not find favour with the House of Lords under the pre-2007 legislation. In the words, again, of Baroness Hale, '[t]he psychiatrist's aim should be to treat the whole patient,' and compulsory treatment was not to be delayed by the rectification of 'largely irrelevant classifications' (*R (B)* v *Ashworth Special Hospital* [2005] UKHL 30, para. 31). It is difficult to see that the change in legislation would alter the court's view in this regard.

Thirdly, the close association between 'appropriate treatment' under s. 3 and treatment that could be compelled as 'appropriate' under s. 58 would largely collapse the distinction between the detention decision and the treatment decision, precisely the distinction that the CPT standard would appear to want to maintain. This is increasingly reflected in ECHR jurisprudence, which now appears to require separate processes for patients to challenge detention and treatment: see *X* v *Finland*, Application No. 34806/04, judgment of 3 July 2012, discussed further at 9.5.3. This approach envisages the possibility that a detained patient would be able successfully to refuse treatment, and would thus appear to run directly counter to Baroness Hale's view that detention without treatment is ethically dubious. The division between the ECHR standards in the two contexts is also relevant. The test of therapeutic necessity under Article 3 of the ECHR applies to compulsory treatment. Detention is instead governed primarily by Article 5, where the mental condition must be of a nature or degree warranting detention, but where therapeutic necessity test has not explicitly been used. Insofar as these standards are different, this is likely to impact on the readings of the domestic legislation, creating a pressure away from an integrated approach.

For all these reasons, and notwithstanding the similar legislative wordings, it would seem unlikely that a close relationship will be found between appropriate treatment under s. 3 and treatment that can be administered under compulsion under Part 4. This returns us to the question of how appropriateness/therapeutic necessity should be understood for purposes of compulsory treatment. The Court of Appeal in *R(N)* v *(M)* [[2002] EWHC 1911 (Admin) went some way to addressing this (para. 19):

> The answer to that question [i.e., whether psychiatric treatment is therapeutically necessary] will depend on a number of factors, including (a) how certain is it that the patient does suffer from a treatable mental disorder; (b) how serious a disorder is it; (c) how serious a risk is presented to others; (d) how likely is it that, if the patient does suffer from such a disorder, the proposed treatment will alleviate the condition; (e) how much alleviation is there likely to be; (f) how likely is it that the treatment will have adverse consequences for the patient; and (g) how severe may they be.

As the Court acknowledges, this is less a standard than a process directed to determining whether a given treatment is medically necessary. Consistent with this, the Court of Appeal has held that the factors in this list are not to be considered sequentially, with each stage needing to be convincingly shown, but instead factors to be considered in an overall assessment of whether a proposed treatment is therapeutically necessary (*R (B)* v *Haddock* [2006] EWCA Civ 961, para. 43). Thus in *Haddock* itself, the appropriate diagnosis of the patient was disputed: B himself said he had no psychiatric disorder; the medical evidence varied between B having a delusional disorder and a personality disorder. While the court rejected B's own view, it did not find it necessary to require a clear diagnosis in order to find the proposed treatment therapeutically necessary (para. 50). Even as a process, it raises a variety of difficulties.

To begin with, the factors identified all require an assessment of likelihood or certainty in an area where certainty is hard to come by. Baroness Hale notes (*R (B)* v *Ashworth* para. 31):

> ...psychiatry is not an exact science. Diagnosis is not easy or clear cut. As this and many other cases show, a number of different diagnoses may be reached by the same or different clinicians over the years.

As has already been noted at 9.3.1, different medications have different effects on different people, and the only way to determine which if any will work may be a matter of trial and error. As discussed in Chapter 6, 6.2.1, the determination of risk is similarly not an exact science. In the view of the Court of Appeal, it would be 'unreal to require psychiatrists, under the umbrella of a requirement of medical or therapeutic necessity, to demonstrate sureness or near sureness of success' (R (B) v Haddock [2006] EWCA Civ 961, para. 41). At the same time, if positive results cannot be predicted with reasonable certainty, can a given treatment in question really be said to be therapeutically necessary? If this matter is viewed as a question of civil rights, can it really be appropriate to engage in a remarkable imposition on bodily integrity based on an optimistic hope?

The uncertainty of psychiatric practice noted by the courts frequently means divergence in professional opinion. The divergent diagnoses noted in Haddock are a not atypical example. At the point of treatment, this disagreement will be relevant if it is between the responsible clinician and the SOAD, since a refusal of the SOAD to sign the s. 58 certificate will mean that the compulsory treatment cannot proceed. The judicial view of the SOAD role in this context appears conflicted. On the one hand, it is clear that the SOAD is to form an independent judgment of the situation (see Wilkinson, paras. 32–3, 71; R (B) v S [2006] EWCA Civ 28). The Court of Appeal has also held, however, that even under the old s. 58 criteria, a SOAD ought to 'have regard for the RMO's greater experience than his of the patient' (Haddock at para. 46). Arguably, the new appropriateness standard under s. 58 makes such deference even clearer under the statute.

Some specific circumstances may affect the appropriateness that treatment be enforced. In Wilkinson, Baroness Hale took the view that people it was right that people with capacity could be compulsorily treated under the MHA 1983, on the basis that to do otherwise would create a pressure to raise the standard of capacity (Wilkinson, para. 80). It is not obvious that this is correct, since as long as people with capacity can refuse physical treatment such an upward pressure will exist in any event. Nonetheless, cases since that time have followed her view, holding that capacity is a relevant factor in determining whether treatment should be compelled under s. 58, but is not in itself determinative: see, e.g., R (PS) v G [2003] EWHC 2335 (Admin), para. 116; R (B) v SS [2005] EWHC 86 (Admin), para. 189; R (B) v SS [2005] EWHC 1936 (Admin), para. 95. This view appears consistent with the current jurisprudence of the ECHR: see Nevmerzhitsky v the Ukraine, Application No. 54825/00, judgment of 12 October 2005.

Whether the position is convincing is a different matter. Certainly here, as in other contexts when capacity has been proposed as a criterion, there is the question of whether it is a sufficiently robust concept, or whether instead it can be manipulated to ensure that specific results are obtained: see, e.g., Chapter 4, 4.4 and Chapter 6, 6.5.1. This reflects long-standing anecdotal accounts from service users: people who consent have capacity and people who do not, do not. The most comprehensive study of the MCA 2005 to date identifies precisely this blurring of capacity determination with the desirability of potential outcomes in decision-making generally under the Act, referring to it as the 'concertina' effect (Williams, 2012: 3.2, 3.4). Insofar as these findings are reflected in psychiatric practice more broadly, it would suggest that safeguards are required for the treatment of allegedly incapable people, to ensure that their 'incapacity' is real, rather than the result of making a decision that is unwise or unpopular in the view of the treating clinician. More controversially, it also raises the question of whether the consent of 'capable' patients should be taken uncritically, as it is now: does their consent in fact reflect the informed choice of a capable patient, or is the patient incapable but acquiescing to treatment? Should consenting patients have the benefit of a SOAD certification or similar process to ensure the appropriateness of the treatment prescribed, at some time during their detention?

The issue of malleability of the category of capacity is relevant for patients who lack capacity, or perhaps who are viewed as capable but consent to treatment. It does not address the situation of the patient who is agreed to be competent but who refuses treatment. Assuming the test of capacity resembles the one in the MCA 2005, this is a person who understands the treatment in question, including the reasonably foreseeable consequences of deciding one way or another or of failing to decide, and can weigh the information as part of a process of making a decision (MCA 2005, s. 3). Regarding this situation, Simon Brown LJ in *Wilkinson* commented (paras. 29–30):

> The precise equivalence under section 58(3)(b) between incompetent patients and competent but non-consenting patients seems to me increasingly difficult to justify.
> If in truth this claimant has the capacity to refuse consent to the treatment proposed here, it is difficult to suppose that he should nevertheless be forcibly subjected to it.

As noted, this does not appear to represent the prevailing judicial view. A capable refusal is instead a factor to be taken into account in deciding whether treatment ought to be enforced.

The actual and active resistance of the patient to the treatment has also been held to be relevant as to whether it ought to be given (see *R (PS) v G* [2003] EWHC 2335 (Admin), para. 117; *R(B) v SS*, [2006] EWCA Civ 28, para. 62). Such resistance raises both theoretical and practical concerns. On the theoretical level, Article 3 of the ECHR requires consideration when behaviour is 'such as to arouse in the victims feelings of fear, anguish and inferiority capable of humiliating and debasing them' (*Kudla v Poland*, Application No. 30210/96, judgment of 26 October 2000, para. 92). Actual resistance suggests the presence of one or more of these emotions. How far this will work to the benefit of patients wishing to avoid treatment is not clear, however, since the prohibition does not extend to suffering that is inevitable as part of a legitimate form of treatment, begging the question of whether the enforced treatment in question is such a legitimate form of treatment. The MCA 2005 allows the overriding of such resistance when treatment is in the best interests of a person lacking capacity, and when the intervention is necessary to prevent harm and is proportionate to the likelihood and severity of the harm (MCA 2005, s. 6). That approach seems less circular, more nuanced, and more defensible than the Strasbourg approach of assessing whether the proposed intervention is a legitimate form of treatment.

The jurisprudence flows from cases where a SOAD certificate has been provided to justify treatment. As noted, this will be the case for a minority of detained patients.

Most detained patients will be within the first three months of their detention, and will therefore be treated under the broader compulsion power of s. 63. As noted, that section contains no substantive criteria for treatment at all. This is not accidental, as the words of the Secretary of State when the three month period of s. 58 was introduced in 1982 make clear (*Hansard*, HL vol. 688, cols 494–5, quoted Jones (2011, para. 1-681)):

> The three-month period is considered appropriate because of the time that it allows for an optimum regime of medication to be identified—or, at least, for certain options to be ruled out before a certificate is needed. Different medications need to be tried before the most suitable is identified.

However much this reflects clinical realities, it does seem to suggest that the intent was that various medications could be used by way of trial and error in the hopes of finding one or a combination that would work, or would work best. As noted in this chapter, it is difficult to see that the administration of a drug can really be said to be therapeutically necessary, when it is doubtful whether it will work. The absence of even an appropriateness standard from treatment under s. 63, and no obvious guidance in the Code of Practice to clarify how discretion to treat involuntarily is to be exercised, does suggest a potential violation of the ECHR.

9.5.3 A right to challenge compulsory treatment?

Mental health legislation has, since 1959, provided a review tribunal structure to challenge detentions. The tribunal however has no jurisdiction over the matters in Part 4 of the MHA 1983. While the tribunal can order the release of a patient detained under s. 3 if no appropriate treatment is available (s. 72(1)(b)(iia)), it cannot make orders as to whether that or any other treatment ought to be enforced on a patient. In principle, decisions to enforce treatment under Part 4 have long been subject to judicial review, and that mechanism has been used to determine for example whether treatments were within or outside the scope of Part 4: see, e.g., *R v Mental Health Act Commission, ex p X* (1988) 9 BMLR 77; *B v Croydon Health Authority* [1995] 1 All ER 683. Such cases did not involve the exercise of discretion as to whether treatment that was within the definitions of the statute ought to be enforced.

For that reason, the case of *R (Wilkinson) v Broadmoor Special Hospital* [2001] EWCA Civ 1545 broke new ground. This case involved a person long detained under Part 3 of the MHA 1983, for whom antipsychotic medication was proposed. A SOAD had certified that such treatment met the conditions of s. 58 as it was then drafted. As such, the treatment fell squarely within the involuntary treatment provisions of the Act; the question was instead whether the treatment ought to be given. The case asked the court to determine whether the treatment would violate Mr Wilkinson's rights under Article 3 of the ECHR. The case itself turned on a set of procedural points, most significantly whether a court could hear oral testimony in a judicial review proceeding (the court held that it could), but the potential of the case stretched well beyond that point.

Wilkinson was heard shortly after the Human Rights Act 1998 had come into effect, and the real issue in the case was how the court should approach allegations that Article 3 rights were being violated. The court held that it was not material whether the case was brought by way of judicial review or civil action for damages. Where a violation of the ECHR was alleged, the court was entitled to reach its own view of the facts, and this included the hearing of oral evidence. Further, the court held that when ECHR rights were at stake, the traditional standards of judicial review were insufficient, and only a full merits review would meet the ECHR standard (*Wilkinson*, paras. 36, 53, 83). For a brief period, it appeared that the stage was set for the development of body of jurisprudence regarding the use of discretion in the enforcement of treatment under the MHA 1983.

This optimism was short-lived. Roughly half a dozen reported cases were brought in the five years following *Wilkinson*. In none was the patient successful, either at first instance or on appeal (see Bartlett, 2011 for discussion). There are no reported cases since that time.

Not merely are the bottom line results uniformly against service users in these cases; the approach of the courts in the post-*Wilkinson* jurisprudence makes it difficult to see how a patient could succeed. The difficulties commence with the court's view of evidence. The courts have held that they should 'pay particular regard to the views of those charged with his care and well-being' (*R (B) v SS (RMO)* [2005] EWHC 86; see also e.g. *R (PS) v G (RMO) and W (SOAD)* [2003] EWHC 2335 (Admin), paras. 82, 84; *Haddock* at para. 14; *R(N) v M* at para. 38). In *Wilkinson* itself, a similarly deferential attitude was adopted to the joint view of the treating physician and the SOAD (at para. 31), but given the attitude of deference to the treating physician's greater experience that the SOAD is meant to adopt after *Haddock* (para. 46), this still leaves the views and evidence of the treating physician subject to particular deference. In human rights terms, this is a problematic starting point, in that it gives the alleged violator of human rights a privileged position in the establishment of whether such a violation has occurred. No doubt treating physicians generally act in good faith and endeavour to present their testimony to the courts honestly, but this is a different question from whether their views ought to be accorded a particularly privileged status in the consideration of evidence.

In the post-*Wilkinson* cases, the views of the treating physician are always preferred to those of the patient's expert witness. The courts justify this deference because of the ongoing relationship between the patient and the treating physician, where the patient's expert will have become acquainted with the patient's situation only recently and have seen the patient only a small number of times: see, e.g., *PS* at para. 88; *R (N)* at para. 38; *R (B) v SS* [2005] EWHC 1936 (Admin), para. 70. This places the patient at a systematic disadvantage, and it seems difficult to see how it can be overcome. The patient is likely to be legally aided, and the number, extent, and scope of examinations of the patient by his or her expert witness is determined by what legal aid will fund. On this basis, it seems that there is no reasonable prospect that the view of the patient's expert will prevail, and if that is the case, it is almost inconceivable that the patient will win.

In a sense, it is difficult to fault the court's approach. If they are to prefer one witness over another, they have to make that determination somehow. Judges are not doctors, and have little background to assess diagnostic or treatment-related testimony offered by medical witnesses. It is nonetheless problematic when the approach, as here, manifestly favours one party to litigation.

The difficulty is premised on the necessity of the court to prefer one view over another. It is not obvious that this is the best approach. The test under *Herczegfalvy* is that the therapeutic necessity of an intervention must be 'convincingly shown to exist', and the court could instead start by taking the view that if reasonable psychiatric opinion differed as to the appropriate intervention, one treatment rather than the other could not be said to be convincingly shown to be therapeutically necessary. In this approach, both (or all) the professional views in question would have to be reasonable, but negligence law already provides a framework to determine such reasonableness and therefore to discount opinions that do not meet the requisite standard. This approach of requiring agreement among professionals was proposed on behalf of the patient in *R (N)* v *M*. It was not successful, in part because it was perceived as using negligence law principles in judicial review, and in part because there was no precedent for the approach either in English or Strasbourg jurisprudence ([2002] EWHC 1911, paras. 113–116; [2002] EWCA Civ 1789, para. 29). The latter point in particular is not convincing. As has been discussed in this chapter, there is little jurisprudence surrounding the meaning or proof of therapeutic necessity in either England or Strasbourg, and there was less in 2002, when *R (N)* was decided. Whatever the court did, it would be making new law. As noted in this section, the court is unlikely to be well-suited to make a determination between conflicting medical evidence, and discussed the approach in fact taken by the court to such determinations systematically favours the treating physician at the expense of the patient in the litigation. The approach proposed in *R (N)* is consistent with an approach that takes the *Herczegfalvy* standard seriously, and avoids this problem of systemically benefitting one party to the litigation. It warranted more careful consideration than it was given.

If the patient's medical witness fares badly in *Wilkinson* hearings, the patient himself or herself fares worse. In none of these hearings did the patient give oral evidence. In *Haddock*, the patient, B, requested to give oral evidence. This was a case where B challenged the accuracy of his medical record, and where his capacity was at issue. Nonetheless, Collins J held that 'it did not seem to me that his evidence would conceivably assist me in reaching my decision' ([2005] EWHC 921 (Admin), para. 14), a view affirmed by the Court of Appeal ([2006] EWCA Civ 961, para. 65). Instead, his witness statement was taken 'at face value'. Nonetheless, while considerable efforts were taken to analyse the medical evidence, B's written evidence was given only one brief mention. The impression given is that the patient has nothing to contribute to a determination of whether or not he or she should be treated against his or her will. In the context of incapacity proceedings, this is no longer acceptable. In cases such as *Shtukaturov v Russia*, Application No. 44009/05, judgment of 27 June 2008 and *Salontaji-Drobnjak v Serbia*, Application No. 36500/05, judgment of 13 January 2010, para. 144, the ECHR has held that a requirement of Article 8 is that the court is required personally to examine the allegedly incapable person. It is not obvious that the Strasbourg court would adopt a different requirement for hearings into involuntary treatment.

In determination of whether a therapeutic necessity is convincingly shown to exist, the English courts have been content to adopt the loosest of legal structures. If a standard of proof were required, the court in *Haddock* said it favoured the balance of probabilities, the unmodified civil standard, but it was hesitant to adopt even this standard: 'It is rather a value judgement as to the future—a forecast—to be made by a court in reliance on medical evidence according to a standard of persuasion.' (para. 42).

In the background of all these cases is a tension about the role of the court in cases of compulsory psychiatric treatment. The *Wilkinson* court took the view that when ECHR rights are at issue, the court is obliged to satisfy itself that any proposed intervention does not violate ECHR rights. Later cases instead return to a much more traditional public law model, with the Court of Appeal in *R (N) v (M)* noting that 'the court's role is essentially one of review' (para. 39; see also *PS*, para. 5), and discouraging the overuse of oral testimony. Once again, that suggests a position of deference to the original decision-maker, the treating physician in this case.

It seems likely that the English position will need to be reconsidered. *X v Finland* (Application No. 34806/04, judgment of 3 July 2012) similarly involved a patient properly detained under domestic mental health legislation, who wished to challenge proposed involuntary treatment. In this case it was treatment with antipsychotic medication for a delusion disorder. In a number of ways, the Finnish legislation resembled the English. Like the English act, detention under the statute allowed treatment without consent (Finnish Mental Health Act (*mielenterveyslaki, mentalvårdslagen*, Act no. 1423/2001) s. 22b). Like the English Act, it contained a treatability requirement as a condition precedent to detention. Where the English Act refers merely to 'appropriate' treatment, however, the Finnish Act was more specific, requiring that 'the person needs treatment for a mental illness which, if not treated, would become considerably worse or seriously endanger the person's health or safety or the health or safety of others' (Finnish Mental Health Act (*mielenterveyslaki, mentalvårdslagen*, Act no. 1116/1990) s. 8). Unlike the English system, all these detentions were scrutinised by an independent body that in this case raised questions that it required to be answered prior to allowing the detention. This scrutiny thus appears from the case to be reasonably serious rather than pro forma. X was able to bring her concerns into the court system, and the appropriateness of the treatment was considered by the Finnish Supreme Administrative Court as part of the assessment of whether she was properly detained.

The European Court of Human Rights nonetheless found a violation of Article 8 regarding the compulsory treatment. While the involuntary treatment had a basis in Finnish law, it was not adequately 'compatible with the rule of law' (para. 217), in that the decision by a treating physician to impose treatment could not be subject to appeal (para. 220):

> The Court considers that forced administration of medication represents a serious interference with a person's physical integrity and must accordingly be based on a "law" that guarantees proper safeguards against arbitrariness. In the present case such safeguards were missing. The decision to confine the applicant to involuntary treatment included an automatic authorisation to proceed to forced administration of medication when the applicant

refused the treatment. The decision-making was solely in the hands of the treating doctors who could take even quite radical measures regardless of the applicant's will. Moreover, their decision-making was free from any kind of immediate judicial scrutiny: the applicant did not have any remedy available whereby she could require a court to rule on the lawfulness, including proportionality, of the forced administration of medication and to have it discontinued.

For the first three months of detention under English law, the compulsory treatment is, as in Finland, solely within the discretion of the treating physician, and after this time, it is at best questionable whether the SOAD system provides a sufficiently meaningful safeguard. In effect, English psychiatrists can, like their Finnish counterparts, 'take even quite radical measures' regardless of the patient's will. As in the Finnish system, there is no routine judicial or similar scrutiny of this power, and given the limitations of the post-*Wilkinson* jurisprudence discussed, it is not obvious that it is an appropriate mechanism to determine the 'lawfulness, including proportionality' of forced medication. Given the extremely few cases where it has been used, and the uniformity of its findings against patients, one must also ask whether it is a meaningful remedy.

9.6 The Convention on the Rights of Persons with Disabilities: A fundamental challenge?

As on so much in mental health law, the United Nations CRPD raises new challenges. At issue are the meaning and scope of Articles 17 (right to integrity) and 25 (right to health). The scope of compulsory treatment that is permitted under these articles is markedly reduced from that contained in the current MHA, if indeed the Convention allows treatment without consent at all.

Article 17 protects the right to integrity. It is a short article:

> Every person with disabilities has a right to respect for his or her physical and mental integrity on an equal basis with others.

Unusually, it is a right not contained elsewhere in international law, and it is therefore not entirely clear what it is meant to cover. During the drafting process of the CRPD, significantly longer versions of the right were discussed that referred to restricting severely or eliminating compulsory treatment, including compulsory psychiatric treatment. None of these drafts succeeded, it would seem because service user organisations were not prepared to allow any text that could be taken to allow any compulsory treatment, and states parties were not prepared to agree to a complete prohibition (see Bartlett, 2012; Lawson, 2006–07; Kayess and French, 2008). The result is that Article 17 lacks a clear definition and scope. This may, perhaps, be a significant own goal by the disability movement. In the words of Kayess and French, '[t]he result is that one of the most critical areas of human rights violation for persons with disability—the use of coercive State power for the purpose of 'treatment'—remains without any specific regulation.' (Kayess and French, 2008: 30). While the minimalism of the current drafting is indeed unfortunate, it does not of course follow that the Article means nothing. The difficulty is that it may be years or even decades before a consensus emerges as to what it does mean.

For interpretation in the short term, Bartlett argues that if the objections to the drafts of states parties to the CRPD did not go far enough, domestic law or practice that does not even conform to those drafts should be taken as violating Article 17 (Bartlett, 2012: 771). This reading would in effect set a floor to Article 17 interpretation, but would allow a more expansive interpretation if a consensus developed in that direction. If that approach holds sway, the MHA provisions remain vulnerable. The draft from the states parties for example would have permitted treatment without consent only in accordance with procedures established by law and with the application of appropriate legal safeguards; as has been discussed, for the roughly 80 per cent of detained patients who are treated in their first three months of detention under s. 63 without the safeguards of s. 58, there are no safeguards or procedures in place at all prior to treatment without consent. It is difficult to see that this would be compliant with the states parties proposals.

Article 25 on the right to health is more direct on the question of consent. Article 25(d) obliges states parties to require health professionals 'to provide care of the same quality to persons with disabilities as to others, including on the basis of free and informed consent…'. This would seem to provide rights specifically against non-consensual treatment.

The rights in both Articles 17 and 25, like so much of the CRPD, are phrased in terms of non-discrimination. It is not that non-consensual treatment is prohibited; it is that it is prohibited in situations where it would not be imposed on people without disabilities. Certainly, that would mean that the overarching provision in s. 63 allowing non-consensual treatment would be in violation; there is nothing that corresponds to such a power for people without mental disabilities. The acceptability of a provision that allowed treatment without consent for people lacking capacity, the standard for intervention in decisions more broadly under the MCA 2005, would depend on the degree to which capacity is itself a discriminatory concept, and thus prohibited by the CRPD: see further Chapter 4, 4.1.1 and 4.7. It is clear that in health care situations where consent is not required for the population as a whole, it is similarly not required for persons with disabilities. At least theoretically, this leaves open the possibility of removing the right of consent in certain circumstances for everyone, including people with disabilities. It is not at all clear how such circumstances would be defined (Emergencies? Life-sustaining treatment? Treatments viewed as desirable by self-styled right-thinking readers of particular tabloid newspapers?), and such an approach would almost certainly be extremely politically contentious. The non-disabled community seems remarkably attached to their civil rights, including the right to consent to medical treatment. That raises an obvious rejoinder, however: if consent rights are so important for the rest of the population, why should we be prepared to override them for the subsection of the population with mental disabilities?

9.6.1 **The right to health**

The considerable bulk of the debate surrounding treatment of people with mental disabilities concerns involuntary treatment. This is understandable: the right to control one's body is a classic civil right, and any interference with that right is likely to be viewed as exceptionally violating by person affected.

It is not, of course, the only health-related issue in mental health law. As noted at the beginning of this chapter, many of the issues that arise in health law generally also arise in mental health law, from issues of information, to regulation of pharmaceuticals, to regulation of research, to regulation by professional organisations of their members, to the effect of the recent structural reforms of the NHS on commissioning of psychiatric services. Space does not allow for a systematic discussion of this array of topics, important though they are.

In closing the chapter, however, it is appropriate to recall that the vulnerability of people with mental disabilities does not manifest itself merely in their being subjected to coercive measures, of which non-consensual treatment is perhaps the clearest example. It also arises in increased ill health, and the failure of health and institutional systems to make available the health care that patients indisputably need. The issue in such provision is often not a matter of whether the patient consents or not; it is a question of whether the service provider is able or prepared to make the service available.

Sometimes, these deficiencies are in mental health care. Prisons are an obvious example where despite significant need, care for basic mental health problems remains undeveloped (HM Chief Inspector of Prisons, 2012: 7). While this is perhaps a particularly clear example, demand also exceeds supply in psychiatric facilities. As noted at 9.3.4, talking therapies are now recommended for the treatment of personality disorder, and moderate to mild depression, and as part of the therapeutic response to schizophrenia. A survey of inpatients undertaken by the CQC in 2009 showed that half of inpatients had wanted such therapy, but only 29 per cent had actually received it. Of those that did receive it, 92 per cent found it helpful, at least to some extent (CQC, 2009), suggesting that better provision might be beneficial for service users without the need to resort to force.

Also of concern is the provision of suitable physical health care for people with mental disabilities. In 2006, the Disability Rights Commission published its report on the physical health and health care provision for people with learning disabilities or mental health problems (Disability Rights Commission, 2006). It found both groups to be at significantly higher risk of major physical health problems than the general population. For people with learning disabilities, these problems included obesity and respiratory disease. For people with mental health problems, they included obesity, smoking, heart disease, respiratory problems, high blood pressure, respiratory disease, diabetes, and stroke (see Table 9.1). People with schizophrenia were found to have twice the incidence of bowel cancer relative to the general population, and women with schizophrenia were 42 per cent more likely to get breast cancer. The age of onset for all these problems was also significantly lower among people with mental disabilities than in the general

Table 9.1 Prevalence of disorders among general population and people with schizophrenia or bipolar disorder, by percent of population

	Heart disease	Stroke	High blood pressure	Diabetes
General population	2.7	0.9	9.7	2.3
People with schizophrenia	4.0	1.7	12.0	6.4
People with bipolar disorder	5.1	1.5	14.7	4.1

(*Source*: Disability Rights Commission 2006, 34)

population, and survival rates worse. In the general population, 8 per cent of people with coronary heart disease died within 5 years of diagnosis. For people with bipolar disorder, this figure was 15 per cent, and for people with schizophrenia, 22 per cent.

The Disability Rights Commission acknowledges that a considerable portion of these inequalities flow from social circumstances, most notably living in poverty, but not all. The disorders in Table 9.1 are all correlated with weight gain, a known adverse effect of psychiatric medications (see 9.3.1). The Commission also found, however, that people with mental disabilities were less likely to receive the standard, evidence-based treatments for their physical illnesses. For example, if they had heart disease, they were less likely than the general population to receive statins to lower their cholesterol. This finding was mirrored in a systematic review by Mitchell, Lord and Malone (2012). The Commission also found that people with learning disabilities were also given standard diagnostic tests (e.g. cholesterol checks, blood pressure checks) less frequently than the general population. Both groups experienced 'diagnostic overshadowing', that is, the attribution of their physical problems to their mental disability (see also Jones, Howard, and Thornicroft, 2008).

These problems were widespread in community settings, but psychiatric inpatient wards were also found to be problematic. Here, the difficulty was that there were few general practitioners, so treatment was likely to be provided by psychiatrists in areas outside their expertise (Disability Rights Commission, 2006: 56). In the view of the Commission, the difficulties span the provision of primary care services: health needs are not recognised, services are not designed to be welcoming to people with mental disabilities, referrals are ineffective, and health promotion is not adequate.

This situation represents more than a mere failure of policy. The right to the best attainable standard of health has long been a part of international law, and is included in Article 25 of the CRPD. Article 25(a) obliges states parties to '[p]rovide persons with disabilities with the same range, quality and standard of free or affordable health care and programmes as provided to other persons'. It is difficult to see that this standard is being met.

10

Control in the Community

10.1 Introduction

English law has historically made a connection between compulsion and incarceration: if any degree of compulsion was to be used in the treatment of a person for mental disorder, it was first necessary to secure the admission of that person into an institution. Outside the asylum, there were no compulsory powers available. The situation changed with the Mental Deficiency Act 1913, which applied only to 'mental defectives'. The Mental Deficiency Act 1913 introduced the concept of guardianship. A guardian was given the powers that a father has over his 14-year-old child. The Mental Health Act (MHA) 1930 made the option of guardianship available for the mentally ill. But thereafter, despite the policy emphasis which was given to care in the community rather than the use of institutional care from 1963 onwards (see Chapter 2, 2.4), there were no further significant legal developments until the mid-1990s, with the introduction of Supervision Registers in 1994 and After Care Under Supervision (ACUS) by the Mental Health (Patients in the Community) Act 1995.

As will be discussed further in this chapter, these initiatives did not go far enough for those who wanted to see legal powers to treat in the community. Pressure for such powers from various quarters, particularly within the psychiatric profession, continued after 1995, and the Labour administration in office from 1997 was also keen to increase the powers of control over patients in the community. After much bluster, and two failed Bills, the passage of the MHA 2007 saw the introduction of the latest set of compulsory powers, in the form of the community treatment order (CTO). As will be seen, the CTO, like ACUS, stops short of giving powers to treat without consent outside a hospital. Albeit similar to ACUS, which was under-utilised, in many other ways, CTOs have proven to be reasonably popular with Responsible Clinicians (RCs), although as will also be seen, the statistics surrounding their use require careful unpacking.

In the absence of specific powers for the use of compulsion outside a hospital, psychiatrists fashioned a *de facto* mechanism out of the powers available to grant a detained patient leave of absence. It has long been possible for a detained patient to be given leave from the hospital at which he or she is currently detained, on conditions set by the RC relating, for example, to place of abode and the acceptance of medication. For detained patients not subject to restrictions, leave of absence can often provide a legal basis for the community-based delivery of a patient's treatment plan which is in many ways is as satisfactory from an RC's point of view as the use, formerly, of ACUS and now, of a CTO. The Code of Practice gives guidance as to when each option is most suitable (DH, 2008: ch. 29), and the success of the CTO is to a considerable extent dependent on this guidance being followed, because the relative absence of formality surrounding the use of leave compared to the complicated and bureaucratic process of consultation and co-decision required in order to make a CTO may offer a more attractive option for RCs, being more simply implemented.

For patients subject to restrictions and housed in high security accommodation, which means that their progression through decreasing levels of security towards eventual discharge has not yet commenced, leave of absence will only rarely, if ever, involve the patient leaving hospital accommodation, but leave is used as a mechanism to move such patients into less secure accommodation on a trial basis. For all restricted patients, leave of absence may only occur with the agreement of the Justice Secretary, who also has powers to transfer a patient as an alternative to granting leave, which will be preferable if it is desirable that the detaining hospital should have full responsibility for the patient. Often, though, the question of whether a high security accommodated restricted patient should be given leave or formally transferred into alternative hospital accommodation involves fine judgments of degrees of improvement in that person's mental condition and of the lessening of the risk he or she poses to others, and there is in reality considerable overlap between these two possibilities. Both transfer and leave are also available for detained patients in respect of whom a need arises to effect their removal into conditions of greater security, and for removals in this direction, too, there is considerable overlap between these two possibilities.

Because, however, leave can offer *a de facto* method of ensuring compulsion in the community both for patients not subject to restrictions, and those who are and who have progressed through lessening levels of security such as to be at the point where discharge has become worthy of serious consideration, it is appropriate to consider it in this chapter, before moving on to consider the long-standing alternative to institutionalisation offered by guardianship, and then the most recent powers to make a CTO. This chapter will also offer a discussion of the powers available in s. 117 of the MHA 1983. Section 117 is concerned with the provision of after-care, comprising treatment and assistance of various kinds to patients discharged from compulsory confinement in a hospital. It will not, however, discuss the main mechanism for the community control of restricted patients, which is conditional discharge. That topic will instead be discussed in Chapter 11. Table 10.1 provides an overview of the various powers that are available.

Local social service authorities (LSSAs) are responsible for guardianship, but CTOs are the responsibility of health services, whilst there is shared responsibility for the provision of after-care under s. 117 of the MHA 1983. In any case, the effective provision of services requires effective inter-agency co-operation at ground level. Such issues have already been discussed in Chapters 2 and 3, but are also an important background consideration for the topics to be discussed here. So too are questions about the broader context in which we should understand the trend which some detect, and which has

Table 10.1 Overview of powers of control in the community

Legal mechanism for control in the community	Eligible	Location of formal criteria	Authorised by	Responsibility for/control over the patient whilst in the community	Can be ended by	Usage in 2011–12
Leave of absence (MHA 1983, s.17)	All detained patients (apart from patients detained under MHA 1983, ss. 35, 36 or 38)	None (but see MHA Code of Practice, Ch. 21)	RC (with the consent of the Justice Secretary if the patient is subject to restrictions)	RC (and Ministry of Justice if patient is subject to restrictions)	RC (or Justice Secretary if patient is subject to restrictions)	Common
Guardianship (MHA 1983, ss. 7, 37)	Those who might otherwise be detained under the MHA 1983	ss. 7, 37, MHA 1983	AMHP/NR (civil patients) or a court (criminal patients)	LSSA/private guardian	RC, LSSA, and (unless the order was made by a court) NR	331 new orders made under Part II, MHA 1983, 8 by a criminal court
Community treatment order (MHA 1983, ss.17A–G)	All detained patients unless subject to restrictions	s. 17A(5), MHA 1983	RC/AMHP (a tribunal may recommend a CTO)	RC or delegated to another mental health professional	RC with the agreement of an AMHP	4,220 new orders made
After-care (MHA 1983, s.117)	All long-term detained patients leaving hospital, whether or not discharged absolutely	None (but service provision should follow an assessment of needs under s. 47, NHSCCA 1990)	N/A (optional unless compliance a condition of discharge, leave or the making of a CTO)	CCG/LSSA	CCG/LSSA (unless patient is on a CTO)	Common
Conditional Discharge (MHA 1983, ss. 42, 73,)*	Patients subject to restrictions	MHA 1983, s. 42 (for Justice Secretary) and s. 73 for tribunals	RC (with consent of Justice Secretary) or a tribunal	RC, Ministry of Justice	Justice Secretary or a tribunal	90 orders made by the Justice Secretary, 371 by tribunal in 2010

*discussed in Chapter 11, 11.3 and 11.5.3.2.

been most vividly described perhaps by Stanley Cohen (1985), involving the shift of compulsion, out of the asylum and into the community (see Chapter 2, 2.4.2).

Should the CTO, for example, be understood in terms of 'surveillance creep', and be situated in the context of, amongst other things; the greater use of electronic tagging of offenders; the creation of powers by s. 123 of the Sexual Offences Act 2003, which enable the police to apply to a magistrates' court for a 'risk of sexual harm order' where it appears that a person has committed two specified sexual offences involving children and there is reasonable cause to believe that it is necessary that the order be made, *without* any requirement that that person has been convicted of the offences he or she is suspected of (which seems to mark a return to the pre-modern era, where less than complete proof would result, not in acquittal as in the modern era where for a conviction there must be proof beyond reasonable doubt, but rather in less than complete punishment: see Foucault, 2003: 6–7); and, as some would argue, such other modern phenomena as the widespread use of CCTV cameras and other high-tech modes of surveillance, website cookies, satellite navigation systems, and so on (Norris and Armstrong, 1999; Gillon and Monahan, 2013)?

For some people, the Orwellian nightmare future is uncomfortably close to modern day realities, and the use of compulsion in the community as part of mental health policy provides a good example of that. As Stanley Cohen famously pointed out, and as current trends in the use of mental health legislation confirm, the use of powers, once confined to institutions, in community settings, has not replaced their institutional use but augmented them, in his terms 'widening the net'. Cohen (1979) suggested in respect of the penal system—which has similarly moved from a simple institutional response (and only the fine as an alternative sanction to imprisonment) to the modern day situation which features a myriad of community-based disposals, alongside the continued use of imprisonment—that what have been known as 'alternatives to custody', now 'community disposals', were better seen, in Foucault's words (1977: 113) as 'hundreds of tiny theatres of punishment'. An offender at home, electronically tagged, for example, is in some sense imprisoned, but the prison now is that person's own home. Does the CTO, along with the conditional discharge of restricted patients, amount, similarly to little more than 'hundreds of tiny theatres of treatment'? Is such a critique strengthened if it can be demonstrated that 'community care' under compulsion often includes requirements to reside in a place where, in reality, the intrusion on the liberty of the individual is, at least in extreme cases, comparable to that imposed by incarceration? Such arguments find support, to some extent, from a roster of authors including, as well as Cohen and Foucault, authors such as Garland (2001) and Lyon (2001, 2003). Today, there is a significant literature on the 'surveillance society', as represented, for example, by the journal *Surveillance and Society*.

Attractive and compelling as such claims may be, however, it is important to remember that the use of compulsion (as opposed to surveillance) in a community setting is far from new, and that the focus and extent of its use is relatively narrow, involving a few thousand individuals out of a population of many millions, and that it can sometimes feel to those who work within the system, in organisations such as the NHS, which are often cash-strapped and under-staffed, that these theoretically-driven critiques of contemporary developments in mental health law policy and practice bear only a passing resemblance to the realities of the situation. It is important to remember, too, that if community-based compulsion, subject to appropriate limits set by human rights law, is working as intended, its effect will be that a significant number of people who would otherwise be institutionalised are, instead, either in their own homes or in some sort of community-based residential provision, and in this important sense compulsion in the community constitutes, in utilitarian terms, a significant benefit to the total sum of human happiness (on the assumption that incarceration reduces the same) or, less prosaically, it means that more people are more free from state intrusion than would otherwise be the case. These are complex issues and we cannot allow them to detain us further here, but they should be borne in mind when considering the broader implications of the law which will be discussed in this chapter.

10.2 Leave and recall

10.2.1 Leave and Part II patients

Leave under s. 17 applies only to detained patients, although informal patients are also routinely given leave of absence as part of their treatment plan, and in either case the provisions of human rights law, and Art. 2 of the ECHR in particular, apply to all patients on leave of absence (*Rabone* v *Pennine NHS Trust* [2012] UKSC 2, see Chapter 7, 7.5), which means that leave given without due consideration of the positive obligation to take reasonable steps to safeguard the life of the patient will render the hospital from which leave has been granted in a situation where it is evident that there is a real and immediate risk to the patient's life, liable under Art. 2 if the patient, as in that case, subsequently commits suicide.

Any detained patient given leave remains 'liable to be detained' at the hospital from which leave has been granted, and so before and during a period of leave the patient is a 'qualifying patient' for the purposes of ss. 130A and 130B of the MHA 1983 (s. 130C(2)(a)) and therefore is entitled to assistance from an Independent Mental Health Advocate (IMHA) (see Chapter 12, 12.9). A patient on leave of absence may not be made subject to a deprivation of liberty under the DOLS powers in the Mental Capacity Act (MCA) 2005 (see Chapter 5) if that is incompatible with a requirement imposed on the patient as a condition of granting leave of absence (MCA 2005, Sch. 1A, paras. 2, 3) or if the deprivation of liberty 'consists in whole or in part of medical treatment for mental disorder in a hospital' (MCA 2005, Sch. 1A, paras. 2, 4; Ministry of Justice (2008b), para. 4.50).

Leave of absence is seen to have a therapeutic and rehabilitative effect. It may also be used on a trial basis when discharge from detention is being contemplated. As such, leave often features as part of a patient's treatment plan, in a variety of forms, including 'ground leave' (freedom to move within specified parts of the hospital and its grounds) (Department of Health (DH), 2008: para 21.4), unaccompanied 'home leave' of various durations, or in the form of short trips out of hospital alone or under the supervision of nursing staff. The managers of the detaining hospital should establish a standardised system for recording leave decisions (DH, 2008: para. 21.21), and the outcome of a period of leave—whether it was successful or not—should be recorded in the patient's notes (DH, 2008: para. 21.22).

As far as patients detained under Part II are concerned, s. 17 gives the responsibility and power for granting leave to the patient's RC, who remains responsible for the patient whilst on leave (DH, 2008: para. 21.23). This power is non-delegable, but may be exercised by another Approved Clinician (AC) acting as RC if the patient's usual RC is not available (DH, 2008: para. 21.6). In practice, RCs tend to give permission in general terms rather than for each trip outside the hospital (Mental Health Act Commission (MHAC), 1991: para. 9.7; and see DH, 2008: paras. 2.16–18), and the decision as to whether leave happens at a particular time or not, or sometimes at all, is in the discretion of nursing staff (MHAC, 2009: para. 2.35). 'Ground leave', which in many instances will only be permitted if the patient is escorted by a member of nursing staff, does not necessarily require the formal use of s. 17 (MHAC, 2009: para. 2.52), although its grant and its planning should nonetheless be subject to formal structures (MHAC, 2009: para. 2.52).

The Code of Practice (DH, 2008: para. 21.8) advises RCs, when considering and planning a leave of absence, to:

- consider the potential benefits and any risks to the patient's health and safety of granting or refusing leave;
- consider the potential benefits of granting leave for facilitating the patient's recovery;
- balance these benefits against any risks that the leave may pose in terms of the protection of other people (either generally or particular people);
- consider any conditions which should be attached to the leave, e.g. requiring the patient not to visit particular places or persons;
- be aware of any child protection and child welfare issues in granting leave;
- take account of the patient's wishes, and those of carers, friends and others who may be involved in any planned leave of absence;
- consider what support the patient would require during their leave of absence and whether it can be provided;
- ensure that any community services which will need to provide support for the patient during the leave are involved in the planning of the leave, and that they know the leave dates and times and any conditions placed on the patient during their leave;
- ensure that the patient is aware of any contingency plans put in place for their support, including what they should do if they think they need to return to hospital early; and

- (in the case of mentally disordered offender patients) consider whether there are any issues relating to victims which impact on whether leave should be granted and the conditions to which it should be subject.

If thought is being given by the RC to granting 'longer-term leave', defined by s. 17(2B) as a period of leave of absence granted or extended which exceeds a total of more than seven consecutive days, he or she should first consider whether a CTO (discussed further at 10.4) should be made instead (DH, 2008: para. 21. 9). Leave of absence under s. 17 should only be used in preference to a CTO if it is the 'more suitable option'. The RC must explain the reason for a decision that it is, and that both options have been duly considered, and all of this must be recorded in that patient's notes (DH, 2008: para. 21.10). The RC must be satisfied in any case that the patient will be able to manage outside the hospital environment (DH, 2008: para. 21.19).

According to the Code, longer-term leave should not be granted if the patient refuses to consent to any necessary consultations with 'carers or other people who would normally be involved in their care' taking place (DH, 2008: para. 20.20). Although this is 'subject to the normal rules of confidentiality' (DH, 2008: para. 20.20), this may cause problems when the patient refuses to agree to the RC consulting with a specific individual for good reason, as in *JT* v *UK* [2000] 1 FLR 909. The European Commission held that the inability of a patient to object to a nearest relative was in breach of Art. 8 of the ECHR, and the government promised to change the law as part of a 'friendly settlement' of that case (see DH, 2006e).

The Department of Health also stated that s. 11 of the MHA 1983 should be interpreted by ASWs (now AMHPs) with due consideration given to the human rights of the patient in the context of admission, and accepted that it is 'also arguable that the issue might arise in other circumstances' (DH, n.d., in MHAC, 2005: para. 130). Although, in the present context, the decision is for an RC rather than an AMHP, here too a patient has no right to make a legitimate objection to consultations that may entail a breach of her Art. 8 rights, and given that the consequence may be continued detention when leave would otherwise be granted, a claim under Art. 5(1)(e) or 5(4) might also, on some fact situations, be feasible. The key to avoiding any breach is to ensure that para. 21.19 of the Code's requirement for the RC to undertake consultations is implemented always with due consideration to the human rights of the patient.

A patient on leave of absence may access the same after-care services under s. 117 (see 10.5) as a patient discharged from detention under ss. 3 or 37 of the MHA 1983 (DH, 2008: para. 21.25), but these services are optional to the patient. Leave may, however, be granted subject to conditions that the RC 'considers necessary in the interests of the patients or for the protection of other persons' (s. 17(1)). One specific condition that is mentioned in the MHA 1983 is that the RC may direct 'escorted leave', under which the patient remains in the custody of a nominated 'officer' on the staff of the hospital or any other person authorised in writing by the hospital managers, if it appears to him or her 'necessary so to do in the interests of the patient or for the protection of other persons' (s. 17(3)). 'Interests' is not defined further and is probably open to a broad definition, whilst 'necessary' is defined by the position as it appears to the RC and not by some objective standard, giving wide scope to the exercise of an RC's discretion. An 'officer', not defined by the Act, nevertheless features often within it. In *R* v *Midlands and North West MHRT, ex p PD* [2004] EWCA Civ 311, 2004 WL 412965, the Court of Appeal, in essence, held that an 'officer' means a person employed at the facility in question, and not any other employee of that Trust.

The *Reference Guide to the Mental Health Act 1983* published by the Department of Health (DH, 2008a) explains that s. 17(3) is intended, inter alia, to 'allow detained patients to have escorted leave on outings, to attend other hospitals for treatment, or to have home visits on compassionate grounds' (2008a: para. 12.43), but might also include home leave under the custody of a relative, for example. The MHAC has reported (2001: para. 4.25) that this does occur, but doubted whether such relatives or friends are aware that they have specific legal powers and duties in respect of the patient. The latest version of the Code of Practice does require that 'responsible clinicians should specify that the patient is to be in the legal custody of a friend or relative only if it is appropriate for that person to be legally responsible for the patient, and if that person understands and accepts the consequent responsibility' (DH, 2008: 21.27). This is a potentially tricky issue. The Cambridge County Court held in *Buck* v *Norfolk and Waveney Mental Health NHS Foundation Trust* [2012] Med LR 266 that no duty of care was owed by a hospital to a bus driver who suffered psychiatric injury when a patient on leave under s.17 threw himself under the driver's bus.

Although of little value as a precedent in and of itself, this decision applied that of the House of Lords in *Mitchell* v *Glasgow City Housing* [2009] UKHL 11; [2009] 1 AC 874; [2009] 2 WLR 481, a case which concerned whether a local housing authority (LHA) owed a duty of care to a tenant to pass on information that he was at risk of violence from a neighbour, which unfortunately transpired, the tenant dying from the injuries inflicted on him. The House of Lords held that there was no duty in such a situation, emphasising that for a duty to arise, there must be an acceptance of responsibility by the duty holder to the person at risk (per Lord Hope of Craighead at para. 29).

Moreover, there was also no question of the harm in *Buck*, unlike in *Mitchell*, being foreseeable: and even then, foreseeability is not sufficient, per se, to trigger a duty of care. Nor did the House of Lords in *Mitchell* find much support for the imposition of legal liability in such a situation on the basis of human rights law, merely reiterating the well-known decision of the European Court of Human Rights in *Osman* v *United Kingdom* (2000) 29 EHRR 245, in which, as the court decided (at para. 116) that for liability under Art. 8 of the ECHR to be found in such circumstances 'it must be established to [the court's] satisfaction that the authorities knew or ought to have known at the time of the existence of a real and immediate risk to the life of an identified individual or individuals from the criminal acts of a third party and that they failed to take measures within the scope of their powers which, judged reasonably, might have been expected to avoid that risk'.

All of this indicates that *Buck* was most probably rightly decided, but that decision does little to assist when a patient on leave is in the custody of a relative or other carer.

The imposition of a duty of care in such circumstances would depend on an application of the same principles. In the situation under discussion, there would be an acceptance of responsibility for the patient by the custodian, and, if the harm which materialised was reasonably foreseeable, the question of whether a duty should be imposed would be a matter of policy rather than legal principle, that is, whether it is 'fair, just and reasonable' (Lord Hope in *Mitchell* at para. 21) that liability should be imposed.

As far as other conditions are concerned, requirements relating to residence and treatment are most common. The patient and other appropriate persons should be given a copy of any conditions (DH, 2008: para. 21.21). As a patient given leave remains 'liable to be detained', the consent to treatment provisions contained in Part IV of the MHA 1983 apply (s. 56(3)). Although this does mean that it is possible, in theory, to administer treatment to a patient with capacity who is refusing consent in the community—the only situation, under the MHA 1983, in which this is the case—the Code of Practice (DH 2008: para. 21.24) advises that 'consideration should be given to whether it would be more appropriate to recall the patient to hospital' if treatment is refused, and there is no data to suggest that patients on leave are being forcibly treated in the community.

Although s. 17 gives the RC a broad discretion, its exercise is subject in practice to the agreement of the detaining hospital and local providers of community services, at least when co-operation, in the form of providing resources or sourcing accommodation outside hospital for example, is required. As the Code of Practice (DH, 2008: para. 21.12) explains,

> the fact that a responsible clinician grants leave subject to certain conditions, eg residence at a hostel, does not oblige the hospital managers or anyone else to arrange or fund the particular placement or services the clinician has in mind. Responsible clinicians should not grant leave on such a basis without first taking steps to establish that the necessary services or accommodation (or both) are available.

On this point, the Code reflects the outcome in *R* v *West London Mental Health NHS Trust, ex parte K* [2006] EWCA Civ 118; [2006] 1 WLR 1865. This case concerned K, a patient with a history of aggression, who had been in Broadmoor for 18 years following his conviction for attempted murder. K's RC was of the opinion that improvements in K's condition (he was diagnosed as suffering from paranoid schizophrenia), following a belated decision by K to accept the antipsychotic medicine clozapine, were such that he could appropriately be transferred into conditions of lesser security on a trial basis using the powers in s. 17. Although one (NHS) Medium Secure Unit (MSU) declined to offer K a bed because of concerns that his improved condition was too recent and of too short a duration for it to be satisfied that the risk of violence to others was manageable, another MSU, in the independent sector, was identified, which was prepared to offer K a bed on a trial basis. A tribunal had also recommended extra-statutorily that K be transferred to an MSU, provided that he remained compliant with his treatment and his improved condition was sustained for a further three or four months. Nonetheless, when the RC applied for funding for the placement in the independent sector MSU, the Trust declined the application.

In reaching this decision, the Trust pointed to the report from the NHS MSU which had declined to offer K a bed, which in its view, based also on advice from its own forensic psychiatrists, demonstrated that he was not ready to move out of high security, and noted that the services available at the MSU were also available at Broadmoor (para. 23). The Trust also took the view that if K were to be transferred, NHS accommodation should first be sought before it would consider funding accommodation for K in the (more expensive) independent sector (para. 27) because there would be continuity of care if K were to be discharged into the community by that NHS MSU, as the same treatment team would manage his care after discharge as had before (para. 35).

K challenged the decision of the Trust, to refuse to fund his transfer, by way of judicial review. The Court of Appeal held that the hospital managers are under duties imposed by the National Health Service Act 1977 (see now National Health Service Act 2006, ss. 3, 3A and 4) to provide inter alia hospital accommodation, and that it is well-established that in the performance of such duties Trusts may take resource considerations into account, and establish priorities for funding (paras. 46, 47, 56), and an 'RMO [now RC] has no power to give directions as to how others are to discharge their functions and section 17 of the MHA cannot be construed as conferring such a power' (para. 54). The court specifically rejected K's argument that the court should find a duty, imposed by s. 17 on hospital managers, analogous to that imposed by s. 117 in the context of after-care (see 10.5), to use reasonable or best endeavours to secure the placement or other service indicated by the RC in the conditions attached to the leave of absence (paras. 56, 61).

The court also made it clear that the Trust, as in this case, is at liberty to decline to fund or otherwise assist in the placement of a person elsewhere under s.17 if it disagrees on clinical grounds with the RC's decision that leave is appropriate (para. 65). The Trust may well consult psychiatrists other than the RC, and 'the knowledge of the RMO [now RC] is not necessarily greater than that of any other medical practitioner responsible for the treatment of any patient' (para. 65). The effect of this decision, when there is a disagreement between the RC and the Trust as to whether leave, or leave on the conditions or in the accommodation proposed by the RC, should be granted, is that the Trust in effect has a power of veto, subject only to the principle that a decision which is so unreasonable that no reasonable decision-maker could reasonably have made it (the 'Wednesbury' principle) will not be allowed to stand. In short, judicial review offers very little prospect of success for an aggrieved patient or RC in this situation.

Furthermore, judging by the case law on the operation of s. 117 (see 10.5) which, although dismissed as irrelevant by the court in K, does seem to raise similar issues under Art. 5 of the ECHR—as in both cases a decision made that the patient need not be detained, made by a person or body entitled to make it, is frustrated by the lack of co-operation of third parties holding a different view of the situation from that person or body—there is little prospect of greater success in using ECHR rights, provided that the criteria laid down in Winterwerp v The Netherlands (1979) 2 EHRR 387 (see Chapter 5, 5.1.1.1) are complied with; and if they are not, the patient is entitled to discharge rather than leave of absence.

Leave may be granted for a limited or unlimited period, and may be renewed in the absence of the patient (s. 17(2)), but a period of leave of absence will end on the expiry without renewal of the authority to detain (s. 17(5)). This means that the maximum period of leave possible under s. 17 is one year (the period of detention for treatment of a renewed s. 3 admission: s. 20(2)). It was accepted, following the decision in *R v Hallstrom, ex p W; R v Gardner, ex p L* [1986] 2 All ER 306 (DC) that it is unlawful to section a patient, or to renew the authority to detain under the procedure found in s. 20, merely to extend a period of leave. The decision in *Hallstrom* ended the practice of using a 'section' as a 'long leash', which had developed after the passage of the MHA 1983 as a way around the historical embargo on compulsory treatment in the community. Although not overruled, the import of this decision has, however, been severely limited by later decisions.

In *Barker v Barking Havering and Brentwood Community Healthcare NHS Trust* [1999] 1 FLR 106, the care plan of B, a patient detained under s. 3, was for graduated, supervised return to the community. She had been granted leave that, at the time that her detention was renewed, allowed her to be absent from the hospital for a number of days each week. B complied with her treatment plan and, on her days in hospital, was assessed rather than treated. She sought judicial review of the decision to renew her detention, on the grounds that the requirements of the relevant section, s. 20(4), were not met. These are, essentially, a repetition of the grounds for initial admission under s. 3. A period of detention cannot be renewed unless the patient is suffering from mental disorder of a nature or degree that makes it appropriate that the patient receive medical treatment in a hospital (s. 20(4)(a)), and that it is necessary for the health or safety of the patient or others that the patient 'should receive medical treatment and that it cannot be provided unless he continues to be detained' (s. 20(4)(c)). Appropriate medical treatment must also be available to that patient (s. 20(4)(d)).

In *Hallstrom*, McCullough J had held that these criteria are not satisfied if, at the time of the renewal, it was not, in the opinion of the RC, necessary that the patient be hospitalised. The Court of Appeal in *Barker* agreed with this, but added the gloss that, although it had to be necessary for the purposes of the renewal of a section under s. 20(4)(c) that a patient 'continues to be detained', this did not mean that it was actually necessary that a patient in B's position needed to be confined to a hospital. It was sufficient that detention would be used as a backstop if the care plan for graduated discharge ran into problems. A similar decision was reached by the Administrative Court in *R v Mersey Health Care NHS Trust, ex p DR* [2002] EWHC 1810, 2002 WL 1654941. DR, a patient detained under s. 3, lived at home on leave as part of her care plan. DR's detention was renewed under s. 20 on the grounds that she had a history of failing voluntarily to take her medication, and so hospitalisation for compulsory treatment was a possibility. She challenged that decision, both on the grounds that there was not, in fact, justification for the decision to renew her detention and as a breach of Art. 5(1)(e) of the ECHR.

The court, following *Barker*, dismissed the first argument on the grounds that the facts showed that treatment in hospital was a significant part of DR's treatment plan. It was further held, although controversially (see MHAC, 2003: para. 9.52 and Figure 20) that the treatment need not be provided on an inpatient basis. This decision was nonetheless followed in *KL v Somerset Partnership NHS Foundation Trust* [2011] UKUT 233 (AAC); [2011] MHLR 194, in which it was held that a community mental health centre (run by the same NHS Trust which provided inpatient mental health services), at which a patient detained under s. 3 but on leave under s.17 attended in order to be given medication, came within the definition of a 'hospital' in s. 145 of the MHA 1983 and therefore the requirements of s. 20(4) were complied with.

In *DR*, the Art. 5 argument was held to be inapplicable, because DR, if detained, would be so under the provisions of the MHA 1983, that is lawfully, and Art. 5 was held not to apply to a patient who is not, in fact, detained. In *R v MHRT and Managers of Homerton Hospital (East London & City Mental Health NHS Trust), ex p CS* [2004] EWHC 2958 (Admin), CS, held under s. 3, had been on leave of absence for three months, and was required to attend the hospital once every four weeks, at which time her progress on leave was monitored by her RC and CS was given encouragement to engage fully with community-based services. CS applied to a tribunal for an order for discharge, which was denied.

On appeal against that decision, CS argued that the facts disclosed that the grounds for detention were no longer made out. Pitchford J found that 'the element of treatment at hospital remained a significant part of the whole' (para. 44), and that, although 'It may be that in the closing stages of the treatment in hospital [the RC's] grasp on the claimant was gossamer thin, but to view that grasp as insignificant is, in my view, to misunderstand the evidence' (para. 46). CS was consenting to her treatment whilst on leave. The court rejected an argument that an order for guardianship or supervised discharge (now a CTO) would be more appropriate than s. 17 leave in such circumstances, in part because 'CS's knowledge of the RC's powers was a significant element in her willingness to accept the treatment plan' (para. 48). This seems to be very close to saying that CS's apparent consent to treatment was, in fact, underwritten by her fear of the legal powers of her RC, and we would add our voices to those who 'are disappointed at this judicial attitude and understanding of the nature of consent to treatment' (MHAC, 2005: para. 4.42).

Although the way that s. 20 has been interpreted in these cases is debatable as a matter of statutory interpretation (Eldergill, 1999), the law as it now stands is reasonably clear. It is *only* when there is *no* intention of hospitalising a patient on leave, and the *only* reason for the extension of a period of detention is to permit continued treatment in the community, that the renewal of authority to detain will be unlawful (for an example of a fact situation in which this was held to be the case, see *R v MHRT and W, ex p Epsom and St Helier NHS Trust* [2001] EWHC Admin 101). This situation may also continue indefinitely, because the court in *CS* (at para. 49) held, understandably, given the uncertain nature of mental disorder, that there was no obligation to state in advance a date at which the detaining section of a person on leave of absence must be ended.

Perhaps all of this is what the MHA 1983 has always provided for, and the decision in *Hallstrom* was routinely over-estimated in its effect on clinical freedom. *Barker* and subsequent case law is clearly in step with the realities of the care programme approach (see Chapter 3, 3.5.1), and with the government's policy of providing for the use of a degree of compulsion in outpatient care (see DH, 2006d). As discussed at 10.4, this policy was realised, most recently, with the introductions of CTOs by the MHA 2007. However, the *Barker* decision defined the scope of s. 17 leave so broadly that it was not apparent what the introduction of CTOs would add to the options available to an RC.

A patient on leave of absence may be recalled to hospital by his or her RC. The powers of recall are contained in s. 17(4). The patient's RC may, by notice in writing to the patient or to the person 'in charge of the patient' (who will be a person who has been appointed under s. 17(3)), revoke the leave of absence and recall the patient to hospital if 'it appears' to the RC 'that it is necessary so to do in the interests of the patient's health or safety or for the protection of other persons'. As with granting leave, this form of words gives a good deal of discretion to RCs. The Code of Practice directs that RCs 'must be satisfied that these criteria are met and should consider what effect being recalled may have on the patient' (DH, 2008: para. 21.31). Failure to take medication as required is frequently a cause for concern, on which the Code (DH, 2008: para. 21.31) advises that 'refusal to take medication would not on its own be a reason for revocation, although it would almost always be a reason to consider revocation'.

These powers must be exercised in compliance with the ECHR, and following the decision in *K v UK* (1998) 40 BMLR 20 (see Chapter 11, 11.3.4), this means that a patient should not be recalled in the absence of 'objective medical evidence' that he or she remains mentally disordered, even where recall is deemed necessary on protectionist grounds. In so far as s. 17(4) does allow recall solely on grounds of public protection, and/or because the RC need not necessarily be a psychiatrist and so a patient may be recalled despite the absence of objective medical evidence of mental disorder, it is arguably incompatible with Art. 5(1)(e), as interpreted by the European Court in *Winterwerp*. The patient is entitled to an explanation of the decision to recall, which should also be recorded in the patient's notes (DH, 2008: para. 21.33). However, unlike the powers to recall a patient subject to a CTO (see 10.4) or a conditionally discharged restricted patient, the use of which triggers the right to apply to a tribunal within one month (see Chapter 11, 11.4.2.1.3), there is no mechanism in the MHA 1983 specifically to review a decision to recall a patient under s. 17(4).

Before its abolition, the MHAC continually expressed concerns over the operation of s. 17, including: withholding of authorised leave by nursing staff as punishment or coercion; failure to appreciate the need for compliance with s. 17 for escorted or short trips out of hospital (MHAC, 1995: para. 9.4); no record of leave having been granted; failure to specify conditions or to consult, or to give the patient and other appropriate persons, such as relatives or professional carers, a copy of the conditions of leave; failure to obtain written permission from the hospital managers before the patient is placed in the custody of someone other than an officer of the hospital (MHAC, 1997: para. 3.4); leave being granted by someone other than the RC (MHAC, 2001: para. 4.59); and leave not being granted solely because of staff or other resource shortages (MHAC, 2003: para. 9.37). A new concern emerged with the expansion of private sector-provided beds for detained patients. In 2005, the MHAC reported (2005: para. 4.38) 'that the use of s. 17 leave may be constrained within some Independent Hospitals because of an understandable reluctance by the relevant commissioning authorities to fund a bed that is not being occupied'. This, as the Commission noted (MHAC, 2005: para. 4.38), may give rise to successful legal challenge under Art. 5(1)(e).

A predominant concern in the MHAC's sixth report (1995) was the use of s. 17 as an alternative to transferring the patient under s. 19. A formal transfer under that section involves the transference of the authority to detain and all ancillary powers between the respective hospitals, but if a patient is transferred under s. 17, the various powers and duties remain with the first hospital. This means that those responsible for the patient's treatment in the hospital to which he or she has been transferred have no original authority over the patient, but the situation had arisen because transfers under s. 17 are typically used to remove acute patients from a district hospital to an MSU, and MSUs had insisted that such transfers occur under s. 17 rather than s. 19, because there were concerns that otherwise district hospitals would refuse to accept the return of patients from MSUs. Nevertheless, some patients had remained 'on leave' for many years in such cases (MHAC, 1995: para. 9.4). Subsequently, Department of Health guidance was issued on the use of s. 17 (DH, 1996), but this did not allay the concerns of the MHAC (1997: para. 3.4.1). Formal leave is required whenever a detained patient leaves a hospital site, even if that is to travel to another site managed by the same NHS trust or to move to accommodation operated on the same site by a different trust (DH, 2008: para. 21.5).

In its final Report (MHAC, 2009) the MHAC noted greater compliance with its own guidance, and with the revised Code of Practice, than had been the case in the past, in terms of documenting the authorisation of leave, and the conditions on which leave was given, and its duration, were sufficiently clear in most (90 per cent) cases (MHAC, 2009: para. 2.31). However, there was still much reason for concern about the operation of s. 17. Copies of paperwork were given to the patient or those into whose custody he or she had been placed only rarely (12 per cent of a sample of 158 cases), despite the clear obligation (found in para. 21.21 of the Code of Practice) to do so; patients were involved in constructing their care plan whilst on leave in only 50 per cent of cases, and in only 55 per cent of cases leave of absence was part of the patient's care plan (MHAC, 2009: para. 2.33). Resource limitations can result in escorted leave being postponed or cancelled (MHAC, 2009: para. 2.37), causing frustration and upset for patients.

On other occasions resource considerations led to a patient's bed being reallocated, even if only very short term leave had been granted, so that the patient has to return to an unfamiliar environment on a different ward, which for some patients acts as an inducement not to seek or take leave. The MHAC discovered that in some institutions escorted leave would only be permitted by nursing staff if the patient agreed to buy the escorting nurse meals during the period of leave, with staff taking the view that patients, in receipt of benefits and with no bills to pay in hospital, were financially better off than staff and so should foot the bill for the costs of being escorted (MHAC, 2009: para. 2.37), in others patients were charged petrol costs for being transported from the hospital to the leave destination if the leave was not classified as therapeutic (MHAC, 2009: para. 2.37). We share the Commission's 'deep concern' about such practices because of the 'inherent risks of perceived or actual exploitation of patients' monies, and potentially compromising relations between patients and staff' (MHAC, 2009: para. 2.37). Although examples of good practice, and the better management of tight resources through transparent procedures, such as initiating waiting lists for leave are also documented by the MHAC (2009: paras. 2.38–39), it is clear that in many institutions the system for granting leave of absence runs in a fairly erratic, and sometimes chaotic fashion, and is significantly hindered by its resource implications.

More recent data on the current operation of s. 17 is hard to come by: the annual reports issued to date by the successor to the MHAC, the Care Quality Commission (CQC) (2010, 2011a, 2013) do not include any sustained discussion of leave of absence, other than to note in passing that there is a continuing correlation between bed over-occupancy and extended leave granted, indicating that leave continues to be used for bed-management, rather than therapeutic reasons, as a mechanism to manage inadequate resources (CQC, 2010, 39–40), and that in at least one hospital a patient's leave will be cancelled if the patient refuses to participate in a limited range of on-ward activities (including art, cookery, and gym) (CQC, 2011a, 41), indicating that, to some extent at least, leave continues to be used to manage the behaviour and compliance of individual patients. As can be seen, leave of absence, although a relatively obscure and under-researched area of mental health law, is heavily implicated in the micro-politics of daily life in our psychiatric institutions.

10.2.2 **Leave of absence for Part III patients**

The provisions of s. 17 do not apply to patients remanded to hospital or made subject to an interim hospital order by a criminal court under ss. 35, 36 and 38 (MHA 1983, s. 40(4)). They do apply to patients detained under s. 37, or an equivalent order such as a transfer from prison without restrictions (s. 55(4)), without modification (MHA 1983, Sch. 1, Part I, para. 1), and to restricted patients with the modifications in s. 41(3) and Sch. 1, Part II, para. 3. A restricted patient may not be given leave of absence without the consent of the Justice Secretary (s. 41(3)(c)(i) and Sch. 1, para. 3(a)), and the provisions relating to longer-term leave (ss. 17(2A) and 17(2B)) do not apply (Sch. 1, Part II, para. 3(aa)).

The policy of the Ministry of Justice was published in 2008 (Ministry of Justice, 2008a) with an updated version published in November 2012 (Ministry of Justice, 2012a). The Mental Health Casework Section (MHCS) housed within the Ministry of Justice aims to respond to requests from RCs to grant leave to a restricted patient within three weeks (Ministry of Justice, 2012a: para. 9). The policy of the Ministry is to give complete discretion regarding ground leave to RCs (Ministry of Justice, 2012a: para. 10), and to respect the discretion of RCs as to whether short term leave is appropriate, including unescorted day leave (2012a: para. 14), but sometimes, for example 'when a patient needs to visit a proposed discharge placement, or where leave at the RC's discretion is not appropriate for reasons of risk or sensitivity' (2012a: para. 5), agreement will be less forthcoming or subject to greater control and more frequent obligations to report back to the Ministry than would otherwise be the case.

RCs have to make a positive case for leave to be granted, including information relating to the assessment of risks and benefits; the place of the proposed leave in the overall treatment plan; the proposed indicators for assessing the success or otherwise of the period of leave; the impact on the patient's victim(s); and the local Victim Liaison Officer (VLO, discussed further later in this section) should be consulted (2012a, para. 8). Generally, leave of more than one night at a time is unlikely to be consented to without prior instances of overnight leave passing without incident (Ministry of Justice, 2008a: para. 13). An up-to-date report on all previous instances of leave must also be provided by the RC (Ministry of Justice, 2012a: para. 25). If, after leave has been granted, the RC revokes his or her consent to it, he or she must inform the MHCS, which will then consider whether the Justice Secretary should also, in the light of the information available, revoke his or her consent (Ministry of Justice, 2012a, paras. 27, 28). It is fair to say that, for the Ministry of Justice, risk management is the main concern and caution threads through the policy as a result.

In *R v SSHD, ex p OS* [2006] EWHC 1903 (Admin), the Secretary of State refused to give permission for OS, detained under ss. 37 and 41 following a conviction for manslaughter, to have leave under s. 17. This was so notwithstanding that OS had been conditionally discharged by a tribunal, which had found that there was insufficient threat to public safety to justify his continued detention. A period of leave under s. 17 was a necessary precursor to the implementation of that decision. The Secretary of State based his decision, in part, on the fact that OS, a foreign citizen, who had been denied asylum and was to be deported, might be tempted to abscond if given leave of absence, and that this, in turn, might lead to OS failing to take necessary medication, thus increasing the risk of harm to the public. The High Court upheld that decision as fair and reasonable on the facts.

There was a similar outcome in *R v Secretary of State for Justice, ex parte PP* [2009] EWHC 2464 (Admin). PP had been made subject to hospital and restriction orders in 1972 following conviction for the rape and manslaughter of a 14-year-old girl, this being the culmination of a long history of sexually violent offending. Apart from one unsuccessful trial leave into conditions of lesser security a decade earlier, PP had spent the best part of four decades in Ashworth hospital. In 2009, when PP was 71 years old, his RC initiated arrangements for his transfer via s. 17 to an MSU on a trial basis. The MSU agreed to take PP, despite acknowledging his high risk of further offending if released from hospital, as he had posed little problem to those responsible for his day-to-day care and management in the past, and was thought to pose little risk in this regard in the future. However, despite the unanimity of the medical views in favour of transfer, the Justice Secretary refused to consent to the proposal and PP sought judicial review.

He challenged the reasons given by the Justice Secretary: that trial leave ten years earlier had ended in failure; that there was no treatment available to PP in the MSU that was not also available in the high security hospital; that PP was himself ambivalent about the move; that PP showed little remorse for his offending; and that PP remained at high risk of reoffending, which put the staff and other patients in the MSU at risk. In deciding that that decision was reasonable, the High Court emphasised that whether or not the Justice Secretary was satisfied that PP would be adequately and safely managed in the MSU 'was a matter of judgment for the Secretary of State. He did not reject any evidence of fact. What he did was to differ from the clinical team on a matter of opinion' (para. 61). If this is the case, then the decision of the Justice Secretary, to refuse to consent, will only rarely be open to successful challenge.

However, the general rules of judicial review must be complied with, which means that all relevant (and no irrelevant) factors should be considered by the Justice Secretary, and adequate reasons for the refusal must be given. *R v Secretary of State for Justice, ex parte X* [2009] EWHC 2465 (Admin) involved a patient initially sentenced to prison for a double murder being before transferred first into high security and, later, medium security hospital accommodation. All involved in X's treatment were in favour of escorted leave, designed to test X's abilities to cope with life outside an institution, being granted, but the Justice Secretary twice refused to consent to this. On the first occasion, no reason was given for the refusal. On the second, it was explained in a letter to the patient's RC from a senior case worker in the Mental Health Unit (MHU, now the MHCS) in the Ministry of Justice that 'The Minister commented that due to the deeply disturbing nature of the crime and importantly, the perspective of the victim's family he would not allow escorted leave' (para. 18).

On this occasion, judicial review of that decision was successful, on the basis that the Justice Secretary's reasons did not demonstrate engagement with 'the nature and scale of any risk which might reasonably be expected to arise if the plan [to used escorted leave] was implemented'. The reasons given did not identify the nature of the risk nor to whom it was posed (para. 49) and 'A fair inference, and in my view the right one, is that the Secretary of State did not ask himself this question at all. In any event, if he did, the answer he gave to it is not clear' (para. 49). Our view is that if the X case had not succeeded, then very, very few cases indeed would succeed. A failure to give any reason at all is indefensible, and a one-sentence explanation of refusal, conveyed as hearsay by a MHCS case worker, is little better.

The Justice Secretary may agree to leave but attach conditions to his or her consent (*R v Secretary of State for the Home Department, ex p A* [2002] EWHC Admin 1618, [2003] 1 WLR 330), and has powers co-existent with the RC to recall a patient under s. 17(4) (MHA 1983, s. 41(3)(c) and Sch. 1, Part II, para. 3(b)). Section 41(3)(d) and Sch. 1, Part II, para. 3(c) provide that s. 17(5) is modified so that a patient given conditional leave of absence either by the RC or the Justice Secretary cannot be recalled to hospital by the RC after the expiration of 12 months from the day on which that leave of absence began, but can be recalled by the Justice Secretary without limit of time. This does not mean, however, that at the expiry of the 12-month period an RC can do nothing. There is always the option of admission of the patient under the *civil* law of compulsory admission, as happened in *R v North West London Mental Health NHS Trust and Ors, ex p S* [1998] 2 WLR 189 (CA), if the criteria for such admission can be made out.

The substantial discretionary powers of the Justice Secretary were challenged in *R v Secretary of State for the Home Department, ex p A* [2002] EWHC Admin 1618, [2003] 1 WLR 330. A, a restricted patient, had been conditionally discharged by a tribunal, but discharge was deferred until suitable accommodation could be found. The Secretary of State had consented to A being given first escorted, and later unescorted and overnight, leave, with A staying at a hostel into which, as part of his care plan, he would eventually move permanently under his conditional discharge. But the Secretary of State refused to consent to A being given leave for a period of six weeks, as a trial of his ability to live long-term in the hostel accommodation. This was because, in the opinion of the Secretary of State, it would, in effect, pass control for A, with a violent history of offending, from the Secretary of State to the RC, and at that time, the Secretary of State was not prepared to do this.

Moreover, leave would, in any case, only be consented to under s. 17, as the court found, in exceptional circumstances (para. 49). The Secretary of State preferred to use the powers to discharge a restricted patient subject to such conditions as he thinks fit, and liable to recall at any time, given to him by s. 42 (discussed in detail at Chapter 11, 11.2.4), as in the view of the Home Office (now the Ministry of Justice), only the RC could attach conditions to leave under s. 17. After some prevarication on the part of the Home Office, A did eventually commence his trial period in the hostel. He nevertheless sought judicial review both of the substantive decision to refuse consent, and of the policy of only using s. 17 for restriction order patients in such narrow circumstances, arguing breaches of Arts. 5(1) and (4) of the ECHR.

The court held, first, that the Secretary of State's reading of s. 17 was incorrect. Because the RC can grant leave with conditions under the section, and the Secretary of State can withhold consent to such leave, it follows that the Secretary of State can determine which conditions, including possibly a condition that he be kept informed of the situation when the patient is on leave, should be attached to leave under s. 17 (para. 41). This, however, has done nothing to change the preference of, these days, the Ministry of Justice, for the use of s. 42 over s. 17, and, according to the Code of Practice, (DH, 2008: para. 21.15) 'The Secretary of State would normally consider any request for section 17 leave for a restricted patient to be in the community for more than a few consecutive nights as an application for conditional discharge'.

This policy preference can impact negatively on the ease and speed with which what in the view of the RC is leave of absence, but in that of the MHCS at the Ministry of Justice is conditional discharge, can be authorised. This is because of the operation of s. 36 of the Domestic Violence, Crime and Victims Act (DVCVA) 2004. Section 36 applies to patients detained under Part III of the MHA 1983 who were charged with any of a wide range of sexual or violent offences (specified in DVCVA 2004, s. 45(2) and Criminal Justice Act 2003, Sch.15) leading to conviction, or a finding of not guilty by reason of insanity, or were found on a trial of the facts following a finding of unfitness to plead to have done the act or made the omission charged as the offence (DVCVA 2004, s. 36(2)). Equivalent provision is made for a patient who on conviction was made subject to a hospital direction coupled with a limitation direction (DVCVA 2004, ss. 39–41A) or who is transferred to hospital from prison (DVCVA 2004, ss. 42–44B) with or without a restriction direction being made (although whether or not there is a restriction determines which regime applies to the patient: the regime described here applies only to patients subject to restriction order, restriction direction, or limitation direction. For the regime which applies for patients not subject to restrictions, see 10.4.1).

When the discharge of such a patient, also being subject to restrictions (DVCVA 2004, s. 36(5)(a),) is being contemplated, the relevant probation board or independent provider of probation services (defined in DVCVA 2004, s. 37(8) as the probation services provider for the area into which the patient will be discharged) 'must take all reasonable steps to ascertain whether a person who appears to the board to be the victim of the offence or to act for the victim of the offence wishes' (DVCVA 2004, s. 36(4)) to make representations regarding whether or not, in the case of a restriction order patient, discharge should be subject to conditions, and if so, what those conditions should include (DVCVA 2004, ss. 36(4)(a), (5)) or to be given information about the conditions that have been attached to discharge (DVCVA 2004, s. 36(4)(b), (6)). This will ordinarily be done by the service provider's Victim Liaison Officer (VLO). If the probation services provider does elicit views from a person appearing to be, or to be acting for, a victim of the offence, those views must be forwarded to the MHCS, being 'the persons responsible for determining the matter' (DVCVA 2004, s.37(2)) in restriction order cases, unless or until the restriction is lifted (DVCVA 2004, s. 37(3)).

The Secretary of State, via the MHCS, must also inform the local probation services provider if considering whether to end a restriction order (DVCVA 2004, s. 37(4)(a)), discharge the patient absolutely or subject to conditions under s. 42 (DVCVA 2004, s. 37(4)(b)) or vary the conditions of a patient already conditionally discharged (DVCVA 2004, s. 37(4)(c)). In addition, if a tribunal receives an application or a reference from the Secretary of State (see Chapter 11, 11.4.2) in respect of a restricted patient to whom s. 36 of the DVCVA 2004 applies, that too must be forwarded to the local probation services provider. That information must then be forwarded to a person who appears to be or represent a victim and who has expressed a wish to be consulted or provided with information at the relevant time (DVCVA 2004, ss. 37(6), (7)). It will be the responsibility of the probation services provider's VLO to carry out these tasks.

The obligations imposed by s. 37 of the DVCVA 2004 are designed to allow victims and their representatives to make informed representations when the release of the patient from hospital or the removal of conditions imposed on discharge are being contemplated. A victim or representative may, however, wish to be informed but not to be involved in the decision-making process. In such circumstances, the information to which the victim or representative is entitled is defined closely by s. 36(6) as 'information about any conditions to which the patient is to be subject in the event of his discharge from hospital', but this should be read subject to the provisions of s. 38.

Section 38 of the DVCVA 2004 applies when a person identified as a victim or victim's representative following the investigations required by s. 36(4) has expressed a wish to be provided with the information referred to in s. 36(6) or has informed the VLO at a later date that he or she wishes to receive the information (DVCVA 2004, s. 38(2)). The

VLO must 'take all reasonable steps to inform that person whether or not the patient is to be subject to any conditions in the event of his discharge' (DVCVA 2004, s. 38(3)(a)). If the patient has been discharged subject to conditions, the detail of any which relate to contact between the patient and the victim or his family must be provided (DVCVA 2004, s. 38(3)(b)). The VLO must also inform the victim if a restriction order is about to be brought to an end, and the date on which it will cease to have effect (DVCVA 2004, s. 38(3)(c)) and may in any case, divulge 'such other information' as the VLO and the probation services provider 'considers appropriate in all the circumstances' (DVCVA 2004, s. 38(3)(d)).

It is not certain what this means. The guidance given to hospital managers, RCs, and AMHPs (as those responsible for administering the system of victim consultation under the DVCVA 2004 in respect of patients not subject to restrictions) advises that victims may also be informed if a patient is given leave in certain circumstances or has absconded from the detaining hospital (DH and Ministry of Justice, 2008: 2.30–32, discussed further at 10.4.1), and the advice given by the Ministry of Justice to the clinical supervisors of conditionally discharged restricted patients also refers to the same two examples (Ministry of Justice, 2009a: para. 15). As the guidance (DH and Ministry of Justice, 2008: 2.30–32) notes, this will 'require close liaison between the VLO and the offender's care team, both in hospital and in the community'. Even so, it will not always be clear that the provision of such information to a victim will do more good than harm: the news that he or she may soon come face to face with the person who offended against them may be terrifying for some victims.

To facilitate the provision of information by the VLO to the victim or representative, the Justice Secretary (via the MHCS) must inform the relevant probation services provider whether the patient is to be discharged; if so whether or not subject to conditions; if conditional, what those conditions are; if the patient is discharged subject to conditions, any variation of those conditions; if the patient is recalled to hospital by the Justice Secretary using the powers of recall contained in s. 42(2) of the MHA 1983; and if the Justice Secretary proposes to bring a restriction order to an end, the date in which it will cease to be in force (DVCVA 200, s. 38(4)). Sections 38(5) and (6) make similar provision for a tribunal to inform the local probation services provider if a restricted patient to whom s. 36 applies makes an application or has his or her case referred to the tribunal and it proposes to discharge the patient, if so whether with conditions attached, and if so, what those conditions are; or, if the patient has been conditionally discharged and the tribunal has varied the conditions, the detail of that variation; or, if the tribunal proposes to take action to end the restriction order, the date on which that order will cease to have effect. If a tribunal recommends to the Justice Secretary that the conditions attached to a patients discharge be varied, or the order for discharge be revoked under s. 42(2), or the restriction order should cease to have effect, and the Justice Secretary acts on such a recommendation, the Justice Secretary must inform the local probation services provider of his or her decision (DVCVA 2004, s. 38(7)).

Section 38B of the DVCVA 2004 further provides that if a restriction order is removed but the accompanying hospital order remains in force, the VLO 'must take all reasonable steps' to notify a person identified as a victim or victim's representative who has expressed a wish to make representations or receive information, of the address of the managers of the relevant hospital and the hospital of the address of that person (DVCVA 2004, s. 38B(2), (3)) to allow the free flow of information between them. A patient in such circumstances will no longer be subject to ss. 37 and 38, but will be subject to the corresponding provisions in respect of unrestricted Part III patients, ss. 37A and 38A (see 10.4.1) (s. 38B(4)). The evidence such as there is, which is more anecdotal than systematic, is that the requirement to consult victims and consider their views has, for some patients at least, increased significantly the time taken by the MHCS to authorise leave of absence (MHAC, 2009: para. 2.47).

The court in *R* v *Secretary of State for the Home Department, ex p A* further held that it is inappropriate for the Justice Secretary to discharge conditionally a patient under s. 42 when he or she has already been discharged conditionally by a tribunal; s. 17 should be used instead (paras. 47, 50). As far as issues of human rights are concerned, the actions of the Secretary of State regarding the implementation of A's leave in this case had, in the view of the court (para. 65), delayed its start by six weeks. In *Johnson* v *UK* (1997) 29 EHRR 296, the European Court held that an unreasonable delay in discharging a person whose mental disorder no longer warranted detention breaches Art. 5(1) of the ECHR. Crane J held that this was the case here, the delay being unreasonable because there was no good reason for it (para. 71).

The court declined to issue a certificate of incompatibility between the MHA 1983 and the Human Rights Act 1998 however, because no specific 'in principle' breach had been argued before it. Crane J did say that 'possibly section 41(3)(c)(i) might be a candidate' (at para. 56) (MHA 1983, s.41(3)(c)(i) is the paragraph in s. 41 which provides that a restricted patient may only be given leave with the consent of the Justice Secretary). There must, in our view, be a very strong possibility that this is correct. In *X* v *UK* (1981) 4 EHRR 181, the European Court held the UK in breach of Art. 5(4) because the final decision regarding the discharge of restricted patients was vested solely in the Secretary of State, with no provision for his or her decisions to be reviewed by a court. The MHA 1983 amended the domestic law accordingly, by giving tribunals co-extensive powers to order discharge (see Chapter 11, 11.5.2). This does not aid a patient such as A, however, who had already been discharged, albeit conditionally and albeit deferred, by a tribunal. There was, as such, no point in A seeking to challenge the refusal to grant leave by applying to a tribunal for discharge. Because there was no other remedy open to him, he was in a situation exactly analogous to the patient in the *X* case, with release from hospital entirely dependent on the discretion of the Justice Secretary, from whose decision there is no right of appeal.

Street (1998: 56) found that 93 per cent of restricted patients had unescorted leave of absence before final discharge, that in the great majority of cases, leave passed without incident, and that around a third of restricted patients discharged from hospital were on leave of absence and living away from hospital at the time. This does not mean that restricted patients are given leave freely—unescorted leave, in particular, will only be granted very close to the end of a period of hospitalisation, during which the patient will have moved into increasingly less secure accommodation—but it does illustrate the widespread use of s. 17 leave.

10.2.3 **Powers to transfer restricted patients between institutions**

The MHA 1983 as originally enacted (and indeed the MHA 1959) gave the Justice Secretary powers in s. 123, to transfer a patient from one high security hospital to another. This power was abolished in 2012 by s. 42 of the Health and Social Care Act 2012, but the explanatory note to that section makes clear that this does 'not affect the power of the managers of high security hospitals themselves to arrange the transfer of patients by agreement with the managers of the receiving hospital'. The Justice Secretary must, however, agree to such a transfer (MHA 1983, s. 19 and Sch. 1, Part II, paras. 2, 5). The Justice Secretary may direct the transfer of any patient subject to a hospital order or a transfer direction, either between special hospitals (in respect of which the patient has no right to be consulted (*R* v *SSHD, ex p Pickering* (1990, unreported) (CA)), or from a high security hospital into less secure accommodation. If the patient is in a high security hospital, it is unlikely that he or she will be discharged into the community. It is MHCS policy that a patient will only be transferred out of a high security hospital on a trial basis in the first instance (Ministry of Justice, 2009b: 1). It is more common that the RC will recommend that he or she be transferred into increasingly less secure accommodation—MSUs and then general NHS hospitals or, perhaps more likely, hostel accommodation—before final discharge.

There is a long-standing problem, that the appropriate transfer of patients out of the high security hospitals into conditions of lesser security has been hindered by the reluctance of MSUs to accept patients (Dell, 1980; Gostin, 1986a; Smith *et al.*, 1991; Home Office and DH, 1992; Dolan and Shetty, 1995; DH, 2000a), with priority given to transfers out of the prison system (Gostin and Fennell, 1992: 211). Dolan and Shetty (1995) found that the average wait for patients judged suitable for transfer was more than a year. There were 349 patients from all three special hospitals awaiting transfer in April 2001, not including those suitable but not officially listed for transfer because there is 'no realistic hope of finding them alternative accommodation' (MHAC, 2001: 5.6). By 2003, 'some acceleration in arranging transfers' had been noted (MHAC, 2003: 12.10). Nonetheless, 'there continue to be a substantial minority of patients who are ready for transfer or discharge, but are waiting Home Office approval, the identification of placements outside the hospital, or an available bed in such a placement' (MHAC, 2003: 12.9), and the experience of those running special hospitals was that, by 2005, it is 'now more difficult than ever' (Mersey Care NHS Trust, 2005: 5) to find medium-secure accommodation able to accept a patient on transfer, albeit that the numbers now in need of transfer seem to be significantly lower than in 2001.

Although more recent data is hard to come by, as the CQC, unlike the MHAC, does not routinely publish this information, delays continue to be reported (Centre for Mental Health, 2011; O'Sullivan and Chesterman, 2007). Tetley, Evershed and Krishnan (2010) found that patients with a personality disorder are particularly difficult to transfer out of high security hospitals, and, confirming earlier research, the main reason for this is the reluctance of MSUs to accept transfers. McClean (2010) found that pathways out of MSUs into low security accommodation are also problematic in operation, with considerable numbers of patients (45 per cent in this hospital) detained in MSUs who could be appropriately accommodated in lesser security accommodation, but MSUs were operating with inexact definitions of 'security' leading to uncertainty as to which accommodation is most appropriate for individuals and unnecessary caution in arranging transfer. In short, it seems as though there is still considerable potential for delay in moving into conditions of lesser security at each stage of the system, from high to medium and from medium to low.

There is little that the patient or his or her RC can do to force the situation. In *R v MHRT and Secretary of State for Health, ex p LH* [2001] 1 MHLR 130 (HC), it was held to be no breach of any ECHR right for the Secretary of State to fail to transfer a patient judged as suitable. It is, however, clear, from *Aerts v Belgium* (2000) 29 EHRR 50, that there is a point when conditions of detention are so unsuitable for the patient in question that a breach of Art. 5(1)(e) will be found. In such a case, a mentally ill person held in unsuitable conditions in prison for seven months until a hospital bed could be located for him successfully brought an action under Art. 5. The CCG of a patient's home area may seek suitable transfer accommodation further afield in an effort to circumvent bed shortages locally, but, as the MHAC noted, and the case of *R v Oxfordshire Mental Healthcare NHS Trust and Oxfordshire Health Authority* [2001] 1 MHLR 140 (HC) demonstrates, 'health authorities [now trusts] appear unwilling to fund expensive placements elsewhere' (MHAC, 1999: para. 5.112).

R v West London Mental Health NHS Trust, ex parte L [2012] EWHC 3200 (Admin); [2013] ACD 15 involved an unusual situation. L, diagnosed as having a dangerous and severe personality disorder (DSPD), had been sentenced to a hospital order following convictions for kidnapping and other offences. No order under s. 41 was attached. L was initially detained in an MSU but because of his violence to others, self-harming, and because he absconded from the MSU on two occasions, on one of which he made his way to the home of a victim of his earlier offence, it was decided to transfer him to Broadmoor high security hospital. Broadmoor's policy is that applications for admission made by MSUs are considered by an admissions panel. L's legal representative sought to attend that panel meeting as an observer (as there was no other mechanism otherwise by which she could attend), but this request was turned down by the hospital. The panel met, and decided that L should be accepted by Broadmoor. The reasons given to the patient were that the panel found (para. 62):

> Overwhelming evidence of a personality disorder, dissocial, borderline and high psycho-pathy; and evidence of self-harm. Fits the DSPD criteria. He did so in the last assessment by DSPD Unit at Broadmoor. To be considered by the DSPD Panel for admission prior to responding to Stockton Hall [the MSU]. A paper review may be sufficient. Unanimous decision of the panel.

Thereafter, L sought judicial review of the transfer decision, arguing that the lack of procedure or regard for the rules of natural justice rendered that decision unlawful.

The High Court noted the lack of legal criteria to be applied when determining if a transfer should take place (para. 131); the potentially adverse consequences of transfer on L's state of mental health and prospects for discharge (paras. 236–91); the inability of the patient to make representations, see all the evidence that panel would consider, or challenge factual inaccuracies (paras. 567–81); before concluding that the common law duty of fairness applied to the decisions of the admissions panel (para. 566) and had not been adhered to in this case (para. 581). The court also found that there would be a breach of Art. 6 in these circumstances unless a patient after transfer has access to judicial review, and that review involved the heightened scrutiny required in cases in which the human rights of the applicant are at issue (para. 839). Although this case involved a patient detained under s. 37 without restrictions, it would seem that the finding in this case should also apply to all other transfers, both of restricted patients and of patients detained under the civil powers found in Part II of the MHA 1983.

10.3 Guardianship

Guardianship is an alternative to compulsory admission to hospital and continuing hospitalisation for persons aged 16 or above (MHA 1983, s. 7(1)). It can therefore be used as after-care and may be suitable for a person leaving compulsory detention (DH, 2008: para. 26.13), although this will be unusual and a CTO (see 10.4) is usually the preferred option. As with admission to hospital under Part II of the MHA 1983, the making of an order does not require the consent of the patient. The basic idea is that a nominated person or body assumes responsibility for the supervision of a patient's care in the community, and, so the Code of Practice suggests (2008: para. 26.22), acts as 'advocate' in securing necessary services for the person subject to the guardianship order, which 'may or may not include specialist medical treatment for mental disorder' (2008: para. 26.2).

There may well be no need for such treatment, as opposed to care, for example, if the person in question has learning disabilities rather than being mentally ill, and it is often for those in the former category that guardianship is best suited. If capacity is an issue, it may be that steps have already been taken under the MCA 2005, such as the appointment of a deputy by the Court of Protection or the appointment of a person to exercise lasting powers of attorney by the patient (Chapter 4, 4.2). This does not necessarily mean that a guardian should not be appointed, although the Code of Practice suggests that there should be no appointment if the patient's welfare can be secured using the general power in s. 5 of the MCA 2005 (see Chapter 4, 4.2) to make various decisions (DH, 2008: para. 26.10), including where the patient should live (2008: para. 26.11).

Consideration should, however, be given to the use of guardianship if the patient, whether or not having capacity, objects to plans made under s. 5 of the MCA 2005, and in particular, if is thought desirable that there should be explicit statutory authority to return the patient to his or her accommodation if absent without leave, or if it is beneficial to vest ultimate authority over the patient in one person (for example if there has 'been long-running or particularly difficult disputes about where the person should live': DH, 2008: para. 26.12). The Code also suggests, though (para. 26.13), that if there are 'finely balanced arguments about where the patient should live', thought should be given to asking the Court of Protection to make a best interests judgment.

If appointed, the powers of the guardian take priority and a person with powers under the MCA 2005 may not make a decision in respect of the patient that conflicts with one made by the guardian (MCA 2005, Sch. A1, paras. 2, 3(2); DH, 2008: para. 26.6). Guardianship should allow the person subject to the order to lead 'as independent a life as possible within the community' (DH, 2008: para. 26.4). Conversely, a guardian may not impose conditions on, or control, the movements of the patient to the extent that he or she is deprived of his or her liberty: if this is the case, deprivation of liberty safeguards (DOLS) should be used instead of guardianship (para. 26.29), although if guardianship is already up and running, it should not necessarily (or even usually) be ended if at a later date it is thought appropriate to use DOLS 'so long as it would not be inconsistent with the guardian's decision about where the patient should live' (para. 26.32), and so long too, as the use of DOLS is not a mechanism to put the patient in same the position as a mental health patient (i.e. a person detained under the MHA 1983) and the patient objects, either to being a mental patient in this sense, or to some or all of the medical treatment which it is proposed that he or she be given (MCA 2005, Sch. A1, paras. 2, 5; Ministry of Justice (2008b): paras. 4.43–4.45).

A patient subject to guardianship may be accommodated in a hospital or other psychiatric facility as an informal patient, but this should not be a requirement imposed by the guardian 'except where it is necessary for a very short time in order to provide shelter while accommodation in the community is being arranged' (DH, 2008: para. 26.33). If a patient is detained under either ss. 2 or 4 of the MHA 1983 this will not affect the continued validity of the guardianship, but if the patient is detained under s. 3, the guardianship will automatically come to an end (DH, 2008: para. 26.34). A patient may be transferred from guardianship into hospital (and vice-versa) under reg. 8 of the *Mental Health (Hospital, Guardianship and Consent to Treatment) (England) Regulations 2008*, SI 1184/2008, as long as the medical recommendations and other requirements of a s. 3 admission are satisfied and the relevant LSSA agrees to the transfer (DH, 2008: para. 26.34).

Under the Mental Deficiency Act 1913, 'idiots', 'imbeciles', 'feeble-minded' persons and 'moral imbeciles' could be taken into guardianship, the effect of which was to give to the guardian the powers of a father over the person subject to the order. The MHA 1959 extended the scope of guardianship to cover mentally ill persons, but s. 34 of that Act maintained the formula whereby a person appointed as a guardian of a mentally disordered person enjoyed 'all such powers as would be exercisable by him in relation to the patient... if he were the father of the patient and the patient were under the age of 14 years'. This would seem to mean, in so far as this issue was given any thought at the time, that a guardian might, amongst other things, consent to medical treatment on behalf of the mentally disordered person.

When the MHA was overhauled in 1983, the opportunity was taken to reword this infantising (and sexist) provision and specify the powers of a guardian with greater clarity and limitation. The White Paper that preceded the reforms of the early 1980s (Department of Health and Social Security, 1981: paras. 43, 44) rejected arguments that guardianship should permit treatment in 'the community' without consent and opted instead for a more restrictive 'essential powers' approach. Accordingly, the MHA 1983 now provides that a guardian has three powers: to require the patient to reside at a specified place; to require that the patient attend at places and times for the purposes of medical treatment, education, occupation, or training; and to require that access to the patient is given to a doctor, AMHP, or other person specified by the guardian (MHA 1983, s. 8(1)). Whether these 'essential powers' do, in fact, contain the essentials of guardianship, which according to the Code of Practice (2008: para. 26.2) 'is to enable patients to receive community care where it cannot be provided without the use of compulsory powers' is at least debatable.

It is accepted law that there is 'no power under the 1983 Act to give treatment to a mentally disordered person who withholds consent [or, presumably, who cannot consent] unless he is [liable to be] detained in hospital' (*R v Hallstrom, ex p W (No. 2)* [1986] 2 All ER 306 (HC) per McCullough J at 313; see also *T v T* [1988] 1 All ER 613 (HC) at 617, per Wood J). In addition, the power to require attendance for treatment, and so on, is not supported by any power to take and convey the patient to the place in question, and although a patient absent from the place where he or she has been required to reside may be deemed by the guardian to be absent without leave and so can be returned by a social worker or police officer if apprehended before the expiry of the guardianship order or six months from the date first absent, whichever is the later (MHA 1983, s. 18(3), (4),(7)), there is no power to detain the patient at the place of residence in question.

If the purpose of guardianship is to give the guardian sufficient powers to ensure and require that patients accept treatment in order to obviate what would otherwise be a need for compulsory detention, then clearly the powers given by s. 8 of the MHA 1983 are not sufficient for that purpose. There is no sanction for a patient who does not comply with the requirements placed on him or her by their guardian. Thus, in practice, the paradoxical situation is that, to be effective, these 'compulsory' powers rely on the co-operation, or at least absence of positive resistance, of patients: this is why the Code of Practice suggests that one situation in which guardianship may be appropriate is when 'the patient is thought to be likely to respond well to the authority and attention of a guardian and so be more willing to comply with necessary treatment and care for their mental disorder' (DH, 2008: para. 26.8). But a person who responds to an attentive authority figure in this way will often do so without the need to invoke formal legal powers. This is the first reason why guardianship under the MHA 1983 failed to live up to expectations.

The second reason is concerned with the criteria for the making of a guardianship order. It is open to a criminal court to make a guardianship order rather than a hospital order (see Chapter 8, 8.4.1), which it can do if of the opinion that to do so is the most suitable method of dealing with the offender (MHA 1983, s. 37(1),(2)), and a guardian willing to act has been identified (s. 37(6)). A guardianship order made by a court takes effect as if had been made under Part II of the MHA 1983 (s. 40(2)). However, courts only rarely make guardianship orders (eight times in 2012 and seven in 2011, with the 19 orders made in 2006 being the highest annual figure in the last ten years (Health and Social Care Information Centre, 2012: table 1)). Rather, guardianship orders are usually made under the civil powers contained in Part II of the MHA 1983. These largely mirror the requirements of admission for treatment under s. 3. Applications may be made by either an AMHP or the patient's NR (s. 11(1)), and must be founded on the written recommendations of two doctors, both of whom must state that the criteria for guardianship are met (s. 7(3)).

The requirements and limitations in ss. 11–13 in relation to admission to hospital for treatment (see Chapter 6, 6.3.2), also apply here, as does the initial time limitation of six months (s. 20(2)(a)), and the pattern of annual renewal thereafter (s.20(2)(b)), with attendant medical reports (but no consultations) under s. 20(6),(8). Differences between the making of a guardianship order and admission for treatment under s. 3 are that it must be necessary for the patient's *welfare* (rather than, in s. 3(2)(b), his or her health or safety) that an application is made (s. 7(2)(b)), which is a much broader, and differently-focused, concept, and there is no requirement that appropriate treatment be available in s. 7. In addition, the medical report required for renewal of the order may be supplied by the GP or other 'nominated practitioner' of the person subject to the order, rather than an AC if the guardian is not an LSSA (ss. 20(6), 34(1)(a)). If an LSSA is guardian, s. 34(1)(b) provides that the report required under s. 20(6) must be supplied by the relevant RC. An order can be discharged by the patient's RC, by the relevant LSSA (but not by a private guardian, if someone other than the LSSA has performed the role) and, except in cases where guardianship was ordered by a court (MHA 1983, s. 40(4) and Sch 1, Part 1), the patient's nearest relative (s. 23) (see Chapter 11, 11.2.3).

As with admission under s. 3, the patient must be suffering from mental disorder (s. 7(2)(a)), although here, obviously enough, it must be of a nature or degree which warrants reception into guardianship rather than hospital. Section 7(2)(a) must be read in the light of s. 1, which incorporates into the criteria for reception into guardianship the requirements of s. 1(2A), (2B)(a) of the MHA 1983, namely that a person with learning disability is only 'mentally disordered' for these purposes if that disability is associated with abnormally aggressive or seriously irresponsible conduct.

This means that the majority of persons with learning disabilities, for whom guardianship was initially designed a century or so ago, who are not normally aggressive or seriously irresponsible, are ineligible for guardianship. This, as Gunn (1986: 147) bluntly noted, is 'a mistake', which was poignantly underlined by the case of Beverley Lewis (Fennell, 1989). In *Re F (Mental Health Act: Guardianship)* [2000] 1 FLR 192, the Court of Appeal confirmed that the criteria for the making of a guardianship order should be construed narrowly, and overruled the High Court, which had found that 'seriously irresponsible' behaviour was exhibited by a person who wished to leave her voluntary residential accommodation and return home against the advice of her carers (see further Sandland, 2000). The opportunity to revisit this situation was not taken by the MHA 2007.

Section 7(5) of the MHA 1983 provides that an application for guardianship must name the proposed guardian, who can be either a LSSA or any other person (including the applicant, so that an AMHP or nearest relative (NR) can both make an application and act as guardian), but s. 7(5) also gives LSSAs a power of veto over an application naming any other person as guardian. It is also to the relevant LSSA that an application for guardianship must be forwarded (s. 8(1), and see reg. 5 of the *Mental Health (Hospital, Guardianship and Consent to Treatment) (England) Regulations 2008*, SI 2008/1184), within 14 days of the second medical recommendation (s. 8(2)). LSSAs must ensure that they have sufficient resources to meet their obligations to oversee guardianship in their area or provide employees to act as guardians (National Health Service Act 2006, Sch. 20, para. 2(2)(a)).

Once an application has been accepted by the relevant LSSA, whether or not it will actually act as the patient's guardian, it is required, under reg. 23 of the 2008 Regs, made by the Secretary of State acting under the powers given in s. 9 of the MHA 1983, to arrange for the patient to be visited by a doctor at least every three months, and by a s. 12-approved doctor at least once every year. The Code of Practice also places certain requirements on LSSAs: to have a system whereby it can accept guardianship applications, monitor the operation of guardianship in its area, make provision for the renewal and/or discharge of guardianship, ensure the suitability of a guardian other than an LSSA, authorise an AC to act as the patient's RC, and ensure that both patients and guardians understand their rights (including the right to apply to a tribunal) and obligations (DH, 2008: para. 26.15).

The third reason why guardianship has been used less than was expected before the passage of the MHA 1983 is that it usually falls to LSSAs to act as guardian (325 out of a total of 331 new cases in 2012 (Health and Social Care Information Centre, 2012: Table 1)) and many, indeed most, are reluctant so to act. More than half of the 682 guardianship cases that were ongoing as at 31 March 2012 were shared between 1 per cent (24/152) of LSSAs (Health and Social Care Information Centre, 2012: 4), and as this suggests, there are very noticeable regional variations in the use of guardianship, with the North West region having 27.2 per cent of all continuing cases, compared to 3 per cent in the East Midlands, 5.4 per cent in the East, and 7.3 per cent in London (although this London figure is an improvement on previous years, in which guardianship was used less than anywhere else in England) (Health and Social Care Information Centre, 2012: 4 and table 3).

In most regions numbers are in single figures and in a sizeable minority of regions, noticeably, but not only, in London boroughs and the South East, no uses, or only one or two uses, were reported (Health and Social Care Information Centre, 2012: Table 5b). There is also significant regional variation in the average length of a period of guardianship, with 63 per cent of guardianship orders still in force a year after being made in the North East and the East Midlands, but at the other end of the spectrum, only 32 per cent were still in force a year later in the South East (Health and Social Care Information Centre, 2012: Table 4). It is not absolutely clear why guardianship has historically and (moreso) presently been used so infrequently, but the limitations on the power of the guardian seem to be one reason. Guardianship should not be used in isolation, but only as part of the broader, comprehensive care plan (DH, 2008: para. 26.4); in the majority of cases, it will be hard to demonstrate what the invocation of guardianship will add to the effective operation of a care plan, in which case, guardianship should not be used (DH, 2008: para. 26.20).

Following a noticeable increase in the use of guardianship, from 41 new cases in 1982–83 to 226 in 1992–93, to 372 in 1995 (MHAC, 1997: para. 8.8), rising to 540 in 2001–02, and peaking with 1,024 individuals subject to a guardianship order on 31 March 2002 (DH, 2002a: Table 1), over the last decade the numbers have continually fallen, with the most drastic fall occurring between 2010, when 439 new cases were opened, to 347 in 2011, falling again to 331 in 2012 (Health and Social Care Information Centre, 2012: Table 1), which is back to where guardianship was in the mid-1990s. It is difficult to unpack this data. In some areas, there is a close correlation between the use of guardianship and the recent introduction of DOLS by the MCA 2005. The North West, for example, makes significant use of guardianship but has one of the lowest rates of applications for DOLS, whereas in the East Midlands, guardianship is used only rarely but the region makes the most use of the DOLS powers (Health and Social Care Information Centre, 2012: 7), although elsewhere neither guardianship nor DOLS, nor community treatment orders (CTOS), in use since 2008, are used frequently. Further research is required in order to offer any more definite analysis.

If, as rarely happens, a private guardian is appointed, he or she will be under the supervision of the LSSA, and must act in accordance with any directions that the LSSA gives him or her, as well as appointing a doctor to oversee the patient's medical treatment, and keeping the LSSA informed of any changes of address of the patient and doctor (2008 Regs, reg. 22). An LSSA or private guardian will also owe a common law duty of care to the patient. Persons subject to guardianship have much the same rights to apply to a tribunal as do other patients subject to Part II of the MHA 1983 (s. 66(1)(c)), which will entail a further layer of paperwork for all concerned (the Secretary of State's powers of referral in s. 67 are also applicable here). From the point of view of an LSSA, it is easy to see how guardianship can be seen to carry all the burdens of compulsory admission to hospital but few of the benefits. Having said that, it does seem that in some areas of the country guardianship is found useful by LSSAs, mainly in respect of elderly people of pensionable age, to buttress the delivery of care (Cox, 1994). This might explain why, in the South East, the average duration of a guardianship order is 41.9 months, compared to a national average of 24.7 months (Health and Social Care Information Centre, 2012: Table 4).

10.4 Community treatment orders

10.4.1 Community treatment orders and their conditions

The so-called 'revolving door' patient has been a long-standing concern for mental health professionals. The term is used to describe those patients who fall into a pattern of acute mental illness—a significant factor in which is often a failure by the patient to take prescribed medication and/or maintain contact with community mental health services—leading to hospitalisation, treatment which improves the patient's condition to the extent that hospitalisation is no longer warranted, discharge, only for the pattern to then begin again.

Various attempts have been made to respond to the problem of the revolving door patient, from the 'long-leash' fashioned by psychiatrists on the basis of s. 17 of the MHA 1983 that was struck down by the High Court in *Hallstrom*, but effectively reinstated by the Court of Appeal in *Barker* in 1999 (see 10.2), to supervision registers, introduced in 1994 but subsequently abandoned, and After Care Under Supervision (ACUS) introduced by the Mental Health (Patients in the Community Act) 1995. The most recent response, introduced by the MHA 2007, is the community treatment order (CTO). A patient subject to a CTO will be subject to Supervised Community Treatment (SCT: this term is used in the Code of Practice and other government literature but not on the face of the Act; we shall use the term CTO). At the time that CTOs were introduced, many were sceptical of their potential, given that the CTO is very similar, in some ways, to ACUS, which was used relatively infrequently. In the event, however, CTOs have proven reasonably and unexpectedly popular, at least with some mental health professionals, although, as will be discussed further, the reasons for this are not clear.

CTOs were finally introduced, following much debate, by s. 32 of the MHA 2007, which inserted new sections 17A–G into the MHA 1983. The CTO is a mechanism to exert some, potentially considerable, control over patients in the community. As with previous attempts to do the same, however, the CTO stops short of permitting the treatment without consent of a person outside a hospital. A CTO can only be made in respect of a person who is detained in hospital for treatment under s. 3 (s. 17A(2)) or ss. 37 or 47 (without restrictions) (Sch. 1, Part 1, para. 1) of the MHA 1983. A person subject to a CTO is known as a 'community patient' (s. 17A(7)). A CTO is an order discharging the patient from hospital (but not from the s. 3 or s. 37 order, which continues to subsist after a CTO has been made: s. 17D(1)) 'subject to his being liable to recall' (s. 17A(1)). An order can only be made by the patient's RC (s. 17A(1)), although a tribunal hearing an application from a patient detained under ss. 3 or 37 may recommend that the patient's RC consider making a CTO (s. 72(3A)(a)).

A community patient is entitled to assistance from an IMHA (s. 130C(2)(c)), and to information, provided by the hospital managers of the responsible hospital, as soon as practicable after a CTO is made (s. 130D(3)(d)), about the purpose and availability of an IMHA (ss.130D(1),(2)(d)). The same information should be conveyed by the hospital mangers to the patient's NR, if there is one, unless the patient objects (DH, 2008: para. 15.29). Hospital managers must also take reasonable steps to ensure that a community patient (s. 132A(1)) and, unless the patient objects, his or her NR (s. 132A(3)), understands the effects and implications of being subject to a CTO and the rights to apply to a tribunal which a community patient has. The CQC has reported (2011a: 26) that 'often' these requirements are not complied with by managers; and too often patients are unsure, either about whether they are subject to a CTO or not, and if so, the significance of that, with little understanding of the conditions attached, the duration of the order, and so on, and with little idea of how to find out.

A community patient is not 'liable to be detained' under the MHA 1983 (s. 17D(2) (a),(b)), or under any other legislation, and the managers of the hospital at which the patient is accommodated when the CTO is made have no authority to detain him or her whilst the CTO is in force (s. 17D(2)(a)). The provisions of s. 20 regarding the renewal of a period of detention under s. 3 do not apply (s. 17D(3)), but whilst the CTO is in force 'authority for his detention shall not expire' (s. 17D(4)). A CTO can in the first instance be of a maximum duration of six months (ss. 17C(a), 20A(1)), but is renewable for a further six months and thereafter annually (s. 20A(3)). Thus, as long as the CTO is renewed, the underpinning s. 3 or 37 admission also continues to subsist. If not renewed, both the CTO and the underpinning treatment order under ss. 3 or 37 shall cease to have effect and the patient 'shall be deemed to be discharged absolutely from liability to recall under this Part of the Act' (s.20B). It is the responsibility of the RC to examine the patient within two months of the expiry of a CTO, and to decide if the criteria for renewal (which mirror those for the making of a CTO in the first place) are satisfied (ss. 20A(4)(a), (6)). If so, the RC must, having first consulted at least two people professionally concerned with the patient's medical treatment (s. 20A(9)) provide a report to the hospital managers (ss. 20A(4)(b),(8)), who must, unless they intend to disagree with the RC and discharge the patient (see Chapter 11, 11.2.2.), in turn inform the patient (s. 20A(5)). The provision of that report by the RC to the hospital managers has the effect of renewing the CTO (s. 20A(10)).

An RC may only make (s. 17A(4)) or renew (DH, 2008: para. 29.12) a CTO if of the opinion that the relevant criteria (see later in this section) are met, and an AMHP agrees in writing with that opinion and states that it is appropriate to make the order. One ongoing cause for concern (CQC, 2013: 79) is that, unlike the situation with admission to hospital, there is no specification of a maximum period between the RC deciding that a CTO should be made and the AMHP agreeing with that decision. The CQC reported in 2010 (CQC, 2010: 103) that in some cases 'considerable time had elapsed' between the RC's decision and the AMHP's agreement, and in its 2011–12 report (CQC, 2013: 79) stated that 'This is still a concern'. Not only does this risk a CTO being out of date before it is even made, but it is also unsettling for patients left in limbo whilst waiting to see if the AMHP confirms the view of the RC.

The CQC's 2009–10 report discussed a case in which the AMHP did not sign the relevant form (Form CTO1) for seven months after it was signed by the RC (CQC, 2010: 103). This seems to us to raise the possibility of a successful claim under Art. 5(1)(e) of the ECHR. The CQC also found examples of an RC signing Form CTO1 to activate the CTO before passing it to the AMHP which, in the view of the CQC (2013: 80), may render any subsequent CTO unlawful, because the RC should not sign the section of the form which activates the CTO unless and until the AMHP has signed it to indicate that he or she agrees with the RC that the CTO should be made. This may not be a particularly strong argument, given that similar submissions in the context of s. 3

admission have proven unattractive to the courts (see Chapter 6, 6.3). The Commission is surely correct, however, in its view that this practice is inappropriate because it 'gives the impression that the doctor has treated the requirement for an AMHP's agreement as a mere formality that can be assumed' (CQC, 2013: 80).

Indeed, AMHPs should not merely 'rubber stamp' RCs' decisions. Instead, even if the criteria lain out are met (DH, 2008: para. 25.24), the AMHP should consider the broader context, including the support structures available to the patient in the community and, controversially perhaps, 'the potential impact on the rest of the patient's family, and employment issues'. The Code (2008: para. 25.25), somewhat opaquely, also requires AMHPs to 'consider how the patient's social and cultural background may influence the family environment in which they will be living and the support structures potentially available. But no assumptions should be made simply on the basis of the patient's ethnicity or social or cultural background'. The CQC (2013: 80) reports examples of cases in which the AMHP's decision and reasoning is not recorded, or inadequately recorded, in the patient's notes, inviting doubts as to whether the AMHP has in fact conducted the enquiries required by the statute and the Code of Practice with sufficient thoroughness: in some cases, it seemed doubtful that enough time had passed between the RC deciding that a CTO is appropriate and its coming into force for such enquiries to have been made.

There is no requirement that the AMHP who gives or withholds agreement under s. 17A(4) has had any prior involvement in the patient's care. The Code (2008: para. 25.26) suggests it could be an AMHP employed by 'any willing LSSA', but if there is no such willing LSSA, then the LSSA which will be responsible for providing after-care services under s. 117 (see Chapter 11, 11.5) should assume responsibility for ensuring that an AMHP is available. Combined with the fact that there is no requirement placed on the AMHP actually to meet the patient, with the CQC providing examples of instances in which 'it is not clear that the AMHP has consulted any wider than reading the medical file and the responsible clinician's statement' (CQC, 2010: 103), the risk of AMHPs in practice doing little more than 'rubber-stamping' is very real.

According to the Code of Practice (2008: para. 25.27), the AMHP has in effect a power of veto over the RC's decision to make a CTO, as, if the AMHP does not agree that the order should be made, 'It would not be appropriate for the responsible clinician to approach another AMHP for an alternative view'. Support for this view is not, however, found on the face of the legislation itself, and it seems that, in practice an RC faced with one recalcitrant AMHP could lawfully seek approval for a CTO from another AMHP, provided that a supportive AMHP could be located, and the RC acted in good faith and reasonably. This could, on the law as it seems to be at present, be an AMHP on the staff of the detaining hospital.

The Code also requires the RC to consult with the patient, his or her NR, any carers, anyone with decision-making authority for the patient under the MCA 2005, and the patient's GP (DH, 2008: para. 25.17). If the patient does not have a GP, he or she should be encouraged to register with a GP practice (DH, 2008: para. 25.17). The provision of treatment to a community patient in some circumstances (see 10.4.4) requires the consent of a Second Opinion Appointed Doctor (SOAD), and if that is the case, the RC should also arrange for a SOAD to certify that the treatment in question should be given before the CTO commences (DH, 2008: para. 25.18).

There are five criteria for the making of a CTO, which are found in s. 17A(5):

(a) the patient is suffering from mental disorder of a nature or degree which makes it appropriate for him to receive medical treatment;

(b) it is necessary for his health or safety or for the protection of other persons that he should receive such treatment;

(c) subject to his being liable to recalled as mentioned in paragraph (d) below, such treatment can be provided without his continuing to be detained in hospital;

(d) it is necessary that the responsible clinician should be able to exercise the power under section 17E(1) below to recall the patient to hospital; and

(e) appropriate treatment is available for him.

As can be seen, these criteria are substantively very similar to those which apply to the decision to admit a patient for treatment under ss. 3 or 37. The distinction between a patient properly detained under s. 3 and one appropriately discharged from hospital but subject to a CTO is not diagnostic—it is not a question of the extent, nature, or degree of the mental disorder from which the patient is suffering—but managerial. In particular, the 'key question', as the Code of Practice (2008, para. 25.7) describes it, in s. 17A(5)(d), of whether a power of recall should necessarily be attached to the discharge of the patient, asks whether the patient is likely to comply with their treatment plan outside hospital. If the patient is likely to comply, then it is difficult to see that a power of recall is necessary. If a patient is unlikely to comply with his or her treatment plan in any case, and so in the opinion of the RC will continue to need to be treated without consent, it is equally difficult to see that a CTO, as opposed to continued hospitalisation, is appropriate.

If discharge from hospital is, in the opinion of the RC, indicated as part of the patient's treatment plan, but there is a 'serious risk of arrangements in the community breaking down or being unsatisfactory' (DH, 2008: para. 28.6) then leave of absence under s. 17 should be preferred, as it should if discharge is on a trial basis (2008: para. 28). On the other hand, the Code of Practice (2008: para. 25.13) further advises that 'A risk that the patient's condition will deteriorate is a significant consideration, but does not necessarily mean that the patient should be discharged onto a CTO. The RC must be satisfied that the risk of harm arising from the patient's disorder is sufficiently serious to justify the power to recall the patient to hospital for treatment'. A CTO, as opposed to simple discharge from hospital, may therefore be inappropriate even if there is some risk of the patient's condition deteriorating after leaving hospital.

Guidance as to the proper operation of s. 17A(5)(d) is given in s. 17A(6), which requires the RC to consider the patient's history of mental disorder and 'any other relevant factors' in order to determine 'what risk there would be of a deterioration in the patient's condition if he were not detained in a hospital (as a result, for example, of his refusing or neglecting to receive the medical treatment he requires for his mental disorder)'. The Code of Practice (DH, 2008: para. 2.11) states that other relevant factors 'are likely to include the patient's current mental state, the patient's insight and attitude to treatment, and the circumstances into which the patient would be discharged'.

In summary, then, the CTO is aimed at that limited constituency of patients detained for medical treatment who would, in the opinion of the RC and the AMHP: (i) be able to go home if they would comply with their treatment plan; (ii) be likely to comply with a community-based treatment plan; but (iii) only if a degree of compulsion is involved and; (iv), who nevertheless may not comply, making it necessary that they be subject to the possibility of recall to hospital; but who (v) are not 'very likely' (2008: para. 28.6) to fail to comply with their treatment plan outside hospital. The RC and the AMHP are therefore called upon to make fine judgments of degree of risk, and although the advice in the Code of Practice is helpful to an extent, the decision as to whether the particular patient presents a 'sufficiently serious...risk of harm' is inevitably fact-specific. One practical upshot of this is that it is very difficult for a person made subject to a CTO, rather than being discharged absolutely, to challenge that decision.

There is a further layer of considerations to be taken into account by the RC and AMHP if the patient is detained by virtue of ss. 37 or 47 of the MHA 1983. Section 36 of the DVCVA 2004 applies if the offence which led to the making of a hospital order is a specified sexual or violent offence (DVCVA 2004, s. 45(2) and Criminal Justice Act 2003, Sch. 15), as a result of the amendment of s. 36(3) of the DVCVA 2004 by Sch. 6, para. 2(2) to the MHA 2007. This means that the procedure for ascertaining, contacting, and inviting representations from and providing information to victims described in relation to restricted patients (see 10.2.2) applies here too. However, as patients without restrictions are not under the control of the MHCS at the Ministry of Justice, the body charged with the responsibility to invite representations and provide information to victims and their representatives is not the Ministry, but the managers of the hospital at which the patient is currently detained or, if already discharged from hospital on a CTO, the 'responsible hospital' (DVCVA 2004, s. 36A(6)), this being the hospital to which the patient will be recalled if the CTO is brought to an end (see further below). It is however possible for hospital managers to delegate their duties under s. 36A to 'any person authorised by them in that behalf' (*Mental Health (Hospital, Guardianship and Treatment) (England) Regulations 2008*, SI 2008/1184, reg. 20).

Guidance for hospital managers and other professionals was published by the Department of Health and Ministry of Justice in 2008 (DH and Ministry of Justice 2008) which advises (2008: para. 2.3) that appropriate delegates 'could include (but is not limited to) their Mental Health Act administrators and their clinical and social work staff'. The hospital managers or their delegates are responsible, for example, for identifying patients subject to s. 36 within the hospital and ensuring that relevant staff such as the patient's RC is aware of their status as a s. 36 patient, and for keeping accurate records of representations that have been made by victims.

The duty to locate victims and ascertain the wishes of victims or their representatives (DVCVA 2004, s. 36(4)), and to transfer information backwards and forwards, including, if the victim does want to be involved or consulted, information as to the name and address of the correspondents (DVCVA 2004, s. 36A(3)) between victims, their representatives, and the hospital managers, as with restriction order patients, is placed on the local probation services provider (DVCVA 2004, s. 36A(2), (3)), which means, as with restricted patients, the probation service provider's VLO. The VLO must also, if the victim(s) or their representatives have indicated that they do wish to make representations or be provided with information, take 'all reasonable steps' to ascertain if the hospital order is still in force, and whether a CTO is also in force and, if the hospital order does remain in force, must notify the hospital managers of that person's wishes and provide that person with the name and address of the hospital (DVCVA 2004, s. 36A(5)).

The VLO should ascertain, specifically, whether the victim or victim's representative wishes to make representations regarding 'what conditions he should be subject to in the event of his discharge from hospital under a community treatment order' (DVCVA 2004, s. 36(5)). When a victim or representative does make representations to a VLO which are then forwarded to the hospital managers, the managers in turn must ensure that the representations are forwarded to the 'persons responsible for determining the matter' (DVCVA 2004, s. 37A(3)). This will be the patient's RC and AMHP (see DH and Ministry of Justice, 2008: paras. 2.20, 2.24, 3.3, and 3.8), although the RC should not delay discharge merely to wait for representations from a victim (DH and Ministry of Justice, 2008: para. 3.2) The RC must inform the managers if he or she is considering discharging the patient (see Chapter 11, 11.2.2), or making or varying the terms of an existing CTO (DVCVA 2004, s. 37A(4)), and should wherever possible do so 'sufficiently far in advance to ensure that victims have a chance to make representations' (DH and Ministry of Justice, 2008: para. 3.1). Section 37A(6) places a similar duty on a tribunal to which the patient has made an application or been referred. On receipt of such information from either source, the managers must, if the victim or representative has communicated either to a VLO (DVCVA 2004, s. 37A(7)(a)) or directly to the hospital (DVCVA 2004, s. 37A(7)(b)) that he or she wishes to make representations before the patient is released from hospital, forward the information received to that person (DVCVA 2004, s. 37A(8)).

The information to be provided, in any case, to a victim or representative who indicates a wish to be kept informed 'is information about any conditions to which the patient is to be subject in the event of his discharge from hospital' (DVCVA 2004, s. 36(6)). To this end, the RC must inform the managers concerning whether: he is to make an order for discharge in respect of the patient under s. 23(2) of the MHA 1983; or make a CTO and if so, on what conditions; or vary the conditions of an existing CTO; or if a CTO is due to expire, the date on which it will do so; or, if having examined the patient under s. 20 of the MHA 1983 for the purposes of ascertaining if the conditions for a renewal are met, is of the view that they are not (DVCVA 2004, s. 38A(2)). Again, a similar duty is placed on a tribunal which receives an application from or reference in respect of an unrestricted patient to whom s. 36 of the DVCVA 2004 applies, to inform the hospital managers if it subsequently discharges the patient (s. 38A(4), (5)). The hospital managers must then forward that information to the victim or representative (ss. 38A(6), (7)).

In addition to information regarding the specific event—the making or varying of a CTO, etc.—the managers have a discretion, as does the MHCS in respect of restricted patients (see 10.2.2), to also pass on 'such other information as the managers of the relevant hospital consider appropriate in all the circumstances of the case' (DVCVA 2004, s. 38A(7)(g)). The guidance issued by the Department of Health and Ministry of Justice (2008a: para. 2.30) explains that this is designed to allow 'hospital managers' discretion to give information intended to reassure victims. It is not intended to permit the disclosure of any information which would otherwise be treated as confidential patient information'. It provides, as illustrations of the possible use of s. 38A(7)(g), disclosing to the victim that the patient has been given leave of absence in a situation where the victim and patient may come into contact whilst the patient is on leave, so that the victim knows that the patient has not absconded (DH and Ministry of Justice, 2008: para. 2.31), or, if a patient has gone absent without leave, informing the victim that steps are being taken to apprehend the patient (para. 2.32). As discussed in the context of restricted patients (see 10.2.2) the decision whether or not to provide such information will often involve fine judgments for the hospital managers.

The guidance further provides that further information over and above this, can with the 'freely given' (DH and Ministry of Justice, 2008: para. 5.5) consent of the patient, be provided and 'this should be encouraged to enable victims and victims' families to be informed about progress, if that is what the victims want' (2008: para. 5.2), as this will reduce victim fears, increase confidence in the working of the criminal justice and mental health systems, improve the patient's prospects for successful rehabilitation (para. 5.3) and reduce the risk of confrontation between victim and patient when the latter is discharged from hospital (para. 5.4).

Once a CTO is made, the patient, as a community patient, will almost certainly be subject to the Care Plan Approach (CPA) (DH, 2008: paras. 25.16–25.23; DH, 2008b: 14, and see Chapter 3, 3.5.1), under which a care co-ordinator should be appointed (DH, 2008: para. 25.16) who may be the RC, but most often will not be. Where there is a transfer of authority, there should be prior consultation between the hospital-based RC and the transferee, who may be an RC working as part of a community-based team, and with the rest of the community team, at an early stage.

Alternatively, the RC in overall charge of the patient's treatment may continue in that role but day-to-day responsibility is allocated to another professional whilst the patient is subject to a CTO. It is also possible under s. 19A of the MHA 1983 to transfer responsibility from one hospital and its RC to another hospital and another RC. Evidence that the arrangements for the transfer of responsibility do not always work well at the local level was published by the Mental Health Alliance in 2010 (Mental Health Alliance, 2010), whilst more recently, the CQC has reported instances when it 'was unclear how and when responsibility was transferred from the inpatient responsible clinician to the community responsible clinician', others when 'There seemed to be no clearly identified process for transferring responsible clinician duties from one doctor to another', and others when 'patient records indicated confusion as to who would manage patients' clinical care in the community' (CQC, 2013: 79), with contradictory statements regarding the identity of a community patient's new RC (2013: 79), in consequence of which 'Several patients interviewed did not know the name of their responsible clinician'. Clearly, this is an unsatisfactory state of affairs, with both professionals and patients unsure about which professionals have legal responsibilities for and to the patient.

A community patient is entitled to access s. 117 after-care services (s. 117(1); see Chapter 10, 10. 5). Section 117(2) imposes a statutory bar on the CCG or local health board which is the main service commissioner in the local area exercising the general discretion given by s. 117, to decide that it is 'satisfied that the person concerned is no longer in need of such services'. Services under s. 117 are, in the main, optional as far as the patient is concerned, but for community patients compulsion will be an element of their community treatment plan. Section 17B(1) contains a mandatory requirement that a CTO 'shall specify conditions to which the patient is subject while the order remains in force', and s. 17B(3) provides that, as a minimum, each CTO 'shall specify–(a) a condition that the patient make himself available for examination under section 20A below; and (b) a condition that, if it is proposed that a certificate under Part 4A of this Act in his case, he make himself available for examination so as to enable the certificate to be given'. The first of these applies to all community patients, the second, which involves the provision of treatment as part of a CTO under powers found in Part 4A of the MHA 1983, applies to nearly all patients, and is discussed further at 10.4.4 in that context.

Additionally, the RC, but only 'with the agreement of' the AMHP, who must be the same AMHP who agreed that a CTO should be made (s. 17B(2)), may specify further conditions thought necessary by the RC to ensure the patient receives medical treatment; prevent the risk of harm to the patient's health or safety; or protect other persons. According to the Code of Practice, this is an exhaustive list of reasons, so that 'Conditions may be set for any or all of these purposes, but not for any other reason' (DH, 2008: para. 25.31). Nonetheless, that leaves the RC with significant discretion to make decisions and attach conditions which impact significantly on the liberty of the community patient. The Code (2008: para. 25.34) provides as examples, conditions 'which might cover matters such as where and when the patient is to receive treatment in the community; where the patient is to live; and avoidance of known risk factors or high-risk situations relevant to the patient's mental disorder'. As with the making of a CTO, there is no requirement in the statute that the patient's consent be obtained in respect of particular conditions, but the Code of Practice (2008, para. 25.32) advises that the patient and 'any others with an interest such as a parent or carer' should be consulted, and any conditions attached, and the reasons for them, should be explained to patients, who should also be provided with 'access to the help they need to be able to comply' (para. 25.35).

Accordingly, and also to incorporate the requirements of human rights law, the conditions should (DH, 2008: para. 25.33):

- be kept to a minimum number consistent with achieving their purpose;
- restrict the patient's liberty as little as possible while being consistent with achieving their purpose;

- have a clear rationale, linked to one or more of the purposes [in s. 17B(2)] and
- be clearly and precisely expressed, so that the patient can readily understand what is expected.

This does not always happen, however. Vague conditions (such as a requirement not to abuse alcohol) have been reported by the CQC (2013: 81) and, more worryingly, so too have conditions which in the view of the CQC amounted to a deprivation of liberty (2013: 82), which are unlawful in the context of a CTO. There is nothing to prevent a community patient being made subject to DOLS under the MCA 2005 in general terms, but paras. 2 and 3 of Sch. 1 to the MCA 2005 provide that any action which it is proposed should be taken using DOLS powers must not be incompatible with a requirement of or condition attached to the CTO. DOLS may also not be used for a community patient if the 'relevant care or treatment consists in whole or in part of medical treatment for mental disorder in a hospital' (MCA 2005, Sch. 1A, paras. 2, 4; Ministry of Justice, 2008: para. 4.50).

10.4.2 **Recall of CTO patients**

There is no clear link in the legislation between compliance with conditions imposed as part of a CTO and the power to recall a community patient to hospital. Generally, failure to comply with a condition is, rather, a fact that may be taken into account by an RC, exercising the power given to him or her by s. 17E(1) of the MHA 1983 to recall a community patient to hospital (s. 17B(6)). There is also a specific power, but not a duty, to recall a community patient if a mandatory condition imposed under s. 17B(3) is breached.

Instead of recalling the patient, the RC can use the power given to him or her by ss. 17B(4) and (5), to ('in writing') vary or (presumably also in writing) suspend the conditions specified in the CTO. There is no requirement that the RC consult the AMHP before so doing, although 'it would not be good practice to vary conditions which had recently been agreed with an AMHP without discussion with that AMHP' (DH, 2008: para. 25.41). These powers are exercisable by the RC at any time, not only when a patient is in breach of condition, but variation or suspension might be a suitable course of action in a specific case of breach. For example, it may be appropriate that the patient move accommodation, or that a condition which is no longer necessary is removed from the CTO. It seems that the power to vary or suspend applies both to any conditions imposed by the RC and the AMHP and to the mandatory conditions that must be included in every CTO by operation of s. 17B(3).

There is a similar issue in respect of CTO patients who have been informally admitted to hospital. Although the powers of recall apply as they do to patients not in hospital, the holding powers given to nursing staff in respect of detained patients by s. 5 of the MHA 1983 do not apply to CTO patients (MHA 1983, s. 5(6)). There is thus no mechanism to use holding powers in respect of a CTO patient who wishes to leave the hospital in circumstances which give cause for concern and which suggest that recall may be appropriate, unless and until the RC can be located, the various consultations carried out, and the paperwork for recall completed. The CQC (2010: 107) has suggested that in such circumstances ward staff may have to rely on common law powers of restrain and detention.

The use of the power of recall is not restricted to situations in which a condition has been breached (s. 17B(7)). Rather, it may be exercised in any situation in which the criteria in s. 17E(1) are met. These enable an RC to recall a patient if '(a) the patient requires treatment for his mental disorder; and (b) there would be a risk of harm to the health of safety of the patient or to other persons if the patient were not recalled to hospital for that purpose'. The 'and' should be noted: these are not alternate criteria: before a patient can be recalled, both must be satisfied. A recall must be done by notice in writing to the community patient (s. 17E(5)) and written notice constitutes authority for the hospital in question to detain the patient (s. 17E(6)). A patient can be recalled to a hospital other than the responsible hospital (s. 17E(3)), and can be recalled if already an informal patient in the hospital to which he or she is recalled (s. 17E(4)).

The patient must be given the opportunity to comply with the condition in question before recall to hospital is considered (DH, 2008: para. 25.49). The patient may also receive inpatient treatment as an informal patient without affecting the continuing validity of the CTO as an alternative to recall. If the RC decides that recall is appropriate, he or she must (unless responsibility for organising recall has by agreement at the local level been allocated to some other person) then organise the recall, giving due consideration to the impact on the patient and their domestic circumstances (DH, 2008: para. 25.54). The recall is only effective when a written notice of recall is served on the patient (para. 25.55), but is immediately effective from that point (para. 25.58).

If the whereabouts of the patient are not known, or if the patient evades delivery by hand, a notice of recall delivered to the patient's last known address is deemed effective 'on the day after it is delivered—that is, the day (which does not have to be a working day) beginning immediately after midnight following delivery' (DH, 2008: para. 25.58). Notice of recall should preferably be delivered by hand rather than through the post (para. 25.57), but if this is not possible, first class post may be used and the recall is deemed effective on the second working day after posting (para. 25.57). Once served with notice of recall, a patient who does not present themselves at the hospital to which recalled is treated as absent without leave (see Chapter 7, 7.5), and can therefore be taken and conveyed to the hospital, and although this should be done in the least restrictive manner (para. 25.60), it will be lawful to use reasonable force to the extent necessary (para. 25.56).

The CQC advises that if the patient is on private premises to which access cannot be gained without force, consideration should be given by the AMHP and RC to seeking a warrant to authorise entry under s. 135(1) of the MHA 1983, which can be issued by a single Justice of the Peace if given 'reasonable cause to suspect that a person believed to be suffering from mental disorder' is, inter alia, 'kept otherwise than under proper control' or is unable to care for himself and is alone in the premises in question. This may be particularly pertinent advice if there are concerns about how the patient will react to being recalled and the notice of recall does not become until midnight of that day effective (if served on the last known address), or for two working days (if sent by post). The procedure thus can create 'a dangerous gap' and at least one patient has committed suicide having received notice of recall through the post (CQC, 2010:105).

The recall of a patient to hospital does not necessarily entail his or her admission as an inpatient. It may be possible to provide treatment, for example, on an outpatient basis (DH, 2008: para. 25.61), and the fact that the patient has been recalled does not in and of itself bring the CTO to an end. Rather, the RC has three options at this point. First, he or she may release the patient from hospital (s. 17F(5)), in which case the CTO carries on as before (s. 17F(7)). This may be appropriate if, following hospitalisation, the patient responds positively and quickly to treatment provided therein (DH, 2008: para. 25.63) or if it transpires that the decision to recall was inappropriate (although if the pre-recall procedures are followed, this should happen only rarely). Secondly, the CTO may be revoked, in accordance with the criteria in s. 17F(4). The RC may revoke the CTO if satisfied that the conditions for detention for treatment found in s. 3(2) of the MHA 1983 are met, and he or she has secured the written agreement of an AMHP (who need not have had any prior involvement in this patient's CTO) with that opinion and that revocation is appropriate (s. 17F(4)(a),(b)). Without the agreement of an AMHP, therefore, the CTO cannot be revoked and will continue in force.

As with the making of a CTO, the Code of Practice advises that if the RC cannot secure the agreement of the AMHP, 'It would not be appropriate for the responsible clinician to approach another AMHP for an alternative view' (DH, 2008: para. 25.69), but this limitation on the discretion of the RC does not appear on the face of the legislation, and as we suggested when discussing the making of a CTO, there may well be situations in which a court would find a revocation to be lawful despite the refusal of one AMHP to agree to it, provided that another AMHP does agree to it and the RC seeking a second AMHP has acted in good faith and reasonably. Once revoked, the authority to detain in s. 6(2) of the MHA 1983 automatically revives by operation of s. 17G(2), the patient reverts to 'liable to be detained' status (s. 17G(3)), and the renewal requirements in s. 20 are reactivated, with the day of revocation marking the beginning of the relevant period for those purposes (s. 17G(5)).

Thirdly, the RC can decide to take neither of these two options. If neither is taken within 72 hours of the time that the patient was detained following recall (s. 17F(8)), the patient must be released (s. 17F(5)), in which case the CTO again carries on as before (s. 17F(7)). The RC has a general discretion to release the patient 'at any time' (s. 17F(5)), although a patient may not be released if the CTO has been revoked (s. 17F(5)), which is understandable, given that the RC will have decided by that point that the patient ought to be detained under s. 3. The hospital managers are charged by the Code of Practice with ensuring that the legal requirements surrounding recall are complied with and so must ensure, for example, that if a CTO is not revoked, the patient is not detained in hospital for longer than 72 hours (DH, 2008: para. 25.71), that all the necessary paperwork is in order (para. 25.72), and that following revocation the patient is referred to a tribunal without delay (para. 25.74). It may be far from easy for the RC to make an informed choice as to which option is to be preferred because, as with the making a CTO in the first place, once the patient has been recalled there may be a transfer of authority, from a community-based RC who made the decision to recall the patient, and a hospital-based RC, who has had little or no involvement with the CTO, who must then decide on the next step, his or her unfamiliarity with the patient and their situation notwithstanding.

There is the possibility, after recall, of transferring the patient to a different hospital (s. 17F(2)), in which case the written notice of recall is also authority for the detention of the patient in that second hospital, and it will be deemed that he had been detained in that second hospital from the time of his return to hospital following recall (s. 17F(3)). If a CTO is revoked after transfer, it shall be deemed that the patient was admitted into the second hospital (s. 17G(4)), and so is now lawfully detained there.

10.4.3 Usage of community treatment orders

At the time of the last edition of the present text, when the introduction of CTOs was being debated, we expressed scepticism about the extent to which the orders would find favour with RCs, given that neither leave of absence nor a CTO allows recall to hospital for non-compliance with treatment per se, and that leave under s. 17 is attended by much less formality than the making of a CTO: there is no legal requirement for an RC contemplating granting leave to consult other persons, as there is with a CTO; the powers to treat outside hospital are greater under s. 17 than under a CTO; and that there is no right to apply to a tribunal following the revocation of leave as there is with the revocation of a CTO. Similar views were expressed when CTOs took their final shape with the MHA 2007 (Bowen, 2007: 73; Gledhill, 2007) and subsequently (Kinton, 2008; Dawson, 2010: para. 14.38).

Yet, despite the predictions, RCs have been prepared to make CTOs, although the data available by the time of writing should be treated with some circumspection. By 31 March 2012, 14,295 CTOs had been made (NHS Information Centre (NHSIC), 2012: 20), although, because of a 'data quality issue' there is no authoritative count of the number of people subject to a CTO on that date: the NHSIC has produced figures of both 6,964 (the total of CTOs made minus those revoked or discharged) (2012: 20) and 4,764 (2012: 21), this latter figure being the number of people reported as being subject to a CTO. As with those subject to detention, two thirds of these were male (NHSIC, 2012: 23), but unlike detained patients, 2 per cent of which are detained in independent sector facilities (NHSIC, 2012: 22), nearly all (99 per cent) of those subject to a CTO had been detained in NHS facilities prior to their CTO being made (NHSIC, 2012: 23). CTOs are almost never used for persons with learning disabilities: only 2 per cent of community patients had been detained under the MHA 1983 with a diagnosis of learning disability as a prime reason for using compulsory powers (NHSIC, 2012: 23), compared to 12 per cent of those detained in hospital (NHSIC. 2012: table 8). They are also used much more frequently for persons detained under s. 3 of the MHA 1983 than for those detained under s. 37. The most common diagnosis by far for people subject to a CTO is schizophrenia, schizoaffective disorder, or other delusional disorder, which accounted for 81 per cent of patients in a sample analysed by the CQC in 2010 (CQC, 2010: 99), with a further 12 per cent suffering from other mood disorders.

The 4,220 orders which were made in 2011–12 constitute a rise of 10 per cent, from the 3,834 made in 2010–11 (NHSIC, 2012: 20), and the NHSIC claims that the general trend is upwards since the introduction of CTOs in 2008–09 (2012: 20). It is perhaps too early to be making such claims without some caveat. The 2010–11 total was down from the 4,107 made in 2009–10, although this was up markedly on the 2,134 made in 2008–09 (2012: 20). However, CTOs were only available from November 2008, and so the figures for that year recorded use over a five- rather than twelve-month period. Extrapolating from the 2,134 CTOs made between November 2008 and April 2009, which marked the start of the data collection year 2009–10, the rate at which CTOs were made was the equivalent of 5,121 orders over a 12-month period. There was thus quite a levelling off as between 2008–09 and 2009–10, with a further 6.6 per cent reduction in 2010–11. At the time of writing, it is only figures for the most recent year, 2011–12, which buck this trend and constitute a genuine increase in the use of CTOs.

The number of recalls to hospital rose from 207 in (the five-month year) 2008–09, to 1,217 in 2009–10, 1,601 in 2010–11, and 2,082 in 2011–12 (NHSIC, 2012: 20), in which year around 70 per cent of recalls resulted in the revocation of the CTO. The number of both revocations and discharges of CTOs has also risen each year: the former from 143 in 2008–09 (the five-month year) to 779 in 2009–10, 1,018 in 2010–11 and 1,469 in 2011–12, the latter from 33 to 1,010 to 1,167 to 1,712 over the same period (NHSIC, 2012: 20). Rising figures are to be expected, because there has, since CTOs were introduced, been a gradual accretion in numbers subject to an order, as many CTOs will be of greater than one year's duration. Of the 14,295 CTOs so far made, 7,731 (51 per cent) have ended, 3,409 of which were revoked and 3,922 discharged.

Firm conclusions about the operation of CTOs cannot yet be drawn. The NHSIC has suggested that the sharp rise in the increase in recalls over the previous year should be seen in the context of the fall in admissions under Part II of the MHA 1983, suggesting that some people who would previously have been subjected to a new admission are now being placed on CTOs and recalled to hospital (NHSIC, 2012: 21). There was a similarly sharp increase in 2011–12, of 481 or 30 per cent (NHSIC, 2012: 20). Although speculative, this is likely to be correct to some extent. The NHSIC also claims that some CTOs will have been revoked following recall on the basis that the patient was not sufficiently well to return to the community (NHSIC, 2012: 21) and this too is likely to explain some, perhaps most, of the recalls.

What is not currently known is whether the powers to make a CTO, and to recall, revocation, and discharge are always being used appropriately. Nor can long-term trends or patterns yet be stated with any certainty. The CQC voiced concerns about the operation of CTOs in its annual reports. It has reported, for example (CQC, 2010: 99), that 30 per cent of a sample of patients it analysed in 2010 did not have a history of non-compliance with medication—this being the patient population at which CTOs were originally targeted—suggesting that there may be 'an extremely unfortunate distortion of Parliament's intention' (CQC, 2010: 99–100) if CTOs are indeed being widely used beyond this target population.

Most CTO patients—around two-thirds, are male. Research commissioned by the CQC and discussed in the 2011–12 report found that white people, who make up an estimated 87.46 per cent of the general population in 2009, constituted 81.3 per cent of the inpatient population in 2010 but only 71.62 per cent of the CTO population across the years 2008–2011. For black people, by contrast, the figures were Black or Black British 2.94 per cent, 9.6 per cent, and 15.02 per cent respectively (CQC, 2013: 89, table 9). Although the data is subject to some limitations, such as not factoring in diagnosis, or medical history including compliance with treatment plan, and does not explain why there is a relationship between ethnicity and the use of a CTO, it is fairly clear that there is a correlation. The CQC also reported very significant variation between Trusts in the use of CTOs, with the Trust making most of use CTOs doing so in 45.5 per cent of all discharges from hospital of eligible patients, and the Trust making the least use of them doing so in only 4 per cent of cases (CQC, 2013: 78). In addition, a number of Trusts who have 'considerable rates of detention under the Act provided nil returns for the use of CTO' (CQC, 2013: 78). It would be interesting to see rates of use of s. 17 leave in Trusts which make little use of CTOs. We suspect that such data may be illuminating.

10.4.4 Treatment of community patients under Part 4A of the Mental Health Act 1983

Alongside its introduction of the CTO, the MHA 2007 also added, as Part 4A of the MHA1983, specific provision relating to the medical treatment of persons subject to a CTO who have not been recalled to hospital (for those who have been recalled, it is Part IV of the 1983 which applies: MHA 1983, s. 56(4)). As with the provision made under Part IV for inpatients, Part 4A is designed to balance the therapeutic benefits to be derived from treatment for mental disorder with the need to offer protection to patients from the imposition of unwarranted treatment. However, as we shall see, reflecting the different context in which it applies, Part 4A has a broader concept of what is deemed 'unwarranted', at least for patients with capacity to give or refuse consent. Part 4A applies to 'relevant treatment', defined in s. 64A as 'medical treatment...for the mental disorder from which the patient is suffering', excluding treatment to which s. 57 applies, as the treatments covered by s. 57 may not be provided outside a hospital.

Relevant treatment may only be provided, first, if there is 'authority' (in the language of the statute: s. 64B(2)(a)) to give it. There will be authority to give the treatment in question, to a person aged 16 or older (s. 64B(1)(b)), if consent has been given for it by a patient with capacity to consent (s. 64C(2)(a): for the situation relating to persons below the age of 16, see ss. 64E and 64F). This means that relevant treatment can never have 'authority' and so cannot be provided to a community patient with capacity in the absence of that person's consent. This prohibition on treatment in the absence of the consent of a patient with capacity applies even to emergency, life-saving interventions (s. 64B(3)(b)(i)).

This is the first major difference between Part 4A and Part IV which, as seen (Chapter 9, 9.4) does allow treatment to proceed when a patient with capacity refuses to consent provided that the safeguards in ss. 58 and 58A are complied with. Unfortunately, the CQC has reported that those responsible for making and implementing CTOs 'often' (CQC, 2011: 8) misunderstand the extent of the powers given by a CTO, and in particular are unaware that a patient with capacity has a right to refuse treatment, and that refusal of treatment per se does not justify recall to hospital (CQC, 2013: 82). There is some mismatch here between the reasons RCs may have for using CTOs and what CTOs are capable of delivering: certainly, the CQC has reported that 'In almost all cases, CTOs are used to try to ensure a patient's compliance with psychiatric medication after discharge from hospital' (CQC, 2010: 107).

If the patient in question lacks capacity to give or refuse consent, or if he or she withdraws consent (ss. 64FA(1),(4)), or loses capacity after having given consent to a treatment plan which has commenced (ss. 64FA(2), (3)), the treatment may then only proceed in accordance with s. 64B (or ss. 64E and 64F if the patient is less than 16 years of age). However, 'if the approved clinician in charge of the treatment considers that the discontinuance of the treatment, or of treatment under the plan, would cause serious suffering to the patient', then he or she may continue to administer it pending compliance with s. 64B (for those aged 16 or above), or s. 64E (for those aged less than 16), or ss. 58 or 58A (which would only apply if the patient was first detained in a hospital) by virtue of s. 64FA(5).

The authority to give the treatment required by s. 64B(2)(a) can be in the form of consent given by a donee of a lasting power of attorney, a deputy appointed by the Court of Protection, or the Court of Protection itself (s. 64C(2)(b)). Section 64C(2)(c) also provides that, in the absence of the consent of a donee, deputy, or the Court of Protection, there will be authority for the treatment given to a patient lacking capacity under the general power to provide relevant treatment to a person lacking capacity under s. 64D or in an emergency situation if s. 64G is complied with. However, all of this applies only if the patient lacks capacity, and so there can only be continuation of treatment under s. 64FA(5) if the patient loses capacity after treatment has commenced. It does not permit the continuation of treatment if the patient has capacity and withdraws consent previously given.

Section 64D permits an AC or a person providing the treatment under the direction of an AC (s. 64D(5)) to give treatment to the patient where he or she has taken reasonable steps to establish whether the patient has capacity to consent (s. 64D(2)) and has formed a reasonable belief that the patient lacks capacity (s. 64D(3)). The person intending to treat must also have no reason to believe that the patient objects to the treatment (s. 64D(4)(a)) (and in reaching a conclusion on that question must consider all the reasonably ascertainable circumstances, including the patient's behaviour, wishes, views, beliefs and values: s. 64J) or, if the patient does object, that it will nonetheless not be necessary to use force to administer it (s. 64D(4)(b)). In addition, that person must ensure that the proposed treatment does not conflict with a 'valid and applicable' advance directive (defined by s. 64D(7)(b) as one valid under the terms of s. 25 of the MCA 2005) or any decision of a donee or deputy (s. 64D(6)).

Section 64G is concerned with emergency situations. It permits the administration of treatment to an adult (s. 64C(2)(c)) or child (s. 64E(6)(b)) community patient who lacks capacity, subject to three conditions being met. The first, found in s. 64G(2) is that the person intending to administer treatment reasonably believes that the patient lacks capacity or competency to consent. The second, found in s. 64G(3), is that the treatment is immediately necessary. Treatment is defined as 'immediately necessary' if: it is immediately necessary to save the patient's life (s. 64G(5)(a)); or, not being irreversible, to prevent a serious deterioration in the patient's condition (s. 64G(5)(b)); or, being neither irreversible nor hazardous, to alleviate serious suffering (s. 64G(5)(c)); or, being neither irreversible nor hazardous, where the treatment represents the minimum intervention necessary to prevent the patient behaving violently or being a danger to him- or herself or others (s. 64G(5)(d)). 'Irreversible' and 'hazardous' are defined in Part 4A in the same way that they are defined (in s. 62(3)) in Part IV (s. 64G(9)). Treatment for ECT which could otherwise only be provided in compliance with s. 58A if the patient were detained in hospital (see Chapter 9, 9.4.3.2) can only be given if the requirements of ss. 64G(5)(a) or (b) are met (s. 64G(6)), but if and when any further forms of treatment are specified under s. 58A(1)(b), all four of the justifications to provide treatment which is immediately necessary will apply (s. 64G(7)), although regulations may make different provision for different treatments (s. 64G(8)).

The third condition, found in s. 64G(4), only applies if it is necessary to use force to administer the treatment in question. If so, it must be the case that the treatment is required to prevent harm to the patient (s. 64G(4)(a)) and the force used must be proportionate to the likelihood of the patient suffering harm, and to the seriousness of that harm (s. 64G(4)(b)).

The securing of 'authority' will be sufficient legal basis on which to provide some, but not all, relevant treatment under s. 64D. If the treatment could, if the patient were detained in hospital, only be given in compliance with the requirements of either ss. 58 or 58A, it can only be provided to a community patient if the certification requirement is also met (ss. 64B(2)(b), 64C(3), and s. 64E(2)(b) for patients younger than 16 years of age). As with Part IV, the certificate, made in accordance with regulations made by the Secretary of State (ss. 64H(2), (9) and see reg. 28 of the *Mental Health (Hospital, Guardianship and Treatment) (England) Regulations*, SI 2008/1184) may authorise a treatment plan, which need not be time-limited, and may authorise two or more different treatments (s. 64H(1)), to be administered at the discretion of the RC or person in charge of the patient's treatment.

The second major difference between Part 4A, as originally enacted, and Part IV was that under Part 4A, even when consent was given by a patient with capacity, a certificated second opinion was required for such treatment whereas under Part IV, as seen in Chapter 9, 9.4.2, the provision of a second opinion by a SOAD, having consulted the appropriate people, would authorise the treatment in the absence of the consent of a patient with capacity. However, this proved an onerous burden on the system for the securing of second opinions. In 2010–11, such cases constituted two thirds of all requests for a second opinion (CQC, 2011: 37 and fig. 6; CQC, 2013: 75) under Part 4A.

It was also unpopular with some patients with capacity, who felt undermined by the need for the use of the certification process even though consent to treatment had been freely given, and with the CQC, which saw SOAD involvement as 'a questionable safeguard for consenting patients and a questionable use of resources' (CQC, 2011: 37), and added to the delays in the certification process in the early months and years after the CTO became available to RCs in November 2008, as the CQC did not have enough SOADs to meet the demand for their services.

In consequence, s. 299 of the Health and Social Care Act 2012 amended s. 64C, adding s. 64C(4A). The situation now is that although certification is still a requirement for such treatment to be given, if the patient has capacity, the certificate can be provided by the AC, who must state in writing that the patient has capacity to consent to the treatment and has consented to it, on a newly created CQC form, form CTO12. This does not prevent the certificate being provided instead by a SOAD under s. 64A(4) using form CTO11, but it is to be expected that SOADs will now be much less involved in the treatment of community patients with capacity, the practical effect of which is that the workload for SOADs providing certificates under Part 4A should become significantly more manageable. There are already signs that this is the case (see statistics later in this section).

There are two situations in which a certificate will not be required at all for the treatment of a patient with capacity. The first is if the treatment is immediately necessary—defined for these purposes by s. 64C(5) in relation to s. 58 treatments, 64C(6) in relation to s. 58A(1)(a) treatments (i.e. ECT) and s. 64C(7) in relation to s. 58A(1)(b) treatments—and the patient consents (s. 64B(3)(b)(i)). The second is if the treatment in question is the administration of medicine to the patient within one month of the day on which the CTO began (s. 64B(4)). Section 64B(4) thus constitutes a 'one month rule', a truncated version of the 'three month rule' which applies to the treatment by the administration of medicine of detained patients (although, as already mentioned, this does not authorise the treatment unless the patient also consents).

When a SOAD certificate is required (as opposed to desirable), which will only be in cases involving a patient lacking capacity to consent to a treatment which would, if the patient were detained, have to be provided under ss. 58 or 58A, it must be signed by a registered medical practitioner who has been appointed for the purposes of Part IV, not being the patient's RC or person in charge of treatment. The person signing thereby certifies that it is appropriate for the treatment to be given, subject to any conditions, and if there are conditions, they are satisfied (s. 64C(4)).

As with the procedure which applies under Part IV, the SOAD must consult two other persons professionally concerned with the patients treatment, neither of which may be the RC or person in charge or treatment, and one of which must not be a doctor (s. 64H(3)). As the CQC (2010: 104) has noted, the Code of Practice (DH, 2008: para. 24.49) inaccurately states that one of the consultees must be a nurse, and the other neither a nurse or a doctor. The SOAD should also see the patient.

This is easily achieved if the patient is detained in hospital, but, adding to delays in the process of certification, CTO patients very often fail to appear at appointed times to meet the SOAD. This meeting must take place in NHS premises and SOADs will not visit patients in their own homes. Since 2010, the policy of the CQC has been that, if the patient misses a SOAD appointment, the matter is handed back to the RC for review, and if the RC continues to consider SOAD certification necessary, he or she must make a fresh application for a SOAD visit (CQC, 2010: 109). This means that a determined patient can easily evade meeting an SOAD and frustrate the intentions of the RC, although this may result in the RC deciding to recall the patient, and has 'inevitably led to a wide use of urgent treatment powers to authorise continuing medication' (CQC, 2010: 110), which is far from satisfactory.

In 2011–12 SOADs completed 3,239 visits to CTO patients (CQC, 2013: 75), 440 fewer than in 2010–11 (CQC, 2013: 75), the decrease reflecting the removal of consenting patients with capacity from the SOAD scheme in June 2012. Although administratively challenging and resource-intensive, and seen as an intrusion on their autonomy by consenting patients and their RCs, SOAD visits to such patients did result in their treatment plan being changed in around 20 per cent of cases and so in practice may have acted as an important safeguard against unwarranted treatment. This rate of alteration was broadly similar to that in cases involving refusing patients with capacity and those lacking capacity to consent (CQC, 2013: 75). There were 284 SOAD visits to refusing patients with capacity in 2011–12 (CQC, 2013: 75), and although a certificate (on form CTO11) can be and is issued in respect of such patients, confirming the opinion of the RC that treatment which the RC wishes to administer is appropriate for the patient whilst in the community, or that there is appropriate treatment which would be available if the patient were admitted under Part 2 of the Act to a hospital, it cannot authorise the treatment if the patient refuses to give consent. Again, the benefit of SOAD involvement with the treatment of such patients is that in a sizeable minority of cases the RC's treatment plan for the patient is amended to make it less intrusive; but the risk is that RCs and others, including the patient, continue to operate on the mistaken belief that the SOAD's certificate authorises the treatment despite the patient's refusal to consent to it.

The 'regulatory authority', that is, the CQC, may require the person in charge of the patient's treatment to provide a report after its administration (s. 64H(4)) and may 'at any time give notice' to that person (s. 64H(7)) that a certificate shall be revoked (s. 64H(5)), in which case the certificated treatment cannot be given after the date specified in the notice unless the person in charge of the treatment 'considers that the discontinuance of the treatment or of the treatment under the plan would cause serious suffering to the patient' (s. 64H(8)). Otherwise, thereafter it will only be lawful to treat that patient further in the community in accordance with the requirements of s. 64B, which means that treatment covered by ss. 58 and 58A cannot be given, and no treatment at all can be given to a patient with capacity who refuses to consent. If the person in charge of the patient's treatment, or his or her RC, wishes to treat further under ss. 58 or 58A, it will be necessary to recall the patient to hospital and revoke the CTO (s. 64H(6)). This power, however, is only rarely used.

10.5 After-care under s. 117 of the MHA 1983

As discussed at Chapter 2, 2.2.2.4, section 117(2) of the MHA 1983 places a duty on CCGs or local health boards to commission (s. 117(2D)), and LSSAs to provide, 'after-care' services to those patients entitled to receive them 'until such time as the clinical commissioning groups or Health Board and [LSSA] are satisfied that the person concerned is no longer in need of such services'. This should be done in co-operation with voluntary agencies (s. 117(2)). As noted, this general discretion to decide that services need no longer be provided does not apply in the case of a community patient (s. 117(2)), who must be provided with services throughout the duration of his or her CTO.

Section 117 applies to a limited constituency of detained patients, comprising those discharged from hospital (although not necessarily immediately) following detention under ss. 3, 37, 45A, 47, or 48 (s. 117(1)). For patients detained under ss. 3 or 37, discharge must be into the community, but for those transferred to hospital from prison under ss. 47 or 48, or made subject to a hospital direction coupled with a limitation direction under s. 45A by a court following conviction, discharge from hospital may result in the patient returning to prison to serve out the rest of his or her sentence. If so, the Code of Practice advises (DH, 2008: para. 27.6) that s. 117 applies 'when patients are released from prison', which must be correct, but there seems to be no good reason why after-care should not be provided to a patient in prison, having been returned there following discharge from hospital. Indeed, our reading of s. 117 is that the duty to provide after-care applies in such circumstances.

Section 117 also applies whether or not discharge is final, and so is relevant when a patient to whom s. 117 applies is given leave of absence or made subject to a CTO (DH, 2008: paras. 21.24, 27.2) or, if subject to restrictions, is conditionally discharged (see Chapter 11, 11.3). Section 117 therefore has no application to informal patients or those detained under ss. 2, 4, 5, or 136, if not subsequently transferred to s. 3. Such patients must rely instead on the general powers to provide services to people living in the community, which are generally not enforceable by individuals (see Chapter 3).

The term 'after-care' is not itself defined nor its components specified in the MHA 1983, but its substance can be determined by reference to those services ordinarily offered or purchased or supplied by CCGs and LSSAs. The Code of Practice (DH, 2008), in para. 27.5, advises that 'After-care is a vital component in patients' overall treatment and care. As well as meeting their immediate needs for health and social care, after-care should aim to support them in regaining or enhancing their skills, or learning new skills, in order to cope with life outside hospital', which gives a good indication of what is entailed, and in para. 27.13 the Code lays out a long list of areas in which after-care could be provided including, as well as those mentioned, help with welfare benefits, employment, or other daytime activity, extending so far as including 'social, cultural or spiritual needs'.

It is clear, too, that s. 117 can be used to provide a package of care which includes housing or other residential accommodation. In *Clunis* v *Camden and Islington Health*

Authority [1998] 2 WLR 902; [1998] QB 978, Bedlam LJ said at (992) that after-care 'would normally include social work, support in helping the ex-patient with problems of employment, accommodation or family relationships, the provision of domiciliary services and the use of day centre and residential facilities', a statement which was subsequently endorsed by Lord Steyn in the House of Lords in *R v Manchester City Council, ex p Stennett* [2002] UKHL 34 (para. 9).

The duty under s. 117 is not to meet all needs for after-care services which the patient may have. The financial and other resources of the potential recipient are relevant to whether a patient is 'in need of' such services under s. 117 (*Tinsley v Sarkar* [2005] EWHC 192), as are the resources available to the provider. In *R v Camden and Islington Health Authority, ex p K* [2001] 3 WLR 553, [2001] MHLR 24 at para. 29 Lord Phillips MR held that 'the nature and extent of [s. 117] facilities must, to a degree, fall within the discretion of the health authority, which must have regard to other demands on its budget' (see also *Brand v The Netherlands*, Application No. 49902/99, judgment on the 1 May 2004, paras. 64 and 65, the court holding that resources are relevant to the question of whether there has been a breach of Art. 5).

That the duties imposed by s. 117 are owed to, and enforceable by, individuals was established in *R v Ealing District Health Authority, ex p Fox* [1993] 1 WLR 373; 3 All ER 170 (HC). Otton J pointed out that s. 117(2) provides that 'it shall be the duty' of (these days) CCGs and LSSAs, in consultation with voluntary agencies, to provide after-care 'for *any person* to whom this section applies' (emphasis added), holding that the duty is not only general, but also entails a specific duty owed to individual patients (at 385). What is less certain is the point at which the duty to a specific individual is triggered. The duty is certainly in play from the moment a patient leaves hospital, when there will be a formal passing of responsibility from the hospital to the CCG and LSSA for subsequent service provision.

Second, it is also clear that there is a duty to make arrangements to enable a conditional or deferred discharge to occur once that has been ordered by a tribunal. Otton J, in *Fox* [1993] 1 WLR 373 (at 387), held that a '[CCG] acts unlawfully in failing to seek to make practical arrangements for after-care prior to [a] patient's discharge from hospital where such arrangements are required by a mental health review tribunal in order to enable the patient to be conditionally discharged from hospital'. In *R v Mental Health Review Tribunal and Ors, ex p Hall* [1999] 1 WLR 1323 (at 1335) Scott Baker J reiterated the same view, as did Lord Phillips MR in *R v Secretary of State for the Home Department and Secretary of State for Health, ex p IH* [2002] EWCA Civ 646 [2002] 3 WLR 967, at para. 96, and from 2008, the Code of Practice (DH, 2008: para. 27.9) requires CCGs and LSSAs to 'do their best' to arrange after-care if a patient is conditionally discharged by a tribunal. The same applies if a tribunal adjourns a hearing in order for the availability of after-care to be investigated (*ex p IH* at para. 98).

Third, however, what is not clear is whether there is any enforceable duty *before* a tribunal or the patient's RC, hospital managers or, in certain circumstances the patient's NR (see Chapter 11, 11.2) orders discharge, or if a tribunal indicates that it is considering discharge and adjourns for investigations to be made. The Code of Practice provides that planning for discharge by CCGs and LSSAs, and for after-care, 'needs to start as soon as the patient is admitted to hospital. CCGs and LSSAs should take reasonable steps to identify appropriate after-care services for patients before their actual discharge from hospital' (DH, 2008: para. 27.8) and 'the responsible clinician should ensure that the patient's needs for after-care have been fully assessed, discussed with the patient and addressed in their care plan' (para. 27.10). Various other people, including the patient's family and informal carers, GP and, if the patient lacks capacity, a donee of a lasting power of attorney or a court-appointed deputy, as well as mental health professionals, an IMHA or IMCA, and those with skills in assisting with providing services such as housing (DH, 2008: para. 27.12) should, as appropriate also be consulted and involved in formulating the patient's care plan.

This is clearly good policy, but the evidence is that it is often not followed in practice: in 2011–12, only 64 per cent of care plans included planning for discharge (CQC, 2013: 21); nor does it seem that the extent of the duty as a matter of law is so extensive. There are some *obiter dicta* to be found in the judgment of Kennedy LJ, in the Court of Appeal in *ex p Hall* at 1353, that there is, or may be, a duty to have in place at least an 'embryonic' care plan before a tribunal hearing, but in the later Court of Appeal decision in *R v Camden and Islington Health Authority, ex p K* [2001] 3 WLR 553, [2001] MHLR 24, Lord Phillips MR had accepted the concession made by counsel for the health authority that 'a health authority has a *power* to take preparatory steps before discharge of a patient' (paras. 20, 29, emphasis added). This view was endorsed by Scott Baker LJ in *R v Doncaster MBC, ex p W* [2004] EWCA Civ 378, [2004] 1 MHLR 201, at para. 49. Scott Baker LJ went on to hold, however, that a health authority's (now CCG's) failure to endeavour to use its s. 117 powers 'in the absence of strong reasons, would be likely to be an unlawful exercise of discretion', which is to effectively turn the power into a duty.

In the later case of *R v Camden LBC, ex p B* [2005] EWHC 1366, Stanley Burnton J referred to these authorities, holding that 'Practicality requires s. 117 authorities to be under a duty before discharge, at least in cases where a tribunal has provisionally decided that a conditional discharge is appropriate' (para. 58), although the s. 117 authority is not fixed with the specific duty to make arrangement until it has been informed that a tribunal has ordered discharge (para. 72). In *R v Islington LBC and Northamptonshire CC, ex parte NM* [2012] EWHC 414 (Admin), a case which involved the duty to assess under s. 47 of the NHSCCA 1990, rather than the duty under s. 117, and involving a person leaving prison rather than hospital, although nothing turns on either of these points, Sales J held that there would be a concrete duty to carry out an assessment of need if the parole board is actively considering the prisoner's release and has called for further information about the services that would be available to that person following release (para. 93), but not before that point.

In the *Doncaster* case in the High Court ([2003] EWHC 192), Stanley Burnton J had held that 'if discharge is not contentious, an authority should if practicable plan after-care before a tribunal hearing in order for it to comply with its section 117 duty on the patient's discharge' (para. 43). The difficulty with this lies in drawing the lines appropriately between cases (i) where discharge is not contentious; (ii) where it is contentious but there is at least some opinion in favour of it; (iii) where there is some lesser prospect of discharge; and (iv) where there is none. In the *Camden* case, the same judge went on to consider whether the reach of the duty was such that those responsible under s. 117 should proactively monitor the progress of patients in hospital, without waiting for a tribunal hearing, in order to ascertain whether there may be a duty to provide services. On this, in the absence of authority, he concluded, *obiter*, that it would be 'inconsistent with the lack of any express duty imposed by s. 117' (para. 62).

It is true that, under the care programme approach (CPA: see Chapter 3, 3.5.1), commissioners of care are required to review the needs of patients continually, even when in hospital (or, indeed, prison), but to demand the investigation of after-care possibilities, when there is very little chance that after-care will soon be required, would be to impose further burdens on the finite resources of CCGs and LSSAs, and other providers of community care, such as CMHTs, for no apparent purpose. Moreover, as Stanley Burnton J noted in *Camden*, services provided under s. 117 are community care services under s. 47 of the NHSCCA 1990, which, as discussed in Chapter 3, 3.3, places a duty on LSSAs to meet the identified needs of persons not only under s. 117 of the MCA1983, but also the other legislation listed in s. 46(3) of the NHSCCA 1990, and 'Parliament could not have intended local authorities to have to devote their resources to making assessments of the possible future needs of persons for such services' (para. 65).

This must, in general terms, be correct, but in our view, at the very least, there *should* be a duty before a tribunal hearing, or when discharge by the RC or hospital managers is in contemplation, to consider into which of the categories mentioned any given case seems likely to fall, and, where the case in question falls into any but the last category, there should be an absolute duty under s. 117. The reason for this is that the nature of the duty before discharge is not to *provide* after-care, but to investigate and report, provisionally, on its suitability and availability for the patient in question. This does not seem to us to be unduly onerous.

Once the duty under s. 117 has been triggered, after-care must be provided. The section uses mandatory language: 'It shall be the duty' to provide after-care. This, however, is not how s. 117 has been interpreted by the courts in a number of cases, which although involving situations in which a patient had sought and been granted discharge by a tribunal, necessitating the making of arrangement for after-care, are relevant to all situations in which s. 117 is in play. The typical situation in the case law has been one in which a tribunal has ordered discharge subject to conditions but it has not been possible for those conditions to be met, either because suitable accommodation or professionals willing to take responsibility for the patient cannot be located.

In the first of these cases, *Fox* [1993] 1 WLR 373, Otton J refused to make an order of mandamus to compel the health authority (now CCG or Health Board) to act, on the grounds that this would be to compel a psychiatrist to treat against his or her clinical judgment (at 387), but he did make it clear that a CCG, faced initially with staff who refuse to treat or otherwise supervise a patient following discharge, 'is under a continuing obligation to make further endeavours to provide arrangements', and it is only when such steps have been taken without success that the CCG should admit defeat. This approach was confirmed in the later Court of Appeal decisions in *ex p K* and *ex p IH*, and, in the latter case, by the decision of the House of Lords ([2003] UKHL 59). In *ex p K*, Lord Phillips MR held (paras. 20, 29) that the duty under s. 117 is to use '*reasonable* endeavours' to make arrangements for discharge, but in *ex p IH*, the same judge, giving the unanimous judgment of the Court of Appeal, held that the duty under s. 117 is to use '*best* endeavours to put in place the necessary aftercare' (para. 96); the same term was used in the House of Lords ([2003] UKHL 59, para. 29, per Lord Bingham). In *Doncaster*, Scott Baker LJ said (para. 50) that, in his view, there is no material distinction between the two terms. Our view is that (i) 'best' entails a more onerous duty than 'reasonable', and (ii) given the importance of the issue, is to be preferred.

Whether a CCG/LSSA has endeavoured sufficiently to meet its statutory obligation will be a question of fact. Has there been sufficient attempt to identify a suitable placement for the patient, or to make necessary arrangements? In some cases, it is the inability to locate professionals willing to take responsibility for the treatment and supervision of the patient in the community that is the problem. On this, in *ex p K*, Sedley LJ explained that (para. 55):

> No judge can realistically sit as a court of appeal from a psychiatrist on a question of professional judgment. What a judge must do is ensure that such judgment, to that extent that its exercise is a public law function, is made honestly, rationally and with due regard only to what is relevant.

If, however, the view that the conditions in question cannot be satisfied 'were shown to have been adopted less as an exercise of professional judgment than as a closing of the ranks against an unwelcome decision of the Mental Health Review Tribunal, the courts would not be powerless to intervene' (para. 53). These dicta were said to apply equally to professional judgments made by social work professionals by Stanley Burnton J in *R v Doncaster MBC, ex p W* [2003] EWHC Admin 192 (para. 45).

There are a couple of points to be made here. First, the dichotomy that Sedley LJ constructs between an exercise of professional judgment (which is permissible) and a closing of ranks in the face of an unwelcome tribunal decision (which is not) is problematic. This is because the first collapses into the second in practice: in all of these cases, a 'closing of ranks' followed, and was intimately related to, an act of professional judgment that a tribunal had made an 'unwelcome' decision. Hence, it will be very difficult, if not impossible, to draw the line where Sedley LJ claims that it can be drawn.

Second, the reference to the court 'not being powerless' is opaque. The High Court can, of course, issue a writ of mandamus, requiring the recipient of the writ to comply with the order of the court. It is clear from the later case of *ex p IH* (see Chapter 11, 11.5.3.2) that, in the view of the House of Lords, the onus is on the tribunal to reconsider the terms of discharge when they prove difficult to implement. In practice, an order of mandamus will be made only in the very rarest of situations—when it is clear that an 'unprofessional' closing of ranks has taken place. The court may not be powerless, but to date, those powers have never been used.

Patients have scored no greater success by invoking their ECHR rights under Art. 5. In *Doncaster*, Scott Baker LJ held that 'the ECHR places no greater obligations upon s. 117 after-care authority than domestic legislation. Provided the authority uses its best endeavours to fulfil the conditions imposed by the tribunal it will meet its obligations both under s. 117 and the Convention' (para. 67). Indeed, even when there is a breach of Art. 5(1)(e) and or (4), it is not clear that a patient will have a remedy against those with duties under s. 117. In *ex p K*, Buxton LJ at para. 49 held that the case law of the European Court demonstrated the possibility of an action, in Strasbourg, against 'the State', but in domestic law, 'the State' in this abstract sense was not a possible defendant. Rather, the nature of the patient's complaint, 'being a complaint about *detention*' (emphasis in original), meant that it had to be targeted against those responsible for that detention—in law, the managers of the detaining hospital. And it seems that there can be no action against the hospital, because s. 6(2) of the Human Rights Act 1998 precludes liability of a state organ (and 'public authority' for the purposes of s. 6(2)) if, by reason of primary legislation, that body could not have acted differently, in which case, there is no remedy against a hospital under Art. 5(4) in domestic law.

In *Doncaster*, the patient argued that, if those with s. 117 duties were responsible for the continued detention of a patient whose discharge had been ordered, it was irrelevant that they were not the detaining authority. This argument chimes with reality. In such a situation, it is those with s. 117 duties who are holding the hospital doors shut, as it were, from the outside to prevent the patient leaving; it is not the hospital that it holding them shut from the inside. But this view was roundly rejected by Scott Baker LJ, holding that 'the respondent did nothing to cause the unlawful detention of W. It neither knowingly tried to nullify the decision of the tribunal nor failed to use its best endeavours to implement the conditions it had directed' (para. 69).

Some may feel that the point is worth taking to Strasbourg. As the European Court has said many times, for example, in *Christine Goodwin v UK* (2002) 35 EHRR 18, [2002] 2 FLR 487, the spirit of the ECHR requires rights that are 'practical and effective, not theoretical and illusory' (para. 74); in this situation, a patient who has been granted discharge by a tribunal may feel, with some justification, that his or her ECHR rights are far from being practical or effective. Moreover, in Strasbourg, issues of how the state constitutes itself and divides responsibility, as Buxton LJ noted, are much less relevant than they are to the domestic courts. But on recent authority (see, for example, *Kolanis*, discussed at Chapter 11, 11.5.3.2), it is perhaps unlikely that patients would score any greater success in Strasbourg than in the domestic courts.

There is one further argument waiting to be made on this issue, which is that those responsible for after-care are 'public authorities' for the purposes of s. 6(1) of the Human Rights Act 1998. Section 6(1) provides that a public authority must act in a way compatible with ECHR rights, and it can be argued that, if a patient's discharge is being blocked by the refusal of psychiatrists, CPNs, or social workers to accept responsibility, then those persons are failing to act in accordance with the patient's ECHR rights. This, in turn, however, depends on such professionals being recognised as a public authority, which s. 6(3) defines to include 'any person certain of whose functions are functions of a public nature'. In *ex p IH*, both the Court of Appeal and the House of Lords declined to rule on this argument, because it was not necessary to do so for the resolution of that case, and so the point must be counted as still open.

The upshot of the jurisprudence to date is that those with s. 117 duties remain free to make a judgment, on professional grounds, that a patient whose discharge has been ordered should not be discharged. Here, in a battle between the patient's RC, or those with s. 117 duties, and a tribunal, the RC and colleagues win. This should be contrasted with the decision of the House of Lords in *R v East London and the City Mental Health NHS Trust, ex p Von Brandenburg* [2004] 2 AC 280. As discussed further in Chapter 11 (11.7.2), it was held in that case that a patient may not be re-admitted at the initiation of his or her RC after discharge by a tribunal in the absence of new circumstances. In that situation, the tribunal wins the battle. The factors relevant to (re-)admission and discharge are not analogous, and it might be argued that the RC's powers in one situation should not necessarily be the flipside of those in the other situation. Nevertheless, there is a sense in which these decisions are anomalous, or perhaps demonstrate that, for RCs, possession remains nine tenths of the law.

Finally, it is worth pointing out that the Court of Appeal in *Clunis v Camden and Islington HA* [1998] 2 WLR 902 held that complainants should not look to the courts to enforce any duty owed under s. 117, unless they have first made a complaint to the Secretary of State to exercise the default powers available in s. 124. These default powers were repealed by s. 66(2) of, and Sch. 10 to, the NHSCCA 1990, although equivalent powers were inserted as s. 7D of the Local Authority Social Services Act 1970 by s. 50 of the NHSCCA 1990. But it is unlikely that a complaint would elicit the outcome that the applicant wants, because the Secretary of State is concerned more with the general provision of services than with access to them by individuals. On the other hand, it may be arguable on appropriate facts that, if the Secretary of State, who clearly is 'the state' for these purposes and who is not precluded in the exercise of his or her discretion to order the discharge of any patient, fails to take steps to enable discharge to occur when it is being blocked by those with s. 117 duties, there is the possibility of a successful challenge, under Art. 5(4), that avoids the difficulties of linking remedy to defendant that vexed Buxton LJ and subsequent courts.

The decision in *R v Manchester City Council, ex p Stennett* [2002] UKHL 34, that services provided under s. 117 may not be charged for (see Chapter 3, 3.2.2.4) raised the stakes for LSSAs, and has led to disputes as to which LSSA is responsible for meeting the s. 117 duty in cases in which this is unclear. The lack of clarity arises from the fact that the duty is placed by s. 117(3) on the CCG or Health Board and LSSA in the area in which the patient 'is resident or to which he is sent on discharge by the hospital in which he was detained'. In *R v MHRT, Torfaen County Borough Council and Gwent AHA, ex p Hall* [1999] 3 ALL ER 132, [2000] 1 WLR 1323 (HC), a patient, H, who, before hospitalisation, had resided in one area, was to be discharged in another area. There was some buck-passing between health authorities (now CCGs) as to which of them was responsible for arranging (and funding) H's care. In the High Court, Scott Baker J held that it is for the service providers in the area in which the patient resided before entering hospital, and no other, to make the necessary arrangements.

The only exception to this, when the duty falls on the authorities in the area to which the patient will be discharged, is when a patient was of no fixed abode at the time of initial detention. But the 'or' in this sentence in s. 117(3) does not imply that any LSSA has a choice in the matter. Rather, the words after the 'or' are designed 'simply to cater for the situation where a patient does not have a current place of residence' ([2000] 1 WLR 1323 at 1335).

The ruling in *Hall* was considered and elaborated on in two more recent decisions, both of the Court of Appeal, *R v Hammersmith and Fulham London Borough, ex parte Hertfordshire County Council* [2011] EWCA Civ 77 and *Sunderland City Council v South Tyneside Council, ex parte SF* [2012] EWCA Civ 1232. In the first of these, JW, who suffered from significant cognitive impairment and Korsakoff's psychosis (a condition which involves memory loss), lived in social housing in the area of LSSA 1. Following an assessment of his needs under community care legislation (see Chapter 3, 3.3.1) he was provided by LSSA 1 with supported accommodation. This was located within the area of LSSA 2. A few days after moving into that accommodation, JW terminated his tenancy with LSSA 1. Several months later, JW was admitted to hospital under s. 3 of the MHA 1983. When it was decided that JW could be discharged from hospital, there was a dispute between LSSA 1 and LSSA 2 as to which of them was responsible for meeting the duty to provide after-care under s. 117.

LSSA 2 argued as JW's placement in its area had been done by LSSA 1, LSSA 1 retained responsibility for JW at the point at which he was admitted to hospital and that, apply-ing *Hall*, this meant that LSSA 1 was responsible for meeting the duty under s. 117, and therefore also for meeting the costs of JW's care (the main component of which was residential facility in the area of a third LSSA). LSSA 1, also relying on *Hall*, repudiated responsibility on the basis that JW, having given up his tenancy with it, was not resident in its area, but rather, in the area of LSSA 2, when admitted to hospital.

LSSA 2 sought judicial review of LSSA 1's decision, but this was dismissed by the High Court and that decision was upheld in the Court of Appeal. Carnwath LJ first confirmed the ruling in *Hall*; that in determining place of residence 'the period of actual detention under the 1983 Act is to be disregarded' (para. 24). He then turned to LSSA 2's argument, that 'If the period of detention under section 3 is to be excluded in order to achieve the statutory purpose, why should one not equally exclude a period of place-ment, for reasons outside the patient's control, in a home such as [that in which JW was placed by LSSA 1 in the area of LSSA 2]?' (para. 47). He held that 'It can be seen as implicit in section 117(3) of the 1983 Act that the area of "residence" is something distinct from the place of detention' (para. 51) and although there are policy reasons in favour of the argument of LSSA 2—namely that it would better achieve the continuity of care which is an important aim of mental health policy to fix responsibility with LSSA 1 in this type of situation, as that LSSA has historically been the patient's community care service provider—'neither counsel was able to offer a legitimate interpretative tech-nique to achieve that result' (para. 52).

On the facts, once JW gave up his tenancy with LSSA 1, it was not possible to say that he was resident in its area. He had lived for around a year in accommodation in the area of LSSA 2. At the point of detention under s. 3 of the MHA 1983 'He had nowhere to live in [the area of LSSA 1]. If anyone had asked him the question, and he had been capable of giving a rational answer to it, "where do you now reside?" on [the date of formal detention], his answer could only have been "[in the accommodation in the area of LSSA 2"]' (para. 31).

The Court of Appeal thus constructed a bright line between formal detention under the MHA 1983, which does not interrupt the continuity of the patient's place of residence before being formally detained, even if the patient has been in hospital for a number of years (as in *Hall*), and any other provision of accommodation, either in the community or, presumably, as an informal hospital inpatient. Such a construction is problematic for reasons beyond impacting negatively on the continuity of care, as the Court of Appeal recognised. So too, as the court discussed (paras. 72–73) has the Law Commission (Law Commission, 2010a). The risk is that a LSSA, LSSA 1, working with tight resources might be tempted to place its mentally disordered clients in community care accommodation outside of its own area, so that if the patient is subsequently detained under the MHA 1983, it will not be responsible for meeting the duty and financial costs of providing that person's care following discharge from hospital. This would be so, even if, in a case such as this, LSSA 2, in discharging its duty under s. 117, provided services to the patient after discharge in the area of LSSA 1, which seems perverse. The Court of Appeal, however, could see no way around that situation faced with the current wording of s. 117.

The 'bright line' policy was challenged in the *Sunderland City Council* case in 2012. This case was in many ways similar to the *Hertfordshire* case. A patient, SF, lived in accommodation (a residential college for autistic students run by a charity) in the area of LSSA 1. Following a suicide attempt, SF was placed by her LSSA (LSSA 1) in accommodation (an NHS Facility) in the area of LSSA 2. As in *Hertfordshire*, this was done in pursuance of LSSA 1's obligations towards SF under community care legislation. It was whilst living in that accommodation that SF was formally detained under s. 3 of the MHA 1983 in a hospital. On the other hand, the fact situation here differed from that in *Hertfordshire* in that, although SF had agreed to her placement in the accommodation (a NHS facility) in the area of LSSA 2, her consent was given in circumstances in which 'it is likely that if she had not given her consent, compulsory powers would have been used' (para. 6). Secondly, unlike JW in *Hertfordshire*, SF had not voluntarily given up her accommodation in the area of LSSA 1. Rather, the college had terminated her course and with it her rights to occupy its halls of residence.

At first instance, the judge took the view that SF's agreement to the move to the accommodation in the area of LSSA 2 was 'close to being involuntary' (para. 11), and unlike the *Hertfordshire* case, here there had not been a 'voluntary surrender' by SF of her accommodation in the area of LSSA 1 (para. 12), concluding on that basis (para. 13) that SF retained her residency in the area of LSSA 1 at all times prior to her detention in hospital. The Court of Appeal overturned this decision, restoring the sharp distinction between formal detention and all other situations in which accommodation is provided. There is, according to Lloyd LJ 'one hard and fast rule imposed as a matter of judicial interpretation of the policy of the legislation, that is to say that the place of detention is not to be regarded as the location of the residence during the period of detention' (para. 20).

Beyond that, it is a matter of ascertaining the facts. Having discussed various formulations of tests of residency in a number of contexts, Lloyd LJ found those of Lord Slynn in *Mohamed* v *Hammersmith and Fulham London Borough Council* [2001] UKHL 57 most helpful. Lord Slynn had explained (at para. 18 in *Hammersmith*) that in the interpretation of such terms as 'is resident' or 'normal residence':

> it is not appropriate to consider whether in a general or abstract sense such a place would be considered an ordinary or normal residence. So long as that place where he eats and sleeps is voluntarily accepted by him, the reason why he is there rather than somewhere else does not prevent that place from being his normal residence. He may not like it, he may prefer some other place, but that place is for the relevant time the place where he normally resides.

Moreover, Lloyd LJ in *Sunderland* (para. 37) did not see the point that JW in *Hertfordshire* had voluntarily given up his tenancy whereas SF in *Sunderland* had been, in effect, evicted, to be a material difference. The fact was that, for whatever reason, in both cases the patient no longer lived in the area of LSSA 1.

This insistence on an absolute and stark difference between a person who consents, however reluctantly and only does so in the shadow of the use of compulsion on the one hand, and a person subject to formal powers of compulsion, goes to some extent against the grain of current thinking. For example, in *Rabone* v *Pennine NHS Trust* [2012] UKSC 2 (discussed further at Chapter 7, 7.5) Lord Dyson in the Supreme Court noted that 'As regards the differences between an informal psychiatric patient and one who is detained under the1983 Act, these are in many ways more apparent than real' (para. 28). In this context, however, the question of compulsion is only relevant insofar as it sheds light on the question of where a person 'is resident', and that in turn is only relevant insofar as it is a mechanism by which to allocate responsibility for particular patients to an identifiable LSSA, recognising that otherwise there is an incentive for an LSSA to seek to evade the imposition of s. 117 duties for resource-related reasons.

As is often the case, then, the real issue is the limited resources available, combined with the relative autonomy of local LSSAs and NHS service providers and commissioners, which puts LSSAs into a competitive and defensive relation to each other. As Lloyd LJ recognised, moving away from the 'absolutist' approach would itself have resource implications, as it would then be necessary to enquire 'as to the circumstances of the voluntary admission which would be difficult to conduct, perhaps some considerable time after the event, would probably be rather undesirable, and would, as it seems to me, hardly be conducive to good administration' (para. 45). This is a valid point, but it is undermined somewhat by the fact that, as seen in Chapter 3, 3. 5.2, the test for residency which applies for the purposes of s. 117 differs from the test for residency which applies for the other, related, legislation, principally the Housing Act 1996, compounding the difficulties for inter-agency co-operation, both within and across provider sectors.

The Law Commission suggested that the 'ordinary residence' test which applies to other community care legislation should apply also to s. 117 (Law Commission, 2011: para. 11.84), and this was accepted by the government, as reflected in cl. 32(2) of the draft Social Care Bill. The Law Commission gave consideration to the future role of s. 117 in a reformed legal framework of community care provision (see Chapter 3), concluding that it should remain as a free-standing duty in more or less its present form, because of its application to a specific group of patients, provided with services 'in order to reduce their chance of being readmitted to hospital' (Law Commission, 2011: para. 11.73), but that it should be re-cast to function also as a 'gateway' into other health-care provision (para. 11.105), and this too is now reflected in cl. 32 of the draft Social Care Bill.

10.6 Concluding comments

This chapter has been drawn into detailed discussion of the extent, scope, and current usage of the various powers by which some degree of compulsion can be imposed on a patient to accept services in the community, and it is sometimes difficult not to allow a focus on the detail to obscure broader questions. It seems appropriate, therefore, that we conclude by attempting to evaluate how the system works, and its broader implications. The major development in recent times has been the introduction of the CTO in 2007, which as seen has subsequently bedded down and it now a fairly well-established part of the landscape of the mental health system.

Despite this, there is a lack of clarity, notwithstanding the attempts to provide it in the Code of Practice, about the interrelation between leave of absence and CTOs, as far as Part II patients not subject to restrictions are concerned, and between leave of absence and conditional discharge, in the case of restricted patients. Moreover, as the CQC (2013: 83) has recently observed, 'Given that the measurement of whether a CTO was suitable would be whether a patient was settled and engaged with treatment, this creates something of a double-bind in terms of discharge criteria, as it is not clear how a patient could ever demonstrate that they were ready to remain in the community without being subject to a CTO'. That is, there is a lack of clarity regarding the purpose of CTOs, and about when a CTO should be brought to an end, with an attendant danger of drift into longer-term use of these powers, in cases when continued use is no longer strictly warranted or necessary but that cannot be demonstrated to the satisfaction of the patient's RC and AMHP.

Such concerns take us back to the 'dispersal of discipline thesis' that was discussed in the introduction to this chapter (10.1). Having now reviewed this area of law, it does seem as though there are significant problems with the application of this thesis to it. This is because, with the exception of guardianship (although even here this is debatable), the powers of compulsion which are available in respect of mentally disordered persons are constructed as by the law as alternatives to (further) hospitalisation. They do not, in other words, constitute a free-standing regime of community-based treatment in the same way as 'community penalties' do in the criminal justice system, which abolished the language of 'alternatives to custody' some time ago for precisely this reason, and in which after-care for those leaving custody is something rather different from a community-based disposal. In the context of mental health, on the other hand, compulsory powers exercisable in the community are designed in the main for those leaving a period of compulsory detention, and are designed to ease that person's passage back into the community. In short, there is an intimate connection between detention in a hospital and powers of compulsion in the community that is lacking in the penal context, and the distinction between community control and after-care is much more poorly delineated in the mental health context.

The fact that there are major structural differences between the mental health and penal systems in terms of how the relation between compulsion in detention and compulsion in the community is constructed gives cause to doubt any 'dispersal of discipline thesis' which is not sensitive to these differences. At the very least, it can be said that if there is such a dispersal, a 'widening of the net' in Cohen's terms, it is happening in different ways, in pursuance of different aims, in different contexts. It also means that it is possible to defend and justify recent developments in mental health law, starting with supervision registers and ACUS in the 1990s and more recently the introduction of CTOs, as being designed to reduce the need for compulsory detention and therefore maximise the freedom of patients, constituting a diminution rather than a dispersal of discipline in the sense meant by Foucault and Cohen. There can be little doubt that a patient at home on leave of absence, or subject to a CTO, has, all things being equal, greater freedom than a person in hospital, given the various rules and regulations, loss of privacy and so on which inevitably accompany a stay in hospital.

The realities of the system, in which, for example, leave under s. 17 of the MHA 1983 seems to be used as much as a bed management tool as it does as part of a care plan for the graduated return of a detained patient to the community, apparently demonstrates not so much a system seeking to 'roll out' social control in community settings, as a cash-strapped hospital system rendering patients subject to community treatment rather than hospitalisation purely on grounds of expediency. The case law concerned with the enforceability of duties under s. 117 of the MHA 1983 demonstrates similarly, that many professionals are reluctant to take control of patients in the community where there are safety- or health-based reasons for preferring hospitalisation. It is also worth mentioning that on the first occasion that a Bill was presented to Parliament proposing reform of mental health law in 2002, it did contain a proposal for a free-standing community-based 'medical treatment order', which would have made the mental health system much more comparable to the penal system in this sense than is currently the case, but that proposal did not eventually see the light of day when a Bill was introduced for the third time, in 2006, because of opposition to it from, amongst other quarters, the psychiatric and legal professions (Royal College of Psychiatrists and Law Society, 2002). If this is a system of social control, it is also a cautious, ambivalent, and sometimes reluctant version of such a system.

On the other hand, not all patients subject to compulsory measures in the community will be at home. A considerable number will be in some sort of state-provided accommodation, as a condition of their freedom from hospitalisation. The CQC in its most recent report (2013: 82) for examples discusses one case, in which a patient was discharged on to a CTO, on the condition, not only that he lived in a specified care home, but also that he keep to a curfew which began at 9.30 pm, and who for reasons of safety of self and other residents was not allowed unsupervised access to his room in the home, which was kept locked. Here, in instances like this, the 'dispersal of discipline' thesis seems much stronger. It is not, as Foucault emphasised, a matter of intention, whether good or bad, but of effect, and in this example very close control is the effect of the CTO. It is important to remember, too, that the control mechanisms discussed in this chapter are not necessarily the only ones available. If a patient lacks capacity, both the general powers and the particular powers to deprive a person of his or her liberty, subject to the DOLS, may also be used.

In addition, it is important to retain a critical perspective on the distinction between 'informal' and 'compulsory'. As is the case with patients informally in hospital under s. 131 of the MHA 1983, who may be technically free from any compulsion but who, if they refused to comply with the regime or attempted to leave the hospital would be placed under compulsory powers of treatment, so too patients who consent to treatment in the community when there is no legal obligation to do so may be genuinely consenting, but may equally be consenting in the knowledge that lack of co-operation will result in greater use of compulsion.

As noted (see 10.2 and 10.5) the Supreme Court in *Rabone* v *Pennine NHS Trust* [2012] UKSC 2 has recently recognised that this distinction is 'in many ways more apparent than real', a fact not lost on those subject to compulsion or the threat, explicit or implicit, of its use. As there is evidence that this issue attaches to leave of absence, guardianship, and CTOs equally, and indeed to persons receiving after-care under s. 117 who are not subject to any specific measures of compulsion, then it follows that 'actual' levels of compulsion, in terms of both depth (in the case of CTOs, for example, where compulsion does not extend to the administration of treatment without consent but where consent may be given in the shadow of compulsory powers) and breadth (so that some patients are technically free of compulsion but in fact feel compelled to accept services in the community as the lesser of two evils) are likely to be greater than official statistics appear to suggest.

The debates around the 'dispersal of discipline thesis' are unlikely to be resolved any time soon. We do know that the effect of recent developments, the introduction of the CTO in particular, as the NHSIC recently noted is that 'it is apparent that increasing numbers of people are being subject to restrictions under the Act' (the NHSIC, 2012: 22). What we do not know, and probably can never know for certain, is whether this means that there is more treatment or more control, and that is because we have never really been able to tell the difference between them with any degree of precision.

11

Ending Compulsion under the Mental Health Act 1983

11.1 Introduction

The ways in which a period of compulsion authorised under the terms of the Mental Capacity Act (MCA) 2005 may be ended has already been discussed (see Chapter 5). This chapter is concerned with the various ways in which a period of compulsion, whether in hospital or in the community, imposed under the terms of the Mental Health Act (MHA) 1983, can be brought to an end. As is clear from the discussion in Chapter 10, for most patients subject to compulsion, its termination is better character-ised as a process rather than an event, and a period or periods of leave, and/or discharge onto a community treatment order (CTO), or less frequently, a guardianship order, or (for restricted patients) an order for conditional discharge, often precedes the final and complete discharge of the patient from liability to recall to hospital. There are a small number of patients, virtually all detained under Part III of the MHA 1983, who will never be discharged from hospital, but most detained patients will be discharged from liability to detention sooner or later, although many of them will be likely to be confined in hospital again at some point in the future.

In general terms, the shift from chronic to acute patients as the main 'clients' of inpatient services, together with the closure of the Victorian asylums and the relocation of psychiatric services into units within general hospitals and into 'the community', means that many patients who would previously have been hospitalised for periods of years, if not decades, now enter hospital, if at all, only for relatively short periods of time. Although there are definitive statistics relating to the discharge of restricted patients, and of patients subject to a CTO, there are no definitive statistics on the use of the powers to discharge patients detained under Part II of the MHA 1983.

We do know, however, from data published by the Care Quality Commission (CQC) that of the 7,768 applications for discharge made to a tribunal by a patient detained under s. 2 in 2011–12, 2,562 were discharged prior to the hearing by their responsible clinician (RC), as were 4,914 of the other 14,674 unrestricted applicants and 83 of the 3,262 applicants subject to restrictions (in respect of whom the RC must obtain the consent of the Justice Secretary: see 11.3.1). In total, 7,559 of the total of 25,704 tribunal applicants were discharged by their RC before the date on which their application was listed for a hearing (CQC, 2013: 17 and table 3). As to be expected by the focus on acute services, this data confirms that many patients can expect to be discharged reasonably soon after their admission—an application by a patient detained under s. 2 must be made within 14 days of that person's admission (ss.66(1)(a), (2)(a)), and the tribunal must sit within seven days of receiving the application—although, equally, many patients will not be discharged for some considerable time, and, in the case of patients subject to restriction, this is likely to be measured in terms of years rather than months.

Despite the removal of (many) chronic patients from long-term detention in a hospital, the number of admissions, both informal and under compulsion has risen year on year (see Chapter 6, 6.3) and our hospitals continue to be overcrowded (see Chapter 2, 2.2.1 and CQC, 2013: 55). One consequence of this, over which there has long been concern, is that patients are discharged from hospital, or given long-term leave of absence, earlier than would otherwise have been the case (Mental Health Act Commission (MHAC), 2001: para. 3.5; CQC, 2013: 55). This is a real cause for concern, because 20 per cent of suicides amongst detained patients occur when the patient is on leave (MHAC, 2001: para. 4.23) and although the suicide rates for inpatients, and for inpatients who have absconded, have fallen year on year throughout this century to date, the same is not true for patients in receipt of mental health services in the community, for whom the figures, rather, show a year-on-year rise from 18 in 2000 to 195 in 2009, although there was a fall, for the first time, to 150 in 2010 (the last year for which data is available at the time of writing) (*The National Confidential Inquiry into Suicide and Homicide by People with Mental Illness, 2012*: 27, 28, 29 and figs. 13, 14, 15).

On the other hand, for many sectioned patients, particularly if held under Part III of the MHA 1983, it will be far from easy to convince professionals, and the Justice Secretary, or a tribunal, that discharge is appropriate. No duty of care is owed by those making discharge decisions, either to the patient (*Clunis* v *Camden and Islington HA* [1998] 2 WLR 902) or third parties (*Palmer* v *Tees HA* (2000) 2 LGLR 69 (CA)) for any harm caused by a patient inappropriately discharged (on the policy basis, that to find the hospital liable would not prevent further incidents of this nature and would detract from its primary functions, and that to issue warnings concerning risk to the public would breach confidentiality: see further Chapter 12, 12.7). If there is a risk to an identifiable individual or class of persons, the situation may be different (*Hill* v *Chief Constable of West Yorkshire* [1989] AC 53), and it is clear that in such a situation the Art. 2 (ECHR) rights of the patient, or any other identifiable person at risk, are at play. In *Osman* v *UK* (2000) 29 EHRR 245 the Court made it clear that the state (here in the form of the hospital) has a positive duty to protect life, although this only applies when the life of an 'identifiable individual or individuals' (para. 116) is at risk from another (and see the decisions in *DCD* v *South Tyneside Health Care NHS Trust, Savage* and *Rabone*, discussed at Chapter 7, 7.5.3).

As can be seen from Table 11.1, there are various persons who may initiate or order the discharge of a sectioned patient: the patient's RC; the managers of the hospital in which the patient is detained; a tribunal; and in some circumstances, the patient's nearest relative (NR). The Justice Secretary has powers both to discharge and to veto

Table 11.1 Overview of powers of discharge

	RC	Hospital Managers	Nearest Relative	LSSA	Justice Secretary	Tribunal
Informal patients*	Yes	Yes	Yes	N/A	N/A	N/A
Pt II liable to be detained	Yes	Yes	Yes**	N/A	N/A	Yes
CTO	Yes	Yes	Yes**	N/A	N/A	Yes
Guardianship	Yes	N/A	Yes	Yes	N/A	Yes
Unrestricted Pt III patients	Yes	Yes	No	N/A	N/A	Yes
Restricted Pt III patients	Yes (with the consent of the Justice Secretary)	Yes (with the consent of the Justice Secretary)	No	N/A	Yes	Yes

*Informal patients may discharge themselves
**Can be overruled by the RC if the patient is 'dangerous'

proposals for discharges of restricted patients that come from the RC or hospital managers. For patients subject to a CTO, discharge from the order and from the underlying section can be ordered by the RC, hospital managers, the NR, and by a tribunal; and for those subject to guardianship, by the RC, the responsible LSSA, or the NR, as well as by a tribunal. These various possibilities will be considered in turn.

11.2 Discharge of Part II patients from hospital, guardianship, or a CTO

11.2.1 Informal patients

There are no special provisions governing the discharge from hospital of informally admitted patients. In theory, informal patients are free to leave at any time, subject to the holding powers contained in s. 5 of the MHA 1983 (see Chapter 6, 6.3), and to the possible making by the hospital managers of an urgent authorisation for a deprivation of liberty under Sch. A1, para. 76(2)(b) to the MCA 2005 if the patient lacks capacity, and the hospital managers, having already made or being about to make an application for a standard authorisation, 'believe that the need for the relevant person to be a detained resident is so urgent that it is appropriate for detention to begin' either before the application for a standard authorisation is made or disposed of, as the case may be (MCA 2005, Sch. A1, paras. 76(2)(b), (3)(b)). However, an informal patient will be ineligible for the use of deprivation of liberty safeguards (DOLS) if, although not formally detained or subject to any other powers of compulsion exercisable in the community, he or she is 'within the scope' of the MHA 1983 (MCA 2005, Sch. 1A, para. 2 and case E, para. 12) and objects to the deprivation of liberty or to some component of the treatment for his or her mental health which that deprivation involves, unless a donee of an LPA or a court-appointed deputy has made a valid decision, in the best interests of the patient (MCA 2005, s. 4), to give consent to the use of DOLS (see Chapter 5, 5.4.6).

As will be discussed shortly, for patients detained under Part II of the MHA 1983, the issue is not whether he or she is discharged from the hospital but whether he or she need be subject any longer to compulsory powers. It is certainly the case that for some patients it is appropriate that they should remain in hospital, but they do not need to remain liable to be detained. For example, a threat to the safety of others may have subsided but the need for treatment may not, or a previously refusing patient may have now agreed to consent to treatment. On the discharge of the detaining section, a patient remaining in hospital acquires informal status (MHA 1983, s. 131(1)).

It is not clear that there is a duty on any person or body to ensure that the patient understands the implications of a change of status from detained to informal. There is a duty, placed on hospital managers, by s. 132 of the MHA 1983 to provide detained patients, as soon as possible following detention, with information regarding the legal basis of detention, the right to apply to a tribunal and the effect, inter alia, of the sections of the Act relating to discharge. But the duty in s. 132 would seem not to apply to a patient discharged onto informal status, as that person would not be 'detained' at that point. The MHA Code of Practice similarly provides that 'Hospital managers should ensure that all relevant patients are aware that they may ask to be discharged by the hospital managers and of the distinction between this and their right to apply for a Tribunal hearing' (DH, 2008: para. 31.10), but again this would not seem to cover a patient once discharged from compulsory detention.

The Code also requires that a decision taken by the hospital managers, whether or not to discharge the patient, is communicated to him or her orally and in writing, as soon as practicable (DH, 2008: para. 31.45), and there is also a duty to explain any change of 'status under the Act', the Code giving the example of a change from detention under s. 2 to detention under s. 3. But there is no explicit mention of any obligation to inform and explain to a patient a change of status from detained to informal. The same is true of the information which an Independent Mental Health Advocate (IMHA) (see Chapter 12, 12.9) shall provide to a patient under s. 130B of the MHA 1983, which is premised on the fact that the patient is a 'qualifying patient', and this does not include a patient in hospital on an informal basis (s. 130C). Nor is there any duty on any person or body to inform an informal patient about the possibility of obtaining assistance in understanding their status from an IMHA for the same reason (see s. 130D). Furthermore, informal patients generally fall outside the remit of the CQC. The situation in England is in sharp contrast to that in Wales, which does recognise the need to provide informal patients with information as to their status and its implications, and which does give such patients access to an IMHA (MHA 1983, ss. 130G, 130J, 130L).

This means that those patients who remain in hospital on an informal basis after formal discharge rely solely on friends and relatives, and the professional ethics and good practice of hospital staff and managers, to protect them from unwarranted hospitalisation. The duty in s. 132 also requires that the patient's NR is also provided with the information which must be given to the patient (unless the patient objects), either at the same time as the information is given to the patient or within a reasonable time thereafter (ss. 132(5), 130D(5), (6)). The involvement of, and legal powers bestowed on, the patient's NR may offer an important brake on unwarranted hospitalisation, but for this to be so there must actually be an NR able and willing to accept that role, sometimes entailing confrontation with the patient's RC and the hospital managers, which is not always the case.

11.2.2 Patients detained under Part II

Hospital managers should monitor the grounds for detention on an ongoing basis, rather than waiting for the operation of the law to bring the question of discharge to the fore (DH, 2008: para. 31.11), but are specifically required by the Code to give specific thought to that question whenever a patient's period of detention is renewed under s. 20, or the patient's NR has given notice of an intention to discharge the patient and a 'barring report' is made by an RC under s. 25 (see 11.2.2.1), or the patient specifically requests a review (DH, 2008: para. 31.11), and, despite the view of the RC that discharge is not then appropriate, the managers 'must always decide whether the patient should be discharged anyway', even if the patient does not desire it (DH, 2008: para. 31.39). There is, however, no mechanism in the MHA 1983 to require a review in these circumstances, and so enforcement of these duties would have to be by way of an application for judicial review and/or invoke human rights law.

Although for most patients, the hoped-for outcome is discharge from hospital, for those detained under Part II of the MHA 1983, and for patients in hospital having been taken their by the police by virtue of the operation of ss. 135 or 136 (see Chapter 6, 6.4.3 and 6.4.4; Chapter 7, 7.3.2), the legal issue is discharge of the authority to detain rather than discharge from hospital. Many patients will be on leave of absence rather than in hospital when discharged from the 'section' on which they are held, and it is from 'liability to detention' that patients are discharged. This means that discharge is not linked directly to the need for hospital treatment and so, for a patient to be discharged the test is whether he or she should remain liable to detention, rather than whether or not he or she should remain in hospital (see *Barker* v *Barking Havering and Brentwood Community Healthcare NHS Trust* [1999] 1 FLR 106 and related cases, discussed at Chapter 10, 10.2.1). Authority to detain a patient held under Part II will cease automatically if the period of detention expires without it being renewed (ss. 2(4), 4(4), 20(1)). It is unlikely that a detention will simply be allowed to lapse (Sackett, 1996: 65).

11.2.2.1 Powers of discharge

A 'section' may be ended at any time by the making in writing of an 'order for discharge' (s. 23(1)) by the RC, hospital managers, or the patient's NR (s. 23(2)(a)). Section 24 gives a medical practitioner (who may be an AC but may equally be any doctor), acting on behalf of an NR considering making an order under s. 23, a right of access in private to the patient, and to records relating to the detention, treatment, and any after-care services provided to the patient. Each person or body empowered to make an order for discharge can act independently of the others. The only caveat on this, imposed by s. 25(1) of the MHA 1983, is that an order for discharge made by a NR is not effective unless 72 hours' notice has been given to the hospital managers. Although s. 25(1) requires that notice must be in writing, there is no prescribed form in the legislation or regulations, but the Code of Practice does contain an illustrative standard form and encourages hospital managers to adopt it or devise something similar (DH, 2008: para. 29.23). In *Re Kinsey* (1999) 21 June, unreported (HC), it was held that notice had not been given to the hospital managers by a NR who handed a letter requesting the discharge of her son to the hospital receptionist, because to be effective, notice must be given to an officer of the hospital appointed for this task.

The reason for the 72-hour delay is to give the RC time to object to the making of the order in the form of a report to the managers 'certifying that in the opinion of that officer the patient, if discharged, would be likely to act in a manner dangerous to other persons or to himself' (MHA 1983, s. 25(1)). If the hospital managers receive such a report (known as a 'barring report') from the RC, they must notify the NR (s. 25(2)); any purported order for discharge made by the NR pursuant to that notice shall be of no effect (s. 25(1)(a)); and the NR may not apply again for the discharge of the patient for six months from the date of the report (s. 25(1)(b)), but is compensated by the fact that he or she may make an application to a tribunal with power to discharge the patient (MHA 1983, s. 66(1)(g): see 11.4.2). Moreover, the sole reason for preventing discharge by the NR is that the patient is dangerous: other factors, such whether the patient's mental disorder makes continued hospitalisation appropriate, are not (*R v Riverside Mental Health Trust, ex parte Huzzey* (1998) 43 BMLR 167 (HC)).

The odds are, however, stacked in favour of the RC, because the hospital managers are, presumably, only required to ensure that the RC's opinion is reasonable, and not necessarily one with which they agree. Nevertheless, there are examples of cases in which hospital managers have not followed the advice of an RC, such as *R v Huntercombe Maidenhead Hospital, ex parte SR* [2005] EWHC 2361, [2006] ACD 17, 2005 WL 2273357. In that case, the decision of the managers to discharge a patient following an application under s. 25 was quashed as perverse, because the managers ignored compelling evidence that the patient was likely to be dangerous. But it is clear that, if the decision of the managers is reasonable, it will also be lawful.

The revised Care Plan Approach (see Chapter 3, 3.5.1) will include most, if not all, patients leaving a period of compulsory detention in hospital. As discussed in Chapter 10 (at 10.5), planning for discharge should begin as soon as the patient has been detained and should involve multiple agencies and actors, including professional and other treatment and/or care providers. However, in 2011–12, only 64 per cent of care plans for Part II patients included planning for discharge (CQC, 2013: 21). As already discussed (10.5), and as will be discussed further at 11.5.3.2 one significant issue affecting the viability of discharge is the availability of suitable provision for the patient in the community, whether in the form of treatment, professionals willing to administer them and to take responsibility for the patient, or accommodation.

11.2.2.2 The discharge decision

There are no criteria governing discharge to be found on the face of the MHA 1983. In consequence, the Act on its face seems to allow a patient to be held for the full duration of a period of detention, even if the grounds for detention can no longer be made out at some earlier point, and similarly to allow the discharge of a patient when those grounds remain. The MHAC's first report (MHAC, 1985: para. 8.13) stated that hospital managers 'have the right and the duty' to end a section as soon as the conditions for admission are no longer met, and in *R v MHRT London South and West Region, ex parte C* [2000] MHLR 220, Scott Baker J (at para. 20) held that an RC has a continuing duty to ensure that the conditions for detention are still met. The fundamental authority is the decision of the European Court in *Winterwerp v The Netherlands* (1979) 2 EHRR 387 (see Chapter 5, 5.1.1) that continued detention is warranted only so long as the detainee remains of unsound mind such as to warrant hospitalisation. In its later decision in *Johnson v UK* (1997) 27 EHRR 296, however, the Court held that discharge need not be immediate if time is required, for example, to organise after-care, clearly accepting that factors other than the patient's soundness of mind are relevant to a discharge decision, and this view is reflected in the Code of Practice made under the MHA 1983 (DH, 2008: para. 31.38).

In *Riverside* Latham J, following the approach in *R v Dr F and DE, ex parte Wirral Health Authority and Wirral Borough Council* [2001] MHLR 6, held that s. 23 bestows a wide discretion which the hospital managers, in this case, had inappropriately fettered. When carrying out a review of a patient's detention, hospital managers should consider the factors in s. 3 (the relevant section in that case), but are not limited to those factors, and should also consider the contents of any report recently made by the RC under s. 25 stating that the patient is dangerous. On this authority, the criteria for discharge under s. 23 seem to comprise, at the least, both those relevant to admission in the first place and those mentioned in s. 25, if s. 25 has been invoked, which only happens rarely. It is appropriate also to consider any other relevant factor: the tone of the judgment in *Riverside* (see para. 20) is very much that the managers can consider any factors felt to be relevant, and are not under a legal obligation, having decided that the patient did not meet the dangerousness criteria, to order discharge (see also *South West London and St George's Mental Health NHS Trust v W* [2002] EWHC Admin 1770).

Whatever the extent of the discretion given by s. 23, it is hedged to some extent by the advice contained in the Code of Practice. Hospital managers are required to have 'sufficient information about the patient's past history of care and treatment, and details of any future plans' (DH, 2008: para. 31.24). This sounds straightforward enough, but according to the Code, the 'main source of this is likely to be the patient's documentation and care plan under the Care Programme Approach (CPA) (or its equivalent)' (2008: para. 31.24), and as already mentioned (Chapter 10, 10.5), around one third of care plans examined by the CQC contained no reference to discharge or planning for it. This is unfortunate because 'the presence or absence of adequate community care arrangements may be critical in deciding whether continued detention (in particular) is necessary' (DH, 2008: para. 31.37, see also 31.36).

Managers should also consider any history of violence or self-harm and must have ensured that a recent risk assessment has been performed, and consider the findings of that assessment (DH, 2008: para. 31.37, see also 31.36). Written reports by the patient's RC (which should include full information about the patient's history, treatment and care plan, and the views of any consultees under s. 20 if the period of detention has been renewed: DH, 2008: 31.30) and 'any other key individuals' such as his or her care co-ordinator, named nurse, social worker, occupational therapist, or clinical psychologist, should also be commissioned and considered (DH, 2008: 31.25), as should the views of any relatives or carers of the patient and others who know the patient well, unless the patient objects, in which case one of the professionals concerned should solicit views from those parties and report them to the managers (DH, 2008: 31.29).

All of this must be considered in the context of the circumstances of the particular patient and so, as with admission, factors such as the patient's willingness to accept treatment as an outpatient and his or her home circumstances, and the availability of suitable accommodation more generally, will impact significantly on the question of whether discharge is appropriate (Dell and Robertson, 1988). The various issues to be considered have been structured in the form of 'readiness for release' scales such as that devised by Eisner (1989) and Hogarty and Ulrich (1972).

11.2.2.3 Managers' panels

The powers of hospital managers to discharge patients may, as in practice is always the case, be delegated to a committee or sub-committee of at least three members (s. 23(4)), with the further stipulation, in the case of NHS Foundation Trusts, that panel members may be members of the trust itself or any of its committees or sub-committees (DH, 2008: para. 31.5), but that, in NHS bodies, including Foundation Trusts, no panel member may be an employee or officer of the Trust (DH, 2008: para. 31.6) and in independent sector hospitals, no panel member may be on the staff of, or person with a financial interest in, the hospital (DH, 2008: para. 31.7). The Code of Practice (DH, 2008: paras. 31.8, 9) further advises that those appointed to these 'managers' panels' (as they are known) should be trained in their role and the workings of the MHA 1983.

If discharge is to be ordered, the decision of a managers' panel to that effect must be unanimous, if a panel of three is sitting (*R v Hospital Managers of Royal Park Hospital, ex parte TT* [2003] EWCA Civ 330,), or have the support of at least three panel members, being in any case a majority of the panel, if the panel has four or more members (DH 2008: para. 31.18). This is a controversial because for a panel of three or four (which is typical) an RC seeking to prevent discharge (as happened in *Royal Park*) need only convince one member of the panel that discharge is not warranted, whereas the patient must convince all panel members (or three out of four) that discharge is appropriate. The Court of Appeal justified this approach on the basis that the starting point is that the RC's views are justified, and so should only be overruled by a unanimous committee (Pill LJ at para. 30), but it is problematic nonetheless. If a preponderance of opinion is in favour of discharge, surely discharge should follow?

Managers' panels are bound by the rules of natural justice and the requirements of human rights law, and so although it is for the managers of the hospital in question to decide on the procedure which their panels will follow 'generally it needs to balance informality against the rigour demanded by the importance of the task' (DH, 2008: para. 31.32). A patient appearing before a managers' panel is entitled under the Code to have a representative of their own choosing 'to help in putting their point of view to the panel' and be supported, if desired, by a relative, friend, or advocate, and should be provided with a copy of the Code (2008: para. 31.32). The NR should be informed of the time and venue at which the panel will convene (DH, 2008: para. 31.28).

The patient's RC should appear before the panel and explain his or her reasons against the patient being discharged, and panels should be conducted so that the patient and others giving views to the panel, if the patient wishes it, can hear each other's submissions and put questions to each other, although the panel should not allow this if it 'believes that would be likely to cause serious harm to the physical or mental health of the patient or any other individual' (DH, 2008: para. 31.34). The patient should also, provided that it is considered safe to do so, be given the opportunity to speak to the panel alone (DH, 2008: para. 31.34).

The patient, and their representative and NR, should be given copies of the reports that the panel is to consider 'as soon as they are available' and 'in good time' unless the panel is of the view that disclosure of the contents of a particular report 'would be likely to cause serious harm to the physical or mental health of the patient or any other individual'. This 'serious harm' test is similar to that which justifies the withholding of documents from a patient by a tribunal (*Tribunal Procedure (First-tier Tribunal) (Health, Education and Social Care Chamber) Rules 2008*, SI 2008/2699, r. 14: see 11.4.3) and should be interpreted by the panel in the same way as r. 14 is interpreted by a tribunal in that context. If a report is not disclosed to the patient, the reason for non-disclosure should be recorded by the panel (DH, 2008: paras. 31.26, 27). Managers' panels 'must give full weight to the views of all the professionals concerned in the patient's care' (DH, 2008: 31.35) and may adjourn to seek further advice if there is a divergence of professional views, as they may if insufficient information upon which to make a decision has been supplied by the time of the hearing (DH, 2008: 31.37). It can be seen that managers' panels, quasi-judicial but relatively invisible, and with no legal professionals involved in their operation, and with no mechanisms for appeal built in, wield a significant amount of power over discharge decision-making.

11.2.3 **Patients subject to a CTO or guardianship**

Section 23 applies also to patients subject to guardianship (s. 23(1)) or a CTO (s. 23(1A)). A patient subject to guardianship may be discharged by the RC, the responsible LSSA, or the patient's NR (s. 23(2)(b)) and a patient subject to a CTO by the RC, managers of the responsible hospital, or the patient's NR (s. 23(3)(b)). As with detained patients, the hospital managers, or LSSA in the case of a person subject to guardianship, may delegate their duties under this section to a panel of at least three members (ss. 23(4), (5)).

The criteria for the discharge of these provisions are no clearer than those relevant to the discharge of patients detained in hospital under Part II of the MHA 1983. As with detained patients, the criteria should be understood as the inverse of those which apply for reception into guardianship, or placement on a CTO. There is no person or body with powers equivalent to the RC of a detained patient to bar an application made for discharge of a guardianship order, but the RC's barring powers in s. 25(1) do apply to an application for discharge of a CTO made by a NR (s. 25(1A)).

11.3 Discharge of Part III patients

11.3.1 Powers of discharge

The powers of discharge in s. 23 apply to patients detained in hospital under s. 37, although subject to the modifications in Sch. 1, Part I, paras. 2 and 8 to the MHA 1983, which disapply the power of the NR to order discharge. For patients subject to s. 41 restrictions, Sch. 1, Part II, para. 7 provides similarly, and also adds the requirement to s. 23(1) that any order for discharge can only be made with the consent of the Justice Secretary. The powers given to the Justice Secretary provide an example of the limitation of medical power and clinical discretion concerning restricted patients, with the implicit message that the clinical gaze fails to consider appropriately all factors relevant to the discharge of presumptively dangerous patients.

The Justice Secretary usually prefers, rather than ordering the discharge of a restricted patient under s. 23, to use the more sophisticated powers available in s. 42 to discharge the patient absolutely or, as is usual in the first instance, conditionally. But here, as under s. 23, there are no detailed criteria on the face of the Act by which to make that decision. A restriction order may be ended 'if the Secretary of State is satisfied that...a restriction order is no longer necessary for the protection of the public from serious harm' (s. 42(1)), in which case the patient is treated as though on a s. 37 order from the date of the discharge of that order (s. 41(5)). This wording is not more closely defined anywhere else, and, according to Stuart Smith LJ in R v Parole Board, ex parte Bradley [1990] 3 All ER 828 at 836, it cannot be elaborated with any degree of precision. A restriction order is not discharged by implication if the Justice Secretary allows the conditions of discharge to lapse (R v Secretary of State for the Home Department, ex parte Didlick [1993] COD 412 (DC)).

There is even less guidance on discharge, which the Justice Secretary may do by warrant 'if he thinks fit' (s. 42(2)). The only judicial consideration of these powers before the coming into force of the Human Rights Act (HRA) 1998 was an obiter comment of Lawton LJ, in Kynaston v Secretary of State for Home Affairs (1981) 73 Cr App R 281 (CA), that a patient who is no longer disordered should be discharged. Now, the requirements of Art. 5(1) of the ECHR and the *dicta* of the European Court in *Winterwerp* (see Chapter 5, 5.1.1) make it clear that the continued detention of a patient depends on evidence of continuing mental disorder; and since the Justice Secretary is given significant powers by the MHA 1983, he or she should not leave matters to be decided at the patient's next tribunal hearing. If he or she has information to suggest that a patient is entitled to discharge, he or she should act on it.

In practice, these decisions are taken by an officer of the Mental Health Cases Section (MHCS) within the Ministry of Justice, which currently has around 60 members of staff. In controversial or otherwise challenging cases, an officer of the MHCS will seek the personal authority of a Ministry of Justice Minister (Ministry of Justice, 2009a: para. 3). The MHCS officer will have information provided by the RC under s. 41(6) of the MHA 1983, which requires the RC of a restricted patient to make yearly reports to the Justice Secretary (although for some patients more frequent reports are required), and which must contain 'such particulars as the Secretary of State may require', or under s. 49(3), which places an equivalent obligation on the RC of a patient transferred from prison to hospital with restrictions.

The purpose of these reports is to prevent the unwarranted detention of restricted patients. The Home Office has issued guidance (Home Office, n.d.), which requires that reports contain information relating to patients' attitudes and motivations, the effects of treatment, and the chances of reoffending, and give reasoned advice on the need for continued detention, and whether detention need be in a special hospital. The main concerns of the Justice Secretary and the MHCS are essentially the same as those that feature in the discharge of patients not subject to restrictions, although, as might be expected, with the emphasis on the degrees of risk to other persons that the patient, if released, might pose (Ministry of Justice, 2009c, para. 5; Green and Baglioni Jr, 1997).

If a patient is able to get to a position in which a decision to discharge can be made, the question arises of whether conditions should be attached. This, like the decision to discharge, is a matter of discretion, but this does not mean that there are no limitations to its exercise. In *Kynaston*, Lawton LJ held that the Home Secretary (now Justice Secretary) should direct the *absolute* discharge of a patient if satisfied that he or she is no longer suffering from mental disorder. In the later Court of Appeal decision in *R v Merseyside Mental Health Review Tribunal, ex parte K* [1990] 1 All ER 694 (discussed further at 11.5.1), it was held that a tribunal can give a conditional discharge to a patient not then suffering from mental disorder, and it would be strange if this power were not also available to the Justice Secretary, given that his or her margin of discretion is wider than that of a tribunal (see 11.5).

A conditional discharge will usually require the patient to reside at a particular location, to attend for treatment (although there are no powers to treat without consent (s. 56(1)(c), and see *R v MHRT, ex p SH* [2007] EWHC 884 (Admin), discussed below in the context of s. 73(4)), and to consent to the supervision of a social worker or probation officer. Although research some time ago (Baxter, 1991) found that a patient conditionally discharged by the Secretary of State could expect to be absolutely discharged around five years later, each case turns on its own facts, and the Ministry of Justice (2009a: para. 72) has explained that:

> The decision on absolute discharge will turn on the extent to which the maintenance of conditions and supervision is seen to be contributing to public safety. Where a patient's offence is assessed as directly linked to his disorder, and he is entirely compliant with treatment which controls that disorder, restrictions may not need to persist for long even where the offence was serious. However where the link is less apparent, or the patient's co-operation with treatment less reliable, it may be necessary to retain conditions for a much longer period.

For example, in *RH v South London and Maudsley NHS Foundation Trust, Secretary of State for Justice* [2010] EWCA Civ 1273, discussed further at 11.5.3.1, a patient's application for absolute discharge was resisted by the Justice Secretary ten years after conditional release from hospital. Conditional discharge, in the first instance, is the norm: the Justice Secretary understandably takes a cautious approach. Only 15 restricted patients were discharged absolutely from hospital in 2011, compared to 94 conditional discharges ordered by the Justice Secretary and 411 ordered by a tribunal (Ministry of Justice, 2012: table 6.6).

11.3.2 Powers of recall

Section 42(3) empowers the Justice Secretary to recall a conditionally discharged patient to hospital at any time unless and until absolutely discharged, at which point the patient will 'cease to be liable to be detained' (s. 42(2)). Patients recalled are entitled to be provided with reasons as soon as possible and, in any case, within 72 hours (DH, 1993a). There are no criteria for the application of s. 42(3), and the fact that these powers are exercisable 'at any time' indicates that recall is not linked to any breach of the conditions of discharge.

Here, as elsewhere, the courts have traditionally been reluctant to fetter the discretion of the Justice Secretary to act on the basis of considerations of public safety. In *R v Secretary of State for the Home Department, ex parte K* [1990] 3 All ER 562, the Court of Appeal held that a conditionally discharged patient can be recalled to hospital even if there is not available to the Home Secretary (now Justice Secretary) evidence that the patient is mentally disordered at that time. The court emphasised that the responsibility to the Justice Secretary was to balance the rights of the patient against the need to protect the public. K challenged that view in the European Court in *K v UK* (1998) 40 BMLR 20. The European Court did not dispute the Court of Appeal's explanation of the considerations properly to be taken into account by the Justice Secretary, but held that there will be, as in that case, a breach of Art. 5(1) of the ECHR when recall is not, except in an emergency situation, based on the 'objective medical evidence' required by *Winterwerp* (see Chapter 5, 5.1.1), which means that there should be no recall (outside an emergency situation) in the absence of 'up to date medical evidence about the applicant's mental health' (*K v UK*, para. 50).

The implication of this, in so far as the Court of Appeal in *ex parte K* suggested that a conditionally discharged patient can be recalled on grounds of public safety even if no longer mentally ill, is that this view should not be taken in future; and in so far as s. 42(3) does allow recall in such circumstances, there is a strong argument waiting to be made that it is in this respect incompatible with Art. 5(1). This seems to be a theoretical rather than live risk, as it is the policy of the MHCS that 'patients will be recalled where it is necessary to protect the public from the actual or potential risk posed by that patient *and* that risk is linked to the patient's mental disorder' (Ministry of Justice, 2009c: para. 5, emphasis in original). The mental disorder which justifies the patient's recall need not be the same mental disorder that led to their initial hospitalisation (*R v SSHD, ex parte L* [2005] EWCA Civ 2, [2006] 1 WLR 88).

The Justice Secretary need not wait until a patient is floridly ill before recalling him or her to hospital. It is sufficient authority for recall that deterioration in the patient's state of mental health is likely, or that there is no deterioration but there is cause for concern about the patient's behaviour. This was established in *R(MM) v SSHD* [2007] EWCA Civ 687 (CA), the Court of Appeal holding that all that is required for lawful recall is that the Justice Secretary 'has to believe on reasonable grounds that something has happened, or information has emerged, of sufficient significance to justify recalling the patient' (para. 50). It is unfortunate that the Court of Appeal did not emphasise the collateral requirement that the reason for recall must also be linked to the patient's mental disorder.

Although an RC has no powers of recall, the decision in *R v North West London Mental Health NHS Trust, ex parte S* [1997] 4 ALL ER 871; [1998] 2 WLR 189 (see Chapter 8, 8.2.2) means that, if the grounds can be made out, there is always the option of sectioning a patient under s. 3 as an alternative to formal recall under s. 42(3); and such a patient remains liable to recall under s. 42(3) during and after discharge from detention under s. 3. As discharge from s. 3 may be ordered by a tribunal, the decisions in these cases effectively allow the Justice Secretary to overrule a tribunal decision, which he or she may want to do given the narrower criteria that are applied by a tribunal and his or her greater concern for public protection. This seems to raise the possibility that a recall in such circumstances would breach Art. 5(4) of the ECHR if there were to have been no change in the patient's condition or circumstances between discharge and recall, which is the basic thrust of the decision of the House of Lords in *R v East London and the City Mental Health NHS Trust, ex parte Von Brandenburg* [2004] 2 AC 280 (see 11.7.2).

On the other hand, if there was objective medical evidence to justify the recall, there could be no breach. It might also be open to a court to hold that there are differences between the considerations relevant to those detained under Part II and s. 37 of the MHA 1983, and those in respect of whom a restriction order is in force—in essence a difference between managing treatment and managing risk (Hudson, 2002)—such as to justify a different weighting of the balance of evidence and different conclusions as to the need to detain in hospital. Something like this line of thinking was adopted by the High Court in *R v SSHD, ex parte T* [2003] EWHC 538, Maurice Kay J holding, at para. 34, that the consideration relevant to the Justice Secretary when deciding whether to impose restrictions on a sentenced prisoner transferred to hospital are not analogous to those relevant to a court contemplating making a hospital order at trial (see Chapter 8, 8.4).

The number of patients recalled after conditional discharge stood at 55 in 1994, rising to around 70 per year around the turn of the century (MHAC, 2005: para. 5.136), with another hike, to 121 in 2003, reaching 196 in 2006. The rate of increase slowed thereafter: there were 210 in 2007, 190 in 2008, 201 in 2009, 211 in 2010, and 209 in 2011 (Ministry of Justice, 2012: table 6.5). An audit of all recalls to Ashworth hospital over the period 1981–91 (Dolan *et al.*, 1993) found that the most common reasons for recall were problems with the provision of suitable community services, especially for persons with alcohol and sexual problems, reoffending by patients, and concerns about public safety.

Offending rates by discharged restricted patients are relatively low. Of the 142 discharged in 1999, only one had been convicted of a grave offence within two years and two within five years, with a further seven convicted of a standard list offence within two years and 19 within five years (Home Office Research, Development and Statistics Directorate, 2005: Table 17). Of all the 1,277 individuals discharged between 1999 and 2005, 14 had committed a grave offence and 63 some other offence within two years of release (Home Office Research, Development and Statistics Directorate, 2009: Table 17). There is evidence to suggest that psychopathically disordered offenders are markedly more likely to reoffend, and for a longer period after discharge, than persons diagnosed as mentally ill, and that conditionally discharged patients are less likely to reoffend than those who are absolutely discharged (Bailey and MacCulloch, 1992), which helps to explain why so few absolute discharges are made.

11.4 Tribunals: Preliminaries and process

Mental health review tribunals (MHRTs) were introduced by the MHA 1959 to provide a mechanism to review the legality of the detention of detained but not informal patients, as well as those subject to guardianship. Tribunals were devised by the Percy Commission (Royal Commission on the Law Relating to Mental Illness and Mental Deficiency, 1957) as a replacement for judicial commitment, which was abolished by the MHA 1959. As the admission process was handed over to social workers and doctors, MHRTs constituted the structural downgrading of legalism, from main player in the admission process to *ex post facto* watchdog.

The Mental Health Bills of 2002 and 2004 would have moved back in the direction of the pre-1959 system, with no long-term compulsion possible without the prior approval of a tribunal, but the slimmed-down proposals published in 2006 abandoned this plan and the MHA 2007 made no major changes to the shape or functioning of the tribunal system, other than extending its reach to cover patients subject to a CTO. On the other hand, the judicial commitment procedure which operated before 1959 'was widely regarded as a "rubber stamp" of little practical value' (per Baroness Hale in *MH* v *SSDH* [2005] UKHL 60 at para. 26) and so its replacement by the tribunal system may actually have increased the extent of the legal limitations on psychiatrists' discretion. Certainly, tribunals do have significant legal powers with respect to the continued detention and discharge of patients. Tribunals had no jurisdiction over restricted patients under the MHA 1959, but this was held to be in breach of Art. 5(4) of the ECHR in *X v UK* (1981) 4 EHRR 181. Under the MHA 1983, *all* detained patients have a right to have their continued detention in hospital reviewed at periodic intervals by a tribunal with the power, indeed, the duty, if the prescribed criteria are met, to discharge the patient. So too do patients subject to guardianship or a CTO, or who, being a patient subject to restrictions, have been conditionally discharged by a tribunal or by the RC with the agreement of the Justice Secretary.

Although the MHA 2007 made only slight and consequential changes to the tribunal system for mental health patients, in the same year the tribunal system in England was overhauled by the Tribunals, Courts and Enforcement Act (TCEA) 2007. The various and manifold independent tribunal systems that were utilised in a wide range of public law contexts, going well beyond the mental health system, were almost all abolished and replaced by a two-tier tribunal structure. The first-tier tribunal (FTT) acts as a court of first instance, and the upper tribunal (UT)—one of the major innovations of the TCEA 2007—has appellate and review functions and may also in certain circumstances use powers of judicial review in respect of FTT decisions. Both tribunals were created by s. 3 of the TCEA 2007. The MHRT's functions were transferred to the FTT by the *Transfer of Tribunal Functions Order 2008*, SI 2008/2833, art. 3 and Sch. 1.

Section 7 of the TCEA 2007 permits the Lord Chancellor, with the concurrence of the Senior President of Tribunals (which is the office created by the TCEA 2007 to have responsibility for the ongoing efficient operation of the tribunal system), to divide both the first and upper tier tribunals into 'chambers' each with a particular specialism. Mental health matters are now allocated to the Health, Education and Social Care 'Chamber' within the FTT (which also hears, for example, applications from those deprived of a licence to operate or manage a care home: see Chapter 3, 3.2.2.1.1). Each Chamber in both the FTT and the UT has its own President (or two job-sharing Presidents) (TCEA 2007, s. 7(2), (4)) and the same person may preside over the same chamber in both the UT and the FTT, but may not preside over two different chambers, in any combination of tiers (s. 7(3)).

The Ministry of Justice (Ministry of Justice, 2008c: 1) reassured those who use the tribunal system that its restructuring has 'few implications for patients or for hospitals or local social services authorities' and 'hearings will remain largely as they are now', and there is much to support this claim: although now a relatively small cog in a much bigger tribunal system—over 90 per cent of the workload of which is concerned with child support and social security disputes, dealt with within the Social Entitlement Chamber (Senior President of Tribunals, 2012: 11)—and although amalgamated with other related tribunals within the Health, Education and Social Care Chamber, the mental health tribunal has its own centre of operations (the Mental Health Administrative Support Centre, situated in Leicester), specialist judges, and other tribunal members, and rules of procedure; and mental health tribunals do indeed function in much the same way as they ever have. On the other hand, the creation of the UT with powers to review or overturn FTT decisions, and the somewhat complex relation between the two tiers, has changed the way in which more difficult cases are dealt with; as such, although things may appear much as before for patients, medical professionals, hospital managers and LSSAs, for lawyers the landscape is markedly changed from the pre-TCEA 2007 situation.

11.4.1 Constitution and appointment

The composition of the FTT and the UT is provided for by the *First-tier Tribunal and Upper Tribunal (Composition of Tribunal) Order 2008*, SI 2008/2835. This is a matter for the discretion of the Senior President of Tribunals. The TCEA 2007 only distinguishes between 'judges' and 'other members' of the tribunal (TCEA 2007, ss. 4, 5). However, in 2009 the Senior President of Tribunals issued a Practice Statement (Senior President of the Tribunals, 2009) which provides, in para. 4, that the FTT should comprise 'a. One judge; and b. One other member who is a registered medical practitioner; and c. One other member who has substantial experience of health, or social care matters'. This continues the pre-2007 format, whereby MHRTs had three members, traditionally known as the 'legal member', 'medical member', and 'lay member'.

By contrast, paras. 3(1) and 2 of the 2008 Order provide that 'The number of members of the tribunal who are to decide any matter that falls to be decided by the Upper Tribunal is one' unless the Senior President of Tribunals decides that two or three tribunal members should sit, and if it is a tribunal of two, both may be Judges of the Tribunal, at the discretion of the Senior President of Tribunals (SI 2008/2835, para. 6). For each tribunal the Senior President of Tribunals must appoint one member to be the 'presiding member' (para. 7), and that person has the casting vote in the event that the tribunal is not unanimous (para. 8). The differences between the structures indicate differences in purpose: the FTT conducts an inter-disciplinary review and is more inquisitorial in structure, whereas the UT is staffed by professional judges and is more court-like. The Senior President and Judges of the UT are obliged to uphold the independence of the judiciary (TCEA 2007, s. 1; Constitutional Reform Act 2005, s. 3(7A), (7B) and Sch. 14).

Judges of the UT are appointed by the Monarch on the advice of the Lord Chancellor (TCEA 2007, Sch. 3, para.1). All other tribunal members are appointed by the Lord Chancellor (on the advice of the Judicial Appointments Commission established by s. 61 of the Constitutional Reform Act 2005) (TCEA 2007, Sch. 2). Sections 50, 55 and Sch.2 of the TCEA 2007 and the *Qualifications for Appointment of Members to the First-tier Tribunal and Upper Tribunal Order 2008*, SI 2008/2692 deal with eligibility for tribunal membership. These provisions require that an FTT judge must generally be a lawyer of five years standing, and an UT judge must have been a judge for at least seven years. Other tribunal members must have relevant experience. Members of the Court of Appeal, High Court judges, circuit judges, and district judges are automatically eligible to sit as a judge of either an FTT or an UT (TCEA 2007, s. 6) and the Senior President of the Tribunal is also a judge of the UT (TCEA 2007, s. 5(1)(a)). An FTT tribunal member may not sit in the UT, but members appointed to the UT may sit in the FTT (TCEA

2007, s. 4(1)(c), (3)(c)). Any chamber President or Deputy President may sit in a tribunal in either tier (TCEA 2007, s. 5(1)(i)). In cases involving restricted patients only judges appointed by the Lord Chancellor to the Restricted Patients Panel may act as the tribunal judge. The Justice Secretary announced in 2010 that salaried mental health judges may now hear cases involving restricted patients, although circuit judges and Recorder QCs would also continue to hear such cases (HC Hansard, 26 July 2010: col. 68WS).

Historically, the mental health tribunal system has suffered from a shortage of persons willing and able to act as tribunal members, particularly medical members, and this was a major cause of delay (Mental Health Review Tribunal Secretariat, 2005: 18). All the evidence at the moment is that the mental health FTT is adequately staffed by judges, and indeed has been able to spare judicial staff on loan to other tribunals within the Chamber (President of Tribunals: 2012: 32). Information about the adequacy of the number of medical members is, however, not given in the Annual Report, and the fact that a considerable number of cases are not being disposed of within target time limits (see further 11.4.4) raises the suspicion that this may still be an issue.

Before 2007, r. 8(2) of the *Mental Health Tribunal Rules 1983*, now abolished, specifically prohibited staff at the facility at which a tribunal applicant is detained, or anyone with a personal connection to the patient or who had recently provided the patient with treatment, from sitting on a tribunal hearing his or her case. There is no equivalent provision in the 2008 Rules, but the rules of natural justice, and the requirements imposed by Art. 6 of the ECHR, perform the same task. The test for bias, both at common law and under Art. 6, was authoritatively stated by Lord Bingham in *Porter* v *Magill* [2001] UKHL 67, [2002] 2 AC 357, [2002] 2 WLR 37, [2002] 1 All ER 465, at para. 103: 'The question is whether the fair-minded and informed observer, having considered the facts, would conclude that there was a real possibility that the tribunal was biased'.

This *dicta* was applied by the Divisional Court in *R* v *MHRT, ex parte M* [2005] EWHC 2791, finding that the test did not prevent the judge who had sentenced the patient from sitting, in *R* v *Midlands and North West MHRT, ex parte PD* [2004] EWCA Civ 311, 2004 WL 412965, finding that it did not prevent a consultant psychiatrist, C, employed by the defendant trust, but who did not work at the hospital in question and had had no contact with the patient, from sitting. The decision in the second case seems reasonable: the trust in *PD* operated over 33 sites across a considerable area of the north-west of England, and had the decision been otherwise, it would have given rise to a new set of logistic problems for the tribunal's administrative staff, which would have been obliged to look further afield to locate medical members deemed sufficiently independent to be acceptable. In the first case, the decision is perhaps more debatable. A tribunal is in no sense an appeal against conviction. But from the point of view of the patient, unease about the impartiality of the tribunal is understandable.

11.4.2 Applications and referrals

The process of making a tribunal application can be complicated, confusing, and intimidating for patients. Although hospital managers are under a duty to 'take such steps as are practicable' to inform detained patients and their NR about their right to apply to an tribunal 'as soon as possible after the commencement of the patient's detention' (MHA 1983, ss. 132(1)(b),(4), 132A(1)), with an equivalent obligation placed on LSSAs in respect of patients subject to guardianship (DH, 2008: para. 26.15), and patients are entitled to assistance from an IMHA (MHA 1983, ss. 130B, 130D; see Chapter 12, 12.9), some will lack the capacity to make an application. There is no specific common law test of capacity in this context, and so the provisions of ss. 2 and 3 of the MCA 2005 would apply. In *MH* v *SSDH* [2005] UKHL 60 at para. 4, Baroness Hale did note in passing that only 'very limited' capacity is required to make a tribunal application.

MH concerned a severely mentally disabled patient, detained under s. 2 of the MHA 1983. The House of Lords held that these mechanisms to provide patients with information and assistance, coupled with the obligation of hospital managers to refer a case to a tribunal when a patient does not take advantage of his or her right to make an application (see 11.4.2.2) means that there is no breach, merely by reason of the patient lacking capacity to make a tribunal application, of Art. 5(4) of the ECHR's requirement that there must be a review of the lawfulness of a patient's detention 'at reasonable intervals' (*Winterwerp* (1979) 2 EHRR 387 at para. 39).

Baroness Hale pointed out that the right given by Art. 5(4) is to 'take proceedings', as opposed to the right of a person detained on a criminal matter, which is to 'be brought promptly before a judge' (Art. 5(3)). Hence, so it was held, there is no absolute obligation to hold a hearing in Art. 5(4). Instead, it is a matter for the patient to decide (para. 22). If the patient lacks capacity to make that decision, this does not mean that the detaining section, here s. 2, breaches Art. 5(4): 'Rather, it leads to the conclusion that every sensible effort should be made to enable the patient to exercise that right if there is reason to think that she would wish to do so' (para. 23).

Baroness Hale further pointed out that the patient's NR and 'other concerned members of the family, friends or professionals, can help put the patient's case before a judicial authority' (para. 27). That was so here, but will not always be so: and the judgment of the House of Lords leaves open the possibility that there will be a breach of Art. 5(4) *in fact* when suitable assistance is not forthcoming for a patient lacking capacity to decide whether or not to make a tribunal application. It is possible that the European Court may be more sympathetic to the plight of patients lacking capacity and hold, as did the Court of Appeal in *MH*, before being overturned by the House of Lords, that, to comply with Art. 5(4), there must be steps taken to 'devise a system in which hospital managers were under a duty to refer incompetent patients admitted under section 2 to an MHRT' (Wall LJ, [2005] 1 WLR 1209, [2004] EWCA Civ 1609 at para. 54).

The risk is, on the one hand, that patients lacking capacity do not have a tribunal hearing, or, if they do, that they are not able to participate effectively in it. In either case, the prospect is disconcerting. A system which does not guarantee the same rights to those lacking capacity as those having it seems increasingly anachronistic, and not easily compatible with the UN Convention on the Rights of Persons with Disabilities (see Chapter 1, 1.6.2) which is why we prefer the approach taken by the Court of Appeal. At present, despite the mechanisms for information provision, many patients do not exercise their right: in 2005 it was reported that 70 per cent of patients detained under s. 2 did not make a tribunal application (MHAC, 2005: para. 4.112). The CQC (2013: 16) has expressed concern that there is no monitoring of the gender and ethnicity of those who do, and those who do not, exercise their right to apply to a tribunal, and in 2013, not for the first time, asked the Ministry of Justice to begin such monitoring.

11.4.2.1 Applications

When a patient is liable to be detained (except under the short-term civil provisions in ss. 5, 135 and 136, or under a remand order or interim hospital order made by a court: ss. 35, 36, 38), the patient or the patient's NR, depending on the circumstances, have a right to test the grounds for the continued (liability to) detention by applying to an tribunal under ss. 66, 69 or 70. Basically, the patient may make a fresh application whenever a significant decision relating to the detention is made. An application must be made within the 'relevant period' (s. 66(1)), which varies according to the event triggering the right to apply. On occasion, both the patient and his or her NR have a right to apply within the same time period, but each can only make one application within each relevant period (s. 77(2)), and there can be no application, except in accordance with the following provisions (s. 77(1)). The detail of entitlement to make an application is as follows.

11.4.2.1.1 *Part II patients*

The position for Part II patients is summarised as follows in Box 11.1:

Box 11.1

PART II PATIENTS APPLICATIONS

The patient alone (s.66(1)(i)) may make an application:

- within 14 days of admission for assessment: s. 66(1)(a), (2)(a);
- within six months of admission for treatment: s. 66(1)(b), (2)(b);
- within six months of receipt into guardianship: s. 66(1)(c), (2)(c);
- within six months of being made subject to a CTO: s. 66(1)(ca), (2)(ca);
- within six months following the revocation of a CTO under s. 17F: s. 66(1)(cb), (2)(cb);
- within six months of transfer from guardianship to hospital: s. 66(1)(e), (2)(e);
- within the period of renewal of detention of a patient detained under s. 3 (which will be six months in the first instance, 12 months thereafter: ss. 20(2)(a), (b),): s. 66(1)(f), (2)(f);
- within the period of renewal of a CTO (which will be six months or twelve months, depending on whether it is a first or subsequent renewal: ss. 20A(3)): s. 66(1)(fza), (2) (fza).

A patient who is returned to hospital or place required to live by a guardian or under the terms of a CTO may also apply within the period of the renewal of the order (ss. 21B(5)(6), 20(2), 66(1)(fa), (2)(f), 21B(6A)(6B), 20A(3), 21B(4A), 66(1)(faa), (2)(fza)).

As for the NR, see Box 11.2:

Box 11.2

APPLICATIONS BY THE NEAREST RELATIVE

NR alone (s. 66(1)(ii)) may make an application:

- within 28 days of a report made by the RC under s. 25 barring discharge by the NR: s. 66(1) (g), (2)(d);
- within twelve months of an order made under s. 29(3)(c) displacing the nearest relative of a person detained under Part II of the MHA 1983, or subject to guardianship or a CTO: s. 66(1)(h), 2(g).

If an application has been made by a patient detained under s. 2, following which a hearing must take place within seven days (see 11.4.1), that hearing must take place within that time period even if the patient is subsequently transferred to s. 3 (*R v SW Thames MHRT, ex parte M* [1998] COD 38 (HC)). But in *R v MHRT, ex parte SR* [2005] EWHC 2923 (Admin) it was held that an application made by a patient who was at that time detained under s. 3, but subsequently, and before that application was heard, was placed on ACUS, had lapsed and a new application was therefore required. The judge, Stanley Burnton J distinguished the decision in the *Thames* case, on the basis that, although s. 72(1) (see 11.5.2.1) treats applications under ss. 2 and 3 of being of the same class, separate provision was made (in s. 72(4A)) for applications from patients subject to ACUS.

However, with the replacement of ACUS by the CTO, this is no longer the case: there is no equivalent to the now-repealed s. 72(4A) and CTO patients have, instead, been brought by the modification of s. 72(1) within the same general class of applicant as those detained under Part II. The implications of this would seem to be that there is no longer a need for a new application to be made. This was the view of the UT in *AA v Cheshire and Wirral Partnerships Trust* [2009] UKUT 195, a case involving an application made by a NR that the FTT held had lapsed when the patient, detained under s. 3, was subsequently discharged subject to a CTO, and in *KF v Birmingham and Solihull Mental Health Foundation Trust* [2011] UKUT 185; and the Code of Practice (DH, 2008: 32.15) seems also to assume that this is now the case. Tribunals have power to permit a document to be amended, and to add a party to proceedings if there has been a change of circumstances (SI 2008/2699, rr.9(1),(2)), which seem to allow an application made by a patient whilst still be detained to be amended to reflect the fact that he or she has subsequently been discharged from hospital subject to a CTO, or guardianship.

11.4.2.1.2 *Patients detained under a hospital order*

Section 66 of the MHA 1983 applies to patients placed under a hospital order by a court in much the same way as it applies to Part II patients (s. 40(4)), although with two modifications. First, there can be no application in the first six months of hospitalisation (or,

in the very rare cases where they are made by a criminal court, a guardianship order),
but the patient may apply within the second six-month period of the order and thereafter annually (MHA 1983, Sch. 1, Part I, paras. 2, 9(a)). Secondly, a nearest relative may
not make an application in the first six months (MHA 1983, Sch. 1, Part I, paras. 2, 9).
An NR may apply in the second six months, and thereafter annually, if the hospital order
is renewed, or if the patient has been made subject to a CTO (s. 69(1)(a)), or within
12 months of such a patient being placed under guardianship, although the patient may
also apply in such circumstances, but most do so within six months (s. 69(1)(b)).

Although the powers of the NR under s. 69 are very similar to those the NR has to
apply in respect of a Part II patient when a report has been furnished under s. 25 barring an application for discharge by the NR under s. 23 (see 11.2.2), the key difference
is that, as the power of the NR to order discharge is disapplied by Sch. 1, Pt. 1, para. 8 of
the MHA 1983 Act if a hospital order has been made, there is never a need for a report
under s. 25 and so dangerousness is never an issue. Hence, a tribunal hearing an application by an NR is not obliged to discharge a patient who can be shown to the satisfaction of the tribunal not to be dangerous, as *is* the case for Part II patients, even where
there is a need for hospitalisation on either or both of therapeutic and protectionist
grounds (see s. 72(1)(b)(iii) and *R v MHRT, ex parte Central and North West London
Mental Health NHS Trust* [2005] EWHC 337).

If a person is treated by operation of s. 41(5) as being subject to a hospital order
because a restriction order ceases to have effect, he or she may apply within the first six
months from the date on which the restriction order ceases to have effect (s. 69(2)(a)).
This is understandable because, in the vast majority of cases, s. 41(5) is triggered by the
Justice Secretary using his or her powers under s. 42(1) to end a restriction order, which
is a good indication that the patient is no longer considered to constitute a serious risk
to other persons. Also, as such, patients will, almost always, have been in hospital for a
considerable period of time, there is no reason why they should have to wait six months
before making an application. Section 69(2) also provides that those in hospital by virtue of an hospital order made under s. 5(2)(a) of the Criminal Procedure (Insanity) Act
1964, which comprises those either found unfit to plead at a criminal trial or found to
be not guilty by reason of insanity (see Chapter 8, 8.2.3 and 8.3), may apply within the
first six months of their detention in hospital, and thereafter annually.

11.4.2.1.3 *Patients subject to restrictions*

There is a different regime for restricted patients, defined by s. 79(1) as including those
subject to a restriction order, limitation direction, or a restriction direction. Section 70
of the MHA 1983 provides that a restricted patient as defined in s. 79 may apply to an
tribunal, first, between six and 12 months into their detention (s. 70(a)), and thereafter in any subsequent 12-month period (s. 70(b)). Not all restricted patients will be
in hospital, because a percentage will have been conditionally discharged. Patients in
this category remain liable to recall until absolutely discharged, and consequently may
apply to a tribunal once in the second 12 months following discharge, and thereafter,
biennially (s. 75(2)). In *Secretary of State for Justice v RB* [2011] EWCA Civ 1608 (CA)

the Court of Appeal noted that this compared unfavourably with the situation for those detained in hospital, who may apply annually, and suggested (paras. 64–65) that this raised difficult questions of compliance with Art. 14 of the ECHR. If recalled to hospital following conditional discharge, the situation is as if a new order has been made and so s. 70 applies (s. 75(1)(b)).

Although the Justice Secretary must refer such cases to a tribunal within one month (see 11.4.2.2), this means that a patient recalled under s. 75 cannot make an application to a tribunal for six months following recall. In *R v Secretary of State for Justice, ex parte Rayner* [2008] EWCA Civ 176; [2009] 1 WLR 310 (CA) it was argued that s. 75 is incompatible with the Art. 5(4) ECHR right to apply speedily to a tribunal. This argument was rejected by the Court of Appeal, which took the view (para. 47) that Art. 5(4) was complied with, provided that the Justice Secretary referred the case quickly (see further 11.4.2.2), and although the referral mechanism alone may not satisfy Art. 5(4), in combination with the right to seek judicial review or commence a habeas corpus action if the Justice Secretary does fail to act quickly—which would permit consideration of the case on its merits and allow the High Court to direct the Justice Secretary to discharge the patient if successful in his or her application—this did together constitute compliance. This must be correct as a matter of ECHR jurisprudence, but it is perhaps nonetheless regrettable that a person recalled under s. 75 cannot make his or her own application to a tribunal to challenge that decision.

11.4.2.2 Referrals

The procedure for making an application to a tribunal is patient-led, and not all patients, whether because of cynicism, fear, apathy, or disorder, will activate it. To ensure that all detained patients are subject to an independent review of the grounds for detention, the MHA 1983 requires hospital managers, or a government minister, according to the circumstances, to refer cases to a tribunal. It also gives the Secretary of State for Health, in s. 67, a wide discretionary power 'if he thinks fit, at any time' to make referrals in respect of any patient detained under Part II, or subject to guardianship or a CTO, or subject to a hospital order without restrictions (MHA 1983, Sch. 1, Part I, para. 1), for the purposes of which an approved clinician (authorised by the patient or his or her representative rather than by the Secretary of State) may visit and examine the patient (s. 67(2)).

Section 67 is a default power and is only rarely used. Referrals usually come from the hospital managers in question, who have their own default duty, in s. 68(6), to refer any Part II patient who has not had their case considered by a tribunal, for whatever reason, in the last three years (or one year if the patient is under the age of 18). This duty is relevant because not every legally significant event triggers the more specific duties found in s. 68. In particular, there is no obligation on managers to refer a case when the authority for detention, or the guardianship order or CTO, as the case may be, is renewed. Hospital managers' duties to refer under s. 68(1) are laid out in Table 11.2.

In addition, a reference will only be possible if neither the patient nor his or her NR has exercised any right either may have under s. 66 (s. 68(3)) to make a tribunal

Table 11.2 Powers and duties to make referrals to a tribunal

	Hospital managers duty to refer within six months: s. 68(1)	Hospital managers duty to refer if no application for three years: s. 68(6)	SS for Health duty	SS for Health power to refer at any time: s. 67(1)	Justice Secretary duty to refer within one month: s. 75(1)	Justice Secretary duty to refer if no application for three years: s. 71(2)	Justice Secretary power to refer at any time: s. 71(1)
Detained under ss. 2, 3	When admitted	Yes	No	Yes	No	No	No
CTO	When order made and when revoked*	Yes	No	Yes	No	No	No
Guardianship	No	Yes	No	Yes	No	No	No
Transferred from Guardianship to hospital under s. 19	When transferred	Yes	No	Yes	No	No	No
Detained under Part III without restrictions	No, unless transferred to hospital from guardianship (Sch.1, Part 1, paras. 1, 10)	No	No	Yes	No	No	No
Detained under Part III with restrictions	No	No	No	No	No	Yes	Yes
Conditionally discharged from detention under Part III and recalled under s. 75	No	No	No	No	Yes	No	No

*If a CTO is revoked, the reference must be 'as soon as possible'.

application within six months (ss. 68(2), (5)). This duty also applies to a patient who makes but withdraws an application, and if that application is withdrawn later than six months after the triggering order was made, the referral must be made 'as soon as possible after that date' (s. 67(4)).

These powers cannot (and will not need to) be exercised if the Secretary of State has already referred the case under s. 67 (s. 68(3)(b)) or if, in the case of a community patient, there has already been a reference under s. 68(7), which requires hospital managers to refer the case to a tribunal 'as soon as possible' after a CTO has been revoked under s. 17F. As with referrals by the Secretary of State under s. 67, a doctor (who may, but need not, be an AC) of the patient's choice may visit and examine the patient, in private, and be given access to the records relating to that person's detention (s. 68(8)).

The Justice Secretary has discretionary powers to refer 'at any time' the case of patients subject to restrictions (s. 71(1)), whether actually 'detained' or not (s. 71(4)). In *R v SSHD, ex parte C* [2002] EWCA Civ 647 these powers were used to refer to a tribunal a patient who had been conditionally discharged, essentially on the grounds that the Home (now Justice) Secretary did not agree with the conditions imposed, viewing them as too lax. This had the effect of voiding the tribunal's decision, which is the effect of any referral made under s. 71 by virtue of s. 73(7). Thus, in the view of the Home Secretary, the tribunal was bound to consider the matter afresh. The patient commenced an action claiming breach of Art. 5(4) of the ECHR, as there was no mechanism to challenge this use of s. 71 and the effect of the referral was that he was not discharged despite the tribunal's decision. The Court of Appeal held that the use of s. 71 in such circumstances is unlawful at common law because it undermined the tribunal's authority (para. 29). Instead, the tribunal should have been 'invited to reconsider' its original decision. There was thus no need for the court to examine the Art. 5(4) issue in connection with this mode of use of s. 71, because it had already been held to be unlawful. Here, as with the requirement that leave is given under s. 17 rather than via s. 42, the courts have prescribed in some detail the limits of the powers open to the Secretary of State, although the precise quality of the difference between a formal referral and an 'invitation to consider' is not readily apparent.

At first instance ([2002] 1 MHLR 100 at 109), Collins J, having held that s. 71 *could* be used in this situation, and where the Secretary of State has information that was not before the tribunal, went on to say that in using it:

> the Secretary of State must form the view that it is probable that the material in question would have affected the result in that it would have decided either that a more onerous condition be imposed or that a conditional discharge would not have been ordered.

Although overruled on the availability of s. 71, these comments nevertheless seem relevant to the question of when the Justice Secretary should 'invite' a tribunal to reconsider its initial decision.

There is a duty placed on the Justice Secretary to make a referral in respect of a detained restricted patient (rather than those 'liable to be detained', which would include conditionally discharged patients and those on leave of absence or absent without leave) whose case has not been considered by a tribunal for three years (s. 71(2)). If a conditionally discharged restricted patient, whether discharged by the Justice Secretary under s. 42(2), or by a tribunal under ss. 73 or 74 (s. 75(1)) is recalled to hospital by the Justice Secretary, he or she must also refer that patient's case to a tribunal within one month of the date on which the patient returned or was returned to hospital (s. 75(1)(a)) so that the recall decision can be scrutinised by a tribunal in accordance with specific criteria, as a safeguard against the possible abuse of power by the Secretary of State, who, as seen, is given powers by the MHA 1983 to recall a patient on the basis of other than medical evidence.

This, as Hale (2010: 258) notes 'was the response to the precise problem raised by the case of *X* v *UK*'. As a 'public authority' under s. 6(3) of the HRA 1998, the Justice Secretary may not now act in a way incompatible with a ECHR right (HRA 1998, s. 6(1)) to the extent possible whilst also complying with domestic legislation. Hence, the *ex post facto* review of a recall decision by a tribunal may satisfy the ECHR but may not satisfy the requirements of the HRA 1998. Once recalled, the right to seek discharge by a tribunal in s. 70 of the MHA 1983 will apply, with the relevant period for the purposes of making an application beginning on the day the patient is recalled (s. 75(1)(b)).

Although the practice of the Justice Secretary is to refer a case under s. 75(1) within 72 hours, in *R* v *Secretary of State for Justice, ex parte Rayner* [2008] EWCA Civ 176; [2009] 1 WLR 310 (CA), a referral in respect of R, a conditionally discharged restricted patient, had been recalled to hospital by the Justice Secretary using the powers in s. 42(3) of the 1983 Act, was not made for seven weeks due to administrative error (para. 7). R sought damages, claiming breach of Art. 5(4), which the Justice Secretary conceded, but he appealed nonetheless because the High Court had interpreted Art. 5(4) as imposing an obligation on the Justice Secretary to make an 'immediate reference' under s. 75(1). In the Court of Appeal, Keene LJ held, at para. 20, that:

> [we] cannot accept that Secretary of State is generally entitled to take the statutory maximum of one month before making a reference. Where the liberty of the subject is at stake and where his action is to be seen as at least a principal method of getting the issue of the lawfulness of detention before a court, the concept of speediness requires a more energetic and rapid approach.

However, Keene LJ did feel that an obligation to refer 'immediately' was not required by Art. 5(4), nor could a specific time frame be identified, preferring instead (at para. 24) to follow Lord Phillips in *R* v *MHRT London South and West Region, ex parte C* [2001] MHLR 110, at para. 42, holding that the question is 'whether there was a failure to proceed with reasonable despatch having regard to all the material circumstances', which should 'normally [be] within a few days' (para. 24), approving the trial judge's view that the case should have been referred within six days (para. 25).

Although the general scheme of this process, as evidenced by s. 77(2), is that there should only be one application per patient per relevant period, the situation can arise when an application and a referral, or two applications, both fall due to be heard at the same time or in close succession. Sometimes both the patient and NR will exercise their right to apply, sometimes delays in the hearing of cases will mean that more than one application falls due to be heard, sometimes a duty to refer will be triggered and the patient makes an application shortly after. It is possible for a tribunal to conjoin two applications and hear them together (SI 2008/2699, r. 5(3)(b)), and it may add a party to proceedings (SI 2008/2699, r. 9(2)), although both applicants (if there are more than one) have full rights to be provided with documentation, representation, and so on under the tribunals' powers, having added a party under r. 9(2), to make consequential directions (r. 9(3)).

Another option, if there are two applications, or an application and a mandatory reference, pending, is to withdraw one application. An application or referral may be withdrawn at any time by the party who made it, in writing, before the hearing or other disposal of the case by the tribunal, or at the hearing, orally, with the agreement of the tribunal (SI 2008/2699, r. 17(1), (2)), with the understandable caveat that withdrawal of a mandatory reference made under ss. 68(1), 71(2) or 75(1) (SI 2008/2699, r. 17(3)) may not be withdrawn, as such referrals are made when a patient's case would not otherwise come before a tribunal. The tribunal must notify the various parties if an application or referral is withdrawn (SI 2008/2699, r. 17(6)).

The 2008 Rules (SI 2008/2699), in r. 17(4), also allow a party which has withdrawn its case to apply, in writing, within 28 days, to the tribunal for it to be reinstated (SI 2008/2699, r. 17(5)). Section 77(2), which provides that if an application is effectively withdrawn, another application may be made within the relevant period (s. 77(2)), may be of more tactical use to patients, given that the relevant period may be a year or even two years in the case of a conditionally discharged restricted patient. The permutations and possibilities mean that there is a tactical aspect to the timing of an application from a purely technical view, in order to ensure that maximum use is made of the tribunal system (Gostin and Fennell, 1992: 77).

11.4.3 Before the hearing

Rule 32(1) of the 2008 Rules (SI 2008/2699) requires that applications to tribunals must be in writing, signed by the applicant or person authorised to act on their behalf, and delivered within the relevant time limit. Both applications (r. 32(2)) and referrals (r.32(2A)) should provide information about the current legal status of the patient, as well their name and address, and that of the NR (if the applicant), and any representative, as well as any other relevant information (r. 32(2)(b), (d)).

An applicant may represent him or herself (SI 2008/2699, r. 11(1)) or may authorise a representative 'whether a legal representative or not' (r. 11(1)) to provide representation, except that another patient who is liable to be detained (which includes patients on leave or conditionally discharged, but not informal inpatients) or subject to guardianship or a CTO may not represent a patient (r. 11(8)). It is the responsibility of that party, or the representative if that person is a legal professional, to inform the tribunal and the other parties of the fact that a representative has been appointed and to provide their contact details (SI 2008/2699, r. 11(2)). If an applicant attends a tribunal accompanied by an unannounced representative, the tribunal has a discretion to allow that person so to act, or to otherwise assist the patient (SI 2008/2699, r. 11(5)). If he or she attends without representation, but has stated a wish to be represented, or lacks capacity to appoint a representative and the tribunal believes that it is in that person's best interests to be represented, the tribunal has a power under r. 11(7), but only to appoint a *legal* representative.

Most applicants appoint a lawyer as representative (Eldergill, 1997: 875, Perkins, 2000). The Law Society runs the Mental Health Accreditation Scheme, under which solicitors, trainee solicitors, solicitors' clerks and fellows and members of the Chartered Institute of Legal Executives (CILEx) and others, subject to approval by the Solicitors Regulation Authority, may apply to be accredited, following some training and practical experience, for the purposes of representing patients before the FTT (Law Society, 2013). Around 80 per cent of legal professionals who represent patients before a tribunal are members of the Mental Health Lawyers Association, which seeks to develop and maintain codes of professional conduct for lawyers appearing before a mental health tribunal. Both patients and NRs are entitled to advice and assistance (*The Community Legal Service (Funding) Order 2007*, SI 2007/2441). The Courts and Tribunals Service has made the applications forms available online. Agreement usually takes about a week, but can be arranged by telephone in emergency situations. Agreement may be refused if it is unreasonable, in all the circumstances, to grant legal aid. As only a relatively small percentage of all patients, and very few restricted patients, are discharged by a tribunal, a strict interpretation of the Regulations might see legal aid frequently being refused, and there are reports that this has happened in the past (Peay, 1989: 47), although it seems that legal aid is now only routinely denied on financial grounds, not least because its provision is a requirement of Art. 5(4) of the ECHR. Once appointed, a representative has the same entitlements as the patient to be supplied by the tribunal and the other parties to the proceedings with all documents relevant to the application (SI 2008/2699, r. 11(4)).

The notification of an intention to make an application triggers the duty of the tribunal to contact the managers of the hospital at which the patient is liable to be detained (SI 2008/2699, rr. 32(5),(6)), and the Justice Secretary, if the patient is a patient subject to restrictions who has been conditionally discharged (r. 32(4)), from which point the 2008 Rules, buttressed by a practice direction made by the Senior President of Tribunals (2012a) specify what amounts to a full exchange of relevant information as between the various parties concerned, during the course of which the RC, relevant nurses, the Justice Secretary (if the patient is subject to restrictions), a social worker, and the NR (except in restricted cases or if the patient does not wish the NR to be involved or if consultation with the NR for these purposes is thought to be inappropriate: Senior President of Tribunals, 2012a: para. 12), as well as course of the tribunal members, should all become apprised of all relevant information, in particular as regard to the patient's health, their treatment, and any risk posed.

If the patient is detained under s. 2, details of the application for admission and the supporting medical recommendations, but not other relevant documents, must be sent or delivered to the tribunal 'immediately' (SI 2008/2699, r. 32(5)). In all other cases (except those involving a conditionally discharge restricted patient), the documents requested from hospitals must be provided 'in any event' within three weeks from the time that a reference was made or the managers received a copy of the application or reference (r. 32(6)). The Justice Secretary must send or deliver the information specified in r. 32(7B) (which concerns the criminal history of the applicant) 'as soon as practicable' (r. 32(7A)), and must do within two weeks if the tribunal has received a reference by virtue of s. 75(1) following the recall of a conditionally discharged restricted patient to hospital (r. 32(7A)(a)), and otherwise within three weeks (r. 32(7A)(b)). If it is an application for discharge from a conditionally discharged restricted patient which is pending, the Justice Secretary must, on receipt of notice by the tribunal of the application, provide the contact details of the patient's RC and 'any social supervisor' immediately (r. 32(4)(a)), and it is the responsibility of the RC, having been contacted by the tribunal, to provide the tribunal with the information it has directed be provided within three weeks (r. 32(4)(b); Senior President of Tribunals, 2012a: paras. 21–26). The RC and social supervisor must send the same information to the Justice Secretary (Senior President of Tribunals, 2012a: para. 24).

On receipt of that information, the tribunal must then give notice of proceedings to relevant parties, including any NHS body with powers to discharge the patient under s. 23, any guardian, the NR (unless the patient, having capacity to do so, objects), the Court of Protection (if any relevant order of that court is in force), and 'any other person who, in the opinion of the Tribunal, should have an opportunity of being heard' (SI 2008/2699, r. 33). This may include a person who is victim, who is given an entitlement to information and to make representations by the Domestic Violence, Crime and Victims Act 2004 (see Chapter 10, 10.2.2.2 and 10.4.1).

Although the general rule is that all documents submitted to the tribunal should be made available by the tribunal to all relevant parties (SI 2008/2699, r. 32(3)), r. 14(7) contains a presumption that 'Unless the Tribunal gives a direction to the contrary, information about mental health cases and the names of any persons concerned in such cases must not be made public'. Beyond this, r. 14 permits a tribunal to make an order prohibiting the disclosure of a particular document or documents, either generally (r. 14(1)(a)), or to a specific person (r. 14(2)) if the tribunal is satisfied both that (i) 'such disclosure would be likely to cause that person or some other person serious harm' and (ii) 'having regard to the interests of justice, that it is proportionate to give such a direction'.

The scope of r. 14(1) varies from that of r. 14(2), because the former 'deals with publicity of the proceedings. Hence the limitation to documents or information "relating to the proceedings"' whereas r. 14(2) is concerned with disclosure to particular persons, normally the patient, and so a broader range of documents—those 'relevant to the proceedings' whether or not actually relied upon at the hearing, are within the scope of the rule (*RM v St Andrew's Healthcare* [2010] UKUT 119 (AAC) per Jacob J at para. 18). The tribunal may also by direction prohibit disclosure of 'any matter likely to lead members of the public to identify any person whom the Tribunal considers should not be identified' (r.14(1)(b)). The Courts and Tribunals Service has, however, made it clear that 'Victims should be made aware that no guarantees can be given that any representations they make will not be disclosed to the patient' (Tribunals Service, 2005: para. 8), although in *Dorset Healthcare NHS Foundation Trust* v *MH* [2009] UKUT 4 (AAC) it was held that r. 14 does not deal with all relevant reasons for non-disclosure, which may be appropriate, for example, to protect the confidentiality of third parties, so that non-disclosure to protect a victim may be justified at common law or under the ECHR, without invoking r. 14 (see further Chapter 12, 12. 2).

If one party forms the view that another party (almost always the patient, but sometimes the NR) should not see a particular document, he or she should not provide it to that other party, but instead send it to the tribunal for it to form a view as to whether disclosure should be prohibited (r. 14(3)). The scope of the test in r. 14 is nowhere closely defined. The current rules contain a reference to proportionality which was lacking from earlier versions, and the current requirement, of 'serious harm', is also clearly intended to tighten up practice (the previous test employed the, much looser, criterion of 'adverse effect on the health or welfare of the patient or others'), but still, there is room for legitimate disagreement as to what does or would constitute serious harm in a given case and what the requirement of proportionality actually amounts to. As was emphasised in *Roberts* v *Parole Board* [2005] UKHL 45, the common law starts from the presumption that disclosure should be permitted, as does Art.5(4) of the ECHR, but as that case also demonstrates, the opinion of the House of Lords (by a 3-2 majority, however) is that those who staff (in that case), the parole board must be trusted to make judgments based on information not available to those it directly concerns, if the public interest requires that, and it seems certain that the same approach would have been taken in that case if the prisoner had been a patient and the parole board had been a mental health tribunal.

The question of when non-disclosure can be justified arose in *RM* v *St Andrew's Healthcare* [2010] UKUT 119 (AAC). In this case, RM, a patient detained under s. 3 was being covertly medicated. When RM applied to a tribunal, the detaining hospital made an application for it to authorise non-disclosure of documents containing this fact to the patient, which was granted by a FTT judge on the basis that the criteria in r. 14(2) were met. There was no doubt the first limb of the test was satisfied, and all agreed that if RM learnt that he was being covertly medicated it would constitute serious harm to him (RM had learnt at an earlier tribunal hearing that covert medication was being administered in his food, to which he had responded by refusing food. His mental condition, schizophrenia, was made worse by the revelation, to the extent that his life had been at risk). The issue was, therefore, whether non-disclosure was a proportionate response to that risk of serious harm. An FTT decided that it was and RM (or rather, his lawyer) appealed.

The UT judge, Jacob J, noted that in *Secretary of State for the Home Department* v *AF (No 3)* [2009] 3 WLR 74 Baroness Hale at para. 105 had held (*obiter*, in a case concerning non-disclosure in a terrorism context) that 'These days, a mental health review tribunal would be unlikely to uphold a non-disclosure claim on the general ground that disclosure would be damaging to the doctor patient relationship. They would want to know precisely what it was in this doctor's evidence that might cause serious harm to this patient or to some other person and to weigh that damage against the interests of fairness'. Applying this, he found that the reasons for non-disclosure did not outweigh the strong interests against it. This is a laudable decision, but surely the question which it raises is, if it is unethical, unfair, and unlawful to keep the fact of covert medication from the patient, how can it be ethical, fair, or lawful (proportionate) to administer that medication, particularly in the knowledge, based on previous revelations of the same, that such a strategy is to put the life of the patient at risk, as well of course as fundamentally undermining the therapeutic relationship between treatment provider and treatment recipient?

It is possible to withhold information from the patient but disclose it, confidentially, to his or her representative, if there is one, and it is in the interests of the patient to do so (SI 2008/2699, r. 14(5), (6)). A representative can be appointed by the tribunal for this purpose (r. 11(7)). It was said in the *Dorset Healthcare* case (para. 28) that 'an undertaking from a solicitor (who owes a duty to the tribunal) will only not be acceptable in quite exceptional circumstances'. This is a pragmatic solution to a moral problem, which in principle clearly satisfies the requirements of Art. 5(4), but it can place a representative in an impossible position vis-à-vis the patient and can cause as many problems as it solves, as was observed by Jacob J in the *St Andrew's* case (para. 27):

> The tribunal may hold a hearing with the patient present. If it does, his legal team will not be able to present the real case. They cannot disclose the covert medication. Nor can the medical witnesses or the tribunal. Everyone in the room will know what the patient does not. They will be reduced to performing a mere mummery. Justice will not be done at the hearing; it will only seem to be done. The real proceedings will have to be conducted out of the patient's sight and knowledge.

Alternatively:

> The tribunal may deal with the real case by way of undisclosed written submissions. If it does, the patient's legal team will be able to present their arguments to the tribunal, but they will not be able to question the witnesses properly. That cannot be done effectively on paper. Or the tribunal may hold all or part of the hearing in the patient's absence. That will make him suspicious, unless the tribunal decides that he should not be told of the hearing. That will require a further order under rule 14(2). Whether the real case is considered on undisclosed written submissions or orally in the claimant's absence, the legal team will have difficulty obtaining instructions. They cannot present his direct response, because they cannot ask for it. They will have to approach the issue obliquely.

These points against non-disclosure and the compensatory mechanism of disclosure to the patient's representative are compelling, and we are pleased that they were decisive in this case, but they will not always be. Admittedly, the issue can be extremely tricky. Nonetheless, we are left wondering if this is a description of the state of mental health law in twenty-first century England or the abstract from Kafka's (2009) famous 1925 novel *The Trial*. Fortunately, it seems that a representative will only rarely face this type of ethical dilemma as, after initial resistance to disclosure of medical reports, particularly from special hospital RCs (Peay, 1989: 66), it is now rarely the case that all documents are not disclosed to patients.

A tribunal will not receive information solely from those exercising the authority to detain the patient. The patient, whether detained in hospital or subject to guardianship or a CTO or is conditionally discharged, is entitled under s. 76 to seek his or her own independent medical report. The purpose of such a report is to provide the patient with advice on whether to make an application to a tribunal, but, of course, if the report is favourable, the patient will want to present it to the tribunal. A doctor 'authorised by or on behalf of a patient', but who must be an RC or an AC, must be given access to the patient in private and may examine records relating to detention and treatment. Although a patient may be denied access to information under r. 14, he or she cannot prevent the disclosure of an unfavourable report that he or she has commissioned, if there is sufficient public interest to justify its disclosure (*W v Edgell and Ors* [1990] 1 All ER 835 (CA)), which means that a report that shows, for example, that a patient is more dangerous than thought to be by the RC or hospital managers can, as in *Edgell*, be disclosed by the person making it, and then onwards to appropriate recipients.

Finally, information is also generated by the medical member of the tribunal. Rule 34 of the 2008 Rules (SI 2008/2699), requires that 'an appropriate member' of the tribunal (who must be the medical member: Senior President of the Tribunals, 2009: para. 5), before the tribunal hearing takes place, 'examine the patient and take such other steps as he considers necessary to form an opinion of the patient's mental condition'. For this purpose, the medical member has rights of access to the patient and his or her records, similar to those of doctors authorised by the patient under s. 76.

If the patient refuses to be examined, the tribunal can exercise its powers under r. 5(3) of the 2008 Rules, to adjourn or stay proceedings. But, ultimately, an FTT may, using r. 7(3), have to refer the case to the UT, which has powers, under s. 25 of the TCEA 2007 equivalent to those of the High Court, inter alia, to require the attendance and examination of witnesses, and to impose sanctions for contempt of court if this is not done. The enforcement of contempt of court allows reasonable and proportionate force to be used. This would be very much the last resort as a mechanism to enforce patient compliance with a medical examination, but on occasion it may be that the tribunal feels that it has no choice, because if it is also clear that the patient does not intend to attend the hearing, it may not go ahead in his or her absence unless there has been a medical examination under r. 34 (r. 39(2)(a)).

The examination required by r. 34 raises issues of due process, because it casts the medical member as both 'witness' and 'decision-maker'. According to the Department of Health (1997: Appendix 13), the medical member should not give his or her opinion to the other members of the tribunal before the hearing, but the risk with this approach is that it is not then heard by the other tribunal members until *after* the hearing, with the applicant neither knowing about it nor having an opportunity to hear it. In *R v Mental Health Review Tribunal, ex parte Clatworthy* [1985] 3 All ER 699 (HC), Mann J held (at 704) that it would be a breach of natural justice for a tribunal to reach a decision based on the opinion of the applicant's condition that the medical member had formed, without that reasoning being made available to the applicant (see also *R v Avon and Wiltshire Mental Health Partnership NHS Trust, ex parte KW* [2003] EWHC 919, 2003 WL 1823101).

This does not mean that the medical member's findings should routinely be made available as evidence and therefore subject to cross-examination. As Gunn (1986c: 251) pointed out, Mann J referred to a tribunal resting its decision on the *opinion* of the medical member. Gunn suggests that this is to blur the opinion–evidence distinction, and it may be that it is only *facts* known to the medical member, rather than his or her opinions, that must be disclosed to the applicant. In *R v Ashworth Hospital Authority, ex parte H* [2002] EWCA Civ 923, at para. 84, Dyson LJ said, *obiter*, that it is 'the substance of the views' of the medical member that must be, other than under exceptional circumstances, disclosed to the patient or his or her representative.

The position of the medical member survived challenge under Art. 5(4) in *R v MHRT, North and East London Region, ex parte H* [2000] CO 2120/2000. The European Court in *DN v Switzerland* Application No. 27154/95 [2001] ECHR subsequently held that there was a breach of Art. 5(4) in the Swiss tribunal system, under which a psychiatrist is both tribunal member and expert witness, because it did not guarantee a patient the independent and impartial hearing required by Art. 5(4). This case was distinguished in *R v MHRT, ex parte S* [2002] EWHC 2522 (QBD), on the basis that, in the English system, the medical member is not an expert witness, and, provided the medical member keeps (or is seen to keep?) an open mind, the requirement for impartiality is not breached.

In the later case of *R v MHRT and SSHD, ex parte RD* [2007] EWHC 781 (Admin) the point of distinction between the English system and that found wanting in the *Switzerland* case was accepted without argument. The issue was whether there was to be superimposed onto the earlier case law a distinction between the medical member's opinion as to the state of mental health of the patient, which, it was argued, could be discussed with the other tribunal members, and the medical member's opinion as to whether the patient should be discharged which, if shared with the other members of the tribunal before the hearing, as happened in that case, would constitute a breach of Art 5(4) of the ECHR.

Munby J held, first, that as the view communicated by the medical member was clearly 'very preliminary' (para. 19), it did not as a matter of fact cross the line between impartiality and pre-judgment, but, secondly in any case:

> There is nothing in rule 11 [now r.34] to disable the medical member from doing what she (like the other members of the Tribunal) would otherwise plainly be entitled to do, namely to discuss all aspects of the case with the other members of the Tribunal before the hearing and to express to them her preliminary views either on the case as a whole or on any particular aspect of the case... The contrary, in my judgment, is simply unarguable.

This is, to date, the last judicial word on the operation of r. 34 and its implications for the human rights of patients.

Research carried out by Richardson and Machin (2000a) suggested that the distinction between witness and judge, and between fact and opinion, is not easily negotiated in practice, that medical members routinely discuss the examination and their opinion based on it with colleagues (2000a: 111–2), that discussions amongst tribunal members only rarely entail consideration of the legal criteria that the tribunal is meant to apply (Richardson and Machin, 2000: 499), and that in all cases in the survey, the tribunal's decision reflected the view of the medical member. Perkins similarly found that 'Evidence was often revealed and considered in a haphazard way' (2000: 2). In a survey carried out by the CQC and the Administrative Justice and Tribunals Council (AJTC) involving 150 tribunal applicants, a quarter were not told by the medical member or anyone of the purpose of the medical examination, and many reported that it was cursory, and often carried out on the day of the hearing (CQC and AJTC, 2011: 19).

This is understandable in terms of the time management of medical members, but it does raise issues about whether tribunals should be able to rely on the medical members' view over those of others who know the patient much better. Richardson and Machin concluded with a call for the role of the medical member to be 'radically reconsidered' (2000: 115), the most radical option being abolition, the alternative being to separate the examination from the hearing by appointing a psychiatrist solely to conduct the medical examination and give evidence on his or her findings to the tribunal, but as seen, this call fell on deaf ears. Our view is that the current situation continues to raise concerns about compliance, both with the spirit of Art. 5(4) ECHR and with the terms of Art. 6, and of natural justice, which are concerned with ensuring a fair, and transparently fair, justice system.

Rule 5(3) of the 2008 Rules (SI 2008/2699) provides that a tribunal may adjourn or postpone a hearing at any time in order to obtain further information or for any other purpose it deems appropriate. A tribunal should normally adjourn if there is any doubt whether conditions that it is considering attaching to an order for discharge can be implemented (*DC* v *Nottinghamshire Healthcare NHS Trust and the Secretary of State for Justice* [2012] UKUT 92 (AAC)), and a decision to order discharge while such doubts still exist will be quashed if unreasonable (*R* v *Secretary of State for the Home Department and Secretary of State for Health, ex parte IH* [2002] EWCA Civ 646 at para. 98; *R* v *MHRT, ex parte East London and the City Mental Health NHS Trust* (QBD (Admin)) [2005] EWHC 2329, 2005 WL 2996870).

In *R* v *MHRT, ex parte B* [2002] EWHC Admin 1553 B claimed that an adjournment, at which he had not been represented, had been improperly authorised. Scott Baker J held (para. 21) that the adjournment demonstrated bad practice, because it did not comply with (what is now) r. 5 of the 2008 Rules. He also stated that an adjournment should specify a specific return date, which had not been the case here, and that the reasons for an adjournment must be given to the patient or his or her legal representative (para. 23). He did find that an adjournment was warranted on the facts (for which, see 11.4.4).

In *R* v *MHRT, ex parte Secretary of State for the Home Department* (1987) *The Times*, 25 March (HC) it was held that what is now r. 5(3)(h) of the 2008 Rules does not permit adjournment in order to see if, with time, the condition of (in that case, a restricted) patient improves (see also *R* v *Nottingham MHRT, ex parte Secretary of State for the*

Home Department (1988) *The Times*, 12 October (HC)). A tribunal should 'give serious consideration' to the possibility of adjournment if the unavailability of medical witnesses for cross-examination 'is likely to be critical to [the tribunal's] ultimate decision' (*R* v *Ashworth Hospital Authority, ex parte H* [2002] EWCA Civ 923, [2003] 1 WLR 127, per Dyson LJ at para. 85).

11.4.4 Haste and delay in the application process

A truncated procedure applies in the case of applications by patients detained under s. 2. As with other applications, there must be a written, signed application containing the information discussed at 11.4.3 (SI 2008/2699, r. 32(5)), but on receipt of an application, the tribunal must fix the date of the hearing to occur within seven days from that date (r. 37(1)), and give at least three days (r. 37(4)(a)) notice of the date, time, and location of the hearing to all those involved and who, in the opinion of the tribunal, should have an opportunity to be heard (r. 33), and those parties are entitled to attend the hearing (r. 36), and those parties should be supplied by the detaining hospital with copies of the admission papers and such information as can reasonably be provided in the time available (r. 32(5)). Documents can be withheld from the patient, as in non-s. 2 applications (r. 32(2)). There has long been evidence (DH, 1992: para. 6), perhaps not surprisingly, that adherence to this timetable can mean hurriedly prepared reports being made available to tribunal members in insufficient time to allow their contents to be digested. Indeed, in Milne and Milne's research into the operation of the MHRT system as it affected one northern hospital in 1988–92, all medical and social work reports bar one were submitted to the tribunal on the day of the hearing (1995: 95).

There are also time limits placed on the hearing of cases referred under s. 75(1), which must be heard no sooner than five weeks but no later than eight weeks after the tribunal received the application (SI 2008/2699, r. 37(2)). There are no time limits imposed by the 2008 Rules on other cases, but the aim is to hear non-restricted cases within nine weeks and those involving restricted patients within 17 weeks of the application or referral being received by the tribunal (Ministry of Justice, 2012b, table 5.1: available as a link from the Annual Statistics).

Historically (see for example DH, 1997; Council on Tribunals, 2000: paras. 2.5–2.9) the mental health tribunal system has been under-funded, under-staffed, and characterised by lengthy delays in the hearing of cases. In the years after the HRA 1998 came into force, patients successfully argued that delays (of four weeks for a s. 2 patient, between nine and 22 weeks for s. 3 patients, and up to 27 weeks in the case a restricted patient) breached Art. 5(4) of the ECHR (see *R* v *MHRT London South and West Region, ex parte C* [2001] MHLR 110; *R* v *MHRT, ex parte KB and Seven Ors* [2002] EWHC Admin 639, a conjoined applicant involving eight patients, and *R* v *MHRT, ex parte B* [2002] EWHC Admin 1553). In *R* v *MHRT and Secretary of State, ex parte KB and Eight Ors* [2003] EWHC Admin 193, all nine of the applicants involved in the above two cases sought damages under s. 9 of the HRA 1998 for their deprivation of liberty, as well as for frustration, distress, damage to mental health, and the loss of the chance of liberty, had the various tribunal hearings taken place earlier than they did. The court dismissed any claim for loss of a chance, but held that the other claims, if proven and, apart from the deprivation of liberty, if proven to be serious, were compensable. Damages of between £750 and £4,000 were awarded to seven of the claimants.

There are other consequences of an ill-functioning tribunal system, as Stanley Burton J noted (para. 8) in *ex parte KB and Seven Ors*:

> delay prolongs the period of uncertainty for the patient. Cancellations of hearings, particularly if repeated, have other consequences: distress and disappointment for the mentally vulnerable patient, the risk of damage to his or her relationship with the psychiatrists and staff of his or her hospital, loss of trust in the tribunal system, and the waste of scarce resources, as where a RC or an independent psychiatrist witness cancels a clinic to accommodate a Tribunal hearing which in the event is cancelled shortly before it is due to take place.

He proceeded to find as fact (para. 114) that the 'the basic responsibility for the delays experienced by patients is that of central government rather than of the regional Chairman or their staff.'

The restructuring of the tribunal system by the TCEA 2007 seems to have improved the situation, but it is still the case that often, hearings take place after the time either required by law or by the targets imposed by the system on itself, and it remains the case that the statutory obligation to comply with the time limits in respect of applications from s. 2 patients has knock-on effects for others held otherwise than under s. 2. In 2010–11 99 per cent, and in 2011–12 99.9 per cent, of s. 2 cases were heard within the seven days required by r. 37(1) of the 2008 Rules (Ministry of Justice, 2012b: table 5.1). But in 2011–12 only 66 per cent of cases involving other non-restricted patients were heard within the target time of nine weeks (although this is up from 51 per cent in 2010–11) and 81 per cent (up from 64 per cent the previous year) of cases involving restricted patients were held within the target time, which is seventeen weeks (Ministry of Justice, 2012b: table 5.1), and as the Senior President of Tribunals has pointed out, this improvement in performance has been achieved notwithstanding 'a range of problems such as the receipt of late reports from doctors and hospitals, last minute cancellation of hearings and poor compliance with case management decisions' (Senior President of Tribunals, 2012: 30). As mentioned at 11.1, many applications do not result in a hearing, which is fortunate in the sense that, without such an attrition rate, the system would not be able to function.

The rate of adjournment stood at 29 per cent of all cases in 2008–09, but this fell to 19 per cent in the following year, and by 2010–11 was down to 7 per cent, which was also the situation in 2011–12 (Ministry of Justice, 2012b: table 1.3). This is an impressive achievement, but because of the increase in the number of tribunal applications over this period (from 15, 367 in 2005 to 29,705 in 2011-12, including 3,901 from CTO patients: CQC, 2013: 17, table 3; 83, table 7), the total number of adjourned cases has risen from 1,300 in 2008–09, to 2,200 in 2011–12 (Ministry of Justice, 2012b: table 1.3). The number of hearings postponed has also fallen in percentage terms, from 18 per cent in 2009–10 to 13 per cent in 2011–12, but again in terms of numbers, this constituted an increase from 3,100 to 4,000 cases (Ministry of Justice, 2012b: table 1.3). The number of hearing applications outstanding at the end of 2011–12 was 4,400, down from 4,500 in 2010–11 and 4,800 in 2009–10 (Ministry of Justice, 2012b: table 1.2). This statistics indicate that the mental health FTT, and the administrative centre in Leicester, is working with increased efficiency, but in a challenging environment in which the call on tribunal resources increases year on year, and the system on present performance cannot yet be considered safe from further claims under Art. 5(4).

11.4.5 **At the hearing**

Neither the TCEA 2007 nor the 2008 Rules (SI 2008/2699) prescribe any formal procedural requirements for the conduct of tribunal hearings, other than requiring that a hearing of the substantive application (but not including a decision to set aside, strike out or review a decision, or an application for permission to appeal: SI 2008/2699, rr. 35(2), (4)) must to take place (r. 35(1)). Indeed, r. 2(2)(b) requires tribunals to avoid 'unnecessary formality' and seek 'flexibility in the proceedings'. Tribunals must, however, comply with the rules of natural justice (*R v Oxford Regional MHRT, ex parte SSHD* [1988] 1 AC 120, [1987] 3 All ER 8, HL), and, as a court and a 'public authority' under s. 6(3)(a) of the HRA 1998, a tribunal must, if possible whilst also acting in accordance with other primary legislation, act in a way compatible with the ECHR rights of applicants (HRA 1998, s. 6(1), (2)).

In *R v MHRT (Northern Region), ex parte N; R v MHRT, ex parte DJ* [2006] QB 468, [2006] 2 WLR 850, [2005] EWCA Civ 1605, the Court of Appeal held that it is the civil law burden of proof—on the balance of probabilities—that applies to all issues upon which a tribunal must make a judgment, and this complies with the requirement found in *Winterwerp* (1979) 2 EHRR 387 at para. 39, that the presence of mental disorder must be 'reliably shown' (para. 78). Richards LJ did, however, point out that 'The more serious the consequences, the stronger the evidence required in practice to prove the matter on the balance of probabilities' (para. 64). Arguably, this is to confuse questions of fact with considerations of proportionality, but in any case this is an important point, not least because tribunals may hear evidence that would not be disclosable in court proceedings, such as hearsay evidence (r. 15(2)), and should therefore guard against the danger of what Munby J at first instance ([2005] EWHC 587 at para. 129) referred to as 'the well-known problem that constant repetition in "official" reports or statements may, in the "official" mind, turn into established fact something which rigorous forensic investigation shows is in truth nothing more than "institutional folk-lore" with no secure foundation in either recorded or provable fact'.

A tribunal hearing has various features that indicate its inquisitorial rather than adversarial nature. For example, there is a requirement that hearings shall take place in private, unless the tribunal considers it in the interests of justice to hold proceedings in public (SI 2008/2699, r. 38(1)), and nearly all do: only 'one at most' out of 600 hearings that took place at Ashworth hospital between January 2000 and January 2003 was held in public (*R v MHRT; Ian Stuart Brady and Secretary of State for the Home Department, ex parte Mersey Care NHS Trust* [2004] EWHC 1749 per Beatson J at para. 1). There was a public hearing, authorised by the UT on appeal from the FTT, in *AH* v *West London Mental Health NHS Trust* [2011] UKUT 74 (AAC), at the request of a restricted patient detained at Broadmoor hospital, who wished to attract publicity to what he perceived as failings and injustices in the mental health system. The UT also permitted press attendance at the hearing. The UT held that the factors to be considered when a tribunal was faced with such a request included: the wishes of the patient; the impact on his mental health of hearing or not hearing his application in public (confirming what had already been said on this in *Brady* per Beatson J at para. 67); any special factors; and whether arrangements for a public hearing can be made without imposing a disproportionate burden on the detaining authority (para. 8). The UT considered the most salient feature in this case to be the special factors which were involved, namely that 'The patient has been kept in detention at public expense over 23 years, often in conditions of high security, and it is only recently that there has been a change in his diagnosis...this potentially gives the case some heightened public significance' (para. 9).

To give effect to this decision, it was necessary for the hearing to take place outside the hospital, at greater expense (estimated at £1,739) than would have been the case had it been held in the hospital in private (£967) or in public (£792). The tribunal found that this was an acceptable additional cost, and that 'considerations of cost must reach a high threshold before they can be regarded as sufficiently disproportionate to permit a restriction of a public hearing' (para. 21). The UT also referred to the 2006 UN Convention on the Rights of Persons with Disabilities, which prohibits discrimination on grounds of disability (Art. 1) and requires 'effective access to justice for persons with disabilities on an equal basis with others' (Art. 13), and to Art. 6 of the ECHR, holding that r. 38 does not breach that Article's requirement of a fair trial, provided that the criteria for permitting a public hearing which it had identified were applied in all cases where there was a request for such (para. 8).

The UT in *AH* further stated that, if there were further applications for a public hearing by patients 'it should be possible for arrangements to be made between the hospital and the Tribunals Service for a hearing at the hospital with a video-link to suitable premises off-site where any interested members of the press or public can view the proceedings' (para. 23), and this arrangement was agreed to in respect of a hearing held in July 2013 concerning a well-known long-term patient at Ashworth hospital, Ian Brady.

Such cases (at the moment anyway) are very much the exception to the norm, and cases involving detained patients routinely take place in the detaining hospital. In 2006, the Council of Tribunals (2006: para. 41), reported 'many of the same issues that we have raised in the past, e.g. the inadequate standard of the tribunal hearing room, delays in the tribunal receiving the papers for the hearing, continuing problems with booking hearing dates in advance, communication difficulties with the secretariat in London', the worst example given is of a tribunal hearing taking place in a hospital lobby; other hearings take place in small and cramped rooms where there may or may not be a table for the tribunal to use (Council on Tribunals, 2000: para. 2.26).

This can undermine both the dignity and the credibility of proceedings. Clearly, the continuing need for improved resourcing for tribunals comes in many and varied forms. The Code of Practice (DH, 2008: paras. 32.33 and 32.34) requires that the 'hearing room should be private, quiet, clean and adequately sized and furnished. It should not contain confidential information about other patients' and that 'The patient should have access to a separate room in which to hold any private discussions that are necessary – for example, with their representative – as should the Tribunal members, so that they can discuss their decision'. HM Courts and Tribunals Service has provided guidance on the location of and facilities required for tribunal hearings (HM Courts and Tribunals Service, 2012).

For patients on a CTO, subject to guardianship, or conditionally discharged, 'the hospital managers should consider whether a hospital venue is appropriate' (DH, 2008, para. 32.35). There is 'anecdotal' evidence that 'a considerable number of CTO patients fail to attend' their tribunal hearing in a hospital (CQC, 2011: 30), which suggests that para. 32. 35 is not always taken as seriously as it should be by the FTT. Although there is the option to adjourn when the patient or some other party does not appear at the hearing, the tribunal may decide that it is necessary to deal with the substantive issue immediately, which it can do in the absence of any party if the tribunal is satisfied that that party has been notified of the hearing, or that reasonable steps to notify that party have been taken, and it is in the interests of justice to proceed despite their absence (r. 39(1)). If the missing party is the patient, the hearing may not take place in their absence unless r. 39(1) is satisfied, and the medical examination required under r. 34 has taken place, and the tribunal is satisfied either that the patient has decided not to attend or cannot attend because of ill health (r. 39(2)). Given the requirements of natural justice and Art. 6 of the ECHR, the tribunal should be as sure as possible that these criteria are met before proceeding in the patient's absence.

Tribunal hearings trade in confidential medical and other information about patients, but also sometimes in matters that attract a public interest. In *Pickering* v *Liverpool Daily Post and Echo Newspapers plc* [1991] 1 ALL ER 622, the House of Lords held that information that a named patient has made a tribunal application, that the application has been or will be heard, and whether the patient was discharged by that hearing, can be made public. Information that discloses the evidential base on which a tribunal reached its decision, or information about any conditions imposed on discharge must remain private. This is understandable, but has the unfortunate consequence that media reports cannot include the reason for a discharge decision, which risks adding to public misunderstanding of the work of the tribunal system. In *R* v *MHRT, ex parte T* [2002] EWHC Admin 247, at para. 37, Scott Baker J held that *Pickering* proved only a general framework and that the tribunal's discretion under r. 38(2) to direct that the tribunal hearing be held in private is not limited by that decision if disclosure of specified information to specified individuals is warranted on the facts—in that case, information as to the conditions attached to discharge being provided to T, a patient's former partner and mother of his child, who had a justified fear of the patient.

He further held that T had no claim under Art. 2 of the ECHR, because her life was found not be at risk, nor under Art. 8(1), because there was insufficient evidence to show that the claimed interference with T's private life had reached the necessary level of severity to engage Art. 8 (para. 47). It is clear, however, that in a suitable case, a third party would be able to rely on Art. 8(1) to found a claim to be entitled to the information in question. On the other hand, any such disclosure is also prima facie a breach of the patient's rights under the same Article (para. 48). The crucial factor, accordingly, is the weighting of the public interest, which can justify the breach in either case. The right of a victim of specified offences to be provided with information or to make representations under the Domestic Violence, Crime and Victims Act 2004 (see Chapter 10. 10.2.2) is also relevant here.

Whether held in public or in private, other parties to the hearing will include the hospital managers and, in the case of a restricted patient, sometimes the Justice Secretary. A failure to notify the Justice Secretary is a breach of natural justice that will vitiate the hearing (*R* v *Oxford Regional MHRT, ex parte SSHD* [1988] 1 AC 120, [1987] 3 All ER 8, per Lord Bridge at 10, see also *R* v *MHRT, ex parte SS* [2004] EWHC 650, 2004 WL 960902). The Justice Secretary will not usually be represented by counsel, except in complicated or controversial cases, for example, where the Justice Secretary and the patient's RC disagree about whether the patient should be discharged (Eldergill, 1997: 164). Richardson (1993: 288) has pointed out that, in cases where the Justice Secretary supplies only affidavit evidence, it will not be possible for that evidence to be cross-examined by the applicant. The evidence for discharge will, of course, always be cross-examined, if only by the tribunal members (SI 2008/2699, r. 16).

In 1989 Peay reported that the lack of a prescribed procedure results in 'stark differences...in the format of hearings' (Peay, 1989: 95). Peay found that some tribunals would hear evidence from the patient, then there would be cross-examination of that evidence by tribunal members and RCs (if the RC was opposed to discharge), followed by a hearing of the case against discharge. Others did not provide RCs with the same opportunities to cross-examine; others heard the RCs' evidence at a much earlier stage. More recently, Perkins (2000: 1) confirmed that 'great variation' continues to be the norm. The point here is not that 'justice by geography' per se is a bad thing; it is also that the order of proceedings can influence the weight given to the various elements of evidence that are presented, and so the chances of discharge. At the risk of undermining the policy that tribunals should be relatively informal affairs, there is a good argument to be made that tribunals should be required to follow what Peay calls 'standard criminal-court procedure' (1989: 95). It is easy for 'informality' to descend into a denial of the due process rights and reliance on unwarranted assumptions (see, for example, *R* v *MHRT, ex parte Kelly* (1997) 22 April, unreported (HC)) that would not be permitted in criminal trials; and tribunal applicants should be in at least as good a position as criminal defendants.

It is also worth noting that Ferencz and Maguire (2000) found, in a small survey, that patients were often dissatisfied with tribunals, irrespective of whether they were formal or informal in procedural terms. The main problems identified were that tribunal hearings were alienating experiences, and tribunal members were often (at least seemingly) uninterested in the patients' side of the story, with patients given little opportunity to speak. Due process is a necessary, but not a sufficient, requirement in this regard. A fundamental problem with greater patient participation, however, is that patients' knowledge of the tribunal process is poor. Dolan *et al.* (1999: 267), for example, found that less than 10 per cent of 80 special-hospital patients surveyed understood the powers of tribunals in respect of their own circumstances.

Similar findings have been reported more recently by the MHAC (2009: 66–67) and the CQC and AJTC (2011). The CQC and AJTC also reported that delays and adjournments were a common frustration for tribunal applicants, and that dissatisfaction with the way in which the pre-hearing medical examination and the hearing itself were conducted and explained to the patient, was fairly common. Without sufficient information to understand tribunal proceedings fully, it is unlikely that levels of patient satisfaction—which research shows are more linked to the way in which the proceedings were conducted than with substantive outcome (Tyler, 1996)—are unlikely to increase.

11.5 Substantive powers of discharge

11.5.1 The powers available to a tribunal

The substantive powers of tribunals are found in ss. 72–75 of the MHA 1983. Section 72 applies to all patients, other than those subject to restrictions, who are dealt with by ss. 73–75. On hearing an application for discharge from a non-restricted detained patient, a tribunal has various options open to it. First, it can confirm the propriety of the situation then pertaining, and make no order. Secondly, it can discharge the patient. Discharge can be immediate or deferred to a future specified date (s. 72(3)). It is not lawful to defer discharge in order to give time to consider whether there is any other lawful basis for the patient's continued detention (*Perkins v Bath District Health Authority* (1989) 4 BMLR 145 (CA)). Although there is no mechanism by which to organise the conditional discharge of an unrestricted patient, a discharge will be appropriately deferred if there is a need to make arrangements for some form of care in the community or suitable accommodation.

On occasion, the conditions that are placed on discharge by a tribunal, or the manner in which those conditions are implemented by those responsible for the care of the patient after discharge, particularly but not exclusively in cases in which the patient lacks capacity, are such that it is clear that discharge from compulsory confinement in hospital does not mean the patient is thereafter at liberty. In *A PCT v LDV and B Healthcare group* [2013] EWHC 272 (Fam) (and see also *A Local Authority v H* [2012] EWHC 49 (COP)) for example, LDV, found to lack capacity, and diagnosed as having learning disabilities and an emotionally unstable personality disorder, and prone to violent outbursts, was discharged from detention under s. 3 by a tribunal, which held that LDV 'needs to be placed in a residential establishment in the community, equipped to meet the needs of a person suffering from mild learning disability with challenging behaviours, and supported by a package of aftercare comprising medical, nursing and social worker oversight and the provision of daycare'.

LDV was placed in accommodation and under a regime which placed very heavy restrictions on her. The accommodation was locked, LDV could only leave with permission of nursing staff, and subject to one to one supervision. LDV would not be allowed to leave the facility if judged to be at particular risk, using restraint if necessary, and was subject to constant observation, personal and property searches, and sedative medication as required by reference to the facility staff's judgement of the level of risk. Not surprisingly, it was held that LDV was deprived of her liberty and so should be made subject to the DOLS, but the point here is that, in this case, the difference between transfer and discharge, and between compulsion and ostensible liberty, is gossamer-thin.

In *LDV*, the tribunal did not specifically recommend, or even envisage, that the arrangements for LDV's after-care would constitute a deprivation of liberty. In *DN v Northumberland Tyne & Wear NHS Foundation Trust* [2011] UKUT 327 (AAC), by contrast, DN, a patient detained under s. 3, appealed against an FTT decision not to discharge him into a situation in which he would be deprived of his liberty under the terms of the MCA 2005 from the outset, arguing that the availability of the DOLS mechanism meant that his continued detention in hospital was no longer appropriate. The FTT based its decision on the fact that three previous attempts to provide the necessary care for DN outside of hospital (which consisted of constant supervision to prevent DN, an alcoholic with consequential mental and physical health problems, from obtaining alcohol) had been unsuccessful.

The appeal was successful, Jacob J holding that 'the evidence showed that [DN] had obtained alcohol when outside the hospital regime previously. However, the [tribunal's] reasons do not explain why the different and stricter regime envisaged by [DN's counsel] might not be more successful' (para. 26). A rehearing of the case by the FTT was ordered. In this case, although it might seem that DN was (if he objected to hospitalisation or treatment) 'within the scope of the Mental Health Act' as defined by Sch. 1A, para. 2 and case E, and para. 12, MCA 2005—being a person in respect of whom (if discharged) an application could be made under one of ss. 2 or 3 MHA 1983, and so ineligible for the use of DOLS—as his need was for 'tactics of general distraction and diversion to prevent [him] obtaining alcohol', this not being a treatment for the purposes of s. 145 of the MHA 1983 (para. 26) and so he was not, in fact, 'within the scope' of the MHA 1983, and so the DOLS were available for use. In any case, the restrictions on the use of the DOLS as an alternative to detention under the MHA 1983 only apply to their use in a hospital, and there is no similar restriction on their use in a care home. As with *LDV*, this case demonstrates that discharge from detention may in fact sometimes be better characterised as a transfer, in terms of the extent to which the person discharged remains in a state of incarceration or deprivation of liberty thereafter (for cases involving patients with capacity, and so outside the scope of the DOLS, see 11.5.3.2).

If a tribunal decides not to order discharge, its third option is to make recommendations to the RC. A tribunal may recommend that the patient be given leave of absence or transferred into guardianship or to another hospital (s. 72(3)(a)), and if this does not subsequently happen, give further consideration to the case (s. 72(3)(b)). A tribunal may not discharge an unrestricted patient because it thinks that the use of CTO would be more suitable for that person (which is somewhat perplexing because as discussed at 11.5.3.2, a tribunal may order the conditional discharge of a patient subject to restrictions, which in effect is very similar to a CTO), but it may recommend that the patient's RC consider making a CTO (s. 72(3A)(a)). If this suggestion is not acted on the tribunal 'may but not must' further consider the case (s. 72(3A)(b)). The difference in wording as between ss. 72(3) and 72(3A) is seems to imply that the tribunal has a discretion to recommend one of the options mentioned in s. 73(3)(a), but if it does so recommend, and this is not done by the RC, the tribunal *must* then give further consideration to the case, at which point it may discharge the patient (*MHRT* v *Hempstock* [1997] COD 443 (HC)). The power to make recommendations can, therefore, be a powerful lever over the care of undischarged patients.

In *MP* v *Mersey Care NHS Trust* [2011] UKUT 107 (AAC) a tribunal concluded that it was not satisfied that the criteria in ss. 72(1)(b)(i) and (ii) continued to be met, and ordered the deferred discharge of MP. Although the tribunal specifically made no recommendations, it did 'invite' MP's RC to 'consider' make a CTO, which the RC did. The CTO took effect before the appointed discharge date. Later, but before the date to which discharge had been deferred, the RC sought and obtained the setting aside of the initial decision, because the effect of the discharge by a tribunal is that a CTO in force at that time automatically comes to an end (s. 17C(b)) which, so the FTT reviewing the original decision decided, had frustrated the purpose of the initial tribunal and constituted an error of law.

That latter decision was subject to consideration by the UT, using its judicial review powers under s. 15 of the TCEA 2007 (see 11.6), the result of which was that the original decision was reinstated. The UT rejected a submission that the initial tribunal should have used the power in s. 72(3A), to recommend that the RC discharge the patient subject to a CTO, because that power is only available if the tribunal decides that the patient is not otherwise entitled to discharge, and here the tribunal was clear that the grounds for continued detention did not exist. The UT also emphasised that an 'invitation' is not a 'recommendation'. This seems to be a sensible solution to a situation in which it would seem that the initial tribunal did have some uncertainty as to how the various elements of the MHA 1983 fit together.

The powers of discharge in s. 72 apply also to patients subject to a CTO (s. 72(1) (c)) or guardianship (s. 72(4)). Discharge from a CTO can be immediate or deferred (s. 72(3)), but there is no equivalent provision in respect of guardianship patients, and so discharge must always be immediate. Similarly, the power to make recommendations applies on an application by a CTO patient (even though, apart from the recommendation to transfer the patient to guardianship, s. 72(3) ill-fits the CTO patient), but there is no power to make recommendations in cases involving guardianship patients.

For restricted patients, other than those subject to a limitation direction or a restriction direction, a tribunal may discharge absolutely (s. 73(1)), or subject to conditions

(s. 73(2)). A conditional discharge, but not an absolute discharge, may be deferred (s. 73(7)). There is no power in s. 73 to make recommendations. Richardson (1993) argued that this means that tribunals are of much less relevance to such patients, who are often held in high security accommodation, and for whom the route back into the community is usually via MSUs and low security provision, because the amount of time spent in custody, as Goffman suggested (see Chapter 3, 3.4), means that it can be hard to assess how the patient might behave outside the institution.

As a consequence, high security patients are often not looking to the tribunal to make a direction for discharge but rather are hoping to speed up the process of transfer into conditions of lesser security, but the tribunal cannot do this. Tribunals can, and do, make extra-statutory recommendations for transfer or leave of absence to be given to high security hospital patients, but such recommendations have 'very little impact unless supported by the RMO [now RC]' (Richardson, 1993: 294). In any case, a restricted patient cannot be transferred or given leave of absence without the consent of the Justice Secretary (s. 41(3)(c)). As with discharge under s. 42(2) (see 11.3.1), the matter will be considered by the Justice Secretary on the advice of the RC, the hospital managers, and possibly others besides, although the decision rests with the Justice Secretary who may choose not to follow the advice of any party, subject to the principles of judicial review and human rights law.

If the patient is subject to a limitation direction or a restriction direction, having entered hospital either by virtue of a 'hybrid order' made by a criminal court under s. 45A or through transfer from prison under either ss. 47 or 48 with restrictions attached under s. 49, a different procedure applies, by virtue of s. 74, even though the effect in hospital is the same as a restriction order (s. 49(2)). This is because such persons will face the prospect of transfer to prison on discharge from hospital (see Chapter 8, 8.4.3). A tribunal hearing an application from a patient to whom s. 74 applies must, after the hearing, notify the Secretary of State whether the patient, if subject to a restriction order made under s. 41, would have been entitled to either absolute or conditional discharge (s. 74(1)(a)); and if the view of the tribunal is that conditional discharge would have been ordered, it may recommend that the patient should continue to be detained in hospital (s.74(1)(b)).

One reason that a tribunal might so recommend is that it views that the illness is in remission, and likely to reoccur if the patient is returned to a prison environment (see, for example, *R v MHRT and SSHD, ex parte Abu-Rideh* [2004] EWHC 1999 (Admin)). In applying the criteria in s. 73(1)(b), therefore, it is appropriate for the tribunal to consider, rather than what would occur if the patient is discharged into the community, what would occur if the patient is discharged from hospital to prison. But it is not legitimate for a tribunal to speculate on whether if so returned, a parole board might decide to release the patient from prison and if so, what conditions the parole board might impose on release, and must make its decision regarding the criteria in s. 73(1)(b) without entering into such speculation (*AC, Partnerships in Care Ltd v SSJ* [2012] UKUT 450 (AAC)). If on the other hand, the tribunal knows that, if the patient is returned to prison there is no prospect of release by the parole board, it may properly take that into account (*Abu-Rideh*).

If the tribunal decides that the patient should continue to be detained in a hospital that is generally what happens. If the patient no longer requires hospitalisation, there are various possibilities. If the transfer was initially made under s. 48 (that is, the transferee was at the time in prison on remand, or as a 'civil prisoner' or held under immigration laws), the Justice Secretary, on notification that the patient is entitled to either version of discharge, 'shall', by warrant, direct that the patient be returned to prison (usually to face the charges for which the patient had been remanded in custody in the first place), unless the tribunal has also made a recommendation under s. 74(1)(b), in which case the Justice Secretary need not issue the warrant of remittance to prison (s. 74(4)). For s. 48 transferees, then, the only outcome of a successful tribunal application or referral will be either return to prison or continued hospitalisation. In 2010, 499 prisoners were transferred to hospital under s. 48 (Ministry of Justice, 2012: table 6.5), and in the same year, 47 of those in hospital as a result of action taken under s. 48 were returned to prison (Ministry of Justice, 2012: table 6.6). As might be expected, the vast majority of s. 48 transferees, in both directions, are male.

For patients transferred to hospital under s. 47, or detained in a hospital by virtue of a hospital direction and a limitation direction under s. 45A (which takes effect as a transfer direction and restriction direction made under ss. 47 and 49: s. 45B(2)(a), (b)), there are more possibilities open. According to the wording of the MHA 1983, a tribunal must, if the criteria for discharge are met (see 11.5.3) direct the discharge of the patient (with or without conditions), but only if the Justice Secretary agrees, and gives notice to that effect to the tribunal within 90 days of being notified that the grounds for discharge have been made out (s. 74(2)).

In *Benjamin and Wilson* v *UK* (2003) 36 EHRR 1, s. 74(2) was held by the European Court to breach Art. 5(4) of the ECHR because the final decision on discharge is not with the tribunal, in consequence of which s. 74(5A) now provides that, if the operation of s. 74(2), coupled with s.74(1)(b) (i.e. there has been a recommendation that the patient should remain in hospital and that has been accepted), the patient can nonetheless apply to the parole board, which has powers to order release, notwithstanding that the restriction direction or limitation direction remains in force. If the parole board makes an order for release, the restriction direction or limitation will cease to have effect. This is, however, a change in form more than substance. Home Office, and now Ministry of Justice, policy has long been that the Secretary of State will refer the case of an offender-patient, even if sentenced to life imprisonment, who is deemed ready to leave hospital by an tribunal, and who has 'passed tariff' for the offence in question, to the parole board, even if he or she does not agree with the tribunal's decision.

Any discharge under s. 74 will take effect as under s. 73 (s. 74(6); s. 73 is discussed further 11.5.3.1), which means that, on absolute discharge, the patient ceases to be liable to be detained and the orders authorising detention automatically cease (s. 73(3)). Hence, there is a possibility that transferred patients may secure early release from custody via a tribunal, if the Justice Secretary consents. If conditional discharge is ordered, the powers discussed, to defer the discharge, to impose and vary conditions, and to recall the patient to hospital, also apply (s. 74(6)).

If the Justice Secretary does not give the notice mentioned in s. 74(2), the hospital managers are placed by s. 74(3) under a duty to transfer the patient back to prison at the end of the 90-day period. For both s. 47 and s. 48 transferees, transfer and restriction directions cease to have effect on the return of the patient to prison (s. 74(5)). This duty, like that of the Justice Secretary in respect of s. 48 transferees, need not be exercised by hospital managers if the tribunal has recommended, under s. 74(1)(b), that a patient entitled to conditional discharge should nevertheless stay in hospital. A tribunal may feel the need to recommend continued detention in hospital because of the overlap of s. 74 with the powers of the Justice Secretary in s. 50. Section 50 empowers the Justice Secretary, on being notified by the patient's RC, any other AC, or a tribunal, that the patient no longer requires treatment in hospital or that there is no effective treatment that can be given, to direct by warrant that the patient be remitted to prison (s. 50(1)(a)). A tribunal might wish to counsel against this, for the reasons discussed. In *R v Nottinghamshire Healthcare NHS Trust, ex parte M* [2002] EWHC Admin 1400 HC, however, it was held that, although the Justice Secretary must take account of any recent tribunal recommendation, he or she is not bound by it, particularly if there has been a subsequent change in circumstances.

On appeal ([2002] EWCA Civ 1728), the Court of Appeal upheld this decision and further stated that the RC, acting under s. 50, does not need to provide the Justice Secretary with a breakdown of all of the various views of those involved in the treatment or assessment of the patient in hospital (in this case, the RC had not informed the Justice Secretary of the views of two professionals, both of whom were of the opinion, not shared by the RC, that the patient would benefit from continued hospitalisation). Pill LJ, at para. 41, held that the RC's duty is to make 'proper enquiries' of colleagues as to whether continued detention in hospital is appropriate before making a recommendation, the extent of which 'disclosure of information will depend on the circumstances of the particular case and will normally be judged as at the moment of decision'. This is a decision for the RC (paras. 39, 40), because 'It is the judgment of the [RC] which is the central feature of the section 50 procedure' (para. 41). This gives RC's considerable powers to sift information before presenting it to the Justice Secretary.

As far as the duty of the Justice Secretary is concerned, 'There will be cases in which circumstances, including information available to the Secretary of State, either in the documents by which the notification is given, or from other sources, create a duty in the Secretary of State to make further enquiries or take further action or both' (para. 47). This did not support M's argument, that he had a right to make representations to the Justice Secretary, particularly when, as in this case, the bone of contention was the issue of treatability. In such a case, the Justice Secretary is entitled simply to act on the clinical recommendation of the RC.

The court dealt briefly with a claimed breach of Art. 8(1) (para. 49):

> the Convention does not render unlawful that interference with private life which inevitability follows from a lawfully imposed custodial sentence. Transfer from prison to hospital and hospital back to prison, as a part of a high-security custodial regime, cannot in present

circumstances be said to breach the Article notwithstanding the differences in medical treatment which may occur.

It might be argued, however, that the pertinent Article here is Art. 5(4), and that here is another example of the Minister having power of veto over a tribunal such as was found to violate Art. 5(4) in *X* v *UK* and *Benjamin and Wilson*. From another point of view, Art. 5(4) has no application here, either because s. 74(1)(b) provides for a recommendation rather than a decision or because the issue is only where a sentenced prisoner should be detained in his best interests, which does not engage Art. 5 at all because, just as under Art. 8, the issue is not one of freedom or detention but only one of the particular form of detention (*Ashingdane* v *UK* (1985) 7 EHRR 528 and *R* v *MHRT and Secretary of State for Health, ex parte LH* [2001] 1 MHLR 130, HC).

The Justice Secretary is also empowered, by s. 50(1)(b), to 'exercise any power of releasing [the patient] on licence or discharging him under supervision' that would have been available to the Justice Secretary had the patient been remitted to prison. These powers comprise, in brief, release on parole or life licence (in the case of prisoners sentenced to life imprisonment), and are found in the Criminal Justice Act 2003 and Powers of Criminal Courts Act 2000. In addition, the Justice Secretary's general power to discharge, by warrant, a restricted patient from hospital absolutely or conditionally under s. 42(2) applies.

Therefore, when notified that the patient satisfies the criteria for discharge, whether absolute or conditional, the Justice Secretary has a choice: to consent to the discharge of the patient into the community by the tribunal, with such conditions as the tribunal sees fit (although, of course, he or she has powers to vary those conditions); to use his or her own powers of discharge; to remit the patient to prison; to accept the recommendation of the tribunal that the patient should remain in hospital; or, if there has been no recommendation under s. 74(1)(b), to do nothing and effect the transfer to prison by default under s. 74(3). Each case inevitably turns on its own facts, but it is Ministry of Justice policy that, as far as the discharge of life-sentence prisoners is concerned, the powers in s. 50(1)(b) are the preferred option over those in s. 42 (see Gunn, 1993: 331–3), other than in exceptional cases, which means release on life licence rather than conditional discharge. The key difference between the two is that, in the former case, liability to recall subsists for the life of the patient, whereas a conditionally discharged patient may apply from between one and two years after conditional discharge for absolute discharge (s. 75(2)), or be absolutely discharged by operation of law, if the restriction order ceases to have effect and the patient has not been recalled to hospital (s. 42(5)).

The policy was challenged in *R* v *SSHD, ex parte Stroud* (1993) COD 75, which elicited from the Home Office (now Ministry of Justice) the explanation of this preference on grounds of public policy—that persons sentenced to life imprisonment should not be able to circumvent the sentence imposed by resort to the MHA 1983, and that a clear policy allowed consistency of decision-making—decisions being taken by the Home Secretary (now Justice Secretary) on the recommendation of the parole board, and in consultation with the Lord Chief Justice and the trial judge, if available. Evidence given on behalf of the Home Office also emphasised that the Home Secretary would consider the use of s. 42 in circumstances under which, for example, the sentencing court had wished to make a hospital order but there was no hospital bed available, or if there had been evidence, not available to the sentencing court, that the patient had been suffering from a mental disorder at the time the offence was committed (Gunn, 1993: 333). In essence, if the Justice Secretary is content that the patient could have been given a hospital order at the time of sentence, s. 42 powers will be used. The High Court in *Stroud* found the policy of the Home Secretary to be unimpeachable and that decision was upheld in the Court of Appeal. Gunn (1993: 333) has pointed out that, because it is not possible for a court to make a hospital order following a murder conviction, one would presume that the Justice Secretary should consider using s. 42 powers in at least some instances involving persons transferred following such a conviction, given the wide range of situations, of varying moral culpability and of risk to the public, caught by that offence.

As to the choice between s. 74 and s. 50 powers of discharge, although there is no clear data, it seems that s. 74 is more frequently used in tribunal cases. Of *all* of the 461 restricted patients conditionally discharged by either a tribunal or by the Justice Secretary in 2010, 371 were discharged by an tribunal, with 90 conditionally discharged by the Justice Secretary (Ministry of Justice, 2012: table A6.6). The Justice Secretary is these days discharging a significantly higher number of patients subject to conditions than was the case a decade ago: in 2000 only 23 patients were discharged through this route, rising to 44 in 2004, but this is to some extent a function of the increased numbers detained: the total number of discharges in 2000 of all restricted patients was 891, in 2010 it was 1,331 (Ministry of Justice, 2012: table A6.6). The number of persons returned to prison to resume a sentence (that is, s. 47 transferees) is somewhat uneven, but here too, and for much the same reasons, the long term trend is up: there were 100 such transfers in 2000, rising to 171 in 2010 (Ministry of Justice, 2012: table A6.6.). It is not clear whether the transfer back to prison of s. 47 patients is achieved by the use of s. 50 or by the use of the default powers of hospital managers in s. 74(3).

The operation of s. 74 contemplates that the option of returning the offender to prison will always be available. But this will not be the case if the prison sentence to which that patient was sentenced expires while he or she remains in hospital on transfer under s. 47. If so, the restriction direction ends and the patient is treated as though on a hospital order without restrictions (ss. 50(2), (3)). Section 74 will therefore not apply to such patients, and s. 72 will apply without modification.

11.5.2 Patients not subject to restrictions: Criteria for discharge

Section 72(1) lays out two avenues of discharge: the first of these is mandatory discharge; the second is discretionary discharge.

11.5.2.1 Mandatory discharge

For patients detained under s. 2, s. 72(1)(a) contains the criteria for discharge, and provides that 'the tribunal *shall* direct the discharge of a patient' if not satisfied that at least one is met. They are as set in Box 11.3.

Box 11.3

SECTION 2 PATIENTS: CRITERIA FOR DISCHARGE

- that he is then suffering from mental disorder or from mental disorder of a nature or degree which warrants his detention in a hospital for assessment (or for assessment followed by a medical treatment) for at least a limited period; *or*
- that his detention as aforesaid is justified in the interests of his own health or safety or with a view to the protection of other persons.

There does not have to be a quantifiable risk before a tribunal can be satisfied that a patient's continued detention is justifiable on grounds of public protection, as long as it is satisfied that there would be 'a substantial and unacceptable' risk to others if the patient were to be released (*R* v *MHRT, ex parte N* [2001] EWHC Admin 1133 per Gibbs J at para. 54).

However, the burden of proof, as a result of the decision of the Court of Appeal in *R* v *MHRT, North and East London, ex parte H* [2001] EWCA Civ 415 and the *Mental Health Act 1983 (Remedial) Order 2001*, SI 2001/3712 (which reversed the existing situation in which the burden of proof was on the patient), is on those seeking to demonstrate that continued detention is warranted. This was a significant change of policy. In cases such as this one, and *R* v *SSHD and SSH, ex parte IH* [2003] UKHL 59 (see 11.5.3.2), in which a tribunal was not satisfied that a patient was not then suffering from mental disorder, but was also not satisfied that he was then so suffering, this change in policy means the difference between detention and release.

Substantively, the criteria for discharge mirror those for admission in the first place, with the substitution of 'justified' in s. 72(1)(a)(ii) for 'ought to be detained' in s. 2(2)(b), although nothing seems to turn on this, and the addition of the word 'then' to the first, medical, limb of the test. This additional 'then' should not be read absolutely literally. In *North and East London* Lord Phillips, giving the judgment of the court, discussed the case of a schizophrenic patient whose condition is in remission whilst in hospital and in receipt of medication, but about whom there were concerns that, if discharged, would be likely to stop taking the necessary medication and hence become a danger to self or others (*R* v *London South and West Region MHRT, ex parte M* [2000] Lloyds Rep Med 143, QB). He said that Art. 5 does not entail that such a patient must always be discharged; instead, each case must be assessed by weighing the interests of the patient against the public interest (para. 33). And although a patient who is not mentally disordered must be discharged in order to comply with Art. 5(1)(e):

> we do not consider that the Convention restricts the right to detain a patient in hospital…to circumstances where medical treatment is likely to alleviate or prevent a deterioration of the condition. Nor is it necessary under the Convention to demonstrate that such treatment cannot be provided unless the patient is detained in hospital.

It is enough that the patient is mentally disordered and detention is 'a proportionate response' to the presence of mental disorder (para. 33).

For patients detained other than under s. 2, and not subject to restrictions, the criteria for mandatory discharge, as for s. 2 patients, largely echo those that apply to admission for treatment. The tribunal must order the discharge of the patient if not satisfied that at least one of the criteria in Box 11.4 are met.

Box 11.4

PATIENTS OTHER THAN DETAINED UNDER SECTION 2: CRITERIA FOR DISCHARGE

- that he or she is then suffering from mental disorder or from mental disorder to 'a nature or degree which makes it appropriate for him to be liable to be detained in a hospital for medical treatment' (s. 72(1)(b)(i)); *or*

- that detention is necessary on grounds of the health or safety of the patient or the protection of other persons (s. 72(1)(b)(ii)); *or*

- that appropriate medical treatment is available for him (s. 72(1)(b)(iia)); *or*

- if the application is made by a nearest relative following the veto by an RC under s. 25 of an order for discharge made by the NR under s. 23, that the patient would be likely to act in a manner dangerous to others or himself or herself if released (s. 72(1)(b)(iii)).

Again, the word 'then' has been added to the criteria, compared with those in s. 3. The criteria in s. 72(1)(b)(iii) are relevant *only* on an application by a NR in respect of a patient detained under s. 3 (*R (MH)* v *Secretary of State For Health, ex parte W* [2004] All ER Digest 188; *R* v *MHRT, ex parte W* [2004] EWHC 3266 (Admin)).

The courts have interpreted these provisions in the manner that is least favourable to the patient. In *R* v *Mental Health Review Tribunal for the South Thames Region, ex parte Smith* (1998) *The Times*, 9 December (HC), it was held that the phrase 'nature or degree' in s. 72(1)(b)(i) should be read disjunctively, so that a patient who suffers from a mental disorder of a 'nature' that makes it appropriate that he or she be hospitalised need not be discharged, even if not then suffering from that disorder to a 'degree' that makes hospitalisation appropriate. This decision is in line with that of the European Court in *Winterwerp*, which used the phrase 'kind or degree' (para. 39), and chimes also with professional concerns, that a patient exhibiting no symptoms of disorder at the time of a tribunal hearing may soon experience acute symptoms if released from hospital prematurely. The court emphasised that there should be some evidence—prior psychiatric history, for example—upon which to base such a view, and it is, indeed, part of the paradox of hospitalisation that the need for it may only be apparent when the individual concerned is not in hospital.

The latest version of the Code of Practice states that 'Nature refers to the particular mental disorder from which the patient is suffering, its chronicity, its prognosis, and the patient's previous responses to receiving treatment for the disorder. Degree refers to the current manifestation of the patient's disorder' (DH, 2008: para. 4.3). The issue of 'degree' is not problematic, but how does a patient demonstrate his or her suitability for discharge when evidence of past disorder is admissible, and when all that those seeking to prevent discharge need demonstrate is that the disorder is of a nature, but not necessarily to a degree, which warrants hospitalisation? Surely, these words should be read conjunctively, requiring a mental disorder of both a nature *and* a degree warranting hospitalisation if discharge is to be denied? The obvious risk of the decision in *Smith* is that patients who, in fact, are no longer disordered, or not disordered sufficiently, to require hospitalisation will be unable to demonstrate this to the satisfaction of the tribunal.

This is what occurred before a FTT in *CM v Derbyshire Healthcare NHS Foundation Trust* [2011] UKUT 129 (AAC), in which a conditionally discharged restricted patient had been recalled because of concerns about his 'chaotic lifestyle' and illegal drug use, and his case was referred to a tribunal by the Justice Secretary. At that point, CM, who had at all times been a 'model patient' and consented always to the administration of antipsychotic medication, whether or not in hospital, had been free of overt symptoms of psychosis for 10 years. His RC and an independent psychiatrist both accepted that CM was not suffering from his mental disorder to a degree warranting hospitalisation (para. 16). Nonetheless, the RC resisted CM's discharge, and the FTT agreed with the RC. This was because CM's disorder was found to be of a nature justifying continued detention. The RC (but not the independent psychiatrist) was of the view that it would be 'very likely indeed' that if CM was discharged he would revert to his 'dysfunctional and chaotic lifestyle' (para. 18). The FTT accepted this, and that it would lead 'eventually' and perhaps 'within a couple of months' to non-compliance with medication (para. 22), and refused to discharge CM. CM appealed to the UT, which noted that the initial risk was of reversion to CM's former lifestyle, within six months according to the RC, and thereafter, that that lifestyle would lead to CM's relapse, noting wryly that 'This would be a lengthy period in view of the meaning of "nature" [in the Code of Practice]' (para. 23) before overruling the decision of the FTT.

We are pleased that the FTT decision in this case was overruled and specifically for the reason given, which was that 'the tribunal was continuing the appellant's detention for the purposes of addressing his drug taking and chaotic lifestyle' rather than his mental disorder (para. 25). But this does not really address the central objection to the disjunctive reading of 'nature or degree'. On the contrary, it highlights the fact that the 'nature' element is somewhat elastic and in practice permits intervention on the basis of mental health legislation for reasons not directly connected to mental health. The UT emphasised that the appeal was allowed because there was little or no prospect of non-compliance with medication and therefore neither of relapse *'in the near future'* (para. 27, emphasised in original). But it seems to us that if there is such a risk, it would be caught by the 'degree' factor in any case: there should be some sign that the patient's disorder is at or approaching a degree which warrants hospitalisation if such a risk is present. As such, and because the requirement in *Winterwerp* is for unsound mind sufficient to 'justify' detention, and we would argue, as has not been done to date before the European Court, that a test that allows nature 'or' degree permits detention when a person's disorder is of a nature but *not* of a degree to justify compulsory hospitalisation, which is outside of the spirit and the letter of the ECHR. In our, perhaps optimistic, view, the preferable and ECHR-compliant wording must be that the mental disorder in question is of both a nature *and* a degree to warrant detention.

The question of when continued detention becomes inappropriate, and thus in breach of s. 72(1)(b)(i), was considered in *R v MHRT and W, ex parte Epsom and St Helier NHS Trust* [2001] EWHC Admin 101, the court holding first, that there is no automatic right to discharge under s. 72 merely because, as in that case, a patient on leave is not actually receiving medical treatment (para. 46); and second a tribunal must so far as possible look to the future as well as to the past in making its decision. Sullivan J said that 'there will come a time when, even though it is certain that treatment will be required at some stage in the future, the timing of the treatment is so uncertain that it is no longer "appropriate" for the patient to continue to be liable to be detained' (para. 52).

In *MD v Nottinghamshire Health Care NHS Trust* [2010] UKUT 59 (AAC) the question was whether it could be said that 'appropriate medical treatment' was 'available' for MD, a patient diagnosed as having an anti-social personality disorder, as required by s. 72(1)(b)(iia) if the patient is to be detained further in hospital. The treatment in question was said to be the nursing care and 'milieu therapy on the ward' (para. 26). Although there is no doubt that such provision can amount to treatment for the purposes of s. 145 and therefore also 'appropriate treatment' for the purposes, inter alia, of s. 72(1)(b)(iia) (see Chapter 9, 9), it is a question of fact in each case, whether or not it can be said that the treatment provisions in the MHA 1983 are being used appropriately or instead functioning as a cover for what, in reality, is containment. The UT did, however, reject arguments (i) that if the purported treatment in question does not reduce the risk posed by the patient and (ii) that if there is no prospect of the patient 'progressing beyond milieu' (para. 35)—i.e. the 'treatment' will never be successful in the sense that it is no longer required—it cannot be defined as treatment as a matter of law (para. 34). On the facts, a FTT and the UT found that that point had not yet been reached.

For patients subject to a CTO, the criteria for mandatory discharge are found in s. 72(1)(c). Again, they mirror the requirements for the making of a CTO. The tribunal must discharge the patient if not satisfied of one or more of the criteria outlined in Box 11.5.

Box 11.5

CTO PATIENTS: CRITERIA FOR DISCHARGE

- that he or she is then suffering from mental disorder or from mental disorder to 'a nature or degree which makes it appropriate for him to receive medical treatment' (s. 72(1)(c)(i)); *or*

- that detention is necessary on grounds of the health or safety of the patient or the protection of other persons (s. 72(1)(c)(ii)); *or*

- that it is necessary that the RC should retain a power to recall the patient to hospital under s. 17E(1) (s. 72(1)(c)(iii)); *or*

- that appropriate medical treatment is available for the patient (s. 72(1)(c)(iv)); *or*

- if the application is made by a nearest relative following the veto by an RC under s. 25 of an order for discharge made by the NR under s. 23 (which would survive the patient subsequently being placed on a CTO by his or her RC), that the patient would be likely to act in a manner dangerous to others or himself or herself if released (s. 72(1)(c)(v)).

Further provision is made regarding the necessity of retaining the power of recall by s. 72(1A), by virtue of which the tribunal 'shall, in particular, consider, having regard to the patient's history of mental disorder and any other relevant factors, what risk there would be of a deterioration of the patient's condition if he were to continue not to be detained in a hospital (as a result, for example, of his refusing or neglecting to receive the medical treatment he requires for his mental disorder)'. For patients subject to guardianship, the substantive criteria for mandatory discharge are contained in s. 72(4). A tribunal may discharge the patient if he or she is not then suffering from mental disorder (s. 72(4)(a)) or it is not necessary for the welfare of the patient or for the protection of others that the patient should remain under guardianship (s. 72(4)(b)).

11.5.2.2 Discretionary discharge

A tribunal should not turn its mind to the possibility of discretionary discharge until it has considered the case for mandatory discharge and rejected it (*R* v *Mental Health Tribunal for the North Wales Region, ex parte P* (20 May 1990) unreported (DC)). There are no powers of discretionary discharge in respect of restricted patients (s. 72(7); *Grant* v *MHRT* (1986) 26 April 1986 (DC)). As far as unrestricted patients are concerned, s. 72(1) gives tribunals a discretionary power to direct the discharge of the patient 'in any case', and the MHA 2007 (in Sch. 10, para. 2) removed the previously applicable criteria, which required tribunals to 'have regard' to whether continued treatment was likely to be beneficial and, in certain circumstances, whether the patient would be able if discharged to care for himself or herself and guard against serious exploitation. Even before the removal of these criteria, however, it had been held, by Lord Clyde in *Reid* v *Secretary of State for Scotland* [1999] 1 All ER 481 (PC) at 504, that the criteria were not exhaustive and a tribunal can consider any factor that may be relevant to the exercise of its discretion. The discretionary powers are used very rarely, however, and the reason is clear, given that a patient unable to make out his or her case on the basis of the criteria for mandatory discharge is prima facie suitable for continued detention or subjection to a CTO.

11.5.3 Discharge of restricted patients

11.5.3.1 Absolute discharge

Section 72(7) disapplies s. 72(1) to restricted patients, except as provided by ss. 73 and 74. Section 73(1) provides that a tribunal *must*, on the application or referral of a patient subject to a restriction order, direct the absolute discharge of that patient, if not satisfied, both that at least one of the criteria in s. 72(1)(b)(i) *or* (ii) *or* (iia) is met *and* 'the tribunal is satisfied that it is not appropriate for the patient to remain liable to be recalled to hospital for further treatment' (s. 73(1)(b)). In *R* v *MHRT, ex parte Secretary of State* [2001] EWHC Admin 849, the High Court quashed the decision of a tribunal to order the absolute discharge of a patient because the tribunal had failed in its reasons explicitly to explain why it had considered that it was not appropriate for the patient to be liable for recall.

The wording of s. 73(1)(b), which was not changed by the Remedial Order of 2001 (which affected only ss. 72(1)(a), 72(1)(b), and 73(1)(a)) is problematic because it remains for the patient to satisfy the tribunal that liability to recall is not appropriate rather than for those opposing discharge to satisfy the tribunal that it is appropriate. This, in our view, is enough to place s. 73(1)(b) in breach of Arts. 5(1) and 5(4).

If the tribunal reaches the conclusion that one or more of ss. 72(1)(b)(i), (ii) or (iia) is met, but decides that the patient should remain liable to recall, it must direct the conditional discharge of the patient (s. 73(2)) (see further 11.5.3.2). If it is the application of s. 72(1)(b)(i) which justifies the patient's discharge; that is, the tribunal concludes that the patient is no longer mentally disordered (whether or not it also concludes that the patient is not dangerous to self or others or that appropriate treatment is not available), or is not mentally disordered to a nature or degree making continued hospitalisation appropriate, the question arises, whether discharge must be absolute, or might also be conditional, and hence making the patient subject to recall.

This was considered by the Court of Appeal in *R v Merseyside MHRT, ex parte K* [1990] 1 All ER 694 (see also *R v MHRT, ex parte SSHD* (2005) EWHC 2468 (Admin)). Some months after K had been conditionally discharged by a tribunal on the grounds that he was not then suffering from a mental disorder, he was convicted of assault and sentenced to six years' imprisonment. In prison, he applied again to a tribunal, for an absolute discharge under s. 75(2), which provides that a conditionally discharged prisoner may apply for absolute discharge when a year has passed since he or she was conditionally discharged, not having been recalled to hospital, and thereafter once every two years. Again, the tribunal found that K was not suffering from a mental disorder, but refused to lift the conditions.

K sought judicial review of both the initial tribunal decision to discharge him conditionally rather than absolutely, and the later decision not to remove the conditions, arguing that, as no longer mentally disordered, he was not a patient within s. 145 (defined as 'a person suffering or appearing to be suffering from mental disorder'), and was therefore entitled to an absolute discharge. The Court of Appeal evaded the difficult question of how mental health legislation can apply to a person who is not mentally disordered. Sir Denys Buckley decided the case on the basis that there had been no decision open to judicial review taken by the second tribunal because that tribunal had not 'discharged' K: he was already discharged. Butler-Sloss LJ, with whom Kerr LJ concurred, merely stated that a patient who has been made subject to restrictions 'remains a patient until he is discharged absolutely', and justified this by reference to the policies behind the MHA 1983, of 'protection of the public' and 'the hoped for progression to discharge of the treatable patient' (at 699), which, so it was implied, would be upset if a patient were to be entitled to absolute discharge as soon after detention as he or she was judged no longer to be mentally disordered. Richardson (1993: 283) argues that this is a 'strained interpretation' and, had the Court of Appeal taken a more autonomy-centred approach, the outcome in *ex parte K* might have been different.

The interpretation of s. 73(2) seems uncontroversial on its face. This is why, presumably, counsel for K felt compelled to look elsewhere, to s. 145(1), in order to raise doubts about the legality of the decision not to discharge K absolutely. Arguments based on the ECHR were made before the court in the later case brought by the same patient to challenge his recall to hospital (*R v Home Secretary, ex parte K* [1990] 3 All ER 562), but these were neatly side-stepped by holding that the House of Lords' ruling in *R v Secretary of State for the Home Department, ex parte Brind* [1990] 1 All ER 649 prevented it from looking to the ECHR, unless the UK statute were to contain ambiguities (although, as a matter of domestic law, how to characterise the relation between ss. 73 and 145 as other than ambiguous is not, in our view, readily apparent).

Subsequently, the HRA 1998 removed such strategies from the courts, and as discussed further at 11.5.3.2, the main thrust of the European Court decisions in *Winterwerp* and *Johnson* (Chapter 5, 5.1.1 and 11.2.2.2) is that, although a person who is no longer mentally disordered may not be detained, and a conditionally discharged patient who is no longer mentally disordered may not be recalled to hospital, this does not mean that a detained patient found not to be suffering from mental disorder at all, or to a nature or degree requiring hospitalisation, is entitled to immediate release; and conditions may be attached to his or her release, as long as there is not an unreasonable delay in release in order for the arrangements in question to be made. The European Court, then, gives no greater entitlement to absolute discharge to a patient free from mental disorder than was given by the Court of Appeal in *ex parte K*. This is unfortunate: it is obviously true that s. 73 reflects both protectionist and beneficent concerns, but all the indicators in the MHA 1983 are to the effect that these concerns are limited in focus, to persons who *are*, as a point of precedent fact, mentally disordered.

The companion case to *ex parte K* is *R v MHRT, ex parte Cooper* [1990] COD 275 (HC), in which it was held that a patient who was no longer dangerous (if he ever had been) was not entitled to absolute discharge solely by virtue of that fact, because the tribunal was not satisfied that the patient should not remain liable to recall on therapeutic grounds. Rose J, relying on the dicta of Butler-Sloss LJ in *ex parte K*—that the policy behind the MHA 1983 is both protectionist and beneficent—saw no reason to limit the scope of the matters to be considered under s. 73(1)(b), and held that a tribunal had no discretion and must order conditional discharge in such a situation. It must be conceded that this is the most straightforward reading of s. 73(1), as a whole, and of s. 73(1)(b) in particular. In *ex parte K*, however, it was the interests of the general public that had to be balanced against K's interest in being free from liability to recall. Accordingly, *Cooper* is the more paternalistic, and in a sense more problematic, decision.

The compatibility between s. 75(3) and the ECHR was returned to in *RH v South London and Maudsley NHS Foundation Trust, Secretary of State for Justice* [2010] EWCA Civ 1273. Before the Court of Appeal, RH argued that s. 75(3) was in breach of Art. 8 of the ECHR, because it places the burden of proof on the patient to demonstrate that absolute discharge should be ordered. The Court of Appeal agreed that Art. 8(1) was in play, but distinguished the decision in *R v MHRT, North and East London, ex parte H* [2001] EWCA Civ 415, in which it had been held that the provisions of s. 72 which, as originally enacted, required the patient to demonstrate that discharge was appropriate rather than requiring those seeking continued detention to prove that it was warranted, breached Art. 5(1) of the ECHR (see 11.5.2.1).

This was not so much because *ex parte H* concerned Art.5 whereas the instant case concerned Art. 8, but on the basis that a patient who seeks removal of his or her restrictions under s. 75(3) will have entered hospital after being sentenced by a criminal court, in which circumstances 'it is neither unfair, nor in any way disproportionate or unnecessary to require him to satisfy the FTT that the order should cease to have effect: i.e. that it is not appropriate for him to remain liable to be recalled' (para. 28). This reasoning may be doubted. As seen above, the criteria in s. 72(1)(b)(i) and (ii) apply equally to *all* patients, whether detained under civil or criminal law powers, and whether or not subject to restrictions: the decision in *ex p H*, as seen above, necessitated the re-wording of s. 72 *and* s. 73. Of course, the concept of proportionality is sensitive to the factual situation, and it may well be 'fair' not to discharge a patient who has entered hospital through Part III of the MHA 1983 when it would be so to discharge a patient held under Part II: but simply a function of the fact that, as a class, Part II patients are less dangerous than Part III patients, which does not provide any basis for a categorical distinction to be made between them in terms of their entitlement to the protection of Art. 5 (and other Articles too), as was made in this case.

If an absolute discharge is granted, the hospital order, and with it, the restriction order, will cease to have effect (ss. 73(3), 75(3)). Absolute discharges without prior conditional discharge are rare. There were only 7 in 2010, and the number has reach double figures only twice since 2004 (Ministry of Justice, 2012, table A6.6). Most absolute discharges follow a period of conditional discharge: there were 96 such absolute discharges in 2003, 74 per cent of which involved patients conditionally discharged sometime in the previous six years (Home Office Research Development and Statistics Directorate, 2005: Table 16, note 4), and 82, 83 and 85 in 2007, 2008 and 2009 respectively (Ministry of Justice, 2012, table A6.6, fn. 4).

The main reason for this is undoubtedly that tribunals, in common with the Justice Secretary, take a cautious approach to the interpretation of s. 73(1)(b), and do so even in the context of applications under s. 75, from patients already discharged, even though s. 75(3) disapplies ss. 73 and 74, so that, strictly speaking, there are no criteria to be applied when an absolute discharge is sought under that section. In *R v MHRT, ex parte C* [2005] EWHC 17, it was said that the lack of criteria for absolute discharge under s. 75 does not render that section incompatible with Arts. 6 and 8 of the ECHR, because any tribunal that did not exercise its powers in accordance with the criteria in s. 73, along with ss. 37 and 41, would be liable to judicial review (paras. 56–67).

11.5.3.2 Conditional discharge and conditions

If a tribunal is not satisfied that a restricted patient should remain in hospital on an application of the criteria in s. 72(1)(b)(i) and (ii), but is also not satisfied that it is appropriate for the patient to be discharged absolutely, which it is required to consider by s. 73(1)(b), it must direct the patient's conditional discharge (s. 73(2)). A conditionally discharged patient is subject to recall by the Justice Secretary using s. 42(3) (s. 73(4)(a)), and must comply with any conditions that are imposed, either by the tribunal on discharge or at a later date by the Secretary of State, who also has powers to vary any condition, however imposed (s. 73(4)(b), (5)). The statute does not require that conditions always be imposed (s. 73(4)(b)), but in *R v MHRT, ex parte Hall* [2000] 1 WLR 1323 (CA), it was held that a tribunal is under a duty to impose such conditions as it decides are necessary, even if it is apparent that meeting the conditions in question may be difficult.

It has been said, by Lord Bridge in *R v Oxford Regional MHRT, ex parte SSHD* [1988] 1 AC 120 [1987] 3 All ER 8, at 11–12, that a tribunal hearing on application must first decide whether one or both of the criteria for discharge in s. 72(1)(b) are met, and only then turn its mind to the issue of whether discharge should be absolute or conditional. Lord Bridge went on to say that the first question 'would inevitably be coloured' by the practical possibility of imposing suitable conditions. In practice, the meeting of the criteria for discharge is intimately related to the practical possibility of attaching conditions to the order.

The conditions that may be imposed are the same as may be imposed on conditional discharge under s. 42 (see 11.3). In *SSHD v MHRT for Wales; SSHD v MHRT for Merseyside RHA* [1986] 3 All ER 233 (HC), Mann J held that a condition of discharge that the patient remain in a hospital is 'inconsistent with the duty to discharge' (at 238). In that case, however, the tribunal sought to effect the transfer of a patient (which it has no power to order) out of a special hospital by way of discharge into conditions of lesser security. The High Court vetoed this creative use of the legislation. This approach was followed in a similar situation in *MP v Nottinghamshire Healthcare NHS Trust, SSHD, SSH* [2003] EWHC 1782.

On the other hand, in *R v Oxford Regional MHRT, ex parte SSHD* [1988] 1 AC 120, [1987] 3 All ER 8, HL, at 12, Lord Bridge said that a condition that a patient reside in a hostel is perfectly acceptable, and such conditions are often attached to the order for discharge. In *R v MHRT, ex parte SSHD, PH* [2002] EWCA Civ 1868, PH, an elderly and physically unwell patient who suffered from chronic paranoid schizophrenia, was conditionally discharged from Broadmoor hospital after 44 years by a tribunal. This was on condition that he live in specialist and secure (although not locked) accommodation with 24-hour supervision, agree to take medication required by his supervising psychiatrist, and that he should not leave his accommodation unless escorted. The Secretary of State sought judicial review of the conditions, essentially arguing that the tribunal had acted *ultra vires* and in breach of Art. 5(1)(e), because the conditions did not amount to discharge and hence the tribunal's decision was, in effect, a decision for transfer.

The High Court rejected these arguments and the Court of Appeal upheld that decision on the basis, first, that the restrictions imposed did not constitute a deprivation, but merely a restriction, of liberty and secondly, following *HM v Switzerland* (2002) 26 February, unreported, that a restriction of liberty designed in the best interests of the patient did not breach Art. 5(1) (para. 17), and that the Secretary of State had failed to demonstrate that this was not the case here, given that the stated intention of the various measures was to monitor and assist PH's discharge out of concern for his own welfare after so long spent in a special hospital. The court did emphasise that every case must be decided on its own facts, but it did specifically overrule the embargo on discharge to hospital accommodation suggested by Mann J in *Merseyside*. The question, rather, is whether or not there is a deprivation of liberty.

In a later case, in which essentially the same conditions were imposed on the discharge of a patient (*R v MHRT, ex parte Secretary of State* [2004] EWHC 2194) Collins J distinguished *PH*, holding that the conditions were unlawful, amounting to a deprivation of liberty, on the basis that, in *PH*, 'the crucial matter was that the restrictive conditions were imposed for PH's own benefit and not for the protection of others' (para. 11), whereas in the case in front of him, they were imposed to protect third parties. Moreover, the consent of the patient to be bound by the conditions could not make the deprivation of liberty lawful; the question is simply whether, as a question of fact, the conditions amount to a deprivation of liberty within the meaning of Art. 5(1) of the ECHR. If so, there will be a detention for the purposes of domestic law and the tribunal will therefore have acted *ultra vires* (*R v MHRT, ex parte G* [2004] EWHC 2193; *IT v Secretary of State for Justice* [2008] MHLR 290; and *Secretary of State for Justice v RB* [2011] EWCA Civ 1608 (CA)).

The second type of commonly made condition mentioned by Lord Bridge in the *Oxford* case, namely a condition that the patient be 'required to submit to treatment' ([1987] 3 All ER 8, at 12), was further discussed in *R v MHRT, ex parte SH* [2007] EWHC 884 (Admin). SH had been discharged from hospital on condition that he live in a named hostel and that 'the patient shall comply with medication prescribed by [a named doctor] or his successor, which is likely to by depot for several years' ([2007] EWHC 884 (Admin), page 1 of transcript). Some time later, SH applied to a tribunal under s. 75(2), requesting that the condition relating to treatment be varied by the tribunal, as permitted by s. 75(3)(a), so that it would no longer apply. SH had capacity and was fully compliant with his treatment. He wished to be able to demonstrate that he would remain compliant without the condition, in order to begin to construct a case, to be made at a future tribunal hearing, that he should be considered for absolute discharge.

The tribunal did not remove the condition, taking the view that SH did not have full insight into his condition, and SH sought judicial review. In the High Court, Holman J was very clear in his view, that, unless the common law right to refuse treatment is taken away explicitly by statute it must be superimposed on the powers to order compliance with conditions given by s. 73(4)(a). Hence, a condition requiring a conditionally discharged patient to submit to medical treatment 'should clearly be read as importing and subject to the absolute right of [the patient] to choose whether to consent' (page 10 of transcript), and 'This approach no doubt requires that a tribunal should not attach a condition in, or similar to, the terms of [the condition requiring SH to comply with treatment] unless there is a proper basis for anticipating that the patient does, and will, consent to the treatment' (page 10 of transcript).

As SH was always clear that he would consent to the treatment provided, the attachment of the condition, and the form of words used, in this case was 'eminently justifiable' (page 10 of transcript), and either did not engage Art. 8 of the ECHR at all, or, if it did, the Art. 8(2) would apply because of the public interest in SH (who had been convicted of manslaughter and sentenced to hospital under ss. 37 and 41) receiving treatment, coupled with the requirement of a tribunal hearing before imposing such a condition and the availability of judicial review provides sufficient safeguard against the abuse of this power.

The situation would be different if the patient, having capacity, refused to consent. If the intention to refuse medication was made plain before or at the tribunal hearing at which conditional discharge is first under contemplation, the tribunal would be in a difficult position, if one of the two criteria in s. 72(1)(b)(i) and (ii) were met, but the tribunal also considered that the patient should be liable to recall to hospital because, as seen, it would have to order conditional discharge, and it seems, following *SH*, 'should not' attach a condition of obligatory submission to treatment in such circumstances. If the refusal came at a later point, after conditional discharge had begun, as in *SH*, it would not be possible to continue treatment beyond that point, nor is refusal of treatment of itself sufficient to justify recall, which depends, instead, on the criteria for recall being satisfied (see the discussion of s. 42(3) at 11.3).

As already mentioned, conditional discharge can be ordered with no conditions attached, and there would seem to be no other option available to a tribunal, if *SH* is correctly decided (which, in our view, it is) in such circumstances. Moreover, if the patient refuses treatment, Art. 8 is clearly engaged if it is given anyway. On this basis Holman J further suggested that if a condition imposing treatment is attached, it should provide clearly on its face that it is 'subject always to his right to give or withhold consent to treatment or medication on any given occasion' (*R v MHRT, ex parte SH* [2007] EWHC 884 (Admin) at page 10 of transcript). This seems to boil down to the fact that a patient has the ability to veto a condition imposing treatment. Given that to refuse treatment in these circumstances is in compliance with and articulates the legal limits placed on conditional discharge, this in itself should not provide a justification to decide against conditional discharge if it would otherwise be granted. The situation would, of course, be different if the patient lacked capacity to consent, if consent was given by some other person or body authorised to give it, such as a donee of a lasting power of attorney, a court-appointed deputy, or the Court of Protection (see Chapter 4, 4.2).

In *R v SSHD and SSH, ex parte IH* [2002] EWCA Civ 646, Lord Phillips MR held that, although it is clear from *Winterwerp* that a patient who is no longer mentally disordered is entitled to discharge, albeit that that may be subject to conditions, the ECHR does not bestow a right to discharge on persons who are mentally disordered but who are, or may be, eligible for release under the domestic scheme by virtue of ss. 72(1)(a)(ii) or (b)(ii), as being no longer sufficiently dangerous that it is necessary he or she remain in hospital. For such individuals, the decision regarding discharge is properly subject to the availability of appropriate provision in the community and considerations of public safety, nor is there any duty on the state to ensure that appropriate community-based facilities exist (paras. 86, 87)—but (at para. 87):

> Available resources may make it possible for essential treatment to be provided to a mental patient in the community in circumstances which will not place in jeopardy either his own

health or safety or the safety of others. In that event it will be a breach of Art. 5(1) to detain the patient in hospital.

A patient who is mentally disordered, who may be released safely using available resources for after-care, must be released, but where there are no such resources available, there is no entitlement to discharge in the first place. In such circumstances, there are no conditions under which discharge would be appropriate, and so treatment in hospital remains appropriate (*R v Ashworth Hospital Authority, ex parte H* [2001] EWHC Admin 901, per Stanley Burnton J at para. 64.)

A conditional discharge may be deferred to allow necessary arrangements to be made to the tribunal's satisfaction (s. 73(7)). This has long between a problematic provision, because the time necessary to make such arrangements can be difficult to predict in advance, and because, before the decision of the House of Lords in *R v SSHD and SSH, ex parte IH* [2003] UKHL 59, in which the court (para. 27) set aside its earlier decision on this point in the *Oxford* case, it was not possible for a tribunal to revisit a decision if the conditions of its implementation proved impossible. In *ex parte IH*, a tribunal attached conditions to the discharge of IH, having decided that although he remained mentally disordered, his mental disorder was not such as to warrant hospitalisation. The conditions were that he reside in suitable hostel accommodation, under the supervision and direction of a named social worker and a named forensic psychiatrist. Unfortunately, the conditions could not be met despite repeated attempts by those responsible for IH's after-care to comply. The consequence was that IH was still in hospital 31 months after his initial hearing (which was adjourned to investigate the possibility of the conditions being met) and 21 months after discharge had been ordered.

IH sought a declaration of incompatibility between ss. 73(2) and/or (7) of the MHA 1983 and Art. 5(1)(e) and 5(4) of the ECHR, in relation to the period from the initial decision to conditionally discharge until the later tribunal decided that he should be detained. Lord Bingham, giving the only opinion, held that there was no breach of Art. 5(1)(e) in such circumstances. The case should be contrasted with *Johnson v UK* (1997) 27 EHRR 296: 'There is a categorical difference, not a difference of degree' between the two cases. In *Johnson*, the patient was found not to be suffering from mental disorder, in which case, 'the alternative, if those conditions proved impossible to meet, was not continued detention but discharge, either absolutely or subject only to a condition of liability to recall' (para. 28). In *IH*, by contrast, 'there was never a medical consensus, nor did the tribunal find, that the *Winterwerp* criteria were not satisfied...the alternative...was not discharge...but continued detention' (para. 28).

Fennell (2005: 98), discussing this case, argued that, because there is rarely a clear statement that a patient is 'cured' of his or her mental disorder, 'the effect of the ruling is to limit significantly the impact of *Johnson*, and the extent to which Article 5 is capable of imposing positive duties on state authorities to provide after-care to facilitate discharge'. Perhaps the ruling is not as narrow as Fennell suggests, however: although the patient in *Johnson* was found, in fact, not to be suffering from mental disorder, there is reason to think that the crucial distinction is not between those who are not mentally disordered and those who are, or who may be. As can be seen, Lord Bingham's point about *Johnson* was that it involved a patient in respect of whom 'the *Winterwerp* criteria were not satisfied'. These criteria do not distinguish the mentally disordered from those who are not, but rather those who do not require hospitalisation for mental disorder from those who do. There must be a mental disorder, which is persisting at the relevant time (these are the first and third criteria respectively), and—the second criterion— 'the mental disorder must be of a kind or degree warranting compulsory confinement' (*Winterwerp*, para. 39). In *R v Doncaster MBC, ex parte W* [2004] EWCA Civ 378, [2004] 1 MHLR 201, Scott Baker LJ held at para. 39, having referred to the speech of Lord Bingham and that of Lord Phillips in the Court of Appeal, that this is the 'fundamental distinction', in which case the *Johnson* category is broader than Fennell suggests.

On the other hand, this seems to mean that the jurisprudence has constructed a very blurred distinction between the two categories. In the Court of Appeal in *ex parte IH*, Buxton LJ (with whom Sedley LJ agreed) said, at para. 42, that when the discharge of a patient not then suffering from mental disorder has had conditions attached, 'the justification for the placing of continued restrictions on the subject relates, and can only relate, to the history of mental illness and, as in *Johnson*, to the prospect of recurrence'. This is clearly correct, and the only way to maintain the distinction between a '*Winterwerp* patient' and a '*Johnson* patient' is to narrow the timeframe, looking only at the present, but not the past or the future. Even then, the question 'is this person mentally disordered such as to justify hospitalisation today?' is by no means always easy to answer.

Be this as it may, when *ex parte IH* reached the House of Lords, Lord Bingham, with the unanimous agreement of the rest of the House, disapproved the approach of Buxton and Sedley LJJ (at para. 28). For him, as seen, there is a 'categorical' difference between the two types of case. In *Doncaster*, Mance LJ held at para. 72 that the test is whether or not 'expected treatment... [is] an essential pre-requisite of discharge from detention'. But, at the margins, the distinction between a patient who is not sufficiently disordered as to necessitate hospitalisation and one who is—both of whom require conditions to be attached to their discharge and to remain liable to recall—can, and will, be hard to detect. And this allows doctors, tribunals, and the courts to hold that a person who does not appear to be mentally ill only appears so because his or her illness is in remission, thus satisfying the *Winterwerp* criteria, as was the case in *Doncaster*, for example. This may be correct as a matter of fact in that case, indeed in many, but it will not always be so, and the risk of detention being wrongly warranted by the law is a real one.

The second key element of Lord Bingham's opinion in *ex parte IH* was his finding that there is 'in principle' no incompatibility between the MHA 1983 and the ECHR on the basis that the tribunal did not have the powers essential to being classified as a court, because (para. 26): 'What Article 5(1)(e) and 5(4) require is that the person of unsound mind compulsorily detained in hospital should have access to a court with power to decide whether the detention is lawful and, if not, order his release. This power, the tribunal had.' A breach of Art. 5(4) was found, however, on the basis that, because of the ruling in the *Oxford* case, the tribunal, having made an order for discharge, was precluded from reconsidering it (para. 27). The Court of Appeal had reached the same conclusion (EWCA Civ 646 at para. 71), and Lord Bingham endorsed the substance of the Court of Appeal's judgment. Hence, the situation now, after an order for deferred conditional discharge has been made, is that the tribunal can, and should, monitor the situation, and if there are problems implementing the conditions within a reasonable period of time, the tribunal should consider whether it should:

- further adjourn in order to seek a resolution of the difficulties;
- amend or vary the conditions;
- order a conditional discharge but with no specific conditions, which nevertheless renders the patient liable to recall by the Justice Secretary if there are problems following discharge: ss. 73(4)(a), 42(3);
- order that the patient continue to be detained in hospital.

Because it was possible to read the MHA 1983 in a manner compatible with these requirements, the court did not make a declaration of incompatibility.

In *Kolanis* v *UK* (2006) 42 EHRR 12, in a very similar fact situation, the European Court, in turn, endorsed the approach taken by the Court of Appeal and House of Lords in *IH*: first, it endorsed the distinction between the situations of a patient found not to be suffering from mental disorder sufficient to necessitate hospitalisation and one who is (para. 69); second, an order for conditional discharge is not necessarily a finding that the patient is no longer mentally disordered, and if the conditions cannot be fulfilled, continued detention does not breach Art. 5(1)(e) per se (para. 70), and in such circumstances there can be 'no question of interpreting Art. 5(1)(e) as requiring the applicant's discharge without the conditions necessary for protecting herself and the public' (para. 71). Third, the absence of a mechanism by which K could exercise her right to challenge her continued detention after conditional discharge had been ordered (a period of a little over a year in this case) did amount to a breach of Art. 5(4) (para. 82), but the Court also seemed to accept that the decision in *IH* had put right any potential future breach of Art. 5(4) (see para. 81). Nonetheless, the law, as it now stands, does not empower tribunals to require compliance with the conditions they impose on discharge, and the practical effect of disagreement between a tribunal and those responsible for making the necessary arrangements will, in most cases, be, as Lord Phillips noted in the Court of Appeal (para. 96), that, after *ex parte IH* as before it, the patient remains in hospital.

Finally, note that although there is a different range of options in respect of patients subject to a limitation direction or a restriction direction (see 11.4.2.1.3), the criteria in s. 73 apply to such patients as they do to patients subject to a restriction order (s. 74(1)(a)).

11.6 Tribunal and decisions

A tribunal need only reach a majority decision (*First-tier Tribunal and Upper Tribunal (Composition of Tribunal) Order 2008*: para. 8). The average tribunal hearing lasts for

100 minutes (MHAC, 2005: para. 4.117), at the end of which the tribunal may, but not must, give a decision orally (SI 2008/2699, r. 41(1)). The CQC and AJTC (2011: 24) in their research found that 'nearly all' hearings concluded with a decision being given in this way, confirming the earlier research of Perkins (2000: 3), that most decisions are made and recorded within 15 minutes of its ending.

The tribunal must in any case provide to each party written reasons for its decisions 'as soon as reasonably practicable' after the hearing, if that amounts to a final disposal of the case (which includes cases in which the tribunal makes a recommendation: r. 42), together with notification of any right of appeal and the time limits in which that must be pursued (r. 41(2)), and must do so within three working days for s. 2 patients and within seven days (not working days) in other cases (r. 41(3)). If the hearing did not lead to a final disposal, there is a discretion to give reasons (r. 41(4)). It is preferable as a matter of policy and for the better comprehension of all parties but in particular the patient, that reasons for an adjournment, for example, should be given.

As with disclosure of documents before a hearing, there is a discretion given to tribunals to decline to disclose full reasons to the patient, and to impose a duty of confidence on other recipients, such as the authorised representative, if there is thought to be a risk to the health or welfare of the patient or others (r. 41(2)(a)). There is an obvious risk that r. 41(2)(a) may be used, in effect, to deprive the patient of his or her right, not only to know the reasons for the decision, but to challenge that decision. Clearly, this is another reason why the appointment of a lawyer (or doctor) as representative is advisable.

Decisions should in their substance address the statutory criteria which apply, although it has been said that 'The Tribunal's reasons must be read as a whole, in a common sense way, not as a legal treatise' (per Sullivan J in *Epsom and St Helier*, at para. 49), and that brevity is acceptable, if the reasons given are clear and reasonable (*R v MHRT, ex parte Mersey Care NHS Trust* [2003] EWHC 1182). An FTT decision that fails to address a relevant statutory factor may be appealed, with permission, to the UT if it raises a point of law, or if not, may be quashed by the UT, using its powers of judicial review. If the decision is that of the UT, it may (in certain circumstances: see below), be the subject of a judicial review application to the High Court (*R v MHRT, ex parte Secretary of State* [2001] EWHC Admin 849, see 11.5.3.1).

A trilogy of cases in the mid-1980s established that a tribunal must do more than simply state that the statutory grounds are met or not met, as was the case in *Bone v MHRT* [1985] 3 All ER 330 (DC). Nolan J referred to a line of case law that showed that 'proper, adequate, reasons must be given' (per Megaw J in *Re Poyser and Mills Arbitration* [1963] 1 All ER 612 (HC) at 616), which are sufficient to 'enable [the parties to the hearing] to know that the tribunal has made no error of law' (per Donaldson P in *Alexander Machinery (Dudley Ltd) v Crabtree* [1974] ICR 120 at 122), holding that merely to rehearse the words of the statute is insufficient. In *R v MHRT, ex parte Clatworthy* [1985] 3 All ER 699 (HC), a tribunal decided not to discharge a patient detained under a hospital order on the grounds that the applicant suffered from 'post-schizophrenic personality disorder'. Although this was contrary to the opinions given to the tribunal by the patient's RC and another doctor, the reasons given did not explain why the tribunal had come to a different clinical view. Mann J quashed the tribunal's decision because the reasons given were 'a bare traverse' of the statutory criteria that 'do not enable one to see why the contentions of [the two doctors] were not accepted' (at 703).

In the third of these cases, *R v MHRT, ex parte Pickering* [1986] 1 All ER 99, a restriction-order patient was not discharged by a tribunal which, by way of giving reasons for that decision, stated that its members were unanimously of the view that the conditions in s. 72(1) were not met; it had noted the 'unhappy history' of the applicant, which included a number of convictions for sexual offences and one for manslaughter, associated with the use of alcohol and considered that the patient might experience stress if released into the community. Forbes J was 'wholly unable to detect' (at 104), from this, which element of which ground in s. 72(1)(b) the tribunal had in mind when refusing the application. Forbes J held that it was 'essential' that the tribunal bear in mind the distinction between the two elements in s. 72(1)(b), that is, the 'diagnostic question' and the 'policy question' (to which should now be added the 'availability of treatment' question), and although the decision of a tribunal does not have to be read 'in the air', but need only be comprehensible to those who know what the issues before the tribunal are (at 102), it was not so in this case. The tribunal must also show that it has grappled with the important issues (at 102; see also *R v North East London Regional MHRT, ex parte T* [2000] CLY 4173 (HC); *R v MHRT, ex parte SSHD* [2003] EWHC 2864 and *R v Ashworth Hospital Authority, ex parte H* [2002] EWCA Civ 923, [2003] 1 WLR 127).

The UT allowed an appeal in *AC, Partnerships in Care Ltd v SSJ* [2012] UKUT 450 (AAC), a case in which the FTT had preferred the evidence of the patient's RC (resisting conditional discharge of a patient detained in hospital under ss. 47 and 49 of the MHA 1983) over that of another psychiatrist (who favoured discharge) on the basis that the RC was more intimately acquainted with the patient's condition. This, said Jacobs J (para. 11) in the UT 'is not of itself a reason for preferring evidence'. On the other hand, if the reasoning of the FTT is clear, and it simply did not agree with the psychiatric evidence, the decision will be allowed to stand (*RH v South London and Maudsley NHS Foundation Trust, Secretary of State for Justice* [2010] EWCA Civ 1273, para. 31). The more surprising the decision adopted by the tribunal, the greater the necessity to explain that decision (*R v MHRT, ex parte East London and City Mental Health NHS Trust* [2005] EWHC 2329 and *R v MHRT, ex parte Li* [2004] EWHC 51 (Admin)).

11.7 Challenging tribunal decisions

11.7.1 Challenges by patients

Most patients do not get the desired result from their tribunal hearing. In 2011–12, of the 5,145 hearings involving s. 2 patients, 603 led to discharge; for other non-restricted patients 8,391 hearings led to 368 orders for discharge and for restricted patients, 2,512 hearings resulted in 773 orders for absolute discharge and 306 for conditional discharge (CQC, 2013: 17 and table 3). For CTO patients, 3,272 hearings resulted in a mere 161 orders for discharge (CQC, 2013: 82 and table 7). Singh and Moncrieff (2009: 16), analysing the results over a ten year period (1997–2007) in one hospital, found that although the number of applications to a tribunal rose from 34 per cent of all patients admitted at the start of the period to 81 per cent by its end, the overall 'success rate' was constant at 12 per cent. This, they suggested, given the backdrop of year-on-year rises in the number of admissions to hospital, indicates that it is easier to detain a patient than formerly, and that tribunals have toughened their approach to granting discharge, which in the opinion of the MHAC, although 'an alarming suggestion' was one 'deserving attention' (MHAC, 2009: 125). In any case, it is not surprising that many patients seek to challenge the decision of a FTT, not to order discharge in their case.

The mechanisms for doing so, at least in the context of mental health law, were significantly altered by the introduction of the two-tier tribunal system by the TCEA 2007, the intention being that the vast majority of disputed FTT decisions should be dealt with by the FTT itself or the UT, rather than involving the courts, and that relatively informal methods of resolving disputes should be used where possible. As discussed further in this section, it is possible to appeal a decision of the FTT to the UT (TCEA 2007, s. 11) and from the UT to the Court of Appeal (TCEA 2007, s. 13), but this will often not be necessary because both the FTT and the UT are given powers to review their own decision.

As far as the FTT is concerned, s. 9(1) of the TCEA 2007 gives the FTT the power to review its own decisions (but only on one occasion: s. 9(10)), either of its own motion (s. 9(2)(a)) or on request from a person entitled by s. 11(1) to appeal against a FTT decision (see the discussion in this section). Following a review, the FTT can correct accidental errors in the decision or in a record of the decision (s. 9(4)(a)); amend the reasons given for its earlier decision (s. 9(4)(b)); or set its original decision aside (s. 9(4)(c)). To set aside an earlier decision, the FTT must be of the view that it is in the interests of justice to do so (SI 2008/2699, r. 45(1)(a)) and rest this view on the fact that there has been some procedural irregularity, including the failure of a party to send or receive a document, or because a party or their representative was not present at the hearings (SI 2008/2699, r. 45(1)(a), (2)). An application to have a decision set aside for one of these reasons must be made within 28 days of that party receiving notification of the tribunal's decision (r. 45(3)).

If an FTT does set aside an earlier decision, it must either make a fresh decision itself (TCEA 2007, s. 9(5)(a)) or refer the case to the UT (s. 9(5)(b)), which must then re-decide the matter referred to it, for the purposes of which it can make any decision which the FTT could make if it were re-deciding the matter itself (TCEA 2007, s. 9(6)–(7)). Section 10 of the TCEA 2007 gives the UT a similar power to that of the FTT to review its own decisions, and to take similar actions following a review.

If a review by an FTT or UT does not resolve the issue to the satisfaction of the aggrieved party, there is the possibility of an appeal but only on a point of law. Permission to appeal must be sought, in writing and within 28 days of that party receiving notification of the decision to be appealed (SI 2008/2699. r. 46(1), (2)) from the FTT or the UT for an appeal to the UT (TCEA 2007, s. 11(4)) or from the UT or Court of Appeal for an appeal to the Court of Appeal: (s. 13(4)) and permission should not be sought from the Court of Appeal unless it has been first refused by the UT (s. 13(5)). The application for permission must identify the alleged error of law and state the result the would-be appellant hopes to achieve (SI 2008/2699, r. 46(5)).

There can be no appeal in respect of an 'excluded decision' of the FTT or UT, as the case may be, defined by ss. 11(1) and 13(1). Section 11(5) lists excluded decisions, the most relevant of which, in s. 11(5)(d), provides that there can be no appeal against a decision of the FTT under s. 9, to review, or not to review, an earlier decision of the tribunal; or to take no action, or not to take any particular action, in the light of a review of an earlier decision of the tribunal; or set aside an earlier decision of the tribunal, or to refer, or not to refer, a matter to the UT. This latter applies even if the initial decision is set aside after the appeal to the UT has begun (s.11(5)(e)). For appeals from the UT to the Court of Appeal, s. 13(6) gives the Lord Chancellor power to make provision that permission to appeal should only be granted if the case either an important point of principle or practice, or there is some other compelling reason to allow the appeal to proceed, and provision to this effect has been made (*The Appeals from the Upper Tribunal to the Court of Appeal Order 2008*, SI 2008/2843). Even if one or the other, or both, of these requirements is met, the UT should be careful only to allow the appeal to proceed on the grounds which raise that issue or those issues, and not on any other (*RH v South London and Maudsley NHS Foundation Trust, Secretary of State for Justice* [2010] EWCA Civ 1273).

If there is an appeal from the FTT, the UT may (but not must), if it finds that the FTT decision involves an error of law, set aside the FTT decision and send the case back, with directions, to the FTT to be re-decided (s. 12(2)(a)), and specify that it should be constituted by tribunal members other than those who made the original decision (s. 12(3)(a)) or decide the case itself (s. 12(2)(b), (4)). The Court of Appeal has similar powers if it concludes that the UT fell into error of law (TCEA 2007, s. 14). Before giving permission to appeal, the tribunal receiving the application must first consider whether it is preferable instead to review the earlier decision (SI 2008/2699, r. 47(1)), giving due consideration to the overriding objective, to deal with cases fairly and justly, avoid unnecessary formality and avoid delay (SI 2008/2699, rr. 47(1), 47(2), 2(1), 2(2)).

In addition, and another innovation introduced by the TCEA 2007, the UT also has a 'judicial review' jurisdiction in respect of decisions of the FTT, allowing it to make any order that the High Court could make when hearing a judicial review application (a mandatory order, a prohibiting order, a quashing order, a declaration,or an injunction: TCEA 2007, ss. 15(1), 17, in the exercise of which it must apply the same principles that would apply in the High Court (ss. 15(4), (5)), and the UT also has the same powers to grant relief, enforceable in the same way, as the High Court (s.15(3)).

The judicial review powers given to the UT by s. 15 may only be exercised if four conditions, found in s. 18, are met, or the UT is authorised to proceed even though not all of them are met (s. 15(2)). The conditions are: (1) that the application asks for nothing more than relief under s. 15 or for permission to apply for such relief, or damages (available under s. 16(6)), interest or costs (s. 18(4)), in other words, the application does not ask for anything other than relief which the UT is able to provide; (2) that the application does not call into question anything done by the Crown Court (s. 18(5)) because 'it would be anomalous to give a tribunal, a superior court of record, supervisory powers over another superior court of record' (TCEA 2007, explanatory notes, para. 132); (3) that the application is within a class specified for this purpose in a direction given in accordance with Part 1 of Schedule 2 to the Constitutional Reform Act 2005 (s. 18(6)) which has been made (see *Practice Direction (Upper Tribunal: Judicial Review Jurisdiction* [2009] 1 WLR 327) and which provides that there may only be an application to the UT to subject an FTT decision to judicial review powers if there is no right of appeal to the UT (see also s. 31A of the Senior Courts Act 1981, which deals with the transfer of cases as between the High Court and the UT); and (4) that the presiding judge is a High Court or Court of Appeal judge (s. 18(8)). If these conditions are met, the UT must decide the substantive application, but if they are not it must transfer the case to the High Court (ss. 18(2), (3)). It was held in *KF* v *Birmingham and Solihull Mental Health Foundation Trust* [2011] UKUT 185 that the UT's judicial review powers did extend to the substantive decisions of FTTs.

The second of these conditions hinted at a problem that subsequently had to be resolved by the Supreme Court, in *R* v *UT, ex parte Rex Cart* [2011] UKSC 28; [2012] 1 AC 663. The issue was whether those decisions of the UT which are not appealable under s. 13 of the TCEA 2007 are open to judicial review in the High Court. The argument against this starts from the observation that the UT is a superior court of record (TCEA 2007, s. 3(5)), and s. 25 of the TCEA 2007 gives the UT 'the same powers, rights and privileges and authority as the High Court'. As a superior court of record, and as a court of the same standing as the High Court, it was not clear if this meant that the UT was outwith the High Court's powers of judicial review.

The Supreme Court held that it was not, but that the High Court's jurisdiction should apply only on limited grounds, which sought, on the one hand, to preserve the integrity and authority of the post-2007 tribunal structure but which, on the other hand, would not do so to the extent that errors of law made by the UT were incapable of being challenged in situations where the UT refused permission to appeal. What was need, according to Lord Dyson, was a mechanism to ensure that 'errors on important points of principle or practice do not become fossilised within the UT system' (para. 130). The Supreme Court held that judicial review should therefore be allowed, but only in the same circumstances that, if permission was granted, a second appeal would be allowed on a point of law, i.e. that it involves an important point of principle or practice or there is some other compelling reason to hear the appeal (Lord Dyson at para. 130, Baroness Hale at para. 57). This is an important decision which preserves the ability of the High Court to review decisions taken by the UT.

11.7.2 Challenges by RCs

An RC, or the detaining hospital, might not agree with a tribunal decision to discharge a patient. As with the patient, an RC, the detaining hospital, and any other party to the

FTT proceedings may seek a review of that decision or permission to appeal against it (TCEA 2007, ss. 9(2), 10(2), 11(2), 13(2)), but RCs have fashioned—and, in *R* v *South Western Hospital Managers, ex parte M* [1994] 1 All ER 161 (HC), the court accepted—an alternative strategy for undermining a tribunal decision, which is simply to readmit the patient: in this case, the patient, discharged from detention under s. 2 by a tribunal, had not left hospital before she was detained under s. 3 at the instigation of her RC.

It should be noted that, after such a readmission, it is again open to a patient to apply for discharge and for a tribunal to order it. In this sense, *ex parte M* built the 'revolving door' into the scheme of the MHA 1983. In addition, it can be argued that, in such a situation, the requirement of Art. 5(4), that the legality of detention should be 'decided speedily by a court' with, as was held in *X* v *UK* (1981) 4 EHRR 181, the power to order discharge, is also undermined by the approach taken that case. In the first edition of this book, we argued that there is a good case for the view that a 'new fact' rule, which functions in many other common law jurisdictions, and holds that a prior decision may not be departed from unless justified by the existence of some new fact, should be introduced in the UK.

The House of Lords confronted these arguments in *R* v *East London and the City Mental Health NHS Trust, ex parte Von Brandenburg* [2004] 2 AC 280, [2003] UKHL 58, [2004] 1 All ER 400, [2003] 3 WLR 1265. A tribunal ordered that a mentally ill patient, B, held under s. 2, be discharged, deferred for seven days so that arrangements could be made for B's after-care. On the sixth day, B's RC arranged for his admission under s. 3. As in *ex parte M*, B was readmitted before he had left the hospital. He sought judicial review of the decision to readmit, and, when that application was dismissed, B appealed.

The House of Lords, in the form of Lord Bingham, held that B's readmission was lawful on the facts: B had assured the tribunal that he would continue to take his medication following discharge, but had, in fact, declined to do so, with the consequence that 'his condition significantly deteriorated' (para. 13). This part of the judgment is not controversial and was applied, after the decision of the Court of Appeal in *Von Brandenburg* ([2001] EWCA Civ 239; [2002] QB 235; [2001] 3 WLR 588) which was similar in essence to that of the House of Lords, by the High Court in *R* v *Oxfordshire Mental Healthcare NHS Trust, ex parte H* [2002] EWHC 465. But both the Court of Appeal and House of Lords moved significantly in the direction of a new fact rule. In the Court of Appeal, Sedley LJ disapproved the view of Laws J in *ex parte M* that an AMHP is not fettered in any way by an earlier tribunal decision (para. 38). In the House of Lords, Lord Bingham held (para. 8) that:

> The regime prescribed by Part V of the 1983 Act would plainly be stultified if proper effect were not given to tribunal decisions for what they decide, so long as they remain in force, by those making application for the admission of a patient under the Act. It is not therefore open to the nearest relative of a patient or an ASW [now AMHP] to apply for the admission of the patient, even with the support of the required medical recommendations, simply because he or she or they disagree with a tribunal's decision to discharge. That would make a mockery of the decision.

He then laid out (at para. 10) something that looks very much like a new fact rule:

> An ASW may not lawfully apply for the admission of a patient whose discharge has been ordered by the decision of a mental health review tribunal of which the ASW is aware unless the ASW has formed the reasonable and bona fide opinion that he has information not known to the tribunal which puts a significantly different complexion on the case as compared with that which was before the tribunal.

Lord Bingham provided 'by way of illustration only' three examples: an AMHP learns of an earlier suicide attempt, unknown at the time of the tribunal, which invalidates an assessment that the patient does not present a serious risk of self-harm; a patient gives assurances that he or she will continue to take medication and then does not, creating a risk to self or others not apparent at the time of the tribunal hearing; or there is a significant deterioration in the patient's condition after a tribunal has ordered discharge (para. 10). In the absence of information not known to the tribunal, then, any application for readmission will be unlawful.

As for the particular duties of the various actors involved, Lord Bingham emphasised that doctors are required only to express a professional opinion, and so any such rule would not, in any case, be relevant. As for AMHPs, ordinarily, in the exercise of his or her duties under s. 13, which requires that the AMHP to be 'satisfied that such an application [for admission to hospital] ought to be made', the AMHP will be or become aware of any relevant tribunal decision. In the Court of Appeal, Sedley LJ perhaps went furthest in the direction of a new fact rule, holding that 'A recent – and often not so recent – order of a tribunal for discharge will always be a relevant fact…it is the duty of the subsequent decision-maker to take it into account; a failure to do so, albeit through ignorance, will vitiate a subsequent decision to seek admission' (para. 41). Lord Bingham 'could not accept' this, however (para. 11): for him, 'if, despite performing these statutory duties in a reasonable way, [the AMHP] does not learn of a tribunal decision, I can see no ground for implying a more far-reaching duty of inquiry not expressed in the statute' (para. 11).

He did accept that where there is a decision to make an application for admission following a tribunal decision to discharge, an AMHP is under a duty to explain to the patient why the tribunal decision will not protect him or her from readmission, but that duty 'must however be limited' and may require an explanation 'in very general terms'. An AMHP cannot be required to make a 'potentially harmful disclosure' to the patient, as, for example, when the AMHP's decision to seek readmission is based on information supplied by relatives of the patient or the patient's doctor, in circumstances under which disclosure would risk undermining a 'continuing and trusting relationship' (para. 12).

Be that as it may, the import of this case is, to some extent, opaque. Both the Court of Appeal (Lord Phillips at para. 30) and House of Lords (Lord Bingham at para. 12) did not accept that the effect of their decisions is that a new fact rule now operates in England and Wales. Both courts attempted to ensure both that AMHPs and RCs are free to act according to their own judgment about the need for admission, and that does not entail a breach of Art. 5(4) of the ECHR, by emphasising that, in cases of disagreement, the tribunal prevails (Lord Phillips in the Court of Appeal at para. 31, cited in the opinion of Lord Bingham in the House of Lords at para. 5). In consequence, the courts end up attempting to articulate a very fine distinction. Sedley, LJ, having explained that, 'while not legally bound in the absence of a change of circumstances by a recent MHRT decision in favour of discharge, those concerned in a s. 3 application cannot lawfully ignore it' (para. 42), noted that 'there may be little practical difference between what [B] has sought [namely to show that a 'new fact' rule exists] and what he has achieved' (para. 39). Certainly, it is debatable whether the average AMHP or mental health professional would feel totally comfortable with this distinction between 'not legally bound' and 'cannot lawfully ignore'.

The Court of Appeal followed its own ruling in *Von Brandenburg* in the later case of *R v Ashworth Hospital Authority, ex parte H* [2002] EWCA Civ 923, [2003] 1 WLR 127 (see also *R v Finnegan and DE, ex parte Wirral Health Authority* [2001] EWCA Civ 1901). In *ex parte H*, a tribunal had made what was later held to be an irrational, and hence unlawful, decision to order the immediate discharge of H. In response, the hospital had begun judicial review proceedings against the tribunal and had re-sectioned H. The High Court held that, if a hospital has substantial grounds for thinking that a tribunal has erred in law, *Von Brandenburg* is distinguishable. This view was rejected by the Court of Appeal (per Dyson LJ at para. 56):

> To countenance such a course as lawful would be to permit the professionals and their legal advisers to determine whether a decision by a court to discharge a detained person should have effect. I cannot think that this is consonant with Article 5.4.

Dyson LJ, in reaching this decision, based his view on a reading of *Von Brandenburg* in which he seems to view that case as though it has introduced a 'new fact' rule. He summed up the *ratio* of that case as follows (at para. 56):

> In the absence of material circumstances of which the tribunal is not aware when it orders discharge, in my judgment it is not open to the professionals, at any rate until and unless the tribunal's decision has been quashed by a court, to resection a patient.

In the light of this, our view is that, matters of legal semantics aside, a new fact rule does now operate in England and Wales. This is surely the most desirable reading of these judgments. And in so far as the ruling in *Von Brandenburg* seems, in theory at least, to leave open the possibility that a discharged patient may be readmitted when there are no new facts justifying that decision (this *must* be the implication of the refusal to recognise the existence of the rule), Dyson LJ's approach is also be to preferred. It is more clearly in line with the requirements of Art. 5(4).

11.8 Concluding comments

This has been a long chapter, and so we shall keep our concluding comments brief. It does seem that the tribunal system is working more effectively than even five years ago, and despite continued reports of delays and last-minute submission of reports by

RCs and hospital managers, recent improvements in this regard have been especially impressive and there is reason to hope that delays will continue to be reduced in the coming years. On the other hand, the current system continues to contain both procedural and substantive provisions—such as rr. 14 and 34 of the Tribunal Rules 2008 in the first case and s. 73(1)(b) of the MHA 1983 in the second—which raise concerns of compliance with the requirements of human rights law.

More generally, the discharge decision, whether taken by an RC, managers' panel, a tribunal, or the Justice Secretary, remains, despite the fairly positive attitude of the UT in *AH* v *West London* (see 11.4.5) towards the public hearing of tribunal applications, relatively invisible. This is of course appropriate in terms of confidentiality, but it is nonetheless problematic in terms of transparency. Such concerns are heightened in cases in which discharge from hospital is subject to conditions imposed on the person discharged, either under the MHA 1983 which amount, in practice, although being defined as a restriction rather than a deprivation of liberty, to continued confinement or, in cases in which the patient lacks capacity, under the DOLS powers, do constitute a deprivation of liberty. Such aspects of discharge cause us to pause and reflect, not for the first time in this book, on the distinction between confinement and being at liberty, between hospital-based and community care, and demonstrate that the distinction can be decidedly problematic, raising again the question of the 'dispersal of discipline' (see Chapter 10, 10.1 and 10.6).

For many patients discharge will come fairly soon after admission, for others discharge will mark the start of a new monitoring regime in the community, but for some patients—those judged unsuitable for discharge by their RC—discharge will be difficult to achieve, or, if it can be achieved, to protect from further action by the RC and other professionals, particularly AMHPs. Despite the (welcome) efforts of the House of Lords in *ex parte IH* (see 11.5.3.2) successfully to salvage the tribunal system for human rights law purposes in situations in which it has proven impossible to comply with conditions imposed on the discharge of a patient, the fact remains that, if the psychiatrists disagree with the tribunal's decision they have an effective power of veto.

Similarly, despite the (equally welcome) efforts of the House in *Von Brandenburg* to comply with the human rights law prohibition on arbitrary confinement, the fact remains that an RC determinedly opposed to discharge will often be able to point to some change in circumstance such as to justify re-sectioning, and the requirement that an AMHP in making a further application for admission following discharge by a tribunal act *bona fide* will be met if there is a genuine difference of opinion. In short, as long as discharge decisions remain within a paradigm dominated by considerations of risk determined by psychiatrists—and we do not argue that such a paradigm is necessarily (wholly) inappropriate—the human rights of those seeking discharge will continue to conflict, at this structural, paradigmatic level, with the agendas of those charged to take discharge decisions. In this conflict, law, paradoxically, is part of the problem and also part of the solution.

12

Legal Responses and Advocacy for Clients

12.1 Introduction

> In conclusion, I may say that this seems to me one of the very cases which Parliament had in mind when they said that such an action as this should not be brought without the leave of the court. It is an unfortunate feature of mental illness that those afflicted by it do not realise the need for their being under the care and control of others. They resent it, much as a small child or a dumb animal resents being given medicine for its own good, and they are apt to turn round and claw and scratch the hand that gives it.
>
> *Richardson* v *London County Council*
> [1957] 1 WLR 751 at pp. 760–1, per Denning LJ

The quotation is shocking to readers at the beginning of the twenty-first century. After 30 years of the politics of disability and patients' rights, Lord Denning's words may sound like reflections of a bygone era; but are they?

As we have seen Chapters 1–11, there is no shortage of law concerning mental disability, contained in the MHA 1983, the MCA 2005, community care legislation and common law. This law is of course relevant only if it contains sufficient substantive bite to create a real standard, and sufficient practical mechanisms in place to ensure that it is followed. The question underlying this chapter is whether the law provides adequate mechanisms for those brought under the mental health system to ensure that they are dealt with consistently with the substantive and procedural rules provided by the law, and whether sufficient recompense is available in the event that the standards are not complied with. In short, can it be said that the law offers a 'level playing field' to people with mental health difficulties?

This returns us to a number of the ongoing themes for this volume. What does 'equal treatment' or 'fairness' mean for people with mental disabilities? If the concern is 'discrimination' on the basis of mental disability, what does that mean? At what point (if any) do the differences that flow from mental disability mean that they must be taken into account by the law, and indeed that it would be discriminatory to fail to account for those differences? And, as always, there is the problem of silence: does the function of the legal system in this area empower people with mental disabilities and encourage

their participation, or is it, like Foucault conceived medicine to be, a language that mar-
ginalises the mad, talking about them rather than involving them?

12.2 Review tribunals

Review tribunals have been discussed at various points in this text (see, primarily,
Chapter 11). The objective here is not to repeat that discussion, but instead to highlight
questions about the limits and efficacy of the tribunal process as a mechanism for mental health service users to seek justice.

   Although review tribunals have substantial powers, their jurisdiction is purely statutory: in matters relating to the MHA 1983, there is no jurisdiction to consider matters
beyond those listed in s. 72. The tribunal system's governing legislation is not geared to
require a patients' rights approach. As discussed in Chapter 6 at 6.3.1, the thresholds for
detention are low and rely on a high degree of discretion by clinical and social services
staff. While tribunals also have a discretion to release patients, even if the confinement
criteria are met (s. 72(1)), this discretion rarely results in an unqualified release. A tribunal can also make recommendations regarding patients, including the grant of a leave
of absence to an unrestricted patient, or the transfer of the patient to another hospital or
into guardianship, or into after care under supervision (s. 72(3)–(3A)), and can further
consider the case in the event that these recommendations are not complied with, but
such recommendations have no formal legal force. Moreover, many issues important to
patients are not within the remit of tribunals. Tribunals have no direct role in adjudicat-
ing whether medical treatment should be enforced, for example, or in considering the
appropriateness of living conditions or administrative restrictions in the facility.

   As we have seen, the success rates before tribunals are limited. Of 16,048 hearings held
in 2011–12, only 773 (4.8 per cent) resulted in an absolute discharge, and an additional
817 (5 per cent) in a conditional, deferred, or delayed discharge (CQC, 2013: table 3).
Such a significant imbalance in outcomes does not necessarily indicate injustice or bias
on the part of tribunals. More than a quarter of people who had applied for a tribunal
in 2011–12 had been released from hospital prior to the hearing, and thus the tribunal
did not proceed. Insofar as it may be assumed that these are people who would have
been successful at the tribunal, it might perhaps be the case that people are generally
being released by responsible clinicians (RCs) when it is suitable to do so. This seems a
particularly coherent speculation given the increasing shortage of beds, and the resulting pressure to find space for incoming patients. Nonetheless, the limited success rates
before the tribunal are notable, and the ethos of the tribunals discussed in Chapter 11
does suggest an approach remarkably sympathetic to the views of the RC.

   The rules governing tribunals do not necessarily work to the benefit of patient rights.
They do contain due process provisions, such as the right to notice (SI 2008/2699, r. 33),
the right to representation (SI 2008/2699, r. 11), and the duty on the tribunal to give
reasons for their decisions (SI 2008/2699, r. 41(2)(b)). Other rules are, at best, problematic. As discussed in Chapter 11 (11.4), rule 34 requires the medical member of

the tribunal to examine the patient prior to the hearing, making that member both witness and judge, raising questions of consistency with Article 5(4) of the ECHR: see *DN* v *Switzerland* (2003) 37 EHRR 21 and Chapter 11. So far, the English courts have not found an ECHR violation on this point: see *R (S)* v *MHRT* (2002) EWHC (Admin) 2522; *R (RD)* v *MHRT* [2007] EWHC 781. The difficulty of the medical member's position is not merely theoretical. In the event that the medical member forms a view as a result of the examination, how is that view to be tested? It is clear that the parties should be informed of any findings from the interview by the medical member and be afforded the opportunity to 'address and comment on' those findings (*R (H)* v *Ashworth Hospital Authority* [2003] 1 WLR 127 (CA), para. 84), but that is not the same as subjecting the views to cross-examination. The government accepted during the process of amending the MHA 1983 that evidence regarding the patient should be provided by independent examiners rather than tribunal members (see Department of Health (DH) and Home Office, 2000: vol. I para. 2.29), but this was not included in the eventual reforms introduced in 2007.

As further discussed in Chapter 11, rule 14 allows the tribunal to prevent disclosure of documents or information to parties (including patients) when disclosure would be likely to cause the individual or another person serious harm, if such non-disclosure is proportionate in the interests of justice. This can therefore drive a wedge between advocate and client. The difficulty was recognised in the Ontario case of *Re Egglestone and Mousseau and Advisory Review Board*, (1983) 42 OR (2d) 268 (at p. 276):

> I would expect that faced with the order made here counsel should obtain the consent of his client to accept the documentary review on this limited basis, otherwise he may not feel at liberty to receive the information at all.

Such instructions in advance cannot be perceived as a solution, however. Either the client refuses the disclosure on this basis, in which case neither advocate nor client will know the information and it is difficult to see how the case can properly be argued; or the client consents, and the advocate will know information which will inform decision-making which the client will not know, furthering the marginalisation and disempowerment of the client. In this latter scenario, the result may be little short of Kafka: the client will be asked for instructions on the conduct of the case, without being able to be told on what basis the instructions are being asked for.

The case law concerning disclosure of potentially sensitive information is mixed. *RM* v *St Andrew's Healthcare* [2010] UKUT 119 (AAC) does create some sort of minimum threshold for disclosure, in situations where ignorance would 'exclude the claimant completely from knowing of the real process that was being followed and allow him to participate only in a pretence of a process' (para. 32). *RM* was an easy case however, in the sense that it did not involve confidentiality rights of third parties. How far it will extend when a privacy interest of a third party exists is less clear. Consider the hypothetical example raised in *Dorset Healthcare NHS Foundation Trust* v *MH* [2009] UKUT 4 (AAC), for example, of family carers who do not wish to take the patient back to live with them but do not wish the patient to be told this, and where in particular their decision flowed from their own health conditions, the details of which of course attract a duty of medical confidentiality. The tribunal notes that 'it is important that all of these rights (i.e., of patient to a fair hearing and of carer to medical confidentiality) are properly considered and maintained' (para. 23). Baroness Hale, speaking *obiter* about such calculations in mental health reviews, notes the need for 'an individualised balancing act carried out after discussion with the patient's own advocate and in the light of the opinions of the patient's own independent medical adviser' (*Secretary of State for the Home Department* v *AF (No 3)* [2009] 3 WLR 74, para. 105). If the refusal of the carers to accept the return of the patient is pivotal to the ongoing detention, however, how is this information less vital than the covert medication in *RM*? If the patient thinks that he or she has a place to go to, and in fact they do not, is this not something that, for the hearing to make sense, they have to be told?

Roberts v *Nottinghamshire Healthcare NHS Trust* [2008] EWHC 1934 (QB) raises the question of access to information outside the context of the review tribunal process. Roberts, an inpatient in a high security facility, sought disclosure of a psychologist's report commissioned by the Trust. There was no active application under s. 72 at that time, and the tribunal therefore rightly concluded it had no jurisdiction to order disclosure. Roberts pursued the matter through a freedom of information request, and was again refused. The High Court upheld this refusal, but rather astonishingly, further refused to provide any substantive reasons for the refusal: its public judgment is entirely about the process, and the substantive reasons for the refusal were kept in a private judgment to be available in the event of an appeal, but not to be seen by Roberts or his solicitors.

Would the response in *Roberts* be different if the request had been in the context of an application to the tribunal under s. 72, and disclosure resisted under rule 14? It is impossible to know, since we do not know the substantive reasons for the refusal in the *Roberts* case. It is however an interesting speculation, since assuming the report was supportive of Roberts' release—a matter implied but never expressly stated in the existing judgment—it would be very helpful to his case for release, written as it was by a professional employed by the detaining institution. While it might or might not be the case that the report would be likely to cause serious harm to the patient or another person, the first requirement of the rule 14 test, that is not in itself determinative. The *Dorset* case makes clear that even in the context of a review tribunal hearing, other interests relating to confidentiality may preclude making the document or information available, when that is consistent with the interests of justice. That said, it is not obvious that the decision in *RM* would stretch so far as to require disclosure, since while the report would be helpful to the patient, it is not obvious that absent disclosure a subsequent hearing would be a mere pretence of process.

12.3 Judicial review

Judicial review, including habeas corpus, might be expected to be a powerful mechanism to challenge decisions made by those implementing mental health services, and certainly there have been some successes in the past.

In principle, habeas corpus will be effective if there is non-compliance with a condition precedent to detention. For example, *Re S-C (Mental Patient: Habeas Corpus)* [1996] QB 599 (CA), involved admission under s. 3 of the MHA 1983, where the approved social worker (now approved mental health professional (AMHP)) consulted with the patient's mother regarding the admission, notwithstanding that she knew that the NR was in fact the patient's father, and that the father objected to the admission (see further Chapter 6, 6.3.2.4). The conditions precedent to the detention had therefore not been complied with, and a writ of habeas corpus issued. Even in this case, however, there was no order for immediate release: the detaining authority was given a week to provide evidence that notwithstanding the failure to comply with the law at the time of the detention, detention could still be justified. A similar delay in permitting enforcement of the writ was provided in *Re Briscoe* [1998] COD 402 (HC). In this way, patients may win in law, but achieve little in practice. The writ did issue immediately in *CX* v *A Local Authority* [2011] EWHC 1918 (Admin), but that was a case where the patient was already on home leave by the time the matter was heard, rendering the whole exercise in the court's view 'symbolic and technical rather than practical and physical' (para. 69).

In any event, the courts have now dissuaded the use of habeas corpus involving judicial review when other legal mechanisms are available, absent circumstances of statutory non-compliance or fraud (see *Barker* v *Barking Havering and Brentwood Community Healthcare NHS Trust* [1999] 1 FLR 106). In practice this would seem to mean that the courts expect most challenges to detention to be brought by way of review tribunal application. This will not suffice entirely however, as the tribunal's role is not to determine whether the initial detention was legal, but whether continued detention is appropriate and legal, that is, they look at the situation on the day of the hearing. If the claim is that the initial detention was illegal, as for example when a s. 3 detention occurs notwithstanding the objection of the nearest relative, habeas corpus remains the appropriate response.

For decisions other than detention, judicial review is in principle available, but as has been seen elsewhere in this book (see, e.g., Chapter 9, 9.5.3 regarding treatment and Chapter 2, 2.5 regarding conditions), applicants have little reason for optimism that they will be successful. The *Wilkinson* decision offered an initial indication that meaningful review of compulsory treatment might be available, but in the subsequent jurisprudence, the patient applicants have been successful in all cases, both at trial, and, where there was an appeal, on appeal. As noted elsewhere, the courts have in this litigation routinely adopted the views of the treating physician, and never the views of the patient's expert witnesses. As discussed in Chapter 9, 9.5.3, it is difficult to see, given the jurisprudential framework of these decisions, how a patient could possibly succeed in challenging a decision to impose compulsory treatment on him or her (see further, Bartlett, 2011).

For matters related to conditions in institutional settings, success for patient applicants has also been minimal. In all the key cases—*R* v *Ashworth Hospital, ex p H* [2001] EWHC Admin 872, [2002] 1 FCR 206 (concerning whether a person with Hepatitis C claiming to be sexually active could have condoms); *R v SSHD, ex p DB* [2006] EWHC 659 (Admin) (whether a male-to-female transsexual could dress as a woman on the wards); *R v Nottinghamshire Healthcare NHS Trust, ex parte G, B and N* [2009] EWCA Civ 795 (concerning the prohibition of smoking in high security hospitals), *R v Ashworth Hospital, ex p Munjaz* [2005] UKHL 58 (departure from Code of Practice policy on seclusion, primarily by vastly reducing the frequency of medical reviews of seclusion) as well as a variety of cases concerning searches—the patient applicants have lost (see further Chapter 2, 2.5).

It is perhaps fair to note that all of these concern high security hospitals—hospitals containing mainly patients admitted through the criminal mechanisms in Part III of the MHA 1983 who are perceived as particularly dangerous. This group has always had particular problems with success in judicial review applications. Prior to 2007, challenges to review tribunal decisions were by way of judicial review. Munro analysed judicial reviews of tribunal decisions from 1998–2008. Of 37 applications by service users (including those admitted under Parts II and III), only 4 were successful. The Justice Secretary initiated review of a decision relating to a detention under Part III in 10 cases in this period, and was successful in every one (Munro, 2008: 270, table 1 and fn 7). While statistics must of course be approached with caution, the unbroken track record of the Justice Secretary in this period is eye-catching.

The third edition of this text spoke with considerable optimism about the possibilities created by the HRA 1998 in the context of judicial review. Certainly, there have been significant victories here that have become engrained into the fabric of mental health law: *R (H) v Mental Health Review Tribunal, North and East London Region* [2001] EWCA Civ 415 (placing the burden of proof in a tribunal hearing on the party wishing to continue the detention, a decision now reflected in MHA 1983, s. 72(1)(c)); *R v Feggetter, MHRC, ex p John* [2002] EWCA 554 (requiring SOADs to provide reasons for their decisions); *R (Brandenburg) v East London and the City Mental Health Trust* [2003] UKHL 58 (concerning the re-sectioning of patients released by review tribunals); and *R (KB) v MHRT and Sec State* [2003] EWHC Admin 193 (regarding delays in the scheduling of tribunal hearings), are obvious examples.

That optimism must now be tempered somewhat. As noted, *Wilkinson*—an obvious point of optimism previously—has fallen flat, and a number of the unsuccessful judicial review applications noted earlier in this section were based on the HRA 1998. If we were anticipating a brave new world of patient rights following that Act, it is difficult to see that it is coming to pass.

The HRA 1998 case law is inevitably influenced by the European Court of Human Rights, and here, too, results have been mixed and the potential for the future uncertain. Certainly, in recent years, the Strasbourg court has discovered that mental disability law exists, and from an entire absence of case law until 1979, the mental disability cases now admitted as not manifestly ill-founded and given a full decision by the court are now a significant number annually, and constitute a substantial and growing jurisprudence. A number of these are potentially very important, for example those concerning guardianship of people deemed to lack capacity (e.g., *Shtukaturov v Russia*, Application no. 44009/05, judgment of 27 March 2008; *Stanev* v *Bulgaria*, Application no. 36760/06, judgment of 17 January 2012; *Đorđovic* v *Croatia*, Application no. 41526/10, judgment of 24 July 2012, concerning freedom from harassment; and *X* v *Finland*, Application no. 34806/04, judgment of 3 July 2012, concerning rights to hearing regarding compulsory treatment). Mental disability has now been incorporated by reference into the non-discrimination provisions in Article 14 of the ECHR (see *Glor* v *Switzerland*, Application no. 13444/04, judgment of 6 November 2009), and in cases regarding mental disability, the Strasbourg court routinely notes the presence of the UN Convention on the Rights of Persons with Disabilities (CRPD) as part of the overall international landscape in which it operates.

At the same time, the Strasbourg court has delivered its share of disappointments. For example, while the court had long held that the continuation of detention of a person of unsound mind under Article 5(1)(e) was dependent on the continuation of a mental disorder, for example, in *Johnson* v *the United Kingdom* (1999) 27 EHRR 296, the court appeared to hold that the cessation of a mental disorder did not provide a right to immediate release. In *Kolanis* v *the United Kingdom* (Application no. 517/02, judgment of 21 June 2005), the court failed to provide a remedy for a patient who was to be released subject to conditions in a situation where the conditions were not fulfilled. Part of the problem for the court is that it cannot easily escape its established jurisprudence. The decision in *Herczegfalvy* v *Austria* (1992) 15 EHRR 437 that treatment which is a 'medical necessity' cannot be inhuman or degrading under Article 3 now seems to warrant re-assessment (see Chapter 9, 9.5.3; Bartlett, 2012a; United Nations Special Rapporteur on Torture, 2013: para. 64). It is not obvious how this can be accomplished in the existing Strasbourg system, however: *Herczegfalvy* is a case that has been taken as foundational for many years. We may, perhaps, have started to see a move at least to amend its meaning in *Gorobet* v *Moldova* (Application no. 30951/10, judgment of 11 October 2011), but it remains to see whether this is a real movement, or confined to the facts of that case (see further Chapter 9, 9.5.1).

12.4 Civil and criminal actions

12.4.1 Controlling the starting gate: s. 139

Section 139 of the MHA 1983 provides:

(1) No person shall be liable, whether on the ground of want of jurisdiction or on any other ground, to any civil or criminal proceedings to which he would have been liable apart from this section in respect of any act purporting to be done in pursuance of this Act or any regulations or rules made under this Act or any regulations or rules made under this Act, unless the act was done in bad faith or without reasonable care.

(2) No civil proceedings shall be brought against any person in any court in respect of any such act without the leave of the High Court; and no criminal proceedings shall be brought against any person in any court in respect of any such act except by or with the consent of the Director of Public Prosecutions.

These subsections do not apply to actions against the Secretary of State, health authorities, or NHS trusts (s. 139(4), as amended by the National Health Service and Community Care Act (NHSCCA) 1990, s. 66(1) and Sch. 9, para. 24(7)), nor to offences for which leave of the Director of Public Prosecutions is already required as condition precedent to prosecution (s. 139(3)). Nonetheless, s. 139 does limit recourse by patients against those who control them, and cases commenced without compliance with that section are a nullity (*Seal* v *Chief Constable of South Wales Police*, [2007] UKHL 31. For this reason, the scope and effects of the section should be analysed with some care.

12.4.1.1 Scope

Section 139 expressly applies to both criminal and civil matters. It does not apply to judicial review (*R* v *Hallstrom, ex p W; R* v *Gardner, ex p L* [1985] 3 All ER 775). The logic here is that notwithstanding that judicial review applications are heard in the civil court structure, they do not determine 'liability' for decisions, but rather correctness of decisions (pp. 783, 784).

The provisions extend, not merely to acts actually done pursuant to the statute but also to acts purporting to be done pursuant to the statute. The leading case here is *Pountney* v *Griffiths* [1976] AC 314 (HL). The case concerned the use of restraint by a nurse in ushering a patient back to his ward at the end of a visit from his family. The patient alleged that he had been assaulted by the nurse, and the nurse, although claiming that he had only lightly brushed against the patient, was duly convicted. The House of Lords held that the conviction could not stand as the events occurred in pursuance of the statute, and therefore there could be no proceedings without leave having first been obtained. The court noted that the detention of an individual in hospital necessarily involved the exercise of control and discipline, as a necessary corollary to the administration of treatment. This would perhaps be uncontroversial if the nurse's version of the facts were accepted; but it is at best doubtful that they were so accepted by the triers of fact at first instance. It is far less obvious that an unprovoked punch, as was the case in the patient's version of events, is appropriately considered part of the exercise of control and discipline. That said, could it be seen to be an act '*purporting* to be done' in pursuance of the legislation? The view of the House of Lords is extraordinarily expansive on the scope of s. 139(1), particularly when combined with the expansive readings of 'medical treatment' which have flowed from s. 145.

The current view is that s. 139 refers only to detained patients, not to those admitted informally (*R* v *Runighian* [1977] Crim LR 361). This authority is merely at the Crown Court level, suggesting some hesitation is appropriate before uncritical reliance is placed upon it. The summary of the case in the *Criminal Law Review* is brief, but it suggests that the decision was reached on the basis that s. 5 of the MHA 1959, now s. 131 of the MHA 1983, did not mandate the admission of informal patients; it merely indicated that the statute did not preclude such admissions. Informal admissions were instead by private arrangement. Such a reading would of course not apply to situations where the statute specifically governs informal patients, such as the treatment safeguards contained in s. 57. More generally, the reading is not obviously consistent with *R* v *Kirklees*

MBC ex parte C [1992] FLR 117, discussed in Chapter 4, where the court appears to see s. 131 and private arrangements as creating separate admission routes, with the bulk of informal patients admitted pursuant to s. 131. Nevertheless, as the possibility of admission pursuant to s. 131 was not disputed in that case, the argument may still be open.

Also problematic will be the issue of when an individual living in the community falls outside the scope of the MHA 1983, so as to render s. 139 inoperative. Clearly, the creation of a plan for after-care pursuant to s. 117 of a person formerly detained under the Act and about to be released will be within the scope of the section. Will the performance of the after-care, as distinct from the formation of the plan for after-care, also fall within the scope of the section? The preferable view would be not, insofar as the individual has been released from the facility and is a regular individual in the community separate from the facility. In reality, such a clean split is unlikely to occur. If the individual is not simply released, but subjected to a community treatment order (CTO) under s. 17A, then the treatment provided would appear to be caught by s. 139. If the discharged individual is not subjected to a community treatment order, he or she may well still be an outpatient. Should outpatients be covered by the section? It would seem not. They have no status under the Act, and it is therefore difficult to see that they can be treated pursuant to it. If an out-patient is actually a detained patient on leave of absence pursuant to s. 17, however, a much closer nexus to the Act is present, and the applicability of s. 139 is considerably more likely.

Prosecutions of offences under the MHA 1983, which already may be only instituted by or with the consent of the Director of Public Prosecutions are not subject to the section (s. 139(3)). This currently applies only to offences under s. 127, concerning ill treatment or wilful neglect of patients.

The section covers not merely events in purported compliance with the legislation, but also with 'any regulations or rules' made under the statute. This extension will be particularly important for matters flowing from review tribunal proceedings which are regulated to a considerable degree by statutory instruments. It is a nice question whether purported reliance on the Code of Practice brings a defendant within the protection of the section. Often, the question will be merely academic, since acts performed within the guidance of the Code will be sufficiently related to some authority in the statute that a plea of *purported* pursuance of the statute will be successful. In the event that informal patients are deemed to be admitted and treated outside the statute, however, there may still be an issue as to whether their admission, treatment, and management as advised in the Code of Practice renders the section applicable. Alternatively, it is perhaps arguable that the applicability of many of the provisions of the Code to informal patients suggests that these patients are treated pursuant to the statute, rather than as a result of the private arrangements by which they were admitted.

Section 139 refers specifically to 'acts' performed in purported pursuance of the statute. It is another nice question as to whether acts include omissions in this context. Jaconelli and Jaconelli (1998:153) argue that it does not. If that is correct, it would be the case that failure to treat would be outside the scope of the section, but maltreatment would be within it. While this seems counterintuitive, the section is quite clear in its reference to 'any act purporting to be done'; it is not obvious that this wording can conveniently include omissions.

The section will, of course, be relevant to patients and former patients who wish to pursue remedies against those administering the legislation. The wording does not limit the category of plaintiff to whom it applies, however. Thus the section will also apply to a plaintiff suing for example on the basis that an individual acted negligently in allowing a detained patient to escape, when that escape results in an assault on the plaintiff: see *In re Shoesmith, In re* [1938] 2 KB 637.

As noted, the section does not apply to judicial review, but it is as yet unclear whether s 139 applies to applications under the HRA 1998. In *Wilkinson*, a majority of the court took the view that it did, at least when the allegations in question were analogous to torts (paras. 54 and 61). The question had not been argued before the court, and Hale LJ expressly indicated that her view in this regard was provisional. An alternative view is found in *R (W)* v *Doncaster Metropolitan Borough Council* [2003] EWHC 192 (Admin). In that case, Stanley Burton J held that section 139 did apply to judicial review cases in which damages were claimed, but distinguished these cases from applications under the HRA 1998 (para. 56):

> I doubt whether liability for the unlawful infringement of the rights of a patient under article 5.1 is precluded by section 139(1) of the MHA. In such a case, the patient has a Convention right to compensation under Article 5.5. Section 3 of the HRA requires the Court to construe legislation in a way that is compatible with that right. Moreover, Parliament did not have breach of the Convention in mind when it enacted section 139(1) of the MHA. Despite the general words of that section, I should have been disposed to read it down so as not to apply to the breaches of Convention rights. The interpretation of general words so as to exclude specific cases that Parliament could not have intended to be included in them is a standard mode of statutory interpretation.

It is submitted that this is the stronger view. While the views in *Wilkinson* extended only to cases which would be tortious absent s. 139, it is the case that some human rights violations may occur without bad faith or a want of reasonable care on the part of the perpetrator. Particularly if the view were to prevail that NHS trusts and government cannot be vicariously liable for the behaviour of those protected by s. 139(1), the financial ramifications for such human rights violations would fall entirely on the patient. For the patient to receive the compensation which is his or her right under Article 5.5, he or she would be required to appeal to the European Court of Human Rights in Strasbourg. The purpose of the HRA 1998 was to make that journey unnecessary. It is difficult to see that it can have been the legislative intent to make it unnecessary for all but psychiatric patients.

The section was challenged before the European Court of Human Rights in *Seal* v *the United Kingdom* (Application no. 50330/07, judgment of 7 December 2010), as a violation of Article 6, the right to a fair hearing. The court held that the legislation was not based on the assumption that those with mental disabilities were likely to be vexatious litigants (para. 77). As will be seen from the domestic jurisprudence cited at 12.7 that is at best a questionable finding. Instead, the court held that the objective of the legislation was to protect individuals making sensitive judgments in a sensitive area of law (para. 77). This was a legitimate aim, and in this case, did not unduly infringe on the applicant's rights.

Curiously, while the applicant in *Seal* cited Article 6 before the domestic courts, he did not cite Article 14, which protects against discrimination in the exercise of ECHR rights. While Article 14 was raised before the European Court of Human Rights, it declined to decide the matter, on the basis that it had not been argued before the domestic courts and therefore domestic remedies had not been exhausted. The point is surely arguable. The Strasbourg court in *Seal* accepted that s. 136 constituted a restriction on access to the legal process; if that discriminates against people with mental disability, a violation of Article 14 would presumably follow. While the point is clearly arguable, its success is not guaranteed. The *Seal* court notes that the object of the provision is not to stop people with disabilities suing, but instead to provide protection for administrative officials (the police, in the facts of *Seal*) making sensitive decisions in a difficult area of law. While this suggests that the court would not find s. 136 to be an example of direct discrimination, it remains debatable whether it remains an example of indirect discrimination: is it a requirement, neutral on its face, that has a differential impact on people of a class protected by Article 14. Indirect discrimination has been taken by the court to be within the conduct prohibited by Article 14 (see, e.g., *DH* v *the Czech Republic*, Application no. 57325/00, judgment of 13 November 2007), so this is certainly arguable. The question would be whether such differential treatment is for a justifiable purpose, and that analysis would presumably resemble the question of whether the restriction was proportionate under the Article 6 claim. If the court followed the same logic it did regarding the Article 6 claim, the discrimination argument would presumably not obviously succeed.

That would be a surprising result. It is clear that people wishing to sue for breaches of the MHA 1983 are at a disadvantage relative to other litigants: whatever the merits of their case, they will require leave. At the very least, that is an additional hurdle that will increase their costs of pursuing their claim. As the Equality and Human Rights Commission argued in *Seal* in Strasbourg, and as the dissenting judges held in the Supreme Court decision in *Seal* here, it is not obvious either that the potential litigants in these cases are unusually prone to vexatious litigation, nor is it obvious that the potential defendants in these cases require greater procedural protection regarding these litigants than such defendants do in other aspects of their professions. Being a police officer, doctor, nurse, or social worker may be difficult and require spontaneous and complicated decision-making; but it is not obviously more difficult in a mental health context than in the other contexts in which such professionals work. And if the mental health context cannot be shown to demonstrate particularly severe difficulties, why would protections in the mental health area be justified, when they are not provided in these other contexts?

12.4.1.2 Leave to commence an action

The immediate effect for a plaintiff or complainant whose action falls within s. 139 is that leave must be sought to commence the action. In the case of a criminal matter, consent must be sought from (or the prosecution instituted by) the Director of Public Prosecutions. For a civil action, it is the leave of the High Court that is required. The requirement for leave to be granted is that the plaintiff demonstrate that the act complained of was done in bad faith, or without reasonable care: s. 139(1).

The section might loosely be understood as creating standards relating both to the defendant's conduct and to the appropriateness of the plaintiff's case. On the one hand, there is a sense that people charged with the administration of the MHA 1983 should not be held liable because they genuinely and in good faith make a mistake in their duties. This approach is manifest, for example, in *Richardson v London County Council* [1957] 1 WLR 751 (at p. 760):

> Parliament has wisely provided that he [the plaintiff] is not to be allowed to bring an action of this kind unless there is substantial ground for believing them [the officers who confined the plaintiff] to have been guilty of want of good faith or want of reasonable care.... [A]lthough these public authorities may have misconstrued the Act and although they may have done things which there was no jurisdiction to do, nevertheless, so long as they acted in good faith and in a reasonable manner, they are to be protected from having actions brought against them.

While the need for 'substantial' grounds must be read in the context of subsequent statutory reform and case law, the remainder of the comment continues to reflect one judicial approach to the section.

The threshold for the granting of leave is significant. Torts of strict liability, including false imprisonment, breach of statutory duty, and battery, do not require proof of intent of the tortfeasor, and the requirement of 'bad faith or without reasonable care' introduces a requirement not contained in these torts themselves. As Jaconelli and Jaconelli (1998: 154) point out, s. 139 must be understood as precluding the pursuit of otherwise winnable cases. This calls into question the reasoning of the ECtHR in *Seal* that 'any request for leave ... would be granted in the case of a well-founded claim' (para. 78).

A similar concern arises for applications relating to the ECHR itself. As noted at 12.4.1.1, there is jurisprudence that s. 139 applies to applications under the HRA 1998 for which damages are sought. Damages are available for ECHR violations, and indeed are specifically provided for in breaches of Article 5 (see Article 5(4)). Consistent with ECHR law, the Privy Council has held that incompatability with domestic law relating to psychiatric confinement will constitute a breach of Article 5 (*A (A Mental Patient) v Scottish Ministers and Advocate-General (Scotland)* [2002] SC (PC) 63, [2002] HRLR 6). No bad faith or want of care is required for such violations, and as violations of Article 5 they create a presumptive right to damages. A requirement of compliance with s. 139 would therefore create a threshold of bad faith or want of reasonable care to access these rights, a threshold that is nowhere contained in the ECHR itself, and must be extremely questionable.

The substantive restrictions of the section will be less likely to be significant when the action is in negligence, since a want of due care forms a part of the action in these cases in any event. Even in these cases however, as Hale (2010: 343) points out, there are residual disadvantages. The plaintiff must receive leave from a High Court judge, even if the claim is in the jurisdiction of the county courts; and at that hearing, they have the burden to show that the case should continue.

The recent trend seems at least at first blush to be to restrict the application of s. 139, and thus to provide the plaintiff with increased access to the courts. This is in part the result of changes to the wording of s. 139(2) in the MHA 1983. Where the MHA 1959 had required a potential plaintiff to demonstrate a 'substantial ground' for the contention that the potential defendant had acted in bad faith or without reasonable care, that requirement was removed from the MHA 1983. The leading case is *Winch v Jones* [1985] 3 All ER 97 (CA). Lord Donaldson MR identified the problems the section is intended to address in the following fashion (pp. 100, 101):

> To be more specific, there are two fundamental difficulties. First, mental patients are liable, through no fault of their own, to have a distorted recollection of facts which can, on occasion, become pure fantasy. Second, the diagnosis and treatment of mental illness is not an exact science and severely divergent views are sometimes possible without any lack of reasonable care on the part of the doctor. The intention of Parliament, as it seems to me, was quite clearly that no one should be prevented from making a valid claim that they have suffered by reason of negligence in the exercise of powers conferred by the Mental Health Acts and that no one should be harassed by an invalid claim.

Thus both the aspects of the section discussed here were noted. His Lordship then addressed the standard by which the court should decide whether leave ought to be granted (p. 102):

> As I see it, the section is intended to strike a balance between the legitimate interests of the applicant to be allowed, at his own risk as to costs, to seek the adjudication of the courts on any claim which is not frivolous, vexatious or an abuse of the process and the equally legitimate interests of the respondent to such an application not to be subjected to the undoubted exceptional risk of being harassed by baseless claims by those who have been treated under the Mental Health Acts. In striking such a balance, the issue is not whether the applicant has established a prima facie case or even whether there is a serious issue to be tried, although that comes close to it. The issue is whether, on the materials immediately available to the court, which, of course, can include material furnished by the proposed defendant, the applicant's complaint appears to be such that it deserves the fuller investigation which will be possible if the intended applicant is allowed to proceed.

While the onus therefore remains on the plaintiff, it is necessary to meet only a relatively low threshold in order for leave to be granted (see also *DD v Durham County Council* [2013] EWCA Civ 96). This is consistent with the procedures for the hearing of the application. Affidavit evidence from both parties may be considered (*Carter v Metropolitan Police Commissioner* [1975] 1 WLR 507), but it is not to be turned into a trial on the affidavit evidence, and Parker LJ in *Winch v Jones* holds that cross-examination on that evidence ought never to be permitted (p. 103). Affidavits might show that 'some allegation made by an intending plaintiff is totally refuted by incontrovertible evidence', but he was unwilling to go much further in interrogating the merits of the case. For Parker LJ the appropriate standard was whether there was a 'reasonable suspicion that the authority had done something wrong' (at p. 103).

12.4.1.3 Section 139 and vicarious liability

In general, employers are liable for the torts of employees acting within the scope of their employment, through the doctrine of vicarious liability. This is of course a separate matter from direct liability of employer in situations where a tort performed by an employee is not involved, such as a failure by an NHS trust to maintain a building adequately, or to provide adequate staffing for a facility. In such situations of direct liability, only the employer will be liable. In situations of vicarious liability, liability will be joint: both employer and employee will be liable, as would be the case when leave is given pursuant to s. 139 and a plaintiff is successful in their suit against the individual doctor or social worker. In most cases, the employer of the doctors and other staff charged with the administration of the MHA 1983 will be a health authority or NHS trust, parties specifically excluded from the protection of s. 139. The question therefore arises as to whether the employers can remain vicariously liable, notwithstanding that leave is not granted under s. 139 to sue the doctor or nurse individually.

The arguments turn on whether vicarious liability is a 'master tort' or a 'servant tort'. If the former, vicarious liability of the employer is based on a theory that the employee acts on express or implied instructions of the employer, and therefore the tort of the employee is equally the tort of the employer. If the latter, the liability is based solely on the tort of the employee, and the liability of the employer is some form of indemnity flowing from the employment relationship.

The standard view in English tort law texts is that vicarious liability is a servant tort (see Rogers, 2010: paras. 20–21). In *Imperial Chemical Industries Ltd* v *Shatwell* [1965] AC 656 (HL) the view was stated by all five Law Lords that unless the servant could be held liable in damages, the employer could not be, and this view was further taken in *Majrowski* v *Guy's and St Thomas's NHS Trust* [2006] UKHL 34. That said, the facts in *Imperial Chemical Industries* were rather unusual, and the point does not appear to be pivotal in *Majrowski*. There are further occasional judicial pronouncements reflecting a master tort approach: see, e.g., *Twine* v *Bean's Express Ltd* [1946] 1 All ER 202; *Norton* v *Canadian Pacific Steamships* [1961] 1 WLR 1057 at p. 1063. The possibility that vicarious liability remains a master tort was specifically left open by Henry J in *Furber* v *Kratter* (1988) unreported (HC), a case involving inappropriate solitary seclusion in a psychiatric facility, allegedly without nursing care and without clothing, or reading or writing material, where leave was sought pursuant to s. 139. If, following the opening left in *Furber*, vicarious liability is perceived as a master tort, the employer might well remain liable, notwithstanding the unavailability of an action against the employee because of s. 139.

This line of argument is complicated by the fact that in some parts of the MHA 1983 duties are vested directly in employees such as AMHPs or medical officers. Specific statutory duties are not generally delegable. It becomes problematic to adopt a theory of implied instructions from employer to employee, when the employee and not the employer is charged with the duties alleged to be violated.

Even if vicarious liability is a servant tort, that does not necessarily end the matter. If, as was argued to be a possibility at the beginning of this section, s. 139 does not alter the substantive law but instead merely removes an action for damages against some people, the tort arguably continues to exist. Just because (in the absence of bad faith or a want of reasonable care) an individual doctor cannot be sued for wrongful confinement, the argument would go, it does not necessarily follow that the tort has ceased to exist, but merely that one of the parties cannot be sued for it (see Jaconelli and Jaconelli, 1998: 159). The issues here would seem to be first, the degree to which s. 139 does in fact affect substantive law; and second, whether the employer can be called upon to indemnify damages for which the employee has not been found liable.

Can this arrangement of split liability reflect the legislative intent of the section? While such an intent may seem improbable, Jaconelli and Jaconelli point to the fact that the sub-section removing health authorities and the Secretary of State from the scope of the provision was drafted as the case of *Ashingdane* v *UK* (1984) 6 EHRR 69; (1985) 7 EHRR 528 neared the European Court of Human Rights, challenging the authority of the predecessor of s. 139. While both the Commission recommendation, reported at (1984) 6 EHRR 69 and the eventual court decision, (1985) 7 EHRR 528, upheld the predecessor of s. 139, it was more reluctant to do so for the health authority and government than it was for individual members of staff. Jaconelli and Jaconelli argue that the exclusion of health authorities and the Secretary of State from the scope of the section is to be read in that context.

This view was adopted by the majority in *Wilkinson* (see paras. 24, 58; para. 42 contra). The argument there does not appear to engage with the principles of tort noted here. The question was further not argued before that court, and was arguably a collateral issue in a case primarily concerned with alleged HRA 1998 violations. It nonetheless provides rather weak authority for the view that hospitals, health authorities, and the Secretary of State are not protected by the terms of s. 139(1), even if this subsection does protect the individuals for whom these bodies are vicariously liable.

12.5 MCA and DOLS

As we have seen, s. 139 of the MHA 1983 creates a two-pronged restriction on litigation. The first is substantive. People (other than NHS Trusts, the Secretary of State, and similar bodies: see s. 139(4)) cannot be held liable absent bad faith or a want of reasonable care. The second is procedural. To sue or to launch criminal proceedings against these people for anything done or purported to be done pursuant to the MHA 1983, leave of a High Court judge is required.

The MCA and the DOLS work rather differently. Applications to the Court of Protection may be made without leave by the person lacking (or alleged to be lacking) capacity, by the parent of such a person if under 18, by the donee of a lasting power of attorney to which the application relates, by any court-appointed deputy to which the application relates, by a person named in an existing order of the court if the application relates to that order, and, if the application relates to the grant of a standard authorisation under the DOLS provisions, by the relevant person's representative (MCA 2005,

s. 50 (1) and (1A)). Otherwise, permission must be sought for the commencement of an application, and in determining whether permission is granted, the court must have regard to (MCA 2005, s. 50(3)):

(a) the applicant's connection with the person to whom the application relates,
(b) the reasons for the application,
(c) the benefit to the person to whom the application relates of a proposed order or directions, and
(d) whether the benefit can be achieved in any other way.

The court has a broad jurisdiction under the MCA 2005 to make declarations as to what is in the best interests of an individual lacking capacity. In principle, this ought to provide a mechanism for those close to the issue to have the merits of a decision assessed where appropriate.

The Court of Protection is a statutory court with a statutory jurisdiction, and does not hear either civil damage claims or criminal prosecutions under the MCA 2005. There are no specific restrictions in the MCA regarding the commencement of such actions that correspond to the leave requirement in s. 139 of the MHA 1983. This situation is more complicated in the case of a person lacking capacity to litigate however, where a litigation friend must be appointed. This may be an inevitable requirement. *Ex hypothesi* the person him- or herself is unable to conduct the litigation, and at least the litigation friend system does allow potentially important issues to be brought before the court for determination. At the same time, it does mean removing the litigation from the claimant him- or herself, so that the litigation becomes about the individual, rather than the individual him- or herself being in control of the litigation.

The MCA 2005 further has a variety of provisions to limit liability of people making decisions under the Act. These generally provide that people who make reasonable efforts to comply with the terms of the Act will not be liable for the decisions they take on behalf of the person lacking capacity: see, e.g., s. 5 (no liability for person acting in what he or she reasonably believes to be the best interests of a person reasonably believed to lack capacity), s. 14(2) (no liability for person acting on basis of a defective LPOA unless person knew of the defect or knew of circumstances that would have terminated the power to act under the LPOA), and s. 26 (no liability for treating unless 'satisfied' that an advance decision refusing the treatment exists; no liability for withholding treatment if reasonably believe an advance decision refusing the treatment exists). The scope of the permitted decisions has been discussed elsewhere in this volume (see Chapter 4), and that discussion will not be repeated here. For present purposes it is relevant to note that the limitations focus on liability for the decision made exercising the powers of the Act. If the implementation of the decision is done negligently, the individual may still be liable for that: see, e.g., s. 5(3). Thus a surgeon will not be liable for decision that a person lacking capacity requires specific surgery, if that decision is taken in reasonable compliance with the Act; the surgeon may still be liable if the surgery is performed negligently.

The Court of Protection further has jurisdiction to make orders relieving the donee of an LPOA of legal liability for his or her actions under the power (MCA 2005, s. 23(3)).

This is consistent with other law relating to trustees and fiduciaries, where the courts enjoy a similar power.

The DOLS have a further protection in paras. 3 and 4 of Sch. A1 to the MCA 2005. These concern acts done in pursuance of an urgent or standard authorisation to detain an individual. So long as the act in question is in compliance with any conditions in a standard authorisation, the person detaining will not incur liability that would not have been incurred if the person detained had been capable and consented to the act.

This is a remarkably loose standard. Conspicuous by its absence is any requirement that the actions of the detaining individual be reasonable, or that they be the least restrictive alternative in the circumstances. The best interests requirement that justifies the grant of the standard authorisation requires that the detention must be to prevent harm to the relevant person, and a proportionate response to the likelihood and severity of the harm, and as this requirement is governed by the overall principles of the MCA 2005, that it is the least restrictive alternative available (see s. 1(6) and Sch. A1, para. 15(4)–(5)). These requirements do not appear to be carried over into the provisions concerning liability of the persons affecting the detention unless specific restrictions and conditions are included in the standard authorisation itself. Instead, it would seem that the limit of what is permitted is what an individual can consent to, and in criminal law, that includes actions resulting in actual bodily harm (see *R* v *Brown* [1993] 2 All ER 75 (HL)). Once again, acts which are themselves negligent continue to attract liability (see Sch. A1, para. 4(1)), so that acts which would be negligent even if performed on a consenting patient would continue to attract liability. Further, the provision only affects acts done for the purpose of the standard or urgent authorisation, and a narrow reading of that would at least protect against a defence for abuse unrelated to the detention. Nonetheless, the result would seem to be a remarkably loose control on the use of both physical and chemical restraints, insofar as they are in implementation of the urgent or standard authorisation.

12.6 Criminal prosecutions

12.6.1 Section 126 of the MHA 1983

Subject to the provisions of s. 139, the regular criminal law continues to apply to those contained in the mental health system. In addition, however, the MHA 1983 provides its own, additional offences in Part IX of the Act.

Section 126 provides penalties of up to two years' imprisonment and an unlimited fine for persons who without lawful authority or excuse possess documents relating to the administration of the MHA 1983 which they know or believe to be false. While the documents to which the section applies are specified in s. 126(3), the class is quite broad, including applications under Part II, medical or other recommendations or reports under the Act, and 'any other document required or authorised to be made for any of the purposes of this Act.' The actual deception by the person creating the document remains under the broader criminal law; this section makes it an offence knowingly to possess such documents.

Section 128 makes it an offence to induce or knowingly assist detained persons to absent themselves without leave. The provision extends not merely to those detained under Part II of the Act, but also to persons detained in a place of safety under s. 137, and also to those subject to guardianship under s. 7. Similarly, the harbouring of individuals absent without leave, or assisting them to prevent their recapture, is made an offence. Section 129 essentially makes it an offence to interfere with inquiries and inspections authorised by the MHA 1983. The interferences prohibited are listed specifically in the section: refusing to allow the inspection of premises; refusing to allow access to or visiting, interviewing, or examination of persons; refusing to produce records and documents; and refusing to withdraw when an interview is permitted under the Act to be held in private.

Section 127 creates a number of offences related to the ill-treatment or wilful neglect of patients. Managers, officers, and staff of hospitals and mental nursing homes can be held liable for ill-treating or wilfully neglecting persons receiving treatment as in-patients of those facilities. These individuals can similarly be held liable regarding ill-treatment or wilful neglect on the premises of outpatients on receiving treatment at the hospital or mental nursing home: s. 127(1). The offences in s. 127(1) are restricted to the staff of the facilities in question. Not so the remaining offences provided in the section. Section 127(2) is broader still:

> It shall be an offence for any individual to ill-treat or wilfully to neglect a mentally disordered patient who is for the time being subject to his guardianship under this Act or otherwise in his custody or care (whether by virtue of any legal or moral obligation or otherwise).

This applies to any individual who cares for another who is mentally disordered, be it through guardianship or otherwise. 'Patient' is defined in s. 145(1) as 'a person suffering or appearing to be suffering from mental disorder'. There is no requirement in that definition that the individual be under medical treatment, in a hospital, or otherwise under the auspices of the MHA 1983. Thus in *R v Newington* (1990) Cr App R 247 (CA), the statute was applied to the owner of a residential home for the elderly. There was no doubt that the section could apply to her, although the mental disorder of the individuals allegedly ill-treated had to be demonstrated (p. 254).

While s. 127(2) will be of particular relevance for those living in the community and in facilities other than those identified in s. 127(1), it is also presumably broad enough to encompass many of the situations contained in s. 127(1). The elements of the offences are nonetheless somewhat different. Section 127(2) requires proof of the mental disorder of the individual, and of a specific relationship between the accused and the individual guardian, custodian, or carer. Section 127(1) requires a patient/staff relationship in a hospital or mental nursing home, and, it would seem from the wording of the sub-section, that the individual is 'receiving treatment for mental disorder'. The current trends in case law would seem to be according a markedly broad interpretation to the phrase 'treatment for mental disorder', suggesting that it may not be a high hurdle for a prosecutor to leap; nonetheless, in the event of ill-treatment of an individual not actually receiving such treatment, s. 127(2) might be considered, in the event that the complainant is mentally disordered and in the care of the potential accused.

Common to all the s. 127 offences is the phrase 'ill-treat or wilfully to neglect'. The leading case on the meaning of this phrase is *Newington*. In that case, the Court of Appeal held that ill treatment should be pleaded separately from wilful neglect, as the latter would require consideration of a particular state of mind, where the former would not (p. 252). The nature of the state of mind was not particularly articulated, as *Newington* was a case of ill-treatment. The court summed up the elements of this aspect of the offence in the following terms (at p. 254):

> In our judgment the judge should have told the jury that for there to be a conviction of ill-treatment contrary to the Act of 1983 the Crown would have to prove (1) deliberate conduct by the appellant which could properly be described as ill-treatment irrespective of whether this ill-treatment damaged or threatened to damage the health of the victim and (2) a guilty mind involving either an appreciation by the appellant at the time that she was inexcusably ill-treating a patient or that she was reckless as to whether she was inexcusably acting in that way.

The court held that a case may be made out notwithstanding no actual injury or unnecessary suffering or injury to health was caused (p. 253). This suggests a relatively wide scope to 'ill-treatment'. Michael Gunn (1990: 361) has suggested that it could well be wide enough to include inadequate feeding or heating, the use of harsh words or bullying. Violence does not necessarily constitute ill treatment if it was used, for example 'for the reasonable control of a patient' (*Newington*, at p. 253). From the earlier case of *R v Holmes* [1979] Crim LR 52, it is clear that the offence can be made out from a single assault; a course of conduct is not necessary.

Proceedings under s. 127 must be instituted by, or with leave of, the Director of Public Prosecutions (DPP): (s. 127(4)). The effect of this provision is to take s. 127 offences outside the scope of s. 139. Thus s. 127 prosecutions may be commenced without proof of bad faith or want of due care.

Local social service authorities are given specific authority to 'institute proceedings' for all the offences in Part IX by s. 130, although this is 'without prejudice to any provision of this Part of this Act requiring the consent of the Director of Public Prosecutions for the institution of such proceedings'. The effect of this caveat is ambiguous. To begin with what is clear, local social service authorities have standing to prosecute the offences under the Act. They must also seek consent of the DPP to institute a prosecution under s. 127, the only section in Part IX where such consent is expressly required. The ambiguity arises in the interface between ss. 130 and 139. Does the authority to 'institute proceedings' mean an authority to institute such proceedings without the leave of the DPP otherwise required by s. 139(2)? The specific maintenance of the role of the DPP 'under this Part' could be taken to imply a modification of that officer's role under s. 139, which is contained in a different part of the Act. On this reading, s. 139 would not apply. At the same time, s. 139(3) specifically exempts from its remit Part IX offences which the DPP must already institute or consent to the institution of. This implicitly brings the remaining Part IX offences under the scope of s. 139(2), and there is nothing which would remove the local social services authority from that sub-section. It is not clear which of these readings the courts would adopt.

In some cases, the issue will be academic. It is difficult to see how leave would be required under s. 139 for an action against an individual who assists another to escape, for example, even given the broadest interpretation of acts 'purporting to be done in pursuance of this Act'. In other cases, the matter will be effectively a procedural nicety. It is difficult to see how an individual who knowingly makes false statements on an admission application can be said to be acting other than in bad faith, suggesting the grant of leave under s. 139 would be a formality. Cases may well be more complicated, however. The obstruction offences contained in s. 129 provide an example. Arguably, these may involve imperfect compliance with the MHA 1983, and a misguided view of the law by the potential defendant. Prima facie, s. 139 might provide a defence, if prosecutions by the local social services authority are in fact covered by that section. The relationship between ss. 130 and 139 is thus not entirely of academic interest.

12.6.2 **Section 44 of the MCA 2005**

Section 44 of the MCA 2005 creates an offence for ill-treating or neglecting a person lacking capacity, or whom the defendant reasonably believes to lack capacity (P). It applies to people who have care of such a person, as well as to donees of lasting powers of attorney created by P and to court-appointed deputies with responsibility for P. The offence is punishable on summary conviction with a term of imprisonment of 12 months or a fine, and on conviction by indictment of imprisonment for five years or a fine.

The reference to ill-treatment and neglect in this section is reminiscent of s. 127 of the MHA 1983, and the discussion of that section above presumably applies to s. 44 as well.

The section is problematic in its reference to a person 'who lacks, or whom D [the defendant] reasonably believes to lack, capacity' (s. 44(1)(a)). The MCA 2005 is based on a decision-specific view of capacity: one might well be capable for some decisions, and not for others. The scope of the offence is thus unclear: what is it, exactly, that P is meant to be incapable of? Is it any incapacity that would trigger the offence? That would seem odd since it would mean that the crime would be committed even if the neglect or ill-treatment occurred in an area where P retained capacity. Thus if P were incapable of some financial decisions, it would seem odd that D could be convicted of neglect flowing from malnutrition, if P continued to have capacity to decide on their choice of food. It surely cannot be correct that D would be guilty of an offence for failing to intervene in an area where D believes (perhaps quite rightly) that P has capacity. Indeed, in such circumstances, there may be little that D can do legally by way of intervention.

At the same time, it seems inappropriate to insist on too close a nexus between the incapacity and the neglect or ill-treatment. If D is hitting P, it would seem unduly arbitrary to have to find a specific iteration of P's incapacity relevant to the situation in order for D to be guilty of an offence under s. 44. Would we say that if P's incapacity were merely relating to consent to medical treatment and financial decisions—issues with no obvious connection to being hit by D—D is not guilty of an offence under s. 44? D would, of course, be guilty of an offence in the general criminal law—hitting anyone is a crime—but it seems counterintuitive that physical assaults on P would not be within a provision meant to prohibit neglect or ill-treatment of people lacking capacity.

The meaning of incapacity in this context was argued at length in *R v Hopkins* [2011] EWCA Crim 1513, where the court indicated that if unconstrained, it would have held s. 44 to be fatally vague, and incompliant with the test of certainty at common law and Article 7 of the ECHR. It held, however, that it was bound by the earlier decision of the Court of Appeal in *R v Dunn* [2010] EWCA Crim 2935, which had held the opposite. The trial judge in *Dunn* had instructed the jury by citing the statutory language that incapacity meant being 'unable to make decisions for himself because of some impairment or disturbance of the function of the mind or brain' (s 2(1)). The judge noted that such incapacity could be permanent or temporary, and that capacity was to be presumed. The Court of Appeal in *Dunn* repeated the relevant sections of the statute, and continued:

> At first blush, and indeed on more mature reflection, these legislative provisions do not appear to be entirely appropriate to defining the constituent elements of the criminal offence of ill-treatment of a person without capacity. By the time sections 2 and 3 are analysed and related to an individual case, they become convoluted and complex when, certainly in relation to a criminal offence, they should be simple. But we pause to remember the purpose of section 44 and the creation of the offence; and bear in mind that everyone, who for whatever reason but in particular the natural consequences of age, has ceased to be able to live an independent life and is a vulnerable individual living in a residential home, is entitled to be protected from ill-treatment if he or she lacks "capacity" as defined in the Act.

This would appear to extend the definition to its broadest—that any neglect or ill-treatment of a person who is incapable of making any decision is within s. 44. As noted, this is a problematic interpretation, given the overall scheme of the MCA 2005, and may warrant re-assessment.

For that reason, it may be prudent for prosecutors to consider a charge under s. 127(2) of the MHA 1983, even when s. 44 of the MCA 2005 might also apply. If P lacks capacity under s. 44, he or she will of necessity have an impairment of, or a disturbance in the functioning of, the mind or brain (MCA 2005, s. 2(1)). The gateway provision for s. 127(2) of the MHA 1983 is that the person subject to the ill-treatment or wilful neglect is a 'patient', meaning a person suffering from or appearing to suffer from a mental disorder (s. 145(1)). It is therefore difficult to imagine victims with s. 44 of the MCA 2005 who are not also within the scope of s. 127(2), and the substance of the crimes—ill-treatment or wilful neglect—is the same. The most significant difference would appear to be that if the prosecutor proceeds by way of summary conviction, the maximum prison sentence under s. 127(2) is six months, where under s. 44 it is one year.

12.6.3 **Other offences**

A variety of offences outside the current MHA 1983 refer specifically to people with mental disabilities. Most notably, ss. 30 to 33 of the Sexual Offences Act (SOA) 2003 prohibit sexual activity with a person with a mental disorder impeding choice. Sections 34 to 37 of the SOA 2003 concern people with any mental disorder (whether or not it impedes choice), prohibiting people from inducing such people to engage in sexual activity, from engaging in sexual behaviour in the presence of such people or causing such people to watch a sexual act. Sections 38 to 44 restrict sexual activity between people with any mental disorder (whether or not it impedes choice) and their care workers. These latter offences include an exception for people in marriages or civil partnerships, or where the sexual relationship pre-dates the care relationship, but these exceptions do not extend to the earlier provisions of the SOA 2003: sex with a person with a mental disorder impeding choice is a crime under the statute, even in the case of relationships that pre-date the incapacity or when the participants are married or civilly partnered.

It is appropriate to close this section by returning to its first point: the broader criminal law also applies to people contained in the mental health system. Thus assaults of patients by staff is not merely an offence under s. 127; it may also give rise to a charge of common assault: see, e.g., *Newington*. A manifest lack of care such as results in the death of a person with mental disorder, unable to care for himself or herself, may result in a conviction for manslaughter in the event that an individual undertakes to provide care to that individual and fails adequately to do so (*R v Stone, R v Dobinson* [1977] 1 All ER 341). Advocates should be aware of such wider possibilities of the criminal law.

12.7 **Civil actions for damages**

Subject again to the provisions of s. 139 of the MHA 1983, the general laws of contract and tort apply to people in the mental health system as much as anywhere else. Contract will be of limited assistance when dealing with NHS trusts and health authorities, for no contract exists between these bodies and their patients (*Pfizer v Ministry of Health* [1965] 1 All ER 152). The same logic would apply to community care facilities, unless the client pays directly for the care received.

Tort, at least in theory, provides a more encouraging line of authorities. Any exhaustive analysis of the torts that might assist people in the mental health system is of course beyond the scope of this book: it could well be a text on its own. That said, advocates should think creatively, and not leap instantly to an action in negligence. Assault or battery may be an effective mechanism to seek redress for inappropriately aggressive behaviour directed at the client by hospital or community care staff. Occupier's liability applies as much in psychiatric facilities as it does elsewhere, providing redress for injury flowing from a person's entry into premises, whether on a short-term or long-term basis. Wrongful confinement may be used to challenge detentions, and has the advantage that once the confinement is shown, it is for defendant to justify their actions. Rather than discuss the variety of torts in a summary fashion, the discussion which follows will instead examine a few more specific difficulties raised in recent mental health litigation. Those issues have tended to arise in the context of negligence law. Negligence also has the advantage that it survives the test under s. 139(1), in that what is alleged is almost by definition a want of reasonable care.

To begin with a basic principle, it is uncontroversial that there is a duty of care between health care professionals such as doctors and nurses, and their patients. The duty arises when the doctor/patient relationship is crystallised, or when the patient is accepted as a patient in a hospital (Jackson, 2010: 103–4). This duty is therefore broad enough to include care both inside and outside psychiatric facilities. This gives the patient the right to expect the standard of care which the 'reasonable doctor' occupying the position of the potential defendant would have provided: general practitioners are subject to the standard of the reasonable general practitioner; psychiatric specialists are subject to the standard of the reasonable psychiatric specialist, and so forth.

In theory, this ought to provide many people in the mental health system with civil redress for medical misadventure or other errors by these professionals. For example, patients given megadoses of cocktails of psychiatric medication (see Chapter 9) might think they can sue in the event that they suffer adverse effects. Until recently, it would be difficult to see that such an action would succeed. The test of whether the standard of care was breached was whether a responsible body of medical opinion would have behaved as the defendant did (*Bolam v Friern HMC* [1957] 2 All ER 118). As megadosing is not uncommon in psychiatric facilities, this test would be difficult to surmount. Recently, however, a caveat has been introduced on the *Bolam* test, by *Bolitho v City and Hackney HA* [1997] 3 WLR 1151, where the House of Lords acknowledged, per Lord Browne-Wilkinson at p. 1159, that the professional views must stand up to objective scrutiny:

> The court has to be satisfied that the exponents of the body of opinion relied upon can demonstrate that such opinion has a logical basis. In particular, in cases involving, as they so often do, the weighing of risks against benefits, the judge before accepting a body of opinion as being responsible, reasonable or respectable, will need to be satisfied that, in forming their views, the experts have directed their minds to the question of comparative risks and benefits and have reached a defensible conclusion on the matter.

The intrusiveness of this revised standard on medical authority is limited. The views of doctors will clearly continue to have considerable sway in court. In megadosing, however, doctors are failing to be governed by the maximum dosages of drugs recommended by the manufacturers of those drugs, maxima presumably based on scientific testing and experimentation. In such extreme situations, *Bolitho* might be invoked to challenge the appropriateness of the doctor's decision. Except in such rather unusual situations, however, a fairly uniform medical view that the doctor's actions were inappropriate would be necessary to found a negligence action; and such uniform views opposing a course of action by a doctor are uncommon.

Megadosing might also be addressed through a negligence action based on insufficient information provision. Informal patients, of course, have the same treatment rights as any other member of the community. That means they must consent to any treatment they are given, assuming they have the capacity to do so (see Chapter 9, 9.2). Similarly, some confined patients are treated on their consent pursuant to s. 58. Treatment on the patient's consent in these contexts must meet the usual common law standard, as established by *Sidaway* v *Governors of Bethlem Royal Hospital* [1985] AC 871, *Pearce v United Bristol Healthcare NHS Trust* [1999] PIQR 53 (CA); *Chester* v *Afshar* [2004] UKHL 41, 2004 WL 2289136 (HL), [2005] 1 AC 134, [2004] 4 All ER 587, [2004] 3 WLR 927.

This means that they must be informed of the major risks and benefits of treatment. The precise scope of this in a megadosing context has yet to be litigated, but it seems at the very least arguable that it would be necessary to disclose that the dosage is in excess of the manufacturer's recommended maximum. Information provision can be a double-edged sword, however, since if the information is provided, including possible adverse effects from the megadose, a court might find that the patient had voluntarily assumed the risk of resulting adverse effects, and no action would therefore lie: *volenti non fit injuria*. It is questionable whether this is an appropriate result. If consenting to the medication is understood by the patient as the only hope for release from the facility, is the consent to the risk 'voluntary' in the sense that ought to invoke the defence?

While the possibilities of negligence law appear promising, a survey of the case law is less encouraging. A Westlaw search under 'negligence' and 'psychiatry' returns relatively few cases, and fewer still where the plaintiff is successful in challenging the care they receive. A number of those successful cases involve care or decisions taken outside the traditional scope of psychiatric care. In *DN* v *Greenwich LBC* [2004] EWCA Civ 1659, for example, the local council was successfully sued for failure properly to assess the child plaintiff's special needs for the purposes of educational placement. Within the realm of traditional psychiatry, *Panther* v *Wharton* QBD No. HQ0000089, 29 Mar 2001, is remarkable as the only case where clinicians are successfully sued for misdiagnosis, and there the sting of the litigation was not so much that a psychiatric disorder was diagnosed but rather that a diagnosis of acute hypersensitivity vasculitis was missed, resulting in a variety of amputations, including a leg below the knee. All the other successful cases involve patients leaving hospitals and injuring or killing themselves (see *Drake* v *Pontefract HA* [1998] Lloyd's Rep. Med. 425 (QBD); *L* v *West Sussex HA* QBD No. 99/TLQ/1022, 7 Feb 2000; and, analogously but instead relying on Article 2 of the HRA 1998, *Savage* v *South Essex Partnership NHS Foundation Trust* [2008] UKHL 74 and *Rabone* v *Pennine Care NHS Foundation Trust* [2012] UKSC 2. In these cases, the negligence claim is essentially that the plaintiff was not sufficiently intrusively treated, sometimes because they were not sufficiently watched and were therefore able to go absent without leave, sometimes because they were inappropriately given leave, and in *Drake*, because they were insufficiently medicated. It should be noted that plaintiffs do not always win on such cases: see, e.g., *D* v *South Tyneside NHS Trust* [2003] EWCA Civ 878; *G* v *Central and NW London Mental Health NHS Trust* [2007] EWHC 3086 (QB), which also involve injuries following departures from hospitals and negligence claims based on allegations of insufficiently intensive controls. It is notable however that, at least in the Westlaw sample, plaintiffs do not succeed on anything else.

Insofar as the Westlaw cases are representative, it provides considerable cause for pause. To begin with, remarkably few cases appear in the data set at all. Either plaintiffs are not successfully suing, or the relevant cases are not being reported. Within the cases that do appear, it may be arguable that tort and similar legal actions have a role in ensuring that patients receive care reaching minimum thresholds of intensity. It is not at all obvious that tort has yet found a role in protecting against over-medication, inappropriate conditions of care, or over-controlling care. Such cases are almost completely absent from the Westlaw database, and in the rare situations where they do appear (*S v SW London and St George's Mental Health Trust* [2011] EWHC 1325 (QB) regarding an allegedly negligent diagnosis of bipolar disorder; *Walker v Semple,* QBD, 30 March 1993, 1993 WL 13725995 regarding an allegedly negligent diagnosis of schizophrenia and hypomania), the patients lose.

The legal relationship between doctor and patient becomes more complex when the doctor is exercising a statutory function under the MHA 1983. Liability for signing a medical certificate as part of a process for involuntary admission will serve as an example. The duty of care of doctors signing medical certificates is an open question: *X (minors) v Bedfordshire County Council* [1995] 3 All ER 353 at p. 384; *Clunis v Camden and Islington Health Authority* [1998] 2 WLR 902 at p. 914. These decisions were somewhat surprising, as the broadly held belief up until the mid-1990s had been that a duty of care did exist, as evidenced by a considerable trail of litigation: see, e.g., *Winch v Jones* (see 12.4.1; leave granted to sue doctor for negligence in confinement); *O'Neill v Morrison* (CA, unreported, 1994) (similar situation, leave refused but no implied doubt as to duty of care); *Buxton v Jayne* [1960] 1 WLR 783 (leave granted to bring action against duly authorised officer of local authority—analogous in the MHA 1959 to the social worker in the MHA 1983—for lack of care in confining plaintiff).

Both *X* and *Clunis* rely for this proposition on the case of *Everett v Griffiths* [1921] 1 AC 631 (HL), where notwithstanding the tentative views of Viscounts Haldane and Cave that such a duty did exist, the fact that no negligence was found in the completion of the medical certificate in question allowed the matter to be left open. A majority of the House of Lords continued to leave the matter open in *Harnett v Fisher* [1927] AC 573, although Lord Atkinson offers the opinion that the doctor signing such a certificate 'is simply engaged as a medical man by a patient to give an opinion as to the patient's state of health, as he would be to diagnose the state of health of any patient who in his daily practice called upon him to prescribe for him.' (p. 596). This suggests that in his Lordship's view, the standard duty of care applied to the duties of a doctor in signing such certificates. The content of these cases may be inconclusive, but reliance upon these cases is not convincing in any event. The statutory regime under consideration was that contained in the Lunacy Act 1890 where the medical certificate was but one piece of evidence necessary to apply for an order for confinement. The order itself was signed by, and was subject to the discretion of, a Justice of the Peace. The removal of this extra layer of bureaucracy is significant. Now, the requisite medical certificates and the application pursuant to ss. 2 or 3 of the MHA 1983 are sufficient for confinement. The certificates therefore have a legal effect that they did not have previously, suggesting a new analysis is necessary.

The obvious starting place for such an analysis is *X* v *Bedfordshire*. In that case, one of the issues was whether the social workers and psychiatrists interviewing children as part of the determination as to whether the children ought to be placed in care gave rise to an action in damages, in the event that it was performed negligently. Lord Browne-Wilkinson, speaking for a unanimous House of Lords, held that it did not, on the basis that such a duty would not be 'just and reasonable' within the meaning of *Caparo Industries plc* v *Dickman* [1990] 2 AC 605. His Lordship reasoned that a complex and interdisciplinary statutory system had been established, in which liability of individuals could not easily be disentangled. Second, child protection proceedings were inherently delicate, involving a complex balancing exercise, and the court should hesitate before criticising the balancing of conflicting priorities by the authorities. Third, liability in damages might induce local authorities to be more cautious and defensive in their approach. Fourth, he held that the fraught relations that often existed between parents of the children concerned and social workers would breed hopeless, vexatious, and costly litigation. He further held that the statutory remedies, although not providing for compensation, did allow for scrutiny of decisions. Finally, he held that the doctors were retained to advise the local authorities, not the plaintiffs, and hence that no patient/doctor relationship was in fact established (pp. 380–84).

A number of these arguments simply do not apply to the doctor or social worker involved in a confinement under the MHA 1983. Certainly, the statutory regime is complex, but the roles of the various professionals is kept distinct. Any negligence or impropriety of these individuals would be clearly definable by reference to the statute. Issues of the delicacy of the proceedings and the risk of vexatious litigation are already dealt with through s. 139, discussed at 12.4.1. Two others can be dismissed relatively briefly. Certainly, the availability of a civil remedy might induce those in charge to 'adopt a more cautious and defensive approach to their duties' (p. 381); but is caution necessarily a bad thing, particularly when considerable violations of civil rights will result from the actions? It should further be recalled that the existence of a duty of care is but one element required for success in a negligence action. A breach of the duty is also necessary, and success on this head will require proof of a want of reasonable care, a criterion already allowing room for error in the event of difficult circumstances. The negligence action is to provide a mechanism to call decision-makers to account, to explain themselves. This is further relevant to the issue of statutory remedies, for as discussed, the review tribunals provided by the statute do not determine the validity of the initial detention, but only the appropriateness of continued detention. The statute does not provide a mechanism for the initial detention to be considered; unlike the child welfare situation, that is left to the broader law of judicial review.

This leaves the most interesting of the grounds for decision in *X*, the question of who is the client of the doctor or social worker. In *X*, Lord Browne-Wilkinson addressed the matter as follows (at p. 383):

> The social workers and the psychiatrists were retained by the local authority to advise the local authority, not the plaintiffs. The subject matter of the advice and activities of the professionals is the child. Moreover, the tendering of any advice will in many cases involve

interviewing and, in the case of doctors, examining the child. But the fact that the carrying out of the retainer involves contact with and a relationship with the child cannot alter the extent of the duty owed by the professionals under the retainer from the local authority. The Court of Appeal drew a correct analogy with the doctor instructed by an insurance company to examine an applicant for life insurance. The doctor does not, by examining the applicant, come under any general duty of medical care to the applicant. He is under a duty not to damage the applicant in the course of the examination: but beyond that his duties are owed to the insurance company and not to the applicant.

The role of the certifying doctors and social worker is by no means as clear cut. Certainly, some doctors or social workers will be brought in for purposes of the certification only, and will have no other professional relationship with the individual. This suggests a relatively close parallel to the doctors and social workers in *X*. Frequently, however, at least one of the certifying doctors will be the patient's general practitioner. In the event that the certificate will involve a readmission, the other doctor may well be the individual's psychiatrist, who may continue to serve in that role following the individual's admission to hospital. In both these cases, the medical professionals signing the certificates are in an ongoing professional relationship with a patient. Can it really be said that the signing of the certificates is severable from the remainder of that relationship, so that it, unlike the programme of treatment of which the admission must form an integral part, is not contained within the doctor-patient relationship?

A finding that the actions of doctors related to medical certification was not within the patient/doctor duty of care would lead to anomaly. Consider a case where a doctor informed a patient that if he or she did not consent to informal admission, the doctor would institute civil confinement. If the patient relied on the doctor and went into hospital as an informal patient, the situation would be analogous to a patient entering hospital for a physical ailment on doctor's advice, and the duty of care would be beyond question. If instead the patient called the bluff of the doctor and the doctor signed the certificate, the duty of care would not exist. The duty would be a function of whether the patient agreed to follow the doctor's advice voluntarily—a most unusual result.

An appeal of *X* v *Bedfordshire* to the ECtHR was successful, for reasons of mixed relevance in the current context (*Z* v *UK*, [2001] 2 FLR 612; (2002) 34 EHRR 3). It was held that the level of abuse to which the children had been subjected constituted a breach of Article 3 of the ECHR, and the consequent failure to provide a domestic remedy in damages constituted a breach of Article 13. As the case did not involve psychiatric care or treatment, the Article 3 violation is of no direct relevance for current purposes, and as Article 5 contains in it an express right to damages, recourse to Article 13 is unlikely to be necessary for psychiatric cases involving wrongful confinement, although there may be relevance for other forms of psychiatric malpractice. The court does not expressly overrule tort law, but instead awards damages for an ECHR breach. The case does not expressly affirm a duty of care in domestic law, therefore, but does provide a salient reminder of the overlapping jurisdiction of the ECHR.

The move towards increasing care in the community similarly raises difficulties relating to the scope of the duty of care and the doctor/patient relationship. The leading case is *Clunis*. In that case, the plaintiff was released from Guy's Hospital in south London. As he wished to live in north London, after-care was arranged by Guy's with a north London hospital, and a Dr Sargeant, a psychiatrist at that hospital agreed to serve as responsible medical officer under the after-care plan. Notwithstanding appointments established for him on 9 October and 13 November 1992, the plaintiff, Clunis failed to attend at the hospital. Dr Sargeant contacted Clunis's last general practitioner, who indicated that Clunis had been removed from his list due to aggressive and threatening behaviour. Dr Sargeant then contacted Guy's Hospital, and social services to arrange a mental health assessment visit. This was to take place on 30 November, but Clunis was not at home at the relevant time, and the assessment therefore did not take place. Dr Sargeant made an appointment to see Clunis on 10 December, which again he did not attend. On 17 December, social services notified Dr Sargeant of a phone call from the police, indicating that Clunis was 'waving screwdrivers and knives and talking about devils'. Later that day, Clunis killed a bystander in an unprovoked attack, by stabbing him with a knife. At trial, a plea of diminished responsibility was accepted, based on a diagnosis of schizoaffective disorder.

Clunis commenced a suit against Dr Sargeant, alleging negligence in her follow up of his care plan. The case is therefore interesting because it lies at the intersection of several issues. First, there is the issue of the duty of care owed by doctors to persons in care in the community in general, and on after-care under s. 117 in particular. Secondly, there is the issue that the negligence alleged was one of omission: the doctor should have intervened more to ensure that appropriate care was given, notwithstanding the inevitable conclusion that Clunis did not, at the time, want the treatment. Finally, there was the issue of whether the action was barred on policy grounds, because it stemmed from Clunis's own criminal act in killing the bystander: *ex turpi causa non oritur actio*. The defendants applied to have the claim struck out as disclosing no cause of action. This was unsuccessful, but their appeal succeeded and the case was dismissed on the basis of the first and third of these issues. In neither case is the reasoning of the court entirely satisfactory.

On the issue of *ex turpi causa*, the court held (at p. 911) that the claim arose out of the commission of a criminal offence:

> In the present case we consider the defendant has made out its plea that the plaintiff's claim is essentially based on his illegal act of manslaughter; he must be taken to have known what he was doing and that it was wrong, notwithstanding that the degree of his culpability was reduced by reason of mental disorder. The court ought not to allow itself to be made an instrument to enforce obligations alleged to arise out of the plaintiff's own criminal act and we would therefore allow the appeal on this ground.

The difficulty with the court's reasoning is that the court conflated the entire action for damages to an action for damages flowing from the death of the bystander. No doubt in monetary terms this was where most of the damages lay; but the failure to provide appropriate medical care would appear to have had adverse effects not directly related to the homicide. Certainly, it would appear that by the morning in question, Clunis was psychotic. The unpleasant experience of having those psychotic delusions before the attack would presumably constitute actionable damage, if the duty of care and breach were successfully shown. There is no reason for those damages to be lost as a result of the *ex turpi* ruling.

Of greater relevance for current discussion is the fact that the Court of Appeal failed to find a duty of care between Dr Sargeant and Clunis. Perhaps unsurprisingly given the lack of express statutory language, the court held that s. 117, the duty to provide after-care services to a formerly detained patient, created a public law duty, rather than a private law action in damages. More problematically, it held (at p. 913–14) that the provision of after-care services under the statute was inconsistent with a coexisting common law duty of care:

> Bearing in mind the ambit of the obligations under s. 117 of the Act and that they affect a wide spectrum of health and social services, including voluntary services, we do not think that Parliament intended so widespread a liability as that asserted by Mr Irwin [counsel for Clunis]. The question of whether a common law duty exists in parallel with the author-ity's statutory obligations is profoundly influenced by the surrounding statutory frame-work....So, too, in this case, the statutory framework must be a major consideration in deciding whether it is fair and reasonable for the local health authority to be held respons-ible for errors and omissions of the kind alleged. The duties of care are, it seems to us, dif-ferent in nature from those owed by a doctor to a patient whom he is treating and for whose lack of care in the course of such treatment the local health authority may be liable.

Certainly, a variety of professional individuals and voluntary agencies may be involved in the patient's after-care. It is not obvious that this should negate a duty of care, how-ever, although the after-care received by a formerly detained patient under s. 117 may well in all outward appearances be similar to the care in the community received by any other patient, only for the latter, the care will be outside the terms of the statute. Precisely analogous arguments to those rehearsed by the court in this case will apply. Therefore, either the court is saying that there is no duty of care between psychiatrists or health authorities and their patients living in the community—a truly startling statement—or it must be asked why the provision of essentially similar services by statutory obligation under s. 117 rather than merely by good practice should *remove* the duty of care.

Perhaps the escape route for the court could have been that Clunis terminated one therapeutic relationship with Guy's upon his release from that facility, and since he never attended an appointment with Dr Sargeant, never commenced a new one. As a result, at the time of the homicide, there was no duty of care in effect: Clunis had slipped through the cracks between therapeutic relationships. Even that is problematic. In gen-eral, the duty of care between hospital and patient arises when there is an express or implied undertaking that the patient will be treated (*Cassidy* v *Ministry of Health* [1951] 1 All ER 574). Such an express undertaking would appear to have existed in this case, and was manifest by Dr Sargeant's continuing, albeit unsuccessful, attempts to establish a therapeutic relationship with Clunis. It is perhaps arguable that the relationship, and hence the duty, did not exist in this case, as it had been repudiated by Clunis's refusal to attend the treatments. While, this is not how the court approached the issue, it is consistent with the decision in *K* v *Central and Northwest London Mental Health NHS*

Trust [2008] EWHC 1217 (QB) where the court declined to strike out a claim based on the provision of s. 117 after-care, on the basis that the question of whether proximity between doctor and patient was sufficient was a matter of fact, to be determined in individual cases.

A broader question arises as to the strategic benefits from a patient's rights perspective of litigation complaining of a doctor's failure to intervene in the life of a patient, either by failing to confine the individual under ss. 2 or 3, or to launch guardianship proceedings under s. 7. Certainly, there is a legal coherence to such actions. If a duty of care exists between doctor and patient, then the patient has a right to expect the doctor to exercise a certain standard of care. Since the doctor's role appropriately includes diagnosis of mental illness and consequent responsibilities under the MAH 1983, it seems tautological that the patient ought to be able to insist that these roles are fulfilled to the appropriate standard of care. The failure to do so, as was alleged in the *Clunis* case, can be tragic; more often it is more mundane, but nonetheless may detract from the longer term quality of life of the patient, and may therefore be actionable. All that is asked, the argument runs, is the exercise of a reasonable professional standard of care. At the same time, such litigation must encourage doctors to err on the side of intervention. As we saw in Chapter 6, 6.2.1, the dangerousness of the mentally ill is significantly over-predicted, and institutionalisation has its disadvantages as well as its benefits. Is it really the case that doctors should be encouraged to intervene more?

12.8 Complaint processes

For much of what clients will want, litigation is not the appropriate model. Not merely is it expensive, it frequently will not provide a remedy to the client's actual problem. There may not be a lot of point to suing because a client is unhappy with the medication they are receiving, or unable for religious or cultural reasons to eat the food served in a hospital, although these may be significant problems for the client. It is not obvious that civil actions would succeed for such problems; and even if they did, they would provide a remedy in damages, not preferable medication or different food. For many such day-to-day difficulties, a direct approach to the doctor or hospital manager may provide the best chance of a resolution to the problem. The presence of an advocate may give the client's concerns increased credence by such authority figures, which may trigger a solution. In other instances, the advocate's negotiation skills may allow otherwise unforeseen solutions to be reached.

Even if the matter is one for which other legal avenues appear appropriate, informal dispute resolution mechanisms should be considered. Thus tribunals tend to be sympathetic to the RC's views of the appropriateness of detention, for example. It may well be the case that some sort of negotiated plan with the RC directed towards release of the client may bring results more effectively than a review tribunal hearing.

Particularly for issues of day-to-day living outside the scope of tribunals, internal complaint processes within the hospital or community care facility might be considered.

A variety of such mechanisms exist. NHS trusts are required to operate complaints processes, headed by a complaints manager. This is a separate structure from the trust's disciplinary system, although the structure of most complaint systems seems to assume that the complaint will be about an individual, rather than an inappropriate policy. Increasingly, these processes will have advocacy programmes running in parallel in the trust, to assist complainants. At their best, these advocacy services will be staffed by people whose knowledge of the workings of the trust will be considerably better than an external advocate, and who may therefore be particularly effective at having the complainant's matter resolved.

In the event that the client is not content with the result of a complaint through one of these internal processes, the complaint may then be forwarded to the Care Quality Commission (CQC). The CQC has a fairly broad authority under the MHA 1983 to visit people detained pursuant to the Act in hospitals and mental nursing homes; and to investigate complaints of detainees under the Act if the complaint has not been adequately dealt with through an internal process (MHA 1983, s. 120). The CQC has powers of investigation—a distinct advantage in ensuring that the substance of a complaint is considered—but its jurisdiction extends only to confined patients, persons on community treatment orders or guardianship. It does not extend to those informally admitted, nor to outpatients, although the CQC does have jurisdiction to investigate complaints relating to events which occurred during a period of detention even if that detention has now ceased.

Complaints may also be lodged with the Parliamentary and Health Services Ombudsman. The Ombudsman has powers of investigation, suggesting that this may be an inexpensive way for a client's concern to be investigated.

There can thus be seen to be a potential overlap between the jurisdictions of the CQC and the Health Services Commissioner. The bodies have informally agreed that matters relating to the circumstances or consequences of detention of psychiatric patients will be dealt with by the former body; otherwise, it will fall to the latter.

Finally, many professionals working in the mental health sector are subject to internal professional disciplinary processes. For example, doctors, nurses, and health visitors are all subject to such professional regulation. In the event that the concern is with the professionalism of such an individual, a complaint to the relevant professional body, be it the General Medical Council or the United Kingdom Central Council for Nursing, Midwifery and Health Visiting, might be considered.

12.9 **Advocacy**

Both the MHA 1983 and the MCA 2005 now require the appointment of advocates to assist people governed by those statutes. These are not lawyers retained for the purposes of individual cases, but rather staff members, generally lay people, who will assist in circumstances specified in the legislation. Sometimes they will be people with personal experience of the mental health system, but this is not a requirement of the legislation.

Independent Mental Health Advocates (IMHAs) are available for the support of persons liable to detention under the MHA 1983, persons subject to guardianship or to a community treatment order under the MHA 1983, persons for whom treatment under s. 57 (most notably, psychosurgery) is proposed, and persons under the age of 18 years for whom treatment with electro-convulsive therapy is proposed (MHA 1983, s. 130C). The services provided include assisting in obtaining information about and in understanding the provisions of the Act relevant to the person's situation (including any restrictions to which he or she is subject pursuant to the MHA 1983), and the legal issues surrounding this or her proposed treatment, and the reasons the treatment is proposed (MHA 1983, s. 130B(1)). The role includes both assisting the service user to understand his or her rights, and helping the service user in exercising those rights (MHA 1983, s. 130B(2)). To that end, the IMHA may interview the service user in private, interview professionals concerned with the service user's care, and, so long as it is done with the capable consent of the service user or does not conflict with an order of the Court of Protection, consider relevant medical or social services records relating to the service user (MHA 1983, s. 130B(3),(4)).

While the IMHA is expected to 'help (by way of representation or otherwise)' the service user in the exercise of his or her rights, the role is not one of a lawyer. Instead, the IMHA's role is much more about assisting the service user to understand his or her situation, and advocate on the service user's behalf within the administrative systems associated with the MHA 1983. In the event that an issue proceeds to the point of litigation, even if only to a review tribunal hearing, a solicitor would normally be sought to represent the service user.

Absent particularly intrusive proposed treatment, IMHA services are not available to informal patients under the MHA 1983. As noted elsewhere in this volume (see Chapter 6, 6.1), the dividing line between informal and detained patients is problematic: informal patients may feel coerced into decisions just as much as detained patients are. These informal but *de facto* coerced patients may be among the most vulnerable in the psychiatric system, yet they are outside the scope of IMHA services.

IMHA services were implemented following the MHA 2007, and thus are relatively new. While it is not yet clear how they are developing, there is reason for cautious optimism. IMHAs will work within one NHS trust—often, indeed, within one hospital—and will therefore know how the administrative systems work, and who to talk to on behalf of the relevant service user. This routine closeness with one institutional framework can however lead to potential difficulties. Does the IMHA understand his or her work as promoting the rights and interests of the service user as perceived by the service user, or because of the ongoing professional relationships that develop with hospital and similar professional staff, can the IMHA come to understand his or her role as a 'go-between' or intermediary between the institution and the service user? In the latter circumstance, the advocacy function of the IMHA is markedly reduced. Indeed, there is the risk that health and social services professionals come to rely on the services of the IMHA to ensure that the service user understands his or her situation, rather than the professional taking the time to ensure the provision of the relevant information him- or herself. If that occurs, the IMHA serves to distance the service user from their care professionals.

This ambiguity seems built into the role of independent mental capacity advocates (IMCAs). The MCA 2005 articulates the specific roles of IMCAs much more specifically than the MHA 1983 does for IMHAs. An IMCA is to represent a person lacking (or allegedly lacking) capacity (P) in the following circumstances:

- when 'serious medical treatment' is proposed for P, and where there is no non-professional carer to be consulted regarding P's best interests (MCA 2005, s. 37). 'Serious medical treatment' is defined as treatment where there is a fine balance between the risks and benefits of treatment, where there is a fine balance as to which among a choice of treatments should be pursued, or treatments which are likely to involve serious consequences for P (*The Mental Capacity Act 2005 (Independent Mental Capacity Advocates) (General) Regulations 2006*, SI 2006/1832, para. 4). Treatment under Part IV of the MHA 1983 is specifically excluded, but of course does come within the purview of an IMHA;

- where it is proposed by an NHS body to admit P to a hospital for a period expected to exceed 28 days or to a care home for a period expected to exceed eight weeks (MCA 2005, s. 38);

- where it is proposed that a social services will provide residential care to P; or where it is proposed to change P's residential care arrangements and there is no non-professional carer to consult about P's best interests regarding the proposed change. These provisions apply when the care in question is expected to extend for eight weeks or more (MCA 2005, s. 39);

- when P is to be deprived of liberty under the DOLS (MCA 2005, ss. 39A–39B); or where the appointment of P's relevant person's representative (see Chapter 5) comes to an end and there is no other appropriate non-professional carer to consult regarding P's best interests (MCA 2005, s. 39C); or where P has a non-paid relevant person's representative and either P or the representative asks to instruct an advocate, or where even without such a request there has been or is likely to be a failure to exercise the right to apply to a court or to request a review when it would be reasonable to do so (MCA 2005, s. 39D). The IMCA's role in these circumstances is further governed by Part 11 of Schedule A1 to the MCA 2005.

The role of an IMCA representing an individual who lacks capacity may be complex. In the context of hearings related to the MHA before review tribunals, it is clear that the lawyer is required to act on the competent instructions of the client, even if those instructions are not in the client's best interests, but has an increasing discretion to act in the best interests of the client in situations where the client lacks capacity (see *AA v Cheshire and Wirral Partnership NHS Foundation Trust* [2009] UKUT 195 (AAC)). This must *a fortiori* be the case for IMCAs, who are under jurisdiction of the MCA 2005 and its general requirement that acts or decisions made on behalf of a person who lacks capacity must be done or made in that person's best interests (s. 1(5)). If this reasoning is pressed to its logical conclusion, however, the role of the advocate is substantially curtailed. If P actually lacks capacity to make the specific decision and to instruct the advocate on the decision, the advocate will presumably be expected to apply the best interests test contained in the MCA 2005 itself, thus mirroring the decision that the decision-maker is to take anyway. Particularly given the increasing prevalence of the objective elements of the best interests test current in the jurisprudence (see Chapter 4, 4.5), this would substantially reduce the advocacy role of the IMCA.

The ambiguity of role does seem however to be built into the role itself. A number of occasions for appointment are triggered by the fact that there is no one other than a professional carer whom it would be appropriate to consult regarding P's best interests. The IMCA in this case appears, at least to a significant extent, to be an information gatherer. That is quite a different role than an advocate, since the information to be gathered relevant to best interests would not necessarily be restricted to matters corresponding to or buttressing arguments for the patient's wishes, and may in fact be undercutting those wishes. It may well be appropriate that this undercutting information form a part of the basis of the decision to be made, but it is odd to view this as 'advocacy'.

12.10 Representing people with mental disabilities

The right of people with mental health difficulties to representation is established in a variety of sources. The *Tribunal Procedure (First-Tier Tribunal) (Health, Education and Social Care Chamber) Rules 2008*, SI 2008/2699, establish a right of a party to representation before those tribunals (r. 11). The representative may be virtually anyone authorised by the party. Legal aid is available for these proceedings (see Chapter 8, 8.4.3).

For litigation before the courts, the usual rules regarding representation apply. The apparent openness of the courts is however subject to the individual's right to participate in litigation. The rule is that a 'patient' may sue or be sued only through a 'litigation friend' (Civil Procedure Rules (CPR), r. 21.2). These take effect if the individual is 'a person who, by reason of mental disorder within the meaning of the Mental Health Act 1983, is incapable of managing and administering his own affairs' (CPR, r. 21.1). The rules adopt the term 'patient', a usage which will be reflected in the discussion which follows. While the patient must be suffering from a 'mental disorder' as contained in the broad definition of s. 1(2) of the MHA 1983, there is no requirement that the individual in question be contained in a psychiatric facility or even under active medical care for their disorder at the time of the litigation. In that sense, 'patient' may be a very misleading term.

The leading case concerning capacity to litigate is *Masterman-Lister* v *Brutton & Co, Jewell & Home Counties Dairies* [2002] EWCA Civ 1889. Consistent with a functional approach to capacity, based on the specific decisions to be made, the court focused particular concern on issues relating to the litigation in question (paras. 18, 75). Kennedy LJ adopted the following articulation of the standards involved (p. 26):

> So the mental abilities required include the ability to recognise a problem, obtain and receive, understand and retain relevant information, including advice; the ability to weigh

the information (including that derived from advice) in the balance in reaching a decision, and the ability to communicate that decision.... [T]he court should have regard to the complexity of decisions under consideration but not to the court's own valuation of the gravity of those decisions because it is not for the court to decide in a non-medical treatment case what is or is not serious in the life of the person before it.

While rule 21.2 of the CPR requires that persons within this class must have a litigation friend, there is no routine mechanism for the prompt and effective enforcement of this provision. Rule 21.3 requires claimants against patients to apply for a litigation guardian in cases where none exists; but it is not necessarily obvious how such claimants will know that the person subject to the proceedings is a patient. This may lead to awkward results, as steps in proceedings taken against patients in contravention of rule 21.3 are of no effect, unless subsequently ratified by the court under rule 21.3(4).

Further, the rules for the appointment of such friends are remarkably lax. For persons wishing to act on behalf of a patient, a court order is often unnecessary (CPR, r. 21.4). Instead, it is sufficient that a 'certificate of suitability' be filed with the court after service on all parties under rule 6.6, to the effect that the individual (CPR, r. 21.4(3):

(a) can fairly and competently conduct proceedings on behalf of the patient; and

(b) has no interest adverse to that of the patient; and

(c) where the patient is a claimant, undertakes to pay any costs in relation to the proceedings to which the patient may become liable, subject to a right to be reimbursed from the assets of the patient.

No evidence of incapacity need be filed with this form. Rule 6.6 further does not require the patient to be served with the form unless the court orders otherwise, although the carer with whom the patient lives must be served. It may well be, therefore, that the patient knows nothing of the litigation. If the patient in fact lacks capacity, this may in some cases have minimal adverse consequences, but this begs the question of whether the patient does in fact lack capacity, and raises questions about the dignity afforded to clients of marginal capacity. Challenges to the appointment of litigation friends under rule 21.7 of the CPR, and appointments by the court under rule 21.6 must be accompanied by evidence, but the nature of that evidence is unspecified, and need not be specifically medical. This absence of judicial process has led to the consistency of the current appointment process with Article 6 of the ECHR being called into question (see *Masterman-Lister*, para. 17).

Advocates should be aware that the authority of the client to conduct proceedings is not merely an issue upon the commencement of proceedings. Indeed, the issue regarding client authority may change over the course of litigation. Thus a client may be capable of providing instructions up to the time of settlement or judgment in a case, but due to specific incapacities may be unable to provide instructions as to how a large sum of damages is to be dealt with. In that event, the appointment of a litigation guardian may become appropriate at that time (*Masterman-Lister*, paras. 27, 83). The authority of a solicitor to act ceases upon a client subsequently becoming a person under disability, and proceedings occurring after that time would seem to be a nullity. In civil actions, the solicitor may become personally liable for costs thrown away by other parties, in the event that the case proceeds after the client becomes a person under disability and without the appointment of a next friend (*Yonge* v *Toynbee* [1910] 1 KB 215).

The effect of the appointment of a litigation friend, or the conduct of the litigation by the Court of Protection, is that the patient, while remaining technically the party in the matter, ceases to be involved in the conduct of the litigation. That role is taken by the next friend. Next friends can be anyone the court sees fit to appoint, although the Official Solicitor often assumes this role. The litigation is of course to be conducted for the benefit of the patient, there is an inevitable loss of control of the litigation by the patient him- or herself. In the event that the loss of capacity is likely to be temporary, it may be worth considering delay of the proceedings until it is regained. In this context, it should be noted that limitation periods do not run against people in their incapacity (Limitation Act 1980, s. 28).

As to the mechanics of representing individuals within the mental health system, Eldergill (1997: ch. 16) provides a valuable 'how to' guide, complete with not merely discussion of general principles, but also checklists, a *pro forma* case summary, and advice on the minutiae of conducting interviews. Quite appropriately, he emphasises the essential similarity between representation in this context with any other form of client advocacy (1997: 884):

> In terms of professional conduct, the principles are the same as for any client attending the office: to serve the client without compromising the solicitor's integrity or his overriding duty to the court and the judicial process. . . . To summarise, the usual principles governing the solicitor-client relationship apply and few problems will arise provided the solicitor is courteous and avoids being patronising.

While this is and must be the overarching principle, as Eldergill acknowledges, representation of this sort of client has its own quirks. Additional patience and empathy may be required to gain the client's trust, to help the client to formulate their wishes and instructions. Particular care may be necessary to explain the situation the client is in. While information about detention and treatment rights is required to be given to clients by s. 132 of the MHA 1983, it would seem that between 20 and 40 per cent of detained patients do not recall what section they were admitted under (see MHAC, 2008; Lomax, 2012). This may be, but is not necessarily, an indictment of those responsible for providing the information. The statute required that the information be given 'as soon as practicable after the commencement of the patient's detention' (s. 132(1)), and thus at a time when the client may well be facing new and frightening surroundings, and a barrage of other information. It is perhaps unsurprising that they do not remember it. Nonetheless, the advocate may have to explain the legal situation, starting at the basics.

As in all relationships with clients, the solicitor should not jump to conclusions about what the client wants. The client may well want to be released from the facility; but alternatively or additionally, the client may want a different treatment regime which, if provided, might make continuation in the facility considerably more palatable or even agreeable. Assuming the client has the capacity to instruct, it is inappropriate that advocates 'second-guess' the client's wishes or instructions due to concerns about whether the instructions are in the client's clinical or social best interests. Virtually all other professionals in the mental health system are professionally obliged to act in the client's best interests: that role is already taken, many times over. In the same way that a solicitor would not second-guess the instructions of other clients, the instructions of these clients should be respected, consistent of course with the solicitor's duty to the court and judicial process. The fact that the client's views should not be second-guessed does not of course mean that the advocate should encourage the client to have a closed mind about other results. An advocate may be able to negotiate a partial solution to a problem, and here as in any other solicitor/client relationship, a partial victory may be preferable to the client than the risk of an all or nothing hearing.

All of this is based on the assumption that the client is able to give competent instructions. What is the role of the advocate if the client does not have this ability? Romano (1997: 750–59) identifies four logically possible responses of the advocate in this situation: follow the client's wishes as if the client is competent; have a guardian appointed; have the advocate act as *de facto* guardian; and withdraw. None of these is ideal; but some are perhaps more problematic than others. In court proceedings, the directions are fairly clear: withdraw until a litigation friend is appointed. The hard line of the court rules does not directly apply to tribunal applications, however, and it seems counterintuitive to remove to a third party the rather specific right to challenge a confinement, for example, which is provided to the patient under the Act. For this reason it is also dubious whether the advocate should act as guardian: it is still not the client making the decisions. In addition, as Romano points out (1997: 755), the role of advocate is different and conflicting from that of guardian:

> While the advocate has an obligation to consult with the client regarding what the advocate should do on his behalf, the guardian's role is to determine the best interests of the client and act accordingly. This shift in responsibility from taking instructions to giving them can result in the advocate disregarding many important ethical rules which should ordinarily govern the advocate-client dynamic.

Arguably, the advocate is in a particularly poor position to fulfil the role of guardian in any event. He or she is unlikely to have known the client prior to the commencement of the professional relationship, and therefore unlikely to be aware of the values of the client when capable. There is real danger here that the advocate will move in directions of which the client may not approve, if they regain capacity.

Continuing based on the client's wishes is also a profoundly problematic option, even in a review tribunal setting where the rules of court do not apply. The difficulty is that continuation with a hearing may have an adverse result. The client has a right to only one hearing per certificate, and if the client is detained under s. 3, it will be six months or a year before the right to another tribunal hearing arises. It is conceivable that a negligence action might lie against a solicitor for the loss of the right to a hearing in this period, in the event that the solicitor proceeded on instructions of an incapable client to a hearing early in the certificate.

That leaves withdrawal, which would seem to be the only appropriate course of action. It, too, is problematic, particularly if the advocate sees what appears to be a winning argument. It also does not preclude the client from proceeding to the tribunal and representing him- or herself. It seems counterintuitive to deny representation to which the client has a prima facie right under the rules of the tribunal, for a hearing that is going to go forward in any event. Withdrawal finally suggests that the client must pass two hurdles to obtain relief from the tribunal: they must not merely convince the tribunal of the justice of their case; but also convince their advocate of their ability to instruct. Care must therefore be taken not to set the standard of capacity to instruct so high as to preclude meritorious cases from reaching the appropriate forum. Yet if the advocate really cannot get proper instructions, it is not obvious what else can be done.

Above all, clients should be treated professionally, with respect, dignity, and emotional commitment.

12.11 Concluding comments

We are now at the end of this book—the time for the reader to look back and to consider where we have been. The legal issues described in this book involve fundamental rights and liberties, and the needs of some of society's most vulnerable people. Conceptually, mental health law contains implied premises as to what it is to be a citizen, what the role of the state is with reference to the vulnerable and the bizarre in society, and what the relative roles of law and medicine are in the regulation and control of deviance. It is a field where what is usually assumed becomes problematic. It has been suggested that the law may have unforeseen effects—some beneficial, some not. Above all, it has been argued that this is an area of considerable legal and social complexity. It is not a realm of simple answers. It is instead a field of considerable difficulty, but a field offering corresponding intellectual rewards. Mediocre advocacy will not suffice. Clients deserve—and need—better. That is the final challenge of this book, to the advocates and potential advocates who read it.

Bibliography

ABDUL-HAMID, W. and COONEY, C. (1997) 'Homelessness, mental illness and the law', *Medicine, Science and Law* 37(4): 341–4.

AHMAD, W.I.U. and ATKIN, K. (1996) *Race and Community Care*, Buckingham: Open University Press.

AKINKUNMI, A. and MURRAY, K. (1997) 'Inadequacies in the Mental Health Act 1983 in relation to mentally disordered remand prisoners', *Medicine, Science and Law* 37(1): 53.

AKRAM, A. and KENT, A. (2010) 'Social Care Needs of Women with Mental Illness' in Kohen, D. (ed.) *Oxford Textbook of Women and Mental Health*, Oxford: OUP.

ALLDERIDGE, P. (1985) 'Bedlam: fact or fantasy?', in W.F. Bynum, R. Porter and M. Shepherd (eds) *The Anatomy of Madness*, Vol. 2, London: Tavistock.

ANDOH, B. (1994) 'Hospital and police procedures when a patient absconds from a mental hospital', *Medicine, Science and Law* 34(2): 130.

ANDOH, B. (2004) 'Absconding from mental hospitals and negligence. (Case comment: D v South Tyneside Health Care NHS Trust) [2004] P.I.Q.R.P12', *Mountbatten Journal of Legal Studies* 8(2): 79–85.

ANON. (1996) 'Why we run for cover', in J. Read and J. Reynolds (eds) *Speaking Our Minds: An Anthology*, Basingstoke: Macmillan.

APPLEBY, L. and BOYINGTON, J. (2005) *Letter regarding prison transfer* (later published together with HM Prison Service, 2006).

ARBER, S., GILBERTY, G.N. and EVANDROU, M. (1988) 'Gender, household composition and receipt of domiciliary services by elderly disabled people', *Journal of Social Policy* 17: 153.

ARMSTRONG, W. (1999) ' "Nature or degree" in the Mental Health Act 1983', *Journal of Mental Health Law* 2: 154–8.

ASSOCIATION OF CHIEF POLICE OFFICERS (2012, 2nd edition) *Guidance on the Safer Detention and Handling of Persons in Police Custody*, London: National Policing Improvement Agency.

ASSOCIATION OF DIRECTORS OF ADULT SOCIAL SERVICES (2011) *Putting People First: 3rd Year Progress*, London: ADASS.

ASSOCIATION OF DIRECTORS OF ADULT SOCIAL SERVICES (2012) *Personal Budgets Survey March 2012 Results*.

ASSOCIATION OF DIRECTORS OF ADULT SOCIAL SERVICES (2012a) *The Case for Tomorrow: Facing the Beyond—A joint discussion document on the future of services for older people*, London: ADASS.

ASTRAZENECA (2012), *Annual Report for 2011*, London: AstraZeneca.

AUDIT COMMISSION (1986) *Making a Reality of Community Care*, London: HMSO.

AUSTIN, C., LE FEUVRE, M., O'GRADY, J., SWYER, B. and VAUGHAN, P. (2003) 'Improving psychiatric information for magistrates' courts', *Justice of the Peace and Local Government Law* 167(1/1): 6–7.

BACH, M. and KERZNER, L. (2010) *A New Paradigm for Protecting Autonomy and the Right to Legal Capacity*, Toronto: Law Commission of Ontario, 2010.

BAILEY J. and MacCULLOCH, M. (1992) 'Patterns of reconviction in patients discharged directly to the community from a special hospital: implications for after-care', *Journal of Forensic Psychiatry* 3(3): 445.

BAKER, E. (1992) 'Dangerousness: the neglected gaoler—disorder and risk under the Mental Health Act 1983', *Journal of Forensic Psychiatry* 3(1): 31.

BAKER, E. (1994) 'Human Rights, *M'Naghten* and the 1991 Act', *Criminal Law Review* 84: 553.

BANNERJEE, S. *et al.* (1995) *Deaths of Detained Patients: A Review of Reports to the Mental Health Act Commission*, London: Mental Health Foundation.

BARHAM, P. (1992) *Closing the Asylum: The Mental Patient in Modern Society*, London: Penguin.

BARNES, M., BOWL, R., and FISHER, M. (1990) *Sectioned: Social Services and the Mental Health Act 1983*, London: Routledge.

BARNETT-CORMACK, S., CAMPBELL, S. NICHOLSON, F. SUMPTER, S., and YOUNG, J. (2012) *Together We Shout*, We are Spartacus http://wearespartacus.org.uk/.

BARTLETT, P. (1997) 'The consequences of incapacity', *Web Journal of Current Legal Issues* 4.

BARTLETT, P. (1999) *The Poor Law of Lunacy: The Administration of Pauper Lunatics in Mid-Nineteenth-Century England*, London: University of Leicester Press/Cassell.

BARTLETT, P. (1999a) 'The asylum, the workhouse and the voice of the insane poor in nineteenth-century England', *International Journal of Law and Psychiatry* 21(3): 1.

BARTLETT, P. (2001) 'English mental health reform: lessons from Ontario?' *Journal of Mental Health Law*: 27–43.

BARTLETT, P. (2001a) 'Legal madness in the nineteenth century', *Social History of Medicine* 14(1): 107–31.

BARTLETT, P. (2003) 'Capacity and confinement: when is detention not detention?', in K. Diesfeld and I. Freckelton (eds) *Involuntary Detention and Therapeutic Jurisprudence: International Perspectives on Civil Commitment*, Aldershot: Ashgate, Dartmouth.

BARTLETT, P. (2003a) 'The test of compulsion in mental health law: capacity, therapeutic benefit and dangerousness as possible criteria', *Medical Law Review* 11: 326.

BARTLETT, P. (2007) *Blackstone's Guide to the Mental Capacity Act 2005*, 2nd edn, Oxford: Oxford University Press.

BARTLETT, P. (2010) 'Sex, Dementia and Care Homes' *Liverpool Law Review* 31: 137–54.

BARTLETT, P. (2011) ' "The necessity must be convincingly shown to exist": standards for compulsory treatment for mental disorder under the Mental Health Act 1983', *Medical Law Review* 19: 514–47.

BARTLETT, P. (2012) 'The United Nations Convention on the Rights of Persons with Disability and Mental Health Law', *Modern Law Review* 75(5):752–78.

BARTLETT, P. (2012a) 'Rewriting Herzcegfalvy' in E Brems (ed) *Diversity and European Human Rights: Rewriting Judgments of the ECHR*, Cambridge: Cambridge University Press.

BARTLETT, P., LEWIS, O., and THOROLD, O. (2006) *Mental Disability and the European Convention on Human Rights*, Leiden: Martinus Nijhof.

BARTLETT, P., LEWIS, O., and THOROLD, O. (2007) *Mental Disability and the European Convention on Human Rights*, Leiden: Brill/Martinus Nijhoff.

BARTLETT, P., MANTOVANI, N. CRATSLEY K., DILLON, C., and EASTMAN, N. (2010) ' "You May Kiss the Bride, But You May Not Open Your Mouth When You Do So": Policies Concerning Sex, Marriage and Relationships in English Forensic Psychiatric Facilities', *Liverpool Law Review* 31(2): 155–76.

BARTLETT, P. and WRIGHT, D. (eds) (1999) *Outside the Walls of the Asylum: The History of Care in the Community 1750–2000*, London: Athlone.

BAXTER, R. (1991) 'The mentally disordered offender in hospital: the role of the Home Office', in K. Herbst and J. Gunn (eds) *The Mentally Disordered Offender*, London: Butterworth-Heinemann.

BEAN, P. (2001) *Mental Disorder and Community Safety*, Basingstoke: Palgrave.

BEAN, P. and MOUNSER, P (1993) *Discharged from Mental Hospitals*, London: Macmillan.

BEAN, P. and NEMETZ, T. (1994) *Out of Depth and Out of Sight*, London: Mencap.

BEAN, P. and NEMETZ, T. (1997) *Final Report to the Mental Health Foundation on the Evaluation of the Southampton MIND Appropriate Adult Scheme*, London: Mental Health Foundation.

BENBOW, S.M. and CRENTSIL, J. (2004) 'Subjective experience of electroconvulsive therapy', *Psychiatric Bulletin* 28: 289–91.

BIRMINGHAM, L., MASON, D., and GRUBIN, D. (1996) 'Prevalence of mental disorder in remand prisoners: consecutive case study', *British Medical Journal* 313: 1521.

BIRMINGHAM, L., MASON, D., and GRUBIN, D. (2000) 'Mental illness at reception into prison', *Criminal Behaviour and Mental Health* 10: 77–87.

BISSETT-JOHNSON, A. and MAIN, S. (2002) 'The Community Care and Health (Scotland) Act 2002 and *Robertson v Fife Council*', *Scottish Law Times* 34: 279–84.

BLACK MENTAL HEALTH UK (2013) *Written Evidence Submitted by Black Mental Health UK to the Home Affairs Committee Investigation into the Independent Police Complaints Commission* [IPCC 23], 13 January 2013.

BLUMENTHAL, S. and WESSELY, S. (1992) 'National survey of current arrangements for diversion from custody in England and Wales', *British Medical Journal* 305: 1322.

BOARDMAN, J. and PARSONAGE, M. (2008) 'The National Service Framework for Mental Health: progress, prospects and priorities', *Journal of Public Mental Health* (7)3: 36–41.

BOAST, N. and CHESTERMAN, P. (1995) 'Black people and secure psychiatric facilities', *British Journal of Criminology* 31(2): 218.

BOBES J. *et al.* (2002) 'Frequency of Extrapyramidal Adverse Reactions in Schizophrenic Outpatients Treated with Risperidone, Olanzapine, Quetiapine or Haloperidol: Results of the EIRE Study', *Clinical Drug Investigation* 22: 609.

BONNIE, R. and MONAHAN, J. (2005) 'From Coercion to Contract: Reframing the Debate on Mandated Community Treatment for People with Mental Disorders', *Law and Human Behavior* 29(4):485–503.

BOTT, E. (1976) 'Hospital and society', *British Journal of Medical Psychology* 49: 97.

BOWDEN, P. (1996) Violence and mental disorder', in N. Walker (ed) *Dangerous People*, London: Blackstone Press.

BOWEN, P. (2007) *Blackstones Guide to the Mental Health Act 2007* Oxford: OUP.

BOWERS, L. (2003) 'Runaway patients', *Mental Health Practice* 7(1): 10–2.

BOWERS, L., ALEXANDER, J., and GASKELL, C. (2003) 'A trial of an anti-absconding intervention in acute psychiatric wards', *Journal of Psychiatric and Mental Health Nursing* 10: 410–6.

BOYNTON, J. (1980) *Report of the Review of Rampton Hospital*, Cmnd. 8073, London: HMSO.

BRABBINS, C.J. and TRAVERS, R.F. (1994) 'Mental disorder among defendants in Liverpool magistrates' court', *Medicine, Science and Law* 31(4): 279.

BRADLEY, LORD (2009) *The Bradley Report: Lord Bradley's Review of People with Mental Health Problems or Learning Disabilities in the Criminal Justice System* London: COI for the Department of Health.

BRIDGES, L. and CHOONGH, S. (1998) *Improving Police Station LegalAdvice*, London: Law Society.

BRITISH MEDICAL ASSOCIATION (2009) *Health care of detainees in police stations*, London: BMA.

BRITISH MEDICAL ASSOCIATION AND ASSOCIATION OF POLICE SURGEONS (1994) *Health Care of Detainees in Police Stations*, London: BMA.

BROOK, R. (1573) *La Grande Abridgement*, 2 vols., n.p.

BROOK, R., DOLAN, M., and COOREY, P. (1999) 'Absconding of patients detained in an English Special Hospital', *Journal of Forensic Psychiatry* 10(1): 46–58.

BROOKE, D., TAYLOR, C., GUNN J., and MADDEN, D. (1996) 'Point prevalence of mental disorder in unconvicted male prisoners in England and Wales', *British Medical Journal* 313:

BROOKER, C., DUGGAN, S., FOX, C., MILLS, A. and PARSONAGE, M. (2008) *Short-changed: Spending on Prison Mental Health Care* London: The Sainsbury Centre for Mental Health 1524.

BROOKER, C. and GOJKOVIC, D. (2009) 'The 2nd national survey of prison in-reach' *Journal of Forensic Psychiatry & Psychology*, 20:S1, S11–28.

BROWN, D., ELLIS, T. and LARCOMBE, K. (1993) *Changing the Code: Police Detention Under the Revised PACE Codes of Practice*, London: HMSO.

BROWN, H. and SMITH, H. (eds) (1992) *Normalisation: A Reader for the Nineties*, London: Routledge.

BROWN, R. (2002). 'The Changing Role of the Approved Social Worker' *Journal of Mental Health Law*, December 2002, 392–8.

BUCHANAN, A. (2002) 'Psychiatric detention and treatment: a suggested criterion', *Journal of Mental Health Law* 6: 35–41.

BURNS, T., *et al.* (2011) 'Pressures to adhere to treatment ('leverage') in English mental healthcare', *British Journal of Psychiatry* 199: 145–50.

BUSFIELD J. (1986) *Managing Madness: Changing Ideas and Practice*, London: Unwin Hyman.

BUTLER, P. and KOUSOULOU, D. (2006) *Women at Risk: The Mental Health of Women in Contact with the Judicial System*, London: The London Development Centre and the Care Service Improvement Partnership.

BUTLER, R. and ROSENTHAL, G. (1985) *Behaviour and Rehabilitation*, Bristol: Wright.

BUTLER, T. (1992) *Changing Mental Health Services: The Politics and the Policy*, London: Chapman and Hall.

BYNUM, W. (1981) 'Rationales for therapy in British psychiatry 1780–1835' in A. Scull (ed.) *Madhouses, Mad-Doctors and Madmen*, London: The Athlone Press.

CAIRNS, R., et al. (2005) 'Prevalence and predictors of mental incapacity in psychiatric inpatients', *British Journal of Psychiatry* 187: 379.

CAIRNS, R., *et al.* (2005a), 'Reliability of mental capacity assessments in psychiatric in-patients' *British Journal of Psychiatry* 187: 372.

CAIRNS, R., *et al.* (2011) 'Judgements about deprivation of liberty made by various professionals: comparison study', *The Psychiatrist* 35:344–9.

CAPE, E. (2002) 'Incompetent police station advice and the exclusion of evidence' *Criminal Law Review* 471–84.

CAPE, E. and HICKMAN, J. (2002) 'Bad lawyer, good defence' *New Law Journal*, 152 (7043), n1194–1195.

CAPLAN, P. (1995) *They Say You're Crazy: How the World's Most Powerful Psychiatrists Decide Who's Normal*, Reading, MA: Addison-Wesley.

CARDINAL, M. (1996) 'The words to say it', in S. Dunn, B. Morrison and M. Roberts (eds) *Mind Readings: Writers' Journeys through Mental States*, London: Minerva.

CARE QUALITY COMMISSION (2009). *National NHS Patient Survey Programme: Mental Health Acute Inpatient Service Users Survey 2009*, London: Care Quality Commission.

CARE QUALITY COMMISSION (2010) *Monitoring the Mental Health Act in 2009/10*, London: Care Quality Commission.

CARE QUALITY COMMISSION (2010a) *Leave of Absence and Transfer Under the Mental Health Act 1983*, London: Care Quality Commission.

CARE QUALITY COMMISSION (2011) *Count Me in 2010: Results of the 2010 National Census of Inpatients and Patients on Supervised Community Treatment in Mental Health and Learning Disability Services in England and Wales*, London: Care Quality Commission and National Mental Health Development Unit 2011.

CARE QUALITY COMMISSION (2011a) *Monitoring the Mental Health Act in 2010/11*, London: Care Quality Commission.

CARE QUALITY COMMISSION (2011b) *Statutory Notification about the Unauthorised Absence of a Person Detained or Liable to be Detained under the Mental Health Act 1983*, London: Care Quality Commission.

CARE QUALITY COMMISSION (2011c) *The Operation of the Deprivation of Liberty Safeguards in England, 2009/10*, London: Care Quality Commission.

CARE QUALITY COMMISSION (2012) *The State of Health Care and Adult Social Care in England: An Overview of Key Themes in Care in 2011/12* London: TSO.

CARE QUALITY COMMISSION (2012a) *National Summary of the Results for the Community Mental Health Survey 2012* available at http://www.cqc.org.uk/sites/default/files/media/documents/20120910_mh12_national_briefing_note_final.pdf

CARE QUALITY COMMISSION (2013) *Monitoring the Mental Health Act in 2011/12*, London: Care Quality Commission.

CARE QUALITY COMMISSION (2013a) *Not Just a Number: Home Care Inspection Programme: National Overview*, London: Care Quality Commission.

CARE QUALITY COMMISSION AND THE ADMINISTRATIVE JUSTICE AND TRIBUNALS COUNCIL (2011) *Patients' Experiences of the First-tier Tribunal (Mental Health)*, London: Care Quality Commission.

CARNAHAN R., *et al.* (2006) 'Increased risk of extrapyramidal side-effect treatment associated with atypical antipsychotic poly-therapy', *Acta Psychiatr Scand* 113: 135–41.

CARSON, D. (1989) 'Prosecuting people with mental handicap', *Criminal Law Review*: 87.

CARSON, D. (1993) 'Disabling progress: the Law Commission's proposals on mentally incapacitated adults' decision-making', 15/5 *Journal of Social Welfare and Family Law*: 304.

CASTEL, R. (1985) 'Moral treatment: mental therapy and social control in the nineteenth century', in S. Cohen and A. Scull (eds) *Social Control and the State*, Oxford: Basil Blackwell.

CAVADINO, M. (1989) *Mental Health Law in Context: Doctor's Orders?*, Aldershot: Dartmouth.

CENTRAL COUNCIL FOR EDUCATION AND TRAINING IN SOCIAL WORK (1993) *Requirements and Guidance for the Training of Social Workers to be Considered for Approval in England and Wales under the Mental Health Act 1983*, CCETSW Paper No.19.27, London: CCETSW.

CENTRE FOR MENTAL HEALTH (2011) *Pathways to Unlocking Secure Mental Health Care*, London: Centre for Mental Health.

CENTRE FOR MENTAL HEALTH, RETHINK AND THE ROYAL COLLEGE OF PSYCHIATRISTS (2011) *Diversion: The Business Case for Action*, London: Centre for Mental Health, Rethink and the Royal College of Psychiatrists.

CENTRE FOR POLICY ON AGEING INFORMATION SERVICE (2013) *Selected Readings: The Personalisation Agenda, Direct Payments and Individual Budgets*, London: Centre for Policy on Ageing.

CENTRE FOR PUBLIC INNOVATION (2005) *Review into the Current Practices of Court Liaison and Diversion Schemes*, London: CPI.

CHADWICK, P.D. (1997) *Schizophrenia: The Positive Perspective*. London: Routledge.

CHEADLE, J. and DITCHFIELD, J. (1982) *Sentenced Mentally Ill Offenders*, London: Home Office Research and Planning Unit.

CHEUNG, P., SCHWEITZER, I., TUCKWELL, V., and CROWLEY, K. (1997) 'A prospective study of assaults on staff by psychiatric inpatients', *Medicine, Science and Law* 37(1): 46.

CLEMENTS, L. (1997) 'Community care: towards a workable statute', *Liverpool Law Review* 19(2): 181.

COCKBURN, P. and COCKBURN, H. (2011) *Henry's Demons Living with Schizophrenia: A Father and Son's Story*. London: Simon and Schuster.

COHEN, J. J. (1999) *Of Giants: Sex, Monsters and the Middle Ages*, Minnesota: University of Minnesota Press.

COHEN, S. (1979) 'The Punitive City: Notes on the Dispersal of Social Control' *Contemporary Crises* 3 (1979) 339–63.

COHEN, S. (1985) *Visions of Social Control*, Cambridge: Polity.

COID, J. (1988) 'Mentally abnormal offenders on remand I: rejected or accepted by the NHS?', *British Medical Journal* 296: 1779.

COID, J., BEBBINGTON, P., JENKINS, R., BRUGHA, T., LEWIS, G., FARRELL, M., and SINGLETON, N. (2002) 'The national survey of psychiatric morbidity among prisoners and the future of prison medical care', *Medicine, Science and the Law* 42(3): 245–50.

COMMISSION FOR HEALTH IMPROVEMENT (2004) *What CHI has Found: Mental Health Trusts*, London: Commission for Health Improvement.

COMMISSION FOR HEALTHCARE AUDIT AND INSPECTION, MHAC, CSIP AND NIMHE (2005) *Count Me In: Results of a National Census of Inpatients in Mental Health Hospitals and Facilities in England and Wales*, London: Commission for Healthcare Audit and Inspection.

COMMISSION FOR HEALTHCARE AUDIT AND INSPECTION (2008), *Count Me In 2008*, London: Healthcare Commission.

COMMISSION FOR SOCIAL CARE INSPECTION (2005) *The State of Social Care in England 2004–5*, London: Commission for Social Care Inspection.

COMMISSION FOR SOCIAL CARE INSPECTION (2006) *Annual Report 2005–6*, London: HMSO.

COMMISSION ON FUNDING OF CARE AND SUPPORT (2011) *Report of the Commission on Funding of Care and Support*, London: TSO.

COMMITTEE ON MENTALLY ABNORMAL OFFENDERS (the 'Butler Committee') (1975) *Report of the Committee on Mentally Abnormal Offenders*, Cmnd 6244, London: HMSO.

COMMON ASSESSMENT FRAMEWORK FOR ADULTS NETWORK (2012) *CAF Lessons Learnt*, available from the CAFAN website at http://www.networks.nhs.uk/nhs-networks/common-assessment-framework-for-adults-learning/caf-lessons-learnt/redesigning-systems-and-services/assessment

COMYN, J. (1822) *Digest of the Laws of England*, 5th edn, 8 vols., A. Hammond (ed.), London: Strahan.

CONFIDENTIAL INQUIRY INTO SUICIDE AND HOMICIDE BY PEOPLE WITH MENTAL ILLNESS (2012) *Annual Report of the Confidential Inquiry into Suicide and Homicide by People with Mental Illness*, Confidential Inquiry into Suicide and Homicide by People with Mental Illness: University of Manchester.

COOKE, D. (1991) 'Treatment as an alternative to prosecution: offenders diverted for treatment', *British Journal of Psychiatry* 158: 785.

CORSTON, BARONESS J. (2007) *A Review of Women with Particular Vulnerabilities in the Criminal Justice System (the 'Corston Report')*, London: HMSO.

COUNCIL ON TRIBUNALS (2000) *Mental Health Review Tribunals: Special Report*, Cm 4740, London: HMSO.

COUNCIL ON TRIBUNALS (2006) *Annual Report 2005–6*, HC1210, London: HMSO.

COURT OF PROTECTION (2011) *Court of Protection Report—2010*, London: Judiciary of England and Wales.

COWAN, D. (1995a) 'Accommodating community care' *Journal of Law and Society* 22(2): 212.

COWAN, D. (1995b) 'Community care and homelessness', *Modern Law Review* 58(2): 256.

COWEN, H. (1999) *Community Care, Ideology and Social Policy*, Hemel Hempstead: Prentice Hall.

COX, B. (1994) *Research on Guardianship for Mentally Ill People*, London: Social Services Inspectorate.

CRAWFORD, D. (1984) 'Problems with assessment of dangerousness in England and Wales', *Medicine and Law* 3: 141.

CRICHTON, J.H.M. and CALGIE, J. (2002) 'Responding to inpatient violence at a psychiatric hospital of special security: a pilot project', *Medicine, Science and Law* 42(1): 30–3.

CROWN PROSECUTION SERVICE (2013) *The Code for Crown Prosecutors*, 7th edn, London: CPS.

CUMMING, E. and CUMMING, J. (1957) *Closed Ranks: An Experiment in Mental Health Education*, Cambridge, MA: Harvard University Press.

CUMMINS, I. (2012) 'Policing and Mental Illness in England and Wales post Bradley' *Policing: A Journal of Policy & Practice* 6(4): 365.

DALLEY, G. (1993) 'Professional ideology or organisational tribalism?', in J. Walmsley, J. Reynolds, P., Shakespeare and R. Wollfe (eds) *Health, Welfare and Practice: Reflecting on Roles and Relationships*, London: Sage.

DAMASIO, A. (1994) *Descartes' Error*, London: Papermac.

DAMASIO, A. (2000) *The Feeling of What Happens*, London: Vintage.

DARTON, R. (2004) 'What types of home are closing? The characteristics of homes which closed between 1996 and 2001', *Health and Social Care in the Community* 12(3): 254–64.

DARTON, R., BÄUMKER, T., CALLAGHAN, L., HOLDER, J., NETTEN, A., and TOWERS, A. (2012) 'The characteristics of residents in extra care housing and care homes in England' *Health and Social Care in the Community* 20(1): 87–96.

DARTON, R., BÄUMKER, T., CALLAGHAN, L., and NETTEN, A. (2011) 'Improving housing with care choices for older people: The PSSRU evaluation of extra care housing' *Housing Care and Support* 14(3): 77–82.

DAWSON, J. (2010) 'Community Treatment Orders' in L. Gostin et al (eds) *Principles of Mental Health Law and Policy*, Oxford: OUP.

DAWSON, J. and SZMUKLER, G., (2006) 'Fusion of mental health and incapacity legislation', *British Journal of Psychiatry* 188:504

DELL, S. (1980) 'Transfer of special hospital patients into National Health Service hospitals', in J. Gunn and D. Farrington (eds) *Abnormal Offenders, Delinquency and the Criminal Justice System*, Chichester: John Wiley.

DELL, S. and ROBERTSON, G. (1988) *Sentenced to Hospital*, Oxford: Oxford University Press.

DENDLE, P. (2007) 'The Zombie as Barometer of Cultural Anxiety' in Scott, N. (ed) *Monsters and the Monstrous: Myths and Metaphors of Enduring Evil*, New York and Amsterdam: Rodopi.

DEPARTMENT FOR CONSTITUTIONAL AFFAIRS (2007) *Mental Capacity Act 2005 Code of Practice*, London: TSO.

DEPARTMENT OF HEALTH (1989) *Caring for People*, London: Department of Health.

DEPARTMENT OF HEALTH (1989a) *Working for Patients*, London: Department of Health.

DEPARTMENT OF HEALTH (1990) *The Care Programme Approach for People with a Mental Illness Referred to Specialist Psychiatric Services*, HC(90)23, London: Department of Health.

DEPARTMENT OF HEALTH (1990a) *Community Care in the Next Decade and Beyond*, London: HMSO.

DEPARTMENT OF HEALTH (1992) *Mental Health Review Tribunals for England and Wales Annual Report 1991*, London: Department of Health.

DEPARTMENT OF HEALTH (1993) *Approvals and Directions for Arrangements from 1 April 1993 Made Under Schedule 8 to the National Health Service Act 1977 and sections 21 and 29 of the National Assistance Act 1948*, LAC(93)10, London: NHS Executive, Department of Health.

DEPARTMENT OF HEALTH (1993a) *Legal Powers on the Care of Mentally Ill People in the Community: Report of the Internal Review*, London: Department of Health.

DEPARTMENT OF HEALTH (1994) *Guidance on the Discharge of Mentally Disordered People and their Continuing Care in the Community*, HSG(94)27, London: Department of Health.

DEPARTMENT OF HEALTH (1995) *Building Bridges: A Guide to Arrangements for Inter-Agency Working for the Care and Protection of Severely Mentally Ill People*, London: Department of Health.

DEPARTMENT OF HEALTH (1995a) *Mentally Disordered Offenders*, produced for LAG and Doughty Street Chambers Conference.

DEPARTMENT OF HEALTH (1996) *The Use of 'Trial Leave' under Section 17 of the Mental Health Act 1983 to Transfer Patients between Hospitals*, HSG (96)28, London: Department of Health.

DEPARTMENT OF HEALTH (1997) *Mental Health Review Tribunals for England and Wales Annual Report 1996*, London: Department of Health.

DEPARTMENT OF HEALTH (1998) *Modernising Mental Health Services: Safe, Sound and Supportive*, London: HMSO.

DEPARTMENT OF HEALTH (1998a) *Modernising Social Services: Promoting Independence, Improving Projection, Raising Standards*, Cm 4169, London: HMSO.

DEPARTMENT OF HEALTH (1998b) *Inpatients Formally Detained in Hospitals under the Mental Health Act 1983 and other Legislation, England: 1987–8 to 1997–8*, London: Department of Health.

DEPARTMENT OF HEALTH (1999) *A National Service Framework for Mental Health*, London: Department of Health.

DEPARTMENT OF HEALTH (1999a) *Reform of the Mental Health Act 1983: Proposals for Reform*, Cm 4480, London: Department of Health.

DEPARTMENT OF HEALTH (1999b) *Report of the Committee of Inquiry into the Personality Disorder Unit, Ashworth Special Hospital* (the 'Fallon Report'), Cm 4194-II, London: HMSO.

DEPARTMENT OF HEALTH (1999d) *Effective Care Co-ordination in Mental Health Services: Modernising the Care Programme Approach*, London: Department of Health.

DEPARTMENT OF HEALTH (1999e) *Still Building Bridges: The Report of a National Inspection of Arrangements for the Inspection of Care Programme Approach with Care Management*, CI 99/3, London: Department of Health.

DEPARTMENT OF HEALTH (1999f) *Modernising the CPA*, London: Department of Health.

DEPARTMENT OF HEALTH (2000) *Report of the Review of Security at the High Security Hospitals*, London: Department of Health.

DEPARTMENT OF HEALTH (2000a) *After-Care Under the Mental Health Act 1983 Section 117 After-Care Services* HSC 2000/003: LAC (2000), London: Department of Health.

DEPARTMENT OF HEALTH (2001) *Guidance on Free Nursing Care in Nursing Homes*, HSC 2001/17, LAC (2001)26, London: Department of Health.

DEPARTMENT OF HEALTH (2001a) *Building Capacity and Partnership in Care: An Agreement Between the Statutory and the Independent Social Care, Health Care and Housing Sectors*, London: Department of Health.

DEPARTMENT OF HEALTH (2002a) *Guardianship under the Mental Health Act 1983 England 2002*, London: Department of Health.

DEPARTMENT OF HEALTH (2003) *Inpatients Formally Detained in Hospitals Under the Mental Health Act 1983 and Other Legislation, NHS Trusts, High Security Psychiatric Hospitals and Private Facilities: 2001–2*, London: Department of Health.

DEPARTMENT OF HEALTH (2004) *Guidance on: National Assistance Act 1948 (Choice of Accommodation) Directions 1992, National Assistance (Residential Accommodation) (Additional Payments and Assessment of Resources)(Amendment)(England) Regulations 2001*, LCA (2004)20.

DEPARTMENT OF HEALTH (2004a) *The National Service Framework for Mental Health: Five Years On*, London: Department of Health.

DEPARTMENT OF HEALTH (2005) *Procedure for the Transfers of Prisoners to and from Hospital under Sections 47 and 48 of the Mental Health Act 1983*, London: Department of Health.

DEPARTMENT OF HEALTH (2005a) *Prison Mental Health Transfers Audit Report*, London: Department of Health.

DEPARTMENT OF HEALTH (2005b) *Delivering Race Equality in Mental Health Care: An Action Plan for Reform Inside and Outside Services and the Government's Response to the Independent Inquiry into the Death of David Bennett*, London: HMSO.

DEPARTMENT OF HEALTH (2006) *Inpatients Formally Detained in Hospitals under the Mental Health Act 1983 and other Legislation, England: 1994–2005 to 2004–5*, London: Department of Health.

DEPARTMENT OF HEALTH (2006a) *The Mental Health Bill: Plans to Amend the Mental Health Act*, Briefing sheet—Professional Roles—A4, April, Gateway ref. 6420, London: Department of Health.

DEPARTMENT OF HEALTH (2006b) *Our Health, Our Care, Our Say: A New Direction for Community Services*, Cm 6737, London: Department of Health.

DEPARTMENT OF HEALTH (2006c) *Form KHO3 Returns*, London: Department of Health.

DEPARTMENT OF HEALTH (2006d) *The Mental Health Bill: Plans to Amend the Mental Health Act 1983*, Briefing sheet—Supervised Community Treatment—A3, April, Gateway ref. 6420, London: Department of Health.

DEPARTMENT OF HEALTH (2006e) *The Mental Health Bill: Plans to Amend the Mental Health Act 1983*, Briefing sheet—Nearest Relative—A5, April, Gateway ref. 6420, London: Department of Health.

DEPARTMENT OF HEALTH (2007) *Guidance on Joint Strategic Needs Assessment*, London: Department of Health.

DEPARTMENT OF HEALTH (2008) *Code of Practice: Mental Health Act*, London: TSO.

DEPARTMENT OF HEALTH (2008a) *Reference guide to the Mental Health Act 1983*, London: TSO.

DEPARTMENT OF HEALTH (2008b) *Refocusing the Care Programme Approach: Policy and Positive Practice Guidance*, London: COI for the Department of Health.

DEPARTMENT OF HEALTH (2008c) 'Impact Assessment of the Mental Capacity Act 2005 deprivation of liberty safeguards to accompany the Code of Practice and regulations' (London: unp.). Available online at http://www.dh.gov.uk/prod_consum_dh/ groups/dh_digitalassets/documents/ digitalasset/dh_084984.pdf; accessed 2 January 2013.

DEPARTMENT OF HEALTH (2009) *Guidance on Direct Payments for Community Care, Services for Carers and Children's Services*, London: COI for the Department of Health.

DEPARTMENT OF HEALTH (2009a) *Common Assessment Framework for Adults: A Consultation on Proposals to Improve Information Sharing Around Multi-Disciplinary Assessment and Care Planning*, London: COI for the Department of Health.

DEPARTMENT OF HEALTH (2009b) *The National Framework for NHS Continuing Healthcare and NHS-funded Nursing Care July 2009* (revised) published online only at http://www.dh.gov.uk/prod_consum_dh/ groups/dh_digitalassets/documents/digita- lasset/dh_103161.pdf

DEPARTMENT OF HEALTH (2009c) *NHS-funded Nursing Care Practice Guide (revised) 2009*, published online only at http://www.dh.gov.uk/en/ Publicationsandstatistics/Publications/ PublicationsPolicyAndGuidance/ DH_106227.

DEPARTMENT OF HEALTH (2009d) *Improving Health, Supporting Justice: The National Delivery Plan of the Health and Criminal Justice Programme Board*, London: COI for the Department of Health.

DEPARTMENT OF HEALTH (2010) *Equity and Excellence: Liberating the NHS* Cm 7881, London: TSO.

DEPARTMENT OF HEALTH (2010a) *Prioritising Need in the context of Putting People First: A Whole System Approach for Eligibility for Social Care* London: Department of Health.

DEPARTMENT OF HEALTH (2010b) *A Vision for Adult Social Care: Capable Communities and Active Citizens*, London: COI for the Department of Health.

DEPARTMENT OF HEALTH (2011) *Safety and Security Directions—Response to Consultation*, published to website only http://www.dh.gov.uk/publications.

DEPARTMENT OF HEALTH (2011a) *Ordinary Residence: Guidance on the Identification of the Ordinary Residence of People in Need of Community Care Services, England*, London: Department of Health.

DEPARTMENT OF HEALTH (2011c) *Membership of National Liaison and Diversion Development Network June 2011*, London: Department of Health.

DEPARTMENT OF HEALTH (2011d) *Good Practice Procedure Guide: The Transfer and Remission of Adult Prisoners under s47 and s48 of the Mental Health Act*, London: Department of Health

DOH, (2011e) *Reference Tables in Support of Annual Mental Health Bulletin*. (London: Health and Social Care Information Centre, 2011). Tables available at http://www.ic.nhs.uk/pubs/mhbmhmds11.

DEPARTMENT OF HEALTH (2012) *Transforming Care: A National Response to Winterbourne View Hospital Department of Health Review: Final Report*, London: Department of Health.

DEPARTMENT OF HEALTH (2012a) *Reforming the Law for Adult Care and Support the Government's Response to Law Commission Report 326 on Adult Social Care*, London: TSO.

DEPARTMENT OF HEALTH (2012b) *Charging for Residential Accommodation Guide*, London: Department of Health.

DEPARTMENT OF HEALTH (2012c) *Fairer Charging Policies for Home Care and other Non-residential Social Services Guidance for Councils with Social Services Responsibilities*, London: Department of Health.

DEPARTMENT OF HEALTH (2012d) *Mental Health Payment by Results Guidance for 2013-14*, London: Department of Health.

DEPARTMENT OF HEALTH (2012e) *Public Health in Local Government: Commissioning Responsibilities*, London: Department of Health.

DEPARTMENT OF HEALTH (2012f) *Bi-annual Analysis of Mental Capacity Act 2005, Deprivation of Liberty Safeguards Assessments (England)—October 2011– March 2012*, London: Health and Social Care Information Centre.

DEPARTMENT OF HEALTH (2012g) *Post-legislative Assessment of the Mental Health Act 2007*.Cm [HC] 8408. London: TSO.

DEPARTMENT OF HEALTH (2013) *Average Daily Number of Available and Occupied Beds Open Overnight by Sector*, available at http://transparency.dh.gov.uk/?p=19745.

DEPARTMENT OF HEALTH (2013a) *Direct Payments for Healthcare: A Consultation on Updated Policy for Regulations*, published online only at https://www.wp.dh.gov.uk/publications/files/2013/03/Direct-payments-for-healthcare-consultation.pdf.

DEPARTMENT OF HEALTH AND DEPARTMENT FOR WORK AND PENSIONS (2002) *Fairer Charging Policies for Home Care and other Non-residential Social Services: Practice Guidance*, London: Department of Health.

DEPARTMENT OF HEALTH AND HOME OFFICE (1992) *Review of Health and Social Services for Mentally Disordered Offenders and Others Requiring Similar Services: Final Summary Report*, Cm 2088, London: HMSO.

DEPARTMENT OF HEALTH AND HOME OFFICE (1996) *Mentally Disordered Offenders: Sentencing and Discharge Arrangements*, Discussion paper, London: Department of Health and Home Office.

DEPARTMENT OF HEALTH AND HOME OFFICE (2000) *Reforming the Mental Health Act* (White Paper), Cm 5016, London: HMSO.

DEPARTMENT OF HEALTH AND HOME OFFICE (2000a) *Reforming the Mental Health Act: Part II High Risk Patients*, Cm 5016-II, London: HMSO.

DEPARTMENT OF HEALTH AND HOME OFFICE (2002) *Consultation on the Draft Mental Health Bill*, London: Department of Health.

DEPARTMENT OF HEALTH AND MINISTRY OF JUSTICE (2008) *Mental Health Act 2007—Guidance on Extension of Victims' Rights to Information under the Domestic Violence, Crime and Victims Act 2004*, London: Department of Health.

DEPARTMENT OF HEALTH AND NATIONAL INSTITUTE FOR MENTAL HEALTH IN ENGLAND (2005) *Offender Mental Health Care Pathway*, London: Department of Health.

DEPARTMENT OF HEALTH AND OFFICE OF THE PUBLIC GUARDIAN (2009) *Deprivation of Liberty Safeguards: A Guide for Hospitals and Care Homes*, London: Department of Health.

DEPARTMENT OF HEALTH AND SOCIAL SECURITY (1971a) *Better Services for the Mentally Handicapped*, London: HMSO.

DEPARTMENT OF HEALTH AND SOCIAL SECURITY (1971b) *Welfare of the Elderly: Implementation of Section 45 of the Health Services and Public Health Act 1968*, Circular 19/71, London: Department of Health and Social Security.

DEPARTMENT OF HEALTH AND SOCIAL SECURITY (1975) *Better Services for the Mentally Ill*, London: HMSO.

DEPARTMENT OF HEALTH AND SOCIAL SECURITY (1980) *Report of the Review of Rampton Hospital*, Cmnd 8073, London: HMSO.

DEPARTMENT OF HEALTH AND SOCIAL SECURITY (1981) *Reform of Mental Health Legislation*, Cmnd 8405, London: HMSO.

DEPARTMENT OF HEALTH AND WELSH OFFICE (1993) *Mental Health Act 1983 Code of Practice*, London: HMSO.

DEPARTMENT OF HEALTH AND WELSH OFFICE (1999a) *Review of the Mental Health Act 1983* (the 'Richardson Report'), London: Department of Health.

DEPARTMENT OF WORK AND PENSIONS (2010) *Disability Living Allowance Reform*, Cm 7984, London: TSO.

DERSHOWITZ, A. (1970) 'The law of dangerousness: some fictions about predictions', *Journal of Legal Education* 23: 24.

DEUTSCH, A. (1973) *The Shame of the States*, New York, NY: Arno.

DHANDA, A. (2008) 'Constructing a New Human Rights Lexicon: Convention on the Rights of Persons with Disabilities', *International Journal on Human Rights* 5:43.

DICKENS, B. (1994) 'Medical consent legislation in Ontario', *Medical Law Review* 2: 283.

DICKENS, G.L. and CAMPBELL J. (2001) 'Absconding of patients from an independent UK psychiatric hospital: a 3-year retrospective analysis of events and characteristics of absconders' *J Psychiatr Ment Health Nurs.* 8(6): 543–50.

DIGBY, A. (1985) 'Moral treatment at the retreat, 1796–1846', in W. Bynum, R. Porter, and M. Shepherd (eds) *The Anatomy of Madness: Volume II—Institutions and Society*, London: Tavistock.

DIGBY, A. (1985a) *Madness, Morality and Medicine: A Study of the York Retreat, 1796–1914*, Cambridge: Cambridge University Press.

DILLON, J. (2003) 'Women in Broadmoor "should not be there" ', *The Independent on Sunday*, 9 March.

DISABILITY ACTION (2009) *Disability Action 2009 Independent Living*, Belfast: Disability Action.

DISABILITY RIGHTS COMMISSION (2006) *Equal Treatment: Closing the Gap*, Stratford: Disability Rights Commission.

DIXON, L., ADAMS, C., and LUCKSTED, A. (2000) 'Update on family psychoeducation for schizophrenia', *Schizophrenia Bulletin* 26: 5–20.

DIXON, L.B. and LEHMAN, A.F. (1995) 'Family interventions for schizophrenia', *Schizophrenia Bulletin* 21: 631–43.

DOCKING, M., GRACE, K., and BUCKE, T. (2008) 'Police Custody as a "Place of Safety": Examining the use of Section 136 of the Mental Health Act 1983', *IPCC Research and Statistics Series, Paper 11*, London: IPCC.

DOLAN, M., COOREY, P. and KULUPANA, S. (1993) 'An audit of recalls to a special hospital' *Journal of Forensic Psychiatry* 4(2): 249–60.

DOLAN, M., GIBB, R. and COOREY, P. (1999) 'Mental health review tribunals: a survey of special hospital patients' opinions', *Journal of Forensic Psychiatry* 10(2): 264–75.

DOLAN, M. and SHETTY, G. (1995) 'Transfer delays in a special hospital population', *Medicine, Science and Law* 35(3): 237.

DONNELLY, M. (2005) 'Treatment for a mental disorder: the Mental Health Act 2001, consent and the role of rights', *Irish Jurist* 40: 220–40

DOWLING, B., POWELL, M., and GLENDENNING, C. (2004) 'Conceptualising successful partnerships', *Health and Social Care in the Community* 12(4): 309–17.

DRENKHAN, K., et al. (2012) 'What is in a name? Preventive Detention in Germany in the Shadow of European Human Rights Law' [2012] Crim LR 167.

DUFF, R. (1986) *Trials and Punishment*, Cambridge: Cambridge University Press.

DUNN, J. and FAHEY, T. A. (1990) 'Police admissions to a psychiatric hospital. Demographic and clinical differences between ethnic groups' *British Journal of Psychiatry* 156: 379–83.

DUNN, S., MORRISON, B., and ROBERTS, M. (eds) (1996) *Mind Readings: Writers' Journeys Through Mental States*, London: Minerva.

DYER, W. (2011) *Criminal Justice Diversion and Liaison Services: Post-Bradley Update on 'Best Practice' Developments*, Durham: North East Offender Health Commissioning Unit.

EASTMAN, N. and PEAY, J. (1998) 'Sentencing psychopaths: is the "hospital and limitation direction" an ill-considered hybrid?', *Criminal Law Review*: 93.

EDGAR, K. and RICKFORD, D. (2009) *Too Little Too Late: An Independent Review of Unmet Mental Health Need in Prison*, London: Prison Reform Trust.

EDMUNDS, R. (1994) 'Locking the mentally ill out of the homelessness legislation', *Journal of Forensic Psychiatry* 5(2): 355–69.

EISNER, H. (1989) 'Returning the not-guilty by reason of insanity to the community: a new scale to determine readiness', *Bulletin of the American Academy of Psychiatry and the Law* 17(4): 401.

ELBOGEN, E. and JOHNSON, S. (2009) 'The Intricate Link between Violence and Mental Disorder' *Arch Gen Psych* 66(2): 152

ELDERGILL, A. (1997) *Mental Health Review Tribunals Law and Practice*, London: Sweet and Maxwell.

ELDERGILL, A. (1999) 'Case note on *Barker v Barking and Brentwood Community NHS Trust and Others*', *Journal of Mental Health Law* 1(1): 68.

ELDERGILL, A. (2002) 'Is anyone safe? Civil compulsion under the Draft Mental Health Bill', *Journal of Mental Health Law* 8: 331–59.

EMERSON, E, et al. (2011) *People with Learning Disabilities in England 2011: Services & Supports*, Stockton on Tees: Learning Disability Observatory.

EUROPEAN COMMITTEE FOR THE PREVENTION OF TORTURE AND INHUMAN OR DEGRADING TREATMENT OR PUNISHMENT (2011), 8th General Report, CPT/Inf (98) 12; rpt in current articulation of CPT Standards, CPT/Inf/E (2002) 1—Rev. 2011.

EVANS, J. and TOMISON, A. (1997) 'Assessment of the perceived need for a psychiatric service to a magistrates' court', *Medicine, Science and Law* 37(2): 161.

EVANS, S., HUXLEY, P., WEBBER, M. et al. (2005) 'The impact of "statutory duties" on mental health social workers in the UK', *Health and Social Care in the Community* 13(2): 145.

EXWORTHY, T. and PARROTT, J. (1997) 'Comparative evaluation of a diversion from custody scheme', *Journal of Forensic Psychiatry* 8(2): 406.

EXWORTHY, T., MOHAN, D., HINDLEY, N., and BASSON, J. (2001) 'Seclusion: punitive or protective?', *Journal of Forensic Psychiatry* 12(2): 423–33.

FALKOWSKI J., WATTS, V., FALKOWSKI, W., and DEAN, T. (1990) 'Patients leaving hospital without knowledge or permission of staff: absconding', *British Journal of Psychiatry* 156: 488.

FANTHORPE, U.A. (1996) 'Walking in darkness', in S. Dunn, B. Morrison and M. Roberts (eds) *Mind Readings: Writers' Journeys through Mental States*, London: Minerva.

FARID, B. (1991) 'Absconders from a district general hospital', *Psychiatric Bulletin* 15: 736.

FARNHAM, F. and JAMES, D., (2001) '"Dangerousness" and dangerous law' *Lancet* 358: 1926.

FARRELL, E. (1997) *The Complete Guide to Mental Health*, London: Vermilion.

FAZEL S., *et al.*, (2009) 'Schizophrenia and Violence: Systematic Review and Meta-analysis' *PLOS Medicine* 6(8): e100012.

FEARON, P, and MORGAN, C. (2006) 'Environmental Factors in Schizophrenia: The Role of Migrant Studies', *Schizophrenia Bulletin* 32:405–8.

FENNELL, P. (1986) 'Law and psychiatry: the legal constitution of the psychiatric system', *Journal of Law and Society* 13(1): 35.

FENNELL, P. (1988) 'Sexual suppressants and the Mental Health Act', *Criminal Law Review*: 660.

FENNELL, P. (1989) 'The Beverley Lewis case: was the law to blame?', *New Law Journal* 139: 559.

FENNELL, P. (1991b) 'Double detention under the Mental Health Act 1983: a case of extra-Parliamentary legislation', 13/3 *Journal of Social Welfare and Family Law*: 194.

FENNELL, P. (1994) 'Statutory authority to treat, relatives and treatment proxies', *Medical Law Review* 2: 30.

FENNELL, P. (1994a) 'Mentally disordered suspects in the criminal justice system', 21/1 *Journal of Law and Society*: 57.

FENNELL, P. (1995) 'The Law Commission proposals on mental incapacity', *Family Law*: 420.

FENNELL, P. (1996) *Treatment Without Consent: Law, Psychiatry and the Treatment of Mentally Disordered People since 1845*, London: Routledge.

FENNELL, P. (2005) 'Convention compliance, public safety, and the social inclusion of mentally disordered people', *Journal of Law and Society* 32(1): 90–110.

FERENCZ, N. and MAGUIRE, J. (2000) 'Mental health review tribunals in the UK: applying a therapeutic jurisprudence perspective', *Court Review* Spring: 48–52.

FERNANDO, S. (2010) *Mental Health, Race and Culture*, (3rd edn) London: Palgrave Macmillan.

FINCH, J. (1984) 'Community care: developing non-sexist alternatives', *Critical Social Policy* 9: 6.

FORRESTER, A. (2002) 'Preventive detention, public protection and mental health' *Journal of Forensic Psychiatry and Psychology* 13: 329.

FORSYTHE, B., MELLING, J., and ADAIR, R. (1999) 'Politics on lunacy: central state regulation and the Devon Pauper lunatic asylum, 1845–1914' in J. Melling and B. Forsythe (eds) *Insanity, Institutions and Society, 1800–1914: A Social History of Madness in Comparative Perspective*, London: Routledge.

Foucault, M. (1965) *Madness and Civilization: A History of Insanity in the Age of Reason*, trans. R. Howard (1973), New York: Random House.

Foucault, M. (1977) *Discipline and Punish: The Birth of the Prison*, London: Allen Lane.

Foucault, M. (1986) *The Foucault Reader*, P. Rabinow (ed), London: Penguin.

Foucault, M. (1988) 'The dangerous individual', in L. Kritzman (ed) *Michel Foucault: Politics, Philosophy, Culture: Interviews and Other Writings*, London: Routledge.

Foucault, M. (2003) *Abnormal: Lectures at the College de France 1974-1975*, trans. Burchell, G., London: Verso.

Foucault, M. (2006) *History of Madness*, trans. Murphy, J. and Khalfa, J., London: Routledge.

Fox, S. (2010) *Liaison and Diversion Healthcare in Police Custody Suites*, London: Home Office Reducing Reoffending Unit.

Freeman, M. (1994) 'Deciding for the intellectually impaired', *Medical Law Review* 2: 77.

Freeman, D. and Freeman, J. (2013) *The Stressed Sex: Uncovering the Truth About Men, Women, and Mental Health*, Oxford: OUP.

Gallagher, P., Barry, P., O'Mahony, D. (2007) 'Inappropriate prescribing in the elderly', *Journal of Clinical Pharmacy and Therapeutics* 32:113–21.

Ganesvaran, T. and Shah, A. (1997) 'Psychiatric inpatient suicide rates: a 21-year study', *Medicine, Science and Law* 37(3): 202–9.

Garcia, I., Kennett, C., Quraishi, M. and Durcan, G. (2005) *Acute Care 2004: A National Survey of Adult Psychiatric Wards in England*, London: Sainsbury Centre for Mental Health.

Gardiner, W. *et al.* (1999) 'Patients' Revisions of Their Beliefs About the Need for Hospitalization', *American Journal of Psychiatry* 156: 1385.

Garland, D. (2001) *The Culture of Control: Crime and Social Order in Contemporary Society*, Oxford: OUP.

Gaskin, C.J., Elsom. S.J., and Happell, B. (2007) 'Interventions for reducing the use of seclusion in psychiatric facilities: Review of the literature' *British Journal of Psychiatry* 191: 298–303.

Gillon, J. and Monahan, T. (2013) *SuperVision: An Introduction to the Surveillance Society*, Chicago: University of Chicago Press.

Glasby, J. and Littlechild, R. (2009) *Direct Payments and Personal Budgets: Putting Personalisation into Practice*, Cambridge: Policy Press.

Glasgow Media Group (1996) *Media and Mental Distress*, G. Philo (ed), London: Longman.

GlaxoSmithKline (2012), *Annual Report for 2011*, London: GlaxoSmithKline.

Gledhill, K. (2007) 'Community Treatment Orders' [2007] *Journal of Mental Health Law* 149.

Glendinning, C. (2008) 'Increasing choice and control for older and disabled people: a critical review of new developments in England', *Social Policy & Administration* 42(5): 451–69.

Glover-Thomas, N. (2002) *Reconstructing Mental Health Law and Policy*, London: Butterworths.

Glover-Thomas, N. (2011), 'The Age of Risk: Risk Perception and Determination following the Mental Health Act 2007' *Medical Law Review* 19:581.

Goffman, E. (1961, republished 1991) *Asylums: Essays on the Social Situation of Mental Patients and Other Inmates*, London: Penguin.

GOLDBECK, R., MACKENZIE, D., and BENNIE, P. (1997) 'Detained patients' knowledge of their legal status and rights', *Journal of Forensic Psychiatry* 8: 573.

GOODING, P. (2012) 'Supported Decision-Making: A Rights-Based Disability Concept and its Implications for Mental Health Law', *Psychiatry, Psychology and Law* DOI: 10.1080/13218719.2012.71 1683.

GOSTIN, L. (1986a) *Institutions Observed*, London: King's Fund.

GOSTIN, L. (2000) 'Human rights of persons with mental disabilities: The European Convention on Human Rights', *International Journal of Law and Psychiatry* 23(2): 125.

GOSTIN, L. and Fennell, P. (1992) *Mental Health: Tribunal Procedure*, London: Longman.

GOVERNMENT STATISTICAL SERVICE (1998) *Health and Personal Social Service Statistics England 1998*, London: HMSO.

GOVERNMENT STATISTICAL SERVICE (2002) *Health and Personal Social Service Statistics England 2002*, London: HMSO.

GOVERNMENT STATISTICAL SERVICE (2006) *Inpatients Formally Detained in Hospitals under the Mental Health Act 1983 and Other Legislation, England: 1994–5 to 2004–5*, Bulletin: 2006/09/HSCIC, London: The Information Centre.

GRAY, N.S., O'CONNOR, C., WILLIAMS, T., SHORT, J., and MACCULLOCH, M. (2001) 'Fitness to plead: implications from case law arising from the Criminal Justice and Public Order Act 1994', *Journal of Forensic Psychiatry* 12(1): 52–62.

GREEN, B. and BAGLIONI Jr, A. (1997) 'Judging suitability for release of patients from a maximum security hospital by hospital and community staff', *International Journal of Law and Psychiatry* 20(3): 323.

GREENBERG, N., LLOYD, K., O'BRIEN, C., MCIVER, S., HESSFORD, A., and DONOVAN, M. (2002) 'A prospective survey of section 136 in rural England (Devon and Cornwall)', *Medicine, Science and Law* 42(2): 129–32.

GREENHALGH, N., WYLIE, K., RIX, K., and TAMLYN, D. (1996) 'Pilot mental health assessment and diversion scheme for an English metropolitan petty sessional division', *Medicine, Science and Law* 36(1): 52.

GREENHALGH, J, et al (2005) 'Clinical and cost-effectiveness of electroconvulsive therapy for depressive illness, schizophrenia, catatonia and mania: systematic reviews and economic modelling studies', *Health Technology Assessment Programme, project 9* Downley: Health Technology Assessment Programme.

GREY, R., et al (2005) 'A survey of patient satisfaction with and subjective experiences of treatment with antipsychotic medication', *Journal of Advanced Nursing* 52: 31–7.

GRIFFITHS, R. (1988) *Community Care: Agenda for Action*, London: HMSO.

GROB, G. (1994) *The Mad Among Us*, New York: Free Press.

GROUNDS, A. (1990) 'Transfers of sentenced prisoners to hospital', *Criminal Law Review*: 544.

GRUBIN, D. (1993) 'What constitutes unfitness to plead?', *Criminal Law Review*: 748.

GUDJONSSON, G. (1992) *The Psychology of Interrogations, Confessions and Testimony*, Chichester: Wiley.

GUDJONSSON, G. (1995) ' "Fitness for interview" during police detention: a conceptual framework for forensic assessment', *Journal of Forensic Psychiatry* 6(1): 185.

GUDJONSSON, G., CLARE, I., RUTTER, S., and PEARSE, J. (1993) *Persons at Risk During Interviews in Police Custody: The Identification of Vulnerabilities*, Royal Commission on Criminal Justice Research Study No.12, London: HMSO.

GUDJONSSON, G., HAYES, G., and ROWLANDS: (2000) 'Fitness to be interviewed and psychological vulnerability: the views of doctors, lawyers and police officers', *Journal of Forensic Psychiatry* 11(1): 74–92.

GUNN, J. and JOSEPH, P. (1993) 'Remands to hospital for psychiatrists' reports: a study of psychiatrists' attitudes to section 35 of the Mental Health Act 1983', *Psychiatric Bulletin* 17: 197.

GUNN, J., MADEN, A., and SWINTON, M. (1991) 'Treatment needs of prisoners with psychiatric disorders', *British Medical Journal* 313: 338.

GUNN, M. (1986) 'Mental Health Act guardianship: where now?', 8/3 *Journal of Social Welfare Law*: 144–52.

GUNN, M. (1986c) 'Case note on *R* v *Mental Health Review Tribunal, ex parte Clatworthy*', 8/4 *Journal of Social Welfare Law*: 249.

GUNN, M. (1990) 'Case note on *R* v *Newington*', *Journal of Forensic Psychiatry* 1: 360.

GUNN, M. (1993) 'Patients subject to restriction direction and release', *Journal of Forensic Psychiatry* 4(2): 330.

GUNN, M. (1994) 'The meaning of incapacity', *Medical Law Review* 2: 8.

GUNN, M.J. and HOLLAND, T. (2002) 'Some thoughts on the proposed Mental Health Act', *Journal of Mental Health Law* 8: 360–72.

HALE, B. (2010) *Mental Health Law*, (5th edn) London: Sweet and Maxwell.

HAM C., and SMITH, J. (2010). *Removing Policy Barriers to Integrated Care in England*. London: Nuffield Trust.

HAMPSON, M. (2011) 'Raising standards in relation to Section 136 of the Mental Health Act 1983' *Advances in Psychiatric Treatment* 17: 365–71.

HARDIE, T., BHUI, K., BROWN, P., WATSON, J., and PARROTT, J. (1998) 'Unmet needs of remand prisoners', *Medicine, Science and Law* 38(3): 233.

HARGREAVES, D. (1997) 'The transfer of severely mentally ill prisoners from HMP Wakefield: a descriptive study', *Journal of Forensic Psychiatry* 8(1): 62.

HARRIS, N. (2011) 'PIP(s) and All' *Journal of Social Security Law* 18(3), 107–10.

HART, L. (1995) *Phone At Nine Just To Say You're Alive*, London: Pan.

HATFIELD, B., HUXLEY, P. and MOHAMAD, H. (1997) 'Social factors and compulsory detention of psychiatric patients in the UK: the role of the approved social worker in the 1983 Mental Health Act', *International Journal of Law and Psychiatry* 20(3): 389–97.

HATFIELD, B., MOHAMAD, H., RAHIM, Z., and TANWEER, H. (1996) 'Mental health and the Asian communities: a local survey', *British Journal of Social Work* 26: 315.

HATTON, C. and WATERS, J (2011) *The National Personal Budget Survey*, Lancaster: In Control and Lancaster University.

HEALTH AND SAFETY EXECUTIVE (2006) *Violence and Aggression Management Training for Trainers and Managers: A National Evaluation of the Training Provision in Healthcare Settings*, Research Report 440, London: HMSO.

HEALTH AND SOCIAL CARE INFORMATION CENTRE (2012) *Guardianship under the Mental Health Act 1983, England, 2012*, London: Health and Social Care Information Centre.

HENSON, J, and IRELAND. J. L. (2009) Patient-to-patient bullying in secure psychiatric services: exploring the value of official records for documenting patient-to-patient bullying *British Journal of Forensic Practice*, 11(2): 10–6.

HERRING, J. (2012) *Medical Law and Ethics*, 4th edn, Oxford: Oxford University Press.

HINES, D. (1999) *Independent Investigation into Complaints Raised by Ian Stewart Brady Relating to His Transfer to Lawrence Ward and Re-feeding at Ashworth Hospital*, London: Department of Health.

HIRST, D. and MICHAEL, P. (1999) 'Family, community and the lunatic in mid-nineteenth-century North Wales' in P. Bartlett and D. Wright (eds) *Outside the Walls of the Asylum*, London: Athlone.

HM CHIEF INSPECTOR OF THE CPS, HM CHIEF INSPECTOR OF PROBATION AND HM INSPECTOR OF CONSTABULARY (2013) *Living In A Different World: Joint Review of Disability Hate Crime*, London: HM Crown Prosecution Service Inspectorate, HM Inspectorate of Constabulary and HM Inspectorate of Probation.

HM CHIEF INSPECTOR OF PRISONS FOR ENGLAND AND WALES (2012) *Annual Report 2011–12*, HC 613 London: TSO.

HM COURTS AND TRIBUNALS SERVICE (2012) *Room Specification Recommendations for Tribunal Hearings*, London: HMC&TS.

HM GOVERNMENT (2007) *Putting People First: A Shared Vision and Commitment to the Transformation of Adult Social Care* London: TSO.

HM GOVERNMENT (2011) *No Health Without Mental Health, a Cross-government Mental Health Outcomes Strategy for People of all Ages*, London: Crown Office for Department of Health.

HM GOVERNMENT (2012) *No Health Without Mental Health: Implementation Framework*, London: Williams Lea for HM Government.

HM GOVERNMENT (2012a) *Caring for our Future: Reforming Care and Support*, Cm 8378, London: TSO.

HM INSPECTORATE OF PRISONS (2007) *The Mental Health of Prisoners: A Thematic Review of the Care and Support of Prisoners with Mental Health Needs*, London: HM Inspectorate of Prisons.

HM INSPECTORATE OF PRISONS (2012) *Thematic Report by HM Inspectorate of Prisons: Remand Prisoners: A Thematic Review*, London: HM Inspectorate of Prisons.

HM PRISON SERVICE (2012) *Prison Service Order 0500: Reception*, London: HMPS.

HM PRISON SERVICE AND DEPARTMENT OF HEALTH (2002) *Mental Health Inreach Collaborative Launch Document*, London: Department of Health.

HM PRISON SERVICE AND DEPARTMENT OF HEALTH (2003) 'Ministerial foreword', in *Prison Health*, London: Department of Health.

HM PRISON SERVICE AND NHS EXECUTIVE (1999) *The Future Organisation of Prison Health Care*, London: Department of Health.

HM PRISON SERVICE PRISON (2006) *Transfer of Prisoners to and from Hospital under Sections 47 and 48 of the Mental Health Act 1983*, Service Instruction 03/2006, London: HM Prison Service.

HM PRISON SERVICE, DEPARTMENT OF HEALTH, AND THE NATIONAL ASSEMBLY FOR WALES (2001) *Changing the Outlook: A Strategy for Developing and Modernising Mental Health Services in Prisons*, London: Department of Health.

HM STATIONERY OFFICE (2004) *Domestic Violence, Crime and Victims Act 2004 Explanatory Notes*, London: HMSO.

HODGSON, J. (1997) 'Vulnerable suspects and the appropriate adult', *Criminal Law Review*: 785.

HOGARTY, G. and ULRICH, R. (1972) 'The discharge readiness inventory', *Archives of General Psychiatry* 23: 419.

HOGGETT, B. (1996) *Mental Health Law*, 4th edn, London: Sweet and Maxwell.

HOLDAWAY, S. (1983) *Inside the British Police*, Oxford: Basil Blackwell.

HOLLOWAY, F. (2005) *The Forgotten Need for Rehabilitation in Contemporary Mental Health Services: A Position Statement from the Executive Committee of the Faculty of Rehabilitation and Social Psychiatry, Royal College of Psychiatrists*, London: Royal College of Psychiatrists.

HOME OFFICE (1990) *Provision for Mentally Disordered Offenders*, Circular 66/1990, London: HMSO.

HOME OFFICE (1991) *Guidance on the Criminal Procedure (Insanity and Unfitness to Plead) Act 1991*, Circular 93/91, London: HMSO.

HOME OFFICE (1992) *Report of the Committee of Inquiry into Complaints about Ashworth Hospital*, 2 vols., Cmnd 2028, London: HMSO.

HOME OFFICE (1996) *Protecting the Public*, Cm 3190, London: HMSO.

HOME OFFICE (1997) *Restricted Patients: Reconvictions and Recalls by the End of 1995*, London: Home Office.

HOME OFFICE (2003) *Prison Population Brief*, London: Home Office.

HOME OFFICE (2003a) *Guidance for Appropriate Adults*, London: Home Office.

HOME OFFICE (2005) *Home Office Circular 24/2005 The Domestic Violence, Crime And Victims Act 2004: Provisions For Unfitness To Plead And Insanity*, London: Home Office.

HOME OFFICE (2006a) *Crime in England and Wales 2005–6*, Bulletin 12/06, London: Home Office Research, Development and Statistics Directorate.

HOME OFFICE (2008) *Police and Criminal Evidence Act 1984 Code of Practice D Code of Practice for the Identification of Persons by Police Officers*, London: The Stationery Office.

HOME OFFICE (2008a) *PACE Review Government proposals in response to the Review of the Police and Criminal Evidence Act 1984*, London: Home Office.

HOME OFFICE (2010) *PACE Review: Summary of responses to the public consultation on the Review of the Police and Criminal Evidence Act 1984*, London: Home Office.

HOME OFFICE (2012) *Revised Code of Practice for the Detention, Treatment and Questioning of Persons by Police Officers Police and Criminal Evidence Act 1984 (PACE)—Code C*, London: Home Office.

HOME OFFICE AND CABINET OFFICE (2002) *Pace Review: Report of the Joint Home Office/Cabinet Office Review of the Police and Criminal Evidence Act 1984*, London: Home Office.

HOME OFFICE AND DEPARTMENT OF HEALTH (1992) *Review of Health and Social Services for Mentally Disordered Offenders and Others Requiring Similar Services*, Cmnd 2088, London: HMSO.

HOME OFFICE RESEARCH, DEVELOPMENT AND STATISTICS DIRECTORATE (2002) *Statistics of Mentally Disordered Offenders 2001*, Bulletin 13/02, London: Home Office Research, Development and Statistics Directorate.

HOME OFFICE RESEARCH, DEVELOPMENT AND STATISTICS DIRECTORATE (2005) *Statistics of Mentally Disordered Offenders 2004*, Bulletin 22/05, London: Home Office Research, Development and Statistics Directorate.

HOME OFFICE RESEARCH, DEVELOPMENT AND STATISTICS DIRECTORATE (2009) *Statistics of Mentally Disordered Offenders 2007 England and Wales*, London: Ministry of Justice.

HOME OFFICE, MENTAL HEALTH UNIT (1997) *Crime Sentences Act*, HO Circular 52/1997, London: Home Office.

House of Commons and House of Lords (2005) *Report of the Joint Scrutiny Committee on the Mental Health Bill*, PP HL (2004–5) 79/HC (2004–5) 95.

Houston, R. (1999) '"Not simple boarding": care of the mentally incapacitated in Scotland during the long eighteenth century', in P. Bartlett and D. Wright (eds) *Outside the Walls of the Asylum*, London: Athlone.

Howard, H. (2003) 'Reform of the insanity defence: theoretical issues', *Journal of Criminal Law* 67(1): 51–67.

Howard, H. (2011) 'Unfitness to plead and the vulnerable defendant: An examination of the law commission's proposals for a new capacity test', *Journal of Criminal Law*, 75(3).

Howlett, M. (1998) *Medication, Non-Compliance and Mentally Disordered Offenders*, London: The Zito Trust.

Hudson, B. (2002) 'Balancing rights and risks: dilemmas of justice and difference' in N. Gary, J. Laing and L. Noaks (eds) *Criminal Justice, Mental Health and the Politics of Risk*, London: Cavendish.

Hume, C. and Pullen, I. (1994) *Rehabilitation for Mental Health Problems: An Introductory Handbook*, 2nd edn, Edinburgh: Churchill Livingstone.

Humphries R., and Curry, N. (2011) *Integrating Health and Social Care: Where Next?*, London: The King's Fund.

Hunter, C. (2007) Denying the severity of mental health problems to deny rights to the homeless *People, Place & Policy Online* 2(1): 17–27.

Hurstfield, J., Parashar, U., and Schofield, K. (2007) *The Costs and Benefits of Independent Living*, London: Office for Disability Issues, Department for Work and Pensions.

Huws, R. and Shubsachs, A. (1993) 'A study of absconding by special hospital patients: 1976 to 1988', *Journal of Forensic Psychiatry* 4(1): 45.

Huws, R., Longson, D., Reiss, D., and Larkin, E. (1997) 'Prison transfers to special hospitals since the introduction of the Mental Health Act 1983', *Journal of Forensic Psychiatry* 8(1): 74.

Huxley, P., Evans, S., Webber, M., and Gately, C. (2005) 'Staff shortages in the mental health workforce: the case of the disappearing approved social worker', *Health and Social Care in the Community* 13(6): 504.

Ilyas, S. and Moncrieff, J. (2012) 'Trends in prescriptions and costs of drugs for mental disorders in England, 1998–2010', *British Journal of Psychiatry* 200: 393–8.

Independent Police Complaints Commission (2012) *Deaths During or Following Police Contact: Statistics for England and Wales 2011/12*, London: Independent Police Complaints Commission.

Ireland, J.L. (2004) 'Nature, extent and causes of bullying among personality- disordered patients in a high-secure hospital', *Aggressive Behavior* 30(3): 229–42.

Ireland, J.L. (2004a) *Patient-to-Patient Bullying in a High Secure Forensic Setting: A Study of Mental Health and Women's Services*, Research funded by National Forensic Mental Health Research and Development Programme, MRD 12/44, London: MRD.

Ireland, J. L. (2006) 'Exploring definitions of bullying among personality disordered patients in a high-secure hospital', *Aggressive Behavior* 32(5): 451–63.

Ireland, J. L. and Bescoby, N. (2004) 'A behavioural assessment of bullying behaviour among personality disordered patients in a high-secure hospital', *Aggressive Behavior* 31(1): 67–83.

IRELAND, J.L. and SNOWDEN, P. (2002) 'Bullying in secure hospitals', *Journal of Forensic Psychiatry* 13(3): 538–54.

JACKSON, E. (2010) *Medical Law: Text, Cases and Materials*, 2nd edn, Oxford: Oxford University Press.

JACONELLI, J. and JACONELLI, A. (1998) 'Tort liability under the Mental Health Act 1983', *Journal of Social Welfare and Family Law* 20: 151.

JAMES, A. (2001) *Raising Our Voices: An Account of the Hearing Voices Movement*, London: Handsell Publications.

JAMES, D. and HAMILTON, L. (1991) 'The Clerkenwell scheme: assessing efficacy and cost of a psychiatric liaison service to a magistrates' court', *British Medical Journal* 303: 282.

JAMES, D., CRIPPS J., and GRAY, N. (1998) 'What demands do those admitted from the criminal justice system make on psychiatric beds?', *Journal of Forensic Psychiatry* 9(1): 74.

JAMES, D., CRIPPS J., GILLULEY P., and HARLOW, P. (1997) 'A court-focused model of forensic psychiatry provision to central London: abolishing remands to prison?', *Journal of Forensic Psychiatry* 8(2): 309.

JAMESON, R. (1996) 'Schizophrenia from the inside', in J. Read and J. Reynolds (eds) *Speaking Our Minds: An Anthology*, London: Macmillan.

JAMISON, K. (1993) *Touched with Fire: Manic-Depressive Illness and the Artistic Temperament*, New York: Simon and Schuster.

JAMISON, K. (1996) *An Unquiet Mind: A Memoir of Moods and Madness*, London: Picador.

JODELET, D. (1991) *Madness and Social Representations*, Hemel Hempstead: Harvester Wheatsheaf.

JOHNSON, C., SMITH, J., CROWE, C. and DONOVAN, M. (1993) 'Suicide amongst forensic psychiatric patients', *Medicine, Science and Law* 33(2): 137.

JOINT FORMULARY COMMITTEE (2012), *British National Formulary*, London: BMJ Group and Pharmaceutical Press.

JONES, K. (1972) *A History of the Mental Health Services*, London: Routledge & Kegan Paul.

JONES, M., and GREY, R. (2008) 'Time to wake up and smell the coffee: antipsychotic medication and schizophrenia', *Journal of Psychiatric and Mental Health Nursing*, 15: 344–8.

JONES, R. (2011) *Mental Health Act Manual*, 14th edn, London: Sweet and Maxwell.

JONES, R. (2011a) 'Hospital bed occupancy demystified' *British Journal of Healthcare Management* 17(6): 242–48.

JONES, R. (2012) *Mental Capacity Act Manual*, 5th edn, London: Sweet and Maxwell.

JONES, S., HOWARD, L., THORNICROFT, G. (2008) ' "Diagnostic overshadowing": worse physical health care for people with mental illness', *Acta Psychiatrica Scandanavica* 118: 169–71.

JUSTICE (1994) *Unreliable Evidence? Confessions and the Safety of Convictions*, London: Justice.

KAFKA. F (2009) *The Trial*, Oxford: Oxford University Press.

KARP, D. (2001) *The Burden of Sympathy: How Families Cope with Mental Illness*, New York: Oxford University Press.

KATSAKOU C. (2011) 'Why do some voluntary patients feel coerced into hospitalisation?', *Psychiatry Research* 187: 275–82

KEMP, V., BALMER, N.J., and PLEASENCE, P. (2012) 'Whose time is it anyway? Factors associated with duration in police custody' *Criminal Law Review*: 736.

KENNEDY, I, *et al.* (eds). (2010). *Principles of Medical Law*, 2nd edn, Oxford: Oxford University Press.

KERNODLE, R. W. (1966) 'Non medical leaves from a mental hospital' *Psychiatry* 29: 25–41.

KERRIGAN, K. (2002) 'Psychiatric evidence and mandatory disposal: Article 5 compliance?', *Journal of Mental Health Law*: 130–8.

KAYESS, R., and FRENCH, P. (2008) 'Out of darkness into light? Introducing the Convention on the Rights of Persons with Disabilities', *HRLRev* 8: 1

KEYWOOD, K. (1996) 'Rectification of incorrect documentation under the Mental Health Act 1983', *Journal of Forensic Psychiatry* 7: 79–91.

KINGHAM, M. and CORFE, M. (2005) 'Experiences of a mixed court liaison and diversion scheme' *Psychiatric Bulletin* 29: 137–40.

Kings Fund and Nuffield Trust (2012) *Integrated Care for Patients and Populations: Improving Outcomes by Working Together*, London: Kings Fund.

KINTON, M. (2008) 'Towards an understanding of supervised community treatment', 17 *Journal of Mental Health Law* 7.

KUTCHINSKY N. (2006) *Development Programme for Extending Offender Healthcare Support: Early Interventions Workstream, Final Report*, London: Revolving Doors Agency.

LACEY, R. (1996) *The Complete Guide to Psychiatric Drugs*, 2nd edn, London: Vermilion.

LAING, J. (1995) 'The mentally disordered suspect at the police station', *Criminal Law Review*: 371.

LAING, J. (1996) 'The proposed hybrid order for mentally disordered offenders: a step in the right direction?', *Liverpool Law Review* 18(2): 127.

LAING, J. (2002) 'Detaining the Dangerous: Legal and Ethical Implications of the Government's Proposals for High-Risk Individuals', *J Crim L* 66:64

LANGAN, J. (2010) 'Challenging assumptions about risk factors and the role of screening for violence risk in the field of mental health', *Health, Risk & Society*, 12: 85–100

LAW COMMISSION (1995) *Mental Incapacity*, LC No. 231, London: HMSO.

LAW COMMISSION (2010) *Consultation Paper No 197 Unfitness to Plead* London: The Law Commission.

LAW COMMISSION (2010a) *Consultation Paper on Adult Social Care* (CP 192), London: TSO.

LAW COMMISSION (2011) *Adult Social Care (Law Comm No 326)* HC 941, London: TSO.

LAW COMMISSION (2012) *Insanity and Automatism: A Scoping Paper* London: Law Commission.

LAW COMMISSION (2012a) *Supplementary Material to the Scoping Paper (July 2012): Insanity and Automatism* London: Law Commission.

LAW REFORM COMMITTEE OF THE BAR COUNCIL AND THE CRIMINAL BAR ASSOCIATION OF ENGLAND AND WALES (2011) *Unfitness to Plead: A Response to Law Commission C.P. 197*, London: Law Reform Committee of the Bar Council and the Criminal Bar Association of England and Wales.

LAW SOCIETY (2002) '*Response to the Draft Mental Health Bill*', London: Law Society (reprinted in *Journal of Mental Health Law* 8: 373–5).

LAW SOCIETY (2013) *Mental Health Accreditation Scheme Guidance*, London: Law Society.

LAWSON, A (2006–07) 'The United Nations Convention on the Rights of Persons with Disabilities: New Era or False Dawn?' 34 *Syracuse J Int'l Law & Com* 563.

LAZLO, A. and KRIPPNER, S. (1998) 'Systems Theories: Their Origins, Foundations, and Development' in J.S. Jordan (ed.) *Systems Theories and A Priori Aspects of Perception*, Amsterdam: Elsevier Science.

LEE, V. and CHARLES, C. (2008) *Research into CPS Decision-making in Cases Involving Victims and Key Witnesses with Mental Health Problems and/or Learning Disabilities*, London: Crown Prosecution Service.

LEECE, J. and PEACE, S. (2010) 'Developing new understandings of independence and autonomy in the personalised relationship', *British Journal of Social Work* 40(6): 1847–65.

LEGGETT J. *et al.* (2007) 'People with learning disabilities' experiences of being interviewed by the police', *British Journal of Learning Disabilities* 35(3): 168–73.

LELLIOTT, P., *et al.* (2002) 'The influence of patient variables on polypharmacy and combined high dose of antipsychotic drugs prescribed for in-patients', *The Psychiatrist* 26: 411–4.

LEUCHT, S, *et al.* (2009) 'How effective are second-generation antipsychotic drugs? A meta-analysis of placebo-controlled trials', *Molecular Psychiatry* 14: 429–47.

LEWES, K. (1988) *The Psychoanalytic Theory of Male Homosexuality*, New York: Simon and Schuster.

LEWIS, B. (1996) 'Therapy Room' in J. Read and J Reynolds (eds) *Speaking Our Minds: An Anthology*, London: Macmillan.

LEWIS, G. (2002) *Sunbathing in the Rain: A Cheerful Book about Depression*, London: Flamingo.

LEWIS, J. (1989) ' "It all really starts in the family": community care in the 1990s', *Journal of Law and Society* 16: 83.

LEWIS, J. and GLENNERSTER, H. (1996) *Implementing the New Community Care*, Buckingham: Open University Press.

LITTLECHILD, B. (1995) 'Reassessing the role of the "appropriate adult" ', *Criminal Law Review*: 540.

LITTLEWOOD, R. and LIPSEDGE, M. (1997) *Aliens and Alienists*, 3rd edn, London: Routledge.

LOCAL GOVERNMENT ASSOCIATION (2012) *White Paper on Social Care and Funding Update LGA On the Day Briefing*, London: LGA.

LOMAX, A (2012) 'Do psychiatric inpatients know their rights? A re-audit on information given to inpatients at a London mental health trust about their rights and admission to hospital', *Medicine, Science and the Law* 52: 36.

LONG, C. and MIDGELY, M. (1992) 'On the closeness of the concepts of the criminal and the mentally ill in the nineteenth century: yesterday's opinion reflected today', *Journal of Forensic Psychiatry* 3(1): 63.

LUENGO-FRENANDEZ, R, LEAL, J., and GRAY, A (2010) *Dementia 2010: The Economic Burden of Dementia and Associated Research Funding in the United Kingdom*, Cambridge: Alzheimer's Research Trust.

LYON, D. (2001) *Surveillance Society: Monitoring Everyday Life*, Buckingham: Open University Press.

LYON, D. (ed.) (2003) *Surveillance as Social Sorting*, London: Routledge.

MACKAY, R.D. (1995) *Mental Condition Defences in the Criminal Law*, Oxford: Clarendon.

MACKAY, R.D. (2002) 'On being insane in Jersey, Part 2: the appeal in *Jason Prior* v *Attorney General*', *Criminal Law Review*: 728–34.

MACKAY, R.D. (2004) 'On being insane in Jersey, Part 3: the case of the *Attorney General* v *O'Driscoll*' *Criminal Law Review*: 291–6.

MACKAY, R. D. (2010) *Unfitness to Plead—Data on Formal Findings from 2002 to 2008* in Law Commission (2010) *Consultation Paper No 197 Unfitness to Plead*, London: The Law Commission.

MACKAY, R. D. (2011) 'Unfitness to Plead-Some Observations on the Law Commission's Consultation Paper', *Criminal Law Review*: 433–44.

MACKAY, R.D. (2012) *The Insanity Defence—Data on Verdicts of Not Guilty By Reason of Insanity from 2002 to 2011* in Law Commission (2012a).

MACKAY, R.D. and GEARTY, C.A. (2001) 'On being insane in Jersey: the case of *Attorney General v Jason Prior*', *Criminal Law Review*: 560–3.

MACKAY, R.D. and KEARNS, G. (1997) 'The trial of the facts and unfitness to plead', *Criminal Law Review*: 644.

MACKAY, R.D. and KEARNS, G. (2000) 'An upturn in unfitness to plead? Disability in relation to the trial of the facts under the 1991 Act', *Criminal Law Review*: 532–46.

MACKAY, R.D. and MACHIN, D. (1998) *Transfers from Prison to Hospital: The Operation of Section 48 of the Mental Health Act 1983*, London: Home Office.

MACKAY, R.D. and MACHIN, D. (2000) 'The operation of section 48 of the Mental Health Act 1983', *British Journal of Criminology* 40: 727–45.

MACKAY, R.D., MITCHELL, B.J. and HOWE, L. (2006) 'Yet more facts about the insanity defence', *Criminal Law Review*: 399–411.

MACLEOD, S. (1996) 'The art of starvation', in S. Dunn, B. Morrison and M. Roberts (eds) *Mind Readings: Writers' Journeys through Mental States*, London: Minerva.

MAGILL, C. and RIVERS, V. (2010) *Prosecution of offenders with mental health problems or learning disabilities*, London: Crown Prosecution Service.

MASON, T. (1992) 'Seclusion: definitional interpretations', *Journal of Forensic Psychiatry* 3(2): 261–9.

MASON, T. (1993) 'Seclusion: an international comparison', *Medicine, Science and Law* 34(1): 54.

MASON, T. and WHITEHEAD, E. (2001) 'Some specific problems of secluding female patients', *Medicine, Science and Law* 41(4): 315–24.

MATHIESEN, T. (1983) 'The future of control systems: the case of Norway' in D. Garland and P. Young (eds) *The Power to Punish: Contemporary Penality and Social Analysis*, London: Heinemann.

MAYS, J. (1995) *In the Jaws of the Black Dogs: A Memoir of Depression*, Toronto: Penguin.

MCCABE, D. (1996) 'No place like home', *Community Care*, 22 August: 27.

MCCLEAN, R. J. (2010) 'Assessing the security needs of patients in medium secure psychiatric care in Northern Ireland', *The Psychiatrist* 34: 432–6.

MCCONVILLE, M. and HODGSON, J. (1993) *Custodial Legal Advice and the Right to Silence*, Royal Commission on Criminal Justice Research Report No.16, London: HMSO.

MCEWAN, J. (2013) 'Vulnerable defendants and the fairness of trials', *Criminal Law Review* 2: 100–13.

MCGOEY, L., and JACKSON, E (2009) 'Seroxat and the suppression of clinical trial data: regulatory failure and the uses of legal ambiguity', *J Med Ethics* 35:107–12.

MCGUE, M., GOTTESMAN, I. and RAO, D. (1985) 'Resolving genetic models for the transmission of schizophrenia', *Genetic Epidemiology* 2: 99.

MCKENZIE, N. and SALES, B. (2008) 'New procedures to cut delays in transfer for mentally ill prisoners to hospital', *Psychiatric Bulletin* 32: 20–2.

McLeod, R. *et al.* (2010) *Court Experience of Adults with Mental Health Conditions, Learning Disabilities and Limited Mental Capacity: Report 1: Overview and Recommendations*, Ministry of Justice Research Series 8/10, London: Ministry of Justice.

Mental Disability Advocacy Center (2006) *Guardianship and Human Rights in Serbia*, Budapest: MDAC.

Mental Disability Advocacy Center (2007) *Guardianship and Human Rights in Bulgaria*, Budapest: MDAC.

Mental Disability Advocacy Center (2007a) *Guardianship and Human Rights in the Czech Republic*, Budapest: MDAC.

Mental Disability Advocacy Center (2007b) *Guardianship and Human Rights in Hungary*, Budapest: MDAC.

Mental Disability Advocacy Center (2007c) *Guardianship and Human Rights in Kyrgyzstan*, Budapest: MDAC.

Mental Disability Advocacy Center (2007d) *Guardianship and Human Rights in Russia*, Budapest: MDAC.

Mental Health Act Commission (1991) *Fourth Biennial Report 1989–91*, London: HMSO.

Mental Health Act Commission (1995) *Sixth Biennial Report 1993–5*, London: HMSO.

Mental Health Act Commission (1997) *Seventh Biennial Report 1995–7*, London: HMSO.

Mental Health Act Commission (1999) *Eighth Biennial Report 1997–9*, London: HMSO.

Mental Health Act Commission (2001) *Ninth Biennial Report 1999–2001*, London: HMSO.

Mental Health Act Commission (2001a) *Deaths of Detained Patients in England and Wales: A Report by the Mental Health Act Commission on Information Collected from 1 February 1997 to 31 January 2001*, London: Department of Health.

Mental Health Act Commission (2003) *Placed Amongst Strangers: Tenth Biennial Report 2001–3*, London: HMSO.

Mental Health Act Commission (2005) *11th Biennial Report 2003–5*, London: HMSO.

Mental Health Act Commission (2008) *Risk, Rights, Recovery: Twelfth Biennial Report, 2005-07*, London: TSO.

Mental Health Act Commission (2009) *Coercion and consent monitoring the Mental Health Act 2007–2009 The Mental Health Act Commission Thirteenth Biennial Report 2007–2009*, London: TSO.

Mental Health Alliance (2010) *Briefing Paper 2 Supervised Community Treatment*, London: Mental Health Alliance.

Mersey Care NHS Trust (2005) *Strategic Business Plan 2004–7 Progress Report*, Paper MC 017/05, Liverpool: Mersey Care Trust

Midelfort, E. (1980) 'Madness and civilisation in early modern Europe: a reappraisal of Michel Foucault', in Malament, B. (ed.) *After the Reformation: Essays in Honor of J.H. Hexter*, Manchester: Manchester University Press.

Milne, E. and Milne, S. (1995) 'Mental health review tribunals: why the delay?', *Journal of Forensic Psychiatry* 6(1): 93.

Milner, G. (1966) 'The absconder', *Comprehensive Psychiatry* 7: 147.

MIND (2004) *The National Service Framework for Mental Health: What Progress Five Years On?*, London: MIND.

Ministry of Health (1963) *Health and Welfare: The Development of Community Care*, London: HMSO.

Ministry of Justice (2008) *Mental Health Act 2007: Guidance for the Courts on Remand and Sentencing Powers for Mentally Disordered Offenders*, London: Ministry of Justice.

MINISTRY OF JUSTICE (2008a) *Leave of Absence for Patients Subject to Restrictions: Guidance for Responsible Clinicians*, London: Ministry of Justice.

MINISTRY OF JUSTICE (2008b) *Mental Capacity Act 2005: Deprivation of Liberty Safeguards—Code of Practice to Supplement the Main Mental Capacity Act 2005 Code of Practice*, London: Ministry of Justice.

MINISTRY OF JUSTICE (2008c) *Changes to the Mental Health Review, Tribunal from November 2008*, London: Ministry of Justice.

MINISTRY OF JUSTICE (2009) *Statistics of Mentally Offenders 2007 England and Wales*: London: Ministry of Justice.

MINISTRY OF JUSTICE (2009a) *Guidance for Clinical Supervisors*, London: Ministry of Justice.

MINISTRY OF JUSTICE (2009b) *Application for Trial Leave or Full Transfer to Another Hospital—Guidance*, London: Ministry of Justice.

MINISTRY OF JUSTICE (2009c) *The Recall of Conditionally Discharged Restricted Patients*, London: Ministry of Justice.

MINISTRY OF JUSTICE (2010) *Breaking the Cycle: Effective Punishment, Rehabilitation and Sentencing of Offenders*, Cm 7972, London: TSO.

MINISTRY OF JUSTICE (2011) *Offender Management Statistics 2010*, London: Ministry of Justice.

MINISTRY OF JUSTICE (2012) *Annual Tables—Offender Management Caseload Statistics 2011*, London: Ministry of Justice.

MINISTRY OF JUSTICE (2012a) *Mental Health Casework Section Guidance—Section 17 Leave*, London: Ministry of Justice.

MINISTRY OF JUSTICE (2012b) *Annual Tribunals Statistics 1 April 2011 to 31 March 2012*, London: Ministry of Justice.

MINISTRY OF JUSTICE (2013) *Story of the Prison Population: 1993–2012 England and Wales*, London: Ministry of Justice.

MINISTRY OF JUSTICE/NATIONAL OFFENDER MANAGEMENT SERVICE (2012) *NOMS Commissioning Intentions 2013-14: Discussion Document*, London: Ministry of Justice.

MINKOWITZ, T. (2010) 'Abolishing Mental Health Laws to Comply with the Convention on the Rights of Persons with Disabilities', in B. McSherry and P. Weller (eds), *Rethinking Rights-Based Mental Health Laws*, Oxford: Hart.

MITCHELL, A., LORD, O., and MALONE, D. (2012) 'Differences in the prescribing of medication for physical disorders in individuals with v. without mental illness: meta-analysis', *British Journal of Psychiatry* 201: 435–43.

MITTMAN, A.S. (2006) *Maps and Monsters in Medieval England*, London: Routledge.

MONAHAN, J. (1981) *Predicting Violent Behavior*, Beverly Hills, CA: Sage.

MONAHAN, J. (1988) 'Risk assessment of violence among the mentally disordered: generating useful knowledge', *International Journal of Law and Psychiatry* 11: 249.

MONAHAN, J., HOGE, S., LIDZ, C., ROTH, L., BENNETT, N., GARDNER, W., and MULVEY, E. (1995) 'Coercion and commitment: understanding involuntary mental hospital admission', *International Journal of Law and Psychiatry* 18(3): 249.

MONAHAN, J., STEADMAN, H.J., SILVER, E., APPELBAUM, P., CLARK ROBBINS, P., MULVEY, E.P., ROTH, L.H., GRISSON, T., and BANKS, S. (2001) *Rethinking Risk Assessment: The MacArthur Study of Mental Disorder and Violence*, Oxford: Oxford University Press.

MONTANDON, C. and HARDING, T. (1984) 'The reliability of dangerousness assessments: a decision making exercise', *British Journal of Psychiatry* 144: 149.

MORGAN, C., and HUTCHINSON, G.(2010) 'The social determinants of psychosis in migrant and ethnic minority populations: a public health tragedy', *Psychological Medicine* 40:705–9.

MORGAN, H. and PRIEST, P. (1991) 'Suicide and other unexpected deaths among psychiatric inpatients: the Bristol confidential inquiry', *British Journal of Psychiatry* 158: 368.

MORRIS, J. (1993) *Independent Lives: Community Care and Disabled People*, London: Macmillan.

MUIJEN, M. (1996) 'Scare in the community: Britain in moral panic', in T. Heller, J. Reynolds, R. Gomm, R. Muston, and S. Pattison (eds) *Mental Health Matters: A Reader*, Basingstoke and London: Macmillan.

MUNRO, P (2008) 'The discreditation of mad people within legal and psychiatric decision making: a systems theory approach'. PhD dissertation (University of Nottingham, School of Law).

MURPHY, E. (1991) *After the Asylums: Community Care for People with Mental Illness*, London: Faber.

NASSER, M. (2010) 'Women, ethnicity and mental health' in Kohen, D. (ed.) *Oxford Textbook of Women and Mental Health*, Oxford: OUP.

NATIONAL APPROPRIATE ADULT NETWORK (2005) *National Standard 1 Recruitment and Selection of Appropriate Adults; National Standard 2 Support, Supervision, Development and Retention of Appropriate Adults*, London: NAAN.

NATIONAL APPROPRIATE ADULT NETWORK (2005a) *National Standard 3 Training*, London: NAAN.

NATIONAL APPROPRIATE ADULT NETWORK (2005b) *National Standard 4 Service Delivery*, London: NAAN.

NATIONAL ASSOCIATION FOR THE CARE AND REHABILITATION OF OFFENDERS (2005) *Findings of the 2004 Survey of Court Diversion/Criminal Justice Mental Health Liaison Schemes for Mentally Disordered Offenders in England and Wales*, London: NACRO.

NATIONAL AUDIT OFFICE (2003) *Ensuring the Effective Discharge of Older Patients from NHS Acute Hospitals*, HC 392, London: National Audit Office.

NATIONAL AUDIT OFFICE (2003a) *A Safer Place to Work: Protecting NHS Hospital and Ambulance Staff from Violence and Aggression: Report Prepared by the Comptroller and Auditor General*, HC 527, London: National Audit Office.

NATIONAL CONFIDENTIAL INQUIRY INTO SUICIDE AND HOMICIDE BY PEOPLE WITH MENTAL ILLNESS (2012) *Annual Report July 2012*, Manchester: University of Manchester Press.

NATIONAL HEALTH SERVICE COMMISSIONING BOARD (2012) *Securing Excellence in Commissioning Primary Care: Key Facts*, London: NHSCB.

NATIONAL HEALTH SERVICE COMMISSIONING BOARD (2012a) *Commissioning Fact Sheet for Clinical Commissioning Groups*, London: Department of Health.

NATIONAL HEALTH SERVICE COMMISSIONING BOARD (2013) *Securing Excellence in Commissioning for Offender Health*, published online only at http://www.commissioningboard. nhs.uk/wp-content/uploads/2013/03/ offender-commissioning.pdf.

NATIONAL HEALTH SERVICE INFORMATION CENTRE (2010) 'Annual analysis of Mental Capacity Act 2005, Deprivation of Liberty Safeguards Assessments (England) 2009–2010' Available online at http://www.ic.nhs.uk/ article/2021/Website-Search?productid=24 97&q=Mental+Capacity+Act+&sort=Relev ance&size=10&page=9&area=both#top.

NATIONAL HEALTH SERVICE INFORMATION CENTRE (2011) 'Annual analysis of Mental Capacity Act 2005, Deprivation of Liberty Safeguards Assessments (England) 2010–11'. Available online at https://catalogue.ic.nhs.uk/publi-cations/mental-health/legislation/m-c-a-2005-dep-lib-saf-ass-eng-2010-11/m-c-a-2005-dep-lib-saf-ass-eng-2010-11-rep.pdf.

NATIONAL HEALTH SERVICE INFORMATION CENTRE (2012) *Inpatients Formally Detained in Hospitals Under the Mental Health Act 1983 and Patients Subject to Supervised Community Treatment— England, 2011-2012, Annual figures,* London: Department of Health.

NATIONAL HEALTH SERVICE INFORMATION CENTRE (2012a) *Abuse of Vulnerable Adults in England 2011-12: Experimental Statistics: Provisional Report,* London: Department of Health.

NATIONAL HEALTH SERVICE INFORMATION CENTRE, (2012c) 'Annual analysis of Mental Capacity Act 2005, Deprivation of Liberty Safeguards Assessments (England) 2011-12'. Available online https://catalogue.ic.nhs.uk/publica-tions/mental-health/legislation/m-c-a-2005-dep-lib-saf-ass-eng-2011-12/m-c-a-2005-dep-lib-saf-ass-eng-2011-12-rep.pdf.

NATIONAL HEALTH SERVICE INFORMATION CENTRE (2013) *Mental Health Bulletin: Annual report from MHMDS returns—England 2011/12, initial national figures: National reference tables* available at http://www.ic.nhs.uk/.

NATIONAL INSTITUTE FOR HEALTH AND CLINICAL EXCELLENCE (2005) *Violence: The Short-term Management of Disturbed/Violent Behaviour in Inpatient Psychiatric Settings and Emergency Departments,* London: NICE.

NATIONAL INSTITUTE FOR HEALTH AND CLINICAL EXCELLENCE (NICE) (2009). *Schizophrenia.* Clinical Guidance 82 London: National Institute for Health and Clinical Excellence.

NATIONAL MENTAL HEALTH DEVELOPMENT UNIT (2010) *Paths to personalisation in mental health: a whole system, whole life framework,* London: Department of Health.

NATIONAL POLICING IMPROVEMENT AGENCY AND DEPARTMENT OF HEALTH (2010) *Guidance on Responding to People with Mental Ill Health or Learning Disabilities,* London: ACPO, NPIA.

NEEDHAM, C. (2011) 'Personalization: from story-line to practice', *Social Policy & Administration,* 45(1): 54–6.

NEMETZ, T. and BEAN, P. (2001) 'Protecting the rights of the mentally disordered in police stations: the use of the appropriate adult in England and Wales', *International Journal of Law and Psychiatry* 24: 595–605.

NETTEN, A., WILLIAMS. J., and DARTON, R. (2005) Care home closures in England: causes and implications *Ageing and Society* 25(3): 319–38.

NEWTON-HOWES, G. and MULLEN, R (2011) 'Coercion in Psychiatry Care: Systematic Review of Correlates and Themes', *Psychiatric Services* 62:465–70.

NHS EXECUTIVE (1999) *Clinical Governance: Quality in the New NHS,* HSC 1999/065, London: Department of Health.

NHS HEALTH ADVISORY SERVICE/ DEPARTMENT OF HEALTH AND SOCIAL SECURITY SOCIAL SERVICES INSPECTORATE (1988) *Report on the Services Provided by Broadmoor Hospital,* HAS/SSI(88) SH 1, London: Department of Health and Social Security.

NORFOLK, G. (1997) 'Fitness to be inter-viewed: a proposed definition and scheme of examination', *Medicine, Science and Law* 37(3): 228.

NORFOLK, SUFFOLK AND CAMBRIDGESHIRE HEALTH AUTHORITY (2003) *Independent Inquiry into the Death of David Bennett,* Cambridge: Norfolk, Suffolk and Cambridgeshire Health Authority.

NORRIS, C. and ARMSTRONG, G. (1999) *The Maximum Surveillance Society: The Rise of CCTV*, Oxford, Berg.

NOTTINGHAMSHIRE NHS TRUST (2011) *Safe Use Of Mechanical Restraint in All Forms*, Nottingham: Nottinghamshire NHS Trust.

OBORNES, A.C., HOOPER, R., SWIFT, C.G. and JACKSON, S.H.D. (2003) 'Explicit, evidence-based criteria to assess the quality of prescribing to elderly nursing home residents', *Age and Aging* 32: 102–8.

OFFICE FOR DISABILITY ISSUES, (2011) *United Kingdom Initial Report on the UN Convention on the Rights of Persons with Disabilities*, London: ODI, 2011.

OKAI, D., *et al.* (2007) 'Mental capacity in psychiatric patients: Systematic review', *British Journal of Psychiatry* 191:291–7.

OLUMUYIWA J. *et al.* (2009) 'Mentally ill prisoners in need of urgent hospital transfer: appeal panels should resolve disputes to reduce delays' 20(1) *The Journal of Forensic Psychiatry & Psychology* 5–10.

ONYETT, S., HEPPLESTON, T., and BUSHNELL, D. (1994) 'A national survey of community mental health team structure and process', *Journal of Mental Health* 3: 175.

O'SULLIVAN, C.J. and CHESTERMAN, L. P. (2007) 'Older adult patients subject to restriction orders in England and Wales: a cross-sectional survey', *Journal of Forensic Psychiatry and Psychology* 18(2): 204–20.

OWEN, G, *et al.* (2009), 'Retrospective views of psychiatric in-patients regaining mental capacity', 195 *British Journal of Psychiatry* 195: 403.

OWEN, S., AVIS, M., and KHALIL, E. (2004) *A Scoping Exercise for a Health Strategy for Women in Custody in England and Wales: Final Academic Report Submitted to the HM Prison Service*, London: Department of Health.

PALMER, C. (1996) 'Still vulnerable after all these years', *Criminal Law Review*: 633.

PAPADOPOULOS, C., ROSS, J., STEWART, D., DACK, C., JAMES, K., and BOWERS, L. (2012) 'The antecedents of violence and aggression within psychiatric in-patient settings', *Acta Psychiatr Scand.* 125(6): 425–39.

PARKIN, A. (1996) 'Where now on mental incapacity?', *Web Journal of Current Legal Issues* 2.

PARSONAGE, M. *et al.* (2009) *Diversion: A Better Way for Criminal Justice and Mental Health*, London: Sainsbury Centre for Mental Health.

PATON, C., *et al.* (2008) 'High-dose and combination antipsychotic prescribing in acute adult wards in the UK: the challenges posed by p.r.n. prescribing', *British Journal of Psychiatry* 192: 435–9.

PEAY, J. (1989) *Tribunals on Trial: A Study of Decision-Making under the Mental Health Act 1983*, Oxford: Clarendon.

PEAY, J. (1997) 'Mentally disordered offenders', in M. Maguire, R. Morgan, and R. Reiner (eds) *The Oxford Handbook of Criminology*, Oxford: Oxford University Press.

PEAY, J. (2003) *Decisions and Dilemmas: Working with Mental Health Law*, Oxford: Hart.

PEAY, J. (2012) *Fitness to Plead and Core Competencies: Problems and Possibilities*, London: LSE Law, Society and Economy Working Papers 2/2012.

PEAY, J. ROBERTS, C. and EASTMAN, N. (2001) 'Legal knowledge of mental health professionals: report of a national survey', *Journal of Mental Health Law* 5: 44–55.

PEGLER, J. (2002) *A Can of Madness*, London: Chipmunka.

PERKINS, E. (2000) *Decision-making in Mental Health Review Tribunals*, London: Department of Health.

PERKINS, R. (1996) 'Choosing ECT', in
J. Read and J. Reynolds (eds) *Speaking
Our Minds: An Anthology*,
London: Macmillan.

PERKS, M. (2010) *Appropriate Adult Provision
in England and Wales: A Report prepared
on behalf of the National Appropriate Adult
Network for the Department of Health
and the Home Office*, London: National
Appropriate Adult Network.

PERRING, C. (1992) 'The experience
and perspectives of patients and care
staff of the transition from hospital to
community-based care', in S. Ramon (ed.)
*Psychiatric Hospital Closure: Myths and
Realities*, London: Chapman and Hall.

PERRUCCI, R. (1974) *Circle of Madness: On
Being Insane and Institutionalized in
America*, New Jersey: Prentice-Hall.

PIERPOINT, H. (2001) 'The performance
of volunteer appropriate adults: a survey
of call outs', *Howard Journal of Criminal
Justice* 40(3): 255–71.

PIERPOINT, H. (2006) 'Reconstructing the
role of appropriate adult in England and
Wales', *Criminology and Criminal Justice*
6(2): 219–37.

PIERPOINT, H. (2011) 'Extending and
professionalising the role of the appropriate adult', 33(2) *Journal of Social Welfare &
Family Law* 33(2) 139–55.

PIRKIS, J. and FRANCIS, C. (2012) *Mental
Illness in the News and Information Media*,
Canberra: [Australia] Department of
Health and Aging.

PLUGGE, E., DOUGLAS, N. and
FITZPATRICK, R. (2006) *The Health of
Women in Prison*, Oxford: Department of
Public Health, University of Oxford.

POLYTHRESS, N.G., BONNIE, R.J.,
MONAHAN, J., OTTO, R., and HODGE,
S.K. (2002) *Adjudicative Competence: The
MacArthur Studies*, New York: Plenum.

PORTER, R. (1987a) *Mind-Forg'd
Manacles: A History of Madness in England
from the Restoration to the Regency*,
London: Athlone Press.

PRIEBE S. *et al.* (2009) 'Patients' views and
readmissions 1 year after involuntary
hospitalisation', *British Medical Journal*
194: 49.

PRIEBE, S. *et al.* (2011) 'Predictors of clinical
and social outcomes following involuntary
hospital admission', *Eur Arch Psychiatry
Clin Neurosci* 261:377–86.

PRIOR, J. (2010) *Attitudes to Mental
Illness 2010 Research Report JN 207028*,
London: Office of National Statistics.

PRIOR, L. (1993) *The Social Organisation of
Mental Illness*, London: Sage.

PRIOR, L. (1996) 'The appeal to mad-
ness in Ireland', in D. Tomlinson and J.
Carrier (eds) *Asylum in the Community*,
London: Routledge.

PRIOR, P. (1992) 'The approved social
worker: reflections on origins', *British
Journal of Social Work* 22: 105.

PRITCHARD, E. (2006) *Appropriate
Adult Provision in England and Wales*,
London: NAAN.

PROCHASKA, F. (1988) *The Voluntary
Impulse: Philanthropy in Modern Britain*,
London: Faber and Faber.

QURESHI, H. (2009) *Report 26: Restraint
in care homes for older people: a review of
selected literature*, London: Social Care
Institute for Excellence.

RAMON, S. (1992) 'The context of hospital closure in the Western world, or
why now?', in S. Ramon (ed.) *Psychiatric
Hospital Closure: Myths and Realities*,
London: Chapman and Hall.

RAY, W., *et al.* (2009) 'Atypical Antipsychotic
Drugs and the Risk of Sudden Cardiac
Death', *New England Journal of Medicine*
360: 225–35.

READ, J. and REYNOLDS, J. (eds) (1996) *Speaking Our Minds: An Anthology*, London: Macmillan.

REED, J. (2002) 'Delivering psychiatric care to prisoners: problems and solutions', *Advanced Psychiatric Treatment* 8(2): 117–25.

REED, J. and LYNE, M. (2000) 'Inpatient care of mentally ill people in prison: results of a year's programme of semistructured inspections', *British Medical Journal* 320: 1031–4.

REES, S. (2009) *Mental Ill Health in the Adult Single Homeless Population: A Review of the Literature*, London: Crisis UK.

RICHARDSON, G. (1993) *Law, Process and Custody: Prisoners and Patients*, London: Weidenfeld and Nicolson.

RICHARDSON, G. (2010), Mental capacity at the margin: the interface between two Acts, *Medical Law Review* 18(1): 56–77.

RICHARDSON, G. and MACHIN, D. (2000) 'Judicial review and tribunal decision making: a study of the mental health review tribunal', *Public Law* Autumn: 494–514.

RICHARDSON, G. and MACHIN, D. (2000a) 'Doctors on tribunals: a confusion of roles', *British Journal of Psychiatry* 176: 110–5.

Rickford, D. (2003) *Troubled Inside: Responding to the Mental Health Needs of Women in Prison*, London: Prison Reform Trust.

RICKFORD, D. and EDGAR, K. (2005) *Troubled Inside: Responding to the Mental Health Needs of Men in Prison*, London: Prison Reform Trust.

RIMER *et al.* (2012), 'Exercise for depression'. Cochrane Database of Systematic Reviews 2012, Issue 7. Art. No.: CD004366. DOI: 10.1002/14651858.CD004366.pub5

ROBERTSON, G., PEARSON, R. and GIBB, R. (1996) 'Police interviewing and the use of appropriate adults', *Journal of Forensic Psychiatry* 7(2): 297.

ROGERS, A. (1990) 'Policing mental disorder: controversies, myths and realities', *Social Policy and Administration* 24: 226.

ROGERS, A. and PILGRIM, D. (2001) *Mental Health Policy in Britain: A Critical Introduction*, 2nd edn, Basingstoke: Palgrave.

ROGERS, A. and PILGRIM, D. (2010) *A Sociology of Mental Health and Illness*, 4th edn, Maidenhead: Open University Press.

ROGERS, T.P., BLACKWOOD, N.J., FARNHAM, F., PICKUP, G.J., and WATTS, M.J. (2009) 'Reformulating fitness to plead: a qualitative study' *Journal of Forensic Psychiatry and Psychology* 20(6): 815.

ROGERS, W. (2010) *Winfield and Jolowicz on Tort*, 18th edn, London: Sweet and Maxwell.

ROMANO, D. (1997) 'The legal advocate and the questionably competent client in the context of a poverty law clinic', *Osgoode Hall Law Journal* 35: 737.

ROSE, N. (1986) 'Law, psychiatry and rights', in P. Miller and N. Rose (eds) *The Power of Psychiatry*, Cambridge: Polity Press.

ROSENHAN, D.L. (1973) 'On being sane in insane places', *Science* 179: 250.

ROSSAU, C. and MORTENSEN, P. (1997) 'Risk factors or suicide in patients with schizophrenia: nested case-study analysis', *British Journal of Psychiatry* 171: 355–69.

ROTH, L., MEISEL, A. and LIDZ, C. (1977) 'Tests of competency to consent to treatment', *American Journal of Psychiatry* 134(3): 279.

ROTHMAN, D. (1971) *The Discovery of the Asylum: Social Order and Disorder in the New Republic*, Boston: Little Brown.

ROTHMAN, D. (1980) *Conscience and Convenience: The Asylum and its Alternative in Progressive America*, Boston: Little Brown.

ROULSTONE, A. and MORGAN, H. (2009) 'Neo-liberal individualism or self-directed support: are we all speaking the same language on modernising adult social care?' *Social Policy & Society* 8(3): 333–46.

ROWLANDS, R., INCH, H., RODGER, W. and SOLIMAN, A. (1996) 'Diverted to where? What happens to the diverted mentally disordered offender', *Journal of Forensic Psychiatry* 7(2): 284.

ROYAL COLLEGE OF PSYCHIATRISTS (2007) *Standards for Medium Secure Units*, London: Royal College of Psychiatrists.

ROYAL COLLEGE OF PSYCHIATRISTS (2011) *Standards on the Use of Section 136 of the Mental Health Act 1983 (England and Wales)CR 159*, London: Royal College of Psychiatrists.

ROYAL COLLEGE OF PSYCHIATRISTS (2011a) *Do the Right Thing: How to Judge a Good Ward. Ten Standards for Adult In-patient Mental Healthcare, Occasional Paper 79*, London: Royal College of Psychiatrists.

ROYAL COLLEGE OF PSYCHIATRISTS (2011b) *Prison Transfers: A Survey from the Royal College of Psychiatrists December 2011*, RCP OP81 London: RCP.

ROYAL COLLEGE OF PSYCHIATRISTS (2011c) *Consultation Response Unfitness to Plead*, London: Royal College of Psychiatrists.

ROYAL COLLEGE OF PSYCHIATRISTS (2012), 'Anti-depressants'. Available online at http://www.rcpsych.ac.uk/expertadvice/treatments/antidepressants.aspx.

ROYAL COLLEGE OF PSYCHIATRISTS AND THE LAW SOCIETY (2002) *Joint Statement on the Reform of the Mental Health Act 1983*, London: Royal College of Psychiatrists and the Law Society.

ROYAL COMMISSION ON CRIMINAL JUSTICE (1993) *Report of the Royal Commission on Criminal Justice*, Cm 2263, London: HMSO.

ROYAL COMMISSION ON LONG-TERM CARE (1999) *With Respect to Old Age: Long-term Care—Rights and Responsibilities* (the 'Sutherland Report'), Cm 4192-I, London: HMSO.

ROYAL COMMISSION ON THE LAW RELATING TO MENTAL ILLNESS AND MENTAL DEFICIENCY 1954–1957 (the 'Percy Commission') (1957) *Report*, Cmnd 169, London: HMSO.

RUSCHENA, D., MULLEN, P., BURGESS, P., CORDNER, S., BARRY-WALSH J., DRUMMER, O., PALMER, S., BROWNE, C. and WALLACE, C. (1998) 'Sudden death in psychiatric patients', *British Journal of Psychiatry* 172: 331.

RUTHERFORD, M. (2010) *Blurring the Boundaries: The convergence of mental health and criminal justice policy, legislation, systems and practice*, London: Sainsbury Centre for Mental Health.

RYAN, S. and WHELAN, D. (2012) 'Diversion of Offenders with Mental Disorders: Mental Health Courts' [2012] 1 *Web JCLI* http://webjcli.ncl.ac.uk/2012/issue1/ryan1.html.

SACKETT, K. (1996) 'Discharges from section 3 of the Mental Health Act 1983: changes in practice', *Health Trends* 28: 66.

SAINSBURY CENTRE FOR MENTAL HEALTH (2009) *Briefing 39: Mental Health Care and the Criminal Justice System*, London: Sainsbury Centre for Mental Health.

SAINSBURY CENTRE FOR MENTAL HEALTH (2009a) *Diversion: A Better Way for Criminal Justice and Mental Health*, London: Sainsbury Centre for Mental Health.

SAINSBURY CENTRE FOR MENTAL HEALTH (2009b) *All-Stages Diversion: a model for the future*, London: Sainsbury Centre for Mental Health.

SAMUEL, M. (2010) 'Glasgow care partnerships scrapped over NHS-council row' *Community Care*, 21 May 2010.

SANDLAND, R. (2000) 'Mental Health Act guardianship and the protection of children', *Journal of Mental Health Law*: 186–95.

SANG, B. (2009) 'Personalisation: Consumer Power or Social Co-Production', *Journal of Integrated Care* 17(4): 31–8.

SCULL, A. (1977) *Decarceration: Community Treatment and the Deviant—A Radical View*, Englewood Cliffs, NY: Prentice Hall.

SCULL, A. (1979) *Museums of Madness*, Harmondsworth: Penguin.

SCULL, A. (1993) *The Most Solitary of Afflictions: Madness and Society in Britain, 1700–1900*, New Haven: Yale University Press.

SCULL, A. (1996) 'Mental patients and the community: a critical note', *International Journal of Law and Psychiatry* 9: 383.

SEDGWICK, P. (1982) *Psychopolitics*, London: Pluto Press.

SENIOR, J., LENNOX, C., NOGA, H., and SHAW, J. (2011) *Liaison and Diversion Services: Current Practice and Future Directions*, Manchester: Offender Health Research Network.

SENIOR PRESIDENT OF THE TRIBUNALS (2009) *Practice Statement: Composition of Tribunals in Relation to Matters that Fall to be Decided by the Health, Education and Social Care Chamber*, London: Ministry of Justice.

SENIOR PRESIDENT OF TRIBUNALS (2012) *Senior President of Tribunals' Annual Report*, London: Ministry of Justice.

SENIOR PRESIDENT OF TRIBUNALS (2012a) *Practice Direction First-Tier Tribunal Health Education and Social Care Chamber Statements and Reports in Mental Health Cases*, London: Ministry of Justice.

SEWELL, H (2008) *Working with Ethnicity, Race and Culture in Mental Health: A Handbook for Practitioners*, London: Jessica Kingsley.

SHAH, A. (1993) 'An increase in violent behaviour among psychiatric inpatients: real or apparent?', *Medicine, Science and Law* 33: 227.

SHAW, J. *et al.* (2008) *An Evaluation of the Department of Health's 'Procedure for the Transfer of Prisoners to and from Hospital under sections 47 and 48 of the Mental Health Act 1983' Initiative October 2008*, Manchester: The Offender Health Research Network.

SHAW, J. *et al.* (2008b) *An Evaluation of the Reception Screening Process Used Within Prisons in England and Wales*, Manchester: The Offender Health Research Network.

SHAW, J. *et al.* (2009) *A National Evaluation of Prison Mental Health In-Reach Services*. Manchester: The Offender Health Research Network.

SHEEHAN, K. and BURNS, T. (2011) 'Perceived Coercion and the Therapeutic Relationship', *Psychiatric Services* 62:471–6

SHILDRICK, M. (2002) *Embodying the Monster: Encounters with the Vulnerable Self*, London: Sage.

SHORT, J. (1995) 'Characteristics of absconders from acute admission wards', *Journal of Forensic Psychiatry* 6(2): 277.

SHORTER, E. (1998) *A History of Psychiatry from the Era of the Asylum to the Age of Prozac* New York: Wiley.

SHUBSACHS, A., HUWS, R., CLOSE, A., LARKIN, E., and FALVEY, J. (1995) 'Male Afro-Caribbean patients admitted to Rampton hospital between 1977 and 1986', *Medicine, Science and Law* 35(4): 336.

SIMMONS, P. & HOAR, A. (2001) 'Section 136 use in the London Borough of Haringey' *Medicine, Science and the Law* 41: 342–8.

SINGH, D. K. and MONCRIEFF, J. (2009) 'Trends in Mental Health Review Tribunal and hospital managers' hearings in north-east London 1997–2007' 33(1) *Psychiatric Bulletin* 15–7.

SINGH, S et al. (2007) 'Ethnicity and the Mental Health Act 1983. Systematic review' British Journal of Psychiatry (Aug, 2007) 99–105.

SINGLETON, N., MELTZER, H., and GATWARD, R. (1998) Psychiatric Morbidity among Prisoners in England and Wales, Office of National Statistics, London: HMSO.

SMITH, A. and HUMPHREYS, M. (1997) 'Physical restraint of patients in a psychiatric hospital', Medicine, Science and Law 37(2): 145.

SMITH, J., DONOVAN, M., and GORDON, H. (1991) 'Patients in Broadmoor hospital from the south-western region: an audit of transfer procedures', Psychiatric Bulletin 15: 81.

SMITH, J.C. (2000) 'Comment on R v Antoine', Criminal Law Review: 621–6.

SMITH, R. (1981) Trial by Medicine: Insanity and Responsibility in Victorian Trials, Edinburgh: Edinburgh University Press.

SOCIAL SERVICES INSPECTORATE AND AUDIT COMMISSION (2001) Delivering Results, London: Audit Commission.

SPANDLER, H. and VICK, N. (2005) 'Enabling access to direct payments: an exploration of care co-ordinators decision making practices', Journal of Mental Health Law 14(2): 145–55.

SPANDLER, H. and VICK, N. (2006) 'Opportunities for independent living using direct payments in mental health', Health and Social Care in the Community 14(2): 107–15.

STEINERT, T. et al. (2010) 'Incidence of seclusion and restraint in psychiatric hospitals: a literature review and survey of international trends' Soc Psychiatry Psychiatr Epidemiol 45(9): 889–97.

STEWART, D. and BOWERS, L (2010) Absconding from Psychiatric Hospitals: A Literature Review, London: Institute of Psychiatry.

STEWART, D., BOWERS, L., SIMPSON, A., RYAN, C., and TZIGGILI, M. (2009) Manual Restraint of Adult Psychiatric Inpatients: A Literature Review, London: City University.

STEWART D, VAN DER MERWE M, BOWERS L, SIMPSON A and JONES J (2010) 'A review of interventions to reduce mechanical restraint and seclusion among adult psychiatric inpatients' Issues Ment Health Nurs. 31(6):413–24.

STILO, S., et al. (2012) 'Social Disadvantage: Cause or Consequence of impending psychosis?', Schizophrenia Bulletin, in press, doi: 10.1093/schbul/sbs112.

STREET, R. (1998) The Restricted Hospital Order: From Court to the Community, Home Office Research Study 186, London: Home Office Research and Statistics Directorate.

STUBBS, B., LEADBETTER, D., PATERSON, B., YORSTON, G., KNIGHT, C., and DAVIS, S. (2009) 'Physical intervention: a review of the literature on its use, staff and patient views, and the impact of training' J Psychiatr Ment Health Nurs. 16(1):99–105.

STURDY, H. and PARRY-JONES, W. (1999) 'Boarding-out insane patients: the significance of the Scottish system 1857–1913', in P. Bartlett and D. Wright (eds) Outside the Walls of the Asylum, London: Athlone.

STYRON, W. (1990) Darkness Visible, London: Cape.

STYRON, W. (1996) 'Darkness visible', in S. Dunn, B. Morrison and M. Roberts (eds) Mind Readings: Writers' Journeys through Mental States, London: Minerva.

SUZUKI, A. (1991) 'Lunacy in seventeenth- and eighteenth-century England: analysis of Quarter Sessions records Part I', History of Psychiatry 2: 437.

SUZUKI, A. (1992) 'Lunacy in seventeenth-and eighteenth-century England: analysis of Quarter Sessions records Part II', *History of Psychiatry* 3: 29.

SUZUKI, A. (1995) 'The politics and ideology of non-restraint: the case of the Hanwell Asylum', *Medical History* 39: 1.

SWIFT. N. P (2012) 'Physical health examination in Section 136 suites' *Adv. Psychiatr. Treat.* 18: 78–9.

SZASZ, T. (1970) *Ideology and Insanity: Essays on the Psychiatric Dehumanisation of Man*, Garden City: Doubleday.

SZMUKLER, G., DAW, R., and DAWSON, J., (2010), 'A model law fusing incapacity and mental health legislation' *Journal of Mental Health Law* (2010) 11–24.

SZMUKLER, G. and HOLLOWAY, F. (2000) 'Reform of the Mental Health Act: health or safety?', *British Journal of Psychiatry* 177: 196–200.

TAXIS, J.C. (2002) 'Ethics and praxis: alternative strategies to physical restraint and seclusion in a psychiatric setting', *Issues in Mental Health Nursing* 23(2): 157–70.

TAYLOR, J. and GUNN, J. (1984) 'Violence and psychosis: 1—Risk of violence among psychotic men', *British Medical Journal* 288: 1945.

TAYLOR, L. (1996) 'ECT is barbaric', in J. Read and J. Reynolds (eds) *Speaking Our Minds: An Anthology*, London: Macmillan.

TAYLOR, N. W. (2009) Case Comment R. v Moyle (Peter Geoffrey): Fitness to plead—whether paranoid delusions may render accused unfit to plead *Criminal Law Review* 586–8.

TAYLOR, P. and GUNN, J. (1999) 'Homicides by people with mental illness: myth and reality', *British Journal of Psychiatry* 174: 9.

TETLEY, A. C., EVERSHED, S., and KRISHNAN, G. (2010) 'Difficulties in the pathway from high to medium secure services for personality-disordered patients' *The Journal of Forensic Psychiatry & Psychology* 21(2): 189–201.

THACKREY, M. and BOBBITT, R. (1990) 'Patient aggression against clinical and non-clinical staff in a VA medical center', *Hospital and Community Psychiatry* 41: 195.

THOMAS, P. (1997) *The Dialectics of Schizophrenia*, London: Free Association Books.

THOMPSON, A., SHAW, M., HARRISON, G., DAVIDON, H., GUNNELL, D., and VEUE, J. (2004) 'Patterns of hospital admission for adult psychiatric illness in England: analysis of hospital episode statistics data', *British Journal of Psychiatry* 185: 334–41.

THOMSON, M. (1996) 'Family, community and state: the micro politics of mental deficiency', in A. Digby and D. Wright (eds) *From Idiocy to Mental Deficiency*, London: Routledge.

THOMSON, M. (1998) 'Community care and the control of mental defectives in inter-war Britain', in P. Horden and D. Smith (eds) *The Locus of Care*, London: Routledge.

THORNICROFT, G. (2006) *Shunned: Discrimination Against People with Mental Illness*, Oxford: Oxford University Press.

THOROGOOD, N. (1989) 'Afro-Caribbean women's experience of the health service', *New Community* 15(3): 319.

TIDMARSH, D. (1978) *Broadmoor Ins and Outs*, unpublished paper presented to the Forensic Section of Royal College of Psychiatrists, Broadmoor Hospital, 23 May.

TOMISON, A. (1989) 'Characteristics of psychiatric hospital absconders', *British Journal of Psychiatry* 154: 368.

Tribunals Service (2005) *New Procedures Concerning the Rights of Access to MHRT Hearings of Victims of Certain Criminal Offences Committed by Patients*, London: Tribunals Service.

Tungaraza, T., *et al.* (2010) 'Polypharmacy and high-dose antipsychotic regimes in the community' *The Psychiatrist* 34: 44–6.

Tungaraza, T., *et al.* (2011) 'Polypharmacy and high-dose antipsychotics at the time of discharge from acute psychiatric wards', *The Psychiatrist* 35: 288–92.

Turner T., Ness, M. N. and Imison, C.T. (1992) 'Mentally disordered persons found in public Places' *Psychological Medicine* 22: 765–74.

Tyler, T.R. (1996) 'The psychological consequences of judicial procedures: implications for civil commitment hearings', in D.B. Wexler and B.J. Winick (eds) *Law in a Therapeutic Key: Developments in Therapeutic Jurisprudence*, Durham, NC: Carolina Academic Press.

United Nations Committee on the Rights of Persons with Disabilities (2011), Concluding observations of the Committee on the Rights of Persons with Disabilities: Tunisia, CRPD/C/TUN/CO/1 (13 May 2011).

United Nations Committee on the Rights of Persons with Disabilities (2011a), Concluding observations of the Committee on the Rights of Persons with Disabilities: Spain, CRPD/C/ESP/CO/1 (19 October 2011).

United Nations Committee on the Rights of Persons with Disabilities (2012), Concluding observations of the Committee on the Rights of Persons with Disabilities: Peru, CRPD/C/PER/CO/1 (9 May 2012).

United Nations High Commissioner for Human Rights (2009), Annual Report 2009, A/HRC/10/48 (26 January 2009).

United Nations Special Rapporteur on Torture, 2013, 'Report of the Special Rapporteur on torture and other cruel, inhuman or degrading treatment or punishment, Juan E. Méndez', General Assembly A/HRC/22/53 (1 February 2013).

Van Dorn, R., Volvka, Johnson, N. (2012) 'Mental Disorder and violence: is there a relationship beyond substance use?', *Soc Psychiatry Psychiatr Epidemiol* 47: 487.

Virtanen, M. *et al.* (2011) 'Overcrowding in psychiatric wards and physical assaults on staff: data-linked longitudinal study' *British Journal of Psychiatry* 198: 149–55.

Walker, N. and McCabe, S. (1973) *Crime and Insanity in England Vol. 1: The Historical Perspective*, Edinburgh: Edinburgh University Press.

Walmsley, J., Atkinson, D., and Rolph, S. (1999) 'Community care and mental deficiency 1913 to 1945', in P. Bartlett and D. Wright (eds) *Outside the Walls of the Asylum*, London: Athlone.

Walsh, E. *et al.* (1998) 'Absconders: characteristics and outcome', *Psychiatric Bulletin* 22: 351–3.

Wand, T., and Chiarella, M. (2006), 'A conversation: Challenging the relevance and wisdom of separate mental health legislation', 15 *International Journal of Mental Health Nursing* 119.

Whelan, R. (1999) *Involuntary Action: How Voluntary is the 'Voluntary' Sector?*, London: Institute of Economic Affairs.

White, C. (2002) 'Re-assessing the social worker's role as an appropriate adult', *Journal of Social Welfare and Family Law* 24(1): 55–65.

White, S. (1992) 'The Criminal Procedure (Insanity and Unfitness to Plead) Act', *Criminal Law Review*: 4.

WILLIAMS, D. (1996) *Deformed Discourse: The Function of the Monster in Medieval Thought and Literature*, Exeter: University of Exeter Press.

WILLIAMS, J. (2000) 'The inappropriate adult', *Journal of Social Welfare and Family Law* 22(1): 43–57.

WILLIAMS, M., LLOYD. K. and HAYRE, C. (2005) 'Mental disordered offenders and prison health care in remand settings', *Prison Service Journal* 162: 24–8.

WILLIAMS, V, *et al.* (2012) *Making Best Interests Decisions: People and Processes*, London: Mental Health Foundation.

WILSON, S. CHIU, K., PARROTT, J. and FORRESTER, A. (2010) 'Postcode lottery? Hospital transfers from one London prison and responsible catchment area' *The Psychiatrist Online* 2010, 34:140–2.

WINSTONE, J. and PAKES, F. (2010) *Liaison and Diversion: Best Practice Assessment*, London: Department of Health.

WINSTONE, J. and PAKES, F. (2010a) *Process Evaluation of the Mental Health Court Pilot: Ministry of Justice Research Series 18/10*, London: Ministry of Justice.

WISH (2011) *Mental Health Liaison and Diversion Schemes in the Criminal Justice System*, London: Wish.

WISTOW, G. (1994) 'Community care futures: inter-agency relationships: stability or continuing change', in M. Titterton (ed.) *Caring for People in the Community*, London: Jessica Kingsley.

WISTOW, G. (1995) 'Coming apart at the seams', *Health Service Journal* 2: 24.

WOLFSON, P., HOLLOWAY, F., and KILLASPY, H. (2009) (eds) *Enabling Recovery for People with Complex Mental Health Needs: A Template for Rehabilitation Services*, London: Royal College of Psychiatrists.

WOOD, C. (2011) *'Personalisation must work for those who need it most…' : Tailor Made* London: Demos.

WRIGHT, D. (1997) 'Getting out of the asylum: understanding confinement of the insane in the nineteenth century', *Social History of Medicine* 10: 137.

WRIGHT, S. (2003) 'Control and restraint techniques in the management of violence in inpatient psychiatry: a critical review', *Medicine, Science and Law* 43(1): 31–8.

ZEDNER, L. (1991) *Women, Crime and Custody in Victorian England*, Oxford: Oxford University Press.

Index